THE INTERNATIONAL HANDBOOK ON PRIVATE ENFORCEMENT OF COMPETITION LAW

The International Handbook on Private Enforcement of Competition Law

Edited by

Albert A. Foer

The American Antitrust Institute, Washington, DC, USA

Jonathan W. Cuneo

Cuneo, Gilbert & LaDuca, LLP, USA

Associate Editors

Randy Stutz

Research Fellow, American Antitrust Institute

Bojana Vrcek

Ph.D., M.E.S., Research Fellow, American Antitrust Institute

Edward Elgar

Cheltenham, UK • Northampton, MA, USA

Published by
Edward Elgar Publishing Limited
The Lypiatts
15 Lansdown Road
Cheltenham
Glos GL50 2JA
UK

Edward Elgar Publishing, Inc.
William Pratt House
9 Dewey Court
Northampton
Massachusetts 01060
USA

Paperback edition 2012

A catalogue record for this book
is available from the British Library

Library of Congress Control Number: 2010925997

FSC
www.fsc.org
MIX
Paper from
responsible sources
FSC® C013056

ISBN 978 1 84844 877 3 (cased)
978 1 78100 528 6 (paperback)

Typeset by Servis Filmsetting Ltd, Stockport, Cheshire
Printed and bound in Great Britain by T. J. International Ltd, Padstow

Contents

PART III EUROPE

PART IV THE AMERICAS

PART V ASIA, AFRICA AND AUSTRALIA

Contributors

Peter Alstergren is an Associate at Advokatfirman Vinge in Sweden
Roberto Amore is an Associate at Freshfields Bruckhaus Deringer LLP in Italy
Giovanni Barone is an Associate at Freshfields Bruckhaus Deringer LLP in Italy
Hilmi Bolatoglu, LLM, is a Competition Expert and Legal Counsel at the Turkish Competition Authority
Adam C. Briggs is an Attorney at Godfrey & Kahn, S.C. in Madison, Wisconsin
Eckart Brödermann, dr. iur., Maître en droit, LLM is a Lecturer at the University of Hamburg and a Managing Partner at Brödermann & Jahn Rechtsanwaltsgesellschaft mbH in Germany
W. Joseph Bruckner is a Partner at Lockridge Grindal Nauen P.L.L.P. in Minneapolis, Minnesota
Alfredo Bullard is a Partner at Bullard, Falla & Ezcurra in Peru
Pedro Callol is a Partner at ROCA JUNYENT in Spain
Scott Campbell is an Associate at Hausfeld & Co LLP in the United Kingdom
Frank S. Chang is a Vice President at Grand Cathay Securities Corporation, a CDFH affiliate in Taiwan
Ma Chunsheng is an Associate at Jun He Law Offices in China
Patrick Clayton is an Associate at Zelle Hofmann Voelbel & Mason LLP in San Francisco, California
John M. Connor is a Professor at Purdue University in Indiana
Craig Corbitt is a Partner at Zelle Hofmann Voelbel & Mason LLP in San Francisco, California
Leonor Cordovil is an Associate Lawyer at Barcellos Tucunduva Advogados in Brazil
Eric L. Cramer is a Shareholder at Berger & Montague, P.C. in Philadelphia, Pennsylvania
Jonathan W. Cuneo is a former Director of the American Antitrust Institute and a Partner at Cuneo, Gilbert & LaDuca in Washington, DC
Brooke Dellavedova is a Principal at Maurice Blackburn Lawyers in Australia
Philipp von Dietze dr. iur., is a Managing Partner at Brödermann & Jahn Rechtsanwaltsgesellschaft mbH in Germany
Cornelius Dube is an Economist at CUTS Centre for Competition, Investment & Economic Regulation in India
Alejandro Falla is a Partner at Bullard, Falla & Ezcurra in Peru
Joost Fanoy is an attorney-at-law with Straatman Koster Advocaten S.V. in the Netherlands
Albert A. Foer is the President of the American Antitrust Institute in Washington, DC
Michal S. Gal is an Associate Professor at the University of Haifa in Israel
Marcus Glader is a Resident Partner at Advokatfirman Vinge in Brussels, Belgium
Joseph Goldberg is a Partner at Freedman Boyd Hollander Goldberg Ives & Duncan P.A. in Albuquerque, New Mexico

Mauro Grinberg is a Partner at Grinberg Cordovil e Barros Advogados in Brazil
Dan Gustafson is a Partner at Gustafson Gluek PLLC in Minneapolis, Minnesota
Michael D. Hausfeld is a Partner at Hausfeld LLP in Washington, DC
Yariv Ilan is a Lawyer at Weinstock, Zecler Attorneys in Israel
Nathalie Jalabert-Doury is a Partner at Mayer Brown LLP in France
Katherine Kinsella is the President of Kinsella Media, LLC in Washington, DC
Robert H. Lande is a Director of the American Antitrust Institute and the Venable Professor of Law at the University of Baltimore School of Law in Baltimore, Maryland
Byung Geon Lee was a Research Fellow at the American Antitrust Institute in Washington, DC
Hwang Lee is an Associate Professor at the Korea University School of Law and Secretary at the Innovation, Competition and Regulation Law Center
Ke Li was a Research Fellow at the American Antitrust Institute in Washington, DC
Lawrence S. Liu is Executive Vice President at the China Development Financial Holding Corporation in Taiwan
Anthony Maton is a Partner at Hausfeld & Co LLP in the United Kingdom
Pradeep S. Mehta is the Secretary General at CUTS International in India
Hiromitsu Miyakawa is an Attorney At Law at Jones Day in Japan
Kasturi Moodaliyar is the Senior Lecturer in Competition Law at the University of Witwatersrand in South Africa
Vince Morabito is a Professor at Monash University in Australia
Kevin J. O'Connor is the Chair of the Antitrust and Trade Regulation Practice Group at Godfrey & Kahn, S.C. in Madison, Wisconsin
Camilla Paoletti is an Associate Lawyer at Barcellos Tucunduva Advogados in Brazil
Hannah L. Renfro is an Attorney at Godfrey & Kahn, S.C. in Madison, Wisconsin
J. Douglas Richards is a Partner at Cohen Milstein Sellers & Toll PLLC in New York City
Jonathan L. Rubin is an attorney in Washington, DC
Matthew R. Salzwedel is an Associate at Lockridge Grindal Nauen P.L.L.P. in Minneapolis, Minnesota
Daan Lunsingh Scheurleer is a Attorney at Law at NautaDutilh N.V. in the Netherlands
Daniel C. Simons is an Associate at Berger & Montague, P.C. in Philadelphia, Pennsylvania
Stacey P. Slaughter is a Partner at Robins, Kaplan, Miller & Ciresi L.L.P. in Minneapolis, Minnesota
Vincent Smith is a former Partner at Hausfeld & Co LLP in the United Kingdom
Laurence T. Sorkin is Senior Counsel at Cahill Gordon & Reindel LLP in New York City
Herman Speyart is an Attorney at Law at NautaDutilh N.V. in the Netherlands
Randy Stutz is a Research Fellow at the American Antitrust Institute in Washington, DC
Bonny E. Sweeney is a Partner at Robbins Geller Rudman & Dowd LLP in San Diego, California
Brendan Sweeney is an Associate Professor at Monash University in Australia
Bojana Vrcek, Ph.D., M.E.S., is a Research Fellow at the American Antitrust Institute in Washington, DC

Zou Weining is a Partner at Jun He Law Offices in China

Shannon Wheatman, Ph.D. is a Vice President at Kinsella Media, LLC in Washington, DC

K. Craig Wildfang is a Partner at Robins, Kaplan, Miller & Ciresi L.L.P. in Minneapolis, Minnesota

Flip Wijers is a Attorney at Law at NautaDutilh N.V. in the Netherlands

Charles M. Wright is a Partner at Siskinds LLP in Canada

Judith Zahid is a Partner at Zelle Hofmann Voelbel & Mason LLP in San Francisco, California

Niv Zecler is a Partner and Founder of Weinstock, Zecler Attorneys in Israel

Preface

A right without a remedy is no right. A famous early statement of this fundamental of the common law came in the English case of *Ashby v. White* in 1703:

> If the plaintiff has a right, he must of necessity have a means to vindicate and maintain it, and a remedy if he is injured in the exercise or enjoyment of it, and, indeed it is a vain thing to imagine a right without a remedy; for want of right and want of remedy are reciprocal. . .[1]

As market economies have displaced various state-dominated regimes, the idea of antitrust has spread remarkably.[2] Temporally, this expansion has been explosive since the fall of the Soviet Union. Its geographic extent is now nearly universal. Today there are well over one hundred jurisdictions in which laws regulate anticompetitive behavior such as collusion or abuse of corporate dominance. Even China, a Communist polity, now has a new and substantial competition law. The principal thrust of the movement toward competition laws has been to create market-based regimes in which most economic decisions are made by private persons and entities complying with (or perhaps manipulating) the laws of supply and demand.

In most of the world's antitrust jurisdictions, ironically, the government itself has maintained a monopoly or virtual monopoly over the implementation of competition law. If there is a violation of competition law, the government decides whether to prosecute. Private parties such as competitors, suppliers, or customers may voice complaints to the government, but they may not initiate their own private actions. And if the government acts, it may fix an identified competition problem, but there will typically be no meaningful way in which private persons who were injured by corporate misbehavior may be made whole. In short, a right to a competitive market is now widely recognized, but private remedies are notoriously difficult to obtain.

This description does not apply equally in all jurisdictions. The US, of course, has evolved an antitrust system in which over 90 per cent of cases are initiated by private

---

1 Ashby v. White (1703), 1 Sm LC (13th Edn 253, 273–74. The quote is from the dissent by Holt CJ, whose opinion was upheld by the House of Lords.

2 We will be using the terms 'antitrust' and 'competition policy' or 'competition law' interchangeably throughout this book. Although 'antitrust' is an American term (and a rather strange one at that, having its birth in the nineteenth century movement against 'trusts' or large holding companies), the term is nevertheless frequently used in other countries that perhaps more readily use terms that include the word 'competition'. Admittedly, competition policy often has a broader meaning than antitrust. The latter technically refers to specific US statutes, the Sherman Act, the Clayton Act, and the Federal Trade Commission Act, whereas the former may refer not only to local statutes or treaties (such as Articles 101 and 102 of the Treaty on the Functioning of the European Union) but may also refer to types of regulation that affect competition (e.g., tax policies, trade policies, intellectual property rights, or sectoral regulations like telecommunications or energy that are often delegated to a specialized government agency) but would not come within what are generally referred to as the US antitrust statutes.

parties. Other nations such as Canada and Australia have substantial private enforcement experience. The European Court of Justice, in the aptly named *Courage* case, recognized the inconsistency between a right to competition and the absence of a remedy, ordering the European Union to ensure that Member States introduce workable private remedies. One justification for this book at this time, then, is that polities around the world are currently in the process of 'taking Courage' by formulating their own approaches to private antitrust enforcement.

Another justification is that surprisingly little empirical literature exists to give guidance to nations contemplating the introduction or expansion of private antitrust enforcement. The US is undoubtedly the leader in private enforcement, but much of the world seems to interpret the US experience as a 'toxic litigation cocktail' to be avoided rather than emulated. One purpose of this book is to set forth a realistic picture of American private antitrust litigation, from the perspective of experienced lawyers who put together and prosecute antitrust cases on behalf of injured parties.

The introductory part of the *Handbook* contains essays by two leading antitrust scholars and a seasoned antitrust practitioner. Robert H. Lande provides an overview of an empirical study of the benefits of private enforcement. John M. Connor, author of *Global Price Fixing*, summarizes the evidence regarding the impact of cartels. Jonathan Cuneo, one of the editors of this *Handbook*, provides an overview of the differing traditions that inform the institutions and practices we will be describing.

The first large section of the *Handbook* consists of eleven chapters that, apparently for the first time, take the development of a US antitrust case from initiation to completion in a systematic way. Each chapter answers a question:

What practices are illegal?
How does a private case get started?
Which claimants may bring a private case?
How does an attorney initiate a private claim?
How may individual claims be aggregated?
What procedural defenses are available, short of a trial?
What devices are available to obtain evidence?
What do you get if you win?
How do you finance private enforcement?
How does private enforcement interact with public enforcement?
What mechanisms make claims distribution workable?

With the US background laid out in depth, the book turns to foreign experiences. We do this through nineteen national chapters written by lawyers and academicians familiar with the local laws and practice. The countries were selected on the basis of their having at least some laws on their books that would appear to provide a private remedy. In many cases these are new laws. In others, the laws have been in effect for varying periods but, for reasons explained in the chapters, they have not proven workable. In a few countries, primarily common law regimes that share much of the same British heritage as the US, there is more of a congruence between law and actual practice.

We approach the countries by geographic region, with each region introduced by an overview that presents generalizations based not only on the chapters that follow but also on information about other countries within the region that are not treated in this volume.

A twelfth question – how can a multi-nation case be settled? – appears in a final section of the *Handbook*, titled 'The Future of Private Enforcement,' followed by a chapter authored by the editors which we call 'Towards An Effective System of Private Enforcement of Competition Law.' Some readers may wish to start with our final chapter, which breaks down the challenge of building an effective private enforcement system into a series of key decision points, indicating the range of solutions that are described in the book and, of course, offering our own policy prescriptions.

The national essays reflect the state of the law as of December 30, 2009. All references to Articles 81 and 82 of the EC Treaty reference Articles 101 and 102 of the Treaty on the Functioning of the European Union ('TFEU') as amended by the Treaty of Lisbon.

* * *

The American Antitrust Institute (AAI) undertook this *Handbook* project in the hope that it will prove useful to governments, NGOs, and others who are trying to develop workable laws and institutions to make private enforcement a reality. The AAI was founded in 1998 as an education, research, and advocacy organization, headquartered in Washington, DC.[3] The AAI is a virtual network of experts representing law, economics, and business acumen, both practitioners and academics, who share a general attitude that antitrust is a good thing and more of it in most situations would be better. This *Handbook*, therefore, reflects all three aspects of the AAI's mission: education, research, and advocacy – in this case advocacy of private enforcement as an essential adjunct to competition laws.

The author of each chapter is identified and relevant personal background is provided in the first footnote of the chapter. The authors were given substantial flexibility to set the tone and outline, although the editorial team asked that most of the same questions mentioned above be addressed to the extent relevant. All chapters were reviewed by a minimum of three editors affiliated with the American Antitrust Institute. We are grateful to the various authors who volunteered their time, energy, and knowledge. Many were drafting in English as a secondary language and no doubt felt that our editorial suggestions put them through an uncomfortable strainer. But even the Anglophones were subjected to a straining process. We appreciate the patience of our authors.

The *Handbook* co-editors-in-chief were Albert A. Foer and Jonathan Cuneo, both of whom have been directors of the American Antitrust Institute since its inception. Foer, the president of AAI, is a former practicing attorney, former senior executive of the Bureau of Competition in the US Federal Trade Commission, and former retail business executive. Cuneo is principal in the Washington law firm of Cuneo, Gilbert and LaDuca, LLP, and a former Counsel to the House of Representatives Subcommittee on Monopolies and Commercial Law.

---

[3] The AAI's website is http://www.antitrustinstitute.org. It contains an archive of all AAI's work product as well as links to antitrust resources.

The two Associate Editors played a crucial role in the project. Dr. Bojana Vrcek, a specialist in European comparative competition law with practical experience in Zagreb and Brussels, wrote the overview of Europe and oversaw the editing of all of the countries outside of the US. Randy Stutz, an experienced antitrust attorney on leave from private practice in the District of Columbia, oversaw the preparation of the US chapters.

During the early phase of this project, a large editorial role was played by Byung-Geon (B.K.) Lee of South Korea (then a Hubert Humphrey Scholar on leave from the Korean Federal Trade Commission). Lee, now returned to a policy post with the KFTC, was the co-author of the overview of Asia and Africa and co-author of the chapter on Korea.

The *Handbook* project was fortunate to have the additional editorial assistance of AAI Research Fellows Ke Li of China (a law student at George Washington University), Nikos Valance (a law student at Fordham with a strong journalism background), Aron Schnur (a law student at Georgetown University), Sandeep Vaheesan (a law student at Duke University), Patrick English (on leave from a law firm), Dae Gunn (D.J.) Jei (also on leave from a law firm), and Irit Dolgin (formerly with the Israeli Antitrust Authority). Logistical support of a highly important nature was provided by Sarah Frey, Communications Director of the AAI. The group functioned as an interactive team, meeting frequently to compare notes and discuss themes and recommendations. For all of us, this has been a special learning experience.

Albert A. Foer
Jonathan Cuneo
Editors-in-Chief

Washington, D.C.
December 30, 2009

PART I

INTRODUCTION

1 Benefits of private enforcement: empirical background[1]

Robert H. Lande[2]

Many commentators, especially members of the defense bar, have criticized the existing United States system of private antitrust litigation. Some assert that private actions all too often result in remedies that provide lucrative fees for plaintiffs' lawyers but secure no significant benefits for overcharged victims.[3] Others suggest that private litigation merely follows an easy trail blazed by government enforcers and adds little of public benefit to government sanctions.[4] Yet others contend that, in light of government enforcement, private cases in the United States lead to excessive deterrence.[5] Further, one common

---

1 This article is a condensation and revision of 'Benefits From Private Antitrust Enforcement: An Analysis of Forty Cases,' 42 USF. L. Rev. 879 (2008), available at http://papers.ssrn.com/sol3/papers.cfm?abstract_id=1090661 (hereafter 'Benefits: An Analysis'). For summaries of the individual case studies analyzed in this article see 'Benefits from Antitrust Private Antitrust Enforcement: Forty Individual Case Studies,' (hereafter 'Benefits: Individual Case Studies'), http://papers.ssrn.com/sol3/papers.cfm?abstract_id=1105523.

2 Venable Professor of Law, University of Baltimore Law School; Board of Directors, American Antitrust Institute. The author is grateful to Thomas Weaver for excellent research assistance.

3 Professor Cavanagh ably summarized this belief: 'Many class action suits generate substantial fees for counsel but produce little, if any, benefit to the alleged victims of the wrongdoing. Coupon settlements, wherein plaintiffs settle for "cents off" coupons while their attorneys are paid their full fees in cash . . . are of dubious value to the victims of antitrust violations . . . [and] defendants are not forced to disgorge their ill-gotten gains when coupons are not redeemed.' Edward Cavanagh, 'Antitrust Remedies Revisited,' 84 Or. L. Rev. 147, 214 (2005) (footnote omitted). However, Professor Cavanagh provides only an anecdote to support these conclusions. He offers no data to show the type of antitrust settlements he describes as typical or to demonstrate how often they result in useless coupons.

4 John C. Coffee, Jr. at one point subscribed to this view, but later concluded the evidence was to the contrary. John C. Coffee, Jr., 'Understanding the Plaintiff's Attorney: The Implications of Economic Theory for Private Enforcement of Law Through Class and Derivative Actions,' 86 Colum. L. Rev. 669 n. 36 (1986) ('Although the conventional wisdom has long been that class actions tend to 'tag along' on the heels of governmentally initiated suits, a recent study of antitrust litigation by Professors Kauper and Snyder has placed this figure at "[l]ess than 20 per cent of private antitrust actions filed between 1976 and 1983."') (citation omitted).

5 As the Antitrust Modernization Commission noted: '[S]ome have argued that treble damages, along with other remedies, can overdeter some conduct that may not be anticompetitive and result in duplicative recovery. No actual cases or evidence of systematic overdeterrence were presented to the Commission, however.' Antitrust Modernization Comm'n, Report and Recommendations, at 247 (2007), available at http://govinfo.library.unt.edu/amc/report_recommendation/amc_final_report.pdf (footnotes omitted). For reasons why 'treble damages' do not lead to excessive deterrence but, on the contrary should be increased, see Robert H. Lande, 'Five Myths about Antitrust Damages,' 40 USF. L. Rev. 651 (2006), available at http://papers.ssrn.com/sol3/papers.cfm?abstract_id=1263478.

criticism of private actions in general – and of class actions in particular – is that they are a form of legalized blackmail or extortion, one in which plaintiffs' attorneys coerce defendants into settlements based not on meritorious claims, but rather on the cost of litigation or fear of an erroneous and catastrophic judgment.[6] These actions also are said to discourage legitimate competitive behavior.[7] For these and related reasons many members of the antitrust community call for the curtailment of private enforcement,[8] some even for its abolition.[9]

Although these criticisms are widespread, they have been made without any systematic empirical basis.[10] Those who point to the alleged flaws of the United Sates system of private antitrust enforcement support their arguments only with anecdotes, many of which are self-serving or questionable. I have never seen these arguments supported with reliable data.

We emphasize that we are not disputing all critics' anecdotes. Private antitrust enforcement, which constitutes in most years more than 90 per cent of antitrust cases in the United States,[11] certainly is imperfect.[12] The point, however, is that nations considering private enforcement should first fairly assess its effects in the United States. They should not confuse anecdotes with data. One factor they should consider carefully is the systematic benefit of private actions to victimized consumers and businesses, and to the economy more generally.

---

[6] See John H. Beisner and Chares E. Borden, 'Expanding Private Causes of Action: Lessons from the US Litigation Experience,' available at www.instituteforlegalreform.com/get_ilr_doc.php?id=1034. However, Beisner and Bordon and others who embrace this view provide no systematic empirical basis for its factual predicates.

[7] AMC Commissioner Cannon wrote: 'Private plaintiffs are very often competitors of the firms they accuse of antitrust violations, and have every incentive to challenge and thus deter hard competition that they cannot or will not meet. . . . [L]itigation is expensive and courts and juries may erroneously conclude that procompetitive or competitively neutral conduct violates the antitrust laws. . . . [P]otential defendants . . . will refrain from engaging in some forms of potentially procompetitive conduct in order to avoid the cost and risk of litigation.' W. Stephen Cannon, 'A Reassessment of Antitrust Remedies: The Administration's Antitrust Remedies Reform Proposal: Its Derivation and Implications,' 55 Antitrust L.J. 103, 106 (1986).

[8] Herbert Hovenkamp, The Antitrust Enterprise: Principle and Execution 59 (Cambridge: Harvard University Press 2005).

[9] See William Breit and Kenneth G. Elzinga, 'Private Antitrust Enforcement: The New Learning,' 28 J.L. & Econ. 405, 440 (1985).

[10] One prominent critic, former ABA Antitrust Section Chair Janet McDavid, candidly admitted this: '[The] issue [of class action abuse] was never directly presented in these cases, but many of these issues arise in the context of class actions in which the potential for abusive ligitation is really pretty extraordinary.' When asked by Professor Andrew Gavil about empirical evidence, McDavid said: 'I'm not aware of empirical data on any of those issues. My empirical data are derived from cases in which I am involved.' Antitrust, Volume 22, Fall 2007, 8, 12–13.

[11] See Sourcebook of Criminal Justice Statistics Online, www.albany.edu/sourcebook/pdf/t5412004.pdf Table 5.41.2004, Antitrust Cases filed in US District Courts, by type of case, 1975–2004.

[12] Government enforcement also is imperfect.

The purpose and design of the study

The article discussed in this chapter is a first step towards providing the empirical data necessary to assess some of the benefits of private enforcement of the United States antitrust laws. It does this by analyzing a group of 40 recent, successful, large-scale private antitrust cases. With the support of the American Antitrust Institute and a variety of research assistants, the authors, Professor Joshua Davis and I, analyzed, inter alia, the amount of money each action recovered for victims, what proportion of the money was recovered from foreign entities, whether the private litigation was preceded by government action, and on whose behalf money was recovered (direct purchasers, indirect purchasers, or a competitor). To our knowledge no similar study has ever been undertaken.

It is important to note that this report does not purport to be comprehensive or in any way definitive. It does not analyze every recent significant private antitrust case, assess a random sample of cases, or even include all of the largest or 'most important' ones.[13] We simply tried to assemble and evaluate 40 of the largest and most successful cases that concluded between 1990 and 2007.[14]

The primary focus of this project, moreover, was not to demonstrate that private litigation often has established important legal precedents: other studies have done this convincingly.[15] Our 'first cut' was, instead, to look for recent private cases that were final, including appeals, and that recovered at least $50 million in cash for victims of anticompetitive behavior. We included only recovered money; products, services, discounts, coupons, and injunctive relief were not included in our results as a 'benefit' of private litigation.[16]

Results of this study

The 40 cases (or groups of cases)[17] analyzed in this report provided a cumulative recovery in the range of at least $18,006 to $19,639 million in allegedly[18] illegally acquired wealth

---

13 For example, we were not able to include an analysis of the consumer class action suits against Microsoft, even though a highly respected journalist reported that together these cases recovered more than $1.5 billion for victims. See Todd Bishop, Todd Bishop's Microsoft Blog, July 7, 2006, available at http://blog.seattlepi.nwsource.com/microsoft/month.asp?blogmonth=7/1/2006&page=4.

14 In one case, the final settlement was approved within this time frame, but the final award of fees and costs to the attorneys did not occur until January, 2008. See In re Auto. Refinishing Paint Antitrust Litig., 2008 US Dist. LEXIS 569 (E.D. Pa. Jan. 3, 2008).

15 For an excellent analysis see Stephen Calkins, Coming to Praise Criminal Antitrust Enforcement, European University Institute 11th EU Competition Law and Policy Workshop (Florence, Italy, June 2–3, 2006). Professor Calkins found that, of leading antitrust cases decided before 1977, 12 were private and 27 were government. Of the leading cases decided in 1977 or later, however, he found that 30 were private cases and only 15 were government cases. Id. at 17.

16 Securities were counted in one case because they had a readily ascertainable market value.

17 To arrive at this number we counted related cases as being a single 'case.' For example, there have been many separate legal actions involving vitamins cartels. However, this report analyzes and counts them all together as one 'case.'

18 For simplicity we are calling all of the charges 'allegations,' even the ones proven in court.

to US consumers and businesses.[19] Of this, more than $5,706 to $7,056 million came from foreign companies that allegedly violated US antitrust laws, in 18 of the 40 cases. Without the private enforcement of the antitrust laws this money would have remained with foreign alleged lawbreakers instead of being returned to US consumers and businesses.[20] It is interesting that of the total amount recovered a large proportion – at least 42 to 46 per cent; $7,631 to $8,981 million – came from the 15 cases that did not follow publicly disclosed United States or EU government enforcement actions.[21] For each of the cases, private plaintiffs appear to have completely uncovered the alleged violations, and initiated and pursued the litigation, with the government following the private plaintiffs' lead or playing no role at all. Another $4,212 million came from cases with a mixed private/public origin.[22] Only about a third of the total private recovery – $6,163 to $6,446 million – occurred in cases that were purely public in origin.

Still other private cases followed a government investigation, but provided significantly greater relief than the government action (if, indeed, a government action was brought), expanded the scope of inquiry and claims, or obtained relief against parties not included in the government actions. There also were cases whose origin we were not able to ascertain.[23] The high proportion of private actions that were filed in the absence of government cases, that had mixed public/private origins, or that significantly expanded the relief obtained through government enforcement alone, is perhaps surprising.

Of the total $18,006 to $19,639 million in recoveries we documented, $12,088 to $13,438 million (67 to 68 per cent of the total), in 32 cases, was recovered by direct purchasers; $1,815 million, in six cases, was recovered by indirect purchasers; and $4,028 to $4,311 million, in six cases, was recovered by competitors.[24] All but six of the cases were class actions.

---

19 We did not change recoveries to 2009 dollars or otherwise correct for the time-value of money. All figures include the awarded attorneys' fees.

Although a United States verdict would produce treble damages for victims, almost all of our cases involved settlements, and in no case did a court determine the percentage overcharge. We know of no way to determine whether any of the settlements exceeded single damages.

20 This project did not select cases on the basis of whether a foreign defendant was likely to be involved.

21 When conduct gave rise to both government and private litigation we tried to ascertain who first uncovered the antitrust violation. For many of the cases our researchers spent dozens of hours on this issue. However, because government records are confidential and the enforcers usually do not reveal or discuss their investigations, we could not always make definitive classifications. Because we had access only to publicly available information some of our classifications could be mistaken. For further discussion of the interplay between public and private enforcement, see Chapter 13 of this *Handbook*.

22 For example In re Polypropylene Carpet Antitrust Litig., 93 F. Supp. 2d 1348 (N.D. Ga. 2000), started as a result of a different private antitrust suit, which led to a government investigation in the polypropylene carpet market, that in turn led to the private litigation analyzed in this Report. See Benefits: An Analysis, supra note 1, Table 5, for other examples.

23 See, for example, the El Paso case summary, Benefits: Individual Case Studies, supra note 1, at 77–87.

24 Direct purchasers are customers who bought a good or service directly from a defendant, and indirect purchasers are customers who purchased a good or service further down the chain of distribution. In the US, in general only direct purchasers and competitors can bring claims for

Some of the cases we analyzed also involved substantial non-monetary relief. For example, one case generated coupons, fully redeemable in cash if not used for five years (however, to be very conservative we did not count any part of this in our 'cash' recovery totals).[25] Another case resulted in a $125 million energy rate reduction for consumers (we did not count this reduction in our benefits total).[26] Some cases involved extremely useful cy pres grants.[27] Many other cases restructured industries in ways that, according to the judge presiding over the litigation, provided improvements for competition even more beneficial than the monetary relief they conferred on the victims. For example, the Visa/MasterCard case was settled in April 2003 for '$3,383,400,000 in compensatory relief, plus additional injunctive relief valued at $25 to $87 billion or more.'[28] Similarly, the NASDAQ case decreased the spreads received by market makers, the Insurance litigation eliminated restrictions on insurance policies, and the NCAA case eliminated caps on pay to college coaches.[29] Further, together the generic drug cases – Buspirone, Cardizem, Oncology (Taxol), Relafen, Remeron, and Terazosin – discouraged collusion between brand name and generic drug manufacturers, saving consumers many hundreds of millions of dollars in lower cost drugs.[30]

Observations

The United States' distinctive system of private antitrust enforcement is substantially underappreciated at home and often seems to be misunderstood abroad. It has produced tremendous benefits for the United States economy – for consumers and for businesses

---

damages under federal law, and indirect purchasers can bring claims for damages only under state law (most, but not all, US states allow indirect purchaser actions). For further discussion of direct and indirect purchaser claims, see Chapter 6 of this *Handbook*.

[25] See Auction House case summaries, Benefits: Individual Case Studies, supra note 1, at 13–18. These coupons traded for a value that reflected their discounted present value. They also comprised 20 per cent of the legal fees paid to prevailing attorneys, who said they will redeem them for cash after the expiration of the mandatory five year waiting period.

[26] See the El Paso summary, in Benefits: Individual Case Studies, supra note 1, at 77–87.

[27] See, for example, the Insurance case, in Benefits: Individual Case Studies, supra note 1, at 110–113. This case resulted in a cash settlement with a creative remedy that: (i) funded the development of a public entity that provides risk management education and technical services to small businesses, public entities, and non profits; and (ii) provided funds to the States to develop a risk database for municipalities and local governments. (*Cy pres* is a type of remedy that is available in some antitrust class actions where there are funds left over after the class members have been compensated, or the funds are insufficient to distribute to the class members in an economically efficient manner. The court has discretion to award these funds to 'the next best' usage consistent with the purposes of the case. See AAI Working Paper 07-11, Albert A. Foer, Enhancing Competition Through the Cy Pres Remedy: Suggested Best Practices, available at www.antitrustinstitute.org/Archives/WP07-11.ashx).

[28] See Wal-Mart Stores, Inc. v. Visa USA & MasterCard Int'l, 396 F.3d 96, 111 (2d Cir. 2005). The case is described in detail by the lead attorney for the plaintiffs, Lloyd Constantine, in *Priceless* (Kaplan Publishing 2009).

[29] See Benefits: Individual Case Studies, supra note 1, at 135–39. This case is described in Arthur R. Kaplan, 'Antitrust as a Public-Private Partnership: A Case Study of the NASDAQ Litigation,' 52 Case Western Reserve L. Rev. 111 (2001).

[30] See Benefits: Individual Case Studies, supra note 1. For further discussion of plaintiffs' remedies, see Chapter 11 of this *Handbook*.

of all sizes. It has helped to deter anticompetitive behavior[31] and to compensate victims of illegal activity. It has enabled US businesses and consumers to protect themselves from economic exploitation, both by those who subvert the free market in general and by foreign cartels in particular.[32] It has saved the US taxpayer tremendous sums in enforcement costs by shifting the enormous burdens and risks of litigating against sophisticated, well-financed lawbreakers from government staff to private plaintiffs' counsel. Although negative assertions about the efficacy of private United States antitrust litigation have been very well publicized, this might well be due in large part to the powerful economic interests that stand to benefit from a curtailment of private antitrust enforcement in the United States and from the prevention of private rights of action for competition law violations in other nations.

As to the possibility of overdeterrence, the United States awards what are nominally 'treble damages' to victorious victims. But in reality, various constraints on recovery mean that, even after nominal trebling of a judgment at trial, plaintiffs likely recover less than single actual damages.[33] Thus, nominal trebling is justified to compensate victims for unawarded prejudgment interest,[34] for difficult-to-quantify and unawarded damages items such as the allocative inefficiency effects of market power[35] and for

---

[31] For a discussion of measuring the deterrence effects of private enforcement, and a comparison of deterrence from private enforcement against DOJ criminal enforcement, see Robert H. Lande and Joshua P. Davis, *Comparative Deterrence from Private Enforcement and Criminal Enforcement of the US Antitrust Laws* (unpublished draft, October 22, 2009) (available from the authors).

[32] See John M. Connor and Robert H. Lande, 'The Size of Cartel Overcharges: Implications for US and E.U. Fining Policies,' 51 Antitrust Bulletin 983 (2007), available at http://papers.ssrn.com/sol3/papers.cfm?abstract_id=988722 (showing that, historically, depending upon the data set used and the methodology employed, cartels in the United States have overcharged an average of 18% to 37%. By contrast, the overcharges of European cartels averaged in the 28% to 54% range, and cartel overcharges within a single European country averaged 16% to 48%).

[33] To the extent the purpose of the remedy is compensation, the 'damages' caused by an antitrust violation should consist of the sum of all relatively predictable harms caused by that violation affecting anyone other than the defendants. Damages should include the wealth transferred from consumers to the violator(s), as well as the allocative inefficiency effects felt by society, whether caused directly, or indirectly via 'umbrella' effects. Plaintiffs' attorneys' fees, the value of plaintiffs' time spent pursuing the case, and the cost to the American taxpayer of administering the judicial system should also be included. When all these adjustments are made it is likely that the United States 'treble' damages remedy actually is less than single damages. See Robert H. Lande, 'Are Antitrust "Treble" Damages Really Single Damages?,' 54 Ohio State L.J. 115, 122–24, 158–68 (1993), available at http://papers.ssrn.com/sol3/papers.cfm?abstract_id=1134822.

[34] In the US, interest is only awarded from the time of a judicial decision and the rate is usually quite low. Id. at 130. For further discussion of pre- and post-judgment interest awards, see Chapter 11 of this *Handbook*.

[35] For an explanation of the allocative inefficiency effects of market power see id. at 119–21, 152–54. Allocative inefficiency is another name for the suboptimal use of societal resources that results from supracompetitive pricing:

> To raise prices a monopoly reduces output from the competitive level. The goods no longer sold are worth more to would-be purchasers than they would cost society to produce. This foregone production of goods worth more than their cost is pure social loss and constitutes the 'allocative inefficiency' of monopoly. For example, suppose that widgets cost $1.00 in a

the value of victims' time expended pursuing litigation.[36] Further, antitrust verdicts producing even nominal treble damages are rare,[37] and we believe that few, if any, of the overwhelming majority of antitrust cases that settle do so for more than one times actual damages.[38]

Moreover, while government criminal and civil actions are essential to deter future antitrust violations, virtually the only way to secure redress for the victims of antitrust violations is through private litigation.[39] Private enforcement at times has substituted for federal and state action entirely when government did not act at all or did not achieve meaningful results. At other times, private actions have complemented governmental enforcement in many situations where the government investigated, prosecuted, and imposed penalties, but was unable to compensate private victims for the harms they suffered as a result of antitrust violations. Private antitrust enforcement also has resulted in restructuring industries or modifying business behavior in ways that have improved efficiency and competitiveness, redounding to the benefit of consumers, the affected industries themselves, and the economy as a whole.[40]

> competitive market (their cost of production plus a competitive profit). Suppose a monopolist would sell them for \$2.00. A potential purchaser who would have been willing to pay up to \$1.50 will not purchase at the \$2.00 level. Since a competitive market would have sold them widgets for less than they were worth to him, the monopolist's reduced production has decreased the consumer's satisfaction without producing any countervailing benefits for anyone. This pure loss is termed 'allocative inefficiency.'

Robert H. Lande, 'The Rise and (Coming) Fall of Efficiency as the Ruler of Antitrust,' 33 Antitrust Bull. 429, 433–34 n. 17 (1988); see also Edwin Mansfield, *Microeconomics: Theory and Applications* 277–92 (W.W. Norton & Co., Inc., 4th ed. 1982) (1970).

[36] See Robert H. Lande, 'Are Antitrust "Treble" Damages Really Single Damages?,' 54 Ohio State L.J. 115, 130–36 (1993), available at http://papers.ssrn.com/sol3/papers.cfm?abstract_id=1134822.

Op. cit. note 33 supra. As the Antitrust Modernization Commission noted: 'Indeed, in light of the fact that some damages may not be recoverable (e.g., compensation for interest prior to judgment, or because of the statute of limitations and the inability to recover "speculative" damages) treble damages help ensure that victims will recover at least their actual damages.' Antitrust Modernization Commission, Report and Recommendations, at 246 (2007) (footnote omitted).

[37] For a list of antitrust verdicts that calculated damages amounts, see Connor & Lande, supra note 32.

[38] For an analysis of this issue see Robert H. Lande, 'Why Antitrust Damage Levels Should Be Raised,' 16 Loyola Consumer L. Rev. 329 (2004), available at http://papers.ssrn.com/sol3/papers.cfm?abstract_id=1118902.

[39] In the United States, State Attorneys General can bring parens patriae actions on behalf of victims located within their states, and the Federal Trade Commission has succeeded in disgorgement actions, but these actions are rare.

[40] As Irwin Stelzer observed, 'An army of private enforcers, enlisting help from attorney-entrepreneurs free to accept cases on a contingency fee basis, freed of "loser pays" obligations, is an important supplement to those limited [government] resources. . . . [S]ome 80 per cent of court decisions establishing important principles (not all of which I find agreeable, I might add) in the competition policy area have resulted from private actions.' Irwin Stelzer, Implications for Productivity Growth in the Economy, notes for talk at Workshop on Private Enforcement of Competition Law, sponsored by Office of Fair Trading, at p. 2 (London, England, Oct. 19, 2006).

In fact, as a practical matter the government cannot be expected to do all or even most of the necessary enforcing of antitrust or competition laws for various reasons including: budgetary constraints;[41] undue fear of losing cases;[42] lack of awareness of industry conditions;[43] overly suspicious views about complaints by 'losers' that they were in fact victims of anticompetitive behavior;[44] high turnover among government attorneys;[45] and the unfortunate reality that government enforcement (or non-enforcement) decisions are at times politically motivated.[46] Not surprisingly, a vigorous private antitrust or competition regime is likely to confer significant benefits over and above those conferred by a system reliant solely upon government enforcement.

In the United States anticompetitive conduct occurs far too frequently and is almost certainly significantly underdeterred[47] – even factoring in the effects of the present system of private litigation. A fortiori this conduct would be even more underdeterred if the United States eliminated or substantially curtailed private enforcement. It would be surprising if firms in other nations were significantly more law abiding than those in the United States, and we suspect that the United States record of underdeterrence of anticompetitive conduct (and undercompensation of victims) exists in many other nations as well.

Each nation of course has unique needs, history, institutions, capabilities and circumstances, and no one ever should advocate 'one size fits all' competition legislation. Nevertheless, every nation without effective private enforcement of its competition laws

---

41 This is especially true in the current climate of tight federal budgets.

42 Professor Calkins notes: 'Governmental agencies also hesitate to litigate because of fear of defeat. Courtroom setbacks can demoralize agency staff, raise questions in the eyes of observers, and impose political costs. Few agency annual reports boast about the well-fought loss, and, in an era in which governmental accountability is fashionable, it is challenging to characterize losses as accomplishments. All too often, agencies worry about their win rates. . . . [A]nd general counsels who are nominated for higher office like to claim that their agency won a high percentage of its cases. Everyone wants a good batting average. Unfortunately, a single loss can ruin a good batting average compiled with few at-bats.' Stephen Calkins, 'In Praise of Antitrust Litigation: The Second Annual Bernstein Lecture,' 72 St. John's L. Rev. 1 (1998) (citations omitted).

43 'Private parties operating in the real markets . . . [will] act on the reality they confront.' Stelzer, supra note 40, at 4. 'The administrators of our antitrust laws might not feel competent to tell what sort of pricing practice is exclusionary or predatory. But the victims most certainly can.' Id. at 5.

44 '[W]ho better to argue that . . . [certain conduct is anticompetitive] than a competitor, injured by illegal anticompetitive practices, conversant in the technical jargon, on the sharp edge of customer relations, well informed on the details and consequences of the dominant firm's practices.' Id. at 5–6.

45 The largest antitrust cases often last for 5–10 years. The government often has trouble retaining a well qualified team throughout this period. Private firms, by contrast, often are able to retain relatively intact teams for longer periods.

46 Irwin Stelzer noted: 'A less obvious but equally important reason that private enforcement is so important is that it is free of direct political influence. In America, administrations come and go, some more given to a jaundiced view of the activities of dominant firms than others, witness the soft settlement worked out with Microsoft when the Bush administration took office and control of the Department of Justice, and its [then] current disinclination to file any §2 cases.' Seltzer, supra note 40, at 6.

47 See Lande, supra note 38, and Connor and Lande, supra note 32.

should seriously consider reform in this area. In doing so, policymakers should understand private enforcement as it actually works in the United States, not a mere caricature, one too often presented by self-interested parties who oppose antitrust enforcement in general.

2 The impact of international cartels

John M. Connor[1]

Introduction

Despite the evident antitrust successes in sanctioning international cartels since 1990, many remain skeptical about whether current enforcement regimes are capable of serving the aims of antitrust. Deterrence is the most commonly accepted legal-economic theory that justifies the passage and enforcement of antitrust laws, and there is emerging evidence that in some jurisdictions it has a strong role as a practical guide to imposing anti-cartel fines.[2] There is also mounting evidence that monetary penalties are at historically high levels in North America and Western Europe, and at low but rapidly accelerating levels in key jurisdictions on other continents. That penalties are by most measures highest in North America is in large part due to the nearly unique availability and widespread use of private rights of action by cartel victims, further amplified by severe penalties for individual cartel executives. Optimal deterrence principles imply that fines, private settlements, and individual criminal penalties are fungible: they are complementary punishments with respect to their ability to raise the expected costs of criminal activity.

While deterrence may have improved marginally since the 1990s, there is a near consensus among scholars of modern international cartels that current competition policies cannot optimally deter cartel behavior because such policies are 'oriented towards addressing harm done in domestic markets . . . [or] merely prohibit cartels without [sufficiently strong] sanctions.'[3] Connor finds that domestic cartel overcharges are so high and conspiracies so durable that current US public and private monetary sanctions provide inadequate *ex post* deterrence;[4] true *ex ante* deterrence[5] is even more remote in

[1] Professor, Purdue University, and Senior Fellow, American Antitrust Institute. Author of *Global Price Fixing* (Springer, 2d ed. 2007).

[2] John M. Connor & Douglas J. Miller, *Determinants of EC Antitrust Fines for Members of Global Cartels,* presented at the Institute of Competition Law's conference on 'New Frontiers of Antitrust' (Paris, February 15, 2010).

[3] Simon J. Evenett, Margaret C. Levenstein & Valerie Y. Suslow, *International Cartel Enforcement: Lessons from the 1990s*, 24 The World Economy 1221, 1221–1245 (2001).

[4] *Ex post* deterrence contemplates the power of penalties by looking backward from the time after which all penalties have been imposed on a criminal; the power is measured by comparing the size of these penalties to the amount gained by the criminal from the crime. In the context of cartel violations, *ex post* deterrence is deemed adequate if all monopoly profits gained from collusion are fully disgorged. Because the *ex post* view of punishment assumes that there is a 100 per cent chance that a crime will be detected and punished, this standard of deterrence is inappropriate for crimes conducted in secret.

[5] *Ex ante* deterrence contemplates the power of penalties by looking forward from the time a would-be conspirator is weighing either forming a new cartel or joining a cartel already operating. This calculus involves comparing the likely future gain from collusion to the expected future penalties, adjusted by the probability of being caught and convicted. If the expected gain equals the

light of the small probability that secret cartel conduct will be detected.[6] International cartels – those with international participation – are more difficult to convict, yet as a group are even more harmful to customer welfare than domestic collusion. *Global* cartels – international cartels that operate across multi-continental markets – typically reap the highest monopoly profits in jurisdictions with weakest anti-cartel enforcement. Moreover, empirical evidence from recent years demonstrates an increasing trend in cartel discoveries and considerable recidivism by corporations for price fixing.[7]

This chapter examines anti-cartel enforcement in selected jurisdictions in all of the world's inhabited continents. Enforcement refers to the antitrust laws, patterns of government sanctions, and the complementary efforts of private actions in the courts. The principal conclusions are as follows. Despite these grave reservations concerning the deterrence power of cartel sanctions, there are indicators that enforcement in North America comes closest to optimal deterrence of illegal cartel conduct. Not only are monetary penalties commensurate with the economic injuries imposed on customers, but also US authorities are nearly alone in handing down long prison sentences for criminal price fixers. The European Union (EU) – both the European Commission (EC) and its National Competition Authorities (NCAs) – has pulled ahead of North America in the size of fines imposed on cartels, yet its fight against cartel violators is hampered by court rules that severely limit the rights of cartel victims to seek compensation in private actions. Moreover, EU law does not permit sanctions to be imposed on cartel managers, nor is this possible in all but a few of its Member States.[8] Cartel enforcement is weakest in Asia, Africa, and Latin America. There are a few rising stars on these continents, but government entities rarely see their efforts complemented by significant private settlements or damages awards to aggrieved cartel victims.

North America: the epicenter of private enforcement

Criminal enforcement

The Antitrust Division of the US Department of Justice (DOJ) pioneered the convictions of international cartels 65 years ago.[9] But for 50 years thereafter, though active with

---

expected adjusted penalty, then *ex ante* deterrence is 'optimal.' Because the probability of detection of hidden cartels is well below 100 per cent, the *ex ante* concept of deterrence requires higher penalties in order to deter a particular cartel violation than does the *ex post* concept.

6 John M. Connor, *Price-Fixing Overcharges: Legal and Economic Evidence*, 22 Research in Law and Economics 59, 59–153 (John B. Kirkwood ed., 2007).

7 From fewer than four discoveries of international cartels per year in the early 1990s, antitrust authorities around the world were investigating or convicting more than 50 cartels per year in 2008. These data also demonstrate more than 200 instances of international-price-fixing recidivism during 1990–2008. John M. Connor, *Latin America and the Control of International Cartels*, Competition Law and Policy in Latin America 291–324 (Oxford: Hart Publishing, Eleanor M. Fox & D. Daniel Sokol eds., 2009), *draft available at* http://papers.ssrn.com/sol3/papers.cfm?abstract_id=1417571.

8 Germany regularly fines managing directors of price-fixing cartels, and the UK and Netherlands are beginning to do so. In Germany and Italy, bid rigging is classified as fraud, which makes imprisonment a possible sanction.

9 John M. Connor, Global Price Fixing 503, xxv (Springer Verlag, 2nd ed. 2008).

respect to domestic cartels, prosecutions of international cartels were almost unheard of. Despite a few losses at trial against alleged international cartelists in the early 1990s, in 1993 the DOJ shifted antitrust resources toward investigating international price-fixing, abetted by enhanced maximum antitrust legal penalties, innovations in detection and investigatory methods, tougher sentencing guidelines, and a new commitment to stiffer prison sentences for cartel executives. This shift in course paid off.

US criminal penalties for hard-core cartels soared after 1995.[10] DOJ prosecutions bifurcated into a large number of cartels with small affected sales and a smaller number of huge international cases. And the biggest of the international cases were *global cartels* – those that spanned at least two and often four continents.[11] Although US companies were the majority of those fined for cartel violations, after 1995 international-cartel fines came to dominate the total fines collected by the DOJ for criminal price-fixing matters.[12] In the same years, the DOJ obtained prison sentences for more than 300 cartel executives, of whom one-sixth were managers of international schemes.[13] Few jurisdictions outside the United States employ prison sentences for price-fixing crimes.

Although no monetary penalties have exceeded treble damages, the United States metes out the most severe corporate and individual punishments of any jurisdiction in the world. The median average for international-cartel penalties in 1990–2008 was 15 to 16 per cent of affected sales in the jurisdiction (and slightly higher in Canada).[14] A superior measure of intensity of penalties would use the cartel's overcharge as a metric; based on about 70 observations, US median penalties amounted to about 70 per cent of the median US overcharge.[15] Although relatively high, optimal monetary penalties ought to be over 300 per cent of a cartel's overcharges.[16]

---

[10] John M. Connor, *Anti-Cartel Enforcement by the DOJ: An Appraisal,* 5 Competition Law Review 89, 89–122 (December 2008), *available at* www.clasf.org/CompLRev/Issues/CompLRevVol5Issue1.pdf. The comments about enforcement in the United States in this section also largely apply to Canada.

[11] Early global-cartel prosecutions include *Lysine, Citric Acid,* and *Vitamins.* John M. Connor, Global Price Fixing 503, xxv (Springer Verlag, 2nd ed. 2008). The definitions used for 'global' cartels – those spanning at least two continents – and 'international' cartels – those spanning at least two nations (defined by reference to nationality of corporate members, determined by location of corporate headquarters or country of incorporation, or by managers' nationalities) – do not necessarily extend to other chapters in this *Handbook.*

[12] John M. Connor, *Cartels & Antitrust Portrayed: Private International Cartels from 1990 to 2008* Slides 59, 61–62 (American Antitrust Institute, Working Paper No. 09-06, 2009), *available at* http://ssrn.com/abstract=1467310.

[13] *Id.* at Slides 84 and 86.

[14] *Id.* at Slide 106. The mean average is much higher – almost 80 per cent of affected sales. *Id.*

[15] *Id.* at Slides 105–106.

[16] As mentioned in footnote 2 above, if criminals are rational actors, optimal (*ex ante*) deterrence requires that expected penalties multiplied by the probability of detection ought to be equal to the expected societal losses from the cartel's illegal price fixing. In this sentence, I assume that cartel managers are good at predicting the additional monopoly profits to be made and at predicting the kind of penalties they might incur. There is some evidence from cartel studies to support these assumptions. Then penalties ought to exceed overcharges for at least two reasons. First, societal losses are greater than the cartel's private gains because the former includes a dead-weight loss and the latter does not. Second, there is also evidence that the probability of detection of cartels

Private enforcement

Unlike any other part of the world, settlements in private antitrust damages suits are the major form of monetary penalties on international cartels in Canada and the United States. The $7.6 billion in international cartel fines collected by the DOJ during 1990–2008 were swamped by the $26.6 billion in private settlements paid to direct and indirect buyers.[17]

Information on public fines is precise, but the outcomes of private suits are difficult to assemble, because most suits end in out-of-court settlements, many of which are not fully reported; very few private suits are resolved in trials with final published judgments.[18] Relative to government fines, antitrust settlement amounts are significantly under-reported. Nevertheless, thorough searches of business and legal news sources turned up satisfactory information on most of the 114 private damages suits against members of international cartels from 1990 to 2007.[19] All but four of the 114 suits in the sample were filed in US or Canadian courts. Information on settlement amounts is available for 92 of the 114 suits, the remainder still being negotiated.

In the United States, private parties have recovered at least $19.7 billion from international-cartel defendants.[20] That includes $13.6 billion in the global cartel cases (of which $3 to $5 billion is from *Vitamins* manufacturers) and $6.0 billion to US plaintiffs injured by North American cartels. In Canada the respective amounts are $164 and $8.7 million. In sum, private plaintiffs in North America were awarded *about five times* the amount collected in fines by the US and Canadian governments.

Evidence that deterrence of cartels is stronger in the United States than elsewhere is inadequate, anecdotal, and hampered by an inability to observe the formation of successful, hidden cartels. Participation by US companies in international cartels is high, but less than the proportional US share of global economic activity might suggest. The number of DOJ cartel cases and number of companies charged has declined during 1990–2008;[21] this could be a result of fewer clandestine cartels (improved deterrence), but could also be attributed to fewer antitrust resources (weaker deterrence). The absolute number of US amnesty applicants and recipients since 1993 exceeds 200, but in the past

---

is less than 33 per cent. If the probability of detection is less than 33 per cent, then the optimal penalties logically must exceed 300 per cent of the gains.

[17] John M. Connor, *Cartels & Antitrust Portrayed: Private International Cartels from 1990 to 2008* Slide 57 (American Antitrust Institute, Working Paper No. 09-06, 2009), *available at* http://ssrn.com/abstract=1467310.

[18] Most large settlements do get reported in the business press or in company financial reports. If the private suit is a class action, there is some information available because many of the opinions of the supervising judges are published on Web-based search engines. The results of suits threatened or launched by firms that opt out of class actions are often unreported in any public source. On the difficulties of gathering information on private antitrust suits, see Robert H. Lande & Joshua P. Davis, *Benefits From Private Antitrust Enforcement: An Analysis of Forty Cases*, 42 U.S.F. L. Rev. 879 (2008).

[19] John M. Connor, *Latin America and the Control of International Cartels* Table 5 (American Antitrust Institute, Working Paper, 2008), *available at* http://ssrn.com/abstract=1156401.

[20] John M. Connor, Global Price Fixing Table 6 (Springer Verlag, 2nd ed. 2008).

[21] John M. Connor, *Anti-Cartel Enforcement by the DOJ: An Appraisal,* 5 Competition Law Review 89, 89–122 (December 2008), *available at* www.clasf.org/CompLRev/Issues/CompLRevVol5Issue1.pdf.

few years has been higher in Europe. Without knowing the relative numbers of cartels operating in each jurisdiction, no deterrence inference is possible. The share of all cartels caught because of the DOJ amnesty program did rise about 60 per cent after the 1993 amnesty program was launched.[22] Another positive sign is that the duration of North American cartels has been relatively short.[23] Finally, although based on a small number of anecdotes, it appears to be true that most executives managing international cartels do consciously avoid meeting in North American venues.

Western Europe: dedicated in principle, slow to implement

The European Commission (EC) began imposing fines on cartels in 1969, with substantial and accelerating fines beginning in the mid-1980s. From 1990–94 to 2006–08, EC fines increased by 29 per cent annually.[24] In 2005, the EC surpassed the DOJ in the annual amount of fines imposed on international cartels, a position it maintained through 2008. Moreover, since 2000 the combined international cartel fines of the EC and the EU's National Competition Authorities (NCAs) have dominated those of other jurisdictions in the world.[25]

By definition, all EC cartel decisions are international.[26] However, it principally tended to target intra-EU cartels until 1997.[27] *Lysine* was the first global cartel fined in the past two decades; the EC began its investigation in June 1997 and issued a decision in June 2000. The *Lysine* fine of US $110 million[28] was the fifth largest ever imposed by the EC. It has fined 89 international cartels $15 billion during 1990–2007, of which 53 were intra-EU and 36 were global. In 2007 the EC had a backlog of over 100 amnesty applications, which makes it likely that large fines by the EC will continue for the next few years. To handle the backlog, in 2009 the EC instituted a process of 'direct settlement' with corporate cartelists that is similar to the DOJ's practice of plea bargaining, in which inculpatory information is exchanged for partial leniency.

Many antitrust specialists are unaware of the recent but accelerating number of

---

22 Nathan H. Miller, *Strategic Leniency and Cartel Enforcement*, 99 American Economic Review 750, 750–68 (2009).

23 John M. Connor, *Cartels & Antitrust Portrayed: Private International Cartels from 1990 to 2008* Slide 44 (American Antitrust Institute, Working Paper No. 09-06, 2009), *available at* http://ssrn.com/abstract=1467310.

24 *Id.* at Slide 67.

25 *Id.* at Slide 70.

26 The EC has jurisdiction over cartels only if substantial inter-state trade can be shown.

27 The EU's first two decisions, *Quinine* and *Dyestuffs,* in 1969 involved global cartels, but there were few such convictions until the *Lysine* decision was announced in 2000. Christopher Harding & Julian Joshua, Regulating Cartels in Europe: A Study of Legal Control of Corporate Delinquency (New York, Oxford University Press, 2003). See *Amino Acids* (Case COMP 36.545/F3) Commission Decision 2001/418/EC (June 7, 2000) [2000] OJ L 152/24; *Quinine Cartel* (Case IV/26.623) Commission Decision 69/240 EEC [1969] OJ L 192/5; *Dyestuffs Cartel* [1969] OJ L 195/11; *In Re Amino Acid Antitrust Litigation*, 1996 WL 164434 (N.D. Ill, Apr. 2, 1996).

28 Note that in this chapter, all monetary amounts are converted to current US dollars. Conversion of a fine occurs on the day a decision is first announced by the referenced antitrust authority. Any subsequent adjustments made to such fines by appeals courts are ignored.

international-cartel prosecutions by NCAs in Europe that are members of the EU-27.[29] Since 1990, each of the members of the EU has had competition laws that are compatible with the EU Treaty. All new members have had to have effective NCAs before joining. Some NCAs predate the Treaty, but all NCAs have developed increasingly convergent anti-cartel laws and policies. For many years, the dividing line between Brussels' anti-cartel activities and those of the NCAs was unclear. Before 1999, an investigation by an NCA that involved some non-domestic firms could be pre-empted by the EC. The devolution of the EC's cartel-prosecution activities to its Member States began in 1999 and became formalized in 2003 with the establishment of the European Competition Network (ECN). Now the NCAs can investigate cartels with significant, but not predominantly, cross-member-state sales. Brussels retains jurisdiction over global cartels and those with large cross-national EU market effects.

The NCAs have become formidable players in the prosecution of international cartels. During 1994–2007, these NCAs fined a total of 112 international cartels, issued six cease-and-desist orders, and were investigating another 20 international cartels in late 2007.[30] The NCAs' total fines amount to $7.4 billion and increased by 39 per cent per year from 1994 to 2008.[31] The total amount of fines imposed is larger than the United States' – an impressive amount given the restricted size of these national economies and the relatively few years of active enforcement.

The first international cartel to be fined by a Member State was *Glass Containers*, a case reported by the national antitrust authority of Italy in June 1997.[32] Italy has been the most aggressive Member State in prosecuting international cartels – 29 in all. The national antitrust authorities in the Netherlands, France, Hungary, and Germany also have become energetic in prosecuting international cartels – 42 cases with fines. All of the Netherlands' authority's cases were launched since mid-2001, shortly after its investigative powers were strengthened. For several years, much of its work was consumed by a major scandal involving bid rigging by more than 2,000 construction companies.

The role of private rights of action in supplementing government fines is extremely limited.[33] The contrast with the size of private settlements in North America is stark. In the European Economic Area (EEA), the EU and its Member States imposed an impressive $21.3 billion in fines on intra-EU international cartels ($15.8 billion) or on global cartels that affected EEA markets ($5.4 billion). In contrast, restitution or private recoveries in Europe amounted to a paltry $200 million or less.[34]

---

29 There are 30 NCAs. Three members of the European Free Trade Association (Norway, Iceland, and Liechtenstein) have agreed by treaty to enforce antitrust laws in a manner consistent with EU law and European Court decisions.

30 John M. Connor, *Latin America and the Control of International Cartels* Table 5 (American Antitrust Institute, Working Paper, 2008), *available at* http://ssrn.com/abstract=1156401. These 138 cartels comprise about one-fourth of the PIC's data set.

31 *Id.* at Slide 69.

32 AGCM, *Produttori di vetro cavo,* 12 June 1997.

33 Ashurst LLP, *Study on the Conditions of Claims for Damages in Case of Infringement of EC Competition Rules,* comparative report for the European Commission (2004), *available at* http://ec.europa.eu/comm/competition/antitrust/actionsdamages/comparative_report_clean_en.pdf.

34 John M. Connor, *Cartels & Antitrust Portrayed: Private International Cartels from 1990 to*

Asia, Africa, and Latin America: green shoots visible

Developments in sanctioning cartels are more recent and spotty on the remaining continents. I provide somewhat more detail on these jurisdictions than those in North America and Europe.

Asia and Oceania

Three Asian nations have active antitrust authorities. The oldest Asian antitrust authority is the Japan Fair Trade Commission (JFTC), established in 1947 during the US occupation.[35] It is the sole enforcer of Japan's Anti-Monopoly Law (AML). Ostensibly an independent agency modeled on the US FTC, for most of its existence the JFTC was overshadowed by more powerful economic ministries. Japan's cartel enforcement differs in many respects from the EU and North American patterns. A very high share of the JFTC's price-fixing cases involve large-scale bid rigging of government tenders. Significant cartel fines[36] were first instituted in 1977; in 1991 and 2006 the surcharge was raised to 6 and 10 per cent, respectively.[37] If a violation is found, these fines are non-discretionary. The JFTC appears reluctant to impose such sanctions, often preferring to issue cease-and-desist orders called 'warnings' or 'guidances.'[38] In 2002 the AML was amended to give the JFTC the right to gather evidence on extraterritorial cartel conduct that affects Japanese markets.[39] As a result, the JFTC subsequently participated in several joint and simultaneous raids with the DOJ and EU. The JFTC adopted a price-fixing leniency program in 2006. While criminal sanctions can be recommended, prison sentences have been rare since 1953 and when imposed are usually suspended.[40]

The Republic of Korea's competition law, the Monopoly Regulation and Fair Trade Act (MRFTA), was passed in 1980; the Korean Fair Trade Commission (KFTC) was

---

2008 Slide 58 (American Antitrust Institute, Working Paper No. 09-06, 2009), *available at* http://ssrn.com/abstract=1467310. In the UK there are more private cases than elsewhere in Europe, but awards remain miniscule by US standards. Barry J. Rodger, *Private Enforcement of Competition Law: The Hidden Story* (2007) (unpublished manuscript).

[35] John M. Connor, *Latin America and the Control of International Cartels* (American Antitrust Institute, Working Paper, 2008), *available at* http://ssrn.com/abstract=1156401; John M. Connor, *Latin America and the Control of International Cartels*, Competition Law and Policy in Latin America 291–324 (Oxford: Hart Publishing, Eleanor M. Fox & D. Daniel Sokol eds., 2009), *draft available at* http://papers.ssrn.com/sol3/papers.cfm?abstract_id=1417571.

[36] Called surcharges, they are technically non-punitive proxies for disgorgement of monopoly profits. Smaller percentages are applied to smaller firms and to non-manufacturing firms. From 1977 to 1991, the surcharge was 1.5 per cent of a participant's affected sales for the most recent three years.

[37] ABA Section of Antitrust Law, Competition Laws Outside the United States, First Supplement (ABA Publishing 2005).

[38] Organisation for Economic Co-Operation and Development (OECD), *Regulatory Reform: Monitoring Review of Japan,* OECD Country Studies 8 (2004), *available at* DAFFE/COMP(2004)11/REV1; Harry First, *Antitrust Enforcement in Japan*, 64 Antitrust Law Journal 137 (1995).

[39] ABA Section of Antitrust Law, Competition Laws Outside the United States 9, First Supplement (ABA Publishing 2005).

[40] James D. Fry, *Struggling to Teeth: Japan's Antitrust Enforcement Regime*, 32 Law and Policy in International Business 825 (July 2001).

created a year later.[41] Although modeled closely on Japan's AML, Korean jurisprudence has been strongly influenced by US and EU competition-law developments.[42] The MRFTA made secret cartels illegal.[43] In 1999, an amendment to the MRFTA contained language that attempts to make cartel behavior a *per se* violation; a guideline issued by the KFTC in May 2002 makes it clear that it intends to apply a *per se* rule to hardcore cartels.[44] The KFTC makes criminal referrals only in hardcore cartel cases.[45] The KFTC decided in 2000 in favor of the legality of extraterritorial prosecutions of cartels, and the first conviction of a global cartel (*Graphite Electrodes*) occurred in 2002.[46] An effective corporate leniency program was instituted in 2001, and the KFTC appears to be the first antitrust authority in the world to offer cash bounties to individuals for information leading to the conviction of cartelists. Imprisonment is possible under the MRFTA, but no prison sentences were imposed until 2007.[47]

Taiwan's Fair Trade Law was enacted with little debate in 1991.[48] Lawrence Liu asserts that it was 'slavishly copied' from Japan's Antimonopoly Law.[49] Cartels among large firms are illegal, but not *per se* illegal.[50] There are many price-fixing exemptions that can be granted by the Taiwan Fair Trade Commission (TFTC), the most dubious being for crisis cartels and small enterprises.[51] Since 2000, Taiwan's antitrust law explicitly endorses extraterritorial prosecutions, but few international cartels have been

---

[41] ABA Section of Antitrust Law, Competition Laws Outside the United States: Volumes I and II (ABA Publishing 2002).

[42] Sang-Seung Yi and Yougjin Jung, *A New Kid on the Block: Korean Competition Law, Policy, and Economics*, 3 Competition Policy International 152, 152–83 (2007), *available at* http://papers.ssrn.com/sol3/papers.cfm?abstract_id=1075324.

[43] OECD, *Korea: Report on Competition Law and Institutions,* OECD 22 (January 2005), *available at* DAFFE/COMP(2005)9.

[44] It is not yet clear whether Korea's courts will agree with the *per se* interpretation of the amendment. OECD, *Korea: Progress in Implementing Regulatory Reform*, OECD Reviews of Regulatory Reform (2007); Woo-Jung Jon, *The Statutory Presumption of Cartel Agreements: Section 19(5) of the Korean Fair Trade Act* (SSRN Working Paper, 2007), *available at* http://ssrn.com/abstract=960103 (concludes that enforcement decisions regarding tacit collusion are also in practice quite similar to those of the EU and the United States).

[45] Sang-Seung Yi and Yougjin Jung, *A New Kid on the Block: Korean Competition Law, Policy, and Economics*, 3 Competition Policy International 152, 152–83 (2007), *available at* http://papers.ssrn.com/sol3/papers.cfm?abstract_id=1075324.

[46] ABA Section of Antitrust Law, Competition Laws Outside the United States 8-9, First Supplement (ABA Publishing 2005).

[47] Korean Fair Trade Commission (KFTC), 2008 Annual Report (2008), *available at* www.ftc.go.kr/eng/.

[48] Lawrence S. Liu, *Fostering Competition Law and Policy: A Facade of Taiwan's Political Economy*, 1 Wash. U. Global Stud. L. Rev. 77 (2002), *available at* http://ssrn.com/abstract=315321; Lawrence S. Liu, *In Fairness We Trust? – Why Fostering Competition Law and Policy Ain't Easy in Asia* (*SSRN Working Paper*, 2004), *available at* http://ssrn.com/abstract=610822 (provides a comprehensive and critical review of the first ten years of the TFTC).

[49] Lawrence S. Liu, *In Fairness We Trust? – Why Fostering Competition Law and Policy Ain't Easy in Asia* (*SSRN Working Paper*, 2004), *available at* http://ssrn.com/abstract=610822.

[50] OECD, *Competition Law and Policy in Chinese Taipei*, OECD (October 2006), *available at* http://www.oecd.org/dataoecd/53/15/38003515.pdf.

[51] Lawrence S. Liu, *In Fairness We Trust? - Why Fostering Competition Law and Policy Ain't Easy in Asia* 55 (*SSRN Working Paper*, 2004), *available at* http://ssrn.com/abstract=610822.

prosecuted.[52] Criminal penalties may be recommended for price fixers, including up to three years' imprisonment, but these are rare in practice.[53]

Australia is a common-law jurisdiction. From 1998 to 2008, the Australian Competition and Consumer Commission (ACCC) fined corporate members of 12 international cartels a total of $95 million. In addition, several managers have been given modest fines. Private suits are permissible, but class actions are rare. One private class action was won by Australian buyers of animal-grade bulk vitamins in 2006 – the first such case in Australia's legal history.[54]

In a global context, the antitrust authorities of Asia (including Oceania) are small players in prosecuting international cartels. During 1990–2007, about 27 Asian-region cartels were investigated or penalized, most of them in markets for intermediate industrial inputs or services.[55] Fifteen were investigated or prosecuted by the KFTC, four by the JFTC, and one by the TFTC. The affected sales of these 27 Asian cartels exceeded $155 billion. In addition to Asian-region cartels, 100 global cartels have been detected, most of which fixed prices in Asia. Affected sales in Asia from global conspiracies were probably in excess of $900 billion.[56] Thus, more than $1.1 trillion in Asian affected sales can be attributed to *known* international cartels with either regional or global geographic scope.[57]

An analysis of a large number of known cartel overcharges, which considers domestic, international and global cartel overcharges from known cartels throughout the world, finds that international cartels operating in Asia generate percentage overcharges equal to the sample mean of all international cartel overcharges: about 29 per cent of affected sales.[58] The sample average overcharges of all global cartels are 10 to 12 percentage points higher than the sample average of all international cartels.[59] Given the above, one may project that international and global cartels have caused at least $500 billion in economic harm to Asian consumers in 1990–2007. Most of these injuries are not being addressed by local antitrust authorities.

Penalties imposed by Asian antitrust authorities on international cartels are sub-optimal. In the aggregate, monetary penalties imposed on international cartels by Asian antitrust authorities in 1990–2007 are at most $1.4 billion.[60] Asian penalties represent

---

52 OECD, *Competition Law and Policy in Chinese Taipei*, OECD (October 2006), *available at* http://www.oecd.org/dataoecd/53/15/38003515.pdf.

53 Lawrence S. Liu, *Fostering Competition Law and Policy: A Facade of Taiwan's Political Economy*, 1 Wash. U. Global Stud. L. Rev. 77 (2002), *available at* http://ssrn.com/abstract=315321.

54 John M. Connor, *Global Antitrust Prosecutions of International Cartels: Focus on Asia*, 31 World Competition 575, 575–605 (2008).

55 *Id.* at Table 1.

56 This projection conservatively assumes that regional affected sales are proportional to GDP.

57 Assuming detection rates of 10 per cent to 33 per cent, 1990–2007 Asian affected sales exceed $4 trillion in current dollars.

58 John M. Connor and Yuliya Bolotova, *A Meta-Analysis of Cartel Overcharges*, 24 International Journal of Industrial Organization 1133 (2006).

59 *Id.* at 1130.

60 John M. Connor, *Global Antitrust Prosecutions of International Cartels: Focus on Asia*, 31 World Competition 575, Table 6 (2008). The degree to which fines, surcharges, and restitution are actually paid is not known.

only 3 per cent of the world total and an even smaller percentage of the prosecuted cartels' affected sales. Most importantly for deterrence, fines are small relative to the harm caused to direct buyers of cartelized products and services in Asia – less than 15 per cent.[61] When one properly considers the probability of detection, actual recoveries are merely 2 to 5 per cent of the optimal penalty. One reason for the low deterrence record of Asian antitrust authorities is their historic tendency to avoid fining *global* cartels. Only two global cartels were penalized by any Asian antitrust authorities: *Vitamins* and *Graphite Electrodes* were surcharged by the KFTC in 2002. Another reason is the absence of private rights of action for Asian buyers harmed by cartels.

Africa

In Africa, only South Africa has a vibrant anti-cartel program that frequently ensnares members of international cartels. The Competition Commission has fined five international cartels a total of $135 million during 2005–2008; there are five more cartels under investigation likely to be fined even higher amounts in 2009–2010. These decisions have been supported by popular opinion and most business organizations. Individual criminal sanctions are possible but rare. Private compensatory suits can be filed, but only a few confidential out-of-court settlements have been reported. Convictions of cartelists will likely soar in the next few years. The Competition Commission initiated a Corporate Leniency Program in 2003. From 2004 to 2006 only six applications were received, but from January 2007 to July 2009, 51 were received.[62]

Latin America

In a global context, the antitrust authorities of Latin America are small players in prosecuting international cartels.[63] During 1990–2007, Latin American antitrust agencies investigated or penalized a total of 21 international cartels, most of them in markets for intermediate industrial inputs or services.[64] The affected sales of these 21 cartels exceed US $20 billion. Of those 21 cartels, 16 operated in Latin America proper; they were investigated or prosecuted by Brazil (eight cartels), Argentina (three), Chile (two), and Mexico, Columbia, and El Salvador (one each). In addition, two global cartels were fined by Brazil and Mexico (*Vitamins* and *Lysine*).[65] The *Vitamins* conviction by Brazil was the result of a long and difficult investigation.

---

[61] *Id.* at Tables 6–7.

[62] Tembinkosi Bonakele, *Evolution of Cartel Enforcement in South Africa,* presentation to the Third Annual Conference on Competition Law, Economics and Policy in South Africa (September 4, 2009) *available at* http://www.compcom.co.za/events/10year.asp.

[63] John M. Connor, *Latin America and the Control of International Cartels* (American Antitrust Institute, Working Paper, 2008), *available at* http://ssrn.com/abstract=1156401; John M. Connor, *Latin America and the Control of International Cartels*, Competition Law and Policy in Latin America 291–324 (Oxford: Hart Publishing, Eleanor M. Fox & D. Daniel Sokol eds., 2009), *draft available at* http://papers.ssrn.com/sol3/papers.cfm?abstract_id=1417571.

[64] John M. Connor, *Latin America and the Control of International Cartels* Table 11 (American Antitrust Institute, Working Paper, 2008), *available at* http://ssrn.com/abstract=1156401.

[65] As of late 2007, at least three more global cartels were under investigation by Brazil's Economic Defense Administration Council (Conselho Administrativo de Defesa Economica or CADE): the *Lysine* cartel had global sales of US $1.9 billion and about US $160 million in

In addition to these 21 prosecuted cartels, another 80 or more global cartels have been detected by other jurisdictions outside Latin America, most of which fixed prices in Latin America.[66] Affected sales in Latin America from known global conspiracies never investigated locally were probably \$100 to \$150 billion.[67]

Private rights of action

In the United States, private parties recovered at least \$19.7 billion from defendants in international cartels during 1990–2008.[68] In Canada and the rest of the world, recoveries during the same period total only \$179 and \$1501 million, respectively. The absolute amounts of recoveries are impressive perhaps, but by themselves say little about cartel deterrence power. There are three ways of measuring the relative size of these private rewards: the ratio of the recovery to the government fine, to affected sales, and to the overcharge.

First, an important fact is that total private damages recouped in 1990–2007 (\$21 billion) is almost as large as the total amount collected worldwide in government fines (\$24 billion).[69] Private settlements announced so far in the United States were *four times* US government fines imposed on international cartels. Second, the median of total monetary penalties as a proportion of affected world-wide sales is 3.3 per cent.[70] Consequently, private recoveries amounted to about 1.6 per cent of affected sales. Third and most relevant for assessing the deterrence value of world-wide cartel penalties is the size of private recoveries relative to damages. In North America, the median international-cartel settlement as a proportion of the overcharge was 103 per cent; for the world as a whole, private settlements recoup only 16 per cent of damages.[71] These cartel settlements are higher than typical domestic price-fixing cases a decade or two ago.[72] Nevertheless, current settlements are still far below the treble damages prescribed

---

Latin America, the *Air-Insulated Switchgear* cartel had about US \$1.8 billion in Latin American affected sales, and the huge *Air Cargo* case with US \$30 to US \$40 billion in Latin American affected commerce.

[66] John M. Connor, *Latin America and the Control of International Cartels* Table 12 (American Antitrust Institute, Working Paper, 2008), *available at* http://ssrn.com/abstract=1156401.

[67] Assuming detection rates are 10 per cent to 33 per cent, total Latin American affected sales of all cartels is somewhere between \$0.5 and \$2 trillion.

[68] John M. Connor, *Latin America and the Control of International Cartels* Table 6 (American Antitrust Institute, Working Paper, 2008), *available at* http://ssrn.com/abstract=1156401.

[69] *Id.*

[70] John M. Connor, *Cartels & Antitrust Portrayed: Private International Cartels from 1990 to 2008* Slide 52 (American Antitrust Institute, Working Paper No. 09-06, 2009), *available at* http://ssrn.com/abstract=1467310. This percentage is overstated because of inflation and the time value of money. Not only is the numerator (settlements) typically paid *seven to ten years after* the cartels' sales revenues are collected, but also the cartelists can invest their illegal profits from the first year of collusion until the year the recovery payments are made.

[71] *Id.*

[72] Mark A. Cohen & David T. Scheffman, *The Antitrust Sentencing Guideline: Is the Punishment Worth the Cost?*, 27 Am. Crim. L. Rev. 331 (1989) (provides a useful historical benchmark. For actual US price-fixing fines from 1955 to 1974, the average fines amounted to only 0.4 per cent of the cartel's affected sales. During 1974–1980, the average price-fixing fines rose to 1.4 per cent of affected commerce). A. Sheer & C. Ho. *Preliminary Review of Sentences Imposed on Organizations*

by US law and the single damages by Canadian law. Moreover, prejudgment interest is not awarded in North American courts, a fact that causes settlements/damages ratios to be seriously overstated.

Private suits are possible in the four Asian/Oceanic jurisdictions discussed above. However, these jurisdictions typically permit only single damages, award only puny damages to successful plaintiffs, restrict discovery, disallow class actions, burden plaintiffs with court costs, delay filings until after official decisions, and have high burdens of proof of damages. In Japan, suits for a maximum of single damages are permitted, but such suits cannot be launched until a JFTC decision of guilt has been rendered. Plaintiffs do not have access to the JFTC's hearing records, and discovery of facts through the Japanese courts appears to be quite limited.[73] Consequently, private cartel damages suits are reported to be rare events that result in very small monetary settlements. In Taiwan, private antitrust suits are permitted for up to single damages, but such suits may not be prosecuted as class actions. Although the rules were relaxed in 2005, the standard of proof required in Taiwanese courts remains a very high hurdle for plaintiffs. In South Korea, plaintiffs in private rights of action also may request up to single damages, and since 2004 they may file cases before the KFTC fines are imposed. Approximately 20 private antitrust suits are filed each year in Korea.[74] Representative actions are permitted for antitrust damages, but not class actions of the US style.[75] Because true class actions are permitted in securities fraud cases, Korea may be the first to change its legal rules in the direction that most resembles that of the United States.

There is very little reporting on the outcomes of private cartel suits outside North America. Information on only three Asian compensatory suits has been found.[76] Although Taiwan's laws on antitrust class actions are ostensibly quite similar to those in North America, in practice few private antitrust suits are successful there.[77] Reasons given include the court costs that must be paid, the absence of civil discovery procedures, and the reluctance of the courts to award large damages.[78] Korea is something of an exception in Asia. About 30 private rights of action for single damages were filed in Korea's courts in 2001–04, and 50 per cent were 'successful' in that they resulted in

---

in 1988, Memorandum to the US Sentencing Commission (August 16, 1989) (survey of 1988 fines that reported average price-fixing fines of only 0.36 per cent of the overcharges).

[73] ABA Section of Antitrust Law, Competition Laws Outside the United States 12, First Supplement (ABA Publishing 2005); Harry First, *Antitrust Enforcement in Japan*, 64 Antitrust Law Journal 137 (1995).

[74] The size of the monetary awards resulting from these suits is not known. A Web search of prominent antitrust law firms by the author found references to activities in Korea with regard to merger cases, but none to Korean-based class actions.

[75] Sang-Seung Yi and Yougjin Jung, *A New Kid on the Block: Korean Competition Law, Policy, and Economics*, 3 Competition Policy International 152, 152–83 (2007), *available at* http://papers.ssrn.com/sol3/papers.cfm?abstract_id=1075324.

[76] John M. Connor, *Latin America and the Control of International Cartels* Table 6, Note C (American Antitrust Institute, Working Paper, 2008), *available at* http://ssrn.com/abstract=1156401.

[77] Lawrence S. Liu, *Fostering Competition Law and Policy: A Facade of Taiwan's Political Economy*, 1 Wash. U. Global Stud. L. Rev. 77, 164–66 (2002), *available at* http://ssrn.com/abstract=315321.

[78] OECD, *Competition Law and Policy in Chinese Taipei*, OECD (October 2006), *available at* http://www.oecd.org/dataoecd/53/15/38003515.pdf.

positive judgments for plaintiffs.[79] In 2007, the Ministry of Defense recovered about $80 million in restitution from an oil cartel.[80] Yet, in general private antitrust litigation 'is not a potent force in Korea' because the law does not allow plaintiffs to seek injunctive relief nor to form class actions.[81] As mentioned above, the one private price-fixing suit won by Australian buyers of animal-grade bulk vitamins in 2006 was the first such case in Australia's legal history.

Private suits are permitted under the laws of five Latin American jurisdictions: Argentina, Brazil, Chile, Mexico, and Peru.[82] However, such suits face so many delays and impediments that exercising these rights is largely theoretical. The principal barriers to launching such suits are the absence of legal traditions and mechanisms for aggregating large numbers of small claims and of something akin to pre-trial discovery. Except for a small number of cases in Brazil, private antitrust suits are practically unknown in Latin America. The absence of private suits outside of North America has a negative effect on deterrence of global cartels, because at most one-third of the global injuries caused by such cartels occur there. At present, buyers in nearly all other parts of the world have no recourse for private compensation in their local court systems.

Concluding observations

International cartelists face investigations, significant fines, and other monetary penalties in a score of national and supranational jurisdictions. Brazil, South Korea, South Africa, Australia, and several Member States of the EU have increasingly aggressive anti-cartel enforcement programs. Criminalization of price-fixing is spreading slowly; individual cartel managers are prosecuted mainly in the United States and Germany and to a lesser extent in Australia, Canada, the UK, the Netherlands, Korea, and South Africa. The world's cartel penalties still originate largely in the three jurisdictions with the greatest experience in combating international cartels: namely, the United States, Canada, and the EU.[83]

Latin American and Asian antitrust authorities play a small role in punishing international cartels, particularly those with a global reach. One reason is the absence of private rights of action or legal impediments to significant compensation for buyers harmed by cartels. This is a pity, because international cartels have had large sales and have caused great economic harm there (Table 2.1). Optimal world-wide cartel deterrence cannot be achieved without more severe cartel penalties in Asia and Latin America.

---

79 OECD, *Korea: Report on Competition Law and Institutions,* OECD 6 (January 2005), *available at* DAFFE/COMP(2005)9.

80 Sang-Seung Yi and Yougjin Jung, *A New Kid on the Block: Korean Competition Law, Policy, and Economics*, 3 Competition Policy International 152, 152–83 (2007), *available at* http://papers.ssrn.com/sol3/papers.cfm?abstract_id=1075324.

81 *Id.* at 159.

82 Daniel A. Crane, *Private Enforcement Against International Cartels in Latin America*, Competition Law and Policy in Latin America 325–349 (Oxford: Hart Publishing, Eleanor M. Fox & D. Daniel Sokol eds., 2009).

83 Japan is an exception. The JFTC is focused almost entirely on domestic bid-rigging schemes. Individual criminal penalties are legally possible but not applied in practice. Only since 2007 or 2008 has the JFTC begun to consider sanctioning companies for price-fixing conduct outside its borders.

Table 2.1 Largest global cartels probably affecting Latin America, 1990–2007, by size of sales

Affected Market	Duration	Rest-of-the-World Sales	Global Penalties
	Months	*$US million*	
Airlines, cargo, fuel surcharge	74	184,585	825.00[p]
Diamonds, rough gem quality	146	131,324	295.00
IATA (Intl. Air Transport Assn.) interline fares	744	79,632	investigation
LCDs (Liquid Crystal Displays), TFP type	24	40332	investigation
Haberdashery (pins, needles, fasteners, ribbons, etc.)	252	17601	221.60
Organic peroxides	323	13460	127.48
Urethane, Polyurethane Plastics	83	10374	23.00
MSG and Nucleotides (IMP, GMP)	49	9855	282.30
Switchgear, air insulated, high voltage, world	255	9300	investigation
DRAMs (digital random access memory semiconductors)	38	8845	1298.00
Vitamins, bulk, sixteen markets	113	8189	7245.00
Carbon Fiber	84	7850	50.50
SRAMs (Static Random Access Memory devices)	95	7451	investigation
Plastic Additives	157	6624	15.50
Steel Tubes, Seamless ('Line Pipe' or 'Oil-Country Tubular Goods')	63	5330	101.50
Hydrogen Peroxide, other industrial bleaches	84	5000	562.90
DVD, '3C' Patent Pool	49	4978	0.41
Switchgear, gas-insulated, high voltage, world	233	3943	974.4
Rubber Processing Chemicals[m]	105	3912	537.00
Bath & kitchen fixtures, high end	84	3192	investigation
Snap buttons, rivets, and other non-zipper fasteners 1	120	2970	216.20
Sherry, DO Committee, ES	876	2833	investigation
Parcel Tankers, Chemical Shipping	50	2775	67.58
Insurance, commercial, brokerage fees, US & UK	45	2500	3413.20
Citric Acid	50	2310	439.99
Polychloroprene Synthetic Rubber (PCP)	31	2093	840.43
Graphite Electrodes	71	1838	1359.75
Methionine	156	1520	568.40
Cathode ray tubes	35	1364	investigation
Zippers	19	1299	9.40
Carbon and Graphite Electrical Products	365	1000	166.25
Diamonds, Industrial	78	1000	40.35
Lysine	35	834	302.15
EPDM synthetic rubber	81	745	255.60
MCAA (monochloroacetic acid)	187	617	329.76
Sorbates	221	475	419.36
Graphite, Isostatic (molded/specialty)	59	472	83.51
Snap buttons, rivets, and fasteners 2	48	450	18.80
Total or median average	84	588,872	21,090

Notes
p) Partial penalties only. Much more to come.

Source: 'Private International Cartels' spreadsheet dated Feb. 12, 2008. Omits some large global cartels for which no reliable affect sales can be estimated.

Despite the higher government fines imposed by the EC and the EU's NCAs, because of the near absence of private rights of action, the EU has not been as successful as North America in imposing monetary penalties that might deter international cartels operating in Western Europe. In the rest of the world private antitrust penalties are negligible. Even from an *ex post* point of view, no international cartel has been required to disgorge 100 per cent of its illegal profits.[84] Therefore, absent government fines far in excess of the current legal maximums, private rights of action are essential to achieving optimal deterrence of international cartels. This statement applies with even greater force to global price-fixing schemes. Without significant increases in cartel detection and in the levels of expected fines or civil settlements, or without expansion in the standing of buyers to seek compensation, international price fixing will remain rational business conduct for decades to come.

[84] John M. Connor, *The Great Global Price-Fixing Conspiracy: Sanctions and Deterrence*, 4 Concurrences: Revue des droits de la concurrences 17, 17–20 (2006).

3 Differing traditions

Jonathan W. Cuneo[1]

Private antitrust enforcement consists of two components: first, a competition law with one or more cognizable offenses; and second, a viable means for private parties to redress those offenses. As this *Handbook* illustrates, it is surely possible to have the first without the second. The United States is historically the center of gravity for both components – antitrust and private rights of action. Even before the sea change in America's trading partners' views of the antitrust laws, foreign interests,[2] including some from Latin America,[3] pursued claims in American courts under the antitrust laws because the United States was the best – if not the only – place to turn to seek legal redress.

So American are the fundamental concepts that both 'trusts' and 'antitrust' are American contributions to the English lexicon. In this context, 'trust' is a nineteenth century term that refers to large agglomerations of economic power under common control. Since passage of the first antitrust act – the Sherman Act in 1890 – the United States has made an at least lip-service commitment to a national policy of free and open competition.

Enforcement of national policies through high-stakes private litigation which carefully balances the rights of aggrieved parties against the due process rights of defendants is also a venerable American tradition. This evenhanded tradition, which includes an independent Federal judiciary, makes large scale litigation possible. The Congressional decision to afford plaintiffs' treble damages and attorneys' fees, as well as joint and several liability and the class device, make many antitrust cases large. In many cases, a cartel's products are distributed in a globalized manner and defendants face governmental investigation as well as private litigation, creating a need for businesses to deal with these risks strategically. Even so, global cartels continue to run amok, as Professor Connor's chapter[4] demonstrates.

For decades, the so-called 'private attorney general' phenomenon appeared to be yet another case of 'American exceptionalism,' as the United States found itself out-of-sync with its most important trading partners. Like jazz, baseball, and Hollywood, however, national commitment to competition is an American export product. The United States

---

[1] Jonathan W. Cuneo, a former Director of the American Antitrust Institute, is a partner in the Washington, D.C., law firm of Cuneo Gilbert & LaDuca, LLP.

[2] Pfizer, Inc. v. Government of India, 434 US 308 (1978).

[3] Minpeco, S.A. v. Hunt, 693 F.Supp. 122 (S.D.N.Y. 1983). A Peruvian company won $197.1 million in damages after the defendants had been found guilty of engaging in price fixing, monopolization and manipulation activities in the world silver markets in violation of the antitrust, commodity and racketeering laws; see generally, Thomas O. Gorman, SEC Actions: A Blog Covering SEC Investigations, Career Highlights (2006), *available at* http://www.secactions.com/pdf/Gorman.pdf.

[4] See Chapter 2, *The Impact of International Cartels.*

does remain virtually alone in some of its procedural innovations, such as treble damages, widespread use of 'opt-out' class joinder devices, and mandatory awards of attorneys' fees to prevailing plaintiffs in antitrust cases, but, as the *Handbook* demonstrates, other countries are beginning to develop effective redress schemes.

The American antitrust private enforcement tradition has deep historical roots in the British Isles; it is intertwined with British history as well as the relations between our countries. In some ways, it is a natural evolution of the traditions that our nation's early colonists imported from England; in other ways, it is a reaction to stifling and anticompetitive British commercial traditions.

The British common law tradition, unlike many civil law traditions, had elements of explicit limitations on central governmental authority. Since English nobles imposed 'checks and balances' on King John at Runnymede through the Magna Carta of 1215, the English monarchy operated under legal limits, increasingly ceding power to Parliament peacefully (with one exception, that is, the Interregnum); and, by 1708, effectively became a constitutional monarchy.[5] In contrast, the French monarchy, which widely exerted dominion over the French economy, met the guillotine in 1793,[6] representing a rejection of sorts of its claims to absolute authority.

The English common law tradition invokes a measure of decentralized dispute resolution. To some extent, courts made determinations by reference to prevailing customs practices and mores that together weave the tapestry of the common law. An essential tradition Americans inherited from their English forbearers is the right of Englishmen (albeit, mostly property owners) to hail one another into court.[7]

Common law antitrust antecedents came from the interplay between the common law and the operation of trade and craft guilds. Through Western Europe, local trade guilds advanced the skills, progress and interests of pre-industrial revolution crafts and trades, but at times sought monopoly status through government decree, local charter or industry standard.[8] Common law monopolization sought to address this at times anticompetitive interaction between merchants and state.[9] Similarly, the 'rule of reason,' sometimes invoked in cases involving agreements to restrain trade, evolved from the

---

[5] In 1708, Queen Anne was the last British monarch to veto an Act of Parliament. 1 David K. Watson, The Constitution of the United States: Its History Application and Construction 355 (Callaghan & Company 1910).

[6] Michel Vovelle, The Fall of the French Monarchy, 1787–1792, 24–25, 32 (Cambridge University Press 1984).

[7] In fact, the Seventh Amendment to the US Constitution provides a right to a jury 'according to the rule of the common law.' US Const. amend VII.

[8] 'Not the shortest and most efficient, but the longest and most labor-consuming process was the prefered technique of production. Advertising was forbidden, and the idea that one master guildsman might produce a better product than his colleagues was regarded as treasonable. In sixteenth century England, when mass production in the weaving trade first reared its ugly head, the guilds protested to the king. The wonderworkshop . . . was thereupon outlawed by His Majesty: such efficiency and concentration of wealth would set a bad precedent.' Robert L. Heilbroner, The Worldly Philosophers: The Lives, Times and Ideas of the Great Economic Thinkers 29 (Simon & Schuster, 6th Ed. 1986).

[9] William Letwin, The English Common Law Concerning Monopolies, 21 U. Chi. L.Rev. 355 (1954); see generally, Stephen F. Ross, Principles of Antitrust Law 12–14 (Foundation Press 1993).

common practice of guild members imposing covenants not to compete on apprentices and subordinates.[10] Thus, primitive common law rules against monopolization and unfair competition took root in the law that colonists imported from England.

The year 1776 was signal in the pre-history of modern antitrust. Through the Declaration of Independence, the American colonies declared that each was an independent state, choosing local control over central control. Among the expressed grievances for that Declaration was that the British would not let the American colonies trade freely with the world, instead insisting that trade be channeled through Great Britain.[11] The economic aspect of the American Revolution was, at least in part, a rebellion against British state-sponsored monopoly trading companies, such as the East India Company, which extracted enormous and unfair prices from colonists. The 1773 'Boston Tea Party,' in which Massachusetts colonists boarded British ships and threw bales of tea into Boston harbor, provoked Parliament to pass its retaliatory and defensive 'Intolerable Acts' that directly led to the Declaration of Independence.[12]

Also in 1776 the Scotsman Adam Smith published the *Wealth of Nations*, the foundational work for free market advocates, setting forth the intellectual case against mercantilist command-and-control economies. Smith argued that free markets would produce optimal results for consumers and ultimately for nations through the operation of the 'Invisible Hand.' Interestingly, Smith noted that guilds frequently served as a hotbed of price fixing: 'People of the same trade seldom meet together, even for merriment and diversion, but the conversation ends in a conspiracy against the public, or in some contrivance to raise prices.'[13]

The debate over the level of government intervention in commerce famously pervaded the early days of the nation. In the years following the Revolutionary War, the thirteen original colonies remained without a central authority and bound themselves together largely through the Articles of Confederation. When that model proved unworkable, the colonists brought forward the Constitution in 1787. Eyeing the pervasive problems that local monopolies had created in England and on the Continent, our Constitutional vessel gave exclusive control over interstate commerce to the federal government.[14]

---

[10] Mitchell v. Reynolds, 24 Eng. Rep. 347 (Q.B. 1711) foreshadowed the modern 'rule of reason' by holding that a restrictive covenant was legal under the common law if it was (1) supported by consideration; (2) voluntary; (3) reasonable in scope; and (4) ancillary to main purpose of the restraint. See Ross, *supra* at 14–15.

[11] In the Declaration of Independence, the colonists held King George accountable 'For cutting off our Trade with all parts of the world' and, at the end of the document, asserted that, 'as Free and Independent States, they have full Power to levy War, conclude Peace, contract Alliances, establish Commerce, and to do all other Acts and Things which Independent States may of right do.' THE DECLARATION OF INDEPENDENCE, para. 18 (US 1776).

[12] The Intolerable Acts served to close off Boston Harbor, until the colonists would pay for the British tea, and to give the royal governor of Massachusetts control over the state legislature. Susan Provost Beller, The Revolutionary War 28 (Benchmark Books 2002).

[13] 1 Adam Smith, An Inquiry into the Nature and Causes of the Wealth of Nations 14 (Adamant Media 2006) (1776).

[14] 'The Congress shall have Power To lay and collect Taxes, Duties, Imposts and Excises, to pay the Debts and provide for the common Defense and general Welfare of the United States. . . . To regulate Commerce with foreign Nations, and among the several States, and with the Indian Tribes. . . .' US CONST. art I, §8.

Thomas Jefferson, the first Secretary of State and Third President, led the intellectual movement for decentralized governance. He argued unsuccessfully to interpose a ban on monopolies in the Bill Of Rights.[15] In contrast, the first Treasury Secretary, Alexander Hamilton, championed a strong central bank and a large role for the central government.

The industrial revolution brought competitive concerns to new levels. Well before the passage of the Sherman Act, the United States Supreme Court faced its first monopolization claim in the landmark case of *Gibbons* v. *Ogden*.[16] Robert Fulton, the inventor of the steamboat, claimed that a charter granted by the State of New York afforded him a monopoly over commercial navigation on the Hudson River – in effect, an exclusive franchise on the lucrative New York and New Jersey commercial river trade. Represented by Daniel Webster (perhaps the most storied advocate in American history), rival operators challenged the state-sponsored monopoly under the interstate commerce clause of the Constitution.[17] Chief Justice John Marshall authored the Court's opinion, stating:

> The appellant contends . . . the [state] laws [affording] the exclusive privilege are repugnant to the Constitution and the laws of the United States . . . This Court is of the opinion that so much of these several laws of the State of New York as prohibits vessels, licensed according to the laws of the United States, from navigating the waters of the State of New York, by means of fire or steam, is repugnant to the said Constitution and void.

The Supreme Court struck down the state-sponsored monopoly not because Congress had passed a law but because it could pass a law, thereby creating the 'dormant' Commerce Clause bar to anticompetitive state regulation of interstate commerce. As *Gibbons* foreshadowed, the industrial revolution transformed the world economy – a global move away from an agrarian and handicrafts economy. Huge industrial combinations were formed to engage in trade with masses of relatively dispersed and powerless buyers and sellers, in many cases through long distance interstate transactions. Centripetal economic forces produced powerful trusts headed by the likes of John D. Rockefeller and J.P. Morgan. A new group of super-wealthy plutocrats emerged, the so-called 'Robber Barons.'

The populist response was Congressional passage of the Sherman Act in 1890, whose major premise was that the states were not powerful enough to regulate trusts by themselves and outlawed monopolies and unreasonable restraints of trade. A key premise of that legislation was that trusts wielded huge economic power and massive political clout; countering this power required multiple, diverse fortified enforcers, including the federal

---

[15] In a letter to James Madison (December 20, 1787), Thomas Jefferson explicitly stated that he wants the Bill of Rights to include 'restriction against monopolies'. Thomas Jefferson, The Essential Jefferson 168 (Jean M. Yarbrough, ed., Hackett Publishing Company 2006).

[16] Gibbons v. Ogden, 22 US 1 (1824).

[17] '[The State] could make the grant for money; and so make the monopoly of navigation over those waters a direct source of revenue . . . But the waters of New York are no more the subject of exclusive grants by the State, than the monopoly of trade, than monopoly of navigation . . . . To all this, no answer is to be given but one, that the concurrent power of the States, concurrent though it be, is yet subordinate to the legislation of the Congress; and that therefore Congress may, whenever it pleases, annul the State legislation. . . .' Daniel Webster, *The Great Speeches and Orations of Daniel Webster* 119 (Edwin Percy Whipple, ed., Little Brown and Company 1914).

government, the states and private plaintiffs. The Sherman Act equipped these enforcers with powerful tools and incentives, providing private enforcers with a federal forum, treble damages and attorneys' fees. These muscular remedies were meant to provide private citizens with the power to hold gargantuan corporations accountable.

The European responses to the industrial revolution were different. Antitrust played no role. On the Continent, rival forms of totalitarian governmental economic control – fascism (which is, after all, an extreme form of state-sponsored capitalism) and communism (which eschews all private property in favor of a collectivist state-controlled regime) battled first with words and then with armed forces. A common theme was a strong central government. Laissez-faire capitalism – with antitrust acting as the umpire – simply did not take root. In Western Europe, state-supported cartels such as I.G. Farben[18] dominated the landscape.

Even in name, post-war capitalist Western Europe did not adopt free market competition as its organizing principle until the Treaty of Rome in 1957.[19] It would take several decades for the free trade principles to overcome manifold barriers – multiple national borders with intercontinental trade barriers, strong protectionist instincts, and differing currencies, to name just three.

After World War II, our European allies and Canada resisted full application of American antitrust laws, both public and private. To our trading partners, the US laws (particularly the Federal antitrust laws) in their extraterritorial application under the 'effects' doctrine, with criminal sanctions, multiple damages, and the hospitality of the United States courts to international disputes, were akin to frightening extraterrestrial beings.

Many American states had passed their own antitrust laws patterned on the federal law. Federal Court was bad enough, but the prospect of being hailed into a state court whose judgments were fully protected by the Full Faith and Credit Clause of the Constitution caused sweaty palms around the world. The application of federal and state antitrust laws replete with criminal sanctions, joint and several liability, treble damages, and per se

---

18 'Criminal and civil proceedings were brought by the United States in March 1942 against Standard Oil Co. (New Jersey) and certain of its subsidiaries charging violations of the Sherman Act based on the agreements between Standard and I. G. Farben. The defendants pleaded nolo contendere to the criminal information and consented to the entry of a decree in the civil case terminating the cartel arrangements.' Herman A. Berman, Cartels and Enemy Property, 11 Law & Contemp. Probs. 110–111 (1945).

19 'The following shall be prohibited as incompatible with the common market; all agreements between undertakings, decisions by associations of undertakings and concerted practices which may affect trade between Member States and which have as their object or effect the prevention restriction or distortion of competition within the common market, and in particular those which: (a) directly or indirectly fix purchase or selling prices or any other trading conditions; (b) limit or control production, markets, technical development, or investment; (c) share markets or sources of supply; (d) apply dissimilar conditions to equivalent transactions with other trading parties, thereby placing them at a competitive disadvantage; (e) make the conclusion of contracts subject to acceptance by the other parties of supplementary obligations which, by their nature or according to commercial usage, have no connection with the subject of such contracts.' Treaty Establishing the European Community as Amended by Subsequent Treaties, Rome, March 25, 1957, Part Three, Title V. 'Common Rules on Competition, Taxation and Approximation of Laws,' Ch. 1, §1, Article 85, *available at* http://www.hri.org/docs/Rome57/.

rules to the participants in the international uranium cartel in the 1970s, members of the North Atlantic ocean shipping trades, as well as entrenched international air carriers in the 1980s were points of friction between the United States and its North American and European allies and trading partners. Diplomatic notes, 'blocking' statutes, 'claw back' provisions, even occasional head of state tête-à-têtes were the order of the day.[20]

In 1947, the Canadian province of Ontario passed the Business Records Protection Act,[21] the first 'blocking statute' – a protectionist provision that essentially made it illegal for domestic corporations to comply with grand jury subpoenas under the American antitrust laws. Others of our trading partners quickly followed suit to directly advance the short-term interests of constituent firms in a mercantilist reprise. The Canadian and British Parliaments joined in, passing nationwide blocking statutes and 'claw back' provisions (allowing defendants who pay treble damages in American courts to recover damages in excess of compensatory damages in the sovereign courts of other countries) in the late 1970s. Australia, South Africa and others followed suit.[22]

Thirty years ago, no futurist or would-be time traveler could have predicted that strong competition policy would become a consensus or that private rights of action would be an American export product. How things have changed! In the developed world, a globalized, post-Cold War now exists that certain types of anticompetitive behavior (most particularly, 'hard core' cartel activity) are injurious.

The European Union, whose member nations once harbored cartel activity, has developed an active antitrust enforcement program that has vigorously pursued cartels and even developed single firm dominance cases that have been a thorn in the side to large American companies, such as Microsoft and Intel! What a role reversal! Several times a year, it seems the financial pages bring new stories of how police forces in Europe, Canada and Asia are executing search warrants to stamp out cartels. New legislation in many countries contemplates international governmental cooperation. 'Positive comity' allows a government antitrust authority in one country to request a second country's antitrust authority to commence an investigation in that country.[23] The European

---

20 In 1982, Laker Airways, parent of the budget airline Skytrain that flew from London to New York, collapsed after the other six airlines that operated between the US and Great Britain 'colluded to oppose' the service while the value of the pound dropped simultaneously. The British courts ruled that the other airlines had applied illegal price pressure on the company; however, in the United States, President Ronald Reagan decided not to seek criminal charges against the airlines. *Low-cost Airline Pioneer Laker Dies*, N.Y. TIMES, Feb. 11, 2006, *available at* http://www.nytimes.com/2006/02/11/world/europe/11iht-web.obit.laker.html.

21 This 'blocking statute' grew out of a United States investigation into the Canadian lumber industry. Jim Walker and Matthew Benjamin, Going it Alone: The Costs Of Unilateral Law Enforcement, 15 Business Crimes Bulletin 1 (2008). Ironically, the authors document that France used its blocking statute for the first time in 2008 with respect to an investigation by the State of California.

22 Countries that had passed blocking statutes to prevent the application of US antitrust judgments include the Philippines, the UK, Canada, Australia, South Africa, and France. ABA Section of Antitrust Law, Antitrust Law Developments 1255 (6th ed. 2007).

23 See Agreement Between the Government of the United States of America and the Commission of the European Communities Regarding the Application of Their Competition Laws (1991); Agreement Between the Government of the United States of America and the

model of enforcement features a strong central authority in contrast to American decentralization.[24]

Western countries other than the United States and Canada are beginning to experiment with private causes of action, as the accompanying chapters amply demonstrate. Under the European model strong government agencies are the primary enforcers, and private enforcers have a backseat role. The private action can either be dependent upon a prior governmental action, or independent.

There are even signs that the American system of aggregating claims is gaining further consideration. The United Kingdom permits 'representative actions.' Class actions, without a predominance requirement, are cropping up above our northern borders in Canada. Other countries are also considering aggregation devices.

And things in the US have changed as well. The antitrust laws of our nation are generally understood to be much kinder and gentler on vertical restraints than they were in the 1960s and 1970s. The London reinsurance market was certainly calmed when the Supreme Court ruled its collective refusals to underwrite certain risks were not a 'boycott' subject to the antitrust laws.[25] Courts have imposed new requirements on certification of damage class actions and are imposing new requirements on pleadings that have cumulatively placed important restraints on private enforcement.[26]

There seems to be an emerging consensus that certain types of anticompetitive conduct are detrimental to society and that government and courts should work together to stamp out these behaviors. It remains to be seen whether private actions – as supplemental to public enforcement – will bloom around the world.

European Communities on the Application of Positive Comity Principles in the Enforcement of Their Competition Laws (1998).

[24] 'In the U.S., the basic antitrust laws are enforced not only by governmental actions for injunctive relief but by criminal penalties and by private suits brought by injured parties (or by states on their behalf) for treble damages injunctive relief and attorney fees. . . . Most US antitrust cases are brought by private parties seeking damages rather than by centralized government agencies.

In the EC . . . virtually all enforcement is done by the European Commission (or national competition agencies) in a way roughly analogous to the Federal Trade Commission in the United States. . . . In recent years, the European Commission has felt growing interest for private law enforcement of EC competition rules but . . . has done very little to overcome the procedural obstacles preventing the development of private antitrust legislation.' Einer Elhauge & Damien Geradin, *Global Antitrust Law and Economics* 4 (Foundation Press 2007).

[25] Hartford Fire Insurance Co., et al. v. California, et al., 509 US 764 (1993).

[26] Sharon L. Gold, Supreme Court Prescribes New Pleading Requirements, 14 August 2009, Wyatt Employment Law Report, *available at* http://wyattemployment.wordpress.com/2009/08/14/supreme-court-prescribes-new-pleading-requirements/.

PART II

EXPERIENCING PRIVATE ENFORCEMENT IN THE US

4 Defining antitrust violations in the US

Bonny E. Sweeney[1]

Introduction

Federal and state governments and private parties have been actively enforcing competition laws in the United States since the passage of the Sherman Act in 1890. In addition to the Sherman, Clayton and Federal Trade Commission Acts, which are the principal federal statutes regulating competition, there are numerous additional federal laws and a multitude of competition laws from every state and the District of Columbia. While the welter of federal statutes, state statutes and judge-made law can be confusing and at times contradictory, there are broad common themes that run through all of these sources of law. First, while there is disagreement about what the primary goal of competition law ought to be,[2] federal and state courts generally agree that these statutes should be interpreted in a manner that 'will yield the best allocation of our economic resources, the lowest prices, the highest quality and the greatest material progress . . . .'[3] For this reason, modern competition law in the United States is concerned with the protection of competition, not competitors (with a few notable exceptions).[4]

A second defining characteristic of United States competition law is the importance of the private plaintiff. Unlike in many other jurisdictions, private parties can sue for redress of antitrust violations. In fact, most antitrust cases in the United States are litigated solely by private parties. While there are many instances of private litigation following government prosecutions or investigations, most private litigation is independent of any government investigation. In some cases, private lawsuits precede government investigations.

The availability of treble damages and the class action mechanism reflects the importance of private actions in ensuring adequate enforcement of the antitrust laws. Many antitrust actions in the United States – particularly price-fixing cases in which individual injuries are typically modest – are pursued as class actions, in which one or a handful of representatives sue on behalf of a much larger group of affected individuals or businesses. Most antitrust class actions are 'opt-out' cases seeking damages. In an

---

1 Bonny E. Sweeney is a partner at Coughlin Stoia Geller Rudman & Robbins LLP in San Diego, California, where she specializes in antitrust class action litigation.

2 *See* Foer, Albert A. (2005), 'The Goals of Antitrust: Thoughts on Consumer Welfare in the U.S.', *available at* http://www.antitrustinstitute.org/archives/files/350.pdf, accessed 16 October 2009.

3 *N. Pac. Ry. Co. v. United States*, 356 US 1, 4 (1958).

4 *Brunswick Corp. v. Pueblo Bowl-O-Mat*, 429 US 477, 488 (1977) (antitrust laws are designed to protect competition, not individual competitors; bowling alleys that complained that rescue of failing competitors diminished their profits did not suffer injury 'by reason of anything forbidden in the antitrust laws'). Some have criticized the Robinson-Patman Act (see discussion below) and similar state laws as inimical to the goals of modern antitrust law because they protect competitors.

opt-out class action, class members do not have to consent to be included in the litigation and usually do not even know of it until the class has been certified and notice has been sent out, at which time they have an opportunity to opt out and bring their own lawsuit. Certification of a lawsuit as a class action places significantly more pressure on the defendant, as a damages class can consist of thousands or even millions of class members.

Federal and state antitrust litigation is also characterized by broad pre-trial discovery. Under federal civil procedure rules, a party can require the other side (or a third party) to produce vast quantities of documents, respond to written questions, and give live testimony under oath. Until recently, a private plaintiff could file an antitrust lawsuit with only the most limited factual allegations, and shortly thereafter begin conducting discovery. While recent Supreme Court decisions have placed limitations on the plaintiff's ability to advance a complaint with only skeletal allegations, the plaintiff's ability to obtain discovery if it can show a plausible factual basis for its allegations remains nearly unfettered. Most states have rules of civil procedure that are similar or in some cases identical to the federal rules, allowing significant pre-trial discovery in state court actions as well.

Finally, at both the federal and state level, competition law is flexible and 'supple enough . . . to take in stride the competitive issues presented by the new economy.'[5] Written for the most part in broad and general terms, federal and state antitrust statutes must be interpreted and filled in by judges, case-by-case. Federal law and the laws of all states except Louisiana are based on a common law system, under which judicial decisions have binding precedential effect on future cases. This feature – in which law is developed case-by-case – facilitates the constant and gradual evolution of competition law doctrine.

This chapter summarizes the principal types of conduct that are subject to scrutiny under United States antitrust laws, and the elements that a private plaintiff must prove under each. While the focus will be on federal law (which is the primary source of competition law in the United States), state law will be discussed briefly, particularly where it diverges from federal law. The chapter is organized along two main themes: (1) joint conduct among two or more actors and (2) unilateral or single-firm conduct. This structure mimics the federal Sherman Act, which separately regulates concerted conduct (under §1) and single-firm conduct (under §2).

Restraints of trade: agreements that restrict competition

Under federal law, agreements that restrict competition are typically evaluated under §1 of the Sherman Antitrust Act, which declares illegal '[e]very contract, combination in the form of trust or otherwise, or conspiracy, in restraint of trade or commerce among the several States, or with foreign nations.'[6] To prevail on a §1 claim, the government must prove three elements: (1) the existence of an agreement between two or more separate

---

[5] Varney, Christine A. (2009), 'Vigorous Antitrust Enforcement in this Challenging Era', *available at* http://www.usdoj.gov/atr/public/speeches/245777.htm, accessed 16 October 2009 (quoting Posner, Richard A. (2001), *Antitrust in the New Economy*, Antitrust Law Journal, 68 (3), 925 (hereinafter, 'Varney Speech').

[6] 15 U.S.C. §1.

parties that (2) unreasonably restricts competition and (3) affects interstate or foreign commerce. A private party must also prove each of these elements, and in addition prove either that he has been 'injured in his business or property' as a result of the unlawful agreement, or that such harm is imminent.[7]

'Contract, combination or conspiracy'

Section 1 is potentially applicable to all types of joint action between two or more separate parties, including overt agreements (such as agreements among members of a joint venture or exclusive dealing contracts) and secret agreements (such as price-fixing cartels). It applies to horizontal agreements (agreements among competitors) and to vertical agreements (agreements between participants in a supply chain, such as a manufacturer and its distributor). It also applies to coerced 'agreements,' such as tying arrangements. Section 1 does not apply to agreements among members of a single corporate entity, such as an agreement between a parent corporation and its wholly-owned subsidiary.[8]

Proving the existence of a 'contract, combination or conspiracy' is often a dispositive issue in cases alleging secret horizontal agreements (price-fixing agreements or agreements to allocate markets or customers among competitors) or challenging vertical price restraints. In these contexts, substantial case law has developed as to what constitutes sufficient proof, and as to appropriate methods of proof.

A plaintiff may prove the existence of a contract, combination or conspiracy through direct or circumstantial evidence. A secret agreement will nearly always need to be proven through circumstantial evidence.[9] The agreement need not be in writing, and it

---

7 Section 4 of the Clayton Act permits 'any person . . . injured in his business or property by reason of anything forbidden in the antitrust laws' to recover treble damages. 15 U.S.C. §15(a). Section 16 of the Clayton Act entitles '[a]ny person . . . upon . . . a showing that the danger of irreparable loss or damage is immediate . . . by a violation of the antitrust laws' to obtain an injunction. 15 U.S.C. §26.

8 In *Copperweld Corp. v. Independence Tube Corp.*, 467 US 752 (1984), the Supreme Court held that a parent corporation and its wholly owned subsidiary are a single entity for antitrust purposes, and so immune from antitrust liability under §1. *Copperweld Corp.*, 467 US at 771. Lower courts have subsequently extended the single-entity defense beyond the context of a parent-subsidiary relationship to include other affiliate relationships. *See, e.g., Jack Russell Terrier Network v. Am. Kennel Club, Inc.*, 407 F.3d 1027, 1035 (9th Cir. 2005) (national breed club and its affiliates not capable of conspiring as separate entities); *Eleven Line, Inc. v. N. Tex. State Soccer Ass'n*, 213 F.3d 198, 205 (5th Cir. 2000) (volunteer sports league and parents of players not found to be conspirators, much less joint venturers); *Chicago Prof'l Sports Ltd. P'ship v. NBA*, 95 F.3d 593, 597-600 (7th Cir. 1996) ('*Bulls II*') ('when acting in the broadcast market the NBA is closer to a single firm than to a group of independent firms'); *Mt. Pleasant v. Associated Elec. Coop., Inc.*, 838 F.2d 268, 271, 276-77 (8th Cir. 1988) (related corporate entities did not have the requisite plurality to form conspiracy). A case currently pending before the US Supreme Court, *American Needle, Inc. v. NFL*, No. 08-661, could determine the extent to which joint ventures can take advantage of the single-entity defense. In *American Needle*, the Seventh Circuit held that the team members of the National Football League acted as a single entity when they collectively licensed their separately owned trademarks, and so were immune from scrutiny under §1 of the Sherman Act.

9 *See, e.g., United States v. Wash.*, 586 F.2d 1147, 1153 (7th Cir. 1978) ('By its nature conspiracy is conceived and carried out clandestinely, and direct evidence of the crime is rarely available.

need not even be express.[10] But there must be sufficient evidence to prove that the parties acted in concert. Specifically, the plaintiff 'must present evidence that "tends to exclude the possibility" that the alleged conspirators acted independently.'[11]

It is not unlawful under the Sherman Act for businesses in a highly concentrated industry to engage in similar or identical behavior, including pricing their products identically, so long as they have not agreed to do so. This conduct – 'conscious parallelism' – can be found unlawful, however, if the plaintiff proves enough additional indicia of agreement – called 'plus factors' – to enable the fact-finder to infer an agreement. The following 'plus factors' are often alleged, in addition to consciously parallel behavior, in support of a conspiracy allegation: (1) evidence that the defendants engaged in behavior that would have been against their self-interest if they had acted alone, but in their self-interest if their competitors engaged in the same conduct; (2) opportunities to conspire; (3) motive to conspire, including poor economic performance prior to the conspiracy; (4) exchange of price information; and (5) structural features that make collusion (that is, an agreement to fix prices, allocate markets or otherwise restrain competition) more likely, such as a limited number of suppliers and a homogenous product.[12]

In its 2007 decision in *Bell Atlantic Corp. v. Twombly*,[13] the Supreme Court clarified the standards for pleading a §1 antitrust conspiracy claim in the context of conscious parallelism. The Court held that allegations of parallel conduct combined with a 'bare assertion of conspiracy' were insufficient, even at the pleading stage, to sustain a complaint:

> [A]n allegation of parallel conduct and a bare assertion of conspiracy will not suffice. Without more, parallel conduct does not suggest conspiracy, and a conclusory allegation of agreement at some unidentified point does not supply facts adequate to show illegality. Hence, when allegations of parallel conduct are set out in order to make a §1 claim, they must be placed in a context that raises a suggestion of a preceding agreement, not merely parallel conduct that could just as well be independent action.[14]

Further, the complaint must include 'plausible grounds to infer an agreement' or 'enough factual matter (taken as true) to suggest that an agreement was made.'[15] The Court concluded that the alleged conspiracy was not plausible because each of the

---

Thus, circumstantial evidence from which the jury could reasonably infer the existence of an agreement is permissible.').

[10] *United States v. General Motors Corp.*, 384 US 127, 142–43 (1966) ('explicit agreement is not a necessary part of a Sherman Act conspiracy').

[11] *Matsushita Elec. Indus. Co. v. Zenith Radio Corp.*, 475 US 574, 588 (1986); *Monsanto Co. v. Spray-Rite Serv. Corp.*, 465 US 752, 768 (1984).

[12] *In re Coordinated Pretrial Proceedings in Petroleum Prods. Antitrust Litig.*, 906 F.2d 432, 445–50 (9th Cir. 1990); *see* Posner, Richard A. (1976), Antitrust Law, Chicago, US: University of Chicago Press. *In re High Fructose Corn Syrup Antitrust Litig.*, 295 F.3d 651, 657 (7th Cir. 2002).

[13] *Bell Atl. Corp. v. Twombly*, 550 US 544 (2007).

[14] *Twombly*, 550 US at 556–57. In *Ashcroft v. Iqbal*, 129 S.Ct. 1937, 1953 (2009), the Court made clear that the *Twombly* standard applies to all civil actions, and not just antitrust cases.

[15] *Twombly*, 550 US at 556. The Court 'retired' the pleading standard of *Conley v. Gibson*, 355 US 41 (1957) which had long held that in a notice pleading case, 'a complaint should not be dismissed for failure to state a claim unless it appears beyond doubt that the plaintiff can prove no set of facts in support of his claim which would entitle him to relief.' *Twombly*, 550 US at 561.

defendants had a rational economic incentive to engage unilaterally in each of the parallel acts alleged by plaintiffs to be suggestive of conspiracy.[16]

Affecting interstate or foreign commerce

The requirement that the challenged agreement affect interstate or foreign commerce is easily satisfied. Even if an agreement is limited by its terms to conduct within a state, it will be found to affect interstate or foreign commerce if the parties or the commerce affected by the restraint have some relation to interstate or foreign commerce.[17]

Unreasonably restrains competition

As the Supreme Court recognized long ago, virtually every commercial contract is, by definition, a 'restraint of trade.' Thus, the Sherman Act only prohibits those agreements that are 'unreasonably restrictive of competitive conditions.'[18] An agreement can unreasonably restrict competitive conditions if it has the effect of raising prices, restricting output, diminishing quality, limiting choice, or creating, maintaining, enhancing or preserving an entity's market power.

Rule of reason vs. per se analysis

In determining whether an agreement unreasonably restricts competition under §1 of the Sherman Act, courts employ one of two standards of analysis. The 'rule of reason' standard, which is used in most cases, analyzes the market and then weighs all of the harmful effects of the restraint against its benefits to determine whether the restraint 'is one that promotes competition or one that suppresses competition.'[19]

To prove a §1 case under the rule of reason standard, the plaintiff must first define the relevant product and geographic markets[20] affected by the challenged restraint, and

---

[16] For a detailed discussion of parallel conduct and the impact of *Twombly* on notice pleading standards, see Chapter 9 of this *Handbook*.

[17] *See, e.g., McLain v. Real Estate Bd., Inc.*, 444 US 232 (1980) (local real estate brokers' agreement to fix the price of sales commissions affected interstate commerce because the commission rates affected local residential real estate sales, which in turn affected interstate demand for financing and title insurance).

[18] *Standard Oil Co. v. United States*, 221 US 1, 58 (1911).

[19] *Nat'l Soc'y of Prof'l Eng'rs v. United States*, 435 US 679, 691 (1978).

[20] Definition of the relevant market is necessary to provide the context in which to assess the competitive effect of the restraint. *Cont'l T.V., Inc. v. GTE Sylvania*, 433 US 36, 53 n.21 (1977). Relevant market analysis is also employed under §2 of the Sherman Act (monopolization), §3 of the Clayton Act (certain tying and exclusive dealing agreements), §7 of the Clayton Act (mergers and acquisitions), the Robinson-Patman Act (price discrimination) and §5 of the FTC Act (unfair methods of competition). The standards for determining the relevant product and geographic markets are nearly identical under these statutes, and courts conducting a relevant market analysis rely on cases decided under each. While a thorough description of relevant market analysis is beyond the scope of this chapter, '[t]he outer boundaries of a product market are determined by the reasonable interchangeability of use or the cross-elasticity of demand between the product itself and substitutes for it.' *Brown Shoe Co. v. United States*, 370 US 294, 325 (1962). A similar test is used to determine the relevant geographic market, which the Supreme Court has described as 'the "area of effective competition . . . in which the seller operates, and to which the purchaser can practicably turn for supplies."' *United States v. Philadelphia Nat'l Bank & Trust*, 399 US 321, 359 (1963); *Brown Shoe Co. v. United States*, 370 US 294, 336–37 (1962) ('The criteria to be used in

demonstrate that the defendant has market power in those markets.[21] Next, the plaintiff must prove that the challenged restraint has a substantial anticompetitive effect.[22] If the plaintiff demonstrates that the agreement has a substantially harmful effect on competition (and not just individual competitors), and in addition demonstrates injury or imminent threat of injury to its business or property, it has established a prima facie case under §1. The burden then shifts to the defendant to proffer a 'procompetitive justification.' In other words, the defendant must show that the restraint benefits competition by, for example, promoting interbrand competition, enhancing efficiency, increasing output, or making available a product or products that would not otherwise be available. If the defendant successfully proffers a non-pretextual procompetitive justification for the restraint, the burden shifts back to the plaintiff to show either that the defendant can advance the proffered procompetitive justification through less restrictive means, or that the anticompetitive harm of the conduct outweighs the procompetitive benefits.[23]

---

determining the appropriate geographic market are essentially similar to those used to determine the relevant product market . . . .').

[21] Market power is 'the ability to raise prices above those that would be charged in a competitive market.' *Nat'l Collegiate Athletic Ass'n v. Board of Regents*, 468 US 85, 109 n. 38 (1984) ('*NCAA*'). Market power can be proven by evidence of a high market share and barriers to new entry. What constitutes a sufficiently high market share to raise competitive concerns has never been definitively answered by the Supreme Court, and varies according to the type of restraint under review. For horizontal restraints, the courts and the enforcement agencies (the Federal Trade Commission ('FTC') and the Antitrust Division of the Department of Justice ('DOJ')) typically require that the competitors whose conduct is being challenged have a combined market share of at least 20 per cent. For vertical restraints like tying arrangements and exclusive dealing, the threshold is at least 30 per cent. For monopolization claims the threshold is generally considered to be 70 per cent. Pearlstein, Debra J. (2002), Antitrust Law Developments, I, US: American Bar Association, pp. 230–232.

Where the plaintiff can prove that the restraint caused 'actual detrimental effects, such as a reduction of output,' no inquiry into market power is required, because the market power inquiry is merely 'a surrogate for detrimental effect.' *FTC v. Ind. Fed'n of Dentists*, 476 US 447, 460–61 (1986) (citation omitted).

[22] *United States v. Topco Assocs., Inc.*, 405 US 596, 606 (1972) (practices that 'in some insignificant degree' restrain competition are not unlawful). The plaintiff must also show that the restraint has a substantially adverse impact on the competitive process, as opposed to a competitor or a group of competitors. *Brunswick Corp.*, 429 US 477.

[23] *Cal. Dental Ass'n v. FTC*, 526 US 756 (1999). In *California Dental*, the Court instructed courts applying a rule of reason analysis to use a 'sliding scale' at each step of the burden-shifting test, so that the degree of proof required depends on the nature of the conduct considered and the degree of proof offered at the previous step. The Court stated that sometimes the analysis can be conducted in 'the twinkling of an eye' and that the analysis can be truncated if at any point the outcome is clear. *Cal. Dental Ass'n*, 526 US at 781 n.15, 780. In *United States v. Microsoft Corp.*, 253 F.3d 34 (D.C. Cir. 2001), a §2 monopolization case, the Court of Appeals for the Second Circuit described a rule of reason analysis that is more structured and sequential than the analysis often employed by courts under §1. Under this approach, after the plaintiff has established that defendant's conduct has caused anticompetitive effects, the burden shifts to the defendant to proffer a procompetitive justification for its conduct. If it succeeds in showing a procompetitive justification, the burden shifts back to the plaintiff to show that the defendant can advance its procompetitive justification through less restrictive means. If plaintiff can meet this burden, it will prevail. If not, plaintiff must then demonstrate that the anticompetitive harm of the conduct outweighs the procompetitive benefits. *Microsoft*, 253 F.3d at 58–59.

A few categories of agreements are deemed so harmful to competition that they are per se unlawful without analysis either of market conditions or their actual competitive effects.[24] Price-fixing, bid-rigging and market and customer allocation agreements among horizontal competitors are per se unlawful.[25] In addition, some restraints can be analyzed either under a rule of reason or a modified per se standard of illegality.

The modified per se standard, also referred to as the 'quick look' rule of reason standard, is more rigorous than the per se standard but less rigorous than a full blown rule of reason analysis. Under a 'quick look,' an analysis of market power is not required because the restraint at issue – typically one that increases price or reduces output – is obviously harmful to competition. On the other hand, the agreement may have some procompetitive benefits, making application of the per se standard inappropriate. For example, the Supreme Court held that a National Collegiate Athletic Association (NCAA) rule limiting the number of football games its member schools could televise was a naked restriction on output that had 'significant potential for anticompetitive effect. . . .'[26] But because the rule was imposed in an industry 'in which horizontal restraints on competition are essential if the product is to be available at all,' application of the per se rule was inappropriate.[27]

Determining which standard of analysis applies has profound implications for private litigation. A full-blown rule of reason analysis requires extensive economic analysis of the relevant product and geographic markets, market power, and the competitive impact of the challenged agreement. This analysis is costly and increases significantly the length and uncertainty of litigation. Thus, a private plaintiff will always attempt to fit its claims within one of the categories of claims that are subject to per se analysis. And the defendant, in turn, will virtually always contend that the case must be analyzed under the rule of reason.[28]

Horizontal restraints

Horizontal restraints are agreements among actual or potential competitors. Vertical restraints, in contrast, are agreements between parties who stand at different levels in a chain of distribution, such as an agreement between a manufacturer and its distributor.

---

[24] A practice that 'appears to be one that would always or almost always tend to restrict competition and decrease output' rather than 'increase economic efficiency and render markets more, rather than less, competitive,' is subject to the per se rule and is deemed illegal without any inquiry into the purported business justifications or the competitive injury. *Broadcast Music, Inc. v. Columbia Broad. Sys., Inc.*, 441 US 1, 19–20 (1979) (citation omitted).

[25] *FTC v. Superior Ct. Trial Lawyers Ass'n*, 493 US 411, 421–23 (1990) (agreement to restrict output); *Arizona v. Maricopa Cty Med. Soc'y*, 457 US 332, 357 (1982) (price fixing); *United States v. Koppers Co.*, 652 F.2d 290, 294 (2d Cir. 1981) (bid rigging); *Palmer v. BRG of Ga., Inc.*, 498 US 46, 49–50 (1990) (agreement to allocate markets).

[26] *NCAA*, 468 US at 104. *See also FTC v. Ind. Fed'n of Dentists*, 476 US 447 (1986) (quick look rule of reason applied to agreement among members of a dentists' association to withhold x-rays requested by insurers evaluating claims).

[27] *NCAA*, 468 US at 100–60.

[28] For further discussion of rule of reason versus per se analysis, see Chapter 5 of this *Handbook*.

Because vertical restraints are almost never analyzed under a per se standard of illegality, the distinction is critical.[29]

Horizontal agreements that may be illegal

CARTELS Cartels – organizations of horizontal competitors that conspire to fix prices, restrict output, rig bids or allocate customers or territorial or product markets – have long been considered the 'supreme evil of antitrust.'[30] In the United States, the only criminal enforcement of antitrust laws is targeted against cartels. Even during periods of relatively relaxed enforcement of the federal antitrust laws, the DOJ's Antitrust Division continued to make cartel prosecution a top priority.[31] Cartel members who fix prices, agree on output restrictions, allocate customers or markets or rig bids are all subject to felony prosecution.[32] Each of these offenses is analyzed under a per se standard of illegality.

Cartels also give rise to a significant percentage of private competition litigation in the United States. Because most cartel behavior is conducted in secret, victims are often unaware of the anticompetitive behavior until a federal criminal investigation is announced. When a criminal investigation becomes public, private individuals and businesses that have been harmed by the cartel's conduct will often file private actions

---

29 As discussed below, some tying arrangements, which consist of a vertical agreement between a supplier and a customer, and hub-and-spoke conspiracies, which consist of both vertical and horizontal agreements, are analyzed under a per se or modified per se standard.

30 *Verizon Commc'n Inc. v. Law Offices of Curtis V. Trinko, LLP*, 540 US 398 (2004).

31 Between 2006 and 2009, federal cartel prosecutions resulted in more than $2 billion in criminal corporate fines and more than 162 years of jail time for offenders. Varney Speech, at 6–7.

32 The Antitrust Division's leniency program, begun in 1978 and modified in 1993 and 1994, enables corporations and individuals to avoid criminal convictions, fines and jail time by being the first to confess participation in a criminal antitrust violation. The leniency applicant must admit participation in a criminal violation of the antitrust laws before receiving a conditional leniency letter, and must demonstrate that it has satisfied its obligation to pay restitution before it will be granted final leniency. The program has been highly successful in encouraging companies and individuals to come forward and report cartel behavior. The Antitrust Division describes the Corporate Leniency Program as the Division's '*most* effective investigative tool' and states that cooperation from leniency applicants 'has cracked more cartels than all other tools at our disposal combined.' Hammond, Scott D. (2005) 'Cracking Cartels With Leniency Program', *available at* http://www.usdoj.gov/atr/public/speeches/212269.htm, accessed 7 October 2009 (emphasis in original).

The leniency program impacts private litigation not only by exposing more cartels; it also sometimes facilitates cooperation with private plaintiffs. A leniency applicant may qualify for detrebling of damages if the applicant cooperates with plaintiffs in their civil action, while the applicant's former co-conspirators will remain liable for treble damages on a joint and several basis. Hammond, Scott D. and B.A. Barrett (2008) 'Frequently Asked Questions Regarding the Antitrust Division's Leniency Program and Model Leniency Letters', *available at* http://usdoj.gov/atr/public/criminal/239583.htm, accessed 21 October 2009. For a discussion of how the leniency program can assist a private plaintiff in deciding whether to bring a case, see Chapter 5 of this *Handbook*; for a discussion of the utility of the leniency program as an evidence gathering tool, see Chapter 10 of this *Handbook*; and for a discussion of how the leniency program impacts the interplay of public and private enforcement generally, see Chapter 13 of this *Handbook*.

– particularly class actions – to recover their damages.[33] In some instances, private litigation precedes the government investigation.[34]

The claim most commonly alleged in private cartel litigation is price-fixing. Because price-fixing agreements are often accompanied by agreements to restrict output or allocate customers or territorial markets, these claims are also common in private litigation. Least common among per se offenses is private litigation challenging bid-rigging. While the DOJ frequently prosecutes businesses and individuals for bid-rigging, the effects are often localized, making nationwide class actions less likely. The episodic nature of bid-rigging may render class certification difficult as well.

JOINT VENTURES Joint ventures are collaborative undertakings among competitors in which otherwise independent firms seek to achieve a specific business objective (or objectives) through partial integration of their resources or risks. Joint ventures are 'more integrated than cartels but less integrated than mergers.'[35] Private parties injured by the formation of a joint venture or by subsequent agreements among venture participants can sue the participants or the joint venture itself under §1 or §2 of the Sherman Act, or under §7 of the Clayton Act.[36] They can also assert state law claims under parallel statutory and common law rules. Most cases are brought under §1.

As with other potentially anticompetitive agreements, the first step in evaluating the legality of a joint venture agreement is determining whether it is subject to a per se or a rule of reason standard. A joint venture (or agreement among participants in the joint venture) is more likely to be assessed under a rule of reason standard if (a) the joint venture requires significant integration of the participants' resources or risk sharing; (b) the challenged agreement constitutes the core activity of a legitimate joint venture or is reasonably related to and reasonably necessary to achieve the procompetitive benefits of a legitimate joint venture activity; (c) the joint venture is of limited duration; (d) the joint venture results in a product that would otherwise not be available; (e) the joint venture

---

[33] The victim of a price-fixing cartel is the customer that paid an inflated price. Because there are many victims, and because individual damages may be relatively modest, most victims pursue recovery through the class action device. Private litigation often begins within weeks or even days of a public announcement of a federal investigation into suspected cartel activity. While the Antitrust Division does not usually announce the inception of a criminal antitrust investigation, pre-dawn raids of targeted companies, often coordinated with antitrust authorities in other countries, are often reported in the press. Such investigations also become public because federal securities laws require publicly held companies to disclose such investigations in their quarterly filings.

[34] *See In re Nasdaq Market-Makers Antitrust Litig.*, 187 F.R.D. 465 (S.D.N.Y. 1998) (private class action litigation preceded any publicly-known government investigation). As another example, the FTC's recent investigation of Intel was preceded by private litigation by Intel's main rival, AMD, and by class action litigation (in addition to enforcement actions in the European Union, Korea and Japan). For further discussion of the interaction of public and private enforcement, see Chapter 13 of this *Handbook*.

[35] *See* Piraino, Jr., Thomas A. (2001), *A Proposed Antitrust Approach to Collaborations Among Competitors*, Iowa Law Review, 86, 1137–1207.

[36] The formation of the joint venture is subject to challenge under §7 if the parties acquire voting securities in the newly formed entity. *United States v. Penn-Olin Chem. Co.*, 378 US 158 (1964).

corrects for a market inefficiency such as free riding; or (f) the challenged agreement does not explicitly set prices or restrict output.[37] In addition, if a joint venture is deemed a single entity – either for all purposes or for purposes of the challenged restraint – it cannot be challenged under §1 of the Sherman Act, and so will be subject to a rule of reason analysis.[38] Merely labeling a collaboration among competitors a joint venture, however, will not protect it from per se illegality under the Sherman Act if it involves joint price-setting or restrictions on output.[39]

As with any other conduct analyzed under the rule of reason, an evaluation of the legality of a joint venture agreement requires a fact-specific analysis. If the agreement has obvious anticompetitive effects or the plaintiff can show that it has already caused anti-competitive harm, the court may apply a 'quick look' rule of reason standard, dispensing with any detailed market analysis.[40] Otherwise, the plaintiff must first define the relevant market (along both product and geographic dimensions) and then demonstrate that the

---

[37] *See, e.g., Broadcast Music, Inc.*, 441 US 1 (agreement by thousands of authors and composers to grant a joint venture a blanket license to all their musical compositions analyzed under a rule of reason standard because the agreement reflected integration of sales, addressed a free-rider problem, and created a product that would otherwise not have been available); *NCAA*, 468 US at 100–01 (NCAA rule limiting member universities' football game telecasts analyzed under quick look rule of reason rather than a per se standard because the 'case involve[d] an industry in which horizontal restraints on competition are essential if the product is to be available at all.'). Most recently, in *Texaco, Inc. v. Dagher*, 547 US 1, 8 (2006), the Court held that a pricing arrangement that Shell and Texaco entered into after they consolidated their operations in the Western United States did not 'fall within the narrow category of activity that is per se unlawful' because the joint venture (already reviewed by the antitrust authorities) had already eliminated all relevant competition between the parties. They had 'agreed to pool their resources and share the risks of and profits from . . . [the joint venture's] activities,' and shared those profits in their role as investors, not competitors. *Texaco, Inc.*, 547 US at 4, 8.

The FTC and DOJ's jointly issued Antitrust Guidelines for Collaboration Among Competitors similarly treat joint ventures differently depending on whether the parties integrate their economic resources and the nature and extent of any efficiencies created by the joint venture. Federal Trade Commission and the United States Department of Justice (2000) 'Antitrust Guidelines for Collaborations Among Competitors', *available at* http://www.ftc.gov/os/2000/04/ftcdojguidelines.pdf, accessed 21 October 2009 (hereinafter, 'Competitor Collaboration Guidelines' or 'Guidelines') at 4 (agreements that 'are reasonably related to, and reasonably necessary to achieve procompetitive benefits from, an efficiency-enhancing integration of economic activity' are analyzed under the rule of reason).

[38] *See Bulls II*, 95 F.3d at 599–600 (whether sports league is a single entity or a joint venture is a question that must be analyzed 'one league at a time and perhaps one facet of a league at a time'); *Copperweld Corp.*, 467 US 752 (a corporate parent cannot conspire with its wholly-owned subsidiary under §1).

[39] *Timken Roller Bearing Co. v. United States*, 341 US 593 (1951). *See also Maricopa Cty Med. Soc'y*, 457 US 32 (agreement among medical doctors to set a maximum fee schedule constituted per se illegal price fixing); *but see Texaco Inc.*, 571 US 1 (legality of joint venture between two previously competing companies that set a single price for jointly-produced product subject to rule of reason, not per se analysis, because the companies participated in the relevant market jointly through investment in joint venture and shared in profits as investors).

[40] *See Ind. Fed'n of Dentists*, 476 US at 460–61 (analysis of market power not necessary where there is proof of actual anticompetitive effect); *Cal. Dental Ass'n*, 526 US at 770 (court of appeals erred in applying quick look analysis where joint venture's advertising restrictions did not have obvious anticompetitive effects).

joint venture has (or will have) market power in that market.[41] If the joint venture meets the threshold market power requirement, the court will then examine the nature of the agreement to determine whether it is likely to cause substantial anticompetitive harm. If yes, then the court will consider any procompetitive benefits proffered by the defendant, and determine whether those benefits can be achieved by a less restrictive alternative.[42]

A party may also look for guidance to the Competitor Collaboration Guidelines, which were issued jointly by the FTC and DOJ in 2000. While the Guidelines are not binding on the courts, they have been cited in some published decisions (though not yet by the United States Supreme Court) and provide a useful framework for analysis because they are based on existing law. The Guidelines explain that the Agencies will challenge agreements 'of a type that always or almost always tends to raise price or reduce output,' such as price-fixing, bid-rigging and market-allocation agreements, under a per se standard of illegality, 'without inquiring into their claimed business purposes, anticompetitive harms, procompetitive benefits, or overall competitive effects.'[43] On the other hand, the Agencies will challenge an agreement 'that is reasonably related' to an 'efficiency-enhancing integration of economic activity' and 'reasonably necessary' to achieve its procompetitive benefits under a flexible rule of reason standard.[44]

Under the Guidelines' flexible rule of reason standard, the Agencies begin their analysis by examining the business purpose of the challenged agreement and inquiring whether the agreement has caused anticompetitive harm. If the nature of the agreement and the absence of market power[45] demonstrate the absence of anticompetitive harm, the Agencies will not challenge the agreement. If the agreement has already caused anticompetitive harm, or if the 'likelihood of anticompetitive harm is evident from the nature of the agreement,' the Agencies will challenge the agreement without a detailed market analysis.[46] If the agreement raises competitive concerns but cannot be analyzed without a detailed market analysis, the Agencies will define relevant markets, calculate market shares and concentration levels, inquire whether the venture and its participants have the 'ability and incentive to compete independently,' evaluate the likelihood and impact of competitive entry, and 'assess any other market circumstances that may foster or impede anticompetitive harms.'[47] If this analysis indicates no potential for anticompetitive harm, the Agencies will discontinue the investigation. Otherwise, the Agencies will

---

41 If the combined market share of the joint venture and its members exceeds 20 per cent that is sufficient to continue the analysis. ABA Section of Antitrust Law (2006), Joint Ventures: Antitrust Analysis of Collaborations Among Competitors, Chicago, US: ABA Publishing, p. 47.

42 *See, e.g., Sullivan v. NFL*, 34 F.3d 1091, 1103 (1st Cir. 1994) ('a given restriction is not reasonable, that is, its benefits cannot outweigh its harm to competition, if a reasonable, less restrictive alternative . . . exists'); *see also Law v. NCAA*, 134 F.3d 1010, 1019 (10th Cir. 1998).

43 Competitor Collaboration Guidelines, p. 8.

44 Competitor Collaboration Guidelines, p. 8.

45 In this initial inquiry, the Agencies may be able to determine that there is no market power without defining a relevant market. For example, if there are no barriers to entry, or there is no plausible market power no matter how the market is defined, the Agencies may discontinue the inquiry without further analysis. Competitor Collaboration Guidelines, p. 10, n. 26.

46 This analysis is similar to the Supreme Court's 'quick look' rule of reason analysis. Competitor Collaboration Guidelines, p. 10.

47 Competitor Collaboration Guidelines, p. 11.

'examine whether the relevant agreement is reasonably necessary to achieve procompetitive benefits that likely would offset anticompetitive harms.'[48]

Two federal statutes – the National Cooperative Research and Production Act (NCRPA)[49] and the Standards Development Organization Advancement Act (SDOA)[50] – provide limited antitrust safe harbors for certain kinds of joint ventures. The NCRPA provides limited antitrust immunity to research and development and production joint ventures that meet its criteria and that register with the DOJ and FTC. A joint venture that meets the NCRPA criteria and files the requisite notice is not subject to the per se standard. Further, if it is adjudged to be in violation of the antitrust laws under a rule of reason standard, it is liable for only actual damages, rather than treble damages. If a private plaintiff unsuccessfully challenges the legality of a qualified NCRPA joint venture, the defendant may recover its attorneys' fees and costs.[51] The SDOA extends the protections of the NCRPA to qualifying standard setting organizations.[52]

CONCERTED REFUSALS TO DEAL Concerted refusals to deal, also known as group boycotts, are agreements among horizontal competitors not to do business with certain other firms or individuals, or to do so only under specified terms. For many years group boycotts were considered illegal per se.[53] Under current law, however, they may be evaluated under either the per se or rule of reason standard, depending on the market power of the defendants, and the purpose and effect of the boycott: 'the per se approach has generally been limited to cases in which firms with market power boycott suppliers or customers in order to discourage them from doing business with a competitor . . . .'[54] A per se approach will also be applied to group boycotts that constitute or enforce a price-fixing agreement or other agreement that is illegal per se.[55]

MERGERS AND ACQUISITIONS While regulation of mergers and acquisitions is mostly left to federal and state antitrust authorities,[56] private litigants may also challenge them under federal and state law. Private plaintiffs may seek injunctive relief preventing or undoing the merger, and may seek damages.[57] The principal statute governing mergers

---

48 Competitor Collaboration Guidelines, pp. 11–12.

49 15 U.S.C. §§4301–4305.

50 15 U.S.C. §4301(a)(7).

51 15 U.S.C. §§4301–4305. Normally, the antitrust defendant must pay its own attorneys' fees and costs, even if it prevails. (The Clayton Act's exception to the 'American Rule' entitles prevailing plaintiffs, not defendants, to attorneys' fees and costs. 15 U.S.C. §15.)

52 15 U.S.C. §4302.

53 *See, e.g., Klor's, Inc. v. Broadway-Hale Stores*, 359 US 207, 212 (1959) (group boycotts 'have long been held to be in the forbidden category' of restraints as to which courts need not inquire into anticompetitive effects).

54 *Ind. Fed'n of Dentists*, 476 US at 458 (quick look rule of reason analysis applied to agreement among a group of dentists not to forward x-rays to insurers).

55 *Superior Ct. Trial Lawyers Ass'n*, 493 US at 436, n. 19 (agreement among lawyers to stop representing indigent clients unless government increased fees illegal per se).

56 The FTC, DOJ and state attorneys general may seek injunctive relief preventing or undoing a merger or acquisition under §16 of the Clayton Act, and may seek damages under §4 of the Clayton Act. 15 U.S.C. §§26, 15.

57 15 U.S.C. §§26, 15.

and acquisitions is §7 of the Clayton Act, which prohibits any merger or acquisition where 'the effect of such acquisition may be substantially to lessen competition, or to tend to create a monopoly.'[58] Plaintiffs can also challenge a merger or acquisition as an unreasonable restraint of trade, monopolization or attempted monopolization under §§1 or 2 of the Sherman Act, and seek damages and injunctive relief under the Clayton Act.[59]

A plaintiff challenging a merger or acquisition must define a relevant market along product and geographic dimensions,[60] identify the market participants, and show that the merger would increase market concentration to a level that would likely have anti-competitive effects, taking into consideration the likelihood of entry by competitors.[61] If the defendant proffers evidence that the merger will create efficiencies and other procompetitive benefits, the plaintiff must show that the anticompetitive effects of the merger would outweigh any procompetitive benefits.[62]

The FTC and DOJ's jointly issued Horizontal Merger Guidelines (published in 1992 and amended in 1997) and Commentary on the Horizontal Merger Guidelines (2006) set forth their merger enforcement policy. As with other agency guidelines, the Horizontal Merger Guidelines, while not binding on the courts, provide a useful framework for analysis. The Horizontal Merger Guidelines describe a process for identifying all participants in the relevant market,[63] determining each participant's

---

[58] 15 U.S.C. §18. Section 7 applies broadly to transactions involving acquisitions of stock, assets or partnership interests, including those transactions which resemble mergers, and those in which only some assets or interests are acquired. *Id.*

[59] 15 U.S.C. §§1, 2, 15, 26.

[60] *United States v. E.I. Du Pont de Nemours & Co.*, 353 US 586, 593 (1957); *Brown Shoe Co.*, 370 US at 324.

[61] While early Supreme Court cases held that mergers resulting in an entity with a market share comprising more than 30 per cent of the relevant market and increasing concentration by more than 33 per cent were illegal (*see, e.g., United States v. Philadelphia Nat'l Bank*, 374 US 321 (1963)), the Court retreated from that position in 1974 (*see United States v. Gen. Dynamics Corp.*, 415 US 486 (1974)), and in recent decades the agencies and lower courts have permitted mergers in markets far more concentrated initially, and in which the merger resulted in far greater concentration. *See, e.g., United States v. Baker Hughes, Inc.*, 908 F.2d 981 (D.C Cir. 1990) (no §7 violation where post-acquisition market share exceeded 75 per cent); DOJ Press Release, Department of Justice Antitrust Division Issues Statement on the Closing of Its Investigation of Arch Wireless' Acquisition of Metrocall Holdings (Nov. 16, 2004) (allowing transaction that would give combined firms about 67 per cent of postmerger national market).

[62] The Merger Guidelines and Merger Commentary make clear that the agencies will consider the nature and extent of any efficiencies created by a merger in analyzing its competitive effects. United States Department of Justice and the Federal Trade Commission (1997) 'Horizontal Merger Guidelines', *available at* http://www.usdoj.gov/atr/public/guidelines/horiz_book/hmg1.html, accessed 21 October 2009, §4. (2006) 'Commentary on Horizontal Merger Guidelines', *available at* http://www.usdoj.gov/atr/public/guidelines/215247.htm, accessed 21 October 2009, pp. 44–59. The Antitrust Modernization Commission Report urged the FTC and the DOJ to give greater weight to certain types of efficiencies, such as research and development expenses in rapidly innovating industries where relative marginal costs are low. (2007) 'Antitrust Modernization Commission, Report and Recommendations', *available at* http://govinfo.library.unt.edu/amc/report_recommendation/amc_final_report.pdf, accessed 21 October 2009, p. 56.

[63] The scope is very broad. Firms that are vertically integrated and produce the relevant

market share,[64] and determining market concentration.[65] They also prescribe methods for analyzing ease of entry by competitors.[66]

In addition to proving all of the elements that a government plaintiff must prove, the private plaintiff challenging a merger or acquisition faces the additional challenge of showing that it has standing. Just as in any other private antitrust action, the plaintiff must show that it has suffered or is likely to suffer antitrust injury as a result of the challenged merger or acquisition.[67] Because of this additional hurdle, competitor challenges to mergers and acquisitions have rarely succeeded since the mid-1980s.[68]

Vertical agreements

Vertical restraints are agreements among firms standing at different levels in the chain of distribution. They may be challenged under §1 (unreasonable restraint of trade) or §2 (monopolization or attempted monopolization) of the Sherman Act. As discussed below, §2 challenges are always assessed under the fact-intensive rule of reason standard of illegality. Until recently, vertical restraints involving concerted conduct and restraints on output or price could be assessed under a per se standard of illegality. Since the Supreme Court's decision in *Leegin*,[69] however, most vertical restraints will likely be challenged under a rule of reason standard.

Vertical agreements that may be illegal

HUB-AND-SPOKE PRICE-FIXING AGREEMENTS The only vertical price restraint that continues to be evaluated under a pure per se standard of illegality is the so-called 'hub-and-spoke' conspiracy. A hub-and-spoke conspiracy is a price-fixing or market allocation cartel involving both vertical and horizontal agreements. At the center, or 'hub', of the

---

product for their own internal use are included, as are firms that produce or sell the product in recycled form. Horizontal Merger Guidelines, §1.31.

[64] Market share is measured by dollar sales, unit sales or physical capacity, depending on which measure is most likely to 'effectively distinguish firms.' Horizontal Merger Guidelines, §1.41.

[65] Horizontal Merger Guidelines, §1.51.

[66] Horizontal Merger Guidelines, §3.0.

[67] *Brunswick Corp.*, 429 US 477 (where acquisition of a competing but failing bowling alley harmed plaintiff by eliminating its opportunity for additional profits, but benefited competition, plaintiff has not shown antitrust injury and has no standing under the antitrust laws); *Cargill, Inc. v. Monfort of Colo., Inc.*, 479 US 104 (1986) (where post-merger conduct did not threaten antitrust injury, rival that challenged merger not entitled to injunctive relief under Clayton Act).

[68] In its 1986 decision in *Cargill, Inc.*, 479 US 104, the Supreme Court denied injunctive relief to a plaintiff rival challenging a proposed merger, holding that the plaintiff had not shown that the merged entity's conduct was likely to cause it antitrust injury, even though both lower courts had found that the merger was illegal under §7 of the Clayton Act. (§7 prohibits a merger where the effect 'may be substantially to lessen competition, or to tend to create a monopoly.' 15 U.S.C. §18.) The competitor–plaintiff's threatened injury of reduced profits (caused by the merged entity's ability to lower prices) did not constitute antitrust injury. *Cargill, Inc.*, at 479 US 114–115. For further discussion of antitrust injury and antitrust standing, see Chapter 6 of this *Handbook*.

[69] *Leegin Creative Prods. v. PSKS, Inc.*, 551 US 877 (2007).

conspiracy is a dominant supplier or distributor, which enters into a series of vertical agreements with its distributors or suppliers (the 'spokes'). Without more, these vertical restraints – even if they dictate prices – are not actionable under §1.[70] If, however, the 'spokes' enter into horizontal agreements with one other to adhere to the vertical restraint (the 'rim' of the conspiracy) the series of agreements are per se unlawful.[71]

RESALE PRICE MAINTENANCE One of the most commonly challenged vertical price restraints is resale price maintenance, in which a manufacturer and its distributor agree on minimum or maximum prices to be charged for the manufacturer's products.[72] Maximum resale price maintenance agreements, under which a manufacturer sets the maximum price that can be charged for its products by its distributors, are analyzed under a rule of reason analysis.[73] Until recently, minimum resale price maintenance agreements were considered so harmful to consumers that they were analyzed under a per se standard of liability. In *Leegin*,[74] however, the Supreme Court reversed 96 years of precedent, holding that minimum resale price maintenance agreements are now subject to the rule of reason.[75] In addition to noting that it has in recent decades reduced the number of practices that are subject to a per se standard of antitrust illegality, the Court reasoned that resale price maintenance policies often have procompetitive benefits, such as promoting interbrand competition by eliminating intrabrand competition.[76]

The *Leegin* decision is controversial and may ultimately be overturned by Congress. As the dissent noted, requiring courts to apply a rule of reason analysis forces the parties to engage in 'one of the most costly procedures in antitrust practice.'[77] As the AAI has testified, the difference between the per se rule and the rule of reason 'generally determines

---

[70] *United States v. Colgate & Co.*, 250 US 300 (1919) (manufacturers may announce pricing policies to their distributors and terminate any distributor that fails to follow the policy without liability under §1, unless the distributor manifests agreement).

[71] *Interstate Circuit, Inc. v. United States*, 306 US 208 (1939); *Toys 'R' Us, Inc. v. FTC*, 221 F.3d 928 (7th Cir. 2000) (where major toy retailer negotiated series of agreements with leading toy manufacturers that they would not sell to discount warehouse club stores, and there was evidence that seven of those manufacturers accepted the restriction on the condition that their competitors would do the same, agreements were illegal per se).

[72] An agreement is an essential element of a claim under §1. Thus, if a manufacturer unilaterally announces a minimum or maximum price for its products, and then terminates distributors that do not comply with the pricing policy, there is no agreement, and hence no liability under §1. *Colgate & Co.*, 250 US 300. (There may, however, be liability under §2 of the Sherman Act.) If, however, the manufacturer demands assent, and receives it, there is an agreement that can be challenged under §1 of the Sherman Act. *See, e.g., Leegin*, 551 US 877 (manufacturer adopted a 'Colgate policy,' that is, a policy stating it would sell its products only to retailers that followed its suggested retail prices, but then took the additional step of demanding a 'pledge' of compliance, which Leegin gave, then broke).

[73] *State Oil Co. v. Khan & Assoc., Inc.*, 522 US 3 (1997) (overturning nearly 30 years of precedent, Court held that maximum resale price maintenance agreements were subject to rule of reason, rather than per se, analysis).

[74] *Leegin*, 551 US 877.

[75] *Id.*

[76] *Id.* at 889–91.

[77] *Id.* at 915–17 (Breyer J., dissenting).

who wins a [resale price maintenance] case.'[78] Since the decision, there have been at least three attempts to pass federal legislation repealing *Leegin* and reinstating the per se rule for resale price maintenance.[79] Equally important, it is likely that some states will subject minimum resale price maintenance agreements to a per se standard of illegality under existing or new state antitrust statutes.[80] With all this uncertainty, and given that the *Leegin* decision does not immunize minimum resale price maintenance agreements from liability, many businesses are reacting with caution to the new rule.

NON-PRICE VERTICAL AGREEMENTS Vertical agreements that do not constrain price are typically assessed under a rule of reason standard of illegality, because of their 'real potential to stimulate interbrand competition.'[81] The most commonly challenged non-price vertical restraints are agreements among manufacturers and their distributors not to permit other entities to distribute the manufacturer's goods (exclusive distributorships) and agreements among manufacturers and their distributors limiting each distributor's customers or geographic sales territory (territorial and customer restrictions).

In determining whether an exclusive distributorship constitutes an unreasonable restraint of trade under the rule of reason, courts will consider the nature and extent of intrabrand competition, the duration of the agreement, and the geographic scope covered by the exclusive distributorship.[82] In assessing the legality of territorial and

---

78 Foer, Albert A. (2005) 'Testimony of Albert A. Foer, President American Antitrust Institute Before the Maryland Senate Judiciary Committee on Senate Bill 239', *available at* http://www.antitrustinstitute.org/archives/files/RPM%20Maryland%20S%20%20239_022520091252.pdf, accessed 21 October 2009.

79 S. 2261, 110th Cong., §1 (2007); S. 148, 111th Cong. §1 (2009); 'The Discount Pricing Consumer Protection Act: Do We Need to Restore the Ban on Vertical Price Fixing?', *available at* http://judiciary.senate.gov/hearings/hearing.cfm?id=3854, accessed 26 October 2009 (Hearing before Senate Judiciary Committee Subcommittee on Antitrust, Competition Policy and Consumer Rights, 111th Cong. (2009)). On July 13, 2009, H.R. 3190, which would reverse the Supreme Court's June 2007 decision in *Leegin*, was introduced in the US House of Representatives, mirroring a bill in front of the US Senate.

80 *See* Barr, Alan M. (2009) 'State Challenges to Vertical Price Fixing in the Post-*Leegin* World', *available at* http://www.ftc.gov/opp/workshops/rpm/may09/docs/abarr.pdf (Federal Trade Commission Hearings on Resale Price Maintenance, statement of Alan M. Barr, Assistant Attorney General, Deputy Chief, Antitrust Division, Office of the Attorney General); Duncan, Richard A. and A.K. Guernsey, (2008) 'Waiting for the Other Shoe to Drop: Will State Courts Follow Leegin?', Franchise Law Journal, 3, 173–184; Wolson, Joshua (2009) 'States Push Back Against Supreme Court's Leegin Decision,' *available at* http://thelegalintelligencer.typepad.com/tli/2009/05/states-push-back-against-supreme-courts-leegin-decision.html, accessed 21 October 2009.

Thirty-seven state attorneys general filed amicus briefs in *Leegin*, asking the Supreme Court to retain the per se standard of illegality for minimum resale price maintenance agreements. Robison, Brian and S. Garcia (2007), *The Supreme Court's Leegin Decision on Resale Price Maintenance: Maintaining Uncertainty*, The Journal of the Antitrust and Unfair Competition Law Section of the State Bar of California, 16 (2) 37–46. Maryland amended its antitrust statute to declare minimum resale price maintenance agreements an 'unreasonable restraint' of trade. S.B. 239 (Md. 2009); H.B. 657 (Md. 2009). Signed into law by Governor Martin O'Malley on April 15, 2009, effective October 1, 2009.

81 *Bus. Elecs. Corp. v. Sharp Elec. Corp.*, 485 US 717, 724 (1988).

82 *United States v. Chicago Tribune-N. Y. News Syndicate*, 309 F. Supp. 1301, 1307–08 (S.D.N.Y.

customer restraints, courts have examined the purpose of the restrictions (for example, a restriction that promotes a legitimate business reason such as improving efficiency, reducing free riding or promoting consumer safety is more likely to be upheld), the effect of the restriction in limiting competition in the relevant market, the market power of the supplier, and the impact on competition.[83]

TYING ARRANGEMENTS A tying arrangement is a vertical 'agreement' between seller and buyer in which the seller agrees to sell a product to the buyer 'only on the condition that the buyer also purchases a different (or tied) product, or at least agrees that he will not purchase that product from any other supplier.'[84] The buyer's agreement, though coerced, is sufficient to satisfy §1's requirement of joint action. In order to prove a tying claim, a plaintiff must show (1) a tie between two separate products or services; (2) that the defendant has appreciable market power in the tying product market; and (3) that the tie has a 'not insubstantial' effect on commerce in the tied product market.[85] Implicit in the first element is the requirement that the buyer was coerced into buying a product he or she did not want, or would have preferred to buy on other terms.

Tying arrangements are usually evaluated under a modified per se standard of illegality. Unlike the standard applied to a horizontal price-fixing agreement, a plaintiff in a tying case must show that the defendant has sufficient market power in the tying product market 'to force a purchaser to do something he would not do in a competitive market.'[86] While the plaintiff must show appreciable market power in the tying product market, however, there is no requirement (in contrast to a rule of reason case) to demonstrate the anticompetitive effects of the tie. Even if the defendant does not have market power in the tying product, however, the plaintiff can still assert a rule of reason claim.[87]

In recent years, courts and commentators have criticized the application of the per se standard in tying cases, citing the procompetitive benefits of some tying arrangements.[88]

1970) (whether territorial scope of agreement was 'arbitrary and unreasonably broad' was fact question); *Paddock Publ'ns v. Chicago Tribune Co.*, 103 F.3d 42, 47 (7th Cir. 1996) (enduring exclusive distribution contracts characterize markets that are recognized as competitive); *Murphy v. Bus. Cards Tomorrow Inc.*, 854 F.2d 1202, 1205 (9th Cir. 1988) (restraint not unreasonable where substantial interbrand competition existed and there were low entry barriers).

[83] *Murphy*, 854 F.2d at 1205 (so long as there is sufficient interbrand competition, negative impact on intrabrand competition irrelevant); *Clairol, Inc. v. Boston Disc. Ctr. of Berkley*, 608 F.2d 1114, 1125 (6th Cir. 1979) (customer restrictions that promoted consumer safety and customer goodwill not unreasonably restrictive); *Bi-Rite Oil Co. v. Ind. Farm Bureau Coop. Ass'n*, 908 F.2d 200, 204 (7th Cir. 1990) (no violation where supplier lacked market power).

[84] *N. Pac. Ry. Co.*, 356 US at 5–6.

[85] *Eastman Kodak Co. v. Image Tech. Servs., Inc.*, 504 US 451, 461–62 (1992); *Jefferson Parish Hosp. Dist. No. 2 v. Hyde*, 466 US 2 (1984).

[86] *Hyde*, 466 US at 13–14 (internal citation omitted). Market power can be demonstrated by a large market share or proof that the defendant offers a unique product that competitors cannot provide. Market power in a tying case will not be inferred from a market share of less than 30 per cent. *Id.* at 26–29.

[87] *Id.* at 21.

[88] *Ill. Tool Works v. Indep. Ink, Inc.*, 547 US 28, 37 (2006) (tracing the history of the Court treatment of tying arrangements and noting that '[t]he assumption that "[t]ying arrangements

The Antitrust Modernization Commission[89] has recommended that all tying cases be evaluated under a rule of reason analysis.[90]

Single firm conduct

Elements of a §2 monopolization claim
Section 2 of the Sherman Act[91] makes it illegal to 'monopolize, or attempt to monopolize, or combine or conspire . . . to monopolize.' A monopoly is illegal only if it was 'willfully' acquired or maintained. 'Willfully' refers to improper conduct that excludes or drives rivals from the market on some basis other than competition on the merits.[92]

In order to make out a monopolization claim, a private plaintiff must prove that the defendant (1) possesses monopoly power in a relevant market; and (2) willfully acquired or maintained that power, instead of acquiring monopoly power through 'growth or development as a consequence of a superior product, business acumen, or historic accident.'[93] Finally, as for any private claim, the plaintiff must prove that it was injured by reason of defendant's monopolization conduct.[94]

Monopoly power in a relevant market To prove that the defendant has monopoly power in a relevant market, the plaintiff must first define the 'relevant market' along both product and geographic dimensions.[95] As with the §1 rule of reason analysis, market

---

serve hardly any purpose beyond the suppression of competition," . . . has not been endorsed in any opinion since.').

[89] Congress established the Antitrust Modernization Commission in 2002 to review federal antitrust law. After several years of hearings and the submission of thousands of pages of written comments, the Commission issued its final Report and Recommendations on April 2, 2007.

[90] Antitrust Modernization Commission, Report and Recommendation, p. 105. The AAI, in contrast, urges retention of the current modified per se rule for tying, with certain caveats. Foer (ed.), 'The Next Antitrust Agenda at 81', *available at* http://www.antitrustinstitute.org/archives/transitionreport.ashx.

[91] 15 U.S.C. §2.

[92] *Aspen Skiing Co. v. Aspen Highlands Skiing Corp.*, 472 US 585, 605 n. 32 (1985).

[93] *United States v. Grinnell Corp.*, 384 US 563, 570–71 (1966).

[94] As in any antitrust case, the plaintiff must also prove that the challenged conduct has an 'anticompetitive effect' or causes 'antitrust injury,' that is, it harms not merely other competitors, but the competitive process itself. *Spectrum Sports, Inc. v. McQuillan*, 506 US 447, 458 (1993) (the Sherman Act is not directed at 'conduct which is competitive, even severely so, but against conduct which unfairly tends to destroy competition itself.'); *Brunswick Corp.*, 429 US at 487–88 (plaintiff must show that the injury caused by defendant's challenged conduct is of 'the type that the statute was intended to forestall').

[95] Definition of the relevant market is often a critical dispute in monopoly cases. *See* Jonathan B. Baker (2007), *Market Definition: An Analytical Overview*, Antitrust Law J., 74 129 ('the outcome of more cases has surely turned on market definition than on any other substantial issues'). In *Microsoft*, 253 F.3d 34 the court defined the relevant market as the licensing of all Intel-compatible PC operating systems worldwide, a market in which Microsoft possessed a 95 per cent market share. The court rejected Microsoft's argument that other products, specifically non-Intel compatible operating systems such as Apple's Macintosh operating system, operating systems for non-PC devices, and middleware, should be included in the market. *Microsoft*, 253 F.3d at 53–54. If the Court had accepted Microsoft's proposed market definition, Microsoft would have prevailed.

definition provides the context in which to evaluate a §2 claim, because the ability of customers to turn to other, competing suppliers restrains a firm from raising prices above competitive levels.[96] The relevant market must include all products 'reasonably interchangeable by consumers for the same purposes.'[97] Products in another market may also be included in the relevant market definition if the producer of those products can quickly and cheaply shift to production of the defendant's product (or a reasonably interchangeable substitute).[98]

Then, having defined a proper relevant market, the finder of fact must determine whether the defendant possesses 'monopoly power'[99] in that market, for example, 'the power to control prices or exclude competition.'[100] Where there is direct evidence that a firm has the power to control prices or exclude competition, monopoly power is clear.[101] Because a plaintiff can rarely rely on direct evidence of monopoly power, however, monopoly power is usually inferred from a firm's possession of a dominant share of a relevant market that is protected from new competitors by barriers to entry.[102] While the Supreme Court has not specified what percentage of the market constitutes a 'predominant share,' the cases suggest that a market share of 70 per cent or more, together with entry barriers, is likely sufficient to establish monopoly power.[103] A plaintiff can prove the existence of entry barriers by showing that a new entrant would have to incur enormous initial capital costs, that regulatory requirements discourage new entry, that the incumbent controls a necessary input or has intellectual property rights necessary

---

[96] *Rothery Storage & Van Co. v. Atlas Van Lines, Inc.*, 792 F.2d 210, 218 (D.D.C. 1986).

[97] *E.I. Du Pont de Nemours & Co.*, 351 US at 395.

[98] *See Rebel Oil Co. v. Atl. Richfield Co.*, 51 F.3d 1421, 1436 (9th Cir. 1995) (explaining 'supply-side substitutability').

[99] Courts have used the terms 'monopoly power' and 'market power' interchangeably, although they arguably carry different burdens of proof. *See, e.g., Grinnell Corp.*, 384 US at 570 (Section 2 violation requires proof of 'monopoly power'); *Hyde*, 466 US at 16–17 (tying arrangement is illegal only if seller has 'market power' in the tying product). *NCAA*, 468 US at 109 n. 38 (in §1 case, Court defined market power as 'the ability to raise prices above those that would be charged in a competitive market') and *E.I. Du Pont de Nemours & Co.*, 351 US at 391 (in §2 case, Court defined monopoly power as 'the power to control prices or exclude competition').

[100] *E.I. Du Pont de Nemours & Co.*, 351 US at 391.

[101] *See, e.g., Am. Tobacco v. United States*, 328 US 781, 789 (1946) (exclusion of competitors supported monopolization finding); *FTC v. Mylan Labs.*, 62 F. Supp. 2d 25 (D.D.C. 1999) (allegations that defendant successfully raised prices above competitive level and constricted supply of two drugs by denying competitor access to essential ingredient sufficient to allege monopoly power), *modified on other grounds*, 99 F. Supp. 2d 1 (D.D.C. 1999); *Rebel Oil Co.*, 51 F.3d at 1434; *Ind. Fed'n of Dentists*, 476 US at 460–61.

[102] *Grinnell*, 384 US at 571 ('existence of [monopoly] power ordinarily may be inferred from the predominant share of the market').

[103] *E.I. Du Pont*, 351 US at 404; *Grinnell Corp.*, 384 US 563 (87 per cent); *Eastman Kodak Co.*, 504 US 451 (80 per cent); *Int'l Audiotext Network v. AT&T*, 893 F. Supp. 1207 (S.D.N.Y. 1994), *aff'd*, 62 F.3d 69 (2d Cir. 1995 ('As a general proposition, a market share of 70 per cent should be an adequate (if barely adequate) basis, at the pleading stage for an inference of power in a relevant market.'). The concept of domination in the European context may be established at considerably lower market shares. *See* Einer Elhauge and Damien Geradin (2007), Global Antitrust Law and Economics, New York, US: Foundation Press, at 270.

to produce the product, or that the incumbent's position in an established network discourages new entry.[104]

Acquired, enhanced or maintained through exclusionary conduct After determining that the defendant possesses monopoly power in a relevant market, the court must then determine whether the defendant has obtained (or maintained) that power *through exclusionary or predatory acts*. As the Supreme Court emphasized recently, the mere possession of monopoly power is not unlawful:

> Simply possessing monopoly power and charging monopoly prices does not violate §2; rather the statute targets 'the willful acquisition or maintenance of that power . . .'.[105]

Determining whether a defendant's conduct in acquiring or maintaining a monopoly is anticompetitive, however, is not easy, because there is no 'general rule for distinguishing between exclusionary acts, which reduce social welfare, and competitive acts, which increase it.'[106]

Examples of potentially exclusionary conduct
Fortunately, while 'the means of illicit exclusion . . . are myriad,' case law has identified certain practices that can constitute exclusionary conduct. Predatory pricing,[107] refusals to deal,[108] product disparagement or displacement,[109] anticompetitive litigation,[110] denial

---

[104] In *Microsoft*, 253 F.3d 34 at 55, for example, the court held that the 'applications barrier to entry' protected Microsoft's monopoly position in the operating system market: because most consumers prefer operating systems for which many applications have already been written, and most developers prefer to write applications for operating systems with a substantial consumer base, rival operating systems cannot easily enter the market (internal citation omitted).

[105] *Pac. Bell Tel. Co. v. Linkline Commc'ns, Inc.*, 129 S. Ct. 1109, 1118 (2009).

[106] *Microsoft*, 253 F.3d at 58.

[107] *Brooke Group Ltd. v. Brown & Williamson Tobacco Corp.*, 509 US 209, 222–23 (1993) (predatory pricing may violate §2).

[108] *See, e.g., Aspen Skiing Co.*, 472 US 585 (Aspen ski resort that operated three of the four area ski resorts violated §2 when it terminated a long-standing joint marketing arrangement with its smaller competitor, and the jury found no business justification for its conduct); *Eastman Kodak Co.*, 504 US 451 (a monopolist's refusal to sell parts to independent service organizations that competed against it in servicing copiers could be a violation of §2); *but see Verizon Commc'ns, Inc.*, 540 US 398 (Verizon's failure to comply with the mandate of the Telecommunications Act of 1996 to share its network with competitors on a non-discriminatory basis did not violate §2.).

[109] *See, e.g., Conwood Co. v. US Tobacco Co.*, 290 F.3d 768, 783–88 (6th Cir. 2002) (distribution of misleading information about competing products, displacement of competitors' advertising, and other conduct violated §2); *Am. Prof'l Testing Serv., Inc. v. Harcourt Brace Jovanovich Legal & Prof'l Publ'ns*, 108 F.3d 1147, 1151–53 (9th Cir. 1997) (distribution of disparaging leaflets about competitor). As the Sixth Circuit noted in *Conwood*, however, these kinds of tortious acts will violate §2 'only in "rare gross cases."' *Conwood*, 290 F.3d 783–84 (quoting 3A Areeda & Turner, Antitrust Law ¶782(a), at 272 (2002)).

[110] *Cal. Motor Transp. Co. v. Trucking Unlimited*, 404 US 508 (1972) (claim for conspiracy to monopolize could be based on concerted action by defendants to file federal and state actions seeking to preclude plaintiff from market).

of access to an essential facility,[111] enforcement of a fraudulently obtained patent,[112] vertical agreements that foreclose competition,[113] tying,[114] bundling,[115] and monopoly leveraging have all been held to constitute exclusionary conduct that can support a monopoly claim under §2.[116]

In some cases, there are relatively precise rules for determining whether a defendant has acquired or maintained a monopoly through anticompetitive conduct. For example, a plaintiff alleging predatory pricing under §2 must meet the exacting standard set by the Supreme Court in *Brooke Group* in 1993. In addition to establishing all of the other elements of a monopoly claim, the plaintiff must prove both that the defendant has set its prices so low that they are below 'an appropriate measure of its . . . costs,'[117] and that there is a 'dangerous probability' that the defendant will recoup the losses it incurs through low pricing by driving out rivals, thereby enabling it to charge monopoly prices.[118]

Though courts, commentators and federal enforcement officials have at times advocated the adoption of a single all-purpose test to determine whether conduct is exclusionary under §2, no single standard has been adopted. Courts and the antitrust enforcement agencies have sometimes used a balancing test derived from the §1 'rule of reason' standard.[119] The Supreme Court, in one case, and several commentators have

---

111 *MCI Commc'ns Corp. v. AT&T*, 708 F.2d 1081 (7th Cir. 1983) (Section 2 violation where a monopolist controlled an essential facility but refused to permit access to competitor).

112 *Walker Process Equip., Inc. v. Food Mach. & Chem. Corp.*, 382 US 172, 176 (1965) (monopolist that knowingly brought infringement action on basis of invalid patent violated §2).

113 *Microsoft*, 253 F.3d 34 (licensing agreements between Microsoft and original equipment manufacturers that contained terms making use of rival browser software difficult or impossible were anticompetitive and violated §2).

114 *Hyde*, 466 US at 9 (tying may violate §2).

115 *LePage's, Inc. v. 3M*, 324 F.3d 141 (3d Cir. 2003) (bundled discounts violated §2).

116 *Image Tech. Servs., Inc. v. Eastman Kodak Co.*, 125 F.3d 1195, 1208–13 (9th Cir. 1997); *but see In re Independent Serv. Orgs. Antitrust Litig.*, 203 F.3d 1322, 1327 (Fed. Cir. 2000) (rejecting monopoly leveraging theory in the absence of below-cost pricing); *Schor v. Abbott Labs.*, 457 F.3d 608, 613–14 (7th Cir. 2006) (same); *Verizon*, 540 US at 415 n. 4 (monopoly leveraging theory inapplicable where no proof of 'dangerous probability of success' in monopolizing second market).

117 *Brooke Group Ltd.*, 509 US at 222–23 (an 'appropriate measure' of cost has been held to be either the defendant's average variable cost, or its marginal cost).

118 *Brooke Group*, 509 US at 222–23.

119 *Microsoft*, 253 F.3d at 58–59. As in a §1 rule of reason case, this balancing approach employs shifting burdens. After the plaintiff has demonstrated that the monopolist's conduct has caused anticompetitive effects in the relevant market, the burden shifts to the monopolist to proffer a 'procompetitive justification' for its conduct, for example, 'a non-pretextual claim that its conduct is indeed a form of competition on the merits,' because, for example, it enhances efficiency or consumer appeal. If the defendant successfully proffers a non-pretextual procompetitive justification, the burden shifts back to the plaintiff to show that the monopolist can advance the proffered procompetitive justification through less restrictive means. If the plaintiff successfully rebuts the monopolist's procompetitive justifications, plaintiff will prevail. If plaintiff cannot rebut defendant's procompetitive justification, it must then demonstrate that the anticompetitive harm of the conduct outweighs the procompetitive benefits.

This balancing approach has been adopted by other courts and advocated by some antitrust enforcers and scholars. *See, e.g., United States v. Dentsply Int'l, Inc.*, 399 F.3d 181, 189, 191–96 (3d Cir. 2005) (using balancing approach); Jacobson, Jonathan M. and S.A. Sher (2006), *'No*

used a 'profit sacrifice' test, which asks whether the defendant is willing to 'sacrifice short-run benefits and consumer goodwill in exchange for a perceived long-run impact on its smaller rival.'[120] The DOJ under a previous administration advocated a 'disproportionality' test, which treats single-firm conduct as exclusionary only if its anticompetitive effects 'substantially outweigh' any procompetitive benefits.[121] This standard has been repudiated by the current Assistant Attorney General for the DOJ's Antitrust Division, who has not proposed a single test for evaluating all conduct under §2, but advocates 'balanced analyses' like the one applied in the *Microsoft* case.[122]

Elements of a §2 attempted monopolization claim

A plaintiff in an attempted monopolization case (just like in a monopolization case) must prove that the defendant 'has engaged in predatory or anticompetitive conduct.'[123] The plaintiff must also prove that the defendant acted with 'a specific intent to monopolize,' and that there was a 'dangerous probability' that the defendant would achieve monopoly power.[124]

In evaluating whether the defendant possessed the requisite intent, evidence that the defendant displayed an intent 'to compete vigorously' is insufficient.[125] Instead, the plaintiff must show a 'specific intent to destroy competition or build monopoly.'[126] Intent may be proven by direct or circumstantial evidence, and must be supported by evidence of conduct corroborating the alleged intent.[127]

The principal factor in assessing whether defendant had a 'dangerous probability of success' is market share. A market share of 50 per cent or more, together with barriers to entry, is often a starting point for this finding. A market share of between 30 and 50 per cent will rarely suffice, and a market share of less than 30 per cent is always insufficient to support a finding of 'dangerous probability of success.'[128]

Price discrimination

The Robinson-Patman Act[129] is the principal federal statute regulating price discrimination. Criticized by many as inimical to the goals of modern competition policy because it

---

Economic Sense' Makes No Sense for Exclusive Dealing, Antitrust Law Journal, 73 (3), 799; *In re Rambus Inc.*, Docket No. 9302; Opinion of the Commission, at 30–31 (FTC Aug. 2, 2006) (using balancing approach); Varney Speech.

120 *Aspen Skiing*, 472 US at 610–11; Melamed, A. Douglas (2005), *Evolving Antitrust Treatment of Document Firms: Exclusionary Conduct Under the Antitrust Laws: Balancing, Sacrifice, and Refusals to Deal*, Berkeley Technology Law Journal, 20, 1247–1267.

121 *See* the now withdrawn United States Department of Justice (2008) 'Competition and Monopoly: Single-Firm Conduct Under Section 2 of the Sherman Act', *available at* http://www.usdoj.gov/atr/public/reports/236681.pdf, accessed 21 October 2009, pp. 45–46.

122 Varney Speech.

123 *Spectrum Sports*, 506 US at 456.

124 *Spectrum Sports*, 506 US at 456.

125 *Spectrum Sports*, 506 US at 459.

126 *Times-Picayune Publ'g Co. v. United States*, 345 US 594, 626 (1953).

127 *William Inglis & Sons Baking Co. v. ITT Cont'l Baking Co.*, 668 F.2d 1014, 1027, 1028 (9th Cir. 1981).

128 Antitrust Law Developments, pp. 312–315.

129 15 U.S.C. §13 *et seq.*

protects competitors and can lead to increased prices to consumers, antitrust law's 'illegitimate child'[130] is still on the books, despite numerous calls for its repeal.[131] Although the FTC and the DOJ both have enforcement authority, the FTC (which is the only federal agency that has enforced the Act since the 1960s) has sharply reduced its enforcement activity under the Act in recent years, bringing only one case since 1992.[132] Hence, it is enforced primarily through private litigation.

The Robinson-Patman Act prohibits a seller from offering different prices to different buyers for commodities of 'like grade and quality,' where the effect of such price discrimination may be to injure competition.[133] Different prices are allowed only if (1) the lower price is available to all buyers;[134] (2) a lower price is justified by lower costs of selling to a particular buyer;[135] (3) a lower price is offered in a good faith attempt to meet competition;[136] or (4) a lower price is justified by a change in market conditions, such as impending bankruptcy or perishability of goods.[137]

There are two kinds of price discrimination claims: primary-line discrimination (involving competition at the seller's level) and secondary-line discrimination (involving competition at the buyer's level). In a primary-line price discrimination claim, a competing seller challenges its rival's pricing policies; in a secondary-line claim, a disfavored buyer (or its customer) challenges the seller's discriminatory pricing.

In sharp contrast to other federal antitrust claims, a secondary-line buyer challenging price discrimination may prove the requisite injury to competition simply by showing its own injury: the statute prohibits price discrimination if its effect 'may be substantially to lessen competition or tend to create a monopoly in any line of commerce, *or to injure, destroy, or prevent competition with any person* . . . .'[138] Thus, a plaintiff can prevail if it can show that a single competitor lost sales as a result of the discriminatory pricing, and need not show injury to competition.[139]

---

130 Hovenkamp, Herbert (2006), Antitrust Law XIV, ¶2300, US: Aspen Publishers, pp. 3–4.

131 Following earlier calls for substantial overhaul of the Act, in 1977, a Department of Justice Report stated that 'serious consideration' should be given to its repeal. In 2007, the Antitrust Modernization Commission recommended that it be repealed in its entirety. Antitrust Modernization Commission Report and Recommendations, pp. 20, 312. The position of the AAI is that the Robinson Patman Act should be revised but not repealed. Foer (ed.), The Next Antitrust Agenda at 130, *available at* http://www.antitrustinstitute.org/archives/transitionreport.ashx.

132 Antitrust Modernization Commission Report and Recommendations, p. 316.

133 15 U.S.C. §13(a).

134 *See, e.g., FTC v. Morton Salt Co.*, 334 US 37, 42 (1948).

135 15 U.S.C. §13(a).

136 15 U.S.C. §13(b).

137 15 U.S.C. §13(a).

138 15 U.S.C. §13(a).

139 *Morton Salt Co.*, 334 US at 49; *Volvo Trucks N. Am., Inc. v. Reeder-Simco GMC, Inc.*, 546 US 164 (2006); *see also, e.g., J.F. Feeser, Inc. v. Serv-A-Portion, Inc.*, 909 F.2d 1524, 1535 (3d Cir. 1990) ('evidence of injury to a competitor may satisfy the component of competitive injury necessary to show a violation of the Robinson-Patman Act'). *Cf. Brunswick Corp.*, 429 US at 488 (the purpose of the antitrust laws is to protect overall competition, not individual competitors). Even if the defendant can show that competition was not harmed, a plaintiff can prevail so long as there was injury to individual buyers. *Chroma Lighting v. GTE Prods*, 111 F.3d 653, 658 (9th Cir. 1977).

In order to recover damages, a secondary-line plaintiff must show that it lost sales or profits as a result of the price discrimination. Merely showing that it paid a higher price than its competitor is insufficient.[140]

The plaintiff alleging primary-line price discrimination must prove, in addition to the four elements required of secondary-line claims (price differential applied to commodities of like grade and quality that are sold in interstate commerce and which differential causes injury), that the differential pricing is *predatory*. That is, the plaintiff must prove 'that the prices complained of are below an appropriate measure of its rival's costs' and that the competitor has a 'reasonable prospect . . . of recouping its investment in below-cost prices . . . .'[141] This standard, nearly identical to the requirements imposed on a plaintiff alleging predatory pricing under §2 of the Sherman Act,[142] has sharply curtailed these cases and 'has largely eliminated calls for further reform regarding primary-line claims.'[143]

State law

All states have their own antitrust laws. Many state antitrust statutes are similar or identical to federal antitrust statutes, and are interpreted by their courts to be consistent with federal law. There are, however, notable distinctions. Many states do not, for example, have monopolization statutes analogous to §2 of the Sherman Act.[144] In at least some of those states, however, monopolies may be challenged under state common law, or under state antitrust statutes that regulate concerted conduct.[145] Another significant difference is in state-law treatment of resale price maintenance. In many states minimum resale price maintenance remains per se illegal even after the Supreme Court's *Leegin* decision; in others, state legislatures are considering or have already enacted statutes directly rejecting *Leegin's* rule-of-reason standard.[146] Another significant difference is state law

In addition, injury can be inferred from proof that a 'favored competitor received a significant price reduction over a substantial period of time.' *Volvo Trucks*, 546 US at 177.

[140] Antitrust Law, XIV, ¶2331, pp. 79–93 (emphasis in original) ('The statute does not prohibit a price discrimination that merely "injures or destroys" the disfavored *purchaser*. Rather, the discrimination must injure or destroy the disfavored purchaser's *ability to compete* with the favored purchaser.') *See J. Truett Payne Co. v. Chrysler Motors Corp.*, 451 US 557, 562 (1981) (to recover damages under §4 of the Clayton Act, plaintiff 'must make some showing of actual injury attributable to something the antitrust laws were designed to prevent').

[141] *Brooke Group*, 509 US at 222, 224.

[142] A plaintiff in a §2 predatory pricing case must also prove below-cost pricing and probable recoupment via supracompetitive pricing. Unlike the Robinson-Patman Act plaintiff, however, the §2 plaintiff must show a 'dangerous probability' of recoupment, instead of a merely 'reasonable prospect.' *Brooke Group*, 509 US at 222, 224.

[143] Antitrust Modernization Commission Report and Recommendations, p. 315.

[144] California, for example, has no §2 analog. *See* Antitrust Law, XIV, ¶2414a, pp. 351–52; *Bondi v. Jewels by Edwar, Ltd.*, 267 Cal. App. 2d 672 (1968) (Cartwright act requires 'combination').

[145] As a practical matter, the absence of a state monopoly statute matters only when a party seeks to take advantage of other features of state law that are different from federal law. For example, a plaintiff may prefer to sue under a state rather than federal antitrust statute because of the availability, in many states, of a damages remedy for indirect purchasers.

[146] *See supra* at n. 80.

treatment of price discrimination. Some states' laws are more aggressively protective of individual competitors. In some states, for example, a primary-line price discrimination plaintiff (claim by a rival seller) need only prove that the defendant sold its goods at a discounted price that was below its fully-allocated cost, as opposed to its marginal or average variable cost (as required under the Robinson-Patman Act).[147] This is a far easier burden for plaintiffs to satisfy. Another significant difference is the treatment of parties who are indirectly injured by antitrust violations. Under federal law, indirect purchasers are barred from recovering their damages under the Clayton Act (though they may still seek injunctive relief). A number of states have explicitly rejected the federal bar to indirect purchaser recovery, adopting 'Illinois Brick repealers' or interpreting their statutes in a manner contrary to federal law.[148]

Exempt industries

Despite broad agreement that the goal of antitrust law is to protect competition rather than competitors, there are currently more than thirty statutory and judge-made exemptions to the federal antitrust laws.[149] Insurance, agriculture, charitable giving, exports, fishing, health care, labor, local governments, college financial aid, medical resident matching programs, small businesses, soft drink distributors, railroads, shippers,

---

[147] Antitrust Law, XIV, ¶2414b, pp. 352–355.

[148] *See* compilation of state laws. Hawxhurst, Gerald E. (2006) 'A State-By-State Look At The Law on Indirect Purchaser Damage Actions', The Journal of the Antitrust and Unfair Competition Law Section of the State Bar of California, 15 (1), 41–58.

[149] The Antitrust Modernization Commission Report, Annex A, identifies the following exemptions:

> **Statutory Exemptions from the Antitrust Laws**: Agricultural Marketing Agreement Act, 7 U.S.C. §§608b–608c; Anti-Hog-Cholera Serum and Hog-Cholera Virus Act, 7 U.S.C. §852; Capper-Volstead Act, 7 U.S.C. §§291–92; Charitable Donation Antitrust Immunity Act, 15 U.S.C. §§37–37a; Defense Production Act exemption, 50 U.S.C. app §2158; Export Trading Company Act, 15 U.S.C. §§4001–21; Fishermen's Collective Marketing Act, 15 U.S.C. §§521–22; Health Care Quality Improvement Act, 42 U.S.C. §§11101–52; Labor exemptions (statutory and non-statutory), 15 U.S.C. §17; 29 U.S.C. §§52, 101–15, 151–69; (and common law); Local Government Antitrust Act, 15 U.S.C. §§34–36; Medical resident matching program exemption, 15 U.S.C. §37b; National Cooperative Research and Production Act, 15 U.S.C. §§4301–06; Need-Based Educational Aid Act, 15 U.S.C. §1 note; Newspaper Preservation Act, 15 U.S.C. §§1801–04; Non-profit agricultural cooperatives exemption, 15 U.S.C. §17; Small Business Act exemption, 15 U.S.C. §§638(d), 640; Soft Drink Interbrand Competition Act, 15 U.S.C. §§3501–03; Sports Broadcasting Act, 15 U.S.C. §§1291–95; Standard Setting Development Organization Advancement Act, 15 U.S.C. §§4301–05, 4301 note; Webb-Pomerene Export Act, 15 U.S.C. §§61–66.
> **Statutory Exemptions Created as Part of a Regulatory Regime**: Air Transportation Exemption, 49 U.S.C. §§41308–09, 42111; McCarran-Ferguson Act, 15 U.S.C. §§1011–15; Motor transportation exemption, 49 U.S.C. §§13703, 14302–03; Natural Gas Policy Act exemption, 15 U.S.C. §3364(e); Railroad transportation exemption, 49 U.S.C. §§10706, 11321(a); Shipping Act, 46 U.S.C. app. §§1701–1719.
> **Judicially Created Exemptions**: Baseball exemption; Filed-rate/*Keogh* doctrine; *Noerr-Pennington* Immunity; State Action Doctrine; Various implied immunities created in specific regulatory settings.

professional baseball teams and local governments all enjoy some measure of protection from federal antitrust liability.

One important statutory exemption is the Capper-Volstead Act of 1922, which immunizes an agricultural co-operative or association from antitrust liability unless it 'monopolizes or restrains trade to such an extent that the price of any agricultural product is unduly enhanced.' The coverage of the Act is broad. It applies to '[p]ersons engaged in the production of agricultural products as farmers, planters, ranchmen, dairymen, nut or fruit growers,' and it allows them collectively to process, prepare for market, handle, and market agricultural products in interstate and foreign commerce.[150]

Enacted in 1922 – when demand for agricultural products was down from its war-time peak – the purpose of the Act was to permit agricultural co-operatives to join together to increase their bargaining strength against large corporate buyers. While antitrust advocates generally view exemptions as contrary to the goals of United States competition policy, there has been little movement in the past to repeal or substantially modify the Act.[151]

More controversially, the McCarran-Ferguson Act exempts a wide swath of insurer conduct from antitrust scrutiny. The Act makes the Sherman, Clayton and FTC Acts inapplicable to the business of insurance, except 'to the extent that such business is not regulated by State law.'[152] With extensive state regulation of insurance, the exemption is broad. The Act does have a limiting provision, however: the Sherman Act still applies 'to any agreement to boycott, coerce, or intimidate.'[153] Numerous attempts to repeal or reduce the scope of the insurance exemption have not yet succeeded, though current efforts may be more successful.[154]

Another important exemption is organized labor. Federal statutes provide that labor unions are not combinations or conspiracies in restraint of trade, and exempt specific union acts, including picketing and boycotts, from the antitrust laws.[155] The exemption does not extend to combinations among unions and non-labor groups. In addition to

---

150 7 U.S.C. §291.

151 Recently, the DOJ and Unites States Department of Agriculture announced that they would hold joint public workshops to address competition issues in agriculture. *See* United States Department of Justice (2009) 'Justice Department and USDA to Hold Public Workshops to Explore Competition Issues in the Agricultural Industry', *available at* http://www.usdoj.gov/atr/public/press_releases/2009/248797.htm, accessed 26 October 2009. It is possible that the Capper-Volstead immunity will be a subject at the workshops.

152 15 U.S.C. §1012(b).

153 *Id.* at §1013(b).

154 Partial repeal of the McCarran-Ferguson Act is, for example, included in a House bill proposing broad health care reform, though the McCarran-related provisions would affect only health and medical malpractice insurance. *See, e.g.*, H.R. 3962, 111th Cong. (1st Sess. 2009) pp. 150–153, introduced October 29, 2009. Additional bills that are more specifically targeted to the McCarran-Ferguson Act have also been introduced, though both also propose only partial repeal and are limited to health and medical malpractice insurance. *See* S. 1681, 111th Cong. (1st Sess. 2009) *and* H.R. 3596, 111th Cong. (1st Sess. 2009).

155 *See* 15 U.S.C. §17 (the labor of a human being is not a commodity or article of commerce and cannot be construed as an illegal combination or conspiracy in restraint of trade); 29 U.S.C. §104 (no court shall have jurisdiction to issue a restraining order or permanent injunction in any case arising out of or involving a labor dispute), 29 U.S.C. §105 (court does not have jurisdic-

the statutory exemptions, courts have held that labor unions and employer groups have limited immunity from federal antitrust laws for conduct that is necessary to make the collective bargaining process work.[156]

Export activities also enjoy limited immunity from antitrust scrutiny under two related statutes, the Foreign Trade Antitrust Improvement Act (FTAIA)[157] and the Export Trading Company Act (ETCA).[158] Under the ETCA, a company engaged in export activities can obtain immunity from federal and state enforcement actions by obtaining a Certificate of Review from the Department of Commerce (which the Department of Commerce issues only with the concurrence of the DOJ). If subsequently sued by a private entity, a company that has obtained a Certificate of Review is entitled to a rebuttable presumption that it has complied with the statute, a shorter statute of limitations for antitrust claims, and a prohibition against treble damages.[159]

The FTAIA makes the Sherman and FTC Acts inapplicable to exporting activities unless those activities have a 'direct, substantial, and reasonably foreseeable effect' on domestic commerce or a domestic firm competing for foreign trade.[160]

Conclusion

The vast body of federal and state antitrust law that has developed in the United States over the past century has been largely driven by private litigation, particularly in recent years. According to some estimates, private lawsuits currently account for roughly 90 per cent of all antitrust litigation in the United States.[161] Private enforcement is robust and effective in the United States because the laws provide standing to injured individuals and businesses, allow recovery of treble damages and attorneys' fees, permit many injured persons and businesses to join together under a class action, and allow liberal pre-trial discovery. And while recent judicial decisions (such as the Supreme Court's *Twombly* decision) have imposed stricter pleading and other requirements on private plaintiffs, there has been no retreat from the legislators' original mandate that private parties play a central role in the enforcement of US antitrust laws.

---

tion to issue restraining order or permanent injunction upon the grounds of a labor dispute that constitutes an unlawful combination or conspiracy).

156 *Brown v. ProFootball, Inc.*, 50 F.3d 1041 (D.C. Cir. 1995).

157 15 U.S.C. §§6(a), 45(a).

158 15 U.S.C. §§4001–4053.

159 15 U.S.C. §§4001–4053.

160 15 U.S.C. §6(a). For further discussion of the FTAIA, see Chapter 9 and Chapter 37 of this *Handbook*.

161 Ernest Gellhorn, William E. Kovacic and Stephen Calkins (2004), Antitrust Law and Economics, St Paul, MN: Thomson West, 5th ed. at 542; Lawrence A. Sullivan and Warren S. Grimes (2006), The Law of Antitrust: An Integrated Handbook, St Paul, MN: Thomson West, 2nd ed. at 954.

5 Pre-claim activities

Craig Corbitt, Judith Zahid and Patrick Clayton[1]

Introduction

The lofty goals of antitrust are not self-executing. They require careful planning and preparation by plaintiffs' counsel and the client. Most antitrust litigation is highly complex, takes years to resolve, and is very expensive. Success in an antitrust case starts with the right plaintiff, with the right claim. This chapter describes how private antitrust litigation typically begins, including client contact and retention, pre-filing investigation, and strategic considerations that typically are considered in determining the specific claims to file, and equally importantly, where to file them.[2]

Meeting clients – class and non-class actions

There are two common ways for the potential antitrust plaintiff and the antitrust lawyer to get together. First, a potential plaintiff who perceives an unfair competition issue may contact an antitrust lawyer, either directly or through a referral from a non-antitrust lawyer, to find out whether there is a basis for a claim. Second, especially in class actions, an antitrust lawyer who is aware of a potential claim may search for a potential plaintiff, subject to certain ethical restrictions discussed below. The former is the more traditional way, while the latter is a more recent trend that sometimes has been met with criticism. Both are central to private antitrust enforcement in the United States.

A variety of individuals and companies may seek out an antitrust lawyer. For example, a project manager who senses that a competitive bidding process is not yielding competitive bids, a company that has been cut off from a supplier or a distribution outlet, a company that believes its larger competitor is engaging in unfair business tactics, or a customer who observes uncannily close price increases by suppliers, all may have reason to contact an antitrust lawyer. Mere perceptions by a market participant of anticompetitive practices often turn out to be just that – perceptions, and are not a good basis for an antitrust suit. An experienced antitrust lawyer usually can determine from an initial interview or after minimal fact investigation that there is no case. Sometimes, however, these competitor perceptions can lead to a very big case, e.g.,

---

[1] Mr. Corbitt and Ms. Zahid are partners, and Mr. Clayton is an associate, in the San Francisco office of Zelle Hofmann Voelbel & Mason LLP. Zelle Hofmann has served as plaintiffs' counsel in some of the cases cited in this chapter. The authors gratefully acknowledge the assistance of Briana James, a law clerk at Zelle Hofmann.

[2] In starting out to build a case, plaintiffs' counsel must consider a broad range of legal and practical issues, many of which arise in earnest at different stages of the litigation process. This chapter touches on many of these concerns, despite their being addressed in detail in other chapters of this *Handbook*. As the reader will come to understand, it is vital that plaintiffs' counsel address these concerns at the outset, no matter how remote they may seem.

Advanced Micro Devices, Inc. v. Intel Corp.,[3] and *Conwood v. United States Smokeless Tobacco Corp.*[4]

Sometimes the potential client is a 'whistleblower,' that is, an insider who observes abusive practices first-hand, and is determined to bring such practices to light, often in hope of a reward.[5]

A potential client may approach an antitrust lawyer, or vice-versa, when antitrust litigation (brought either by the government or private plaintiffs) has already commenced, and the client has potential claims similar to those already being litigated. When the existing litigation is a class action, a large company with substantial purchases from one or more defendants (usually direct purchases) may be advised by an antitrust lawyer to 'opt out', i.e., remove itself from the class, and either negotiate its own settlement without initiating litigation, or file its own individual action against the same defendants, which usually proceeds alongside the class action in the same court. Opt-out plaintiffs, especially those with whom the defendants want to maintain an ongoing business relationship, can often recover more money on their own than if they had remained in the class. Fee agreements between law firms and opt-out plaintiffs are typically wholly or partially contingent on a successful outcome. Because of the size of potential recoveries by opt-out plaintiffs and the corresponding potential for large fees, law firms, even quite large ones, often seek out and contact potential opt-out plaintiffs in the hopes of representing them.[6]

The potential plaintiff often initially contacts a lawyer or a law firm that he or she has previously used in connection with other legal matters. If that lawyer is not experienced in antitrust prosecution, the matter is likely to be referred to an antitrust specialist, sometimes in return for a referral fee.[7] An antitrust practitioner's demonstrated track record of success can lead to new clients and cases.

Class action lawyers sometimes are approached by a potential client in the first instance, but more often lawyers who specialize in class actions actively seek out potential clients to act as class representatives, either by contacting other lawyers who may provide a referral or by initiating direct contact with the potential client. Class action lawyers often race to sign up class representatives as quickly as possible in order to increase their chances of being appointed by the court as class counsel, also known as the lead or co-lead counsel in the litigation. This position is highly sought-after by class action lawyers because of the potential for significantly higher fees. Class counsel 'must fairly and adequately represent the interests of the class,'[8] which means running all aspects of the case from the pleading stage through discovery and trial or settlement,

---

3 Civil Action No. 05-441, D. Del. (unlawful monopolization case, settled before trial by Intel in November 2009 for $1.25 billion plus business considerations).

4 290 F.3d 768 (6th Cir. 2002), *cert. denied*, 537 US 1148 (2003) (judgment entered after jury trial of $1.1 billion in treble damages in unlawful monopolization case).

5 *See, e.g., Sabry Lee, Inc. v. Genera Corp., et al.*, Case No. 08-CV-05758 (C.D. Cal.) (Sept. 3, 2008) (price-fixing claim against group of after-market auto parts makers where plaintiff was a former distributor allegedly terminated for refusing to go along with the conspiracy).

6 For further discussion of opt-out claims, see Chapter 8 of this *Handbook*; for a discussion of notice in the context of opt-out claims, see Chapter 14 of this *Handbook*.

7 ABA Model Rules of Professional Conduct, Rule 1.5(e), applies to referral fees.

8 F.R.Civ.P. 23(g)(4).

and supervising the other law firms representing the class. Especially in a large case, there may be a number of other law firms simultaneously representing the class, under lead counsel's direction. In addition to the increased workload, being appointed lead counsel carries with it increased responsibility for funding the litigation, which can run into millions of dollars and greatly increase the potential risk. The involvement of multiple law firms spreads the risk among plaintiffs' counsel.

The relevant criteria for appointment of lead counsel are set forth in Rule 23(g) of the Federal Rules of Civil Procedure. They place a premium on 'the work counsel has done in identifying or investigating potential claims in the action,' along with counsel's knowledge, experience, resources, and other factors.

Many firms specialize in representing plaintiffs in class actions, and are commonly called 'class action firms.' Usually such firms are small, with a handful or at most a few dozen lawyers, compared with the large multi-national law firms with hundreds of lawyers that typically represent corporate defendants. Some firms regularly represent both class plaintiffs and opt-out plaintiffs (although not in the same case), and a few firms also represent defendants as well as plaintiffs in class action and other matters.

Rival class action firms often compete for appointment as class counsel. A group of firms may form an alliance in order to present an agreed-upon choice to the court, in return for promises by the selected firm or firms to favor its allies with work assignments, thereby increasing their potential fees. A class action firm that has done more of the initial investigation, signed up more class representatives, has a track record of success, is able to fund the litigation, or is located in the venue where the litigation is or is likely to be pending, is often rewarded by its peers with support for the lead counsel application. The court usually, but not always, will accept this 'private ordering.' Sometimes rival groups will submit applications to be appointed, accompanied by attacks on the qualifications of their rivals.

Courts may also appoint interim class counsel. This role grants leadership status when multiple actions are pending and classes have not yet been certified. Interim class counsel is generally appointed in instances where a large number of actions have been consolidated or are otherwise pending before a single court.[9]

Class action plaintiffs can be either 'direct purchasers' or 'indirect purchasers.' Direct purchasers, as the name implies, are those that bought directly from the alleged cartel members or abusive monopolist, while indirect purchasers typically have bought from resellers, and tend to be consumers and businesses which do not resell the product at issue.[10] Indirect purchaser plaintiffs may not have bought the allegedly price-fixed product separately, but instead bought a product into which the product at issue was a component, e.g., a personal computer sold with Microsoft Windows.[11]

---

[9] *In re TFT-LCD (Flat Panel) Antitrust Litigation*, M:07-CV-01827 (N.D. Cal. filed April 20, 2007); *In re Flash Memory Antitrust Litigation*, 4:07CV000086 (N.D. Cal. filed January 5, 2007). For further discussion of the appointment of class counsel, see Chapter 8 of this *Handbook*.

[10] Indirect purchasers at an intermediate level also have standing under 'Illinois-Brick repealer' state laws, but such claims are more difficult to pursue because of the complexity of proving that the overcharges they paid were not passed on to downstream purchasers.

[11] For a detailed discussion of issues affecting direct and indirect purchasers, see Chapter 6 of this *Handbook*.

The Supreme Court's decision in *Illinois Brick v. Illinois*[12] barred indirect purchasers from recovering under federal antitrust law. However, a number of state legislatures and appellate courts reacted to that decision by permitting indirect purchasers to sue under their respective state laws, and the right of states to enforce their laws was upheld by the Supreme Court in *California v. ARC America Corp.*[13] For many years, it was common for direct purchaser cases to be heard in federal court and indirect purchaser cases to be heard in state court. That changed with the enactment by Congress of the Class Action Fairness Act, which expanded the jurisdiction of federal courts to cover most large indirect purchaser class actions.[14] As a result, direct purchaser class actions under the Sherman Act and indirect purchaser class actions under state antitrust laws now commonly end up before the same federal court, and separate lead counsel are usually appointed for each group.[15]

Indirect purchaser litigation is usually more complex than direct purchaser litigation, both because the laws of a number of different states may be at issue, and because it may be challenging to prove how much of the overcharge was 'passed through' from the direct purchasers to end-user consumers and businesses. Federal judges who are familiar with *Illinois Brick*'s admonition about the complexity of indirect purchaser cases, and who have little or no experience with such cases, may be more hostile to class certification. Defendants in a few cases also have successfully challenged the standing of consumers who purchased the product at issue as a component of another product.[16] On the other hand, it is usually easier for antitrust class action lawyers to find appropriate indirect purchasers to represent, since they are more abundant. The potential class-wide damages may be much greater in an indirect than in a direct purchaser class action, because large

---

12 431 US 720 (1977).

13 490 US 93 (1989).

14 28 U.S.C. §§1332(d), 1453, and 1711–1715.

15 This trend has led some commentators, including the Antitrust Modernization Commission, to advocate the repeal of *Illinois Brick* and the symmetrical decision in *Hanover Shoe, Inc. v. United Shoe Machinery Corp.*, 392 US 481 (1968), which prohibits antitrust defendants from asserting that the direct purchaser 'passed on' overcharges to indirect purchasers, so that damages can be allocated between the various vertical plaintiff groups. *Antitrust Task Force Hearing on the 'Findings and Recommendations of the Antitrust Modernization Committee,'* 2007 WLNR 8780237 (May, 9 2007). For further discussion of the Class Action Fairness Act, see Chapter 7 and Chapter 8 of this *Handbook*.

16 *See In re Dynamic Random Access Memory (DRAM) Antitrust Litig.*, 516 F.Supp.2d 1072 (N.D. Cal. 2007) ('*DRAM I*') and 536 F.Supp.2d 1129 (N.D. Cal. 2008) ('*DRAM II*'). In the *DRAM I* and *DRAM II* decisions, the district court held that the indirect-purchaser plaintiffs who bought technology products containing DRAM did not have standing to maintain a class action against the defendant manufacturers of DRAM. The court applied the United States Supreme Court's *Associated General Contractors* ('AGC') factors (see fn. 42 *infra*) to the state-law claims of the indirect-purchaser plaintiffs and concluded that the indirect-purchaser plaintiffs who purchased computers or other products in which DRAM was a component lacked standing as a matter of law, because they did not 'participate' in the same market as the defendants who manufactured and sold DRAM chips. *DRAM II*, 536 F.Supp.2d at 1141. The *DRAM* decision is on appeal. Other courts have reached a contrary result, *e.g.*, *In re Graphics Processing Units Antitrust Litig*, 527 F.Supp.2d 1011, 1097–98 (N.D. Cal. 2007); *In re TFT-LCD Antitrust Litig.*, 586 F.Supp.2d 1109, 1123 (N.D. Cal. 2008).

direct purchasers frequently opt out of the class, and because the direct purchasers are often foreign companies that resold to consumers in the United States.[17]

For the typical cartel-based class litigation, the total number of indirect purchaser class action cases filed is usually much higher than the total number of direct purchaser cases. This is true not only because it is easier to sign up an indirect purchaser plaintiff, but also because cases are usually filed initially in many district courts around the country because of the various state laws at issue. Direct purchaser cases tend to be fewer in number, but unless the industry is such that there are only a small handful of direct purchaser plaintiffs (e.g., the *Intel* and *Microsoft* cases), there are almost always multiple direct and indirect cases filed. When there is more than one federal district court involved, the cases will be consolidated in one court before one federal judge by the United States Judicial Panel on Multidistrict Litigation.

Ethical restrictions and fee arrangements

When the client contacts the lawyer or law firm in the first instance, the principal ethical issue that needs to be addressed is the potential for conflicts of interest. The American Bar Association's Model Rules of Professional Conduct should be consulted, along with the ethical rules of the particular states where the lawyer practices or where the case may be filed, which usually are similar but may have slight variations.[18] Generally, conflicts rules prohibit lawyers from representing clients which have adverse or potentially adverse relationships with each other, unless each gives informed consent in writing. Larger law firms typically have a computerized system in place to identify potential adverse client relationships in order to ensure that they do not run afoul of this rule. With the increased mobility of lawyers from firm to firm, unforeseen conflicts may arise due to a lawyer's prior representation of an adverse client at another firm. Often this issue can be addressed through the creation of an ethical 'wall' between the affected lawyer and the rest of his or her new firm. Under certain circumstances, however, this conflict will be imputed to his new firm and lead to the entire firm's disqualification.[19]

When the lawyer contacts a potential class representative or other potential client, the same conflicts rules apply, plus an additional ethical consideration, the rules against client solicitation.

Generally, a lawyer may solicit an existing client but is severely restricted from directly

---

17 For example, in the *In re TFT-LCD* litigation, plaintiffs allege a price-fixing conspiracy among producers of LCD panels manufactured abroad, many of which were sold directly to other non-US manufacturers, who assembled the panels into finished products such as televisions that were sold in the United States. Defendants have asserted that under the Foreign Trade Antitrust Improvement Act (FTAIA), 15 U.S.C. §6a, indirect purchasers in the United States cannot recover based on these foreign direct purchases. The FTAIA is discussed in greater detail below.

18 ABA Model Rules of Professional Conduct, Rule 1.7(a), applies to conflicts of interest involving current clients. *See also* ABA Model Rule 1.8, which provides more specific conflicts rules for current clients.

19 *Schiessle v. Stephens*, 717 F.2d 417 (7th Cir. 1983); *In re Compact Disc Minimum Price Antitrust Litigation*, 2001 WL 243494 (D. Me. 2001); *Central Milk Producer Co-op. v. Sentry Food Stones, Inc.*; 573 F.2d 988 (8th Cir. 1978); *Pfarr v. Island Services Co., Inc.*, 124 F.R.D. 24 (D.R.I. 1989); *Fred Webner, Inc. v. Shell Oil Co.*, (E.D. Mo. 1977).

contacting potential clients with whom there is no prior relationship.[20] However, a lawyer may ask existing clients or colleagues in other firms to refer potential plaintiffs, and may even advertise in order to attract potential plaintiffs (attorney advertising is more common in product defect or other mass tort litigation than it is in antitrust litigation).[21]

Shortly after discussing any possible claim with a potential client, counsel should address options for fee arrangements. At one end of the spectrum are pure by-the-hour agreements, and at the other are 'fee upon success,' or straight contingent fee agreements, where the lawyer advances all costs and does not recover anything unless the client or class recovers something. Between these two extremes are so-called 'blended' fee agreements, which can contain a mix of reduced-rate hourly billing and sliding-scale 'percentage-of-recovery' arrangements that are tied to case milestones (pre-filing, post-complaint, pre-summary judgment, pre- and post-trial, etc.).

Antitrust cases today often cost millions of dollars to litigate and may not reach a resolution for five to ten years. To spread the risk in class actions, groups of plaintiffs' law firms often form joint ventures or de facto working groups, sometimes but not always by written agreement, in order to litigate a case together and share the risks and costs. A plaintiffs' law firm or group of firms must be confident that it has sufficient resources, in both lawyers and money, to staff and fund lengthy and costly litigation that may drag on for many years. There is certainly a greater risk assumed by the plaintiff's attorney who sues a corporate giant for unlawful monopolization or takes on a large industry for price fixing, compared with the attorney who files a duplicative, tag-along action along with dozens of others, without giving any serious thought to running the case themselves. Such 'tag-along' firms may be assigned work and assessed money toward costs, but at a greatly reduced level. Lead counsel are subject to court orders and must see the case through to the end even if it turns out to be a poor investment, but tag-along firms usually can decide well before then to cut their losses and stop working on the case.

For plaintiff cases brought by individual firms on a non-class basis, sometimes a straight hourly fee plus expenses agreement is reached. Since antitrust cases are very expensive but also, however, potentially very lucrative, the client and the lawyer often negotiate a 'blended' fee that may call for client payment of costs plus a reduced hourly rate, with a contingent fee depending on results. Some large opt-out cases, however, have been undertaken by law firms on a straight contingent fee basis, which can result in very large fees when tens of millions of dollars are recovered.[22]

---

[20] ABA Model Rules of Professional Conduct, Rule 7.3, applies to direct contact with prospective clients.

[21] In 2007, at least four partners in the prominent national plaintiffs' securities litigation firm formerly known as Milberg Weiss were indicted on federal charges of participating in a scheme to pay millions of dollars in secret kick-backs to several individuals in exchange for them serving as named plaintiffs in more than 225 class-action and shareholder derivative-action lawsuits that were filed across the United States. The case shined a spotlight on the potential for abuse in recruiting class representatives. *See, e.g.*, United States Attorney's Office, Central District of California, Press Release, 'Melvyn Weiss, Co-Founder of Milberg Weiss Law Firm, Indicted In Secret Kickback Scheme Involving Named Plaintiffs In Class Action Lawsuits' (Sept. 20, 2007).

[22] For further discussion of fee arrangements and the funding of cases, see Chapter 12 of this *Handbook*.

Investigative tools

A plaintiff's antitrust attorney should investigate and consider multiple factors before agreeing to represent either an individual client or a proposed class representative. First and foremost, the plaintiff's attorney must determine if it is a good case. Experience with similar cases helps greatly in this judgment, but even for an experienced antitrust lawyer it is not always obvious that the case is worth undertaking. In part this is because the antitrust laws have been established largely through decisions of the Supreme Court and lower federal appellate courts, and those decisions may change over time or be inconsistently applied by federal district courts. The circuit where the case is filed, and even the identity of the district judge, can make a huge difference in the outcome. Even a seemingly strong case on the merits may be uneconomical to pursue, at least on a contingent fee basis, because the damages are not high enough, the anticipated expenses for discovery and experts are too high, or the case is otherwise too risky to pursue on a contingent fee basis. Despite the pressure in class actions in particular to get a case on file as soon as possible, the prudent antitrust lawyer will carefully consider the relevant facts and law before filing it, and thoroughly research unsettled legal issues.

A successful antitrust attorney must become as knowledgeable as possible about the particular market and industry involved in the case. It is critical that the attorney gathers and analyzes information on the market, the industry players and channels of distribution, pricing and market trends, and volume of commerce, both foreign and domestic. Discovery of unusual market conditions or pricing trends, for example, can validate a client's or an attorney's suspicions that anticompetitive behavior is taking place. Unnatural price increases or supply restrictions, the consolidation of participants or the dominance of one participant, and high barriers to enter a market are all factors that lend themselves to imperfect competition. Some of this information can be collected online, or purchased from third party vendors that specialize in tracking and analyzing prices in a particular market. Developing this pre-filing body of information can take many months in some cases, and cost tens of thousands of dollars.

Information should be obtained from a variety of sources. The starting place, particularly in a non-class case, is with the client. The plaintiff's attorney should gather all documents and information in the client's custody and thoroughly explore any potential weaknesses. A potential plaintiff that is a competitor or terminated distributor of the proposed defendant will certainly be attacked by the defendants as having brought on its own problems through mismanagement or worse, and the evidence pertaining to this defense must be thoroughly and candidly reviewed with the client. Class representatives on the other hand, particularly consumers, are unlikely to have much relevant information beyond being able to substantiate their purchases of the product at issue. This information should also be gathered before the case is filed. Occasionally, class representatives also have dubious backgrounds and can be disqualified, thus any prior litigation history, arrest records, etc. should be explored.

The Internet is another primary investigatory tool. With just an online connection, attorneys and their staffs can investigate industries and markets around the world, and can quickly and inexpensively gather information about market participants, pricing history, supply shortages, capacity constraints, product demand, and a host of other relevant issues. The plaintiff's law firm should diligently scour the websites of US and international competition regulators as well as news websites and financial websites such as Bloomberg or Market Watch. In addition, for a relatively small investment, lawyers can subscribe to international news services which also provide inside reports on industries in which the antitrust violation is believed to have occurred. The exponential growth of online information has substantially increased the ability of antitrust lawyers to gather relevant information before filing a case and make more informed decisions about strategy.

Expert economists are another critical resource in antitrust litigation. It is very important for the plaintiff's lawyer to retain a good economist as quickly as possible when it appears that litigation will be commenced. Preferably this will be done before filing the lawsuit. A number of economists specialize in competition economics, or more generally in industrial organization, and are experienced expert witnesses. Some are generally known to be more sympathetic to plaintiffs' cases than others. In addition to providing the theoretical and factual support to the underlying allegations of the case and the potential damages, economists typically provide opinions on whether common issues predominate over individual issues for purposes of class certification, and on the appropriate measure and amount of damages. In big cases, several testifying economists and other experts may be retained for different issues. Testifying expert economists are usually supported by large staffs at economic consulting firms, which 'crunch the numbers' to support the testimony. The total expenses for economic advice and testimony over the course of the litigation can easily be millions of dollars. Unlike the lawyers, these economists cannot work on a contingent basis, lest they be accused of being biased for having a financial incentive in the outcome of the case (under ethical rules, lawyers cannot split fees with non-attorneys).[23]

It is a good (but expensive) idea to seek advice from an economist before filing a case. For example, economists can assist in determining whether a suspected market is conducive to collusion, whether pricing history is suspect, whether a suspected monopolist has sufficient market power in a definable relevant market, or whether there is a pro-competitive rationale for the defendants' conduct, and can otherwise assist in formulating the liability case. Industry experts, along with economists, can help analyze the various products in a market, the distribution channels, manufacturing processes and costs, and can identify potential roadblocks, such as atypical product specifications or potential problems in proving pass-through to indirect purchasers.

Plaintiffs' attorneys also sometimes hire private investigators prior to filing a suit. These investigators can conduct informal interviews of ex-employees or industry participants, or uncover evidence of relevant concealed activities. Care must be taken to stay within ethical rules in these situations.

Private investigators are particularly susceptible to violations arising from conversations with parties represented by opposing counsel or using improper surveillance methods. Counselors who hire private investigators must remain cognizant of the laws and principles that guide the conduct of undercover investigations.[24] The attorney

---

23 *See* ABA Model Rule 5.4.

24 *See* ABA Model Rule 4.2 ('In representing a client, a lawyer shall not communicate about the subject of the representation with a person the lawyer knows to be represented by another lawyer in the matter, unless the lawyer has the consent of the other lawyer or is authorized to do so

remains responsible for controlling investigations, and repercussions of an investigator's unethical behavior may be imputed to the attorney.[25]

News travels fast in the antitrust plaintiffs' community when a government agency announces that it is investigating suspected anticompetitive activity, when a news outlet reports a rumor of anticompetitive activity, or when a company announces in a regulatory filing that it has been subpoenaed in connection with an antitrust investigation. This information is readily available online. The activities of the Department of Justice (DOJ), the Federal Trade Commission (FTC), and state attorneys general can be monitored through news sites and the receipt of electronic alerts through various e-mail-based services. News of a 'dawn raid' or other coordinated activity by the DOJ, the European Commission (EC) and/or other competition regulators around the world including the Canadian Bureau of Competition, Japanese Fair Trade Commission (JFTC), and the Korean Fair Trade Commission (KFTC) often leads to attempts by plaintiffs' lawyers to quickly get cases on file. These agencies also report the status of their investigations online. The public companies being investigated by a governmental entity typically disclose this news in corporate press releases, and in Securities and Exchange Commission (SEC) and other regulatory filings.[26]

The announcement that a company is cooperating with the DOJ under the Antitrust Criminal Penalty Enhancement and Reform Act of 2004 (ACPERA) also draws the particular attention of plaintiffs' attorneys. ACPERA was designed to give leniency to a company that has engaged in criminal anticompetitive behavior but has voluntarily come forward and reported the activity.[27] The news of such cooperation can validate a plaintiff's attorney's belief that there is an underlying conspiracy, and can also suggest that in a subsequent lawsuit, cooperation by the defendant may be available. Under ACPERA, an amnesty applicant that cooperates with private litigants can avoid treble damages and joint-and-several liability in private litigation. Even though the appropriate level and the timing of such cooperation have not been clearly defined by the statute or

---

by law or a court order.'); *see also, e.g.*, N.J.S.A. §2A'156A-1 *et seq.* and 18 Pa. Cons. Stat. Ann. §5702 *et seq.* (wiretapping and electronic surveillance control acts).

[25] *In re Complaint of PMD Enterprises, Inc.*, 215 F.Supp.2d 519, 527 (D. N.J. 2002) (revocation of attorney's pro hac vice admission was appropriate sanction after attorney's private investigator engaged in improper ex parte conversation with members of opponents' litigation control group).

[26] Government agencies have the primary advantage over private litigants in that once they have the appropriate level of suspicion – for the US DOJ it is 'the belief that a crime has been committed' (*Antitrust Grand Jury Practice Manual*, Vol. 1, Ch. I.B.1.) – they may launch an investigation, which immediately allows them access to the internal workings of a company. The European Commission's unannounced inspections (intriguingly referred to as 'dawn raids') have been instrumental in breaking open many of the international cartels that plaintiffs' attorneys learn about and ultimately litigate here in the U.S.

Because the illegal operations of the cartelists and monopolists are inherently kept secret, learning the details of a violation of the antitrust laws can be one of the biggest challenges for antitrust practitioners. Making this challenge more difficult is the fact that the anticompetitive activities at the heart of today's cases now span continents and reside in multiple levels of huge, international corporations. For cartels in particular, the details of 'who met with who?' and 'what was agreed to?' are jewels of knowledge that are sometimes never fully uncovered by regulatory bodies or teams of plaintiffs' attorneys.

[27] ACPERA is currently due to expire in June 2020.

case law, there is a reasonable expectation that when a named defendant is identified as being the ACPERA applicant, that cooperation will be forthcoming.[28]

News of such government raids or investigations usually prompts plaintiffs' lawyers to do some independent analysis to see whether there is a basis for a lawsuit. However, more than a raid or an announced grand jury investigation is required before a case can be filed. Courts have held such news to be an insufficient basis standing alone to sustain a complaint against a motion to dismiss.[29]

In earlier years, class actions filed in response to announcements of government investigations or even findings of liability were not filed as quickly and frequently as they are today. Counsel would usually wait to see what developed from a government investigation before filing. For example, everyone in the plaintiffs' bar knew in 1999 that the government was investigating Microsoft and that a lengthy monopolization trial was underway in the federal district court, yet only one class action, in California state court, was on file. After Judge Jackson announced his findings against Microsoft in the government's case, however, dozens of cases were filed around the country within weeks.[30] Ten years later, with a faster flow of information (facilitated by the Internet, e-mail notices of case filings and government action, actions of foreign regulatory investigations and access to foreign periodicals) and more competition among plaintiffs' lawyers, there is a tendency to pull the trigger much faster, sometimes, regrettably, with insufficient grounds to do so.

Nevertheless, the criticism from some quarters that class action lawyers merely piggy-back on the efforts of government agencies is misguided. Many successful cases have not depended on prior government action at all, while in others the recoveries by private plaintiffs were well above the fines obtained by the government.[31]

After the case is filed, the plaintiff's lawyer must continue to regularly monitor reports of government actions against the suspected cartelist or monopolist. News of indictments or fines can bolster a case already on file. However, certainly not all regulatory investigations lead to guilty pleas, corporate fines, or criminal indictments. And, for those that do, the events often occur a substantial time after an investigation has been opened and after litigation has been filed. Even following the news of an investigation, counsel often must engage in years of aggressive and expensive litigation before a government action is concluded.[32]

---

28 For a discussion of the utility of the leniency program and ACPERA as evidence gathering tools, see Chapter 10 of this *Handbook*; for a discussion of how the leniency program and ACPERA impact the interplay of public and private enforcement generally, see Chapter 13.

29 *See, e.g., In re Graphics Processing Units Antitrust Litig.*, 253 F.R.D. 478, 482 (N.D. Cal. 2008); *In re Static Random Access Memory (SRAM) Antitrust Litig.*, 580 F.Supp.2d 896, 902 (N.D. Cal. 2008).

30 *Microsoft Corp. Antitrust Litg.*, No. 00-5594 (Hennepin Co. Dist. Ct., Minnesota); *Microsoft Corp. Antitrust Litig.*, No. CL 82311 (Polk Co. Dist. Ct., Iowa); *Microsoft Corp. Antitrust.*, No. 05-CV-010927; *Microsoft Cases,* J.C.C.P. No. 4106.

31 *See, e.g.,* Robert H. Lande & Joshua P. Davis, *Benefits From Private Enforcement: An Analysis Of Forty Cases*, 42 University of San Francisco Law Review 879 (2008).

32 Parallel government activities do not always benefit plaintiffs in an antitrust case. They can lead to disruptions to private actions, such as government interventions, discovery stays, and potential weakening of a private action if the government ends its investigation without any

The presence or absence of prior government action can influence the courts in their decisions. One federal court noted in its decision denying class certification that, unlike Microsoft cases in which very similar classes had been certified, in the case at hand the government had dropped its investigation without bringing any charges.[33]

Financial considerations

In addition to the extraordinary but necessary cost of expert economists discussed above, discovery costs for document review and depositions in antitrust cases are enormous. Antitrust cases have always been notorious for massive and expensive discovery. The shift to discovery of electronic information has made the once dirty and time-consuming work by junior associates of digging through hundreds of boxes in dusty warehouses seem quaint, but ironically has largely increased the cost of document review. Now, document productions consist of massive production of electronic information, comprised of e-mails and similar electronic information. This requires the plaintiffs to invest in sophisticated and expensive electronic databases for document review. Some larger plaintiffs' firms have internal systems for such review, but in most cases the law firms hire third party vendors to provide this service, at a cost that can range into millions of dollars. Due to the international scope of some of today's cartel cases, these documents are often in multiple foreign languages, so they require costly translation software, paid interpreters, or teams of bilingual attorneys and paralegals. The sheer volume of these document productions, which may involve millions of pages and are measured in gigabytes or even terabytes, requires many months for review.

Dozens or even hundreds of contract attorneys are sometimes hired by plaintiffs' firms. This is a risk-reducing strategy because the firm has no obligation to retain the contract lawyer beyond the duration of the review. Usually, the hourly rates for contract attorneys that class counsel claim in fee petitions are well above the out-of-pocket payments to those attorneys or to the agencies that supply them.

The global scope of today's cartels also increases the cost of litigation. Antitrust actions now typically involve multiple global companies, which makes the task of obtaining discovery that much more difficult and expensive. Hundreds of depositions are often taken in major antitrust cases, sometimes requiring travel throughout the world. Costs for court reporters and videographers can be thousands of dollars for each deposition taken. In addition, dozens of companies are often subpoenaed as third parties, either

---

indictments or guilty pleas. The government can also negotiate terms of pleas that limit the scope of the conspiracy and create somewhat artificial boundaries within a private litigation. Private party discovery can also be severely limited by prior government investigations. For example, companies that have been subpoenaed by a grand jury must produce documents to the US DOJ. These productions are negotiated and limited according to discussions had with the government representatives. When that finite universe is produced to the DOJ, it often serves as the benchmark for what private plaintiffs will first receive pursuant to a request for production of documents in their litigation. Since the documents are already collected by these companies, they can usually be produced quite quickly, but plaintiffs will fight an uphill battle to supplement such productions for any reason down the line – whether to increase the time period, learn of how the original production was queried, expand on a particular request, or the like.

[33] *GPU*, *supra* note 13 at 482. For further discussion on how plaintiffs' attorneys may obtain evidence, see Chapter 10 of this *Handbook*.

to obtain facts that bear on the liability allegations or, particularly in indirect purchaser cases, to obtain purchase and sale information relevant to establishing pass through and damages.

The out-of-pocket costs associated with conducting discovery and working with experts in major antitrust cases can easily amount to several million dollars.[34] In class actions and other contingency cases, these and all litigation costs are borne entirely by the plaintiffs' attorneys.

Each firm that participates in a large contingency antitrust case is expected to contribute regularly to a common litigation fund, from which expert and discovery costs are paid. These assessments have become increasingly larger, making it more difficult for smaller firms to keep up. Plaintiffs' attorneys that win court-appointed leadership roles can be expected to pay hundreds of thousands more dollars to the common fund than their co-counsel. Although they are rewarded with significantly higher fees if the case is successful, they are also the ones left holding the bag if the case does not reach a favorable resolution. Experts, court reporters, and document vendors expect to get paid, win or lose.

In addition to providing financial support, a plaintiffs' law firm in a class action is often expected to provide attorney power to help fuel large discovery efforts. Attorney reviewers are regularly needed to donate substantial hours to the electronic discovery review, which also can be particularly taxing on smaller firms.

Defining the claims to be asserted

After the client has been retained, the fee agreement has been signed, the legal and factual investigation has commenced, and the financial risks have been assessed, the final step before actually starting the litigation is to decide how to define the claims to be asserted.

Most private antitrust cases fall into one of two categories: claims against a group of firms, operating as a *cartel* in restraint of trade, or claims against a single firm, operating as a *monopoly* in restraint of trade.[35] The Sherman Act makes both illegal, and the Clayton Act confers upon certain victims the right of private enforcement to collect damages, and enjoin future harm.[36] Other kinds of anticompetitive activity such as tying arrangements, vertical dealer terminations, and price discrimination are also outlawed by antitrust law, but private challenges to these activities are relatively rare.[37] The statutes, however, tell the antitrust plaintiff only part of the story.

The sweeping language in §1 of the Sherman Act – '[e]very contract, combination . . .

---

[34] *See, e.g., Microsoft I-V*, J.C.C.P. No. 4106 (document production costs and the costs for experts and consultants were $853,110.39 and $6,088,480.74, respectively).

[35] *See* 15 U.S.C. §§1, 2.

[36] *See* 15 U.S.C. §§15, 26.

[37] Private plaintiffs can sue to block mergers under §7 of the Clayton Act, but damages are not recoverable in such cases. Normally merger cases are brought by the Department of Justice or the FTC. However, companies that can afford to pay for them sometimes bring them in a private capacity, and it is not unheard of for law firms to file on behalf of smaller plaintiffs on a contingent basis. Attorneys' fees are awarded by statute to a successful plaintiff, and the cases sometimes are settled through payment by the merging defendants to the plaintiff to drop the case.

or conspiracy, in restraint of trade . . . is declared to be illegal' – has been narrowed by a century of precedent that limits the category of forbidden contracts, combinations, and conspiracies to only those that *unreasonably* restrain trade.[38] In a similar fashion, the courts read §15 of the Clayton Act, which declares that 'any person who shall be injured in his business or property by reason of anything forbidden in the antitrust laws may sue therefore in any district court,' with the gloss that 'any person' means 'any person *with antitrust standing*.'[39] Thus, a lavish body of antitrust jurisprudence fleshes out these statutes' bare language.[40]

Just as the antitrust law has refined the definitions of who may sue for what, it has also drawn distinctions regarding the antitrust plaintiff's burden of proof. The elements of a typical cartel claim are: (1) existence of a contract, combination, or conspiracy; (2) that unreasonably restrained trade; (3) affecting interstate commerce; and (4) causing antitrust injury to the plaintiff.[41]

Yet not all claims are created equal. Some cartel claims – those alleging agreements among horizontal competitors to fix prices or to divide markets – fall into the category of automatic, or 'per se,' illegal conduct. These practices, the courts have concluded, 'lack any redeeming virtue,' and 'always or almost always tend to restrict competition and decrease output.'[42] Accordingly, the antitrust plaintiff alleging, for example, that a group of competitors entered into a horizontal price-fixing conspiracy need only prove the existence of the conspiracy in order to establish that the conspiracy was an unreasonable restraint of trade. The plaintiffs must still prove injury and damages in order to prevail.

By contrast, the balance of cartel claims (vertical price-fixing agreements, exclusivity arrangements, group boycotts, tying, etc.), and all monopoly claims, proceed under a 'rule of reason' or other non-per se test of illegality.[43] This means that the antitrust

---

38 *See Standard Oil Co. v. United States*, 221 US 1 (1911); *State Oil Co. v. Khan*, 522 US 3 (1997).

39 *See Associated General Contractors of California, Inc. v. California State Council of Carpenters,* 459 US 519 (1983) (describing five-factor test to satisfy antitrust standing); *Illinois Brick Co. v. Illinois*, 431 US 720 (1977) (limiting right to seek federal antitrust damages to plaintiffs who purchased directly from defendants).

40 For further discussion of antitrust standing, see Chapter 6 and Chapter 9 of this *Handbook*.

41 *See, e.g., William O. Gilley Enterprises, Inc. v. Atlantic Richfield Co.*, 561 F.3d 1004, 1009 (9th Cir. 2009); *cf. Cost Management Services, Inc. v. Washington Natural Gas Co.*, 99 F.3d 937, 949–950 (9th Cir. 1996) (identifying the elements of typical monopoly claim as: (1) possession of monopoly power in the relevant market; (2) willful acquisition or maintenance of such power; and (3) causing antitrust injury to the plaintiff).

42 *Leegin Creative Leather Products, Inc. v. PSKS, Inc.*, 551 US 877, 127 S.Ct. 2705, 2713 (2007).

43 Certain cases are judged under various other tests that have been articulated by the Supreme Court and appellate courts. *See, e.g., California Dental Ass'n v. F.T.C.*, 526 US 756, 770 (1999) (explaining the abbreviated or 'quick-look' analysis under the rule of reason); *Brooke Group Ltd. v. Brown & Williamson Tobacco Corp.*, 509 US 209, 222–223 (1993) (describing analysis for predatory pricing claims as requiring (1) below-cost pricing by a competitor and (2) a dangerous probability that the competitor will recoup its investment in below-cost prices); *Continental T.V. Inc. v. GTE Sylvania Inc.*, 433 US 36, 49 (1977) (under the rule of reason, 'the factfinder weighs all of

plaintiff alleging, for example, that firms in a vertical distribution chain agreed to set minimum prices must not only prove the existence of the agreement, but must then prove that, under the circumstances, the conspiracy worked an unreasonable restraint of trade. That is, the plaintiff must foreclose the possibility that the pro-competitive effects of the agreement outweigh the anticompetitive effects.

While the bumper-sticker phrase 'rule of reason = plaintiff loses' has been disproved in several high-profile antitrust cases proceeding under the rule,[44] the underlying sentiment highlights the special care with which a rule of reason claim must be prosecuted. Although the rule of reason is described as the 'standard' antitrust approach, with the per se rule as the exception, in practice, horizontal price-fixing cartel conspiracy claims under the per se rule dominate the antitrust docket – both in terms of private enforcement, as well as government prosecution.[45] The reason for this is clear: with fewer elements to prove, the risk analysis favors the plaintiff and increases the defendant's potential exposure to an adverse outcome. Therefore, the first task of the antitrust plaintiff's lawyer is to determine whether the per se rule will apply and, if not, evaluate the added complexity that will attend a claim proceeding under the rule of reason or other, more stringent standard of proof.[46]

Anticipating defenses

With the claim in mind, the antitrust plaintiff must anticipate the roadblocks the defendants are likely to mount at the pleading stage, and how to overcome these obstacles. The responsive Rule 12(b) motion seeking dismissal of the complaint is a standard feature of antitrust litigation. The grounds for a motion to dismiss the complaint are varied but familiar, and include: not plausible (*Twombly v. Bell Atlantic*);[47] not connected to this country (FTAIA); not justiciable (preemption); and not the right plaintiff (*AGC*). The well-pleaded antitrust complaint anticipates and neutralizes, as much as possible, each of these grounds.

In *Twombly*, the Supreme Court used the context of a Sherman Act cartel claim to refine the 'notice pleading' standard applicable to all civil complaints under Rule 8:

> While a complaint attacked by a Rule 12(b)(6) motion to dismiss does not need detailed factual allegations, a plaintiff's obligation to provide the 'grounds' of his 'entitlement to relief' requires more than labels and conclusions, and a formulaic recitation of the elements of a cause of action will not do. Factual allegations must be enough to raise a right to relief above the speculative level. [internal citations omitted].

---

the circumstances in deciding whether a restrictive practice should be prohibited as imposing an unreasonable restraint on competition.').

44 *See, e.g.*, the *Microsoft* private antitrust cases.

45 *See, e.g.*, US Attorneys' Manual, Title 7, Antitrust Resource Manual, §8 ('The most common violations of the Sherman Act – and the violations most likely to be prosecuted criminally – are price fixing, bid riggings, and territorial or customer allocation among competitors (commonly described as "horizontal agreements").').

46 For further discussion of the elements of an antitrust claim and rule of reason versus per se analysis, see Chapter 4 of this *Handbook*.

47 550 US 544, 555 (2007).

Twombly directs the courts to review the allegations of a complaint and determine whether the plaintiff has 'nudged' its claims 'across the line from conceivable to plausible.'[48] The courts have been grappling with this new standard ever since.[49]

'Plausibility' under *Twombly* is often in the eye of the (district judge) beholder. Clearly, the more factual detail included in a complaint the better – yet even this aphorism does not explain fully the outcome of recent *Twombly* motions in antitrust cases. Consider the orders on motions to dismiss in the remarkably similar cases of *In re LTL Shipping Services Antitrust Litig.*[50] and *In re Rail Freight Fuel Surcharge Antitrust Litig.*[51] Both complaints alleged that a group of shippers (truckers and railroads, respectively) with dominant market shares conspired to coordinate near-lock-step fuel surcharges levied on the plaintiff customers. To support these allegations, the plaintiffs in both complaints noted the defendants' membership in industry trade groups and the habit of posting surcharge announcements on the web.

The district courts split in their rulings on the defendants' respective *Twombly* motions to dismiss. The *LTL* court concluded that, '[i]n sum, Plaintiffs' allegations do not show enough facts for the Court to find that agreement was plausible,'[52] whereas the *Railroad* court held that, '[t]he direct purchaser plaintiffs have provided robust factual details in their complaint supporting their "independent allegation of actual agreement" from which the Court can infer that it is plausible that an actual agreement existed.'[53] In light of the striking similarity of the complaints, these outcomes are difficult to reconcile.

The presence of government investigative activity has similarly proven to be an unreliable indicator of how a court will rule on a *Twombly* motion. Thus, despite the fact of multiple enforcement proceedings against several defendants by the Department of Justice, the Securities and Exchange Commission, and the Internal Revenue Service, the court in *In re Municipal Derivatives Antitrust Litig.* dismissed the complaint.[54]

Yet where plaintiffs alleged a price-fixing conspiracy by makers of 'flash' memory chips, and noted that many of the defendants were already under government investigation for price fixing other kinds of memory chips, the court denied the *Twombly* motion: 'At bottom, while these facts may not prove the existence of a conspiracy with respect to NAND flash memory, they are properly pleaded for the purpose of establishing the plausibility that such a conspiracy existed.'[55] Only the most basic insights for the anti-

---

48 *Id.* at 570.

49 *See also Ashcroft v. Iqbal*, 129 S.Ct. 1937 (2009), holding that the *Twombly* pleading standard applies to all civil complaints under Fed. R. Civ. P. 8.

50 Case No. 1:08-MD-01895, 2009 WL 323219 (N.D. Ga. Jan. 28, 2009).

51 587 F.Supp.2d 27 (D.D.C. 2008).

52 *LTL*, 2009 WL 323219 at *17.

53 *Rail Freight*, 587 F.Supp.2d at 34 (internal citation omitted); *see also In re Hawaiian & Guamanian Cabotage Antitrust Litig.*, 647 F.Supp.2d 1250 (W.D. Wash. 2009) (dismissing complaint under *Twombly* standard where allegations centered on parallel movements in fuel surcharges).

54 620 F.Supp.2d 499, 514 (S.D.N.Y. 2009) ('Named Plaintiffs' citations to these investigations do not constitute factual averments of a §1 claim that would allow such a claim to survive a motion to dismiss.').

55 *In re Flash Memory Antitrust Litig.*, 643 F.Supp.2d 1133, 1149 (N.D. Cal. 2009); *see also In re Chocolate Confectionary Antitrust Litig.*, 602 F.Supp.2d 538, 576 (M.D. Pa. 2009) (denying

trust plaintiff can be salvaged from the *Twombly* landscape, but they bear great importance: investigate and plead every fact available, and be satisfied that the complaint is 'plausible' as the courts of the relevant venue understand and apply the standard.

While *Twombly* is probably the most-often cited grounds for a motion to dismiss, the rise of a global economic system has resulted in an increase in the filing of motions to dismiss based on the once-obscure Foreign Trade Antitrust Improvements Act (FTAIA).[56] The statute should be consulted whenever any potential antitrust claim will name a non-US defendant. 'The FTAIA seeks to make clear to American exporters (and to firms doing business abroad) that the Sherman Act does not prevent them from entering into business arrangements (say, joint-selling arrangements), however anticompetitive, as long as those arrangements adversely affect only foreign markets.'[57]

The statute itself is a muddle of double-negatives and exceptions that has been politely described as 'inelegantly phrased.'[58] The Supreme Court has summarized FTAIA as 'removing from the Sherman Act's reach, (1) export activities and (2) other commercial activities taking place abroad, unless those activities adversely affect domestic commerce, imports to the United States, or exporting activities of one engaged in such activities within the United States.'[59]

In considering a potential antitrust claim that involves a non-US party, there are two alternative paths for avoiding the application of an FTAIA dismissal. The first, and simplest, path to avoidance is to bring the claim within the 'import trade or import commerce' exception, whereby the antitrust defendants, although located and acting abroad, are alleged to have imported goods or services into the US.[60]

The second, and more complicated, path to avoidance is to plead that the foreign conduct of the defendants, although not directly involving defendants' importation of good or services into the US, nonetheless '(1) has a "direct, substantial, and reasonably foreseeable effect" on domestic commerce, and (2) "such effect gives rise to a [Sherman Act] claim."'[61] This 'domestic effects' exception analysis is elaborate, and discussed in greater detail later in this *Handbook*. The preliminary consideration to keep in mind, however, is that the link between defendants' foreign conduct and the domestic effects must be clear and strong.[62]

Moreover, where the US market for a good or service is just one of many affected by a foreign, global conspiracy, many courts have been hostile to allow the antitrust claim to go forward.[63] These cases should cause the antitrust plaintiff contemplating a claim

---

motion to dismiss where complaint detailed the Canadian government's investigation of defendants, because '[d]efendants' alleged conduct in Canada enhances the plausibility of the alleged US price-fixing conspiracy.').

56 15 U.S.C. §6a.

57 *F. Hoffmann-La Roche Ltd. v. Empagran S.A.*, 542 US 155, 161 (2004).

58 *Carpet Group Intern. v. Oriental Rug Importers Ass'n, Inc.*, 227 F.3d 62, 69 (D.N.J. 2000).

59 *Empagran*, 542 US at 161.

60 *See Carpet Group*, 227 F.3d at 71 (holding that claims against foreign association of importers and wholesalers of oriental rugs invoked the import trade or commerce exception).

61 *Empagran*, 542 US at 158–159 (quoting 15 U.S.C. §6a(1)(A), (2)).

62 *See US v. LSL Biotechnologies,* 379 F.3d 672, 680 (9th Cir. 2004) (discussing meaning of 'direct' effect).

63 *See, e.g., Dee-K Enters., Inc. v. Heveafil Snd. Bhd.*, 299 F.3d 281, 295 (4th Cir. 2002)

involving a non-US defendant to evaluate whether the claim will reasonably fall within an exception to the FTAIA.[64]

In the same vein, certain other statutes and legal doctrines can frustrate attempts to sue non-US defendants that are directly or indirectly controlled by a foreign state.[65]

While the presence of a non-US defendant in a potential antitrust claim should trigger research as to the effect of the FTAIA and other legal defenses to the claim, the presence of a defendant subject to some type of federal regulation or oversight should alert the antitrust plaintiff to the possibility of antitrust preemption. Several industries enjoy some form of immunity from private antitrust claims under a grant of express antitrust preemption. For example, agricultural producers are free to form cooperative organizations for purposes of marketing such goods because of the Capper-Volstead Act, which places such conduct beyond the reach of the antitrust laws.[66] The airline industry, as a result of de-regulation in the late 1970s, also enjoys limited immunity from state-law claims relating to the rates, routes, or service of an airline under the Airline Deregulation Act;[67] however, this immunity does not extend to *federal* antitrust claims.

In other circumstances, the courts have held that a regulatory system works an implied preemption of antitrust laws in favor of the regulated entity. In *Credit Suisse Securities (USA) LLC v. Billing*,[68] the Supreme Court held that an antitrust claim against securities brokers was preempted due to a 'plain repugnancy' between the antitrust laws and the specific regulations of brokers under the securities laws. The Court applied a four-factor analysis for determining if the goals of the securities laws and the antitrust claim could be reconciled. Concluding that reconciliation was not possible, the Court held that the more general antitrust laws had to yield to the specific securities regulation.[69]

Closely related to the concept of implied preemption is the filed rate doctrine. This judicially-created rule provides that a carrier whose rates are subject to certain federal regulation cannot be sued for antitrust damages arising from those rates.[70] The doctrine applies to some federally-regulated railroads and motor carriers, electricity wholesalers and pipeline operators, and telecommunications providers.

The rationale for applying the filed rate doctrine to dismiss rate-challenging lawsuits is

---

(affirming judgment for foreign defendants because under the domestic effects test, 'these links to the United States are mere drops in the sea of conduct that occurred in Southeast Asia (and around the world)'), *cert denied*, 539 US 969 (2003).

[64] For further discussion of *Twombly*, the FTAIA and procedural defenses generally, see Chapter 9 of this *Handbook*; for a discussion of how the FTAIA has served as an obstacle to the United States becoming a single forum for private claims in the context of global cartels, see Chapter 37 of this *Handbook*.

[65] *See, e.g.*, Foreign Sovereign Immunities Act, 28 U.S.C. §1602 *et seq.; Mannington Mills v. Congoleum Corp.*, 595 F.2d 1287, 1293 (3rd Cir. 1979) (explaining concept of 'foreign sovereign compulsion doctrine,' as concerning immunities arising when a foreign government compels a business to violate US antitrust laws).

[66] *See* 7 U.S.C. §291.

[67] 49 U.S.C. §41713(b)(1)

[68] 551 US 264, 127 S.Ct. 2383 (2007).

[69] *Id.* at 2392.

[70] *See Keogh v. Chicago and Northwestern Ry.*, 260 US 156, 163–164 (1922) (announcing the doctrine); *Square D Co. v. Niagara Frontier Tariff Bureau, Inc.*, 476 US 409 (1986) (upholding the doctrine).

two-fold: first, it prevents the carriers from collecting different rates among like customers. Second, it preserves the exclusivity of the regulatory agency's power to determine rate reasonableness by placing the rate-making process beyond the reach of the courts. Courts hearing antitrust and other substantive law claims against regulated carriers look at whether granting relief will require the court to determine the reasonableness of a rate subject to federal regulation. If so, the filed rate doctrine bars the claim.[71]

The common theme across the various antitrust preemption doctrines is that the courts will engage in a close analysis before concluding that an antitrust claim is preempted. Moreover, often there are significant exceptions and limitations on such preemption. If relevant, the antitrust plaintiff should dig deep into the preemption issue to locate these exceptions and limitations in order to keep the claim viable.

Another type of challenge interposed by defendants at the pleading stage with some frequency relates to the antitrust standing of the plaintiff to bring the claim. This type of challenge is typically shorthanded as an '*AGC*' motion, stemming from the Supreme Court's decision in *Associated General Contractors of California, Inc. v. California State Council of Carpenters*.[72] There, the Court held that a trade union did not have standing to pursue an antitrust claim alleging that a contractors' association conspired to restrain the union's activities. The Court balanced five factors, summarized as: '(1) the nature of the plaintiff's alleged injury; that is, whether it was the type the antitrust laws were intended to forestall; (2) the directness of the injury; (3) the speculative measure of the harm; (4) the risk of duplicative recovery; and (5) the complexity in apportioning damages.'[73]

The typical *AGC* motion is now most often seen in antitrust claims brought on behalf of *indirect* purchasers (who cannot sue under the Sherman Act) in federal court but based on state antitrust law. *AGC*, a case interpreting federal antitrust law, has been held to apply to the standing requirements of some states' antitrust laws.[74] Yet even this application of federal standing law to state substantive claims is the subject of controversy, creating an unsettled area of law.[75] The antitrust plaintiff considering a claim under state substantive law (usually an indirect purchaser claim) must investigate whether *AGC* may apply to the particular state statute, and whether, if so, the five-factor *AGC* analysis weighs in favor of standing.

Deciding where to file the case

Antitrust cases can be filed in any federal district court.[76] As a practical matter, though, cases are usually filed where the plaintiff is located if it is a non-class case, unless the law

---

71 *See E. & J. Gallo Winery v. EnCana Corp.*, 503 F.3d 1027 (9th Cir. 2007) (holding that filed rate doctrine is limited to claims involving rates subject to federal agency's jurisdiction, but does not apply to rates beyond the jurisdiction of the federal agency).

72 459 US 519 (1983).

73 *American Ad. Mgmt., Inc. v. General Tel. Co. of Cal.*, 190 F.3d 1051, 1054 (9th Cir. 1999) (citing *AGC*, 459 US at 535).

74 *See In re Flash Memory Antitrust Litig.*, 2009 WL 1096602 at *12 (N.D. Cal. Mar. 31, 2009).

75 See note 17 *supra*.

76 15 U.S.C. §7; *Blumstock Bros. Advertising Agency v. Curtis Pub*, 252 US 436, 440 ('The Sherman Anti-Trust Act [*sic*] created a cause of action in favor of any person to recover by suit in

is more favorable in another location.[77] Sometimes a defendant is strongly identified with its principal place of business, e.g., Microsoft and the State of Washington, and the plaintiffs' lawyer probably will want to avoid bringing the case in that jurisdiction.

Although the law is theoretically the same in all federal district courts, certain districts and circuits have a reputation for being more plaintiff-friendly than others. Often this is based on a track record of success by plaintiffs' lawyers in a particular court, or on more favorable appellate decisions by the circuit court of appeals in charge of those districts. Plaintiffs' lawyers in both class and non-class cases should give careful thought to selecting the most favorable venue.

Would-be class actions are often filed in multiple district courts around the country, often depending on the locations of the law firms filing them. When this happens, the United States Judicial Panel on Multidistrict Litigation, colloquially called the MDL Panel, which consists of district judges from various parts of the country, will choose one district court in which to centralize them. Just as plaintiffs will advocate assignment to a district perceived as more plaintiff-friendly, defense counsel will advocate assignment to a more conservative venue. Groups of plaintiffs' lawyers often will form alliances to back a particular destination over another, in return for promises of support for a significant role in the leadership of the case. The MDL Panel considers a number of factors in making its decision, including convenience of the parties and potential witnesses, how many cases have been filed in each of the various districts, whether significant activity already has occurred in one of the candidate transferee courts, the experience of the district judge who potentially may supervise the case, and the relative volume of complex cases already on file in the various districts.[78]

---

any District Court'); *see also* 15 U.S.C. §15, the Clayton Act: 'any person who shall be injured in his business or property by reason of anything forbidden in the antitrust laws may sue therefore in any district court'.

[77] *AMD v. Intel* was filed in the district court in Delaware even though both companies are located in the Bay Area, presumably because AMD thought that the applicable law was more favorable in light of *United States v. Dentsply Int'l, Inc.*, 399 F.3d 181 (3d Cir. 2005) and *LePages, Inc., v. 3M Company, Inc.*, 324 F.3d 141 (3d Cir. 2003).

[78] *See* John G. Heyburn II, *A View from the Panel: Part of the Solution*, 82 Tul. L. Rev. 2225 (2008), in which the chair of the Panel reviews the trends and explains the process by which the Panel makes its decisions. For further discussion of the Judicial Panel on Multidistrict Litigation, see Chapter 7 and Chapter 8 of this *Handbook*.

6 Parties entitled to pursue a claim

Eric L. Cramer and Daniel C. Simons[1]

Introduction

Antitrust violations often reverberate widely throughout a market and the economy more generally, impacting a myriad of market participants in a broad variety of ways. Hence, for a single violation, there may be multiple victims, each with potentially cognizable antitrust claims.

Under the literal and broad terms of the US antitrust laws, all persons or entities suffering harm to their 'business or property'[2] due to anticompetitive conduct theoretically have a claim to recover three times their damages resulting from that conduct.

However, the courts have placed prudential limits on both the types of entities that can bring suit for violations of the Sherman Act and the circumstances under which such suits can be brought. These limitations come in the form of a multi-pronged test that examines the claimant, the linkage between the alleged harm and the challenged conduct, the type of claim asserted, and, in certain circumstances, the complexity of the proof needed to prove the claim. Because of this test, determining whether a plaintiff has standing to bring an antitrust claim can sometimes present complex and difficult issues,[3] and thus has generated a myriad of decisions over the years.

Chief among the restrictions on who can bring a claim is the need for the private antitrust plaintiff to demonstrate 'antitrust injury.' For that, the law first looks to see if a private plaintiff has sustained the type of injury the antitrust laws are meant to prevent.[4] Second, the plaintiff's injury must flow from that which makes the defendant's acts unlawful.[5] This portion of the test asks whether the alleged injury is connected to the purposes of the antitrust laws: the protection of competition.[6] A showing of antitrust injury – or the threat of such injury – flowing from the antitrust violation is a prerequisite for obtaining damages or injunctive relief under the federal antitrust laws.

Antitrust injury alone, however, is not sufficient to entitle a plaintiff to treble damages under §4 of the Clayton Act, 15 U.S.C. §15. An antitrust violation can send 'ripples' of harm throughout various levels and segments of the economy. Courts have observed that permitting multiple damage claims for similar injuries arising from an antitrust violation could lead to duplicative recoveries or complex proceedings to apportion damages among claimants. Therefore, the Supreme Court has required a claimant to

---

1 Eric L. Cramer and Daniel C. Simons are, respectively, a shareholder and an associate at Berger & Montague, P.C. Both focus their practices on antitrust and complex litigation.

2 15 U.S.C. §15.

3 Arroyo-Melecio v. Puerto Rican Am. Ins. Co., 398 F.3d 56, 72 (1st Cir. 2005) ('in many ways the standing question is the most difficult issue in [a] case').

4 Brunswick Corp. v. Pueblo Bowl-O-Mat, Inc., 429 US 477, 489 (1977).

5 Id.

6 II Phillip E. Areeda & Herbert Hovenkamp, Antitrust Law ¶362 (1995).

meet several 'prudential' factors before it is allowed to bring a claim for treble damages under the Clayton Act.[7] Those plaintiffs who meet these factors are said to possess 'antitrust standing.'

One group of claimants has almost universally been recognized to have antitrust standing for both injunctive relief and money damages: those who purchased a product whose price was artificially inflated by alleged anticompetitive conduct *directly* from the accused monopolist or cartel member, *i.e.*, 'direct purchasers.' Direct purchasers typically claim harm and seek damages measured by overcharges, which are measured as the difference between the price actually paid to the defendant for the affected product and the price that would have prevailed but for the illegal conduct.[8] Thus, the recovery sought by direct purchasers is directly related to the harm to competition due to anticompetitive practices, *i.e.*, the higher prices that flow from competitive restrictions. In addition, because the harm is direct, it is nearly always found to 'flow' from the antitrust violation. For reasons discussed below, direct purchasers are the only purchasers in the chain of distribution entitled to recover overcharges resulting from antitrust violations under federal law. As a result, they are permitted to recover the entire overcharge, without a set-off reflecting the extent to which the direct purchaser may have 'passed on' the overcharge down the chain of distribution or benefitted economically from the challenged conduct.

In contrast with direct purchasers, *indirect* purchasers must show a sufficient causal nexus between the anticompetitive conduct and their injuries before they are granted antitrust standing. Even then, standing is almost always restricted to equitable relief. The corollary to the Supreme Court's ruling allowing direct purchasers to recover the entire overcharge is that indirect purchasers are not entitled to monetary relief under the Sherman Act.[9] However, indirect purchasers are permitted to recover damages under the laws of many states.[10]

Those in competition with a monopolist or cartel are also commonly permitted to pursue claims to recover for injuries they may have suffered due to the anticompetitive conduct. However, a competitor cannot merely show that its business or market share was adversely impacted by an anticompetitive practice. Even if the defendant otherwise violated the antitrust laws, if the competitor's claimed harm constituted losses incurred as a result of competition on the merits, there can be no antitrust injury.[11]

Finally, several other types of claimants have appeared as plaintiffs in antitrust suits alleging harm flowing from antitrust violations, including shareholders of corporations, suppliers, employees, terminated distributors, unions, trade groups, and others. Antitrust

---

7 Associated Gen. Contractors of Cal. v. Cal. State Council of Carpenters, 459 US 519 (1983).

8 See, e.g., American Bar Ass'n, PROVING ANTITRUST DAMAGES 171 (1996) ('the plaintiff's damages depend on the difference between the actual price paid and the competitive price, or the price that would have been charged absent the illegal agreement.').

9 Ill. Brick Co. v. Illinois, 431 US 720 (1977) (disallowing damage claims by indirect purchasers); Hanover Shoe, Inc. v. United Shoe. Mach. Corp., 392 US 481 (1968) (reaffirming that direct purchasers are entitled to recover and banning defense that they passed on any overcharge downstream).

10 See infra Indirect Purchasers.

11 See infra Competitors.

standing for such claimants is sometimes granted, and sometimes, not depending on the nature of the claim and the relationship of the alleged harm to the violation.

This chapter *first* discusses the *sine qua non* of any private antitrust claim: antitrust injury. *Second*, the chapter looks at the standing requirements for those seeking injunctive relief under the federal antitrust laws. *Third*, we explore the necessary showing for standing to bring damage claims.[12] *Fourth*, we observe that direct purchasers are frequently granted antitrust standing, and catalog the few scenarios where antitrust purchaser recoveries have been questioned. *Fifth*, standing of indirect purchasers to pursue claims is examined, as well as possible exceptions to the federal bar on indirect purchaser damages actions and potential other means of recovery (including recovery under state law). *Sixth*, we discuss antitrust standing issues concerning competitors bringing claims, and the types of recoveries they have standing to seek. And, *finally*, we canvass the various other types of plaintiffs that have brought antitrust suits, and discuss how courts have dealt with each group's standing to bring antitrust claims.

Antitrust injury: harm to competition, not competitors

As the oft-quoted adage goes: the antitrust laws were designed for the protection of competition, not competitors.[13] The idea behind this proposition is that antitrust laws are not intended to protect competitors for their own sake. Rather, antitrust is concerned about the loss of competitors in a market only where that loss harms consumer welfare through higher prices, restricted output, or reduced choice.[14]

The Supreme Court elaborated on this principle in *Brunswick Corp. v. Pueblo Bowl-O-Mat, Inc.*[15] In that case, the owner of a handful of bowling alleys alleged that a rival's purchase of a large number of bowling centers violated the antitrust laws because it substantially lessened competition in certain regions. The plaintiff sought as damages the income it had lost to the alleged monopolist due to the violation. The Supreme Court found that the plaintiff could not recover because there was no demonstration that the defendant's conduct had created any anticompetitive effects and thus its 'injury was not of the type that the statute was intended to forestall.'[16] Moreover, the plaintiff was seeking damages *because* the challenged acquisitions actually preserved otherwise failing bowling alleys and thus preserved competition and decreased market concentration. Because the plaintiff's claimed harm flowed from the promotion of competition and not

---

[12] See supra n.7.

[13] Brown Shoe v. United States, 370 US 294, 320 (1962).

[14] 'Congress designed the Sherman Act as a "consumer welfare prescription."' Reiter v. Sonotone Corp., 442 US 330, 343 (1979) (quoting Robert H. Bork, The Antitrust Paradox 66 (1978)). See also Broadcom Corp. v. Qualcomm Inc., 501 F.3d 297, 308 (2007) ('The primary goal of antitrust law is to maximize consumer welfare by promoting competition among firms.'). Other scholars have countered that the primary goal should not be end-user welfare, but rather, 'protect[ing] the people by protecting the competitive process.' Gregory J. Werden, Monopsony and the Sherman Act: Consumer Welfare in a New Light, 74 Antitrust L.J. 707, 735 (2007); see also Albert A. Foer, The Goals Of Antitrust: Thoughts On Consumer Welfare In The US, in Philip Marsden (ed.), Handbook of Research in Trans-Atlantic Antitrust 566, 566–593 (2006).

[15] 429 US 477 (1977).

[16] Id. at 487–88 (internal quotes and citation omitted).

its elimination, allowing the plaintiff to recover would have been contrary to the very purpose of the antitrust laws – the protection of competition, not competitors.[17] As a result, to bring an antitrust claim, a plaintiff has to demonstrate, as a threshold matter, that it sustained 'antitrust injury,' defined as injury of the type of harm the antitrust laws were intended to prevent, and which flows from that which makes defendants' acts unlawful.[18]

Accordingly, a plaintiff must demonstrate not only harm to itself, but that the harm suffered resulted from conduct that diminished competition and harmed consumer welfare generally.[19] Indeed, '[w]henever the plaintiff and consumers have divergent rather than congruent interests, there is a potential problem in finding "antitrust injury". . . . When the plaintiff is a poor champion of consumers, a court must be especially careful not to grant relief that may undercut the proper functions of antitrust.'[20] Harm to competition is typically in the form of higher prices, reduced output, or reduced choice.[21]

To show antitrust injury, some courts have imposed an additional requirement that the plaintiff must be a participant in the market in which the alleged restraint was carried out.[22] However, if 'two markets are so closely related', anticompetitive behavior in the first market may give rise to antitrust injury for participants in another market.[23]

Establishing antitrust injury is only a first step in determining whether the plaintiff is an appropriate party. A plaintiff must also meet additional requirements to establish that it has standing to seek injunctive relief or money damages for violations of the Sherman Act. These requirements are discussed below.

Standing for injunctive relief

The right to injunctive relief is established by §16 of the Clayton Act, 15 U.S.C. §26:

> Any person, firm, corporation, or association shall be entitled to sue for and have injunctive relief . . . against threatened loss or damage by a violation of the antitrust laws, . . . when and under the same conditions and principles as injunctive relief against threatened conduct that will cause loss or damage is granted by courts of equity, under the rules governing such proceedings[.][24]

---

17 Id. at 488.

18 Id. at 489.

19 See supra n.14 and accompanying text.

20 Ball Mem'l Hosp. v. Mut. Hosp. Ins., 784 F.2d 1325, 1334 (7th Cir. 1986).

21 NicSand, Inc. v. 3M Co., 507 F.3d 442, 451–52 (6th Cir. 2007) (harm to competition deemed absent because plaintiff alleged harm flowing from lower prices); Yellow Page Solutions, Inc. v. Bell Atl. Yellow Pages Co., No. 00-Civ.-5663(MBM), 2001 US Dist. LEXIS 18831, at *34 (S.D.N.Y. Nov. 19, 2001) (antitrust plaintiff's claim for lost profits fails unless plaintiff also shows harm to competition); Cancall PCS, LLC v. Omnipoint Corp., No. 99-Civ.-3395(AGS), 2000 WL 272309, at *6 (S.D.N.Y. Mar. 10, 2000) (dismissing antitrust claims for want of allegation that 'consumers in general were charged higher prices').

22 See, e.g., Legal Econ. Evaluations, Inc. v. Metro. Life Ins. Co., 39 F.3d 951, 956 (9th Cir. 1994) (no antitrust injury because 'the asserted harm to competition takes place in different markets' than alleged injury).

23 Sanner v. Board of Trade of Chicago, 62 F.3d 918, 929 (7th Cir. 1995).

24 15 U.S.C. §26.

A plaintiff seeking an injunction must show antitrust injury, as well as (1) a threatened loss or injury cognizable in equity (2) proximately resulting from the alleged antitrust injury.[25]

Thus, whereas a plaintiff seeking damages under §4 of the Clayton Act must demonstrate damage to 'business or property,' injunctive relief is available merely upon a showing of a '*threatened* loss or damage.'[26] And because the harm need not specifically be to 'business or property,' the threatened harm may not even be economic at all; it simply must result from an antitrust violation.

The distinction between damage to 'business or property' and the lesser showing of 'threatened loss or damage' is rooted in more than simply linguistic differences between §§4 and 16 of the Clayton Act. The right to obtain treble damages is restricted due to the prospect of overlapping or duplicative recoveries and the potential need for complex proofs to sort them out. These concerns are absent in the injunction context, however. As to the possible multiplicity of claims, 'one injunction is as effective as 100, and, concomitantly, . . . 100 injunctions are no more effective than one.'[27]

Of course, a plaintiff seeking an injunction must still demonstrate antitrust injury.[28] Thus, in *Cargill*, the plaintiff, a would-be competitor, was denied an injunction because the harm it alleged – the defendants' decision to lower prices resulting in the plaintiffs' loss of profits – was not a cause of concern under the antitrust laws.[29] By contrast, direct purchasers are permitted to seek injunctive relief flowing from the charging of allegedly 'supra-competitive prices.'[30]

Moreover, the threatened harm must be proximately caused by the antitrust violation. Like §4 of the Clayton Act, §16 requires that the threatened harm come about '*by* a violation of the antitrust laws,'[31] which has been read to require a showing of proximate causation.[32] Thus, despite the 'relaxed' requirements for injunctive relief (as compared to damages claims), inability to show proximate causation can still doom a potential antitrust action.[33]

---

25 McCarthy v. Recordex Serv., Inc., 80 F.3d 842, 856 (3d Cir. 1996).

26 Cargill, Inc. v. Monfort of Colo., Inc., 479 US 104, 112 (1986) (emphasis added).

27 Id. at 111 n. 6. As discussed elsewhere in this chapter, it is for this reason that an indirect purchaser plaintiff has traditionally been allowed to pursue claims for injunctive relief for violations of the antitrust laws even though it is barred from seeking money damages. See infra Indirect Purchasers.

28 Cargill, 479 US at 111–112.

29 Id. at 115.

30 See, e.g., In re Rail Freight Fuel Surcharge Antitrust Litig., 593 F. Supp. 2d 29, 41 (D.D.C. 2008).

31 15 U.S.C. §26 (emphasis added).

32 In re Warfarin Sodium Antitrust Litig., 214 F.3d 395, 399–401 (3d Cir. 2000); Catlin v. Wash. Energy Co., 791 F.2d 1343, 1350 (9th Cir. 1986); Mid-West Paper Prods. Co. v. Cont'l Group, Inc., 596 F.2d 573, 591–92 (3d Cir. 1979); Reibert v. Atl. Richfield Co., 471 F.2d 727, 731 (10th Cir. 1973).

33 See, e.g., Pocahontas Supreme Coal Co., Inc. v. Bethlehem Steel Corp., 828 F.2d 211, 220 (4th Cir. 1987) (affirming denial of injunction because claimed harm 'too attenuated to be considered proximate'); Catlin, 791 F.2d 1350–51 (Reinhardt, J. concurring) (injunction appropriately denied where plaintiff did not establish causation).

Section 16 also requires that the plaintiff show that it would be entitled to an injunction under traditional principles of equity.

Standing for damages claims

Demonstrating standing to obtain antitrust damages, in contrast, requires a somewhat greater showing than is required for an injunction. As the Supreme Court has explained, '[a] showing of antitrust injury is necessary, but not always sufficient, to establish standing under §4 [of the Clayton Act], because a party may have suffered antitrust injury but may not be a proper plaintiff under §4 for other reasons.'[34]

The nature of some of those limitations appeared in the Supreme Court's decision in *Hawaii v. Standard Oil Co.*,[35] where the court denied the State of Hawaii standing to seek damages for harm to its 'general economy' as the result of an antitrust violation. The Court found the alleged harm was 'no more than a reflection of injuries to the "business or property" of consumers, for which they may recover themselves under §4.'[36] Even a 'lengthy and expensive trial' could not address the potential problems of 'double recovery' inherent in permitting such a claim.[37]

The potential for double recovery and complex proofs again proved to be determinative in *Illinois Brick Co. v. Illinois*.[38] There, the Court disallowed treble damage claims by indirect purchasers because of the risk of duplicative recovery by both direct and indirect purchasers flowing from a single overcharge by the alleged violator.[39] That, and the unwieldy and expensive proofs that would be involved in attempting to allocate damages among direct and indirect purchaser plaintiffs, led the Court to adopt a rule barring indirect purchasers from recovering damages under the antitrust laws. Instead, the Court hewed to the rule it had announced in *Hanover Shoe, Inc. v. United Shoe Machinery Corp.*,[40] that direct purchasers – those most likely to 'effectively enforce[]' the antitrust laws – were the appropriate plaintiffs to bring damages claims.[41]

The 'direct purchaser rule' of *Illinois Brick* applies only to claims by downstream purchasers in the chain of distribution and has not been held to restrict all damages claims by consumers. For instance, in *Blue Shield of Virginia v. McCready*, the Court allowed a claim for treble damages by a patient seeking reimbursement from her health plan for her psychologist's services. McCready claimed that her health plan was restraining trade in the psychotherapy services market, by providing reimbursement only for psychiatric therapy (or psychological therapy administered through a physician's office). None of the factors of *Hawaii* or *Illinois Brick* prohibited McCready's claim even though McCready was not a 'direct purchaser' from her health plan. Moreover, although the excluded

---

34 Cargill, 479 US at 110.

35 405 US 251 (1972).

36 Id. at 264.

37 Id. Of course, this is not to say a state can *never* be a proper plaintiff to recover antitrust damages. For instance, if a state or its agent had directly purchased goods or services from a cartel, it would have standing as much as any other direct purchaser. These were exactly the facts in Chattanooga Foundry & Pipe Works v. Atlanta, 203 US 390 (1906).

38 431 US 720 (1977).

39 Id. at 730–31.

40 392 US 481 (1968).

41 Ill. Brick, 431 US at 735.

psychologists and McCready's employer (who paid for the health plan) might also have standing, the plan was purchased for McCready's benefit, and thus she had standing as a consumer.[42] She faced a 'Hobson's choice' between foregoing treatment by a psychologist or foregoing reimbursement. This rendered her injury 'inextricably intertwined' with the injury the alleged conspirators sought to inflict on the market.[43]

After *McCready*, the Supreme Court further explicated the requirements for standing to bring a treble damages claim in *Associated General Contractors of California v. California State Council of Carpenters.*[44] *First*, the Court emphasized the need for a 'causal connection' between the asserted violation and the alleged harm.[45] *Second*, the Court repeated its focus on the 'nature of the plaintiff's alleged injury,' and that it must comport with the antitrust laws' purpose of 'assur[ing] customers the benefits of price competition' and 'protecting the economic freedom of participants in the relevant market.'[46] *Third*, it examined the 'directness or indirectness of the asserted injury,' and whether the injury and alleged restraint were directly connected or attenuated by 'several somewhat vaguely defined links.'[47] *Fourth*, the Court looked for more 'immediate victims of coercion by defendants,' whose injuries would be 'direct' and who would hold a right to obtain damages of their own. *Fifth,* the Court referred to the potentially speculative nature of the harm alleged.[48] *Finally,* the Court expressed concern about keeping the 'scope of complex antitrust trials within judicially manageable limits,' avoiding 'duplicate recoveries on the one hand,' and 'the danger of complex apportionment of damages on the other.'[49]

The courts of appeal have each construed the *Associated General* factors as guidelines, but not a comprehensive 'checklist.' For instance, in *In re Lower Lake Erie Iron Ore Antitrust Litigation,*[50] the Third Circuit noted that the various factors should be 'weighed and balanced,' with no 'specific weight' assigned to any particular factor.[51] The

---

42 McCready, 457 US at 480.

43 Id. at 483–84

44 459 US 519 (1983).

45 Id. at 537. The Court offered no precise test for causation, instead referring to the general law of proximate cause on torts. This generally means that the violation was a material factor in causing the plaintiff's injury, and that the plaintiff's injury was foreseeable by the alleged violator. See Nelson v. Monroe Reg'l Med. Ctr., 925 F.2d 1555, 1563–64 (7th Cir. 1991).

46 Associated Gen., 459 US at 538 (citations omitted).

47 Id. at 540.

48 Id. at 542.

49 Id. at 543–44. Different circuits enumerate the factors in different ways. See, e.g., In re Lower Lake Erie Iron Ore Antitrust Litig., 998 F.2d 1144, 1165–66 (3d Cir. 1993) (five factors). The Serpa Corp. v. McWane, Inc., 199 F.3d 6, 10 (1st Cir. 1999) (grouping factors under six headings); Andrx Pharms., Inc. v. Biovail Corp., 256 F.3d 799, 806–817 (D.C. Cir. 2001) (five factors); Am. Ad Mgmt., Inc. v. Gen'l Tel. Co., 190 F.3d 1051, 1054 (9th Cir. 1999) (same); Paycom Billing Servs., Inc. v. MasterCard Int'l, Inc., 467 F.3d 283, 290–291 (2d Cir. 2006) (four factors).

50 998 F.2d at 1166.

51 Id.; see also Paycom, 467 F.3d at 291 ('the weight to be given the various factors will necessarily vary with the circumstances of particular cases') (alteration in original; citation omitted); Am. Ad Mgmt., 190 F.3d at 1055 ('To conclude that there is antitrust standing, a court need not find in favor of the plaintiff on each factor . . . . Generally no single factor is decisive[,]' but noting 'great weight' is given to the nature of plaintiff's injury) (internal quotes and citations omitted).

court then took each of the factors in turn and assessed how well the plaintiffs and their asserted injuries fit with each factor.[52]

Over time, courts of appeal began to view these factors not only as a gauge of standing, but as part of an effort to find 'efficient enforcers' of the antitrust laws.[53] That is, courts now use these factors to test the strength of the plaintiffs' motivation and ability to enforce the antitrust laws. With that in mind, we turn to the various types of plaintiffs that have appeared in private antitrust litigation over the years, and discuss how their ability to establish injury and standing has fared.

Direct purchasers

It is by now well-settled that the prototypical 'efficient enforcers' of the antitrust laws are the entities or persons that purchase directly from the alleged violator of the antitrust laws, *i.e.*, the 'direct purchasers.'[54] Direct purchasers are 'the immediate buyers from the alleged antitrust violators.'[55] It is so well established, in fact, that direct purchasers need not show they are 'efficient enforcers' under the facts of any particular case; it is simply presumed.[56]

The foundations for the status of direct purchasers to bring antitrust damages claims were set over one hundred years ago in *Chattanooga Foundry & Pipe Works v. City of Atlanta*,[57] where the plaintiff city claimed injury in its 'business or property' because an illegal conspiracy among the defendants 'led [the city] to pay more than the worth of the pipe.'[58] The Supreme Court agreed, concluding, 'A person whose property is diminished by a payment of money wrongfully induced is injured in his property.'[59]

Direct purchasers' standing to bring damage claims was reaffirmed and bolstered by the Court's decision in *Hanover Shoe, Inc. v. United Shoe Machinery Corp.*[60] There, the defendant had argued that the plaintiff, who purchased directly from the defendant, should not be entitled to recover because it had 'passed on' any overcharge to the plaintiff's own customers in the distribution chain.[61] The Court began with the notion that '[t]he general

---

52 Lower Lake Erie, 998 F.2d at 1167–1171. Notably, even if one factor weighed against standing, the court balanced it against the other factors as a whole, rather than treating each factor as a necessity. See id. at 1170 ('complex apportionment is not a sufficient reason to deny standing').

53 Paycom, 467 F.3d at 290; Abraham v. Intermountain Health Care, Inc., 461 F.3d 1249, 1268 (10th Cir. 2006); Todorov v. DCH Healthcare Auth., 921 F.2d 1438, 1449 (11th Cir. 1991).

54 Blue Shield of Va. v. McCready, 457 US 465, 474 (1982) (direct purchasers are plaintiffs most likely to 'press their claims with . . . vigor').

55 UtiliCorp, 497 US at 207; In re Mercedes-Benz Anti-Trust Litig., 364 F. Supp. 2d 468, 478 (D.N.J. 2005). For the sake of simplicity, we speak of the direct purchaser as the potential plaintiff and the seller as the violator. However, if the violation alleged involves monopsonistic conduct, potential plaintiffs include the seller who was forced to part with his goods at too low a price. E.g., Mandeville Island Farms Inc. v. Am. Crystal Sugar Co., 334 US 219 (1948).

56 See, e.g., Del. Valley Surgical Supply, Inc. v. Johnson & Johnson, 523 F.3d 1116, 1121–23 (9th Cir. 2008). One of the authors of this chapter (Mr. Cramer) was counsel for the direct purchaser class plaintiffs in this case.

57 203 US 390 (1906).

58 Id. at 396.

59 Id.

60 392 US 481 (1968).

61 Id. at 488.

tendency of the law, in regard to damages at least, is not to go beyond the first step.'[62] Rejecting the notion that the possibility the purchaser passed on an overcharge requires recognition of the 'pass on' defense, the Court noted that '[a] wide range of factors influence a company's pricing policies.'[63] If the 'passing-on' defense were recognized, an antitrust plaintiff seeking to recover damages would need to retain an economist to compute what the plaintiff's sales prices and volumes would have been absent the challenged conduct – a task which 'would normally prove insurmountable,' requiring 'additional long and complicated proceedings involving massive evidence and complicated theories.'[64] Also, if a direct purchaser would be subject to a defense that it passed on the overcharge to its own customers, the damage claim would keep running down the distribution chain to the 'ultimate consumers' who only buy a tiny amount of the affected product and 'would have only a tiny stake in a lawsuit and little interest in attempting a class action.'[65] As a result, the Court held that the direct purchaser had a claim for the entire amount its price was inflated due to the anticompetitive conduct, i.e., the entire overcharge.[66]

Having allowed damage claims by direct purchasers even if the plaintiffs had passed on all or part of their overcharge, the Court in *Illinois Brick* barred *indirect* purchasers from seeking some or all of those same damages under Clayton Act §4.[67] The Court understood that an overcharge could cause 'ripples of harm,' affecting parties throughout the distribution chain, but nonetheless limited the reach of §4 of the Clayton Act to the first-level, *i.e.*, direct, purchaser. The direct purchaser could thus recover the entire amount of the overcharge despite the 'pass on' or other effects of the challenged conduct on the business of the direct purchaser,[68] but, as noted above, more attenuated purchasers down the chain of distribution could not recover for any harms flowing from the anticompetitive conduct, in light of the potential for double recovery and the complex proof needed to allocate injuries to purchasers along the distribution chain.[69] In sum, only direct purchaser damages claims were allowed.[70]

---

[62] Id. at 490 n. 8 (internal quotes omitted).

[63] Id. at 492.

[64] Id. at 492–93.

[65] Id. at 494.

[66] Id.

[67] Ill. Brick, 431 US at 729–30.

[68] Courts interpreting *Hanover Shoe* and *Illinois Brick* have made clear that those decisions prohibit not only use of the 'passing on' defense, but also the subtle variation thereon that the direct purchasers somehow benefitted from the anticompetitive conduct (like increased revenues from reselling goods at the artificially inflated price). See Sports Racing Servs., Inc. v. Sports Car Club of Am., Inc., 131 F.3d 874, 884–885 (10th Cir. 1997) (rejecting argument that plaintiff benefitted from alleged violation and therefore lacked injury because '[t]hat reasoning is directly contrary to the Supreme Court's holding in *Hanover Shoe*. *Hanover Shoe* precludes the argument that [plaintiff] did not suffer cognizable antitrust injury merely because it passed overcharges on to its customers or otherwise was shielded from competition by the defendants' anticompetitive behavior'); Meijer, Inc. v. Abbott Labs., 251 F.R.D. 431, 435 (N.D. Cal. 2008); In re Relafen Antitrust Litig., 346 F. Supp. 2d 349, 369 (D. Mass. 2004). The authors of this chapter were counsel to the plaintiffs in the latter two cases.

[69] Ill. Brick, 431 US 720.

[70] Id. at 724 ('a direct purchaser suing for treble damages under §4 of the Clayton Act is injured within the meaning of §4 by the full amount of the overcharge paid by it').

Direct purchaser claims were not at issue in *Associated General*, but the Court seems to have taken pains to reinforce the primacy of direct purchasers to private antitrust enforcement. *First*, in describing the nature of harms most closely associated with the purposes of the Sherman Act, the Court stated that 'the Sherman Act was enacted to assure customers the benefits of price competition, and our prior cases have emphasized the central interest in protecting the economic freedom of participants in the relevant market.'[71] *Second*, in describing the types of claims associated with complex apportionment and duplicative recovery, the Court pointed to the *indirect purchaser* damages claims it had banned in *Illinois Brick*, reaffirming impliedly that direct purchaser claims would yield no such complexities.

The Supreme Court further expanded on purchaser standing in *Reiter v. Sonotone Corp.*,[72] where an attempt was made to cabin purchaser standing to businesses and foreclose claims by purchasing consumers. The defendants had argued that a consumer could not be injured in her 'business or property' because a consumer had no 'business' to injure. The Court disagreed, finding it was precisely for consumers that the Sherman Act was enacted:

> We described the Sherman Act as 'conceived of primarily as a remedy for "[t]he people of the United States as individuals," especially consumers,' and the treble-damages provision of the Clayton Act as 'conceived primarily as "open[ing] the door of justice to every man . . . and giv[ing] the injured party ample damages for the wrong suffered."'[73]

Thus, even if the purchaser is a consumer 'injured only in terms of . . . a wrongful deprivation of [] money because the price . . . was artificially inflated by reason of [the] anticompetitive conduct,' that is sufficient injury under the Clayton Act.[74]

Direct purchaser claims: overcharge damages

The form of damages most frequently sought by direct purchasers is an 'overcharge,' that is, the difference between the price actually paid to the antitrust defendant for the affected product and the price which would have prevailed but for the illegal conduct.[75]

Overcharges are intended to reflect the very essence of the societal harm done to the general economy: injuries flowing from the higher prices the cartel or monopolist was able to impose due to its anticompetitive activity. 'Since the very purpose of antitrust

---

71 Associated Gen., 459 US at 538.

72 442 US 330.

73 Id. at 343 (quoting Brunswick Corp., 429 US at 486 n.10).

74 Id. at 342. The Supreme Court did not address whether the direct purchaser rule applied to Reiter, nor what effect that rule might have on Reiter's ability to bring a claim (noting only that whether a person or entity was a 'direct purchaser' and whether that same person or entity suffered 'antitrust injury' were distinct questions). See id. at 337 n. 3. Later decisions have made clear that a consumer must still satisfy *Illinois Brick*. See, e.g., Campos v. Ticketmaster Corp., 140 F.3d 1166, 1169, 1171–72 (8th Cir. 1998) (recognizing that consumers could sue under Reiter, but barring consumers who were indirect purchasers from recovering damages).

75 See supra n. 7 and accompanying text. See also PROVING ANTITRUST DAMAGES 202 ('Overcharge damages can be calculated . . . by determining a hypothetical competitive price, subtracting it from the actual price, and multiplying the resulting number by the quantity actually purchased.').

law is to ensure that the benefits of competition flow to purchasers of goods affected by the violation, buyers have usually been preferred plaintiffs in private antitrust litigation, and a purchaser's standing to recover for an overcharge paid directly to an illegal cartel or monopoly is seldom doubted.'[76] Thus, injuries in the form of overcharges are 'of the type the antitrust laws were intended to prevent and that flows from that which makes defendants' acts unlawful.'[77]

Damages for supra-competitive prices from non-conspirators

While direct purchaser standing is generally recognized, one form of damage claim has generated some controversy among courts: damages sustained due to high prices charged by sellers who did not join a conspiracy.

Suppose, for instance, Firms A, B, and C – the only sellers in the market – entered into a conspiracy to fix prices above competitive levels. A purchase from any one of the conspirators is made at supra-competitive prices and thus gives rise to antitrust damages.

However, if Firms A and B conspire, but not Firm C – prices set by all three may still be at supra-competitive levels. This is because Firm C prices its product in relation to the prevailing market price. As Firms A and B are conspiring, this leaves Firm C free to raise its prices as well under the 'umbrella' of the artificially inflated prices caused by the conspiracy between A and B. Given that Firm C can be expected to set its price as high as the market will profitably allow, it will do so. Purchasers from Firm C may have overpaid, and ostensibly should be able to sue the conspirators for such overcharges if they flow from the illegal conduct.

Many courts have recognized that such claims for 'umbrella damages' are merely another form of the anticompetitive harm that can result from a conspiracy in restraint of trade, and have held such overcharges are recoverable.[78] Other courts have barred

---

[76] In re Cardizem CD Antitrust Litig., 105 F. Supp. 2d 618, 650–651 (E.D. Mich. 2000) (internal quotes and citations omitted).

[77] Cordes & Co. Fin. Servs. v. A.G. Edwards & Sons, Inc., 502 F.3d 91, 107 (2d Cir. 2007) (quoting Brunswick Corp., 429 US at 489). See also In re Warfarin Sodium Antitrust Litig., 214 F.3d 395, 401 (3d Cir. 2000) ('The excess amount paid by' purchasers (there, indirect purchasers) was 'not only . . . "inextricably intertwined" with the injury [the monopolist] aimed to inflict [on its competitor], the overcharge was the aim of [the] preclusive conduct. It is difficult to imagine a more formidable demonstration of antitrust injury.'). For further discussion of forms of damages and calculating damages, see Chapter 11 of this *Handbook*.

[78] See, e.g., Loeb Indus., Inc. v. Sumitomo Corp., 306 F.3d 469 (7th Cir. 2002); Lower Lake Erie, 998 F.2d 1144; In re Beef Indus. Antitrust Litig., 600 F.2d 1148, 1166 n. 24 (5th Cir. 1979); In re Online DVD Rental Antitrust Litig., No. M 09-2029 PJH, 2009 US Dist. LEXIS 111602 (N.D. Cal. Dec. 1, 2009) ('the court is not persuaded that there is a categorical bar precluding the umbrella liability theory' in direct purchaser case); In re Relafen Antitrust Litig., Master File No. 01-12238-WGY, Order at 2 (D. Mass. Dec. 19, 2003) (Young, C.J.); In re Ariz. Dairy Prods. Antitrust Litig., 627 F. Supp. 233, 236 (D. Ariz. 1985); In re Uranium Antitrust Litig., 552 F. Supp. 518, 525 (N.D. Ill. 1982); Oberweis Dairy v. Assoc. Milk Producers, 553 F. Supp. 962, 973–74 (N.D. Ill. 1982); Pollock v. Citrus Assoc. of New York, 512 F. Supp. 711, 719 (S.D.N.Y. 1981); Strax v. Commodity Exch., 524 F. Supp. 936, 939–40 (S.D.N.Y. 1981); In re Bristol Bay, Alaska Salmon Fishery Antitrust Litig., 530 F. Supp. 36, 38–39 (W.D. Wash. 1981); Wash. v. Am. Pipe & Constr. Co., 280 F. Supp. 802, 806–807 (W.D. Wash. 1968). See also II PHILLIP

such recoveries, determining that, under the facts of those cases, the harm is too far removed from the alleged violation, that there is a risk of duplicative recoveries, or that there would be a need for complex reapportionment of damages.[79]

Some courts have expressed concerns about the difficulty of proving the price the non-conspirator would have charged absent the alleged conspiracy.[80] But, this raises an issue about the ability to calculate damages and should provide no basis for disallowing recovery entirely. Moreover, computing the price the non-conspirator actually charged and what it would have charged absent the conspiracy is not materially different from evaluating the price a conspirator would have charged in the but-for world.[81] Finally, other courts have expressed concerns about imposing liability on defendants for harm from which they received no direct benefit.[82] But courts have long held that antitrust violators must bear the full extent of the injuries they caused, regardless of whether the violators directly profited.[83]

Rather than creating a default rule, in our view, recovery of 'umbrella damages' from non-conspirators should be assessed on a case-specific basis, as required by *Associated General*.

Direct purchasers: standing in cases alleging fraud on the patent office

Despite the long tradition of recognizing direct purchaser standing, a question has recently arisen as to whether direct purchasers have standing to pursue antitrust claims predicated on the fraudulent procurement of a patent.

In *Walker Process Equip., Inc. v. Food Mach. & Chem. Corp.*,[84] the Supreme Court held that one who enforces a patent procured through fraud on the US Patent and Trademark Office 'must answer under [Sherman Act §2] and §4 of the Clayton Act in treble damages *to those injured* by any monopolistic action taken under the fraudulent patent claim.'[85]

AREEDA, ANTITRUST LAW §347 (2007) (LEXIS Ed.); American Bar Ass'n, PROVING ANTITRUST DAMAGES 192 (1996) ('the weight of authority seems now to be on the side of recognizing the claim for damages.').

79 See, e.g., Mid-West Paper Prods., 596 F.2d at 583; FTC v. Mylan Labs., 62 F. Supp. 2d 25, 39–42 (D.D.C. 1999); Antoine L. Garabet, M.D., Inc., v. Autonomous Tech. Corp., 116 F. Supp. 2d 1159, 1168–70 (C.D. Cal. 2000); In re Vitamins Antitrust Litig., 2001 WL 855463, at *3–4 (D.D.C. Jul. 2, 2001); In re Folding Carton Antitrust Litig., 88 F.R.D. 211, 218–220 (N.D. Ill. 1980).

80 E.g., Mid-West Paper Prods., 596 F.2d at 584.

81 See Loeb, 306 F.3d at 491 ('One need only know two pieces of information: the amount of cathode purchased by [the plaintiff] and the amount of cathode purchased and sold by those who sold cathode to [the plaintiff]. From there, reasonable estimates of damages are the order of the day.'); Uranium, 552 F. Supp. at 525 (calculating but for prices of nonconspirators 'is no more problematic than determining damages in any price-fixing case' and '[i]n the most pedestrian price-fixing case, the trier of fact must calculate the price the defendants would have charged but for the conspiracy'); AREEDA, ANTITRUST LAW §347.

82 See, e.g., Folding Carton Antitrust Litig., 88 F.R.D. at 220.

83 AREEDA, ANTITRUST LAW §347.

84 382 US 172 (1965).

85 Walker Process, 382 US at 176 (emphasis added).

However, two district court decisions – *In re Remeron Antitrust Litigation*[86] and *In re DDAVP Direct Purchaser Antitrust Litigation*[87] – have held that purchasers did *not* have standing to pursue such claims.

These district courts offered no reason why the direct purchasers had failed to sustain antitrust injury, nor was any showing made that purchasers could not meet the *Associated General* factors for *Walker Process* claims. Instead, invoking patent law rules restricting the bases for challenging patents and cases limiting competitor standing to those competitors that could actually enter the market absent the challenged conduct, these courts ruled that only a competitor against whom a patent was enforced has standing to bring such an antitrust claim.

The Second Circuit in *DDAVP* reversed the district court's denial of direct purchaser standing. It applied the factors from *Associated General*, finding that the direct purchasers were 'efficient enforcers under any formulation,'[88] and that there is no reason antitrust law would deny them standing. Recognizing that increasing the number of possible challengers to a patent's validity might disturb incentives for innovation, the court nonetheless held that that consideration was outweighed by the 'potential "to leave a significant antitrust violation undetected or unremedied."'[89] Noting that the patent at issue in *DDAVP* had been found in a previous case to have been obtained through inequitable conduct and was therefore unenforceable, the court upheld the direct purchaser plaintiffs' antitrust standing.[90]

The decision in *DDAVP* comports with basic antitrust principles. The direct purchasers seek to vindicate the harm done to the economy through a defendant's monopolistic conduct and pricing.[91] A competitor could not, even in theory, bring a claim for overcharges as a purchaser could. A competitor would instead seek lost profits.[92] Thus, to have standing, the competitor must show that its attempts to compete were somehow inhibited by the presence of the fraudulent patent, *i.e.*, that the fraudulent patent was somehow enforced against it, causing it to lose sales.[93]

The cases denying standing commit a two-fold mistake. *First*, they 'mistakenly appl[y]

---

86 335 F. Supp. 2d 522 (D.N.J. 2004). However, the court did permit the plaintiffs to pursue a claim for a scheme to monopolize that included the alleged 'Walker Process violation' as part of the scheme.

87 No. 05-cv-2237-CLB, 2006 US Dist. LEXIS 96201 (S.D.N.Y. Nov. 2, 2006), rev'd 585 F.3d 677 (2d Cir. 2009). The authors were counsel for the direct purchaser class plaintiffs in Remeron and are currently representing the direct purchaser class plaintiffs in DDAVP.

88 Id. at 689.

89 Id. at 691 (quoting Associated Gen'l, 459 US at 542).

90 DDAVP, 585 F.3d at 691.

91 Glaberson v. Comcast Corp., Civ. A. No. 03-6604, 2006 WL 2559479, at *7 (E.D. Pa. Aug. 31, 2006) ('Plaintiffs' injuries, which consist of overcharges, are distinct from [the excluded competitor's] injuries, which likely consist of lost profits.'); In re Cardizem CD Antitrust Litig., 200 F.R.D. 297, 309–310 (E.D. Mich. 2001) (explaining that direct purchasers claim overcharges, while excluded competitors would seek 'lost sales and lost profits').

92 See DDAVP, 2009 WL 3320504, at *8.

93 See, e.g., Indium Corp. of Am. v. Semi-Alloys, Inc., 566 F. Supp. 1344, 1350 (N.D.N.Y. 1983), modified in part, 591 F. Supp. 608 (N.D.N.Y. 1984). See also Indium, 591 F. Supp. at 614 ('it would be a mistake to interpret "enforcement" too narrowly, and thereby limit the remedy of a Walker Process type antitrust action').

the antitrust rules for competitor standing to cases involving consumer standing.'[94] Unlike a purchaser, a competitor must seek lost profits and therefore must show that the use of the patent somehow caused it to lose business. Hence, there must be enforcement which affects the competitor plaintiff. This concern, however, does not apply to purchasers, who are harmed whenever the patent is unlawfully used to impede competition and artificially inflate prices.

Second, these cases take rules for standing to initiate a challenge under *patent law*[95] and improperly import those standards into *antitrust* standing analysis. But this conceives of antitrust claims that include *Walker Process* allegations as a kind of patent claim: the very error which the Seventh Circuit made – and the Supreme Court reversed, in *Walker Process*.[96] As one court has explained:

> Viewed properly as an antitrust claim, there is little reason to think that standing requirements for *Walker Process* claims differ from standing requirements in more conventional antitrust actions.[97]

Direct purchaser claims: reduction in output and quality

Rather than proving it paid too high a price, a purchaser may also suffer cognizable antitrust injury by showing that it was directly affected by a reduction in output or product quality. The reduction in output is itself harmful to competition, as reduced volume can also lead to increased prices and reduced consumer choice. Reduced quality that results from collusion or monopolization can likewise constitute a cognizable anticompetitive effect, as a reduction in quality means that the purchaser is getting less value for the same money – with effects similar to a price increase.[98] Thus, purchaser claims can be based on losses of consumer choice or reduction in quality, as well as price increases.[99]

---

[94] See I Herbert Hovenkamp, Mark D. Janis, & Mark A. Lemley, IP and Antitrust §11.4b (Supp. 2008) (emphasis added).

[95] E.g., Amana Refrigeration, Inc. v. Quadlux, Inc., 172 F.3d 852, 855 (Fed. Cir. 1999); Lang v. Pac. Marine & Supply Co., Ltd., 895 F.2d 761, 763–64 (Fed. Cir. 1990).

[96] See Food Mach. & Chem. Corp. v. Walker Process Equip., Inc., 335 F.2d 315, 316 (7th Cir. 1964), rev'd, 382 US 172 (1965). The Court of Appeals had affirmed dismissal of the antitrust claims, reasoning that the suit sought the cancellation of a patent, and standing to seek such relief was then restricted to the US government.

[97] Molecular Diagnostics Labs. v. Hoffmann-LaRoche, Inc., 402 F. Supp. 2d 276, 280–81 (D.D.C. 2005); see also In re Netflix Antitrust Litig., Nos. C 07-00643 WHA, C 07-01266 WHA, C 07-01978 WHA, 2007 WL 1725422 (N.D. Cal. Jun. 14, 2007) (permitting purchaser standing for Walker Process allegations).

[98] Int'l Bhd. of Teamsters Local 734 Health & Welfare Trust Fund v. Philip Morris Inc., 196 F.3d 818, 823 (7th Cir. 1999) (Easterbrook, J.) ('Paying too much, or getting an inferior product for the same money, or getting a product that causes deferred injury . . ., causes a loss of one's money, which is "property."'); AD/SAT v. Associated Press, 181 F.3d 216, 230 (2d Cir. 1999) (equating injury to competition with 'higher prices or reduced output or quality' (quoting III Areeda, Antitrust Law ¶652; Mathias v. Daily News, L.P., 152 F. Supp. 2d 465, 478 (S.D.N.Y. 2001) ('the prototypical example of antitrust injury is an allegation by consumers that they have had to pay higher prices (or experienced a reduction in the quality of service) as a result of a defendant's anticompetitive conduct').

[99] See, e.g., Nelson, 925 F.2d at 1563–64 (patients alleged standing because illegal conduct led them to be deprived of treatment by physicians of their choice); Ross v. Bank of Am., 524 F.3d

Indirect purchasers

An indirect purchaser is one who is not the 'immediate buyer[] from the alleged antitrust violator[],'[100] or who '[does] not purchase [the affected product] directly from the [antitrust] defendant[.]'[101]

In contrast with direct purchasers, indirect purchasers are barred from pursuing treble damage claims under Clayton Act §4 due to the *Illinois Brick* doctrine.[102] Thus, if a direct purchaser suffered an overcharge and passed that overcharge on to its own customers, the latter lack standing to sue for damages under the Clayton Act. Unlike *Associated General*, which requires a factual, case-by-case analysis for standing, the rule in *Illinois Brick* establishes a legal bar. The Supreme Court found that the presence of more direct victims, and the complications of apportioning overcharges between direct and indirect purchasers, mandated the bar.

Nevertheless, the Court in *Illinois Brick* stated that there are potential exceptions providing for indirect purchaser standing to pursue damage claims under the federal antitrust laws.

First, an indirect purchaser plaintiff may have standing if it was committed to what the Supreme Court referred to as a 'preexisting cost-plus contract' with the direct purchaser, in which the indirect buyer 'commit[s] to buying a fixed quantity.'[103] Critical to this potential exception is the requirement of a 'cost plus' arrangement, under which 'a product is sold at a specified markup above the seller's own cost.'[104] Importantly, the indirect purchaser must also have bound itself to purchase a 'fixed quantity' of the affected good. The buyer is thus pre-committed to pay a set markup on a set number of goods. A 'requirements contract,' however – under which the buyer commits to buy all (or a set share) of its needs for a product from a particular seller – does not satisfy the 'cost plus' exception.[105]

217, 223–25 (2d Cir. 2008) (where conspiracy imposed certain terms into credit card agreements, injury could be based on fact cardholders would be deprived of the choice of a card without such a term). Although Ross dealt with Article III standing, the concept applies to antitrust standing as well.

100 Kansas v. Utilicorp United, Inc., 497 US 199, 207 (1990).

101 California v. ARC Am. Corp., 490 US 93, 97 (1989). See also Del. Valley Surgical Supply, Inc., 523 F.3d at 1124–25 (noting that indirect purchasers purchased through, and were invoiced by, wholesalers). In contrast, a direct purchaser buys from the antitrust violator without any intermediary. See, e.g., In re Lorazepam & Clorazepate Antitrust Litig., 202 F.R.D. 12, 23 (D.D.C. 2001) (class members afforded standing as direct purchasers 'to the extent that they purchased directly from [the defendant] for their own account[,]' i.e., they were billed by and paid the defendant directly); McCarthy v. Recordex Serv., 80 F.3d 842, 852 (3d Cir. 1996) (purchaser using a buying agent which 'received a flat monthly fee, unrelated to the quantity of toilets ordered, and kept no inventory' meant that the purchaser, rather than the buying agent, would have standing).

102 Ill. Brick, 431 US 720.

103 Id. at 736.

104 Mid-West Paper Prods., 596 F.2d at 577.

105 UtiliCorp., 497 US at 217 (contract for requirements of natural gas failed to meet exception); Lefrak v. Arabian Am. Oil Co., 487 F. Supp. 808, 823 n. 21 (E.D.N.Y. 1980). Requirements contracts 'often create uncertainty as to meaning and effect' and 'are designed to avoid the exactness imposed by the Supreme Court for determining the existence of a cost plus contract.' Id. By the same token, a purchase order placed under a requirements contract dated after the

The viability of this exception was thrown into serious doubt by the Supreme Court's decision in *Kansas v. Utilicorp United, Inc.*,[106] where the Court denied an indirect purchaser standing even though it had allegedly absorbed 100 per cent of the price increase. In the wake of *Utilicorp*, some courts have expressly questioned whether the 'cost plus' exception still exists at all.[107]

Second, the indirect purchaser may be permitted to sue in lieu of the direct if the antitrust defendant owns or controls the direct purchaser.[108] The 'owned and controlled' exception is limited, however, to 'relationships involving such functional economic or other unity between the direct purchaser and either the defendant or the indirect purchaser that there effectively has been only one sale.'[109]

There are other instances where *Illinois Brick* does not apply. When an ostensible direct purchaser is also a member of the antitrust conspiracy, many courts have recognized that it is the first innocent purchaser that has antitrust standing.[110] This is less an exception to *Illinois Brick* than a proper understanding and application of the rule. In such instances, the first-level party purchasing from a member of a conspiracy is the true direct purchaser. Indeed, the fundamental tenet underlying *Illinois Brick* – the effective enforcement of federal antitrust laws – would be stood on its head were this not the rule. Otherwise, no innocent purchaser could maintain a claim.

Finally, an indirect purchaser may acquire standing to sue for damages by receiving

---

anticompetitive conduct at issue will not likely fall within the 'cost plus' exception. This is not the sort of preexisting, fixed quantity contract the court spoke of in Illinois Brick.

106 497 US 199 (1990).

107 McCarthy v. Recordex Serv., 80 F.3d 842, 855 (3d Cir. 1996) ('The vitality of the "pre existing cost plus contract" exception is doubtful, however, in light of Utilicorp.').

108 Id. at 736 n.16.

109 Jewish Hosp. Assn. v. Stewart Mech. Enterps., 628 F.2d 971, 975 (6th Cir. 1980). Similarly, in Royal Printing Co. v. Kimberly-Clark Corp., those indirect purchaser plaintiffs who could demonstrate that the wholesaler was a subsidiary of the defendant could proceed; plaintiffs who had purchased through an independent wholesaler, however, were denied suit. 621 F.2d 323, 326–28 (9th Cir. 1980).

110 Paper Systems, Inc. v. Nippon Paper Indus. Co., Ltd., 281 F.3d 629, 631–32 (7th Cir. 2002); Lowell v. Am. Cyanamid Co., 177 F.3d 1228, 1233 (11th Cir. 1999) ('Illinois Brick is inapplicable to the present case where the complaint alleges a vertical conspiracy with no pass-on.'); In re Brand Name Prescription Drugs Antitrust Litig., 123 F.3d 599, 604 (7th Cir. 1997) (Posner, C.J.) ('[A]ny indirect-purchaser defense would go by the board, since the [plaintiffs] would then be direct purchasers from the conspirators.'); Ariz. v. Shamrock Foods Co., 729 F.2d 1208, 1212–14 (9th Cir. 1984); Fontana Aviation, Inc. v. Cessna Aircraft Co., 617 F.2d 478, 481 (7th Cir. 1980); *see also* II Phillip E. Areeda, Antitrust Law ¶346h, at 369 (2d ed. 2000) ('Whether one adopts a coconspirator exception or regards this situation as outside Illinois Brick's domain, there is no tracing or apportionment to be done.'); In re Wyoming Tight Sands Antitrust Cases, 695 F. Supp. 1109, 1117 (D. Kan. 1988) (noting that it is not an '"exception" at all' to grant standing if 'the direct purchaser participated in the allegedly illegal activities, the indirect purchaser would be the proper plaintiff'). Cf. Dickson v. Microsoft Corp., 309 F.3d 193 (4th Cir. 2002) (dicta that exception would apply in price fixing cases).

A number of courts require that the middleman co-conspirator must be named as a defendant before standing may be conferred upon the middleman's customers. McCarthy, 80 F.3d at 854–55; Campos, 140 F.3d at 1171 n. 4; In re Midwest Milk Monopolization Litig., 730 F.2d 528, 529–30 (6th Cir. 1984); Beef Indus. Antitrust, 600 F.2d at 1163.

an assignment from a direct purchaser.[111] Any assignment of an antitrust claim must be 'express' and specifically refer to the antitrust claims.[112] Once an assignment is in place, the indirect purchaser 'stands in the shoes' of the direct purchaser, and has standing to the same extent as the assignor.[113]

It is unlikely any further exceptions to *Illinois Brick* will be recognized by the courts. The Supreme Court has cautioned lower federal courts against creating new exceptions to the *Illinois Brick* rule:

> The rationales underlying *Hanover Shoe* and *Illinois Brick* will not apply with equal force in all cases. We nonetheless believe that ample justification exists for our stated decision not to carve out exceptions to the [direct purchaser] rule.[114]

Indirect purchasers: injunctive relief

Illinois Brick was fundamentally a decision addressing §4 of the Clayton Act, which governs damages. In *Cargill,* the Supreme Court distinguished between a competitor's ability to seek treble damages and a plaintiff's right to seek an injunction. This distinction applies with equal force to indirect purchasers. None of the underlying rationales of *Illinois Brick* – such as, *e.g.*, the complications in allocating damages to different levels of the distribution chain, or the problems inherent in allowing duplicative recovery – prohibits an indirect purchaser from seeking *injunctive* relief. As the Third Circuit explained:

> [I]n contrast to the treble damage action, a claim for injunctive relief does not present the countervailing considerations such as the risk of duplicative or ruinous recoveries and the spectre of a trial burdened with complex and conjectural economic analyses that the Supreme Court emphasized when limiting the availability of treble damages.[115]

Hence, indirect purchasers are generally permitted to seek injunctive relief,[116] provided they meet the other requirements to establish standing to seek such relief outlined above.[117]

---

[111] Gulfstream III Assocs., Inc. v. Gulfstream Aerospace Corp., 995 F.2d 425, 437 (3d Cir. 1993) (Greenberg, J. writing opinion for court) ('There is no serious doubt that an antitrust claim can be expressly assigned.'); In re Fine Paper Litig., 632 F.2d 1081, 1090 (3rd Cir. 1980); La. Farmers' Protective Union, Inc., v. Great Atl. & Pac. Tea Co. of Am., Inc., 131 F.2d 419, 423 (8th Cir. 1942).

[112] Gulfstream III, 995 F.2d at 440.

[113] Cordes, 502 F.3d at 101 ('[assignees] Cordes and Creditors Trust stood before the district court in the shoes of [assignors] Western Pacific and EqualNet'); Meijer, Inc. v. Warner Chilcott Holdings Co. III, 246 F.R.D. 293, 296 (D.D.C. 2007); In re Urethane Antitrust Litig., 237 F.R.D. 440, 448 (D. Kan. 2006).

[114] Utilicorp, 497 US at 216 (internal quotation marks omitted). For instance, one court declined to create an exception for the medical device industry, where certain indirect purchasers purportedly purchased the product in question under contracts with the manufacturers setting forth some terms of the sale, but nevertheless bought through middlemen. Del. Valley, 523 F.3d at 1122.

[115] Mid-West Paper Prods., 596 F.2d at 590.

[116] Id. at 592; see also Dickson, 309 F.3d at 214 n.24; Campos, 140 F.3d at 1172 ('Indirect purchaser status does not bar the plaintiffs from seeking injunctive relief under §16 of the Clayton Act.').

[117] See supra Standing for Injunctive Relief.

Indirect purchasers: restitution and disgorgement

Barred from seeking damages, some indirect purchasers have attempted instead to seek monetary relief in equitable forms, such as in the form of restitution or disgorgement, under §16 of the Clayton Act. These remedies, in essence, seek to force the defendant to give up allegedly ill-gotten gains.

However, plaintiffs' pursuit of these remedies has not fared well. In *In re Multidistrict Vehicle Air Pollution Litigation*,[118] the Ninth Circuit, while recognizing that 'restitution is indeed an equitable remedy,' barred it as a vehicle for monetary relief under §16:

> [Section] 16 limits the equitable remedies available under its terms to those against 'threatened loss or damage.' Here, the 'reimbursement' would be awarded for the loss which has already occurred, at the time the car owner paid to have his vehicle retrofitted; it would not be relief 'against threatened loss or damage.' Recovery for past losses is properly covered under §4; it comes under the head of 'damages.'[119]

In other words, the court viewed a claim for 'reimbursement' as little more than a prohibited damages claim in equitable clothing. Moreover, courts have been skeptical of using equitable theories as a basis for damage claims because the practice would run afoul of the duplicative recovery concerns of *Illinois Brick*.[120]

Indirect purchasers: recovery under state law

While the federal antitrust laws bar damages recovery for indirect purchasers, indirect purchasers may be able to recover damages resulting from anticompetitive conduct under the laws of various states.

The ruling in *Illinois Brick* prohibiting indirect purchaser damage claims was criticized for limiting the 'broad objective[]' of the antitrust laws: 'to compensate victims of antitrust violations' – including consumers – 'and to deter future violations.'[121] As Justice Brennan noted in his dissent, 'the brunt of antitrust injuries is borne by indirect purchasers, often ultimate consumers of a product, as increased costs are passed along the chain of distribution.'[122] In contrast, the 'middlemen' may 'have little incentive to sue suppliers so long as they pass on the bulk of the illegal overcharges.'[123] Calculating and then allocating damages between direct and indirect purchasers was said to be no more difficult or complex than other antitrust issues.[124] Some of these criticisms have either not been borne out by the facts (*e.g.*, there is little evidence that direct purchasing middlemen are failing to bring cases that indirect purchasers would have brought), or fail to grapple with some of the procedural and other hurdles that sometimes impede indirect purchaser

---

118 538 F.2d 231 (9th Cir. 1976).

119 Id. at 234.

120 Mylan Labs., 62 F. Supp. 2d at 41–42. For further discussion of equitable remedies for antitrust violations, see Chapter 11 of this *Handbook*.

121 Ill. Brick Co., 431 US at 748 (Brennan, J. dissenting).

122 Id. at 749 (Brennan, J. dissenting).

123 Id. (Brennan, J. dissenting).

124 Id. at 758–60 (Brennan, J., dissenting).

cases. For instance, in antitrust cases involving 'inputs,' such as, *e.g.*, hydrogen peroxide, sorbates, high fructose corn syrup, or lysine, because of the diffusion of the harm, absent a direct purchaser capable of standing in and recovering for all of the overcharges caused by the anticompetitive conduct, there would for all practical purposes be no one to recover for the vast bulk of the harm caused.

Nevertheless, in light of criticisms of *Illinois Brick*, a number of states passed '*Illinois Brick* repealer' acts, designed to give consumers standing even if they did not purchase directly. It is estimated that approximately 70 per cent of the American population lives in states where a right of action is permitted by some or all indirect purchasers.[125]

The Supreme Court grappled with the repealer statutes in *California v. ARC America Corp.*[126] Notwithstanding its decision in *Illinois Brick*, and despite the possibility of duplicative recoveries, the Court found that states were not barred from enacting laws to afford standing to indirect purchasing consumers.

The *Illinois Brick* repealer statutes take several different forms. Many states simply permit indirect purchaser plaintiffs to pursue damage claims. For instance, California's Cartwright Act explicitly permits suits by '[a]ny person who is injured in his or her business or property by reason of anything forbidden or declared unlawful by this chapter, regardless of whether such injured person dealt directly or indirectly with the defendant.'[127] Likewise, in the wake of *Illinois Brick*, the Minnesota legislature amended its antitrust act to specify that a plaintiff can sue for a violation of the antitrust law whether 'injured directly or indirectly.'[128] Other states authorize such damage claims

---

125 Antitrust Modernization Comm'n, Report and Recommendations, at 279 n. 22 (Apr. 2007).

126 490 US 93 (1989).

127 CAL. BUS. & PROF. CODE §16750(a). See also, e.g., ALA. CODE §6-5-60; ARIZ. REV. STAT. ANN. §44-1408; D.C. CODE ANN. §28-4509; HAW. REV. STAT. §480-13; IDAHO CODE §48-113; 740 ILL. COMP. STAT. 10/7(2) (authorizing private suits but providing 'no person other than the Attorney General of this State shall be authorized to maintain a class action in any court of this State for indirect purchasers asserting claims under this Act'); ME. REV. STAT. ANN., tit. 10, §1104(1); MICH. COMP. LAWS. ANN. §445.778; MINN. STAT. §325D.57; MISS. CODE ANN. §75-21-9; NEV. REV. STAT. §598A.210; N.M. STAT. ANN. §57-1-3A; N.Y. GEN. BUS. LAW §340(6) (authorizing individual claims; see infra n.139 and accompanying text regarding class claims); N.C. GEN. STAT. §75-16 (as construed in Hyde v. Abbott Labs., Inc., 473 S.E.2d 680 (N.C. Ct. App. 1996)); N.D. CENT. CODE §51-08.1-08(3); R.I. GEN. LAWS §6-36-12(g); S.D. CODIFIED LAWS §37-1-33; WIS. STAT. ANN. §133.18(1). The West Virginia statute is silent on the matter, but its Attorney General has promulgated a legislative rule extending standing to 'any person who is injured directly or indirectly by reason of a violation of the West Virginia Antitrust Act.' W. VA. CODE R. §142-9-2. Cf. In re New Motor Vehicles Canadian Exp. Antitrust Litig., 350 F. Supp. 2d 160, 173–74 (D. Me. 2004); In re Chocolate Confectionary Antitrust Litig., 602 F. Supp. 2d 538, 582 n.55 (M.D. Pa. 2009). Other states simply subsume indirect purchaser recovery under their general consumer protection or unfair trade laws, which is generally outside the scope of this chapter.

128 MINN. STAT. §325D.57. *See also* State by Humphrey v. Philip Morris, Inc., 551 N.W.2d 490, 497 (Minn. 1996) ('After Illinois Brick was decided . . . Minnesota acted to change its law to allow anyone to sue in antitrust.').

only if brought by the Attorney General or another government authority,[129] or if the government is the indirect purchaser.[130]

In states where no specific statute is in force, courts have sometimes permitted indirect purchaser damage claims nevertheless.[131] The Tennessee Supreme Court, for instance, interpreted its state statute, which gave a right of action to '[a]ny person who is injured or damaged' by an antitrust violation, as 'affording a remedy to the ultimate victims of the antitrust conduct.'[132] It deemed them to be 'the real victims of the antitrust violations,' with 'the true incentive to bring suit.'[133]

On the other hand, courts in several states have adopted *Illinois Brick* and barred indirect purchaser claims. For instance, Florida courts have adopted the policy of *Illinois Brick* in construing their own state antitrust law.[134] In *Free v. Abbott Laboratories*,[135] the Fifth Circuit predicted Louisiana would follow a similar path.[136] Some courts have pointed to the legislature's failure to enact *Illinois Brick* repealer legislation as an indication that indirect plaintiffs ought not to have standing.[137] Other state legislatures have commanded their courts generally to follow federal antitrust law, which the courts have read to adopt *Illinois Brick*.[138]

In New York, indirect purchasers are barred from bringing private class actions to recover treble damages.[139] Some states are said to not explicitly provide for private antitrust damage actions.[140]

---

129 E.g., COLO. REV. STAT. §6-4-111; Siena v. Microsoft Corp., 796 A.2d 461, 464–65 (R.I. 2002) (Rhode Island Attorney General may bring suit on behalf of indirect purchasers). *See also* 740 ILL. COMP. STAT. 10/7(2) (indirect purchasers can sue, and Attorney General can bring class action); Gaebler v. N.M. Potash Corp., 676 N.E.2d 228, 230 (Ill. Ct. App. 1996) (construing this provision to preclude private class actions for indirect purchasers).

130 E.g., MD. CODE ANN. COM. LAW §11-209(b)(2); Davidson v. Microsoft Corp., 792 A.2d 336, 341 (Md. Ct. App. 2002) (governments permitted to sue whether they dealt 'directly or indirectly' with defendant, but noting legislature had rejected a bill that would have repealed *Illinois Brick* generally).

131 E.g., Freeman Indus., LLC v. Eastman Chem. Co., 172 S.W.3d 512, 517–20 (Tenn. 2005); Bunker's Glass Co. v. Pilkington, 47 P.3d 1119, 1124 (Ariz. App. 2002). See also Elkins v. Microsoft Corp., 817 A.2d 9, 16–20 (Vt. 2002) (indirect purchaser standing existed under Vermont law even prior to passage of repealer statute).

132 Freeman, 172 S.W.3d at 517, 520.

133 Id. at 520.

134 E.g., Mack v. Bristol-Myers Squibb Co., 673 So. 2d 100, 110 (Fla. Dist. Ct. App. 1996). Nevertheless, indirect purchasers may still seek to recover under Florida's Deceptive and Unfair Trade Practices Act, FLA. STAT. §§501.201, et seq. See In re Wellbutrin XL Antitrust Litig., Civ. A. No. 08-2433, 2009 US Dist. LEXIS 66676, at *49–54 (E.D. Pa. Jul. 31, 2009).

135 176 F.3d 298 (5th Cir. 1999).

136 Id. at 299. Accord New Motor Vehicles, 350 F. Supp. 2d at 170; FTC v. Mylan Labs., Inc., 99 F. Supp. 2d 1, 6–8 (D.D.C. 1999).

137 Vacco v. Microsoft Corp., 793 A.2d 1048, 1059–60 (Conn. 2002).

138 Major v. Microsoft Corp., 60 P.3d 511, 513 (Okla. Ct. Civ. App. 2002).

139 Sperry v. Crompton Corp., 863 N.E.2d 1012, 1013 (N.Y. Ct. App. 2007).

140 In re K-Dur Antitrust Litig., 2008 US Dist. LEXIS 71767, at *22–23 (D.N.J. Feb. 25, 2008) (Orlofsky, J. Special Master) ('Pennsylvania has no general antitrust statute, nor any statute creating a private right of action against restraints of trade. Plaintiffs have not cited, nor have I located, any case awarding damages under Pennsylvania law for antitrust violations.'). See also XF Enterprises, Inc. v. BASF Corp., 47 Pa. D.&C. 4th 147, 150, 2000 WL 33155746 (Pa. Com.

Do the *Associated General* factors apply to a damages claim brought under a state *Illinois Brick* repealer statute?

Although *Illinois Brick* repealers may avoid the total bar to recovery that exists under federal law, some courts have found that indirect purchasers may nonetheless be too remote from the anticompetitive conduct to recover, even under a repealer statute. Thus, in *In re Dynamic Random Access Memory Antitrust Litigation* (DRAM),[141] the court recognized that California's Cartwright Act contained an *Illinois Brick* repealer. It stated:

> However, while the Cartwright Act directly contradicts federal law insofar as indirect purchaser standing is generally concerned, it does not follow from this either that indirect purchaser status is itself sufficient under California law to establish antitrust standing, or that California law necessarily eschews the general test for antitrust standing as set forth in [*Associated General*]. For as defendants point out, the question whether indirect purchasers have standing under state law, and the question whether antitrust plaintiffs – which may include indirect purchasers – have antitrust standing for a particular claim, are two 'analytically distinct' issues.[142]

The court pointed to a California decision which suggested that, the repealer notwithstanding, California's antitrust standing rules were in flux.[143] Thus, according to the *DRAM* court, an indirect purchaser must still meet 'efficient enforcer' factors like those announced *Associated General*, even when pursuing an antitrust claim for damages under California state law.[144]

Judge Hamilton's opinion quickly drew fire from a fellow jurist. Judge Alsup, writing in *In re Graphics Processing Units Antitrust Litigation* (GPU),[145] refused to follow *DRAM*, sagely observing that '*Associated General Contractors* arose under the federal Clayton Act. It is far from clear that *Associated General Contractors* should be automatically read into the substantive antitrust law of each and every state.'[146] Judge Alsup continued:

> Standing under each state's antitrust statute is a matter of that state's law. It would be wrong for a district judge, in *ipse dixit* style, to bypass all state legislatures and all state appellate courts and to pronounce a blanket and nationwide revision of all state antitrust laws. The rule urged by the defense may (or may not) be sound policy but that is a matter for the state policy makers to decide, not for a federal judge to impose by fiat.[147]

Pl. 2000). But see Collins v. Main Line Bd. of Realtors, 304 A.2d 493, 498 (Pa. 1973) (suggesting record in that case did 'not provide any legal basis for an award of damages,' but not stating a rule that such damages are never available).

[141] 516 F. Supp. 2d 1072 (N.D. Cal. 2007).

[142] Id. at 1087.

[143] Id. at 1087–88 ('[t]he exact parameters of "antitrust injury" under [the Cartwright Act] have not yet been established through either court decisions or legislation'), quoting Cellular Plus, Inc. v. Superior Court of San Diego County, 18 Cal. Rptr. 2d 308, 313 (Cal. Ct. App. 1993).

[144] See also In re Intel Corp. Microprocessor Antitrust Litig., 496 F. Supp. 2d 404, 409 (D. Del. 2007) ('[I]t is appropriate to apply the AGC factors if not directly, at least as a guide, in evaluating Class Plaintiffs' state law antitrust claims.').

[145] 527 F. Supp. 2d 1011 (N.D. Cal. 2007).

[146] Id. at 1025.

[147] Id. at 1026. See also In re TFT-LCD Antitrust Litig., 586 F. Supp. 2d 1109, 1123 (N.D. Cal. 2008) ('The Court agrees with Judge Alsup that it is inappropriate to broadly apply the AGC test to plaintiffs' claims under the repealer states' laws in the absence of a clear directive from those

Judge Alsup acknowledged that two states – Iowa and Nebraska – had adopted the *Associated General* test as their own for purposes of antitrust standing,[148] but declined to adopt the *Associated General* test on behalf of any other state.[149]

Some state courts have expressly considered – and rejected – application of the *Associated General* standing factors in the context of state antitrust claims.[150]

Other courts, however, have referenced those factors when evaluating whether a plaintiff has antitrust standing. As one court reasoned, the *Illinois Brick* repealer simply removed the absolute bar, but 'd[id] not address the standing issue,' which must be resolved through the application of a test like *Associated General*.[151] Notably, the court viewed itself as bound by statute to give 'due deference to interpretations given by the federal courts to comparable antitrust statutes.'[152]

This issue is currently before the Ninth Circuit in the *DRAM* case, which accepted the indirect purchaser plaintiffs' interlocutory appeal. The American Antitrust Institute (AAI) has filed an *amicus curiae* brief supporting reversal.[153] AAI argued that under *Erie Railroad Co. v. Tompkins*,[154] the role of federal courts is to apply existing state law policies articulated by the respective state legislatures, and not to create new rules of law in derogation of such policies.[155] This issue is noteworthy, in part, because the *Illinois Brick* repealer acts, including California's, were specifically passed to abrogate the federal indirect purchaser bar with its attendant concerns of complexities of proof, and to permit

---

states' legislatures or highest courts.'); Moniz v. Bayer Corp., 484 F. Supp. 2d 228, 231 (D. Mass. 2007); D.R. Ward Const. Co. v. Rohm & Haas, Co., 470 F. Supp. 2d 485, 500–02 (E.D. Pa. 2006) (doubting Associated General applies to Vermont's antitrust statute).

148 GPU, 540 F. Supp. 2d at 1097 (citing Southard v. Visa U.S.A., Inc., 734 N.W.2d 192, 199 (Iowa 2007) and Kanne v. Visa U.S.A., Inc., 723 N.W.2d 293, 302–03 (Neb. 2006)).

149 Id. See also In re Flash Memory Antitrust Litig., 43 F. Supp. 2d 1133, 1152 (N.D. Cal. 2009) (declining to adopt AGC factors for any states other than Iowa, Nebraska, and California). The court observed that one intermediate court appeared to use the *Associated General* factors, suggesting California would adopt them as well.

150 Teague v. Bayer AG, 671 S.E.2d 550, 557 (N.C. Ct. App. 2009) ('We hold the [Associated General] factors do not apply in determining which indirect purchasers have standing to sue under the North Carolina antitrust statutes.'); Lorix v. Crompton, 736 N.W. 2d 619, 627–28 (Minn. Aug. 2, 2007).

151 Stark v. Visa U.S.A. Inc., No. 03-055030-CZ, 2004 WL 1879003, at *4 (Mich. Cir. Ct. July 23, 2004). See also Duvall v. Silvers, Asher, Sher & McLaren, M.D., 998 S.W.2d 821, 824–25 (Mo. Ct. App. 1999) (referencing Associated General's requirement for directness of injury, but not adopting multi-factor test); County of Cook v. Philip Morris, Inc., 817 N.E.2d 1039, 1043–46 (Ill. App. Ct. 2004) (incorporating remoteness analysis and dismissing Illinois antitrust claim); Ho v. Visa U.S.A., Inc., No. 112316/00, 2004 N.Y. Misc. LEXIS 577, at *2–3 (N.Y. Sup. Ct. Apr. 21, 2004) (applying Associated General factors to indirect purchasers). One trial court referenced the Associated General factors, but indirect purchaser standing was not before the court; as the opinion notes, the plaintiff had 'not actually acquired the product or service that is alleged to be tainted by unlawful trade.' Fucile v. Visa U.S.A. Inc., No. S1560-03 CNC, 2004 WL 3030037, at *1–2 (Vt. Sup. Ct. Dec. 27, 2004).

152 Stark, 2004 WL 1879003, at *4.

153 Brief for the American Antitrust Institute as Amicus Curiae in Support of Appellants and Reversal, In re Dynamic Random Access Memory (DRAM) Antitrust Litigation, Appeal No. 08-16478 (9th Cir.), filed Mar. 5, 2009 ('AAI DRAM Br.').

154 304 US 64 (1938).

155 AAI DRAM Br. at 5–9.

indirect purchasers to recover.[156] The *Associated General* standard, on the other hand, 'essentially applies the same considerations that underlay the *Illinois Brick* rule, which were obviously rejected by the repealer states.'[157] How federal courts interpret and apply state antitrust laws is of increasing concern now that many state law antitrust class actions are removed to federal court under the Class Action Fairness Act (CAFA).[158] Thus, there is the increased danger of impediments being erected in federal court that hinder the enforcement of state antitrust laws and policies.

Competitors

Competitors have been recognized as among the classic groups of plaintiffs authorized to bring antitrust suits.[159]

Like any other antitrust plaintiff, competitors must establish antitrust injury, *i.e.*, they must show 'injury of the type the antitrust laws were intended to prevent and that flows from that which makes defendants' acts unlawful.'[160] In other words, the competitor plaintiff must show harm from conduct that impedes competition and should 'reflect the anticompetitive effect either of the violation or of the anticompetitive acts made possible by the violation.'[161] Competitor plaintiffs must also demonstrate that their asserted claims satisfy the factors enumerated in *Associated General*.

Thus, a competitor plaintiff cannot survive merely by showing that it lost profits or business as a result of ostensibly anticompetitive activity.[162] After all, the antitrust laws are designed to preserve and foster competition, not inhibit it. 'The antitrust laws . . . were enacted for the "protection of competition, not competitors."'[163] Antitrust law 'ensure[s] competition in general' and is 'not narrowly focused to protect individual competitors . . . .'[164]

Following these general rules, courts have been hostile to claims for lost business brought by competitors if the defendant's actions were actually favorable to consumers or consumer welfare generally – a point which was dispositive in *Brunswick*.[165]

For instance, in *Cargill, Inc. v. Monfort of Colorado, Inc.*, a plaintiff competitor could not show antitrust injury where a merged company (presumed to be illegal) threatened to engage in vigorous price competition, which would have allegedly caused the plaintiff to lose substantial profits. The plaintiff's threatened injuries flowed from the defendant's

---

156 AAI DRAM Br. at 9–16.

157 Id. at 17.

158 Pub. L. 109-2, 119 Stat. 4 (2005). For further discussion of CAFA, see Chapter 7 and Chapter 8 of this *Handbook*.

159 '[G]enerally only competitors and consumers will suffer antitrust injury . . . .' Carpet Group Int'l v. Oriental Rug Imps. Ass'n, Inc., 227 F.3d 62, 77 (3d Cir. 2000).

160 Brunswick Corp., 429 US at 489 (1977); see also Atl. Richfield Co. v. US Petroleum Co., 495 US 328 (1990).

161 Brunswick Corp., 429 US at 489.

162 Atl. Richfield, 495 US at 338; Cargill, 479 US at 115.

163 Brunswick Corp, 429 US at 488.

164 Capital Imaging Assocs., P.C. v. Mohawk Valley Med. Assoc., Inc., 996 F.2d 537, 543 (2d Cir. 1993).

165 See Brunswick Corp., 429 US at 488–89; see also supra notes 15–20 and accompanying text.

offer of its products at low prices, but as long as those prices were not predatory, that was not 'activity forbidden by the antitrust laws.'[166] As a result, in *Cargill*, the competitor plaintiff had not alleged cognizable antitrust injury.

Likewise, lower courts have disallowed competitor claims arising out of the operation of competition rather than its suppression. In *NicSand, Inc. v. 3M Co.*,[167] the plaintiff alleged that a monopolist gave customers up-front cash payments and signed them to multi-year contracts.[168] As to the cash payments (which were discounts) and multi-year provisions (which allowed the purchasers to 'buy in bulk' and thus earn a lower price), the court reasoned 'cutting prices in order to increase business often is the very essence of competition' and penalizing such activity would 'chill the very conduct the antitrust laws are designed to protect.'[169] According to the court, the exclusive supplier arrangements were not part of the defendant's anticompetitive design, but in fact had arisen due to customer demand (and the plaintiff had previously enjoyed their operation). Accordingly, the competitor plaintiff had not alleged cognizable antitrust injury.

In sum, a competitor plaintiff must allege an injury that parallels the harm done to consumers, rather than simply bemoan lost profits or income to itself.

Competitors: new entrants to the market

A frequent question that emerges is when a plaintiff, rather than claiming that it was forced out of the market, asserts that it is being kept from entering the market in the first place. To be sure, 'the law does not condone the purchase of protection from uncertain competition any more than it condones the elimination of actual competition.'[170] However, the prospective competitor must do more than simply claim it wishes to compete. 'A "nascent" business – one that is merely a gleam in the eye and a hope in the heart of its promoters – does not possess the property to which antitrust injury can be done.'[171] Hence, 'most courts . . . have required a company that has not actually entered the market to show that it intended to enter and was prepared to do so within a reasonable time.'[172]

---

[166] 479 US at 115–116.

[167] 507 F.3d 442 (6th Cir. 2007).

[168] Id. at 451–54.

[169] Id. at 452 (quoting Matsushita Elec. Indus. Co. v. Zenith Radio Corp., 475 US 574, 594 (1986)).

[170] XII Herbert Hovenkamp, Antitrust Law ¶2030b at 213 (2d ed. 2005). Accord United States v. Microsoft Corp., 253 F.3d 34, 79 (D.C. Cir. 2001) (en banc); Sullivan v. Nat'l Football League, 34 F.3d 1091, 1100 (1st Cir. 1994); Engine Specialties Inc. v. Bombardier, Ltd., 605 F.2d 1, 9 (1st Cir. 1979).

[171] Bourns, Inc. v. Raychem Corp., 331 F.3d 704, 712 (9th Cir. 2003).

[172] Grip-Pak, Inc. v. Ill. Tool Works, Inc., 694 F.2d 466, 475 (7th Cir. 1982). See also Bourns 331 F.3d at 711 (noting plaintiff's intent but that it was 'unprepared to enter the business'); Andrx Pharms., 256 F.3d at 808 (plaintiff '*can* allege facts sufficient to indicate its intent and preparedness') (emphasis in original); Jayco Sys., Inc. v. Savin Bus. Mach. Corp., 777 F.2d 306, 313 (5th Cir. 1985) ('Where a business expansion . . . is contemplated, there must be a showing of intent to expand and of preparedness for the expansion.') (internal quotations and citation omitted); Huron Valley Hosp., Inc. v. City of Pontiac, 666 F.2d 1029, 1033 (6th Cir. 1981) (citations omitted).

Other types of antitrust claimants

Although competitors and purchasers are among the most common antitrust plaintiffs, the courts have never foreclosed other members of the public from bringing suit. As the Supreme Court long ago observed:

> The [Clayton Act] does not confine its protection to consumers, or to purchasers, or to competitors, or to sellers. . . . The Act is comprehensive in its terms and coverage, protecting all who are made victims of the forbidden practices by whomever they may be perpetrated.[173]

Shareholders

One of the earliest cases relating to antitrust injury denied standing to shareholders seeking relief due to harms done to the corporation. The court in *Loeb v. Eastman Kodak Co.*[174] reasoned that any injuries sustained were borne by the corporation itself, which was capable of vindicating its own interests if it so chose. By contrast (foretelling the remoteness factors which later came into play in *Associated General*), the shareholder's interest was only 'indirect, remote, and consequential.'[175]

Suppliers

Courts have been divided on whether suppliers to market participants have standing to pursue antitrust claims.

Of course 'a seller may well have a claim if victimized by a price-fixing ring composed of buyers that lowered the market price: in such a case the seller is a participant in the very market where competition is impaired.'[176]

However, a different result pertains if the anticompetitive conduct targets the downstream market rather than upstream. Thus, if the supplier's customer fails (or loses business, curtailing purchases from the supplier) because of an antitrust violation, 'usually the conduct was deemed an antitrust violation because of the threat to the customer, not the supplier.'[177] Hence, the customer – *i.e.*, the excluded rival – would have antitrust standing, but not the supplier.[178]

To like effect, no standing was found for a landlord who wanted to supply real estate to a retailer's rivals, but could not because that retailer had previously leased the property and left it vacant and refused to surrender the lease, diminishing the rental value of all of the rental spaces on the property.[179] Applying *Associated General*, the court found such an injury too remote to confer standing on the landlord wishing to supply space to

---

173 Mandeville Island Farms, Inc. v. Am. Crystal Sugar Co., 334 US 219, 236 (1948).

174 183 F. 704, 709 (3d Cir. 1910).

175 Id. at 709. Loeb was specifically cited in Associated General as an example of an injury deemed too 'remote.' 459 US at 533–34. Courts applying the Associated General factors have accordingly denied standing to shareholders as well. E.g., Meyer Goldberg, Inc. of Lorain v. Goldberg, 717 F.2d 290, 294 (6th Cir. 1983) (sole shareholder of bankrupt corporation lacked antitrust standing).

176 SAS of P.R. v. P.R. Tel. Co., 48 F.3d 39, 44 (1st Cir. 1995). See also Mandeville Island, 334 US at 236; Beef Indus., 600 F.2d 1148; II Areeda & Hovenkamp, Antitrust Law ¶375b.

177 SAS of P.R., 48 F.3d at 44.

178 See id.

179 Southaven Land Co. v. Malone & Hyde, Inc., 715 F.2d 1079, 1085–88 (6th Cir. 1983).

the potential rival. Consumers and market participants were more immediately affected and could bring suit if they chose.[180] Also, the asserted injury – the diminution in rental values at the shopping center – was considered too speculative.

Thus, some courts have stated that '[s]uppliers to direct market participants typically cannot seek recovery under the antitrust laws because their injuries are too secondary and indirect to be considered "antitrust injuries."'[181]

However, the view is not unanimous. In *Chemi SpA v. GlaxoSmithKline*,[182] the court permitted the supplier of an excluded rival to sue. The court viewed the injury as one the Sherman Act was designed to forestall: 'In our view the antitrust laws are intended to provide a remedy to the manufacturers and sellers of a product where the monopoly was specifically designed to prevent the sale of that very product in the marketplace.'[183]

Terminated dealers and distributors

Another recurring fact pattern is where a manufacturing company has been acquired by (or otherwise fallen prey to) a monopolist. The manufacturer may have contracted with dealers and distributors to disseminate the former company's product to the public. However, once acquired by a monopolist, the distributors are cut off, as the monopolist begins to use its own distribution channels. The dealer or distributor attempts to sue the monopolist.¶

Such attempts often fail because this is not deemed to be 'antitrust injury' associated with the anticompetitive harm – higher prices or reduced output. 'Dealers in this situation lack standing because their particular injury was not caused by an exercise of the defendant's newly acquired power to raise prices . . . Instead, the dealer's injury was caused by the manufacturer's decision to terminate their relationship, something the manufacturer could have just as well done without having monopoly power.'[184] In contrast, distributors and consumers buying from the monopolists *would* have antitrust injury, because they are paying higher prices due to the reduction in competition.

Employees

As with suppliers (employees are suppliers of labor), employee standing depends on the type of claim being pressed. An employee would be entitled to sue were there a conspiracy between the employer and others to suppress wages or fix other conditions of

---

180 See id. at 1087.

181 Serfecz v. Jewel Food Stores, 67 F.3d 591, 597 (7th Cir. 1995); see also R.C. Dick Geothermal Corp. v. Thermogenics, Inc., 890 F.2d 139, 148 (9th Cir. 1989); Asahi Glass Co., Ltd. v. Pentech Pharms., Inc., 289 F. Supp. 2d 986, 990–91 (N.D. Ill. 2003) (Posner, J., sitting by designation) (denying standing to supplier of prospective generic product); Delco LLC v. Giant of Md., LLC, Civ. No. 07-3522 (JBS), 2007 WL 3307018, at *10 (D.N.J. Nov. 8, 2007).

182 356 F. Supp. 2d 495 (E.D. Pa. 2005).

183 Id. at 501.

184 Port Dock & Stone Corp. v. Oldcastle Northeast, Inc., 507 F.3d 117, 123 (2d Cir. 2007); see also Atl. Richfield Co. v. USA Petroleum Co., 495 US 328, 345–46 (1990); Norris v. Hearst Trust, 500 F.3d 454, 465–66 (5th Cir. 2007); The Serpa Corp., 199 F.3d at 11–12; Florida Seed Co. v. Monsanto Co., 105 F.3d 1372, 1375 n. 3 (11th Cir. 1997); John Lenore & Co. v. Olympia Brewing Co., 550 F.2d 495, 500 (9th Cir. 1977).

employment.[185] Thus, in *Eichorn v. AT&T Corp.*,[186] employees were granted standing to challenge a 'no hire' agreement – an agreement among competitors not to hire a particular set of prospective employees – which suspended competition for their technical services. Quoting Areeda and Hovenkamp, the Court concluded:

> Antitrust law addresses employer conspiracies controlling employment terms precisely because they tamper with the employment market and thereby impair the opportunities of those who sell their services there. Just as antitrust law seeks to preserve the free market opportunities of buyers and sellers of goods, so also it seeks to do the same for buyers and sellers of employment services. It would be perverse indeed to hold that the very object of the law's solicitude and the persons most directly concerned – perhaps the only persons concerned – could not challenge the restraint.[187]

In contrast, employees may not sue for injuries sustained in the market into which their employers sold product. Thus, former employees of a car dealership driven out of business by an antitrust conspiracy were denied standing in *Peck v. General Motors Corp.*[188]

Unions and trade associations

Likewise, unions generally do not have standing for injuries sustained by their members. Indeed, enhanced competition – and the consequent drive by manufacturers to lower prices by reducing production costs – may be in tension with a union's *raison d'être* of increased wages and benefits for its members.[189] Thus, if the claim is for lost work or reduced wages, the injury may not be one that the antitrust laws were meant to prevent. This is particularly true if the employees themselves lack standing.[190] However, when the claimed injury is that the union purchased products that were the subject of anticompetitive conduct, standing has been upheld.[191]

Trade associations have had mixed success as antitrust plaintiffs. While some courts have permitted them to seek an injunction for harm sustained by their members,[192] US law does not generally allow such entities to recover damages sustained by their members.[193] The claim is deemed to belong to the affected members, who would be able to

---

185 See AREEDA AND HOVENKAMP, ANTITRUST LAW ¶377a.

186 248 F.3d 131 (3d Cir. 2001).

187 Id. at 141 (quoting AREEDA & HOVENKAMP, ANTITRUST LAW ¶377c); see also Doe v. Ariz. Hosp. & Healthcare Ass'n, No. CV 07-1292-PHX-SRB, 2009 US Dist. LEXIS 42871, *19–23 (D. Ariz. Mar. 19, 2009) (allowing claims by proposed class of nurses alleging that Defendants fixed the price of their wages below competitive levels).

188 894 F.2d 844 (6th Cir. 1990). See also G.K.A. Beverage Corp. v. Honickman, 55 F.3d 762, 766 (2d Cir. 1995) ('merely derivative injuries sustained by employees, officers, stockholders, and creditors of an injured company do not constitute "antitrust injury" sufficient to confer antitrust standing').

189 Associated Gen., 459 US at 539.

190 See supra Employees.

191 See, e.g., In re Warfarin Sodium Antitrust Litig., 391 F.3d 516, 531 (3d Cir. 2004).

192 See, e.g., Associated Gen. Contractors v. Otter Tail Power Co., 611 F.2d 684, 690 (8th Cir. 1979) (association could sue for injunction as representative of its members).

193 See, e.g., Southwest Suburban Board of Realtors, Inc., v. Beverly Area Planning Ass'n, 830 F.2d 1374, 1379–80 (7th Cir. 1987) (trade group denied standing because conduct aimed at

sue in their own right either individually or as part of a class. This stands in contrast to proposals within the European Union that would permit certain damage claims for anticompetitive conduct by consumer groups, but not by their constituent members.[194]

Conclusion

The list of potential claimants under the antitrust laws is as long and varied as the means by which the antitrust laws can be violated. But there are limits. To have a cognizable claim, a plaintiff would need to first and foremost establish that it has suffered the requisite type of injury, namely an antitrust injury.

---

its 'member brokers'). Of course, members may assign their claims to the association. See, e.g., Jefferson County Pharm. Ass'n, Inc. v. Abbott Lab., 460 US 150 (1983).

[194] See Commission of the European Communities, 'White Paper on Damages Actions For Breach Of The EC Antitrust Rules' (Apr. 2, 2008), at 4 *available at* http://ec.europa.eu/competition/antitrust/actionsdamages/files_white_paper/whitepaper_en.pdf; see also Chapter 38 of this *Handbook*.

7 Initiation of a private claim

Michael D. Hausfeld[1]

Introduction

Although the initiation of a private claim in the United States appears relatively straightforward – a plaintiff prepares, files, and serves a complaint – this process actually involves a number of important choices on the part of a litigant:

- Should the case be in court at all, or is some alternative forum preferable? This chapter discusses options such as complaining to the Federal Trade Commission or Department of Justice, pursuing arbitration, or attempting to negotiate a pre-litigation settlement.
- If the dispute or claim is to be in court, should it be filed in state or federal court? This chapter provides an overview of why one or the other might be more appropriate.
- What venue should be selected? This chapter explores requirements for jurisdiction and venue, the role of the multidistrict litigation process, and considerations about when to invoke the process and what factors to emphasize.
- Are US courts even available? This chapter examines limitations on the right of foreign plaintiffs to take advantage of the US court system.
- What are the procedural requirements for initiating a claim? This chapter concludes by summarizing the necessary contents of a complaint and the rules of service.

Considering alternatives to courts

Before initiating a private claim, an injured party may consider several alternatives to filing suit in court. Possibilities include lodging complaints with the Federal Trade Commission, the Department of Justice or state regulators, seeking arbitration or engaging in pre-litigation settlement negotiations.

Federal Trade Commission

The Federal Trade Commission was initially established for the purpose of addressing economically ambiguous conduct that could not be effectively regulated by conventional judicial procedures.[2] For this purpose the Commission has the power not only to seek injunctions and issue cease and desist orders, but also to use its rulemaking authority to address competitive problems on a more general basis.[3] This rulemaking authority

---

[1] Chairman, Hausfeld LLP. Brent Landau, Faris Ghareeb, and Carina Clark assisted in the preparation of this chapter.

[2] David Balto, *Returning to the Elman Vision of the Federal Trade Commission: Reassessing the Approach to FTC Remedies*, 72 Antitrust L.J. 1113 (2005).

[3] *Id.* at 1114–17; 15 U.S.C. §§46, 57a.

is unique to the Commission in its role as a competition enforcer, as the Department of Justice does not possess this ability.

Since its establishment, the Commission has been granted the additional power to seek equitable remedies including restitution, rescission, or disgorgement of funds.[4] It still, however, lacks authority to impose criminal penalties or civil fines.[5]

The Commission is not a forum in which an aggrieved party can bring a private claim. Individuals or entities can make their competition concerns known to the Commission, but ultimately the decision whether to pursue the matter, and how to pursue it, is left with the Commission.[6] And the appropriateness of using the Commission's powers to secure compensation for parties injured by competition violations has been a subject of controversy, with recent policy statements suggesting that it will be used sparingly in the future.[7] Factors that the Commission will consider prior to seeking such remedies include the blatancy of the violation and remedies available through other means such as private actions.[8]

Department of Justice

Unlike the Federal Trade Commission, the Antitrust Division of the Department of Justice is capable of bringing both civil and criminal actions against potential violators of competition laws.[9] Much like the Commission, however, the Division does not provide a forum for the resolution of private claims. While the Division may certainly act on information it receives from the general public, news stories, or other federal agencies, the ultimate decision on what cases to bring is left to its discretion.[10]

The Division's civil investigations are often resolved by entry of a consent decree.[11] In the criminal context, the Division will bring charges for those antitrust violations that courts have deemed to be *per se* illegal.[12] This includes violations for price fixing, bid rigging, or market allocation.[13] Charges can be brought against both the offending

---

4 *Id.* at 1120; 15 U.S.C. §53(b).

5 Meghan K. Woodsome & Katherine S. Dumouchel, *Antitrust Violations*, 46 Am. Crim. L. Rev. 275, 305 (2009).

6 Peter C. Ward, *Federal Trade Commission: Law, Practice and Procedure* §1.02[4], 1–9 (1986).

7 FTC Policy Statement on Monetary Equitable Remedies in Competition Cases, 68 Fed. Reg. 45,820 (Aug. 4, 2003), *available at* http://www.ftc.gov/os/2003/07/disgorgementfrn.htm.

8 *Id.* at 1122; FTC Policy Statement on Monetary Equitable Remedies in Competition Cases, 68 Fed. Reg. 45,821 (Aug. 4, 2003), *available at* http://www.ftc.gov/os/2003/07/disgorgementfrn.htm.

9 *See* Ward, *supra* note 6, at 1.02[4], 1–9.

10 Mark R. Joelson, *An International Antitrust Primer* 31 (Kluwer Law International 2006).

11 *See id.* at 31.

12 Edward Cavanagh, *Antitrust Remedies Revisited*, 84 Or. L. Rev. 147, 149 (Spring 2005); *see* Gary R. Spratling, Deputy Assistant Attorney General Antitrust Division, *Transparency in Enforcement Maximizes Cooperation from Antitrust Offenders*, Address Before the Fordham Corporate Law Institute 26th Annual Conference on International Antitrust Law & Policy (Oct. 15, 1999), *available at* http://www.usdoj.gov/atr/public/speeches/3952.htm (last visited July 30, 2009).

13 An Antitrust Primer for Federal Law Enforcement Personnel (Revised: April 2005), *available at* http://www.usdoj.gov/atr/public/guidelines/209114.htm (last visited October 17, 2009).

company as well as responsible persons in an individual capacity.[14] If convicted, both the company and its individual officers are subject to significant fines, and the individuals may also receive a prison sentence.[15]

As with the Federal Trade Commission, there is no guarantee that the Division will act on reports of anti-competitive activity. Even if it does, the resolution may result in the cessation of harmful conduct but it will not directly lead to restitution for aggrieved consumers. However, actions brought by the FTC or the Division could be used to bolster a private claim for civil damages. They could also lead to a quicker cessation of anticompetitive activity than may be accomplished through the courts.

State regulators

Like the federal government, states also have the ability to initiate actions under both federal and state antitrust law. These rights are typically exercised by state attorneys general on behalf of three constituencies: (1) the proprietary claims of state agencies, divisions, and programs, (2) consumers, using the state's *parens patriae* authority, and (3) the state's general economy.[16] Additionally, states often work together to coordinate their antitrust enforcement efforts through the Multistate Antitrust Task Force of the National Association of Attorneys General.[17]

When bringing claims on behalf of consumers, states can pursue both injunctive relief and damages under either federal or state law. When bringing such suits, states exercise their *parens patriae* authority, which derives from different sources depending on whether or not the claims are brought under federal or state antitrust law. If a state brings a federal claim, then its *parens patriae* authority comes directly from Title III of the Hart-Scott-Rodino Act.[18] This authority, however, is limited to claims that fall under the purview of the Sherman Act.[19] As a result, due to the Supreme Court's decision in *Illinois Brick*, states may bring a federal antitrust claim on behalf of direct purchasers but not indirect purchasers.[20] This limitation has significant impact on a state's *parens patriae* authority because ultimate consumers are usually indirect purchasers. However, if the claims do satisfy the federal requirements, then the state's attorney general may seek treble damages on behalf of all natural persons who reside in the state.[21]

When bringing suit on behalf of natural persons, the state must notify all persons on whose behalf it is suing, and it must give them an opportunity to opt out of the case.[22]

---

14 *See* Joelson, *supra* note 10, at 32; Anne K. Bingaman, Assistant Attorney General Antitrust Division, & Gary R. Spratling, Deputy Assistant Attorney General Antitrust Division, *Criminal Antitrust Enforcement*, Joint Address Before the Antitrust Section of the American Bar Association Criminal Antitrust Law and Procedure Workshop (Feb. 23, 1995), *available at* http://www.usdoj.gov/atr/public/speeches/95-02-23.txt (last visited July 30, 2009).

15 *Id.*

16 Jonathan M. Jacobson, *Antitrust Law Developments*, American Bar Association 723–24 (Sixth ed. 2007).

17 *Id.* at 724.

18 15 U.S.C. §§15c–15h.

19 *Id.*

20 Illinois Brick Co. v. Illinois, 431 US 720, 733 n.14 (1977).

21 15 U.S.C. §15c(a)(1).

22 15 U.S.C. §§15c(b)(1), (2).

Individuals who are covered by the lawsuit and who elect not to opt out will be prohibited from suing for damages under §4 of the Clayton Act.[23] While there is no requirement for class certification in a *parens patriae* lawsuit,[24] settlements still require court approval.[25]

As an alternative to bringing suit under federal law, most state attorneys general may sue to enforce state antitrust laws.[26] States that allow indirect purchasers to bring state law antitrust claims can also include such purchasers within the scope of their *parens patriae* state law actions.[27] State attorney generals may also act as *parens patriae* to prevent actual or threatened harm to a state's general economy.[28] As with federal regulators, however, whether and when to bring such a claim is at the discretion of public officials.[29]

Arbitration

Consent is necessary from both sides in order to arbitrate an antitrust dispute. This consent will often be found in the form of a pre-existing arbitration clause in a contract between the parties. Assuming such a clause exists, the process commences with the service of a notice of arbitration in the manner provided by the rules applicable to the contract.[30] Such notices usually include some detail regarding the claims being brought and the relevant facts.[31]

Some arbitration clauses purport to bar arbitrations on behalf of a class, and courts are split on whether these provisions improperly prevent plaintiffs from vindicating their statutory rights when they are bringing an antitrust claim.[32] The First and Ninth Circuits have invalidated class bars, whereas the Third, Fourth, Fifth, Sixth, Seventh, Eighth, and Eleventh Circuits have upheld them.[33] Meanwhile, the Supreme Court recently agreed to hear a case raising the issue of whether a plaintiff has a right to pursue class arbitration when the agreement is silent about that right.[34]

If an opposing party refuses to arbitrate, the claimant must file a motion to compel

---

23 15 U.S.C. §15c(b)(3).

24 Pennsylvania v. Budget Fuel, 122 F.R.D. 184, 185 (E.D. Pa. 1988).

25 15 U.S.C. §15c(c).

26 *See* Jacobson, *supra* note 16, at 729.

27 *Id.*

28 15 U.S.C. §18a; State of Conn. ex rel. Blumenthal v. BPS Petroleum Distributors, Inc., 1991 WL 177657 (D.Conn 1991).

29 For a discussion of the interplay between *parens patriae* actions and private class actions, see Chapter 13 of this *Handbook*.

30 *Arbitration Procedures: The Rules of the Road in Arbitrating Antitrust Disputes*, 19-FALL Antitrust 15 (Fall, 2004).

31 *Id.*

32 Bryon Allyn Rice, *Enforceable or Not? Class Action Waivers in Mandatory Arbitration Clauses and the Need for a Judicial Standard*, 45 Hous. L. Rev. 215, 226 (2008).

33 *See* Kristian v. Comcast Corp., 446 F.3d 25 (1st Cir. 2006); Ingle v. Circuit City Stores, 328 F.3d 1165 (9th Cir. 2003); Johnson v. W. Suburban Bank, 225 F.3d 366, 369 (3d Cir. 2000); Snowden v. CheckPoint Check Cashing, 290 F.3d 631, 638–39 (4th Cir. 2002); Carter v. Countrywide Credit Indus., Inc., 362 F.3d 294, 298 (5th Cir. 2004).

34 Stolt Nielsen SA et al. v. Animalfeeds International Corp., Case No: 08-1198.

arbitration in an appropriate forum, which might be a state or federal court.[35] If a respondent argues that an arbitration provision does not cover antitrust disputes, a court decides whether a particular claim is arbitrable unless the contract itself demonstrates a clear intent by the parties for the arbitrators to determine arbitrability.[36] When faced with broad arbitration clauses, courts often defer to the arbitrators on this issue.[37]

If some parties or claims are not subject to the arbitration agreement, they may not participate in the proceedings.[38] While courts may elect to stay related proceedings while an arbitration is underway, it is also possible that litigation in state or federal court could proceed simultaneously with arbitration.[39] This can be problematic in a large antitrust case in which allegations of a wider conspiracy involving several parties may implicate evidence from co-conspirators not subject to the arbitration.[40]

Because courts are split on the authority of arbitrators to order third-party production of evidence prior to an arbitral hearing, a claimant's ability to present a full case can be severely limited.[41] Some federal courts have acknowledged these issues and excused claimants from their obligation to arbitrate.[42]

The discovery process in arbitration is less formal and less structured than in court.[43] While some arbitration agreements will provide for more detailed discovery procedures, including those that will comport with the Federal Rules of Civil Procedure, most are more limited.[44]

Once an arbitral award is rendered, it will be set aside by a court only in 'very unusual circumstances.'[45] Judicial review of an arbitrator's findings of facts and conclusions of law is also very limited, and even a serious error will not be overturned if it appeared that the arbitrator was acting honestly and within the scope of his authority.[46] An example of an award that might be overturned is one that violates a well-defined and dominant public policy, or one that directs the parties to violate the antitrust laws.[47]

Pre-litigation settlement

Pre-litigation settlement is frequently a potential option for individual plaintiffs or a proposed class. The motivation to settle on the part of a defendant will depend on a variety

---

35 19-FALL Antitrust 15.

36 *Id.*

37 *Id.* at 17.

38 *Id.* at 16.

39 *Id.*

40 *Id.*

41 *Id.* at 16, 18; *compare* Hay Group, Inc. v. E.B.S. Acquisition Corp., 360 F.3d 404, 412–13 (3d Cir. 2004) ('The power to require a non-party "to bring" items "with him" clearly applies only to situations in which the non-party accompanies the items to the arbitration proceeding'), *with* In re Security Life Ins. Co. of Am., 228 F.3d 865, 870–71 (8th Cir. 2000) ('implicit in an arbitration panel's power to subpoena relevant documents for production at a hearing is the power to order the production of relevant documents for review by a party prior to the hearing').

42 Jung v. Ass'n of Am. Med. Colleges, 300 F. Supp. 2d 119 (D.D.C. 2004).

43 19-FALL Antitrust at 17.

44 19-FALL Antitrust at 17.

45 First Options, Inc. v. Kaplan, 514 US 938, 942 (1995).

46 Associated Coal Corp. v. United Mine Workers of Am., Dist. 17, 531 US 57, 62 (2000).

47 19-FALL Antitrust at 21.

of factors, including the strength of the case of the party threatening litigation, the relationship between the parties, and the volume of business that may have been affected by anti-competitive activity.

On behalf of a class, plaintiffs' lawyers can negotiate a potential agreement with defendants before any filings are made, and plaintiffs' lawyers can then file a settlement class action for certification.[48] Whether this is done at the same time as the filing of a complaint or subsequent to it, the parties ask the court for an order that simultaneously approves the settlement and certifies the class.[49] A court must review the terms of the settlement to ensure that it was fairly negotiated and is in the best interest of the class.[50] For certification of a settlement class, the class must satisfy all requirements set forth in Federal Rule of Civil Procedure 23 except for the manageability requirement.[51] According to the Supreme Court's ruling in *Amchem*, the remaining Rule 23 requirements, including predominance, typicality, and commonality, will demand 'undiluted, even heightened, attention in the settlement context.'[52]

Where a case is contemplated by individual plaintiffs, the parties can enter into a prelitigation settlement that is never seen by anyone and does not require judicial approval.[53] Parties negotiating such a settlement might consider entering into a tolling agreement during the course of the negotiations so that the statute of limitations does not run if the dispute cannot be resolved.[54]

Choosing between state and federal court

Once a potential litigant has decided to pursue a claim in court, it must choose between filing a complaint in state or federal court. Because federal courts have exclusive jurisdiction over Sherman Act claims, historically most antitrust cases were filed in federal court. However, some state laws allowed indirect purchasers to sue in cases when they would not have a federal claim. And state courts have sometimes been perceived as more friendly to plaintiffs.[55] With the recent passage of the Class Action Fairness Act, nearly all antitrust class actions, including indirect purchaser cases, are now heard in federal court, as discussed in more detail below.

---

[48] Martin H. Redish & Andrianna D. Kastanek, *Settlement Class Actions, The Case-or-Controversy Requirement, and the Nature of the Adjudicatory Process*, 73 U. Chi. L. Rev. 545, 553 (Spring 2006).

[49] *Id.*

[50] Fed. R. Civ. Proc. 23(e).

[51] Amchem Products, Inc. v. Windsor, 521 US 591 (1997).

[52] *Id.* at 621. For further discussion of class action requirements under Federal Rule of Civil Procedure 23, see Chapter 8 of this *Handbook*.

[53] Scott A. Moss, *Illuminating Secrecy: A New Economic Analysis of Confidential Settlements*, 105 Mich. L. Rev. 867, 883 (2007).

[54] For a discussion of pre-litigation settlements involving global cartel claims, see Chapter 37 of this *Handbook*.

[55] *See generally* Thomas E. Willging & Shannon R. Wheatman, *An Empirical Examination of Attorneys' Choice of Forum in Class Action Litigation* (Fed. Judicial Ctr. 2005).

Federal court

Federal courts have exclusive jurisdiction over private cases brought under federal antitrust law.[56] A federal claim, however, must involve conduct affecting interstate commerce.[57] The conduct itself need not constitute interstate commerce so long as there is a substantial and adverse effect on interstate commerce, or at least the potential for such harm.[58]

Because federal courts have exclusive jurisdiction, Sherman Act claims, even when accompanied by state law claims, may not be brought in state court, and if a plaintiff attempts to do so a defendant may either seek to remove the case from state to federal court or file a motion to dismiss for lack of subject matter jurisdiction.[59] But the reverse is not true: if a case presents both federal and state claims, a federal court can exercise supplemental jurisdiction over the state law claims.[60] In its discretion, the court may continue to do so even if the federal claims have been dismissed.[61]

Moreover, the Class Action Fairness Act ('CAFA') provides for federal jurisdiction over many class actions based entirely on state law. CAFA was designed to address perceived abuses associated with class actions filed in state courts, particularly suggestions that state courts were sometimes biased against out-of-state defendants and made judgments that imposed their view of the law on residents of other states in cases of national importance.[62]

Under CAFA, federal courts have jurisdiction if the amount in controversy exceeds $5 million and any member of the proposed class (A) is a citizen of a state different from any defendant; (B) is a foreign state or citizen or subject of a foreign state and any defendant is a citizen of a state; or (C) is a citizen of a state and any defendant is a foreign state or a citizen or subject of a foreign state.[63]

CAFA includes several exceptions. A federal court may decline to exercise jurisdiction if more than one-third but less than two-thirds of class members and the primary defendants are citizens of the forum state.[64] And it must decline to exercise jurisdiction if (A) more than two-thirds of class members are citizens of the forum state, at least one defendant from whom significant relief is sought and whose alleged conduct forms a significant basis for the claims is a citizen of the forum state, and principal injuries occur in the forum state, or (B) two-thirds or more of class members and the primary defendants are citizens of the forum state.[65]

---

56 15 U.S.C. §4; 15 U.S.C. §15(a).

57 15 U.S.C. §1.

58 McLain v. Real Estate Board of New Orleans, 444 US 232 (1980).

59 28 U.S.C. §1441; Dzik & Dzik, P.C. v. Vision Service Plan, 1989 WL 3082 (Tenn.App. 1989).

60 28 U.S.C. §1367(a).

61 28 U.S.C. §1367(c).

62 P.L. 109-2, §2(a)(4).

63 28 U.S.C. §1332(d)(2).

64 28 U.S.C. §1332(d)(3).

65 28 U.S.C. §1332(d)(4). For further discussion of the Class Action Fairness Act, see Chapter 8 of this *Handbook*.

State court
Provided that CAFA does not apply and that no federal claims are included, a plaintiff may elect to bring a claim in state court. State antitrust and consumer protection laws are generally similar to their federal counterpart, and many require harmonization with federal law.[66]

There are some differences, however, such as states that provide for full consideration damages, i.e. damages that account beyond the 'actual damage' to the injured party, or states that require a showing of concerted conduct.[67] Significantly, some state laws allow indirect purchasers to seek antitrust damages, which is not permitted under the Supreme Court's interpretation of the Sherman Act in *Illinois Brick*.[68] Pre-CAFA, almost all indirect purchaser cases were brought in state court, resulting in similar claims pending in multiple courts. Today, a single federal court might handle pretrial proceedings for consolidated indirect purchaser claims arising entirely under the laws of various states.[69]

Selecting a venue
After determining to file in the federal system, a plaintiff must decide which federal court venue to select. A federal court must have jurisdiction over the defendants and it must be an appropriate venue.

Generally, a federal court has personal jurisdiction when a defendant has sufficient minimum contacts with that forum,[70] though all jurisdictions can and some do impose additional requirements.[71] Also, some federal courts have interpreted §12 of the Clayton Act[72] to confer personal jurisdiction over an antitrust defendant anywhere in the United States, based on that defendant's contacts with the United States as a whole, rather than with any particular jurisdiction.[73]

If all defendants reside in the same state, then venue is proper in a federal court in that state.[74] If not, venue is proper where a substantial part of the events or omissions giving rise to the claim occurred or, if there is no district where the action may otherwise be

---

[66] *See, e.g.*, In re Relafen Antitrust Litig., 221 F.R.D. 260, 278 (D. Mass. 2004); D.R. Ward Construction Co. v. Rohm & Haas Co., 470 F.Supp.2d 485 (E.D.Pa.2006).

[67] *See, e.g.*, Kan. Stat. §50-115 (allowing full consideration damages); Cal. Bus. & Prof. Code §16720 (requiring concerted conduct).

[68] Illinois Brick Co. v. Illinois, 431 US 720 (1977); California v. ARC America Corp., 490 US 93 (1983).

[69] *See, e.g.*, In re Intel Corp. Microprocessor Antitrust Litig., 496 F.Supp.2d 404 (D. Del. 2007).

[70] International Shoe Co. v. Washington, 326 US 310 (1945).

[71] *See, e.g.*, N.Y. C.P.L.R. §302.

[72] 15 U.S.C. §22.

[73] *Compare* In re Auto. Refinishing Paint Antitrust Litig., 358 F.3d 288, 298 (3d Cir. 2004) (basing jurisdiction on nationwide contacts) *and* Action Embroidery Corp. v. Atlantic Embroidery, Inc., 368 F.3d 1174 (9th Cir. 2004) (same) *with* Daniel v. Am. Bd. of Emergency Med., 428 F.3d 408, 427 (2d Cir. 2005) (rejecting this interpretation) *and* GTE News Media Services, Inc. v. BellSouth Corp., 199 F.3d 1343 (D.C. Cir. 2000) (same).

[74] 28 U.S.C. §1391(b)(1).

brought, where any defendant may be found.[75] Additionally, an alien may be sued in any district in the United States.[76]

This means that for an antitrust claim involving a product sold throughout the United States, almost any federal district will be a potentially appropriate venue. Choosing one of these districts for filing involves consideration of the multidistrict litigation process and several other factors.[77]

Judicial Panel on Multidistrict Litigation

When similar cases are pending in multiple federal courts, the Judicial Panel on Multidistrict Litigation may transfer them to a single district for coordinated or consolidated pretrial proceedings.[78] Generally, a party involved in one or more of the cases files a motion to transfer the actions to a particular district; other parties may support or oppose transfer or propose a different transferee court.[79] After a hearing, the Panel – which consists of seven district and appellate judges – renders its decision.[80] Subsequently filed, or 'tag-along,' cases are later transferred to the selected court as well.[81]

When the cases are ready for trial, they are remanded to the courts in which they were originally filed; a transferee court does not have authority to assign a case to itself for trial.[82] Also, the filing of a consolidated complaint in the transferee court will not automatically waive remand rights.[83] But there appears to be no case law addressing a situation where multiple nationwide class actions are filed in several jurisdictions and consolidated beyond pretrial proceedings – i.e., answering the question whether duplicative class actions are each remanded to their transferor courts or whether they are tried together in some forum.

In any event, parties may consent to have the transferee court preside over trial.[84] This may be desirable because of the experience gained by the transferee court during pretrial proceedings, promoting efficiency and possibly facilitating settlement.[85]

Considerations

Selecting a venue can involve considerations about applicable law, judges, and jury pools, among other factors. Different judicial circuits may have adopted different approaches on various legal issues, such as what type of conduct constitutes an antitrust violation,

---

75 28 U.S.C. §§1391(b)(2), (b)(3).

76 28 U.S.C. §1391(d).

77 For a discussion of procedural defenses challenging the legal sufficiency of a claim based on improper venue or lack of personal jurisdiction, see Chapter 9 of this *Handbook*.

78 28 U.S.C. §1407(a).

79 *See* 28 U.S.C. §1407(c)(ii); J.P.M.L. R. 7.2.

80 *See* 28 U.S.C. §§1407(c), (d).

81 J.P.M.L. R. 7.5.

82 Lexecon Inc. v. Milberg Weiss Bershad Hynes & Lerach, 523 US 26 (1998).

83 In re Propulsid Prod. Liab. Litig., 208 F.R.D. 133, 141–42 (E.D. La. 2002).

84 In re Carbon Dioxide Indus. Antitrust Litig., 229 F.3d 1321, 1326–27 (11th Cir. 2000).

85 *See Manual for Complex Lit. (Fourth)* §20.132 (2008). For further discussion of the Judicial Panel on Multidistrict Litigation, see Chapter 8 of this *Handbook*.

the proper tests to be used, or the standards for class certification.[86] If an action is based on state law but is heard by a federal court, state law governs substantive matters and federal law governs procedural matters.[87] If an action is transferred by the Judicial Panel on Multidistrict Litigation, the law of the transferee court governs pretrial proceedings but the law of the transferor court will govern trial.[88]

Considering these factors when selecting a forum is both legal and ethical.[89] As Justice Harlan recognized in 1965, 'litigants often choose a federal forum merely to obtain what they consider the advantages of the Federal Rules of Civil Procedure or to try their cases before a supposedly more favorable judge.'[90] There are some limitations, however, such as a procedural rule allowing courts to impose costs on a plaintiff who withdraws a case in one forum or before one judge and then refiles elsewhere.[91]

Suits by foreign plaintiffs

Whether US courts are open to a foreign antitrust plaintiff depends in part on whether US law or foreign law claims are being asserted.

US law claims and the FTAIA

The Foreign Trade Antitrust Improvements Act ('FTAIA') lays out the conditions under which conduct involving trade or commerce with foreign nations can fall under the authority of the Sherman Act. The FTAIA has two main requirements: first, that the conduct has a 'direct, substantial, and reasonably foreseeable effect' on domestic commerce, and second, that the act must rise to the level of a Sherman Act claim.[92] In *Empagran*, the Supreme Court expounded on this doctrine when it held that there is no subject matter jurisdiction under the FTAIA where a plaintiff's injury abroad is independent of anti-competitive effects in the United States.[93]

The Supreme Court ruled that the text and legislative history of the FTAIA demonstrate that only foreign conduct which has a direct, substantial, reasonably foreseeable, and harmful antitrust effect domestically may be subject to the Sherman Act.[94] The Sherman Act does not prevent American exporters or firms doing business abroad from 'entering into business arrangements, however anticompetitive, as long as those arrangements adversely affect only foreign markets.'[95]

The *Empagran* case was remanded to the D.C. Circuit, which held that a plaintiff's

---

86 *Compare* Le Page's Inc. v. 3M, 324 F.3d 141 (3d Cir. 2003) *with* Cascade Health Solutions v. PeaceHealth, 502 F.3d 895 (9th Cir. 2007) to see contrasting treatments of bundled discounts.

87 *See* Erie v. Tompkins, 304 US 64 (1938).

88 *See, e.g.*, In re Temporomandibular Joint (TMJ) Implants Prods. Liab. Litig., 97 F.3d 1050, 1055 (8th Cir. 1996).

89 *See* Alan B. Morrison, *Removing Class Actions to Federal Court: A Better Way to Handle The Problem of Overlapping Class Actions*, 57 Stan. L. Rev. 1521, 1521–22 (2005).

90 Hanna v. Plumer, 380 US 460, 475 (1965) (Harlan, J., concurring).

91 *See* Fed. R. Civ. P. 41(d).

92 15 U.S.C.A. §6a.

93 F. Hoffmann-LaRoche Ltd. v. Empagran S.A., 542 US 155 (2004).

94 *Id.* at 161–62.

95 *Id.* at 161.

injury must be 'proximately' caused by anti-competitive US effects, and that 'arbitrage effects' were not sufficient to meet this standard.[96]

Significantly, the FTAIA explicitly excludes domestic commerce and import commerce from its scope. As a result, the common law 'effects test' still applies to foreign import commerce.[97] The effects test, as applied by the Supreme Court, holds as a 'well established' principle that US antitrust laws apply to 'foreign conduct that was meant to produce and did in fact produce' substantial effects in the relevant US market.[98]

Foreign law claims in US courts

There are several hurdles that must be overcome by foreign claimants who wish to bring foreign law claims in US courts. The ability of foreign plaintiffs to bring an EU-law claim was recently tested in the *Air Cargo* case pending in the United States District Court for the Eastern District of New York.[99] That court discussed several potential barriers to such claims, including the issues of *forum non conveniens* and international comity.

International comity is very case specific. Some examples of its application include situations where a foreign sovereign would bar a foreign claim, or where the adjudication of claims involves the application of unsettled foreign law.[100]

Analysis of *forum non conveniens* involves a three-step inquiry.[101] The first step involves 'assess[ing] the amount of deference to be accorded to the plaintiffs' choice of forum.'[102] There is usually a 'strong presumption' in favor of the plaintiff's choice.[103] The greatest deference is typically afforded to a plaintiff's choice of its home forum.[104] With respect to non-US plaintiffs, however, 'less deference' is afforded to a foreign plaintiff's choice of a United States forum.[105]

After completing this deference analysis, the second step is determining whether an adequate alternative forum exists. In *Air Cargo*, EU plaintiffs recognized that EU member state courts were empowered to hear their claims, but were concerned that these EU courts lacked the procedural mechanisms necessary to provide effective redress to individual plaintiffs in an antitrust suit.[106] The judge sympathized with these concerns, but ultimately ruled that the likelihood that a forum would grant a party the damages they sought was not relevant.[107] The mere 'power' or ability of another court to award

---

[96] Empagran S.A. v. Hoffmann-LaRoche Ltd., 417 F.3d 1267 (D.C. Cir. 2005).

[97] Daseul Kim, *'Perfectly Properly Triable' in the United States: Is Extradition a Real and Significant Threat to Foreign Antitrust Offenders?*, 28 Nw. J. Int'l L. & Bus. 583, 592 (2008).

[98] *Hartford Fire*, 509 US at 796. For further discussion of the FTAIA, see Chapter 9 of this *Handbook*; for a discussion of how the FTAIA has served as an obstacle to the United States becoming a single forum for private claims in the context of global cartels, see Chapter 37 of this *Handbook*.

[99] In re Air Cargo Shipping Services Antitrust Litigation, Case No: 06-1775.

[100] *Id.* at Docket No. 787.

[101] *Id.*; Iragorri v. United Technologies Corporation, 274 F.3d 65 (2d Cir. 2001).

[102] *Iragorri*, 274 F.3d at 70–73.

[103] Piper Aircraft Co. v. Reyno, 454 US 235, 255 (1981).

[104] *Id.* at 255–56.

[105] *Id.*

[106] *Air Cargo*, Docket No. 787.

[107] *Id.*

damages in such a case was sufficient to establish the existence of an adequate alternative forum, even if that power had never before been exercised.[108]

If the court determines that an adequate alternative forum does in fact exist, then its third step is to weigh a variety of public and private interest factors to determine the appropriateness of each forum. Such private factors include: (1) the interests of the litigants in having the case tried in a particular forum; (2) the relative ease of access to sources of proof; (3) the availability of compulsory process for attendance of unwilling witnesses; (4) the cost of obtaining attendance of willing witnesses; and (5) all other practical problems that make trial of a case easy, expeditious, and inexpensive.[109]

Issues of particular concern include the enforceability of a US court's judgment applying foreign law or the enforceability of a class action judgment in forums that lack such a mechanism.[110] The relevant public interest factors include: (1) court congestion; (2) the interest of forums in having local disputes decided at home; and (3) the interest in having the issues of law decided by courts of the nation whose law is involved.[111] One particular public interest concern raised by the magistrate judge in *Air Cargo* was the risk of being faced with undecided foreign law issues.[112]

It should also be noted that in the Supreme Court's *Empagran* decision, the Court frowned upon the possibility of analyzing foreign antitrust laws or comparing them to domestic policies to ensure that comity is upheld. The Court stated that such a process could 'threaten interference with a foreign nation's ability to maintain the integrity of its own antitrust enforcement system.'[113] The Court explained that even if US and foreign laws were identical with respect to their views on an issue such as price-fixing, they may still differ with respect to the type and scope of the appropriate remedy.[114] In the Court's view, this could result in an overall reduction of antitrust enforcement by decreasing the incentives for conspirators to enter into national amnesty programs.[115]

Preparing and serving a complaint

Once a forum has been selected, a case is initiated by the filing of a complaint.[116] Particular courts may have individual rules about how complaints should look and what information they must contain, but generally complaints identify the parties, describe the bases for personal and subject matter jurisdiction, allege the relevant facts, set forth the legal claims for relief, and indicate whether a jury trial is demanded.[117]

Complaints in federal court 'must contain sufficient factual matter, accepted as true, to "state a claim to relief that is plausible on its face." A claim has facial plausibility when

---

108 Capital Currency Exch. v. Nat'l Westminister Bank PLC, 155 F.3d 603, 609 (2d Cir. 1998).

109 *Gilbert*, 330 US at 508.

110 *Air Cargo*, Docket No. 787.

111 *Gilbert*, 330 US at 508–09.

112 *Air Cargo*, Docket No. 787.

113 542 US at 168–69.

114 *Id.* at 169.

115 *Id.* For a discussion of procedural defenses challenging the legal sufficiency of a claim based on principles of international comity or *forum non conveniens*, see Chapter 9 of this *Handbook*.

116 Fed. R. Civ. P. 3.

117 *See, e.g.*, N.D. Cal. Civ. Local R. 3-4 to 3-6.

the plaintiff pleads factual content that allows the court to draw the reasonable inference that the defendant is liable for the misconduct alleged.'[118] Thus, '[t]hreadbare recitals of the elements of a cause of action, supported by mere conclusory statements, do not suffice.'[119]

After receiving a complaint, a federal court issues a summons, which a plaintiff must serve along with a copy of the complaint on each defendant within 120 days, though additional time is allowed for service on foreign defendants.[120] Then, a defendant has 20 days to answer or move to dismiss, or 60 days if it agrees to waive service.[121]

---

[118] Ashcroft v. Iqbal, 129 S. Ct. 1937, 1949 (2009) (quoting Bell Atlantic Corp. v. Twombly, 550 US 544, 570 (2007)).

[119] *Id.* (citing *Twombly*, 550 US at 555).

[120] Fed. R. Civ. P. 4(c), (m).

[121] Fed. R. Civ. P. 12(a).

8 Aggregation of claims

J. Douglas Richards[1]

Introduction

Competition law violations ordinarily cause widespread injuries to many participants in a market. In cases brought by overcharged purchasers, injuries suffered by any one purchaser, standing alone, are usually too small to make independent pursuit of an individual damage claim cost-effective. It is therefore indispensible, if private civil damage claims are to vindicate the objectives of competition law effectively, that claims asserted in multiple courts on behalf of multiple plaintiffs must be combined into one or more cases, with some form of orderly, consolidated leadership being established to prosecute the consolidated civil claims. In the absence of established procedures for such consolidation, the multiplicity of individual claims and duplicative costs of various kinds would overwhelm any possibility of feasible private enforcement.

In the United States, there are three basic procedural mechanisms for the consolidation of competition law claims, pertaining, respectively, to: consolidation of cases into one court; establishment of common leadership of the consolidated cases; and common resolution of the consolidated claims in a class action. In Parts A through C below, we address each of those three basic components of the process for aggregation of competition law claims in the United States. In Part D, we then briefly discuss other, less common procedures for common resolution of claims, which also can be available, at least in theory, in competition law cases in the United States.

A. Consolidation of cases – the Judicial Panel and CAFA

There are a vast number of courts in which claimants can initiate competition law cases in the United States. Claims asserted under the competition laws of the United States may be asserted in any of the ninety-four federal judicial districts that exist in the states and territories of the United States. Although claims under United States competition law cannot be pursued in state courts, there exist parallel bodies of state law under which competition law claims are brought, as to which one also can file claims in the diverse

[1] J. Douglas Richards joined Cohen Milstein Sellers & Toll, PLLC, as the managing partner of its New York office in 2009. Prior to joining the firm, he specialized in antitrust class actions for approximately ten years as a partner at two other leading plaintiffs' class action firms, Pomerantz Haudek Block Grossman & Gross and Milberg Weiss. Mr. Richards served for more than two years in 1997–2000 as Deputy General Counsel of the Commodity Futures Trading Commission. Before working for the Commission, Mr. Richards was a litigation partner for more than eight years with O'Sullivan Graev & Karabell (which merged into O'Melveny & Myers in 2002 and became its New York office). While with O'Sullivan, he participated in diverse commercial litigation including antitrust cases such as *In re Beer Industry Antitrust Litigation*, 86 CV 2400 (E.D.N.Y.), in which he was a lead trial counsel for defendant Stroh Brewery Company and successfully obtained a directed verdict for it after a two-week jury trial. Mr. Richards has broad experience with the litigation of antitrust and trade regulation matters at the trial and appellate levels.

state courts.[2] If distinct cases had to be pursued simultaneously in all of those innumerable courts based on a common competition law violation with nationwide effects, the resulting procedural complications and duplication of effort would make efficient and effective private enforcement extremely difficult, if not impossible.

The primary procedure in the United States for preventing judicial chaos stemming from parallel claims in different federal district courts is the statutory mechanism for consolidation of multidistrict litigation (MDL) by the Judicial Panel on Multidistrict Litigation (the Judicial Panel), which is embodied in 28 U.S.C. §1407 and in rules promulgated thereunder by the Judicial Panel. Whenever cases that involve common questions of fact are pending in multiple federal districts, parties to those cases are entitled to make a motion under MDL procedures to have all of the cases transferred to a single judicial district, for coordination of all pretrial proceedings. Such motions are heard by the Judicial Panel, which holds hearings periodically throughout the year at various locations, and then determines whether to transfer all cases to a single district for pretrial proceedings. The United States Supreme Court has held that cases that survive pretrial proceedings must be sent back to the original transferor districts for trial.[3] In practice, however, the vast majority of cases are disposed of prior to being sent back to the transferor district, whether through pretrial proceedings or through settlement in those cases that survive pretrial proceedings.

The Judicial Panel is generally perceived among practicing attorneys to function smoothly and efficiently, and to eliminate undue complication fairly effectively when multiple federal cases are filed. Although some recent commentary attempts to make systematic sense of the criteria that have governed MDL decisions by the Judicial Panel,[4] the prevailing consensus among practicing class action attorneys is that the Judicial Panel's choice of transferee forum is often driven in part by opaque judicial politics and is highly unpredictable.

Regardless of the criteria that determine Judicial Panel decisions, MDL procedures have been very effective in consolidating cases and avoiding duplication of effort. When making arguments for tort reform in the United States, supporters of reform often cite the large number of class action cases filed against a defendant in the wake of an antitrust violation, in an effort to exaggerate an appearance of duplicative burdens from multiple class action cases. However, where multiple cases filed in federal court are concerned, Judicial Panel procedures function very well as the first step toward consolidation of large numbers of parallel class actions into a small number of related cases, heard at the same time by a single judge as to all pretrial matters. For example, although data

---

2 State antitrust claims can be and often are pursued by distinct groups in parallel to Federal antitrust claims in the United States, because the United States Supreme Court has held that state antitrust laws are not 'preempted' by federal antitrust law. *California v. ARC America Corp.*, 490 US 93 (1988).

3 *Lexecon, Inc. v. Milberg Weiss Bershad Hynes & Lerach*, 523 US 26 (1998).

4 *See* Daniel A. Richards, *Note, An Analysis of the Judicial Panel on Multidistrict Litigation's Selection of Transferee District and Judge*, 78 Fordham L. Rev. 311 (Oct. 2009) (describing trends in the Judicial Panel's selection of transferee district and judge and arguing that factors that influence the Judicial Panel's decisions differ depending on the nature of the claims and the various other issues).

gathered by the Federal Judicial Center for the years 2002–2006 showed an average of more than seventy-eight antitrust class action cases filed each year, the bulk of that number was attributable to duplicative cases that were subsequently consolidated through Judicial Panel procedures into less than nine multidistrict class action cases per year.[5] Within the class action bar, few would question the effectiveness or desirability of consolidating pretrial proceedings in a single court to avoid unnecessarily duplicative legal processes.[6]

A more recent and controversial set of procedures applies to parallel federal and state cases under the Class Action Fairness Act (CAFA), enacted in 2005.[7] Proponents of CAFA had argued, in a way that raised concerns in the minds of many that it might undermine the principles of 'federalism' under the United States Constitution, that state courts were inappropriate forums to handle cases of 'national importance.'[8] To address this and related concerns, CAFA was enacted to provide that most class action cases may be removed, by either the plaintiffs or the defendants, from state court to federal court. The primary exceptions – 'home state' and 'local controversy' cases in which most or all parties reside in a single state – are seldom applicable, especially in antitrust class actions. After CAFA, nearly all antitrust class actions may successfully be removed to the federal courts, and may then be consolidated into a single forum pursuant to the Judicial Panel procedures discussed above. Many have criticized CAFA for removing many actions brought under state law to the federal courts, because doing so shifts much of the primary responsibility for construing many state laws to federal courts, thereby intruding on traditional state prerogatives.[9] There can be little question, however, that CAFA has succeeded in sharply reducing the number of cases in which the pendency of state court class actions prevented effective consolidation of all related class actions into a single forum pursuant to longstanding Judicial Panel procedures.[10]

B. Common case leadership

Even with cases being consolidated by the Judicial Panel under MDL procedures, multidistrict litigation would remain chaotic if there were no procedural mechanism for the appointment of common leadership for closely related cases. Federal judges presiding in class action cases have broad authority, under Rule 23(d) of the Federal Rules of Civil Procedure, to 'prescribe measures to prevent undue repetition or complication in presenting evidence or argument,' and under Rule 23(g) to appoint class counsel. Broader guidance to federal courts, concerning how and why to establish common leadership among class counsel, also is set forth in §21.27 of the Manual for Complex Litigation

---

[5] *See* AMERICAN ANTITRUST INSTITUTE, THE NEXT ANTITRUST AGENDA: THE AMERICAN ANTITRUST INSTITUTE'S TRANSITION REPORT ON COMPETITION POLICY TO THE 44TH PRESIDENT 228–29 (2008).

[6] For further discussion of consolidation and the Judicial Panel, see Chapter 7 of this *Handbook*.

[7] Pub. L. No. 109-2, 119 Stat 4 (2005).

[8] CAFA, §2(a)(4)(A), 119 Stat. at 5.

[9] *See e.g.*, Jay Himes, *The Class Action Fairness Act: A Wolf in Wolves' Clothing*, Class Action Litigation Report, 10 CLASS 452 (May 8, 2009).

[10] For further discussion of CAFA, see Chapter 7 of this *Handbook*.

(Fourth) (the Manual). Although the Manual makes clear in its introduction that it 'is not, and should not be cited as, authoritative legal or administrative policy,' litigants and federal courts turn to it routinely for guidance and for persuasive material to justify rulings that litigants seek and that federal courts make on the appointment of class counsel and similar matters.

The policy cornerstone of common, court-appointed representation is that those who 'represent' absent parties in litigation must 'fairly and adequately represent the interests of the class.' This requirement has its roots in fundamental constitutional principles of due process. In *Hansberry v. Lee* the United States Supreme Court made clear that the constitutional requirement of due process of law forbids the courts from binding non-parties to the results of a representative case purportedly brought on their behalf unless they are adequately represented in the proceedings.[11] Such adequate representation exists only when the governing procedure 'fairly insures the protection of the interests of absent parties who are to be bound by it.'[12] The Supreme Court elaborated on those basic principles in the class action context in *Amchem Prods., Inc. v. Windsor*.[13] In *Amchem*, the Court characterized the question of adequacy of representation as one concerning representational adequacy of the named party, stating that the adequacy inquiry under Rule 23 'serves to uncover conflicts of interest between named parties and the class they seek to represent.'[14] Since *Amchem*, it has been recognized increasingly that inquiries concerning adequacy of representation also must be applied to class counsel, who often play the primary leading role in the conduct of a class action, and not only to the named plaintiffs. Accordingly, in 2003, Rule 23 of the Federal Rules of Civil Procedure (Rule 23) was amended to focus the inquiry concerning fairness and adequacy of representation on the attorney who is appointed to represent the class, and not only the named party. The notes of the Advisory Committee to the 2003 amendments to Rule 23 state that the 'new' Rule 23(g) 'responds to the reality that the selection and activity of class counsel are often critically important to the successful handling of the class action' and 'will guide the court in assessing proposed class counsel as part of the certification decision.'

Rule 23 states various criteria that 'must' be applied by the court in appointing class counsel, including such factors as the work done by candidate counsel in identifying or investigating the potential claims, counsel's past experience in handling class actions, complex litigation and similar claims, counsel's knowledge of the applicable law, and the resources that counsel will bring to bear in representing the class. Often, however, several firms that wish to be appointed by the court as lead counsel will be comparably qualified where such criteria are concerned. Courts are understandably reluctant to draw fine and sometimes unseemly distinctions based on such criteria, in what is sometimes referred to disparagingly as a 'beauty contest' among fully qualified law firms, especially when, as is often the case, a district court has no substantial past experience with some of the lawyers or national law firms in question. In practice, therefore, as the Manual recognizes, courts

---

11 311 US 32 (1940).
12 *Id.* at 42.
13 521 US 591 (1997).
14 *Id.* at 626.

most commonly follow the so-called 'private ordering' approach toward selection of lead counsel for the class, in which '[t]he lawyers agree who should be lead class counsel and the court approves the selection after a review to ensure that the counsel selected is adequate to represent the class interests.'[15]

This general deference toward 'private ordering' often engenders highly politicized maneuvering among plaintiffs' class action attorneys, in which support is built for particular firms' appointment as lead counsel largely through concerted filings by competing groups of attorneys and various commitments made within each of the competing groups; as the Manual recognizes, '[c]ounsel may agree to designate a particular lead class counsel in exchange for commitments to share the legal work and fees.'[16] Often these private negotiations succeed only in narrowing the field of candidates to two or three competing groups, with proposed leadership for each. Courts will then either choose one group's proposed leadership candidates, or, at least as often, will choose co-lead counsel from the multiple groups that remain in contention with one another after efforts at further 'private ordering' have reached an impasse. Such decisions play a useful role in assuring that the skills, talents and resources of all plaintiffs' counsel are brought to bear inclusively for the benefit of the class, rather than having the chosen lead counsel view its role as an exclusive prerogative from the standpoint of its own narrower interests. Nonetheless, particularly since the custom in most cases is for lead counsel to decide how any aggregate fee award for class counsel is to be divided at the end of a case, the process whereby 'private ordering' takes place can be a divisive and competitive one for all of its participants, and can have weighty consequences to the profitability of participation in the case on the part of each of the various class counsel who remain involved.[17]

C. Common claim resolution

Once related cases have been consolidated, and once common attorney leadership has been established for a case under the procedures described above, it remains necessary under United States law to determine the circumstances under which the named parties before the court may resolve claims asserted by others who have been injured by the same antitrust violation. Those circumstances are defined in the United States courts principally by Rule 23, which separately states the somewhat different prerequisites that apply to class actions that seek to recover damages, and those that seek only injunctive relief.

Class actions seeking damages

Rule 23, which was first adopted in 1938, attempts to articulate necessary prerequisites for a case to proceed as a class action. Up until 1966, the only type of common resolution of damage claims that was permitted in the federal courts by Rule 23 was the so-called 'spurious class action,' which 'generally functioned as a permissive joinder ("opt in")

---

[15] Manual, §21.272.

[16] *Id.*

[17] For further discussion of appointment of class counsel in the context of how a case begins, see Chapter 5 of this *Handbook*.

device,'[18] similar to a mass action.[19] In 1966, however, in what was characterized by the Supreme Court as a 'most adventuresome' innovation at the time,[20] Rule 23 was amended to provide for civil damage judgments that would be binding 'on all class members save those who affirmatively elected to be excluded' – the so-called 'opt out' class action. The 'opt-out' class action facilitates aggregation of competition law claims by greatly reducing the transaction and information costs of common representation. Instead of all class members being required to agree in advance to be bound by a judgment in the common proceeding, representative parties may pursue claims on behalf of an entire class, with all class members being bound by the resulting judgment or settlement unless they affirmatively make a decision to 'opt out' of the class.

Even prior to development of the 'opt out' class action, United States law recognized that such representative litigation must be subject to various limitations if the interests of the absent class members are to be adequately protected. For example, in *Hansberry v. Lee*, the United States Supreme Court stated broadly that any procedural system for representative litigation of claims must 'insure that those present are of the same class as those absent and that the litigation is so conducted as to insure the full and fair consideration of the common issue.'[21] The pertinent requirements for representation in an 'opt out' class action seeking damages have subsequently been set forth comprehensively in Rule 23. Those requirements are generally referred to as: (a) numerosity; (b) commonality; (c) typicality; (d) adequacy of representation; (e) predominance; and (f) superiority.

a. Numerosity The first requirement that must be satisfied if a case is to proceed as a class action is that 'the class is so numerous that joinder of all members is impracticable.'[22] In most competition law class actions brought on behalf of overcharged purchasers, this requirement is easily satisfied because the class will consist of hundreds, thousands or even millions of purchasers in a marketplace during the class period who were similarly affected. In some industries, however, the number of direct purchasers who are entitled to sue for competition law violations under federal antitrust law will be unusually small. For example, in cases seeking to recover overcharges for prescription drugs, it has occasionally been suggested that there are as few as thirty true direct purchasers from defendant manufacturers.[23] This is somewhat smaller than the number that is conventionally referenced as a benchmark for numerosity, which is forty.[24] Nevertheless, if smaller numbers of class members are widely dispersed geographically, they still may satisfy the numerosity requirement, since one element of the numerosity analysis involves considerations of judicial economy stemming from the consolidation of widely disparate individual actions into a single case.[25] Thus, classes of as few as thirty plaintiffs have been

---

18 *Amchem*, 521 US at 615.
19 *See* 'Other procedures' discussed *infra*.
20 *Amchem*, 521 US at 615.
21 *Hansberry*, 311 US at 43.
22 Rule 23(a)(1), Fed. R. Civ. P.
23 *See Meijer, Inc. v. Warner Chilcott Holdings Co.*, 246 F.R.D. 293, 305–07 & n. 13 (D.D.C. 2007).
24 *Labauve v. Olin Corp.*, 231 F.R.D. 632, 665 (S.D. Ala. 2005)(citing cases).
25 *Meijer*, 246 F.R.D. at 306–07.

held to satisfy the numerosity requirement when the plaintiffs have been geographically dispersed.[26]

b. Commonality The second requirement is that 'there are questions of law or fact common to the class.'[27] Because the same course of conduct in a competition law case generally has broad effects on prices market-wide, this requirement is nearly always satisfied by the need to establish that an unlawful course of conduct has occurred. This requirement is therefore non-controversial in nearly all competition law class actions.

c. Typicality The third requirement is that 'the claims or defenses of the representative parties are typical of the claims or defenses of the class.'[28] This requirement seeks to make certain that those who wish to act as class representatives have no divergent interests that could cause them to sacrifice the interests of other class members in order to favor their own interests. In cases brought by classes of overcharged purchasers, all class members usually have been injured in the same way, as a result of increased price levels in the relevant market. Unlike in many other kinds of class actions, therefore, typicality usually is not a major obstacle to the pursuit of a class action in a competition law case brought by overcharged purchasers.

Nevertheless, in some competition cases class members have been injured under different transactional circumstances, such as purchases under different types of contracts, or purchases in materially different markets. Such situations can give rise to divergences of interest within the class, stemming from ways in which the claims of the class representative are atypical. For example, in *Deiter v. Microsoft Corp.*, the named plaintiffs, who were individual direct purchasers of computer software from Microsoft, sought to represent a class that included both individual direct purchasers and businesses who purchased software directly from Microsoft pursuant to its 'Enterprise Program.'[29] Such 'Enterprise Purchasers,' unlike the individual purchasers, purchased bundles of 250 or more software licenses at individually negotiated prices that were 'unique to each transaction.' Because the types of transactions and markets in which the two groups of purchases participated were very different, the court found that proof of the named plaintiffs' claim would do little to establish liability on the claims of 'Enterprise Purchasers.' The court therefore excluded 'Enterprise Purchasers' from the class on grounds that the named plaintiffs' claims were not 'typical' of claims asserted on behalf of that portion of the class.

d. Adequacy of representation The fourth requirement is that 'the representative parties will fairly and adequately protect the interests of the class.'[30] This requirement tends to overlap substantially with the 'typicality' requirement discussed above, since divergent interests stemming from representation by an atypical class member are often

---

26 *Id.*
27 Rule 23(a)(2), Fed. R. Civ. P.
28 Rule 23(a)(3), Fed. R. Civ. P.
29 436 F.3d 461 (4th Cir. 2006).
30 Rule 23(a)(4), Fed. R. Civ. P.

the reason for any inadequacy of representation by that class member.[31] Thus, the Second Circuit has identified the *sine qua non* of adequate representation to be 'the alignment of interests of class members,' which is essentially indistinguishable from the analysis applicable to 'typicality.'[32] As the Supreme Court pointed out in *Amchem*, however, adequacy of representation 'also factors in competency and conflicts of class counsel.'[33] For example, in the highly-publicized class actions against Christie's and Sotheby's for fixing auction commissions, counsel for clients in United States domestic auctions were found not to provide adequate representation as to clients who made purchases in foreign auctions; the structure of their compensation as class counsel for United States auction clients gave rise to a 'structural conflict' on their part that ultimately led them to attempt to compel class members to give up claims arising from foreign auctions for no compensation.[34]

e. Predominance The fifth requirement, that 'questions of law or fact common to the members of the class predominate over any questions affecting only individual members,'[35] is by far the most legally controversial requirement for a class action in competition law cases seeking damages. In several prominent cases in recent years, conservative judges have begun to scale back on the scope of competition law class actions, often by finding that the predominance requirement has not been met. In the course of doing so, as shown below, some courts in recent years have created legal confusion about basic principles governing the predominance requirement.

I. EXTENT OF JUDGE'S FACT-FINDING ROLE To determine whether 'common questions' predominate over 'individual questions,' all that Rule 23 asks a court to do is to identify the merits 'questions' that are to be tried in a case, and to weigh those that are common to multiple class members against those that affect 'only individual members' of the class. It does not ask the court to resolve those questions on their merits, nor does it ask the court to determine which side of the disputed issues is correct. Language in the recent appellate case law clearly recognizes that to do so is inappropriate.

First, in *In re New Motor Vehicles Canadian Export Antitrust Litig. (New Motor Vehicles)*, the First Circuit recognized that 'the validity of plaintiffs' theory is a common disputed issue' and that '[i]t will be for the fact finder to decide whether this theory is persuasive.'[36] The First Circuit explained that a court deciding class certification should not be making such 'persuasiveness' determinations with regard to 'hard factual proof,' but instead should only scrutinize the plaintiffs' arguments for a satisfactory 'explanation of how the pivotal evidence behind plaintiffs' theory can be established.'[37]

---

31 *See Amchem*, 521 US at 626 n. 20 (pointing out that adequacy of representation tends to 'merge with' typicality analysis).

32 *Wal-Mart Stores, Inc. v. Visa U.S.A. Inc.*, 396 F.3d 96, 113 (2d Cir. 2005).

33 *Amchem*, 521 US at 626 n. 20.

34 *In re Auction Houses Antitrust Litig.*, 138 F. Supp. 2d 548, 551 (S.D.N.Y. 2001), *aff'd*, 2002 US App. LEXIS 15327 (2d Cir. 2002).

35 Rule 23(b)(3), Fed. R. Civ. P.

36 522 F.3d 6, 29 (1st Cir. 2008).

37 *Id.*

Second, in *In re Initial Public Offering Securities Litig. (IPO)*, the Second Circuit carefully addressed the statement of the Supreme Court, in *Eisen v. Carlisle & Jacquelin*, that '[w]e find nothing in either the language or history of Rule 23 that gives the court any authority to conduct a preliminary inquiry into the merits of the suit in order to determine whether it may be maintained as a class action.'[38] The Second Circuit noted that this observation was made 'in a case in which the district judge's merits inquiry had nothing to do with determining the requirements for class certification.'[39] Consistently with *Eisen*, the Second Circuit in *IPO* emphasized that in making determinations concerning whether the requirements of Rule 23 are satisfied, 'a district judge should not assess any aspect of the merits unrelated to a Rule 23 requirement.'[40]

Third, in *In re Hydrogen Peroxide Antitrust Litig.*, the Third Circuit stated that 'Plaintiffs' burden at the class certification stage is not to prove' its case, but that, instead, 'the task for plaintiffs at class certification is to demonstrate that the element of antitrust impact is capable of proof through evidence that is common to the class rather than individual to its members.'[41] Likewise, later in its *Hydrogen Peroxide* opinion, the Third Circuit stated that 'the question at [the] class certification stage is whether, if such impact is plausible in theory, it is also *susceptible to proof* at trial through available evidence common to the class.'[42] Thus, with regard to the key question of predominance, the question is only whether antitrust impact in the case is 'capable' of or 'susceptible' to available proof through common evidence, not whether the element of antitrust impact has been proved on the merits or whether the Court finds the plaintiff's evidence on that issue to be more persuasive than the defendants' opposing evidence. In determining whether impact is 'capable' of or 'susceptible' to proof through common evidence, *Hydrogen Peroxide* makes clear that the touchstone is to identify 'the method or methods by which plaintiffs propose to use the evidence to prove impact at trial.'[43] In that respect, the Third Circuit in *Hydrogen Peroxide* echoes the First Circuit's ruling, in *New Motor Vehicles,* that the court is required only to ascertain that there is a satisfactory 'explanation of how the pivotal evidence behind plaintiff's theory can be established.'[44]

Emphasizing such language in these recent opinions of the Courts of Appeals, those supporting a more traditional interpretation of the governing legal standards continue to argue that in inquiring into the predominance of common questions to support a class action, a court should not attempt to determine the persuasiveness of a plaintiff's common proof. Because the predominance inquiry does not ask the court to answer the common questions, to attempt to answer those questions in the context of class certification would violate the Second Circuit's admonition – which comes directly from the

38 471 F.3d 24 (2d Cir. 2006) (citing *Eisen v. Carlisle & Jacquelin*, 417 US 156, 177 (1974)).
39 *Id.* at 33.
40 *Id.* at 41.
41 552 F.3d 305, 311–12 (3d Cir. 2008).
42 *Id.* at 325 (emphasis added).
43 *Id.* at 312.
44 *See also, Hydrogen Peroxide*, 552 F.3d at 312 (quoting from *New Motor Vehicles* that 'a district court must formulate some prediction as to how specific issues will play out in order to determine whether common or individual issues predominate . . . .').

Supreme Court's mandate in *Eisen* – that 'a district judge should not assess any aspect of the merits unrelated to a Rule 23 requirement.'

Unfortunately, however, other language in these decisions has confused some courts and attorneys into believing that a court deciding class certification is now permitted to determine broadly whether it is persuaded by all of the plaintiffs' methods of common proof, thereby transforming the court's role from that of merely identifying common and individual questions in a case into the much more problematic role of determining the correct answers to key merits questions. Those who advocate this transformational view of the case law emphasize language from *Hydrogen Peroxide*, for example, in which the Third Circuit states that 'the court must resolve all factual and legal disputes relevant to class certification, even if they overlap with the merits.' Those taking the more transformational view contend that such language requires a court, in effect, to determine at the time of class certification whether the plaintiffs' proposed common proof of their case is correct or incorrect, by a standard of the preponderance of the evidence. The effect of such an interpretation of the recent case law would be revolutionary, because it would effectively call for the court to stop class action cases from going to a jury even when there are 'genuine issues of material fact' that would preclude summary judgment, in effect substituting a court's own evaluation of key merits questions for that of the jury.[45]

However, careful reading of recent Court of Appeals case law shows that this revolutionary view is incorrect, where the 'predominance' element of class certification analysis is concerned. To be sure, all of the recent Court of Appeals case law has stated unequivocally that in order to certify a class a court must make either 'findings' or 'determinations' that the prerequisites to class certification are satisfied. However, one must consider the substance of the specific class action requirements in question. In the *IPO* case, for example, the Second Circuit illustrated its statements with regard to the need for 'determinations' by reference to the requirement of numerosity, stating that 'in considering whether the numerosity requirement is met, a judge might need to resolve a factual dispute as to how many members are in a proposed class. Any dispute about the proposed class must be resolved. . . .'[46] This is true of the numerosity requirement, which on its face calls for the court to determine how numerous the class members are. Some other class action requirements, similarly, call for a court to make outright determinations of fact. For example, the requirement of adequacy of representation requires that the court find the representation to be in fact adequate.

By contrast, the key point, which has been sometimes lost sight of by those who wish to interpret recent Court of Appeals authority in a way that hinders class actions, is that, unlike Rule 23 requirements like numerosity or adequacy, the requirement of

---

45 In most American lawsuits that seek recovery of damages (as distinguished from equitable relief such as an injunction, which is always decided by the judge), questions of material fact are generally to be determined by the jury. At least formally, the role of the judge in deciding cases is limited to determining whether to dismiss a case based on some form of deficiency as a matter of law (under Rule 12 of the Federal Rules of Civil Procedure) and whether to grant so-called 'summary judgment' to one side or the other (under Rule 56 of the Federal Rules of Civil Procedure) on the basis that there is no 'genuine issue of material fact' that requires determination by a jury.

46 *IPO*, 471 F.3d at 40.

predominance does not ask a court to determine whether proposed common methods of proof are correct or incorrect, persuasive or unpersuasive. Instead, all it asks the court to do is to determine that common questions are presented and that the plaintiff genuinely has common methods of proof. Once that key point is grasped, it becomes clear that recent Court of Appeals case law is far less transformational than some have contended, in light of the fact that the class action prerequisites that call for the court to make actual fact determinations – such as numerosity and adequacy – are not commonly the primary controversies on class certification in the first instance. Instead, the primary controversy at the time of class certification nearly always centers on the predominance of common questions. Those questions need not be answered in order for a court to determine that they are common questions. Accordingly, for a court in the context of the predominance inquiry to determine whether the plaintiffs' proposed common proof is correct or incorrect would violate the Second Circuit's admonition in *IPO* – which comes directly from the Supreme Court's authority in *Eisen* – that 'a district judge should not assess any aspect of the merits unrelated to a Rule 23 requirement.'

II. NOT 'EVERY CLASS MEMBER' MUST BE INJURED Within virtually any large class in a competition law class action, there will be a small number of overcharged purchasers who, for idiosyncratic reasons, were not injured by the challenged conduct. For example, subjective preferences of some class members will sometimes cause a small number of plaintiffs to pay a higher price for a product, even if the same product is available for a lower price elsewhere. If it were necessary to determine for every class member whether such circumstances are present for that class member, that would be, by definition, a 'question affecting only individual members' of the class, which could cause individual questions to 'predominate' over common questions. Recent case law reveals stark disagreement concerning whether it is necessary to determine which class members may be subject to such idiosyncratic defenses.

Until recently, there was a broad judicial consensus that the presence within a class of a small proportion of class members who were not injured for idiosyncratic reasons would not preclude class certification.[47] Recently, Judge Richard Posner, who was one of the founders of the conservative 'law and economics' movement at the University of Chicago and is influential in competition law circles, has expressed continuing support for this traditional view.[48]

---

[47] *See e.g., In re NASDAQ Mkt.-Makers Antitrust Litig.*, 169 F.R.D. 493, 523 (S.D.N.Y. 1996) (Even if it could be shown that some individual class members were not injured, class certification, nevertheless, is appropriate where the antitrust violation has caused widespread injury to the class.); *In re Cardizem CD Antitrust Litig.*, 200 F.R.D. 297, 321 (E.D. Mich. 2001) (courts have routinely observed that the inability to show injury as to a few does not defeat class certification where the plaintiffs can show widespread injury to the class); *In re Warfarin Sodium Antitrust Litig.*, 212 F.R.D. 231, 252 (D. Del. 2002) (a class can be certified even where some individual, absentee class members may later prove not to be injured); *In re Northwest Airlines Corp. Antitrust Litig.*, 208 F.R.D. 174, 223 (E.D. Mich. 2002) (the 'impact' element of an antitrust claim need not be established as to each and every class member; rather, it is enough if the plaintiffs' proposed method of proof promises to establish 'widespread injury to the class' as a result of the defendant's antitrust violation.).

[48] *Kohen v. Pacific Investment Management Co. LLC*, No. 08-1075 (7th Cir. July 7, 2009) (Posner,

However, in *New Motor Vehicles*, the First Circuit held that the plaintiffs' methods of proof were required to 'include some means of determining that each class member was in fact injured,' and that the plaintiff was required to show 'that *all* consumers would pay more' as a result of the challenged antitrust violation.[49] Pursuant to that holding, the district court subsequently granted a motion to dismiss the case on that basis, finding itself to be bound by its interpretation of the First Circuit's ruling that the plaintiffs were required to 'establish that *all* class members paid a higher price.'[50] However, under the First Circuit's opinion (as interpreted in that case by the district court) it is difficult to see how one could often have a successful antitrust class action in that Circuit, because, as Judge Posner recognizes in *Kohen*, it is 'inevitable' that a few class members in any large class will not have been injured.

This view recently expressed by the First Circuit, which could make class actions impossible in many cases, is inconsistent with basic principles concerning the burden of proof. All that plaintiffs in an antitrust class action are required to prove with regard to the fact of injury is that it is more likely than not that each class member was injured. Such a showing establishes the requisite *prima facie* case of injury as to each class member. If that showing is based on common proof, then common issues predominate, and it is a question for trial whether the proof is persuasive. Even if some small number of unidentified class members could be shown by the defendants not to have been injured, plaintiffs, at class certification, need only offer common proof that carries the burden of establishing a *prima facie* case of injury as to all class members. In an individual case, it would suffice to establish a case of such *prima facie* injury if the plaintiff were to establish that the vast majority of persons in his position were injured. There is no reason why that same proof should not be sufficient to establish a *prima case* of injury for all class members.[51] To require that each plaintiff specifically prove that he or she was one of the vast majority of class members that were injured would effectively apply a heightened standard of proof, by requiring a plaintiff to eliminate even the smallest of possibilities that he or she might not have been injured. To the extent that a contrary view was expressed by the First Circuit in *New Motor Vehicles,* it is inconsistent not only with the weight of authority, but with basic principles governing the burden of proof in civil litigation in the United States.

III. QUESTIONS AFFECTING 'ONLY INDIVIDUAL CLASS MEMBERS' In recent years, courts and parties often have questioned the predominance of common questions, not by

J.) (stating that the 'possibility or indeed inevitability' that a class 'will often include persons who have not been injured by the defendants' conduct . . . does not preclude class certification).

49 522 F.3d 6, 27–29 (1st Cir. 2008).

50 *In re New Motor vehicles Canadian Export Antitrust Litig.*, MDL No. 1532, slip op at 22–23 (D.Me. July 2, 2009) (emphasis in original).

51 Of course, a defendant may be able to rebut this prima facie case by showing that particular class members were not injured. However, this should not defeat class certification. *See Blackie v. Barrack*, 524 F.2d 891, 906 n. 22 (9th Cir. 1975) (The right of rebuttal . . . does not preclude the predominance of common questions. . . . The fact that a defendant may be able to defeat a showing of causation as to a few individual class members does not transform the common question into a multitude of individual ones; plaintiffs satisfy their burden of showing causation as to each by showing [generalized damage] as to all.).

arguing that truly 'individual' issues predominate, but only that the case includes important issues that are not common to the class as a whole. For example, when confronted with state law antitrust claims from many different states, courts have sometimes viewed such differences in state law as weighing against a finding of predominance. To reason in that fashion, however, is inconsistent with the clear language of Rule 23(b)(3), which clearly states that 'individual' issues, for purposes of a predominance analysis, are 'questions affecting only individual members' of the class. A difference between the laws of multiple states clearly is not a question 'affecting only individual members' of a class. On the contrary, each state's laws in such a case typically affects many thousands, if not millions, of class members. When engaging in a 'predominance' analysis, it is important to recognize that questions that affect broad subgroups within the class – whether they be questions of law or of fact – should count on the 'common' side of the balance, and not the 'individual' side, even though they may be questions that are not common to the entire class. They nonetheless are not questions 'affecting only individual members' of the class.

f. Superiority The last requirement for class actions seeking to recover damages under Rule 23(b)(3) is that 'a class action is superior to other available methods for fairly and efficiently adjudicating the controversy.' Rule 23 identifies a number of criteria for a court to consider in making that determination. However, given the breadth of the superiority question, that portion of Rule 23(b)(3) provides little in the way of concrete guidance for a court to consider. In substance, the 'superiority' requirement functions as a catch-all that permits a court to consider additional criteria that seem important to it in any particular case, without being rigidly bound by the more specific criteria that precede it. In practice, most United States courts tend to focus on the more specific criteria for class certification that are previously stated in Rule 23 and that are discussed above, rather than on a free-ranging 'superiority' analysis.

One prominent exception, however, is Judge Easterbrook's opinion in *In re Bridgestone/Firestone, Inc. Tires Prods. Liab. Litig.*, in which the Seventh Circuit prohibited class treatment of a nationwide case under state laws on policy bases having little, if any, grounding in specific Rule 23 requirements, such as that to consolidate all of the state law claims in a single federal class action reflected 'the model of the central planner' and did violence to 'principles of federalism' by 'keep[ing] the litigation far away from state courts.'[52] For a period of time, that decision and the principles articulated in it made it substantially more difficult to persuade federal judges to certify classes in cases arising under multiple state laws. However, reasoning such as that embodied in Judge Easterbrook's opinion should be less viable in the wake of CAFA, since Congress has made its own policy determination in CAFA that claims should be consolidated into the federal courts regardless of federalism concerns, as referenced in Part A above. It would hardly be fair or reasonable to require that nearly all state law class actions be removed to federal court for consolidation, pursuant to CAFA and the MDL procedures described above, and then to deny class certification on the basis that the case then involves multiple state laws that are better considered by state courts. No court seems

---

[52] 288 F.3d 1012, 1020 (7th Cir. 2002).

yet to have opined, however, concerning the impact of CAFA on the persuasiveness of Judge Easterbrook's opinion in *Bridgestone*.

Class actions seeking injunctive relief

The first four criteria for damage class actions that are discussed above – numerosity, commonality, typicality and adequacy – are also applicable to classes seeking injunctive relief. Instead of predominance and superiority, however, the additional requirement for a class action seeking injunctive relief is that the defendant 'has acted or refused to act on grounds that apply generally to the class, so that final injunctive relief or corresponding declaratory relief is appropriate with respect to the class as a whole.'[53] In most antitrust class actions, if the substantive legal requirements for an injunction are satisfied in a case, this requirement that the class be generally affected will be satisfied as well. Thus, although there is frequent dispute in cases concerning whether the requirements for injunctive relief are satisfied as to any plaintiff, it is rare for the requirement of broader impact on the class to be separately disputed in the context of a class action for injunctive relief.[54]

D. Other procedures

In addition to class actions under Rule 23, which are by far the most common procedural method of aggregating competition law claims in the United States, competition law claims are sometimes aggregated through: (1) opt-out procedures; (2) mass actions; (3) *parens patriae* cases brought by state attorneys general; and (4) disgorgement claims by the FTC.

Opt-out cases

Under Rule 23, any class member who 'requests exclusion' from the class will not be bound by a judgment in the class action. Commonly, large purchasers with extraordinarily large claims will request exclusion (thereby 'opting out') from the class. The right to opt out of the class action is one of the most fundamental assurances of ultimate fairness in class actions, because if a class member is dissatisfied with his or her representation in the class action, he or she may opt out and pursue an individual case instead. Because such an assurance of fairness is effective only if the class member has notice of what is happening in the class action, Rule 23(b) mandates that class members must be notified at the time of class certification of their right to opt out of the class in any class action seeking damages, while Rule 23(e) permits the court, in its discretion, also to require further notice of the right to opt out at the time of any settlement. If a class member receives such notice and does not exercise his or her right to opt out on a timely basis, the class member will then be bound by the judgment or settlement in the case, unless defense counsel and the court agree otherwise.[55]

The time at which such opt-outs occur and the nature of their impact on the class action case vary greatly. Individual class members sometimes opt out of the class at the

---

53 Rule 23(b)(2), Fed R. Civ. P.

54 For a detailed discussion of injunctive relief generally, see Chapter 11 of this *Handbook*.

55 For further discussion of the notice requirement, see Chapter 14 of this *Handbook*.

very outset of the proceedings and then commence their own actions, which then usually are coordinated with the pending class action, with most motions, discovery proceedings and other events in the case proceeding in parallel with those that take place in the class action. In other cases, individual class members will remain in the class until a settlement is proposed, and will then either threaten to opt out of the class, or formally do so, in order to negotiate their own, independent settlement(s) with the defendant. In the latter case, there is sometimes said to be a serious 'free rider' problem stemming from the fact that the opt-outs benefit from the work done by class counsel, but usually do not share in the obligation to pay class counsel's fees. There is some legal authority for a court to address such problems by mandating that the opt-out pay some portion of its recovery to class counsel.[56] However, whether and to what extent a presiding court has authority to provide such relief is an unsettled legal question. In light of that lack of clarity, some believe that 'free rider problems' have undermined the effectiveness of some competition law class actions to so great an extent as to prevent particular types of meritorious competition law class actions from being brought and effectively prosecuted.[57]

Because of the size of the claims held by such 'opt-outs,' representation of large opt-outs from a class action can be a profitable endeavor for the attorneys who represent the opt-outs. Some competition law attorneys specialize in representing such opt-outs, rather than representing the class in class action cases. Within limits, the governing ethical rules even permit attorneys to advertise for the representation of opt-outs from class actions.

Mass actions

In cases in which a class action is unavailable in the United States – such as when it is clear that common questions do not 'predominate' over individual questions – cases often will nonetheless be consolidated and have common leadership appointed, in accordance with the procedures described in parts B and C above, consisting entirely of plaintiffs who participate directly as named parties. For example, in some types of personal injury cases where the plaintiffs' injuries and their means of causation are widely divergent, plaintiffs' attorneys will often aggregate dozens or even thousands of claims in a so-called 'mass action,' with proceedings being consolidated in a single location pursuant to Judicial Panel procedures. Section 22 of the Manual for Complex Litigation (Fourth) suggests a wide variety of procedures for such cases, which differ in various ways from the procedures that apply to class actions.

Due to the high transaction and information costs associated with aggregation of most competition law claims by very numerous overcharged purchasers, it is unusual

---

56 *See In re Linerboard Antitrust Litig.*, 333 F. Supp. 2d 343 (E.D. Pa. 2004).

57 For example, in competition law class actions brought by so-called 'indirect purchasers' under state competition law against pharmaceutical companies, a large proportion of the class typically consists of so-called 'third party payors' who share the cost of overcharges that are paid for prescription drugs in the United States as a consequence of various types of competition law violations. Certain attorneys have become sufficiently adept at persuading third party payors to opt out of settlements in such cases, at the time when a settlement is proposed, that it is often suggested that many qualified law firms that otherwise would pursue such cases have ceased pursuing them altogether, as a consequence of 'free rider' problems stemming from opt-outs sharing in the benefits from class counsel's work, without class counsel being permitted by the courts to share fairly in the fees awarded by the courts for the performance of that work.

for such 'mass action' procedures to be applied in a competition law case. Instead, such procedures are much more commonly associated with personal injury cases involving jet crashes, chemical spills, explosions, harmful medications, product liabilities and the like. However, competition law cases by large corporate plaintiffs that do not lend themselves to class action treatment, such as individual antitrust claims by competitors or very large purchasers, may occasionally be aggregated by means of 'mass action' procedures. Likewise, it is possible, at least in principle, for the number of opt-outs from a class action to cause the case to function as much like a mass action as a class action. As in class actions, the courts have authority to appoint lead counsel and committees of counsel to coordinate and lead the representation of similarly-situated parties. Thus, even in the absence of a class action, much of the same machinery for claims aggregation that exists in class actions often still applies. The primary thing that is missing in a 'mass action,' as distinguished from a 'class action,' is the ability to bind absent parties who do not affirmatively 'opt out' of the litigation.

Parens patriae *cases*

Under 15 U.S.C. §15c, and counterpart provisions that exist in the laws of most states, state attorneys general have so-called *parens patriae* authority to bring suit under the antitrust laws on behalf of their citizens, thereby, in effect, aggregating the claims of their citizens. However, there are substantial legal and practical impediments to the effectiveness of such proceedings. From a legal standpoint, nearly all *parens patriae* authority to sue under the competition laws is limited to authority to represent the natural persons in the state in question, and does not extend to the representation of corporations, partnerships or proprietorships. Because corporations and other business enterprises frequently comprise a large proportion of those who are overcharged as the consequence of a competition law violation, this limitation significantly curtails the effectiveness of *parens patriae* remedies in competition law cases.

From a practical standpoint as well, the *parens patriae* authority of state attorneys general has sometimes been criticized as ineffective. For example, Judge Posner has recently argued that state attorneys general in the United States not only lack the resources that would be necessary for them to enforce competition laws effectively, but also that they are sometimes 'excessively influenced by interest groups that may represent a potential antitrust defendant's competitors.'[58] On the basis of such criticisms, Judge Posner has made the radical recommendation from a policy standpoint that state attorneys general be 'stripped of their authority to bring antitrust suits, federal or state, except under circumstances in which a private firm would be able to sue . . . .'[59] This is highly unlikely to occur, and much of Judge Posner's criticism of attorney general *parens patriae* authority seems exaggerated. Nevertheless, there is no question that state attorneys general are insufficiently funded for their enforcement efforts alone to be an effective deterrent against competition law violations.[60]

---

[58] Richard A. Posner, Antitrust Law 281 (2nd ed., 2001).

[59] *Id.*

[60] For further discussion of the *parens patriae* authority, see Chapters 7 and 13 of this *Handbook*.

FTC disgorgement claims

Although the issue is not entirely clear, the Federal Trade Commission (FTC) may have authority, in competition cases brought pursuant to section 13(b) of the FTC Act, 15 U.S.C. §53(b), to seek monetary equitable remedies, including disgorgement and restitution.[61] The FTC has exercised that authority in a number of competition cases over the last few decades.[62] Thus, disgorgement and restitution in cases brought by the FTC are additional legally available methods for aggregation of antitrust claims in the United States. Nevertheless, the FTC has made clear that it does 'not view monetary disgorgement or restitution as routine remedies for antitrust cases,' and that it 'will continue to rely primarily on more familiar, prospective remedies, and seek disgorgement and restitution in exceptional cases.'[63] Moreover, the FTC clearly does not have the resources that would be necessary in order for it to operate as the primary enforcer of private claims for injuries from antitrust violations. Recognizing that fact, the FTC has stated that 'it is important and beneficial that there be a number of flexible tools, as well as a number of potential enforcers, available to address competitive problems in a particular case.'[64] At least for the foreseeable future, the primary method of aggregating civil competition law claims in the United States will not be government disgorgement or restitution remedies, but instead will be private antitrust litigation, including class actions.

---

[61] The authority of the FTC to seek disgorgement was recognized by a federal district court in *F.T.C. v. Mylan Labs., Inc.*, 62 F. Supp. 2d 25 (D.D.C. 1999). However, that court recognized that the section of the FTC Act that the agency relied upon in that case 'does not authorize the FTC to seek monetary remedies.' *Id.* at 36. Instead, the court found the authority to exist only because 'the defendant cite[d] no relevant case law that prohibits the FTC from seeking disgorgement.' *Id.* at 37. Accordingly, some commentators have questioned whether the FTC has genuine legal authority to seek monetary remedies that would effectively aggregate the claims of injured private parties.

[62] Federal Trade Commission, Policy Statement on Monetary Equitable Remedies in Competition Cases, 68 Fed. Reg. 149 (Aug. 4, 2003).

[63] *Id.*

[64] *Id.*

9 Procedural defenses short of trial

Jonathan L. Rubin[1]

Introduction

Defendants in civil antitrust lawsuits brought in the US federal courts have several opportunities short of a trial on the merits by which to dispose of claims against them. This chapter concerns three categories of defenses: i) challenges to the court's subject matter jurisdiction, ii) defenses available by pre-answer motion, and iii) pretrial summary proceedings and affirmative defenses. The chapter that follows after this one deals with discovery issues under the Federal Rules of Civil Procedure.

Rule 12 of the Federal Rules of Civil Procedure[2] gives defendants 20 days after being legally notified of the suit filed against them (the 'service of process'[3]) within which to serve the plaintiffs with a 'responsive pleading' answering the allegations in the complaint. The responsive pleading also must allege affirmative defenses the defendant intends to raise. The time to respond to a complaint may be extended to 60 days (or 90 days for defendants not found in any US judicial district) if the defendant acknowledges notice of the suit and waives objections to the form or manner of service of process.[4]

In practice, however, a responsive pleading is only rarely filed within the initial time limits that run from the time of service of process. Defendants more often opt to toll the time to respond through the use of Rule 12(b), which permits a defendant to interpose a pre-answer motion to dismiss raising the defenses enumerated in Rules 12(b)(1)–(7). The list is non-exhaustive. Generally speaking, Rule 12(b) defenses require little or no inquiry beyond the pleadings, self-authenticating documents, or matters of public record. The first of these defenses, in Rule 12(b)(1), is lack of subject matter jurisdiction. This concept can be particularly important in international antitrust cases, because the authority of US federal courts to hear antitrust suits arising from conduct that does not have a direct, substantial, and reasonably foreseeable effect on US domestic commerce, or that solely causes independent, non-US economic harm, is circumscribed by statute.

---

1 The author is an attorney and Ph.D economist and specializes in antitrust litigation and counseling. The author is solely responsible for the contents of this chapter. Jonathan Rubin may be contacted at JRubinUS@att.net.

2 The Federal Rules of Civil Procedure, which govern procedure, practice and evidence in the federal courts, are referred to hereinafter as the 'Rules' or 'Rule ___.' The federal courts also promulgate 'Local Rules' that codify the customary practice before that particular court for implementing the Rules. Congress authorizes the federal judiciary to promulgate the Rules in the Rules Enabling Act, 28 U.S.C. §§2071–2077. Effective December 1, 2007, the Rules underwent a plenary revision in style and the sample Forms were rewritten. Practitioners should be aware of numbering changes when conducting legal research on a particular Rule.

3 Service of process customarily consists of a summons issued by the court clerk and a complete copy of the complaint or petition personally delivered to an individual defendant or to the agent designated by a defendant business entity.

4 Rule 12(a)(1)(A)(ii).

Dismissal for lack of subject matter jurisdiction differs from dismissal based on the other defenses that may be raised on a Rule 12(b) pre-answer motion in two important respects. First, because courts are never permitted to adjudicate claims for which subject matter jurisdiction is lacking, Rule 12(h)(3) requires the court to dismiss an action at *any time* it is determined that it lacks subject matter jurisdiction. Thus, determinations of subject matter jurisdiction may arise not only on a Rule 12(b) motion but at any stage of the litigation. Second, because courts cannot adjudicate claims over which subject matter jurisdiction is lacking, dismissal on Rule 12(b)(1) grounds does not have the effect of a final decision on the merits of the claim, as does a final order of dismissal on other grounds, such as Rule 12(b)(6) grounds of failure to state a justiciable cause of action. Accordingly, Rule 12(b)(1) challenges to subject matter jurisdiction are treated separately in Section 1 of the chapter.

Section 2 addresses the remaining procedural defenses permitted to be raised in a Rule 12(b) pre-answer motion. Two of these defenses – failure to state a claim upon which relief may be granted (Rule 12(b)(6)) and failure to join a required party to the lawsuit (Rule 12(b)(7)) – may, but need not be, raised in a Rule 12(b) pre-answer motion because they cannot be waived. A claim that the complaint fails to state a claim upon which relief may be granted is a demurrer, which tests the sufficiency of the pleaded allegations or challenges the plaintiff's legal right to prosecute the claim on the facts alleged. Rule 12(b)(6) and (7) defenses also may be raised for the first time later in the litigation, for example, in any pleading allowed by Rule 7(a), in a motion for judgment on the pleadings under Rule 12(c), or at trial, and may be heard and ruled upon at the court's discretion any time up to and including at trial.

The remaining defenses that may be raised in a pre-answer motion, listed in Rules 12(b)(2)–(5), are challenges to the court's jurisdiction over the defendant's 'person,'[5] improper venue,[6] and challenges to the issuance of the court's summons or to the manner in which it was served upon the defendant.[7] These defenses may be waived if not raised in a timely manner, so they are customarily raised in a Rule 12(b) pre-answer motion.

Section 3 of the chapter discusses the defensive use of summary proceedings for summary judgment or pre-trial adjudication of affirmative defenses. A defendant can prevail on summary judgment if the parties' submissions demonstrate the absence of any disputed material issue of fact for determination at trial. A non-exhaustive list of affirmative defenses, which are also frequently determined on a motion for summary judgment, is set out in Rule 8(c).[8]

---

5 Rule 12(b)(2).

6 Rule 12(b)(3).

7 Rules 12(b)(4) and 12(b)(5).

8 The enumerated defenses are: accord and satisfaction; arbitration and award; assumption of risk; contributory negligence; discharge in bankruptcy; duress; estoppel; failure of consideration; fraud; illegality; injury by fellow servant; laches; license; payment; release; res judicata; statute of frauds; statute of limitations; and waiver.

1. Dismissal for lack of subject matter jurisdiction

In the US system, a federal court is a forum of limited jurisdiction with authority under Article III of the Constitution to hear only live 'cases or controversies' involving specifically enumerated federal subject matter.[9] Federal courts require statutory or common law authority to hear and decide the dispute before them. These requirements delineate the subject matter jurisdiction of the federal courts.

A lack of subject matter jurisdiction may never be waived by any party, nor may a party be estopped from asserting it or consent to submit to jurisdiction where none exists. Thus, while subject matter jurisdictional challenges may be raised by a Rule 12(b)(1) pre-answer motion well before trial, the defendants may also move for dismissal or suggest a lack of subject matter jurisdiction at any time the claim is pending, either before trial, at trial, or on appeal.

Rule 8(a)(1) specifies that a statement of a claim for relief must contain 'a short and plain statement of the grounds for the court's jurisdiction . . . .' This jurisdictional pleading requirement applies only to subject matter jurisdiction, and not to jurisdiction over the person, or *in personam* jurisdiction.[10]

There are four statutory grounds for subject matter jurisdiction:

- Federal question jurisdiction;
- Diversity of citizenship jurisdiction;
- Admiralty jurisdiction; and
- Supplemental jurisdiction.

Private federal civil antitrust claims are properly based on federal question jurisdiction, but in appropriate circumstances diversity jurisdiction may provide an additional statutory basis for jurisdiction, or establish federal jurisdiction over antitrust claims based on state law, including certain class actions. Antitrust claims do not arise in admiralty. The balance of this section is devoted to challenges to federal question, diversity, and supplemental subject matter jurisdiction.

The plaintiff bears the burden of establishing subject matter jurisdiction (even though it is challenged in the defendant's motion).[11] *Facial* challenges to subject matter jurisdiction may be determined on a Rule 12(b)(1) pre-answer motion or a Rule 12(c) pre-trial motion for judgment on the pleadings. In reviewing a facial challenge on a Rule 12(b)(1) motion, the court is limited to the allegations in the complaint (which are presumed to be true), the documents referred to in or attached to the complaint, and matters of public record.[12]

In reviewing a *factual* challenge to subject matter jurisdiction, the court is not limited to the allegations in the complaint and the presumption of truthfulness does not attach

---

[9] State trial courts, by contrast, are considered courts of 'general jurisdiction,' with presumptive common law jurisdiction to hear all civil disputes concerning persons, properties or activities affecting the state.

[10] *See* Caribbean Broadcasting System, Ltd. v. Cable & Wireless PLC, 148 F.3d 1080, 1090 (D.C. Cir., 1998) (antitrust plaintiff not required to plead the basis of *in personam* jurisdiction).

[11] Kokkonen v. Guardian Life Ins. Co. of America, 511 US 375 (1994).

[12] Gould Electronics Inc., v. U.S., 220 F.3d 169, 176 (3d Cir. 2000).

to the complaint. The challenge is raised as an affirmative defense subject to proof on a Rule 56 motion for summary judgment or at trial. An allegation that the suit is barred because the statute of limitations lapsed before the complaint was filed is an example of a factual challenge to subject matter jurisdiction.

a. Challenges to federal question jurisdiction
Congress in 28 U.S.C. §1331 authorizes the federal district courts to hear 'all civil actions arising under the Constitution, laws, or treaties of the United States.'[13] This jurisdiction also encompasses claims arising under federal common law, such as contract disputes with the federal government.[14] The broad grant of federal subject matter jurisdiction in §1331 overlaps with other statutes, in which jurisdiction is granted to the district courts to hear particular private causes of action in specific areas of federal law. In the field of antitrust, 28 U.S.C. §1337 authorizes the district courts to hear 'any civil action or proceeding arising under any Act of Congress regulating commerce or protecting trade and commerce against restraints and monopolies. . . .'[15] In addition, §4 of the Clayton Act, 15 U.S.C. §15, provides that:

> any person who shall be injured in his business or property by reason of anything forbidden in the antitrust laws may sue therefor in any district court of the United States in the district in which the defendant resides or is found or has an agent without respect to the amount in controversy, and shall recover threefold the damages by him sustained, and the cost of suit, including a reasonable attorney's fee. . . .

The statute thus grants an express private right of action in a district court for treble damages plus a reasonable attorney's fee to 'any person' injured in his 'business or property' by reason of conduct 'forbidden in the antitrust laws.' An antitrust treble damages complaint that states, 'This court has subject matter jurisdiction over the federal antitrust claims asserted in this action under §4 of the Clayton Act, 15 U.S.C. §15, and Title 28 U.S.C. §§1331 and 1337,' satisfies the pleading requirement of Rule 8(a)(1) for a 'short and plain statement of the grounds for the court's jurisdiction,' provided the balance of the pleading purports to set forth one or more claims based on conduct 'forbidden in the antitrust laws.'

Substantive antitrust violations include price fixing or cartelization, or the allocation of product lines, territories, customers, or market share, forbidden by §1 of the Sherman Act, 15 U.S.C. §1, or monopolization, monopoly maintenance, or attempted monopoly, forbidden by §2, 15 U.S.C. §2. Other substantive violations for which a private cause of action is available include price discrimination in the sale of goods in violation of §2 of the Clayton Act, 15 U.S.C. §13, commodity prices, discounts or rebates conditioned on an agreement not to deal with competitors in violation of §3 of the Clayton Act, 15 U.S.C. §14, or damages legally caused by an unlawful merger in violation of §7 of the Clayton Act, 15 U.S.C. §18.[16]

Plaintiffs sometimes seek an injunction to prevent a threatened antitrust injury.

---

13 28 U.S.C. §1331.
14 Up State Federal Credit Union v. Walker, 198 F.3d 372, 375 n. 4 (2nd Cir., 1999).
15 28 U.S.C. §1337(a).
16 For further discussion of substantive antitrust violations, see Chapter 4 of this *Handbook*.

Section 16 of the Clayton Act, 15 U.S.C. §26, authorizes private parties to 'sue for and have injunctive relief . . . against threatened loss or damage by a violation of the antitrust laws. . . .' In the event of an emergency, a plaintiff may be heard on the need for an immediate court order to prevent some imminent, irreparable harm to persons or property due to a threatened antitrust violation.[17]

i. Statute of limitations Several statutes limit federal question jurisdiction over private antitrust actions. For example, §4B of the Clayton Act, 15 U.S.C. §15b, provides that private antitrust causes of action 'shall be forever barred unless commenced within four years after the cause of action accrued.'

Rarely is a statute of limitations defense unambiguously borne out by the allegations pleaded in the complaint, so the defense is usually factual rather than facial, and, therefore, not determinable on a Rule 12(b)(1) pre-answer motion. The defense is ordinarily litigated as an affirmative defense and proven by admissions from the plaintiff or other evidence that the claim is time-barred.

ii. Insufficient effect on US domestic commerce or imports A claim that the cause of action is barred by §7 of the Sherman Act, 15 U.S.C. §6a, also known as the Foreign Trade Antitrust Improvements Act of 1982 ('FTAIA'), on the other hand, is a challenge to federal question subject matter jurisdiction that may be determined on a defendant's Rule 12(b)(1) pre-answer motion to dismiss.[18] The FTAIA provides that the Sherman Act shall not apply to conduct involving trade or commerce with foreign nations, other than import transactions, unless i) such conduct has 'a direct, substantial, and reasonably foreseeable effect' on domestic or import commerce or on the export business of a domestic person and ii) the effect is of a kind that the antitrust laws consider harmful.

The FTAIA's domestic-injury requirement had been the subject of a split in authority among the Circuit Courts of Appeals,[19] but in a series of decisions arising out of the global vitamins cartel that came to light in the 1990s, the courts, including the US Supreme Court, significantly clarified the pleading requirements for foreign parties suing

---

[17] 15 U.S.C. §9; *see also* Rule 65. For further discussion of antitrust remedies, see Chapter 11 of this *Handbook*.

[18] Dicta in a recent decision by a Ninth Circuit panel observed that '[i]t is unclear . . . whether the FTAIA is more appropriately viewed as withdrawing jurisdiction from the federal courts . . . or as simply establishing a limited cause of action requiring plaintiffs to prove . . . an [additional] element of the claim.' *In re:* Dynamic Random Access Memory (DRAM) Antitrust Litigation, 546 F.3d 981, 985, note 3 (9th Cir. 2008) (alteration added). The court's observation is based on a mistaken interpretation of the basis of the Second Circuit's decision in *In re*: Elevator Antitrust Litigation, 502 F.3d 47 (2nd Cir. 2007), in which the court affirmed dismissal of the complaint on Rule 12(b)(6) grounds. The court's holding in that case, however, was expressly limited to the failure of the pleadings to 'state a claim,' obviating the need for the court to 'consider the extraterritorial reach of the Sherman Act' under the FTAIA. *Id.* at 52, note 8. The *DRAM* panel's misreading of the *Elevator* holding caused it to see confusion over whether a challenge on FTAIA grounds is properly raised on a Rule 12(b)(1) motion where none, in fact, exists.

[19] *See* F. Hoffmann-LaRoche, Ltd. v. Empagran SA, 542 US 155, 161 (2004) (citing cases).

for, or being sued for, a violation of US antitrust law. The case was brought as a class action on behalf of both US-domestic and non-US direct purchasers of vitamins against foreign and domestic vitamin manufacturers for injury caused by a global price-fixing conspiracy conducted largely outside the US and supra-competitive prices in the world-wide market. The defendants moved to dismiss the claims brought by non-US purchasers, five vitamin distributors located in the Ukraine, Australia, Ecuador and Panama, on the grounds that the FTAIA makes the Sherman Act inapplicable to conduct involving non-import foreign trade or commerce. The defendants argued that, because the non-US plaintiffs had not purchased vitamins in the US, the conduct did not satisfy the domestic-injury requirement. The district court agreed, and dismissed the Sherman Act claim against them for lack of subject matter jurisdiction.

On appeal, the District of Columbia Circuit reversed, reinstating the foreign purchasers' claim, finding that the allegations of injurious anticompetitive effects of the foreign conduct in both US and non-US markets were sufficient to bring the claim within the domestic-injury requirement in the FTAIA. In *F. Hoffmann-LaRoche, Ltd. v. Empagran S.A.*,[20] the US Supreme Court, on a limited set of facts, reversed, holding that the foreign purchasers' claims did not meet the domestic-injury requirement. The facts were limited to circumstances in which '[t]he price-fixing conduct significantly and adversely affected both customers outside the United States and customers within the United States, but the adverse foreign effect was independent of any adverse domestic effect.'[21] The Court framed the basic question thus:

> Why is it reasonable to apply this law to conduct that is significantly foreign *insofar as that conduct causes independent foreign harm and that foreign harm alone gives rise to the plaintiff's claim?*[22]

Finding no good reason, the Court vacated the DC Circuit's order that reinstated the case. At the same time, however, the Court made note of its maintained assumption that the anticompetitive conduct 'independently caused foreign injury; that is, the conduct's domestic effects did not help to bring about that foreign injury.'[23] Because it reviewed a limited set of facts, the Court did not consider the plaintiffs' related, alternative claim that the domestic US effects were linked to the foreign injury, which could not have been inflicted but for the harm to the domestic US economy. The plaintiffs contended that, because vitamins are fungible and readily transportable, cross-border price differentials would be arbitraged away, the defendants could not have maintained their international price-fixing arrangement, and the plaintiffs would not have suffered their foreign injury. The plaintiffs argued that such causation-in-fact was sufficient to bring their claim within the scope of the FTAIA domestic-injury exception.

The Supreme Court declined to consider this argument because the DC Circuit had not considered it. The Court instructed the DC Circuit on remand, however, to decide whether the plaintiff's alternative (and more economically realistic) scenario should

---

20 542 US 155 (2004).
21 *Id.* at 164.
22 *Id.* at 166.
23 542 US at 175.

bring the foreign conduct within the exception to the FTAIA's exclusion of non-import foreign trade from the Sherman Act.

On remand, the DC Circuit found that the plaintiffs had painted

> a plausible scenario under which maintaining super-competitive prices in the United States might well have been a 'but-for' cause of the [plaintiff's] foreign injury. . . . [H]owever, 'but-for' causation between the domestic effects and the foreign injury claim is simply not sufficient to bring anti-competitive conduct within the FTAIA requirement. The statutory language – 'gives rise to' – indicates a direct causal relationship, that is, proximate causation, and is not satisfied by the mere but-for 'nexus' the [plaintiffs] advanced in their brief. This interpretation of the statutory language accords with principles of 'prescriptive comity' – 'the respect sovereign nations afford each other by limiting the reach of their laws.'[24]

The court held that while supra-competitive US pricing may have facilitated the defendants' scheme, it was not alleged that US domestic effects of the defendants' conduct proximately caused the foreign plaintiffs' injuries. As a consequence, the law in the DC Circuit provides that district courts have subject matter jurisdiction over foreign antitrust injury claims based on a Sherman Act violation only if the injury is alleged to have been proximately caused by the US domestic anticompetitive effects.

The court distinguished its result from *Caribbean Broadcasting System, Ltd. v. Cable & Wireless PLC*,[25] in which the DC Circuit expressly found that the FTAIA exception applied to a non-US plaintiff seeking redress against a non-US defendant for economic harm occurring outside the US. The defendant, a commercial radio station operator, stood accused of misrepresenting the reach of its signal for the purpose of monopolizing the US and non-US radio advertising markets for Caribbean-area advertisers. The court distinguished *Caribbean Broadcasting* from *Empagran* on the ground that the US domestic effect, excessive prices paid by US radio advertisers, was sufficient to bring the case within the scope of the FTAIA requirement. A more cogent basis on which to distinguish *Caribbean Broadcasting*, however, is that *Caribbean Broadcasting* involved a competing radio station that claimed injury from being excluded from business with US domestic advertisers, so the US domestic effects 'gave rise to,' or proximately caused, the non-US harm. By contrast, *Empagran* involved a suit by non-US direct purchasers in non-US markets in transactions that can fairly be characterized as 'wholly foreign.'

The rule that an overlapping, global, or interrelated market, without more, does not satisfy the requirement that US domestic effects 'give rise to' the complained-of harm has since been followed in the Second,[26] Eighth[27] and Ninth[28] Circuits.

Even where the plaintiff is a competitor in a global relevant geographical market in which worldwide anticompetitive conduct is alleged, jurisdiction over foreign antitrust injury is unlikely to lie on that basis alone. Thus, the district court in *Intel Corp.*

---

24 Emparan SA v. F. Hoffmann-LaRoche, Ltd., 417 F.3d 1267, 1270–71 (D.C. Cir. 2005) cert. denied 126 S.Ct. 1043 (2006) (citations omitted).

25 148 F.3d 1080 (DC Cir. 1998).

26 Sniado v. Bank Austria AG, 378 F.3d 210 (2nd Cir. 2004).

27 *In re*: Monosodium Glutamate Antitrust Litigation, 477 F. 3d 535 (8th Cir. 2007).

28 *In re*: Dynamic Random Access Memory (DRAM) Antitrust Litigation, 546 F.3d 981 (9th Cir. 2008).

Microprocessor Antitrust Litigation[29] found that harm occurring outside the US was beyond the reach of the Sherman Act. The market in that case was the world supply of x-86 microprocessors, the brains of the personal computer, in which Intel and AMD constitute a duopoly. AMD fabricates its products in Germany and assembles them in Asia. In its complaint against Intel, AMD alleged that Intel's business practices throughout the world were designed to prevent AMD from expanding its worldwide market share or operating at efficient minimum scale.

Intel asserted that AMD was, in part, seeking relief for business practices that affected the sale of AMD's microprocessors in foreign countries, foreign claims outside of the domestic-injury requirement of the FTAIA. In response, AMD argued that the US market was but an integral part of the world market, and that Intel had kept AMD from selling microprocessors in foreign markets with the purpose and effect of weakening AMD as a domestic rival. 'Intel has necessarily had to cut AMD off from business opportunities throughout the market, including opportunities with foreign customers.'[30]

The court, however, observed that the direct effects requirement meant that the effects in the US had to be an immediate consequence of the alleged anticompetitive conduct abroad with no intervening developments. 'AMD's chain of effects [was] full of twists and turns, which themselves [were] contingent upon numerous developments,'[31] including the use of profits from foreign sales to shore up US domestic marketing. The court agreed with Intel that the 'simultaneous, direct foreign and direct domestic effects, with the plaintiffs' antitrust claim arising from those direct domestic effects,'[32] that characterized *Caribbean Broadcasting* did not obtain where 'the foreign harm . . . arises from the effects of the alleged foreign conduct and there is no direct link between the foreign conduct and the domestic antitrust injury.'[33] The court then struck the allegations of AMD's complaint that claimed injury due to lost sales to European and Japanese computer manufacturers, the interference with product launches by those manufacturers, lost sales to non-US distributors selling to non-US markets, and interference with sales to European-based retailers.

It is worth noting that not all FTAIA jurisdictional challenges are reviewed as facial challenges, but may require a factual record. In *Sun Microsystems Inc. v. Hynix Semiconductor Inc.*,[34] for example, where the defendants in a global DRAM-memory chip price-fixing scheme moved to dismiss from US litigation transactions made by the plaintiffs' foreign affiliates, the court ruled that 'if plaintiffs can articulate and prove a legal theory that . . . they stand in the shoes of or are the alter ego of their foreign affiliates as well as a factual basis for such a claim, the court would be permitted to find that proximate cause under the FTAIA is necessarily satisfied, and that jurisdiction exists.'[35] The court denied the motion and moved the case into the discovery phase, without prejudice to a renewed defense motion on the same grounds after discovery. Ultimately, however,

---

29 452 F.Supp.2d 555 (D. Del. 2006).
30 *Id.* at 560 (citation omitted).
31 *Id.*
32 *Id.* at 562.
33 *Id.*
34 534 F.Supp.2d 1101 (ND Cal. 2007).
35 *Id.* at 1116.

the plaintiff was unable to establish that it 'stands in the shoes of its foreign subsidiaries,' so the court viewed the foreign purchases 'as foreign transactions made by independent subsidiary entities' that did not satisfy the jurisdictional requirements of the FTAIA.[36]

iii. Express antitrust immunities and exemptions Numerous other statutes and common law doctrines limit the reach of the antitrust laws by providing an express immunity or exemption for particular industries or commercial activities, giving rise to additional challenges to federal question subject matter jurisdiction in the appropriate circumstances.

In the agricultural field, the Clayton Act §6, 15 U.S.C. §17, permits, among other things, the operation of non-profit, non-stock agricultural or horticultural mutual assistance organizations. The Capper-Volstead Agricultural Producers' Associations Act, 7 U.S.C. §§291–92, allows agricultural producers to act in concert for the purpose of 'collectively processing, preparing for market, handling, and marketing' products, and to have 'market agencies in common.' The Capper-Volstead Cooperative Marketing Act of 1926, 7 U.S.C. §§451–457, authorizes the acquisition and exchange of past, present, and prospective pricing, production, and marketing data among agricultural producers and associations.

Similarly, under the Export Trading Company Act of 1982, 15 U.S.C. §§4001–4003, a certificate of review issued by the Secretary of Commerce with the concurrence of the Attorney General provides limited antitrust immunity for specific export trade, export trade activities, and methods of operation. The Webb-Pomerene (Export Trade) Act, 15 U.S.C. §§61–66, immunizes the formation and operation of associations by competing businesses to engage in collective export sales, excluding anticompetitive effects within US domestic commerce or injury to domestic competitors of the export trade association members.

Collective activity by employees relating to a dispute concerning terms or conditions of employment and legitimate objectives of labor organizations are immune from the antitrust laws by virtue of the Clayton Act §20, 29 U.S.C. §52. The Norris-LaGuardia Act of 1932, 29 U.S.C. §§101–115, provides that US courts may not issue restraining orders or injunctions against certain labor union activities, for example, on the grounds of a threatened antitrust violation.

The McCarran-Ferguson Act, 15 U.S.C. §§1011–15 exempts the 'business of insurance' from the antitrust laws to the extent 'regulated by state law,' except for acts of 'boycott, coercion or intimidation.' The Fishermens' Collective Marketing Act, 15 U.S.C. §§521–22, permits fishermen to act together for the purpose of catching, producing, and marketing their products. The Newspaper Preservation Act of 1970, 15 U.S.C. §§1801–04, provides a limited antitrust exemption for joint operating arrangements between newspapers that share production facilities and commercial operations. The Sports Broadcasting Act of 1961, 15 U.S.C. §§1291–95, exempts certain agreements

---

36 Sun Microsystems, Inc. v. Hynix Semiconductor, Inc., Order Granting Motion to Dismiss; Denying Motion to Exclude; and Granting Summary Judgment in Part and Denying Summary Judgment in Part, No. 06-1665-PJH (N.D. Cal., March 31, 2009). For a discussion of how the FTAIA has served as an obstacle to the United States becoming a single forum for private claims in the context of global cartels, see Chapter 37 of this *Handbook*.

among professional sports teams to negotiate through their leagues for the sale of television rights. Still other laws exempt certain joint research activities, local governments, and joint purchasing in national emergencies. All of these provisions are part and parcel of substantive US antitrust law that may arise in litigation as facial or factual challenges to subject matter jurisdiction.

b. Challenges to diversity jurisdiction

Although federal question jurisdiction customarily provides the jurisdictional basis for antitrust matters, federal subject matter jurisdiction also exists for claims arising under state antitrust laws, including certain state antitrust class actions, if the applicable requirements of diversity of citizenship or supplemental jurisdiction are met. Plaintiffs may wish to plead a state cause of action because it affords them greater rights than are available under federal law. Diversity of citizenship jurisdiction is discussed in this subsection, and supplemental jurisdiction is discussed in the following subsection.

Under 28 U.S.C. §1332(a) federal courts have original jurisdiction over state claims in four situations:

- a case between citizens of different US states;
- between citizens of a state and a citizen or subject of a foreign state;
- between citizens of different states in which foreign citizens are additional parties; or,
- between a foreign state as plaintiff and citizens of a US state.

The concept of 'citizenship' for diversity purposes requires an individual to be domiciled in the state, amounting to physical presence with the intent to reside in the state indefinitely. A US citizen domiciled abroad is not a 'citizen of a state' nor a subject or citizen of a foreign state, so such an individual may not bring suit in the federal courts based on diversity jurisdiction.[37] On the other hand, Subsection 1332(a) provides that 'an alien admitted to the United States for permanent residence shall be deemed a citizen of the State in which such alien is domiciled.' A corporation is a citizen of each state in which it is incorporated plus the state in which it has its one principal place of business. Courts look either to the location of the corporation's headquarters (taking a corporate 'nerve center' approach[38]), the place where the bulk of the corporate assets are found, or both.

All diversity claims must satisfy both the technical rules for diversity of citizenship and an amount in controversy requirement, which should be alleged as a 'short and plain statement of the grounds for the court's jurisdiction,' as required by Rule 8(a)(1). Diversity of citizenship requires 'complete diversity,' that is, all plaintiffs must have citizenship different from all defendants. Jurisdiction fails if any defendant shares citizenship with any plaintiff. The complaint should allege the citizenship of each individual party, the state of incorporation and principal place of business of each corporate party, and that the amount in controversy in each claim of each plaintiff exceeds US $75,000,

---

37 Coury v. Prot, 85 F.3d 244, 248 (5th Cir. 1996).

38 *See* Metropolitan Life Ins. Co. v. Estate of Cammon, 929 F.2d 1220, 1222 (7th Cir. 1991).

exclusive of interest and costs. A failure to allege jurisdictional facts in sufficient detail to establish complete diversity or the amount in controversy is grounds for a Rule 12(b)(1) pre-answer motion to dismiss for lack of subject matter jurisdiction.

Congress made major changes in diversity jurisdiction for class actions commenced on or after February 18, 2005. A new Subsection 1332(d) provides more generous jurisdictional standards for class actions that relax the complete diversity requirement and permit plaintiffs to aggregate their claims to meet a total amount in controversy threshold of US $5,000,000. Sections 1332(d)(2)(A)–(C) provide that diversity for class actions is satisfied if any class member is a citizen of a different state from any defendant, any class member is a foreign state or a citizen of a foreign state and any defendant is a citizen of a US state, or any class member is a citizen of a US state and any defendant is a foreign state or citizen. However, Subsection 1332(d)(4) requires the court to decline jurisdiction where more than two-thirds of the class members are citizens of the forum state and any significant defendant is also a citizen of that state. Under Subsection 1332(d)(3) the court may decline to exercise jurisdiction where more than one-third but less than two-thirds of the class members and the primary defendants are citizens of the forum state, based on six factors enumerated in the statute. Subsection 1332(d)(9) excludes certain securities and corporate law class action claims. State law class actions based on diversity jurisdiction that do not satisfy all the standards of §1332 may be challenged on subject matter jurisdiction grounds.

c. Challenges to supplemental jurisdiction

Supplemental jurisdiction is not an independent basis for subject matter jurisdiction, unlike federal question or diversity jurisdiction. It arises only when jurisdiction already exists for one or more of the other claims in the complaint, in which case the pleader is permitted to litigate non-federal claims related to the same 'case or controversy.'[39] Supplemental jurisdiction, authorized by Congress in 28 U.S.C. §1367 in 1990, codifies the common law doctrines of pendant and ancillary jurisdiction.[40]

Supplemental jurisdiction will fail if the original action is based on diversity jurisdiction and the exercise of supplemental jurisdiction would contradict the requirements of diversity, except in exceptional circumstances.[41] Where the claims conferring original federal jurisdiction are dismissed, whether the claims based on supplemental jurisdiction may or must be dismissed depends on the reasons for dismissal. If the original federal subject matter jurisdiction was lacking, the supplemental claims must be dismissed. If dismissal relates to the merits of the federal claims, the district has discretion to decline to continue to exercise jurisdiction.[42]

2. Pre-answer defenses

This section begins by discussing challenges available to achieve dismissal of a complaint for failure to state a claim upon which relief may be granted, focusing on the significance

---

39 28 U.S.C. §1337(a).

40 *See* Peacock v. Thomas, 516 US 349, 355 n. 5 (1996). Practitioners should be aware that some features of prior law in this area were abrogated by the statute.

41 28 U.S.C. §1367(b).

42 28 U.S.C. §1367(c)(3).

of the *Bell Atlantic Corp. v. Twombly*[43] and *Ashcroft v. Iqbal*[44] decisions on the applicable pleading standards for antitrust claims. The remainder of the section considers the other procedural defenses that may be raised in a pre-answer motion.

a. Rule 12(b)(6) pre-answer motion to dismiss for failure to state a claim upon which relief may be granted

As a practical matter, Rule 12(b)(6) pre-answer motions to dismiss for failure to state a claim arise in nearly every case. Rule 12(b)(6) codifies the common law plea of demurrer, that is, that the complaint fails 'to state a claim upon which relief can be granted.' It tests the legal sufficiency of the claim to screen out lawsuits 'that are fatally flawed in their legal premises and destined to fail. . . .'[45] Dismissal on these grounds is warranted when a claim either i) asserts a legal theory that is not cognizable as a matter of law, or ii) fails to allege sufficient facts to support a cognizable legal claim.

i. Non-cognizable claims Some defenses that do not challenge subject matter jurisdiction are nonetheless based on a limitation of the applicability of the antitrust laws. In industries in which competitive conduct is regulated defendants may claim an implied antitrust immunity (as distinct from an express statutory immunity or exemption) or, in a §2 monopolization claim, the lack of any antitrust duty to deal.[46]

Implied antitrust immunity may arise where regulatory statutes are silent with respect to antitrust but courts determine that application of the antitrust laws to conduct closely supervised by a regulatory body should be implicitly precluded. The US Supreme Court re-formulated the standard for implied immunity in the 2007 case of *Credit Suisse Securities (USA) LLC v. Billing*.[47] The case involved a Sherman Act §1 claim by a putative class of investors seeking to recover for injuries allegedly sustained as a result of anticompetitive agreements among major underwriters regarding the terms of sale for initial public offerings. Summarizing its view of prior securities industry cases, the Court identified the following factors as critical to finding sufficient incompatibility between the securities laws and the antitrust complaint in any given case:

> (1) the existence of regulatory authority under the securities law to supervise the activities in question; (2) evidence that the responsible regulatory entities exercise that authority; and (3) a resulting risk that the securities and antitrust laws, if both applicable, would produce conflicting guidance, requirements, duties, privileges, or standards of conduct.[48]

---

43 550 US 544 (2007).

44 556 US ____, 129 S.Ct. 1937 (2009).

45 Advanced Cardiovascular Systems, Inc. v. Scimed Life Systems, Inc., 988 F.2d 1157, 1160 (Fed.Cir. 1993).

46 By an express statutory immunity, Congress divests the district courts of subject matter jurisdiction over immune activities or parties, so it is properly raised in a Rule 12(b)(1) motion. The resolution of an implied immunity defense, by contrast, requires, at a bare minimum, the factual background alleged in the complaint. If the facts alleged establish an implied immunity, the complaint should be dismissed under Rule 12(b)(6).

47 551 US 264, 127 S.Ct. 2383 (2007).

48 127 S.Ct. at 2392.

In reference to previous occasions on which the Court found an antitrust claim non-cognizable on the grounds of implied immunity by virtue of the securities laws, the Court noted that 'the possible conflict [between antitrust and securities regulation] affected practices that lie squarely within an area of financial market activity that the securities law seeks to regulate.'[49] As with other of its recent pronouncements in the field, the Supreme Court in *Credit Suisse* incrementally limited the reach of the antitrust laws by re-calibrating the standard applicable to the decision before it (in this case, the well-established 'clear repugnancy' test governing antitrust immunity implied by a regulatory regime).

Implied immunity may be unavailable if an 'antitrust savings clause' is enacted in the regulatory enabling legislation. But, at least four legal avenues other than implied immunity also may bar an antitrust claim against a regulated entity, even where Congress includes an antitrust savings clause. The first is the so-called 'state action doctrine.' This rule, originating in *Parker v. Brown*,[50] emerges from federalism to protect the activities of the states. The state action doctrine shields certain anticompetitive conduct when the conduct is (1) in furtherance of a clearly articulated state policy, and (2) actively supervised by the state. This protection is available to officials and agencies of the states and may be available to many lower-level functionaries and public–private activities.

The second defense is the 'filed rate doctrine,' adopted in *Keogh v. Chicago & N. W. Ry. Co.*,[51] and reaffirmed in *Square D Co. v. Niagara Frontier Tariff Bureau, Inc.*,[52] which bars antitrust claims which seek remedies that are incompatible with the rate approval process of a regulatory agency.

Third, the doctrine of primary jurisdiction directs a district court to defer an antitrust claim where the case 'requires resolution of issues which, under a regulatory scheme, have been placed within the special competence of an administrative body.'[53] '[I]n such a case the judicial process is suspended pending referral of such issues to the administrative body for its views.'[54]

Finally, limitations on the cognizability of antitrust claims against regulated entities may arise from the alteration of the market environment induced by regulation or deregulation. Thus, in *Town of Concord, Ma. v. Boston Edison Co.*,[55] the First Circuit did not say either that the antitrust laws did not apply to the electrical wholesale market or that they applied less stringently, but rather that the regulatory scheme itself made 'a critical difference in terms of antitrust harms, benefits, and administrative considerations.'[56]

In *Verizon Communications Inc. v. Law Offices of Curtis V. Trinko, LLP*,[57] the Supreme

---

49 *Id.*
50 317 US 341 (1943).
51 260 US 156 (1922).
52 476 US 409 (1986).
53 Ricci v. Chicago Merc. Exch., 409 US 289 (1973).
54 United States v. Western Pacific R. Co. 352 US 59, 64 (1956), citing General American Tank Car Corp. v. El Dorado Terminal Co., 308 US 422, 433 (1940).
55 915 F.2d 17 (1st Cir. 1990), cert. denied, 499 US 931 (1991).
56 915 F.2d, at 23.
57 540 US 398 (2004).

Court relied on this perspective to shield newly deregulated telephone companies from the application of §2 of the Sherman Act. The deregulatory legislation imposed duties on regional monopoly telephone carriers to interconnect with rival firms. In the Court's view, this governmental scheme would have been 'a good candidate for implication of antitrust immunity,'[58] but an antitrust savings clause prevented this. Nonetheless, the Court found that the investment disincentives of imposing an antitrust duty on telephone carriers to share their infrastructure were in tension with the underlying purposes of the antitrust laws. Moreover, regulatory redress was available and was obtained on the basis of the defendant's failure to abide by mandated interconnection duties. The Court also noted the prospect of inconsistent decisions in the area by antitrust courts throughout the country. Consequently, in a decision that appears to have narrowed the range of circumstances in which monopolists may be compelled by antitrust law to deal with rivals, the Court declined to recognize a cause of action for an incumbent telephone carrier's failure to fulfill its statutory duties. The Court concluded that the firms had not violated any duty to deal that was or should be imposed by the antitrust laws, rendering the plaintiff's claim non-cognizable.

ii. Non-justiciable claims By virtue of the act of state and political question doctrines, or for considerations of international comity, a private antitrust action may be non-justiciable and subject to dismissal on a Rule 12(b)(6) pre-answer motion. These defenses were raised by the defendants and discussed in detail in *Refined Petroleum Products Antitrust Litigation*,[59] in which US domestic oil companies stood accused of participating with the Organization of Petroleum Exporting Countries ('OPEC') in the planning and execution of output restrictions and other concerted conduct prohibited by §1 of the Sherman Act. The defendants, arguing that the court may not find unlawful the conduct of a sovereign state and that the case presented a non-justiciable political question of foreign policy reserved to the Executive branch, submitted a Rule 12(b)(1) motion to dismiss for lack of subject matter jurisdiction. The plaintiffs instead urged the court to treat the matter as a Rule 12(b)(6) motion to dismiss for failure to state a claim for which relief may be granted.

The court observed that, in deciding a Rule 12(b)(1) motion to determine whether the court has the constitutional or statutory power to adjudicate a case (i.e. subject matter jurisdiction), the court may consider the pleadings, undisputed facts evidenced in the record, and disputed matters of fact that the court has resolved. The burden of proof rests with the party asserting jurisdiction (ordinarily, the plaintiffs, but on removal from state court, the party seeking removal), and a dismissal on jurisdictional grounds alone does not constitute adjudication on the merits. By contrast, in deciding a Rule 12(b)(6) motion to determine whether the complaint states a cognizable and justiciable claim for relief, the court may only consider the pleadings, documents central to the claim, and matters of public record. The burden of proof is on the defendant, and a final order of dismissal has the effect of an adjudication on the merits.

---

58 540 US at 406.

59 2009 WL 81923 (SD Tex. Jan 9, 2009).

The court quoted the Supreme Court's decision in *Baker v. Carr*[60] distinguishing between these two categories of defenses:

> First: That the facts and injury alleged, the legal bases invoked as creating the rights and duties relied upon, and the relief sought, fail to come within that language of Article III of the Constitution and of the jurisdictional statutes which define those matters concerning which United States District Courts are empowered to act;
>
> Second: That, although the matter is cognizable and facts are alleged which establish infringement of appellants' rights . . . the court will not proceed because the matter is considered unsuited to judicial inquiry or adjustment.
>
> We treat the first ground of dismissal as 'lack of jurisdiction of the subject matter.' The second we consider to result in a failure to state a justiciable cause of action.[61]

Accordingly, the *Petroleum Products* court treated the defendant's act of state and political question defenses as an attack on the justiciability of the plaintiffs' claim rather than an attack on subject matter jurisdiction.

Although adopting the approach urged by the plaintiffs, the court ruled that the defendants had met their burden on both grounds. The act of state doctrine is a 'principle of decision' binding on federal and state courts that arises only when the outcome of the case turns upon the effect of official action by a foreign sovereign.[62] The doctrine bars courts from having to declare invalid the official act of a foreign sovereign performed within its own territory.[63] Because the §1 claim in *Petroleum Products* could not 'be resolved without the court having to rule on the legality of governmental acts and agreements that foreign sovereign members of the alleged conspiracy made with respect to crude oil production in their own territory,' and the complaint did not state a claim that the defendants *alone* had violated §1, the act of state doctrine rendered the claim non-justiciable.

The court also invoked the political limitations of the judiciary by finding that 'to determine the legality of crude oil production decisions of foreign sovereigns would express a lack of respect for the Executive Branch because of its longstanding foreign policy that issues relating to crude oil production by foreign sovereigns be resolved through intergovernmental negotiation.'[64] The political question doctrine counsels courts against entering at the will of litigants into a delicate area of foreign policy which the executive and legislative branches have chosen to approach with restraint.[65]

iii. Failure to allege facts sufficient to state a cognizable legal claim Two recent US Supreme Court decisions, *Bell Atlantic Corp. v. Twombly*,[66] decided May 21, 2007, and *Ashcroft v. Iqbal*,[67] decided May 18, 2009, strengthened the interpretation of the pleading requirements of Rule 8(a)(2) for stating a claim in antitrust and other federal civil cases.

---

60 369 US 186 (1962).
61 369 US at 698–89.
62 2009 WL at *8 (citations omitted).
63 *Id.*
64 *Id.* at *23.
65 *Id.* at *24 (citation omitted).
66 550 US 544 (2007).
67 556 US ____, 129 S.Ct. 1937 (2009).

As a consequence, private plaintiffs now bear a greater obligation at the inception of their lawsuit to allege facts reasonably confirmable by discoverable evidence and, based on a coherent antitrust and economic theory, reasonably sufficient, if proven, to establish the grounds for the plaintiffs' claimed right to compensatory and treble damages for an antitrust injury. Naturally, defendants in antitrust cases have been placing increasing emphasis on challenging the plaintiffs' right to seek relief on the basis of the facts alleged in the complaint.

In *Bell Atlantic Corp. v. Twombly*[68] the Court's stated intention was to 'address the proper standard for pleading an antitrust conspiracy through allegations of parallel conduct,'[69] and to take a 'fresh look at [the] adequacy of pleading when a claim rests on parallel conduct.'[70] The plaintiffs were a putative class of consumers alleging that the defendants, the regional US Bell telephone monopolies, had agreed to – and did – refrain from expanding into one another's service regions in order to maintain an anti-competitive market allocation and exclude competitive, third-party potential entrants, in violation of §1. The plaintiffs also alleged that, in so doing, defendants acted against their individual economic self-interests. The Supreme Court in *Twombly* found that the allegations in the plaintiffs' amended complaint did not adequately establish grounds entitling plaintiffs to a claim for relief. An allegation of parallel conduct in a §1 case, without more, the Court held, does not suffice to state a claim. '[S]uch a claim requires a complaint with enough factual matter (taken as true) to suggest that an agreement was made.'[71]

The Court likened the plaintiffs' claim to a claim alleging parallel pricing, which by itself neither proves an unlawful §1 agreement[72] nor is sufficient to overcome a defendant's motion for summary judgment.[73] Indeed, the amended complaint in *Twombly* was ideal for illustrating the principle that oligopolistic interdependence does not support an inference of agreement in the legal sense. Both before the 1996 deregulatory telecommunications legislation and afterward, the regional telephone companies each occupied in their own regions optimal, jointly profit-maximizing monopoly positions from which none of the companies would have had an economic incentive to deviate, and for the maintenance of which no prohibited agreement would have been necessary. To allege that the defendants had acted against their own self-interest after passage of the Act in

68 550 US 544 (2007).

69 550 US at 553.

70 *Id.* at 561, n. 7.

71 *Id.* at 556.

72 Theatre Enterprises, Inc. v. Paramount Film Dist. Corp., 346 US 537, 540 (1954) ('To be sure, business behavior is admissible circumstantial evidence from which the fact finder may infer agreement . . . [but the Court] . . . has never held that proof of parallel business behavior conclusively establishes agreement or, phrased differently, that such behavior itself constitutes a Sherman Act offense'), citing Interstate Circuit, Inc. v. United States, 306 US 208 (1939), United States v. Masonite Corp. 316 US 265 (1942), United States v. Bausch & Lomb Optical Co., 321 US 707 (1944), American Tobacco Co. v. United States, 328 US 781, and United States v. Paramount Pictures, Inc., 334 US 131 (1948).

73 Matsushita Electric Industrial Co. v. Zenith Radio Corp., 475 US 574, 588 (1986) ('conduct as consistent with permissible competition as with illegal conspiracy does not, standing alone, support an inference of antitrust conspiracy').

circumstances where it appeared they had simply chosen to continue in a position upon which it was difficult or impossible to improve did not supply sufficient grounds to infer that the defendants had entered into an unlawful agreement.

Twombly was decided in light of settled precedent that to survive a defense motion for summary judgment in a parallel pricing case (and, perforce, to make out a *prima facie* case at trial), the plaintiff must present additional evidence beyond mere parallel conduct that tends to contradict tacit, lawful oligopoly conduct in order to create a factual issue on whether there was an agreement. In connection with summary proceedings, ambiguous evidence of parallel conduct must be accompanied by what the courts have recognized as 'plus factors,' evidence '"that tends to exclude the possibility" that the alleged conspirators acted independently.'[74] Although the question in *Twombly* of whether the pleaded allegations of parallel conduct in the amended complaint were sufficient to state a §1 claim was decided against this background, the Court did not look to the plus factor paradigm to address what it framed as a separate issue here. Instead, it looked to the general requirements of Rule 8(a)(2), which calls for 'a short and plain statement of the claim showing that the pleader is entitled to relief.' Following a pattern seen in several recent decisions, the Court proceeded from first principles, modified the applicable standard, and then applied the modified standard to decide the case before it.

The plus factor paradigm in any case would have been inadequate for the Court's purposes of articulating pleading standards for §1 driven by the evidentiary requirements for proving unlawful collusion. The plus factor approach treats all evidentiary factors more or less equally.[75] The Court's *Twombly* analysis, by contrast, distinguishes between four categories of evidence of agreement: i) direct evidence of the agreement itself, ii) unambiguous circumstantial evidence of an agreement, iii) ambiguous evidence of an agreement, and, iv) 'labels and conclusions' and formulaic recitations of the elements of a claim.

The *Twombly* Court held that 'a plaintiff's obligation to provide the "grounds" of his "entitle[ment] to relief," requires more than labels and conclusions, and a formulaic recitation of a cause of action's elements will not do.'[76] Under the 'Rule 8 entitlement requirement'[77] a complaint requires '[f]actual allegations . . . enough to raise a right to

---

74 *Id.* quoting Monsanto Co. v. Spray-Rite Serv. Corp., 465 US 752, 764 (1984).

75 *See* William E. Kovacic, 'The identification and proof of horizontal agreements under the antitrust laws,' 38 *Antitrust Bull.* 5, 35 (Spring, 1993) ('. . . [C]ourts rarely attempt to rank plus factors according to their probative value or to specify the minimum critical mass of plus factors that must be established to sustain an inference that the observed market behavior resulted from concerted conduct rather than from "consciously parallel" choices.').

76 550 US at 555 (citation omitted, alteration in original).

77 The Court cited Dura Pharmaceuticals, Inc. v. Broudo, 544 US 336 (2005) for the 'Rule 8 entitlement requirement.' *Dura* involved securities fraud litigation in which the plaintiffs' alleged injury was having paid an inflated price for shares compared to what the price would have been in the absence of the fraud. The Supreme Court held that the purchase of shares, the market price of which fluctuates for a variety of reasons, does not cause injury, so the complaint lacked the required allegation of 'loss causation.' Reversing the Ninth Circuit, the Court held that a complaint lacking the necessary elements of a cause of action is insufficient under Rule 8, because it fails to give adequate notice of the grounds for the plaintiffs' entitlement to relief.

Table 9.1 Summary of Twombly standard

Nature of the Allegation	Type of Inference Required	Applicable Standard
1. Direct evidence of agreement	No inference	Plausible
2. Communications and other unambiguous circumstantial evidence of agreement	Ordinary inference from circumstantial evidence	Plausibly suggestive
3. Parallel conduct and other ambiguous circumstantial evidence of agreement	Inference from economic data or market behavior	Plausibly suggestive when placed in context
4. Labels and conclusions	No inference warranted	Not creditable

relief above the speculative level,'[78] and 'something more . . . than . . . a statement of facts that merely creates a suspicion [of] a legally cognizable right of action.'[79] The 'threshold requirement [is] that the "plain statement" possess enough heft to "sho[w] that the pleader is entitled to relief."'[80]

Thus, the Court explained that the Rule 8 entitlement requirement requires allegations to be weighed in terms of plausibility, suggestiveness and discoverability. Suggestiveness calls for allegations that cross the 'boundary . . . between the factually neutral and the factually suggestive . . .' to enter 'the realm of plausible liability.'[81] Plausibility demands that grounds for entitlement be alleged with 'enough facts to state a claim to relief that is plausible on its face.'[82] And the discoverability component hinges entitlement to relief on a 'reasonable expectation that discovery will reveal relevant evidence.'[83]

With respect to allegations of conspiracy under §1, the *Twombly* standard requires plausible direct evidence of agreement, circumstantial evidence 'plausibly suggesting' agreement,[84] or parallel conduct 'placed in a context that raises a suggestion of a preceding agreement.'[85] 'A blanket assertion of entitlement to relief' and 'labels and conclusions' are not entitled to credit as well-pleaded facts. This flexible standard is summarized in Table 9.1.[86]

The most frequent forms of direct evidence of agreement in private §1 claims are guilty pleas in criminal prosecutions and the admissions recited in deferred prosecution agreements. Unambiguous circumstantial evidence is indirect evidence, such as evidence of secret communications or clandestine meetings of the conspirators or of documents that appear to further a common scheme or purpose, which is probative of agreement and also

78 550 US at 555.
79 *Id.*
80 *Id.* at 557 (citation omitted, second alteration in original).
81 550 US at 557 n. 5. The word 'plausible' appears fifteen times in the opinion as a noun, adverb, and adjective, excluding quoted instances.
82 *Id.* at 570.
83 *Id.* at 556.
84 550 US at 557.
85 *Id.*
86 The table is a heuristic construct intended to summarize the author's analysis of the decision.

tends to exclude the hypothesis of non-cooperation, justifying an inference of agreement. By contrast, evidence of parallel conduct or other economic data may be ambiguous on the issue of agreement, that is, as consistent with agreement as it is with oligopolistic interdependence.[87] In singling out this category of evidence for special treatment, the *Twombly* decision serves as the vehicle for the incorporation into antitrust of the principle that economic evidence of this kind often requires interpretation and factual context to show that it rejects the hypothesis of a Nash non-cooperative equilibrium before an inference of agreement is justified. Standing apart from a sufficiently suggestive context, such evidence is what the *Twombly* court labeled 'factually neutral' on the issue of agreement. The flexible plausibility standard, therefore, accommodates the practical distinction between allegations of non-economic, circumstantial evidence of agreement and economic evidence of a market outcome probative of agreement only if inconsistent with non-cooperation. Finally, allegations that are conclusions and labels do not constitute grounds for relief.

Under this standard, the *Twombly* plaintiffs' allegations that the defendants engaged in a 'contract, combination or conspiracy' and 'agreed not to compete with one another' were merely legal conclusions resting on the prior allegations or, in terms of the foregoing taxonomy, category 4 allegations not entitled to the presumption of truth.[88] 'The nub of the complaint,' the Court observed, 'is the [defendants'] parallel behavior.'[89] But, applying the standard for category 3 to those allegations, the *Twombly* Court concluded that the complaint had not 'nudged [the] claims across the line from conceivable to plausible' by pleading a sufficiently suggestive context.

The alleged parallel conduct lacked a suggestive context even though the plaintiffs had alleged a widely recognized plus factor, that the defendants' conduct was contrary to their individual economic self-interests. Had the alleged plus factor been instead category 2 circumstantial evidence of agreement, the parallel conduct would have been more suggestive and plausible grounds for relief likely would have been stated. But, plaintiffs apparently knew of no category 2 evidence. The Court's implicit conclusion was that the complaint did not allege facts that were inconsistent with non-cooperative equilibrium in the US telephone market, despite the alleged plus factor. Indeed, the defendants' *ex ante* occupancy of allocated monopolies fails to suggest that refraining from competition was necessarily against their individual economic self interests. Under the circumstances, the Court deemed plaintiffs' assertion in this regard as conclusory and not entitled to the presumption of truth, placing it in category 4.

The Court cited three factual scenarios that might provide plausibly suggestive context for a claim based on parallel conduct. The first is 'parallel behavior that would probably not result from chance, coincidence, independent responses to common stimuli, or mere interdependence unaided by an advance understanding among the parties.'[90] The

---

[87] *See In re*: High Fructose Corn Syrup Antitrust Litigation, 295 F.3d 651, 655 (2002) ('The evidence upon which a plaintiff will rely will usually be . . . of two types – economic evidence suggesting that the defendants were not in fact competing, and noneconomic evidence suggesting that they were not competing because they had agreed not to compete.')

[88] 550 US at 565.

[89] *Id.* at 566.

[90] 550 US at 557, n. 4 quoting 6 P. Areeda & H. Hovenkamp, Antitrust Law ¶1425, at 167–185 (2d ed.2003).

second is 'conduct [that] indicates the sort of restricted freedom of action and sense of obligation that one generally associates with agreement.'[91] Finally, 'complex and historically unprecedented changes in pricing structure made at the very same time by multiple competitors, and made for no other discernible reason'[92] would also provide a suitable context. These allegations supporting a plausible inference of conspiracy are likely to supplant plus factors as the focus of §1 claims based on circumstantial evidence for the simple reason that what must be alleged also must be proven.

The *Twombly* decision adds significant precision to the analysis of proof of agreement in circumstantial §1 cases and, as such, is an important antitrust precedent. But, the decision is also an important civil procedure precedent, in which the Court articulated a more granular pleading standard based on the character of the evidence being described. For complaints alleging direct evidence or unambiguous circumstantial evidence that posseses a reasonable hope of being discovered (i.e. category 1 and 2 allegations) the existing pleading standard remains largely unaffected. But, in complaints describing ambiguous circumstantial evidence and stating conclusory assertions of liability, that is, allegations in categories 3 and 4, grounds for entitlement to relief are unlikely to be stated unless the ambiguous evidence can be situated in a suggestive factual context.

It bears mention that, in spite of the Court's claim to the contrary, a pleading standard that differentiates conclusions and allegations of indeterminate evidence from allegations of standard direct and circumstantial evidence does not follow directly from the Court's precedent or the general standards of pleading. For half a century, the requirements of Rule 8(a)(2) have described a 'notice pleading' standard based on 'the accepted rule [of *Conley v. Gibson*] that a complaint should not be dismissed for failure to state a claim unless it appears beyond doubt that the plaintiff can prove no set of facts in support of his claim which would entitle him to relief.'[93] By singling out for special treatment indeterminate and factually neutral circumstantial allegations, the *Twombly* standard is inconsistent with this part of the long-standing *Conley* rule. Repudiating this part of *Conley*, the Court declared that the 'no set of facts' language 'ha[d] earned its retirement,'[94] and observed that the language 'ha[d] been questioned, criticized, and explained away long enough,' and '[wa]s best forgotten as an incomplete, negative gloss on an accepted pleading standard. . . .'[95]

In *Erickson v. Pardus*,[96] decided two weeks after *Twombly*, however, the Court was quick to reaffirm the undisturbed portion of *Conley* and its continued fidelity to the

---

91 *Id.* quoting Blechman, 'Conscious Parallelism, Signalling and Facilitating Devices: The Problem of Tacit Collusion Under the Antitrust Laws', 24 *N. Y. L. S. L. Rev.* 881, 899 (1979).

92 *Id.* quoting Brief for Respondent (Twombly) at 37.

93 *Conley v. Gibson*, 355 US 41, 45–46 (1957). Bills have been introduced in the House and Senate to repeal *Twombly* and restore the *Conley* 'no set of facts' standard. *See, e.g.*, Notice Pleading Restoration Act of 2009, S. 1504, 111th Cong. (1st Sess. 2009) ('A bill to provide that Federal courts shall not dismiss complaints under rule 12(b)(6) or (e) of the Federal Rules of Civil Procedure, except under the standards set forth by the Supreme Court of the United States in Conley v. Gibson, 355 US 41 (1957)').

94 *Id.*

95 550 US at 563.

96 551 US 89, 127 S.Ct. 2197 (2007).

concept of notice pleading. Quoting from *Twombly*, which in turn quoted from *Conley*, the Court's Per Curiam order reiterated that a pleading need only '. . . give the defendant fair notice of what . . . the claim is and the grounds upon which it rests.' A more direct declaration of fidelity to the part of the *Conley* notice pleading standard that survived the Court's repudiation of the neighboring 'no set of facts' formulation is difficult to imagine. Thus, rather than signaling a retreat from the essential standard of notice pleading, *Twombly* more profitably may be conceived as applying the notice pleading standard with greater rigor to the 'short and plain statement . . . showing that the plaintiff is entitled to relief' called for by Rule 8(a)(2). It does so using a plausibility standard with two effects. A substantive effect through the Rule 8 entitlement requirement calls for allegations that show a cognizable narrative of 'loss causation' connecting a wrongful act by a defendant with a remediable injury to the plaintiff. A procedural effect is exerted through evidentiary standards that no longer tolerate complaints that describe facts merely consistent with a claim or allege more factually neutral evidence or conclusions of liability, requiring instead that a pleading allege suggestive and discoverable grounds for the plaintiff's entitlement to relief. The Court took up the subject of civil pleading standards again in *Ashcroft v. Iqbal*,[97] which confirmed that *Twombly*, as an 'interpretation and application of Rule 8,' 'expounded the pleading standard for "all civil actions."'[98] The *Iqbal* Court offered the following guidance for implementing the *Twombly* standard:

> Determining whether a complaint states a plausible claim for relief will . . . be a context-specific task that requires the reviewing court to draw on its judicial experience and common sense. . . . [A] court considering a motion to dismiss can choose to begin by identifying pleadings that, because they are no more than conclusions, are not entitled to the assumption of truth. While legal conclusions can provide the framework of a complaint, they must be supported by factual allegations. When there are well-pleaded factual allegations, a court should assume their veracity and then determine whether they plausibly give rise to an entitlement to relief.

Iqbal involved a civil claim against US government officials for prisoner abuse and discrimination which alleged that the Attorney General and FBI Director personally 'knew of, condoned, and willfully and maliciously agreed to subject [the plaintiff]' to harsh conditions of confinement 'as a matter of policy, solely on account of [his] religion, race, and/or national origin and for no legitimate penological interest.'[99] The Court held that '[u]nder *Twombly*'s construction of Rule 8,' these allegations 'are conclusory and not entitled to be assumed true.'[100] As to the remaining allegations describing the conduct of the officials inflicting the discrimination, while arguably consistent with an intent of the two named defendants to discriminate, the Court concluded that the plaintiff needed 'to

---

[97] 556 US ____, 129 S.Ct. 1937 (2009). The Court had already expanded the *Twombly* analysis to §2 of the Sherman Act, *see* Pacific Bell Telephone Co. v LinkLine Comm'ns, Inc., 556 US ____, 129 S.Ct. 1109, 1123 (2009) ('[i]t is for the District Court on remand to consider whether the amended complaint states a claim [for predatory pricing] upon which relief may be granted in light of the new pleading standard we articulated in *Twombly*').

[98] 129 S.Ct. at 1953 quoting Rule 1.

[99] 129 S.Ct. at 1951.

[100] *Id.*

allege more by way of factual content to "nudg[e]" his claim of purposeful discrimination "across the line from conceivable to plausible."'[101]

The *Twombly* plausibility standard suggests that Rule 12(b)(6) motions to dismiss claims based on circumstantial grounds for relief should identify and discredit conclusory allegations and then test whether the remaining allegations describe sufficiently suggestive facts to state grounds for relief. Facts that are equally as consistent with an entitlement to relief as not, such as parallel conduct, state grounds for relief only if pleaded in a sufficiently suggestive factual context.[102]

iv. Dismissal for lack of standing The final Rule 12(b)(6) pre-answer motion discussed in this section seeks dismissal on the grounds that the plaintiffs do not have 'antitrust standing' to bring their claim. Section 4 of the Clayton Act provides that 'any person who shall be injured in his business or property by reason of anything forbidden in the antitrust laws may sue therefor.'[103] The dual purpose of this provision is to deprive violators 'of the fruits of their illegality and to compensate victims of antitrust violations for their injuries.'[104] However, courts have never read §4 to grant a private treble damage suit to every person to have incurred an economic loss as the result of an antitrust violation, nor does it 'encompass every harm that can be attributed directly or indirectly to the consequences of an antitrust violation.'[105] A plaintiff may satisfy the constitutional requirement of injury in fact yet not necessarily be a proper party to bring a private antitrust action. 'Harm to the antitrust plaintiff is sufficient to satisfy the constitutional standing requirement of injury in fact, but the court must make a further determination whether the plaintiff is a proper party to bring a private antitrust action.'[106] The party invoking federal jurisdiction bears the burden of establishing standing.[107]

b. Rule 12(b)(7) pre-answer motion to dismiss for failure to join a required party
Rule 19 covers certain circumstances in which a non-party to the litigation may be necessary and indispensable to the proper adjudication of the controversy. Rule 19(a)(1)(A) addresses a person in whose 'absence, the court cannot accord complete relief among existing parties,' and Rule 19(a)(1)(B) protects unrepresented interests in the subject of the action where adjudication would i) 'as a practical matter impair or impede the person's ability to protect the interest,' or ii) leave the party 'subject to a substantial risk of incurring double, multiple, or otherwise inconsistent obligations because of the interest.' The absence of a required party is typically raised by a Rule 12(b)(7) motion to dismiss

---

101 *Id.* at 1952 quoting *Twombly*, 550 US at 570 (alteration in original).

102 *Twombly* and *Iqbal* have already been cited in thousands of reported cases, including opinions issued by the 1st, 2nd, 3rd, 6th, 7th, 9th and Federal Circuit Courts of Appeal.

103 15 U.S.C. §15.

104 Pfizer Inc. v. Gov't. of India, 434 US 308, 314 (1978) (internal quotation marks and citations omitted).

105 Associated General Contractors of California, Inc. v. California State Council of Carpenters, 459 US 519, 529 (1983).

106 *Id.* at 535, n. 31.

107 For further discussion of antitrust standing, see Chapter 6 of this *Handbook*.

for failure to join a party under Rule 19, but may also be raised in any responsive pleading. Although an objection that a required party has not been joined may be properly denied for lack of timeliness if it is raised too late in the proceedings, it is not among the Rule 12(b) defenses that is waived if not raised in a Rule 12(b) pre-answer motion (if one is filed) or in the responsive pleading (if a Rule 12 motion is not filed). The burden of persuasion lies with the party seeking dismissal to demonstrate that the non-party is a required party.

The Rule sets out a two-part analysis. First, the court will determine whether the person is essential to the litigation. If so, and joinder of the party is feasible, the court must issue an order joining the party. If the person is required but for some reason cannot be joined, the court must then use the factors outlined in Rule 19(b)(1)–(4) to 'determine whether, in equity and good conscience, the action should proceed among the existing parties or should be dismissed.' The application of Rule 19 is highly fact specific, and courts may examine both legal and factual elements of the court's ability to accord complete relief or the impairment of a non-party's interest in the litigation.

c. Rule 12 motions objecting to personal jurisdiction, venue and service of process

The second category of procedural defenses are the three kinds of issues raised by pre-answer motions under Rules 12(b)(2)–(5), objections to personal jurisdiction, venue and service of process. These defenses may be waived if not raised in a timely manner, or may be deemed waived by implication, if the defendant's conduct is inconsistent with the objection. These defenses must be raised in a Rule 12 motion if one is filed or in the responsive pleading if one is not.

i. Dismissal for lack of personal jurisdiction Individual parties may be dismissed from a lawsuit if the exercise of the court's jurisdiction over the 'person' of the defendant does not meet the due process standards of the Fifth and Fourteenth Amendments of the US Constitution. However, when a case is dismissed for lack of personal jurisdiction, the plaintiff is not precluded from refiling the lawsuit in a forum where personal jurisdiction over the defendant lies. The practical consequence of the exercise of personal jurisdiction over a defendant is to require the defendant to travel to the court to defend the action. For most civil actions the limitations on the exercise of personal jurisdiction by state courts are guided by the same considerations of due process, so Rule 4(k) equates the territorial limits of effective service of process in the federal court with the limits of personal jurisdiction of the courts of the state in which the federal court sits, with a special provision for Rule 19 parties, third parties, and interpleaded parties, which may be served anywhere within one hundred miles of the federal court, irrespective of any limitation on the state courts. The Rule also allows for personal jurisdiction over certain parties that have sufficient contacts with the US as a whole.[108]

In the case of corporations, private antitrust suits present an exception to the general rules of personal jurisdiction by virtue of §12 of the Clayton Act, 15 U.S.C. §22, which permits private antitrust defendants to be sued and served in any judicial district 'where it may be found or transacts business.' The appellate courts are split on the extent to

---

[108] Rule 4(k)(2).

which federal 'nationwide service of process' statutes obviate considerations of due process, with some courts holding that the plaintiffs' choice of forum must still be fair and reasonable even where Congress has authorized nationwide personal jurisdiction.[109] Service of process in non-US jurisdictions ordinarily requires compliance with international treaties or service of process in accordance with the customs of the non-US jurisdiction.

Objections to personal jurisdiction may be waived if not raised in a timely manner, that is, in a Rule 12(b)(2) motion to dismiss for lack of personal jurisdiction (if a Rule 12(b) motion is filed) or in the responsive pleading. The federal appellate courts are split as to whether a defendant contesting personal jurisdiction who simultaneously pleads a counterclaim is deemed to have waived objection to personal jurisdiction. The burden of persuasion lies with the party asserting that the court has jurisdiction. There is no required order for the court's determination as between an objection to subject matter jurisdiction and an objection to personal jurisdiction.[110]

The three kinds of jurisdiction over 'persons or things' are: i) personal, or *in personam*, jurisdiction, ii) attachment, or quasi *in rem*, jurisdiction, and iii) jurisdiction over an object or land, or *in rem* jurisdiction. At least one form of personal jurisdiction must be established over each defendant in the lawsuit. Private antitrust litigation ordinarily requires *in personam* jurisdiction over the defendant. If no form of jurisdiction has been acquired, the court will typically dismiss the action.

The due process analysis considers the contacts of the defendant with the forum state and the quality of the notice to the defendant. The most common means of satisfying the due process requirement are:

- The defendant's consent to personal jurisdiction;
- Service of process on a defendant found within the state; and
- Service of process on a defendant outside the state where the defendant has sufficient contacts with the forum state.

In general, parties to a contract may consent by agreement to personal jurisdiction in a specified forum. Parties that waive objection to personal jurisdiction because they fail to timely object may also be deemed to have consented. A defendant that objects to personal jurisdiction consents to be bound by the court's determination of whether personal jurisdiction exists.[111]

Because the Rules encourage waiver of service of process, they encourage defendants to consent to personal jurisdiction implicitly. Where a defendant submits a written waiver of service of process and, therewith, waives objections to personal jurisdiction, the time to respond to the complaint will be enlarged from 20 to 60 days.[112]

A defendant found within the state may be in transit and need not necessarily reside in

---

[109] *See, e.g.*, Peay v. BellSouth Medical Assistance Plan, 205 F.3d 1206, 1210 (10th Cir. 2000) (nationwide service of process proper where defendants 'have adequate contacts [within] the United States as a whole').

[110] Ruhrgas AG v. Marathon Oil Co., 526 US 574 (1999).

[111] Insurance Corp. of Ireland v. Compagnie des Bauxites di Guinee, 456 US 694 (1982).

[112] Rule 4(d)(1).

the state or be regularly found there.[113] However, persons induced to travel to the forum state by coercion or fraud will not be subject to personal jurisdiction.[114] Defendants not found within the forum state may nonetheless be subject to the court's personal jurisdiction if the party has sufficient minimum contacts of such a nature so as not to offend 'traditional notions of fair play and substantial justice.'[115]

ii. Motion to dismiss or to transfer for improper venue Venue refers to the appropriate federal district in which to bring a lawsuit, and should be proper even where subject matter and personal jurisdiction are satisfied. The general criteria for federal court venue are set forth in 28 U.S.C. §1391. Section 1391(a) covers cases in which federal jurisdiction is based on diversity of citizenship, and §1391(b) covers non-diversity cases. Both provisions emphasize where the defendant resides, where the events giving rise to the lawsuit took place, and where a defendant is subject to personal jurisdiction.

Defendants have available two types of challenges to improper venue. A Rule 12(b)(3) motion to dismiss for improper venue invokes the common law principle of *forum non conveniens*, as described, for example, in *Gulf Oil Corp. v. Gilbert*.[116] The second kind of challenge to improper venue is a motion to transfer pursuant to the authority granted to the court by 28 U.S.C. §1404, which provides that '[f]or the convenience of parties and witnesses, in the interest of justice, a district court may transfer any civil action to any other district or division where it might have been brought.' However, 28 U.S.C. §1406(a) directs 'a district court in which is filed a case laying venue in the wrong division or district shall dismiss, or if it be in the interest of justice, transfer such case to any district or division. . . .' Finally, §1406(b) provides that '[n]othing . . . shall impair the jurisdiction of a district court of any matter involving a party who does not interpose timely and sufficient objection to the venue.' That is, objections to venue, like objections to personal jurisdiction, may be waived if not timely raised. Courts are split on which party bears the burden of proof when venue is challenged, but the majority view is that the party that has chosen the forum bears the burden for establishing proper venue. The procedure for resolving objections to venue is the same as that for determining issues of personal jurisdiction.[117]

iii. Dismissal for insufficient process or service Rules 12(b)(4) and 12(b)(5) provide related but different procedures for objection to the basis on which the defendant was served with the court's process. Rule 12(b)(4) is used to challenge the sufficiency of the form of the process, rather than the manner or method by which it is served. By contrast,

---

113 Rule 4(e)(2).

114 *See, e.g.*, Amusement Equipment, Inc. v. Mordelt, 779 F.2d 264, 271 (5th Cir. 1985). For further discussion of personal jurisdiction, see Chapter 7 of this *Handbook*.

115 International Shoe Co. v. Washington, 326 US 310 (1945).

116 330 US 501, 503 (1947) ('[T]he defendant, invoking the doctrine of forum non conveniens, claimed that the appropriate place for trial is Virginia where the plaintiff lives and defendant does business, where all events in litigation took place, where most of the witnesses reside, and where both state and federal courts are available to plaintiff and are able to obtain jurisdiction of the defendant.').

117 *See* Gulf Ins. Co. v. Glasbrenner, 417 F.3d 353, 355 (2nd Cir. 2005). For further discussion of venue, see Chapter 7 of this *Handbook*.

Rule 12(b)(5) challenges the mode of delivery or the lack of delivery of the summons and complaint.[118]

Service of process – *i.e.*, the delivery of the summons and complaint – may be deficient if the forms are not properly issued or the summons sets forth the wrong name or is not sealed by the clerk of court. Such defects are challenged by way of a Rule 12(b)(5) motion to quash. Unless a party is able to demonstrate actual prejudice, however, courts will often overlook technical defects on the face of the service of process.

Similarly, the mode of delivery may be deficient if it is made at the wrong place, served on an incompetent, minor, or non-agent of the defendant, or not accomplished within 120 days after commencement of the action. Ordinarily, the appropriate defense is a Rule 12(b)(4) or (5) motion to quash for insufficient process or service, rather than a motion to dismiss. Mislabeling the motion under the wrong provision of the rules will ordinarily not be fatal to the defense. Where there is a reasonable chance that service of process is likely to be able to be accomplished on a second attempt, courts are more likely to quash service of process rather than dismiss the action.

In general, objections to service of process will be waived if not raised in a Rule 12(b) pre-answer motion (if one is filed) or else in the responsive pleading. However, where it is shown that the defendants never received actual notice of the complaint, defendants will be able to raise the failure of service of process in opposition to a motion for default. When service of process is challenged, the plaintiff has the burden to demonstrate proper service and process. An executed return of service constitutes *prima facie* evidence that service was properly effectuated, but it is not conclusive if the defendant can adduce evidence challenging the affidavit or return. A well-founded objection to service of process must be specific, must describe any prejudice suffered by the defendant, and must demonstrate how service of process was defective under the requirement of Rule 4. Dismissal for failure of service of process is usually without prejudice to permit the plaintiff to re-attempt service of process.

3. Summary proceedings

Summary proceedings may be non-evidentiary or evidentiary. A defendant may move for dismissal or judgment through a Rule 12(c) motion for judgment on the pleadings, provided the pleadings are closed and the motion is based on admitted allegations or a facial infirmity in the pleadings.[119] The court may also consider matters of which it may take judicial notice, but without reference to any other extrinsic evidence. Where the pleadings must be supplemented by extrinsic evidence in order to demonstrate the defendant's entitlement to dismissal or judgment, such as through affidavits, discovery materials, and other evidence, the appropriate vehicle is a motion for summary judgment.[120]

Parties may seek through summary proceedings to have the court determine specific

---

118 Davies v. Jobs & Adverts Online, GMBH, 94 F.Supp.2d 719 (E.D. Va. 2000).

119 Rule 12(c). A motion for judgment on the pleadings, provided it is brought 'early enough not to delay trial,' is also the appropriate means by which to raise the defense of failure to state a claim on which relief may be granted, if that defense has not previously been raised in a pre-answer motion or in the pleadings. If a defendant's motion for judgment on the pleadings on these grounds is deemed untimely, the defendant may still raise the defense at trial.

120 Rule 56; *see also* Rule 12(d).

legal or factual issues, adjudicate a particular claim, or dispose of an entire case. Thus, defendants may raise the affirmative defenses generally not permitted to be raised in a Rule 12(b) pre-answer motion, but which must be alleged in a responsive pleading. Cases that survive a defendant's motion for summary judgment frequently stand considerably improved chances of being voluntarily settled.

a. Motion for judgment on the pleadings

A Rule 12(c) motion is appropriate any time after the pleadings are closed, even before discovery, but must be raised 'early enough not to delay trial.' However, a Rule 12(c) motion made before an answer is filed is premature, and will be treated as a Rule 12(b) pre-answer motion. A Rule 12(c) motion for judgment on the pleadings may not be used to raise defenses that have been waived because they were not raised in a pre-answer motion. The motion is well founded if the movant can demonstrate that no material facts remain for determination at trial based on the pleadings or matters of which the court may take judicial notice. If a Rule 12(c) motion is granted, the prevailing party is entitled to a judgment in its favor.

The legal standard applicable to a Rule 12(c) motion mirrors that of a Rule 12(b)(6) motion to dismiss. Thus, well-pleaded allegations of the non-moving party are accepted as true subject to the stipulations regarding conclusory or factually neutral allegations introduced by the Supreme Court in the *Twombly–Iqbal* modification to the federal civil pleading standards discussed above in connection with Rule 12(b) pre-trial motions.

b. Rule 56 Motions for summary judgment or adjudication of issues

A Rule 56 motion for summary judgment may be brought by either the plaintiffs or the defendants. Rule 56(b) provides that '[a] party against whom relief is sought may move at any time, with or without supporting affidavits, for summary judgment on all or part of the claim.' Thus, defending parties may move for summary judgment at any time, although the Circuits are split as to whether a Rule 56 motion filed before an answer is filed tolls the time for filing an answer.[121] Rule 56 establishes the procedure by which a party may request or oppose judgment on one, some, or all of the issues in the case, and it allows for an interlocutory determination on liability even where only the amount of damages would remain as a genuine issue.

i. Standard of review The legal standard for summary judgment is similar to the requirements for judgment as a matter of law under Rule 50 (the equivalent of a motion for a directed verdict), which should be granted 'if, under the governing law, there can be but one reasonable conclusion as to the verdict.'[122] The test is whether a reasonable jury could return a verdict in the non-moving party's favor. While a Rule 50 motion is brought during trial and raises the question of whether the case should be submitted to the jury, a Rule 56 motion for summary judgment is brought before trial, and raises the question of whether there is a need to convene a trial at all.

The court may enter summary judgment when no genuine issue exists as to any

---

[121] *See, e.g.*, Rashidi v. Albright, 818 F.Supp. 1354 (D.Nev. 1993).

[122] Anderson v. Liberty Lobby, Inc., 477 US 242, 250–51 (1986).

material fact, entitling the moving party to judgment as a matter of law. In contrast to a Rule 12(b)(6) pre-answer motion, where the well-pleaded allegations are assumed true and evaluated for their legal sufficiency, the court on summary judgment may consult the pleadings, any affidavits, depositions, interrogatory answers, admissions, Rule 26 disclosures or other material to determine whether a genuine issue exists for trial. The evidence of the non-moving party will be assumed to be true, and doubts about the evidence will be resolved against the moving party. In ruling on a Rule 56 motion for summary judgment, the court's role is never to weigh the evidence, the credibility of witnesses, or to resolve disputed issues of fact, and it should not venture beyond the threshold question of whether a genuine issue exists regarding a material fact that requires a trial.[123]

A 'genuine issue' exists where the evidence submitted could support a finding by a rational factfinder in favor of the non-moving party.[124] A fact is 'material' if, under the applicable substantive law, the fact might affect the outcome of the suit.[125]

ii. Burden of production A moving party may submit a written motion on its own, or supplement it with pleadings, affidavits, discovery materials, transcripts of oral testimony from other proceedings, or matters of which the court may take judicial notice. In general, the evidence must be of a character that is admissible at trial. However, parties frequently rely on affidavits that would not be admissible without the testimony of the affiant, although Rule 56(e)(1) requires that affidavits 'set out facts that would be admissible in evidence.' Similarly, a document referred to in an affidavit must be attached as 'a sworn or certified copy.'

Rule 56(e)(2) provides that a party opposing summary judgment may not rely on allegations or denials in its pleadings, but is required to produce affidavits or other evidence that 'set out specific facts showing a genuine issue for trial.' As the Supreme Court noted in *Matsushita Elec. Indus. Co. v. Zenith Radio, Corp.*,[126] '[w]hen the moving party has carried its burden under Rule 56(c), its opponent must do more than simply show that there is some metaphysical doubt as to the material facts. . . . Where the record taken as a whole could not lead a rational trier of fact to find for the non-moving party, there is no genuine issue for trial. . . .'[127]

iii. Summary judgment in antitrust cases The Court's *Matsushita* decision in 1986 ushered in a period of more frequent use of summary judgment to dispose of antitrust cases. Prior to that, statements such as the Supreme Court's admonition in *Poller v. CBS*[128] that 'summary judgment procedures should be used sparingly in complex antitrust litigation' led to considerable reluctance by courts to dispose of antitrust cases on summary judgment. But, the *Matsushita* Court's observation that 'antitrust law limits the range of ambiguous evidence in a §1 case,' created a special burden for antitrust

---

123 *Id.*
124 Matsushita Elec. Indus. Co. v. Zenith Radio Corp., 475 US 574, 586 (1986).
125 *Anderson*, 477 US at 248.
126 475 US 574, 585 (1986).
127 *Id.*
128 368 US 464, 473 (1962).

plaintiffs seeking to survive summary judgment, particularly in §1 conspiracy cases based on circumstantial evidence. The Court stated:

> To survive a motion for summary judgment or for a directed verdict, a plaintiff seeking damages for violation of §1 must present evidence 'that tends to exclude the possibility' that the alleged conspirators acted independently.[129]

It should be emphasized that *Matsushita's* 'more likely than not' standard sets out a limited special rule for what is necessary in §1 cases in addition to ambiguous evidence of conspiracy, such as parallel conduct, for a plaintiff to survive summary judgment, and it should not be read more broadly so as to impinge on the province of the jury or the preponderance of the evidence standard by which a private antitrust plaintiff ordinarily must prove its case. The *Matsushita* decision has given rise to the practice of producing evidence of 'plus factors' in connection with summary judgment motions, evidence that tends to bolster the inference of conspiracy in light of inconclusive or ambiguous evidence of parallel conduct. As described by one court, a plus factor refers to 'any showing . . . that "tend[s] to exclude the possibility of independent action."'[130]

In cases involving direct evidence of a §1 conspiracy or concerning other kinds of antitrust violations, the effect of *Matsushita* is more limited, but it still imposes a requirement that 'the nonmoving party's inferences be reasonable in order to reach the jury.'[131] *Matsushita* remains particularly relevant when there is a question regarding the plausibility of the plaintiff's economic theory. In addition to establishing plus factors to bolster ambiguous evidence, the *Matsushita* Court observed that where 'the factual context renders [the] claim implausible – if the claim is simply one that makes no economic sense – [plaintiffs] must come forward with more persuasive evidence to support their claim than would otherwise be necessary.'[132] Disclaiming any special burden on antitrust plaintiffs, the Supreme Court in *Kodak* observed that:

> *Matsushita* demands only that the nonmoving party's inferences be reasonable in order to reach the jury, a requirement that was not invented, but merely articulated, in that decision. If the plaintiff's theory is economically senseless, no reasonable jury could find in its favor, and summary judgment should be granted.[133]

Procedurally, the moving party carries its *prima facie* burden on summary judgment by demonstrating an absence of evidence supporting the non-moving party's claims or defenses. The burden of production then shifts to the non-moving party to show that a genuine issue of material fact remains for resolution by the jury.

---

129 *Matsushita*, 475 US at 588.

130 Williamson Oil Co., Inc. v. Philip Morris USA, 346 F.3d 1287, 1301 (11th Cir. 2003) quoting City of Tuscaloosa v. Harcros Chems., Inc., 158 F.3d 548, 571 n. 35 (11th Cir. 1998).

131 Eastman Kodak Co. v. Image Tech. Servs., Inc., 504 US 451, 468 (1992).

132 *Matsushita*, 475 US at 589.

133 *Kodak*, 504 US at 469.

10 Obtaining evidence

Joseph Goldberg and Dan Gustafson[1]

Introduction

This chapter discusses the pretrial discovery process in civil litigation only – either public or private. Also, it focuses only on litigation in the federal court system and not in the state court or administrative agency systems. The omission of discussion of state court civil litigation is explained by two factors. *First*, most states model their rules governing civil litigation after the federal rules, and, therefore, the description of discovery in federal litigation provides substantial insight into the processes in many of the state civil litigation systems. *Second*, under the Class Action Fairness Act,[2] much of the civil antitrust cases previously litigated in state courts are now being filed in or removed to federal court.

Certain attributes of civil antitrust litigation make the pretrial discovery process particularly important. *First*, much activity by firms in the marketplace raising antitrust concerns is covert. For example, cartel behavior is very often hidden by the cartel participants and so civil discovery is an important tool for uncovering that activity.[3] *Second*, antitrust litigation almost invariably calls for the use of expert consultants and expert testimony. For example, expert economists and statisticians often testify in antitrust litigation to prove both liability and damages. This extensive use of experts in civil antitrust litigation implicates the 'expert' provisions of the federal rules governing pretrial discovery. *Third*, civil antitrust litigation often involves claims for very large amounts of damages. The stakes of civil antitrust litigation are increased by the mandatory trebling of any damages awarded by the jury under the Clayton Act.[4] Because of these high stakes, plaintiffs and defendants have an incentive to aggressively use pretrial discovery procedures to uncover relevant information.

Theory of the Federal Rules of Civil Procedure: overview

With a few exceptions, the Federal Rules of Civil Procedure govern the procedure in all civil actions in the United States district courts. The stated purpose of the Federal Rules – the administration of a 'speedy' or 'inexpensive' determination reaching 'justice'[5]

---

[1] Joseph Goldberg is a partner at Freedman Boyd Hollander Goldberg Ives & Duncan. Dan Gustafson is a partner at Gustafson Gluek PLLC. They thank Karla Gluek who contributed significantly to this chapter.

[2] 28 U.S.C. §1332(d) (2005).

[3] Of course, public agencies involved in criminal antitrust enforcement also have powerful tools available for uncovering covert anticompetitive behavior, including the availability of federal and state investigative agencies. In addition, public enforcement agencies have civil discovery tools available (such as civil investigative demands).

[4] 15 U.S.C. §15(a) (1982).

[5] *See* Fed. R. Civ. P. 1.

– is the touchstone for the administration of the discovery process in federal court litigation.

The Federal Rules govern the disclosure of discoverable information by all parties to federal court litigation. The Rules provide for initial disclosures,[6] expert disclosures[7] and pretrial disclosures.[8] These disclosures are required without formal discovery requests by the opposing party.

The Federal Rules also provide for formal discovery requests in which one party specifically requests certain information from another party. These can be in the form of depositions;[9] written interrogatories;[10] production of documents, electronically stored information and tangible things; entering onto land for inspection and other purposes;[11] physical and mental examinations;[12] and requests for admissions.[13] Each of these methods of discovery and the advantages or disadvantages to a plaintiff in a civil litigation is discussed in further detail below.

The discovery rules as they are now implemented in Fed. R. Civ. P. 26–37 provide the parties with the means to find out where the information relevant to the claims and defenses in the litigation is located; narrow the issues that are relevant to the litigation; and obtain that evidence for trial. Again, going back to the purpose of the Federal Rules of Civil Procedure, this reinforces the securing of a 'just, speedy and inexpensive determination.'[14]

Investigation/pre-filing discovery[15]

a. Public enforcement agencies

Both the Antitrust Division of the United States Department of Justice ('DOJ') and the Federal Trade Commission ('FTC') have public enforcement responsibilities. Often, private antitrust litigation follows on public enforcement efforts, and, as mentioned above, occasionally, public enforcement is stimulated by private litigation.[16]

---

6 Fed. R. Civ. P. 26(a)(1).
7 Fed. R. Civ. P. 26(a)(2).
8 Fed. R. Civ. P. 26(a)(3).
9 Fed. R. Civ. P. 27–32.
10 Fed. R. Civ. P. 33.
11 Fed R. Civ. P. 34.
12 Fed. R. Civ P. 35.
13 Fed. R. Civ P. 36.
14 The enactment of Rules 26–37 changed pre-existing discovery practices in federal courts. *See Hickman v. Taylor*, 329 U.S. 495, 500 (1947); *see also* 8 Charles Alan Wright, Arthur R. Miller & Richard L. Marcus, *Federal Practice and Procedure* §2001 (2d ed. 1994) (discussing the purposes and problems of discovery).
15 For further discussion of pre-filing investigation in the context of building a case, see Chapter 5 of this *Handbook*.
16 An example of this latter occurrence is the public enforcement that came from the filing of the *Nasdaq Market-Makers Antitrust Litigation. See In re Nasdaq Market-Makers Antitrust Litig.*, MDL No. 1023 (S.D.N.Y). The private cases were filed first, and the information uncovered in that private litigation resulted in public enforcement that resulted in a substantial restructuring of the Nasdaq organization. *See also* Arthur M. Kaplan, *Antitrust as a Public-Private Partnership: A Case Study of the NASDAQ Litigation*, 52 Case Western Res. L. Rev. 111 (2001). For further

The federal public enforcement agencies are severely restricted in sharing information obtained through their investigative powers with private individuals (not subject to the enforcement action)[17] and experience is consistent with those restrictions. That does not mean, however, that there is not communication between public enforcement agencies and private litigants with both mutually beneficial results and some tensions. For example, frequently private litigants voluntarily provide information to the DOJ or the FTC. Private litigants often gain helpful information from publicly available information resulting from public investigations, through indictments, criminal plea agreements, allocutions and proffers.[18]

b. Amnesty program

The Antitrust Division of the DOJ has a policy of according leniency to corporations reporting their illegal activity at an early stage, if they meet certain conditions. 'Leniency' means not charging such a firm criminally for the activity being reported. The policy also is known as the 'corporate amnesty' policy.

While this program encourages violators of the federal antitrust laws to reveal their illicit behavior, the threat of private antitrust litigation that may follow from any DOJ investigation could decrease incentives for early cooperation. In response to this concern, Congress passed the Antitrust Criminal Penalty Enhancement and Reform Act of 2004 (ACPERA), which provides that corporations that successfully enter the program will only have to pay the actual damages (as opposed to treble damages) plus attorneys' fees, costs, and interest.[19] This limitation applies to antitrust violations litigated under both federal and state law and immunizes program participants from joint and several liability for the acts of their co-conspirators.[20] Significantly, the Act requires the trial court to

---

discussion of the interaction between public and private enforcement, see Chapter 13 of this *Handbook*.

[17] *See e.g.* Fed. R. Crim. P. 6(e) (generally prohibiting the disclosure of grand jury proceedings); 5 U.S.C. §552(b)(7) (exempting from the Freedom of Information Act 'records and information compiled for law enforcement purposes, but only to the extent that the production of such law enforcement records or information (A) could reasonably be expected to interfere with enforcement proceedings; . . . or (D) the identity of a confidential source, including a State, local or foreign agency or authority or any private institution which furnished information on a confidential basis, and, in case of a record or information compiled by criminal law enforcement authority in the course of a criminal investigation or by an agency conducting a lawful national security intelligence investigation, information furnished by a confidential source. . . .').

[18] On the other hand, the public enforcement agencies occasionally will seek to delay discovery in private litigation on their claim that discovery in the private litigation will unduly interfere with the public agency's investigation. This claim will likely put the public agency and the private litigants (or at least the private plaintiffs) at odds with each other. *See In re Flash Memory Antitrust Litigation*, No. C 07-0086, 2007 WL 3119612 (N.D. Cal. Oct. 23, 2007) (recognizing that it is well established that the government may intervene in a civil action for the purpose of limiting discovery when there is a parallel criminal proceeding involving a common question of law or fact).

[19] Antitrust Criminal Penalty Enhancement and Reform Act of 2004, Pub. L. No. 108-237, §213(a)–(b), 118 Stat. 665, 66–67 (2004).

[20] 'Joint and several liability' means that each member of a cartel or co-conspirator to an anticompetitive conspiracy is liable for the injured plaintiff's full damages. Although the injured plaintiff may not recover more than the judgment amount, joint and several liability can place great pressure on each co-conspirator. For example, if there are three co-conspirators and the

certify that corporations seeking to limit damages under the Act also have cooperated with the civil plaintiffs by providing them with documentation and reasonable access to potential witnesses. In addition, the Act does not apply to Attorney General lawsuits.

Under ACPERA, in order to obtain the amnesty benefits, an amnesty defendant must:

(a) have a currently effective antitrust leniency agreement with the DOJ, and
(b) cooperate with private plaintiffs in the prosecution of the civil antitrust lawsuit.[21]

The court in which the civil action proceeds determines whether the amnesty defendant has provided satisfactory cooperation, after considering plaintiffs' submission regarding the cooperation.

In 2008, the DOJ clarified the leniency policy by establishing a list of 'Frequently Asked Questions Regarding the Antitrust Division's Leniency Program and Model Leniency Letters.'[22] The ACPERA was recently extended for one year and future hearings are likely to reveal information about its impact prior to further extensions.[23]

c. Talking with employees/former employees of possible antitrust violators

Prior to filing a lawsuit alleging antitrust violations, a lawyer for a party may wish to obtain more information by communicating with employees or former employees of the company that is suspected of committing antitrust violations. The lawyer may also have learned about the illegal activity from employees or former employees who came forward with the information.

Many states have rules governing lawyers' conduct that limit the contact that attorneys can have with employees or former employees of an adverse party. Violations of those rules may result in disqualification of counsel to participate in the litigation against the company for which the employees or former employees worked and other possible sanctions.[24]

---

plaintiff settles with two of them, each for $100,000, and the jury after trial against the third co-conspirator finds damages in the amount of $500,000, the remaining co-conspirator (because of joint and several liability) is liable for the full amount of the damages, trebled, minus the settlement amounts; or $1,300,000. For further discussion of joint and several liability, see Chapter 11 of this *Handbook*.

21 Antitrust Criminal Penalty Enhancement and Reform Act of 2004, Pub. L. No. 108-237, §213(a)–(b), 118 Stat. 665, 66–67 (2004).

22 US Dep't of Justice, Frequently Asked Questions Regarding the Antitrust Div.'s Leniency Program & Model Leniency Letters, *available at* http://www.usdoj.gov/atr/public/criminal/239583.htm (last visited Aug. 5, 2009).

23 For a discussion of how the leniency program and ACPERA can assist a private plaintiff in deciding whether to bring a case, see Chapter 5 of this *Handbook*; for a discussion of how the leniency program and ACPERA impact the interplay of public and private enforcement generally, see Chapter 13 of this *Handbook*.

24 *See, e.g., In re Potash Antitrust Litig.,* No. 3-93-197, 1993 WL 543013, *16–17 (D. Minn. Dec. 8, 1993); *compare Camden v. Maryland,* 910 F.Supp. 1115 (D. Md. 1996) (disqualifying counsel for ex parte contact with former employee), *with In re EXDS, Inc.,* No. C05-0787, 2005 WL 2043020 (N.D. Cal. Aug. 24, 2005) (denying motion to disqualify counsel).

Rule 4.2 of the ABA Model Rules of Professional Conduct ('Model Rules')[25] reads:

> In representing a client, a lawyer shall not communicate about the subject of the representation with a person the lawyer knows to be represented by another lawyer in the matter, unless the lawyer has the consent of the other lawyer or is authorized to do so by law or a court order.[26]

This Rule and similar rules adopted by individual states raise concern when counsel wants to talk with an employee or former employee of a corporation. Is that employee represented by counsel if the corporation is represented by counsel? Most states look at the employee's role within the corporate structure.

There are various tests that states apply to determine whether Rule 4.2 is violated by communications with an employee. One test is referred to as the 'control group' test in which opposing counsel cannot communicate with employees in the corporation's '"control group" – *i.e.*, the most senior corporate managers – without the corporate attorney's consent.'[27] This view holds that only the employees with the power to control the corporation may properly be equated with the corporation.[28]

A second test was described in official Comment [4] to Rule 4.2 of the ABA Model Rules of Professional Conduct (1995). This test would prohibit communications about the matter in dispute by a lawyer for one party with persons having a managerial responsibility on behalf of the organization and with any person whose act or omission in connection with the matter may be imputed to the organization or whose statement may constitute an admission on the part of the organization.[29] The test often turns on the meaning of 'admission.' Various courts have applied different meanings, causing confusion as to what is permissible and what is not.[30]

In February 2002, the ABA revised Comment [4] (now Comment [7]) to Rule 4.2 to prohibit communications only with:

> [A] constituent of the organization who supervises, directs or regularly consults with the organization's lawyers concerning the matter or has authority to obligate the organization with respect to the matter or whose act or omission in connection with the matter may be imputed to the organization for purposes of civil or criminal liability.[31]

---

25 Since there is no single, federal rule governing this conduct and since the ABA Model Rules are widely adopted by the states, we use these Model Rules as the discussion reference.

26 Model Rules of Prof'l Conduct R. 4.2.

27 *See* Ellen J. Messing & James S. Weliky, *Contacting Employees of an Adverse Corporate Party: A Plaintiff's Attorney's View*, 19 Lab. Law. 353, 354–55 (2004).

28 *Id.*

29 *Id.* at 355–56 (citing Model Rules of Prof'l Conduct R. 4.2 cmt.4 (1995)); *see also* Mich. Rules of Prof'l. Conduct R. 4.2 cmt.

30 Messing & Weliky, *supra* note 27, at 356–57; *compare Orlowski v. Dominick's Finer Foods, Inc.*, 937 F.Supp. 723, 730 (N.D. Ill. 1996) (prohibition should be read narrowly to permit broad access to witnesses), *with In re Air Crash Disaster near Roselawn*, 909 F.Supp. 1116, 1121 (N.D. Ill. 1995) (broad prohibition because 'virtually every employee may conceivably make admissions binding on his or her employer.').

31 Messing & Weliky, *supra* note 27, at 357.

Several states have now adopted the ABA's 2002 changes to the Model Rules and Comments and have either adopted or proposed changes identical to or substantially similar to those in the new Comment [7].[32]

Do these rules, however, apply equally to former employees? The specific language of the rules and comments does not appear to encompass former employees. The 2002 version of Comment [7] to Model Rule 4.2 clearly states that '[c]onsent of the organization's lawyer is not required for communication with a former constituent.'[33] The Comments caution, however, that a lawyer must not try to obtain any privileged communications or information from the former employee.[34]

When deciding whether to communicate with employees or former employees of the opposing party, it is important to remember that whether a court will find the communication permissible is a fact-intensive determination, and the standard varies from state to state.[35] As such it is difficult to generalize about what communications will be allowed and what communications will be prohibited. These concerns arise in almost every antitrust case as these types of cases usually involve pre-filing investigations and often deal with information that is emanating from a former employee of one of the companies in question.

d. Initial expert analysis

Prior to filing a lawsuit, the plaintiff may want to retain an expert to do a preliminary analysis of the marketplace and an initial scope of damages. This expert may or may not ultimately be disclosed as a 'testifying expert' for the plaintiff. Unless the party has definitely determined at the outset that the expert hired to do the initial analysis will not be the testifying expert, the party should treat this expert as a potential witness and remember that materials given to the expert may become discoverable by the other party later in the litigation if the expert consultant is disclosed as a testifying expert or the expert's analyses or opinions become part of the basis for allegations in the complaint.

Prior to filing the lawsuit, an expert in a potential antitrust action can provide useful information as to the relevant marketplace. The expert can analyze the market and determine what products are in the market and what products are not. The expert can analyze how large the marketplace is and the amount of sales that may have been involved in the antitrust activity. The expert can provide an analysis of the behavior of the actual and potential competitors in the marketplace, whether characteristics of the marketplace and the behavior of the firms in the marketplace are consistent or not with the exercise of market power and whether the pricing in the marketplace appears to reflect a competitive market or whether the pricing supports a claim for antitrust violations. The expert

---

32 *Id.* at 358.

33 *Id.* at 363.

34 *Id.*; Model Rules of Prof'l Conduct R. 4.2 cmt.7; *see also Smith v. Kalamazoo Ophthalmology*, 322 F. Supp. 2d 883, 888 (W.D. Mich. 2004) ('A majority of courts that have considered the issue have held that Rule 4.2 does not bar *ex parte* communications with an adversary's former employees who are not themselves represented in the matter.' (citations omitted)).

35 *See, e.g., US v. W.R. Grace,* 401 F. Supp. 2d 1065, 1067 (D. Mont. 2005); *In re Complaint of PMD Enters., Inc.,* 215 F. Supp. 2d 519, 526–27 (D.N.J. 2002) (applying New Jersey's version of Model Rule 4.2); *Camden,* 910 F.Supp. at 1116.

can also analyze the possible overcharge that occurred to the consumer as a result of the anticompetitive conduct and whether that overcharge is likely to be generally spread throughout the potential class.

This type of information would provide the plaintiff's counsel with important information to determine whether the market conditions and competitive activity would support the claims of antitrust violations and what the scope of damage might be in the case. It also may alert the plaintiff and plaintiff's counsel to possible pitfalls or problems in their lawsuit that might deter them from filing the suit or at least provide them with the knowledge of what issues might arise. Given the recent establishment of heightened pleading requirements in federal antitrust cases,[36] plaintiffs may wish to include information derived from any such expert analyses or opinions in support of the allegations in the complaint.

e. FOIA requests/state law equivalent

Also prior to initiating a lawsuit, the plaintiff or plaintiffs' counsel may want to issue Freedom of Information Act requests to federal agencies seeking relevant public information.[37] The Freedom of Information Act[38] ('FOIA' or 'the Act') generally provides that any person has a right, enforceable in court, to obtain access to federal agency records, except to the extent that such records (or portions of them) are protected from public disclosure by one of nine exemptions or by one of three special law enforcement record exclusions.[39]

Obtaining certain records from a governmental agency may be a beneficial investigative tool. For example, if a party wants to assert that a company misused its patent to keep a generic manufacturer off the market in violation of the antitrust laws,[40] it may be useful to see what records were submitted to the Patent Office by the company or the generic manufacturer.

Not all records are accessible. For example, Exemption 4 of the Act protects 'trade secrets and commercial or financial information obtained from a person [that is] privileged or confidential.'[41] This exemption is intended to protect the interests of both the government and submitters of information by allowing submitters to voluntarily provide the government with useful and reliable commercial or financial information with the assurance that the government will protect the information from being released. This exemption may come into play in the example of the FOIA request to the Patent Office.

---

36 *See Bell Atlantic Corp. v. Twombly,* 550 US 544 (2007); *Ashcroft v. Iqbal,* 556 US ___, 129 S. Ct. 1937 (2009). For further discussion of *Twombly* and *Iqbal*, see Chapter 9 of this *Handbook*.

37 Most states have some sort of Freedom of Information Act or Public Records Act that provides a method by which citizens may request access to government records. Again, these are subject to exemptions similar to the Federal FOIA and, therefore, have somewhat limited utility. *See, e.g.,* Minnesota Data Practices Act, Minn. Stat. §13.03; New York State Freedom of Information Law, N.Y. Pub. Off. Law §§84–90 (2008).

38 5 U.S.C. §552 (2000 & Supp. IV 2004).

39 US Dep't of Justice, Guide to the Freedom of Information Act – Introduction, *available at* http://www.usdoj.gov/oip/foia_guide07/introduction.pdf (last visited Aug. 5, 2009).

40 *See, e.g., In re Wellbutrin SR Antitrust Litig.,* Nos. 04-5525, 04-5898 & 05-396, 2006 WL 616292 (E.D. Pa. Mar. 9, 2006).

41 5 U.S.C. §552(b)(4).

The information that a company submits to the Patent Office might be considered 'trade secret' and thereby would be excluded from disclosures made pursuant to a FOIA request.

Another example of a useful FOIA request prior to filing a lawsuit would be a request for documents related to the initiation of any enforcement action against the company that is the subject of the potential antitrust lawsuit. In this case, however, Exemption 7 of FOIA may come into play.

Exemption 7 of FOIA protects from disclosure 'records or information compiled for law enforcement purposes.' There are, however, several exceptions to this exemption.[42]

Written discovery

Fed. R. Civ. P. R. 26 sets forth the parties' duties to disclose and other general provisions governing discovery. Rule 26 describes the requirements of initial disclosures, expert disclosures, pretrial disclosures and the timing for making those disclosures. It also identifies the scope of such discovery. Fed. R. Civ. P. 26(b)(1) sets forth the scope of discovery in civil matters:

> Parties may obtain discovery regarding any non-privileged matter that is relevant to any party's claim or defense – including the existence, description, nature, custody, condition, and location of any documents or other tangible things and the identity and location of persons who know of any discoverable matter.[43]

Rule 26 goes on to note that, 'For good cause, the court may order discovery of any matter relevant to the subject matter involved in the action.'[44] Relevant subject matter includes information that may not be admissible at trial but that may reasonably lead to the discovery of admissible evidence.[45]

a. Rule 26 initial disclosures

Rule 26(a)(1) of the Federal Rules of Civil Procedure requires the parties to make certain initial disclosures unless exempted by Rule 26(a)(1)(B) or otherwise stipulated or ordered by the court. Without waiting for a discovery request, a party must provide to the other parties at a time early in the litigation:

(i) The name and, if known, the address and telephone number of each individual likely to have discoverable information – along with the subjects of that information – that the disclosing party may use to support its claims or defenses, unless the use would be solely for impeachment;

(ii) A copy – or a description by category and location – of all documents, electronically stored information, and tangible things that the disclosing party has in its

42 5 U.S.C. §552(b)(7); *see* US Dep't of Justice, Guide to the Freedom of Information Act – Exemption 7, *available at* http://www.usdoj.gov/oip/foia_guide07/exemption7.pdf (last visited Aug. 5, 2009).

43 Fed. R. Civ. P. 26(b)(1).

44 *Id.*

45 *Id.*

possession, custody, or control and may use to support its claims or defenses, unless the use would be solely for impeachment;

(iii) A computation of each category of damages that the disclosing party is claiming, and that party must make available for inspection and copying, the documents or other evidentiary material, unless privileged or protected from disclosure, on which each computation is based, including materials bearing on the nature and extent of injuries suffered; and

(iv) For inspection and copying as under Rule 34, any insurance agreement under which an insurance business may be liable to satisfy all or part of a possible judgment in the action or to indemnify or reimburse for payments made to satisfy the judgment.[46]

The plaintiff in an antitrust action likely will not have a lot of information to disclose at the time of initial disclosures. Most of the relevant information is going to be in the hands of the defendants. Plaintiffs may be aware of names of company executives who have been indicted or charged with antitrust violations and as such would indicate those individuals under Fed. R. Civ. P. 26(a)(1)(A)(i). Plaintiffs also may be able to identify generally the types of documents that may be relevant, but most of the relevant documents will likely be in the possession of the defendant in antitrust cases. In a price-fixing case, for example, plaintiffs likely will have invoices or other documents that will demonstrate that they purchased the products at issue and may provide some evidence of the prices charged for those products. Again, however, much of that information will be found in defendants' records. Part (iii) of Rule 26(a)(1)(A) asks for a computation of damages. Generally speaking, this information simply is not available at the time of initial disclosures. Computation of damages in antitrust cases often requires a statistical analysis of defendants' records and cannot be computed without those records. As such, plaintiffs usually will respond that damages will be in the form of overcharges paid by the plaintiffs on the products that were the subject of the anticompetitive activity, and detailed computations will be provided pursuant to expert testimony.[47]

Finally, Part (iv) of Rule 26(a)(1)(A) also is not particularly relevant to plaintiffs in an antitrust action. As the plaintiff is seeking damages and is generally not subject to a judgment, there is no insurance relevant to plaintiffs in these cases. Where the defendant has relevant insurance and that requirement is not waived or limited by court order, the policy must be made available for inspection or copying. There is no general rule or custom as to whether or not a corporation will have insurance that would pay for damages that may arise from an antitrust case. It must be determined on a case by case basis by the defendants, who must decide whether their insurance policies would apply to any damages that may be awarded.

The Federal Rules require that the initial disclosures be made within 14 days after the parties' Rule 26(f) conference.[48] The parties may stipulate or the court may order that

46 Fed. R. Civ. P. 26(a)(1)(A)(i)–(iv).

47 For further discussion of calculating plaintiffs' damages, see Chapter 11 of this *Handbook*.

48 Rule 26(f) requires that the parties meet and confer as soon as practicable (but in no event less than 21 days prior to the initial scheduling conference with the court) to discuss the nature of the claims and defenses, the possibility for settlement, the initial disclosures, and the development

initial disclosures be made at some other time. A party may also object during the Rule 26(f) conference that initial disclosures are not appropriate in this action, in which case the party must state the objection in the proposed discovery plan. 'In ruling on the objection, the court must determine what disclosures, if any, are to be made and must set the time for disclosure.'[49] While the Federal Rules do call for these initial disclosures, including in antitrust cases, courts often do not strictly enforce these disclosure requirements in antitrust cases.

The initial disclosures under Rule 26(a)(1)(A) must be 'based on information then reasonably available' to a party.[50] A party is 'not excused from making its disclosures because it has not fully investigated the case or because it challenges the sufficiency of another party's disclosures or because another party has not made its disclosures.'[51] That being said, the information available to an antitrust plaintiff will vary widely depending on the complexity of the issues, the number of defendants, the number and location of witnesses and documents, among other things.

Under Rule 26(e), these initial disclosures must be supplemented or corrected if the party learns that the disclosure is incomplete or incorrect. These corrections or supplementations must be made in a 'timely manner.'[52]

b. Interrogatories

Interrogatories are another method of discovery. These are formal written discovery requests that one party makes to another party seeking written responses, the answers to which are sworn to by the responding party and constitute evidentiary admissions.

When answering interrogatories, a party must answer in writing and the answers must be under oath signed by the party providing the information.[53] It is not sufficient for the attorney to sign the answers to interrogatories. Interrogatories must be answered by individuals that have the knowledge or information to provide the answer. Interrogatories that are directed to companies or other entities should be responded to by an officer, agent or employee who has the requisite knowledge.[54] A party may object to interrogatories but must state the objection with specificity and must include all grounds to support the objection.[55] Typical objections include assertions that the interrogatory is vague or ambiguous, overly broad, unduly burdensome, seeks privileged information and is outside the scope of Rule 26.

Fed. R. Civ. P. 33 addresses Interrogatories specifically. As set forth in that Rule, a party is limited to serving no more than 25 written interrogatories on any other party

---

of a discovery plan. The discovery plan should include the parties' views and proposals on the timing of initial disclosures (if different from what is provided for by the rules), what discovery may be needed and when it should be completed, whether discovery should be conducted in phases, electronically stored discovery, issues relating to the privilege or work product protections, among other things.

49 Fed. R. Civ. P. 26(a)(1)(C).
50 Fed. R. Civ. P. 26(a)(1)(E).
51 *Id.*
52 Fed. R. Civ. P. 26(e).
53 Fed. R. Civ. P. 33(b)(5).
54 Fed. R. Civ. P. 33(b)(1)(B).
55 Fed. R. Civ. P. 33(b)(4).

unless the parties agree to a different number or a court order permits additional interrogatories.[56] This limitation includes subparts, so a party may not attempt to circumvent this limitation through formal labeling. [57] Rule 33 and Rule 26 thus work together to encourage parties to be selective in determining both the amount and scope of information they seek through interrogatories. For this reason, interrogatories are best used to obtain specific, objective information. For example, interrogatories asking for names, titles, dates or the identification of specific documents can be useful. Interrogatories that are not as specific or narrowly focused can elicit vague answers that are usually qualified with so many objections that they become almost meaningless.

A party may ask 'contention' interrogatories, in which it seeks all facts that the opposite party possesses that support or refute any claims or defenses in the litigation. The party may follow that up by asking for all documents that support the opposite party's response to that 'contention' interrogatory. For example, a plaintiff may ask the defendants to 'identify all facts that support the defendant's affirmative defense.' The plaintiff may also ask for all documents that support its affirmative defense. These interrogatories may be effective in forcing a party to identify what the real claims at issue are and what evidence it has to support those claims. Often courts will set a deadline by which both parties will have to respond to 'contention' discovery. This deadline is frequently extended beyond the 30-day deadline set forth in Fed. R. Civ. P. 33(b)(2) to give the parties until further along in the discovery process (or even until the end of discovery) to respond.

Under Fed. R. Civ. P. 33(d), a party may opt to produce business records in lieu of responding to interrogatories under certain conditions.[58] The production of documents or the identification of documents instead of a response has advantages and disadvantages. On one hand, identifying or producing documents in response to an interrogatory puts the burden on the requestor to uncover the answer within those documents. This is not to say that a responding party can hide the answer among a mass of documents, most of which are not responsive to the interrogatory. Most courts in these circumstances will require the responder to identify the responsive documents.[59] On the other hand, merely identifying the documents or producing the documents rather than responding does not allow the responding party to craft the answer in the light most favorable to itself.

c. Request for production of documents

Another means of obtaining discovery is through requests for the production of documents. Fed. R. Civ. P. 34 permits a party to serve upon another party a request to produce (or permit for inspection, copying, testing or a sample) any designated documents or

---

56 Fed. R. Civ. P. 33(a)(1).

57 *Id.*

58 Fed. R. Civ. P. 33(d).

59 *Graske v. Auto-Owners Ins. Co.*, 647 F. Supp. 2d 1105 (D. Neb. Aug. 13 2009) (recognizing that 'if a party responds to interrogatories pursuant to Rule 33(d), it must specify the documents from which the responses to the interrogatories can be derived in sufficient detail to enable the interrogating party to locate the documents as readily as the responding party could.') (citing Fed. R. Civ. P. 33(d)); *see also In re Sulfuric Acid Antitrust Litig.*, 231 F.R.D. 320, 326 (N.D. Ill. 2005) (finding that it is not sufficient for a responding party to simply direct the interrogating party to a mass of business records).

electronically-stored information or any designated tangible thing.[60] In collusion cases, defendants' internal documents, obtained through discovery, are often a primary source of evidence of defendants' collusive behavior. Documents or electronically-stored information include writings, drawings, graphs, charts, photographs, sound recordings, images and other data or data compilations.[61] In antitrust litigation, document requests are a primary means of pretrial discovery and are typically served during the first wave of discovery. It is through such document requests that an antitrust plaintiff may obtain a defendant's transactional data that often is important in estimating damages. Again, however, the scope of documents or other information that may be sought by a party is limited by Rule 26.[62]

Rule 34 is limited to parties and itself does not require a non-party to respond to a request for production of documents. Rule 45, however, allows for such discovery from a non-party and will be discussed in more detail below.

There is no limit set forth in the Federal Rules on the number of document requests that a party can serve (although some courts place limits on the extent of discovery under Rule 34 in their local court rules), and a party responding to the request must either state that inspection will be permitted or a copy produced or else object to the request. If a party objects to one part of the request it must still produce documents in response to the non-objectionable portions of the request.[63]

Rule 34 requires only the production of those documents or information that is in the responding party's possession, custody or control.[64] The question of what is meant by 'possession, custody or control' has been addressed by several courts in various situations. Possession and custody includes both actual and constructive possession and custody. Control includes situations where the responding party has the legal right to obtain the documents, regardless of whether the document is actually in the party's possession.[65] For example, a party can be required to produce a document that is not in its direct possession but is in the possession of its legal counsel, its insurance company or its other agents.[66]

In an antitrust case, the plaintiff is often suing large corporations that have many organizational divisions or entities. The question of whether the party has possession, custody or control will often arise in the context of whether the duty to search and produce responsive documents extends beyond the accused organizational entity to related entities. If the facts suggest that one of the corporate entities essentially controls

---

60 Fed. R. Civ. P. 34(a)(1)(A) & (B). As noted, Rule 34 also permits requests for items other than documents or electronically-stored information. This is not as likely to come into play in an antitrust case as it would in, for example, a patent case, where the design of the product is at issue. Rule 34 also allows for the inspection, among other things, of land or other property. Fed. R. Civ. P. 34(a)(2). This is also an unlikely request in an antitrust case.

61 *Id.*

62 Rule 26 was amended in 2006 to provide additional guidance on electronically stored discovery, which will be discussed in more detail below.

63 Fed. R. Civ. P. 34(b)(2)(B) & (C).

64 Fed. R. Civ. P. 34(a)(1).

65 8A Wright, Miller & Marcus, *supra* note 14, §2210.

66 *Id.*

the other, the court will likely find that the party is in 'control' of the documents held at the related corporation for purposes of Rule 34.[67]

Similarly, the question in antitrust cases will often arise with regard to documents of a former employee of a party corporation. Courts have generally found that corporations do not have control over former employees but may require the corporations to make inquiries of former employees.[68]

A party responding to document requests may object to all or part of any request for production of documents. Common objections to document requests include an objection that the documents are not in the party's possession, custody or control or are no longer in existence; that the request is unduly burdensome, overly broad or vague; and that the documents requested are privileged. Again, these objections must specify which part of the request is objectionable. The responding party must reply within 30 days after service of the request and must either produce the documents or identify a time and place for inspection and/or copying of the documents.[69] A responding party must also produce the documents in their native format or must organize and label them to correspond to the categories in the request.[70] The production of electronically-stored documents is discussed below.

d. Electronic discovery

Electronic discovery or e-discovery is an area that has been much discussed and written about. As originally adopted, Rule 34 addressed discovery of 'documents' and 'things.'[71] In 1970, the Rule was amended to include discovery of 'data compilations.'[72] This amendment anticipated the rise in the use of computerized technology and included in Rule 34 a means for discovery of computerized information. In 2006, Rule 34 was again amended to further take into account the issues raised by electronically-stored information, including stored electronic data and stored electronic documents.[73] The 2006 amendments make clear that discovery of electronically stored information 'stands on equal footing with discovery of paper documents.'[74] The Comments state, '[t]he change clarifies that Rule 34 applies to information that is fixed in a tangible form and to information that is stored in a medium from which it can be retrieved and examined.'[75] As such, requests for production of documents under Rule 34 should be understood to encompass, and the response should include, electronically-stored information unless otherwise specified.

Rule 26(f) was amended to direct the parties to meet and confer prior to a Rule 26(f) conference to discuss any issues about the disclosure or discovery of electronically stored information, including the form or forms in which it should be produced.[76]

---

67 *Id.*
68 *Id.*
69 Fed. R. Civ. P. 34(b)(2)(A).
70 Fed. R. Civ. P. 34(b)(2)(E)(i).
71 Fed. R. Civ. P. 34 cmt. 2006 Amendment.
72 Fed. R. Civ. P. 34 cmt. 1970 Amendment.
73 *Id.*
74 *Id.*
75 *Id.*
76 Fed. R. Civ. P. 26(f)(3)(C); *See also* Fed. R. Civ. P. 26(f) cmt. 2006 Amendment.

In reality, and as the Comment states, the issues to be addressed during the Rule 26(f) conferences relating to e-discovery depend on the nature and extent of the contemplated discovery and the parties' information systems.[77] The Comment encourages parties to discuss those issues prior to the conference and become familiar with the systems at issue so the parties can develop a discovery plan that takes into account the capabilities of the various systems.[78] Such pre-conference meet-and-confers among the parties are especially helpful in antitrust cases where the parties tend to include large firms and where there will be extensive electronic discovery. Typically, issues discussed at these meet-and-confers include, among other things: (i) the nature, extent and identification of information systems and databases; (ii) the format of production of electronic documents, such as 'native', 'tiff', 'pdf', etc.; (iii) the extent of 'metadata'[79] produced with electronic documents and whether the documents will be 'searchable'; (iv) search parameters, including identification of document custodians and locations and electronic search terms; and (v) the medium of production (i.e., electronic files, disks, hard-drives, etc.). Often, it is helpful for the parties to have individuals who are familiar with the various computer systems utilized by the parties or who possess particular IT expertise involved in these early discussions.[80] Often, these discussions result in agreed-on protocols governing this facet of discovery. At least one state, Maryland, has adopted a suggested Protocol for Discovery of Electronically Stored Information.[81]

In addition to meet-and-confers among the parties as to electronic document production (e.g. emails), it is also helpful to discuss production of the relevant parties' electronic transaction data. Often, in antitrust cases, these data sets are large and can be complex. Almost invariably, they are referred to the parties' economic or statistical experts for analysis. Typically, parties discuss and seek to reach agreement on issues with respect to transaction data, such as: (i) the existence of 'data dictionaries' or other documents that would assist in identifying what information is in particular fields in the data; (ii) the existence of 'cross-walks' or other documents that would assist in identifying products, customers and locations; and (iii) the availability of party IT personnel for informal consultation on data questions. Sometimes, such agreements are incorporated into an agreed protocol.

Rule 26(b)(2) was amended to address the specific limitations on e-discovery. Rule 26(b)(2)(B) states:

---

[77] Fed. R. Civ. P. 26(f) cmt. 2006 Amendment.

[78] *Id.*

[79] Metadata is structured information about an electronic file that is embedded in the file but not normally visible when viewing a printed or on screen rendition of the document, and which describes the characteristics, origins, usage and validity of the electronic file. *See* The Sedona Conf. Working Group on Elec. Doc. Retention & Prod., *The Sedona Glossary: for E-Discovery & Digital Information Mgmt.*, 33 (Conor Crowley & Sherry Harris eds., 2d ed. 2007), *available at* http://www.thesedonaconference.org/dltForm?did=TSCGlossary_12_07.pdf.

[80] In 2006, Rule 16(b) was also amended to alert the court to the possible need to address the handling of discovery of electronically stored information at the pretrial conference. Fed. R. Civ. P. 16(b)(3)(B)(iii).

[81] *See* D. Md., Suggested Protocol for Discovery of Electronically Stored Information ('ESI'), *available at* http://www.mdd.uscourts.gov/news/news/ESIProtocol.pdf (last visited Aug. 5, 2009).

> A party need not provide discovery of electronically stored information from sources that the party identifies as not reasonably accessible because of undue burden or cost. On motion to compel discovery or for a protective order, the party from whom discovery is sought must show that the information is not reasonably accessible because of undue burden or cost. If that showing is made, the court may nonetheless order discovery from such sources if the requesting party shows good cause, considering the limitations of Rule 26(b)(2)(C).[82]

As the Comments make clear, the determination of whether the information is reasonably accessible or not is made on a case by case basis. 'It is not possible to define in a rule the different types of technological features that may affect the burdens and costs of accessing electronically stored information.'[83] The Comments also make clear that '[a] party's identification of sources of electronically stored information as not reasonably accessible does not relieve the party of its common-law or statutory duties to preserve evidence.'[84] Again, it is beneficial for the parties to discuss whether a party believes the information sought will be reasonably accessible at the outset of the case so those issues can either be agreed upon by the parties or brought before the court.

Finally, Rule 37(e) was amended in 2006 to protect a party from sanctions for failing to provide electronically stored information 'lost as a result of the routine, good faith operation of an electronic information system.'[85]

The Comments to the Rule confirm that 'The good faith requirement . . . means that a party is not permitted to exploit the routine operation of an information system to thwart discovery obligations by allowing that operation to continue in order to destroy specific stored information that it is required to preserve.'[86]

In other words, if, for example, a system has an automatic purge of information after 30 days, a party must take steps to disengage that feature if failure to do so would result in the loss of otherwise discoverable information. If a party is able to do so but does not do so, it may be found to have not acted in good faith and thus sanctions may be appropriate. Again, what type of automatic purging of information or destruction of information occurs in a party's computer systems should be discussed early in the litigation so it can be addressed by agreement either of the parties or the court.

e. Requests for admissions

Fed. R. Civ. P. 36 governs requests for admissions. Rule 36 allows a party to serve on another party a written request to admit the truth of any matter that is otherwise discoverable under Rule 26(b)(1) relating to: '(a) facts, the application of law to facts or opinions about either; and (b) the genuineness of any described documents.'[87]

Requests for admissions are not as commonly used as interrogatories, depositions or requests for production of documents but can help narrow the disputed issues for a hearing or trial. Rule 36 requires that if a party cannot admit the information set forth in the request, that the party must 'specifically deny it or state in detail why the answering party

---

82 Fed. R. Civ. P. 26(b)(2)(B).
83 Fed. R. Civ. P. 26(b)(2) cmt. 2006 Amendment.
84 *Id.*
85 Fed. R. Civ. P. 37(e).
86 Fed. R. Civ. P. 37(f) cmt. 2006 Amendment.
87 Fed. R. Civ. P. 36(a)(1).

cannot truthfully admit or deny it.'[88] Unlike interrogatories, which allow the responding party to craft the answer, requests to admit are closed-ended questions that are crafted by the requesting party. An admission in response to a request is conclusive and that issue need not be proven any further at the hearing or trial.[89] As such, requests for admission carefully propounded and properly responded to can be a powerful tool for a litigant. Often, requests for admission are employed to establish foundation facts for important documents anticipated to be used at trial, thereby avoiding burdening the trial with detailed and repetitive evidentiary foundation testimony. The federal rules do not limit the number of requests to admit although local rules or court orders may do so.

A party that does not respond to a request for admission is deemed to have admitted the request.[90] However, apart from admitting or denying, a responding party may object to the request for admission based on Rule 26(b) relevancy grounds; defective drafting grounds, such as overly broad, vague, or compound, among others; or based on a legal privilege. A party may also respond that he or she lacks the information or knowledge to admit or deny the request. The responding party, however, has to state that it made a reasonable inquiry and that the information it knows is insufficient to enable it to admit or deny.[91] A responding party may not object solely on the ground that the request presents a genuine issue for trial.[92]

f. Third party discovery

A party may also seek formal discovery from a non-party, or third party, to the litigation in the form of depositions or document requests. This can only be accomplished through the service of a subpoena on a third party, which is governed by Fed. R. Civ. P. 45. A subpoena can command the person to whom it is directed to attend and testify at a deposition (or trial); to produce designated documents, electronically stored information or tangible things in that person's possession, custody or control; or to permit the inspection of premises.[93] A party may not serve interrogatories or requests for admission on a third party.

A subpoena for attendance at a hearing or a trial must be issued from the court for the district where the hearing or trial will be held. A subpoena for attendance at a deposition must be issued from the court for the district where the deposition is going to take place. Finally, a subpoena for production or inspection of documents or tangible things must be issued from the court for the district where the production or inspection is to be made, unless the request is included on a subpoena to command attendance at a deposition, trial or hearing.[94]

A subpoena must also be accompanied by one day of witness fees and mileage to cover the cost of traveling to the hearing or trial.[95]

---

88 Fed. R. Civ. P. 36(a)(4).
89 Fed. R. Civ. P. 36(b).
90 Fed. R. Civ. P. 36(a)(3); 8A Wright, Miller & Marcus, *supra* note 14, §2259.
91 Fed. R. Civ. P. 36(a)(4).
92 Fed. R. Civ. P. 36(a)(5).
93 Fed. R. Civ. P. 45(a)(1)(A)(iii).
94 Fed. R. Civ. P. 45(a)(2).
95 Fed. R. Civ. P. 45(b)(1).

The court that issued the subpoena must quash or modify the subpoena if: (1) the subpoena fails to allow a reasonable time to comply; (2) the subpoena requires a person who is not a party nor a party's officer to travel more than 100 miles from where the target of the subpoena resides, is employed, or regularly transacts business in person; (3) the subpoena requires disclosure of privileged or other protected matter, if no exception or waiver applies; or (4) the subpoena subjects a person to undue burden.[96]

As with production under Rule 34, a person responding to a subpoena requesting documents must produce the documents as they are kept in the ordinary course of business or must label them to correspond to the categories in the demand.[97] Similarly if the subpoena does not specify the form of production for electronic documents, the producing party must produce the information in the form in which it is ordinarily maintained or in a reasonably usable form.[98] Again, as under Rule 34, a person need not provide discovery of electronically-stored information from sources that the person identifies as not reasonably accessible because of undue burden or cost.[99]

g. Supplements to discovery

A party has a continuing obligation to supplement discovery responses in a timely manner as the litigation progresses.[100] This duty to supplement applies if the party learns that in some material respect the disclosure or response is incomplete or incorrect and if additional or corrective information has not otherwise been made known to the other party during the discovery process.[101] Under Rule 26(e)(2), expert disclosures must be supplemented no later than the pretrial disclosures called for under Rule 26(a)(3) – at least 30 days before trial, unless otherwise agreed to or ordered by the court.

Depositions[102]

Fed. R. Civ. P. 30 governs depositions by sworn oral examination.[103] Depositions by oral examination are a useful and often utilized discovery tool.[104] They allow a party to

---

96 Fed. R. Civ. P. 45(c)(3)(A).

97 Fed. R. Civ. P. 45(d)(1)(A).

98 Fed. R. Civ. P. 45(d)(1)(B).

99 Fed. R. Civ. P. 45(d)(1)(D).

100 Fed. R. Civ. P. 26(e).

101 Fed. R. Civ. P. 26(e).

102 Another method of formal discovery is depositions upon written questions. *See* Fed. R. Civ. P. 31. The difficulty with written depositions is that counsel cannot ask follow-up questions based on answers given as all of the questions have to be submitted ahead of time. Similarly, it is difficult to anticipate what areas would be fruitful for cross examination without knowing how the witness is going to answer the direct examination questions. For these reasons and given the efficacy of other means of discovery, depositions on written questions are rarely used.

103 *See* Fed. R. Civ. P. 30. Fed. R. Civ. P. 28 identifies persons before whom a deposition may be taken, distinguishing between depositions taken in the United States and outside the United States. Within the United States, a deposition must be taken before an officer authorized to administer oaths and take testimony either by federal law or by the law in the jurisdiction the deposition is taking place or a person appointed by the court where the action is pending. The term 'officer' as defined in Rule 28, applies to Rules 30, 31 and 32. *See* Fed. R. Civ. P. 28(a)(2).

104 A party seeking to depose an individual or corporation must provide written notice to the deponent and all other parties to the litigation. The notice must state the time and place of the

question individuals (and corporations, as will be discussed below) to determine what information witnesses know and do not know. Depositions are a way to obtain information in a more spontaneous setting, in that the witnesses must answer the questions posed in the deposition without consulting with their counsel or counsel for the opposing party. They also allow the examiner to ask follow-up questions in response to any given answer. These are discovery techniques that are not available through interrogatories or requests for admissions. The examining party also preserves testimony of witnesses that can later be used to impeach a party if they provide inconsistent testimony at trial or in future depositions. Depositions are the best way to discover what the strengths and weaknesses of each party's case are likely to be.

The scope of depositions, like all discovery in civil cases, is limited by Rule 26(b). As such, deposition questions are limited to any non-privileged matter that is relevant to any party's claim or defense and, for good cause shown, the court may order discovery of any matter relevant to the subject matter involved in the action.[105] A party may take the deposition of any person, including a party, without leave of court, except under certain limited situations. Leave of court is required if (i) the deposition would exceed the deposition limit established by the Rules or by agreement of the parties or order of the court, (ii) the deponent has already been deposed or (iii) the deposition is sought before the parties have conferred pursuant to Rule 26(d).[106] A party must also seek leave of court to depose a person confined in prison.[107]

Because each deponent ordinarily can only be deposed once in his or her individual capacity, when to take a deposition of an individual is a strategy decision. Sometimes an early deposition may be useful to help facilitate crafting more useful interrogatories or document requests as the witness can help solidify the facts. Early depositions may also provide more accurate testimony as they will occur closer in time to the events at issue. Also, depending on the answers to the deposition questions, they may help facilitate an early settlement. Often, however, in antitrust cases, the plaintiff will want to obtain documents requested in discovery requests from the defendants prior to taking depositions. This will allow the plaintiff to better identify the key employees or decision makers that may have participated in the antitrust conduct. In cartel cases it will also

---

deposition and, if known, the deponent's name and address. Fed. R. Civ. P. 30(b)(1). If a party wants a deponent to bring documents or other tangible items to a deposition, a subpoena duces tecum must be served on the deponent and a list of the documents or other items sought must be attached or, if the deponent is a party, the notice must include a Request for Production of Documents, pursuant to Rule 34. Fed. R. Civ. P. 30(b)(2). The party issuing the notice of deposition may specify the location of the deposition (if the deposition is not of a non-party, and the location is not limited by the requirement of Rule 45, set out above). If, however, the deponent believes that the location of the deposition is unreasonable, the deponent may seek a protective order from the court pursuant to Rule 26(c). Fed. R. Civ. P. 26(c)(2). Often, however, the issue of location of depositions will be discussed early in the litigation and may even be part of the Rule 26(f) conference and the parties will reach agreement on where the deposition will occur. For example, the parties may agree that the depositions will occur where the deponent is located or they may agree that the depositions will occur where counsel is located.

105 Fed. R. Civ. P. 26(b)(1).

106 Fed. R. Civ. P. 30(a)(1) & (2).

107 Fed. R. Civ. P. 30(a)(2)(B).

assist the plaintiff in better understanding the methods used to implement any collusive agreements and thereby assist in framing the information that should be sought through further written discovery or by deposition. Depositions also allow plaintiffs to obtain, prior to trial, testimony by defendants' witnesses on key documents that will be used at trial, as well as testimony to be used at trial by witnesses who cannot be compelled to appear at trial. They also may help identify any weaknesses in the plaintiff's clams or the defendant's defenses. This allows the parties then to gather further evidentiary support to shore up their cases.

Rule 30 limits the number of depositions that any party can take to ten unless the parties agree otherwise and the court so orders.[108] Often in complex antitrust cases, the parties enter into agreements that expand the number of depositions available to each side. Any limitation on the number of depositions may counsel in favor of waiting until after some written discovery is complete so as to not 'waste' depositions on individuals that do not have relevant information. Rule 30(d)(1) limits a single deposition to one day of seven hours unless otherwise stipulated to or ordered by the Court. However, the Court can allow additional time if needed to fairly examine the witness or if the deposition has been impeded or delayed.[109]

Rule 30(b)(6) depositions

A party may also notice a deposition of an entity, such as a corporation. Obviously, a corporation itself cannot appear at a deposition so the question becomes what individual should appear at the deposition on behalf of a corporation. Rule 30(b)(6) addresses depositions of corporations, partnerships, associations, governmental agencies, or other entities. The rule provides that the notice naming one of these entities as the deponent must also describe with reasonable particularity the matters that are going to be the subject of the deposition questions.[110] The named entity must then designate one or more officers, directors or managing agents, or other persons who consent to testify on its behalf. It may also set out the matters on which each person designated will testify.[111] The rule requires that the person designated must testify about information known or reasonably available to the organization; and such testimony is binding on the corporation.[112]

These Rule 30(b)(6) deponents therefore must be prepared to testify about the subject matters for which they are designated. There is no limit on the number of individuals a corporation can designate to testify on the subject matters identified in the notice. However, regardless of the number of individuals designated, a single Rule 30(b)(6) deposition will only count as one deposition for purposes of the deposition limits.[113] However, again, Rule 30(d) limits a single deposition to seven hours.[114] Courts have found that the Comments to Rule 30(b)(6) do not mean that each designated witness can

---

[108] Fed. R. Civ. P. 30(a)(2)(A)(i).

[109] Fed. R. Civ. P. 30(d)(1).

[110] Fed. R. Civ. P. 30(b)(6).

[111] *Id.*

[112] *Id.*

[113] Fed. R. Civ. P. 30 cmt. 1993 Amendments; *see also In re Sulfuric Acid Antitrust Litig.*, No. 03-C-4576, 2005 WL 1994105, at *3 (N.D. Ill. Aug. 19, 2005).

[114] Fed. R. Civ. P. 30(d)(1).

be deposed for seven hours, as this would reward parties that issue very broad Rule 30(b)(6) notices that would require multiple designees.[115]

If, during the course of the deposition, it becomes clear that the designated witness is not knowledgeable about the subject matter for which he or she is designated, the party noticing the deposition may request that the deponent corporation produce a different witness and, if need be, may move to compel the production of a different witness.

The fact that a witness is designated as a Rule 30(b)(6) witness for a corporation does not preclude the parties from taking that person's deposition a second time in his or her individual capacity.[116] This situation may arise when an individual is designated for a single topic listed in the Rule 30(b)(6) deposition notice, but the plaintiff also wants to depose that individual as to his or her knowledge of other areas of the litigation as well. During the Rule 30(b)(6) deposition, the plaintiff is not permitted to ask questions beyond the subject matters for which that individual is designated under the Rule 30(b)(6) notice. Therefore, that individual must also be served with an individual deposition notice if plaintiff wishes to pursue different subject matters. Often, counsel will try to work out a process in which the individual deposition of the person takes place at the same time or immediately following the Rule 30(b)(6) deposition so the individual does not have to appear more than once.

Trial depositions

There are two types of depositions that may be used in trial. If counsel knows that a person is going to be unavailable to testify at trial, the party may take a trial deposition. Although the rules for depositions still apply to a trial deposition, the strategy is different. Unlike a deposition taken during the course of discovery, where the purpose is fact-finding, a trial deposition should mirror what would occur if that witness appeared live at the trial. As such, generally, neither counsel would typically ask questions where the answers were unknown, as they would not want to be surprised at trial. This type of deposition is less about fact-finding and more about eliciting facts that help support the claims or defenses for the party calling the witness. If the witness is hostile, the examiner will ask leading questions, as would occur at trial.

Rule 32 of the Federal Rules of Civil Procedure sets out the parameters of using a deposition in a court proceeding. The rules provide that a deposition may be used against a party when the party was present or represented at the deposition or had reasonable notice of the deposition.[117] Rule 32(a)(2)–(8) discusses the ways in which a deposition may be used at trial. For example, a deposition may be used at a hearing or trial to contradict or impeach the testimony given by a deponent as a witness.[118] A deposition may also be used at a hearing or trial if the witness is unavailable to appear at trial.[119]

---

115 *See In re Rembrandt Techs.,* No. 09-CV-00691, 2009 WL 1258761, at *14 (D. Colo. May 4, 2009) (limiting the Rule 30(b)(6) deposition topics and expanding the seven hour limitation for the Rule 30(b)(6) deposition to ten hours regardless of the number of designees required to testify on those topics).

116 *See* Fed. R. Civ. P. 30(b)(6).

117 Fed. R. Civ. P. 32(a)(1)–(8).

118 Fed. R. Civ. P. 32(a)(2).

119 Fed. R. Civ. P. 32(a)(4) explains when a witness may be considered unavailable, including

If the witness is unavailable, either a trial deposition may be used or a previously taken 'discovery' deposition may be used. If a party offers only parts of a deposition, the adverse party may offer other parts of the deposition of that same witness.[120]

Any objection that may be made to testimony if the witness was appearing live at the trial may also be made to testimony being offered through the deposition.[121]

Expert discovery

Parties often hire experts to assist them in the preparation of their cases or in the presentation of testimony at trial. There are different types of experts and the federal rules acknowledge these differences. One type of expert is a testifying expert. This expert will actually provide a report that includes the expert's opinions that will be served upon all other parties in the litigation.

In antitrust cases, experts in the fields of economics, statistics and econometrics are often employed, as well as experts in the industries or markets involved in the litigation. Often these experts are found in litigation consulting firms[122] or from academic ranks or from the industries involved. Since experts do not testify as to percipient facts but rather to their expert opinions, they may be – and invariably are – paid for their testimony. Since expert opinions in antitrust cases often involve complex computer modeling employing large volumes of data, these expert fees – both for the testifying experts and the people who assist them – can amount to sizeable sums, often in the millions of dollars.

Parties also hire non-testifying consultants to assist in either the preparation of the case or the initial investigation of the case (as discussed above).[123] Non-testifying consultants do not provide written reports or depositions, and their opinions and work product are not discoverable unless used by a testifying expert. In antitrust cases, the parties will often utilize testifying economic and statistical experts to opine on liability, causation and damages issues, the industry and relevant markets. These experts may utilize non-testifying consultants and assistants to help in preparing their analyses.

Sometimes a party will have employees that would be considered 'experts' in their field. Rule 702 of the Federal Rules of Evidence ('FRE') defines what is considered 'expert testimony.' FRE 702 states that:

> If scientific, technical or other specialized knowledge will assist the trier of fact to understand the evidence or to determine a fact in issue, a witness qualified as an expert by knowledge, skill,

---

because the witness is deceased, otherwise unable to attend for enumerated reasons, or, on motion and notice, in the interests of justice in exceptional circumstances.

[120] Fed. R. Civ. P. 32(a)(6).

[121] Fed. R. Civ. P. 32(b).

[122] There are large and small litigation consulting firms. The larger firms (such as LECG, CRA and Compass/Lexecon) tend to be defense oriented and the smaller firms (such as Nathan Associates, InfoTech, or ERS Group) often consult with plaintiffs or defendants. Most of the litigation consulting firms have arrangements with college and university professors to work with the consulting firms on assignments as testifying experts.

[123] For further discussion of the use of experts during the initial investigation of the case, see Chapter 5 of this *Handbook*.

> experience, training, or education, may testify thereto in the form of an opinion or otherwise, if (1) the testimony is based upon sufficient facts or data, (2) the testimony is the product of reliable principles and methods, and (3) the witness has applied the principles and methods reliably to the facts of the case.[124]

FRE 701 states:

> If the witness is not testifying as an expert, the witness' testimony in the form of opinions or inferences is limited to those opinions or inferences which are (a) rationally based on the perception of the witness, (b) helpful to a clear understanding of the witness' testimony or the determination of a fact in issue, and (c) not based on scientific, technical, or other specialized knowledge within the scope of Rule 702.[125]

Therefore, FRE 701 and 702 should guide the determination of whether an employee's opinions fall within the definition of 'expert testimony' that must be disclosed.

Fed. R. Civ. P. 26(a)(2) sets out the requirements for disclosure of expert testimony and Fed. R. Civ. P. 26(b)(4) discusses the discovery of information from either testifying or non-testifying experts.

Rule 26(a)(2) requires a party to disclose to the other parties the identity of any witnesses that may be used at trial to present evidence under Federal Rules of Evidence 702 (Testimony by Experts), 703 (Bases of Opinion Testimony by Experts) or 705 (Disclosure of Facts or Data Underlying Expert Opinion).[126] Rule 26 requires that the disclosure be made through a written report that is prepared and signed by the expert, if the expert is going to provide expert testimony in the litigation. The written report must contain a complete statement of all opinions the witness will testify to and the basis and reasons for those opinions. The report must also contain the data or other information considered by the expert in forming those opinions, any exhibits that the expert will use to summarize or support the opinions, the expert's qualifications (including a list of all publications authored in the previous ten years), a list of all other cases in which the expert has testified as an expert at trial or by deposition in the past four years and a statement of the compensation to be paid for the study and testimony in the case.[127]

Rule 26 requires that these disclosures be made at the times and in the sequence that the court orders, or absent an order or stipulation, at least 90 days before the date set for trial or, if the evidence is solely to contradict or rebut evidence on the same subject matter identified by another party, then within 30 days after the other party's disclosure.[128] The timing and sequence of disclosing expert reports, pursuant to Fed. R. Civ. P. 26(a)(2), are usually set out in the court's scheduling order. Often, the party with the burden of proof on any issue will be required to submit its expert disclosures first, usually shortly after the close of discovery, with response expert reports from the opposing side due sometime thereafter (for example, 30–60 days after the initial reports), and sometimes the courts

---

124 Fed. R. Evid. 702.
125 Fed. R. Evid. 701.
126 Fed. R. Civ. P. 26(a)(2)(A); *see also* Fed. R. Evid. 702, 703 & 705.
127 Fed. R. Civ. P. 26(a)(2)(B).
128 Fed. R. Civ. P. 26(a)(2)(C).

will allow reply expert reports (for example, 30 days or so after the rebuttal reports). Parties usually discuss the timing and sequence of the expert disclosures and reports during their initial meet-and-confer prior to the Rule 26 conference and either will agree to a schedule or submit competing proposals to the court.

Rule 26(b)(4) addresses depositions of expert witnesses.[129] Rule 26(b)(4) permits the deposition of an expert that has been identified as one whose opinions may be presented at trial, but it requires that the deposition occur only after the report has been provided.[130]

A party may not discover facts known or opinions held by a consultant who has been retained by a party but who is not identified as an expert who will testify at trial. Rule 35(b) may provide the only limited exception to this limitation on discovery, allowing discovery from non-testifying consultants on a showing of exceptional circumstances under which the party cannot obtain facts or opinions on the same subject matter by other means.[131]

The scheduling for deposing testifying experts is often set forth in the court's scheduling order and usually follows along the same schedule as the expert reports. Often, the schedule will provide for the deposition of experts following submission of their expert reports but prior to either the rebuttal or reply report. So, for example, the party with the burden of proof will submit the expert report and that expert will be deposed prior to the opposing party's submission of the rebuttal report. Once the expert rebuttal report is submitted the rebuttal expert will be deposed prior to the submission of the reply report. Sometimes courts will defer all depositions until all reports are submitted.

Finally, parties have a duty to supplement expert reports or testimony if appropriate.[132] Therefore, if the expert learns new information or new facts that he or she considers in forming his or her opinions, then the party must disclose that new information or new facts. If that information changes the expert's opinion, those new opinions must be disclosed. Rule 26(e)(2) sets a time limit on making such additions or changes, requiring that new information be disclosed by the time the party's pretrial disclosures are due under Rule 26(a)(3), no later than 30 days prior to trial, unless otherwise agreed or ordered by the court.[133]

Daubert

In *Daubert v. Merrell Dow Pharmaceuticals, Inc.*,[134] the United States Supreme Court replaced the pre-existing and restrictive 'general acceptance' test of admissibility of expert testimony under *Frye v. United States*.[135] While still recognizing that the judge

---

129 Fed. R. Civ. P. 26(b)(4).

130 *Id.*

131 Fed. R. Civ. P. 26(b)(4)(B).

132 Fed. R. Civ. P. 26(e)(2) ('For an expert whose report must be disclosed under Rule 26(a)(2)(B), the party's duty to supplement extends both to information included in the report and to information given during the expert's deposition.').

133 *Id.*; *see also* Fed. R. Civ. P. 26(a)(3)(B).

134 509 US 579 (1993).

135 293 F. 1013 (D.C. Cir. 1923). The *Frye* test limited admissibility of expert opinions to those that were accorded widespread acceptance within the relevant discipline.

plays a 'gatekeeper' role in ensuring that only expert opinions and testimony that will be of assistance to the jury will be admitted, the Supreme Court in *Daubert* liberalized the standards of admissibility.[136] *Daubert* established a three-part test: (1) is the expert qualified to testify competently on the matters at hand? (2) is the methodology employed by the expert sufficiently reliable? (3) will the testimony assist the trier of fact to determine a fact in issue?[137]

Since expert testimony plays a significant role in antitrust cases and since antitrust plaintiffs often rely on expert testimony to establish essential elements of their claims (such as damages and causation and sometimes liability), *Daubert* challenges to exclude expert testimony have quickly become a staple of antitrust litigation practice. While the Supreme Court clearly indicated that it was 'liberalizing' the rules of admissibility of expert opinions and the Advisory Committee to the Federal Rules of Evidence has stated explicitly that 'rejection of expert testimony is the exception rather than the rule,'[138] there is some reason to believe that the increasing frequency of *Daubert* challenges is having an adverse impact on the successful prosecution of private plaintiffs' civil antitrust actions.[139]

The trial judge's 'gatekeeper' role under *Daubert* is not intended to replace the adversary system.[140] The focus is on the expert's methodology and not on the conclusions of the experts.[141] Therefore, so long as the expert's methodology is reliable, the court need not resolve disputes between the plaintiff's and the defendant's experts as to conclusions. That is for the jury to decide.

Often, an antitrust plaintiff will employ expert testimony to prove damages.[142] Where an expert's opinion on damages is challenged under *Daubert*, the courts need to be especially wary of excluding the expert opinions. The United States Supreme Court has recognized a lenient standard for the admission of evidence estimating antitrust damages because the 'wrongdoer is not entitled to complain that [damages] cannot be measured with the exactness and precision that would be possible if the case, which he alone is

---

136 *See Daubert*, 509 US at 588. *See also Estate of Bud Hill v. Conagra Poultry Co.*, 1997 WL 538887 at * 3 (D. Ga. 1997) (*Daubert* 'relaxed the standard for admitting scientific evidence.').

137 509 US at 589.

138 Fed. R. Evid. 702, Notes of Advisory Committee on 2000 Amendments.

139 *See* James Langenfeld and Chris Alexander, *Daubert* Challenges of Antitrust Experts, *available at* http://www.antitrustinstitute.org/node/11022. But, many courts have rejected *Daubert* challenges in antitrust cases. *See e.g. In re Ready-Mixed Concrete Antitrust Litig.*, 261 F.R.D. 154, 164–65 (S.D. Ind. Sept. 9, 2009); *In re Scrap Metal Antitrust Litig.,* No. 1:02 CV 0844, 2006 WL 2850453 at *16 (N.D. Ohio, Sept. 30, 2006). *See also In re High Pressure Laminates,* No. 00 MDL 1368, 2006 WL 931692, at *1 (S.D.N.Y. April 7, 2006); *In re High Fructose Corn Syrup Antitrust Litig.*, 295 F.3d 652, 660–61 (7th Cir. 2002); *In re Linerboard Antitrust Litig.*, 497 F. Supp. 2d 666 (E.D. Pa. 2007); *In re Mercedez-Benz Antitrust Litig.,* No. 99-4311, 2006 WL 2129100, at *7–9 (D.N.J. July 26, 2006); *In re Bulk Popcorn Antitrust Litig.*, 792 F.Supp. 650, 652 (D. Minn. 1992).

140 *United States v. 14.38 Acres of Land*, 80 F.3d 1074, 1078 (5th Cir. 1998).

141 *Daubert,* 509 US at 595.

142 For further discussion of plaintiffs' proof of damages, see Chapter 11 of this *Handbook*.

responsible for making, were otherwise.'[143] This more lenient standard of proof may make a *Daubert* challenge as to expert opinions on damages more difficult.[144]

Typically, *Daubert* challenges are brought at the close of expert discovery (which itself is often deferred until after the close of fact discovery). Often, the trial judge will hold an evidentiary hearing to evaluate the expert opinions, although such an evidentiary hearing is not required. Occasionally, *Daubert* challenges are brought as to expert opinions at the class certification stage. Often, these *Daubert* challenges at class certification have been rejected as premature,[145] but because of more recent decisions requiring district courts to resolve more factual controversies at class certification,[146] the courts may be more receptive to considering *Daubert* challenges at this early stage.[147]

Compelling discovery – motion practice

Despite the guidance set forth in the Federal Rules of Civil Procedure, parties often do not agree on what are appropriate discovery requests or discovery responses. The Federal Rules of Civil Procedure set forth a mechanism for addressing these discovery disputes. Initially, however, if the responding party receives a discovery request that it believes to be overly broad or outside the scope of discovery or, alternatively, if the requesting party receives discovery responses that it believes are inadequate, the parties may be able to resolve the disputes without formal motion practice.

The parties should, prior to involving the court through formal motions to compel or motions for protective order, attempt to meet and confer regarding the discovery at issue and see if they can reach a mutually agreeable solution. Indeed, the federal rules

---

143 *Story Parchment v. Pasterson Parchment Paper Co.*, 282 US 555, 562 (1931); *see also Bigelow v. RKO Pictures, Inc.*, 327 US 251, 264 (1946); *Metrix Wareouse, Inc. v. Daimler-Benz AG*, 825 F.2d 1033, 1043 (4th Cir. 1987).

144 *See In re Polypropylene Carpet Antitrust Litig.*, 996 F.Supp. 18, 29 (1997).

145 *See, e.g., Bert v. AK Steel Corp.*, No. 1:02-CV-00467, 2006 WL 1071872, at *7 (S.D. Ohio Apr. 24, 2006) ('In ruling on Plaintiffs' class certification motion, the Court need not determine whether or not Dr. Bradley's opinion can survive a *Daubert* challenge'); *Nichols v. Smithkline Beecham Corp.*, NO. CIV.A. 00-6622, 2003 WL 302352 (E.D. Pa. Jan. 29, 2003) ('At [the class certification] stage of the proceeding the Court does not consider whether an expert witness's opinion would be admissible pursuant to *Daubert*. . . .'); *In re Monosodium Glutamate Antitrust Litig.*, 205 F.R.D. 229, 234–35 (D. Minn. 2001) ('Even assuming that there are problems with Dr. Beyer's methodology, however, Defendants' attack on that methodology is premature. The *Daubert* inquiry requires a more searching analysis than is appropriate at this preliminary stage') (citations omitted).

146 *In re Hydrogen Peroxide Antitrust Litig.*, 552 F.3d 305, 209 (3d Cir. 2008) (finding that class certification is proper only if the court is satisfied, after 'a rigorous analysis' of the 'factual and legal allegations' that Rule 23 is met) (*citing Gen. Tel. Co. of Sw. v. Falcon*, 457 US 147, 161 (1982); *Newton v. Merrill Lynch, Pierce, Fenner & Smith, Inc.*, 259 F.3d 154, 166 (3d Cir. 2001)); *In re Initial Public Offering Securities Litig.*, 471 F.3d 24, 42 (2d Cir. 2006) (disavowing the suggestion that an expert's testimony may establish a component of a Rule 23 requirement simply by being not fatally flawed. A district judge is to assess all of the relevant evidence admitted at the class certification stage and determine whether each Rule 23 requirement has been met, just as the judge would resolve a dispute about any other threshold prerequisite for continuing a lawsuit).

147 *See In re Fed Ex Ground Package Sys., Inc. Employment Practices Litig.*, NO. 3:05-MD-527RM (MDL-1700), 2007 WL 3027405, at *4 (N.D. Ind. 2007) (noting that a 'more relaxed' Rule 702 standard may be appropriate at class certification stage).

and many local rules require that the parties meet and confer prior to bringing a motion, and if they fail to do so the motion can be denied on that basis alone.[148] At the very least, the parties may be able to narrow the issues of dispute prior to bringing a motion so that neither the parties nor the court will have to expend resources on discovery disputes that may easily be resolved through a meet-and-confer process.

If, however, the parties have attempted to resolve the discovery disputes but are unable to do so, then a party may move for an order compelling the disclosure of discovery requested.[149] Specifically, Rule 37 provides for motions to compel in situations where a party fails to make a disclosure required by Rule 26(a). It also provides that a party seeking discovery may move for an order compelling an answer, designation, production or inspection if (1) the deponent fails to answer a question during a deposition (either oral or written), (2) an entity fails to make a designation under Rule 30(b)(6) or 31(a)(4), (3) a party fails to answer an interrogatory or (4) a party fails to respond that an inspection will be permitted or fails to permit an inspection requested under Rule 34.[150]

If the court grants the motion to compel, the court must, after giving the parties an opportunity to be heard, require the losing party, deponent or attorney whose conduct or advice necessitated the motion to pay the movant's reasonable expenses incurred in making the motion, including attorney's fees.[151] A party will not be awarded these costs if the movant did not in good faith try to obtain the discovery prior to making the motion or if the opposing party's non-disclosure, response or objection was substantially justified or if other circumstances make the award unjust.[152]

If, after the court orders that the discovery be responded to or produced, the party still refuses to provide the information, the court may impose sanctions on that party.[153] Rule 37(b)(2) sets out the various sanctions that a court may impose for failure to comply with an order compelling discovery, including: (1) directing that the matters or facts that were the subject of the order compelling discovery be taken as established for purposes of the litigation; (2) prohibiting the non-compliant party from supporting or opposing designated claims or defenses or from introducing designated matters into evidence; (3) striking pleadings in whole or in part; (4) staying further proceedings until the order is complied with; (5) dismissing the action or proceeding in whole or in part; (6) rendering default judgment against the non-compliant party or (7) treating as contempt of court the failure to comply with the order.[154] These sanctions can be imposed against the parties but can also be imposed against the parties' attorneys.[155]

---

148 Fed. R. Civ. P. 37(a)(1); *see also, e.g.*, D. Minn. LR 37.1; *see also Use Techno Corp. v. Kenko USA, Inc.*, No. 06-02754, 2007 WL 3045996, at *1 (N.D. Cal. Oct. 18, 2007) (denying motion to compel for failure to demonstrate good faith attempt to meet and confer).

149 Fed. R. Civ. P. 37(a)(1).

150 Fed. R. Civ. P. 37(a)(3)(A)–(B).

151 Fed. R. Civ. P. 37(a)(5)(A); *see also* Fed. R. Civ. P. 26(c)(3) (Expenses awarded with regard to motions for protective orders are also governed by Rule 37(a)(5).).

152 Fed. R. Civ. P. 37(a)(5)(A).

153 Fed. R. Civ. P. 37(b).

154 Fed. R. Civ. P. 37(b)(2).

155 Fed. R. Civ. P. 37(b)(2)(C) ('. . . the court must order the disobedient party, the attorney advising that party, or both to pay the reasonable expenses, including attorney's fees, caused by the failure. . . .').

Limits on discovery

a. Protective/confidentiality orders

As indicated throughout this chapter, there are limits on discovery. The Federal Rules limit the scope of discovery as discussed above. The Rules also recognize that discovery can be unduly burdensome and can be used to embarrass or harass the responding party. The Rules recognize that discovery sought may require that trade secret information or other confidential or commercially sensitive information be produced. In those situations, a party may seek a protective order to prevent the disclosure of the information or to protect the information from being publicly disclosed.

Rule 26 provides that a party from whom discovery is sought may move for a protective order in the court where the action is pending, or for a deposition in the court for the district where the deposition will be taken.[156] Again, the motion must confirm that the parties have met and conferred in good faith in an effort to resolve the dispute.[157] The court may, for good cause shown, issue an order to protect a party from annoyances, embarrassment, oppression or undue burden or expense by: (a) forbidding the disclosure or discovery; (b) specifying the terms, including the time and place, for disclosure or discovery; (c) prescribing a discovery method other than the one selected by the party seeking discovery; (d) forbidding inquiry into certain matters or limiting the scope of disclosure or discovery; (e) designating the persons who may be present while the discovery is conducted; (f) requiring that a deposition be sealed and opened only on a court order; (g) requiring that a trade secret or other confidential research, development or commercial information not be revealed or be revealed only in a specified way; and (h) requiring that the parties simultaneously file specified documents or information in sealed envelopes, to be opened as the court directs.[158]

Often, the parties will discuss and try to stipulate to the entry of a protective order or confidentiality order prior to the initiation of discovery. These types of protective orders or confidentiality orders will try to address the parties' interest in protecting trade secret and other confidential commercial information. If the parties can agree on a proposed order, courts will often just enter it prior to the start of discovery. If the parties do not agree on the language of a proposed protective order, often the parties will submit competing proposed protective orders and the court will enter one or the other or its own protective order. The entrance of a protective order prior to the start of discovery will expedite the discovery process at the outset as it will provide comfort to the parties that their trade secrets or confidential information will be protected.

b. Privilege logs

The Federal Rules also recognize that certain information is subject to privileges and as such, does not have to be produced. Rule 26(b)(1) states that discovery is limited to 'non-privileged matter.' The laws of evidence have determined what information is

---

156 Fed. R. Civ. P. 26(c)(1).
157 *Id.*
158 *Id.*

considered privileged.[159] Generally, privileges may apply to communications that occur in furtherance of certain relationships (e.g., doctor and patient, lawyer and client) that have been found to warrant various forms of protection.[160]

Among the common privileges asserted in litigation are the attorney–client privilege and work product protection. If a party has communications with his or her attorney that are intended to be confidential, those communications are privileged and do not need to be produced or disclosed during discovery, except under very limited circumstances. Similarly, if counsel for a party creates a document as part of the litigation that contains the mental thoughts or impressions of the attorney, then that document, or portions of the document that reflect the attorneys mental thoughts or impressions, may be protected from disclosure by the 'work product' exception to discovery.[161]

A party that is withholding information based on privilege that would otherwise be discoverable must expressly make the claim and describe the nature of the documents, communications or tangible things not produced or disclosed, and must do so in a manner that will enable the other party to assess the claim.[162] Generally, parties will provide to the other parties a 'privilege log' which will identify the type of document being withheld and the stated privilege. Often, the log will include the types of document, the names of the author and recipients, the date of the documents and a general description of the nature of information. The issue of whether or not a privilege log complies with Rule 26(b)(5) will frequently be the subject of meet-and-confers among the parties and may result in motions to compel a more complete privilege log to allow the requesting party to assess whether the claim of privilege should be challenged.

c. Expert stipulations

Another limitation that may be agreed upon by the parties is the scope of discovery relating to expert witnesses. Often, parties will agree to and enter into a stipulation limiting the materials that the parties need to produce to opposing parties with respect to their expert witnesses. For example, the parties may agree that they will not have to produce drafts of written expert reports or that they will not have to produce communications between the attorneys and the testifying experts. Although arguably this information otherwise must be produced under Fed. R. Civ. P. 26(a)(2), the parties may agree not to require its production in order to facilitate communication between the attorneys and the expert witnesses that the parties have retained.

There are proposed amendments to Fed. R. Civ. P. R. 26 to provide for expert stipulations. The amendments would provide that for witnesses that are required to provide a written report, unless stipulated or otherwise ordered by the court, the Rule 26(a)(2)(A) disclosure must state:

---

159 *See* Fed. R. Evid. 501.

160 *See Perrigon v. Bergen Brunswig Corp.*, 77 F.R.D. 455, 458 (D.C. Cal. 1978) ('The law of privilege is not just a rule governing the admissibility of evidence. Its primary purpose is to protect the confidentiality of certain communications where such confidentiality serves broad societal goals.').

161 *See generally* Fed. R. Evid. 502 (setting forth the provisions that apply when information protected by the attorney–client privilege or work product doctrine is disclosed).

162 Fed. R. Civ. P. 26(b)(5).

(i) the subject matter on which the witness is expected to present evidence under Federal Rule of Evidence 702, 703, 705; and
(ii) a summary of the facts and opinions to which the witness is expected to testify. [163]

The proposed amendments would also provide for protection for draft reports of expert witnesses and communications between a party's attorney and an expert witness.[164]

d. In camera proceedings

Occasionally, the court may decide that it needs to see the documents that are at issue either with respect to whether or not they are properly the subject of a motion to compel (i.e., they truly do fit within the scope of discovery) or to assess whether or not the documents should be withheld on privilege grounds. The court may issue an order that the party opposing production of certain information or documents produce those documents to the court in camera, which means that the party will have to produce those documents to the court only and the court will review the documents to assess whether the documents should be produced or whether the documents are privileged. The court may also have the parties pay for a special master to review the documents for the court and make a recommendation as to whether the documents should be produced. As a practical matter, the more often the parties come before the court on discovery disputes, generally the more frustrated the court gets with the parties' inability to work through these issues. This may play a role in whether or not a court decides to appoint a special master at cost to the parties. If the parties are constantly before the court on discovery disputes and the court believes that the parties are not trying to resolve these issues on its own, it may believe that the parties will be more likely to resolve the disputes if they are required to pay a special master to resolve them rather than being able to simply go to the court for relief. Parties should generally try to resolve discovery disputes and only resort to motion practice on those issues that are critical to the case; otherwise the parties will lose credibility with the court if it believes they are unwilling to try and reach resolution on any discovery disputes.

Conclusion

Given the stakes and nature of antitrust litigation, pretrial discovery plays a significant role in this type of litigation. The formal categories of discovery are established by the federal rules. And, while the federal rules regime relies on lawyer initiative, the discovery and discovery disputes are subject to court supervision and control. While the object of the federal rules is to encourage full pretrial disclosure of relevant information or information that likely would lead to relevant evidence, the recent, more restrictive trend of the courts in applying the discovery rules may have an adverse impact on plaintiffs, who rely substantially on discovery to get at the evidence that will reveal covert anticompetitive activity.

---

[163] ABA, Proposed Amendments to the Fed. R. Civ. P., *available at* http://www.abanet.org/litigation/committees/expertwitnesses/docs/1008_rule26.pdf.
[164] *Id.*

11 Plaintiffs' remedies

W. Joseph Bruckner[1] *and Matthew R. Salzwedel*[2]

Introduction

Unlike most of the world, the United States has long maintained that private victims of anticompetitive conduct are entitled and should be encouraged to seek private redress for violations of the antitrust laws, distinct from the civil and criminal fines and penalties imposed and collected by governments. The deterrence value of private antitrust enforcement is discussed throughout this *Handbook*, but the incentivizing force behind that deterrence – plaintiffs' remedies – is discussed here.

This chapter begins by discussing the linchpin of the US system of private antitrust remedies, the treble damages award, as well as attendant considerations including joint-and-several liability, measurement and distribution of damages, and the availability of pre- and post-judgment interest, attorneys' fees, and costs. The chapter concludes by discussing various equitable remedies and related issues.

Single versus treble damages

One of the primary economic deterrents of the American antitrust laws is the ability of successful plaintiffs to recover statutorily mandated awards of treble (three times) actual damages, in addition to whatever other legal or equitable relief they may receive under the law.

The Sherman Antitrust Act of 1890 itself does not authorize a private right of action or an award of treble damages to persons injured by a violation of its terms; instead, §4 of the Clayton Antitrust Act of 1914[3] establishes a private right of action, including an award of treble damages: 'Any person who shall be injured in his business or property by reason of anything forbidden in the antitrust laws may sue therefor . . . and shall recover threefold the damages by him sustained, and the cost of suit, including a reasonable attorney's fee.'[4]

In interpreting the Clayton Act's treble-damages provision, the Supreme Court of the United States has acknowledged two primary reasons for awarding civil plaintiffs treble damages for violations of the antitrust laws: (1) to punish past violations of the

[1] W. Joseph Bruckner is a partner at Lockridge Grindal Nauen P.L.L.P., in Minneapolis, Minnesota.

[2] Matthew R. Salzwedel is an associate at Lockridge Grindal Nauen P.L.L.P., in Minneapolis, Minnesota. The authors would like to thank Devona Wells for her research assistance in preparing this chapter.

[3] The Clayton Antitrust Act of 1914, in its entirety, is codified at 15 U.S.C. §§12–27 (2009). Section 4 of the Clayton Act is codified at 15 U.S.C. §15 (2009).

[4] Clayton Act, 15 U.S.C. §15(a) (2009); *see also* Volvo Trucks N. Am., Inc. v. Reeder-Simco GMC, Inc., 546 US 164, 176, 126 S. Ct. 860 (2006) (treble damages may be recovered for violations of the Robinson Patman Act); Kristian v. Comcast Corp., 446 F.3d 25, 47 (1st Cir. 2006).

law; and (2) to deter future antitrust violations.[5] Because of the quasi-punitive nature of treble damages, a number of federal courts have concluded that parties cannot – even knowingly and voluntarily – contractually waive their ability to pursue awards of treble damages.[6] In addition, the jury is not told that its award of damages will be trebled; the court automatically multiplies the jury's damages award by three.[7]

Because of the availability of treble damages under the Clayton Act, punitive damages are not otherwise available under the Sherman or Clayton Act.[8] In addition, plaintiffs generally are only entitled to treble damages for either (1) overcharges paid[9] or lost profits attributable to defendants' antitrust violation; or (2) the deprivation to the value of a business as the result of the defendant's anticompetitive conduct, but not both.[10]

---

[5] Agency Holding Corp. v. Malley-Duff & Assocs., Inc., 483 US 143, 151, 107 S. Ct. 2759 (1987); Mitsubishi Motors Corp. v. Soler Chrysler-Plymouth, Inc., 473 US 614, 635, 105 S. Ct. 3346 (1985) ('The treble-damages provision wielded by the private litigant is a chief tool in the antitrust enforcement scheme, posing a crucial deterrent to potential violators.') (citing Perma Life Mufflers, Inc. v. Int'l Parts Corp., 392 US 134, 138–39, 88 S. Ct. 1981 (1968)), *overruled on other grounds*, Copperweld Corp. v. Independence Tube Corp., 467 US 752, 104 S. Ct. 2731 (1984)). *But cf.* Atl. Richfield Co. v. USA Petroleum Co., 495 US 328, 331 n.1, 110 S. Ct. 1884 (1990) (stating that the treble-damages provision of the Clayton Act is a 'remedial provision').

[6] Kristian v. Comcast Corp., 466 F.3d 25, 47–48 (1st Cir. 2006) (citing Mitsubishi Motors Corp. v. Soler Chrysler-Plymouth, Inc., 473 US 614, 637 n.19, 105 S. Ct. 3346 (1985)) (noting that other circuit courts also have disapproved of waiver of statutory remedies for antitrust violations (citing Gaines v. Carrollton Tobacco Bd. of Trade, Inc., 386 F.2d 757, 759 (6th Cir. 1967))).

[7] Pollock & Riley, Inc. v. Pearl Brewing Co., 498 F.2d 1240, 1242 (5th Cir. 1974).

[8] Brown v. Presbyterian Healthcare Servs., 101 F.3d 1324, 1332 (10th Cir. 1996) (citing McDonald v. Johnson & Johnson, 722 F.2d 1370, 1381 (8th Cir. 1983)). *See also* Hawaii v. Standard Oil Co., in which the US Supreme Court held that although a state may sue to recover three times the actual damages it has suffered from an alleged antitrust violation, the same as any citizen, it cannot also recover antitrust damages for harm to 'its general economy' because such recovery 'would open the door to duplicative recoveries.' The Court observed that if 'general economy' damages under the antitrust laws were allowed, 'we should insist upon a clear expression of a congressional purpose to make it so, and no such expression is to be found in §4 of the Clayton Act.' Haw. v. Standard Oil Co., 405 US 251, 263–64, 92 S. Ct. 885 (1972).

[9] S. Pac. Co. v. Darnell-Taenzer Lumber Co., 245 US 531, 38 S. Ct. 186 (1918); In re Linerboard Antitrust Litig., 305 F.3d 145, 159–60 (3d Cir. 2002); Paper Sys. Inc. v. Nippon Paper Indus. Co., 281 F.3d 629, 631–32 (7th Cir. 2002); Hasbrouck v. Texaco, Inc., 842 F.2d 1034, 1043 (9th Cir. 1988).

[10] L.A. Mem'l Coliseum Comm'n v. Nat'l Football League, 791 F.2d 1356, 1374 (9th Cir. 1986). The US Supreme Court has held that only direct purchasers may recover monetary damages under the Clayton Act for violations of the Sherman Act. Illinois Brick Co. v. Illinois, 431 US 720, 735, 97 S. Ct. 2061 (1977) ('[T]he antitrust laws will be more effectively enforced by concentrating the full recovery for the overcharge in the direct purchasers rather than by allowing every plaintiff potentially affected by the overcharge to sue only for the amount it could show was absorbed by it.'). Similarly, the Court has held that a defendant may not defend such a claim by demonstrating that the plaintiff had passed on any overcharges to indirect purchasers and consumers. Hanover Shoe, Inc. v. United Shoe Mach. Corp., 392 US 481, 494, 88 S. Ct. 2224 (1968). Indirect purchasers still may sue for injunctive relief under the Clayton Act. In addition, several states allow monetary recovery by indirect purchasers for violations of the states' own antitrust and unfair trade practices statutes. For further discussion of direct and indirect purchaser standing, see Chapter 6 of this *Handbook*.

Joint and several liability

In cases in which multiple defendants have been shown to have engaged in a conspiracy with anticompetitive effects, it is well established that each defendant is liable, not only for the injury caused by its own conduct, but also jointly and severally for the injuries caused by the illegal acts of its coconspirators.[11] An antitrust action is a tort action, and, as such, co-conspiring joint tortfeasors are jointly and severally liable for the entire amount of damages caused by their acts.[12] Like the availability of treble damages for successful antitrust plaintiffs, defendants' joint and several liability for antitrust violations is another strong deterrent to anticompetitive conduct.[13]

Damages measured

Determining with precision the exact amount of damages resulting from violations of the antitrust laws is nearly impossible in most large antitrust cases. As a result, federal courts permit antitrust plaintiffs substantial leeway in calculating and showing their damages.[14]

'An antitrust plaintiff seeking treble damages under section 4 of the Clayton Act must prove an antitrust violation, fact of damage or injury, and measurable damages.'[15] A plaintiff's damages calculation, therefore, consists of two related damage components – the fact of injury or damage, and the measure of damage.[16]

First, a plaintiff must show 'the fact of damage,' that is, injury to the antitrust plaintiff, which courts sometimes deem to be the predicate 'injury in fact.'[17] 'The fact of damage requirement is one of causation; the plaintiff must show that the defendant's unlawful conduct was a material cause of injury to its business.'[18] 'The fact of injury may be established by inference or circumstantial evidence.'[19]

---

[11] In re Cotton Yarn Antitrust Litig., 505 F.3d 274, 284 (4th Cir. 2007) (quoting Wilson P. Abraham Constr. Corp. v. Tex. Indus., Inc., 604 F.2d 897, 904 n.15 (5th Cir. 1979)); In re Uranium Antitrust Litig., 617 F.2d 1248, 1257 (7th Cir. 1980); *see also* Paper Sys. Inc. v. Nippon Paper Indus. Co., 281 F.3d 629, 632–33 (7th Cir. 2002).

[12] *E.g.*, Wainwright v. Kraftco Corp., 58 F.R.D. 9, 11–12 (N.D. Ga. 1973). Soon after the Sherman Act was enacted, courts 'treated antitrust violations as akin to torts' and applied joint-and-several liability as a remedy for plaintiffs. Burlington Indus. v. Milliken & Co., 690 F.2d 380, 391 (4th Cir. 1982). Recently, the Antitrust Modernization Commission also supported the continuation of joint-and-several liability in antitrust cases with some modifications. *See* Antitrust Modernization Comm'n, Report & Recommendation at 44 (Apr. 2007).

[13] Paper Sys. Inc. v. Nippon Paper Indus. Co., 281 F.3d 629, 631–33 (7th Cir. 2002).

[14] Eleven Line, Inc. v. N. Tex. State Soccer Ass'n, Inc., 213 F.3d 198, 207 (5th Cir. 2000).

[15] Danny Kresky Enter. Corp. v. Magid, 716 F.2d 206, 209 (3d Cir. 1983).

[16] In re New Motor Vehicles Canadian Exp. Antitrust Litig., 522 F.3d 6, 19 n.18 (1st Cir. 2008); Nichols v. Mobile Bd. of Realtors, Inc., 675 F.2d 671, 675–76 (5th Cir. 1982).

[17] Zenith Radio Corp. v. Hazeltine Research, Inc., 395 US 100, 114, n.9, 89 S. Ct. 1562 (1969); Am. Seed Co. v. Monsanto Co., 271 Fed. Appx. 138, 140 (3d Cir. 2008) (citing Bogosian v. Gulf Oil Corp., 561 F.2d 434, 454 (3d Cir. 1977)); In re New Motor Vehicles Canadian Exp. Antitrust Litig., 522 F.3d 6, 19 n.18 (1st Cir. 2008); Robinson v. Tex. Auto. Dealers Ass'n, 387 F.3d 416, 422 (5th Cir. 2004); In re Cardizem CD Antitrust Litig., 200 F.R.D. 326, 339 (E.D. Mich. 2001).

[18] El Aguila Food Prods., Inc. v. Gruma Corp., 131 Fed. Appx. 450, 452 (5th Cir. 2005).

[19] In re Cardizem CD Antitrust Litig., 200 F.R.D. 326, 339 (E.D. Mich. 2001); *see also* Cont'l Ore Co. v. Union & Carbon Corp., 370 US 690, 700, 82 S. Ct. 1404 (1962).

Second, the plaintiff must establish the 'measure of damage,'[20] which is the amount of damages directly flowing from the predicate fact of damage.[21] Once a plaintiff shows 'fact of damage,' his burden of persuasion in proving the amount of damages is relaxed,[22] and he must only satisfy a relaxed just-and-reasonable-inference standard in measuring damages.[23] To this end, a plaintiff is entitled to offer evidence of damages, and, after hearing such evidence, a 'jury is entitled to award damages in an antitrust case based on expert testimony.'[24]

Just-and-reasonable standard[25]

Courts substantially relax the proof required for showing the measure of plaintiff's damages 'to facilitate the policy of the antitrust laws.'[26] According to the United States

---

[20] Blades v. Monsanto Co., 400 F.3d 562, 566 (8th Cir. 2005) (citing Amerinet, Inc. v. Xerox Corp., 972 F.2d 1483, 1490 (8th Cir. 1992)).

[21] Zenith Radio Corp. v. Hazeltine Research, Inc., 395 US 100, 114 n.9, 89 S.Ct. 1562 (1969) (stating that an antitrust plaintiff's 'burden of proving the fact of damage under §4 of the Clayton Act is satisfied by its proof of *some* damage flowing from the unlawful conspiracy; inquiry beyond this minimum point goes only to the amount and not the fact of damage').

[22] El Aguila Food Prods., Inc. v. Gruma Corp., 131 Fed. Appx. 450, 452 (5th Cir. 2005); Eleven Line, Inc. v. N. Tex. State Soccer Ass'n, Inc., 213 F.3d 198, 206-07 (5th Cir. 2000); Pierce v. Ramsey Winch Co., 753 F.2d 416, 435 (5th Cir. 1985); In re Plywood Antitrust Litig., 655 F.2d 627, 635 (5th Cir. 1981).

[23] In re Plywood Antitrust Litig., 655 F.2d 627, 635 (5th Cir. 1981) (quoting Malcolm v. Marathon Oil Co., 642 F.2d 845, 858 (5th Cir. 1981) (citing Terrell v. Household Goods Carriers' Bureau, 494 F.2d 16, 23–24 (5th Cir. 1974)); Lehrman v. Gulf Oil Corp., 464 F.2d 26, 46 (5th Cir. 1972); *see also* Eleven Line, Inc. v. N. Tex. State Soccer Ass'n, Inc., 213 F.3d 198, 207 (5th Cir. 2000) (highlighting that once the fact of antitrust damage is shown, a more relaxed burden of proof arises for showing the amount of damages than would justify an award in other civil cases) (citing Pierce v. Ramsey Winch Co., 753 F.2d 416, 434 (5th Cir. 1985)); Allied Accessories & Auto Parts Co. v. Gen. Motors Corp., 901 F.2d 1322, 1326 (6th Cir. 1990) ('While the damages may not be determined by merely speculation or guess, it will be enough if the evidence shows the extent of damages as a matter of just and reasonable inference, although the result be only approximate. The wrongdoer is not entitled to complain that they cannot be measured with the exactness and precision that would be possible if the case, which he alone is responsible for making, were otherwise.') (quoting Allied Accessories & Auto Parts Co. v. Gen. Motors Corp., 825 F.2d 971, 974 (6th Cir. 1987)) (quoting Story Parchment Co. v. Paterson Parchment Paper Co., 282 US 555, 563, 51 S. Ct. 248 (1931))).

[24] In re Scrap Metal Antitrust Litig., 527 F.3d 517, 533 (6th Cir. 2008) (citing Texaco Inc. v. Hasbrouck, 496 US 543, 572, 110 S. Ct. 2535 (1990)). Expert testimony and analysis is not required as a matter of law to be part of a plaintiff's proof of damages, but it is almost universally offered as a matter of practice.

[25] In addition to the relaxed standard for measuring antitrust damages, a plaintiff need only show that the antitrust violation was a material cause of the plaintiff's injury and resulting damages and need not show that the antitrust violation was the sole cause of the plaintiff's injury and resulting damages. *See, e.g.*, L.A. Mem'l Coliseum Comm'n v. Nat'l Football League, 791 F.2d 1356, 1366 (9th Cir. 1986) (citing Zenith Radio Corp. v. Hazeltine Research, Inc., 395 US 100, 114 n.9, 89 S. Ct. 1562 (1969)); William Inglis & Sons Baking Co. v. ITT Cont'l Baking Co., 668 F.2d 1014, 1051 (9th Cir. 1981)). Finally, a plaintiff's profitability does not preclude a damages award. *See* Image Tech. Servs., Inc. v. Eastman Kodak Co., 125 F.3d 1195, 1222 (9th Cir. 1997) (holding that plaintiffs demonstrated that, although plaintiffs remained profitable, defendants' anticompetitive replacement-parts policy handicapped plaintiffs' growth) (citation omitted)); Pierce v. Ramsey Winch Co., 753 F.2d 416, 436–37 (5th Cir. 1985) (noting that a plaintiff can establish antitrust injury by showing that it would have earned an even higher profit but for the antitrust injury).

[26] Malcolm v. Marathon Oil Co., 642 F.2d 845, 858 (5th Cir. 1981) (citing Ford Motor Co.

Supreme Court, '[a]ny other rule would enable the wrongdoer to profit by his wrongdoing at the expense of his victim.'[27]

In *J. Truett Payne Co. v. Chrysler Motors Corp.*, for example, the United States Supreme Court, in explaining its 'traditional rule excusing antitrust plaintiffs from an unduly rigorous standard of proving antitrust injury,' articulated the reasons for its willingness to accept a degree of uncertainty in proving a plaintiff's measure of damages. The Court recognized the difficultly in determining actual damages in antitrust cases as opposed to other civil causes of action, such as personal injury cases: [28]

> The vagaries of the marketplace usually deny us sure knowledge of what the plaintiff's situation would have been in the absence of the defendant's antitrust violation. But our willingness also rests on the principle articulated in cases such as *Bigelow* [*v. RKO Radio Pictures*], that it does not 'come with very good grace' for the wrongdoer to insist upon specific and certain proof of the injury which it has itself inflicted.[29]

In *Bigelow*, the Court concluded that not allowing a jury to make 'a just and reasonable estimate' of damages based on direct, as well as inferential, proof could preclude recovery for an antitrust plaintiff, and thereby incentivize future antitrust wrongdoing by defendants.[30]

Courts will affirm an award of damages based 'on a plaintiff's estimate of sales it could have made absent the antitrust violation,'[31] despite the inherent imperfections in such an estimate. Indeed, '[t]he antitrust cases are legion which reiterate the proposition that, if the fact of damages is proven, the actual computation of damages may suffer from minor

---

v. Webster's Auto Sales, Inc., 361 F.2d 874, 887 (1st Cir. 1966)); Hobart Bros. Co. v. Malcolm T. Gilliland, Inc., 471 F.2d 894, 903 (5th Cir. 1973); J. Truett Payne Co. v. Chrysler Motors Corp., 451 US 557, 566, 101 S. Ct. 1923 (1981); In re Scrap Metal Antitrust Litig., 527 F.3d 517, 533 (6th Cir. 2008).

[27] Bigelow v. RKO Radio Pictures, Inc., 327 US 251, 264, 66 S. Ct. 574 (1946).

[28] J. Truett Payne Co. v. Chrysler Motors Corp., 451 US 557, 565, 101 S. Ct. 1923 (1981); *see also* Texaco Inc. v. Hasbrouck, 496 US 543, 572–73, 110 S. Ct. 2525 (1990).

[29] J. Truett Payne Co. v. Chrysler Motors Corp., 451 US 557, 566–67, 101 S. Ct. 1923 (1981) (quoting Hetzel v. Balt. & Ohio R. Co., 169 US 26, 39, 18 S. Ct. 255 (1898) (quoting US Trust Co. v. O'Brien, 143 N.Y. 284, 289, 38 N.E. 266, 267 (1894)); Story Parchment Co. v. Paterson Parchment Paper Co., 282 US 555, 563, 51 S. Ct. 248 (1931).

In *Bigelow*, the Supreme Court permitted an award of damages based on the difference in movie-theater receipts before the defendant unlawfully distributed films and fixed admission prices and the receipts after the plaintiff could no longer show certain new films. *See* Bigelow v. RKO Radio Pictures, Inc., 327 US 251, 261–63, 66 S. Ct. 574 (1946); *see also* Zenith Radio Corp. v. Hazeltine Research, Inc., 395 US 100, 123, 89 S. Ct. 1562 (1969) (stating that '[t]rial and appellate courts alike must also observe the practical limits of the burden of proof which may be demanded of a treble-damage plaintiff who seeks recovery for injuries from a partial or total exclusion from a market; damage issues in these cases are rarely susceptible of the kind of concrete, detailed proof of injury which is available in other contexts.').

[30] Bigelow v. RKO Radio Pictures, 327 US 251, 264, 66 S. Ct. 574 (1946); *see also* Pac. Coast Agric. Exp. Ass'n v. Sunkist Growers, Inc., 526 F.2d 1196, 1207 (9th Cir. 1975).

[31] Conwood Co. v. US Tobacco Co., 290 F.3d 768, 794 (6th Cir. 2002) (citation omitted).

imperfections.'[32] Additionally, '[a] plaintiff need not calculate a specific damage figure so long as he proposes an acceptable method for calculating damages.'[33] The amount of damages, however, must not be a product of 'speculation or guess work.'[34]

In determining whether the amount of plaintiff's claimed damages are just and reasonable, federal courts generally apply one or more of four measure-of-damages tests: (1) the yardstick lost-profits method; (2) the violation-free-market method; (3) regression analysis; and (4) the before-and-after method.

Yardstick lost-profits method The yardstick lost-profits method attempts to calculate damages by analyzing the profits of business operations in an industry closely comparable to the plaintiff's industry, or prices charged for products comparable to the conspiratorially affected products, but in markets or industries not affected by the conspiracy.[35] In employing the yardstick lost-profits method of calculating damages, however, the plaintiff 'bears the burden to demonstrate the reasonable similarity of the business whose earning experience he would borrow.'[36]

Violation-free-market method The violation-free-market method attempts to measure antitrust damages by estimating the amount of sales the plaintiff could have made (or what prices would have been for a particular product) absent the defendant's antitrust violation[37] by (1) constructing an 'offense-free' world; and (2) using and evaluating that 'offense-free' world to determine what would have happened in the particular market 'but for' the defendants' anticompetitive conduct.[38]

Regression analysis Another generally accepted method of measuring antitrust damages is a statistical analysis known as multiple- or variable-regression analysis.[39]

---

[32] In re Scrap Metal Antitrust Litig., 527 F.3d 517, 533 (6th Cir. 2008); Conwood Co. v. US Tobacco Co., 290 F.3d 768, 795 (6th Cir. 2002) (quoting South-East Coal Co. v. Consol. Coal Co., 434 F.2d 767, 794 (6th Cir. 1970)).

[33] Rodney v. N.W. Airlines, Inc., 146 Fed. Appx. 783, 791 (6th Cir. 2005).

[34] In re Linerboard Antitrust Litig., 497 F. Supp. 2d 666, 675 (E.D. Pa. 2007) (quoting In re Lower Lake Erie Iron Ore Antitrust Litig., 998 F.2d 1144, 1176 (3d Cir. 1993)); *see also* Blanton v. Mobil Oil Corp., 721 F.2d 1207, 1216 (9th Cir. 1983); MCI Commc'ns Corp. v. Am. Tel. & Tel. Co., 708 F.2d 1081, 1161 (7th Cir. 1983)).

[35] Conwood Co. v. US Tobacco Co., 290 F.3d 768, 793 n.8 (6th Cir. 2002); Eleven Line, Inc. v. N. Tex. State Soccer Ass'n, Inc., 213 F.3d 198, 207 n.17 (5th Cir. 2000); Lehrman v. Gulf Oil Corp., 500 F.2d 659, 667 (5th Cir. 1974).

[36] Eleven Line, Inc. v. N. Tex. State Soccer Ass'n, Inc., 213 F.3d 198, 208 (5th Cir. 2000); *see also* Lehrman v. Gulf Oil Corp., 500 F.2d 659, 667 (5th Cir. 1974).

[37] Conwood Co. v. US Tobacco Co., 290 F.3d 768, 794 (6th Cir. 2002) (citing J. Truett Payne Co. v. Chrysler Motors Corp., 451 US 557, 565, 101 S. Ct. 1923 (1981)).

[38] LePage's Inc. v. 3M, 324 F.3d 141, 165 (3d Cir. 2003) (citing Callahan v. A.E.V., Inc., 182 F.3d 237, 254–58 (3d Cir. 1999); Rossi v. Standard Roofing, Inc., 156 F.3d 452, 484–87 (3d Cir. 1998)); Conwood Co. v. US Tobacco Co., 290 F.3d 768, 793 n.8 (6th Cir. 2002); Eleven Line, Inc. v. N. Tex. State Soccer Ass'n, Inc., 213 F.3d 198, 207 n.17 (5th Cir. 2000).

[39] Conwood Co., v. US Tobacco Co., 290 F.3d 768, 793 (6th Cir. 2002); Petruzzi's IGA Supermarkets, Inc. v. Darling-Delaware Co., 998 F.2d 1224, 1238 (3d Cir. 1993); In re Flat Glass Antitrust Litig., 191 F.R.D. 472, 485–86 (W.D. Pa. 1999) (discussing multiple-regression analysis), *cited in* In re Linerboard Antitrust Litig., 305 F.3d 145, 153 (3d Cir. 2002).

> Multiple regression analysis is a statistical tool for understanding the relationship between two or more variables . . . . [It] is sometimes well suited to the analysis of data about competing theories in which there are several possible explanations for the relationship among a number of explanatory variables . . . . [It] may also be useful (1) in determining whether a particular effect is present; (2) in measuring the magnitude of a particular effect; and (3) in forecasting what a particular effect would be, but for an intervening event.[40]

In general, regression analysis attempts to estimate a plaintiff's damages by determining the effect that two or more independent variables have on a single dependent variable.[41] For example, regression analysis can be used to estimate the effect of an antitrust violation on prices charged during the violation period by attempting to hold constant all other material 'non-violation' variables that also affected prices during the same period. In 1993, the United States Court of Appeals for the Third Circuit observed that multiple regression analysis is considered a reliable method to measure antitrust damages.[42]

Before-and-after method The before-and-after method of measuring antitrust damages (sometimes also called the 'before-during-after' method) attempts to measure damages by comparing the plaintiff's profits or defendant's prices charged during some period shown to be free of the antitrust violation (perhaps before the violation commenced, after its cessation, or during a break-down in the midst of an otherwise ongoing violation) to prices charged or profits earned during the violation period.[43] But the before-and-after theory is not easily applied to a plaintiff who is driven out of business by anticompetitive conduct, because it often cannot easily compile a subsequent earnings record to estimate its lost profits. In such circumstances, a yardstick lost-profits method sometimes is used.[44]

---

[40] In re Linerboard Antitrust Litig., 203 F.R.D. 197, 219 (E.D. Pa. 2001), *quoted in* In re Linerboard Antitrust Litig., 497 F. Supp. 2d 666, 670 n.8 (E.D. Pa. 2007).

[41] Eng'g Contractors Ass'n of S. Fla. Inc. v. Metro. Dade County, 122 F.3d 895, 917 (11th Cir. 1997); *see also* Piggly Wiggly Clarksville, Inc. v. Interstate Brands Corp., 100 Fed. Appx. 296, 299 (5th Cir. 2004); Conwood Co. v. US Tobacco Co., 290 F.3d 768, 793 n.8 (6th Cir. 2002); Gutierrez v. Johnson & Johnson, 2006 WL 3246605, *5 (D.N.J. Nov. 6, 2006); In re Polypropylene Carpet Antitrust Litig., 93 F. Supp. 2d 1348, 1359 (N.D. Ga. 2000); In re Flat Glass Antitrust Litig., 191 F.R.D. 472, 486 (W.D. Pa. 1999) (citing Daniel L. Rubinfeld, *Reference Guide On Multiple Regression*, Reference Manual on Scientific Evidence at 419 (1994)); In re Aluminum Phosphide Antitrust Litig., 893 F. Supp. 1497, 1504 (D. Kan. 1995).

[42] Petruzzi's IGA Supermarkets, Inc. v. Darling-Delaware Co., 998 F.2d 1224, 1238 (3d Cir. 1993); *see also* Conwood Co. v. US Tobacco Co., 290 F.3d 768, 793 (6th Cir. 2002); City of Tuscaloosa v. Harcros Chems., Inc., 158 F.3d 548, 566 (11th Cir. 1998) (citing Askew v. City of Rome, 127 F.3d 1355, 1365 n.2 (11th Cir. 1997)).

[43] In re Scrap Metal Antitrust Litig., 527 F.3d 517, 529 (6th Cir. 2008); Conwood Co. v. US Tobacco Co., 290 F.3d 768, 793 n.8 (6th Cir. 2002); Eleven Line, Inc. v. N. Tex. State Soccer Ass'n, Inc., 213 F.3d 198, 207 n.17 (5th Cir. 2000) (quoting Lehrman v. Gulf Oil Corp., 500 F.2d 659, 667 (5th Cir. 1974)).

[44] Eleven Line, Inc. v. N. Tex. State Soccer Ass'n, Inc., 213 F.3d 198, 207 n.17 (5th Cir. 2000) (quoting Lehrman v. Gulf Oil Corp., 500 F.2d 659, 667 (5th Cir. 1974)). In *Eleven Line, Inc.*, the court observed that, while the before-and-after method and the yardstick lost-profits method are common ways to quantify antitrust damages, different damages measures may be appropriate,

Distribution of damages

In antitrust cases involving multiple plaintiffs, the distribution of damages (whether through settlement or jury verdict) depends on the number of plaintiffs and the degree to which each plaintiff was damaged by defendants' conduct in relation to the other plaintiffs. In antitrust class or mass actions, for example, total damages may be distributed to the various class members or individual plaintiffs based on matrices comparing a given class member's or plaintiff's total purchases or sales to those of all other class members or plaintiffs.

In general, however, courts do not permit the 'fluid recovery' method of distributing damages. 'Fluid recovery refers to the distribution of unclaimed or unclaimable funds to persons not found to be injured but who have interests similar to those of the class.'[45] Fluid recovery, for example, is not allowed in the United States Court of Appeals for the Second Circuit.[46] The United States Court of Appeals for the Ninth Circuit, however, appears to allow fluid recovery only 'where conventional methods of proof are unavailable and, even then, only in an extraordinary circumstance.'[47]

The concept of 'fluid recovery' as a method for *distributing* damages, which generally is not allowed, should not be confused with the concept of a court or jury finding class-wide impact from an antitrust violation and *awarding* 'aggregate' or class-wide damages as a result. The United States Court of Appeals for the Sixth Circuit has held that '[d]amages in an antitrust class action may be determined on a classwide, or aggregate, basis, without resorting to fluid recovery where the [evidence] . . . provide[s] a means to distribute damages to injured class members in the amount of their respective damages.'[48]

Thus, for example, in a class action recovering damages for a price-fixing conspiracy, class members claiming against a recovery fund must demonstrate (usually to class plaintiffs' court-appointed class counsel or a court-appointed claims administrator) that

---

depending on the facts of the particular case 'so long as the estimates and assumptions used [in the chosen method of showing antitrust damages] rest on adequate data.' 213 F.3d at 207.

[45] In re Scrap Metal Antitrust Litig., 527 F.3d 517, 534 (6th Cir. 2008) (quoting In re NASDAQ Market-Makers Antitrust Litig., 169 F.R.D. 493, 525 (S.D.N.Y. 1996) (citing Schwab v. Philip Morris USA, Inc., 2005 WL 3032556, *1 (E.D.N.Y. Nov. 14, 2005))). Fluid recovery is conceptually distinct from a *cy pres* distribution. A *cy pres* distribution may be used to distribute damages that for one reason or another have not been claimed by members of a class. *See* Six (6) Mexican Workers v. Ariz. Citrus Growers, 904 F.2d 1301, 1307 (9th Cir. 1990) (holding 'that the district court properly considered cy pres distribution for the limited purpose of distributing the unclaimed funds').

[46] Gutierrez v. Wells Fargo & Co., 2009 WL 1247040, *3 (N.D. Cal. May 5, 2009) (quoting Eisen v. Carlisle & Jacquelin, 479 F.2d 1005, 1018 (2d Cir. 1973) ('allowing gross damages by treating unsubstantiated claims of class members collectively significantly alters substantive rights under the antitrust statutes' and 'is clearly prohibited by the Enabling Act')).

[47] Gutierrez v. Wells Fargo & Co., 2009 WL 1247040, *3 (N.D. Cal. May 5, 2009) (citing In re Hotel Tel. Charges, 500 F.2d 86, 89–90 (9th Cir. 1974)). In *Gutierrez*, the district court pointed out that such an extraordinary circumstance would be 'where a defendant has not preserved its records so as to allow a more precise calculation of damages.' *Id.*

[48] In re Scrap Metal Antitrust Litig., 527 F.3d 517, 534 (6th Cir. 2008) (quoting In re NASDAQ Market-Makers Antitrust Litig., 169 F.R.D. 493, 526 (S.D.N.Y. 1996)).

they purchased a product or products whose price is shown to have been affected by the antitrust violation, and that they purchased the product during the violation period.

Prejudgment interest allowed only on a finding of defendants' bad faith and material delay
In addition to authorizing awards of treble damages, the Clayton Antitrust Act, as amended in 1982, allows awards to successful plaintiffs of prejudgment interest, but only on a finding of bad faith on the part of defendants that caused a material delay in the adjudication of the dispute.

If the court finds such limited circumstances exist, the court may award prejudgment interest 'on actual damages for the period beginning on the date of service [of the complaint] . . . and ending on the date of judgment, or for any shorter period therein, if the court finds that the award of such interest for such period is just in the circumstances.'[49] Because the bar is set high for a plaintiff to show that it is entitled to an award of prejudgment interest, it appears that no court to date has awarded prejudgment interest to a successful antitrust plaintiff.[50]

Postjudgment interest
In addition to prejudgment interest, an antitrust plaintiff also may obtain an award of postjudgment interest. Congress intended postjudgment interest to compensate a successful antitrust plaintiff for being deprived of compensation between the entry of judgment and the subsequent payment of the judgment by the defendant.[51] Postjudgment interest on a judgment generally begins to run from the date judgment is entered, rather than the date of the jury's verdict.[52]

Indemnification or contribution
The Clayton Antitrust Act does not provide for contribution, *i.e.*, the right of a joint tortfeasor to recover from other joint tortfeasors, nor does the common law provide a right of contribution among joint tortfeasors. The United States Supreme Court has held that it will not find such a right by implication in cases arising under the Sherman and Clayton Antitrust Acts because there is no indication that Congress considered contribution among joint violators under the US antitrust laws.[53]

---

49 Clayton Act, 15 U.S.C. §15(a)(1–3) (2009). *See* Masters v. Wilhelmina Model Agency, Inc., 473 F.3d 423, 435–36 (2d Cir. 2007); Fishman v. Estate of Wirtz, 807 F.2d 520, 561 (7th Cir. 1986); In re Linerboard Antitrust Litig., 504 F. Supp. 2d 38, 64–66 (E.D. Pa. 2007) (court found plaintiffs' damages claim for 'opportunity costs' akin to prejudgment interest and therefore not allowed absent finding of bad faith and material delay).

50 *See* Zapata Gulf Marine Corp. v. Puerto Rico Maritime Shipping Auth., 133 F.R.D. 481, 487 n.4 (E.D. La. 1990) (noting that neither the court nor the parties cited any case where court awarded prejudgment interest under 15 U.S.C. §15(a)).

51 H.J. Inc. v. Flygt Corp., 925 F.2d 257, 261 (8th Cir. 1991) (citation omitted).

52 Kaiser Aluminum & Chem. Corp. v. Bonjorno, 494 US 827, 835, 110 S. Ct. 1570 (1990). The postjudgment interest rate is set by statute. It is calculated from the date of judgment, and the rate is 'equal to the weekly average 1-year constant maturity Treasury yield' as set by the Federal Reserve System. 28 U.S.C. §1961.

53 Tex. Indus., Inc. v. Radcliff Materials, Inc., 451 US 630, 635–36, 101 S. Ct. 2061 (1981). *See generally* Chemung Canal Trust Co. v. Sovran Bank/Md., 939 F.2d 12, 17 (2d Cir. 1991). In

Fees[54]

Many antitrust cases are brought on a contingency-fee basis. Under a contingency-fee arrangement, attorneys representing a successful plaintiff or plaintiff class (through pre-trial settlement or jury verdict) generally will advance on their clients' behalf the time and costs for prosecuting the litigation and, if successful, will receive a percentage of the common-damages fund awarded to the plaintiff or plaintiff class (for example, in price-fixing direct-purchaser antitrust class actions).

Some larger single-plaintiff cases, however, may be brought under an hourly-fee or other attorney-fee arrangement. For example, a large plaintiff that files its own lawsuit in conjunction with a class action, in which the plaintiff would have qualified for class membership but chose to opt out, may decide to pay its attorneys to prosecute its tag-along action on an hourly basis.

The general 'American Rule' for awards of attorneys' fees provides that, absent statutory or other similar authority, a civil plaintiff generally may not ask the court to order the opposing party to pay the plaintiff's attorneys' fees, even if the plaintiff ultimately prevails in the litigation.[55]

The Clayton Antitrust Act, however, provides a statutory exception to the American Rule and specifically mandates that a losing defendant must pay the attorneys' fees of a successful plaintiff: 'Any person who shall be injured in his business or property by reason of anything forbidden in the antitrust laws may sue therefor . . . and shall recover threefold the damages by him sustained, and the cost of suit, *including a reasonable attorney's fee*.'[56] Under the Clayton Act, therefore, an award of attorneys' fees to a successful antitrust plaintiff is mandatory[57] and, like awards of treble damages, may not be waived by agreement of the parties (for example, through agreements to arbitrate their antitrust claims).[58]

What is more, an antitrust plaintiff need not be entirely or even substantially successful in the litigation to obtain an award of attorneys' fees. In 1990, for example, the United

2007, the congressionally chartered Antitrust Modernization Commission recommended that Congress enact legislation allowing non-settling defendants to seek contribution from other non-settling defendants to the extent a plaintiff has collected a disproportionate share of its judgment from one or more of the non-settling defendants. Two of the twelve Commissioners declined to join the Commission's recommendation; one Commissioner believed that current policy better furthers the goal of deterrence by destabilizing cartels and discouraging their formation. Antitrust Modernization Commission, *Report & Recommendations* at 252–55 (Apr. 2007). To date, no such legislation has been enacted, and the rule barring a right of contribution among co-defendants in antitrust cases remains in effect.

54 For further discussion of attorneys' fees in the context of financing private enforcement, see Chapter 12 of this *Handbook*.

55 Alyeska Pipeline Serv. Co. v. Wilderness Soc'y, 421 US 240, 247, 95 S. Ct. 1612 (1975); Fleischmann Distilling Corp. v. Maier Brewing Co., 386 US 714, 718, 87 S. Ct. 1404 (1967); Arcambel v. Wiseman, 3 US (3 Dall.) 306 (1796); Goldberger v. Integrated Res., Inc., 209 F.3d 43, 47 (2d Cir. 2000); Kelco Disposal, Inc. v. Browning-Ferris Indus., 845 F.2d 404, 410 (2d Cir. 1988).

56 Clayton Act, 15 U.S.C. §15 (2009) (emphasis added).

57 Hasbrouck v. Texaco, Inc., 879 F.2d 632, 635 (9th Cir. 1989) (citing Twin City Sportservice, Inc. v. Charles O. Finley & Co., 676 F.2d 1291, 1312 (9th Cir. 1982)).

58 Kristian v. Comcast Corp., 466 F.3d 25, 53, 64 (1st Cir. 2006).

States Court of Appeals for the Fifth Circuit concluded that a successful plaintiff need only show (1) defendant's violation of the antitrust laws; and (2) the predicate 'fact of damage' to recover attorneys' fees from the losing defendant.[59] Therefore, 'the actual recovery of compensatory damages [is] irrelevant to the recoverability of attorneys' fees.'[60] The Supreme Court of the United States has similarly held that the Clayton Antitrust Act authorizes fees 'for legal services performed at the appellate stages of a successfully prosecuted private antitrust action.'[61]

The United States Court of Appeals for the Ninth Circuit has pointed out the significant benefit afforded to the general public by awarding attorneys' fees to a successful plaintiff: The purpose of requiring an award of attorneys' fees under the Clayton Act 'is to insulate treble damage recovery from expenditures for legal fees, consistent with section [4 of the Clayton Act's] purpose to encourage private persons to undertake enforcement of antitrust laws.'[62] Shifting the payment of attorneys' fees from a successful plaintiff to a losing defendant also serves to deter future antitrust violations.[63]

Awarding attorneys' fees to a successful plaintiff, however, should not result in a windfall to successful plaintiffs' counsel.[64] To guard against the potential for excessive attorneys' fee awards, for example, federal courts will judge the amount of 'reasonable'[65] fees requested by plaintiffs' counsel not based on the actual amount paid by a plaintiff to his attorneys but instead on the market rate for similarly situated attorneys in the particular legal market, however defined.[66]

---

[59] Sciambra v. Graham News, 892 F.2d 411, 415 (5th Cir. 1990) (citing Ala. v. Blue Bird Body Co., 573 F.2d 309, 317 (5th Cir. 1978)); Terrell v. Household Goods Carriers' Bureau, 494 F.2d 16, 20–22 (5th Cir. 1974).

[60] Sciambra v. Graham News, 892 F.2d 411, 415–16 (5th Cir. 1990).

[61] Aspen Highlands Skiing Corp. v. Aspen Skiing Co., 738 F.2d 1509, 1527 (10th Cir. 1984) (quoting Perkins v. Standard Oil Co., 399 US 222, 223, 90 S. Ct. 1989 (1970)) (citing Alexander v. Nat'l Farmers Org., 696 F.2d 1210, 1211–12 (8th Cir. 1982)); Moore v. James H. Matthews & Co., 682 F.2d 830, 839 & n.11 (9th Cir. 1982); Carpa, Inc. v. Ward Foods, Inc., 536 F.2d 39, 55–56 (5th Cir. 1976); 2 S. Speiser, Attorneys' Fees § 14:6 (1973)).

[62] Hasbrouck v. Texaco, Inc., 879 F.2d 632, 639 (9th Cir. 1989) (quoting Twin City Sportservice, Inc. v. Charles O. Finley & Co., 676 F.2d 1291, 1312 (9th Cir. 1982)).

[63] Sciambra v. Graham News, 892 F.2d 411, 416 (5th Cir. 1990) (quoting Farmington Dowel Prods. Co. v. Forster Mfg. Co., 421 F.2d 61, 90 (1st Cir. 1970)) (citing Tic-X-Press, Inc. v. Omni Promotions Co., 815 F.2d 1407, 1423–24 (11th Cir. 1987)); Illinois v. Sangamo Constr. Co., 657 F.2d 855, 859–60 (7th Cir. 1981) (quoting Farmington Dowel Prods. Co. v. Forster Mfg. Co., 421 F.2d 61, 90 (1st Cir. 1970)).

[64] La. Power & Light Co. v. Kellstrom, 50 F.3d 319, 328 (5th Cir. 1995) (citing Hensley v. Eckerhart 461 US 424, 430 n.4, 103 S. Ct. 1933 (1983)); *see also* City of Riverside v. Rivera, 477 US 561, 580, 106 S. Ct. 2686 (1986) (quoting S. Rep. No. 94-1011 (1976), *reprinted in* 1976 U.S.C.C.A.N. 5908, 5913)).

[65] The hourly fee of only the senior-most partners of a law firm does not constitute a reasonable hourly billing rate. *See* In re Rite Aid Corp. Sec. Litig., 396 F.3d 294, 306 n.14 (3d Cir. 2005) (citing Gunter v. Ridgewood Energy Corp., 223 F.3d 190, 195 n.1 (3d Cir. 2000)); In re Cendant Corp. PRIDES Litig., 243 F.3d 722, 732 n.11 (3d Cir. 2001).

[66] La. Power & Light Co. v. Kellstrom, 50 F.3d 319, 328 (5th Cir. 1995) (citing Blum v. Stenson, 465 US 886, 895–96, 104 S. Ct. 1541 (1984)); Blanchard v. Bergeron, 489 US 87, 93, 109 S. Ct. 939 (1989) (stating that '[s]hould a[n] [attorney's] fee agreement provide less than a reasonable fee . . ., the defendant should nevertheless be required to pay the higher [market-based] amount').

In *Hasbrouck v. Texaco*, the United States Court of Appeals for the Ninth Circuit noted that reasonable attorneys' fees could exceed the agreed-on contingency-fee arrangement between the plaintiff and his attorneys.[67]

Courts have employed several methods to calculate a reasonable attorneys' fee to be awarded to a successful plaintiff. The most common methods of determining a reasonable attorneys' fee are: (1) the percentage-of-the-fund method; (2) the lodestar method; (3) the lodestar cross-check method; and (4) the *Johnson-Kerr* method. These methods are discussed more fully in Chapter 11 of this *Handbook*, which addresses the funding of private antitrust litigation.

Costs

In addition to authorizing an award of attorneys' fees, the Clayton Antitrust Act also authorizes recovery of a successful antitrust plaintiff's costs: '[A]ny person who shall be injured in his business or property by reason of anything forbidden in the antitrust laws may sue therefor . . . and shall recover threefold the damages by him sustained, *and the cost of suit*, including a reasonable attorneys' fee.'[68] The recovery of costs also is discussed more fully in Chapter 11.

Equitable remedies

Injunctive relief

Permanent injunctive relief Section 16 of the Clayton Antitrust Act specifically authorizes an award of injunctive relief: 'Any person, firm, corporation, or association shall be entitled to *sue for and have injunctive relief*, in any court of the United States having jurisdiction over the parties, against *threatened loss or damage* by a violation of the antitrust laws . . . .'[69]

Injunctive relief, therefore, is available to an antitrust plaintiff as an equitable remedy, even if the plaintiff has not yet suffered any actual antitrust damages.[70] In circumstances such as these, where a plaintiff has not yet suffered any damages, a plaintiff 'need only demonstrate a significant threat of injury from an impending violation of the antitrust laws or from a contemporary violation likely to continue to recur.'[71]

---

[67] Hasbrouck v. Texaco, Inc, 879 F.2d 632, 639 (9th Cir. 1989).

[68] Clayton Act, 15 U.S.C. §15 (2009) (emphasis added).

[69] Clayton Act, 15 U.S.C. §26 (2009) (emphasis added); *see also* Cargill, Inc. v. Monfort of Colo., Inc., 479 US 104, 110–11, 107 S. Ct. 484 (1986); In re New Motor Vehicles Canadian Exp. Antitrust Litig., 522 F.3d 6, 12 (1st Cir. 2008); Rosebrough Monument Co. v. Mem'l Park Cemetery Ass'n, 666 F.2d 1130, 1147 (8th Cir. 1981).

[70] Cargill, Inc. v. Monfort of Colo., Inc., 479 US 104, 111, 107 S. Ct. 484 (1986); Zenith Radio Corp. v. Hazeltine Research, Inc., 395 US 100, 130, 89 S. Ct. 1562 (1969); In re New Motor Vehicles Canadian Exp. Antitrust Litig., 522 F.3d 6, 12 (1st Cir. 2008) (citations omitted).

[71] Zenith Radio Corp. v. Hazeltine Research, Inc., 395 US 100, 130, 89 S. Ct. 1562 (1969) (citing Swift & Co. v. United States, 196 US 375, 396, 25 S. Ct. 276 (1905)); Bedford Cut Stone Co. v. Journeymen Stone Cutters' Ass'n, 274 US 37, 54, 47 S. Ct. 522 (1927); United States v. Or. State Med. Soc'y, 343 US 326, 333, 72 S. Ct. 690 (1952); United States v. W. T. Grant Co., 345 US 629, 633, 73 S. Ct. 894 (1953)); *see also* Cargill, Inc. v. Monfort of Colo., Inc., 479 US 104, 111, 107 S.

Injunctive relief is intended to provide a private plaintiff with important non-monetary relief; but, like awards of treble damages, it also is vital to enforcing the antitrust laws and deterring future antitrust violations. As such, injunctive relief generally is applied flexibly, with 'adjustment and reconciliation between the public interest and private needs as well as between competing private claims.'[72]

It is plaintiff's burden to show the presence of the threat of injury sufficient for an award of injunctive relief.[73] A plaintiff attempting to establish a claim for injunctive relief must demonstrate 'a "cognizable danger" of injury, not just a "mere possibility."'[74]

The broader range of anticompetitive conduct subject to injunctive relief was recognized by the United States Court of Appeals for the First Circuit in *Cia. Petrolera Caribe, Inc. v. Arco Caribbean, Inc.* There, the court concluded that Congress empowered a broader range of antitrust plaintiffs to seek injunctive relief than it did plaintiffs seeking money damages by providing for less exacting standards for showing an entitlement to injunctive relief.[75] According to the First Circuit, a plaintiff seeking injunctive relief must only show 'a threat of injury rather than an accrued injury.'[76]

The distinction between the proof required for an award of injunctive relief as opposed to an award of money damages also took center stage in *Ocean State Physicians Health Plan, Inc. v. Blue Cross & Blue Shield*, where the United States Court of Appeals for the First Circuit held that, although a jury could find no damages on an antitrust claim, that jury finding still 'arguably requires the lower court to [independently] consider awarding injunctive relief.'[77]

Preliminary injunctive relief As opposed to permanent injunctive relief, which a court typically awards at the end of the litigation, courts also may grant requests for preliminary injunctions. A preliminary injunction is considered an extraordinary equitable remedy and, therefore, the antitrust plaintiff's 'right to relief must be clear and unequivocal.'[78]

Ct. 484 (1986); In re New Motor Vehicles Canadian Export Antitrust Litig., 522 F.3d 6, 13 (1st Cir. 2008) (quoting Mid-West Paper Prods. Co. v. Cont'l Group, Inc., 596 F.2d 573, 591 (3d Cir. 1979)); Rosebrough Monument Co. v. Mem'l Park Cemetery Ass'n, 666 F.2d 1130, 1147 (8th Cir. 1981).

[72] Zenith Radio Corp. v. Hazeltine Research, Inc., 395 US 100, 131, 89 S. Ct. 1562 (1969) (citing Hecht Co. v. Bowles, 321 US 321, 329–30, 64 S. Ct. 587 (1944)).

[73] In re New Motor Vehicles Canadian Exp. Antitrust Litig., 522 F.3d 6, 14 (1st Cir. 2008) (citations omitted).

[74] Datagate, Inc. v. Hewlett-Packard Co., 941 F.2d 864, 870 (9th Cir. 1991) (quoting TRW, Inc. v. FTC, 647 F.2d 942, 954 (9th Cir. 1981)); *see also* Lake Hill Motors, Inc. v. Jim Bennett Yacht Sales, Inc., 246 F.3d 752, 755 (5th Cir. 2001) ('Likewise, a plaintiff seeking injunctive relief under §16 of the Clayton Act can only obtain that relief when they show a significant threat of some injury to their business or property from a violation of the antitrust laws.' (citing McCormack v. Nat'l Collegiate Athletic Ass'n, 845 F.2d 1338, 1341 (5th Cir. 1988); Cargill, Inc. v. Monfort of Colo., Inc., 479 US 104, 113, 107 S. Ct. 484 (1986) (same))).

[75] Cia. Petrolera Caribe, Inc. v. Arco Caribbean, Inc., 754 F.2d 404, 407–08 (1st Cir. 1985); *see also* In re New Motor Vehicles Canadian Export Antitrust Litig., 522 F.3d 6, 13 (1st Cir. 2008).

[76] Cia. Petrolera Caribe, Inc. v. Arco Caribbean, Inc., 754 F.2d 404, 408 (1st Cir. 1985).

[77] Ocean State Physicians Health Plan, Inc. v. Blue Cross & Blue Shield, 883 F.2d 1101, 1106 (1st Cir. 1989).

[78] SCFC ILC, Inc. v. Visa USA, Inc., 936 F.2d 1096, 1098 (10th Cir. 1991) (citing GTE Corp. v. Williams, 731 F.2d 676, 678 (10th Cir. 1984)); Penn v. San Juan Hosp., Inc., 528 F.2d 1181, 1185

Courts in antitrust cases have differed on the elements of, and the level of proof required for, a preliminary injunction. In 1986, the United States Supreme Court concluded that to obtain preliminary injunctive relief a plaintiff must allege a threatened loss or damage of the type the antitrust laws were designed to prevent and that flows from that which makes defendants' acts unlawful.[79] Twenty-one years later, however, the United States Court of Appeals for the Second Circuit appeared to apply a relaxed standard for preliminary injunctive relief, concluding that an antitrust plaintiff must simply show irreparable harm as a result of the defendants' conduct,[80] in addition to a likelihood of success on the merits of the litigation.[81]

The United States Court of Appeals for the Seventh Circuit, in contrast, has varied in its treatment of requests for preliminary-injunctive relief. In 1999, in *Allied Signal v. B.F. Goodrich Co.*, the Seventh Circuit held that a plaintiff seeking preliminary-injunctive relief first must show that he was likely to prevail on the merits of the litigation and had suffered irreparable harm for which there was no adequate remedy.[82] If the plaintiff

---

(10th Cir. 1975); Matzke v. Block, 542 F. Supp. 1107, 1112–13 (D. Kan. 1982); *see also* Grand River Enter. Six Nations, Ltd. v. Pryor, 481 F.3d 60, 66 (2d Cir. 2007) (citing Moore v. Consol. Edison Co., 409 F.3d 506, 510 (2d Cir. 2005)).

[79] Cargill Inc. v. Monfort of Colo., Inc., 479 US 104, 109, 107 S. Ct. 484 (1986) (citing Brunswick Corp. v. Pueblo Bowl-O-Mat, Inc., 429 US 477, 489, 97 S. Ct. 690 (1977)).

[80] Grand River Enter. Six Nations, Ltd. v. Pryor, 481 F.3d 60, 66 (2d Cir. 2007) (explaining that, to satisfy the irreparable-harm requirement, an antitrust plaintiff must demonstrate that, absent a preliminary injunction, it will suffer "'an injury that is neither remote nor speculative, but actual and imminent,' and one that cannot be remedied 'if a court waits until the end of trial to resolve the harm'" (quoting Freedom Holdings, Inc. v. Spitzer, 408 F.3d 112, 114 (2d Cir. 2005) (quoting Rodriguez v. DeBuono, 175 F.3d 227, 234 (2d Cir. 1999)))).

[81] Grand River Enter. Six Nations, Ltd. v. Pryor, 481 F.3d 60, 66 (2d Cir. 2007) (quoting Brooklyn Legal Servs. Corp. v. Legal Servs. Corp., 462 F.3d 219, 225 (2d Cir. 2006)).

[82] AlliedSignal, Inc. v. B.F. Goodrich Co., 183 F.3d 568, 573 (7th Cir. 1999) (citing Doran v. Salem Inn, Inc., 422 US 922, 931, 95 S. Ct. 2561 (1975)); Roth v. Lutheran Gen. Hosp., 57 F.3d 1446, 1453 (7th Cir. 1995). Previously, Judge Richard Posner introduced a mathematical formula to guide the analysis of whether or not to grant a preliminary injunction: $P \times Hp > (1 - P) \times Hd$. Under this formula, a preliminary injunction should be granted only if the harm to the P (plaintiff) if the injunction is denied multiplied by the probability that the denial would be an error (so that P would win at trial) exceeds the harm to the defendants if the injunction is granted, multiplied by the probability that granting the injunction would be an error. Judge Posner opined that this formula was not offered as a new legal standard but was intended to assist with the analysis of a preliminary injunction by presenting succinctly the factors that the court must consider in making its decision and by articulating the relationship among the factors. *See* Am. Hosp. Supply Corp. v. Hosp. Prods. Ltd., 780 F.2d 589, 593 (7th Cir. 1986); *see also* Gen. Leaseways, Inc. v. Nat'l Truck Leasing Ass'n, 744 F.2d 588, 590 (7th Cir. 1984) (citing Libertarian Party v. Packard, 741 F.2d 981, 984–85 (7th Cir. 1984) (holding that a preliminary injunction requires analysis of the harm to the plaintiff and the harm to the defendant from denial or grant of the injunction, respectively, the likelihood of the plaintiff prevailing on the merits when the case is tried, and the effect on the public of granting or denying the preliminary injunction)); Roland Mach. Co. v. Dresser Indus. Inc., 749 F.2d 380, 386–87 (7th Cir. 1984) (holding that an antitrust plaintiff must show that (1) he has no adequate remedy at law; (2) he will suffer irreparable harm if the preliminary injunction is not granted; and (3) he has some likelihood of succeeding on the merits; then, the court will determine the likelihood of success on the merits in determining whether to grant a preliminary injunction).

In contrast, the United States Court of Appeals for the Sixth Circuit has held that a preliminary-injunction analysis weighs whether (1) the plaintiff is likely to prevail on the merits; (2) whether

makes that preliminary showing, the court then applies a sliding-scale analysis that balances the harms to the parties with the public's interest.[83]

In 1988, however, the United States Court of Appeals for the Ninth Circuit held that a party seeking a preliminary injunction must show either (1) a likelihood of success on the merits and the possibility of irreparable injury; or (2) the existence of serious questions going to the merits and the balance of hardships tipping in its favor.[84] According to the Ninth Circuit, either test requires a plaintiff to show a significant threat of irreparable harm to the plaintiff.[85]

Declaratory relief

Although a plaintiff might not always recover money damages for allegedly anticompetitive conduct, he may be entitled to declaratory relief to determine his rights in relation to another party.[86]

In 1980, for example, the United States Court of Appeals for the Ninth Circuit acknowledged that 'the strong policy favoring enforcement of the antitrust laws may stay its application where the plaintiff seeks only to disentangle itself from an agreement which has a substantial anti-competitive effect on commerce.'[87] In *Beacon Theatres, Inc. v. Westover*, the United States Supreme Court recognized that plaintiffs may bring an action for declaratory judgment under the antitrust laws; however, the defendant was still entitled to a jury trial on the issue of antitrust liability.[88]

Limitation periods

The Clayton Antitrust Act provides for a four-year statute of limitations for claims under the several civilly enforceable antitrust laws: '[A]ny action to enforce any cause of action under [15 U.S.C.] shall be forever barred unless commenced within four years after the cause of action accrued.'[89] Courts generally consider the four-year limitations period in the Clayton Act to be procedural, not substantive, which means that it can be varied by agreement of the parties.[90]

But because Congress in the Clayton Act provided for a four-year statute of limitations in civil antitrust actions, that limitations period is definitive, and provides the

---

the plaintiff would suffer irreparable injury if the court does not grant the injunction; (3) whether a preliminary injunction would cause substantial harm to others; and (4) whether a preliminary injunction would be in the public interest. *See* Samuel v. Herrick Mem'l Hosp., 201 F.3d 830, 833 (6th Cir. 2000) (citing Glover v. Johnson, 855 F.2d 277, 282 (6th Cir. 1988)).

83 Am. Hosp. Supply Corp. v. Hosp. Prods. Ltd., 780 F.2d 589, 593–94 (7th Cir. 1986).

84 US v. BNS Inc., 858 F.2d 456, 464 (9th Cir. 1988) (citing Apple Computer, Inc. v. Formula Int'l Inc., 725 F.2d 521, 523 (9th Cir. 1984)).

85 US v. BNS Inc., 858 F.2d 456, 464 (9th Cir. 1988) (citing Oakland Tribune, Inc. v. Chronicle Pub. Co., 762 F.2d 1374, 1376 (9th Cir. 1985)).

86 THI-Hawaii, Inc. v. First Commerce Fin. Corp., 627 F.2d 991, 996 (9th Cir. 1980).

87 THI-Hawaii, Inc. v. First Commerce Fin. Corp., 627 F.2d 991, 996 (9th Cir. 1980) (citing Phillip E. Areeda & Donald E. Turner, Antitrust Law ¶348a (1978)); *cf.* Florists' Nationwide Tel. Delivery Network v. Florists' Tel. Delivery Ass'n, 371 F.2d 263 (7th Cir. 1967).

88 359 US 500, 504, 79 S. Ct. 948 (1959).

89 Clayton Act, 15 U.S.C. §15(b) (2009); Zenith Radio Corp. v. Hazeltine Research, Inc., 401 US 321, 338, 91 S. Ct. 795 (1971).

90 In re Cotton Yarn Antitrust Litig., 505 F.3d 274, 287–89 (4th Cir. 2007).

exclusive limitations period for civil antitrust claims, subject to very limited exceptions.[91] The United States Court of Appeals for the Fourth Circuit, for example, has held that an arbitration agreement between the parties may reduce the four-year limitations period to as short as one year, noting that the Clayton Act does not prevent parties from agreeing to a contractually shortened limitations period.[92]

Accrual

The predicate question that naturally arises in determining the effect of the Clayton Act's four-year statute of limitations is: when does a civil antitrust cause of action accrue, triggering the commencement of the statute's four-year statute of limitations?

The Supreme Court of the United States has held that an antitrust claim accrues 'when a defendant commits an act that injures a plaintiff's business'[93] and where the injured plaintiff is aware, or should be aware, of the existence and source of her injury.[94] Generally, this means an antitrust plaintiff must file its claim within four years following the defendant's injurious act, where the plaintiff was or should have been aware of the existence and source of the injury.[95] Important exceptions to this general rule are discussed more fully below.

Laches

The equitable doctrine of laches is similar to, but legally and factually distinct from, a statute of limitations. Laches may apply to bar an antitrust claim where it would be inequitable to permit a claim to be enforced because of a change in the condition or relations of the property or parties. It is possible, but not likely, that laches could bar an antitrust claim even though the statute of limitations for the claim has not yet expired.[96] For example, in *Kloth v. Microsoft Corporation*, the United States Court of Appeals for the Fourth Circuit concluded that the district court did not abuse its discretion in dismissing plaintiffs' claims for injunctive relief based on the doctrine of

---

[91] Holmberg v. Armbrecht, 327 US 392, 395, 66 S. Ct. 582 (1946) (citing Herget v. Cent. Nat. Bank & Trust Co., 324 US 4, 65 S. Ct. 505 (1945)).

[92] In re Cotton Yarn Antitrust Litig., 505 F.3d 274, 287-88 (4th Cir. 2007). For a discussion of defendants raising limitation periods as a procedural defense, see Chapter 9 of this *Handbook*.

[93] Rotella v. Wood, 528 US 549, 554, 120 S. Ct. 1075 (2000); Zenith Radio Corp. v. Hazeltine Research, Inc., 401 US 321, 338, 91 S. Ct. 795 (1971); Morton's Mkt., Inc. v. Gustafson's Dairy, Inc., 198 F.3d 823, 827 (11th Cir. 1999) (quoting Zenith Radio Corp. v. Hazeltine Research, Inc., 401 US 321, 338, 91 S. Ct. 795 (1971)), *amended in part*, 211 F.3d 1224 (2000); In re Cotton Yarn Antitrust Litig., 505 F.3d 274, 287–90 (4th Cir. 2007); Sanderson v. Spectrum Labs, Inc., 227 F. Supp. 2d 1001, 1011 (N.D. Ind. 2000).

[94] Oshiver v. Levin, Fishbein, Sedran & Berman, 38 F.3d 1380, 1386 (3d Cir. 1994) (noting that a different rule for determining the time of accrual for a cause of action would require an insufficient degree of diligence on the part of the potential claimant).

[95] Morton's Mkt., Inc. v. Gustafson's Dairy, Inc., 198 F.3d 823, 827 (11th Cir. 1999) (citing Clayton Act 15 U.S.C. §15(b)).

[96] Holmberg v. Armbrecht, 327 US 392, 396, 66 S. Ct. 582 (1946) (citing Galliher v. Cadwell, 145 US 368, 373, 12 S. Ct. 873 (1892)); *see also* S. Pac. Co. v. Bogert, 250 US 483, 488–89, 39 S. Ct. 533 (1919).

laches, noting that plaintiffs did not pursue their equitable claims for injunctive relief with diligence.[97]

Tolling

Pendency of government action The Clayton Antitrust Act authorizes the tolling of a private civil antitrust action while the government (usually the United States Department of Justice or United States Attorneys) pursues a criminal or civil cause of action against the targeted defendants.[98] The Clayton Act provides:

> Whenever any civil or criminal proceeding is instituted by the United States to prevent, restrain, or punish violations of any of the antitrust laws, but not including an action under section 15a of this title, the running of the statute of limitations . . . *shall be suspended during the pendency thereof and for one year thereafter* . . . .[99]

This tolling provision applies to 'all proceedings in the government action until its termination in a final decree disposing of all issues.'[100]

In 1970, the United States Court of Appeals for the Second Circuit determined that the pendency of a government action continues until such time that a judgment or decree becomes final so that the government and defendants are satisfied (to the extent possible) with the result of the litigation and have decided to not appeal.[101] Consequently, according to the Second Circuit, 'only after the time to appeal has expired can private litigants rely on the irrevocability of determinations made in the [pendent] government action.'[102] Finally, a plaintiff's right to toll the statute of limitations during the pendency of a government action does not depend on the government's success (or lack thereof) in proving its allegations.[103]

There are several reasons why the statute of limitations for a private antitrust claim is tolled during the pendency of a government criminal or civil-enforcement action. Tolling during the pendency of a government action seeks to balance competing policy objectives of the antitrust laws, namely (1) retaining private antitrust litigation as a tool for

---

[97] 444 F.3d 312, 325–26 (4th Cir. 2006).

[98] Clayton Act, 15 U.S.C. §16(i) (2009); *see also* In re Scrap Metal Antitrust Litig., 527 F.3d 517, 536–37 (6th Cir. 2008).

[99] Clayton Act, 15 U.S.C. §16(i) (2009) (emphasis added). Congress intended the pendency-of-government-action provision in the Clayton Act to replace 'diverse state laws with a uniform federal rule requiring that private antitrust actions be brought within four years of accrual or within one year after a government enforcement action ceased to pend.' Russ Togs, Inc. v. Grinnell Corp., 426 F.2d 850, 853 (2d Cir. 1970) (citing S. Rep. No. 619 (1955), *reprinted in* 1955 US Code Cong. & Admin. News, pp. 2332–33)).

[100] Russ Togs, Inc. v. Grinnell Corp., 426 F.2d 850, 854 (2d Cir. 1970).

[101] Russ Togs, Inc. v. Grinnell Corp., 426 F.2d 850, 857 (2d Cir. 1970).

[102] Russ Togs, Inc. v. Grinnell Corp., 426 F.2d 850, 857 (2d Cir. 1970) (citing Twentieth Century-Fox Film Corp. v. Brookside Theatre Corp., 194 F.2d 846, 857-58 (8th Cir. 1952)).

[103] Leh v. Gen. Petroleum Corp., 382 US 54, 65–66, 86 S. Ct. 203 (1965) (citing Minn. Mining & Mfg. Co. v. N.J. Wood Finishing Co., 381 US 311, 316, 85 S.Ct. 1473 (1965)).

effective enforcement of the antitrust laws;[104] and (2) providing certainty in applying the statute's tolling provision to avoid overly prolonged antitrust litigation.[105]

Tolling during the pendency of a government action, however, is not without limits. In 2007, for example, the United States Court of Appeals for the Fifth Circuit stated that the leeway accorded to antitrust plaintiffs as a result of tolling during the pendency of a government action should not be interpreted to allow plaintiffs to '"sit on their rights" and to assert, years after the traditional statute of limitations has run, "claims so much broader than those asserted by the government that they open entirely new vistas of litigation."'[106]

Equitable tolling and the fraudulent-concealment doctrine In general, equitable tolling[107] prevents the statute of limitations for an antitrust claim from barring the claim even if the plaintiff fails to bring the claim within four years after the date the claim accrued.[108]

The equitable-tolling doctrine extends the Clayton Antitrust Act's four-year statute of limitations starting from the date the operable facts supporting plaintiff's claims either *actually* become apparent to the plaintiff, or the date where the operable facts *should have* become apparent to a reasonably prudent person in the plaintiff's position.[109]

Equitable tolling may toll the four-year statute of limitations in several circumstances. Equitable tolling may extend the applicable statute of limitations where the defendants actively misled plaintiffs by fraudulently concealing their unlawful conduct. Equitable tolling also may save an otherwise time-barred claim where the plaintiff in an extraordinary circumstance has been prevented from asserting his rights. Finally, equitable tolling

---

[104] Novell, Inc. v. Microsoft Corp., 505 F.3d 302, 320 (4th Cir. 2007), *cert. denied* 128 S. Ct. 1659 (2008) (quoting Minn. Mining & Mfg. Co. v. N.J. Wood Finishing Co., 381 US 311, 318, 320 (1965)).

[105] Novell, Inc. v. Microsoft Corp., 505 F.3d 302, 320 (4th Cir. 2007), *cert. denied* 128 S. Ct. 1659 (2008) (citing Greyhound Corp. v. Mt. Hood Stages, Inc. 437 US 322, 335, 98 S. Ct. 2370 (1978)).

[106] Novell, Inc. v. Microsoft Corp., 505 F.3d 302, 322 (4th Cir. 2007), *cert. denied*, 128 S. Ct. 1659 (2008) (quoting In re Microsoft Corp. Antitrust Litig., 2005 WL 1398643, *5 (D. Md. June 10, 2005)).

[107] In 1998, the United States Court of Appeals for the Tenth Circuit stated that '"tolling" means "to suspend or stop temporarily," whereas the phrase, "a cause of action accrues" refers to "when a suit may be maintained thereon." Also, the federal equitable tolling doctrine "is at times misnamed because it often provides a rule for determining when the limitation period accrues."' Sterlin v. Biomune Sys., 154 F.3d 1191, 1195 n.8 (10th Cir. 1998) (quoting Ebrahimi v. E.F. Hutton & Co., 852 F.2d 516, 520 n.6 (10th Cir. 1988)).

[108] Forbes v. Eagleson, 228 F.3d 471, 486 (3d Cir. 2000) (citing Oshiver v. Levin, Fishbein, Sedran & Berman, 38 F.3d 1380, 1387 (3d Cir. 1994)).

[109] Zenith Radio Corp. v. Hazeltine Research, Inc., 401 US 321, 338, 91 S. Ct. 795 (1971); In re Scrap Metal Antitrust Litig., 527 F.3d 517, 536 (6th Cir. 2008); Forbes v. Eagleson, 228 F.3d 471, 486 (3d Cir. 2000) (noting that equitable tolling differs from the discovery rule in that equitable tolling centers on a plaintiff's cognizance of the facts supporting the plaintiff's cause of action rather than the plaintiff's cognizance of actual injury. Equitable tolling, therefore, presumes accrual while the discovery rule is meant to determine the accrual date of a claim to determine when the statute of limitations begins to run) (quoting Oshiver v. Levin, Fishbein, Sedran & Berman, 38 F.3d 1380, 1390 (3d Cir. 1994)).

may save an otherwise time-barred claim where the plaintiff timely asserted its rights but mistakenly did so in the wrong judicial forum.[110]

One of the circumstances where equitable tolling may apply to save an otherwise time-barred antitrust claim, or to extend the statute of limitations beyond four years from the date the claim accrued, is where the defendant fraudulently concealed its unlawful anticompetitive conduct from the plaintiff.[111] The fraudulent-concealment doctrine seeks 'to prevent a defendant from "concealing a fraud, or . . . committing a fraud in a manner that it concealed itself until such time as the party committing the fraud could plead the statute of limitations to protect it."'[112] In general, 'acts of fraudulent concealment by the [antitrust] defendant toll the limitations period for as long as theconcealment continues.'[113] But 'a plaintiff seeking to invoke the doctrine of fraudulent concealment in order to toll the statute of limitations in an antitrust case must prove "affirmative acts" of concealment; "concealment by mere silence is not enough."'[114]

To show the existence of fraudulent concealment sufficient to equitably toll the running of the four-year statute of limitations, an antitrust plaintiff must show that (1) the defendant concealed from him the existence of his cause of action;[115] (2) he remained

---

[110] Oshiver v. Levin, Fishbein, Sedran & Berman, 38 F.3d 1380, 1387 (3d Cir. 1994) (citing Sch. Dist. of City of Allentown v. Marshall, 657 F.2d 16, 19–20 (3d Cir. 1981)); *see also* Miller v. Beneficial Mgmt. Corp., 977 F.2d 834, 845 (3d Cir. 1992); Smith v. Am. President Lines, Ltd., 571 F.2d 102, 109 (2d Cir. 1978)).

[111] The equitable fraudulent-concealment doctrine is read into every federal statute of limitations. *See* Holmberg v. Armbrecht, 327 US 392, 396, 66 S. Ct. 582 (1946).

[112] State of N.Y. v. Hendrickson Bros., Inc., 840 F.2d 1065, 1083 (2d Cir. 1988) (quoting Bailey v. Glover, 88 US (21 Wall.) 342, 349 (1874)); *see also* In re Cotton Yarn Antitrust Litig., 505 F.3d 274, 287–91 (4th Cir. 2007) (citing Holmberg v. Ambrecht, 327 US 392, 397, 66 S. Ct. 582 (1946)); Supermarket of Marlinton, Inc. v. Meadow Gold Diaries, Inc., 71 F.3d 119, 122 (4th Cir. 1995)).

[113] In re Scrap Metal Antitrust Litig., 527 F.3d 517, 536 (6th Cir. 2008) (citing Norton-Children's Hosps., Inc. v. James E. Smith & Sons, Inc., 658 F.2d 440, 443 (6th Cir. 1981)).

[114] In re Scrap Metal Antitrust Litig., 527 F.3d 517, 538 (6th Cir. 2008) (quoting Pinney Dock & Transp. Co. v. Penn Cent. Corp., 838 F.2d 1445, 1467 (6th Cir. 1988)).

[115] In 1995, the United States Court of Appeals for the Fourth Circuit observed that different federal circuit courts of appeals apply different standards to determine if antitrust plaintiffs have satisfied the first element of the fraudulent-concealment doctrine. *See* Supermarket of Marlinton v. Meadow Gold Dairies, 71 F.3d 119, 122 (4th Cir. 1995). These differing standards are: (1) the self-concealing standard; (2) the separate-and-apart standard; and (3) the affirmative-acts standard. *Id.* The self-concealing standard is satisfied simply by showing that a self-concealing antitrust violation has occurred. *Id.* (citing N.Y. v. Hendrickson Bros., Inc., 840 F.2d 1065, 1084 (2d Cir. 1988)). The separate-and-apart standard, however, requires the plaintiff to provide evidence separate and apart from the acts of concealment involved in the defendants' antitrust violation, namely, that defendants affirmatively acted to conceal the plaintiff's claim. *Id.* (citation omitted). Finally, the affirmative-acts standard requires the plaintiff to show that the defendant affirmatively acted to conceal its antitrust violation but the plaintiff's proof may include acts of concealment involved in the antitrust violation itself. *Id.* (citing Texas v. Allan Constr. Co., 851 F.2d 1526, 1532 (5th Cir. 1988)). *See generally* Conmar Corp. v. Mitsui & Co. (U.S.A.), 858 F.2d 499, 505 (9th Cir. 1988) (holding that more than passive concealment is required to toll the statute of limitations unless the defendant had a fiduciary duty to disclose information to the plaintiff (citing Volk v. D.A.

ignorant of his potential claim within the four years before he filed his claim; and (3) his continuing ignorance was not attributable to any lack of diligence on his part.[116]

The latter element – the plaintiff's due diligence – is particularly important. In 1997, the United States Supreme Court held, citing a litany of cases, that a plaintiff who is not reasonably diligent cannot rely on the fraudulent-concealment doctrine to equitably toll the statute of limitations.[117]

Continuing-violation injury In addition to tolling during the pendency of a government action, and equitable tolling (including the fraudulent-concealment doctrine), the statute of limitations for a civil antitrust claim may be tolled if the defendant has engaged in a continuing antitrust violation.

In 1997, in *Klehr v. A.O. Smith*, the United States Supreme Court observed that:

> Antitrust law provides that, in the case of a 'continuing violation,' say, a price-fixing conspiracy that brings about a series of unlawfully high priced sales over a period of years, 'each overt act that is part of the violation and that injures the plaintiff,' *e.g.*, each sale to the plaintiff, 'starts the statutory period running again, regardless of the plaintiff's knowledge of the alleged illegality at much earlier times.'[118]

The United States Supreme Court also has distinguished a continuing antitrust violation from a distinctly new violation, stating that 'the commission of a separate new overt act

---

Davidson & Co., 816 F.2d 1406, 1416 (9th Cir. 1987)); Rutledge v. Boston Woven Hose & Rubber Co., 576 F.2d 248, 249–50 (9th Cir. 1978).

[116] Hamilton County Bd. of Comm'rs v. Nat'l Football League, 491 F.3d 310, 315 (6th Cir. 2007) (quoting Dayco Corp. v. Goodyear Tire & Rubber Co., 523 F.2d 389, 394 (6th Cir. 1975) (citing Pinney Dock & Transp. Co. v. Penn Cent. Corp., 838 F.2d 1445, 1465 (6th Cir. 1988)); Supermarket of Marlinton v. Meadow Gold Dairies, 71 F.3d 119, 122 (4th Cir. 1995) (citing Weinberger v. Retail Credit Co., 498 F.2d 552, 555 (4th Cir. 1974)); State of N.Y. v. Hendrickson Bros., Inc., 840 F.2d 1065, 1083 (2d Cir. 1988) (citation omitted); Baskin v. Hawley, 807 F.2d 1120, 1131 (2d Cir. 1986) (claim for pension benefits); Cerbone v. Int'l Ladies' Garment Workers' Union, 768 F.2d 45, 48 (2d Cir. 1985) (employment-discrimination claim); *see also* Pinney Dock & Transp. Co. v. Penn Cent. Corp., 838 F.2d 1445, 1465 (6th Cir. 1988); In re Beef Indus. Antitrust Litig., 600 F.2d 1148, 1169 (5th Cir. 1979).

[117] Klehr v. A.O. Smith Corp., 521 US 179, 194–95, 117 S. Ct. 1984 (1997) (noting that many antitrust cases require due diligence by the plaintiff or that the plaintiff could reasonably have known of the offense, and none state to the contrary) (quoting 2 Phillip E. Areeda & Herbert Hovencamp, Antitrust Law ¶338 at 152 (1995)) (citing Irving Scher, Antitrust Adviser §10.27, p. 10–62 (4th ed. 1995)); Conmar Corp. v. Mitsui & Co., 858 F.2d 499, 502 (9th Cir. 1988); Texas v. Allan Constr. Co., 851 F.2d 1526, 1533 (5th Cir. 1988); Pinney Dock & Transp. Co. v. Penn Cent. Corp., 838 F.2d 1445, 1465 (6th Cir. 1988); N.Y. v. Hendrickson Bros., Inc., 840 F.2d 1065, 1083 (2d Cir. 1988); Berkson v. Del Monte Corp., 743 F.2d 53, 56 (1st Cir. 1984); Charlotte Telecasters, Inc. v. Jefferson-Pilot Corp., 546 F.2d 570, 574 (4th Cir. 1976).

[118] Klehr v. A.O. Smith Corp., 521 US 179, 189, 117 S. Ct. 1984 (1997) (quoting 2 Phillip E. Areeda & Herbert Hovencamp, Antitrust Law ¶338b at 145 (1995) (footnote omitted)) (citing Zenith Radio Corp. v. Hazeltine Research, Inc., 401 US 321, 338, 91 S. Ct. 795 (1971)); Hanover Shoe, Inc. v. United Shoe Mach. Corp., 392 US 481, 502 n.15, 88 S. Ct. 2224 (1968); DXS, Inc. v. Siemens Med. Sys., Inc., 100 F.3d 462, 467 (6th Cir. 1996); *see also* In re Cotton Yarn Antitrust Litig., 505 F.3d 274, 287–91 (4th Cir. 2007); Midwestern Mach. v. N.W. Airlines, 392 F.3d 265, 269 (8th Cir. 2004).

generally does not permit the plaintiff to recover for the injury caused by old overt acts outside the limitations period.'[119]

In 2006, the United States Court of Appeals for the Tenth Circuit set forth the requirements in that circuit for extending the statute of limitations as the result of a continuing antitrust violation: '1) It must be a new and independent act that is not merely a reaffirmation of a previous act; and 2) it must inflict new and accumulating injury on the plaintiff.'[120] Similarly, in 1999, the United States Court of Appeals for the Eleventh Circuit pointed out that:

> an act constitutes a 'continuing violation,' if it injures the plaintiff over a period of time. Even though the illegal act occurs at a specific point in time, if it inflicts 'continuing and accumulating harm' on a plaintiff, an antitrust violation occurs each time the plaintiff is injured by the act.[121]

For the purpose of determining the point when the statute of limitations recommences, the focus should generally be on the timing of the defendant's overt acts, rather than the effects of the overt acts.[122] In 2004, the United States Court of Appeals for the Eighth Circuit, for example, concluded that the continuing-violation theory can apply only where the violator 'actively reinitiates the anti-competitive policy and enjoys benefits from that action.'[123] The Eighth Circuit further noted that the distinction between a new and a continuing violation 'allows the statute of limitations to have effect and discourages private parties from sleeping on their rights.'[124]

---

119 Klehr v. A.O. Smith Corp., 521 US 179, 189, 117 S. Ct. 1984 (1997) (citing Zenith Radio Corp. v. Hazeltine Research, Inc., 401 US 321, 338, 91 S. Ct. 795 (1971), Pa. Dental Ass'n v. Med. Serv. Ass'n, 815 F.2d 270, 278 (3d Cir. 1987), Hennegan v. Pacifico Creative Serv., Inc., 787 F.2d 1299, 1300 (9th Cir. 1986), Nat'l Souvenir Cent., Inc. v. Historic Figures, Inc., 728 F.2d 503, 509 (D.C. Cir. 1984)); Imperial Point Colonnades Condo., Inc. v. Mangurian, 549 F.2d 1029, 1034–35 (5th Cir. 1977); Crummer Co. v. Du Pont, 223 F.2d 238, 247–48 (5th Cir. 1955)). *Cf.* 2 Phillip E. Areeda & Herbert Hovencamp, Antitrust Law ¶338b at 149 (1995).

120 Champagne Metals v. Ken-Mac Metals, Inc., 458 F.3d 1073, 1088 (10th Cir. 2006) (quoting Kaw Valley Elec. Co-op. Co. v. Kan. Elec. Power Co-op., Inc., 872 F.2d 931, 933 (10th Cir. 1989)).

121 Morton's Mkt., Inc. v. Gustafson's Dairy, Inc., 198 F.3d 823, 828 (11th Cir. 1999) (quoting Hanover Shoe, Inc. v. United Shoe Mach. Corp., 392 US 481, 502 n.15, 88 S. Ct. 2224 (1968)).

122 Varner v. Peterson Farms, 371 F.3d 1011, 1019 (8th Cir. 2004) (quoting DXS, Inc. v. Siemens Med. Sys., Inc., 100 F.3d 462, 467 (6th Cir. 1996) (citing Peck v. Gen. Motors Corp., 894 F.2d 844, 849 (6th Cir. 1990)).

123 Midwestern Mach. v. N.W. Airlines, 392 F.3d 265, 271 (8th Cir. 2004).

124 Midwestern Mach. v. N.W. Airlines, 392 F.3d 265, 271 (8th Cir. 2004).

12 Funding litigation

K. Craig Wildfang and Stacey P. Slaughter[1]

Fee arrangements in funding antitrust cases are varied. In the United States, for example, contingent fees, hourly fees, and alternative billing arrangements have all been used to finance antitrust lawsuits in private enforcement actions. This chapter focuses on the various types of fee arrangements utilized in funding antitrust and competition lawsuits in private enforcement actions. This chapter focuses on American fee models, specifically the history of contingency fees, along with a brief analysis of other fee models. This chapter also discusses the typical costs associated with antitrust litigation, which are a significant factor in funding such litigation. Cost plays a role in budget considerations for the litigation, and vary depending on the stage of the litigation. Finally, this chapter discusses some of the noteworthy damage recoveries and attorney's fees obtained in private enforcement antitrust actions.

History of funding litigation in the US through contingent fees

The contingent fee system developed from the once-prohibited practice of selling speculative judgment proceeds to a disinterested party, in consideration for funding the underlying litigation.[2] Commonly known as 'champerty,' the prohibition on such bargains between plaintiffs and disinterested third parties existed as early as thirteenth-century England when feudal lords and magnates could take advantage of

---

[1] K. Craig Wildfang is a partner at the law firm of Robins, Kaplan, Miller & Ciresi L.L.P. Before joining the firm's antitrust practice, Mr. Wildfang served as Special Counsel to the Assistant Attorney General for Antitrust, United States Department of Justice in Washington, DC from 1993 to 1996. Stacey P. Slaughter is also a partner at the law firm of Robins, Kaplan, Miller & Ciresi L.L.P., where she focuses on antitrust litigation and complex business and financial litigation. Members of the Minnesota bar, the authors are currently counsel for a class of merchant plaintiffs challenging, inter alia, horizontal fixing of interchange fees by Visa, MasterCard, and their member banks. *Photos Etc. Corp. v. Visa U.S.A., Inc.*, No. 305-CV-1007 (D. Conn. filed June 22, 2005). That case and other cases filed later were consolidated under MDL 1720 by the Judicial Panel on Multi-District Litigation by order dated October 19, 2005, and transferred to the Honorable John Gleeson in the US District Court for the Eastern District of New York. By Order dated February 24, 2006 the Court appointed the authors' firm co-lead counsel for the Class Plaintiffs. The named Class Plaintiffs are Plaintiffs Photos Etc. Corporation; Traditions, Ltd.; Capital Audio Electronics, Inc.; CHS Inc.; Coborn's Incorporated; Crystal Rock LLC; D'Agostino Supermarkets; Discount Optics,Inc.; Jetro Holdings, Inc. and Jetro Cash & Carry Enterprises, LLC; Leon's Transmission Service, Inc.; Parkway Corp.; and Payless ShoeSource, Inc. (collectively the 'Merchant Plaintiffs'), Affiliated Foods Midwest Cooperative, Inc.; National Association of Convenience Stores; NATSO, Inc.; National Community Pharmacists Association; National Cooperative Grocers Association; National Grocers Association; and National Restaurant Association (collectively the 'Trade-Association Plaintiffs'). Special thanks for attorneys Mathew Korte and Courtney Thompson for their assistance with this chapter.

[2] Stephen Landsman, 'The History of Contingency and the Contingency of History,' 47 DePaul L. Rev. 261, 262 (1998).

the poor, thus abusing the legal system in such a way as to further their own power or property.[3] As the American legal system began to take shape after separating from England, a prominent concern was to guarantee that both the rich and the poor had access to the courts and were assured an opportunity to avail themselves of the assistance of counsel.[4] The major purpose of the attorney contingency fee was to provide court access and assistance of counsel, regardless of a person's financial situation.[5] While the champerty prohibition still existed in form, this acceptance was a drastic departure from traditional English common law foundations that forbade any such 'contingency fees.'[6] The departure from the traditional English model began as early as late colonial America. The contingency fee's purpose was magnified throughout the early and mid-nineteenth century when many people who settled on land, believing they had good title, were later removed by the true landowners and could not afford to defend themselves.[7] Moreover, during the Industrial Revolution, the number of transportation and work-related accidents increased, but people who were injured could not afford legal representation.[8] Consequently, the increase in such claims forced the American Bar Association to accept the contingency fee as a valid system for lawyers' compensation.[9] By the mid-to-late nineteenth century, contingency fees were well-accepted.[10]

By the late nineteenth and early twentieth centuries, contingency fees began to become popular in various fields. Professor Peter Karsten notes that even before 'some of their high courts had sanctioned contingency fees, the American public was putting them to increasing numbers of use.'[11] For instance, Professor Karsten observes that the following situations had begun to involve contingency fee arrangements:

> Minority stockholders and dissident stock subscribers suing corporations, importers and customs brokers suing the federal government, depositors suing banks, creditors suing insolvent railroads and manufacturing firms, merchants and traders reporting depredations and losses at the hands of either Indian tribes or others before federal Claims Commissions, passengers and crews suing steamship companies, urban park commissioners seeking to clear title to park land, county commissioners and state auditors suing for title to land from those without proper title, subordinate government entities suing higher ones over tax revenues, towns and counties suing to halt the issuance or transfer of railroad bonds, as well as bondholders suing counties and municipalities to collect on these bonds.[12]

---

3 *Id.* at 263.

4 *Id.*

5 David A. Root, 'Attorney Fee-Shifting in America: Comparing, Contrasting, and Combining the "American Rule" and "English Rule",' 15 Ind. Int'l & Comp. L. Rev. 583, 593 (2005).

6 Peter Karsten, 'Enabling the Poor to Have Their Day in Court: The Sanctioning of Contingency Fee Contracts, A History to 1940,' 47 DePaul L. Rev. 231, 232 (1998).

7 Kristin Porcu, 'Protecting the Poor: The Dangers of Altering the Contingency Fee System,' 5 Suffolk J. Trial & App. Advoc. 149, 152–153(2000).

8 Angela Wennihan, 'Let's Put the Contingency Back in the Contingency Fee,' 49 SMU L. Rev. 1639, 1645–1646 (1996).

9 Root, *supra* note 5, at 593.

10 Karsten, *supra* note 6, at 249. (Supreme Court Chief Justice Morrison once called a contingency fee arrangement 'a legitimate and honorable professional assistance').

11 *Id.* at 248.

12 *Id.*

Contingency fee contracts, therefore, had begun to garner widespread use and binding recognition even before official sanctioning.[13] Despite the general approval of these contingency fee contracts, certain fields of law were deemed outside the bounds of contingency fees: alimony as part of the divorce, criminal matters,[14] securing 'a discharge for one who had been drafted during the Civil War,' or lobbying of legislators for purely private interests.[15]

Contingency fees saw some official sanctioning by a Congressional Act in 1915. The 1915 law 'limited the contingency fees of attorneys representing Southerners claiming damages for depredations or uncompensated takings' that occurred during the Civil War.[16] Nevertheless, many high courts found the limitations unconstitutional, thereby showing the 'clear evidence of the propensity of jurists by [the early 20th century] to treat [contingency] arrangements as part of the legal landscape and as the bread and butter of a large segment of the profession, to be defended when contravened by either the client or the defendant.'[17]

Nevertheless, not all courts were willing to sanction contingency fee agreements as written, and legal fictions were used to work around this restriction. For example, some of these courts voided clauses involving an 'attorney's promise to pay all of the costs associated with the suit.'[18] In Massachusetts, contingency fee arrangements were only tolerated if the agreement did not contain a 'no-win, no-fee' clause (even though all parties understood that the client would not pay if the action was unsuccessful).[19]

Today, contingency fee agreements have the official sanction of the American Bar Association. Rule 1.5 of the ABA's Model Rules of Professional Conduct allows for contingency fee arrangements, provided that they are reasonable and placed in writing. However, all courts retain the discretion and final determination for reasonableness of attorney fees.[20] In fact, courts may require attorneys to provide detailed justifications for their fees, or risk the court reducing the fee proportionally to the amount the court determines the attorney has proven reasonable.[21] For example, when determining the reasonableness of attorney fees drawn from a common class fund, the Third Circuit has held that courts should consider (1) the size of the fund created and the number of persons benefitted; (2) the presence or absence of substantial objections by members of the class to the settlement terms and/or fees requested by counsel; (3) the skill and efficiency of the attorneys involved; (4) the complexity and duration of the litigation; (5) the risk of nonpayment; (6) the amount of time devoted to the case by plaintiff's counsel; and (7) the awards in similar cases. [22]

---

13 *Id.* at 249.

14 Porcu, *supra* note 7, at 154.

15 Karsten, *supra* note 6, at 249.

16 *Id.*

17 *Id.* at 250.

18 *Id.* at 253.

19 *Id.*

20 Porcu, *supra* note 7, at 155–156; *see also In re Relafen Antitrust Litig.*, 231 F.R.D. 52 (D. Mass. 2005).

21 Porcu, at 153.

22 *In re Rite Aid Corp. Sec. Litig.*, 396 F.3d 294, 301 (3rd Cir. 2005) (citing *Gunter v. Ridgewood Energy Corp.*, 223 F. 3d 190, 195 (3rd Cir. 2000)). *See also Segen v. Optionsxpress Holdings, Inc.*,

Contingency fee advocates often point to the fact that such a fee structure represents the freedom to contract.[23] The ability to freely contract for services enables the market to function most efficiently.[24] Some courts have been reluctant to lower attorneys' contingency fees on the grounds that, 'absent fraud or overreaching, the attorney-client contract for legal services should not be intruded upon by the State.'[25] Nevertheless, courts routinely do reduce contingency fees. Attorneys and judges alike seem to believe it is within the power of the court to reduce a contingency fee when it seems excessive, as a means of administering justice and simultaneously disciplining a potentially unscrupulous attorney.[26] This power to reduce excessive-seeming fees is regarded as 'inherent' and 'equitable.'[27]

Considerations before funding a contingent fee case

Antitrust fee arrangements have seen many different shapes, forms, and sizes. Funding private antitrust cases typically depends on whether the client is a plaintiff or a defendant in the case. A defendant in an antitrust case usually pays attorneys' fees on a per diem, or billable hour, basis. Although plaintiffs also pay attorneys' fees by the hour in some circumstances, this arrangement is rare. More often, plaintiffs fund antitrust litigation using some form of contingent fee arrangement in which the attorneys' fees are paid if the plaintiff ultimately prevails in the lawsuit. If the plaintiff does not prevail, then he does not pay attorney's fees or the defendants' expenses.[28]

When a law firm agrees to represent a client on some type of alternative fee arrangement, it will consider several factors. These factors include '(1) the likelihood of a favorable outcome, (2) the time frame in which the recovery is likely to occur, (3) the probable amount of recovery, and (4) the percentage contracted for.'[29] In reality, these factors may vary and other considerations may come into play, including a weighing of a particular attorney or firm's expertise, the other cases that the firm or attorney is handling, and the needs of the particular client. Due to the professional expertise such weighing involves,

---

631 F.Supp.2d 465, 466 (D. Del. 2009) (reducing requested attorney fees from 33 per cent down to 8 per cent of the recovery).

[23] Angela Wennihan, 'Let's Put the Contingency Back in the Contingency Fee,' 49 SMU L. Rev. 1639, 1650; *see also* Stephen D. Annand & Roberta F. Green, 'Legislative and Judicial Controls of Contingency Fees in Tort Cases,' 99 W. Va. L. Rev. 81, 94 (1996) (citing Henry H. Drummonds, 'The Law and Ethics of Percentage Contingent Fees in Oregon,' 72 Or. L. Rev. 859, 872 n.56 (discussing the enforcement of contingent fees under contract theory).

[24] Wennihan, *supra* note 23, at 1650.

[25] *Id.* at 1650.

[26] *Id.* at 1665.

[27] *Id.* at 1665 (quoting Note, 'Judicial Power over Contingent Fee Contracts: Reasonableness and Ethics,' 20 Case W. Res. L. Rev. 523, 523 (1980)).

[28] Root, *supra* note 5, at 583, 589, 597–98; Virginia G. Maurer, Robert E. Thomas, Pamela A. DeBooth, 'Attorney Fee Arrangements: The US And Western European Perspectives,' 19 Nw. J. Int'l. L. & Bus. 272, 293, 306 (1999).

[29] Drew C. Phillips, 'Contingency Fees: Rules & Ethical Guidelines,' 11 Geo. J. Legal Ethics 233, 237 (1998) (citing Stephen Gillers, 'Regulation of Lawyers,' Problems of Law and Ethics 140 (1995)).

'. . . in most cases, the lawyer is far better equipped than the client to evaluate the criteria that should determine whether or not to take a case on a contingent basis.'[30]

Certain fixed costs and expenses are associated with litigating a private antitrust case. As part of its retainer agreement with the client, the law firm will address how such costs will be paid. The litigation costs typically range from small expenses such as photocopying and mail service, to larger expenses such as expert fees and travel. These expenses are 'out of pocket.' In other words, the law firm will have to pay the expenses as they come due, regardless of whether or when there will be a favorable recovery in the case.

When a law firm considers whether to accept a case on an alternative fee basis, it must evaluate what the estimated costs of the case will be. The following items are merely examples, not an exhaustive list, of the larger costs typically associated with litigating a case: electronic document retrieval, storage or hosting, and production; expert fees; deposition stenographer hourly reporting fees; deposition transcript costs; travel expenses; and legal research using electronic search services.[31]

In cases in which multiple law firms agree to represent a plaintiff – or more typically, several plaintiffs – on an alternative fee basis, the firms divide the costs of the litigation and the attorneys' fees ultimately recovered.[32] This assessment is sometimes based on a lodestar value, which is discussed in more detail below. Simply put, the costs and fees are assessed and distributed equitably, based upon the number of hours that each law firm works on the case. Thus, at the end of the case, the attorney's fees would be distributed to the various law firms based upon the lodestar value.

Finally, in some cases, insurance policies may cover the attorney's fees and expenses for litigation.[33] Generally, if a business has purchased a general liability insurance policy, part of the policy's coverage may go towards attorneys' fees. Individuals, unless they have the risk of suit in a professional capacity, do not often purchase general liability insurance in the United States. However, in England, legal expenses insurance can be purchased by individuals to protect against the 'loser pays' rule, whereby a losing plaintiff or defendant has to pay the full amount of her opponent's fees in addition to her own.[34] This type of insurance is described as being 'non-existent in America.'[35]

---

30 Phillips, *supra* note 29, at 238.

31 The federal tax laws impose an additional hurdle by treating expenses and costs that a plaintiffs' attorney advances as 'loans' to the client or putative class of clients. These expenditures are therefore not deductible from income as business expenses for the attorney when they are incurred. In complex cases, these expenses can run into the millions of dollars and financing them can pose a formidable challenge.

32 For a discussion of recovery of attorney's fees and costs in the context of plaintiffs' remedies, see Chapter 11 of this *Handbook*.

33 This subject is worthy of its own separate article and will not be discussed at great length here.

34 Root, *supra* note 5, at 601.

35 *Id.*

Recoverability of costs[36]

The Clayton Act provides a successful plaintiff the right to recover its costs of suit in addition to a reasonable attorney's fee.[37] However, questions sometimes arise as to what costs are recoverable. Courts have differed regarding whether discovery-deposition costs, as opposed to costs of depositions used by a plaintiff at trial, for example, are recoverable under the Clayton Act.[38] In 2002, the United States Court of Appeals for the Eleventh Circuit affirmed a district court decision that a plaintiff may recover the costs for such discovery depositions of potential witnesses listed on the losing party's witness list, in addition to the costs for expedited transcripts.[39]

With regard to the similar question of whether expert-witness fees are recoverable costs under the Clayton Act, in 1986 the United States Court of Appeals for the Fifth Circuit held that a prevailing party's recovery of private expert witness fees is limited to general cost recovery statutes, including 18 U.S.C. §1821, and that the Clayton Act does not authorize the recovery of expert witness fees in excess of that amount.[40] The Fifth Circuit stated that 'Congress knows full well how to provide for the recovery of excess expert witness' fees as costs. That Congress did not do so in 15 U.S.C. §15 is clear.'[41]

While the Clayton Act provides a successful plaintiff the right to recover its costs of suit, the Act grants no such right to a successful defendant. In *J.T. Gibbons, Inc. v. Crawford Fitting Co.*, the Fifth Circuit denied a prevailing defendant's request for an award of fees and costs because, by definition, defendants do not fall within the plaintiffs-only provision in the Clayton Act for the shifting of attorney's fees.[42]

That the Clayton Antitrust Act does not permit awards of attorney's fees to successful defendants, however, does not completely foreclose the ability of a defendant to obtain an award of attorney's fees under other federal statutory authority addressing baseless or frivolous litigation. For example, a prevailing antitrust defendant, the same as any other defendant, can recover attorney's fees on appeal if the court of appeals determines that the losing plaintiff filed 'a frivolous appeal.'[43] In addition, a prevailing defendant could

---

[36] Joseph Bruckner and Matthew Salzwedel, who authored Chapter 11 of this *Handbook*, contributed research and text to this section of this chapter.

[37] 15 U.S.C. §15 (2009).

[38] Maris Distrib. Co. v. Anheuser-Busch, Inc., 302 F.3d 1207, 1225 (11th Cir. 2002) (citing Hall v. Ohio Educ. Ass'n, 984 F. Supp. 1144, 1146 (S.D. Ohio 1997)).

[39] Maris Distrib. Co. v. Anheuser-Busch, Inc., 302 F.3d 1207, 1225–1226 (11th Cir. 2002) ('Although we do not believe that the costs associated with expedited trial transcripts should be allowed as a matter of course, lest litigation costs be unnecessarily increased, the district court found that expedited transcripts were necessary in this case given its length and complexity.').

[40] *J.T. Gibbons, Inc. v. Crawford Fitting Co.*, 790 F.2d 1193, 1194–1195 (5th Cir. 1986) (citing *Berkey Photo, Inc. v. Eastman Kodak Co.*, 603 F.2d 263, 309 n.75 (2d Cir. 1979)); *Ott v. Speedwriting Publ'g Co.*, 518 F.2d 1143, 1149 (6th Cir. 1975); *Illinois v. Sangamo Constr. Co.*, 657 F.2d 855, 864–865 (7th Cir. 1981)).

[41] *J.T. Gibbons, Inc. v. Crawford Fitting Co.*, 790 F.2d 1193, 1195 (5th Cir. 1986) (citing *Int'l Woodworkers of Am. v. Champion Int'l Corp.*, 790 F.2d 1174, 1181 (5th Cir. 1986)).

[42] *J.T. Gibbons, Inc. v. Crawford Fitting Co.*, 790 F.2d 1193, 1194–1195 (5th Cir. 1986).

[43] *Olympia Co. v. Celotex Corp.*, 771 F.2d 888, 892–893 (5th Cir. 1985) (award made against a party-appellant) (citing 28 U.S.C. §1912, Fed. R. App. P. 38; 28 and U.S.C. §1927 (2009)).

possibly obtain an award of attorney's fees using other methods, such as a request for sanctions under Federal Rule of Civil Procedure 11, or the federal frivolous-litigation statute, 28 U.S.C. §1927, which specifically authorizes an award of attorney's fees against an opposing party's attorneys.

Types of fee arrangements

The most common fee arrangement in a private antitrust action is the contingency fee.[44] As fee arrangements are often privately negotiated, public data on this subject in the US is scarce. In the American Antitrust Institute's Private Enforcement Project study,[45] 30 of the 40 cases analyzed are included in the tables highlighting the percentage of recovery awarded as attorney's fees.[46] These cases are all contingent-based; the remaining cases' fee structures are not otherwise discussed or disclosed. In addition to the contingent fee arrangement, the incentive-based fee arrangement, the 'billable hour,' the task-based arrangement, the flat fee arrangement, mixed arrangements and the attorney investment arrangement have all been utilized in some form in antitrust cases. These arrangements are discussed below.

100 per cent contingent agreements

This type of arrangement is the commonly understood 'no-win, no-pay' system. This arrangement is common in large, class-action suits, including antitrust lawsuits.[47] In this type of arrangement, attorneys accept 'the case in return for a percentage of any award or settlement.'[48] ABA Model Rule of Professional Conduct 1.5 allows for these types of arrangements, provided that:

> A contingent fee agreement shall be in a writing signed by the client and shall state the method by which the fee is to be determined, including the percentage or percentages that shall accrue to the lawyer in the event of settlement, trial or appeal; litigation and other expenses to be deducted from the recovery; and whether such expenses are to be deducted before or after the contingent fee is calculated. The agreement must clearly notify the client of any expenses for which the client will be liable whether or not the client is the prevailing party. Upon conclusion of a contingent fee matter, the lawyer shall provide the client with a written statement stating the outcome of the matter and, if there is a recovery, showing the remittance to the client and the method of its determination.[49]

Several advantages to this type of agreement exist. First, and most importantly, this arrangement provides the opportunity for greater access to justice for disadvantaged plaintiffs.[50] Plaintiffs can pursue worthy cases without a large, up-front fee arrangement.

---

44 Sarah Northway, 'Non-Traditional Class Action Financing and Traditional Rules of Ethics: Time for A Compromise,' 14 Geo. J. Legal Ethics 241, 245 n.30 (2000).

45 Robert H. Lande & Joshua P. Davis, *Benefits from Private Antitrust Enforcement: An Analysis of Forty Cases*, (2007).

46 *Id.* at Tables 6A–6C.

47 Paula Batt Wilson, 'Attorney Investment in Class Action Litigation: The Agent Orange Example,' 45 Case W. Res. L. Rev. 291, 291(1994).

48 *Id.* at 297.

49 ABA Model Rule of Professional Conduct 1.5 (2004)

50 Wennihan, *supra* note 23, at 1649–1651.

Second, contingency fee agreements promote progressive litigation.[51] This advantage was noticed by the Supreme Court in *Deposit Guar. Nat'l Bank of Jackson, Miss. v. Roper,* where the Court described the role of the contingency fee agreement as an effective tool in vindicating smaller aggregated claims unremedied by the regulatory action of government, thus creating a 'private attorney general.'[52] Examples of other progressive litigation include the abolition of government immunity in some states, the right of parents to recover for the wrongful death of an unborn child, and liability lawsuits which have removed harmful products such as flammable children's pajamas, cars that explode on impact, and harmful contraceptive devices.[53] Third, contingency fee agreements help align the interests of the attorney and client by providing shared incentives and shared risks.[54] Fourth, contingency fee agreements that are based upon a percentage of recovery are easier to compute than other common alternative fee arrangements.[55]

Although the contingency fee system opens the justice system for many people, some critics have identified disadvantages of the traditional contingency fee agreement. First, while the client and attorney share a similar end goal of a successful action, their interests are not completely aligned. For instance, 'the attorney may want to settle early for a guaranteed fee rather than invest additional hours in the case. Those hours might result in a marginally greater recovery for the client, or alternatively, in the loss of the case altogether.'[56] However, professional responsibility requirements to the client must ultimately motivate the litigation.

Second, as the critics note, contingency fees may result in windfall profits for the attorney. For example, an attorney may accept a case with very little risk and very little work required, but with a large potential damage amount. In such a situation, the attorney may collect a 'windfall' amount.[57] Nevertheless, such fee arrangements are subject to checks and balances. Courts often act as gatekeepers to ensure that attorneys do not recover 'windfall' amounts. In the *In re Visa Check/MasterMoney Antitrust Litigation*, for example, Judge Gleeson concluded that the plaintiff attorneys' fee request was 'excessive' and 'absurd.'[58] Plaintiffs' counsel had requested fees at 18 per cent of the clients' monetary relief, or around $609,012,000.[59] After applying a

---

51 *Id.* at 1651.

52 445 US 326, 388 (1980).

53 Wennihan, *supra* note 23, at 1651.

54 Michael McKee, Rudy Santore, and Joel Shelton, 'Contingent Fees, Moral Hazard, and Attorney Rents: A Laboratory Experiment,' 36 J. Legal Stud. 253, 269–271 (2007).

55 Wilson, *supra* note 47, at 308.

56 *Id.* at 300.

57 *Id.* at 309.

58 *In re Visa Check/MasterMoney Antitrust Litig.*, 297 F. Supp.2d 503, 522 (Dec. 19, 2003). In his book about the lawsuit, attorney Lloyd Constantine argues that his fee request for the attorneys on the case was justified. Lloyd Constantine, *Priceless* 224–227 (2009). Mr. Constantine recounts the measures that he and colleagues took to present the attorney's fees to Judge Gleeson, including cutting attorney hours that were billed for excessively long days. 'In this exercise, my hours were cut for numerous days when I traveled to San Francisco and worked through the night; that is, after my drink in the Redwood Room of the Clift Hotel.' *Id.* at 225.

59 *In re Visa Check/MasterMoney Antitrust Litig.*, 297 F. Supp.2d at 522.

six-factor test to determine an appropriate fee, Judge Gleeson awarded $220,290,160.44 in reduced fees.[60]

Nevertheless, the vast number of cases in which a court reduces contingency fees when the plaintiff is an individual are personal injury cases. These are difficult to compare in size, scope, and damages award amounts to the numbers in even a small antitrust claim. The similarity that exists is that in either type of case, if a court believes the fee is excessive then the court retains the authority to reduce that fee. Attorneys may preempt this problem by scaling back on an original contingency percentage when the higher-than-expected recovery is returned. In 2007, a report by the American Antitrust Institute's Private Enforcement Project found that, in antitrust cases in which attorney's fees are near the standard one-third amount, the recovery is smaller.[61] For cases where the recovery is between $100 and $500 million, the percentage of attorney's fees drops proportionally.[62] Of the five cases with recoveries greater than $500 million included in the study, four had attorney's fee percentages between 5.2 and 13 per cent. The perceived (and proportional) fairness of the fees guides the court in its determination, whether plaintiffs are injured individuals or members of a large class. Professional associations also recommend limits on such recoveries. The ABA Rules attempt to regulate contingent recoveries by requiring all fees to be 'reasonable.'

A third criticism of the contingency fee model is the increase in litigation that it may engender.[63] However, such criticism is largely unfounded.[64] In fact, as discussed later, the process that attorneys undertake to evaluate a case, as well as the costs associated with litigating a case, often serves as an inherent check on unfettered litigation.[65]

Despite the criticism, a percentage-based contingency fee model has become a widely-used and accepted method for funding private enforcement antitrust litigation. As the court commented in *Wal-Mart Stores, Inc. v. Visa U.S.A. Inc. and MasterCard Int'l, Inc.*, the trend has been towards applying the percentage-based method because 'it directly aligns the interests of the [party] and its counsel and provides a powerful incentive for the efficient prosecution and early resolution of litigation.'[66]

---

60 Mr. Constantine, who disagreed with the Court's fee calculation, argues that Judge Gleeson actually awarded a 3.5 multiplier of the $62,940,045.84 amount submitted as the lodestar in the fee application. *Id.* at 232.

61 Lande & Davis, *supra* note 45, Table 6A (2007).

62 *Id.* at Table 6B.

63 Wennihan, *supra* note 23, at 1658.

64 Wennihan, *supra* note 23, at 1659 (citing Stephen Budiansky, et al., 'How Lawyers Abuse the Law,' US News & World Rep., Jan. 30, 1995, at 5056 for the fact that personal injury contingency litigation remained constant from 1975 to 1990, and has fallen since 1990).

65 *Id.* at 1659 ('[T]he lawyer acts as a buffer between the plaintiff and defendant by not accepting baseless claims because it is not in her own economic best interest to do so.') (citing Philip H. Corboy, 'Contingency Fees: The Individual's Key to the Courthouse Door,' 1976 Litig. 27 (1975–1976); Root, *supra* note 5, at 596 ('[T]he lawyer who takes a certain percentage of the proceeds from a victorious case will screen out those cases lacking sufficient merit to avoid the opportunity cost of wasting his time and resources. Coinciding with this "screening out" argument, others argue that contingency fees actually decrease the amount of frivolous litigation by changing the lawyer's incentives.').

66 396 F.3d 96, 121 (2nd Cir. 2005); See also *In re Lease Oil Antitrust Litig. (No. II)*, 186 F.R.D. 403, 444 (S.D. Tex. 1999) (commenting upon the strong trend toward the percentage method).

Incentive-based fee arrangement

This type of arrangement 'creates an incentive for the attorney to obtain a favorable result at a lower cost to all clients in a manner not unlike the contingent fee arrangements for plaintiff clients.'[67] Under an incentive-based fee arrangement, an attorney's fees are dependent upon the result – the more favorable the settlement or judgment, the more fees collected by the attorney.[68] Thus, in this type of arrangement, an 'attorney is given an incentive to resolve the lawsuit for the lowest possible cost to the client.'[69] Furthermore, the 'client benefits either from low fees and/or settlement costs due to a favorable resolution of the case or from reduced fees if the settlement or judgment is not favorable.'[70]

The 'billable hour'

The traditional 'billable hour' method gained popularity in the mid-1960s.[71] This method is the simplest to calculate. The fee is computed by taking the number of hours worked multiplied by the attorney's hourly billing rate.

This type of arrangement was originally thought to improve 'fairness.' Calculating a fee based on 'the hours of work that a lawyer put[s] into a task was an objective way to measure the amount a client should owe.'[72] Thus, this hourly rate is perceived as the 'fair value' of services provided to a client.

Nevertheless, one of the biggest disadvantages of this billing system is the potential of an unnecessary increase in litigation costs. This system rewards inefficiency, because 'the more hours worked, the more fees are generated.'[73] Furthermore, the hourly billing method leads to a bigger and very obvious problem: litigation is unpredictable, and the hourly billing method does not have a mechanism to control costs. Finally, the billable hour method does not solve some of the problems identified earlier. People who may not otherwise have access to the court system because they cannot afford it will not be able to fund litigation this way. Moreover, even people who have the funds may not be willing to invest the funds to pursue viable but nevertheless high-stakes, cutting edge legal issues.

Task-based and flat fee arrangements

Task-based fee systems are based on the completion of various tasks instead of an hourly or contingent agreement. Tasks may be 'defined as narrowly as a specific deposition or as broadly as completion of fact research and case analysis.'[74] Fees for each task can be negotiated, 'creating an incentive for the attorney to perform efficiently.'[75]

---

67 Stephen W. Jones and Melissa Beard Glover, 'The Attack on Traditional Billing Practices,' 20 U. Ark. Little Rock L.J. 293, 304 (1998).

68 *Id.* at 304–305.

69 *Id.* at 305.

70 *Id.*

71 *Id.* at 293–299.

72 *Id.* at 294.

73 *Id.* at 295.

74 *Id.* at 306.

75 *Id.*

Flat fee agreements are exactly that – a fee is 'charged for handling a matter from beginning to end.'[76]

Mixed arrangements
While the above fee arrangements can be used as the sole type of fee agreement for a specific matter, many fee arrangements in complex litigation are a blending of various types of arrangements. A common 'blend' is the partial contingent agreement. In such an agreement, the attorney will be paid a reduced hourly fee, in exchange for an amount from the final judgment. In such a system, for example, an attorney may charge reduced fees, in exchange for 10 per cent of the final settlement or judgment.

Attorney investment
An attorney investment arrangement involves an attorney advancing a share of the litigation expenses in exchange for a specified return on investment to be allocated from the amount approved for attorney's fees following judgment or settlement.[77] However, the setting of attorney's fees by fixing a rate of return on an initial investment is uncommon, perhaps as a result of professional responsibility rules dictating that fees must be 'reasonable.'[78] Setting a fixed rate of return on an investment before any recovery is had may obstruct the process of fairness, as compared to a contingency fee, which may have a greater claim to reasonableness due to its proportionality, whether or not a recovery ultimately covers the expenses advanced. Though the attorney-investment model exists, due to its high-profile difficulties in the *Agent Orange* litigation,[79] attorneys may be wary to utilize it, especially since the contingency fee method is accepted as the norm in class action litigation. The most famous situation involving attorney investment involved the aforementioned *Agent Orange* cases.

1. The Agent Orange example The plaintiffs in the *Agent Orange* cases adopted an attorney investment fee model after lengthy and 'tortuous' attempts to finance the massive, complex litigation.[80] This case was initiated in 1979 by plaintiff Edward J. Gorman and his attorney Victor J. Yannacone, Jr.[81] Eventually, Yannacone was replaced by a three-member Plaintiffs' Management Committee ('PMC').[82] After the court 'threw the plaintiffs' camp into a "near-panic" by setting a trial date which gave the parties less than seven months to complete pre-trial investigation and preparation of the case,' the PMC sought help.[83] Nine members of a new PMC 'executed an agreement

---

76 *Id.*
77 Wilson, *supra* note 47, at 311–312.
78 Model Rule 1.8(g) ('A lawyer shall not acquire a proprietary interest in the cause of action or subject matter of litigation the lawyer is conducting for a client except that the lawyer may:
(1) acquire a lien granted by law to secure the lawyer's fee or expenses; and
(2) contract with a client for a reasonable contingent fee in a civil case.')
79 Wilson, *supra* note 47.
80 *Id.* at 311.
81 *Id.*
82 *Id.*
83 *Id.*

requiring six members to advance $200,000 each for litigation expenses.'[84] These new 'investor-attorneys,' in exchange for the investment, would receive $600,000 from the amount of approved attorney's fees if the case was successful, and also 50 per cent of the remaining amount to be divided equally among the investors.[85] Of the other 50 per cent of the remaining amount, 30 per cent would be divided according to hours expended on the case, and 20 per cent would be divided based on majority vote.[86]

After the court expressed 'serious doubt about its legality and propriety,' the PMC members executed a new agreement.[87] The new agreement left unchanged the percentage on the return on investment (300 per cent), but allowed for an increase of $50,000 per contributing attorney.[88] The new agreement, however, eliminated the earlier provisions regarding the percentage distributions for the amount remaining after remuneration to the investor-attorneys, and substituted 'division among all PMC members "in the proportion the individual's and/or firm's fee award bears to the total fees awarded."'[89]

2. Ethical considerations of attorney-investors One of the biggest ethical issues raised by attorney investment concerns litigation objectives. A primary premise of American law is that the client defines the objectives of the litigation. In a situation where the attorney holds a financial investment in a case, and in class actions in general, the attorneys 'function essentially as entrepreneurs who bear a substantial amount of the litigation risk and exercise nearly plenary control over all important decisions in the lawsuit.'[90]

Other conflicts may also arise in attorney-investor agreements. Financial conflicts may arise in cases where an attorney has a financial investment in a case and exercises such great control over day-to-day litigation decisions. These problems may be further exacerbated when a client has difficulty getting information from the attorney about a case or has difficulty dismissing an attorney.[91] Specifically, the attorney may be guided by his financial considerations instead of the client's wishes. The Fifth Circuit phrased the issue as follows: 'Whenever an attorney is confronted with a potential for choosing between actions which may benefit himself financially and an action which may benefit the class which he represents there is a reasonable possibility that some specifically identifiable impropriety will occur.'[92] In *Agent Orange*, the Second Circuit stated:

> Given the size and complexity of the litigation, it seems apparent that the potential for abuse was real and should have been discouraged. . . . The conflict obviously lies in the incentive provided to an investor-attorney to settle early and thereby avoid work for which full payment may

---

84 Wilson, *supra* note 47, at 312.
85 *Id.*
86 *Id.*
87 *Id.*
88 *Id.*
89 Wilson, *supra* note 47, at 312.
90 *Id.* at 316.
91 *Id.*
92 *Id.* at 317.

> not be authorized by the district court. Moreover, as soon as an offer of settlement to cover the promised return on investment is made, the investor-attorney will be disinclined to undertake the risks associated with continuing the litigation. [93]

Thus, the investor-attorney model leads to serious potential conflicts. In *Agent Orange*, the Second Circuit refused to accept the PMC's attorney-investment agreement. Nevertheless, some legal scholars have suggested that the PMC fee arrangement used in the *Agent Orange* example should be essentially 'institutional[ized] . . . by creating a risk multiplier for expenses. Giving attorneys a risk premium for expenses advanced, as well as for fees, would increase the attorney's recovery and theoretically minimize the effect of champerty in inducing settlement.'[94]

Other investors

In recent years, the litigation funding industry has grown, especially with regard to plaintiff's personal injury cases.[95] There are now companies that exist to invest money in litigation, by advancing those funds to the attorney or plaintiff involved in the contingency fee case, and negotiating the type of return on that investment.[96] It appears that, though the majority of such investments are also structured on a percentage-based contingency fee recovery,[97] some negotiate a flat fee, based on the specific rate of return on that initial investment.[98] For example, a litigation funding company may loan an attorney money for costs of the litigation, and the attorney, upon recovery, will repay the amount loaned, plus a fee.[99] Some companies attach a high interest rate, such as 50 per cent, on the money that was initially loaned to the plaintiff.[100] If the plaintiff does not recover any damages from the litigation, the investor recovers nothing, thus participating in the risk involved.[101]

The increase in funding arrangements such as these is more common in the personal injury arena now, probably due to the much smaller amount of money needed to advance the costs of such a lawsuit. If companies such as these continue to grow, non-lawyer investors may be able to fund large antitrust class action litigation. Proponents of the increase in litigation funding point to the fact that it increases legal access and thereby 'evens the playing field on an economic level in a way that traditional banking institutions cannot.'[102] Most banks regard litigation, with its accompanying uncertainties, as

---

93 *Id.* at 318.
94 *Id.*
95 *See* Susan Lorde Martin, 'The Litigation Financing Industry: The Wild West of Finance Should Be Tamed Not Outlawed,' 10 Fordham J. Corp. & Fin. L. 55, 55 (2004).
96 Douglas R. Richmond, 'Other People's Money: The Ethics of Litigation Funding,' 56 Mercer L. Rev. 649, 650 (2005).
97 Martin, *supra* note 95, at 55.
98 Richmond, *supra* note 96, at 650.
99 *Id.*
100 Martin, *supra* note 95, at 56.
101 *Id.*
102 Christy B. Bushnell, 'Champerty Is Still No Excuse in Texas: Why Texas Courts (And The Legislature) Should Uphold Litigation Funding Agreements,' 7 Hous. Bus. & Tax. L.J. 358, 364 (2007).

too risky a venture for investment.[103] Additionally, attorneys have been unable in most instances to borrow money to fund a lawsuit from a bank, due to the ethical restrictions on the division of fees and the possibility of accidental partnership formation with non-lawyers.[104]

Court factors in awarding attorney's fees

The 'lodestar' method

A common method for calculating attorney's fees in class actions is the 'lodestar' method. The lodestar method was developed in the Third Circuit, and has now been approved by most circuit courts in the United States.[105] In using this method, '[t]he court multiplies the number of hours reasonably worked on a client's case by a reasonable hourly billing rate for such services based on a given geographical area, the nature of services provided, and the experience of the attorneys' to create an objective 'lodestar.'[106] Courts then utilize multipliers to adjust the fee subjectively for various situations, such as high-risk litigation.[107]

Despite the popularity of the lodestar method, some critics cite drawbacks to this system. Criticisms of this method 'involve its asserted. . .

> . . . incentives to pad billable hours, its burden on the parties and the court, and the fact that its guarantee of fees in successful cases may cause attorneys to reject a favorable settlement for the class. In 1985, the Third Circuit . . . formed a Task Force to address the 'widespread belief that the deficiencies of the current system either offset or exceed its benefits.' Specifically, the Third Circuit Task Force 'concluded that the lodestar formula increases the use of judicial resources, encourages attorneys to bill excessive hours, and discourages early settlement.[108]

Other commentators have noted the drawbacks from a different perspective:

> In some cases, plaintiffs' attorneys can be tempted to negotiate early with the defense counsel about settlement. The ensuing pre-litigation work becomes merely a 'meaningless exercise' to bill additional hours after a settlement has been agreed upon in actuality. In this way, the lodestar approach can produce structural, de facto collusion between the plaintiff's attorney and defendants. In this scenario, the defendant makes a low settlement offer and then cooperates with the plaintiff's attorney to allow the latter to accumulate hours, which are deducted from the class recovery at no additional cost to the defendant. 'At no point must either side actually link the fee award and the settlement size in their negotiations – the law does this for them by tying fee awards to hours billed rather than settlement size.'[109]

Thus, this method can 'award a settling attorney the same fee award she would receive if she litigated a much higher recovery for the plaintiffs at trial.'[110] As a consequence,

---

103 *Id.* at n.43.
104 Wilson, *supra* note 47, at 342.
105 *Id.* at 305.
106 *In re Rite Aid,* 396 F.3d at 305–306.
107 Wilson, *supra* note 47, at 305–306.
108 *Id.* at 307.
109 *Id.* at 307–308.
110 *Id.* at 308.

the lodestar approach of setting fees can be 'too vulnerable to collusive settlements.'[111] Therefore, attorneys get no compensation for accepting additional risk by litigating the case, and the lodestar method encourages attorneys to accept large settlements, even if a litigated recovery could be greater.[112]

Nevertheless, these criticisms have not deterred courts from applying the lodestar method in a number of cases. For example, in *Kenny A. ex rel. Winn v. Perdue*, the court awarded $10.5 million in attorney's fees which included an upward adjustment under the lodestar method. [113] In support of the 75 per cent upward adjustment from the requested fees, the court praised the plaintiff's counsel for their skill, expertise, and professionalism, stating:

> [T]he evidence establishes that the quality of service rendered by class counsel, including their extraordinary commitment of capital resources, was far superior to what consumers of legal services . . . could reasonably expect to receive for the rates used in the lodestar calculation. . . .[114] The Court is unaware of any other case in which a plaintiff class has achieved such a favorable result on such a comprehensive scale.[115]

Often in antitrust cases, courts will also utilize the lodestar method in order to verify the reasonableness of the percentage-based attorney fee request.[116] For example, the court in *In re Relafen Antitrust Litigation* granted $22.3 million in attorney's fees (one-third of the recovery) after conducting a lodestar cross-check.[117] The court, citing precedent granting percentage-based fees in excess of four times the lodestar value, stated that the fee request was reasonable as a matter of law.[118] Again, the court praised plaintiff's counsel for their work.

The Goldberger factors[119]

In 2003, the court in the *In re Visa Check/MasterMoney* antitrust litigation applied the six-factor *Goldberger* test utilized by the Second Circuit in determining the appropriate amount of attorney's fees.[120] In applying the *Goldberger* factors, 'the key consideration in

---

111 *Id.*

112 *Id.*

113 454 F.Supp.2d 1260 (N.D. Ga. 2006), *aff'd by* 532 F.3d 1209 (11th Cir. 2008).

114 Id. at 1288.

115 Id. at 1290. See also *Rodriguez v. West Publishing Corp.*, 563 F.3d 948 (9th Cir. 2009) (antitrust suit appropriately applying the lodestar method was remanded for consideration of attorney fees in light of conflict of interest resulting from incentive agreements).

116 *In re Insurance Brokerage Antitrust Litig.*, 2009 WL 411856, *4 (D.N.J. Feb. 17, 2009) ('While either the lodestar or percentage-of-recovery method should ordinarily serve as the primary basis for determining the fee, the Third Circuit has instructed that it is sensible to use the alternative method to double check the reasonableness of the fee.').

117 231 F.R.D. at 81-82.

118 *Id.* at 82. See also *Wal-Mart,* 396 F.3d at 123 (approving a percentage-based fee 3.5 times the lodestar value as reasonable).

119 Joseph Bruckner and Matthew Salzwedel, who authored Chapter 11 of this *Handbook*, contributed research and text to the paragraphs discussing the Johnson-Kerr method of calculating attorney's fees in this section of this chapter.

120 *In re VISA Check/Mastermoney Antitrust Litig.*, 297 F. Supp. 2d 503, 521 (E.D.N.Y. 2003) (citing *Goldberger v. Integrated Res., Inc.*, 209 F.3d 43, 50 (2d Cir. 2000)).

awarding fees is what is reasonable under the circumstances.'[121] This included weighing (1) the time and effort expended by counsel, (2) the size of the lawsuit and its complexity; (3) the risk involved; (4) the level of the representation; (5) the size of the requested fee relative to the settlement obtained; and (6) relevant public policy considerations.[122] In the *In re Visa Check/MasterMoney Antitrust Litigation* suit, the court found that although the suit went on for many years,[123] was of a significant size and complexity,[124] involved substantial risk,[125] and was excellently represented by plaintiffs' counsel,[126] the request for fees was 'excessive.'[127] Nevertheless, the *Goldberger* factors 'compel[led]' the court to an 'award of an extraordinary fee.'[128] The court emphasized that the size of the settlement obtained made 'even the exorbitant fee . . . award[ed] seem[] small in comparison.'[129] Finally, the public policy considerations merited a 'substantial fee award,'[130] due to the 'significant and lasting benefits for America's merchants and consumers'[131] arising out of the litigation. The court's ultimate award of $220,290,160.44 in fees represented 6.511 per cent of the Fund.[132]

The United States Supreme Court, however, has been critical of courts applying tests similar to the *Goldberger* factors. In reference to the *Johnson-Kerr* method of calculating attorney's fees, an approach originating in the Fifth Circuit in which courts generally consider the following non-exclusive factors: (1) the time and labor required;[133] (2) the novelty and difficulty of the questions involved;[134] (3) the skill requisite to perform the legal service properly;[135] (4) the preclusion of other employment by the attorney due to acceptance of the case; (5) the customary attorney fee;[136] (6) whether the fee is fixed

---

121 *Id.* at 521.
122 *Id.* at 521.
123 *Id.* at 523.
124 *Id.* at 523.
125 *Id.* at 523.
126 *Id.* at 524.
127 *Id.* at 522.
128 *Id.* at 523.
129 *Id.* at 524.
130 *Id.* at 524.
131 *Id.* at 524.
132 *Id.* at 524.
133 The major consideration in determining the amount of a fee award is the result achieved. *See Hensley v. Eckerhart*, 461 US 424, 436, 103 S. Ct. 1933 (1983) ('most critical factor is the degree of success obtained').
134 *See, e.g.*, *In re Linerboard Antitrust Litig.*, 2004 WL 1221350, *10 (E.D. Pa. June 2, 2004) (finding an antitrust class action 'is arguably the most complex action to prosecute') (quotation omitted); *In re Motorsports Merch. Antitrust Litig.*, 112 F. Supp. 2d 1329, 1337 (N.D. Ga. 2000); *In re Shopping Carts Antitrust Litig.*, 1983 WL 1950, *7 (S.D.N.Y. Nov. 18, 1983) (stating that 'antitrust price fixing actions are generally complex, expensive and lengthy').
135 The caliber of opposing counsel is relevant in assessing the quality of counsel's work. *See, e.g.*, *In re Equity Funding Corp. Sec. Litig.*, 438 F. Supp. 1303, 1337 (C.D. Cal. 1977); *J.N. Futia Co. v. Phelps Dodge Indus., Inc.*, 1982 WL 1892 (S.D.N.Y. Sept. 17, 1982).
136 The customary fees paid in contingent fee, non-class actions are also a factor in this analysis. *See, e.g.*, *In re Remeron Direct Purchaser Antitrust Litig.*, 2005 WL 3008808, *16 (D.N.J. Nov. 9, 2005). Some private contingent cases (*i.e.*, non-class action cases, and therefore not subject to court approval) provide for fees equaling 30–40 per cent of the recovery. *See, e.g.*, *In re M.D.C.*

or contingent; (7) time limitations imposed by the client or the circumstances; (8) the amount involved and the results obtained; (9) the experience, reputation, and ability of the attorneys;[137] (10) the 'undesirability' of the case; (11) the nature and length of the professional relationship with the client; and (12) awards in similar cases,[138] the Court noted that this method gives little guidance to federal district courts in setting attorney's fees with 'sometimes subjective factors [that] place unlimited discretion in trial judges and [produce] disparate results.'[139]

Recovery awarded as attorney's fees in antitrust cases

In 2007, a report of the American Antitrust Institute's Private Enforcement Project analyzed 40 recent private antitrust enforcement cases and the results obtained in the cases. Table 1 of the Report indicates that the recoveries in private cases for the 40 cases analyzed ranged from $36 million to $5,600 million.[140] Attorney's fees recoveries ranged in percentage from 5.2 per cent in a case with a $552 million recovery, to 33.3 per cent, in several cases with recoveries ranging from $50 million to $220 million.[141]

Recoveries exceeding $500 million

Five antitrust cases that reported the attorney's fees percentage of recoveries exceeded $500 million: [142] *In re Visa/MasterMoney* (6.5 per cent of $3,383 million);[143] *Auction Houses* (5.2 per cent of $552 million);[144] *El Paso* (6 per cent of $1,427 million);[145] *Fructose* (25 per cent of $531 million);[146] *In re NASDAQ* (13 per cent of $1,027 million).[147]

Holdings Sec. Litig., 1990 WL 454747, *7 (S.D. Cal. Aug. 30, 1990); *Phemister v. Harcourt Brace Jovanovich, Inc.*, 1984 WL 21981, *15 (N.D. Ill. Sept. 14, 1984).

137 *In re Agent Orange Prod. Liab. Litig.*, 611 F. Supp. 1296, 1313 (E.D.N.Y. 1985); *In re Ashanti Goldfields*, 2005 WL 3050284, *4 (E.D.N.Y. Nov. 15, 2005).

138 *Brown v. Phillips Petroleum Co.*, 838 F.2d 451, 454–455 (10th Cir. 1988); *Kerr v. Screen Extras Guild, Inc.*, 526 F.2d 67, 69–70 (9th Cir. 1975) (citing *Johnson v. Ga. Highway Express, Inc.*, 488 F.2d 714, 717–719 (5th Cir. 1974)); *cf. United Steelworkers of Am. v. Phelps Dodge Corp.*, 896 F.2d 403, 406 & n.3 (9th Cir. 1990) (noting that the factors from *Kerr* are used in preliminary determinations of the lodestar).

139 *Pa. v. Del. Valley Citizens' Council for Clean Air*, 478 US 546, 563, 106 S. Ct. 3088 (1986).

140 Lande & Davis, *supra* note 45, at Table 1.

141 *Id.* at Tables 6A–6C.

142 *Id.* at Table 6C.

143 *In re Visa Check/MasterMoney Antitrust Litig.*, 297 F. Supp.2d 503, 522 (Dec. 19, 2003).

144 *In re Auction Houses Antitrust Litig.*, 164 F. Supp.2d 345 (S.D.N.Y. 200), *aff'd*, 2002 US App. LEXIS 15327 (2d Cir. 2002) and *Kruman v. Christie's Int'l PLC*, 284 F.3d 384 (2d Cir. 2002).

145 *Sweetie's v. El Paso Corp.*, No. 319840 (S.F. Super. Ct.); *Continental Forge Co. v. Southern Ca. Gas Co.*, No. BC237336 (L.A. Super. Ct.); *Berg v. Southern Ca. Gas Co.*, No. BC241951 (L.A. Super. Ct.); *City of Long Beach v. Southern Ca. Gas Co.*, No. BC247114 (L.A. Super. Ct.); *Phillip v. El Paso Merchant Energy L.P.*, No. BC265905 (L.A. Super. Ct.); *Phillip v. El Paso Merchant Energy LP*, No. GIC 759425 (San Diego Super. Ct.); *Phillip v. El Paso Merchant Energy LP*, No. GIC 759426 (San Diego Super. Ct.).

146 *In re Fructose Antitrust Litig.*, MDL No. 1087, Master File No. 94-1577 (C.D. Ill.).

147 *In re NASDAQ Market-Makers Antitrust Litig.*, MDL No. 1023, No. 94 Civ. 3996 (S.D.N.Y. 1998).

Fructose and *In re NASDAQ* had the highest percentages.[148] In *In re Fructose*, the attorneys received attorney's fees that equaled 25 per cent of the recovery amount.[149] *In re Fructose* involved allegations of price fixing among the major manufactures of fructose. No indictments were ever brought, even though the government convened a grand jury. Moreover, the private enforcement class action lasted for 10 years before finally settling for $531 million. Of this damages recovery, $100 million was paid by a foreign entity, A.E. Staley Manufacturing.[150] The payments to the class members themselves were larger than average – over $10 million per class member in some cases – due to the relatively small number of fructose purchasers.[151] The case established important precedent in antitrust and civil conspiracy, and the court may have awarded the higher percentage of the fund to class counsel due to the ability of counsel, which the court frequently praised.[152] In *In re NASDAQ*, the attorneys recovered fees that equaled 13 per cent of the recovery amount.[153] Here, the class received aggregate settlements of approximately $1.027 billion, all in cash.[154] Because the size of the attorney's fees was a modest percentage of the settlement, class members received $896,233,301.[155]

Recoveries between $100 million and $500 million

In the eight antitrust cases in which the damages recovered ranged from $100 million to $500 million, the percentage of attorneys' fees recovered ranged from 20 per cent to 33.3 per cent.[156] These cases include *Buspirone* (33.3 per cent of $220 million);[157] *Cardizem* (30 per cent of $110 million);[158] *DRAM* (25 per cent of $326 million);[159] *Flat Glass* (32 per cent of $122 million);[160] *Linerboard* (30 per cent of $202 million);[161] *Lease Oil* (25 per cent of $193 million);[162] *Paxil* (20 & 30 per cent of $165 million);[163] and *Relafen* (33 per cent of $250 million).[164] In *Paxil*, the plaintiffs received a 'megafund' settlement of over $165 million, on behalf of direct and indirect purchasers of Paxil, with a claim that the

---

148 Lande & Davis, *supra* note 45, at Table 6C.
149 *Id.*
150 *Id.* at Case 14 Summary.
151 *Id.*
152 *Id.*
153 *Id.* at Table 6C.
154 *Id.* at Case 21 Summary.
155 *Id.*
156 *Id.* at Table 6C.
157 *In re Busiprone Antitrust Litig.*, MDL Docket No. 1413, 85 F.Supp.2d 340 (S.D.N.Y. 2002).
158 *In re Cardizem CD Antitrust Litig.*, MDL No. 1278, 105 F.Supp.2d 682 (E.D. Mich. 2000).
159 *In re Dynamic Random Access Memory Antitrust Litig.*, Master File No. M-02-1486PJH, MDL No. 1486 (N.D. Ca.).
160 *In re Flat Glass Antitrust Litig.*, DL 1200, Master Dkt. No. 97-0550 (W.D. Pa.).
161 *In re Linerboard Antitrust Litig.*, 2005 WL 1221350 (E.D. Pa. June 2, 2004).
162 *In re Lease Oil Antitrust Litig. No. II*, 186 F.R.D. 403 (S.D. Tex. 1999).
163 *Stop & Shop Supermarket Co., et. al. v. SmithKline Beecham Corp.*, 2005 WL 1213926, E.D.PA. May 19, 2005, at *17–18; *Nichols v. SmithKline Beecham Corp.*, 2005 WL 950616, Apr. 22, 2005, at *20.
164 *In re Relafen Antitrust Litig.*, Civ. Action No. 01-12239, 231 F.R.D. 52 (D. Mass. 2005).

defendant Smithkline Beecham Corporation had abused its patent approval process in order to maintain its monopoly over the drug.[165] Because plaintiffs in the two cases were able to coordinate discovery, plaintiffs were able to achieve both a timely result and the favor of the court.[166] The court awarded 20 and 30 per cent of the respective settlements to counsel, due to the case's complexity and the attorneys' skill and efficiency.[167] In *Linerboard*, the class received a cash settlement of $202.5 million, representing approximately 42–55 per cent of plaintiffs' alleged damages.[168] Counsel received 30 per cent of that settlement in fees.[169] In determining the fee award, the court emphasized both the 'superb' lawyering demonstrated and the groundbreaking nature of this private enforcement action, as the class did not benefit from an earlier government investigation in its case.[170]

Recoveries less than $100 million

In the 17 antitrust cases in which the damages recovered were less than $100 million, the attorney's fees ranged from 7 per cent to 33.3 per cent of recovery.[171] These cases are *Airline Ticket Commission* (33.3 per cent of $86 million);[172] *Augmentin* (20 per cent and 25 per cent of $91 million);[173] *Automotive Refinishing Paint* (32 per cent of $67 million);[174] *NCAA* (26.8 per cent of $74 million);[175] *Remeron* (33.3 per cent of $75 million);[176] *Platinol* (33.3 per cent of $50 million);[177] *Taxol* (30 per cent of $66 million);[178] *Drill Bits* (30.8 per cent of $53 million);[179] *Polypropylene Carpet* (33.3 per cent of $50 million);[180] *Sorbates* (22-33 per cent of $96 million);[181] *Terazosin* (33.3 per cent of $74 million);[182] *Microcrystalline Cellulose* (33.3 per cent of $50 million);[183] *Specialty Steel* (30 per cent of

165 Lande & Davis, *supra* note 45, at Case 27 Summary.
166 *Id.*
167 *Id.*
168 *Id.* at Case 18 Summary.
169 *Id.*
170 *Id.*
171 Lande & Davis, *supra* note 45, at Table 6C.
172 *In re Airline Ticket Comm'n Litig.*, 1996 US Dist. LEXIS 20361.
173 *Ryan-House et al. v. GlaxoSmithKline plc*, C.A. Doc. No. 2:02cv442 (E.D. Va. 2004) and *SAJ Distributors, Inc. and Stephen L. LaFrance Holdings, Inc. v. SmithKline Beecham Corp.*, Doc. No. 2:04cv23 (E.D. Va. 2004).
174 *In re Automotive Refinishing Paint Antitrust Litig.*, 2004 US Dist. 29162 (E.D. Pa. Oct. 13, 2004).
175 *Law v. National Collegiate Athletic Assoc.*, 902 F. Supp. 1394 (D. Kan. 1995); *aff'd*, 134 F. 3d 1010 (10th Cir. 1998).
176 *In re Remeron Antitrust Litig.*, 2005 US Dist. LEXIS 27013 (D.N.J. 2005).
177 *North Shore Hematology & Oncology Assoc. v. Bristol-Myers Squibb Co.*, Civil Action No.:04cv248 (2004).
178 *Oncology & Radiation Associates v. Bristol-Meyers Squibb Co.*, Case No. 1:04CV00248 (D.C.C.).
179 *Eagle Resources, et. al., v. Baker Hughes Inc., et. al.,* No. 4:91cv00627 (Docket) (S.D.Tex. Mar. 11, 1991).
180 *In re Polypropylene Carpet Antitrust Litig.*, 93 F.Supp.2d 1348 (N.D. Ga. 2000).
181 *In re Sorbates Direct Purchaser Antitrust Litig.*, 2002 WL 31655191 (N.D. Cal.).
182 *Terazosin Hydrochloride Antitrust Litig.*, Case No. 99-MDL-1317 (S.D. Fla.).
183 *In re Microcrystalline Cellulose Antitrust Litig.*, 218 F.R.D. 79 (2003).

$50 million);[184] *Lysine* (7 per cent of $65 million);[185] *Commercial Explosives* (30 per cent of $77 million);[186] *Graphite Electrodes* (15 per cent of $47 million).[187]

Tax implications

Finally, brief mention of tax considerations is appropriate. A Circuit Court split exists regarding the appropriate tax treatment of contingent attorney's fees contained within a recovery.[188] Some of the Circuits have held that contingent attorney's fees contained within a recovery are part of one's taxable gross income, while others have determined that these fees are not part of gross income.[189] Whether one's fees will be included in gross income will depend on the jurisdiction. An attorney and client could take the tax treatment of their jurisdiction into account when structuring a settlement, although timing may matter in that calculation.[190] Litigation, especially large-scale litigation, can take several years. This fact alone can significantly impact tax liability and should be considered when assessing fees, expenses, and the ultimate recovery.[191]

Conclusion

Although contingent and other alternative fee arrangements have their detractors and critics, such arrangements permit important antitrust work to proceed in private enforcements, which might not occur otherwise. Moreover, courts have typically embraced alternative fee arrangements in antitrust cases, where the issues are complex and require skilled attorneys to handle them.

---

184 *Transamerican Refining Corp. v. Dravo Corp., et. al,* No. 4:88CV00789 (S.D.Tex. 1988) (settlement 1992).

185 *Amino Acid Lysine Antitrust Litigation*, 918 F.Supp. 1190 (N.D. Ill. 1996).

186 *In re Commercial Explosives Litig.*, 945 F. Supp. 1489 (D. Utah 1996).

187 *In re Graphite Electrodes Antitrust Litig.*, 2003 WL 22358491 (E.D. Pa. 2003).

188 Kristina Maynard, 'The Fruit Does Not Fall far from the Tree: the Unresolved Tax Treatment of Contingent Attorney's Fees,' 33 Loy. U. Chi. L.J. 991, 993 (2002) (Explaining that the Seventh Circuit held that contingent attorney's fees incurred in obtaining a taxable recovery must be included in taxpayer's gross income. The Third, Fourth, Ninth, Tenth, and Federal Circuits all have held that a taxpayer's gross income includes contingent legal fees paid to obtain a taxable recovery. The Fifth, Sixth, and Eleventh Circuits have held that such fees are not gross income to the taxpayer.).

189 Lande & Davis, *supra* note 45, at Table 6C.

190 *See* Edward A. Morse, 'Taxing Plaintiffs: a Look at Tax Accounting for Attorney's Fees and Litigation Costs,' 107 Dick. L. Rev. 405, 424 (2003).

191 *Id.* at 431.

13 Interaction of public and private enforcement

Kevin J. O'Connor, Hannah L. Renfro and Adam C. Briggs[1]

Introduction

One of the unique features of the American system of antitrust enforcement is the multiplicity of potential plaintiffs, governmental and private, authorized to challenge allegedly unlawful conduct under federal and state antitrust law.[2] Not only do the United States Department of Justice (DOJ) and Federal Trade Commission (FTC) maintain overlapping antitrust enforcement authority,[3] but other federal agencies also possess the authority to block business transactions in certain industrial sectors.[4] In addition, state attorneys general and private plaintiffs are empowered to sue under federal and state antitrust law. Although similar to their federal equivalent, state antitrust laws often present potential plaintiffs with remedies beyond those obtainable under federal law.[5]

In short, the United States antitrust enforcement system has evolved into a system including multiple enforcers, each possessing concurrent enforcement authority: two federal antitrust agencies, other federal agencies reviewing industry-specific transactions, fifty state attorneys general, and thousands of private parties. However, except for certain non-antitrust federal agencies, all federal litigants operate in an integrated federal court system under a single body of federal precedent.[6] Even most state antitrust laws

[1] Kevin J. O'Connor is a shareholder with Godfrey & Kahn, S.C., and chairs the firm's Antitrust and Trade Regulation Practice Group. Before joining Godfrey & Kahn, O'Connor headed the Wisconsin Department of Justice's Office of Consumer Protection and Antitrust. While an Assistant Attorney General in Wisconsin DOJ, O'Connor also chaired the National Association of Attorneys General's Multistate Antitrust Task Force. He has exhaustive experience in private and public antitrust actions. Hannah L. Renfro and Adam C. Briggs are attorneys with Godfrey & Kahn, S.C. and members of the firm's Antitrust and Trade Regulation Practice Group.

[2] *See* International Competition Policy Advisory Committee, Final Report (Feb. 28, 2000), *available at* http://www.usdoj.gov/atr/icpac/finalreport.htm, accessed 28 July 2009, ch. 3, p. 146 [hereinafter ICPAC]. (No other legal system in the world distributes decision-making power for competition policy issues so widely.)

[3] The DOJ has exclusive federal governmental authority to enforce the Sherman Act and shares federal authority to enforce the Clayton Act with the FTC. *See* ABA Section of Antitrust Law (6th ed. 2007), Antitrust Law Developments, Chicago, IL: American Bar Association, pp. 691–92 [hereinafter ALD VI].

[4] 15 U.S.C. §21(a) provides the Federal Communications Commission (FCC), the Secretary of Transportation, and the Federal Reserve Board with limited Clayton Act authority. *See generally* ALD VI, *supra* note 3, p. 691. The ICPAC report focused its discussion on several agencies including the Surface Transportation Board (STB) (railroads), the FCC (telephone), and the US Department of Transportation (airlines). ICPAC, *supra* note 2, pp. 148–51.

[5] *See* ALD VI, *supra* note 3, ch. 7.

[6] For example, the FCC and the STB review mergers in their respective industry sectors under 'public interest' standards subject to little or no oversight by the federal antitrust agencies.

are guided by federal precedent either by statute or state decisional law.[7] Consequently, while American antitrust law has not evolved linearly, the decisional law of the past century guides virtually all antitrust actions, regardless of the identity of the plaintiff in a particular action. Simply put, it was not apparent in 1890 that this degree of convergence would be possible over 100 years later. This chapter explores that convergence from a practical perspective.

Varying remedies

In general, each category of antitrust enforcers can seek various remedies unavailable to other enforcers. For example, the DOJ has criminal enforcement authority and civil authority to seek injunctions and forfeitures, but not damages on behalf of injured parties.[8] The FTC may seek injunctive relief, administrative relief, and, more recently, disgorgement of profits.[9] State attorneys general as *parens patriae* may seek direct damages on behalf of 'natural persons' and injunctive relief under federal law.[10] Forty-seven states and the District of Columbia also have authority under state laws to seek some form of criminal penalty;[11] at least twenty-one states and the District of Columbia permit indirect purchasers to recover damages for state antitrust violations;[12] and virtually all states have the authority to recover direct damages on behalf of state agencies.[13]

Varying incentives and concerns

In addition to varying remedies, prospective plaintiffs often have varying incentives and concerns. Private plaintiffs and their counsel are often most interested in obtaining

---

47 U.S.C. §214(a); 47 U.S.C. §310(d); 49 C.F.R. §1180.1 (2008). The benchmark for the FCC in 47 U.S.C. §214(a) for license transfers and acquisitions is 'the present or future public convenience and necessity.' The FCC test in 47 U.S.C. §310(d) is the 'public interest, convenience, and necessity.' The STB in 49 C.F.R. §1180.1 interprets the 'public interest' standard as a balancing test that weighs the potential benefits to applicants and the public against the potential harm to the public.

7 *See* ALD VI, *supra* note 3, p. 624.

8 For a detailed discussion of the DOJ's civil and criminal remedies, *see id.*, pp. 687–724.

9 *See id.* pp. 656–64. An example of the FTC seeking disgorgement of profits can be found in the case of *In Re Lorazepam & Clorazepate Antitrust Litig.*, 205 F.R.D. 369, 2002–1 Trade Cas. (CCH) ¶73,649 (D.D.C. 2002), where the FTC, along with several states, agreed to settle with drug manufacturer Mylan Laboratories, Inc. in litigation where Mylan was accused of attempting to monopolize the markets for generic anti-anxiety drugs. The settlement provided over $71 million to consumers who purchased the drugs during the relevant period and a total of $100 million in disgorgement of Mylan's profits. Disgorgement can complicate damages awards and a disgorgement may mean that plaintiffs' lawyers do not receive the portion of the damages they would otherwise receive.

10 *See* ALD VI, *supra* note 3, pp. 724–25. For a detailed discussion of state *parens patriae* power, *see Pennsylvania v. Playmobil USA*, 1995–2 Trade Cas. (CCH) ¶71,215 (M.D. Pa. 1995); *New York v. Reebok Int'l*, 903 F. Supp. 532 (S.D.N.Y. 1995); *In re Mid-Atlantic Toyota Antitrust Litig.*, 560 F. Supp. 760 (D. Md. 1983).

11 *See* ABA Section of Antitrust Law (4th ed. forthcoming), State Antitrust Practice and Statutes, Chicago, IL: American Bar Association, introduction.

12 *See id.*

13 *See* ALD VI, *supra* note 3, pp. 725–26. For further discussion of remedies, see Chapter 11 of this *Handbook*.

monetary damages and related, usually contingent, fee awards. State antitrust enforcers may be particularly sensitive to the effects of antitrust violations on the local and state level. Bid-rigging on state and local contracts, for example, may not only impose costs on local government but also have more macro-level implications by undermining the government's competitive bidding process. Similarly, a merger of large companies that operate in a local market is likely to be of acute concern to state antitrust enforcers because of the direct impact on the community.[14] Finally, states are particularly attentive to recovering damages for their own citizens, especially in cases involving indirect purchasers who cannot recover damages under federal law.

Of course, when state attorneys general seek damages on behalf of their citizens or attempt to block a merger in federal court, their actions are governed by federal antitrust statutes and decisional law.[15] But when state attorneys general or private plaintiffs seek remedies under state antitrust law or state law applies to an action removed to federal court,[16] the same principles generally apply. Virtually all state antitrust provisions are patterned after or analogous to the Sherman Act, and many state statutes provide that the state antitrust provisions shall be interpreted consistently with federal precedent.[17] Therefore, the decisional law of the past century guides virtually all antitrust actions, regardless of the identity of the plaintiff in a particular action.

Public enforcers often initiate cases before private plaintiffs

A common pattern for the interaction of private and public cases begins where a government enforcement agency initiates an investigation or even obtains indictments or guilty pleas. When the fact of the investigation or preliminary outcome becomes public in some form, 'follow on' class actions are often filed in federal and state courts seeking damages for direct and indirect purchasers.[18] In many cases, these follow on actions are filed as soon as possible after a government investigation is made public, which may

---

14 In 1998, several states worked closely with the DOJ Antitrust Division in reviewing the proposed merger of Waste Management, Inc. and United Waste Services, Inc. The merger ultimately was cleared, but only after divestiture relating to numerous local solid waste disposal markets. *See* Antitrust Merger Challenges, DOJ Antitrust Division, United States and Commonwealth of Pennsylvania v. USA Waste Services, Inc., United Waste Systems, Inc., and Riviera Acquisition Corp. (8/22/97), *available at* http://www.usdoj.gov/atr/public/4523h.htm, accessed 27 July 2009 (merger challenge by United States and States of Ohio, Arizona, California, Colorado, Florida, Commonwealth of Kentucky, States of Maryland, Michigan, New York, Commonwealth of Pennsylvania, States of Texas, Washington, and Wisconsin). At one point in the review of this merger, the federal enforcers were prepared to resolve the case with divestitures affecting only the largest local markets. States not in those markets insisted that additional divestitures be discussed because of the likely impact on other local markets.

15 Even in the seminal case establishing the state attorneys general's authority to seek divestiture in merger cases notwithstanding a decision by the federal agencies to not challenge the merger, the states were held to be governed by the same substantive merger law. *See generally California v. American Stores Co.*, 495 US 271 (1990).

16 Barry Hawk and Laraine Laudati (1996), 'Antitrust Federalism in the United States and Decentralization of Competition Law Enforcement in the European Union: A Comparison', Fordham International Law Journal 20 (1), 18–49, p. 21.

17 ALD VI, *supra* note 3, pp. 623–24.

18 *See* the following section, Private Plaintiffs Take the Lead in Initiating Some Cases, *infra*.

maximize an opportunity to act as lead counsel for the lawyers who file suit first.[19] This rush occurs even though plaintiffs are generally protected from the running of the statute of limitations in such cases.[20]

Follow on private plaintiffs may be able to take advantage of factual developments and legal judgments established in government actions without having to expend the resources to duplicate the government's investigative and enforcement efforts. Section 5 of the Clayton Act provides that certain final judgments or decrees entered against a defendant in a government criminal or civil proceeding brought under the antitrust laws may be used in a subsequent private antitrust action as '*prima facie* evidence against such defendant . . . as to all matters respecting which said judgment or decree would be an estoppel as between the parties in the government suit.'[21] Moreover, even though a judgment under a federal antitrust law is not proof of a violation under a parallel state antitrust law, the factual development from a federal action (based on federal law) can be employed in a subsequent state action.

At the same time that private plaintiffs may rely on judgments from governmental actions, the defendants' liability in a follow on private action is generally unaffected by amounts paid out to government enforcers through civil forfeitures, damages, or criminal fines. Moreover, private plaintiffs can often obtain treble damages awards and attorneys' fees, and rarely face any real risk of paying defendants' attorneys fees.[22]

Perhaps in part because of these advantages of a follow on or private suit, a very active plaintiffs' antitrust bar has emerged. The bar is comprised of large firms and solo practitioners specializing in private-plaintiff antitrust claims and, in many cases, the individual firm or attorney represents various plaintiffs in massive nationwide class actions.[23] There are firms that represent both plaintiffs and defendants in antitrust cases, but some of these must deal with the concomitant difficulties associated with practicing under two different business models. Perhaps most notably, it is typical for members of the plaintiffs' antitrust bar to represent clients on a contingency fee basis while members of the defense bar charge hourly fees.

The *DRAM* case exemplifies how a large-scale, privately-initiated antitrust suit can follow closely in the tracks of a government-led enforcement effort. In that case,[24] the DOJ obtained criminal indictments and guilty pleas against several dynamic random

---

[19] Some critics of this rush to the courthouse have argued that plaintiffs file baseless, duplicative actions as soon as the investigation is announced regardless of whether the private plaintiff has obtained anything more 'than the fact of the investigation and conclusory allegations of collusive conduct.' Steven F. Cherry and Gordon Pearson (2007), 'Why *Twombly* Does (and Should) Apply to All Private Antitrust Actions, Including Alleged Hard-Core Cartels', Antitrust Source, 7 (2), 1–7, p. 6.

[20] Section 5(i) of the Clayton Act tolls the statute of limitations while some government suits are pending.

[21] ALD VI, *supra* note 3, pp. 977–78.

[22] *See* Robert H. Lande and Joshua P. Davis (2008), 'Benefits From Private Antitrust Enforcement: An Analysis of Forty Cases', University of San Francisco Law Review, 42 (4), 879–918.

[23] *See, e.g., California v. Infineon Technologies AG*, No. 06-4333 (N.D. Cal. filed July 14, 2006), in which there are 21 law firms involved representing over 21 parties.

[24] *Id.*

access memory (DRAM) producers and their executives.[25] A number of private class actions on behalf of indirect purchasers quickly followed, attempting to rely on the early groundwork completed by the federal enforcers. Almost three years later, 41 states filed antitrust claims for civil damages against a cartel of DRAM manufacturers for price-fixing over a period of several years.

While the inception of the private claims in the *DRAM* case demonstrates how the plaintiffs' bar can coalesce around a national assortment of direct and indirect purchasers, the difficulties these private plaintiffs have encountered demonstrate that private enforcers face their own unique legal challenges. In *DRAM*, in fact, the federal judge presiding over the consolidated multidistrict litigation concluded that indirect purchasers, who had purchased products *containing* DRAM but had not purchased DRAM itself, could not survive a motion for judgment on the pleadings under a number of state-based *Illinois Brick* repealer statutes because they did not 'participate' in the DRAM market at issue in the case.[26] (The trial court's decision, not incidentally, is contrary to substantial authority that an indirect purchaser can recover for damages stemming from overcharges for incorporated products.[27])

In addition, in the *Vitamins* indirect purchaser litigation, the DOJ similarly led the enforcement effort followed by a number of private indirect purchaser actions. Only after the DOJ obtained guilty pleas, and while the private actions were still pending, did a collection of state attorneys general eventually join with private plaintiffs' counsel in negotiating a comprehensive settlement. Despite the significant 'overlap' among federal, state, and private enforcement actions, government and private enforcers coordinated on litigation strategies and settlement negotiations. Coordination between private plaintiffs and state attorneys general was particularly extensive and effective.[28] Indeed this state–private cooperation yielded $305 million dollars in settlement agreements for indirect, private purchasers.[29]

Applicability of rulings in prior government cases

Follow on private-plaintiff lawsuits are facilitated by the applicability of rulings in prior government cases, which is provided for under federal law. Section 5(a) of the Clayton Act essentially allows private plaintiffs to shorten the relative distance between filing and collecting on an antitrust claim by 'piggyback[ing] on public enforcement outcomes and work product'.[30] Even those commentators seemingly opposed to private plaintiffs' 'parasitic' or 'piggyback' use of prior rulings in government antitrust cases will not deny

---

25 Press Release, US Dept. of Justice (Sept. 15, 2008), 'Infineon Technologies AG Agrees to Plead Guilty to Participating in DRAM Price-Fixing Conspiracy', *available at* http://www.usdoj.gov/atr/public/press_releases/2004/205437.pdf, accessed 28 July 2009.

26 *In re Dynamic Random Access Memory (DRAM) Antitrust Litig.*, 536 F. Supp. 2d 1139 (N.D. Cal. 2008).

27 *See, e.g.*, *In re Linerboard Antitrust Litig.*, 305 F.3d 145 (3d Cir. 2002); *Holder v. Archer Daniels Midland Co.*, No. 96-2975, 1998 WL 1469620 (D.C. Super. Nov. 4, 1998); *Comes v. Microsoft Corp.*, 646 N.W.2d 440 (Iowa 2002).

28 Kevin O'Connor (2001), 'Is the *Illinois Brick* Wall Crumbling?', Antitrust, 15 (3), 34–38, p. 37.

29 *Id.*

30 David Rosenberg and James P. Sullivan (2006), 'Coordinating Private Class Action and

its 'obvious efficiency' for private plaintiffs and for the antitrust enforcement system as a whole.[31] As one critic – Professor Richard Epstein – concedes, the current policy allows plaintiffs and their counsel to review the content of prior rulings before committing their own resources to the task of private recovery. Regardless of whether, as some argue, this policy creates negative externalities,[32] the availability of the 'piggyback' option remains a key part of antitrust enforcement in the US.

In most cases, §5(a) allows prior rulings to have conclusive and controlling effects over subsequent private actions under the collateral estoppel doctrine.[33] Under the collateral estoppel doctrine, a judgment in one case is conclusive on the issues litigated in that case between those parties, and a party from that earlier case is precluded from re-litigating the issues from that case in a different, subsequent legal action involving the same parties. A plaintiff's successful 'offensive' use of collateral estoppel can obviate the need for virtually any fact-finding or judgments on the merits.[34] Where the same underlying facts are at issue, federal courts give the preclusive effect to a state court judgment to the extent permitted by that state's law.[35]

Moreover, even where the requirements of collateral estoppel are not satisfied, §5(a) still offers an invaluable advantage to private antitrust plaintiffs. Specifically, antitrust plaintiffs may use prior government rulings to establish their *prima facie* case, essentially arriving at the courthouse steps with a rebuttable presumption of having proved their case.[36] The ready-made *prima facie* case dramatically reduces the amount of resources that a plaintiff or a group of plaintiffs must commit to survive initial dispositive motions. While such plaintiffs still carry a heavy burden of proving that they were specifically injured by the anticompetitive conduct alleged, it is cheaper and easier to prove one has been injured by an anticompetitive scheme when the existence of that scheme is assumed from the start.

Generally, consent judgments and *nolo contendere* pleas[37] arising from federal government antitrust actions will not shift burdens or otherwise reduce plaintiffs' burdens in

---

Public Agency Enforcement of Antitrust Law', Journal of Competition Law and Economics, 2 (2), 159–187, p. 161.

31 Richard Epstein (2008), 'The Coordination of Public and Private Antitrust Actions, in OECD Policy Roundtables: Private Remedies 2007', *available at* http://www.oecd.org/dataoecd/24/62/39892177.pdf, accessed 27 July 2009.

32 Ilya R. Segal and Michael D. Whinston (2006), 'Public vs. Private Enforcement of Antitrust Law: A Survey', *available at* http://ssrn.com/abstract=952067, p. 12, accessed 27 July 2009.

33 Julian O. Von Kalinowski (2d ed. 2006), Antitrust Laws and Trade Regulation, New York, NY: Matthew Bender, §169 [hereinafter Von Kalinowski]. Section 5(a) was legislatively expanded in 1980 to recognize, by statute, that virtually all government antitrust rulings other than FTC rulings can have a collateral estoppel effect over privately-initiated antitrust actions. *Id.*

34 Collateral estoppel may also be employed to defend against an antitrust claim. 'Defensive use [of collateral estoppel] occurs when a defendant seeks to prevent a plaintiff from asserting a claim the plaintiff has previously litigated and lost against another defendant.' *Parklane Hosiery Co. v. Shore*, 439 US 322, 326 n.4 (1979).

35 Von Kalinowski, *supra* note 33, at §169.05.

36 *Id.*

37 A *nolo contendre* plea is a 'no contest' plea in which the defendant declines to contest or admit that he or she is guilty of the charges against him or her.

private antitrust actions.[38] For any other government decision or decree exhibiting key criteria, however, private plaintiffs can take full advantage of the collateral estoppel or *prima facie* effect.

'Under the doctrine of nonmutual offensive collateral estoppel, "a litigant who was not a party to a prior judgment may nevertheless use that judgment 'offensively' to prevent a defendant from relitigating issues resolved in the earlier proceeding."'[39] For collateral estoppel to apply, several factors must be met. First, the judgment in favor of the government on which the private plaintiff wants to rely must be 'final.' This means the judgment must be fully litigated and completed at the trial court and appellate levels.[40] In other words, no aspect of the government's case may remain unresolved for the judgment to be 'final.'[41]

Second, the judgment must have been obtained in a suit brought by the United States via the DOJ or FTC. However, '[i]t has also been held that an appellate court judgment affirming and enforcing an FTC order is not admissible as prima facie evidence in a private suit since appellate review is instituted by the defendant, a private party, and accordingly is not a proceeding brought by the United States.'[42]

Third, the judgment must have been obtained in an action arising under federal antitrust laws. This requirement is generally construed to include actions arising under the Sherman Act, Clayton Act, and Wilson Tariff Act, but the FTC Act is not included.[43]

Fourth, as noted above, the judgment cannot be a consent decree entered prior to taking testimony. This provision applies to *nolo contendere* pleas as well. If some testimony has been taken in a case, however, any resulting consent decree may have *prima facie* effect. In other words, the consent decree can be used as evidence that the defendant violated the antitrust laws. Similarly, defendants' guilty pleas are excluded from this provision.[44] The law is less clear on whether judgments arising from stipulated facts are also considered consent decrees and thus excluded from the *prima facie* effect.[45]

Fifth, the government judgment must assert an antitrust violation. In *Wendkos v. ABC Consolidated Corp.*, an FTC judgment that did not specify whether it related to violations of the FTC Act or one of the enumerated 'antitrust laws' was not given any *prima facie* effect in a subsequent private action.[46]

While not an enumerated criterion, it also bears noting that government judgments will only carry a *prima facie* or collateral estoppel effect in a subsequent private plaintiff's

---

38 Some FTC decisions may carry a *prima facie* effect for purposes of §5(a), however.

39 *Discover Financial Services v. Visa USA. Inc.*, 598 F. Supp. 2d 394, 398 (S.D.N.Y. 2008) (quoting *Parklane Hosiery Co. v. Shore*, 439 US 322, 326 (1979)).

40 Von Kalinowski, *supra* note 33, §169.02.

41 *Fifth & Walnut, Inc. v. Loew's Inc.*, 176 F.2d 587, 593 (2d Cir. 1949); Von Kalinowski, *supra* note 33, §169.02.

42 Von Kalinowski, *supra* note 33, §169.02[b][1].

43 *Id.*; Lawrence A. Sullivan and Warren S. Grimes (2d ed. 2006), Law of Antitrust: An Integrated Handbook, St. Paul, MN: Thomson/West, §17.8.

44 Thomas V. Vakerics (2009), Antitrust Basics, New York, NY: Law Journal Press, §3.03[3][a].

45 Von Kalinowski, *supra* note 33, §169.02.

46 379 F. Supp. 15, 21 (E.D. Pa. 1974).

favor as to issues that have been fully addressed by the adjudging court.[47] Issues that might have been adjudicated but were not cannot give rise to any outcome-determinative effect in a follow on action.[48] In addition, temporal and geographical limitations on prior judgments may limit their applicability to future plaintiffs.[49]

Limits on private plaintiffs' use of materials and information acquired in the government's suit

While the availability of collateral estoppel and *prima facie* treatment affords advantages to plaintiffs, these procedural advantages are not limitless in their value. In follow on actions attempting to rely on prior criminal proceedings, for example, plaintiffs may have limited access to key information and may not even be able to review key judgments and decrees because of secrecy relating to ongoing investigation of other criminal activities.

A full transcript of grand jury testimony in a federal government antitrust investigation might be of immense value to a civil plaintiff, but few plaintiffs attempting to obtain such testimony for follow on actions are able to meet the stringent 'particularized need' standard required to obtain it.[50] Since grand jury testimony is presumptively secret, follow on private plaintiffs rarely have the benefit of any such testimony when pursuing their own claims.[51] Since private plaintiffs also face increasingly demanding standards for detailed notice pleading (see *Twombly* discussion, *infra*), grand jury secrecy constitutes a more significant hurdle for private enforcers than their government counterparts.

Furthermore, guilty pleas in the antitrust context often relate only to narrow pieces of larger conspiracies, and accordingly represent only a portion of a plaintiff's overall case.

To be sure, government antitrust defendants are well aware of the risks that await them after government proceedings conclude. Nothing prevents government defendants from negotiating for settlements that are of as little value as possible to any other private party. Still, as Von Kalinowski notes, the very threat of follow on plaintiffs' lawyers opportunistically cashing in on the government's work serves an important social purpose: taxpayers save money on antitrust enforcement when government defendants feel compelled to negotiate consent decrees that carry collateral estoppel or *prima facie* effects.[52]

Private plaintiffs take the lead in initiating some cases

'The genius of the US legal system is that it allows private parties to remedy wrongs, hold tortfeasors accountable, and deter future violations without government action. Congress intended no less in enacting the Sherman and Clayton Acts. . . .'[53] Among

---

47 Von Kalinowski, *supra* note 33, §169.04.

48 *Id.*

49 *Id.*

50 *See Douglas Oil Co. v. Petrol Stops Northwest*, 441 US 211 (1979).

51 Federal Rule of Criminal Procedure 6(e)(2)(B) (imposing secrecy on grand jury testimony and proceedings).

52 Von Kalinowski, *supra* note 33, §169.01.

53 William J. Blechman (2007), 'Why *Twombly* Does Not (and Should Not) Apply to Hard-Core Cartels', Antitrust Source, 7 (1), 1–9, p. 7.

critics of the US private enforcement model, the stereotypical follow on plaintiff is merely a disgruntled competitor incapable of competing with the defendant in a free market and resorting to opportunistic but meritless private antitrust claims against a government-penalized competitor to secure a windfall or more favorable market conditions.[54] Another popular archetype is the indirect purchaser seemingly happy with her computer and indifferent to anyone's litigation costs until a clever plaintiff's attorney convinces her that she can get some easy money by putting her name on a complaint against a foreign electronics supplier already prosecuted by a government agency.

In many cases, however, private plaintiffs have superior or timelier information by virtue of being direct market participants. 'Private parties have superior information about potential violations and the resulting harm' thanks to their crucial possession of 'decentralized knowledge' unavailable to the government.[55] Because they are sometimes better positioned to uncover antitrust violations, private plaintiffs are not always relegated to follow on status. As recent research has demonstrated, private plaintiffs have led the way more frequently than previously realized. Professors Robert Lande and Joshua Davis discovered in their 2008 research that more than one third of the largest 40 privately-initiated antitrust suits studied were not preceded by government action.[56] While 'piggybacking' remains common, it is far from the only type of private action that is brought.

Indeed, in some cases it may be the government itself 'piggybacking' on private investigative and enforcement efforts. As Lande, Davis, and other commentators have noted, the *Visa/MasterMoney* case involved private-plaintiff efforts upon which government enforcers subsequently relied.[57]

Advantages of private enforcement

Whether subsequently used by the government or not, these private actions represent a sizeable component of US government enforcement policy. Focusing on the 40

[54] Cherry and Pearson, *supra* note 19, p. 6 (criticizing private plaintiffs who race to the courthouse to file what turn out to be entirely baseless complaints based on 'vague press reports' immediately following the heels of a government action against the same defendants); Lande and Davis, *supra* note 22, pp. 883–89 (summarizing criticisms of private antitrust enforcement); *see also* Interview with J. Thomas Rosch, Commissioner, Federal Trade Commission (2009), Antitrust, 23 (2), 32–45, p. 43. In this interview, FTC Commissioner Rosch noted that while he witnessed abuses in treble damages class actions, the private bar also can play an important role in protecting consumers and courts should consider the most effective way of curing the abuses without adversely affecting private antitrust actions that curb anticompetitive conduct. He stated: 'What happens is that by shrinking substantive antitrust principles, which we've seen in *Credit Suisse* and *Trinko* for example, out of a concern about private litigation, that can slop over into public enforcement and it can hobble public enforcement as well. I don't think that's a sound way to address concerns about private treble class action abuses. Rather, I think a much sounder way is for the Supreme Court to consider remedying those abuses directly, head on.'

[55] Segal and Whinston, *supra* note 32, p. 4.

[56] Lande and Davis, *supra* note 22, p. 898, Table 3. The 40 cases were merely representative of large cases won by or settled to the benefit of the plaintiffs bringing the action.

[57] *See, e.g., In re Visa Check/MasterMoney Antitrust Litig.*, 297 F. Supp. 2d 503, 524 n.31 (E.D.N.Y. 2003) (noting that the 'government piggybacked on Class Counsel's efforts').

largest antitrust actions between 1998 and 2008, Lande and Davis found that private plaintiffs recovered between $7.631 and $8.981 billion from the 15 cases that did not follow or arise simultaneously with a government action.[58] Instead, the government followed the private plaintiffs' suit or the government did not commence an action at all. By enabling these actions to proceed from inception to completion, federal and state governments effectively achieved billions of dollars in recovery in just a ten year period, along with some measure of accompanying deterrence, without spending any taxpayer dollars.[59] By including a 'private' component, US antitrust policy effectively outsourced a portion of its enforcement role and gave taxpayers a massive return on essentially no investment. As Lande and Davis assert, these cases 'have saved the United States taxpayer tremendous sums in enforcement costs by shifting the enormous burdens and risks of litigating against sophisticated, well-financed lawbreakers to private plaintiffs' counsel.'[60] Moreover, the authors found that fines resulting from private actions are a greater deterrent than fines or criminal prosecutions imposed by the US DOJ.[61]

However, it deserves noting that participants in the DOJ's Antitrust Division's Corporate Leniency Program are eligible for relief from the full amount of damages which a private plaintiff would otherwise be entitled to recover. The leniency program grants amnesty from criminal prosecution to the first member of an illegal conspiracy that reports the illegal conduct to the government and cooperates with the ensuing investigation. The Antitrust Criminal Penalty Enhancement and Reform Act (ACPERA) of 2004 limits the civil liability of the amnesty program's participants.[62] Participants' damages in a follow on private lawsuit are limited to the actual damages incurred by the antitrust plaintiff. This means that under ACPERA, the plaintiff cannot recover treble damages from a participant in the leniency program, which is intended to incentivize those involved in illegal activity to report the criminal activity.[63]

The vast availability of 'private attorneys general' able to take the lead on antitrust enforcement prevents the dilution of public enforcement through budgetary constraints and electoral politics. Government enforcers operate on fixed budgets and have strong normative and pragmatic disincentives to pursue cases they are unlikely to win.[64] State and federal prosecutors shy away from hard-to-prove cases not only because they have fewer resources, but also because they often have rational but 'selfish' motives to 'bring cases that the agency will win' and burnish their own credentials accordingly.[65] To 'pick

---

[58] Lande and Davis, *supra* note 22, pp. 897–99. That amount is cash and does not include 'products, services, discounts, coupons, [or] injunctive relief.' *Id.*, p. 891.

[59] *Id.*, p. 898.

[60] *Id.*, p. 905.

[61] *Id.*, p. 895.

[62] Pub. L. 108-237 (2004), 118 Stat. 665 (2004).

[63] For a discussion of how the leniency program and ACPERA can assist a private plaintiff in deciding whether to bring a case, see Chapter 5 of this *Handbook*; for a discussion of the utility of the leniency program and ACPERA as evidence gathering tools, see Chapter 10 of this *Handbook*.

[64] Lande and Davis, *supra* note 22, p. 906.

[65] Sullivan and Grimes, *supra* note 43, §17.1c.

and choose' the low hanging fruit makes too much sense for an agency and its individual attorneys.[66]

Nor can these government officials be expected to be impervious to political pressures. As many legal commentators and historians have long noted, government-led antitrust enforcement came to a standstill during the presidency of Ronald Reagan, did not approach the pre-Reagan level until the second term of the Clinton presidency, and has arguably never risen all the way to its pre-Reagan levels.[67] Turnover among state attorneys general (who are sometimes referred to as 'governors in training') can similarly affect state-level enforcement.

Finally, no discussion of this subject would be complete without noting that the interest of some states in the Microsoft litigation originated in the perceived weakness of the decree negotiated by DOJ and Microsoft in 1994–95.[68] In 1998, several states began investigating Microsoft shortly after the entry of the federal decree and eventually began pressing the DOJ to join them in bringing a broader case against Microsoft that would address a wide array of conduct. Although the remedy obtained was not wholly effective, the Court of Appeal's decision on liability is an important statement of the applicability of the antitrust laws to a significant industry.[69]

Difficulties faced by private plaintiffs

While private plaintiffs have been a part of US national and state-level antitrust enforcement for over a century, and can derive advantages from the collateral estoppel and *prima facie* effects of prior rulings, they also bear their own unique difficulties.

First, while the government possesses the statutory standing to enforce its own laws, private antitrust plaintiffs must prove that they have standing to sue based on their actual connection to the alleged wrongdoing. Antitrust standing is among the most debated but least settled areas of US antitrust law, and the hurdles imposed by this amorphous standing doctrine have limited the access of competitor plaintiffs to legal relief.[70] Among the most slippery elements required to prove antitrust standing is proving antitrust injury.

Antitrust injury is 'injury of the type the antitrust laws were intended to prevent and that flows from that which makes defendants' acts unlawful.'[71] This means the alleged injury must be proximately caused by the anticompetitive conduct that is the subject of the lawsuit. In *Blue Shield of Va., et. al, v. McCready*, the US Supreme Court explained that the standard did not require fixed indicia on price or output.[72] But a plaintiff must

---

66 *Id.*

67 *See* Ernest Gelhorn, William E. Kovacic and Stephen Calkins (5th ed. 2004), Antitrust Law and Economics in a Nutshell, St. Paul, MN: Thomson/West, Section XIII.A.1; Lande and Davis, *supra* note 22, p. 915.

68 *See United States v. Microsoft Corp.*, 159 F.R.D. 318, 330–38 (D.D.C.) (finding proposed consent decree was not in the public interest because it failed to address all of Microsoft's alleged anticompetitive behavior and did not have an effective monitoring mechanism), *rev'd and remanded,* 56 F.3d 1448 (D.C. Cir. 1995).

69 *United States v. Microsoft Corp.*, 253 F.3d 34 (D.C. Cir.), *cert. denied*, 534 US 952 (2001).

70 Sullivan and Grimes, *supra* note 43, §17.1a.

71 *Atlantic Richfield Co. v. USA Petroleum Co.*, 495 US 328, 334 (1990).

72 457 US 465, 482 (1982).

show that its injury-in-fact was 'inextricably intertwined with the injury' the defendants sought to cause.[73]

While this discussion does not attempt to recapture the entire history of the antitrust injury doctrine, the key limitation preventing many private plaintiffs from reaching trial is the requirement that a plaintiff show injury not just to itself, but to competition in the relevant market.[74] Accordingly, mere allegations of lost profits or constrained production are not sufficient to establish standing.[75] While individual plaintiffs may have superior information about the harms they themselves have sustained, demonstrating harm to the market through discovery but before trial can sometimes prevent otherwise viable antitrust claims from being asserted.[76]

In addition, the controversial US Supreme Court *Twombly* case and its progeny further raise the bar for private plaintiffs.[77] Under *Twombly*, private antitrust plaintiffs bringing §1 claims must plead the conspiratorial activity in sufficient detail just to survive a motion to dismiss.[78] This recent holding represents a key victory for defendants who can now effectively subject any private plaintiff to a more stringent notice-pleading requirement through a motion to dismiss before such a plaintiff can even obtain basic discovery.

Accordingly, even as private plaintiffs can avoid some of the burdens carried by government enforcers, they must satisfy a range of other requirements before presenting their claims to a jury, much less obtaining discovery.

Coordinated action among private and public plaintiffs

Given the multiplicity of enforcers and the varying incentives each is given under the American system, it is unlikely that any serious antitrust violation will not be the subject of at least one, and probably several, overlapping lawsuits. For example, after the members of the vitamin price-fixing cartel were prosecuted criminally by the DOJ, they were subsequently subjected to follow on private civil suits in federal court for damages incurred by direct purchasers in addition to private and state suits for damages incurred by indirect purchasers.[79] This pattern of litigation raises issues about litigation costs and optimal procedures for resolving overlapping claims.[80] On the other hand, the multiplicity of antitrust enforcers does minimize the possibility that valuable cases will be overlooked. To the extent the system encourages the filing of cases with little or no merit

---

73 *Id.* at 484.

74 *See Brunswick Corp. v. Pueblo Bowl-O-Mat*, 429 US 477 (1977).

75 *Id.*

76 For further discussion of standing and antitrust injury, see Chapters 6 and 9 of this *Handbook*.

77 *Bell Atlantic Corp. v. Twombly*, 550 US 544 (2007).

78 *Id.* at 555–57.

79 Harry First (2001), 'The Vitamins Case: Cartel Prosecutions and the Coming of International Competition Law', Antitrust Law Journal, 68 (3), 711–34, pp. 712–19; Joel M. Cohen and Trisha Lawson (2001), 'Navigating Multistate Indirect Purchaser Lawsuits', Antitrust, 15 (3), 29–33, p. 31; Michael L. Denger and D. Jarrett Arp (2001), 'Does Our Multifaceted Enforcement System Promote Sound Competition Policy?', Antitrust, 15 (3), 41–46, p. 41.

80 *See, e.g.*, Cohen and Lawson, *supra* note 77, p. 33.

(something the authors do not concede),[81] the courts are given an opportunity to dismiss those cases at various stages of the litigation, thereby creating precedents that enhance the transparency of American antitrust law. Professor Jean Burns takes the argument even further and asserts that 'by bringing inconsistency, unpredictability, and flat-out contradictions into the law, federalism enhances antitrust jurisprudence,' reminding us that we do not yet have all the answers about appropriate antitrust policy and that reasonable minds can and do differ about the appropriate goals of antitrust policies.[82]

Overlapping representation results in part from the interplay of *parens patriae* authority and private class actions. Some of the differences between the states and private plaintiffs' ability and incentive to bring cases are discussed here.

Parens patriae actions

Federal law allows the federal government and certain private plaintiffs to sue for violations of antitrust law, but also allows state attorneys general to file antitrust claims for monetary damages on behalf of 'natural persons' under *parens patriae* authority found in §4(c) of the Clayton Act.[83]

Under this authority, a state attorney general acts much like a class representative in a private class action suit, but need not obtain 'certification,' nor prove that she is a proper representative for a class of aggrieved consumers.[84] State attorneys general also have authority to initiate actions on behalf of the state as a purchaser of goods and services.[85]

When undertaken in conjunction with private class actions, this federally-derived *parens patriae* authority allows for the overlap of concurrently pending cases, ostensibly pursued on behalf of many of the same consumers. While defendants face additional

---

81 The American Antitrust Institute has found:

> The frivolous litigation myth is premised on the idea that plaintiffs will bring weak claims in order to obtain settlements and that defendants will settle such claims in order to avoid the costs of discovery . . . or the small risk of 'massive exposure' that may accompany class actions as a result of treble damages, joint and several liability, and fee shifting . . . Both theories are seriously flawed.
>
> * * *
>
> Beyond the flawed theory, the claim of widespread frivolous antitrust litigation is unsupported in fact. It is not simply that there are no empirical studies to support the claim; there are apparently no good examples of settlements of frivolous antitrust suits. And absent such settlements, class action plaintiffs have nothing to gain by bringing such suits. The evidence suggests that if there is a problem with class action settlements in antitrust cases, it is that plaintiffs sometimes settle strong cases for too little, not weak cases for too much. In sum, there is simply no basis to believe that frivolous antitrust class actions are a significant problem.

American Antitrust Institute (2008), 'The Next Antitrust Agenda: The American Antitrust Institute's Transition Report on Competition Policy to the 44th President of the United States', pp. 231–34.

82 Jean Wegman Burns (2000), 'Embracing Both Faces of Antitrust Federalism: *Parker* and *ARC America Corp.*', Antitrust Law Journal, 68 (1), 29–44, pp. 41, 42. A debate on the role of concentration in antitrust analysis was the focus of a proceeding under the auspices of the ABA Antitrust Section. Report of the Task Force on Fundamental Theory (July 2001).

83 15 U.S.C. §15(c). For an introduction and explanation of the *parens patriae* authority generally, see Chapter 7 of this *Handbook*.

84 *New York v. Reebok Int'l*, 96 F.3d 44, 46 (2d Cir. 1996).

85 *Georgia v. Pennsylvania R.R. Co.*, 324 US 439 (1945).

challenges in this 'overlap' environment, state attorneys general and private plaintiffs often find that coordinating two overlapping actions poses challenges of its own.

Unlike private plaintiff actions, for example, federally-initiated *parens* actions are limited to damages to natural persons (not businesses) who were direct purchasers, arising from Sherman Act violations.[86] However, should plaintiffs falling within the permitted scope of such a *parens* action obtain relief through the attorney general, they may not separately seek duplicative relief as private plaintiffs.[87] The recovery is essentially the same for plaintiffs in a *parens* action and a private action. The main distinction is that private plaintiffs' attorneys usually take a contingency fee out of the total damages awarded while attorneys general will receive their attorney fees as a separate damages award from the defendant(s). Likewise, plaintiffs who have already obtained private relief may not be included in damages calculations in a *parens* action.[88] States can also seek civil penalties through *parens* actions, which are unavailable to private plaintiffs.

While these *parens* actions sometimes precede private class actions, in other cases a private class will be certified before the filing of a federally-derived *parens* claim, effectively making the *parens* action subordinate to the private class as a potential judgment creditor. While this diminished stature as a potential creditor might seem to remove the largest incentive to bring a *parens* action, a state attorney general electing to proceed with such a case may simply conclude that the certified class is not sufficiently representative of the full population of injured parties, and may also be responding to political incentives.

Notably, nearly half of all states also provide statutory authority for their attorneys general to initiate *parens* actions in state court, in some instances with fewer restrictions than the federal *parens* authority.[89] While such state-derived *parens* actions may still be removed to a multi-district litigation (MDL) forum under the preemptive federal procedural code,[90] these state *parens* actions are not subject to the Class Action Fairness Act (CAFA).[91] In instances in which state *parens* actions come first, private plaintiffs may view the existence of a state-driven action as a source of additional leverage to obtain a more favorable settlement upon attaining certification.

A practical example of the ways in which overlapping private and *parens* actions can add complexity is settlement. When a private class action and a state *parens* action addressing the same anticompetitive conduct proceed to settlement, states may assert that their *parens* claims are separate and superior to the claims of the private class.[92]

---

86 *See* 15 U.S.C. §15(c); *see also Illinois Brick Co. v. Illinois*, 431 US 720 (1977).

87 15 U.S.C. 15c(b)(3).

88 *Id.* at §15c(a)(1)(A).

89 *See, e.g.,* Conn. Gen. Stat. §35-32(c) (2009) (allowing attorney general to initiate *parens* actions on behalf of 'persons,' not just 'natural persons').

90 *Parens* actions may also be removed to federal court on diversity grounds, depending on a court's determination of whether diversity exists among the defendants and the real parties in interest. *See Hood v. F. Hoffmann-La Roche, Ltd.*, __ F. Supp. 2d __, 2009 WL 2371341, *4–6 (D. D.C. Aug. 4, 2009).

91 The Fifth Circuit recently cautioned, however, that a state *parens* case may not avoid CAFA's reach if it were not 'truly' a *parens* action but something else in disguise. *Louisiana ex rel. Caldwell v. Allstate Ins. Co.*, 536 F.3d 418 (5th Cir. 2008).

92 *See In re Compact Disc*, No. 00-1361 (D. Me. Oct. 21, 2002) (class definition in settlement agreement excluded natural persons in plaintiff states).

Twombly may alter the nature of private enforcement's interactions with state *parens* enforcers. *Twombly*, discussed *supra*, holds antitrust plaintiffs to a more stringent standard of articulating details about an alleged anticompetitive act before being permitted to proceed to discovery.[93] As private plaintiffs may be less equipped than before to survive preliminary motions to dismiss and obtain discovery, states may play a greater role in coordinating precomplaint investigations with private plaintiffs.

Private class actions

A recent study of private antitrust enforcement found that the 'growth [of private antitrust cases] is fuelled by extraordinary increases in the number of antitrust class action lawsuits filed in recent years.'[94] The authors of this study found that class actions now constitute 70 per cent of antitrust cases, while they constituted only 15 per cent of antitrust cases ten years ago.[95] While many class actions are duplicative (i.e., not each case represents different anticompetitive conduct engaged in by a different defendant), this trend is significant.

To maintain an antitrust class action, a plaintiff must meet the same requirements of any class action brought under Federal Rule of Civil Procedure 23 or a state equivalent. Most states have laws allowing class actions and most of them track Rule 23 of the Federal Rules.[96]

> Careful application of Rule 23 accords with the pivotal status of class certification in large-scale litigation because 'denying or granting class certification is often the defining moment in class actions (for it may sound the "death knell" of the litigation on the part of the plaintiffs, or create unwarranted pressure to settle nonmeritorious claims on the part of the defendants).'[97]

To satisfy the requirements under Rule 23(a): (1) the class must be sufficiently numerous that joinder of all the class members is impracticable, (2) there must be questions of law or fact common to the class, (3) the claims of the party or parties representing the class must be typical of the class claims, and (4) the representative party or parties must adequately represent the interests of the class. In addition to the numerosity, commonality, typicality, and adequacy of representation requirements, Rule 23(b) also requires the plaintiff to show that (1) requiring individual suits by the putative class members would create the risk of inconsistent rulings, or that a ruling on one individual class member's claim may be dispositive of other class members' claims and thus 'substantially impair[ing] or imped[ing] their ability to protect their interests'; (2) the party

---

93 *See Twombly*, 550 US at 544.

94 Joseph Ostoyich, David Emanuelson, and Parker Normann (2009), 'More of the Same: Growth in Private Antitrust Litigation and Cutbacks by the US Supreme Court', p. 46, The Antitrust Review of the Americas, *available at* http://www.globalcompetitionreview.com/reviews/9/sections/27/chapters/351/more-same-growth-private-antitrust-litigation-cutbacks-us-supreme-court/, last accessed 24 August 2009.

95 *Id.*

96 The nuances of state class action law, of which there are many, are beyond the scope of this chapter.

97 *In re Hydrogen Peroxide Antitrust Litig.*, 552 F.3d 305, 310 (3d Cir. 2008) (quoting *Newton v. Merrill Lynch, Pierce, Fenner & Smith, Inc.*, 259 F.3d 154, 162 (3d Cir. 2001).

against whom the putative class seeks relief has acted or refused to act on grounds generally applicable to the class, 'so that final injunctive relief or corresponding declaratory relief is appropriate respecting the class as a whole'; or (3) common questions of law or fact predominate over individual questions, and that proceeding by way of class action would be 'superior to other available methods for fairly and efficiently adjudicating the controversy.' In analyzing whether the class action is superior to alternative legal routes of remedying the anticompetitive conduct at issue, some courts have deferred to pending *parens patriae* actions.[98]

The Class Action Fairness Act of 2005 (CAFA) decreased the likelihood that private parties can maintain a class action in state court. Now, defendants can remove to federal court a class action based on state law claims if: '(1) minimal diversity exists between members of the plaintiff class and the defendants; (2) the aggregate value of the individual class members' claims exceeds $5 million dollars; (3) the number of putative class members exceeds 100; and (4) the defendants are not "States, State officials, or other government entities."'[99] CAFA does not, in practice, apply to *parens patriae* actions brought by state enforcers. This means that these cases can stay in state court while (perhaps overlapping) private class actions may be removed to federal court.[100]

Since states' *parens patriae* authority generally extends only to natural persons, and does not include businesses, only private lawyers can ordinarily bring actions on behalf of direct purchasers or intermediate indirect purchasers. It is not just state attorneys general who can represent government entities in class actions. In most states, private class actions could include state agencies as part of the class, although most plaintiffs' lawyers simply exclude all governmental entities. With respect to cases representing consumer indirect purchasers, state *parens actions* generally take priority over private actions. States can seek certain remedies, such as civil penalties, that private plaintiffs cannot.

Overlapping lawsuits: case examples

The issues surrounding overlapping private–public lawsuits are best illustrated through actual examples of concurrent, or even competing, enforcers choosing alternative paths.

Hartford Fire Insurance Co. v. California[101] is an example of a case which the DOJ Antitrust Division declined to investigate despite a direct request to do so by several states.[102] In the face of federal inaction, 19 states sued 32 insurers, reinsurers, and an important trade association of insurers, alleging boycotts of certain types of business and municipal insurance. The states were particularly sensitive to these violations because

---

98 ALD VI, *supra* note 3, p. 906. For a detailed discussion of the Rule 23 requirements, see Chapter 8 of this *Handbook*.

99 *Id.*, p. 882.

100 For further discussion of CAFA, see Chapters 7 and 8 of this *Handbook*.

101 509 US 764 (1993). There are numerous additional examples that could be cited in industries as diverse as national debit cards, cable television, and retail grocery. *See generally* ALD VI, supra note 3, ch. 15.

102 In 1987, several states asked the DOJ Antitrust Division to investigate the property and casualty insurance industry, including several syndicates of Lloyd's of London. The Division declined to do so. *See* Michael F. Brockmeyer (1988), 'State Antitrust Enforcement', Antitrust Law Journal, 57 (1), 169–78, p. 170 n.4.

their own municipalities and governmental agencies were unable to obtain liability insurance from the domestic commercial property and casualty insurers, allegedly due to a conspiracy among domestic insurers, domestic and foreign reinsurers, and the trade association representing the domestic industry. In other words, although the conspiracy was international in scope, the effects of the conspiracy were felt most acutely at the local level. Ultimately, the states prevailed on three important issues in the Supreme Court, including the issue concerning the ability of US courts to reach the conduct of foreign reinsurers operating largely outside of the United States. The case settled for important structural relief.[103]

Many of the international cartel cases now resulting in antitrust enforcement by the DOJ Antitrust Division are premised on the precedent established by *Hartford Fire Insurance*.[104] Had the system not provided concurrent authority to the states (and private plaintiffs who represented various affected classes of injured parties), not only would the conspiracy have continued, but an important piece of decisional authority would not have been created.

Similarly, *In Re NASDAQ Market-Makers Antitrust Litigation* is another high-profile example where private plaintiffs acted despite the inaction of federal enforcers.[105] In this litigation, private plaintiffs sued several NASDAQ market-makers after learning about a potential bid-rigging activity first exposed in a business journal.[106] The activity essentially involved a 'rounding up' of specific bid/ask spreads, which resulted in substantially higher spreads (and higher broker/dealer profits) than with comparable securities traded on other markets.[107] At the time, the settlement ($1.027 billion) was apparently the largest antitrust recovery in history. Both the DOJ and the Securities and Exchange Commission began formal investigations of the activity only after the private suits had already been filed, and not without questioning whether collusion could have occurred as a matter of economic theory.[108] In fact, the federal district court approving the settlement emphasized that the private plaintiffs '[awoke] the federal government to . . . price collusion that the government had previously ignored,' and 'pulled the laboring oar in advancing this case.'[109]

---

[103] The structural relief included transforming the Insurance Services Office, the principle trade association of commercial insurers, from an organization dominated by the industry into one controlled by non-industry board members. Also, two independent organizations were created from resources contributed by the defendant insurers and reinsurers to provide key services to governmental entities seeking to insure outside of the commercial market. *See* Michael L. Weiner (1993), 'Developments at the Division, in the Court, and in Congress: The Increasing Internationalization of Antitrust', Antitrust, 8 (1), 31–34, p. 31 (discussing the case and settlement).

[104] *Hartford Fire Insurance Co. v. California*, 509 US 764 (1993). *See* O'Connor, *supra* note 28, pp. 34, 38. *See also* Robert Skitol and James Meyers, 'Ten Milestones In Twentieth-Century Antitrust Law and Their Importance to the Decade Ahead', Antitrust Report, 2000 (1), 6 (listing *Hartford Fire Insurance* as a 'milestone case' in the field of antitrust law).

[105] 184 F.R.D. 506 (S.D.N.Y. 1999).

[106] Arthur M. Kaplan (2001), 'Antitrust as a Public-Private Partnership: A Case Study of the NASDAQ Litigation', Case Western Reserve Law Review, 21 (1), 111–32.

[107] *Id.*

[108] *Id.*, p. 116 n.17 and accompanying text.

[109] *Id.*, p. 112 n.4 and accompanying text (citing Affidavit of Columbia Professor John C. Coffee, Jr., ¶24). In more colorful language, the private parties' role was described as 'not a case

These examples illustrate how the American system can generate opportunities for the courts to develop important precedents even where the national enforcers choose not to act. This constant testing of facts against theory facilitates the emergence of a meaningful consensus or, at least, a sharpening of the antitrust dialogue. The various circuit courts of appeal rely on reported decisions from each other as persuasive but not controlling precedent, facilitating a convergence of national antitrust enforcement policy and highlighting the outstanding areas of doctrinal differences. The concurrent enforcement system in the United States allows the United States to assume a leadership role not only because it is a leader in governmental enforcement,[110] but because its system generates a wide range of decisional law and allows most parties entitled to relief under the antitrust laws to commence an action for recovery.

None of this is meant to assume away the relative merits of more centralized enforcement systems: less complexity, greater predictability due to fewer decisionmakers, more uniformity, and lower compliance/litigation costs. However, decentralized systems tend to generate more case law and fewer false negative enforcement decisions because there is no monopolization of the enforcement decision-making apparatus. While it is not possible to quantify these costs and benefits in a meaningful manner, it is possible to appreciate the dynamic nature of the American system even while we attempt to minimize the costs associated with it.

Coordination problems and solutions

Private plaintiffs and public enforcers practice under and are guided by substantially the same substantive law, and frequently represent, or at least attempt to represent, overlapping groups of individuals, businesses, and other entities that claim to be injured by violations of the antitrust laws. But, as discussed throughout this chapter, private plaintiffs and public enforcers operate according to varying incentives, are subject to varying constraints, and are entitled to varying remedies. As a result of these differences, there may be tensions between the private plaintiffs and public enforcers. To best achieve the overarching objective of stopping the alleged anticompetitive conduct and providing relief to victims of the conduct, private plaintiffs and public enforcers should coordinate their efforts as much as possible. At the very least, they should communicate on a consistent basis and determine at what points and for what litigation tasks the private plaintiffs and public enforcers can coordinate.

Generally, there are three phases to a civil lawsuit in which issues arise about coordination between private plaintiffs and public enforcers: (1) investigative and precomplaint case strategy; (2) litigation; and (3) settlement or arbitration. What follows is a description of best practices for coordination between private plaintiffs and public enforcers.

1. The investigative and precomplaint case strategy phase An issue that arises in this phase is whether public enforcers, when in the process of investigating or developing

where plaintiffs' counsel can be cast as jackals to the government's lion, arriving on the scene after some enforcement or administrative agency has made the kill.' *Id.* at 112.

[110] *See* First, *supra* note 79, pp. 731–32.

enforcement actions, should encourage private class counsel to represent parties not represented by the government. Where the investigation is confidential, the government will be precluded from sharing information with private parties. But where there are no confidentiality concerns, the government may find it beneficial to encourage the involvement of private parties, especially if the governmental entity is facing budget constraints. Not only does a private lawsuit mean that the anticompetitive conduct with which the government is concerned may be stopped, but private counsel may be able to identify for the government additional cases for investigation. As discussed in Chapter 9, *Twombly* and its progeny pose challenges to private parties who may be unable to meet the stricter pleading standard set forth in that case. After *Twombly*, there may be cases in which private plaintiffs should, or must, cede to the government, as the *Twombly* standard does not apply to governmental actions.

Another issue that arises in this initial, investigative phase is whether state enforcers should bring overlapping actions where there is no concern about the quality of representation in the private action and there is no specific need for governmental involvement (for example, where specific injunctive relief – conduct or structural – which is more likely to be sought and obtained by government plaintiffs, is not at issue). In such cases, the governmental entity considering suit should determine whether an overlapping suit – even an investigation – is worth the resources. State attorneys general must consider public finance and budgetary constraints. Of course this is not to suggest that private plaintiffs all have access to unlimited resources – they too may be constrained with limited funds to devote to an antitrust lawsuit that will likely require retaining experts, reviewing enormous amounts of discovery, taking and defending numerous depositions, and engaging in extensive briefing on complex matters. But the source of and method of addressing financial constraints differ in the private and public realms.

There are distinct advantages to overlapping suits, and there are circumstances under which they should be pursued. The government can add credibility to an action while the private bar can perhaps bring greater resources. In addition, the parties can avoid future potential conflicts in class actions involving both direct and indirect purchasers.

In practice, governmental agencies may want to reserve the initiation of an overlapping suit for compelling cases. State enforcers may also wish to adopt selection criteria for bringing indirect purchaser cases. In addition, state enforcers may assign highest priority to cases in which there is a need for specific injunctive relief; there are insufficient – if any – private plaintiff or adequate class counsel; the anticompetitive conduct at issue is egregious; or no other governmental entity has dealt with the conduct.

In the event the government decides to pursue an investigation in anticipation of bringing suit, the public and private parties should discuss how to proceed most efficiently, including at settlement. Private plaintiffs and public enforcers should discuss as soon as practicable a case management strategy.

2. Litigation phase There are several principles that private plaintiffs and public enforcers may employ to guide a coordinated action. First, private plaintiffs and public enforcers should enter into common interest agreements as soon as practicable to protect joint work product.[111] This should be completed as soon as possible to allow the maximum confidentiality protection. Second, counsel for the class and the government should, if they have not already, adopt a litigation strategy that will maximize the recovery for injured parties they are representing. That litigation strategy should include an optimal combination of cases to file in federal and state courts, which should consider limitations imposed by CAFA, state indirect purchaser and class certification law, among a host of other issues that invariably affect any litigation and complex antitrust litigation suits in particular.

Third, private plaintiffs and public enforcers should coordinate discovery as much as practicable. Discovery can be enormously expensive and time consuming.[112] Without coordination, these efforts may be unnecessarily duplicated by the public and private plaintiffs.

Fourth, private plaintiffs and public enforcers should communicate with each other about litigation schedules, significant deadlines, and components of the case in which each can utilize the other's assistance. For example, the public and private plaintiffs should be prepared to assist each other with amicus briefs on matters in which they have a mutual interest.

Fifth, the parties should consider and discuss any other time saving measures. The parties should not hesitate to raise these issues as they arise over the course of litigation.

3. Settlement/arbitration phase As with the other phases discussed above, coordination is essential during settlement or arbitration. Where the private and public lawsuits represent overlapping classes or groups of injured parties, the private plaintiffs and public enforcers should coordinate to the extent possible a settlement or arbitration negotiation strategy. In private actions in which government enforcers are able to get involved but have not done so, class counsel should consider inviting the government to become part of the settlement or arbitration process. According to David Rosenberg and James Sullivan, '[c]oordinating public and private litigation and settlement decisions is . . . crucial to the effective enforcement of antitrust laws' to ameliorate the 'overbearing

---

[111] Parties involved in the same or a related case who share a common interest in the litigation may enter into a common interest agreement, which can be a useful tool. Assuming all of the particular elements required by the applicable state law are met, a common interest agreement allows parties represented by separate counsel to exchange verbal and written information in furtherance of the parties' common interest without waiving the attorney–client privilege or work product protection.

[112] In *Twombly*, the Supreme Court emphasized the expensive discovery costs associated with litigating an antitrust suit. 550 US at 558–59, citing the following: William H. Wagener (2003), 'Modeling the Effect of One-Way Fee Shifting on Discovery Abuse in Private Antitrust Litigation', New York University Law Review, 78 (5), 1887–1928, pp. 1898–99 (discussing the unusually high cost of discovery in antitrust cases); Federal Judicial Center (4th ed. 2004), Manual for Complex Litigation, Washington DC: Government Printing Office, §30, p. 519 (describing extensive scope of discovery in antitrust cases); Memorandum from Paul V. Niemeyer, Chair, Advisory Committee on Civil Rules, to Hon. Anthony J. Scirica, Chair, Committee on Rules of Practice and Procedure (May 11, 1999), 192 F.R.D. 354, 357 (2000) (reporting that discovery accounts for as much as 90 per cent of litigation costs when discovery is actively employed).

litigation costs and excessive sanctions' that, according to the authors, accompany private antitrust class actions.[113]

A final aspect of this third phase is the *cy pres* doctrine. This doctrine is applied in antitrust class actions 'where direct distribution of the damages awarded to all the class members is not feasible, permitting funds to be distributed in the next best fashion in order to benefit the intended class as closely as possible and to avoid retention of ill-gotten gains by defendants.'[114]

Where *cy pres* is part of a settlement agreement, the private and public plaintiffs should consider several guiding principles:

- the first priority in a damages award in an antitrust case is to return the damages to the injured class members;
- *cy pres* should be used only if the class is so large compared to the size of the fund that the transaction costs render a distribution of cash infeasible;
- if a *cy pres* award is made, there must be an adequate nexus between the nature of the claim and the uses to which the *cy pres* funds will be put;
- where the fund is sufficiently large, a foundation-like process should be used to oversee the selection of the recipients and their expenditures; and
- if the fund is not sufficiently large, plaintiffs should present one or more candidates for the court to select based on detailed proposals by the candidates.

The United States' model of private and public enforcement maximizes the opportunities for injured parties to recover from anticompetitive conduct.

Qualitative and quantitative results of multiple layers of enforcement

It is precisely the concurrent enforcement system that allows time-honored theories to be tested against the facts of particular cases (which carries qualitative and quantitative elements). Qualitatively, the concurrent enforcement system allows private parties, through litigation, to test theories adopted by the federal government in previous cases[115] or in guidelines.[116] Even bedrock doctrine, such as the *per se* illegality of horizontal price-fixing,[117] has subsequently been 'clarified' in private litigation.[118] Perhaps the most prominent example of an attempt to test theories adopted by the federal government is the attempt by a number of states to obtain injunctive relief against Microsoft beyond

---

113 Rosenberg and Sullivan, *surpa* note 30, p. 162.

114 Albert Foer (2007), 'Enhancing Competition Through the Cy Pres Remedy: Suggested Best Practices', AAI Working Paper No. 07-11, *available at* http://www.antitrustinstitute.org/Archives/WP07-11.ashx, accessed 27 July 2009 (quotation marks omitted).

115 *Compare United States v. Arnold, Schwinn & Co.*, 388 US 365 (1967), *with Continental T. V. v. GTE Sylvania*, 433 US 36 (1977). *GTE Sylvania* is, of course, viewed as a seminal case in antitrust jurisprudence. *See, e.g.,* Thomas B. Leary (2002), 'The Essential Stability of Merger Policy in the United States', Antitrust Law Journal, 70 (1), 105–42, p. 110.

116 *See, e.g., United States v. Baker Hughes Inc.*, 908 F.2d 981 (D.C. Cir. 1990) (citing, somewhat critically, the FTC/DOJ Horizontal Merger Guidelines with respect to the importance of entry in merger analysis).

117 *See, e.g., United States v. Socony-Vacuum Oil Co.*, 310 US 150 (1940).

118 *See, e.g., Broadcast Music, Inc. v. Columbia Broadcasting System, Inc.*, 441 US 1 (1979).

what had already been obtained by the DOJ and several other states through negotiation. Whatever one thinks of the merits of the litigating states' position, their persistence is likely to generate significant decisional law on the appropriate antitrust remedies in an ever-evolving and expanding industry.[119]

Quantitatively, in 2008, the DOJ Antitrust Division filed 19 civil cases in federal courts: 15 merger challenges, two pursuant to Sherman Act §1, and two 'other' civil cases.[120] The Antitrust Division also filed 54 criminal cases in 2008.[121] Additionally, the FTC filed four non-merger and 22 merger challenges.[122] State antitrust enforcers account for a large percentage of antitrust cases filed (in state and federal courts) in an average year.[123] As the Antitrust Modernization Commission pointed out in its 2007 report, there are both vocal critics and proponents of state enforcement.[124] However, the Commission concluded that the benefits of state enforcement outweigh the costs:

> State antitrust enforcement can benefit consumers by obtaining treble damages for consumers and supplementing federal enforcement. The states have unique authority to recover antitrust damages for their consumers and local government purchasers. The vast majority of state enforcement activity over the past fifteen years has involved areas in which state enforcers may have a comparative advantage in terms of knowledge – that is, with respect to local markets, local competitive effects, and local government purchasers. During the same time period, the states' enforcement efforts have targeted most frequently those antitrust violations most likely to cause significant consumer harm, such as price-fixing, bid-rigging, and market allocation.[125]

As a result, the Commission did not recommend elimination of state enforcement but instead recommended mechanisms for state and federal enforcers to coordinate their efforts to best protect competition without imposing unnecessary costs on businesses and taxpayers.[126]

Aside from governmental enforcement of the antitrust laws, there were 1,287 private antitrust actions in federal court in 2008, accounting for 96.1 per cent of the total number

---

[119] *See generally* Robert Pitofsky (2002), 'Antitrust Remedies in the 21st Century: Too Many Actions? Too Much – or Still Too Little – Recovery?', Antitrust Source, 1 (5), 1–16, p. 11 (indicating a judicial decision would be useful regarding appropriate relief given the governments' victory in the Court of Appeals).

[120] *See* Appropriation Figures for the Antitrust Division, *available at* http://www.usdoj.gov/atr/public/10804a.htm, accessed 27 July 2009 (links to information on FTC and DOJ caseload, staff, and budget information).

[121] *Id.*

[122] FTC Competition Enforcement Database, *available at* http://www.ftc.gov/bc/caselist/index.shtml, accessed 27 July 2009.

[123] Although state antitrust cases are more difficult to track, a review of the ALD Annual Supplements and various NAAG publications supports this assertion, even counting multistate complaints filed in federal court as one complaint, though such complaints may assert claims under state law that alternatively could have been filed in multiple state courts. *See generally* ABA Section of Antitrust Law (2008), Annual Review of Antitrust Law Developments, Chicago, IL: American Bar Association, pp. 183–90 (previous issues offer similar discussions of the annual number of state enforcement actions).

[124] US Antitrust Modernization Comm'n, Report and Recommendations 185–87 (2007).

[125] *Id.* at 186.

[126] *Id.* at 186–203.

of antitrust cases filed.[127] Since 1975, private antitrust actions have accounted for 83.4 per cent to 96.6 per cent of all antitrust actions filed.[128] The number of antitrust actions filed by private parties in state courts is not tabulated, although it appears that private plaintiffs increasingly are using state fora to obtain damages in indirect purchaser cases.[129]

Although this volume of antitrust filings is somewhat misleading (in that separate cases brought by various enforcers often allege overlapping violations as they seek varying remedies), it does indicate that the system produces numerous opportunities for courts to apply the general precepts of competition law to particularized facts.

The multiple layers create a unique antitrust enforcement landscape

It is undoubtedly true that this diversity of potential enforcers motivated by varying incentives has resulted in an active antitrust litigation environment in the United States. Whether this environment results in a greater degree of enforcement than would be optimal from some perspectives is a valid concern.[130] It certainly is not the case that the optimal number of enforcers approaches infinity. Some commentators have suggested eliminating the competition enforcement authority of a number of federal agencies because they apply 'soft' competition standards to mergers in specific industry sectors and have only limited expertise in competition analysis. The ICPAC report singles out the overlapping authority of these sectoral agencies and the federal antitrust agencies as a 'defect' of the American system.[131] In addition to the increased transaction costs and the relative lack of antitrust expertise in the sectoral agencies, critics of the current system point to the broad 'public interest' standard that governs agency review of these transactions.[132] This standard imports non-competition criteria into the analysis, thereby allowing some transactions to be evaluated on grounds inconsistent with those governing other industries. These criticisms are well taken, and underscore that in any system of concurrent enforcement, the potential enforcers ought to be governed by a single set of competition standards, preferably reviewable in an integrated court system.

Moreover, a system of multiple potential enforcers applying the same law has produced numerous opportunities for federal and state courts to rule on antitrust questions, creating a rich trove of antitrust decisional law, at least in comparison to other enforcement regimes. Even in those instances where a state or private enforcer unsuccessfully

---

127 Bureau of Justice Statistics, Sourcebook of Justice Statistics Online: Antitrust Cases Filed in US District Courts by Type of Case, 1975–2008, *available at* http://www.albany.edu/sourcebook/pdf/t5412008.pdf.

128 *Id.*

129 *See generally* O'Connor, *supra* note 28, p. 34; First, *supra* note 79 (discussing vitamins indirect purchaser litigation).

130 *See* Douglas H. Ginsburg and Scott H. Angstreich (2000), 'Multinational Merger Review: Lessons from Our Federalism', Antitrust Law Journal, 68 (1), 219–38, p. 220. *See also* Speech, Ky P. Ewing, Jr. (Oct. 27, 2000), 'Suggestions for a Framework for Governmental Discussion About Antitrust Procedures and Principles', Fourth Annual Competition Conference, The European University Institute, Fiesole, Italy.

131 ICPAC, *supra* note 2, ch. 3, p.144.

132 *See, e.g.,* Milton A. Marquis, 'DOJ, FTC and FERC Electric Power Merger Enforcement: Are There Too Many Cooks in the Merger Review Kitchen?,' Loyola University Chicago Law Journal, 33 (4), 783–90, pp. 788–89.

litigates an alleged violation, the end result can be the development of useful or even significant case law.[133]

Conclusion

The American system of antitrust enforcement is strengthened by concurrent enforcement. Antitrust litigation in multiple jurisdictions and by numerous plaintiffs produces tangible benefits in the number of reported decisions and facilitates the continual and transparent evolution of the law. There are several benefits to an enforcement system that produces a wealth of litigation. One premier benefit is that litigation requires parties and courts to apply the broad language of the antitrust laws to the specific facts at issue. As case law develops, parties are provided more guidance on the contours of what constitutes illegal anticompetitive conduct. This guidance assists firms, and individuals avoid liability with knowledge of what conduct violates the antitrust laws. It also assists litigating plaintiffs because they have a more specific framework on which to base their claims.

Because consensus in antitrust principles emerges from continued discussion about the application of national laws to specific cases, a system of concurrent enforcement is apt to enhance, not discourage, the process of convergence. This issue is relevant whether one is a believer, non-believer, or agnostic regarding the welfare advantages of current antitrust policy in the United States or elsewhere.

On a broader level, there is intuitive appeal to the argument that a common international set of competition rules and enforcement policies will reduce uncertainty and enhance economic efficiency. Divergent standards for vertical agreements, unilateral conduct by dominant firms, and mergers (especially mergers) almost certainly entail real net economic costs, especially in the mature economies of North America, Europe, and Japan.

Notwithstanding the benefits of maintaining an international antitrust enforcement system where substantive antitrust policy continually is tested against the facts of particular cases, much could be gained from enhanced coordination on the procedural front, especially with respect to merger enforcement. The methods used by states in the United States to coordinate and streamline merger enforcement with each other and with the federal agencies can be a useful starting point for a discussion about improvements in the international enforcement system.

---

133 *See, e.g., New York v. Kraft Gen. Foods*, 862 F. Supp. 1030 (S.D.N.Y. 1993) (New York unsuccessfully challenged Nabisco acquisition after DOJ chose not to act); *Continental T.V. v. GTE Sylvania*, 433 US 36 (1977) (private plaintiff's unsuccessful challenge to location clause resulted in precedent virtually eliminating the applicability of the per se rule to non-price vertical restraints).

14 Class notice and claims administration

Katherine Kinsella and Shannon Wheatman[1]

Much has been written and discussed about the negative aspects of the American class action model.[2] Indeed, the US class action device is far from perfect, and other countries are taking steps to avoid the abusive aspects of class actions in their construction of statutes to govern collective actions. There is, however, an important aspect of the US model that is clearly worth consideration. Over the past 70-plus years, federal and most state laws have evolved safeguards to protect the due process rights of class members. Due process rights are fundamentally at issue in US class actions when notice is required to inform class members about class certification and/or settlement and when a judgment has awarded class-wide relief.

The emergence of a global economy now requires US courts to face the dilemma of securing the due process rights of class members around the world.[3] In US class action law, which has been carefully crafted to protect the rights of class members, notification plays a prominent role. Although additional international concerns with class actions may remain, the notice provisions required by Rule 23 of the Federal Rules of Civil Procedure[4] could provide a model for the development of notice standards in other countries.

In 1938, Rule 23 was included in the new Federal Rules of Civil Procedure. The role of notice in class actions was expanded in 1966 when Rule 23 was modified to include the 'best notice practicable' standard. Class action notice provisions advanced even further in 2003 when Rule 23 was amended to require plain language.[5] Rule 23 requires close judicial scrutiny over the entire class action process including an explicit standard ('fair, reasonable, and adequate') for approving a settlement.[6] In addition, when class actions settle in federal court, the Class Action Fairness Act (CAFA), enacted by Congress in

---

[1] Katherine Kinsella is the President and Shannon Wheatman, Ph.D. is a Vice President of Kinsella Media. They are leading, nationally and internationally recognized experts in the design, preparation, and dissemination of legal notice in class actions and bankruptcies.

[2] For a response to these negative critiques, see Chapter 1 of this *Handbook*.

[3] The authors have worked on numerous class actions that included foreign claimants, for example: Authors Guild, Inc. v. Google Inc. No. 05-8136 (S.D.N.Y. 2009); In re Int'l Air Transp. Surcharge Antitrust Litig., No. 06-1793 (N. D. Cal. 2008); In re TJX Cos. Retail Sec. Breach Litig., No. 07-10162 (D. Mass. 2008); In re Parmalat Sec. Litig., No. 04-1653 (S.D.N.Y. 2007); In re Royal Ahold Sec. & ERISA Litig., No. 03-1539 (D. Md. 2006); Galanti v. The Goodyear Tire & Rubber Co., No. 03-0209 (D.N.J. 2004); In re Western Union Money Transfer Litig., No. 01-0335 (E.D.N.Y. 2003); In re Holocaust Victim Assets Litig., No. 96-4849 (E.D.N.Y. 1999); Ahearn v. Fiberboard Corp., No. 93-0526 (E.D. Tex. 1994); and Continental Casualty Co. v. Rudd, No. 94-0458 (E.D. Tex. 1994). [Citation reflects the year the notice program was implemented.]

[4] Fed. R. Civ. P. 23(c)(2).

[5] *Id.*

[6] Fed. R. Civ. P. 23(e).

2005, is intended to further enhance the due process protection for class members by allowing scrutiny of class action settlements by federal and state attorneys general or regulatory authorities.[7]

Notifying class members about a lawsuit and giving them an opportunity to be heard is meant to solve many problems inherent in class actions. Beginning with the landmark ruling by the US Supreme Court in *Mullane v. Central Hanover & Trust Company,* US class action jurisprudence has repeatedly confirmed that notice plays a critical role in due process:

> an elementary and fundamental requirement of due process in any proceeding which is to be accorded finality is notice reasonably calculated, under all the circumstances, to apprise interested parties of the pendency of the action and afford them an opportunity to present their objection.[8]

It has been said that notice helps to 'democratize' the class action procedure.[9] Notice provides the mechanism for class members to act. Every class member has an equal right to participate in the class action but those rights and how to act on them can only be given through proper notification. Notice in Rule 23(b)(1) and (b)(2) classes, where money damages are not involved, does not include a right to exclude oneself (opt-out) and is given at the court's discretion when appropriate under the circumstances of the case. However, notice is mandatory in Rule 23(b)(3) classes where money damages are involved.[10] In situations where the litigation is moving towards trial the notice typically is disseminated at least 30 days before the start of the trial. If the litigation is being settled the notice will be disseminated shortly after the court grants preliminary approval to the settlement.

This chapter provides an overview of the notification requirements under Rule 23 and offers insights into how courts and practitioners should evaluate a notice program to ensure that it adequately reaches class members with information that is easily digested and acted upon. The authors explain how a notice program is designed and executed. The chapter concludes with a discussion about administering a class action.

Individual notice

Individual notice is sent directly to the class member via first class mail (in the form of a letter or postcard) or electronic mail. The US Supreme Court, in *Eisen v. Jacquelin,* made clear that individual notice must be provided to all class members who are identifiable through reasonable efforts, regardless of the cost.[11] '[W]hat is "the best notice practicable

---

7 The Class Action Fairness Act of 2005, §§1712–1715 (2005).

8 Mullane v. Cent. Hanover Bank & Trust Co., 339 US 306, 315 (1950).

9 *See* Benjamin K. Kaplan, *Continuing Work of the Civil Committee: 1966 Amendment of the Federal Rule of Civil Procedure (I)*, 81 Harv. L. Rev. 356, 392 (1967).

10 Rule 23(b)(1) is utilized to avoid prejudices that would result in inconsistent adjudication if individual actions were allowed, 23(b)(2) is used when plaintiffs are seeking declaratory or injunctive relief, and 23(b)(3) is suitable when a class action is superior to other available methods and common questions predominate over individual ones. Herbert B. Newberg & Alba Conte, 2 Newberg on Class Actions §4:1 (4th ed., West 2002).

11 Eisen v. Jacquelin, 417 US 156, 173 (1974).

under the circumstances" and what constitutes "reasonable effort" is a determination of fact to be made in the individual litigation.'[12] The individual notice concept continued to evolve in *Jones v. Flowers,* in which the US Supreme Court held that due process dictates that reasonable steps be taken to deal with undelivered mail.[13]

In referencing the notice requirements of Rule 23, the court in *In re Nissan Motor Corporation Antitrust Litigation* stated, 'The United States Supreme Court has declared that subdivision (c)(2) expresses an "unambiguous requirement" that "individual notice must be provided to those class members who are identifiable through reasonable effort."'[14] The Court in *Nissan* went on to explain '[o]bviously, the word "reasonable" cannot be ignored. In every case, reasonableness is a function of anticipated results, costs, and amount involved.'[15] Generally, the cost of providing notice to a class that is certified for trial falls upon the plaintiffs.[16] However, the court can order that the defendant bear some of the costs of identifying potential class members.[17] When a class action is being certified for settlement purposes only, typically the defendants will either separately pay for the costs of notice or the money will be deducted from the settlement fund.

Paid media notice

The key question in any notice program is what constitutes 'the best notice practicable'? When comprehensive mailing lists of class members exist, direct mail (by post or email) should be the primary method used for notification. When comprehensive mailing lists are unavailable or cannot be compiled through reasonable effort then 'notice by publication will suffice under Rule 23(c)(2) and under the due process clause.'[18] In *In Re Domestic Air Transportation Antitrust Litigation* the court held, '[i]f class members . . . cannot be identified, there is no other requirement of mandatory individual notice, and the Court must exercise its discretion to provide the best notice practicable under the circumstances.'[19]

The overarching goal of any notice program is to effectively reach the class so that class members have a 'meaningful' opportunity to be heard.[20] Rule 23 can 'comport with constitutional standards of due process only if there is a maximum opportunity of notice to the absentee class members . . . .'[21] Each class action requires a notice program tailored to the specifics of the case. Factors such as the distribution or consumption of a product or service, the number of readily identifiable class members, the anticipated class size, the

---

12 In re 'Agent Orange' Prod. Liab. Litig., 100 F.R.D. 718, 729 (E.D.N.Y. 1983) (internal citations omitted).

13 Jones v. Flowers, 547 US 220, 225 (2006).

14 In re Nissan Motor Corp. Antitrust Litig., 552 F.2d 1088, 1097 (5th Cir. 1977) (internal citations omitted).

15 *Id.* at 1099.

16 *Eisen*, supra note 11, at 177.

17 Oppenheimer Fund, Inc. v Sanders, 437 US 340, 350, 355–56, 358 (1978).

18 Carlough v. Amchem Prods., Inc., 158 F.R.D. 314, 325 (E.D. Pa. 1993) (citing Mullane, 339 US 306, 317–18 (1950)).

19 In re Domestic Air Transp. Antitrust Litig., 141F.R.D. 534, 555 (N.D. Ga. 1992).

20 Armstrong v. Manzo, 380 US 545, 552 (1965) (due process requires an opportunity to be heard 'at a meaningful time and in a meaningful manner').

21 Greenfield v. Villager Indus., Inc., 483 F.2d 824, 831 (3d Cir. 1973).

demographics of class members, and the geographic location of class members influence the direction and scope of a notice program.

Both direct and indirect purchasers form distinct classes in many antitrust cases. Direct purchasers, which are often businesses that may have registered agents authorized to receive notice, are usually 'readily identifiable' and can be reached through direct mailed notice. The names and addresses of indirect purchasers, who are typically consumers of a particular product or service, whether an individual or entity, are not usually known. While there are many ways to communicate information, paid media is usually the basic component of a notice plan intended to reach unidentifiable class members. It is targetable to specific demographic groups, measured by accredited marketing research firms for audience reach and frequency of exposure, and contractually guaranteed to appear on a certain date.

In selecting media vehicles for notice, it is important to rely on an expert in analyzing demographics and media usage – skills that attorneys are not trained in and usually do not have – to help guide the selection. An expert can help ensure that the notice program has the optimal media or mixture of media that is necessary to strike an adequate balance between cost efficiency and reach effectiveness. Cost efficiency is critical in any large media campaign. Of course, the overall cost of class notice depends on the size and geographic location of class members. However, a national notice program relying entirely on paid media in the US is costly and frequently runs to over a million dollars.

Identifying a target demographic and selecting media Demographics of class members guide the selection of media in a class action notice program. Individuals within the general population consume media differently based on income, gender, age, education, and other factors. Notice programs therefore must establish a clear demographic target or targets in order to select media to reach a specific audience. How a product or service was used or how a product exposure occurred, by or to whom, where and over what period of time, provides critical information in identifying the demographic characteristics and geographic distribution of class members. This research establishes the parameters for identifying and locating class members and shapes the notice program.

In the US as well as many other countries throughout the world, accredited media and marketing research firms provide syndicated data on audience size, composition, and other factors pertaining to major media, including broadcast, print, and outdoor advertising. They provide a single source measurement of major media, products, services, and in-depth consumer demographic and lifestyle or psychographic characteristics. These research companies regularly survey consumers nationally through in-person interviews and questionnaires.

There are literally hundreds of information sources throughout the world combining the measurement of media with product usage. In the US, the leading survey company for single-source measure is GfK MRI (MRI).[22] MRI's parent company, GfK Group, is conducting similar cross-media research in eight countries throughout Europe along with print and other media surveys in at least ten more. Target Group Index (TGI) is a global network of single-source market research surveys in over 60 other countries on

---

22 *See* Mediamark Research, Inc., http://www.mediamark.com (last visited Dec. 7, 2009).

six continents.[23] Additionally, the Nielsen Company conducts audience or marketing research in over 100 countries and is one of the leading providers of audience measurement in television and the Internet worldwide.[24] Whether one is using television in the UK, magazines in Germany, newspaper in Japan, or the Internet in Australia, there is an accredited media company providing research on relevant audiences.

Demographic profiles of individuals who use a specific service or product can be constructed from these surveys. For example, the data allow notice and media experts to identify the demographics of consumers who are cell-phone users, homeowners, cigarette smokers, insurance policyholders, or prescription drug purchasers. In many instances, product usage by brand or type is available.

In addition, the media habits of these product users or demographic targets can be further evaluated. It can be determined if they are light newspaper readers, heavy television viewers, moderate Internet users, and so forth. A media expert can compare different types of media for audience penetration and cost. For example, TV penetration of a particular target audience can be compared to that of radio, magazines, and newspapers. In addition, the data is indexed by media vehicle – a specific television show, radio program, or magazine – with respect to its penetration of the target audience. This information provides direction to the media selections and ensures that the media used actually reaches the target audience.

For example, in the class action *In Re International Air Transportation Surcharge Antitrust Litigation*, the classes involved international travelers who had traveled on British Airways or Virgin Atlantic, which included people living predominantly in the US and the UK.[25] Kinsella Media consulted several research sources in order to determine the appropriate vehicles to carry the notice. The TGI survey of the UK provided the demographic characteristics and the media usage of the class members there as well as the readership of UK publications. ComScore, an international provider of digital marketing data, provided rankings and audiences for websites visited by class members.[26] This audience data revealed which media vehicles provided the most efficient means of reaching class members (in this case newspapers and travel websites), as well as how many insertions were necessary to adequately reach a substantial number of them.

Measuring media-based notice There are a number of ways to measure media penetration. Two of the most basic are reach and frequency. Reach is the estimated percentage of a target audience reached through a specific media vehicle or combination of media vehicles. Frequency is the estimated average number of times an audience is exposed to an advertising vehicle carrying the message. Reach and frequency calculations are estimates within a standard margin of error that provide the advertiser with a reliable basis upon which to judge penetration of target audiences by media.

Software programs created by the media industry allow media planners to calculate reach and frequency estimates. Statistical formulas factor out duplication of readership

---

23 *See* Global TGI, http://www.tgisurveys.com (last visited Dec. 7, 2009).

24 *See* Nielsen, http://www.nielsen.com (last visited Dec. 7, 2009).

25 Declaration of Katherine Kinsella, *In re* Int'l Air Transp. Surcharge Antitrust Litig. No. 06-1793 (N.D. Cal. Sept. 18, 2008).

26 *See* ComScore, http://www.comscore.com (last visited Dec. 7, 2009).

or viewership among the target audience and allow calculation of reach and frequency as well as other media measurements. This allows determination of the net audience reach of a media schedule using various kinds of print, online, and broadcast media.

Reach and frequency targets depend upon a number of factors that guide how extensive a paid media program should be within the context of what is reasonable and practicable. Among the factors are the type of relief sought (injunctive relief or damages, whether direct or cy pres/fluid recovery), the seriousness of the tort, the size of the settlement, and the percentage of the class to be reached through media versus direct mail.

Determining the adequacy of notice

Rule 23 and the relevant case law do not define what constitutes adequate notice. However, the guarantee of due process that is inherent in the Fifth and Fourteenth Amendments of the US Constitution provides valuable information on the minimum notice required.[27] The Fifth Circuit has explained, 'The essence of due process is that "deprivation of life, liberty or property by adjudication be preceded by notice and opportunity for hearing appropriate to the nature of the case."'[28] The Seventh Circuit has added, 'due process requires notice reasonably calculated to provide actual notice of the proceeding and a meaningful opportunity to be heard.'[29]

To demonstrate to a court that a notice program satisfies due process, the program should provide certain objective and quantifiable elements, for example, the size of the class and the percentage of class members reached through direct notice. In particular, a notice program directed to unidentified class members should: (1) identify the demographics of class members and establish a target audience, (2) outline the methodology for selecting the media and other plan elements and how they relate to product usage or exposure, and (3) provide results that quantify for the court the adequacy of the notice based upon recognized tools of media measurement.

In cases where there is a measurable demographic target available through survey data and the reach and frequency can be accurately measured, the notice expert should use these estimates to demonstrate to the court what percentage of a target audience was reached and how many opportunities class members had to see the notice. In situations where a measurable target demographic is not available because of limitations on survey data, the notice expert must demonstrate to the court the rationale for selecting the media and why it is effective in reaching class members. A demographic analysis can provide reasonable guidance to a notice expert in determining what media is best to reach the class. For example, in a class composed of highly educated people, without any other discerning demographic characteristics, such an analysis might show that newspapers would likely be the best choice.

In the international class action *In re Holocaust Victims Assets Litigation*, it was not possible to measure media against Jewish or Roma (Gypsy) people, two principal target audiences.[30] However, the team of notice administrators constructed a multi-faceted

[27] *See* Zadvydas v. Davis, 533 US 678, 693, 121 S.Ct. 2491, 150 L.Ed.2d 653 (2001).

[28] In re Nissan Motor Corp. Antitrust Litig., 552 F.2d 1088, 1103–04 (5th Cir. 1997) (citing Mullan v. Central Hanover Bank & Trust Co., 339 US 306, 313 (1950)).

[29] Nazarova v. INS, 171 F.3d 478, 482-83 (7th Cir.1999).

[30] In re Holocaust Victim Assets Litig., No. 96-4849 (E.D.N.Y. 1999).

program that included paid media in Jewish publications and in countries where there were Jewish concentrations, worldwide press outreach in 40 countries that contained target audiences, outreach through Jewish social service networks and religious organizations, as well as in-country in-person outreach to Roma people through field coordinators and social service organizations. Reports from the administrators meticulously chronicled all aspects of the notice program, quantifying efforts and results that demonstrated its success.

Content and design of notice 'It is in the government's interest that class members meaningfully understand their rights and make knowing, intelligent and voluntary choices.'[31] The 2003 plain language amendment to Rule 23 grew out of a desire to ensure that class members were fully informed of their rights.[32] During the rule-making process the US judicial branch's Advisory Committee on the Federal Rules of Civil Procedure asked the Federal Judicial Center (FJC) to conduct research and develop illustrative plain language notices.[33] The Advisory Committee notes accompanying the revised rules discuss the importance of plain language:

> The direction that class-certification notice be couched in plain, easily understood language is a reminder of the need to work unremittingly at the difficult task of communicating with class members. It is difficult to provide information about most class actions that is both accurate and easily understood by class members who are not themselves lawyers. Factual uncertainty, legal complexity, and the complication of class-action procedure raise the barriers high.[34]

According to the FJC, the first impression of any notice must 'persuade the readers that they have a stake in the class action and that they will be able to comprehend the notice.'[35] The notice must clearly describe all of the rights and options available to class members (such as filing a claim, appearing in court, objecting to the settlement, or opting out of the class[36]) as well as the binding nature of any judgment on anyone who fails to opt out of the class.[37] Rule 23 also requires that class members be notified of an attorney

---

31 Orantes-Hernandez v. Meese, 685 F.Supp. 1488, 1499 (C.D. Cal. 1988).

32 *See* Kinsella Media, LLC & Rust Consulting, Inc., *Plain Language Primer*, *available at* http://www.kinsellamedia.com (last visited Dec. 7, 2009).

33 The FJC is the research and education agency of the federal judicial system. More information on the research that was done by the FJC on the model notice project can be found at http://www.fjc.gov. *See also* Shannon R. Wheatman, *The Effects of Plain Language Drafting on Layperson's Comprehension of Class Action Notices* (2001) (Ph.D. dissertation, University of Georgia). This dissertation was based on research that was done at the FJC on the model notice project.

34 Fed. R. Civ. P. 23(c)(2)(B) advisory committee notes.

35 *See* FJC website, *supra* note 33.

36 Rule 23(e)(4) allows the court to condition settlement approval on the defendant's willingness to provide a second opportunity to opt out. The court knows it is key for class members to understand the terms of the settlement before their individual right to file their own lawsuit is terminated.

37 'Surely "the best notice practicable under the circumstances" cannot stop with . . . generalities. It must also contain an adequate description of the proceedings written in objective, neutral terms, that . . . may be understood by the average absentee class member.' *In re* Nissan Motor Corp. Antitrust Litig., 552 F.2d 1088, 1104 (5th Cir. 1977).

fee motion by class counsel and be given an opportunity to object to it.[38] This transparency of attorneys' fees is also recommended by *The Manual for Complex Litigation, Fourth*, a reference guide for judges and practitioners.[39]

Class Action Fairness Act

In 2005, CAFA imposed new notice requirements and increased judicial scrutiny of coupon settlements (which usually give class members a coupon for future services or products with the defendant's company) and attorneys' fees.[40] In federal court, CAFA requires defendants to give notice of a proposed class action settlement to certain state and federal government officials. Attorneys general and regulatory agencies now have a chance to comment on class action settlements providing yet another opportunity to safeguard the rights of class members. CAFA provides very detailed and comprehensive requirements for notice to regulating authorities, which must be undertaken within ten days of filing a proposed settlement. The governing court is prohibited from approving the settlement before 90 days after this notice has been given.

Administering a class action

Any class action settlement requires the terms of the settlement to be carried out: disseminating class notice via mail, email, or other means to class members; answering class members' questions via phone, email, website, or correspondence; receiving and processing claims, with whatever specific parameters each settlement requires; calculating awards; distributing settlement benefits; and reporting to the parties. The parties can retain a settlement administrator to manage some or all of these processes, as well as to offer consultative expertise. Notice experts also may be retained by the parties to work closely with the settlement administrator to ensure that the court-approved notice program is properly implemented.[41] While hired by one or more of the parties to the lawsuit, the settlement administrator generally works according to the terms of the settlement agreement, accepting only the joint direction of the parties in resolving matters not made clear by the settlement agreement. At one or more key points in the administration of the settlement, the settlement administrator typically provides a detailed summary of its actions to the court and the parties in the form of one or more affidavits or declarations. Such reporting is most often submitted prior to the hearing at which the court determines whether to grant the class action final approval, but may also be done after each phase of administration or as a final accounting.

The basic methods of administering a class action settlement with a substantial international contingent do not vary significantly from settlements with primarily US-based classes. However, such an administration requires the parties and administrator to consider up-front some key components to provide the class with clear and easily understandable information and to minimize the risk of objections – in short, to ensure the settlement is given its best chance at court approval.

---

38 Fed. R. Civ. P. 23(h).

39 Manual for Complex Litigation (Fourth), §21.312 (2004).

40 *Supra* note 7.

41 The notice expert firm may or may not be affiliated with the claims administration firm.

Most obvious of the issues to be addressed when dealing with a class containing foreign claimants is offering notice, claim forms, and other information (via printed, online, and recorded means as well as live customer service) in various languages, all while containing costs as much as is practicable.

Language issues

Typically, an administrator works with the parties to format the approved notice so it can be mailed or emailed to a list of known class members. When administering settlements with large numbers of foreign claimants, the parties or administrator must arrange for the translation of materials into the necessary additional languages. In most cases, more than just the notice itself must be translated: claim forms, website copy, and telephone scripts must also be considered for translation. Sufficient time and a contract with a reputable firm that is capable of translating legal material are paramount, and in-country native translators are preferred. A critical issue is the existence of terms such as 'class action,' which are not part of the language in certain countries, either as specific words or as legal concepts. This can cause confusion among class members unless carefully explained. In such cases, a glossary should be prepared and agreed to for all terms to be used in class member communications for clarity as well as for consistency.

Recently, in *Authors Guild, Inc. v. Google Inc.,* a worldwide consumer class action, notice was published in 216 countries in 72 languages, with direct notice and a settlement website with online claim features in 36 languages.[42] Ensuring the consistency and accuracy of all materials in multiple languages, across multiple forms of media including communication with in-country organizations assisting with notice requires adherence to a translation protocol.

Data concerns

Perhaps less obvious but of utmost importance in notification and ongoing settlement administration is data management, which includes strict adherence to privacy laws. An administrator often receives class member data (such as name, address, and other information relevant to the settlement). Crossing national borders necessitates knowledge of and adherence to a multitude of data privacy laws. The European Union and its member countries as well as other nations around the world have unique requirements for the treatment of personal information, which may differ from US law.

The parties and an administrator of a settlement whose sphere intersects with differing privacy laws must consider strategies to avoid violating any privacy law. Partnership with firms located in each relevant country can be an effective strategy in dealing with privacy issues. In the administration of the *Google* settlement, hundreds of copyright organizations, publisher associations and author groups worldwide were contacted to ask for assistance with giving direct notice to the class which obviated the need for the release of any personal information to the administrator.[43]

---

[42] The notice program in Authors Guild, Inc. v. Google Inc., 05-8136 (S.D.N.Y.) was implemented and is pending final court approval as of the publishing of this *Handbook*.

[43] *Id.*

Communicating with class members

Increasing use of the Internet benefits international administration. While accommodations should be made for printed materials and customer service in multiple languages, settlement websites can incorporate translated information to accommodate class members' needs at their convenience, regardless of time zones, toll-free telephone numbers, or delays allowed for international mail service. Approximately 30 times as many class members filed claims online as filed through traditional paper claims in the aforementioned *Google* settlement.[44]

A typical settlement website includes a summary of the case information including the terms of the settlement, answers to frequently asked questions, links to settlement documents such as the long-form notice, claim form, and settlement agreement, and, increasingly, the functionality to submit questions or claim forms online. By utilizing these features, many of the cost-prohibitive and time-consuming aspects of settlement administration are bypassed.

Despite this increasingly online experience, an administrator must continue to work with more traditional methods of communication. Toll-free telephone support is complicated when dealing with class members in different countries: a toll-free number established for the US cannot receive calls from most foreign nations, necessitating multiple numbers to cover all affected countries (each possibly with different instructions, such as dialing codes or geographic limitations). There are certain exceptions to this rule, however, such as 'freephone' numbers that will work across numerous European and other countries.

Once callers dial the administrator's office, Interactive Voice Response (IVR) – that is, pre-recorded messaging set up in a series of menus – allows for cost-effective administration in any language. Because many callers' questions or needs are satisfied through this automated messaging, the need for live operators in many languages is greatly reduced or eliminated. Voicemail can be utilized in those less-commonly requested languages to allow fluent operators to make callbacks rather than sit available for extended periods of time awaiting calls.

Claims processing

The administrator also facilitates the processing of claims. Settlement structures and funds vary greatly, so this process can be as simple as logging receipt of a claim or as complex as reviewing claim information such as receipts, proof of ownership documents, or financial transaction records. Similarly, benefits may be pre-determined awards (i.e., $5 per claimant) or require complex calculations based on pre-existing and/or class member-provided documentation.

Once the settlement has received final approval and the calculation of awards is completed, an administrator disseminates the settlement benefits to eligible class members. Most often, benefits are remunerated in the form of checks, but can take the forms of coupons, vouchers, or even products, depending on the settlement. The distribution phase of administration includes both the printing and mailing of checks and follow-up processing including handling of undelivered checks, re-mailing of checks to

---

44 *Id.*

better addresses, reissuing checks when necessary, and distribution account management. Typically, this process lasts 180 days, at which point any remaining, unused or unclaimed funds are handled in accordance with the settlement agreement or the parties' joint instruction.

Conclusion

Notice 'provides the structural assurance of fairness that permits representative parties to bind absent class members.'[45] The 'assurance of fairness' can only be achieved if the class is adequately reached with a notice that is easy to understand and act upon. The ability to act upon the notice requires proper administration of the class action. Administrators have the important task of ensuring that the voice of class members is heard by answering class member inquiries and processing claims, objections, and opt-outs.

The ongoing international dialogue regarding how to move forward with aggregate litigation has already played out in the US. Those experiences have had an impact on other countries' development of aggregate litigation laws and procedures, which can be seen most prominently in Canada.[46] Many other countries are on the brink of where the US was back in 1965, the year before the opt-in procedure was replaced with the current opt-out procedure. The structural dynamics of US class action law, particularly as they apply to notice and due process, are quite sound and worthy of consideration. Developing mechanisms to ensure proper notification of class members will allow countries to harness the legal virtues of class actions and contain many of its vices.

In the US, a specialized service industry came into existence in order to effectively implement the class action rule. It required the generation of expert services that could identify and locate class members, give them fair notice, and administer their claims. It is likely that other jurisdictions contemplating class action reform would have to generate similar institutions to help service this process.

---

45 Amchem Prods., Inc. v. Windsor, 521 US 591, 627 (1997).

46 The Supreme Court in Canada, in Canada Post Corp. v. Lepine, SCC 16 (S.C. 2009) 'emphasized the vital importance of clear notices and adequate mode of publication' as being an important requirement in recognizing a judgment within Canada.

PART III

EUROPE

15 Overview of Europe

Bojana Vrcek[1]

Introduction

Private antitrust litigation in Europe is undergoing an important evolution toward the provision of actions for damages, but there is significant variation in practice among the nations, even where laws already exist. Almost none of the European jurisdictions have mechanisms in place to make damages actions effective. None of the EU Member States has active private enforcement for collective redress. Rules regarding access to evidence, pre-trial discovery, and statutes of limitations are mixed, but overall are not very helpful for private antitrust claimants. The concrete success on the EU level has been achieved due to steady efforts made by the European Commission, which recognized that competition policy is more than imposing fines and breaking cartels.[2] Fines do not deliver compensation for the harm suffered by victims, and therefore effective private remedies are needed for redress to be awarded by the national courts.

The European Commission supported an external study[3] which analyzed whether and which national legal orders provide for private damages actions. The study found that between May 1, 2004, and the end of 2007, 96 damages actions were filed in the EU Member States. Those were concentrated in only ten Member States. Sixty-one of those cases related to vertical restrictions, and none of the 96 resulted in damages being awarded. On the other hand, between January, 1990, and November, 2008, there were 516 'formal official investigations' of suspected international cartels, with the most affected sales occurring in the European Union.[4] Presumably, cartels are creating huge overcharges in Europe, creating victims who have no means of recompense. According to the impact assessment study accompanying the *White Paper on Damages Actions for breach of the EC antitrust rules* (White Paper),[5] the lack of effective instruments for obtaining compensation may well cost European consumers and businesses more than 20 billion Euros per year.

The European Commission has been prepared to launch the legislative proposal which would introduce an EU-wide system of damages actions. However, the Commission's initiatives are facing strong opposition from European industry, which is claiming that

---

1 Ph.D., Attorney at Law, Research Fellow, American Antitrust Institute, bojana_vrcek@yahoo.de.

2 Neelie Kroes, Speech/09/486, Consumer welfare: more than a slogan, Opening address at conference: 'Competition and Consumers in the 21st Century'.

3 CEPS, EUR and LUISS, Making antitrust damages actions more effective in the EU: welfare impact and potential scenarios, Final report Brussels, Rome and Rotterdam, 21 December 2007, p. 39.

4 See John M. Connor, *Cartels & Antitrust Portrayed: Private International Cartels from 1990 to 2008,* AAI Working Paper#09-06, pp. 4 and 8.

5 European Commission White Paper on Damages Actions for Breach of EC Antitrust Rules, COM(2008)165 final, 2 April 2008.

the legislative act would constitute a radical shift from the current legal traditions and bring new uncontrollable risks for them to face. Therefore the initiation of the EU legislative process has been temporarily stopped while a political consensus is under development.

EC competition rules and importance of ECJ rulings

Nothing in the EC Treaty specifies that damages should be available to those who suffer as a result of competition law infringements. Articles 81 and 82 of the EC Treaty[6] are directly applicable and create rights for individuals that national courts must protect. Moreover, these Treaty provisions have supremacy over national legislation. However, the EC Treaty itself is silent on the question of remedial rights. This gap was plugged by the case law of the European Court of Justice (ECJ) in the 2001 case of *Courage v. Crehan*,[7] holding that competition damages should be available for breaches of EC competition rules.[8] The ECJ held that the full effectiveness of Article 81 EC and, in particular, the practical effect of the prohibition laid down in Article 81 (1) EC would be put at risk if it were not open to any individual to claim damages for losses caused to him by a contract or by conduct liable to restrict or distort competition. In 2006, the ECJ repeated almost verbatim paragraphs 26 and 27 in its judgment *Vincenzo Manfredi v Lloyd Adriatico Assicurazioni*[9] that 'any individual can claim compensation for the harm suffered where there is a causal relationship between that harm and an agreement or practice prohibited under Article 81 EC'.

The fact is that EC competition rules provide rights to individuals but the remedies must be provided by and under national law. Articles 81 and 82 of the EC Treaty contain the basic competition rules applicable in the European Union. Article 81 (1) EC prohibits agreements between undertakings which have as their object or effect the prevention, restriction, or distortion of competition within the European Union, and Article 82 EC prohibits the abuse by one or more undertakings of a dominant position within the common market. Where the agreements or abusive practices at issue are capable of affecting trade between the Member States, Articles 81 and 82 EC are enforceable by the national courts of the Member States. Apart from the establishment of an infringement of Articles 81 and 82 EC, everything else is presently regulated by 27 different national laws. A single major legislative initiative undertaken at the EU level was needed to foster debate on how to make private enforcement of EC competition rules happen. Since the decentralization of the application of Article 81 EC and the publication of

---

[6] On 1 December 2009, the Treaty of Lisbon came into effect, amending the Treaty Establishing the European Community (EC Treaty) that is now called the Treaty on the Functioning of the European Union (TFEU). Therefore, all references to Articles 81 and 82 of the EC Treaty now reference Articles 101 and 102 TFEU.

[7] *Courage Ltd v Bernard Crehan and Bernard Crehan v Courage Ltd and Others*, case C–453/99, [2001] ECR I–6297.

[8] The principle was established in the *Frankovich* case (*Francovich and Bonifaci v. Italy* (joined cases C–6 and 9/90) ECR I–5357, ¶42) guaranteeing that damages for loss resulting from a breach of EC law shall be awarded pursuant to national law. This starting-point concerned the claim of loss suffered as a result of inadequate implementation of directives in national law. See in detail Assimakis P Komninos, *EC Private Antitrust Enforcement*, Hart Publishing, 2008, pp. 165–167.

[9] Joined Cases C–295–298/04, [2006] ECR I–6619.

the Commission's Green Paper, the debate on private enforcement has obtained a new quality, both in depth and intensity.

The debate was foreshadowed in 2003 by the implementation of Regulation 1/2003,[10] one of the main objectives of which was to facilitate private enforcement of EC competition rules.[11] Recital 7 of the Regulation explicitly acknowledges the importance of a private right of action:

> National courts have an essential part to play in applying the Community competition rules. When deciding disputes between private individuals, they protect the subjective right of infringements. The role of national courts here complements that of the competition authorities of the member states. They therefore are allowed to apply Article 81 and 82 of the Treaty in full.

However, when all the hurdles, costs and risks of going to court to claim damages are considered, there is today little opportunity to gain relief, apart from whatever benefits a public competition authority in its discretion can bestow. Some of the main obstacles to private enforcement are lack of clarity in the substantive law, uncertainty as to how to prove damage and the limited amount of damages likely to be awarded, the cost of proceedings, delays in the judicial process, and a general unfamiliarity of Member States' courts and practitioners with competition cases.

Traditionally, private antitrust actions for damages have played a very limited role in the enforcement of the EC competition rules. The EC competition law has been regarded to be of a public law nature, partly as a result of administrative enforcement systems in which competition law rules are embedded[12,] and partly because of implications of competition laws which European countries thought would be best reserved for governmental authorities. The reason that breaches of antitrust law are still seldom pursued privately in Europe is the failure to recognize antitrust law as the basis of private law and the market economy. The lack of an effective collective redress mechanism in many Member States is a major obstacle in this respect.

The EC competition rules have been primarily enforced by the EU bodies, notably by the European Commission and European Courts. In recent years the European Commission has stepped up its fight against price-fixing cartels, and has imposed very substantial fines for cartel violations. The success of the fight against cartels has been boosted by the EC Leniency Program. As awareness of the ubiquity of cartels

---

[10] Council Regulation 1/2003 on the Implementation of the Rules on Competition Laid Down in Articles 81 and 82 of the Treaty, OJ L 1, 4.1.2003 p. 1–25.

[11] See speeches of EU Commissioners for Competition Mario Monti, Effective Private Enforcement of EC Antitrust Law, Speech 01/258 held at the 6th EU Competition Law and Policy Workshop, Florence, 1–2 June 2001. M. Monti, Private Litigation as a key Complement to Public Enforcement of Competition Rules and the First Conclusions of the Implementation of the new Merger Regulation, Speech 04/403 held at the IBA 8th Annual Competition Conference, Fiesole, Italy, 17 September 2004; Neelie Kroes, SPEECH/05/613, Neelie Kroes, Damages Actions for Breaches of EU Competition Rules: Realities and Potentials, Opening speech at the conference 'La réparation du préjudice causé par une pratique anti-concurentielle en France et à l'étranger: bilan et perspectives, Cour de Cassation, Paris, 17 October 2005.

[12] See Clifford A. Jones, Private Antitrust in the Global Market, An Essay on 'Swimming without getting wet', in: Mario Monti et al., *Festschrift für Carl Baudenbacher*, Nomos, 2007, 443, p. 448.

and their impact on consumers and businesses has grown, attention has increasingly focused on the desirability of national regimes facilitating the award of compensation to victims of anticompetitive conduct. The big question is no longer whether, but how and when.

Green and White Papers on damages actions

Following the ECJ's rulings the European Commission undertook actions that should make the remedial right become a reality across the EU. The European Commission recognizes that its public enforcement agenda cannot be achieved by the competition authorities alone, and is therefore actively encouraging the use of private competition law remedies before the national courts. The European Commission chose to take on a very difficult set of issues in its *Green Paper on Damages actions for breach of the EC antitrust rules* (Green Paper),[13] highlighting and discussing a few of the most essential elements of damages action, which are further discussed in the related *Commission Staff Working Paper*.[14] The Commission presented four policy options for the discussion relating to the passing-on defense and indirect purchaser standing.

With the publication in 2008 of the White Paper, the European Commission suggested a number of legal and procedural innovations to encourage greater private enforcement. The White Paper is accompanied by a Commission Staff Working Paper on Damages actions for breach of the EC antitrust rules[15] and Impact Assessment Report.[16] The model the White Paper is suggesting is a European model that should reflect legal traditions of the Member States and not rely on the US system. The proposals of the White Paper, reflecting public comments in response to the Green Paper, were more conservative than some of the recommendations in the Commission's earlier Green Paper. According to the White Paper victims have the right to full compensation, private enforcement should be a complement to, and not a substitute for, a vigorous public enforcement, and private enforcement must reflect European norms and values as opposed to those of other jurisdictions. In that sense, the White Paper proposes no opt-out class actions system, no discovery system, and no treble damages. The Commission is clearly wary of the perils of over-enforcement.

European Parliament initiatives

In March 2009, the European Parliament adopted a resolution[17] in support of the White Paper on damages actions. Parliamentary committee debates on the White Paper

---

13 European Commission (COM(2005)672, SEC(2205)1732), Green paper – Damages actions for breach of the EC antitrust rules (19 December 2005).

14 European Commission (COM(2005)672), Commission Staff Working Paper – Annex to the Green paper – Damages actions for breach of the EC antitrust rules (19 December 2005).

15 Commission Staff Working Paper SEC(2008)404, 2 April 2008.

16 Impact Assessment Report SEC(2008)405, 2 April 2008 which draws on the findings of an external impact study undertaken by the Centre for European Policies Studies, in association with Erasmus University Rotterdam and Libera Università Internazionale degli Studi Sociali Guido Carli, Making antitrust damages actions more effective in the EU: welfare impact and potential scenarios, as of 21 December 2007.

17 European Parliament resolution of 26 March 2009 on the White Paper on damages actions for breach of the EC antitrust rules, available at: www.europarl.europa.eu.

resulted in the proposal of a report by the ECON Committee. The ECON Committee recognizes that an integrated or horizontal approach to collective redress: (i) does not necessarily require adoption of a single instrument, and (ii) must not delay or avoid the development of proposals and measures identified as necessary for the full enforcement of EU competition law. Among the most-discussed issues in the Parliament was the relationship between the collective redress mechanisms suggested in the competition White Paper and the options presented recently in a document known as the Green Paper on Consumer Collective Redress. A major difference between the two initiatives is that the consumer Green Paper only covers redress for consumers, whereas the redress mechanisms suggested in the competition White Paper are designed to benefit both consumers and businesses. Whereas the White Paper focuses strictly on competition law infringements and seeks to address the problems faced by the victims of these infringements, the consumer Green Paper deals with compensation for a very broad range of issues such as unsafe products, misleading advertising and other consumer related matters.

The Commission proposal for an EC directive

Although the draft legislation had not been published as of this writing, the European Commission has announced that it is preparing a proposal for a Council directive. The legislative proposal was finalized during the term of Commissioner Neelie Kroes and is ready to be adopted by the next administration. The President of the European Commission, José Manuel Barroso, has declared that he is committed to more effective enforcement of competition law and that he puts EU consumers firmly at the centre of EU projects.[18] Following those statements, it is generally expected that a legislative package will be enacted in the near future. The exact legal basis for the proposal has yet to be determined. The Commission recommendations in a directive are expected to leave a great deal of discretion to national judges for implementation. While the flexibility provided by this discretion may be desirable for achieving an appropriate balance between the need for evidence and the danger of overbroad discovery obligations, such flexibility may be achieved only if predictability and certainty are sacrificed. Thus, depending on how national judges will interpret the Commission's recommendations, European litigants may notice little change or may experience something approaching American-style pre-trial discovery.

A yet-unfinished text of the proposal for a Council directive on private enforcement has made its way into the public domain. It appears to have been formulated on the grounds of the White and Green Papers of the European Commission as well as comments the Commission received in a public discussion. The Commission's intent is both to achieve the full effectiveness of Articles 81 and 82 EC, and to supplement public enforcement. Important guidance will be in particular rules on disclosure of relevant evidence, group actions and representative actions, as well as defense of passing-on of overcharges. There is also a *novum* for most of the European civil laws, according to which the Commission

---

[18] José Manuel Barroso, President of the European Commission, Meglena Kuneva, Commissioner for consumer protection, Empowering consumers means a more prosperous Europe, in European press on world consumer rights day, 15 March 2008.

suggests that the infringing undertaking bear the burden of proof and demonstrate that it did not act intentionally or negligently. The Commission opts for full compensation, which means compensation of actual loss and lost profit (*damnum emergens* and *lucrum cessans*). The directive is expected to set out a framework that the Member States must work within, although they will have a certain range of leeway on how to implement the directive's requirements in their compliant statutes.

Looking for solutions to avoid the US 'opt-out' style class actions because of concerns that they could 'lead to excesses', the Commission's White Paper proposes consumer 'opt-in' class actions and 'representative actions'. The representative action would be brought by designated entities such as consumer associations, state bodies or trade associations and they could recover all of the losses for their members. The step further was made in the draft Article 5 (4) Directive Proposal according to which members of the designated entities would be automatically represented. If they do not want to participate, they have to opt out. This solution should be a major step forward for European collective redress.

Conditions of liability and rules of evidence

Legal basis

In most European jurisdictions conditions of liability largely follow the general provisions of tort law provided in national civil codes. Several Member States have included an express statutory basis in competition laws. Germany incorporated a legal basis for action for damages in §33 (3) of the Act against Restraints of Competition with alleviations for plaintiffs compared to general tort law. Another example is Romania where, pursuant to Article 61 of the Competition Law, a party having suffered losses as a result of an anti-competitive act (direct or indirect purchasers) has the right to be indemnified for such losses by the infringing party following a private damages claim. In countries where there is no explicit statutory basis, such as Belgium, general law is applicable, which may include contractual claims for damages and claims based in tort.

Forum

The forum for competition cases varies by country. It is noteworthy that several Member States have assigned responsibility over private antitrust cases to a limited number of specialized courts. In England & Wales, for example, the relevant court is the High Court. The Chancery Division had been created to strengthen the expertise among judges who are dealing with competition cases.[19] The High Court has jurisdiction to hear all claims based on EC and UK competition rules. Moreover, with the entry into force of the Enterprise Act 2002, so-called 'follow-on' damages claims may be brought in the High Court. In addition, the Competition Appeal Tribunal (CAT), a specialized jurisdiction to deal with competition cases, can hear some damages follow-on actions. Stand-alone

[19] The Civil Procedure Rules require competition proceedings to be brought in or transferred to the Chancery Division of the High Court (Law 3/1991, 10 January 1991, Unfair Competition Act 1991).

cases cannot currently be brought before the CAT.[20] In France, Decree n° 2005–1756 of 30 December 2005 has nominated 16 courts to specialize in competition matters, which have been given exclusive authority over private antitrust matters.

Standing

In Europe all market participants, including direct and indirect suppliers and purchasers and competitors, natural and legal persons, have standing to sue, provided that the alleged infringement of Article 81 or 82 EC is likely adversely to affect (or already has affected) the legitimate interests of the plaintiff. Under the doctrine of direct effect in Community law, a plaintiff who can show injury caused by an infringement has a private right of action which is coextensive with the substantive reach of the directly effective competition rules of the EC Treaty. In this regard, under the EC regime, the principal limitation on who can sue for damages will be the plaintiff's evidence of causation. Indeed, the ECJ ruled on standing in *Courage v. Crehan* and found that not only third-party competitors, but 'any individual', including co-contracting parties, have standing to sue. However, many national laws still have restrictive rules on standing for damages actions which are interpreted very narrow by the national courts. Therefore it is important that the new EU legislative framework does not limit standing to only certain classes of antitrust victims.[21]

Permitting indirect purchaser suits is logically necessary for the jurisdictions of Member States. The position of consumers is not clear in many jurisdictions. Although being most often those who are harmed, consumers are facing high hurdles before national courts.[22]

Fault

To establish liability for damages all jurisdictions require proof of an infringement of competition law, damage and a causal link. Many jurisdictions also require fault to be shown. In others there is a presumption of fault, either rebuttable or irrebuttable, once a violation of competition law has been found, or the violation is in itself considered to establish fault.

All jurisdictions provide for tort principles of joint and several liability of infringers for the damages. There have been fears that leniency applicants will be more exposed than their co-defendants to damages actions and that this may jeopardize further success of the EC and national leniency programs. Therefore the Commission is proposing

[20] Very few such cases (e.g., *Arkin v. Borchard Lines and others* [2000] EuLR 232 (Comm Ct), *Hendry, Williams and others v. The World Professional Billiards and Snooker Association* [2002] UKCLR 5) and *Attheraces Ltd. v. The British Horse Racing Board* [2006] ECC 12/103, [2005] EWHC 3015 (Ch.)) have reached trial in the High Court.

[21] See Jakob Rüggenberg and Maarten Pieter Schinkel, Consolidating Antitrust Damages in Europe: A Proposal for Standing in Line with Efficient Private Enforcement, World Competition 29 (3): 395–420, 2006, p. 398.

[22] In Italy, one of the first important cases was the *Motor Insurance* case where the court denied standing to consumers claiming damages against insurance companies engaged in a cartel which exchanged information on car accident insurance. The Corte di Cassazione confirmed the decision that consumers lack standing in competition cases and that competition law aims to protect competitors and not consumers.

that protection against disclosure should apply to all statements submitted by leniency applicants, regardless of whether or not the application is accepted. Furthermore, the Commission is considering a proposal for limitation of civil liability for successful leniency applicants. Almost none of the Member States has statutory provisions on the interaction between leniency programs and damages actions.[23] Contribution, which is not allowed in US antitrust cases, is common in Europe, permitting defendants to recover proportionately from fellow-defendants, and thereby mitigating the leverage that claimants may have over particular defendants within the joint and several liability framework.

Pass-on defense and indirect purchasers

There is no consistent regulation of passing-on in the different Member States.[24] However, the passing-on defense has been recognized widely in national courts. While exclusion of indirect purchasers is not permissible due to the principle of direct effect of EC law from *Courage v. Crehan,* which suggests that 'any individual' may pursue a private action for breach of competition laws, there is no explicit indirect purchaser rule in any of the Member States.

Rules of evidence

Access to evidence

The European Commission suggested in the White Paper that claimants should meet several conditions before obtaining a disclosure order from the court. First, the claimant must establish a threshold of plausibility in the initial factual pleading. Second, the plaintiff must demonstrate that the evidence sought is unavailable through other means. Third, the plaintiff must specify sufficiently precise categories of information, documents or other means of evidence relevant to the claim. At the core of the recommendation is reliance on the 'central function of the court' to control discovery: disclosure measures could only be ordered by judges and would be subject to strict and active judicial control as to their necessity, scope and proportionality. In fact, the proposal may not be altogether different from the system in the United States, depending both in the US and Europe on how judges actually fulfill their role; however in most European countries, there is no doubt that the absence of discovery procedures constitutes today one of the major obstacles to antitrust damages actions.

Actions for damages in antitrust cases normally require the investigation of a much broader set of facts and issues than in ordinary civil litigation cases. All of our country chapters have reported that the powers of the courts to order the production of documents are very limited and not sufficient for providing claimants with access to crucial

---

[23] An exception is the German Leniency Notice (Notice no. 9/2006 of the Bundeskartellamt on the immunity from and reduction of fines in cartel cases – Leniency Programme as of 7 March 2006) which explicitly says that the notice has no effect on the private enforcement of competition law.

[24] It has been argued that there should be no legal barriers for the ECJ to forbid the passing-on defense in antitrust litigations. See Clifford Jones, *Private enforcement of antitrust law in the EU, UK and USA*. Oxford University Press, 1999, pp. 366–369.

evidence. This is particularly problematic with regard to stand-alone cases that do not depend on the findings of fact and law previously made in a case brought by a competition authority.

Very few Member States have mandatory pre-trial disclosure requirements. Pre-trial discovery possibilities are provided in the jurisdictions of England and Wales, Sweden, Ireland and also Cyprus. The Civil Procedure Rules of England and Wales, the most liberal in Europe, provide for the standard disclosure of all documents supporting or adversely affecting the parties' positions, and for the possibility of additional specific disclosure. A party who is 'likely' to be a party to an action may apply for pre-action disclosure against a party who is also 'likely' to be a party to that same action before the claim is issued. The applicant must specify the documents or class of documents to be provided and the documents requested must not be over and above those which the respondent would be required to disclose if the respondent were a party to proceedings. The request for pre-action disclosure may be made by 'would be' defendants as well as claimants.

More typical may be the case of Sweden, where a court may issue an order, subject to a conditional fine, requiring anybody to produce any potentially relevant documentary material in its possession. However, a private party would have difficulty making use of such an order because the requesting party must specify what written document it seeks and what the document is intended to prove; requests will not be allowed to be used for 'fishing expeditions.' Trade secrets are exempted from discovery unless extraordinary reasons justify disclosure, and finally the court may not order the production of a document subject to a legal privilege.

Perhaps more stringently, the procedural laws of Germany, France and Spain do not provide for any pretrial discovery in the common law sense, and the courts of those Member States may order the production only of documents that a party has specifically identified. The extreme case may be Belgium, where discovery as such does not exist. Each party can produce documents it deems necessary. During the trial, the court can order parties and third parties to submit specific evidence if there are serious, specific and concurring suspicions that the party or third person has a document that would contain proof of a relevant fact.[25] The plaintiff will have to convince the court that such specific documents exist, before the court can decide to order its production.

The difficulty for a plaintiff to obtain evidence of an alleged antitrust violation is less pronounced in follow-on actions, where there is a prior decision from the European Commission or a national competition authority (NCA) finding an infringement. There may also arise confidentiality issues as was the case in *Spanish Banks*[26] and *Akzo*[27], where only the European Commission could have full access to a document and see its content, while parties could only know about the existence of the document.[28]

In subsequent civil proceedings for damages before a national court, a claimant can rely on an infringement decision by the Commission as binding proof of the violation. The claimant must still produce proof of causation and the amount of damages, and

---

25 Art. 871, arts 877–882 Judicial Code.

26 AEB (*Spanish Banks*) ECJ July 16, 1992, 1992 ECR I-4785.

27 AKZO National Chemicals, CFI Oct. 30, 2003, T-125/03 R.

28 See Roundtable OECD and European Commission, DAF/COMP(2006)34, p. 55.

most of the relevant evidence should be in the claimant's possession. However, the court may have to stay its proceedings until any appeals from the ruling are resolved by the Community Courts. The issue of confidentiality of materials that may be exchanged between the public enforcement agencies and courts has not yet been resolved in a satisfactory way.

Because of the discovery problems, stand-alone cases have been rare. An example of how difficult it is for such an action to be successful is the Irish case of *Meridian Communications Limited and Cellular 3 Limited v Eircell Limited,*[29] brought in 2000. The action was heard in the High Court for over 94 days before being dismissed. By the time the Supreme Court appeal came to the hearing, the company's assets had been exhausted and the action proceeded no further. The litigation also brought an end to the attempt by Meridian Communications Limited and Cellular 3 Limited to enter the Irish mobile telephony market.[30]

Burden of proof

The question of the burden of proof in national proceedings for the application of Articles 81 and 82 EC is regulated by Article 2 of Regulation 1/2003. Pursuant to this provision, a party alleging the infringement of Article 81 (1) or 82 EC shall bear the burden of proof. However, Article 2 Regulation 1/2003 EC deals only with the burden of proof, whereby levels of proof are decided individually by the national courts.

In that respect, requirements differ among the Member States. German courts have overcome a narrow interpretation of causation.[31] The Landgericht Dortmund awarded €1.6 million damages in a vitamins case to the non-resident plaintiff from Switzerland, and this was the first damages award in the vitamin cartel[32] case. This case is particularly significant because it was brought by a Belgian firm, Cartel Damage Claims (CDC),[33] that had purchased the claims from third parties that had suffered damage,[34] reflecting

---

29 [2002] 1 IR 17, per Justice O'Higgings J., High Court. See James O'Reilly, Observations on Aspects of Commission 'Green Paper on Damages Action for Breach of EC Antitrust Rules' and the Accompanying 'the Commission Staff Working Paper', p. 5, available at: http://ec.europa.eu/comm/competition/antitrust/others/actions_for_damages/143.pdf.

30 See Emil Paulis European Commission Remarks on: What are the problems with EC Antitrust Damage Actions in Europe? Does the private pillar require reinforcement? Speech at the IBA and European Commission Conference on Cartel enforcement and Antitrust damage actions in Europe, Brussels, 9 March 2007.

31 The Landgericht Berlin held in the *Max Boegl v. Hanson* case (*Max Boegl Bauunternehmung v. Hansen Germany*, Judgment of the Berlin Landgericht as of 27 June 2003) that 'purchasers of cement at cartel prices could not claim damages unless they had been individually targeted by a market-sharing cartel'.

32 Judgment of the Landgericht Dortmund as of 1 April 2004, Az. 13 O 55/02 Kart.

33 Cartel Damage Claims (CDC) is a Belgian limited liability company founded in 2002 to be the first company in Europe to understand damages claims based on antitrust law infringements as a self-contained and marketable asset. CDC bundles the interests involved and creates individual incentives for market participants to contribute to private antitrust enforcement on a Europe-wide basis. One of the first activities of the company was to acquire and enforce damages claims against the participants of the German cement cartel. See http://www.carteldamageclaims.com.

34 However Landgerichts Mannheim and Mainz refused to award damages in similar cases. See Frank Röhling & Thomas Lübbig, Several German courts of first instance decide on

experimental efforts to find ways to finance group actions within a culture that still seems to view class actions and contingency fees in a negative light.[35]

In most notable cases in Spain such as *Antenna 3 v. La Liga National De Fútbol Profesional* and *Euskaltel* and *Tenaria v. Sogeceable* and *Audiovisual Sport*, both of which were stand-alone actions, the damages claim has been rejected. The Spanish courts found that the caual link between the damage suffered and the infringment had not been proven and the damage suffered had not be properly quantified.

In England and Wales, the burden of proof falls on the party seeking to make out its case. For infringement actions, the burden of proof will rest with the claimant but section 58A of the Competition Act 1998 provides that OFT infringement decisions are binding on the CAT as proof of the infringement. English courts require a high standard of proof suggesting that a high degree of probability should be required in Article 81 EC cases.[36]

Binding effect of final infringement decisions

The Commission is proposing that a final decision on Article 81 or 82 EC taken by a NCA in the European Competition Network (ECN)[37] should be accepted in every Member State as irrefutable proof of the infringement in subsequent damages cases. Under these circumstances the defendant will have the opportunity of persuading the courts of its position. This solution would reduce legal certainty and have a strong encouraging effect for claimants considering a private action.

Currently only German law contains an explicit rule on binding effect. Under German law, for follow-on actions, final decisions of the German Federal Cartel Office, of the European Commission and of competition authorities (or the court acting as such) of another Member State of the European Union finding an infringement of Article 81 or 82 EC or the German Competition Act are binding on the court in respect of finding an infringement.[38] Binding force applies only with respect to the infringement and does not concern causality and damages. The general principle is that the plaintiff has the burden of proof of all facts upon which the claim is based. Some jurisdictions permit enforcement officials to participate in the damages case before the court. In Germany, for example, members of staff of the Bundeskartellamt are allowed to take an active part in the court proceedings. On the other hand in Turkey, although providing explicit statutory provision for damages actions, plaintiffs still face difficulties, as the Supreme

damages claims brought by the customers of the vitamins cartel (Vitaminpreise), 1 April 2004, e-Competitions, N°329.

[35] Following the ECJ's interpretation of the EC competition rules, the courts of England and Wales have not contested either the right to be awarded damages or other remedies such as injunctive relief arising from infringements of competition laws.

[36] See *Shearson Lehman Hutton Inc v Maclaine Watson & Co Ltd* [1989] 3 CMLR 429 (QB). In detail see A. P. Komninos, *EC Private Antitrust Enforcement*, Hart Publishing, p. 226.

[37] The European Competition Network (ECN) has been established as a forum for discussion and cooperation of European competition authorities in cases where Articles 81 and 82 EC are applied. The ECN provides means to ensure their effective and consistent application. Through the ECN, the competition authorities inform each other of proposed decisions and take on board comments from the other competition authorities. In this way, the ECN allows the competition authorities to pool their experience and identify best practices.

[38] Section 33(4) The Act against Restrains of Competition (GWB).

Court requires a final infringement decision of the Turkish Competition Authority (TCA).[39]

Damages

The White Paper recommends that compensation for a competition injury be limited to single damages, but that there be recovery of interest. The Commission chose to leave the question of the damages calculation to Member States. The White Paper recommends the recovery of interest from the date of infringement which, depending on interest rates, whether interest is compounded, and the length of the potential process, could result in large awards that may equal or exceed double damages. In order to provide advice to national courts and parties involved in antitrust damages actions, the Commission is preparing non-binding guidance for the quantification of harm in antitrust damages actions. Such guidance paper will be based on an external study on 'Quantifying antitrust damages' prepared by economists and a multijurisdictional team of lawyers for the European Commission.[40] The guidance will contain information on economic models and methods of calculation of harm caused by anticompetitive practices. It is expected to be a useful learning tool for the courts which is even not available to the US courts.

The nature of damages in all countries is compensatory and no exemplary or punitive damages are available. All jurisdictions provide for monetary compensation in the form of redress. Damages for breach of competition rules have been awarded in several Member States, notably in England and Wales, Germany, Italy, France, Spain, Netherlands, Sweden. In Germany compensatory and restitutionary damages including lost profits are available.

The principles of tort law ensure that injured parties have the right to be compensated for damage on the condition that they can prove the existence of the damage, its quantification, and the causal link with the fault of the defendant. In addition, the Commission endorses a rebuttable presumption that an illegal overcharge has been passed on in its entirety. Indirect purchasers will benefit from this proposal and this solution may encourage consumer litigation. The national courts must be trusted to deal with all issues of the passing-on defence.

---

[39] The first case seeking damages claims arising from an abuse of a dominant position was decided in 1999. On appeal, the Supreme Court reversed the judgment and instructed the lower court to seek whether there was a decision of the Turkish Competition Authority establishing the infringement or whether there was an application of the plaintiff pursuing that decision. The TCA rejected the application and the plaintiff lost his claim. The important decision was decided by the Supreme Court in 2002. The trial court granted double damages to the car dealer whose contract was terminated by the manufacturer. On appeal, the Supreme Court again reversed the judgment, reasoning that there was not a TCA decision establishing the infringement. See in detail Bolatoglu, infra. See also UNCTAD, The effects of anti-competitive business practices on developing countries and their development prospects, Hassan Qaqaya Q and George Lipimile (Eds), *Estimation of antitrust damages and its effects on antitrust policy in developing countries: A case study of a Turkish Yeast Cartel*, 2008, p. 550.

[40] 'Quantifying antitrust damages', Towards non-binding guidance for courts, Study prepared for the European Commission, Oxera and a multijurisdictional team of lawyers led by Dr. Assimakis Komninos, available at http://ec.europa.eu/competition/antitrust/actionsdamages/quantification_study.pdf.

Group litigation

Europe-wide proposal

The European Commission is aware that since many direct purchasers pass on some element of their damages to the level in the supply chain below them, consumers are almost always the ultimate victims of anti-competitive behaviour. As a general rule, consumers individually suffer only small injuries that by themselves cannot justify the expenses of an antitrust suit. Therefore an appropriate collective redress mechanism is essential to make compensation for antitrust damage possible for consumers.[41]

The White Paper suggests a combination of two complementary mechanisms of collective redress (i) opt-in collective actions, in which injured parties expressly decide to combine their individual damages claims into one single action, and (ii) representative actions, which can be brought only by qualified entities certified by the Member States on behalf of defined groups of injured parties. The Commission does not address the issue of multi-jurisdiction litigation and it is unclear how the courts will handle this issue. It will likely be challenging to coordinate 'representative' and 'opt-in' actions occurring more or less simultaneously in multiple countries.

Collective actions can be brought jointly by any injured parties and are strictly based on the opt-in mechanism. Representative actions can only be brought by entities which fulfill eligibility conditions set and controlled by the Member States and which represent legitimate interests of defined groups of injured parties. These can be, for example, consumer organizations, trade associations or public bodies such as an ombudsman. The White Paper says that the notion of 'qualified entities' should be interpreted widely. All consumer and trade associations should be considered as eligible for the function of 'qualified entity.'[42] The Commission is actively seeking for consumers to be involved in competition policy. The European Commission's Directorate General for Consumer Policy adopted in March 2007 a new Consumer Policy Strategy for 2007–2013, setting out objectives and priorities for the future. The strategy stressed:

> If consumers are to have sufficient confidence in shopping outside their own Member State and take advantage of the internal market, they need assurance that if things go wrong they have effective mechanisms to seek redress. Consumer disputes require tailored mechanisms that do not impose costs and delays disproportionate to the value at stake.[43]

---

[41] According to the Cross Border Injunctions Directive 98/27/EC (Directive 98//27/EC, 1998 OJ L166 51) consumer associations or public entities ('qualified organizations') can bring injunctive actions to stop violations of national laws implementing an array of consumer protection provisions. The Cross Border Injunctions Directive opens the door to representative actions as it provides for consumer associations to enjoin violations regarding misleading advertising, consumer credit practices, television broadcasting, package holidays, advertising of medicines and unfair terms in consumer contracts. However, organizations cannot seek damages under the Injunctions Directive.

[42] Commission Staff working paper accompanying White Paper (SEC(2008)404, 2 April 2008), para. 51.

[43] Brussels, 13 March 2007, COM(2007)99 final 'Communication from the Commission to the Council, The European Parliament and the European Economic and Social Committee', EU Consumer Policy strategy 2007–2013, Empowering consumers, enhancing their welfare, effectively protecting them.

Although the importance of introducing effective private antitrust remedies has been widely recognized within the European Commission,[44] it was reported in late March, 2010, that due to business opposition the EU directive has been postponed in order to permit extended consultations with stakeholders.[45] We cannot predict how much this will delay the process or alter the outcome.

National developments

Approximately half of the Member States provide for the possibility of aggregating claims. Most of the European national provisions can be classified as representative actions. In the last few years, several Member States have introduced class action laws. None of these laws or proposed laws closely resembles class actions as experienced in the US system, in that they generally work on the opt-in principle and lack adequate financial incentives for bringing a class action. There are two countries in Europe that have introduced an opt-out model class action mechanism, namely Portugal and Denmark. In Denmark there is a dual system which consists of both opt-in and opt-out representative actions. Opt-in repreesntation is available to everybody and the action can be brought either by an individual or by a consumer organization. On the other side, opt-out representation is available only to a consumer ombudsman who acts as a public authority. The opt-out model has reputedly proved to be a strong and effective instrument in Denmark so far.[46]

Although representative action by consumers' organizations is authorized in several countries, the experience to date has generally been dismal, reflecting the many obstacles that must be overcome. Most commonly, legislation gives consumers' associations standing to represent consumers' interests, as in the Netherlands and France, but not much has been achieved. In England and Wales the representative party action has long been recognized, and the Civil Procedure Rules (CPR) provide for group litigation orders. Since 'group actions' were introduced in 2000 there were 60 such cases filed in seven years.[47] The absence of awards appears to be the consequence of a thriving practice of settlement rather than the failure of claims.

Of particular interest is the experience of the UK Consumers' Association in *Consumers Association v. JJB Sports PLC*,[48] involving a claim for damages on behalf of consumers who had bought football replica shirts overpriced because of price-fixing. The

---

44 See speeches of John Dalli, European Commissioner for Health and Consumer Policy, meeting of the American Chamber of Commerce, Brussels, 23 March 2010; speech of Alexander Italianer, Director-General, DG Competition, European Commission at the International Forum Competition Law of the Studienvereinigung Kartellrecht, Challenges for European Competition Policy, 9 March 2010.

45 See Financial Times, EU competition proposals delayed, by Nikki Tait, 29 March 2010.

46 Henrik Øe, Danish Consumer Ombudsman, Damages actions for breach of competition rules, Competition and Consumers in the 21th Century, available at http://ec.europa.eu/competition/consumers/events/2009/Henrik_OE.pdf.

47 Michael Hausfeld and Andrea L. Hertzfeld, A Victim's Culture, European Business Law Review, (2007) 18 EBLR 1209–1475, p. 1229.

48 Notice of a claim for damages under s. 47B of the Competition Act 1998, Case No: 1078/7/9/07.

case resulted in a settlement approved by the CAT where JJB Sports agreed to directly compensate any consumer who was party to the action with £20 and £10 to those who did not opt in but could prove purchase of a shirt sold at the overcharged prices. This first consumer representative claim was brought under section 47B of the Competition Act 1998 on the opt-in basis, and although it resulted in redress, it shows that the procedural challenges of the opt-in system, such as the limitation on bringing the claim only on behalf of named consumers and not on behalf of businesses or consumers at large, combined with disproportionate costs and time, are too high to encourage representative actions.

Some Member States such as Germany, Austria and Netherlands provide for the possibility of assigning claims. This has become common for general damages claims of consumers represented by a consumers' organization in Austria.[49] German law itself does not provide for a class action device. There are other instruments of collective litigation, most notably complaints by interest groups or associations (*Verbandsklagen*) which have a long history in Germany whereby the right of action will be granted to associations promoting an industrial interest.[50] The ruling of the Supreme Court in a cement case allows actions by private plaintiffs that others can join by affirmative consent. The Supreme Court (Bundesgerichtshof, BGH) has paved the way for collective actions in its ruling of 7 April 2009 in *Cartel Damage Claims v. Dyckerhoff AG*. Rejecting a motion to dismiss the claims, the BGH confirmed that actions based on 'bundled' damages claims assigned to a single plaintiff are permissible under German law, thus allowing actions similar to opt-in class actions.[51] On the same basis, CDC launched another damages suit against six makers of hydrogen peroxide in a Dortmund court in March 2009, seeking damages of EUR 430 million incurred by the pulp and paper companies as a result of cartel activity. The six defendants, except the successful leniency applicant, were previously fined by the European Commission.

A French case shows the difficulties that consumers may encounter when claiming damages in the absence of a true representative action. The largest French consumers' organization. L'UFC-Que Choisir, filed a claim against three French mobile telecommunications operators that had been fined by the Competition Council for price conspiracy in the period from 2000 to 2002.[52] Out of the several million telephone customers, 200,000 actively expressed their intention to launch an action by registering on the consumers' association's website, but only approximately 12,000 claims could actually be brought before the Paris Commercial Court (Tribunal de Commerce de Paris) in October 2006. The claim was rejected on the grounds that the association had made illegal, i.e. legally unethical, solicitations to collect mandates from victims in order to bring this representative action What, we might ask, would be the motivation of a consumers' association to spend its time and money on behalf of just a small number of members who opt in, without any advertising to alert them of the opportunity?

---

49 See Ashurst Study, p. 46.
50 Section 13 of the Unfair Competition Act.
51 Decision of 7 April 2009 – KZR 42/08.
52 See http://www.cartelmobile.org.

Costs of litigation

All EU jurisdictions hold that all costs of litigation can be recovered and that the losing party pays both parties' costs. This rule is widely regarded as a significant obstacle to private antitrust actions. The Commission encouraged Member States to reflect on their costs regimes so as to facilitate meritorious antitrust litigation. It is unclear whether the recommendation will result in a shift away from the 'loser pays' rule. Several countries such as Italy, UK, Sweden, Hungary, Finland, Poland and Slovenia require that the cost recovery be reasonable.[53] Generally, class members can be held responsible for the costs of a lost case.[54] As the UK Government recognizes,[55] adversarial civil litigation is inherently risky and can be very costly. A good illustration is a UK case involving an unsuccessful predatory pricing action against a shipping conference where in the end the plaintiff had to pay several millions of pounds in costs.

In competition cases in the US, the availability of contingency fees facilitates the prosecution of actions for damages. Most of the EU countries do not allow contingency fees, but several provide for the possibility of enhancement of attorneys' fees above the basic amount charged.[56] For example, English law allows conditional fee arrangements, in which a successful attorney can earn a basic fee and an agreed-upon 'success fee' uplift of up to 100 per cent of the basic fee. In both Germany and Spain, contingency fees were traditionally not permissible, but this situation appears to be changing. A bill revising the prohibition on contingent fee agreements has been introduced in the German Parliament as a result of a decision by the country's Constitutional Court, and the Spanish Supreme Court held last December that the ban on contingency fees was anticompetitive. Finally, in France contingency fees which represent a supplement to an attorney's general fee are permitted.

A number of countries are now exploring whether contingency fees should be permitted in the context of collective litigation. In the UK, legal aid, which funded group actions in the 1990s, has been almost completely replaced by conditional fee agreements (CFAs) and after-the-event insurance policies. Lawyers who are representing claims grouped under the Group Litigation Order (GLO) do not share in the proceeds of a claim. Under the conditional fee arrangement, the lawyers are entitled to a 'success fee,' which is limited to a maximum of double their normal fees. In its 2005 report, the Civil Justice Council urged that some type of contingency fee was necessary to fund multi-claimant litigation.[57]

Settlements

There have been only limited data available on settlements. It is known, however, that several settlements have been concluded after damages claims were filed in UK, Dutch or German courts. In Germany, a settlement has been reached in the damages claim filed against members of the Hydrogen Peroxide cartel before German courts. The Belgian company CDC was claiming the largest amount ever in cartel damages claims before the

---

53 See Ashurst Study, p. 94.

54 See Glader and Alstergren, infra.

55 Ministry of Justice, The Government's Response to the Civil justice Council's Report: 'Improving Access to justice through Collective Actions', July 2009, point 10.

56 See Ashurst Study, p. 116.

57 Civil Justice Council, Annual Report 2005, p. 26.

German courts, amounting to EUR 643 million, from Evonik Degussa, Solvay, Kermira, Arekma, Akzo and FMC. The settlement was reached only with a whistle-blower Evonik Degussa.

In a worldwide settlement reached between passengers and British Airways and Virgin Atlantic and approved under US law before the US courts, the affected passengers have until 2012 to claim refunds for their loss from a fuel surcharge price fixing agreement.[58] In that case over 211,000 claims have been processed, 170,000 of which originated with UK consumers and businesses. The case is apparently a precedent for the effective participation of consumers in the private enforcement of competition law, and a clear indication that European consumers can be made aware of their losses caused by antitrust violations. Another settlement was reached following governmental investigations by the EC, the Office of Fair Trading in the UK, and the US DOJ of a price-fixing conspiracy involving the leading manufacturers of marine hose. Based on the global settlement reached with Parker ITR,[59] any of Parker ITR's customers is able to claim compensation in respect of their losses arising from the cartel, irrespective of where they reside or where the marine hose was bought. The settlement also provides for Parker ITR's co-operation in bringing claims against the other cartelists.[60] Experience in the US suggests that as private enforcement becomes more prevalent in Europe, nations will have to find ways to facilitate the settlement of claims both within the national context and within a more global context, recognizing that many cartels operate in a multitude of states.

Limitation periods

Statutory provisions regarding limitation periods vary among the Member States. Most of the Member States provide for a combination of subjective and objective statutes of limitation where the expiry of the objective period precludes the plaintiff from filing a claim. For example, in Germany, the limitation period is three years from knowledge of infringement and (without knowledge) ten years from the arising of damage or 30 years from infringement. The limitation period stops running when the competition authority institutes proceedings for infringement of competition law.

Some countries use subjective periods which start running on the day the potential plaintiff discovered or should have discovered the damage. A few Member States have objective limitation periods which begin to run on the day of infringement notwithstanding the plaintiff's awareness of infringement. The Commission is proposing a new limitation period of at least two years which should start once the infringement decision on which a follow-on claimant relies has become final.

Forum shopping and 'torpedoes'

Complex multi-jurisdictional litigation will inevitably raise issues of forum shopping in Europe. Council Regulation (EC) 44/2001[61] (Brussels Convention) is the most

---

58 The webpage http://www.airpassengerrefund.co.uk was set up for victims to opt in.

59 See http://www.marinehoseclaims.com.

60 See more on global settlements Lawrence T. Sorkin, Private Remedies: Where are the global antitrust settlements?, infra.

61 Council Regulation (EC) No 44/2001 of 22 December 2000 on jurisdiction and the recognition and enforcement of judgments in civil and commercial matters, 2001 OJ L 12/1.

important legislation for those involved in European cross-border litigation. The Brussels Convention transformed and harmonized jurisdictional rules in Europe and paved the way for ready enforcement of judgments.[62] However, procedural heterogeneity and differences between the substantive national rules can create inconsistencies that will foster forum shopping among the Member States. The potential is greatest in cases where anti-competitive effects are Community-wide or within at least a few Member States. Parallel or consecutive proceedings have proved to be an obstacle to efficient procedures. Under Article 28 of Regulation 44/2001 where related actions are pending in the courts of different Member States, national courts other than the one first seised may stay proceedings or decline jurisdiction. The key shortcoming which arises due to Regulation 44/2001 is the potential delay caused by 'torpedoes', i.e., the launching of litigation by defendants in one jurisdiction with the object or effect of causing a mandatory stay of anticipated litigation in one or more other jurisdictions.

To date, the English courts have often been preferred by plaintiffs for the following reasons: the disclosure rules in England allow greater discovery than continental laws and damages awards by English courts are thought to be higher than those granted by continental courts. Furthermore, the UK courts have proven appealing to European claimants because they have decided that they are able to accept damages claims based on breaches of competition law outside the UK. The *Provimi*[63] ruling allowed damages claims against Roche and Aventis, two of the parties found by the European Commission to have been members of the Vitamins[64] cartel. The High Court held that as long as it has jurisdiction over one of the claimants in an action, it will accept related claims of an outside company to be brought in the same suit. This ruling makes it possible for claimants to file a claim in the English courts when the defendants are not domiciled in the UK, and where the plaintiff is also a non-UK-based company and has purchased the vitamins outside the UK. With these features, the UK system provides a strong incentive for defendants to settle early for a relatively low amount.

Conclusion

Private rights of action are granted in most of the EU Member States, but jurisdictions vary with regard to how difficult it is to bring private action for damages. The current positions of the EU and national laws show that there is a substantial diversity amongst the European national standards and that, whatever the theoretical rights, competition damages actions are uncommon. Recent legal developments have begun to facilitate the bringing of private antitrust actions in Europe, and it can reasonably be expected that, in the next few years, private enforcement of the Community competition rules will grow. Without effective private enforcement, firms may consider that their conduct either will not be detected or will not result in substantial penalties. Administrative penalties which are currently the main method of enforcing European competition law are a blunt

---

[62] Another international treaty is the Lugano Convention on jurisdiction and the enforcement of judgements in civil and commercial matters of 16 September 1988 which applies to jurisdictional issues involving certain countries such as Switzerland.

[63] *Provimi Ltd. v. Roche Products Ltd. et al.* (2003), QBD, approved judgment at 6.5. 2003, The High Court, 28 April 2003.

[64] Case COMP/E- 1/37.512 – Vitamins of 21 November 2001, 2001 OJ L 6/1.

instrument since those who suffered from an infringement are not compensated. None of the jurisdictions reported a successful stand-alone case. This shows that despite legislative reforms that have been made, the obstacles to bringing a stand-alone action are still too high.

There have not been any antitrust damages cases filed before the Bulgarian, Cypriot, Czech, Estonian, Lithuanian, Slovak, Luxembourg and Maltese courts, but these are not generally states in which public enforcement of competition law has progressed very far. More broadly, the main reason for the low level of private enforcement in Europe appears to be that victims of competition law breaches find it too difficult to enforce their rights and bring their cases to court in a successful manner. In order to encourage private enforcement, further legislative reforms are needed, both on the EU and national levels.

Any EU-wide system of collective redress should at the very least require a formal opt-out mechanism. Indeed, there is every reason to give the instruments to European private market participants which will enable them to act effectively against market power that harms European consumers. Indeed, private entrepreneurs and investors are often more likely to properly assess existing market situations and understand just what steps are best taken to improve consumer welfare.

Although one might believe that an EU directive would achieve significant uniformity among the Member States for effective class or group actions, this is for the future to determine. The Member States will retain a great deal of autonomy in the means of implementation of a directive. A proper set of European minimum standards would reduce inconsistencies. The right balance between public and private competition enforcement is critically important for the EU jurisdiction.[65]

Private antitrust enforcement brings clear benefits to society in terms of direct savings for customers and end consumers, deterrence of infringements, the promotion of economic efficiency and pro-competitive conduct and a greater potential for just compensation. Modern competition policy sees consumer welfare as its primary goal. Thus the consumer is given the right to defend himself against negative effects of competitive constraints by means of private enforcement. Finally, more competition law enforcement will foster a competition culture which is a much desired goal still to be accomplished in most of the Member States. As the Competition Commissioner Neelie Kroes stated, 'Justice is a core value of the EU Member States societies and victims of competition law infringements have been waiting too long for that justice. They are still waiting.'[66]

---

[65] See Spencer Weber Waller: Towards a Constructive Public-Private Partnership to Enforce Competition Law. World Competition Law and Economics Review, 29 (3), 2006, pp. 367–381.

[66] Neelie Kroes, European Commissioner for Competition Policy, Collective Redress – delivering justice for victims, Address at ALDE Conference, European Parliament, Brussels, 4 March 2009, SPEECH/09/88 of 4 March 2009.

16 England and Wales

Vincent Smith,[1] *Anthony Maton*[2] *and Scott Campbell*[3]

Introduction

In the past two to three years in England and Wales significant strides have been taken towards the formation of a nascent claimant's bar. This progress is attributable to a number of important common law, regulatory, ethical and commercial developments which have made it increasingly practical for both: (a) claimants (individual consumers and businesses) to seek compensation for the losses they have sustained as a result of anti-competitive practices; and (b) lawyers seeking to specialize in holding participants in anti-competitive practices to account to practice. Within this context, a number of the major developments in England and Wales are set out below.

1. How does a damages action get started?

a. Meeting clients and ethical restrictions

Overarching duties In England and Wales, a solicitor's conduct is governed by the *Solicitors' Code of Conduct 2007 ('Code of Conduct')*. Rule 1 of the *Code of Conduct* prescribes a core set of duties that a solicitor will be subject to in all circumstances. These duties include a duty to uphold the rule of law and the administration of justice, to act

---

[1] Vincent Smith is a former Partner with Hausfeld & Co LLP in London focusing on UK and European claimant and complainant competition matters. He joined the firm from the Office of Fair Trading ('OFT') where he was Senior Director for Competition and Director of its Competition Enforcement Division from 2003. He led the OFT's 180-strong competition function, having overall responsibility for its work in combating cartels and other anti-competitive practices and for its merger control duties as well as oversight of its developing enforcement policy – for example on case prioritization. From 2002–2003, he was the OFT's Director of Competition Policy Co-ordination and Deputy Director of the division with prime responsibility for the OFT's input to the EC 'modernization' of competition enforcement.

[2] Anthony Maton is a Partner specializing in competition and financial services litigation in the European Office of Hausfeld & Co LLP in London. He has extensive experience of complex international dispute resolution including litigation, arbitration and mediation in a number of different jurisdictions. He has acted for governments, in regulatory investigations, for multinationals and for private business, and has worked in the USA and extensively throughout Europe, the Middle East and the Gulf.

[3] Scott Campbell is an Associate in the London office of Hausfeld & Co LLP, focusing on UK and European claimant and complainant competition dispute resolution matters. He joined the firm in May 2007 from the London office of Latham & Watkins, where his practice focused on merger control, regulatory competition law and defendant competition matters. To date, he has experience of matters relating to the transport, energy, media and technology, pharmaceuticals, financial services, telecommunications and retail sectors.

with integrity, to act in a way where a solicitor's independence is not compromised, to act in the best interests of the client, to provide a good standard of service to clients, and to behave in a way that instils public confidence in the legal profession.[4] Thus, any conduct by a solicitor designed to solicit potential clients must comply with these duties.

Publicity Any publicity designed to solicit clients with potential claims will be subject to the conditions contained in Rule 7 of the *Code of Conduct*. This rule provides that publicity should not be misleading or inaccurate.[5] Stationery, advertisements, brochures, websites, directory entries, media appearances, promotional press releases and direct approaches to clients (in person, in writing or via email) are considered forms of publicity under the terms of the provision.[6] Publicity aimed at a jurisdiction outside England and Wales must be compliant with Rule 7 (and where applicable, Rule 15.07 which deals with publicity by overseas practices) and the laws in that jurisdiction governing publicity by lawyers.[7] Furthermore, in addition to a solicitor's own duty not to contravene the provisions contained in Rule 7, he must not authorize others to conduct publicity in a way which would contravene the provision.[8] Rule 7 also prohibits the making of unsolicited approaches to members of the public (commonly referred to as 'cold-calls').[9] Although the rules governing English and Welsh solicitors' ability to advertise their services with a view to attracting new clients are extensive, they do not act as a significant bar to building groups of claimants in the context of competition litigation.

b. Investigative tools

It is not a *sine qua non* of a private claim for damages that a prior investigation has been conducted by a national competition authority or the European Commission. It is entirely legitimate, under English law, for claimants to bring a stand-alone action for damages in relation to a contravention of UK or EU competition law before the High Court.

However, there are a number of potential advantages to pursuing a follow-on claim based on the regulatory decision of a governmental authority. Firstly, competition authorities will be in a much stronger position than individual claimants to obtain the information required to establish allegations of unlawful conduct. For example, ss 26–28 of the Competition Act 1998 ('Competition Act') provide the OFT with specific powers to obtain information from parties who are the subject of a complaint – including the power to search and enter into private premises – in order to prove any allegation of unlawful conduct. Furthermore, competition authorities will have the means and

---

4 Rule 1, *Solicitors' Code of Conduct 2007*.

5 Rule 7.01, *Solicitors' Code of Conduct 2007*. Rule 7.02 further highlights that publicity related to charges must be clearly expressed. Additionally, the Guidance to Rule 7 provides that where a firm's website or emails include financial promotions, the firm will need to be authorized by the Financial Services Authority.

6 Rule 7.06, *Solicitors' Code of Conduct 2007*. Rule 7.07 continues on to provide detailed guidance as to what information should be provided on letterheads, websites and emails.

7 Rule 7.04, *Solicitors' Code of Conduct 2007*.

8 Rule 7.05, *Solicitors' Code of Conduct 2007*.

9 Rule 7.03(1), *Solicitors' Code of Conduct 2007*.

resources that an individual claimant would not have to collate market information and to commission research into relevant markets.[10] For an individual claimant to undertake such a task would not only be difficult, but prohibitively expensive.

Secondly, the binding nature of OFT and European Commission decisions on national courts appreciably simplifies what is required from claimants in order to pursue a claim for damages. Pursuant to Article 16 of Regulation 1/2003, national courts of the EU Member States will be bound by decisions taken by the European Commission in respect of allegations of breach of EU competition law (insofar as the decision in question relates to addressees of the Commission's decision). Similarly, with respect to the domestic regime, ss 58 and 58A of the Competition Act provide that national courts are bound by decisions made by the OFT with respect to a breach of UK competition law (subject to any subsequent appeals by the addressees of the decision). Thus, in follow-on claims, a claimant would only need to establish issues pertaining to causation and the quantum of the loss, thereby appreciably reducing the time and cost which would otherwise be involved if it had to bring a stand-alone action for damages before the civil courts.

Nonetheless, it is clear that provisions making decisions of competition authorities binding on English courts will be interpreted narrowly. The House of Lords has made it clear in the case of *Crehan v Inntrepreneur Pub Company*[11] that while national courts are generally under a duty of sincere cooperation and legal certainty with regards to decisions by the European Commission, they are not bound to follow such decisions in each and every instance, but only in relation to the same agreement between the same parties as was the subject of the regulatory authority's decision. Thus, if a court is faced with a dispute involving entirely different parties, the Commission's decision will not be binding, even if the conduct concerned relates to the same product or market. The Commission's decision may nevertheless be persuasive to a Court's finding and may, thus, still enhance a claimant's follow-on claim for damages.[12]

Additional evidence requirements

I. FOLLOW-ON ACTIONS In order to bring a follow-on action in England and Wales, a claimant will need to bring additional evidence before the Court which would not otherwise be available from the public action. For the purposes of causation, this will require evidence necessary to prove the link between the breach and the loss (as so required under tort and contract law). For the purposes of quantum, this will require economic evidence, such as financial data and invoices, in order to prove how much was spent and/or lost by the claimant.

II. STAND-ALONE ACTIONS In some cases the action may only technically be a stand-alone action, in that there is either an ongoing Commission/OFT

---

10 Ward, T. and K. Smith (2005), *Competition Litigation in the UK*, London: Sweet & Maxwell.

11 [2006] UKHL 38.

12 Although that case specifically addressed decisions made by the European Commission, it is likely that a court would follow the same principles insofar as would concern decisions by the OFT and/or other national competition authorities.

investigation which is anticipated to disclose a cartel, and which will cause the action to be stayed, or there are criminal or regulatory findings in another jurisdiction which will allow the action to be pleaded. In some cases it is strategically important to file a claim form at an early stage, even before a regulatory investigation has been completed, if there is a threat of a rival claim being filed in a jurisdiction other than England and Wales.

In cases where there is no such government action, it may be possible to settle with one of the cartelists on the basis that they will produce evidence of the cartel. Failing that, enough evidence will be required in order for the pleading in the case to be adequate and survive attack. The most common route to this will be where documents have been produced under pre-action disclosure. Pre-action disclosure, which is governed by the English courts' Civil Procedure Rules ('CPR'), provides a means for claimants to obtain copies of documents from the intended defendant to properly assess whether or not proceedings should be commenced.

c. Amassing sufficient evidence

The burden of proof rests with the claimants to demonstrate that on a high balance of probabilities[13] it has suffered loss as a result of the anti-competitive conduct of the defendant(s). The claimants' burden of proof is often alleviated by the existence of a relevant regulatory decision on which it can rely. Indeed decisions of the European Commission and of the OFT are binding on the courts of England and Wales in as far as the liability of the addressees of the decision is concerned. Claimants must also demonstrate a causal link between the anti-competitive behaviour found in the regulatory decision and the damage they claim to suffer. However, in the context of a stand-alone case without the benefit of a regulatory decision, the practicalities of reaching the requisite standard of proof that an infringement has occurred can be onerous (bearing in mind it is axiomatic that cartels tend to conceal evidence of their existence). In any event, the wide-ranging standard disclosure of documents governed by CPR Rule 31 applies to competition cases as set out below.

2. Who may pursue a claim?

The principle that breaches of EU competition law give rise to claims for damages and other relief in English courts has been clearly established at least since the 1983 decision of the House of Lords in *Garden Cottage Foods Ltd. v Milk Marketing Board.*[14] Therefore a party who has suffered a loss as a result of an infringement of competition law can seek to pursue a claim for damages either in the Chancery Division of the High Court or before the Competition Appeal Tribunal ('CAT').

There are broadly two categories of claimants who may bring an action for damages in respect of anti-competitive conduct. These are third parties to infringing agreements and parties to infringing agreements.

---

13 *Arkin v Borchard Lines Ltd and Others* (*No. 4*) [2003], England and Wales Court of Appeal, Civil 655.

14 [1984] AC 130.

a. Third party claimants
A third party who has not been privy to an infringing agreement, but has suffered due to other parties entering into such agreements, can bring a claim against the infringing parties. Potential third-party claimants may include:[15]

i. Direct purchasers – direct purchasers would clearly have a claim against infringing parties.
ii. Indirect purchasers – indirect purchasers may also have a claim against infringing parties where direct purchasers who have had to pay a higher price for goods than they otherwise would have, in turn increase prices to their own customers.
iii. Competitors – competitors of infringing parties may have a claim against these parties due to losses suffered from their infringing behaviour (in particular, exclusionary conduct). These losses may be both actual and potential.
iv. Suppliers – suppliers to infringing parties may have an actionable claim for damages due to the lost sales resulting from an artificial reduction in output by the parties.
v. Other members of the public – customers who would have bought goods had the prices not been so high may also suffer losses giving rise to a potential claim. However, the burden of evidencing a claim of this sort would likely be too onerous.
vi. Designated consumer bodies – under s 47B of the Competition Act, consumer bodies designated by the secretary of state may bring representative actions before the CAT on behalf of two or more consenting consumers suffering loss flowing from one and the same competition infringement (although this procedure does not apply to businesses). At the moment, the UK Consumers' Association, (otherwise known as '*Which?*') is the only designated body under this procedure.

b. Parties to the anti-competitive conduct
In the case of *Crehan v Courage*,[16] the European Court of Justice ('ECJ') found that English courts had erred in holding that damages would not be available, as a matter of principle, to parties to anti-competitive agreements. It was held that damages could be claimed by a party to an anti-competitive agreement so long as that party did not bear a 'significant responsibility' for the infringement. Thus, damages may now be available under English law even to parties who are privy to an illegal undertaking.

Limitations to claims: The passing-on defence A claimant may be precluded from seeking damages if it is deemed that the 'passing-on' defence is applicable under English law, and that the particular defence applies to the case. The rationale underlying the passing-on defence is that a claimant should not be allowed to seek compensation for a loss which it does not actually suffer. Thus, the defence would be applicable in cases where claimants pass on any or all of their losses to customers by way of higher prices, such that the claimant actually suffers a much lower degree of loss, and in certain instances, no loss at all.[17]

---

[15] See generally, Ward and Smith, above n 10, 264–5.
[16] Case C-453/99 [2002] QB 507.
[17] See Mobley S, T. Cassels, K. Jones, M. Garcia and S. Mann (2007), 'England and Wales' in 'Private Anti-Trust Litigation in 19 Jurisdictions Worldwide', *Global Competition Review* 33.

The applicability of the defence under English law was raised in an interlocutory application for security for costs in *BCL Old Co Ltd v Aventis SA*.[18] In that application, two of the defendants argued that the claimant should be safeguarded from pursuing its claim as it had passed on its losses to other purchasers by way of higher prices. The court held that the applicability of the passing-on defence under English law raised 'novel and important issues' and 'would be an important consideration to potential claimants when considering whether to issue proceedings in the future'.[19] However, the court deemed it unnecessary to consider the issue in an interlocutory application, arguing that the issue should only be assessed when all the relevant facts had been determined.[20]

3. In what forum does a plaintiff initiate a claim?

While EU law provides claimants with rights and protections, remedies for all actions must be provided by and under the national law of each Member State.[21] All private claims arising from a breach of UK or EU competition law should thus be brought before the courts of England and Wales.

As discussed earlier, claimants can initiate a private claim for breach of UK or EU competition law in either the Chancery Division of the High Court or the CAT. The most appropriate forum in which a claimant should pursue its claim will depend on a variety of factors, including whether the claimant wishes to bring the case on a 'stand-alone' or 'follow-on' basis, the nature of the relief being sought, the level of expertise which the claimant is seeking from a court, and the time and cost which the claimant is willing to invest in litigation.

a. High Court: Chancery Division

An action may be brought before the Chancery Division of the High Court on a 'stand-alone' or 'follow-on' basis. The High Court is the only available avenue for a claimant where there has been no prior infringement decision by a national competition authority in the matter or the relief sought extends beyond a claim for damages (for example, the claimant wishes to seek an injunction or a declaration).[22]

In circumstances where there has been a prior infringement decision by a national competition authority, a claimant may elect to bring a 'follow-on' action either in the High Court or before the CAT.

b. Competition Appeal Tribunal

Section 47A of the Competition Act provides that where an adverse decision has been made by the CAT, the OFT, or the Competition Commission (and the decision is no longer appealable) in respect of the Chapter I and II prohibitions or Articles 81 and 82 EC,[23] a claimant may pursue a follow-on claim for damages (or some other claim for a

---

18 [2005] CAT 2.

19 *BCL Old Co Ltd v Aventis SA* [2005] CAT 2, [33], [38].

20 *BCL Old Co Ltd v Aventis SA* [2005] CAT 2, [37].

21 Ward and Smith, above n 10, [7-008].

22 Case C–453/99 *Courage v Crehan* [2001] ECR 1–6297, [26].

23 On 1 December 2009, the Treaty of Lisbon came into effect, amending the Treaty Establishing the European Community (EC Treaty) that is now called the Treaty on the Functioning of the

sum of money) before the CAT. The CAT is more likely to be the forum of choice for claimants bringing follow-on actions due to the flexibility with which issues of evidence may be dealt, and the specific expertise that the tribunal has in the area of competitions law. Since 1998, eleven damages claims have been lodged with the CAT.

c. Other jurisdictions and consolidation

Claimants involved in multi-jurisdictional claims may also elect to bring their proceedings before the courts and tribunals of England and Wales, as it is now possible for such claims to be consolidated and heard in a single claim. Under the Jurisdiction Regulation,[24] where an infringement involves a number of parties in different jurisdictions, the case should ordinarily be brought in the jurisdiction in which the defendant is domiciled. Nonetheless, actions may, for example, be brought in the jurisdiction in which a tort takes place instead.[25]

Furthermore, it is possible to bring all actions into the same jurisdiction where the claims are 'so closely connected that it is expedient to hear and determine them together to avoid the risk of irreconcilable judgments resulting from separate proceedings'.[26] In terms of seising the jurisdiction of the English High Court to exercise the right to claim for damages arising from competition law breaches, the judgment in *Provimi Ltd v Aventis Animal Nutrition SA*[27] suggests that English courts are likely to interpret their jurisdiction broadly. The competition issue in *Provimi* was whether companies which had purchased cartel-affected products across Europe could choose to proceed against an English implementing subsidiary of a cartelist in respect of all European losses instead of having to pursue separate claims in multiple jurisdictions. The court held that where a subsidiary of a cartelist has implemented a cartel in England, the English High Court has jurisdiction to hear claims by other European purchasers against the English subsidiary, even if there is no direct contractual relationship between the purchasing company and the English subsidiary. Nonetheless, as the court held in *SanDisk Corporation v Koninklijke Philips Electronics NV*,[28] there must be some connection to England and Wales before the English court will assert its jurisdiction. In that case, the court decided that it did not have jurisdiction to hear the claim since no immediate damage had been caused to SanDisk in England, and none of the alleged conduct amounting to an abuse of a dominant position had originated in England.[29] Thus, in light of the *Provimi* and *SanDisk* judgments, it appears that the English High Court is likely to cast its jurisdiction widely so long as there is a real connecting link between the parties to the claim and England and Wales.

European Union (TFEU). Therefore, all references to Articles 81 and 82 of the EC Treaty now reference Articles 101 and 102 TFEU.

[24] Art 3, Council Regulation (EC) No. 44/2001 of 22 December 2000, L 12/1, 16.1.2001, p. 1.

[25] Art 5, Council Regulation (EC) No. 44/2001 of 22 December 2000.

[26] Art 6(1), Council Regulation (EC) No. 44/2001 of 22 December 2000.

[27] [2003] EWHC 961 ('*Provimi*').

[28] [2007] EWHC 332 (Ch) ('*SanDisk*').

[29] It would be beyond the scope of this chapter to discuss issues relating to the applicable law in multi-jurisdictional claims. However, it is sufficient to say that even if an English court asserts its jurisdiction over such a claim, it will still need to decide upon the appropriate law to be applied in the case.

4. How may claims be aggregated?

a. Representative actions

CPR Rule 19.6 allows one or more claimants with the 'same interest' in a claim to initiate proceedings in the High Court as representatives of any other person having that same interest. This provision also allows the court to order that the claim be continued.

Representative actions may – at least theoretically – be a preferential avenue for a claimant if there are other claimants with a similar interest in the claim, as a representative judgment is binding on those with the 'same interest'. This mechanism is the closest approximation to a US style opt-out class action available in the English legal system. Nonetheless, representative actions have been relatively infrequently used due to the 'same interest' requirement of Rule 19.6 being notoriously difficult to satisfy. In a strike-out application arising from *Emerald Supplies Limited v British Airways PLC*,[30] the claimants sought to bring their claim as a representative action, thereby seeking to act as representatives of all 'direct and indirect purchasers of airfreight services'. However, the Chancellor of the High Court, Sir Andrew Morritt, held that because it was impossible to say of a given person that he was a member of the class represented at the time the claim was issued, Rule 19.6 did not permit the claimants to represent that class as a whole. He also decided that the declaration sought could not be equally beneficial to all members of the class, as there was an 'inevitable conflict' between some of those represented who might have claims against others in the class.

Contrasting the position of the English courts with those in the US, he said that it was for Parliament to deal with the issues raised by representative actions rather than courts, and not for lawyers to use Rule 19.6 to accommodate such cases. He further ruled that the criteria for inclusion in the class of claimants cannot be satisfied at the time the action is brought, as this was dependent on the action itself succeeding. The Rt. Hon Lady Justice Arden granted the claimants permission to appeal this decision before the Court of Appeal in December 2009 and the Court's judgment is still pending.

b. Group claims

As discussed earlier, s 47B of the Competition Act provides claimants with an avenue to bring their claims as a group. One such claim was that of *Consumers' Association v JJB Sports Plc* 3,[31] in which the Consumers' Association brought an action on behalf of consumers who had been overcharged by JJB Sports on England and Manchester United football shirts. In a settlement agreed between the parties and approved by the CAT by an order of Lord Carlisle of Berriew QC dated January 14, 2008, JJB Sports agreed to directly compensate any customers who were parties to the action with £20. Other affected customers who were not parties to the Consumers' Association's action could, on production of the relevant replica shirt, reclaim either £10 if the label was still intact or £5 if it was not. These customers were required to have their replica shirts indelibly marked and sign a document waiving the right to further legal action against JJB Sports.

---

30 [2009] EWHC 741 (Ch).

31 [2009] CAT 3.

c. Group Litigation Orders

Group Litigation Orders ('GLO') were introduced in May 2000 in response to the problems associated with bringing a representative action before the High Court. GLOs provide for the case-management of all claims raising 'common or related issues' of law or fact, pursuant to the provisions outlined in CPR Rule 19.11. This test is substantially broader than the 'same interest' test and provides the court with wide discretionary powers with which it can manage grouped claims. GLOs are likely to become an important tool for courts to manage claims in the future.[32]

Indeed, a GLO was used successfully in the case of *Sempra Metals Limited (formerly Metallgesellschaft Limited) (Respondents) v Her Majesty's Commissioners of Inland Revenue and another (Appellants)*,[33] which followed the referral of Sempra's case to, and the decision of, the ECJ. The ECJ held that Sempra must be provided with a remedy in English law to enable it to recover an amount equal to interest on the amounts paid to HMRC under the UK's Advance Corporation Tax Regime ('ACT'). A significant number of similar claims were subsequently brought in the High Court following the ECJ's decision. Those claims were grouped under a GLO, known as the ACT Group Litigation Order. Sempra was the test claimant on the question of whether companies such as Sempra should recover interest at a compound rate or, as HMRC maintained, a simple rate on the amounts paid by way of ACT.

d. Public interest litigation

As stated above, claimants may also bring a representative damages action before the CAT under the provisions of s 47B of the Competition Act. However, the circumstances in which claimants may pursue a representative action under s 47B are considerably more limited than would be the case before the High Court – s 47B only allowing a government approved 'specified body' to bring a damages action before the CAT on behalf of a group of named consumers. Claimants may also apply to the CAT for interim relief such as an injunction.

Additionally, s 47B does not allow for a claim to be brought on a stand-alone basis. Thus, if there has been no prior infringement decision by a national competition authority, a group of claimants wishing to initiate a representative action will have to do so in the High Court. Furthermore, the requirement that a representative action may only be brought on behalf of named consumers, and cannot be brought on behalf of businesses or consumers at large, has been the subject of much criticism and has prompted calls for reform from several quarters. Indeed, the Consumers' Association has stated it is unlikely to pursue a representative claim again due to the disproportionate cost and time required to do so. This reaction is likely to be born of the fact that while the Consumers' Association ultimately settled the case with JJB on behalf of consumers, creating a settlement fund worth £18,000, the legal costs incurred by the Consumers' Association are likely to be in the region of several hundred thousand pounds.

In light of these perceived deficiencies in the English group litigation system, on December 12, 2008, the Civil Justice Council ('CJC') – a non-departmental public body

---

32 Mobley et al., above n 17, 30.

33 [2007] UKHL 34.

established under the Civil Procedure Act 1997 with responsibility for overseeing and co-ordinating the modernisation of the civil justice system in England and Wales – published its final recommendations to improve access to justice for consumers and small businesses in collective claims for compensation in its paper 'Improving Access through Collective Actions – Developing a more Effective and Efficient Procedure for Collective Actions'.

This is the most recent set of recommendations published by the CJC relating to collective claims and will be submitted to the Lord Chancellor and Secretary of State for Justice as formal advice. While most elements of a new collective action procedure could be introduced by the Civil Procedure Rule Committee, it is considered desirable that any new action be introduced by primary legislation. The CJC had previously published, on February 8, 2008, research into the need to improve consumer redress, and on August 5, 2008, its initial set of recommendations designed to improve access to justice for consumers and small businesses in collective claims, which indicates the considerable body of research and consultation that has resulted in the CJC's final recommendations as to the future for collective claims.

The CJC formulated eleven recommendations in total. In particular, the CJC recommended:

- increasing the types of representative bodies that can bring claims, including individual representative claimants or defendants, designated bodies, and ad hoc bodies;
- making the judiciary the 'gatekeeper' of the collective action procedure;
- permitting claims to be brought on an 'opt-out' or 'opt-in' basis subject to court certification and where it is in the interests of justice to do so; and
- changing the law to permit the award of aggregate damages. Unallocated damages from an aggregate award should be distributed by a trustee of the award according to general trust law principles. In appropriate cases, such a *cy-près* distribution could be made to a charitable foundation or trust.

The CJC's recommendations are a significant contribution to the debate as to how consumers and small businesses can have improved access to justice. The CJC's work responds to the widely-held perception that individual consumers and small businesses often find the complexity and cost present in the current system of civil justice a barrier to the exercising of their rights to obtain access to the courts.

On July 20, 2009, the Government responded to the CJC's recommendations and broadly rejected the CJC's recommendation of a generic right of collective action. The Government would prefer that such rights should be considered and, where appropriate, introduced in respect of specific 'sectors' (such as competition, personal injury and consumer claims) and the issue of who may bring a collective claim (in terms of criteria and methods of authorization) should also be decided on a sectoral basis. The Government concluded that rights of collective action should be introduced only where there is evidence of need and following an assessment of the economic and other impacts and consideration of alternative approaches. In particular, the Government favours consideration of regulatory options (such as allowing regulators to order the payment of compensation) before introducing court-based options. Finally, the

Government noted that there is not necessarily a clear-cut distinction between opt-in and opt-out models for collective actions and that there are several options depending on the stage of proceedings at which the class is closed. Some of these may combine the features and benefits of both models. In the light of these conclusions, the Government will develop a framework document setting out the issues to be addressed when introducing a right of collective action with options and, where appropriate, a preferred approach.

e. Is there joint and several liability?

In cartel cases (and joint dominance cases), liability is almost inevitably found on a joint and several basis in the High Court and the CAT. Therefore, a claimant may bring an action for damages against one cartelist for the entirety of losses arising from the anti-competitive conduct of all known cartelists during the time of the defendant's participation in the cartel.

5. What procedural defences are available short of a trial?

a. Default judgment

CPR Part 12 allows a default judgment to be obtained without a trial where a defendant has either (i) failed to file an acknowledgement of service within the required time; or (ii) filed an acknowledgement of service but then failed to file a defence within the required time.

b. Summary judgment

CPR Part 24 allows the court to give summary judgment against a claimant or a defendant on the whole of a claim or on a particular issue if it considers that the claimant or defendant has no real prospect of victory on the claim or issue and there is no other compelling reason why the case or issue should be disposed of at trial.

6. What devices are available to obtain evidence?

a. Evidence gathering

In England and Wales, standard disclosure requires the parties to litigation to disclose to one another the documents on which they rely, documents which are adverse to their own case, documents which adversely affect another party's case and documents which support another party's case. It is also possible in certain circumstances to apply for pre-action disclosure and disclosure from third parties. It is arguable therefore in stand-alone cases, where a claimant wishes to take action in respect of a suspected cartel that is not subject to a regulatory decision, it may be prohibitively difficult to particularise a case adequately before even moving to the disclosure stage. Note that in the CAT disclosure is subject to directions of the Tribunal under Rule 19(2)(K) of the CAT Rules and is therefore not automatic.

Communications containing legal advice between a party to the litigation and its solicitor are protected by legal professional privilege. Communications between a solicitor, client or a third party in connection with litigation that is in contemplation or has commenced also benefits from this privilege. Without prejudice communications (in other words, privileged documents that relate to all negotiations genuinely aimed at a settlement between the parties) are additionally outside the jurisdiction of the court.

In English procedure, witness evidence is typically provided in the form of a witness statement given to the other party before trial, augmented by oral evidence at the trial, typically in the form of a cross-examination. The English court has the power to compel any witness within its jurisdiction to give evidence and the Hague Convention of 18 March 1970 on the Taking of Evidence Abroad in Civil or Commercial Matters procedures allow evidence to be taken abroad in certain circumstances.

b. Experts

Expert evidence is admissible in court and is frequently relied upon as evidence; parties usually appoint (and pay for) experts to give reports or testimony to the court on technical issues with the court's permission. Permission of the court is always required either to call an expert or to put an expert's report in evidence. The English courts have been left to determine ad hoc the relevant expertise and the qualifications for the provision of the expertise. It is for the parties to the litigation to decide who will give the expert evidence, although the quality of that evidence is only likely to be tested by the opposing litigant's cross-examinations.[34]

7. What practices are illegal and what are the elements of proof?

Article 81(1) EC provides insofar as material:

> The following shall be prohibited as incompatible with the common market: all agreements between undertakings decisions by associations of undertakings and concerted practices which may affect trade between Member States and which have as their object or effect the prevention, restriction or distortion of competition within the common market, and in particular those which:
> (a) directly or indirectly fix purchase or selling prices or any other trading conditions;
> (b) limit or control production, markets, technical development, or investment;
> (c) share markets or sources of supply;
> (d) apply dissimilar conditions to equivalent transactions with other trading parties, thereby placing them at a competitive disadvantage;
> (e) make the conclusion of contracts subject to acceptance by the other parties of supplementary obligations which, by their nature or according to commercial usage, have no connection with the subject of such contracts.

Article 53 of the EEA Agreement is to similar effect. The Chapter I prohibition contained in s 2 of the Competition Act introduces a prohibition in materially the same terms as Article 81(1) EC, save that it is only necessary under the Competition Act to establish an effect on trade within the United Kingdom or a part of it rather than an effect on interstate trade.

Article 82 EC provides insofar as material:

---

[34] See Blom-Cooper, L (ed.) (2006) *Experts in the Civil Courts*, Oxford: Oxford University Press, 1.26.

> Any abuse by one or more undertakings of a dominant position within the common market or in a substantial part of it shall be prohibited as incompatible with the common market insofar as it may affect trade between Member States.
> Such abuse may, in particular, consist in:
> (a) directly or indirectly imposing unfair purchase or selling prices or other unfair trading conditions;
> (b) limiting production, markets or technical development to the prejudice of consumers;
> (c) applying dissimilar conditions to equivalent transactions with other trading parties, thereby placing them at a competitive disadvantage;
> (d) making the conclusion of contracts subject to acceptance by the other parties of supplementary obligations which, by their nature or according to commercial usage, have no connection with the subject of such contracts.

Article 54 of the EEA Agreement is to similar effect. The Chapter II prohibition contained in s 18 of the Competition Act introduces a prohibition in materially the same terms as Article 82 EC, save that it is only necessary under the Competition Act to establish an effect on trade within the United Kingdom or a part of it rather than an effect on interstate trade.

As a matter of European Community law, a claim for damages before the courts of a Member State arising from a breach of EU or UK competition law must according to the principle of effectiveness be available to an injured party, whether a direct or indirect purchaser, under the heads of actual losses and loss of profits including interest, caused by such a breach.[35]

In the absence of European Community rules governing the matter, it is for the domestic legal system of each EU Member State to designate the courts and tribunals having jurisdiction and to lay down the detailed procedural rules governing actions for safeguarding rights which individuals derive directly from European Community law, provided that such rules are not less favourable than those governing similar domestic actions (principle of equivalence) and that they do not render practically impossible or excessively difficult the exercise of rights conferred by Community law (principle of effectiveness).[36] In English law, a breach of the duty imposed by Article 81(1) or Article 82 EC is categorized as a breach of statutory duty,[37] subject however to the principles of equivalence and effectiveness.

In terms of evidencing loss, the Commission's Staff Working Paper annexed to the Commission's Green Paper on Damages Actions for Breach of the EC Anti-Trust Rules states:

> Typically the measure of loss which shall be compensated in an antitrust damages case is taken to be the difference between the claimant's actual position and the situation he would have been in 'but for' the illegal conduct (the counterfactual). The former encompasses actual losses as well as profits that have not been gained, while the latter refers to the hypothetical situation in which the claimant would be had no competition law infringement occurred. The loss is thus compensated if the claimant is put into the financial situation he would have been

---

35 See Cases C–295–298/04 *Manfredi v Lloyd Adriatico Assicurazioni SpA* [2006] ECR I–6619, [95].

36 See Case C–453/99 *Courage v Crehan* [2001] ECR I–6297, [29].

37 See *Garden Cottage Foods Ltd. v Milk Marketing Board* [1984] AC 130, 141 (per Lord Diplock).

in 'but for' the infringement. A number of methods are used to establish this 'but for' scenario, for example the prices, profits, costs, and the market situation etc., that would have prevailed in the absence of the infringement, to allow a comparison between the hypothetical and the actual situation.

The most commonly claimed types of antitrust damages are likely to be overcharges (that is, increased prices in case of cartels or excessive prices in case of a dominant position) and damages claimed for other anti-competitive conduct (that is, predatory pricing or refusal to supply) which has led to lost net profits to a continuing business or even lost going concern value of a terminated business.

The 'lost going concern value' was the measure favoured by the Court of Appeal in *Crehan v Inntrepreneur Pub Company*.[38]

8. What do plaintiffs get if they win?

a. Single v treble or punitive damages

In England and Wales, treble damages are not available. In general, English courts seek to apply the general principles of foreseeability and quantum applicable in tort claims where loss of profit is claimed (which are likely to form the bulk of cartel damages claims).

On this basis, the most common damages claims in the English courts are for 'compensatory damages' – that is damages which compensate a claimant for loss (whether financial or not) suffered as a result of wrongdoing.[39] It seems clear from the High Court's ruling in *Devenish Nutrition Ltd v Sanofi-Aventis SA* that 'exemplary damages' – damages additional to an award which fully compensates the claimant for his loss, and which are intended to punish and deter – will not be available in follow-on actions for breach of antitrust law based on the court's determination that to do so would breach the principle of *ne bis in idem*, which dictates that (i) a person should not be sanctioned more than once for the same illegal conduct; and (ii) Article 16 of Regulation 1/2003,[40] which dictates that Commission decisions will be binding on national courts, and thus a court will be precluded from making a decision counter to one already taken by the Commission in respect of the same facts.[41] Nonetheless, it remains to be seen whether exemplary damages will be awarded in stand-alone cases – where no prior infringement decision or fine will have been imposed by a regulatory authority.

b. Damages calculation

As stated above, English damages rules are designed to put claimants in the position they would have occupied had the breach from which their loss flows not been committed (plus interest and costs).

---

38 [2006] UKHL 38.

39 This should be distinguished from 'user damages' – damages assessed by reference to the fair price for the use of what has been taken from the claimant without the claimant having to show he has suffered actual outlay.

40 OJ L 1, 4.1.2003, pp. 1–25.

41 [2007] EWHC 2394 (Ch.), [52], [53].

c. Pre-judgment interest
Simple interest is generally available in the High Court, and is to be awarded on all or any part of the damages awarded for all or any part of the period from the date that the infringement occurred up to the date of the judgment. The CAT may include, in any sum awarded for damages, interest on all or any part of the damages in respect of which the award is being made. Depending on the duration of the infringement, awards of pre-judgment interest can be substantial and can act as an effective equivalent to treble damages. It is arguable that complex interest should be awarded in cartel cases, but this has yet to be tested before the courts.

d. Indemnification or contribution
Members of a hard-core cartel who have rigged bids, allocated markets, or fixed prices have clearly conspired and agreed to act in such a way as to achieve a desired outcome. As such, the members of a cartel have each contributed to damages suffered to specific markets and their participants. On this basis, under s. 1(1) of the Civil Liability (Contribution) Act 1978, if a claim is brought against one member of a cartel, a right of contribution arises with regard to the other cartel members as a result of their joint and several liability for the cartel activity.

e. Fees
As a general rule in the civil courts of England and Wales, the losing party will be ordered by the court to pay the successful party's legal costs. The CAT has the power to make orders it thinks fit in relation to the payment of costs by one party or another in respect of the whole or part of the proceedings. Solicitors (and, indeed, barristers) may be keen to represent consumers, small businesses or even larger business seeking to bring a follow-on damages claim under a conditional fee agreement allowing a fee-uplift due to the potentially high likelihood of eventual success in follow-on actions.

f. Equitable remedies

(i) Injunctive relief In the English civil courts, it is possible to seek interim injunctions, for instance to prevent a defendant from continuing to infringe competition law to the detriment of the applicant until such time as there can be a full trial of the issues. The court must not attempt to decide the claim on the affidavits or witness statements; it is enough if the claimant can show that there is a serious question to be tried.[42] If the claimant satisfies the test, the grant or refusal of an injunction is a matter for the exercise of the court's discretion on the balance of convenience. However, the court will not grant an injunction if damages would be a sufficient remedy instead, and will also consider whether more harm will be done by granting or refusing an injunction.

(ii) Restitution In *Devenish Nutrition Limited v Sanofi-Aventis SA (France)*,[43] the Court of Appeal held that the claimants were not entitled to restitution and were

---

42 *American Cyanamid Co v Ethicon [1975]* AC 396.
43 [2008] EWCA Civ 1086.

confined to seeking compensation for their losses. The majority of the Court of Appeal held that the Court was bound by its previous decision in *Stoke-on-Trent City Council v W & J Wass Ltd*[44] as to the categories of tort for which gains-based damages could be recovered. These categories did not include breach of statutory duty, the cause of action relied upon by Devenish. In any event, even if it had not been bound by this precedent, the Court found that restitution would only be available in 'exceptional circumstances', and that that condition was not satisfied in that case because compensatory damages would have been an adequate remedy for Devenish.

(iii) Declaratory relief The High Court has general jurisdiction to grant declaratory relief under CPR Part 40.20. Within the limits of their general jurisdiction and subject to any express statutory provision to the contrary, the courts have discretion to grant declarations upon any matter whatsoever.[45]

(iv) Limitation periods In England and Wales, the time limit in which to institute proceedings is six years for actions founded on tort.[46] The time limit starts on the date the wrongful act caused the damage in question, subject to fraud, concealment and mistake.[47] In *National Grid v ABB Limited*,[48] the High Court indicated that follow-on claims for damages would not necessarily be stayed in the event of an appeal against a regulatory authority's decision insofar as concerns an infringement. It is, thus, simply a matter of case management as to what stage the claim will be allowed to proceed pending the outcome of any appeal.

Claimants have two years in which they bring follow-on claims for damages before the CAT.[49] The time limit in which claimants may bring a claim may be extended in the event of an appeal against the regulatory authority's infringement decision depending on whether the appeal is in respect of the substance of the decision or the infringement. In *BCL Old Co Limited v BASF*, the Court of Appeal clarified that time will be prevented from running where a defendant appeals against the substance of a regulatory authority's infringement decision. However, it will not stop running where a defendant is solely appealing against a regulatory authority's fine.[50]

(v) Distribution of damages In England and Wales, it is only possible for named claimants in litigation to make claims in respect of their own losses. Therefore the courts cannot create aggregated pools of damages, and there exists no active equivalent to a US-style *cy-près* fund.

However, novel mechanisms for the distribution of damages have arisen from private settlements of claims based on breaches of competition law. For example, in 2007 a

---

44 [1998] 1 WLR 1406.

45 See Zamir and Woolf (2001), *The Declaratory Judgment*, London: Sweet & Maxwell (3rd ed) [3.005].

46 Section 2, Limitation Act 1980.

47 Section 32(1), Limitation Act 1980.

48 [2009] EWHC 1326.

49 Rule 13, Competition Appeal Tribunal Rules 2003.

50 [2009] EWCA Civ 434.

£73.5 million settlement was reached on behalf of UK air passengers in the price-fixing class action lawsuit brought against British Airways and Virgin Atlantic in the US.[51] Under the terms of the settlement, passengers who purchased tickets from either airline for specified long-haul flights between August 11, 2004 and March 23, 2006 are able to claim a partial refund. Passengers who purchased tickets from the airlines in the UK are entitled to a refund of 33.3 per cent of the fuel surcharge they paid on each flight segment purchased. Passengers who purchased tickets in the US will receive their partial refund (also 33.3 per cent of the fuel surcharge paid on each flight segment) in dollars rather than pounds out of a separate $73 million US settlement fund. This unprecedented settlement represents the first instance in which such a case has been resolved simultaneously under UK law and US law and has provided compensation to classes of purchasers from both the US and the UK.

More recently, Parker ITR S.r.l. ('Parker') has made a global offer to settle claims arising from the marine hose cartel to all purchasers of marine hose on the basis of settlement terms. The offer to settle applies not only to all purchasers of marine hose from Parker but also to all other purchasers of marine hose from Parker's co-cartelists or companies that operated the Parker business prior to January 31, 2002. However, the settlement terms differ depending on whether purchases were from Parker or not.

In return for giving up rights to litigate against Parker, purchasers can claim against the settlement fund. An independent expert assisted by an independent economist will determine how much of the fund goes to each claimant but there is a presumption that direct Parker purchasers will be entitled to 16 per cent of purchases during the settlement period unless they passed on the loss. Purchasers settling with Parker will also benefit from Parker's cooperation in the form of production of witnesses, interviews, depositions and documents in relation to proceedings against other cartelists and a guarantee against payment of adverse costs in civil damages proceedings against those other cartelists.

9. How does the plaintiff's lawyer finance private enforcement?

The Consumers' Association has stated in response to the OFT's November 2007 publication '*Private Actions in Competition Law: Effective Redress for Consumers and Business*' that:

> Whilst a system is in place for an approved body to bring an action on behalf of consumers – in fact, this is the system we are using to take action against JJB Sports for the price-fixing of replica football shirt case – this system has limitations and in some ways favours the cartel and not the consumer. The OFT is hoping to iron out these imbalances through the recommendations it has announced.[52]

To this end, the OFT has recommended: modifying restrictions which limit the funding of actions, to ensure that claimants can find lawyers willing to represent them; encouraging

---

[51] Fortson, Danny, 'UK Businesses Braced for Class Action Suits after BA and Virgin Pay Out $200m', *The Independent* (16 Feb 2008) available at www.independent.co.uk/ news/business/news/uk-businesses-braced-for-class-action-suits-after-ba-and-virgin-pay-out-200m-783077.html.

[52] Which?, 'Cartel Victims need Better Rights: OFT Wants Better Redress for Price-Fix Victims' (27 November 2007) available at www.which.co.uk/news/2007/11/cartel-victims-need-better-rights-126297.jsp.

the courts to consider limiting risks of claimants having to pay the other side's costs in appropriate cases; and ensuring that funding is available for meritorious cases which would not otherwise be brought. In order to achieve some of these advances, legislation may be required. However, in the absence of government action, there are certain mechanisms available to cartel victims not only to fund the pursuit of a claim but also to mitigate the potential costs risks of launching an unsuccessful claim.

a. Indemnification

The adverse costs rule risk can be alleviated by an insurer who will insure the client against the risk of paying these adverse costs up to a limit or cap. This is called after the event insurance ('ATE'). The cost of ATE – provided it is reasonable and proportional – is recoverable from defendants when a claim is successful. Insurers will make an assessment of the level of premium appropriate on a case by case basis. It is also possible to defer insurance premiums so that they are not payable until after judgment and so that the premium is only payable in the event that the claim is successful. This means that if the claim is lost, the insurer pays the defendant's legal costs and disbursements. If the claim is won, the claimants pay the premium which is recoverable from the defendants (so in reality, the claimants pay nothing). If the claim is lost, the insurer cannot recover its premium from the defendant and, depending on the policy, may not recover a premium from the claimant either.

It is also possible for professional litigation funders (non-lawyers) to provide capital to fight litigation in return for a proportion of the claimant's eventual recovery on success. These arrangements have to be structured carefully in order to avoid the breach of various ethical rules. In particular, the claimant, not the funder, should give instructions to the solicitor, and the funder's stake in the proceeds should not be disproportionate or, as a general rule, exceed the claimant's share. Such arrangements are becoming more widespread and the number of funders in the English market continues to grow.[53]

The Court of Appeal has examined the question of third party litigation funding in some detail, in *Arkin v Bouchard Lines Ltd.*[54] The claimant, Mr Arkin, had availed himself of a Conditional Fee Agreement ('CFA' – see more below) arrangement with his solicitors due to his limited means. He also had the benefit of professional third party funding for his case which allowed him to pursue his claim of a breach of competition law against Bouchard Lines Ltd to judgment. Under those funding arrangements the professional funders had no role in the decision-making process in the case but they were kept informed of developments, and their approval of any proposed settlement was required. The professional funders agreed to remuneration of 25 per cent of recoveries from the litigation up to £5m and 23 per cent thereafter. Mr Arkin's claim was ultimately unsuccessful, therefore his solicitors could not recover their fees under the CFA, nor could his professional funders recover the costs support of £1.3 million they had provided to Mr Arkin to pursue his claim. The defendants' total costs in the case were around £6 million and they sought recovery of those costs from Mr Arkin's third party funders. Therefore

[53] See, eg, the case of *Moore Stephens v Stone & Rolls Limited* [2008] EWCA Civ 644, a prominent example of funded complex litigation.

[54] [2005] 1 WLR 3055 ('*Arkin*').

a question arose as to whether a professional funder would be liable for the costs of the other side where that side was successful in the claim? The Court of Appeal held that the funder was liable for the successful party's costs, but only subject to the financial cap of the amount of funding provided (£1.3 million in *Arkin*).

In the Court of Appeal's earlier judgment in *R (Factortame) v Secretary of State*,[55] it was held that so long as a funder did not interfere in an improper way with the conduct of the litigation in question, the agreement to fund the litigating party would be enforceable. Therefore, the judgments in *Arkin* and *Factortame* indicate that so long as the funder does not interfere in the conduct of the litigation, such arrangements are valid and enforceable. On a practical level, third party funding is likely to grow in prevalence as a means to bring otherwise prohibitively expensive litigation, including group litigation in competition matters.

b. Attorney's fees including the availability and usage of conditional fee agreements

The normal model of charging for litigation in England and Wales is on an hourly rate basis, payable by clients monthly. The rules in England and Wales do not allow solicitors to act on a contingency basis, that is, to take a percentage of damages if successful. However, the rules allow solicitors to act on CFAs. Under a CFA, the solicitor agrees to charge on an hourly rate basis with an uplift to that rate expressed on a percentage basis (up to 100 per cent), but agrees to charge only if successful. This fee is recoverable from the defendants.

10. How does private enforcement interact with public enforcement?

As set out above, there is a very clear interaction between public and private enforcement in follow-on damages actions – such actions are primarily reliant on the evidential decision published by the regulator. However, in private actions for damages following on from cartel decisions in England and Wales, the regulator will not provide claimants in follow-on litigation with evidential materials going beyond its published decision (although this is unlikely to be problematic as the decision is effectively a coherent presentation of those underlying evidential materials). Nonetheless, the binding nature of regulatory infringement decisions on the courts of England and Wales (as well as the courts of other Member States of the EU) is a powerful weapon in the private litigant's arsenal in litigating against cartelists. Indeed, the fact that a cartelist may be a beneficiary of a leniency program will not protect it from private litigation flowing from the infringement decision of which it is an addressee under the principle of joint and several liability.

Policy developments proposed by the European Commission are likely to lead to legislative changes that will improve claimants' access to compensation for their losses. At a European level, following the publication of its White Paper on Damages Actions for Breach of the EC Antitrust Rules, the European Commission is likely soon to publish a proposal for a directive on rules governing damages actions for infringements of Articles 81 and 82 EC. It is understood that one of its key proposals is that group and representative actions (possibly akin to GLOs and representative actions in England and Wales)

55 [2002] 3 WLR 1104 ('*Factortame*').

should be available throughout the EU. If, as indicated in the Commission's White Paper, representative actions are opt-out in nature (whereby persons or businesses falling into a defined group need not actively be named in a claim but simply represented by a qualified entity, such as a trade association), such a proposal would be a major advance in the effectiveness of EU collective redress mechanisms. This advance – if coupled with proposed solutions to the inequality of the evidential burden in cartel cases and the complexity of issues surrounding the passing-on of cartel overcharges and proposals to set minimum standards for limitation periods – would represent a significant spur in the development of effective collective redress throughout the EU.

Turning to England and Wales, one of the greatest hindrances to the development of an efficient system of domestic collective redress is the non-existence of an opt-out method of collective litigation. The OFT, the European Commission and the CJC have all proposed solutions to this challenge while the European Commission is proposing legislation to allow for the creation of qualified entities to conduct representative actions on an opt-out basis and to make the decisions of national competition authorities binding throughout the EU. Taken together, the proposals of public policy makers and the innovations in case funding and collective redress mechanisms devised by private practitioners are likely to facilitate the continued development of private actions for damages arising from competition infringements in the courts of England and Wales.

17 France

Nathalie Jalabert-Doury[1]

Introduction

In France, private enforcement actions in the antitrust field are dealt with under general tort law rules. Claims are brought pursuant to article 1382 of the Civil Code, which provides that any act which causes damage to another person obliges the party at fault to compensate the victim.

For years, antitrust enforcement was essentially public, with the *Autorité de la Concurrence* (the French Competition Authority or FCA) and the European Commission (EC) being empowered to investigate and impose injunctions and fines on companies participating in antitrust violations. An agency of the Ministry of Economy, the *Direction Générale de la Concurrence, de la Consommation et de la Répression des Fraudes* (DGCCRF) is also empowered to investigate and settle minor cases. However, none of these authorities is empowered to grant damages.

In the past decade, private enforcement actions have developed and are today more numerous than they used to be. But so far, private enforcement remains limited in France, primarily due to restrictions of French judicial procedures concerning access by private parties to evidence, and the absence of any true group or representative actions.

However, the European Commission is advocating the merits of private enforcement to Member States and has made a series of recommendations to promote effective access to justice for victims of competition law infringements – the latest being a draft proposal for a directive on rules governing damages actions for infringement of European competition law which goes far beyond the present French private enforcement system.[2]

At the national level, several proposals have also been made to foster effective mechanisms for full compensation, such as introducing group actions.[3]

All these proposals are on the table but, so far, they have not led to laws or pending legislative proposals. The EC draft proposal for a directive might very well push matters in this direction, but it is uncertain that French law would be amended until an EC directive were adopted and in force. As this draft directive advocates a high level of private enforcement, it may take some time to be adopted and may still undergo significant amendments.

---

1 Attorney At Law, Carreras, Barsikian, Robertson & Partners, Paris.

2 European Commission, *Proposal for a Council Directive on rules governing damages actions for infringement of Articles 81 and 82 of the Treaty*, unpublished.

3 See Conseil de la concurrence, *Avis du 21 Septembre relatif à l'introduction de l'action de groupe en matière de pratiques anticoncurrentielles*, in which the French Competition Authority expresses its support for such a reform; see also the legislative proposal by Mr Luc Chatel on collective consumer actions, which was postponed and then set aside by the Government, Proposed Law N°3055 dated 26 April 2006.

1. How does a damages action case get started?

a. Meeting clients and ethical restrictions

The legal profession is strictly regulated in France. Lawyers being representatives of the law, they are subject to strong ethical rules. As a result, a lawyer must be solicited by a client in order to identify a potential antitrust claim and develop a relationship with the client. The client may inform other victims of the name and contact information of the lawyer, but the lawyer may not solicit other victims to join the action.

Violation of the prohibition on client solicitation is a criminal offence, punishable by a fine of € 4,500 (€ 9,000 for a repeated offence) and/or up to six months in prison.[4] The prohibition applies to any form of personalized offer sent to a potential client.

In 2005, a group of lawyers created a web site by the name of classaction.fr and offered consumers the opportunity to join actions led by these lawyers on consumer issues. The web site was condemned for illicit solicitation by the *Tribunal Correctionnel* (Criminal Court) of Paris, this decision being confirmed by the *Cour de Cassation* (Supreme Court).[5]

b. Investigative tools

i. Follow-on actions Prior or simultaneous governmental action is not a *sine qua non* to a damages action.[6] However, the likelihood of succeeding in a potential claim may be enhanced by a prior competition authority decision in several ways.

The French Competition Authority's decisions are not binding on courts as they relate to different matters (administrative decisions enforcing competition rules on the one hand, disputes between private parties on the other hand).

A prior competition authority decision will nonetheless pave the way for the court on technical issues such as the relevant market and can provide the legal reasoning to conclude that a given behavior qualifies as an infringement. Moreover, in practice, a prior FCA decision will have strong evidential value before courts and the plaintiff will not need to provide the court with as much evidence if evidence can be derived from the competition decision itself.

However, it must be stressed that a prior competition decision does not give direct and immediate access to the government's case file or the evidence collected by the French Competition Authority, which are covered by the principle of confidentiality of the investigation.

Pursuant to article L.463-2 of the *Code de commerce* (Commercial Code), when a case is brought before the Competition Authority the complainant has access to all the contents of the file other than documents containing business secrets. However, pursuant to article L.463-6, the disclosure by one of the parties of information regarding another

---

[4] Article 66-4 of Law n°71-1130 dated 31 December 1971. National Bar Rules, articles 10.1 and 10.2 also prohibit such solicitation and may lead to disciplinary measures (warning, blame, temporary or permanent removal).

[5] 1ère Civ, 30 septembre 2008 n°06-21400.

[6] In some cases, no governmental action is possible. For restrictive practices, no prior public action is available, enforcement being limited to the private sphere (see 7 below).

party or a third party, which could only be obtained by access to the file, is punishable by one year's imprisonment and a fine of €15,000. Accordingly, the complainant normally cannot use such information to bring a follow-on action.[7] Several means may nonetheless be implemented in order to obtain access to these documents for the purpose of a follow-on action (see below).

ii. Stand-alone actions The main obstacle when bringing a stand-alone action relates to the burden of proof. Pursuant to article 9 of the *Code de procedure civile* (Civil Procedure Code), each party must prove the facts necessary to support its claim, and no discovery process exists in order to supplement the evidence gathered by the plaintiff.

Several procedural means may nonetheless be used in order to collect additional evidence. Notably, article 145 of the Code of Civil Procedure enables a would-be plaintiff to ask the Court, *ex parte*, to issue a formal request for evidence to the would-be defendant. These formal requests are made by a bailiff who registers the statements and evidence presented by the company concerned. The bailiff has the power neither to search the company nor to force production of documents. In practice, this procedure may help supplement the evidence amassed by the plaintiff in cases where the plaintiff is able to identify precisely the information to request.[8]

c. Amassing sufficient evidence

The burden of proof consists of three elements for antitrust private enforcement actions. The plaintiff must prove (i) a breach of competition law; (ii) damage or prejudice to the plaintiff; and (iii) a direct causal link between the breach and the harm.

The first decisions of French courts on private enforcement claims reveal that they are requiring a high standard of proof on all three elements of this burden, particularly on the latter two.[9]

Once the action is established, the procedural preparation for cases allows the exchange of arguments and evidence among parties. The intervention of the court in this process is generally limited unless specific requests are made (as detailed below).

A plaintiff may also endeavor to amass sufficient evidence out of court. Any piece of evidence regularly obtained may be produced before a court.

Another request that can be made to the court is to ask for an advisory opinion from the French Competition Authority or the European Commission on a specific competition law matter (see below). In such instances, the Competition Authority may carry out investigations (notably through hearings and written requests for information) in order to provide an opinion on the specific facts of the case.[10]

---

7 See Annual Report of the French Competition Authority 2005, Etude Thématique, p. 145.

8 It is not necessary to identify precisely the document but rather the type of documents likely to contain the information sought (i.e. 'all the correspondence between two companies over a given period of time').

9 See for example the *Arkopharma* and *Juva* decisions in footnote 11.

10 For instance, see French Competition Authority, *Avis n° 05-A-20 du 9 novembre 2005 relatif à une demande présentée par le tribunal de grande instance de Paris concernant un litige opposant la société Luk Lamellen à la société Valeo, available at* www.autoritedelaconcurrence.fr.

2. Who may pursue a claim?
To pursue a claim, a party must have an interest in the case, that has to be personal (the prejudice has been suffered by the plaintiff), existing and real (the prejudice has already materialized), and legitimate.

a. Direct purchasers
Direct purchasers normally have a sufficient interest to pursue a claim against anticompetitive practices by their suppliers. However, the prejudice they may claim is limited to the damage they effectively suffered. Notably, if the price increase was passed on to customers, this reduces or may even annul any prejudice.

Following the vitamins cartel case, a customer of cartel members pursued a claim before French courts asserting that the cartel resulted in price increases which could not entirely be passed on to consumers. This claim was rejected for failure to provide sufficient and accurate evidence that the claimant suffered prejudice directly caused by the cartel offence at hand, whereas the claimant presumably could have passed on a price increase that was applied by all the industry.[11]

b. Indirect purchasers
Although there does not seem to be published precedent in the antitrust field, an indirect purchaser can generally claim damages from a supplier as a secondary victim, provided that a distinct and personal prejudice can be evidenced (for example a passed-on price increase and subsequent margin loss).

c. Competitors
Competitors also normally have a sufficient interest to file a claim. These private enforcement actions have grown considerably in the past few years, notably with respect to exclusionary behavior.

d. Suppliers
Actions by suppliers are less frequent than actions by customers, but they also normally have an interest in asking for compensation for damage caused, for example, by purchasers in dominance or by a purchasing cartel.

e. Others
A party to a restrictive agreement is also entitled to bring a claim, as decided by the European Court of Justice.[12] However, litigants may not profit from their own unlawful conduct, such that damages are unavailable when a party is found to bear significant responsibility for the distortion of competition.

---

[11] Nanterre Commercial Court, 11 May 2006, *Arkopharma*; Paris Commercial Court, 26 January 2007, *Juva Santé et Juva Production SED c/ Société Hoffmann La Roche AG*.

[12] ECJ, 20 September 2001, *Courage Ltd v Bernard Crehan and Bernard Crehan v Courage Ltd and Others*, Case C–453/99.

3. In what forum does a plaintiff initiate a private claim?

a. Civil and commercial courts

First, the *Tribunaux de commerce* (Commercial Courts) have jurisdiction on disputes between persons engaged in commerce, on disputes concerning commercial companies and concerning acts of commerce. Other disputes are heard by the *Tribunaux de Grande Instance* (main civil courts) except for minor claims (handled by *Tribunaux d'Instance*).

Pursuant to article 42 of the Code of Civil Procedure, the territorially competent court is, unless otherwise provided, that of the place where the defendant is domiciled. If there are several defendants, the plaintiff may choose to bring the case before a court where one of them is domiciled.

It shall be noted that, pursuant to article L.420-7, cases relating to the application of national antitrust law and Articles 81 and 82 of the EC Treaty[13] are allocated to specialized chambers within a limited number of courts at the two first levels of judicial review. More precisely, specialized chambers within eight different main civil courts and within eight Commercial Courts, with extended territorial jurisdiction, will rule on disputes involving competition rules, while only the *Cour d'appel de Paris* (Appeal Court of Paris) will review their decisions.[14]

Pursuant to EC Regulation 44/2001,[15] which is applicable to all cases brought before a Member State court by persons domiciled in a Member State, the claimant may either bring the case in the Member State where the harmful event caused by a breach of competition law occurred or may occur, or in the Member State where the defendant or one of the defendants is domiciled.

Additionally, specific provisions apply to French nationals: articles 14 and 15 of the *Code civil* (Civil Code) provide that French courts may always have jurisdiction when the claimant is French in cases involving an international contract or a fault committed abroad, even when the defendant is not a French national.

b. Criminal courts

Under article L.420-6 of the French Commerce Code, it is also a criminal offense for a natural person to fraudulently, personally and decisively take part in the conception, organization or implementation of an infringement to competition rules.

However, the status of complainant before criminal courts is not satisfactory compared to a civil or commercial action. First, the criminal procedure is not led by the complainant but by the prosecution. Second, criminal courts are focused on establishing and

---

13 On 1 December 2009, the Treaty of Lisbon came into effect, amending the Treaty Establishing the European Community (EC Treaty) that is now called the Treaty on the Functioning of the European Union (TFEU). Therefore, all references to Articles 81 and 82 of the EC Treaty now reference Articles 101 and 102 TFEU.

14 Changing *rationae loci* jurisdiction for disputes related to the application of competition rules raises complex issues of allocation of jurisdiction, notably for mixed cases involving both competition issues and non-competition issues; see for example Main Civil Court, Béthune, 4 April 2007, *SA Quaron c/ Roquette Frères*.

15 Council Regulation (EC) No 44/2001 of 22 December 2000 on jurisdiction and the recognition and enforcement of judgments in civil and commercial matters, OJ L 012, 16.01.2001, pp. 0001–0023.

sanctioning the infringement, the allocation of damages being only an ancillary mission of theirs.[16] As a result, private enforcement claims rarely begin before criminal courts.

A criminal complaint may lead to police investigations including searches and seizures within business premises and homes.

c. Administrative courts

Administrative courts have jurisdiction for claims relating to acts or contracts involving public authorities or parties acting with powers of public authority. Any act by a public authority must comply with French and EC competition laws.

There are no specialized administrative courts for the application of competition law (as is the case with civil and commercial courts).

Administrative courts also have jurisdiction for actions brought by public entities to obtain compensation and/or the annulment of the subsequent contract in cases of bid-rigging. Several claims have been lodged by the French railway company in the past years, with success.[17]

d. Arbitration

Compensation may also be sought in arbitration proceedings. The Paris Court of Appeal has ruled that arbitrators have jurisdiction to decide upon the existence and consequences of an infringement of EC and national competition law.[18]

Arbitration courts do not have investigative authority, but may request the parties to produce evidence and utilize their broad interpretative powers to draw conclusions from a refusal by a party.

4. How may claims be aggregated?

a. Collective claims

Group actions do not exist under French law. However, calls for reform introducing group actions have been made and the French Competition Authority is in favor of such a reform as well.[19]

Moreover, pursuant to the draft proposed EC directive, Member States would have to ensure that two or more injured parties who suffered harm caused by the same infringement of competition law could jointly bring a group action for damages.[20] If adopted, the directive would thus require significant amendments to French procedure rules, which so far do not allow treating the action of different plaintiffs as one single action or joinder of an existing action as provided in Article 5 of the draft directive.

---

16 Article 475-1 of the Criminal Procedure Code.

17 See Administrative Supreme Court, 19 December 2007, *SNCF v. Campenon*; 19 March 2008, *SNCF v. Fougerolle Ballot* and *SNCF v. Dumez*.

18 Paris Court of Appeal, 19 May 1993, *Labinal*.

19 French Competition Authority, *Avis du 21 Septembre relatif à l'introduction de l'action de groupe en matière de pratiques anticoncurrentielles*.

20 European Commission, *Proposal for a Council Directive on rules governing damages actions for infringement of Articles 81 and 82 of the Treaty*, article 4, unofficial and unpublished draft.

b. Representative claims

Representative claims may be brought by a consumers' association if the association is registered and recognized as representative on a national level and mandated in writing by at least two consumers who suffered individual damage caused by the same business practice (article L.422-1 of the Consumer Code).

In such a case, the association merely exercises the individual right of action of each consumer in a single claim. The allocated damages, if any, are granted to the individual consumers and not to the association, and no allocation of attorneys' fees appears in published decisions. Costs should be allocated to consumers individually as this is a representative action, but this remains unclear. In addition, the association may be held liable under its mandate towards consumers should its action fail (including for legal costs to be borne by consumers).

Consumer mandates can be solicited neither by means of a public appeal on radio or television, nor by means of advertising, by tract or personalized letter. For instance, a representative claim lodged by UFC Que Choisir, a consumers' association, on behalf of 3,606 consumers following the *Mobile Telephony Case* where the National Competition Authority heavily condemned the three major mobile operators in France for an agreement to stabilize market shares,[21] was rejected on the grounds that the association had made illegal solicitations to collect mandates from victims in order to bring this representative action.[22]That case is rather emblematic of the difficulty to ensure private enforcement under French present rules where numerous claims of limited amounts are involved. An appeal is presently *sub judice*.

The EC draft proposal for a Council directive, if adopted, would require significant amendments to the French rules on representative claims. The draft directive indeed provides for a representative action, allowing registered associations to file an action which would represent all those who may have claims and are entitled to damages. The merits of the EC proposal is that it is based on registered associations, as it exists in French law, but the directive – if adopted – would nonetheless require a significant evolution of our procedural rules, which are based on a totally different approach.

c. Public interest litigation

Duly declared associations whose statutory purpose includes the protection of consumers' interests may introduce claims on facts causing a direct or indirect prejudice to the collective interest of consumers (article L.421-1 and 2 of the Consumer Code). This allows associations to initiate cases and obtain the termination of the wrongful conduct, but such actions rarely lead to significant damages, as the association may only claim compensation for the collective prejudice of its members, but not the individual prejudice of each of them (see above).

If the claim succeeds, the consumers' association can also recover costs and part of its attorney fees (see however below).

---

[21] € 534 million were imposed on the three mobile operators, Decision n°05-D-65 dated 30 November 2006.

[22] Paris Commercial Court, Paris, 6 December 2007, *UFC Que Choisir v Bouygues Telecom*.

Moreover, pursuant to legal provisions on restrictive practices (see below), the French Minister of the Economy has a specific right of action before civil and commercial courts to have such practices ordered to cease, have unlawful clauses or contracts declared void in respect of such practices, and request reimbursement of the sums improperly paid or any other form of compensation to the injured persons, as well as the imposition of a civil fine (article L.442-6 III Commercial Code). This is an independent right of action, the object of which is to ensure the protection of the proper functioning of the market and competition.

d. Is there joint and several liability?

Pursuant to settled case law, conspirators in an act causing damage may be jointly liable to compensate for such damage, with a right of contribution against co-defendants in case one of them is called to pay more than the share he shall contribute.[23]

5. What procedural defenses are available short of trial?

French courts may deliver preliminary rulings useful for the discussion of substantive issues such as a ruling on liability before assessing damages, but they rarely deliver rulings on procedural issues preventing a full trial. The only significant exception to this is in jurisdictional issues, for which courts may deliver a preliminary ruling limited to the subject.

In any event, parties are invited to plead on the whole case pending the decision of the court whether to deliver a preliminary ruling or a full decision.

6. What devices are available to obtain evidence?

a. Evidence gathering

With regards to evidence, the *actori incumbit probatio* principle applies and any form of evidence is admissible, as long as it has been regularly obtained (see above).

i. Exchange of evidence between parties Documents in the possession of the other party may be requested, but parties are under no obligation to submit to such requests. The requesting party may ask the court to order the communication of such documents (article 142 Civil Procedure Code), but these requests are rarely granted by courts due to the *actori incumbit probatio* principle.

ii. Requests to the Court The court has the authority to order *sua sponte* any legally appropriate investigative measures.[24]

Notably, courts can be requested to order communication of documents held by the parties, third parties (article 139 Civil Procedure Code) as well as public bodies, including the French NCA (article 11 Civil Procedure Code). This procedure is, however, rarely implemented by courts.

---

23 For an example, see Paris Court of Appeal, *Speedy France*.
24 *Ibid.* article 10.

iii. Request to the public bodies including the NCA A law of 17 July 1978[25] provides for a general right of access to documents held by the French administration. Such a right applies to official records and reports held by the competition authorities,[26] and shall be denied only when the disclosure of the documents would obstruct the proper functioning of procedures engaged in by the administration or contain information covered by privilege, such as the principle of secrecy of criminal investigations (if a criminal procedure is launched).

If documents are not available, it is possible to ask the *Commission d'Accès aux Documents Administratifs (Agency for access to documents)*, to deliver a public but non-binding opinion on the case. This Agency has already delivered several opinions in favor of would-be plaintiffs who were denied a right of access by the competition authorities.

b. Searches
Civil and commercial courts do not have the power to order searches in the context of a private claim.

c. Experts
Where necessary, the court may appoint an independent registered expert to deliver an opinion on a specific matter.[27] The judge is not bound by the findings or conclusions of the expert,[28] whose role it is to provide guidance to the court. In practice however, courts rely to a large extent on the technical assessments made by registered experts.

Experts are very commonly appointed in damages actions for infringement of competition law, particularly in order to quantify the damage suffered by the plaintiff.[29] The expert will investigate the factual issues listed in the court's appointment order, on an *inter partes* basis, and will submit his final report after hearing the observations of the parties.

The plaintiff may also appoint a private expert if the court does not appoint a registered expert, or as a preliminary step in order to obtain such an appointment. Private experts' opinions produced by the parties have less evidential value than a registered expert's opinion.

7. What practices are illegal and what are the elements of proof?
As a preliminary matter, it should be noted that pursuant to article 3(1) of EC Regulation 1/2003,[30] courts of the Member States must apply Article 81 EC to agreements, decisions by associations of undertakings and concerted practices which may affect trade between

---

25 Loi n°78-753 du 17 juillet 1978 portant diverses mesures d'amélioration des relations entre l'administration et le public et diverses dispositions d'ordre administratif, social et fiscal.

26 Conseil d'Etat, 1st March 2004, *Société civile de moyens Imagerie Médicale du Nivolet.*

27 Code of Civil Procedure, article 232 *et seq.*

28 *Ibid.*, article 246.

29 For instance, see Paris Court of Appeal, 30 September 1998, *Labinal*; and 22 October 2001, *UGAP/CAMIF.*

30 Council Regulation (EC) No 1/2003 of 16 December 2002 on the implementation of the rules on competition laid down in Articles 81 and 82 of the Treaty (Text with EEA relevance), OJ L 1, 4.1.2003, pp. 1–25.

Member States, when they apply national competition law to such agreements, decisions or concerted practices. Similarly, when the courts apply national competition law to any abuse prohibited by Article 82 of the EC Treaty, they must also apply Article 82 EC.

Pursuant to Article 3(2) of Regulation 1/2003, the application of national competition law may not lead to the prohibition of agreements, decisions and concerted practices which may affect trade between Member States, but do not restrict competition within the meaning of Article 81(1) of the EC Treaty, or which fulfill the conditions of Article 81(3) of the EC Treaty[31] or are covered by a Regulation for the application of Article 81(3) of the EC Treaty.

a. Horizontal and vertical restraints

Pursuant to article L.420-1 of the Commercial Code, concerted practices, agreements, and explicit or tacit understandings are prohibited, even through the direct or indirect intermediation of a company in the group established outside France, when they are designed for or may have the effect of preventing, restricting or distorting competition in a given market. This is especially true when they tend to:

- limit market access or free competition by other undertakings;
- hinder the free market determination of prices by artificially promoting increases or reductions;
- limit or control production, market outlets, investments or technical progress or
- share markets or supply sources.

The following elements must be proved by the claimant in order to establish the existence of a prohibited agreement: (1) an agreement or a concerted practice (2) between two or more entities (3) having a restrictive object or effect.

Cartels, concerted practices and anticompetitive agreements between third parties are the hardest cases to deal with under private enforcement mechanisms due to the difficulty of collecting evidence in such cases.

b. Single firm conduct

Article L.420-2 of the Commercial Code prohibits abuses of a dominant position. The analysis of a claim requires the prior definition of the relevant market, which is defined as the area in which the demand for and supply of products or services that are considered to be economic substitutes by consumers actually overlap. As a dominant position is not prohibited *per se*, it must further be proven that the dominant company has adopted behavior that has the object or likely effect of preventing, restricting or distorting competition. For instance, practices such as predatory pricing, refusal to sell, discriminatory pricing or tie-in sales are prohibited when implemented by a dominant company.

---

[31] Which exempts from the application of Article 81(1) EC agreements, decisions and concerted practices which contribute to improving the production or distribution of goods or to promoting technical or economic progress, while allowing consumers a fair share of the resulting benefit, provided they do not impose on the undertakings concerned restrictions which are not indispensable to the attainment of these objectives or afford such undertakings the possibility of eliminating competition in respect of a substantial part of the products in question.

Furthermore, article L.420-2(2), prohibiting the abuse of the economic dependency of a customer or a supplier, applies specifically to vertical relationships. Practices such as a refusal to sell, tie-in-sales or discriminatory selling, as well as the termination of established business relations for the mere reason that the client or supplier has refused to agree to unjustified commercial conditions, amount to abuses of economic dependency.

Economic dependency cases are very frequently dealt with before courts as sufficient evidence is generally available to the victim. Dominance cases generally require more detailed evidence, as well as detailed technical assessments, making them sometimes easier to deal with before competition authorities rather than courts.

c. Restrictive practices

Under articles L 440-1 et seq. of the French Commercial Code, a number of business practices such as imposition of disproportionate obligations on a trading partner, brutal termination of commercial relationships, etc are also considered restrictive. These provisions are not enforced by the FCA but by civil and commercial courts, which have full jurisdiction to order compensation for the prejudice suffered by the victims.

d. What industries are exempt?

State-owned companies, as well as companies enjoying exclusive or special rights from Member States (companies assuming obligations of general interest, such as universal postal or telecommunication services), complicate the filing of a private action at two levels. First, they raise complex jurisdiction issues (whether civil and commercial courts or administrative courts have jurisdiction). Also, such companies raise substantive difficulties, as Article 86 of the EC Treaty[32] provides that competition law applies to these companies only insofar as it does not obstruct the performance of their mission of general interest.

8. What do plaintiffs get if they win?

a. Single versus treble or punitive damages

There are no treble or punitive damages under French law. Compensation is only granted in proportion to the actual loss (*damnum emergens*) and the loss of profit (*lucrum cessans*).

A group of law professors suggested in a 2005 report to the Minister of Justice that punitive damages should be awarded when the defendant has manifestly committed a deliberate fault, especially when the defendant benefited from such a fault.[33] However, no action has been taken so far on the basis of this report and the legal and business community has voiced significant concerns on the introduction of punitive damages, our system being based on the principle that the victim is only entitled to recover for the damage effectively suffered.[34]

---

[32] After entering into effect the Treaty on the functioning of the European Union (TFEU) all references to Article 86 of the EC Treaty reference Article 106 TFEU.

[33] Avant-projet de réforme du droit des obligations Catala, 2006, article 1371.

[34] For instance, see R. Saint Esteben, *Pour ou contre les dommages et intérêts punitifs*, Petites Affiches, 20 January 2005, p. 53.

b. Damage measure

Any type of damage, including material, moral, loss of chance and loss of profits, may be compensated as long as it is direct and certain. Moral damage and loss of chance are, however, very complex to quantify, frequently limiting compensation of that damage.

Besides this principle, there is no specific method of damages calculation; the calculation is made on a case by case basis. Damages are frequently awarded, notably in follow on actions, but generally much less than the amounts claims.

c. Prejudgment interest

In all matters, the award of compensation involves interest at the statutory rate,[35] even failing a claim in this respect or a specific provision in the judgment. Unless otherwise provided by legislation, interest runs from the declaration of the judgment unless the judge rules to the contrary, which is extremely rare.

Compound interest may be awarded at the request of the claimant.

d. Indemnification or contribution

A defendant can join a third party to the action as a co-defendant in order for the latter to contribute to the damages awarded to the victim if the third party contributed to such damage.

e. Fees

Pursuant to article 696 of the Code of Civil Procedure, judicial costs – such as the cost of an expert ordered by the court – are borne by the losing party, unless the judge, by a reasoned decision, imposes the whole or part of them on another party.

Moreover, pursuant to article 700 of the same Code, the judge may order the party bearing the judicial costs or the losing party to cover other legal expenses incurred by the other party such as lawyers fees.[36] The amount set by the judge pursuant to this provision is usually less than the costs effectively incurred.

f. Equitable remedies

In emergency situations, the court may order all measures that are not reasonably challenged by the defendant or which the existence of the dispute justifies.[37]

Moreover, even where confronted with a serious challenge by the defendant, the court may order protective measures or measures to restore the original situation of the parties if they are necessary to avoid imminent damage or to abate a manifestly illegal nuisance.[38]

For instance, pursuant to these provisions, a French court ordered a telecom operator to stop tying its own Wireless Application Protocol portal to the mobile phones it

---

[35] See *décret n° 2009-138 du 9 février 2009 fixant le taux de l'intérêt légal pour l'année 2009*. In 2009, the statutory rate was 3.79%.

[36] Article 700 of the Code of Civil Procedure.

[37] Code of Civil Procedure, articles 808 (applicable in civil courts) and 872 (applicable in commercial courts).

[38] Code of Civil Procedure, articles 809 (applicable in civil courts) and 873 (applicable in commercial courts).

marketed, and to provide untied devices, enabling competitors to provide their own WAP portal.[39]

g. Limitation periods

Pursuant to article 2270-1 of the Civil Code, tort liability claims are barred after ten years from the manifestation of the injury or its aggravation.

9. How does the plaintiff's lawyer finance private enforcement?

Lawyers' fees may generally be freely determined between the lawyer and client (by the hour/for a set price), but true contingency fee agreements are prohibited.[40] It is permitted, however, to set a part of the lawyer's fees in proportion to the damages awarded.[41]

10. How does private enforcement interact with public enforcement?

a. Initiation of cases

The French Competition Authority may initiate cases before courts, including criminal courts, for the application of article L.420-6 of the Commerce Code (see above).

The Minister of Economy may also initiate cases before courts for restrictive practices (see above).

Courts are not empowered to refer or initiate cases in front of the French Competition Authority, but they may request an advisory opinion (see above).

b. Extraterritoriality

French courts have jurisdiction to allocate damages for prejudice suffered in France or by French nationals (see above). These claims are mainly dealt with under EC and French law, which apply to any competitive restraint producing its effects in France, notwithstanding any contrary contractual provision.

According to settled case law, if a claim is filed by a French national in a French court concerning prejudice suffered abroad to which different laws would apply, the court would apply the foreign law.

c. Extent of cooperation of private and public officials

Significant cooperation has developed between courts and the competition authorities (EC Commission and FCA) first through EC mechanisms[42] and later through initiatives from the French authority.

---

[39] CA Paris, 30 May and 13 July 2000, *Wappup.com v Itineris*.

[40] National Bar Rules, article 11.

[41] Artificial fixed fees (for example € 1) would presumably be considered as a circumvention of the prohibition of *quota litis*, but the Supreme Court ruled that there is no condition in the law that the contingent part remains inferior or proportionate to the fixed part, Supreme Court, 10 July 1995, n°93-20.290.

[42] See notably the 2004 EC Notice on cooperation between the EC Commission and national courts.

As mentioned above, the EC Commission and the FCA may intervene as amicus curiae and courts may themselves ask for information and advisory opinions from these competition authorities.

d. Effect of binding decisions of a national authority and local jurisdictions, administrative court and civil court, or (EU-only) of European Commission and national competition authorities

Pursuant to Article 16 of Regulation 1/2003 EC, national courts cannot make decisions on practices under EC Treaty Articles 81 or 82 running contrary to decisions adopted by the EC Commission.

The same is not true for the FCA's decisions, which are not binding on national courts.[43] However, in practice, courts rely to a significant extent on decisions of the FCA, and this alleviates somewhat the burden of proof on the plaintiff.

e. Interplay with leniency programs of the national authority and local jurisdictions or (EU-only) of the European Commission and national competition authorities

Where a company is granted leniency, the FCA will be reluctant to provide assistance to the plaintiff on private enforcement issues in order not to undermine the attractiveness of its leniency program, which only provides for immunity or reduction of fines.[44]

In this respect, the French NCA specified in its annual report for 2005[45] that the effectiveness of leniency programs could characterize a legitimate right to not produce evidence requested by courts. Legal privilege and business secrecy are also considered to be legitimate impediments.

The French Competition Authority is similarly reluctant to refer cases for criminal action against individuals working for companies admitted to leniency.

Conclusion

The French system can certainly be improved in order to allow for a more effective private enforcement of competition rules, and the release of the draft EC directive may, in itself, be considered as an indication that private enforcement systems such as the French one may not appropriately ensure the full effectiveness of EC competition rules.

However, the prospect of bringing US style class action raises strong objections both from the business community as well as from the legal community considering that our procedural system is far different: actions are individual, damages are strictly limited to the prejudice suffered, and lawyers are prevented from intervening on a purely contingency basis.

We shall rapidly see whether the EC is able to set and advocate a median position, on which Member States can agree and move forward.

---

[43] And vice versa: see Paris Court of Appeal, 17 March 1998, *Syndicat des pharmaciens de l'Aveyron*.

[44] Article L 464-2 of the Commercial Code and Procedure Guidance of the FCA on the French leniency program, 2 March 2009.

[45] Annual Report 2005, *Etude thématique*, p.145.

18 Germany

Philipp von Dietze and Eckart Brödermann[1]

Introduction

Private enforcement of antitrust law is both a long-standing practice and a new phenomenon in German case law. The reason for such an astonishing statement is simple. Antitrust law in Germany covers three areas: prohibition of cartels, prohibition of the abuse of a dominant market position and merger control. In the past, German courts have had many opportunities to deal with private actions of companies claiming that other companies have abused their dominant position by, for example, refusing to supply, refusing access to an essential facility or predatory pricing, while actions against members of cartels have been very rare. The public has seen several such actions in German courts: against the vitamin cartel (*Hoffmann-La Roche*), which was settled out of court; against a cartel of cement manufacturers, which is still pending, and recently a new action filed against the members of a hydrogen peroxide cartel.

Actions for damages have significant hurdles to overcome. The reform of the German Act against Restraints of Competition (i.e. the *Gesetz gegen Wettbewerbsbeschränkungen*, hereinafter referred to as GWB) in 2005 lowered some of these hurdles. However, in Germany and other European countries, the legal framework still does not provide for an effective legal regime of private enforcement of damages claims against members of cartels. For this reason, the European Commission in 2005 issued the *Green Paper on Damages Actions for Breach of EC Antitrust Rules*[2] and, after in-depth consultation, in April 2008 published a subsequent *White Paper on Damages Actions for Breach of the EC Antitrust Rules*[3] comprising concrete recommendations for a harmonized European private law to serve as a unified base for effective private enforcement of damages claims against cartels. The European Commission is making efforts to propose a directive on rules governing damages actions for infringements of Articles 81 and 82 of the EC Treaty.[4] A brief insight into a draft proposal shows that the European Commission is taking steps towards the US American approach, in particular by introducing opt-out collective actions and disclosure burden which are a close resemblance to their US models, the class action and pre-trial discovery provisions.[5]

---

1 Philipp von Dietze and Eckart Brödermann are managing partners of the German law firm Brödermann & Jahn Rechtsanwaltsgesellschaft mbH.

2 European Commission, COM(2005)672, 19.12.2005.

3 European Commission, COM(2008)165 final, 2.4.2008.

4 On 1.12.2009, the Treaty of Lisbon came into effect, amending the Treaty Establishing the European Community (EC Treaty) that is now called the Treaty on the Functioning of the European Union (TFEU). Therefore, all references to Articles 81 and 82 of the EC Treaty now reference Articles 101 and 102 TFEU.

5 European Commission, Proposal for a Council Directive on Rules governing Damages Actions for Infringements of Articles of 81 and 82 of the Treaty (draft of 2009, no concrete date), not officially published.

This chapter focuses on relevant issues potential plaintiffs should bear in mind if they want to bring a private damages action. The analysis covers the essential substantive and procedural aspects of current German private antitrust enforcement rules in the GWB. In view of the initiatives taken by the European Commission and the legislative measures which are likely to follow, the field of antitrust damages suits should not be regarded as static. Rather, it should be seen as 'work in progress', one which requires updated awareness and knowledge of changes in the relevant laws.

1. The start of a private antitrust case

Any work of a lawyer requires clients. In Germany, soliciting clients is restricted by the German professional regulation.[6] A simple example of such restrictions is the one that an outside counsel is not permitted to contact the in-house lawyer of a company which is known to have suffered substantial losses from price fixing by a cartel and to propose initiation of a lawsuit against the members of this cartel.

Private plaintiffs who suffered harm caused by a breach of German or EC antitrust laws can bring an action for damages against the infringer in German courts. Such private antitrust litigation for damages can be brought independently of public enforcement actions (stand-alone actions)[7] or following a successful prosecution by a public enforcement agency (follow-on actions).[8] Stand-alone actions generally pose substantial risks for the plaintiff, in particular in respect of the high costs and the long duration of litigation as well as the burden of proof which is not in favor of private plaintiffs. Follow-on actions as an effective procedural tool were introduced through §33 (4) GWB which was supplemented into the GWB on the basis of experiences of established court practice prior to the GWB reform: i.e. civil courts treated statements by cartel authorities essentially as prima facie evidence.[9] Such decisions of cartel authorities are binding upon German courts with regard to the existence of an infringement.

In addition to claims for damages, a company which believes itself to be a victim of an abuse of a dominant position may file for an injunction to prohibit the dominant company from continuing its abusive conduct. Customers of a firm which is a member of a price-fixing cartel may also file for a similar injunction. To date, however, there are no known cases in which a company with such a claim has successfully forced another company through an interim measure to lower prices. In a stand-alone action, the plaintiff (and the court) would have no means to examine whether competitors have fixed prices. Consequently, any such interim measure has to be issued by the cartel

---

[6] The most important ones are the Federal Lawyer Regulations (*Bundesrechtsanwaltsordnung*, BRAO), the Professional Regulations for Lawyers (*Berufsordnung*, BORA), the Specialist Lawyer Regulations (*Fachanwaltsordnng*, FAO) as well as the Lawyers Fee Act (*Rechtsanwaltsvergütungsgesetz*, RVG).

[7] Section 33 (1), (2) and (3) GWB.

[8] Section 33 (4) GWB.

[9] See *Wurmnest*, A New Era for Private Antitrust Litigation in Germany? A Critical Appraisal of the Modernized Law against Restraints of Competition, in: German Law Journal, Vol. 06 No. 08/2005, pp. 1173–1189, 1185. *Cf. Rolf Hempel*, Private Follow-on Klagen im Kartellrecht, in: WuW 2/2005, p. 137.

authorities[10] and is therefore not available to private plaintiffs. Under German law, the customer is entitled to file an application with the cartel authorities to request such an interim measure which is governed by public law.

With respect to follow-on actions, specific legislation was introduced to regulate the statutory period of limitations for actions which largely follows the general rules for limitation of actions in the BGB (the German Civil Code, *Bürgerliches Gesetzbuch*, BGB).[11] Section 33 (5) GWB provides for suspension of the running of this general limitation period if a German cartel authority initiates an infringement proceeding. The same applies to antitrust investigations launched by the European Commission or a cartel authority of another EC Member State. The suspension terminates six months after the competition authority has made a final decision or ended the investigation by other means.[12] This specific legislation allows potential plaintiffs to await the outcome of public enforcement, which may last for several years, before filing their actions for damages in German courts.

2. Who may pursue a claim?

In Germany a private damages action can be filed by affected parties or an association with legal capacity. Moreover, a third party to whom damages claims have been assigned from other cartel victims can also file a damages action, which will be discussed below in Part 5.

a. Affected parties

The 7th Amendment of the GWB introduced a new term, 'affected parties,' to limit the scope of potential plaintiffs. Any affected party (*Betroffener*) may demand (i) removal of an anticompetitive measure carried out by a party which has infringed the provisions of GWB, Article 81 or 82 of the EC Treaty (*Beseitigung*); (ii) injunctive relief (*Unterlassung*) from the party which has infringed cartel laws; or (iii) injunctive relief from the party which has infringed the decision of the cartel authority.[13] An 'affected party' is defined as a 'competitor (*Mitbewerber*) or other market participant (*sonstiger Marktbeteiligter*) impaired by the violation of competition law.'[14] However, the wording of the provision does not give a clear definition of the scope of the 'affected parties', especially with respect to the question whether an indirect effect of the price fixing and/or indirect damage are already sufficient in order for the party in question to be deemed as 'affected'.[15] Therefore, it is still an open question whether, in cases of horizontal cartels, indirect purchasers, i.e. entities which have purchased goods or services at inflated prices

---

10 According to §48 GWB, the cartel authorities in Germany are the Federal Cartel Office (*Bundeskartellamt*), the Ministry of Economy and Technology (*Ministerium für Wirtschaft und Technologie*) and the highest regional authorities (*oberste Landesbehörde*) established according to the specific state laws.

11 *Cf.* §§194–213 BGB. See further below at Part 8 b) (dd).

12 *Cf.* §33 (5) GWB in conjunction with §204 (2) BGB.

13 Section 33 (1) Sentence 1 GWB.

14 Section 33 (1) Sentence 3 GWB.

15 *Lübbig*, Münchener Kommentar: Europäisches und Deutsches Wettbewerbsrecht (Kartellrecht), Band 2, Beck 2008, §33 GWB, Rn. 48.

in downstream markets, are also entitled to claim damages against the suppliers which have formed the cartel.[16]

b. Association with legal capacity

The 7th Amendment of GWB extended the scope of potential plaintiffs to associations with legal capacity (*rechtsfähiger Verband*) to act as an abstract 'affected party.'[17] Under the GWB, such an association with legal capacity can both file a competition-related action and require the economic benefit of the illegal gains (*Herausgabe der Vorteilabschöpfung*) to the Federal Treasury.[18]

An association with legal capacity is legally defined in §33 (2) GWB. The definition requires first the 'legal capacity' of an association, but no specific limitation of legal forms, so that it can be an association of companies subject to private law, a chamber of industry and commerce, i.e. an entity existing under public law, as well as a craft guild.[19] Among other[20] requirements, the association shall serve to advance 'the interests of commerce and freelancers as well as professionals', and shall have a considerable number of members who trade in the same or similar products on the same market.[21] It is important to note that a 'consumer protection association' cannot be qualified as an association within the meaning of §33 (2) GWB, and therefore cannot file a private damages action.

In practice, actions by such associations are rare, since – as outlined before – the outcome of the proceeding, i.e. the payments by the convicted cartel member, flows directly to the Federal Treasury. The 'best case' scenario for such an association would be to be reimbursed for its legal expenses by the losing party, i.e. the member of the cartel which has been sued, or – to the extent the losing party has not reimbursed the costs – by the Federal Cartel Office.[22] Obviously, the present legal situation does not provide sufficient incentive to go to court.

3. In what forum does a plaintiff initiate a private claim?

Private antitrust litigation is normally brought in the German civil courts.[23] The Regional Courts (*Landgericht*, LG) are exclusively competent for any civil litigation arising from infringements of competition law.[24] The geographical competence of the courts within

---

16 *Wurmnest*, A New Era for Private Antitrust Litigation in Germany? A Critical Appraisal of the Modernized Law against Restraints of Competition, in: German Law Journal, Vol. 06 No. 08/2005, pp. 1173–1189, 1181.

17 See §33 (2) GWB, *Cf. Lübbig*, Münchener Kommentar: Europäisches und Deutsches Wettbewerbsrecht (Kartellrecht), Band 2, Beck 2008, §33 GWB, Rn. 68.

18 Section 34a (1) GWB.

19 See Decision of Federal Court of Justice (BGH) of 14 March 2000, in: WuW 07-08/2005, pp. 737–739, DE-R 485–487. *Cf Lübbig*, Münchener Kommentar: Europäisches und Deutsches Wettbewerbsrecht (Kartellrecht), Band 2, Beck 2008, §33 GWB, Rn. 72.

20 More see *Lubbig*, Münchener Kommentar: Europäisches und Deutsches Wettbewerbsrecht (Kartellrecht), Band 2, Beck 2008, §33 GWB, Rn. 72.

21 Section 33 (2) GWB.

22 See §34a GWB.

23 An exception to the general exclusive forum competence of civil courts refers to social insurance cases; see further §87 Sentence 3 GWB, *cf. Bechtold*, Kommentar zum GWB, Beck 2008, 5. Edition, §87 Rn. 13.

24 Section 87 GWB.

Germany for competition-related claims is generally determined by the criteria of the German Code of Civil Procedure (*Zivilprozessordnung*, ZPO). As regards appeals arising from damages claims as such, special cartel law panels at the Higher Regional Courts (*Oberlandesgericht*) shall be organized and hold exclusive competence.[25] Further appeals on questions of law only (*Revision*) will be decided by the panel for cartel law at the Federal Court of Justice.[26]

The issue over jurisdiction for damages claim matters in the European Community is determined by the Brussels Regulation,[27] according to which the court where the defendant has its seat has jurisdiction (Article 2 Brussels Regulation). Furthermore, antitrust damages claim actions may also be filed in courts located where the damage allegedly occurred (Article 5 No. 3 Brussels Regulation). The place where the damage occurred is deemed to be the place where the market is distorted by the price-fixing of the cartel members. However, this specific jurisdiction rule shall, however, only apply if the defendant is domiciled in an EU Member State.

Example: a cartel consists of two companies, one of them having its seat in Germany, the other in the United Kingdom. The cartel has fixed prices in the German market. Both companies may be sued in Germany – the German company according to Article 2 of the Brussels Regulation and the UK-domiciled company according to Article 5 No. 3 of the Brussels Regulation. However, on the basis of the well-known judgment of the European Court of Justice in the *Shevill* case,[28] the action against the UK-domiciled company may only aim to collect compensation for damage suffered in the German market while the action against the German company may recover compensation for damage suffered worldwide. The *Shevill doctrine* restricts an action filed with courts competent on the basis of Article 5 No. 3 of the Brussels Regulation to the damage suffered on the market in the Member State of the court, while an action filed with courts competent on the basis of Article 2 of the Brussels Regulation is not restricted in any way regarding the damage suffered.

As a cartel consists of at least two companies, it may often occur that these companies have their seats in different Member States. Article 6 of the Brussels Regulation opens up a way to sue them in the court of a state where either one of them is domiciled. This clause does not apply for companies which have no seat within the EU.

4. Applicable law

Filing an action with a German court does not mean that the court will apply German civil law. The question regarding which law shall be applied is answered by the rules of conflict of law (international private law). Since 16 January 2009 these rules have been set forth in the Rome II Regulation.[29]

Antitrust cases are dealt with in Article 6 paragraph 3 Rome II, which provides that

---

25 Section 91 GWB.

26 Section 94 GWB.

27 Council Regulation (EC) No 44/2001 of 22.12.2000 on jurisdiction and the recognition and enforcement of judgments in civil and commercial matters, OJ L 12, 16.1.2001, pp. 0001–0023.

28 ECJ, 7 March 1995, Case C–68/93, *Shevill v. Press Alliance SA* [1995] ECR I–415.

29 Regulation (EC) No 846/2007 of the European Parliament and of the Council of 11.7.2007 on the law applicable to non-contractual obligations (Rome II), OJ L 199, 31.7.2007.

the law applicable to a non-contractual obligation based on a restriction of competition shall be the law of the country where the market is, or is likely to be, affected. This otherwise very simple rule evidently would seem to make the lawyer's work difficult when filing suit for compensation for damage suffered in more than one national market because of the evident need to invoke more than one substantive national law. Fortunately, the need to facilitate the antitrust enforcement (and the lawyer's work) was recognized by lawmakers, and the statute provides in Article 6 paragraph 3 letter b Rome II that the plaintiff may choose the court and its respective law for damage suffered in other national markets. This shall apply, however, only if the Member State's market in which the action is filed is amongst those directly and substantially affected by the restriction of competition and when at least one of the defendants has its seat in the place of the court.

Forum shopping is still possible under the regime of Rome II. Plaintiffs may evaluate the substantive law of all Member States in which a member of a cartel has its seat. They may then sue all members of a cartel at one court (Article 6 Brussels Regulation) and thereby choose the substantive law of that court for all damage, including damage suffered in other national markets.

One remark to US defendants: a US company may only be sued in Germany if it has a subsidiary or at least some assets (including receivables) in Germany.[30] The question of the applicable law is governed by Article 6 (3) (a) Rome II. According to this provision, different substantive laws may apply depending on which national markets are affected by the anticompetitive conduct (including US law for damage suffered in the US market).

One remark to US plaintiffs: a US plaintiff has the same rights as any European plaintiff.

5. How may claims be aggregated?

Under the GWB, collective claims for injunctive relief against violations of antitrust law are only available to certain associations and representative bodies, while claims for damages can only be filed by those who actually suffer the harm. However, a third party who acquires the assignment of damages claims from other cartel victims can also file a damages action under the general civil law,

Despite the unavailability of class actions in German law, the bundling and collective enforcement of damages claims can be done via third parties. That means a third party collects the assignments of damages claims of cartel victims and files the damages action against the cartel members. If successful, the third party holds a certain percentage of the awarded compensation. The admissibility of such collective actions in Germany was confirmed by the German Federal Court of Justice on 7 April 2009 when it affirmed the admissibility of a bundled claim against six cement companies seeking at least euro 114 million in damages.[31] The claimant, Cartel Damages Claims SA (CDC), is a Belgian company specially set up to pursue antitrust claims which acquired the damages claims of 36 customers of the alleged cartel participants. The CDC has also brought another

---

[30] See §23 ZPO (the German Civil Procedure Code, *Zivilprozessordnung*, ZPO).

[31] See Decision of Federal Court of Justice of 7 April 2009 (File No. KZR 42/08).

action in the German court,[32] on behalf of 32 European paper and pulp manufacturers, against six members of a hydrogen peroxide cartel in Europe, seeking around €643 million in damages.[33] Another example is Talionis International GmbH, a German limited liability company,[34] which collects assignments of private damages claims of companies and private customers who have been victims of a cartel and will transfer their claims to Talionis International for a symbolic amount. Talionis International bundles the claims of as many damaged parties as possible and enforces such claims at its own risk and costs. For example, after the German Cartel Office imposed a penalty of €57.6 million against 12 paper wholesalers in 2004 and this decision was confirmed by the German Federal Court of Justice in 2007, Talionis International made an effort to collect assignments of printing plants and enterprises that were damaged due to the above paper wholesalers' cartel. The claims pool was closed on 31 March 2009 and now no information is available whether an action has been filed in a German court. It remains to be seen whether this model will succeed in practice.

The European Commission may try to implement a combination of two complementary mechanisms for collective redress, namely group action and representative action.[35] The so-called 'group action' shall be an action brought by two or more parties which suffered harm caused by the same antitrust law infringement. Further claimants are free to join the group (opt-in model). In the 'representative action', the qualified entities such as consumers' associations shall be entitled to bring damages actions on behalf of the injured parties. It is the task of these qualified entities to make known the representative action and to distribute the amounts awarded by the courts. Injured parties may choose not to be represented by the qualified entity, and in such cases are not bound by the court decision (opt-out model). Both approaches would be totally new for the German civil procedural law.

It remains to be seen whether the European Commission will succeed, since political and economic pressure groups actively try to prevent such legislative measures.

6. What procedural defenses are available short of trial?

In respect of procedural defenses, the potential claimant should pay attention to the limitation of actions which could favor the defendant. For both sides, there are still possibilities of settlement following a model suit and dispute resolution through arbitration.

a. Limitation of actions

The general rules in the BGB provide the statute of limitations for a competition related claim. A damages claim must be filed within three years from the end of the year in which the right to damages arises and the plaintiff either has knowledge of both

32 Regional Court Dortmund (Landgericht Dortmund), File No. 13 O 23/09 [Kart].

33 See press release of CDC, available at www.carteldamageclaims.com/presse/20090423_CDC_PressRelease.pdf.

34 See www.talionis.de.

35 European Commission, Proposal for a Council Directive on Rules governing Damages Actions for Infringements of Articles of 81 and 82 of the Treaty (draft of 2009, no concrete date), not officially published, see recital 7 and Article 4 and Article 5.

the circumstances underlying the claim and the identity of the defendant or does not know of them through gross negligence, which generally also applies to the limitation of actions for injunctive relief.[36] If damages cannot be quantified before the time limit ends, the plaintiff can file a declaratory action (*Feststellungsklage*) to stop the time limit from expiring and thereby preserve its claim.[37] Furthermore, §33 (5) GWB supplements a rule with the suspension of the running of the limitation period when either German cartel authorities initiate proceedings for a breach of domestic competition law or Articles 81 and 82 EC, or if the EC Commission or a cartel authority of another EU Member State institutes proceedings for a breach of Articles 81 and 82 EC. The suspension will end six months after the final adjudication of any of the investigating authorities.[38] For the limitation of actions for injunctive relief, the general civil law rules apply.[39]

b. Arbitration clause

An alternative way to resolve competition-related disputes is arbitration. Prior to 1998, arbitration agreements with respect to disputes arising out of cartel agreements, cartel decisions or civil actions for damages pursuant to old §33 GWB were permissible but subject to a significant practical limitation.[40] Since the modernization of German arbitration law in 1998, all disputes arising from infringement of German and EC competition law can be settled by means of arbitration.[41] It was held that judicial control over arbitral awards through applications to set aside and resist enforcement of awards constitutes sufficient policing of competition law.[42]

c. Settlement following a model suit

It is also possible under the German law that the potential claimants and defendants agree to have a settlement of competition-related disputes following the outcome of

---

36 Sections 195, 199 (1) No. 1 and 2 as well as 5 BGB.

37 Section 256 ZPO.

38 Section 33 (5) Sentence 2 GWB in conjunction with §204 (2) BGB.

39 See §§195, 199 BGB, cf. *Emmerich*, in: Immenga/Mestmäcker (eds.) Kommentar zum Deutschen Kartellrecht GWB, Beck 2007, 4. Edition, §33 Rn. 93. However, §199 BGB only provides for the longest limitation of actions for injunctive relief. The decision practices of German courts have developed a short time limit of 4 to 6 weeks. An application for injunctive relief would be rejected by a court if it was not filed within this short time limit. There is also a little difference between the court practices of various regions in Germany. The northern German courts would allow a longer period of 6 or 8 weeks, while the southern only 4 weeks (see e.g. Decision of First Regional Court Munich as of 19 February 2009 (LG München I, File No. 7 O 1686/09).

40 The limitation, in old §91 GWB, was that an arbitration agreement was void if it did not confer a right on each party to request a decision through the courts instead of an arbitral tribunal. It was considered that confidential arbitration did not provide a sufficient check against anti-competitive conduct. *Cf. Schmidt*, in: Immenga/Mestmäcker (eds.) Kommentar zum Deutschen Kartellrecht GWB, Beck 2007, 4. Edition, §87 Rn. 61.

41 Section 1030 (1) ZPO. Cf. *Rehbinder*, in: Immenga/Mestmäcker (eds.) Kommentar zum Deutschen Kartellrecht GWB, Beck 2007, 4. Edition, §130 Rn. 343.

42 *Schmidt*, in: Immenga/Mestmäcker (eds.) Kommentar zum Deutschen Kartellrecht GWB, Beck 2007, 4. Edition, §87 Rn. 75.

a so-called 'model suit'. A 'model suit' (*Musterprozess)* is a judicial proceeding which essentially has similar facts as the case claimants and defendants agreed to settle.[43] A model suit can serve as a procedural example or guide for other similar actions in respect of both procedural costs and court decision. To avoid further legal costs for both sides, the potential claimants and defendants could have a settlement agreement based on the result of the 'model suit' (*Musterprozessvereinbarung*). This method leads to settlement efficiency, but shall not be tantamount to the extension of the *res iudicata* effect to all similar cases.[44]

7. What devices are available to obtain evidence?

a. General

The rules of evidence in German civil procedural law apply to private antitrust litigation. Generally, the plaintiff bears the burden of proof for the claim, while the defendant shall provide evidence supporting his defense against the claim. Permissible forms of evidence include visual inspection by the court (*Augenschein*), witnesses, experts, documents, interrogation of the parties and official information.[45] The general requirement for admissibility of evidence is that the court must be convinced of the veracity of every single fact.[46]

Under German law, common law-style cross-examination usually does not occur. The German Code of Civil Procedure does not provide for pre-trial or other discovery procedures. The German courts have limited power to force the submission of evidence, or to take evidence that has not been previously offered by one of the parties. Exceptionally, under certain circumstances, the court can require *ex officio* one of the parties or a third party to disclose documents in their possession to which a party to the litigation has made reference in its pleadings,[47] or it may upon request of one party request the other party to disclose a document if the requesting party has a substantive legal right of access to that document.[48]

b. Antitrust litigation

It is often very difficult for a plaintiff in private antitrust litigation to gather evidence to prove its claim. To a certain extent, German competition law compensates for this deficiency by providing several statutory presumptions which serve to improve the plaintiff's position by either shifting the burden of proof to the defendant or lowering the required standard of proof. For instance, in cases involving the abuse of a dominant position the burden of proof of a justification should generally be shifted to the defendant.[49] For

---

43 See *Zöller*, Zivilprozessordnung, 27. Edition, 2009, §325 Rn. 43b.

44 See *Zöller*, Zivilprozessordnung, 27. Edition, 2009, §325 Rn. 43b.

45 See §§371 et seq. ZPO.

46 Section 286 ZPO, *cf.* Thomas/Putzo, Kommentar zur ZPO, 30. Edition, 2009, §286 Rn. 6.

47 Section 142 ZPO.

48 Section 422 ZPO.

49 *Cf.* §20 GWB, see *Wulf-Henning Róth*, Private Enforcement of European Competition Law – Recommendations flowing from the German Experience, in: Jürgen Basedow (ed.), Private Enforcement of EC Competition Law, Kluwer Law International, 2007, pp. 61–81, 77.

example, in the case of an essential facility,[50] the dominant undertaking will have to bring forward an adequate justification for non-access to an infrastructure such as a telecommunication net or grid net.[51] Under §20 (4) Sentence 2 GWB there is a statutory presumption that an anticompetitive hindrance exists, if a dominant undertaking regularly offers goods or services occasionally below its cost price, unless the defendant can provide an objective justification for doing so. §20 (5) GWB puts the burden of proof on the defendant to disprove the existence of abusive practices if the plaintiff (i.e. either the offending firm's competitor or relevant representative associations) pleads 'specific facts' which, in light of 'general experience,' allow for the conclusion that a dominant undertaking has misused its market power. In such a case, the burden falls on the defendant to clarify and justify those aspects of its business activities which are being challenged.

Furthermore, another improvement is §33 (4) GWB, which makes the final decisions of the German competition authority, the European Commission and competition authorities of other EU Member States binding on the German courts in competition-related civil proceedings. This binding effect constitutes the same legal elements of follow-on actions and it is expected to stimulate private antitrust litigation. However, the binding effect only relates to the declaration of the infringement of competition law, but not to the causal relationship or amount of damages, which shall be subject to the assessment of the court.[52] Also, this binding effect only applies to claims for compensation but not to claims for injunctive relief.[53]

The European Commission may try to introduce the 'disclosure of evidence', under which, once the claimant in an antitrust damages action has presented reasonably available facts and evidence showing plausible grounds to suspect that it has suffered harm caused by an anticompetitive infringement, the court shall order the defendant or third parties to disclose evidence. The right to obtain disclosure shall also be available to the defendant. If this effort of the European Commission succeeds, it will bring significant effects to the private damage action in Germany.

8. What do plaintiffs get if they succeed?

The answer seems to be simple: they obtain injunctive relief or compensation for damage they have suffered. If, however – as outlined above – an association sues a member of a cartel with regard to profits it made on the basis of price-fixing, such profits have to be paid directly to the Federal Treasury.

a. Injunctive relief

§33 GWB provides for the right to claim for injunctive relief. In Germany, injunctive relief aims to stop current and prevent future infringements. Injunctive relief can

---

[50] The European Commission has defined an essential facility as 'a facility or infrastructure, without access to which competitors cannot provide services to their customers, and which cannot be replicated by any reasonable means'. The German definition in §19 (4) No. 4 GWB shall be interpreted in compliance with the European definition.

[51] Section 19 (4) No. 4 GWB.

[52] *Bechtold*, Kommentar zum GWB, Beck 2008, 5. Edition, §87 Rn. 35.

[53] *Id.*

be awarded provided that there are sufficient grounds for the expectation of future infringement of competition law. Future infringements may take the form of an active infringement or a failure to remedy a persisting source of harm. An action for injunctive relief can include a claim to remedy future consequences where a persisting infringement is established and still impairing the plaintiff, such as a continuing exclusion from a particular market.[54]

b. Damages compensation

i. Calculation of damages and the passing-on defense Section 33 (3) GWB provides for the right of compensation for all damage incurred provided that the violation of German or European cartel laws had been committed negligently or by willful act. Obviously, price fixing is conduct which fully meets this requirement.

The calculation of the amount of damages is based on the regular rules governing civil damages actions in BGB.[55] In general, damages are assessed on the basis of the impairments suffered by the plaintiff. When calculating damages, the courts can use all information available to compare the plaintiff's actual position following the harmful conduct with the hypothetical position which would have existed had the harmful event not occurred (*Differenzhypothese*). If the calculation of damages proves difficult, the courts can estimate the amount of damages.[56] Nevertheless, the calculation of accurate damages is often very difficult or even impossible in competition-related claims,[57] particularly with regard to establishing hypothetical market prices as a basis for the calculation of damages in, for example, case claiming an abuse of dominant position under §19 GWB or Article 82 EC Treaty.[58] In order to facilitate the assessment and enforcement of damages claims, the 7th Amendment of the GWB allows the courts to take into account, when assessing and estimating the amount of damages under the provisions of §287 ZPO, the proportion of the profit which the undertaking has derived from the infringement.[59]

Another issue relevant to the calculation of damages is the passing-on defense that was very controversial during the legislative debate surrounding the 7th Amendment of the GWB. The passing-on defense can be understood as the right of a defendant to argue that the claimant's loss has been reduced or negated by the claimant having passed on to the consumer (the indirect purchaser) all, or a proportion of, any overcharge resulting from the defendant's action. Thus, damages are calculated based on the actual loss rather than the entire amount of overcharge.

---

54 *Emmerich*, in: Immenga/Mestmäcker (eds.) Kommentar zum Deutschen Kartellrecht GWB, Beck 2007, 4. Edition, §33 Rn. 90.

55 Section 249 et seq. BGB.

56 Section 287 ZPO.

57 *Bechtold*, Kommentar zum GWB, Beck 2008, 5. Edition, §33 Rn. 28.

58 This is the so-called difference hypothesis, an arithmetical comparison between the financial position after the harmful infringement and the financial situation which would have existed had the harmful infringement not occurred. For more see *Bechtold*, Kommentar zum GWB, Beck 2008, 5. Edition, §33 Rn. 28.

59 Section 33 (3) Sentence 3.

While legal experts insist that the mitigation of damages for 'passing on' contradicts the purpose and intent of legislation prohibiting cartels,[60] the German courts have previously held differing opinions on the issue.[61] Finally, §33 (3) Sentence 2 GWB was enacted, addressing the 'passing on' issue as follows: 'If a good or a service was purchased at an inflated price, the existence of damage is not precluded because the good or the service was resold.' This rule has been interpreted by some scholars as an exclusion of the passing-on defense.[62] Actually, this issue is probably more complex, since the wording of §33 (3) Sentence 2 GWB does not explicitly preclude the possibility of a passing-on defense.

From the legislations' point of view, the issue of the passing-on defense concerns actually not the question of damages calculation, but the question of 'adjustment by benefit' (*Vorteilsausgleichung*).[63] Under the German civil law as well as in private antitrust litigation, the damages shall be assessed on the basis of actual loss and the rules against unjustified enrichment apply. The exclusion of the passing-on defense serves to avoid the infringer keeping the benefit gained through anticompetitive behavior. However, this exception might lead to unjustified enrichment by the claimant, if he does not suffer any damage because the excessive prices have been transferred through downstream resale. In case of conflict between these two arguments, it shall be clear that civil damages actions shall not have punitive function. In this respect, the fines and penalties which are imposed by a public enforcement agency on cartel members fulfill the punitive function.[64] Given that, the interpretation of the newly implemented §33 (3) Sentence 2 GWB remains open. At least, however, this provision would enable the court – on a case-by-case basis – to exercise its own discretion with regard to the question whether a claim shall be rejected because the plaintiff has not suffered any damage.

As far as the burden of proof is concerned, it is the opinion of the legislator that the tortfeasor, namely the defendant, bears the burden of demonstration and proof of all the facts that may be considered in the context of reduction of damages.[65]

ii. Types of damages and interest Indemnification of damage can be awarded in the form of restitution in kind, which can take any form necessary to restore the

---

60 *Hempel*, Privater Rechtsschutz im deutschen Kartellrecht nach der 7. GWB-Novelle, in: WuW 4/2004, pp. 362–374, 369–370. Also *cf. Emmerich*, in: Immenga/Mestmäcker (eds.) Kommentar zum Deutschen Kartellrecht GWB, Beck 2007, 4. Edition, §33 Rn. 54.

61 See OLG Karlsruhe, WuW/E DE-R p. 1229 (1231) – *Vitaminpreise*; LG Mannheim, GRUR 2004 p. 182 (184). For more see *Wurmnest*, A New Era for Private Antitrust Litigation in Germany? A Critical Appraisal of the Modernized Law against Restraints of Competition, in: German Law Journal, Vol. 06 No. 08/2005, pp. 1173–1189, 1183.

62 *Bechtold*, Kommentar zum GWB, Beck 2008, 5. Edition, §33 Rn. 26.

63 *Emmerich*, in: Immenga/Mestmäcker (eds.) Kommentar zum Deutschen Kartellrecht GWB, Beck 2007, 4. Edition, §33 Rn. 53.

64 *Lübbig*, Münchener Kommentar: Europäisches und Deutsches Wettbewerbsrecht (Kartellrecht), Band 2, Beck 2008, §33 GWB, Rn. 102.

65 See Beschlussempfehlung und Bericht des Ausschusses für Wirtschaft und Arbeit, BT-Drucks. 15/5049 of 9. March 2005, p. 48; *cf* also Bundeskartellamt, Private Kartellrechtsdurchsetzung Stand, Probleme, Perspektiven (discussion paper of 26 September 2005), p. 10.

situation to what it would have been without the infringing conduct.[66] If restitution in kind is impossible, pecuniary compensation shall be awarded by virtue of §251 BGB. This means that the German law provides only compensation for damage incurred. After having won the suit (and being paid by the losing defendant accordingly) the claimant shall be financially in the same position which would have occurred if the defendant had not violated the law. Consequently the German law rejects any kind of punitive damages.

In settling damages, the fines and penalties imposed by competition authorities shall not be offset, since this would hinder the injured plaintiff's ability to obtain compensation for harm suffered from the infringement. The competition authorities shall consider the damages already paid to the plaintiff when confiscating profits or imposing fines on the infringer.[67] Punitive damages violate the German 'ordre public'.[68]

In competition related claims, as in general civil actions, interest that is proven to be part of the damages is recoverable. However, in a general civil action, statutory interest is awarded from the moment of default in payment. §33 (3) Sentences 4 and 5 GWB introduce rules of prejudgment interest which favor the plaintiff, that mean that under the GWB statutory interest will be awarded from the moment the damage occurs. Compound interest is excluded from being recoverable.[69]

c. *Recovery of legal costs*

According to the general rule in §91 (1) ZPO the losing party has to bear the costs of the litigation.[70] The winning party can recover the costs which are necessary for bringing or defending the action.[71] If the plaintiff partly loses its case, the legal costs will be proportionally allocated based on the degrees of success.[72] The lawyers' fees of the winning party shall be paid by the losing party, however, but at no higher rate than the statutory limit.[73] That means that a party and his lawyer can agree on fees at a higher level than the statutory level. However, the winning party can only get recovery of his lawyer's fees up to the limit of the statutory level. Costs spent to avoid litigation or prepare a formal warning letter do not qualify as 'costs' in terms of §91 ZPO. These costs must be claimed as part of the damages in the party's substantive claim.[74]

---

66 *Bechtold*, Kommentar zum GWB, Beck 2008, 5. Edition, §33 Rn. 25.
67 Section 34 (2) GWB.
68 Federal Court of Justice, File No. IX ZR 49/91.
69 Section 289 BGB.
70 *Putzo*, in Thomas/Putzo, ZPO, 30. Edition, 2009, §91 Rn. 9.
71 Section 91 (1) Sentence 1 ZPO.
72 Section 209 ZPO.
73 *Putzo*, in Thomas/Putzo, ZPO, 30. Edition, 2009, §91 Rn. 19. The statutory lawyers' fee is set by the Lawyers Fee Act (*Rechtsanwaltsvergütungsgesetz*, RVG).
74 Palandt, Beck'scher Kommentar zum Bürgerlichen Gesetzbuch, Beck 2007, Vorb. v §249 Rn. 90.

9. How does the plaintiff's lawyer finance private enforcement?

a. Litigation costs

Litigation costs mainly consist of two parts: court fees and out-of-court costs. Court fees include public-law costs of the judiciary and the costs of court disbursements such as witnesses and experts, mail charges and transport costs.[75] In civil proceedings court fees have to be paid by the plaintiff up front.[76] Out-of-court costs are mainly the lawyers' fees and expenditures and the parties' costs.

The amount in dispute plays an essential role in the calculation of litigation costs. Consequently, the newly supplemented §89a GWB provides for the possibility of having court fees and lawyers' fees assessed on the basis of a reduced 'reasonable value of claim.' These cost reductions are only available if the party concerned makes a plausible argument that full payment of court fees would endanger its economic standing. Once such an application has been submitted, the court may order that the court fees for the submitting party are to be assessed on the basis of a proportion of the amount in controversy, and shall be considered reasonable by reference to the party's economic situation. This order also applies to the calculation of attorneys' fees and leads to a corresponding reduction.[77]

Under certain conditions, parties can request public legal aid (*Prozesskostenhilfe*).[78] The court decides on such requests in a special procedure without a hearing.[79] However, private legal aid insurance in Germany does not cover the costs of competition-related litigation.[80]

b. Contingent fee

An important issue for both clients and lawyers is contingency fees. This refers to agreements between lawyers and clients whereby the lawyer will be paid either a fixed amount of money or a percentage of the proceeds if successful, but nothing in the event of failure, as well as to agreements whereby the lawyer is in any event paid the statutory fees but is entitled to an extra fee if successful (*palmarium*).[81] Under German law, contingency fees are generally prohibited for litigation.[82] This has been changed partly through the amendment of the German Lawyers' Fee Act, according to which contingency fee agreements will be allowed but only under very limited circumstances.[83] A contingency fee agreement may only be on an individual basis and only be entered into under the

---

[75] *Putzo* in Thomas/Putzo, ZPO, 30. Edition, 2009, before §91 Rn. 3 and 4.

[76] Sections 61 (1) No. 1, 65, 68 GKG (the Law governing Court Costs).

[77] Section 89a (1) GWB.

[78] See §§114 et seq. ZPO.

[79] Section 127 (1) ZPO.

[80] See §4 (1) e) (75) of the General Policy Conditions of Defence Insurance, §3 (2) e) (94) of the General Policy Conditions of Defence Insurance. Cf. Gerod/Schmidt, Rechtsanwaltsvergütungsgesetz, 18. Auflage 2008, §4a RVG Rn. 3 et seq.

[81] *Hartung/Holl*, Anwaltliche Berufsordnung, BRAO §49 b Rn. 30.

[82] Section 49 b (2) of the Federal Lawyer Regulations (*Bundesrechtsanwaltsordnung*, BRAO).

[83] For more details see §4a of the German Lawyers Fee Act (*Rechtsanwaltsvergütungsgesetz*, RVG), amended by the amendment Act of 12.6.2008.

condition that the client, in the event of a lack of contingency fee agreement, might be deterred from filing the litigation by reason of his economic circumstances. If these conditions are met, an agreement may be reached that no or less than the statutory fees shall be paid in the event of failure of litigation while an adequate supplement is to be paid for success.[84] From today's perspective it does not appear that such exceptional contingency agreements will be of relevance in private antitrust litigation since companies generally will not be able to argue that they cannot afford their lawyers' fees.

10. How does private enforcement interact with public enforcement?

In general, public enforcement should aim to clarify and develop antitrust prohibitions and deter and punish violations, whereas private actions for damages should aim for compensation.

a. Effect of public antitrust enforcement on private actions for damages

Successful public antitrust enforcement is expected to encourage private actions for damages because they not only prove the existence of the antitrust violation, but they also very likely generate useful evidence of causation and harm for the plaintiff in a follow-on action. The binding effect of the finding of a violation in public enforcement proceedings stimulates follow-on actions. §33 (4) GWB provides for such binding effect, not only for final decisions of the German competition authority, but also for final decisions of the European Commission and other EU Member States. The fines imposed by a competition authority are of a punitive nature and shall not affect the amount of pecuniary compensation available in successful claims for private damages. In the event that the competition authority confiscates thė illegally gained profits obtained through anticompetitive conduct, the amount of damage compensation paid to the private plaintiff or of fines imposed by competition authority shall be subtracted from the illegal gains.[85]

b. Effect of private actions for damages on public antitrust enforcement

Since follow-on actions for damages are much easier to bring than stand-alone actions, potential plaintiffs are eager to push competition authorities to investigate cases of alleged competition infringement. Accordingly, German competition authorities can initiate public proceedings against infringement either on their own initiative or by acting on a complaint.[86]

Another impact of private damages actions is the public leniency program. Under the Guideline of Leniency Program, published by the Federal Cartel Office, undertakings that participate in or have participated in secret cartels can obtain immunity from fines or a fine reduction in exchange for cooperating with the authorities in the detection and collection of evidence regarding the cartel.[87] It is generally alleged that providing

---

84 Section 4a (1) of the German Lawyers Fee Act.

85 Section 34 (2) GWB.

86 Section 54 (1) GWB.

87 Notice no. 9/2006 of the Bundeskartellamt on the immunity from and reduction of fines in cartel cases – Leniency Programme – of 7 March 2006.

admitted violators of competition laws with immunity from damages or any reduction of their liability in follow-on actions for damages appears unnecessary and unjust.[88]

Conclusion

The recent amendments to German antitrust law (GWB) and to European law (Brussels Regulation and Rome II) have facilitated private antitrust enforcement in Germany, but substantial hurdles remain. The White Paper of the European Commission[89] has illustrated the willingness of the Commission to provide the instruments for effective private enforcement of antitrust law. The legal community is currently awaiting the European Commission's proposal for a legally binding directive on damages claims based on violations of EC antitrust law. Whether this directive reflects the US approach to private enforcement or develops a unique European method will be the most discussed issue in the near future.

---

[88] *Wils*, The Relationship between Public Antitrust Enforcement and Private Actions for Damages, in: World Competition 32, No. 1/2009, pp. 3–26, 25.

[89] European Commission, White Paper on damages actions for breach of the EC antitrust rules, COM(2008)165 final, 2.4.2008.

19 Italy

Giovanni Barone and Roberto Amore[1]

Introduction

The level of private antitrust enforcement in Italy has been gradually increasing over the last few years thanks to consistent promotion and public debates at both the EU and national levels, leading to a greater awareness of the remedies available through private actions. This trend was somewhat reinforced by the landmark judgment of the Supreme Court (ruling in Plenary Session) in the *Unipol* case of 2005,[2] which finally clarified that, in addition to competitors and intermediate customers, final consumers may also bring private lawsuits in Italy under either Italian or EU competition law. Ever since then, extensive discussions and proposals have taken place on the introduction of a new law regulating collective or 'class' actions in Italy, which could also be utilized in relation to antitrust cases. The adoption of such a law has been delayed and hampered by widespread public criticism, including resistance by the main industry federation. The frequent turnover of the Italian Government, leading to shifts in legislative priorities, further compounded the delay until January 2010, when the new law finally entered into force.

Private antitrust claims in Italy, particularly follow-on damages actions based on cartel infringements, may also increase in the future as a result of the rising application of the Leniency Program introduced by the Italian Antitrust Authority (*Autorità Garante della Concorrenza e del Mercato*, hereinafter 'IAA') in 2007, which is expected to lead to greater detection of cartel activity in the coming years.

Conversely, follow-on litigation in relation to abuse of dominance cases may be negatively affected by the fact that in recent years the IAA has resolved the vast majority of its abuse of dominance cases through the 'commitments procedure', first introduced in Italy in 2006.[3] The use of this procedure results in some sort of settlements agreed between the IAA and the investigated party without formal findings of infringements, which plaintiffs could rely on in follow-on suits. In practice, however, since the commitments procedure binds the allegedly infringing party to pro-competitive measures shortly after the opening of an investigation by the IAA, potential plaintiffs (whether damaged competitors, intermediate customers or final consumers) may in some cases be satisfied with the effects of the agreed commitments and refrain from bringing private actions (particularly

[1] Attorneys-at-law, Freshfields Bruckhaus Deringer LLP, Rome. The opinions expressed in this chapter are those of the authors and do not necessarily reflect the positions of the firm.

[2] Corte di Cassazione (*Sezioni Unite*), judgment n. 2207 of February 4, 2005, *Unipol Assicurazioni c. Ricciardelli.*

[3] Such procedure was introduced through Law n. 248 of August 4, 2006 which inserted Article 14-*ter* into Italian Competition Law n. 287/1990, adopting similar provisions to Article 9 of EC Regulation n. 1/2003, although indicating that the commitments must be offered within three months from the launch of the investigation.

when the potential plaintiff filed the initial complaint giving rise to the IAA investigation). Accordingly, the role of the IAA seems to be gradually changing from that of a pure watchdog to a *de facto* regulator, especially in relation to those cases in which the commitments assessed by the IAA did not fully match the type of harm initially alleged in its decision to launch the investigation or went beyond what was necessary to curb such harm, as happened in a recent and much debated case.[4]

Private antitrust actions may be brought in Italy under both EU and Italian competition law and before different courts, depending on which law an action is brought under. The litigation is governed by general civil law and procedure. As for the remedies available, plaintiffs may opt for damages, declaratory relief (e.g. seeking the nullity of a contract) and/or interim measures, although in the last case the requisite legal standard is particularly high. With regard to criminal sanctions, under Italian law antitrust infringements may give rise to criminal liability only in very limited and exceptional cases.[5]

All in all, although the number of cases is growing, the relevant jurisprudence has not been fully consistent and does not yet provide definitive guidelines or assurances to market players willing to act before national courts to defend their interests.

This chapter aims to summarize the main procedural and substantive issues that arise in private antitrust disputes in Italy, while explaining the remedies available as well as the main features of the Italian class action legislation which entered into force in January 2010.

1. How does a private antitrust action case get started?

Private antitrust actions in Italy may begin from previous cases decided by the European Commission or the IAA (follow-on damages claims) or through the autonomous initiative of a plaintiff irrespective of a pending public case (stand-alone litigation). Previous or simultaneous governmental action is not a *conditio sine qua non*, although it is preferred, as in most cases it may help lower the plaintiff's burden of proof and possibly expedite the case. Indeed, as under Italian law private antitrust disputes in Italy are generally regulated by ordinary tort rules,[6] the parties to proceedings are required to

---

4 See IAA decision n. 19021 of October 23, 2008, case A391 – *Servizi di soccorso autostradale*, then annulled in appeal by judgment n. 4994 of May 8, 2009 by Tribunale Amministrativo Regionale per il Lazio, which is the first instance administrative court competent to review IAA decisions.

5 For example, this could be the case in relation to bid-rigging conduct in the context of public procurement (classified by Articles 353 and 354 of the Italian Criminal Code as '*Turbata libertà degli incanti*'). This conduct basically concerns any material restrictions to the freedom of action imposed on, or agreed by, parties participating in public tenders. Also 'private bid-rigging' may become criminally relevant to the extent that a public official is involved.

6 *Ex multis*, Corte di Cassazione (*Sezioni Unite*), judgment n. 2207 of February 4, 2005, cited above; Corte di Cassazione, judgment n. 2305 of February 2, 2007, *Fondiaria-SAI Assicurazioni c. Nigriello*; Corte d'Appello di Roma, judgment of January 20, 2003, *Albacom c. Telecom Italia*; Corte d'Appello di Torino, judgment of July 6, 2000, *Indaba Incentive Company c. Juventus FC*. *Contra*, Corte d'Appello di Napoli, judgment of July 12, 2007, *P.Z. c. R.*, in which the court indicated that the liability of an insurer for having applied a 'cartelized' price to a consumer had a '*contractual* nature.'

submit evidence of the facts (and rights) that they allege. This may prove to be very burdensome in the event of stand-alone antitrust actions (especially in relation to cartel cases), as relevant information and documents may not be held by the plaintiff. Previous or simultaneous governmental action may thus ease this task.

a. Locus standi and statute of limitation

General procedural rules of tort and contract litigation also apply in relation to *locus standi*. A plaintiff can file an action for damages or interim measures only if it has a legal interest in it, as customarily required by Italian procedural law. In order to succeed, the plaintiff must show that it has been directly harmed by particular anticompetitive conduct. A direct causal link must be demonstrated between an intentional or negligent violation of the competition rules and the damage suffered.[7]

The notion of 'direct causal link' has been interpreted broadly by the Italian Supreme Court (*Corte di Cassazione*). As mentioned, the landmark judgment in *Unipol* issued by the Supreme Court in 2005[8] clarified that final consumers may also bring private antitrust lawsuits, as competition laws aim to protect all market participants and they too may suffer damage from antitrust wrongdoings. This decision overruled previous jurisprudence by the Supreme Court from 1999[9] and 2002,[10] which had indicated that competition rules are primarily designed to benefit undertakings and secure the constitutional principle of freedom of private enterprise. Under the old approach, the Supreme Court had denied standing to consumers, holding they were only indirect beneficiaries of competition rules.

Like other tort actions in Italy, private antitrust actions must be brought within five years of the facts leading to the alleged damage, which in antitrust cases could generally be identified with the date on which the alleged infringement ended. However, another general provision of Italian civil law specifies that the five-year statute of limitations starts running only 'from the day on which the right at issue can be exercised'. On this point, in a recent judgment on a follow-on case from the motor insurance cartel sanctioned by the IAA in 2000, the Supreme Court clarified that for private antitrust actions the five-year period does not start running until the plaintiff can 'reasonably perceive' that certain conduct could be in violation of antitrust law and thus give rise to tort liability.[11] It would then be for the defendant to prove that under such basis the statute of limitations had already expired.

Conversely, if the action is based on contractual liability and not on tort, then a 10-year limitation period ordinarily applies.

---

[7] As will be further explained below (see footnote 24), under Italian tort law the alleged damage for which the plaintiff seeks compensation must be 'unjust'.

[8] Corte di Cassazione (*Sezioni Unite*), judgment n. 2207 of February 4, 2005, *Unipol Assicurazioni c. Ricciardelli*.

[9] Corte di Cassazione, judgment n. 1811 of March 4, 1999, *Montanari c. Cassa Risparmio Genova e Imperia*.

[10] Corte di Cassazione, judgment n. 17475 of December 9, 2002, *Axa Assicurazioni c. Larato*.

[11] Corte di Cassazione, judgment n. 2305 of February 2, 2007, *Fondiaria-SAI Assicurazioni c. Nigriello*. See also Corte di Cassazione, judgment n. 355 of January 10, 2008, *Consorzio Tutela Formaggio Grana Padano c. Valgrana*.

b. Competent courts

When an action is brought under Article 81 or 82 of the EC Treaty,[12] the ordinary rules of Italian civil procedure apply, giving local courts of first instance (*Tribunali ordinari*) jurisdiction over private antitrust claims.[13] Appeals against first instance judgments may be lodged with the competent Court of Appeal (*Corte d'Appello*). Finally, judicial review of issues of law decided by the Courts of Appeal lies with the Italian Supreme Court in Rome (*Corte di Cassazione*). Conversely, private actions based on alleged infringements of Italian antitrust rules (Article 2 or 3 of Law n. 287 of 10 October 1990, hereinafter 'Law 287/90') must be brought directly before the competent Court of Appeal, which under Article 33 of the same law has jurisdiction to hear nullity actions and claims for damages, as well as to grant interim relief if specifically required.[14] These judgments may be challenged directly before the Supreme Court on issues of law only. Thirdly, special jurisdictional rules apply in relation to collective/class actions, as will be illustrated in Section 6 further below.

This 'multiple court' system may lead to inefficiencies as well as potential jurisdictional conflicts and overlaps,[15] as the boundaries of applicability of EU competition rules are not always clearly distinguishable from those of domestic competition rules.[16] However, the risk of decisions conflicting on substantive issues may be avoided to some extent by a stay of one of the overlapping proceedings.

With regard to jurisdiction, Italian courts are competent to hear cases against non-Italian defendants in at least two situations:

(i) under Article 5.3 of EC Regulation n. 44/2001 before the Italian court(s) of the place where the harmful event occurred or may occur; or
(ii) under Article 6.1 of EC Regulation n. 44/2001 if the action against a non-Italian defendant is closely connected with an action against a defendant domiciled in Italy, in which case all defendants may be sued together before the competent Italian court.

c. Legal fees and costs

With regard to legal fees, under Italian law it is normally for the losing party to pay all costs related to the proceedings, including court fees as well as legal fees and expenses incurred by the prevailing party. The measure of such costs and fees is decided by the

---

[12] On December 1, 2009, the Treaty of Lisbon came into effect, amending the Treaty Establishing the European Community (EC Treaty) that is now called the Treaty on the Functioning of the European Union (TFEU). Therefore, all references to Articles 81 and 82 of the EC Treaty now becomes references to Articles 101 and 102 TFEU.

[13] Corte d'Appello di Milano, Order of May 24, 2007, *Gas Intensive c. Trans Tunisian Pipeline*; Tribunale di Milano, Order of December 5, 2005, *Il Numero Italia e Directory Assistance Company c. Telecom Italia*. However, if the value of the claim is below 5,000 Euro, then the Justice of the Peace (*Giudice di pace*) has jurisdiction in first instance and the *Tribunale ordinario* on appeal.

[14] See Corte d'Appello di Milano, Order of January 10, 2006, *Exergia c. Trans Tunisian Pipeline*.

[15] For a reasoned critique of such system, see S. Rosso, *Ways to promote workable private antitrust enforcement in Italy*, in *World Comp.*, 2009, p. 305.

[16] See Tribunale di Milano, Order of December 5, 2005 cited in footnote 13 above.

court itself in the context of the final judgment, and as a matter of practice is generally lower than the actual value of fees requested by the (attorneys of the) prevailing party. If the claimant obtains only a partial judgment in its favor or if the court considers that the issues of law at stake were novel or particularly complex (as it is not uncommon in antitrust cases), the award of costs may follow a different pattern, e.g. costs may be split proportionally between the litigating parties.[17]

Contingency fees in favor of the attorneys assisting the plaintiffs used to be expressly prohibited in Italy and were introduced for the first time only in mid-2006. Since then, however, this and other measures contained in Law Decree n. 233 of 4 July 2006 and intended to stimulate competition between lawyers have been severely criticized by a part of the legal community in Italy, and it is now being discussed in legislative circles whether to abrogate or at least modify these new measures. With particular regard to contingency fees, a low percentage cap may be introduced.

2. Substantive issues of damages actions

As mentioned, from a substantive standpoint, private antitrust actions in Italy may be pursued in connection with either Article 81/82 of the EC Treaty or violations of Law 287/90, particularly Articles 2 and 3 which prohibit anticompetitive agreements,[18] concerted practices and abuses of dominant position.[19,20] Moreover, under Italian procedural law, negative declaratory actions are also possible, through which an alleged cartelist or dominant firm may seek a judicial declaration that a certain practice did not amount to an antitrust violation or that no damage arose from that conduct.[21] Overall,

---

[17] As in other European countries, Italian law provides for public legal aid in civil proceedings in favor of individual plaintiffs (not companies or associations) who cannot otherwise afford legal fees only upon the existence of strict conditions, namely that (i) the individual requesting public legal aid has a personal (or family) annual income of less than 10,600 Euro, and (ii) upon a preliminary review, his/her legal case at issue is not manifestly unfounded.

[18] With particular regard to anticompetitive agreements, private actions may be brought in relation to both horizontal and vertical agreements; in the former situation it would more often be an action for damages and/or interim measures, while in the latter case it may also aim for declaratory relief seeking the nullity of the vertical agreement or clause.

[19] Merger control cases are unlikely to generate private antitrust actions. It is actually debated whether private litigation could arise from cases in which the merged parties did not comply with a previous IAA decision, such as a decision through which the IAA blocked the merger or issued conditional clearance. While in a case of 2004 the Milan Court of Appeal indicated that the IAA has exclusive competence to verify compliance with its merger control decisions (Corte d'Appello di Milano, order of June 3, 2004, *Moto c. Autogrill*), it is arguable that private damages actions could nonetheless be brought against non-compliant merging parties.

[20] With regard to consumer protection in the strict sense, we note that a detailed analysis of the rules on unfair commercial practices under Legislative Decree n. 206/2005, Legislative Decree n. 145/2007 (implementing Article 14 of Directive 2005/29/EC that amended Directive 84/450/EEC on misleading advertising) and Legislative Decree n. 146/2007 (implementing Directive 2005/29/EC on unfair business-to-consumer commercial practices and amending Directives 84/450/EEC, 97/7/EC, 98/27/EC and 2002/65/EC and EC Regulation n. 2006/2004) is beyond the scope of this chapter.

[21] Tribunale di Milano, judgment of May 8, 2009, *ENI et al. c. Pirelli Tyre et al.* (hereinafter 'the *ENI* Case'). In this case, some companies of the ENI group engaged in the production of specific synthetic rubbers acted before the Court of Milan to obtain a negative finding that, *inter alia*,

however, the majority of the private antitrust actions brought in Italy are damages actions. As will be explained below in the Remedies section, damages may include any cost incurred by the victim (generally the plaintiff), including both for direct damage and loss of profits.

For the sake of completeness, damaged competitors may ground their claims not only on infringements of EU or Italian antitrust rules, but also on the unfair competition rules provided by Article 2598 of the Italian Civil Code (ICC), which, unlike antitrust rules, cannot be relied upon by consumers. Under Article 2598, paragraph 3, of the ICC an undertaking behaves unfairly towards its competitors and may be liable for damages if it adopts any practices not complying with the principle of 'professional fairness' (*correttezza professionale*) and which is capable of causing detriment to its competitor(s). The enforcement of this provision, however, has not proven to be straightforward and uniform. In relation to below-cost selling, for example, a new approach on unfair competition practices was taken by the Supreme Court in 2006,[22] which links the application of antitrust and unfair competition laws. This new approach was however criticized, and there are still doubts whether such interpretation of Article 2598 n. 3 of the ICC will hold. According to the previous and more consolidated case law, unfair competition conduct in breach of Article 2598, paragraph 3, of the ICC constitutes a different type of infringement from that of antitrust rules, being more focused on the actual effects of the defendant's conduct vis-à-vis a single competitor rather than on the overall impact on the market.

Finally, in addition to these provisions, Article 2597 of the ICC applies to legal monopolies, imposing a general duty to conclude contracts with third parties upon their request and under non-discriminatory conditions. However, the practice has shown that it is difficult to obtain judicial injunctions against alleged monopolists.[23]

a. Legal bases for actions

Antitrust damages actions brought by private parties, whether individuals or corporations, can be based upon Italian tort or contract law, centered around Articles 2043 and 1218 of the ICC respectively, although the case law has generally considered them as tort litigation. Regardless of the alternative legal basis, the plaintiff must prove that (i) the defendant breached antitrust law; (ii) the plaintiff suffered damage; and (iii) there was a causal link between the defendant's conduct and the alleged harm.

---

a cartel in the Butadiene Rubber (BR) and Emulsion Styrene Butadiene Rubber (ESBR) market ascertained by the European Commission in 2006 had not produced anticompetitive effects on the market and, consequently, no damage had occurred to the tire manufacturers summoned in the proceedings. Other BR/ESBR producers also intervened in the proceedings *ad adiuvandum* some of the ENI claims. This judgment of first instance dated May 8, 2009 is, however, under appeal before the Milan Court of Appeal at the time of this publication.

[22] Corte di Cassazione, judgment n. 1636 of January 26, 2006, *Universo c. RCS*.

[23] For one such negative example, see Tribunale di Napoli, order of May 21, 2004, *Farmacie Petrone c. Pfizer Italia*, concerning a case of refusal to supply pharmaceuticals. As a result of the Court of Naples' rejection of the plaintiff's request for an injunction under Article 2597 of the ICC, Farmacie Petrone then started a new action under Article 3 of Law 287/90 before the Milan Court of Appeal, and this time obtained the interim measure (Corte d'Appello di Milano, Order of July 23, 2005, *Farmacie Petrone c. Pharmacia Italia e Pfizer Italia*).

If the action is based on tort law, the (alleged) damage has to be 'unjust'[24] and the plaintiff must prove intentional or negligent misconduct by the defendant, which is a subjective inquiry. Italian scholars and case law are divided on what constitutes such misconduct in anticompetitive activities.[25] On the one hand, it can be argued that certain *per se* antitrust violations or the breach of statutory provisions may imply negligence (objective negligence theory). On the other hand, the presumption of negligence provided for by Article 2600 of the ICC in relation to unfair trade practices could be applied by analogy to antitrust claims.[26]

b. Causal link

With respect to the requirement of causal link between the alleged anticompetitive conduct and harm suffered by the plaintiff, it is worth noting that, under Italian law, actions based on tort or contractual liability are of a compensatory nature. As a result, only victims who have actually suffered damage could successfully bring such actions. The causal link must be verified on a case-by-case basis according to the general principles on compensation provided by the ICC,[27] i.e. the damage must be an immediate and direct consequence of the alleged breach of competition law.

With regard to the notion of causality, according to Italian case law '. . . the causality nexus must be construed as to comprise . . . also the indirect damages that represent a normal effect on the basis of the principle of the so-called causal regularity . . .'.[28]

With respect to causation and with particular regard to follow-on private actions related to cartel cases, the Supreme Court recently held that a presumption may exist of a direct link between a cartel and the damage suffered by consumers, because downstream contracts between cartel participants and consumers are normally the means by

---

24 'Unjust damage' means that the infringing conduct must have injured a legally protected right or interest of the plaintiff. In antitrust actions under either Italian or EU competition law, this element is normally satisfied on showing that there has been a restriction of the constitutionally protected 'right to competition' of the plaintiff, whether a competitor or a customer of the infringing party.

25 For a brief overview of this issue, see M. Barcellona, *Funzione compensativa della responsabilità e private enforcement della disciplina antitrust*, Contratto e Impresa 1/2008, p. 123 and ff.; P. Fattori – M. Todino, *La disciplina della concorrenza in Italia*, Il Mulino (2004), p. 434 and ff.; M. Tavassi – M. Scuffi, *Diritto processuale antitrust*, Giuffrè (1998), p. 310 and ff.

26 Article 2600 of the ICC, titled 'Compensation for damages' states that '[a]nyone who performs acts of unfair competition with fraud, malice, or negligence, is liable for damages . . . . When acts of unfair competition are ascertained, negligence is presumed'. While Article 2600 applies to unfair competition acts pursuant to Article 2598 of the ICC (which can be enforced by harmed competitors, not consumers – see above) it is arguable that antitrust violations also may fall within this provision and accordingly could be challenged by harmed competitors under this legal basis. See also the works of M. Barcellona, P. Fattori – M. Todino, and M. Tavassi – M. Scuffi cited in footnote 25 above.

27 In particular, Article 1223 of the ICC provides that the measure of damages arising from missing or delayed performance of any obligation must include the loss sustained by the creditor and the lost profits as far as they are the direct and immediate consequence of the non-performance or delay.

28 *Ex multis*, Corte di Cassazione, judgment n. 16163 of December 21, 2001, *Anas c. Luraghi*; judgment n. 5913 of May 9, 2000, *Calvi c. Frangipane*; and judgment n. 3536 of March 24, 2000, *Venier c. Cassa Risparmio di Udine e Pordenone*.

which the cartel is put into effect.[29] In this case, however, the Court expressly noted that the presumption in favor of the plaintiff is rebuttable, particularly with regard to the causal link between the conduct and the alleged damage. It is clear that the plaintiff's burden of proof becomes much higher (see *infra*) in cartel cases in which the IAA (or another public authority) has not issued a decision, because in such cases, beside the amount of the damages and the related causal link with the (allegedly) illicit conduct, which the plaintiff would have to prove anyway, the same plaintiff would first need to prove the existence of a cartel. On the other hand, after a public authority has ascertained the existence of a cartel and closed the investigation, the plaintiff may be able to prove the existence of the antitrust infringement by (i) relying on prior findings of the public authority (which however are not formally binding, as we will specify later), (ii) providing a copy of the contract or agreement it entered into with one or more of the cartel participants, and (iii) providing a reasonable estimate of the overcharges paid as a result of the cartel.

Despite the recent extension of the notion of causality by the Supreme Court, which opened to final consumers and, to a lesser extent, indirect victims the possibility of bringing private damages claims, the proof of such a causal link and the measure of the related damages (discussed below) remain difficult as they require an in-depth economic analysis. Indeed, this is often the main deterrent against private antitrust litigation.

c. Examples of recent damages cases in Italy

Despite the relatively young age of antitrust legislation in Italy (enacted in 1990) as well as the fact that many cases are settled out of court, in recent years there has been a growing number of judgments in which damages were awarded in the context of private antitrust actions. What follows is a brief outline of the most important damages cases until now.

In the *International Broker* case of 2008, the Rome Court of Appeal awarded damages for the loss of profits suffered as a result of price alignment by the main oil refining companies operating in a specific local market in a cooperative joint venture for the production and distribution of bitumen.[30]

In the *Avir/ENI* case of 2006, the Milan Court of Appeal awarded damages upon finding that the incumbent gas operator in Italy had abused its dominant position by imposing unfair prices.[31]

In the *Inaz Paghe* case of 2004, damages were awarded to a software provider that had been boycotted by national and local employment consultant associations in retaliation for encroaching on activities allegedly reserved for authorized employment consultants.[32]

In the *Bluvacanze* case of 2003, damages were awarded to a travel agent that had been

---

[29] Corte di Cassazione, judgment n. 2305 of February 2, 2007, *Fondiaria-SAI Assicurazioni c. Nigriello*.

[30] Corte d'Appello di Roma, judgment of March 31, 2008, *International Broker*.

[31] Corte d'Appello di Milano, judgment of September 16, 2006, *Avir/ENI*.

[32] Corte d'Appello di Milano, judgment of December 10, 2004, *Inaz Paghe c. Associazione nazionale consulenti del lavoro*, then upheld by the Supreme Court (Corte di Cassazione, judgment n. 3640 of February 13, 2009, *Associazione nazionale consulenti del lavoro c. INAZ Paghe*).

boycotted by three major tour operators in retaliation for aggressive discounts the agent had offered to its customers.[33]

In the *Albacom*[34] (2003) and *Telsystem*[35] (1996) cases, before the Courts of Appeal of Rome and Milan respectively, damages in tort were awarded to potential new entrants whose market access had been hindered by the former telecom monopolists' refusals to supply them with services they needed in order to enter the relevant telecoms market.

In the *Valgrana* case of 2002, damages were awarded to a producer of Grana Padano parmesan cheese which was found to be harmed as a result of illegitimate output-limitation decisions adopted by the *Consortium for the Protection of Grana Padano*, of which the plaintiff was a member.[36]

Finally, in several cases before local courts, damages or restitution were awarded to a number of consumers who had paid higher premiums for their motor vehicle insurance as a result of a national cartel between insurance companies ascertained by the IAA (Decision n. 8546 of July 28, 2000, case I-377–*RC Auto*).[37]

Except for the various insurance and telecom cases as well as the *INAZ Paghe* case (all of which followed on IAA decisions), most of the other cases were stand-alone actions in which the final amount of damages awarded was somewhat limited.

3. Antitrust actions under contract law

As mentioned, private antitrust actions in Italy may in certain cases be grounded on principles of contract law, particularly claims seeking the declaration of nullity of an agreement in whole or in part. In an action seeking nullity of the whole contract, the plaintiff relies on Article 1418 of the ICC, either claiming the agreement is in breach of a mandatory provision (e.g. the EU or Italian antitrust rules mentioned above) or that its *causa* or subject matter is unlawful.[38] In the event of partial nullity (e.g. nullity of the clause which fixes the price), the claimant would seek the application of Article 1419 of the ICC in order to show that such clause was not severable from the rest of the contract

33 Corte d'Appello di Milano, judgment of July 11, 2003, *Bluvacanze c. I Viaggi del Ventaglio, Turisanda e Hotelplan Italia*.

34 Corte d'Appello di Roma, judgment of January 20, 2003, *Albacom c. Telecom Italia*.

35 Corte d'Appello di Milano, judgments of July 18, 1995 and December 24, 1996, both in the *Telsystem c. SIP-Telecom Italia* case.

36 Corte d'Appello di Torino, judgment of February 7, 2002, *Valgrana c. Consorzio tutela formaggio Grana Padano*, then confirmed by Corte di Cassazione, judgment n. 355 of January 10, 2008.

37 *Ex multis*, Giudice di Pace di Bitonto, judgment of May 21, 2007, *Manfredi c. Lloyd Adriatico Assicurazioni*; Corte d'Appello di Napoli, judgment of May 3, 2005, *Nigriello c. SAI Assicurazioni*. This judgment was, however, overruled by the Supreme Court on the basis of the fact that the lower court had dismissed the insurance company's defense of 'lack of causation' without proper examination, and misapplied the five-year statute of limitations (Corte di Cassazione, judgment n. 2305 of February 2, 2007, *Fondiaria-SAI Assicurazioni c. Nigriello*).

38 Article 1418 of the ICC provides that any contract that is contrary to mandatory provisions shall be void, unless the law provides otherwise. According to the same provision, a contract can also be rendered void by, among other things, the unlawfulness of its cause or, in particular circumstances, its motives (i.e. whenever the parties concluded the contract exclusively pursuant to a common and illegal motive).

and that the nullity of the individual clause should thus extend to the entire contract. In both cases, the declaratory action may be coupled with either a direct damages claim[39] or a claim for restitution of what has been unduly paid on the basis of a right – i.e. a contractual provision – later declared void.

When bringing a contractual claim in court, the plaintiff must only prove the objective element on which the action is based (e.g. nullity of the agreement, failure to comply with the obligations of fairness and good faith, detrimental effect on the contractual balance), while for the subjective element Article 1218 of the ICC provides a rebuttable presumption of negligence by the infringing party.

4. Evidence

As far as evidence is concerned, ordinary civil litigation rules apply to antitrust disputes, placing each party under an obligation to submit evidence of the facts that it alleges. Specifically, the plaintiff must prove the facts upon which the action is based and the defendant, in challenging the relevance of these facts or the merits of the case, must give evidence substantiating any such argument.[40] In this respect, all evidence normally admitted in civil proceedings, including witness testimonies (oral and written), documents and expert opinions, is also admissible in private antitrust actions.

In follow-on claims, documents coming from the previous or simultaneous proceedings before a public authority could theoretically be used by the plaintiff in the private action only if the latter was a direct participant in the public proceedings and had thereby gained access to such documents.

If the plaintiff intends to secure evidence from the defendant prior to trial, fearing that such evidence may no longer be available at a later stage, it may request from the competent court a pre-emptive injunction against the defendant, ordering for example an on-site inspection or the submission of specific documents or information. In practice such requests are hard to obtain and must be thoroughly reasoned. Similar 'exhibition orders' may also be sought by the plaintiff in the course of the proceeding, although this does not amount to a formal full discovery process as is applicable in the US or UK.[41]

---

39 Article 1338 of the ICC states that any party to a contract who knew or should have known that the contract was invalid and did not inform the other party of this invalidity is obliged to pay the other party the damages suffered as a consequence of having entered into an invalid contract.

40 It remains to be seen whether, as a follow-up to the European Commission's White Paper on Damages Actions of April 2008 and the expected EC directive on this matter, Italian legislation could be amended so as to facilitate the plaintiff's burden of proof in case of follow-on actions relying on previous decisions by the same Commission or the IAA.

41 In private actions based on the illegal use of intellectual property rights, plaintiffs enjoy more power to obtain disclosure orders against defendants than in regular civil proceedings. Indeed, Article 121 of the so-called 'Industrial Property Code' (Legislative Decree n. 30/2005, as subsequently amended to be compatible with Directive 2004/48/EC of April 29, 2004 'on the enforcement of intellectual property rights') allows for the parties to obtain exhibition orders from the court in order to obtain relevant documents and information from the opponent. In particular, the claimant will need to (i) provide circumstantial evidence that his claim is well-founded, and (ii) indicate what documents or information held by the opponent would support his claim. In such actions, the standard of proof for the claimant in order to obtain disclosure of information is lower that in regular civil proceedings (as antitrust actions would be), given that he only has to provide a serious indication of the validity of his claim.

Moreover, with particular regard to private actions related to cartel cases, in the absence of relevant case law it is unclear – and unlikely in our opinion – whether Italian courts could order disclosure of confidential documents of the defendant(s) or, more generally, documents used by the latter in a public antitrust proceeding in order to obtain immunity or a reduction of fine under the relevant Leniency Program.[42]

Otherwise, Italian courts can only hear evidence presented by the litigants and do not have (nor frequently use) major *ex officio* investigative powers. Among such powers, the most relevant in the present context are the rights to:

- order on-site inspections;
- appoint a relevant expert, which in antitrust actions may be an economist or accountant[43] (in such cases the court will have to provide clear instructions and guidelines for the tasks at issue and the parties will be able to appoint their own experts in order to comment on or criticize the findings of the expert instructed by the court);
- request information from public authorities, including the IAA or the European Commission; and
- either *ex officio* or upon specific request by a party, order one or more parties to the proceedings (or a third party) to submit relevant documents or information that is necessary to the decision.

When requesting information from public authorities, the court could make such a request of the IAA where the latter has already reached a decision on a specific case.[44] In practice, however, this tool is rarely used, as information concerning IAA proceedings is normally supplied by the parties themselves. In one 2007 case before the Naples Court of Appeal,[45] the court went as far as concluding that, in damages actions following cartel decisions by the IAA, a plaintiff may prove the causal link between the defendant's infringement and the damage suffered simply by presenting a copy of the relevant IAA decision, although – as a matter of law – IAA decisions do not constitute binding

---

42 In this regard, please note that even the European Commission's draft proposal for Council Directive on rules governing damages actions for infringements of Article 81 and 82 of the Treaty, which otherwise seems to somehow promote the use of disclosure orders, states that 'Member States shall ensure that national courts at no point in time order the disclosure of corporate statements or settlements submissions'. The draft proposal also adds that 'Member States shall ensure that national courts refrain, to the extent necessary, from ordering disclosure upon application by a competition authority that has shown to the court that disclosure would undermine an ongoing investigation concerning a suspected infringement of Article 81 or 82 of the Treaty'. Even more explicitly, the 2004 Commission Notice on the co-operation between the Commission and the courts of the EU Member States in the application of Articles 81 and 82 EC provides that 'the Commission will not transmit to national courts information voluntarily submitted by a leniency applicant without the consent of that applicant'.

43 See for example the *Telsystem* case discussed further below.

44 In the *International Broker* case, cited above, upon request of the Rome Court of Appeal, the IAA disclosed to the court the minutes of a hearing of the defendants' representatives as well as the documents seized in a dawn raid at the defendants' premises.

45 Corte d'Appello di Napoli, judgment of July 12, 2007, *P.Z. c. R.*

precedents for civil courts.[46] On this same matter the Supreme Court recently indicated that IAA decisions may represent a 'preferential evidentiary tool' in the context of private actions, which in turn may lead to a reversal of the burden of proof.[47] Nonetheless, in a more recent judgment on the *INAZ Paghe* case, the Supreme Court restated that civil courts are not bound by IAA decisions and that new facts and evidence contradicting such decisions may still be assessed in private enforcement proceedings.[48]

Conversely, decisions by the European Commission under Article 81/82 EC have a stronger – albeit in our opinion still not formally binding – influence on Italian judges, as Article 16 of EC Regulation n. 1/2003 provides that national courts cannot take decisions 'running counter' to previous Commission decisions on the same antitrust matter.[49] In the recent *ENI* case,[50] however, the Court of Milan pushed this provision even further when it declared ENI's claim on the absence of effects by the cartel inadmissible on the assumption that it was going against a cartel decision by the European Commission on the same matter. This argument was made by the court to avoid examining the same facts from the outset (rather than examining them and then possibly deciding in line with the European Commission), but this '*escamotage*' does not seem to reflect what Article 16 of EC Regulation n. 1/2003 intended to achieve.[51] Indeed, the judgment by the Court of Milan has been appealed on this and other points by a number of parties before the Milan Court of Appeal, where the proceedings are currently pending.

Finally, it is worth noting that if a private antitrust action is somewhat simultaneous to a parallel public proceeding conducted by the IAA (or just concluded by the IAA but then appealed to the competent administrative courts for judicial review), Italian law does not provide for a mandatory stay of the private proceedings,[52] although in practice it could happen that the civil judges informally discuss the matter with the IAA or the administrative court at issue to avoid conflicting or overlapping decisions.

---

[46] See Corte di Cassazione, judgment n. 2305 of February 2, 2007, *Fondiaria-SAI Assicurazioni c. Nigriello*.

[47] See Corte di Cassazione, judgment n. 3638 of February 13, 2009, *Certel et al. c. ENEL*. See also Corte d'Appello di Milano, order of April 19, 2005, *Alice c. Auditel*.

[48] Corte di Cassazione, judgment n. 3640 of February 13, 2009, *Associazione nazionale consulenti del lavoro c. INAZ Paghe*.

[49] In particular, the fact that national courts cannot 'run counter' to previous Commission decisions in relation to Articles 81/82 of the EC Treaty does not necessarily mean that national courts are strictly bound by these decisions – i.e. they should be allowed to examine new facts and/or evidence that were not disclosed to (or simply not at stake in) the administrative proceedings before the Commission, and rule accordingly. On this point see A. Komninos, *Resolving Jurisdictional Issues*, unpublished paper for the *Joint Training Programme for Judges*, London, February 2010; and W. Wils, *The relationship between public antitrust enforcement and private actions for damages*, in *World Comp.*, 2009, p. 16.

[50] See footnote 21 above.

[51] This view was also shared by judge G. Muscolo (from the Court of Rome) in her paper *Le azioni civili nelle corti europee e italiane – Alcune questioni sulla prova del danno*, prepared for a speech at a IAA conference on private antitrust enforcement held on February 12, 2010.

[52] *Inter alia*, Corte di Cassazione, judgment n. 9384 of June 11, 2003, *Liquigas c. Girelli*; Corte d'Appello di Milano, order of 3 June 2004, *Moto c. Autogrill*.

5. Remedies and defenses

Under Italian and EU competition law, antitrust plaintiffs may sue for damages or declaratory relief (e.g. seeking the nullity of a contract), and may also seek interim measures in summary proceedings.

a. Damages

As mentioned above, in order for a private damages action based on tort law to be successful, a plaintiff must demonstrate that:

- there has been an infringement of Italian or EU competition law (a prior decision by the IAA or European Commission on the same facts may facilitate this from a factual standpoint but is not conclusive on the existence of damages);
- the infringement caused unjust harm and there is a direct causal link between the violation and the damage suffered; and
- there was intent or negligence on the part of the defendant.

The substantive issues related to these elements have already been illustrated above.

With regard to the measure of damages, the plaintiff bears the burden of proving both the existence and extent of the claimed damage, although under Italian procedural law the court may also decide this upon an equitable basis where practical problems of determination arise.[53] Damages may include compensation for both direct damage (*danno emergente*), including expenses for bringing the action and legal fees, and loss of profit (*lucro cessante*), which may also comprise loss of chance/opportunity. For example, in the *Telsystem*[54] and *Albacom*[55] cases mentioned above the loss of chance was duly assessed when calculating the damages caused by the incumbent telecom operator's refusals to supply the plaintiffs with services they needed to enter the relevant markets.

In particular, in the landmark *Telsystem* judgment of 1996,[56] the Milan Court of Appeal identified the value of lost investments as direct damage, while the loss of profit was essentially calculated on the basis of the profits that would have reasonably accrued to the victim in the period in which it could not enter the market (more than one year in this case). For this purpose, through the appointed independent expert the Milan Court of Appeal identified a 'virtual market position' that the plaintiff would have achieved without illicit obstacles created by the incumbent operator, taking into account the size of the plaintiff, its competence and promptness in marketing services, as well as its organizational ability (which were eventually reduced from what had been originally

---

[53] See for example Corte d'Appello di Milano, judgment of July 11, 2003, *Bluvacanze c. I Viaggi del Ventaglio, Turisanda e Hotelplan Italia*, where the Court calculated the 'reputational damage' upon an equitable basis (whilst the amount of direct damage and loss of profit was determined on the basis of the specific circumstances of the case).

[54] Corte d'Appello di Milano, judgments of July 18, 1995 and December 24,1996, both in the *Telsystem c. SIP-Telecom Italia* case.

[55] Corte d'Appello di Roma, judgment of January 20, 2003, *Albacom c. Telecom Italia*.

[56] Corte d'Appello di Milano, judgments of July 18, 1995 and December 24, 1996, both in the *Telsystem c. SIP-Telecom Italia* case.

claimed).[57] In the *Albacom* case the Rome Court of Appeal used the plaintiffs' market shares in an adjacent market as a proxy for determining the competitive position that they could have achieved in the absence of the illicit conduct; then in order to quantify damages the Court proportionally multiplied such estimated market shares by the revenues generated by the incumbent operator in the relevant market at issue.

In cases of exclusionary conduct such as these two telecoms cases and some others that followed, damages were calculated as the difference between the current economic condition of the victim and the condition in which it would have been without the illicit conduct (but for causation[58]), provided that all other economic and market conditions are the same. In the *Bluvacanze* case, the court determined the damages on the basis of the plaintiff's sales before and after the illicit conduct, multiplying them by the margins agreed between the same plaintiff (a travel agent) and the defendants (the boycotting tour operators).[59]

In summary, a competitor that suffered from exclusionary conduct by a dominant company might recover any of the following damages:

- for direct damage resulting from lost investments and/or legal expenses incurred in all proceedings against the defendant;
- lost profits due to a delayed entry into the relevant market;
- loss of chance to develop significant commercial know-how and expertise; and/or
- loss of corporate reputation among customers and sector operators.

In this latter regard, in the *Gruppo Sicurezza* case,[60] a security service provider claimed damages against the Rome-Fiumicino airport operator, alleging exclusionary abuse (unlawful interference with the plaintiff's customers, which led them to terminate the contracts they had entered into with the plaintiff). Gruppo Sicurezza was eventually awarded damages to compensate its loss of profit as well as the harm to its reputation. Reputational damages (of 50,000 Euro) were also awarded, albeit on an equitable basis, in the *Bluvacanze* case just mentioned above.[61]

In the dominance case of *Avir v. ENI*, also of 2006 and concerning a type of abuse involving excessive prices charged by the main gas operator in Italy, the plaintiff was awarded restitution of the overcharges in addition to damages.[62]

Conversely, in private actions following findings by a public authority of cartels or

---

[57] Overall, damages eventually awarded by the Milan Court of Appeal amounted to 3.85 billion lire (including legal fees), i.e. approximately 2 million Euro.

[58] See *inter alia* Blair-Page, *Speculative Antitrust Damages*, in *Wash. Law Rev*. 1995, p. 428.

[59] Corte d'Appello di Milano, judgment of July 11, 2003, *Bluvacanze c. I Viaggi del Ventaglio, Turisanda e Hotelplan Italia*. A similar 'before and after' method for calculating damages was used in the *INAZ Paghe* case (Corte d'Appello di Milano, judgment of December 10, 2004, *Inaz Paghe c. Associazione nazionale consulenti del lavoro*).

[60] Corte d'Appello di Roma, judgment of January 8, 2004, *Gruppo Sicurezza c. Aeroporti di Roma*.

[61] Corte d'Appello di Milano, judgment of July 11, 2003, *Bluvacanze c. I Viaggi del Ventaglio, Turisanda e Hotelplan Italia*.

[62] Corte d'Appello di Milano, judgment of September 16, 2006, *Avir c. ENI*.

concerted practices, the trend has been to measure damages as the overcharge paid by the direct purchaser as a result of the collusion.[63]

As a general rule, no punitive or treble damages are provided by Italian law. However, in a surprising judgment of 2007, a lower civil court in Bitonto held that, when calculating damages, the deterrent effect should also be considered (despite this normally being the domain of antitrust authorities in the context of public enforcement).[64] This judgment came in the civil proceeding related to the landmark *Manfredi* judgment at the EU level,[65] following a referral under Article 234 of the EC Treaty by the same *Giudice di Pace* of Bitonto. As a result, the local judge awarded damages that not only reflected the loss suffered by the plaintiff but also set off any economic benefit gained by the defendant, an insurer that had participated in a price-fixing cartel in the motor vehicle insurance market. In applying such a mechanism, the court ultimately awarded double damages.

However, given the peculiar circumstances of this case (including the small amount of damages at stake, i.e. less than 1,000 Euro) and the low level of the court at issue, it is unlikely that this judgment will have any persuasive authority in the future. Furthermore, in the *Ciancarelli* case of 2007, [66] the Supreme Court clarified that even in those cases where the courts are allowed to decide upon an equitable basis, the damages awarded must be proportionate and there cannot be treble (i.e. punitive) damages. Compensation must be strictly related to the actual or reasonably estimated damage suffered by the plaintiff and the criteria set forth by the court must be straightforward and very much based on the evidence provided by the parties during the proceedings, thus definitely not speculative.

b. Passing-on defense

A 'passing-on' defense would appear to be admissible in Italy pursuant to general burden of proof rules. Indeed, such a defense was expressly referred to in the 2000 judgment by the Turin Court of Appeal in the *Juventus* case,[67] holding that an alleged victim cannot successfully claim damages if it has passed them on to third parties, including final consumers. Moreover, according to this judgment and general principles of Italian tort law, where it is found that the plaintiff has contributed to the loss with its negligent conduct, damages may be reduced proportionately. Defendants may thus make use of a further defense beside the 'passing-on'.

It should be noted that the passing-on theory is not necessarily used only by defendants. For instance, in the *ENI* case currently pending before the Milan Court of Appeal, the passing-on argument is being used as an offensive maneuver (rather than defensively)

---

[63] Corte di Cassazione (*Sezioni Unite*), judgment of February 4, 2005 n. 2207, *Unipol Assicurazioni c. Ricciardelli.*

[64] Giudice di Pace di Bitonto, judgment of May 21, 2007, *Manfredi c. Lloyd Adriatico Assicurazioni.*

[65] Court of Justice of the European Union, judgment of July 13, 2006, case C–295 to 298/04, *Manfredi et al. c. Lloyd Adriatico Assicurazioni et al.*

[66] Corte di Cassazione, judgment n. 23304 of November 8, 2007, *Telecom Italia c. Ciancarelli.*

[67] Corte d'Appello di Torino, judgment of July 6, 2000, *Indaba Incentive Company c. Juventus FC.* See also Corte d'Appello di Cagliari, judgment of January 23, 1999, *Unimare c. Geasar*, relating to an alleged abuse of dominance in relation to ground-handling services in Olbia Airport in Sardinia.

by some of the synthetic rubber producers acting as plaintiffs or interveners, claiming, *inter alia*, to have caused no direct damage to the tire manufacturers (summoned as defendants) and arguing that the latter passed on price increases (if the court were to find any) to their own customers.

c. Interim injunctions

The victim of an infringement of Article 81/82 EC or Article 2/3 of Law 287/90 may request an interim injunction in order to prevent further damages as a consequence of the illicit conduct. In several cases, national courts have confirmed the availability of 'cease and desist' injunctions, mainly in the context of national competition law rather than EU law.[68] On the other hand, peremptory injunctions which would modify existing legal relationships between the parties or impose a duty to enter into a new contract may be refused.[69] However, in an order of July 2005 in the *Farmacie Petrone/Pfizer* case,[70] the Milan Court of Appeal found that Pfizer's refusal to supply certain drugs to the wholesaler amounted to an abuse of dominant position under Italian competition law and, accordingly, it ordered Pfizer to supply the wholesaler. Nevertheless, in November 2005,[71] the same Court of Appeals clarified and limited the scope of this injunction to cover only the wholesaler's needs for the national market.

Interim measures based on Italian competition law may be requested from the competent Court of Appeal, while requests based on Article 81/82 EC must be addressed to the local first instance tribunal (or the *giudici di pace* if the claim is worth less than 5,000 Euro). Since 2006, the IAA has also been competent to issue interim measures in antitrust cases (not only *ex parte* but also *ex officio*). Although this would occur in the context of public enforcement, any such interim measure would ultimately benefit private parties injured by the alleged antitrust violation.

In all cases, the applicant for an interim measure must prove (i) a *prima facie* infringement of the relevant competition rules (*fumus boni iuris*);[72] and (ii) that if interim measures are not adopted, the length of ordinary proceedings would likely cause serious and irreparable harm to the applicant (*periculum in mora*). In this latter regard, the applicant's likely exit from the relevant market deriving from the alleged antitrust infringement has

---

68 *Inter alia*, Corte d'Appello di Milano, Order of July 13, 1998, *Tramaplast c. Macplast*; Corte d'Appello di Milano, Order of September 29, 1998, *Inaz Paghe c. Consiglio nazionale consulenti del lavoro*.

69 *Inter alia*, Corte d'Appello di Milano, Order of June 3, 1995, *Novamont c. CEIT*, which overruled on appeal a previous decision of the same court in the same case (order of April 29, 1995). Most recently, Tribunale di Milano, order of February 16, 2010, *NewsCorp e SKY Italia c. Publitalia*, concerning the allegedly unfair and anticompetitive refusal by Publitalia to let SKY Italia advertise its TV programs on Mediaset's leading DTTV channels (Mediaset being part of the same corporate group of Publitalia). However, for the sake of completeness, we note that collective claims brought by registered consumers' associations pursuant to Article 140 of the Consumer Code (see Section 6 below) may to some extent be aimed at obtaining peremptory injunctions.

70 Corte d'Appello di Milano, Order of July 23, 2005, *Farmacie Petrone c. Pharmacia Italia e Pfizer Italia*.

71 Corte d'Appello di Milano, Order of November 10, 2005, *Farmacie Petrone c. Pharmacia Italia e Pfizer Italia*.

72 The *prima facie* infringement may even derive from pre-contractual negotiations (e.g. Corte d'Appello di Milano, Order of October 8, 1994, *Telsystem c. SIP*).

been considered by Italian courts as a possible indicator of the existence of serious and irreparable harm.[73]

Where possible, applicants for interim measures under antitrust rules tend to additionally allege that the same facts also amount to a breach of Italian law on unfair trade practices (Articles 2598 ff. of the ICC),[74] as Italian judges are more accustomed to such legislation. Therefore, obtaining the relevant injunction may ultimately prove easier.

d. Declaratory relief

With regard to declaratory relief, Italian courts may be asked to declare as null and void contracts or clauses which infringe EU or Italian competition law.

In this regard it is worth noting that while Article 81 EC and Article 2 of Law 287/90 expressly state that any forbidden agreements are void, Article 82 EC and Article 3 of Law 287/90 do not formally do so. However, it is generally accepted that the contracts through which a dominant firm abuses its dominant position (or those that are directly affected by the abuse) are void, as both Articles 81 and 82 EC and their Italian equivalents (Articles 2 and 3 of Law 287/90) are considered 'public policy' rules.[75]

Whether the whole or a part of the agreement will be declared null and void essentially depends on (i) the type of violation alleged; and (ii) whether the alleged anticompetitive clauses are severable from the rest of the agreement, in light of the relevant contract negotiations.[76] This severability rule may not apply and the whole agreement not be affected where the infringing clauses declared void are by law replaced by applicable mandatory provisions.

For example, in the *Avir/ENI* stand-alone case of 2006, the Milan Court of Appeal found that the pricing clauses of gas supply agreements, through which ENI had imposed excessive prices by leveraging its market power, were null and void as they were contrary to Italian law expressly prohibiting excessive prices by a dominant company (i.e. Article 3 of Law 287/90).[77]

Conversely, general rules of Italian civil law suggest that a private antitrust action seeking a permanent order to carry out specific performance may not be admissible. Generally, the order by a national court to perform a specific act is issued only as an interim measure, as illustrated above. In its final judgment on the merits, the court

---

[73] *Inter alia*, Corte d'Appello di Roma, Order of August 18, 2000, *Albacom c. Telecom Italia*.

[74] *Inter alia*, Tribunale di Milano, order of October 26, 2009, *NewsCorp e SKY Italia c. Publitalia*; Tribunale di Roma, order of March 31, 2000, *RAI-TV c. RTI*.

[75] See for instance P. Giudici, *Private Antitrust Law Enforcement In Italy*, *The Competition Law Review* 1(1), August 2004, pp. 61–85. On the other hand, it might be argued that if the abusive conduct does not generate, nor is actually related to, a contractual obligation, the nullity of the anticompetitive practice itself will not be at stake and the damaged party should base its claim merely on tort liability under Article 2043 of the ICC (see also P. Iannuccelli, *Il Private Enforcement del diritto della concorrenza in Italia, ovvero può il diritto antitrust servirsi del codice civile?*, in *Rivista delle Società* 2006, p. 739).

[76] This latter issue would essentially have to be decided under Article 1419 of the ICC which provides that, in the event of nullity of one clause of an agreement, the whole agreement would be null and void only if it can be shown that the parties would not have entered into the agreement without the void clause.

[77] Corte d'Appello di Milano, September 16, 2006, *Avir c. ENI*.

generally has no power to order a permanent injunction, except in limited circumstances (e.g. the conduct at issue was contemplated in the pre-contractual negotiations).

6. Aggregating claims

Article 140 of Legislative Decree n. 206/2005 (the so-called 'Consumer Code')[78] provides that consumers' associations with a nationwide presence registered with the Ministry of Economic Development (formerly the Ministry of Productive Activities) can bring private actions on behalf of the final consumers they represent. Pursuant to Article 140, consumers' associations are allowed to request injunctions in order to stop the illicit conduct or, based on recent case law, injunctions imposing particular duties on the defendants which might benefit final consumers.[79] Conversely, under Article 140, consumers' associations are not entitled to obtain damages, thus ruling out that this provision could be used for compensation purposes.

At the end of December 2007, the Italian Parliament passed the 2008 Budget Law, adding Article 140-*bis* to the Consumer Code which for the first time in Italy introduced the possibility of initiating class actions for damages in relation to all civil suits.[80] However, while this legislation originally provided that class actions could be initiated from June 2008, a series of subsequent interventions ultimately postponed the start-up date to January 1, 2010. Under the last amended text, the law has (almost) no retroactive effect, going back only as far as August 15, 2009.[81] Interestingly, the elimination of the retroactive effect coupled with the postponement of the law may have saved financial institutions from onerous litigation related to recent financial setbacks.

Under the current text of the law, both individual consumers and groups of consumers will be able to obtain a declaratory judgment setting out the right to obtain compensation and a refund of sums paid, whilst under the previous text the standing to bring such claims had been granted only to entities such as consumers' associations and other consumer groups, or investors' groups/associations, to be considered by the court as sufficiently representative of collective interests.[82] However, since Article 3(a) of the Consumer Code

---

[78] Article 140 of the Consumer Code basically reproduces Article 3 of Law n. 281/1998 which regulated consumers' and final users' rights before implementation of the Consumer Code.

[79] *Inter alia*, Tribunale di Torino, judgment of November 20, 2006, *Associazione Movimento Consumatori c. Wind Telecomunicazioni*, later confirmed by Corte d'Appello di Torino, judgment of February 24, 2009; see also Tribunale di Roma, judgment of April 20, 2008, *Movimento Consumatori e Unione Nazionale Consumatori c. SKY Italia*.

[80] Law 244/2007 of December 24, 2007 added a new statutory provision (n. 140-*bis* titled 'collective damage action') to the Consumer Code.

[81] This is an important amendment introduced by Law n. 99/2009, effective from August 15, 2009. In amending Article 140-*bis*, Law n. 99/2009 provides that 'Article 140-bis should be applied only to illegal conducts that took place after implementation of the present law', which literally means that Article 140-*bis* will apply to conducts that took place after the entry into force of Law 99/2009, thus as of August 15, 2009. However, it is commonly accepted that the Italian legislator meant to introduce the above mentioned amendment directly in the text of Article 140-*bis*, therefore by 'implementation of the present law' referring to entry into force of Article 140-*bis* itself, i.e. as of January 2010.

[82] For a brief overview of the old text of Article 140-*bis* of the Consumer Code, see F. Arossa and G. Rosato, Freshfields Bruckhaus Deringer LLP, *Recent developments in class action and third party funding of litigation*, February 2008, (see www.freshfields.com/publications/pdfs/2008/

defines consumers and users as 'any physical individual who is acting for purposes falling outside the scope of his business or profession', it is not clear whether Italian class action legislation will actually apply to claims brought by individuals acting *within* the scope of their businesses or professions – including their employment contracts.

Under the current law, class actions can be brought only before the *tribunale ordinario* of the regional capital where the company is legally resident – with some Regions being aggregated under the same capital – making a total of eleven competent courts in Italy.[83]

With regard to the specific rights that can be enforced under Article 140-*bis*, these are:

- contractual rights of a plurality of final consumers and users against the same undertaking/professional, including rights stemming from standard form contracts (where the consumer is usually not in a position to negotiate the terms and conditions of the same);
- rights of final consumers or users of a particular product against the producer, regardless of any direct contractual relationships;
- consumers' rights arising from unfair commercial practices or anti-competitive conduct.

In all the above-mentioned cases, consumers' claims must be 'identical', meaning that, in order for the court to admit the class action, the extent and kind of damages claimed by class members must be common.[84]

In fact, once the claim is filed, the judicial procedure will basically consist of two steps, the first of which will consist of a 'filtering' process, a particular *ad hoc* mechanism that has been introduced specifically for class actions to allow the court to assess the admissibility of the claim. The claim will be deemed inadmissible if (i) it is groundless; (ii) there is a conflict of interest; (iii) there is no commonality of interests between the class members; or (iv) the plaintiff does not appear to be able to adequately represent the interest(s) of class members. Interestingly, the court may also decide to suspend the procedures if a case on the same matter is pending before an independent authority (such as the IAA) or an administrative court.

If the action is declared admissible, the claimant must proceed with suitable promotion to inform all potential class members of the collective action, including members of consumers' associations, enabling them to 'opt in' within the applicable deadline and

---

feb20/21722.pdf); see also J. Isted, N. Goeke and M. Raja, Freshfields Bruckhaus Deringer LLP, *Class action in the EU: a threat to the life sciences industry?*, December 2008 (see www.freshfields.com/publications/pdfs/2008/dec08/class_actions.pdf).

[83] Namely the Tribunale di Bari for Puglia, Tribunale di Bologna for Emilia-Romagna, Tribunale di Cagliari for Sardinia, Tribunale di Firenze for Tuscany, Tribunale di Genova for Liguria, Tribunale di Milano for Lombardy, Tribunale di Napoli for Basilicata, Calabria and Campania, Tribunale di Palermo for Sicily, Tribunale di Roma for Abruzzi, Lazio, Marche, Molise and Umbria, Tribunale di Torino for Piedmont and Valle d'Aosta, Tribunale di Venezia for Friuli-Venezia Giulia, Trentino-Alto Adige and Veneto.

[84] With this regard, the recent amendments to Article 140-*bis* introduced in August 2009 basically exclude the possibility of starting a class action for environmental and health damages.

according to the criteria set forth by the court in the admissibility decision – basically the court is supposed to specify what are the main features of the claim, the rights being relied upon and, most of all, what are the elements that would allow a consumer to fall within or outside the scope of the class action. In order to quickly reach consumers potentially interested in joining the claim, the court is also called upon to indicate the most suitable media to advertise the collective action.

Indeed, unlike the US class action rule and, most interestingly, the European Commission's draft proposal for a Council Directive on rules governing damages actions for infringements of Article 81 and 82 of the Treaty, the Italian class actions law provides for an 'opt-in' system, meaning that the right to compensation following a successful action will only extend to those individuals who expressly joined the action. Moreover while opting-in consumers will of course be bound by the results of the action (and will not be able to bring other related actions, whether individually or collectively), those consumers who chose not to participate in the class action will be free to bring separate actions.

In the second phase of the judicial procedure, the court will hear the parties and take a final decision, either directly determining damages for class members or defining the criteria for liquidating damages (which supposedly each claimant should then ask for in a separate actions). With particular regard to calculation of damages, under the current text of the law the court's assessment is to be made upon an equitable basis (pursuant to Article 1226 of the ICC), thus somehow lowering the standard of proof for the plaintiff, which will not need to prove the exact amount of damage suffered.[85] With regard to legal fees and costs related to the proceedings, as previously mentioned with regard to standard individual civil actions, they are usually for the losing party to pay, but the measure of such costs and fees is in any case established by the court itself in its final decision. Finally, the court may suspend the execution of the decision, in light of the total amount to be paid by the defendant, the number of claimants and the potential risks related to a hypothetical subsequent recovery of the sums paid should the decision be overruled.

As a general remark, after two years of parliamentary discussions and active debate in the business and legal communities, the introduction of the new class action legislation should be considered favorably, as it puts Italy up to speed with other EU Member States, such as France, Germany, Spain and the Netherlands, that allow collective actions, in one form or another, to be brought in courts. At the time this chapter is being finalized, while the new law has been in effect for only three months, it appears that five class actions have been lodged, three of which have already been cleared by the court to go to trial.[86]

---

[85] It remains to be seen if and to what extent the Italian courts will be willing to apply, whether or not through external economic consultants, the recent report on the quantification of damages in antitrust cases, prepared for the European Commission by Oxera and a group of economic consultants and lawyers (see Oxera, *Quantifying antitrust damages – towards non-binding guidance for courts*, December 2009, available at http://ec.europa.eu/competition/antitrust/actionsdamages/quantification_study.pdf).

[86] Two of these three cases have been brought against the two largest Italian banks, Intesa Sanpaolo and Unicredit, in relation to a claim on overdraft charges, following on an opinion (not amounting to a formal decision) by the IAA in December 2009.

However, at this early stage some concerns remain as to how Italian courts will react to the introduction of this new judicial tool. First of all, as of today it seems that none of the eleven Italian courts competent for judging on class actions has yet set up any special sections or *ad hoc* panel for this purpose, thus casting doubts on their ability to promptly handle the complexity of aggregated claims. Furthermore, the 'filtering' process to be carried out by the courts, as currently structured, gives plenty of scope for judicial discretion. Finally, it is still not clear how Article 140-*bis* will interact with the specific rules for class actions against public institutions and entities in charge of public services, which are currently limited to peremptory injunctions against the public administration, thus not allowing damages actions in the same context.[87]

Conclusion

Contrary to general belief, private antitrust enforcement in Italy has been gradually increasing over the last few years and the recent introduction of class action legislation may very much have a significant impact in private lawsuits based on Italian or EU competition laws. Overall, however, antitrust law in Italy and across the EU has traditionally had more of a public than private nature, given the widespread negative effects that antitrust infringements are able to cause. Moreover, many Italian judges are not (yet) very familiar with antitrust matters and until now have mostly refrained from awarding multi-million damages judgments even in interesting cases of anticompetitive practices already ascertained by the IAA.

As illustrated in this chapter, although the number of private actions in Italy is growing, the relevant jurisprudence is not yet fully consistent and does not provide definite assurances to market players willing to act before national courts to defend their interests. Moreover, the length of civil proceedings before Italian courts, the complexity of the procedural rules and, in the absence of disclosure-type rules like in the US or UK, the difficulty in gathering the necessary evidence to bring successful antitrust lawsuits may still deter private parties from bringing stand-alone damages actions. The absence of any form of punitive damages would also appear to render the Italian system less attractive to potential plaintiffs, particularly where forum-shopping is somewhat possible. It thus remains to be seen when and how future legislation that has been discussed at European level to further promote damages actions (i.e. the draft EC directive on damage claims mentioned above) will actually be adopted, when and how it will be implemented in Italy and in the other Member States, and how the relevant changes will be used in practice. In any case, it is very likely that any such legislation will provide not only clearer guidelines to the legal community but also further stimulus to, and public awareness of, private antitrust actions.

Based on the current trends in public antitrust policy in Italy, it is possible that in the next few years private antitrust claims in this country will mainly be follow-on damages

---

[87] The rules on class actions against the public administration were introduced by Legislative Decree 198/2009 of December 12, 2009. Interestingly enough, these rules apply not only to public administrations in the strict sense but also to public services providers (thus also including services in regulated industries such as electricity, gas, water, etc.). However, Legislative Decree 198/2009 does not formally exclude that damages actions against the providers of such services might still be brought under Article 140-*bis* of the Consumer Code.

actions based on cartel infringements, which may increase in the future as a result of successful implementation of the Italian Leniency Program. However, this possible increase in follow-on damages actions related to cartel cases may in its turn have a negative impact on the number of leniency applications lodged with the IAA, with the consequence of creating an opposite effect in view of further actions in the future. It may thus be opportune to adopt appropriate legislation in this regard, either at EU or directly at Italian level, as also discussed in recent public conferences on private antitrust claims organized by the IAA.

On the other hand, considering that in recent years the vast majority of abuse of dominance cases pursued by the IAA have been promptly resolved through the 'commitments procedure', follow-on litigation related to dominance cases may decrease.

Overall, in conclusion, it would seem that for a definite and consistent increase of private antitrust litigation in Italy, representing a sort of 'second generation' set of cases, new appropriate legislation is needed at EU or Italian level, or – alternatively – another one or two landmark judgments in important national cases, which would create further thrill in the business and legal communities.

20 Netherlands

Daan Lunsingh Scheurleer, Herman Speyart, Flip Wijers and Joost Fanoy[1]

Introduction

As in most countries, adherence to competition law is enforced in the Netherlands through public enforcement by the European Commission or the Dutch Competition Authority (*Nederlandse Mededingingsautoriteit,* hereinafter NMa), and through private damages claims before civil courts.

National Dutch competition law, which is laid down in the Dutch Competition Act (DCA), is largely copied from European legislation. The mechanisms for private enforcement, however, are not; it follows from European case law that the private enforcement of competition law is expressly left to the Member States.

Historically, the private enforcement of claims based on infringement of competition rules has not been widespread in the Netherlands. That changed somewhat following the introduction of the DCA in 1998, but that led to only a limited increase in such claims. To date, such claims are still scarce. An often used explanation for this scarcity is that it is rather complicated to establish the amount and scope of the damage suffered and to provide sufficient proof of such damage.

1. How does a damages action case get started?

a. Meeting clients and ethical restrictions

A plaintiff's attorney can identify clients with potential antitrust claims in a number of ways, depending upon the specific circumstances of the case.

If an antitrust violation has been established in a competition authority decision with respect to companies supplying specific sectors or clients, it is easy to identify potential claimants, either directly or through an industry sector organization.

If the potential claim relates to consumer goods, an attorney may appear on a consumer television show and describe the claim, enabling prospective clients to sign up, most often via the website of the consumer television programme.

Under Dutch Bar rules, lawyers may also advertise and set up websites where potential plaintiffs can register. Under the same rules, however, attorneys are not allowed to commission third parties for signing up clients. The rules on fee agreements will be discussed below. Getting victims to sign up for a claim was extensively done in the Dexia securities collective action which led to a €1 billion settlement in 2007.

---

[1] Daan Lunsingh Scheurleer, Herman Speyart and Flip Wijers are attorneys-at-law with NautaDutilh N.V., Amsterdam, the Netherlands. Joost Fanoy is an attorney-at-law with Straatman Koster Advocaten S.V. in Rotterdam, the Netherlands.

b. Investigative tools

i. Follow-on actions Government action is not a *sine qua non* for private litigation but greatly facilitates such litigation because:

(i) The Dutch civil discovery rules are limited, while both the NMa and the European Commission have extensive powers to conduct searches, seize documents and demand information; and
(ii) European Commission or NMa decisions finding antitrust infringements are binding upon Dutch civil courts, based on (a) Dutch rules of civil procedure as far as NMa decisions are concerned and (b) Article 16 (1) of Regulation (EC) 1/2003 as far as European Commission decisions are concerned.

Although such decisions establish the existence of an infringement, plaintiffs must still prove (i) the extent of their damage, (ii) the causal link between the wrongful conduct and the damage, and (iii) the attribution of the wrongful conduct to the defendant.

ii. Stand-alone actions In a stand-alone action, there is no competition authority decision to be relied upon. The plaintiff must therefore assert and, if denied by the defendant, prove all facts necessary to establish liability, including the existence of the infringement. Therefore, witnesses may need to be examined and expert evidence may need to be furnished at a later stage of the proceedings. These discovery mechanisms are described below.

c. Amassing sufficient evidence

A damages action begins, like other civil actions, with the service of a complaint and summons on the defendant and the filing of these documents with the appropriate court. There are no specific pleading standards in civil competition cases: the complaint must state the facts that support various elements of the claim for damages. The amount of evidence needed to prove the claim varies from case to case, but should support the various elements of the unlawful act.

2. Who may pursue a claim?

Any party alleging to have suffered damage as a result of an antitrust infringement may initiate proceedings before a Dutch civil court, regardless of whether such party is a direct or indirect purchaser, competitor or supplier of the alleged infringer. Pursuant to Article 3:303 of the Dutch Civil Code (DCC), however, the plaintiff must have a sufficient interest in a legal action in order to have standing to bring it. Such an interest is generally presumed, but is rebuttable.

3. In what forum does a plaintiff initiate a private claim?

a. Claims for damages

A private claim for damages of less than EUR 5,000 must be brought in a specific section of the court of first instance that is competent to hear the case (see below), which is referred to as the 'cantonal section'. In such proceedings, the parties may represent themselves. Claims exceeding this threshold must be brought in the regular civil section of the same court, where representation by an attorney is required. There is a legislative initiative to raise the threshold to EUR 25,000.

If the defendant is an EU individual or company, the competent court of first instance is the court of first instance in the district in which the defendant is domiciled or has its corporate seat. Pursuant to Article 101 of the Dutch Code of Civil Procedure (DCCP), however, a consumer's claim may also be brought in the district in which the plaintiff is domiciled. If the defendant is not an EU individual or company, any Dutch court of first instance may accept jurisdiction if the claim is based upon an unlawful act and this act can be located in the Netherlands.

b. Claims for declaratory relief

These claims must be brought in the civil section of the competent court of first instance. Such claims need not to be attached to a claim for damages and can be filed separately. They can be useful to obtain actual relief or to obtain damages in a separate follow-on procedure. In practice, declaratory relief is difficult to obtain, because courts expect parties to request such relief from the NMa or from the European Commission.

4. How may claims be aggregated?

a. Representation by a foundation, association or public body

US-style class actions do not exist in the Netherlands. The DCC, however, does allow for collective actions. Pursuant to §3:305a DCC, a foundation or association whose purpose, as laid down in its articles of association, is to protect the interests of a specific group of persons may bring a collective action on behalf of those persons against one or more wrongdoers. This is only permitted if the interests protected are similar in nature. Such an action may also be brought by legal entities governed by public law (Article 3:305b DCC) and certain consumer interest organizations that have been placed by an EU Member State on a list maintained by the EU for this purpose (Article 3:305c DCC). All such entities will be referred to below as 'representative organizations.'

The representative organization may file any cause of action and seek to recover any type of relief (including a declaratory judgment on liability for damages), with one important exception: monetary relief. The main reason for this exception is that in order for damages to be awarded, certain issues can only be dealt with on an individual basis, such as causation and whether the circumstances causing the damage can be imputed to the injured party. However, recovery of damages in an individual action is facilitated if the representative organization obtains a favorable judgment (which will usually be for declaratory relief), because the issue of liability will have already been decided.

While legal mechanisms are available to circumvent the prohibition against collectively claiming monetary damages, each of them has its own drawbacks. For example, the issuance of powers of attorney by the injured parties to the representative organization to claim damages on their behalf does not eliminate the need to demonstrate individual causation. The same applies if the injured parties transfer their claims to the representative organization. As a consequence, these mechanisms are not often used. Nevertheless, a well-argued collective claim based on §3:305a DCC is generally regarded by defendants as a serious threat.

Dutch law also provides for a specific mass claim procedure in which parties agreeing to settle a mass damages claim may apply for court endorsement of a specific settlement, the effect of this endorsement being that the settlement becomes binding upon absent claimants unless they opt out. This procedure will be discussed in more detail below.

b. Joint writ of summons

Aggregation of claims is also possible where multiple plaintiffs jointly file one complaint, a claim is brought by one plaintiff acting for multiple injured parties on the basis of powers of attorney or where multiple claims have been transferred to one plaintiff.

c. Joint and several liability

The DCC provides for joint and several liability. In cases of multilateral anticompetitive behavior, such liability can be based on the collective nature of the antitrust infringement in question.

5. What procedural defences are available short of trial?

Dutch law recognizes several defences a defendant may invoke before the court decides on the merits of a collective action.

a. Amicable resolution of dispute

Before starting a collective action, a representative organization is obliged to attempt to resolve the dispute out of court (Article 3:305a (2) DCC). Absent such attempt, the action will be dismissed if this admissibility defence is raised by the defendant. In practice, this obligation has proved to be little more than a formality and consists of a simple request to settle.

b. Denial of class

An often used defence against a collective action is that the interests of the members of the class are insufficiently similar to justify such an action. Absent a sufficient similarity of interests, the representative organization lacks standing. Both Dutch case law and legal scholars are divided on the question of whether this defence can be raised and decided upon prior to the submission of any substantive defences. Because of this uncertainty, a defendant who challenges a plaintiff's standing in the pre-trial phase runs the risk of this being regarded as his full and final defense and being precluded from subsequently submitting any substantive defences. Consequently, even though it would be more cost effective to deal with the standing issue before litigating the case on its merits, in practice this does not occur.

c. Jurisdiction

Another possible defense is that the court lacks jurisdiction. The defendant is required to raise this defense either prior to submitting his answer or in his answer.

d. Lis pendens and connectivity

If a collective action involving the same cause of action and the same plaintiff and defendant is first brought in another jurisdiction and then, in the Netherlands, a Dutch court will, at the defendant's request, stay the proceedings until the foreign court has either accepted or declined jurisdiction. Such a request can, depending on whether any of the following provisions is applicable, be based on Article 27 of Regulation (EC) 44/2001, Article 21 of the Lugano Convention or Article 12 DCCP. This rule aims to prevent conflicting judgments. If the foreign court accepts jurisdiction, the Dutch court will decline it and vice versa.

If a related collective action (an action involving the same cause of action but not the same parties) is pending in a different jurisdiction, a Dutch court may stay the proceedings if requested by the defendant under Article 28 of Regulation (EC) 44/2001 or Article 22 of the Lugano Convention, where applicable. These provisions also allow a Dutch court to refer the Dutch action to the courts of the foreign jurisdiction, provided that the legislation of that jurisdiction allows the two actions to be joined. For purposes of these provisions, actions are deemed to be related when they are so closely connected that it is expedient to hear and determine them together to avoid the risk of irreconcilable judgments resulting from separate proceedings.

e. Summary proceedings

Under Dutch law, both the plaintiff and defendant may petition for provisional measures, such as an order enjoining the other party from engaging in certain activities. Such measures may also be requested through a collective action under Article 3:305a DCC and can be brought either as a sub-action in main proceedings or in separate summary proceedings. A judgment ordering provisional measures will not be issued if the plaintiff fails to demonstrate such urgency that he cannot await the final judgment in main proceedings. In deciding whether to grant interim relief, the court must make a preliminary assessment of the likelihood that the plaintiff will ultimately prevail in main proceedings. It is not possible to seek declaratory relief in summary proceedings.

6. What devices are available to obtain evidence?

a. Discovery

Dutch law does not provide for document discovery procedures similar to those available in the US. Limited discovery, however, is available. Requests for discovery have always been dealt with by the courts in a rather restrictive manner, in order to avoid fishing expeditions. However, in recent years the courts seem to have become less strict in dealing with these requests. The starting point for this is Article 21 DCCP, requiring the parties to completely and truthfully disclose facts relevant to the decision of the case.

Article 843a DCCP provides that a party may request the production of certain sufficiently identifiable documents if he has a legitimate interest in obtaining a copy thereof. In addition, the document must concern a legal relationship – either contractual or based on an unlawful act – to which he is a party. An order to produce such documents will not be granted if the information requested can also be obtained through other means, such as witness testimony. A request for the production of documents may be refused for compelling reasons, such as to protect trade secrets. A person subject to professional secrecy obligations may refuse to produce a document if the information contained therein was obtained in the performance of his professional activities.

It may be argued that the evidence to which a decision of the European Commission or NMa explicitly refers should be discoverable in follow-on litigation and that decisions on related confidentiality issues should be left to the Dutch courts.[2] Additionally, at the request of a party or on its own initiative, a court may order the disclosure of books, records and documents that a company is required to draw up or retain under Dutch law (Article 162 DCCP).

The DCCP also provides for pre-trial witness hearings which are aimed at allowing the plaintiff to determine whether he actually has a case.

b. Access to Commission and NMa files

As indicated above, the NMa has powers to conduct dawn raids, seize documents and demand information. These powers are similar to those conferred upon the European Commission by Regulation (EC) No 1/2003.[3]

Access by private parties to a case file held by the NMa is governed by the Dutch Public Information Act (DPIA), while access to a case file held by the Commission is covered by Regulation (EC) No 1049/2001.[4] Both instruments contain various exceptions, relating, inter alia, to trade secrets and the interest of effective prosecution, which in practice restrict a plaintiff's access to the file.[5]

c. Experts

At the request of a party to the litigation or on its own motion, a court may appoint experts to issue an opinion on certain issues identified by the court. The parties are obliged to cooperate with the experts in their information-gathering; the failure to do so may result in the court drawing conclusions it considers appropriate. Prior to submitting his final report to the court, the expert must allow the parties to the litigation to comment on a draft of the report.

7. What practices are illegal and what are the elements of proof?

Under Dutch law there is no explicit statutory basis for an antitrust damages claim. Such claims must therefore be brought under a general statutory cause of action, such as unlawful acts or contractual liability.

---

2 Preliminary advice of the Dutch Civil Law Association, W.A.J. van Lierop and E.H. Pijnacker Hordijk, Privaatrechtelijke aspecten van het mededingingsrecht.

3 Council Regulation (EC) No 1/2003 of 16 December 2002 on the implementation of the rules on competition laid down in Articles 81 and 82 of the Treaty (Text with EEA relevance) OJ L 1, 4.1.2003, pp. 1–25.

4 Council Regulation (EC) No 1049/2001 of the European Parliament and of the Council of 30 May 2001 regarding public access to European Parliament, Council and Commission documents, in OJ 31.05.2001, No L 145, pp. 43–8.

5 See, for the Dutch decisional practice, NMa Decision of 25 June 2007 in Case 6112 – Martens and Van Oord; NMa Decision of 13 December 2007 in Case 6074 – Broadcast Partners; NMa Decision of 25 June 2008 in Case 6386 – Topherstel and Focwa; NMa Decision of 16 December 2008 in Case 6386 – Automark II and NMa Decision of 9 July 2009 in Case 6407 – Heijmans & IBC. These decisions have not been appealed. Reference is made, as far as access to the European Commission files is concerned, to Case T–403/05 *MyTravel Group v. Commission*, Case T–198/03 *Bank Austria v. Commission*, Case T–2/03 *Verein für Konsumenteninformation v. Commission*, Joined Cases T–391/03 and T–70/04 *Franchet and Byk v. Commission* and Case T-380/08, *Netherlands v. Commission (Bitumen Cartel)*.

a. Unlawful acts

The main statutory basis for antitrust claims is the general provision on unlawful acts (Article 6:162 DCC). An unlawful act is defined in paragraph 2 of that provision as:

> the violation of a right or an act or omission infringing a duty imposed by law or by a rule of unwritten law pertaining to proper social conduct.

An infringement of the applicable antitrust provisions of Articles 81 (restrictive agreements) and/or Article 82 (single-firm abuse of dominance) EC[6] constitutes a breach of a duty imposed by law and is therefore an unlawful act. The same applies to an infringement of the equivalent domestic prohibitions contained in Articles 6 and 24, respectively, DCA.

Although claims deriving from any type of infringement of Articles 81 and 82 EC and their Dutch equivalents are possible, whether vertical or horizontal, claims based on horizontal multilateral infringements and single-firm conduct are more likely to occur because the European Commission and the NMa traditionally focus on horizontal infringements, creating greater opportunities for follow-on claims of this type.

b. Unjust enrichment

The second statutory basis is unjust enrichment, as set out in §6:212 DCC. Under this provision:

> a person who has been unjustly enriched at the expenses of another must, to the extent this is reasonable, repair the damage up to the amount of his enrichment.

An action based on unjust enrichment may be appropriate, for example, (i) to recover an overcharge attributable to bid rigging, (ii) in cases of excessive pricing by a dominant company, or (iii) to obtain repayment of a penalty imposed on one of the members of a cartel for breach of a void cartel agreement.

c. Contractual liability

Where the plaintiff had a contractual relationship with the defendant for the provision of goods or services subject to price-fixing, it may be argued that, had it been known the prices were inflated due to price-fixing, the contract would not have been entered into. This may allow for an action to nullify the contract, resulting in obligations for both parties to undo actions already taken pursuant to the contract and pay damages, if applicable. The nullification of a contract has retroactive effect.

8. What do plaintiffs get if they win?

Damages for an infringement of the antitrust rules are governed by the same rules as those applicable to damages awarded in other actions brought on the basis of an

---

[6] On December 1, 2009, the Treaty of Lisbon came into effect, amending the Treaty Establishing the European Community (EC Treaty) that is now called the Treaty on the Functioning of the European Union (TFEU). Therefore, all references to Articles 81 and 82 of the EC Treaty now reference Articles 101 and 102 TFEU.

unlawful act or breach of contract. Therefore, the starting point in determining the amount of damages is putting plaintiffs in the same position in which they would have been had the infringement not occurred.

Punitive damages cannot be awarded in the Netherlands. The damages awarded in antitrust actions mainly compensate material loss, which may include both actual out-of-pocket loss and loss of profit. Although compensation for emotional damage is theoretically possible, it is very unlikely to be awarded in an antitrust action. Damages are generally awarded in the form of a direct monetary payment, but the court has discretion to order payment in a different form. Material loss can also include any reasonable costs incurred by the plaintiff in trying to mitigate further damage or obtain compensation out of court. In addition, the plaintiff is entitled to statutory interest on losses, which can include prejudgment interest. In calculating the damages to be awarded, any benefits gained by the injured party as a result of the infringement may be set off against the amount of his loss. A Dutch court has great discretion in determining the amount of damages to be awarded. The court may estimate damages when the amount of actual damages cannot be precisely calculated.

Collective settlements

Although US-style class actions do not exist in The Netherlands, US-style class settlements do. Articles 7:907–910 DCC and 1013–1018 DCCP were enacted pursuant to the 2005 Act on the Collective Settlement of Mass Claims that covers the court approval of a collective settlement (the Act). If parties agree to settle their disputes out of court, they can apply to the court to declare the settlement fair and binding even on non-parties to the agreement, on an opt-out basis. The Act has proven to be a big success and is perceived to be an efficient instrument in arriving at global settlements. Its main features are as follows. Defendants and representative organizations can try to reach a settlement out of court. It is not possible, however, to put pressure on a defendant who is unwilling to settle as it is under the US class action regime through the initiation of a damages class action.

If and when the parties succeed in reaching an out-of-court settlement, they can jointly petition the court to approve it. The Amsterdam Court of Appeal has exclusive jurisdiction in first and final factual instance over such cases, so that it can develop case management expertise in this field.

The Act introduces the damage scheduling approach, under which compensation is awarded to claimants not on the basis of their personal characteristics, but rather on the basis of the characteristics of various classes of claimants. The agreement should describe the class and the various sub-classes and give information about (i) the number of class members (by estimation), (ii) the amounts of compensation, (iii) eligibility for compensation, (iv) the method of determining the compensation amount and finally (v) the method of obtaining payment. The parties must be able to explain to the court how they divided the money between the sub-classes or different types of plaintiffs.

The collective settlement must be published in a newspaper and everyone who is included within one of the categories of the settlement has the opportunity to opt out within a certain period of time. The notice requirement that applies twice (see below) has to be met on an individual basis, which is a significant difference from North American style class action regimes and has cost consequences/implications. It is, however, important to mention that notice to known injured parties can be given by ordinary mail; and that the first announcement may be by advertisement only, if the court approves this.

The requirements that must be met in order to obtain court approval are, among others: (i) the compensation amount may not be unreasonable, (ii) the defendant's performance must be sufficiently guaranteed, (iii) the representative organization must sufficiently represent the class and (iv) the number of class members must be sufficient to warrant certification (numerosity). It is possible to see the sufficient representation test as a Dutch-style 'adequacy of representation test', although it must be stressed that under this Dutch test, counsel to the representative organization does not have to meet quality requirements as is required under the US regime, nor is its counsel court-appointed.

When considering whether or not to approve a settlement, the court has to take into account the nature, cause and amount of loss, the simplicity and expediency of the payment method, the defendant's asset base, the nature of the legal relationship between the defendant and the class members and the availability of insurance. The opt-out period for class members must be at least three months. The opt-out period for the defendant may continue no longer than six months after the expiry of the opt-out period for the class members. It is important to note that the defendant is only entitled to opt out if this is explicitly stipulated in the agreement. Defendants may wish to do so if too many injured parties opt out from the settlement. The Netherlands is among the first EU countries to take steps to facilitate the settlement of mass damages claims using such an opt-out regime.

If a settlement is approved, it will be filed with the court registry, where it will be available for inspection and where copies may be obtained by interested parties. All known injured parties will be sent a copy of the decision by ordinary mail. In addition, the decision and such other information as the court sees fit will be published in at least one national newspaper, to be determined by the court. The court may order that the decision also be published or communicated by other means which allows for flexibility and case-tailored approaches.

If the court decides to approve the settlement, every person who is included in one of the categories of the settlement and does not opt out on time is bound by that settlement, even if he or she does not know about it. In other words, class members become parties to the settlement agreement by operation of law and are entitled to receive payment of the stipulated compensation amount. There is no possibility for appeal, and only the petitioning parties can jointly and under restricted conditions present their case to the Supreme Court. In practice, this system does not offer a realistic possibility of appeal but does offer a realistic option for a final solution.

The court's power to interfere with the content of the settlement is limited: it can only do so if the amount of compensation awarded under the agreement or the process of determining the compensation is unfair. However, case law shows that the court can exercise certain discretionary powers.

This system has proven to be a success. To date, six collective settlements have been brought before the Amsterdam Court of Appeal, five of which have been declared binding, such as the EUR 1 billion settlement in the widely reported Dexia investment products case affecting 300,000 potential claimants and also the widely reported USD 340 million Shell oil recategorization settlement. The latter settlement applies to investors in 105 jurisdictions who purchased their shares on non-US markets but excludes US persons and entities.[7] The fifth collective (securities) settlement, which was declared binding on July 15, 2009 includes US persons and entities.[8] None of the collective settlements that have been brought before the Amsterdam Court of Appeal are related to antitrust claims.

9. How does a plaintiff's lawyer finance private enforcement?

a. Fee shifting

The Dutch courts apply a 'loser pays' rule. However, the amount is determined on the basis of a special tariff system used by the courts which usually results in a fraction of the actual cost of legal representation.

b. Attorneys' fees

Generally, lawyers in the Netherlands charge on the basis of an hourly fee. An additional success fee may be agreed. It is prohibited for attorneys' fees to be made entirely dependent on their obtaining a favorable judgment in the litigation. Thus, true contingency arrangements are not permitted. However, the parties may agree to a fixed fee that will cover the attorney's fees, at a reasonable rate plus a percentage of the result. If the plaintiff is a private individual with an income below certain levels, state-funded legal aid may be available. However, the fees available under this scheme are fairly limited, and do not secure access to the type of specialist legal aid which is required for the bringing of antitrust damage claims.

10. How does private enforcement interact with public enforcement?

Based on Article 16 (1) of Regulation (EC) No 1/2003, a decision of the European Commission is binding on the Dutch national civil courts with respect to the same parties and the same subject. The same is true of decisions of the NMa once they have become irrevocable after administrative and appellate remedies have been exhausted. Thus, a decision of the NMa or the European Commission will constitute binding evidence of wrongful conduct in a civil suit for damages. This is true for both the factual findings and the legal conclusions in the decision.

A disadvantage of not awaiting the outcome of a NMa or European Commission investigation is in many cases that the plaintiff will find it difficult to prove that an infringement of the competition rules has occurred.

In *Vreugdenhil/Bloemenveiling*,[9] for example, the Dutch Supreme Court held that 'the Court of Appeal should have conducted an extensive investigation in the form of a market analysis in order to arrive at a well-founded judgment'.

This means that the plaintiff must provide a comprehensive market analysis to support its claims. This will be problematic since the facts for doing so will not be easily available.

---

7 For more information see www.shellsettlement.com.

8 For more information see www.vediorsettlement.com.

9 Dutch Supreme Court, 3 December 2004, *Vreugdenhil/Bloemenveiling*, NJ 2005, 118.

A decision of the NMa or European Commission will contain all elements of fact and law required to establish the existence of an infringement. In the Netherlands, there are a number of cases which indicate that the availability of a preliminary NMa report (which is the equivalent of a European Commission Statement of objections) or of decision was or would have been very useful.[10]

On the other hand, awaiting an NMa or European Commission decision creates a risk of running afoul of the five-year statute of limitations for bringing a civil damages claim. The five-year period starts to run from the date on which the injured party became aware of the damage and the responsible party. In *CEF/Bestuurders*, the Rotterdam Court of First Instance held that the statute of limitations began to run upon media coverage of a dawn raid by the NMa, as the plaintiff could then have been aware of the person responsible for the damage.[11] Therefore, as soon as such a dawn raid takes place, a potential plaintiff should perform an act of interruption of the statute of limitations, such as writing a letter for the purpose of commencing proceedings.

The NMa operates a leniency programme pursuant to which voluntary statements and cooperation with a NMa investigation can result in immunity from fines or in their reduction. However, that program does not provide immunity from private claims or reduce damages recoverable in private actions.

Under a special procedure applied by the NMa to facilitate the processing of an unusually large number of bid-rigging cases in the construction sector, the NMa granted a fixed time reduction percentage to those defendants which did not contest the NMa's factual findings, thereby facilitating follow-on actions. In another isolated case relating to allegedly excessive fees charged by the PIN debit card payment processor Interpay, the NMa dropped its charges in administrative appeal due to the fact that proving the case would have required extensive economic research and that Interpay had entered into a covenant with retailers agreeing to lower its fees with retroactive effect from a certain date onwards.

Future perspectives

It is hard to predict what the future will bring. Case law is scarcely available. However, one successful claim may prompt others to follow the same route. What is clear though is that the European Commission seeks to facilitate damages actions for breach of the EC antitrust rules. On April 3, 2008, the Commission published a White Paper on this topic. Interested parties have been able to comment on the White Paper. This resulted in a draft Council directive pursuant to which, if adopted, Member States must, to the extent not already available, introduce the possibility of opt-in collective actions to allow victims to recoup that loss from the undertaking(s) which infringed the law. This means that the actual loss suffered and the loss of profit must be compensated. A claim for punitive damages will not be allowed. A passing-on defence will be possible and the Council directive even provides for the presumption that under certain circumstances, the

---

[10] Alkmaar Court of First Instance, 5 February 2003, *WINO/PO Wieringen c.s;*, Alkmaar Court of First Instance, 28 January 2004, *PO Wieringen c.s./VEBEGA*; Maastricht Court of First Instance, 2 July 203, *Province Limburg/X*, LJN AI 0281 and Utrecht Court of First Instance, 27 August 2003, *Inexco/Laurens*, LJN AI 16398.

[11] Rotterdam Court of First Instance, 7 March 2007, *CEF/Bestuurders*, LJN BA 0926.

overcharge has been passed on. There will be no need to re-litigate this issue of infringement of the law where decisions by the national competition authorities will be binding on the national court deciding on the damages claims. The draft directive also provides for a rather extensive disclosure obligation, provided that a victim is able to demonstrate (i) sufficient relevance of the information requested to the claim for damages, (ii) that the request for information does not result in a fishing expedition and (iii) the victim is unable to produce the evidence itself.

Dutch law is to some extent already in line with the draft Council directive. Although the possibility to collectively claim for damages will be welcomed, it is hard to predict whether it will often be used. The main reason for this is that the opt-in aspect requires an active approach by the victims of the infringement. On the other hand, more extensive access to information, together with the binding effect of a final decision by the national competition authorities, will certainly lower the threshold for bringing a collective claim.

21 Spain

Pedro Callol[1]

Introduction

Private antitrust damages litigation has been rare in Spain thus far. However, recent developments on the legislative front, along with concerted efforts by the European and Spanish authorities, are expected to increase the number of private damages actions in years to come.

a. The 1989 Competition Act

Spain, led by the EU modernization effort,[2] has recently adopted legislation that facilitates claims for antitrust damages. The legislation includes Law 15/2007 (Competition Act), which was approved on July 3, 2007 and became law on September 1, 2007. The Competition Act abrogated Law 16/1989 (1989 Competition Act), which had been approved on July 17, 1989. The Competition Act brings Spanish competition law in line with EU competition law after the passing of Regulation 1/2003.[3]

The question of private antitrust damages, like the question of private litigation in general, may be approached from two perspectives, each determining the law applicable

[1] Admitted to practice in Spain and the UK (currently non-practising solicitor); law graduate, University of Chicago Law School (Fulbright Scholar) and College of Europe, Bruges. I would like to acknowledge valuable comments kindly provided by my colleague Gonzalo Serrano. Any responsibility for errors or omissions is mine.

[2] It is worthwhile citing as key elements in this EU law driven push the case law of the European Court of Justice (ECJ), notably in the Judgments of the ECJ of September 20, 2001, *Courage v. Crehan*, case C–453/99 and of July 13, 2006, and *Manfredi v. Lloyd Adriatico Assicurazioni SpA*, case C–295/04; the Commission Green Paper on Damages actions for breach of the EC antitrust rules (SEC(2005)1732)/* COM(2005)0672 final. More recently, see also the White Paper on Damages Actions for Breach of the EC antitrust rules, COM(2008)165, April 2, 2008. Although not directly focused on antitrust damages claims, it is also worthwhile mentioning EC Regulation 1/2003, of December 16, 2002, on the implementation of the rules on competition laid down in Articles 81 and 82 of the Treaty, cited, and the regulatory package accompanying Regulation 1/2003. The direct effect of Articles 81(1), 81(2) and 82 EC Treaty has long been a well established principle (*e.g.*, Judgments of the ECJ of January 30, 1974, *BRT/SABAM*, case C–127/73 and of March 18, 1997, *Guérin Automobiles v. Commission*, case C–282/95 P). But the more recent decentralization in the application of Article 81(3) (previously the monopoly of the European Commission) has given an important push to the application of European competition law by national courts and the bringing of cases before them by private parties. Ultimately, this should doubtless lead to an increase in the number of antitrust damages cases brought before national courts and more effective handling by those courts. On December 1, 2009, the Treaty of Lisbon came into effect, amending the Treaty Establishing the European Community (EC Treaty) that is now called the Treaty on the Functioning of the European Union (TFEU). Therefore, all references to Articles 81 and 82 of the EC Treaty now reference Articles 101 and 102 TFEU.

[3] Regulation 1/2003, of December 16, 2002, on the implementation of the rules on competition laid down in Articles 81 and 82 of the EC Treaty, O.J. L 1, January 2003, pp. 1–25.

to the underlying conduct. First, there is business conduct that does not affect trade between Member States and is therefore governed exclusively by Spanish law. Second, there is conduct that does affect trade between Member States and is governed concurrently by both Spanish law and EC law (the Treaty of Rome[4] or EC Treaty, and derivative legislation).

Under the 1989 Competition Act, legal actions for damages arising out of violations could take place only after a final decision (i.e., a decision by the Competition Authority which, if it is appealed, is confirmed by the highest possible judicial authority available in the case), holding that a breach of the antitrust rules has occurred.[5] This requirement, however, only applied to conduct in violation of the 1989 Competition Act, and not to conduct which violated Article 81 or 82 of the EC Treaty. In other words, under the 1989 Competition Act, a final declaration of illegality by the highest available judicial authority in the case was necessary to initiate a private claim for antitrust damages, as long as the alleged violations occurred under Spanish law (i.e., the violation did not impact trade between Member States).

In practice, the above meant that stand-alone actions were not possible for infringements of the 1989 Competition Act.[6] Follow-on actions were available, but extremely difficult because administrative decisions by the Spanish Competition Authority (SCA) had to be reviewed by courts first. Given that court proceedings can take several years, particularly if judicial decisions in the first judicial instance are appealed, private actions for antitrust damages often had to wait for many years until the appeal system was exhausted (usually until the Supreme Court had made a decision). This helps explain the scarcity of judicial decisions adjudicating antitrust damages claims under the 1989 Competition Act.

Some scholars suggested that a proper interpretation of Article 13(2) of the 1989 Competition Act, considering its goal of protecting the right to a defence and effective redress (including effective compensation for damages) would weigh in favor of admitting private actions for antitrust damages prior to a final finding of illegality.[7] This interpretation, however, has been rejected by the courts. The scarce case law in the field of private antitrust damages under the 1989 Competition Act has clearly confirmed that an exhaustion of possible appeals available in court was a *conditio sine qua non* for a private damages action.

An example of this is the ruling in *Antena 3 v. National Professional Football League*.[8] The *Antena 3* case was a rare decision under the 1989 Competition Act. It awarded

---

4 Treaty establishing the European Community, OJ C329, 24 December 2002.

5 Article 13(2), 1989 Competition Act.

6 Stand-alone actions under Article 81 or 82 EC Treaty may in theory have been possible given that national courts had acknowledged already under the 1989 Competition Act the direct effect of those Community provisions. In practice, however, there are no reported stand-alone damages decisions for breach of Articles 81, 82 EC Treaty under the 1989 Competition Act.

7 See e.g., R. E. CÁCERES (2004), 'El Resarcimiento de Daños y Perjuicios derivado de ilícitos antitrust: problemática que plantea y posibles soluciones.' Gaceta Jurídica 230, pp 63–76. See also I. R. DIAZ (2003), 'El ilícito antitrust como ilícito desleal. El resarcimiento de daños y perjuicios.' Gaceta Jurídica 228, pp 32–51.

8 Decision of the Court of first instance n. 4 of Madrid, of June 7, 2005, *Antena 3 v. National Professional Football League*.

damages totalling €25.5 million to the plaintiffs. The case originated in a dispute over broadcasting rights for football events, an important business sector in Spain and one where antitrust concerns are at the forefront. In brief, the Spanish professional football league association (LNFP) entered into agreements with all regional broadcasting stations and with Canal Plus, a pay-TV operator, to share the broadcasting rights for premium events for eight consecutive years for Spain, excluding other entities (*i.e.*, open-TV stations Antena 3 and Telecinco) from the deal. These agreements were the basis of two successive complaints by each of Antena 3 and Telecinco before the SCA. The SCA found that the agreements in question constituted abusive conduct and violated the rules on anticompetitive agreements.[9] This declaration by the SCA was later confirmed by the courts on review until a *final* decision was reached by the Supreme Court.[10] Hence, the antitrust infringement that served as a basis for a claim for private antitrust damages had been declared illegal first by an administrative decision and then confirmed on review by all the available appellate judicial resources up to the Supreme Court.[11] Consequently the Court of first instance dealing with the private antitrust damages claim by Antena 3 had no trouble acknowledging that the requirement set out in Article 13(2) of the 1989 Competition Act had been satisfied and the court awarded damages of €25.5 million.[12]

Another rare example of antitrust damages granted as a result of a breach of the 1989 Competition Act is the damages award in the *Sugar Producers* cartel.[13] In this case, the existence of a cartel had also been declared by the Competition Authority and by all the courts on review up to the Supreme Court. The Court expressly acknowledged the possibility for a defendant in an antitrust damages case to rely on the 'passing-on' defense. The expert economic evidence was also considered key to deciding the case. The case was entirely decided on the basis of the claimant's expert evidence because the expert evidence of the defendant, stating that no damage was caused, was considered as not credible.

The situation regarding private damages claims for breaches of Articles 81 and 82 of the EC Treaty under the 1989 Competition Act was, at least in theory, more favorable

---

9 It was found that using the market power in the upstream market of football broadcasting rights by the Football League, by granting long-term licenses, disrupted competition in the open-TV market, blocking access to the image rights to Telecinco and Antena 3 (Article 6 of the 1989 Competition Act); also, the long-term exclusivity clauses (8 years) contained in licensing agreements preventing Telecinco and Antena 3 from gaining access violated the rules on anticompetitive agreements (Article 1 of the 1989 Competition Act).

10 Decision of the Supreme Court 2003/6409 of June 9.

11 The principle was also admitted in *obiter dicta* of some relevant Court of first instance cases (Order of May 18, 2006, *Euskaltel v. AVS and Sogecable*). Incidentally, the Order of May 18, 2006, cited, limited the prior declaration principle *ex* Article 13(2) 1989 Competition Act to actions for damages, while holding that commercial courts, and not just the Competition Authority, were also competent to declare infringements of the 1989 Competition Act in cases brought before them (a principle that would later be codified in the laws of procedure under the Competition Act, see below).

12 The antitrust damages Decision of June 7, 2005, cited, was later reversed by a higher court on appeal (Decision of December 18, 2006, of the *Audiencia Provincial de Madrid*). The latter Decision is currently pending review by the Supreme Court.

13 Decision of October 9, 2009 of the *Audiencia Provincial*, on damages in the *Sugar Producers* cartel.

than the situation regarding private damages claims for breach of substantive provisions of the 1989 Competition Act. The requirements for a final decision for intra-State violations under Article 13(2) of the 1989 Competition Act did not apply to damages claims for breach of Articles 81 and 82 EC Treaty. Also, Spanish courts had accepted the direct effect of Articles 81 and 82 of the EC Treaty[14] (this direct effect, although well established under EC law, required some time for national courts to accept expressly[15]). Hence, the courts should have had no trouble in dealing with antitrust damages claims under the 1989 Competition Act for breaches of Articles 81 or 82 of the EC Treaty. Again, however, there are very few precedents on how the matter was dealt with prior to the current Competition Act. There is a reported case where Conduit, an Irish telecommunications provider, claimed damages against Spanish telecommunications incumbent Telefónica, which had denied Conduit access to data necessary to compete in the directories services market.[16] The infringement of Article 82 of the EC Treaty was claimed, but only indirectly. The primary legal basis relied on in that case was Article 15(2) of the Spanish Unfair Trade Act,[17] which characterizes as unfair the reliance on an advantage in the market procured by violating laws or trade regulations. In this case the plaintiff argued breach of the Unfair Trade Act for reliance on a market advantage procured by a violation of Article 82 EC Treaty. The claim for damages was partially successful (only a fraction of the claimed amount was obtained) and Telefónica was ordered to pay damages amounting to €639,000 under the Unfair Trade Act. It is a good example of damages for breach of Article 82 EC Treaty (certainly the best one available under the 1989 Competition Act), even if the direct legal basis was a breach of the Unfair Trade Act. The use of the Unfair Trade Act may have been an attempt by the plaintiff to prevent a judge in a court of first instance from rejecting the case for failure to use a specific legal basis to claim damages, in the absence of a final declaration by the Supreme Court pursuant to the rule *ex* Article 13(2) 1989 Competition Act already explained. In our view, it should have been possible to rely directly on a breach of Article 82 EC Treaty (by invoking the case law and principles stemming from EC law), but the plaintiff might have thought that the Unfair Trade Act, which contains a specific provision for damages awards, provided a more straightforward basis for the claim under the national law then in force.

In summary, the procedural limitations under the 1989 Competition Act were the following:

---

[14] The Supreme Court had accepted this principle in decisions such as those of June 2, 2000, *DISA*, 540/2000; March 15, 2001, *Petronor*, 232/2001; and March 2, 2001, *Mercedes Benz*, 202/2001. Regarding abuse of a dominant position, see the *Euskaltel* case, cited, an interesting precedent from a lower court.

[15] A provision of Community law is said to have direct effect when that provision meets the requirements to be invoked by individuals before national courts. A Community law provision has direct effect if it is drafted in a clear and unambiguous way, it is unconditional and its operation is not dependent on any further action being taken by Community or national authorities (Decision of the ECJ of February 5, 1962, *Van Gend en Loos*, case C–26/62, [1963] ECR 1).

[16] Decision of the Commercial Court of first instance n. 5 of Madrid of November 11, 2005, 85/2005, *Conduit v. Telefónica*, confirmed by Decision of the Audiencia Provincial of Madrid of May 25, 2006, 73/2006.

[17] Law 3/1991, of January 10, on Unfair Trade.

- Damages claims for breach of the 1989 Competition Act met with a high procedural barrier under Article 13(2) of the 1989 Competition Act, *i.e.*, the requirement that a final decision by the ultimate court available to review the case (normally the Supreme Court) confirm the antitrust infringement prior to initiating a private claim for damages. This made private antitrust damages claims very difficult and extremely rare.
- The requirement under Article 13(2) of the 1989 Competition Act did not apply to damages claims for breach of the EC competition rules. In some instances, private damages claims were attempted using the Unfair Trade Act, which contained a specific legal basis for damages awards. This succeeded in at least one case (*Conduit*).

The current Competition Act has put an end to the old procedural rule by eliminating the requirement for a final decision under Article 13(2) 1989 Competition Act, thereby making private antitrust damages claims easier. Numerous other procedural improvements have also been enacted and are expected to make damages claims more attractive and feasible.

b. The current Competition Act

The Competition Act and the creation of specialist commercial courts (by Law 22/2003, on July 9, 2003), have brought with them important innovations. The Competition Act became enforceable on September 1, 2007 and there have been no reported judicial decisions adjudicating on damages claims under the Competition Act thus far. The description below details the requirements for private antitrust damages litigation in Spain and reflects the current status of the Competition Act and its applicable procedural rules. It is likely that these requirements will evolve as a body of relevant case law develops.

Substantive rules regarding determination of liability and calculation of damages remained largely the same following the introduction of the Competition Act. The general rules on contractual and non-contractual liability stem from principles of Roman law.

As set out above, the Competition Act has eliminated the procedural rule, established under Article 13(2) of the 1989 Competition Act, which required a final decision (and exhausted appeals) in a public enforcement proceeding before a private civil claim for antitrust damages could be initiated. The transitional rules for application of the Competition Act state that any proceedings initiated under the 1989 Competition Act, subsequent to the implementation of the procedural rules contained in the Competition Act, should, nonetheless, follow the rules of procedure of the 1989 Competition Act.[18] This rule should in our view be interpreted as not applying to private damages claims, *i.e.*, private damages claims introduced subsequent to the implementation of the Competition Act for breaches of the substantive law provisions of the 1989 Competition Act should not be governed by the procedural rules contained in Article 13(2) of the 1989 Competition Act. This interpretation is based, first, on the literal wording of the first

[18] First transitional rule of the Competition Act.

transitional rule, which refers to 'penalty proceedings'[19] (i.e., punishing administrative proceedings), whereas damages claims are always brought as civil actions in Spain. For the same reason, a claim for damages should be considered as a 'new' action, so that it is possible to construe the statutory language under the Competition Act to understand that an action that is started anew under the Competition Act is not bound by Article 13(2) of the 1989 Competition Act, even if the underlying facts occurred prior to the Competition Act taking effect.

Consequently, it appears logical to conclude that no civil action brought in Spain claiming damages for anticompetitive conduct should henceforward be required to comply with the burdensome rule *ex* Article 13(2) 1989 Competition Act. This development alone should facilitate antitrust damages claims generally.

The elimination of the rule under Article 13(2) of the 1989 Competition Act is an additional incentive for private enforcement of the Spanish antitrust rules, because a company or person harmed by anticompetitive conduct is now allowed simultaneously to request *(i)* a declaration of violation of competition law and *(ii)* a claim for damages.[20]

1. Jurisdiction requirements

The rules regarding international jurisdiction are complex and, particularly in the case of international cartels, would require detailed analysis on a case-by-case basis. Generally speaking, under the Spanish rules on jurisdiction, Spanish courts will have jurisdiction over antitrust damages claims in the following cases:[21]

- When the defendant is domiciled in Spain.
- When the parties have expressly or implicitly submitted themselves to the jurisdiction of the court. This could happen, for instance, when there is a prior arrangement between the parties to resolve disputes between them before the Spanish courts or when the defendant does not contest the jurisdiction of the court once it has been served with a lawsuit.
- It is likely that some claims related to agreements under Article 81 of the EC Treaty and/or Article 1 of the Competition Act must be decided as contractual disputes. In that case, Spanish courts have jurisdiction over the claims if the contract was entered into in Spain or must be performed in Spain.
- In cases of non-contractual liability, typically harm is alleged by parties injured in abuse of dominance cases and cartel cases by the infringer. Spanish courts have jurisdiction when the alleged anticompetitive conduct took place in Spain or when both the infringing party and the aggrieved party are domiciled in Spain.

2. Competent courts

Once it has been decided that Spanish courts have jurisdiction over a given damages claim, it is necessary to ascertain which courts within the Spanish system will provide the

---

19 '*Procedimientos sancionadores*'.

20 On the other hand, an interpretation of the Competition Act which strictly preserves legitimate expectations acquired under the 1989 Competition Act would favour the opposite outcome. It will be for the courts to decide on this point.

21 Article 22 of Organic Law 6/1985, governing the judicial branch.

appropriate forum. In 2003, a reform of the law governing the judicial branch created the commercial courts of first instance.[22] This reform granted such courts jurisdiction over all matters related to competition. In the future, as discussed, it appears more likely that private parties may decide to sue in court, requesting simultaneously the finding of a breach of antitrust provisions (under the Competition Act and/or under the rules of the EC Treaty) and damages as a result of the breach. The commercial courts of first instance are empowered to adjudicate both claims. However, a recent Order by an appellate court on jurisdiction matters has decided that civil courts (as opposed to commercial courts) can also be competent to adjudicate on damages claims if the damages claim is filed on the basis of a prior finding of an antitrust infringement.[23] This suggests that commercial courts are competent to grant damages when the damages claim is joined together with the claim requesting a finding that an antitrust infringement has taken place. If the damages claim is a separate claim as a result of a previous finding of the infringement, then civil courts have jurisdiction under the mentioned case law.[24]

Decisions on damages claims by the courts of first instance may be appealed before the appellate courts (*Audiencias Provinciales*, which are the appellate courts in Spain). Ultimately, decisions may be reviewable on points of law before the Supreme Court, subject to the appropriate procedural conditions and limitations.

3. *Standing to sue*

In Spain, parties that hold a right or an interest in the subject matter of a legal action generally have standing to sue.[25] Thus parties who have suffered harm as a result of anticompetitive conduct may initiate court proceedings seeking redress. Direct purchasers and, generally, parties directly harmed by anticompetitive conduct of any kind (*e.g.*, a company suffering a refusal to supply) are allowed to sue for damages. Spanish law does not contain any rule barring or limiting indirect purchasers' capacity to appear as claimants in damages cases. In this regard, Spanish law is consistent with the case law of the European Courts in *Crehan* and *Manfredi*.[26] However, the possibilities of success on the merits of damages claims brought by indirect purchasers may depend on the application of the substantive requirements, particularly on issues such as causation. These are discussed below.

As for the possibility of class actions in Spain, there is no Spanish law specifically allowing them. However, the law on civil procedure provides a number of devices that, in some circumstances, may bridge the gap.

First, the civil procedure rules enable a group of consumers or users affected by harmful conduct (*e.g.*, antitrust infringement) to band together as plaintiffs in a civil proceeding whenever that group of consumers is determined or can be easily determined.

---

22 *Juzgados de lo mercantil.* Reform introduced by Organic Law 8/2003 of 9 July, inserting Article 86 *ter* into Organic Law 6/1985, cited.

23 Court Order of the Audiencia Provincial de Madrid of April 10, 2008, *Vodafone*, 83/2008.

24 The same applies to follow-on actions subsequent to findings of an infringement under the Unfair Trade Act (Court Order of February 4, 2008, *Nestlé*, 67/2008).

25 Article 10 of Law 1/2000, of January, 7 on Civil Procedure: '*serán considerados partes legítimas quienes comparezcan y actúen en juicio como titulares de la relación jurídica u objeto litigioso.*'

26 Judgements of the ECJ in the *Courage* and *Manfredi* cases, cited.

Also, the law requires that the majority of the affected persons join together to file the lawsuit.[27] Consumers or users who did not initially join the group filing the damages claim may subsequently do so provided that they can prove a direct and legitimate interest in the subject matter of the lawsuit.[28] This should not be problematic, given that those users or consumers should find themselves in an identical position to those constituting the group that initially filed the claim. The system in Spain is an opt-in system, meaning that those who do not expressly opt in are not deemed represented.

Second, the law on civil procedure confers a distinct and privileged role on consumers' associations incorporated with a view to defending the collective interests of their members. When those injured by a harmful event are a group of consumers or users whose identity is determined or can be easily determined, the standing to sue to uphold the interests of those affected is vested either in a relevant consumers' association, or in the affected individuals themselves. However, if it is not easy to determine the group of affected consumers or users, the standing to sue is entrusted exclusively to a relevant consumers' association representing those individuals.[29] Once a complaint has been certified, it is publicized in order to enable any users or consumers not yet parties to the case to join in defence of their interests. In cases where the individuals affected are determined or are easy to determine, those affected may intervene at any stage after the aforementioned publicity, but they may only participate in the stage of the proceedings then reached. Thus if a third party joins at the final stage of the proceeding, it is entitled to act in court only within the part of the procedure still remaining prior to the judgement. In contrast, if the individuals affected are not easily identifiable, then the civil proceedings may be stayed for up to two months and, after such period, those individuals who have not intervened and joined may no longer participate in the process.[30]

Consumers' associations having standing to sue on behalf of consumers must be founded in compliance with the rules contained in the Consumer Protection Act.[31] In particular the association must be independent to be recognized as a lawful consumers' association. Independence means that the association may not have as members any companies acting for profit, nor may it receive any aid or financial support from companies that supply goods or services to users or consumers. Legally recognized consumers' associations may not issue any communications or publicity promoting consumer goods and may not sponsor or provide their images or names to any corporate communications related to the promotion or advertising of consumer goods or services. Generally, they may not engage in any activities unrelated to consumer protection, except in some limited fields such as training and education. On the other hand, consumers' associations may be shareholders of companies, but only in those whose corporate purpose is limited to activities that are instrumental and/or related to the purposes of consumers' associations

---

[27] Article 6.7 of the Law on Civil Procedure, cited.

[28] Article 13 of the Law on Civil Procedure, cited.

[29] Article 11 of the Law on Civil Procedure, cited.

[30] Article 13 of the Law on Civil Procedure, cited.

[31] The rules are contained on Royal Decree 1/2007, of November 16, approving the text of the Act for the defence of consumers and users and other complementary laws (*Real Decreto Legislativo 1/2007, de 16 de noviembre, por el que se aprueba el texto refundido de la Ley General para la Defensa de los Consumidores y Usuarios y otras leyes complementarias*).

(*e.g.*, companies devoted to the education and training of users and consumers or to the defence of the interests of users and consumers).[32]

4. Rules of evidence

All available evidence (documents of all types, experts, witnesses, etc.) which supports proving the facts is generally acceptable under Spanish law provided it has been lawfully obtained. In the case of expert evidence, the standard rule is that an expert must sign a written report and submit it as an addendum to the main complaint filed in court.[33]

The possibilities for discovery (as understood under US law) are scarce under Spanish law. There are some limited rules which may enable a plaintiff to prepare a legal action by asking questions of the counterparty or requesting that the judge solicit evidence from it, provided there is some circumstantial or initial evidence that warrants such a petition. These rules are interpreted restrictively though and thus there are few possibilities of getting useful evidence through these procedures.[34]

A question that may arise is whether it is possible to use evidence collected during administrative antitrust proceedings for private litigation cases. In principle one would expect that this type of evidence should be accepted in court. Documents regarded as confidential in the antitrust proceedings will not be released to the other parties in accordance with the rules of confidentiality in the file.[35] However once a document is treated as non-confidential and is therefore open to other parties through the administrative file, then it may be produced before a court in a damages claim. The same principle applies to leniency applications which will ultimately be accessible in the administrative file as well, subject to any applicable confidentiality rules. Verbal leniency applications or corporate statements may be viewed by parties other than the leniency applicants in administrative antitrust proceedings, but they may not be reproduced. Therefore it is less obvious whether subsequent court proceedings could rely on them. At a minimum a claimant could resort to including a witness who viewed and/or took notes of the evidence accompanying the leniency application.[36] There is, however, no case law yet on these questions, so it remains to be seen what the courts' stance will be.

Finally, attorney–client communications are privileged under Spanish law provided they contain advice which is given for the purpose of representing or defending the client. Generally speaking, this has been accepted by the Spanish Competition Authority[37] relying on authority coming from the European Courts. Privileged documents should not appear in any administrative file. That being said, the law on privilege and particularly how the presence of privileged documents affects the Competition Authority's

---

32 Articles 27 and 28 of Royal Decree 1/2007, cited.

33 Articles 335 and following of the Civil Procedure Act.

34 Articles 256 and 328 Civil Procedure Act. These rules are devised with a view to intellectual property cases (counterfeiting cases), more than other types of cases such as damages claims.

35 Article 42 Competition Act.

36 See Articles 65 and 66 of the Competition Act, Article 51 of Royal Decree 261/2008, of February 22, implementing the Competition Act and paragraphs 28 and following of the NCC Guidelines for leniency applications (www.cncompetencia.es/Portals/0/PDFs/indicaciones%202%20programa%20clemencia%20_8_.pdf).

37 Decision of July 22, 2002, *Pepsi-Cola v. Coca-Cola*, exp. R508/02.

discovery powers in the course of dawn raids is developing law. One would expect that Spanish courts should uphold the principle, rooted in Article 24 of the Constitution, that attorney–client communications are privileged. A recent landmark judgment of September 30, 2009 has decided, for the first time under the new Competition Act, on the issue of legally privileged documents in the context of surprise 'dawn raids'.

The judgment of the High Court (*Audiencia Nacional*) of September 30, 2009 expressly acknowledges the existence of the client–attorney privilege in Spain. However, the High Court, faced with the petition to quash the entire surprise inspection in view of the fact that privileged documents had been seized, rejected the petition. The High Court stated that the client–attorney privilege is embedded in the fundamental rights of legal defence but it also said (more or less explicitly) that even if privileged documents are seized, as long as they are not used, this should not impinge upon the fundamental rights of defence.

In our view, this ruling encroaches upon the case law of the Court of First Instance of the EU (see, in particular, the *AKZO* case).[38]

In the *AKZO* case, the Court concluded, building on previous case law, that a company may refuse to allow Commission officials to take even a 'cursory look' at one or more specific documents which it claims to be covered by legal professional privilege, provided the company concerned considers that such a cursory look is impossible without revealing the content of those documents and that it gives the inspectors appropriate reasons for its view.[39]

In the event of disagreement between the inspectors and the inspected company regarding whether or not a given document should be deemed confidential, the CFI in the *AKZO* case establishes the following procedure: in such a case the document at stake should be placed in a sealed envelope and later remove it with a view to a subsequent resolution of the dispute.[40]

The High Court in the *Stanpa dawn raids* case has apparently ignored the reasoning stemming from the *AKZO* case, since it has upheld the seizure of all documents provided they are not 'used' and, therefore, cannot cause a harm to the rights of defence.

5. *Substantive rules applicable to antitrust damages claims*

a. Distinction between contractual and non-contractual liability In cases where the anticompetitive conduct causing the harm is based on an agreement in violation of Article 81(1) of the EC Treaty or Article 1.1 of the Competition Act, the consequence under both Article 81(2) of the EC Treaty and Article 1.2 of the Competition Act is to nullify the contract or agreement. In that case, the rule under Spanish law is *restitutio in integrum* or restitution of things to the status they were in, as if there had never been a contract.[41]

In all other cases, where no contractual relationship binds the company responsible

---

[38] Judgement of the CFI of September 17, 2007, *AKZO v. Commission*, Joined Cases T–125/03 and T–253/03, [2007] ECR II-3523.

[39] ¶82, *AKZO* case, cited.

[40] ¶83, *AKZO* case, cited.

[41] Articles 1300 and following of the Civil Code.

for the anticompetitive conduct and the party suffering the harm, the applicable rules are those of non-contractual liability. Non-contractual liability is governed in Spain by the law on torts contained in Article 1902 of the Civil Code, the origins of which are traced back to the *Lex aquiliana* under Roman law. There is a large body of legal doctrine and case law applying Article 1902 of the Civil Code, which is one of the legal provisions most relied upon under Spanish civil law.[42] Below we attempt to briefly outline the requirements for a finding of liability under Article 1902 of the Civil Code by referring to both the general legal doctrine and the case law, with specific reference to the *Antena 3* antitrust damages case, cited, which was decided on the basis of both Articles 13(2) of the 1989 Competition Act and Article 1902 of the Civil Code.

The requirements for a finding of liability under Article 1902 of the Civil Code are:

I. ACTION OR OMISSION BY THE ALLEGEDLY LIABLE PARTY The anticompetitive conduct must result from an illegal agreement or an illegal unilateral practice. A defendant may argue that the anticompetitive conduct is the result of an omission of a duty of care (e.g. a sophisticated form of abuse declared anticompetitive which the defendant claims he could not foresee). However this is irrelevant for the application of Article 1902 of the Civil Code because it covers both actions and omissions.

II. ILLEGALITY OF THE CAUSE OF HARM This will normally be established by the finding of the antitrust infringement.

III. HARM AND MITIGATION Actual harm must be proved. In antitrust cases this will largely be a matter of evidence, but there must be harm that is capable of being compensated so that liability can be attached. Also, the aggrieved party must take reasonable steps to mitigate the harm. A defense that the harm has been passed on (called the passing-on defense) is available under the principles governing Article 1902 of the Civil Code. The burden of proof that the harm has been passed on rests with the party asserting it. As indicated above, all types of evidence generally accepted in other jurisdictions are acceptable under Spanish law, along with numerous statutory restrictions on subjects such as impartiality, witness age and sanity, and the validity of document collection methods among others. Witnesses can be cross-examined. However the US discovery mechanism is not available in Spain.[43]

IV. NEGLIGENCE OR WILFUL INTENT Traditionally, negligence or wilful misconduct is required for a finding of liability. The party found responsible for an infringement of the antitrust laws must be found to have negligently or intentionally infringed the antitrust laws. Another issue is whether the party claiming damages may be, to an extent, responsible for the damage incurred. This discussion is related to the issue of mitigation.

---

42 CASTAN, Derecho civil español, común y foral, Tomo 4, p. 940.

43 Article 328 of the Law on Civil Procedure, cited, provides for a right of parties to request documents from the other party. But the parties must show which document they are seeking and what the contents are. It is more a means of verification of the existence of given documents; therefore it is not discovery in the common law sense.

Courts are willing to find that the negligence or intention causing the harm may not be attributed to one party alone, and that it should be shared between the parties.

This raises the question of whether joint and several liability exists when various parties are held to be responsible for an antitrust infringement (e.g., a cartel case). Under Spanish law joint and several liability would enable the party harmed by a cartel to claim the total amount of the damages award against one of the parties responsible for the antitrust breach. The party to whom the claim is addressed may later claim back its respective shares against the remaining entities liable for the harm.[44]

The general principle under Spanish civil law is that joint and several liability cannot be presumed, but rather must be expressly established.[45] Using the example of a cartel, joint and several liability is not expressly established regarding the cartel members. Nonetheless, the courts have developed a doctrine that if anticompetitive harm is caused by joint conduct of multiple parties (e.g., multiple parties agreeing to set prices) and it is not possible to discern the actual degree of causality that can be attributed to the conduct of each party, then the parties can be declared by the judge jointly and severally liable.[46] In our view, this doctrine is applicable to antitrust damages cases. Notably, in the case of cartels, members of the cartel may be regarded as jointly and severally responsible under the case law discussed.

V. A CAUSAL LINK BETWEEN THE ANTICOMPETITIVE CONDUCT AND THE HARM In the very few antitrust damages claims adjudicated by Spanish courts, this requirement was not given much attention. The courts have found it self-evident in those cases and presumed that the harm was caused by the anticompetitive conduct.

b. What damages can be claimed under Spanish law The Court of first instance in the *Antena 3* case reminds us that, under general tort law, the claimant can assert both harm suffered as a result of the anticompetitive conduct (*damnum emergens*) as well as loss of profit (*lucrum cessans*).[47]

The key issue is the evaluation of both the actual harm and the loss of profit. To this end, Spanish courts rely on expert economic evaluations, which must be introduced by the parties. The *Antena 3* case shows that these evaluations are absolutely essential, from the judge's standpoint, to the success of damages claims in the antitrust field. A judge values their discussion of whether harm exists and, if so, how great that harm is. In the *Antena 3* case, the higher court reversed the damages award by the court of first instance because the economic evaluation submitted by the plaintiff was untenable and unrealistic. The quality of the economic evidence in this type of case is a key factor before Spanish courts. The *Antena 3* case indicates that Spanish courts will show great reluctance in relying on estimations that are not based on provable facts.

---

44 Articles 1137 and following of the Civil Code.

45 Article 1137 of the Civil Code.

46 See, for instance, Decisions of the Supreme Court 276/2006, of 17 March and 413/2004, of 24 May.

47 That is the principle codified by Article 1106 of the Civil Code.

c. *Statute of limitations*

I. NON-CONTRACTUAL DAMAGES CLAIMS In the absence of Community rules governing statutory limitations on antitrust damages actions, Member States are responsible for establishing the limitation periods, subject to the principles of equivalence and effectiveness.[48]

According to the Spanish Civil Code, the limitation period for a non-contractual damages action is one year.[49] Pursuant to the Civil Code, the one year limitation period starts to run once the victim has knowledge of the harm suffered.[50]

The question may arise over what happens in cases where the victim has knowledge of the alleged antitrust infringement and the possible harm but, at the same time, the relevant Competition Authority (be it the SCA or the European Commission) is in the process of reviewing the alleged cartel (or abuse of dominance).[51] The answer to this question may be found in the case law. The Spanish Supreme Court has developed the so-called 'accomplishment theory', which states that the limitation period of a damages action only starts to run when the action is capable of being successful, *i.e.* the victim who has knowledge of the harm should have a viable basis for claiming damages before the court in the form of an official antitrust decision.[52] Under this theory, it can be argued that an action for damages, at least in complex cases, would only be viable once the illegality of harmful antitrust infringements has been found by the relevant Competition Authority.

In a recent damages case[53] that reached the Spanish Supreme Court, the claimant filed an action for damages after a finding by the European Commission that certain dumping measures in the pharmaceutical industry were illegal. It was the same claimant who filed the administrative anti-dumping proceedings before the European Commission, more

---

48 See *Manfredi* case, cited, paragraphs 77–82.

'As was pointed out in paragraph 62 of this judgment, in the absence of Community rules governing the matter, it is for the domestic legal system of each Member State to lay down the detailed procedural rules governing actions for safeguarding rights which individuals derive directly from Community law, provided that such rules observe the principles of equivalence and effectiveness.' (¶77).

'A national rule under which the limitation period begins to run from the day on which the agreement or concerted practice was adopted could make it practically impossible to exercise the right to seek compensation for the harm caused by that prohibited agreement or practice, particularly if that national rule also imposes a short limitation period which is not capable of being suspended.' (¶78).

49 Article 1968, second paragraph, of the Civil Code, in connection with article 1902 of the same Code.

50 Article 1968, second paragraph, of the Civil Code.

51 Note that, with regard to EC competition law infringements, the European Commission suggests, in such cases, that 'a new limitation period of at least two years should start once the infringement decision on which a follow-on claimant relies has become final'. See §2.7 *in fine* of the European Commission's White Paper on damages actions for breach of the EC competition, in connection with Chapter 8 of the Commission staff working paper on EC antitrust on EC antitrust damages actions.

52 See e.g., Judgment of the Supreme Court of 8 June 2007, case 625/2007.

53 See Judgment of the Supreme Court of October 2, 2008, case 870/2008.

than one year after the claimant had been aware of the alleged illegality. The defendant alleged the expiration of the one year limitation period. On appeal the Spanish Supreme Court, by applying the 'accomplishment theory,' ruled that the damages action was only possible after the illegality was determined by the European Commission and therefore the limitation period had not expired. This is good authority, particularly in complex cases, that the one year limitation period would start to run only when the relevant administrative body, *i.e.* the Competition Authority (or a commercial court in the case of a direct action) issues its decision finding the existence of an antitrust infringement. Only then would it be viable for the injured party to file a claim for damages.

6. Damages actions with contract relationships

Agreements in violation of EC or Spanish antitrust laws are void. Pursuant to the Civil Code, the legal consequence of the nullity of anticompetitive agreements is the restitution of the goods and amounts of money that were the subject matter of the contested agreement.[54] The limitation period for claiming damages is fifteen years from the day when the courts declare the relevant agreement null and void.[55]

7. Costs of antitrust damages claims in Spain

Contingency fees have been possible in Spain since 2008, when the Supreme Court held that a prohibition of contingency fees would be restrictive of competition.[56] Regarding legal costs, the principle in Spain is that the losing party is also ordered to pay the legal costs, which are reviewed by the judges to avoid abuse. This means that the losing party pays expenditures related to witnesses and experts, attorneys' fees, as well as other necessary expenses. However, judges step in to make sure the costs incurred are reasonable, which in practice means that a successful plaintiff may often not recover full costs.

It is possible under Spanish law to reach a settlement between the parties where the claimant agrees to abandon its damages action in exchange for a settlement payment.[57] There was a settlement reached between Jazztel and Telefónica according to which Jazztel would discontinue various claims against Telefónica in exchange for the latter paying EUR 10 million. Apparently there was a settlement between Gas Natural and Iberdrola as well.

8. The prospect of antitrust damages claims in Spain

At the time of writing this chapter, there are no reported judicial decisions on antitrust damages in Spain under the new Competition Act. The general expectation is that the abrogation of Article 13(2) of the 1989 Competition Act should facilitate antitrust damages claims: the length and costs of litigation are considerably reduced when it comes to establishing breaches of the national antitrust laws and there will be more incentive for private parties to litigate because now private parties can petition that the courts declare

---

[54] Article 1303 Civil Code.

[55] Article 1964 Civil Code. It must be borne in mind, however, that if the plaintiff wants to have a contract to which he is party annulled, the limitation period for claiming annulment is four years (Article 1301 Civil Code).

[56] Decision of the Supreme Court of October 21, 2008, case 5837/2005.

[57] Articles 1809 and following of the Civil Code.

an infringement of the Competition Act and grant damages simultaneously. The creation of the commercial courts with jurisdiction on competition related matters should result (it is hoped) in a higher degree of specialization and therefore higher efficiency and reliability in dealing with antitrust damages claims.

The European Commission was preparing but withdrew a draft directive on rules governing damages actions for infringements of Articles 81 and 82 of the EC Treaty. Since a subsequent draft is widely anticipated, it may be useful to comment on the withdrawn draft in terms of its implications for Spain. The purpose of this directive was to harmonize a number of procedural rules across Member States with a view to facilitating damages claims in Europe. Bearing in mind the embryonic stage at which the directive stands, below is a short analysis of its main points.

First, most of the principles and requirements of the directive appear to have already been addressed by Spanish law. Spanish law provides for full compensation of actual loss and loss of profit (Article 1 draft directive); standing to sue, group actions and 'qualified entities' for standing-to-sue purposes (Articles 3, 4 and 5); and passing-on defenses (Article 12). The limitation period rule in the draft directive (Article 14) already seems to be addressed under Spanish law as well, even in non-contractual liability cases where the short statute of limitations (one year) has been generously interpreted by the courts to ensure feasibility of damages claims (see discussion on those topics above).

The issue of fault described under Article 11 of the draft directive should not be a burden to antitrust damages claimants under Spanish law because courts are likely to find the existence of intent (either intention or negligence) in an antitrust breach.

Other matters, such as the rules on discovery and on pending international litigation between different parties from those of the proceeding brought before the Spanish courts, may require further legislative action in Spain before they can be fully realized.

It may be concluded that the road to ensuring the viability of antitrust damages claims in Spain has been long and painful. However, a number of legal reforms and case law developments, although still in the making, have helped put in place the rules necessary to allow for the possibility of effective recovery in Spain.

The future now depends on the determination of affected parties to litigate as well as the responsiveness of the system to those claims. Both will be important and integral parts of competition enforcement.

22 Sweden

Marcus Glader[1] *and Peter Alstergren*[2]

Introduction

Since 1993, the Swedish Competition Act has expressly provided that private parties may bring damages claims for competition law violations. This damages provision has not only survived subsequent legislative amendments, it has also been modified to increase the possibilities of bringing such actions. In 2003, Sweden also enacted the Group Proceedings Act, which allows private group actions for damages.

Despite these legislative tools, private damages case law based on competition law violations remains very sparse. Most of the few private damages cases that have made it to court have been settled out of court.[3] At present only a single case, which related to an abuse of a dominant position, has resulted in court-awarded damages under the Competition Act's damages provision (currently under appeal). However, a number of damages actions based on cartel violations are pending, and many expect private damages to play a more important role in the future.

This chapter outlines the Swedish legislative framework for private enforcement of competition law, discusses the interaction between public and private competition law enforcement, and describes the types of private actions (including group actions) that are available. Practical considerations relating to gathering evidence, standards of proof and the determination of damages are also addressed. Finally, we conclude by commenting on the European Commission's (Commission) recent regulatory initiatives from a Swedish perspective.

1. The role of attorneys

There are no general limitations under the Code of Conduct of the Swedish Bar Association (or the official Commentary thereto) governing how an attorney may solicit

---

1 Resident partner, Advokatfirman Vinge, Brussels, Belgium.

2 Associate, Advokatfirman Vinge, Stockholm, Sweden.

3 See *e.g.* Stockholm City Court, T 8-1319-94, *Privpak AB v. Posten Distribution AB*, where the plaintiff claimed approximately SEK 78 million from the state-owned postal operator based on an abuse of dominance claim (withdrawn following a settlement); T 8-738-96, *CityMail Sweden AB v. Posten Sverige AB*, where the plaintiff claimed approximately SEK 68 million from the state-owned postal operator based on an abuse of dominance claim (withdrawn following a settlement); T 8-1093-98, *BK Tåg AB v. Statens Järnvägar*, where the plaintiff claimed approximately SEK 30 million in damages from the state-owned railroad operator based on an abuse of dominance claim (withdrawn following a settlement); T 8122-00, *Weba Kemi AB v. Arla ekonomisk förening*, October 9, 2002, where the court dismissed, on substantive grounds, an action for damages due to a claimed breach of the two primary prohibitions under the 1993 Competition Act; and T 17228-99, *Powerpipe Holding AB v. ABB Asea Brown Boveri Ltd*, February 4, 2003, where the plaintiff, among other things, claimed approximately SEK 315 million in damages based on the defendant's participation in a European-wide cartel (a settlement was reached and legalized by the court).

existing or potential clients. Thus, an attorney is generally free to approach potential clients proposing to bring a private action for damages. The only relevant exception is that members of the Swedish Bar may not solicit clients in a manner that takes advantage of someone's distress (*i.e.* 'ambulance chasing'), but this seems unlikely to be relevant for damages claims due to competition law infringements.

An attorney's fees must be reasonable based on, among other things, the scope, nature, degree of difficulty and importance of the assignment, the attorney's skills and proficiency, and the results of the attorney's labor. Fees shall generally be based on an hourly rate or a fixed fee. The Swedish Bar's rules generally do not accept contingency fees arrangements whereby an attorney enters into a risk sharing agreement with a client based on the outcome of the case. Risk sharing agreements may be permitted only where 'particular reasons' make it necessary. This would be the case where it otherwise would be difficult for the client to gain access to justice or where the assignment is part of a cross-border dispute and a risk sharing agreement has been concluded for the dealings outside of Sweden and this agreement constitutes a prerequisite for the attorney's assignment. In addition, in cases brought under the Group Proceedings Act, risk sharing agreements concluded between the plaintiff(s) and an attorney can be approved by a court.[4]

2. Legislative framework

a. The basic damages provision

The Swedish competition legislation dates back to July 1, 1993 and the implementation of the 1993 Competition Act (1993:20). In anticipation of Swedish membership of the EU, the Act was modeled after the then applicable EC competition law framework. As noted in the introduction, private litigation was foreseen and facilitated by the inclusion of a specific damages provision. The 1993 Competition Act was continually amended and updated, and in 2005 several amendments were implemented to increase the incentives to bring private actions. The rules on standing were expanded to include all persons and entities that had suffered losses (whereas previously, standing was restricted to 'companies and contracting parties'), the statutory limitation period was extended (from five to ten years) and an express right to base claims on violations of Articles 81 and 82 of the EC Treaty[5] was included (whereas previously, the 1993 Competition Act only referred to the corresponding national provisions as the basis for such claims).[6]

The current Competition Act (2008:579) (Competition Act) entered into force on November 1, 2008. The Act's damages provision (Chapter 3 §25) provides that if an undertaking 'intentionally or negligently infringes any [of the Competition Act's two

---

4 Sections 38–41 of the Group Proceedings Act (2002:599). A court may approve the agreement if it is reasonable with regard to the nature of the substantive matter. However, a court is prevented from approving a risk agreement if the fees are based solely on the value of the subject matter of the dispute.

5 On December 1, 2009, the Treaty of Lisbon came into effect, amending the Treaty Establishing the European Community (EC Treaty) that is now called the Treaty on the Functioning of the European Union (TFEU). Therefore, all references to Articles 81 and 82 of the EC Treaty now reference Articles 101 and 102 TFEU.

6 See Government Bill 2004/05:117, pp. 25–30, 33–36 and 70–71.

primary prohibitions or] Article 81 or 82 in the EC Treaty, the undertaking shall compensate the damage that is caused thereby.' This applies without any industry-specific exemptions. As the Competition Act does not go further and comprehensively regulate private enforcement, this provision must be interpreted in conjunction with Swedish civil procedural law and tort law in the context of private damages actions.

b. Prohibited practices

The Competition Act includes two primary prohibitions: a ban on anticompetitive agreements or concerted practices (Chapter 2 §1) and a ban on the abuse of a dominant position (Chapter 2 §7). These prohibitions are practically identical to Articles 81 and 82 of the EC Treaty. In theory, damages claims may be based on any competition law infringement, regardless of whether it stems from a horizontal or vertical relationship or whether it occurs in the context of a contractual agreement. In practice, however, only damages actions alleging cartel activity or the abuse of a dominant position have been brought before Swedish courts.

c. Standing

The Competition Act does not contain any express provisions on standing. Swedish courts will therefore determine standing by looking at the underlying purpose of the act and the general principles of tort law. In essence, the scope of potential claimants is limited by the need to show an identifiable and indemnifiable injury as well as a causal link between the injury and the competition law violation.[7]

Competitors operating in the same market as the infringer or companies that operate in upstream or downstream markets are typically entitled to bring damages claims, provided they have suffered economic losses as a result of an infringement. Nothing prevents a contracting party to an anticompetitive agreement from claiming damages against its counterparty. Public authorities have also been entitled to seek damages when, for example, a public procurement was affected by bid-rigging. In such instances it is possible for public authorities to claim damages not only from the company with which the procuring authority entered into a contract, but also from other cartel members.[8] Finally, end-consumers may likewise be entitled to damages, even if they have not been in a direct contractual relationship with the infringing undertaking, so long as they can show a concrete injury caused by the violation.[9]

d. Limitation period

According to the Competition Act (Chapter 3 §25), the right to damages lapses 'if no action is brought within ten years from the date when the damage was caused.'[10]

---

7 See Wetter, Carl, J. Karlsson and M. Östman (2009), Konkurrensrätt – en kommentar (4 ed.), Thomson Reuters, p. 865.

8 See *e.g.* Svea Court of Appeal, T 9597-04, *Skanska Sverige AB v. Linköpings kommun et al.*, July 5, 2006, where the court concluded that all members of a tender cartel may be liable to pay damages to a procuring municipality.

9 See Wetter (note 7 above), pp. 865–866.

10 The statutory limitation period was extended from five to ten years on August 1, 2005. For claims that arose before this date, the five year limitation period applies. This could be compared

The only way to interrupt the period of limitation is consequently to bring a legal action.[11] Other ways of interrupting the period of limitation that generally are applicable to tort or contractual claims (*e.g.* serving the debtor with a written demand) do not apply.

Additionally, the statute provides that the limitation period starts to run when the 'damage was caused'.[12] This may have practical consequences where damages arise at a later point in time than when the tortuous act took place and in cases of continuing infringements where damages also arise continuous (*i.e.* 'new and additional' losses arises over time). In *Europe Investor Direct AB et al. v. VPC*[13] (described below), the court concluded that an abuse of dominance through a refusal to supply had led to profit losses for the claimant. The court estimated these losses for each relevant year. Since any damages that had accrued prior to December 5, 2000 were subject to the statute of limitations,[14] the court, for that particular year, made an estimation of how much of the annual losses had been incurred after the cut-off date.

e. Choice of forum

Two principal fora are available for a private damages claim. First, under general procedural law, a plaintiff may bring suit in the competent court for tort claims, which is the district court where the defendant resides.[15] Where the plaintiff seeks to bring a group action pursuant to the Group Proceedings Act (described below), such matters are handled by specifically designated district courts in each Swedish county.[16]

Second, under a special forum provision in the Competition Act (Chapter 3 §26), Stockholm City Court is always deemed competent to hear actions for damages for competition law violations. A consideration for a plaintiff contemplating opting for Stockholm City Court is that this court is generally deemed to be better versed in competition law issues as decisions by the Swedish Competition Authority (SCA) are generally appealed to the court and assigned to its specific division for competition law cases.[17]

In either instance, appeals are heard by one of five Swedish Courts of Appeal,

---

to the rules on administrative fines, where the statutory limitation period runs from the time when the infringement *ceased* (Chapter 3 §20).

11 It follows from general legal principles that an action is deemed to be brought on the date when the prospective plaintiff submits a summons application to a court. See *e.g.* Government Bill 1979/80:119, p. 56.

12 The statutory text quoted above is the most authoritative translation of the Competition Act. The Swedish wording reads that the right to damages lapses '*om talan inte väcks inom tio år från det att skadan uppkom*'. In our view, the translation of the word '*uppkom*' to 'was caused' is slightly misleading. A more precise translation would be 'occurred' or 'arose'.

13 Stockholm City Court, joined cases T 32799-05 and T 34227-05, *Europe Investor Direct AB et al. v. VPC AB*, November 20, 2008.

14 Prior to August 1, 2005, the statutory limitation period was five years. See note 10 above.

15 See Chapter 10 of the Code of Judicial Procedure (1942:740).

16 Section 3 of the Group Proceedings Act.

17 Certain decisions by the SCA are nevertheless appealed to other courts: (i) the Competition Act lists certain types of cases that are appealed to or heard by the Market Court as the sole judicial instance; and (ii) decisions taken by the SCA that are governed by administrative law where appeals are heard by the County Administrative Court in Stockholm as the court at first instance.

depending on which court has appellate jurisdiction over the district court where the action was filed. Further appeals may be heard by the Supreme Court.

Outside the realm of traditional court proceedings, the Arbitration Act provides that arbitrators 'may rule on the civil law effects of competition law as between the parties.'[18]

3. Public vs. private enforcement

The SCA is entrusted with the public enforcement of the Competition Act. Any investigation and subsequent action by the SCA may cover infringements of the two Swedish primary prohibitions as well as infringements of Articles 81 and 82 of the EC Treaty.

The public enforcement remedies available to the SCA include injunctions ordering an undertaking to terminate a competition law infringement (Chapter 3 §1) and decisions to accept voluntary commitments to bring a perceived infringement to an end (Chapter 3 §4). However, the SCA does not have authority to issue administrative fines unless the company accepts such a fine (Chapter 3 §§16–18). In disputed cases, the SCA must bring an action seeking administrative fines before Stockholm City Court, which may subsequently be appealed to the Market Court.[19]

The public and private components of the Competition Act's two primary prohibitions are generally enforced independently and the SCA will not directly assist a private party seeking to obtain damages caused by a competition law infringement.

Nevertheless, given private plaintiffs' often limited access to evidence, prior or simultaneous public action may, in practice, be a pre-condition to a successful private action, particularly in cartel cases. As will be explained, private litigants can make use of the public procedures in different ways.

4. Private actions

Plaintiffs have several procedural alternatives for bringing damages claims and/or claims for equitable relief.

a. Stand-alone actions

The formal requirements for initiating a private action for damages are fairly easy to meet.[20] If the requirements are satisfied, the district court will issue a writ of summons calling upon the defendant to answer the case. However, the court shall *ex officio* (without a prior motion or request) dismiss a summons application if it is manifest that

---

[18] Section 1 of the Arbitration Act (1999:116).

[19] The Swedish Market Court is a specialized court that handles cases related to the Competition Act as well as cases under the Marketing Act (2008:486) and other consumer and marketing legislation. The Market Court is the highest court of appeal for these cases. The court consists of a chairman and a vice chairman plus five special members. The chairman, the vice chairman and one of the special members are lawyers with experience as judges while the other special members are experts in economics.

[20] Chapter 42 §1 of the Code of Judicial Procedure. A summons application must state a distinct claim, a detailed account of the circumstances invoked as the basis of the claim, a specification of the evidence offered and what shall be proved by each item of evidence adduced and the circumstances rendering the court competent to handle the case (unless this is apparent from what is otherwise stated in the summons application).

the case cannot proceed due to a procedural impediment. The court may also (without a prior motion or request) decide to dismiss the case without issuing a writ of summons if the plaintiff's statement does not constitute a legal basis for the case or if it is otherwise clear that the case is unfounded.[21]

Accessibility of evidence is a key consideration for a prospective private plaintiff in determining whether to initiate a damages action. The investigative tools available to a private party for gathering evidence are far more limited than those available to the SCA. Stand-alone actions are therefore unlikely to be brought unless the potential plaintiff already possesses evidence considered sufficient to prove the claim. In this respect, it is unsurprising that the only private Competition Act claim to result in court-awarded damages was an abuse of dominance case, as an injured party is more likely to possess relevant evidence in an abuse of dominance case than in a cartel case.

In *Europe Investor Direct AB et al. v. VPC*,[22] the plaintiff was a group of companies processing and selling various forms of investor information. The plaintiff brought a damages claim against VPC (now Euroclear Sweden), the Swedish central securities depository, for terminating the supply of address information for shareholders in listed companies. Stockholm City Court found for the plaintiff, concluding that VPC was a monopolist in the market for the supply of information contained in share registers of listed companies and, as such, had abused its dominant position by refusing to continue the supply. The plaintiff was awarded damages of approximately SEK 3.9 million plus interest as well as compensation for litigation costs. The judgment has been appealed and will be heard by Svea Court of Appeal.

In this case, the facts appear to have been generally undisputed, which probably contributed to the plaintiff's successful action. The plaintiff had purchased the relevant information for several years, but was unable to do so during a period of approximately five years when VPC's price quotes were substantially higher than what the plaintiff had previously paid. Eventually, the plaintiff purchased the requested information for a price that VPC said corresponded to its costs for supplying it. The main issue was whether VPC's conduct should be classified as a competition law violation. The court characterized VPC's behavior in its entirety as a refusal to supply and concluded that VPC had no objective justifications for its 'constructive' refusal.

With respect to the alleged damages, the court found that it was shown that the plaintiff had suffered losses as several of its customers had refrained from using its services due to the gradual decrease in quality resulting from unavailability of the address information. As the court considered VPC's behavior abusive, the plaintiff was also deemed to have suffered damage indemnifiable under the Competition Act (although the size of this loss was disputed). The measure of damages in the case will be commented on further below.

Another interesting abuse of dominance case is *Scandinavian Airlines System v. Staten genom Luftfartsverket*.[23] This case did not involve damages under the Competition Act,

---

[21] Chapter 42 §§4–5 of the Code of Judicial Procedure.

[22] Stockholm City Court, joined cases T 32799-05 and T 34227-05, *Europe Investor Direct AB et al. v. VPC AB*, November 20, 2008.

[23] Norrköping District Court, T 2746-96, *Scandinavian Airlines System v. Staten genom Luftfartsverket*, December 22, 1999, and Svea Court of Appeal, T 33-00, *Staten genom*

but repayment of discriminatory charges as a matter of contract law. The plaintiff, the airline operator SAS, brought an action against LFV (the state-owned airport operator) requesting that certain clauses in two agreements between SAS and LFV regulating airport fees at Arlanda airport be declared null and void on the ground that the clauses breached the competition law abuse prohibition. On this basis, SAS additionally sought repayment, as a matter of contract law, of the excess airport fees it considered that it had paid during the contract period (in other words, a performance claim connected to the declaratory claim). Svea Court of Appeal found for the plaintiff, concluding that the 1993 Competition Act was applicable to the agreements and that LFV had abused its dominant position by charging higher airport fees to SAS than other airlines (which amounted to illegal price discrimination). As the clauses were held invalid, SAS was entitled to repayment of parts of the airport fees it had paid during the period covered by the contracts in question. The repayment amounted to approximately SEK 400 million plus interest as well as compensation for litigation costs. The repayment constituted the difference between what SAS had in fact paid and what it would have had to pay had LFV charged SAS the same fees that were applied to other airlines. As other airlines were charged according to a tariff schedule (which LFV had implemented a few years after the disputed agreements with SAS were entered into), the sum was fairly easily calculated and not disputed as such.

b. Follow-on actions

A prior or simultaneous public action by the SCA can have tremendous evidentiary value in a private action. The SCA has extensive powers to investigate potential infringements and may require undertakings or other parties to disclose documents or other materials (Chapter 5 §1).[24] The SCA may also require persons who can give relevant testimony to appear at hearings and, subject to prior authorization by Stockholm City Court, it may inspect the premises of an undertaking or the private premises of a board member or employee of an undertaking (Chapter 5 §§3–5). Such requests and orders may also, in most cases, be made subject to a conditional fine (Chapter 6 §1).[25] Materials compiled or

---

Luftfartsverket v. Scandinavian Airlines System, April 27, 2001. On appeal, the Supreme Court did not issue a writ of *certiorari*.

24 This does not include documents with content protected by legal privilege (Chapter 5 §11). See also Stockholm City Court, Ä 10773-03, *Konkurrensverket v. Nynäs AB et al.*, July 14, 2003, where the court concluded that a letter drafted by a foreign lawyer working as a solicitor in Scotland (and being a member of the Law Society of Scotland) was protected by legal privilege. The solicitor who had drafted the document was deemed comparable to a Swedish attorney.

25 In addition, under a broadly worded statute from 1956 (the Act on obligation to supply information concerning prices and competition conditions (1956:245)), the SCA may, subject to a conditional fine, require any business proprietor to submit information relating to conditions of competition. Most recently, the SCA issued such a request against Apoteket AB (the state-owned retail pharmacy operator) after the company had refused to voluntarily supply information concerning its business which the SCA had requested during a general market survey of the conditions for the distribution and sale of pharmaceuticals triggered by the then imminent deregulation of the Swedish pharmacy market. See SCA, dnr 340/2007, *Apoteket AB*, September 24, 2007. The SCA eventually withdrew its formal request after the company supplied the requested information (decision in the same case, April 24, 2008).

prepared by the SCA in the course of an investigation can serve as evidence in a private follow-on action concerning the same conduct.

Furthermore, despite the fact that previous court decisions are not binding in subsequent proceedings, and each court under Swedish procedural principles is entirely at liberty to evaluate all evidence in order to determine what has been proven at the case at hand,[26] as a practical matter the outcome of the public action is highly relevant to the question of whether an alleged competition law infringement in fact occurred. In practice a final judgment by the Stockholm City Court or the Market Court regarding the same matter will be guiding in subsequent private follow-on actions.

Follow-on actions were recently initiated in the wake of the SCA's *Asphalt cartel* case. After conducting multiple dawn raids in 2001, the SCA brought an action against several defendant construction companies accused of distorting competition in the asphalt market through market sharing, price-fixing and other illegal practices. In parallel with the SCA's action, nine Swedish municipalities have reportedly[27] commenced damages actions against the construction companies in various district courts. The follow-on actions were initiated before the SCA's public action had been finally settled, but were stayed pending the final judgment of the Market Court.[28] The actions are now expected to continue.

General procedural rules allow for courts to order a stay of proceedings where private plaintiffs initiate a damages action before the final outcome of a prior or simultaneous action by the SCA is clear (*e.g.* due to limitation periods). A court may stay a proceeding if it is of 'extraordinary importance for the adjudication of a case that an issue sub justice in another court proceeding, or in a proceeding of another kind, be determined first.'[29] Due to reasons of judicial economy, a stay of proceedings in these instances is often in the interests both of the plaintiff and the court (and possibly also the defendant).

c. Joined public/private actions

Since the implementation of the 1993 Competition Act, private parties have been able to bolster a contemplated damages action by intervening in a public enforcement action. Under general procedural rules, anyone who can show probable cause that the matter at issue will bear on its legal rights or obligations may intervene in litigation, whether on

---

[26] For example, nothing prevents the Market Court, subsequent to a public enforcement action brought by the SCA, from finding that an undertaking has abused its dominant position through a refusal to supply while a district court, deciding on a private follow-on action for damages based on the same refusal, may find that no such abuse has occurred. This may relate not only to points of facts, but also to points of law.

[27] SCA background note on the *Asphalt cartel* case published in connection with the Market Court's judgment (see SCA press release, May 28, 2009).

[28] Market Court, MD 2009:11, *NCC AB et al. v. Konkurrensverket*, May 28, 2009. The court imposed record-level administrative fines of approximately SEK 277 million on five of the defendant companies. In addition, administrative fines of SEK 222.5 million were awarded against three defendant companies that did not appeal the judgment of the court at first instance. See Stockholm City Court, T 5467-03, *Konkurrensverket v. Kvalitetsasfalt i Mellansverige AB et al.*, July 10, 2007.

[29] Chapter 32 §5 of the Code of Judicial Procedure.

the side of the plaintiff or the defendant.[30] This may be the case, for example, where the judgment will have evidentiary value in another case in which the intervening party has an interest. A typical example would be when the intervening party has initiated a private damages claim with respect to an agreement and/or practice that is being examined in a SCA public action for administrative fines.[31] In such cases, the intervener may provide evidence and make submissions in the public proceedings.[32]

For example, in *BK Tåg AB v. Statens Järnvägar*,[33] an abuse of dominance case, the private action was settled out of court after the SCA had successfully obtained administrative fines of SEK 8 million from the state-owned rail operator with the private action plaintiff having intervened on the SCA's side in the public proceedings.[34]

In addition, the 2008 Competition Act introduced a new procedural path that allows private parties to litigate with the SCA in the same proceedings. If the SCA brings an action for administrative fines before Stockholm City Court, the court may decide, if appropriate, that a private damages action shall be joined with a public action for administrative fines (Chapter 8 §7). When making its decision, the court shall consider whether a joinder of actions would achieve an efficient and expeditious resolution of the proceedings. In the event the continuous joint handling of the cases gives rise to significant inconveniences, the court may subsequently order the cases to be separated. Final judgments by the Stockholm City Court in joined cases may be appealed to the Market Court.

The main purpose of allowing private damages claims to be joined with public actions is to enhance the efficiency of the sanction system laid down in the Competition Act.[35] The SCA may benefit from being assisted by a company that has incurred losses due to the challenged behavior. For a private plaintiff, a joint action may reduce the time and cost of bringing a damages action. In addition, such cooperation with the SCA would give the plaintiff access to useful information.

d. Actions for equitable remedies

While any damages claim will have a declaratory element, it is also possible for a private party to bring an action solely seeking a declaratory judgment.[36] For example, a plaintiff

---

[30] Chapter 14 §§9-13 of the Code of Judicial Procedure. See also *e.g.* Market Court, MD 1997:16, *City Mail Sweden AB*, October 13, 1997, where the court took an expansive view of the procedural rules governing intervention in cases brought by the SCA.

[31] Intervention has been allowed in several cases for administrative fines brought by the SCA. See *e.g.* Stockholm City Court, T 8-1264-94 *Konkurrensverket v. Posten Sverige AB*, December 23, 1997; Market Court, MD 2000:2, *Statens Järnvägar v. Konkurrensverket*, February 1, 2000; and Stockholm City Court, T 31862-04, *Konkurrensverket v. TeliaSonera Sverige AB* (pending). See also Market Court, MD 2001:4, *Konsortiet Scandinavian Airlines System v. Konkurrensverket*, February 27, 2001, where intervention was allowed in a case where the SCA sought an injunction.

[32] See Wetter (note 7 above), pp. 965–967.

[33] Stockholm City Court, T 8-1093-98, *BK Tåg AB v. Statens Järnvägar*.

[34] For the public actions brought by the SCA, see Stockholm City Court, T 8-103-96, *Konkurrensverket v. Statens Järnvägar*, December 8, 1998, and Market Court, MD 2000:2, *Statens Järnvägar v. Konkurrensverket*, February 1, 2000.

[35] See Government Bill 2007/08:135, pp. 98–100 and 283.

[36] Chapter 13 §2 of the Code of Judicial Procedure.

may request a court to declare that the defendant is liable to pay damages due to a competition law infringement but leave the quantum of damages to be dealt with in a subsequent proceeding.[37]

In addition to such general equitable remedies, the Competition Act provides for a specific, subsidiary right for private parties to bring an action before the Market Court requesting an injunction against a competition law infringer (Chapter 3 §2). Such an injunction would require the infringement to end, either by forcing the infringer to terminate or correct improper behavior (*e.g.* to cease applying a particular contract term) or by imposing a positive obligation (*e.g.* establishing an obligation to supply). The injunction can also be made subject to a conditional fine (Chapter 6 §1).

The scope for such injunctive relief under the Competition Act is nevertheless limited. It is a subsidiary right reserved for undertakings (not private individuals) and it can be exercised only after a party has filed a complaint with the SCA and the SCA has decided not to take action.[38] Because the Market Court is the exclusive forum for these actions, they cannot be handled together with a private action for damages, which has to be brought before a district court or Stockholm City Court.

In *Skyways Express AB v. Marknadsföringsbolaget Nya Norrköping AB et al.*,[39] the airline Skyways Express sought, among other things, an injunction prohibiting Norrköping municipality from granting any further economic aid to the competing airline Cimber Air. The basis for the request was that the aid violated Article 81 or 82 of the EC Treaty and/or the corresponding provisions in the Competition Act. The district court and, on appeal, the appellate court both dismissed the request, holding that the courts were not authorized to order such an injunction as the 1993 Competition Act specifically named the SCA and the Market Court as the appropriate fora. In this respect, no material legislative changes have been made in the current Competition Act. As a consequence, private damages and private injunctions must be pursued through separate actions.

5. Several parties and group proceedings

a. Several parties

Under general procedural law, several plaintiffs' tort claims against the same defendant(s) may be joined in one proceeding if the claims are based essentially on the same grounds.[40]

---

[37] See *e.g.* Stockholm City Court, T 8122-00, *Weba Kemi AB v. Arla ekonomisk förening*, October 9, 2002, where the plaintiff only requested that the court should declare that the defendant was liable to pay damages for infringing §§6 and 19 of the 1993 Competition Act (corresponding to Chapter 2 §§1 and 7 of the current Competition Act).

[38] Injunctions are also barred where the SCA has applied Article 13 of Council Regulation (EC) No 1/2003 (OJ L 1, 4.1.2003, p. 1) and rejected the complaint because the Commission or the competent authority of another EU Member State has received a complaint regarding the same practice and has already dealt with it.

[39] Norrköping District Court, T 2522-06, *Skyways Express AB v. Marknadsföringsbolaget Nya Norrköping AB et al.*, February 15, 2007, and Göta Court of Appeal, Ö 638-07, *Skyways Express AB v. Marknadsföringsbolaget Nya Norrköping AB et al.*, May 22, 2007. On appeal, the Supreme Court did not issue a writ of *certiorari.*

[40] See Chapter 14 of the Code of Judicial Procedure.

If an action for damages is brought against several defendants, damages shall be claimed from, and determined individually for, each of the defending parties.

With respect to the responsibility of the defendants, two or more companies that are liable for the same injury are generally held jointly and severally liable.[41] A company that has paid damages to an injured party has a right of recourse against other liable parties to the extent that it has paid more than the damages that have been individually determined.

b. Group proceedings

Group actions (a similar, but not identical, concept to US class actions) are governed by the Group Proceedings Act which entered into force on January 1, 2003. This Act is not limited to particular types of cases, and a group action can thus be brought for any claim that is eligible for consideration by a district court, including private competition law cases.

According to a recent report by the Swedish Justice Department[42] only ten group actions have been initiated since the enactment of the Group Proceedings Act, none of which concerned competition law infringement claims. Despite the low number, the report concluded that the Act helped promote individuals' access to courts, because several of the initiated actions would probably not have otherwise been pursued. In practice it is consumer claims – typically low-value claims spread among a large number of individuals – that are most frequently pursued as group actions.

Under the Group Proceedings Act, a group action may be instituted in three different ways: (i) as a *private group action*, which may be brought by a natural person or legal entity; (ii) as an *organization action*, which may be brought by a non-profit association that, in accordance with its rules, protects consumers' or wage-earners' interests; or (iii) as a *public group action*, which may be brought by an authority expressly permitted by the government to institute public group actions.[43] Notably, the SCA has not been granted the authority to institute public group actions.[44]

Irrespective of the type of group action, five cumulative conditions must be fulfilled. A group action will only be heard if: (i) the action is founded on circumstances that are common or similar among group members; (ii) a group proceeding would not be inappropriate due to distinctions or differences among various group members' claims; (iii) the majority of group members' claims cannot be pursued equally well through personal actions; (iv) the group, taking into consideration its size, ambit and otherwise, is appropriately defined; and (v) the plaintiff is appropriate to represent the members

---

41 See Chapter 6 of the Tort Liability Act (1972:207).

42 Ds 2008:74, October 28, 2008.

43 See §§1 and 4–6 of the Group Proceedings Act.

44 It was discussed however, in connection with the amendments made in 2005 to the 1993 Competition Act, whether or not the SCA should be granted the authority to institute public group actions. Such authority was not granted, *inter alia* because it was thought that the SCA's resources should be focused on public competition law enforcement and not be spent on assisting individual parties seeking restitutionary damages for competition law infringements. No other public authority was authorized to institute public group actions for competition law infringements. See Government Bill 2004/05:117, pp. 30–33.

of the group in the proceedings.[45] In its report, the Justice Department concluded that courts have had difficulty applying the prerequisites, resulting in a somewhat less efficient outcome than initially hoped.

Under the Group Proceedings Act, a group action is defined as an action brought by a plaintiff as the representative of several persons (without a power of attorney for the lawsuit). The outcome has legal effects for group members although they are not parties to the case.[46]

The court hearing the case will nevertheless rule on the individual group members' claims and right to damages. Normally, this is unproblematic due to the five prerequisites for instituting a group proceeding accounted for above. Generally, the individual claims are identical, easily ascertainable or could be estimated to a reasonable amount. However, the claims of the individual group members do not necessarily have to be identical and individual members may have to provide individual evidence to support their claim and/or the size of the losses suffered. The court hearing the case may split a group action into one or more sub-groups in order to conduct an action on a particular issue or a part of the substantive matter that only applies to the rights of particular members of the group.[47]

The final judgment (or court sanctioned settlement) is legally enforceable by or against all individuals that are members of the group (as comprised at the time of the judgment).[48] As the Group Proceedings Act is based on an opt-in system, the group will comprise only those members that declare themselves willing to join. Technically, anyone who does not make such a declaration before a deadline set by the court is deemed to have stepped out of the group.[49] Failure or refusal to opt into a group does not lead to any negative legal consequences as the group action will not create any form of estoppel against a subsequent individual claim.

6. Standard of proof and evidence

a. Standard of proof

The general rules on standard of proof applicable in tort cases apply to cases concerning private enforcement of competition law. The plaintiff bears the burden of proof with respect to all elements of the claim. In particular, it must show that: (i) an infringement has occurred (through the intent or negligence of the infringing party); (ii) indemnifiable damage has occurred; and (iii) a causal link exists between the infringement and the damage.[50] The standard of proof here requires that the relevant facts be 'proven' or 'shown'. This is a lesser standard than 'beyond a reasonable doubt' but does not involve a 'balance of probabilities' exercise. Under general procedural principles, once the plaintiff has discharged its burden of proof, the burden shifts to the defendant.

---

45 Section 8 of the Group Proceedings Act.
46 Section 1 of the Group Proceedings Act.
47 Section 20 of the Group Proceedings Act.
48 Sections 26 and 29 of the Group Proceedings Act.
49 Section 14 of the Group Proceedings Act.
50 See Wetter (note 7 above), p. 865.

Further, a private party bringing a Competition Act claim has the same burden of proof as the SCA in bringing a public enforcement action.[51] Thus, the principles that have evolved on the burden and standard of proof applicable to the Swedish and EC primary competition law prohibitions apply.

b. The use of evidence in Swedish proceedings

The general rules of evidence apply to private actions for competition law infringements. As a private damages claim is a case amenable to settlement, it is the parties' responsibility to provide the evidence that they wish the court to consider. A party may, in principle, rely on any documents, statements or testimony it wishes to present. Expert testimony from economic and legal scholars is regularly used in Swedish competition law proceedings. In addition, physical inspections can be undertaken during the course of trial with the judges and parties' representatives being present. A court will only reject evidence if it finds that a circumstance that a party offers to prove is without importance in the case, or that an item of evidence offered is unnecessary or evidently should be of no effect. Live testimony is preferred over written statements as written statements will be allowed only in exceptional circumstances.[52]

Further, Swedish courts have a wide margin of appreciation to evaluate any evidence in determining whether a party has discharged its burden of proof. The general rule on evidence provides that '[a]fter evaluating everything that has occurred in accordance with the dictates of its conscience, the court shall determine what has been proved in the case.'[53] This rule is supplemented with specific provisions such as that no proof is required regarding legal standards (*jura novit curia*). Other specific provisions apply as to the effect of certain kinds of evidence, such as witnesses, documentary evidence, physical inspections, and experts. These supplemental and specific rules are, however, relatively straightforward and rarely limits the ability of private parties to present evidence, or the courts' ability to take the evidence presented into account when determining what has or has not been proved in the case at hand.

Courts also have the option to occasionally appoint their own expert(s) in order to determine an issue the appraisal of which requires special professional knowledge. In those instances, if the court finds it necessary to call upon an expert, the court may either obtain an opinion on the issue from a public authority or officer or commission any other expert(s) 'known for their integrity and their knowledge of the subject' to deliver an opinion.[54]

c. Order to produce evidence

Broad pre-trial discovery is not available under Swedish procedural law. However, a Swedish court may issue an order, subject to a conditional fine, requiring anybody

---

[51] See *e.g.* Market Court, MD 2007:26, *Övertorneå kommun et al. v. Ekfors Kraft AB et al.*, November 15, 2007, where two Swedish municipalities sought an injunction against a local electricity provider (*i.e.* it was a subsidiary action brought in the Market Court after the SCA decided not to take any action regarding the municipalities' complaint).

[52] See Chapter 35 of the Code of Judicial Procedure.

[53] Chapter 35 §1 of the Code of Judicial Procedure.

[54] Chapter 40 §1 of the Code of Judicial Procedure.

(including a third party) to produce any potentially relevant documentary material in its possession.[55]

In practice, plaintiffs have difficulties making use of this possibility. First, the requesting party must specify what written document it seeks and what the document is intended to prove. In other words, the applicant must know exactly which documents to request and be able to identify them. Such requests cannot therefore be used for more general requests or 'fishing expeditions' for evidence. Second, trade secrets[56] do not have to be disclosed unless extraordinary reasons justify disclosure. Third, a court may not order the production of a document subject to legal privilege.[57] Finally, the intended recipient of the order must be afforded an opportunity to respond to the request. Further, if it is feared that evidence may be destroyed or otherwise distorted, the applicant may petition the court for suitable interim measures to protect the material.[58]

Konkurrensverket v. Posten Sverige AB[59] may be mentioned as an example of the practical difficulties of securing such an order. In the case, the private postal operator CityMail (which had intervened on the SCA's side in a public proceeding) requested that the state-owned postal operator should be ordered to produce a cost estimate that had been reported in a newspaper article. However, in view of the defendant's denial that it possessed the cost estimate in question, the Market Court considered that it lacked a sufficient basis to grant the request.

d. Access to the SCA's case file

In follow-on actions, a private party may potentially rely on documents in the SCA's case file. As mentioned above, the SCA has extensive powers to investigate potential competition law infringements, but during an SCA investigation, documents and information in the case file are generally subject to absolute secrecy.[60]

Once the investigation has ended (*e.g.* through a decision by the SCA to close the investigation or to bring an action for administrative fines), this absolute protection ends. Any individual (including foreigners) may then, under the constitutional principles guaranteeing public access to information, request material gathered, created, received or held by the SCA. This includes information provided to the SCA by a leniency applicant. Access shall be granted unless the information is subject to confidentiality protection under the Publicity and Secrecy Act.[61] While business secrets (typically competitively

---

55 See Chapter 38 of the Code of Judicial Procedure.

56 A 'trade secret' is generally defined as information concerning the business or industrial activities of a business proprietor that is being kept secret and the disclosure of which is likely to cause competitive harm. See §1 of the Act on the Protection of Trade Secrets (1990:409).

57 Only independent lawyers can be members of the Swedish Bar and as such be covered by the rules of legal privilege. It follows that any documents or correspondence drawn up by in-house counsel are not covered by legal privilege. Cf. note 24 above concerning the extension of legal privilege to foreign (independent) lawyers deemed comparable with Swedish independent lawyers and the Court of First Instance's judgment in joined cases T–125/03 and T–253/03, *Akzo Nobel Chemicals Ltd and Akcros Chemicals Ltd v. Commission of the European Communities* [2007] ECR II–03523.

58 Chapter 15 §3 of the Code of Judicial Procedure.

59 Market Court, dnr A 3/98, *Konkurrensverket v. Posten Sverige AB*, June 30, 1998.

60 Chapter 17 §3 of the Publicity and Secrecy Act (2009:400).

61 Chapter 2 §§1–2 of the Freedom of the Press Act (1949:105).

sensitive information or other sensitive information such as business structures, etc.) are covered under the Publicity and Secrecy Act,[62] the SCA's file will nonetheless contain other information that may prove useful to a private party. The SCA could refuse access to applications or statements by an individual or a company, if it can be assumed that the individual or company would suffer considerable harm or significant injury if the information is made public.[63]

Understandably these relatively wide constitutional principles guaranteeing public access to information could potentially cause leniency applicants to be hesitant about providing information to the SCA. Further, as court proceedings are generally necessary in order for the SCA to seek administrative fines (with the exception of accepted such fines) and the information submitted in those proceedings is governed by the same legislative framework as described above, a leniency applicant will always enter the process knowing that potential private plaintiffs may be able to access sensitive information concerning the infringing actions or behavior.

The Swedish leniency system was first implemented on August 1, 2002 through an amendment to the 1993 Competition Act (and revised through the implementation of the current Competition Act). Since then, only two leniency applications have been submitted that have resulted in an active cartel being disclosed and successfully charged by the SCA.[64] Whether or not the seemingly poor result that the Swedish leniency program so far has yielded can be partly attributed to potential leniency applicants' hesitance to provide information is a matter for discussion.

7. Damages and litigation costs

a. Single damages

As discussed above, an undertaking that intentionally or negligently commits a competition law infringement is obliged to compensate the damage that is caused thereby (Chapter 3 §25). This accords with Swedish tort law principles, which afford plaintiffs compensatory relief in the form of single damages.

For the same reasons, and because no express legislation suggests otherwise, it seems clear that a defendant can rely on a passing-on defense under Swedish law. Because damages are considered restitutionary, an infringing undertaking is only liable for damages *actually* caused.[65]

---

62 Chapter 30 §1 of the Publicity and Secrecy Act. Cf. note 56 above regarding the general definition of trade secrets.

63 Chapter 30 Section 3 of the Publicity and Secrecy Act.

64 See Stockholm City Court, T 11660-03, *Konkurrensverket v. Keyvent AB et al.*, March 14, 2005, and SCA, dnr 237/2007, *Rundvirke Poles AB*, June 30, 2009 and the SCA's press release thereto (July 8, 2009). Further, in the *Asphalt cartel* case, the SCA did not bring an action against one of the participating companies (as a way to grant the company a full reduction of its fines) due to its cooperation with the authority during the investigation (see SCA press release, March 21, 2003). The actual disclosure of the *Asphalt cartel* was, however, made by whistleblowers in the infringing companies (see SCA press release, October 24, 2001).

65 See Wahl, Nils (2000), Konkurrensskada, Elanders Gotab, p. 312, and Wetter (note 7 above), p. 866 note 251.

b. Measuring damages

Compensation is assumed to cover 'pure economic losses' such as loss of profits due to reduced revenues or increased costs, and other losses due to the distortions caused by infringement. The compensation should, in theory, restore the injured party to the position it would have occupied had the infringement not occurred. Courts must therefore consider the injured party's actual economic status compared to a hypothetical scenario in which the infringement did not occur.[66]

Naturally, calculating such losses is often difficult. Various methods have been developed such as a 'before-and-after approach', benchmarking, cost-based models, statistical analyses and simulation models.

General procedural rules permit a court to determine damages by estimating a reasonable amount where either full proof cannot be presented at all, or only with difficulty, or where the costs or inconvenience of fully proving the damages would be disproportionately high considering the scope of the harm and the amount of compensation sought.[67] Given the difficulties involved in proving the extent of the injury, commentators have suggested that the incentive for private competition law enforcement would be low without this kind of relaxation of the burden of proof.[68]

In *Europe Investor Direct AB et al. v. VPC*[69] (described above), the plaintiff used the 'before-and-after approach' to calculate the lost profit caused by the alleged infringement. Stockholm City Court noted that this method may be appropriate where it is not possible to draw direct comparisons with a competing business in attempting to estimate losses. According to the court, the plaintiff had nevertheless failed to prove its claimed losses. The court therefore resorted to its own generalized estimation of the appropriate compensation to be awarded. This estimation was based, among other things, on the plaintiff's revenues, costs and potential cost savings from the challenged business practices.

A successful plaintiff has the right to full compensation interest under the Interest Act. The interest will amount to the Swedish Central Bank's reference rate plus eight percentage points and accrue on the amounts due from the 30th day following the day on which a damages claim has been submitted in writing to the liable party, or at the latest from the date a summons application is served on the defendant.[70]

c. Litigation costs

The general rule in tort cases is that the losing party shall reimburse the winning party's litigation costs. If a case concerns several claims and the outcome is split, each party must bear its own costs, or one party will be awarded an adjusted amount. Where there is a split outcome and the costs attributable to each component of the case are distinguishable, liability for costs will be allocated accordingly.[71]

---

66 See Government Bill 1992/1993:56, pp. 96–97. See also Wetter (note 7 above), pp. 870–872.

67 Chapter 35 §5 of the Code of Judicial Procedure.

68 See Wahl (note 62 above), p. 385.

69 Stockholm City Court, joined cases T 32799-05 and T 34227-05, *Europe Investor Direct AB et al. v. VPC AB*, November 20, 2008.

70 Sections 4 and 6 of the Interest Act (1975:635).

71 See Chapter 18 of the Code of Judicial Procedure.

Compensation for litigation costs shall cover the expenses, including attorney fees, which have been reasonably incurred for preparing the trial and presenting the action. Compensation will also be awarded for the time and effort expended by the party due to the litigation. A court shall *ex officio* consider to what extent the claimed costs have been reasonably incurred to safeguard the party's interests and may order a downward adjustment where appropriate.[72]

The Group Proceedings Act contains additional rules that apply in the context of group actions.[73] For example, if the defendant has been ordered to compensate the plaintiff (*i.e.* the representative of the group members) for litigation costs but is unable to pay, the group members are liable to pay these costs. The same applies to certain costs that the plaintiff incurs in connection with risk sharing agreements.

8. Extraterritoriality

The Competition Act's two primary prohibitions are broadly worded. For example, the prohibition against anticompetitive agreements or concerted practices is applicable to any agreement that to an appreciable extent distorts competition in the whole or a part of the Swedish market, even if the agreement or the parties to the agreement do not otherwise have any connection to Sweden.[74]

The Competition Act itself does not limit its extraterritorial application. Consequently, a private enforcement action could arguably be initiated and/or defended by foreign parties in Sweden solely because an agreement or practice breaches the two primary Swedish prohibitions and affects the Swedish market.[75] However, according to the preparatory works for the 1993 Competition Act, it was noted that practical considerations and international law rules limit the applicability of national law and, more specifically, it was asserted that the extraterritorial application of the Competition Act should be assessed in light of the efficiency principle.[76] As for the forum issue, Stockholm City Court is always deemed competent to deal with actions for damages due to the special forum provision in the Competition Act (Chapter 3 §26).

Case law on this extraterritoriality is sparse, but the issue was touched upon in connection with a private damages claim against ABB following the European *Pre-Insulated Pipe Cartel* case.[77] ABB initially requested that the case be dismissed for lack of

---

[72] Chapter 18 §8 of the Code of Judicial Procedure.

[73] Sections 33–36 of the Group Proceedings Act.

[74] See Wetter (note 7 above), p. 100.

[75] Cf. Wetter (note 7 above), pp. 101–102, where the authors argue, possibly *de lege ferenda* and with a reference to the *Wood Pulp* case (see note 75 below), that a condition for the application of the Competition Act, apart from at least a *prima facie* distortion on competition in Sweden, should be that a prohibited measure at least partly shall have been *implemented* in Sweden.

[76] See Government Bill 1992/1993:56, p. 73, Government Bill 1999/2000:140, p. 181 and Swedish Governmental Official Reports 2000:4, pp. 106, 171–172. Cf. the *Wood Pulp* case where the territorial principle was referred to as the jurisdictional basis for applying EC competition law to concerted practices between undertakings established in non-member countries. See European Court of Justice, joined cases 89, 104, 114, 116, 117 and 125 to 129/85, *A. Ahlström Osakeyhtiö and others v. Commission of the European Communities* [1988] ECR 05193.

[77] See the Commission's decision in Case No IV/35.691/E-4: – Pre-Insulated Pipe Cartel (OJ L 24, 30.1.1999, p. 1).

jurisdiction. Stockholm City Court applied Article 5.3 of the Lugano Convention[78] and held that it was authorized to consider the part of the claim concerning damages that had arisen in Sweden, but not those that had occurred outside Sweden. On appeal, the Svea Court of Appeal upheld the lower court's decision, noting that it was apparent from the Commission's previous decision in the cartel case that harmful effects of the cartel had encompassed the entire European market and thus had also affected competition in the Swedish market.[79]

Conclusion

As elsewhere in Europe, Sweden has experienced few cases involving private claims for damages resulting from competition law violations. There are several possible explanations.

Damages claims for competition law violations are a relatively new phenomenon, and it will take time to create awareness among potential claimants. In the corporate context, there also seems to be a lingering resistance in the business community to pursuing such claims against its fellow members, particularly following public enforcement actions. However, indications suggest that such notions are fading, and many are instead equating this type of harm with more traditional forms of damages. This development is likely to continue, if the number of successful claims increases going forward. Moreover and potentially more importantly, significant legal, economic and practical impediments to private enforcement remain. In particular, the high costs incurred by the losing party in combination with the difficulty of amassing evidence are likely to discourage prospective claimants.

The European Commission's initiative to propose a Council directive on private damages no doubt would have gone in the direction of facilitating private action. Judging from an internal draft,[80] the reforms that the Commission had in mind would require significant changes to the Swedish and other national legal systems. From that perspective it is not surprising that the Commission initiative was received with skepticism. It now seems the Commission's plan has come to a halt and the initiative will have to come from the European Parliament. Although it is uncertain what the outcome, if any, will eventually be, it seems useful to consider some of the key aspects of what the Commission had in mind.

First, making the finding of an infringement of Article 81 or 82 by any national competition authority or review court in the EU binding on Swedish courts would create a significant exception to the principle that Swedish courts are entirely at liberty to evaluate all evidence in order to determine what has been proven. However, the practical impact

[78] Convention on jurisdiction and the enforcements of judgments in civil and commercial matters, done at Lugano on September 16, 1988. Article 5.3 provides that '(a) person domiciled in a Contracting State may, in another Contracting State, be sued . . . in matters relating to tort, delict or quasi-delict, in the courts for the place where the harmful event occurred.'

[79] Stockholm City Court, T 17228-99, *Powerpipe Holding AB v. ABB Asea Brown Boveri Ltd*, May 3, 2000, and Svea Court of Appeal, Ö 3787-00, *ABB Asea Brown Boveri Ltd v. Powerpipe Holding AB*, January 22, 2001.

[80] Internal draft Proposal for a Council Directive on rules governing damages actions for infringements of Articles 81 and 82 of the Treaty (not dated).

could be less dramatic, given the high evidentiary significance that Swedish courts normally would give to such decisions today. The impact would also depend on the extent to which claimants would find it attractive to bring claims in Sweden based only on those infringements that were subject to foreign national procedures.

Secondly, implementation of an opt-out system for certain authorized organizations in place of the opt-in regime currently employed by the Swedish Group Proceedings Act would potentially facilitate the ease and effectiveness with which such organizations can bring damages actions. However, to the extent an opt-in regime would remain for groups of private claimants, it is unlikely that such changes would significantly affect the scope for corporate group actions.

Thirdly, the Commission's intention was to extend the means through which private plaintiffs could access relevant evidence. In 2004, the Swedish government considered measures that were similar to those now being called for by the Commission. A public inquiry resulted in a proposal for a system that mirrors Sweden's intellectual property regime.[81] The Swedish government did not endorse that proposal. If accepted, the Commission's model could achieve a similar result through different means, ultimately resulting in a far-reaching deviation from traditional Swedish procedure.

[81] Under various Swedish intellectual property statutes, a court can order an investigation at the premises of the defendant, executed by the Swedish Enforcement Authority (*i.e.* the bailiff), to seek evidence that could verify or disprove the alleged infringement. See Swedish Official Reports 2004:10, pp. 103–125 and Government Bill 2004/05:117, pp. 39–45.

23 Turkey

Hilmi Bolatoglu[1]

Introduction

Turkey utilizes a dual system of administrative and private antitrust enforcement. Although the Turkish Competition Authority (TCA), a government agency established pursuant to The Act on the Protection of Competition[2] (Competition Act), plays a central role in this dual system, private actions for damages also have very strong statutory roots which make private enforcement potentially important for Turkish competition law. Provisions regarding damages actions in the Competition Act depart from the general rules of the Code of Obligations both in proving injury and in calculating damages.[3] Competition infringements may be classified as a new and unique statutory cause of action other than those codified in the Code of Obligations.[4]

Provisions concerning substantive issues such as restrictive agreements, abuse of dominant position and merger control in the Competition Act are adapted from the competition law area of the *acquis communautaire*[5] of the European Community (EC).[6] However, the Turkish Parliament has followed the US example in damages actions, explicitly codifying rules similar to those found in the Clayton Act. Interestingly, this adaptation includes relief in the form of treble damages,[7] a concept not previously recognized in Turkish liability law.[8] As the EC law does not have Community-wide legal provisions governing damages in private actions, adaptation of the US approach might be regarded as a significant contribution to the effectiveness of private enforcement. Thus, the Competition Act seems divided between the EC and US approaches. This dichotomy

---

[1] Competition Expert & Legal Counsel, Turkish Competition Authority; LL.M. University of Illinois College of Law (2006). The views submitted in this work are those of the author and do not represent any official position of the Turkish Competition Authority.

[2] Act No. 4054 of 13.12.1994.

[3] I.Y. Aslan (2007), Competition Law, Bursa: Ekin, p. 783.

[4] Act No. 818 of 22.04.1926.

[5] *Acquis communautaire* is an expression that describes the entire body of European laws. This includes all the treaties, regulations and directives passed by the European institutions as well as judgments laid down by the European Court of Justice. Source: http://news.bbc.co.uk/2/hi/in_depth/europe/euro-glossary/1216329.stm.-glossary/1216329.stm. On 1.12.2009, the Treaty of Lisbon came into effect, amending the Treaty Establishing the European Community (EC Treaty) that is now called the Treaty on the Functioning of the European Union (TFEU). Therefore, all references to Articles 81 and 82 of the EC Treaty now reference Articles 101 and 102 TFEU.

[6] For a comparative analysis, see generally: G. Oz (1999), Competition Law and Practice in Turkey, European Competition Law Review, Vol. 20, Issue 3, pp.149–158.

[7] M. Topcuoglu (2001), Collaborative Conducts Restricting Competition Between Undertakings and Legal Consequences, Ankara: Competition Authority, p. 306.

[8] M.N. Aksoy (2004), Private Law Consequences of Competition Infringements, Ankara: Competition Authority, p. 53.

may cause debates on certain points, such as using the presumption of concerted practice which is rooted in EC case law in an action for treble damages.

On the other hand, decisions of the TCA are subject to judicial review in the Council of State,[9] which is the highest administrative court in the Turkish legal system. This has raised discrepancy concerns, as nullity claims[10] or damages actions are subject to the jurisdiction of the civil courts of law. For example, in a controversy concerning whether the civil court should wait for the outcome of the action for annulment of the decision of the TCA, the Supreme Court has decided affirmatively. In this regard, a divided judicial structure has also crippled efforts on the private enforcement scheme.

Over the last decade, private actions for damages have been very rare and, as of June 2009, no damages award has survived appeal. Some scholars believe that the infrequency and poor success rate of litigation is primarily attributable to competition law being almost unknown to the legal community and the injured parties, leading to a significant degree of under-enforcement.[11] These phenomena are also attributable to the framework of the Competition Act, which includes provisions strongly supporting private actions, yet is designed to be enforced by an administrative agency. Moreover, the lengthy average duration of cases both in civil courts and in the Council of State also contributes to the abstention of potential plaintiffs from suing. Last but not least, relatively high litigation costs may be another drawback for private enforcement.

Despite the lack of successful damages actions, nowadays private litigation draws more attention than in the past decade. There are some pending cases which have not been resolved yet by the trial courts. Nevertheless, the TCA may still play a significant role in promoting private actions by guiding and encouraging the legal community while the European Commission and EU Member States struggle to develop private remedies.

1. How does a damages action case get started?

a. Meeting clients and legal restrictions

An attorney involved in an incipient antitrust private damages action in Turkey must comply with certain norms while obtaining clients. Article 55 of the Attorneyship Act[12] prohibits advertising and client soliciting, stating 'it shall be prohibited for attorneys to behave or to act in a manner that might be deemed advertisement and especially to use

---

[9] Article 55 of the Competition Act.

[10] Antitrust rules can be used in a defensive or offensive manner. Damages actions are deemed offensive while nullity claims concerning agreements that breach antitrust rules constitute defensive use. For example, in *Hall v. United States* 92 US 27 (1875), the Supreme Court said: '. . . In the light of these authorities, it is clear that if Hall did contract with Roach, as he alleges he did, the contract was an utter nullity. In the view of the law, it created no obligation, and conferred no rights as to either of the parties.' Parties may claim that the contract in question is null and void. For a detailed discussion on nullity see generally: O.B. Gurzumar (2002), 'The Invalidity Regime to which the Agreements Contrary to Article 4 of the Act on the Protection of Competition are Subject', Competition Journal 12, 3–76.

[11] See Aslan, *supra* note 3, p. 785.

[12] Act No.1136 of 19.03.1969.

titles other than the title of attorney and academic titles on their signboards and printed papers in order to find a client.'

Moreover, Chapter II of the Code of Conduct of the Union of Turkish Bar Associations ('Code of Conduct') prohibits attorneys from engaging in any behavior that amounts to solicitation for legal work. This includes the use of exorbitant business cards, signboards or letterheads, or the making of public announcements like TV, newspaper or radio advertisements. Reasonable means of self-introduction, such as web pages that comply with the principles set forth under the Code of Conduct, are permissible.

b. Stand-alone/follow-on actions

Article 57 of the Competition Act creates a stand-alone cause of action over which the civil courts have complete jurisdiction.[13] However, the Supreme Court has consistently required a TCA decision establishing infringement of the Competition Act before allowing a prospective plaintiff to proceed with a damages claim. The Turkish Supreme Court has ruled that an action for damages should be preceded by a TCA decision establishing the infringement. Although no provision in the Competition Act assigns the duty to determine infringements exclusively to the TCA, the Supreme Court's approach has compelled trial courts to dismiss stand-alone actions for damages. For example, in the *Etibank* case,[14] the 19th Civil Law Chamber of the Turkish Supreme Court, in reversing a lower court decision, emphasized that a decision of the Competition Authority must be obtained before a judgment relating to Article 57 of the Competition Act can be entered.

Three years later, in the *Ford* case,[15] the same chamber of the Supreme Court affirmed its position. Again reversing a lower court judgment that awarded double damages to the plaintiff, the 19th Chamber stressed '. . . since it is determined by the decision of the TCA that the defendant's behaviors did not violate the Competition Act, conditions are not met for granting damages pursuant to Article 58 of the aforesaid Act.'[16] With this ruling, the Supreme Court implicitly refused the discretion of trial courts over determination of competition infringements and TCA decisions gained a binding power over the civil courts.

In its *Turk Telekom*[17] decision, the 19th Chamber of the Supreme Court again followed its precedents and required that the TCA decision and final stance of its judicial review be sought.

The Supreme Court's approach has been criticized.[18] Some commentators argue that

---

[13] N. Inan (2002), 'The Role of the Courts of Law in Enforcement of the Competition Act', paper given at the Ankara Bar Association International Law Congress, panel on Intellectual Property and Competition Law, Ankara, p. 615; G. Oz (2000), Abuse of Dominant Position in EC and Turkish Competition Law, Ankara: Competition Authority, p. 186.

[14] The Turkish Supreme Court, 19th Civil Law Chamber, E:1999/3350 K:1999/6364, 01.11.1999.

[15] The Turkish Supreme Court, 19th Civil Law Chamber, E:2002/2827 K:2002/7580, 29.11.2002.

[16] *Id.*

[17] The Turkish Supreme Court, 19th Civil Law Chamber, E:2007/3229, K:2007/10677, 29.11.2007.

[18] For criticism of this approach, see Gurzumar, *supra* note 10, p. 46; K. C. Sanli (2003), 'Tort Liability in Turkish Competition Law' in 1st Symposium on Recent Developments in Competition

even absent specific provisions, plaintiffs might still bring damages actions by relying on the general rules of tort law,[19] as do plaintiffs in most EC Member States.[20]

The author is of opinion that although there are difficulties in proving infringements and in gathering sufficient evidence, stand-alone actions should be supported as they may prove an efficient tool for deterrence in addition to affording redress.[21]

2. Standing

The standing of the claimant is, in principle, subject to the rules of the Code of Civil Procedure. Article 38 of the Code of Civil Procedure provides rules on one's ability to initiate or be a party to a lawsuit. Thus, a prospective plaintiff has virtually no procedural restrictions in bringing a damages action. Further considerations eventually fall under the substantive questions of the case.[22]

The concept of 'standing has an entirely different meaning in antitrust law.'[23] In an antitrust damages case, a strong connection between the protected legal interest and the plaintiff must exist. Because no particular competition case has addressed standing, relevant decisions of the Turkish Supreme Court should be taken into account indicatively.[24] In a recent decision, the General Assembly of Civil Law Chambers of the Turkish Supreme Court ruled as follows:

Law, Ankara: Competition Authority, 244. Despite being of the opinion that there is no statutory requirement for the civil courts to wait for a decision of the TCA, Aslan proposes a model rule to this effect as he favors legislative intervention to the potential problems of concurrent proceedings. See Aslan, *supra* note 3, p. 799.

[19] See Aslan, *supra* note 3, p. 783; See Topcuoglu, *supra* note 7, p. 297.

[20] A. Jones and B. Sufrin, 2008, EC Competition Law, Oxford: Oxford University Press, p. 1303.

[21] Green Paper – Damages Actions for Breach of the EC Antitrust Rules, COM(2005)672 final, 4; Private Actions in Competition Law: Effective Redress for Consumers and Business Recommendations from the Office of Fair Trading, 2007, 12; A. Renda, *et al.* (2007), Making antitrust damages actions more effective in the EU: Welfare Impact And Potential Scenarios, http://ec.europa.eu/competition/antitrust/actionsdamages/files_white_paper/impact_study.pdf, accessed 5 June 2009, p. 153.

[22] Compare: G. Cumming, *et al.*, (2007), Civil Procedure Used for Enforcement of EC Competition Law by the French, English and German Civil Courts, Alphen aan den Rijn: Kluwer Law International, p. 230.

[23] C.A. Jones (1999), Private Enforcement of Antitrust Law in the EU, UK and USA, Oxford: Oxford University Press, p. 159. 'The label "antitrust standing" has traditionally been applied to some of the elements of this inquiry. As commentators have observed, the focus of the doctrine of "antitrust standing" is somewhat different from that of standing as a constitutional doctrine. Harm to the antitrust plaintiff is sufficient to satisfy the constitutional standing requirement of injury in fact, but the court must make a further determination whether the plaintiff is a proper party to bring a private antitrust action.' *Associated Gen. Contractors v. Carpenters*, 459 US 519 (1983), footnote 31. Similarly, standing in a damages case originating from the Competition Act differs from the meaning referred to in Article 36 of the Turkish Constitution.

[24] According to settled case law of the Turkish Supreme Court, regardless of other parameters, standing means an established connection between the claimant and the damaged legal interest that is protected by the law. See for example: 3rd Civil Law Chamber, E:2001/10432 K:2001/10922, 24.12.2001; 3rd Civil Law Chamber, E:2002/2772 K:2002/3152, 01.04.2002; 11th Civil Law Chamber, E:2002/12537 K:2003/5170, 20.05.2003; 1st Civil Law Chamber, E:2007/10610 K:2007/10509, 05.11.2007.

> . . . [T]he issue of standing is not a question of the procedural law but a question of substantive law, which relates to the essence of the subjective right in trial. Therefore, lack of standing is not a demurrer . . . but a substantial point of objection which can be raised by the parties at every stage and which must be considered by the court *ex officio.*[25]

Indeed, Article 58 of the Competition Act states that those who suffer from prevention, distortion or restriction of competition may claim damages. The notion that a 'sufferer' may recover bears a striking similarity to comparable language in §4 of the Clayton Act, which provides standing for any person injured.[26] In this regard, many scholars are of opinion that Article 58 should be interpreted in favor of direct and indirect purchasers and competitors.[27] However, the scope of the term 'sufferer' must ultimately be clarified by the courts.

a. Direct purchasers

The Supreme Court has confirmed that persons who purchase directly from the violator have clear standing under Article 58 of the Competition Act.[28] However, no court has addressed standing of consumers in an antitrust damages case.

b. Indirect purchasers

The Turkish courts have not yet addressed the question of indirect purchaser standing. Commentators have suggested that the law supports recognizing a broad circle of claimants, including indirect purchasers.[29]

The question of indirect purchasers' standing closely relates to the availability of a passing-on defense to defendants.[30] US antitrust case law has denied defendants the use of the passing-on defense,[31] and whether EC competition law will follow the so-called *Illinois Brick* rule[32] has been the center of debate.[33] The *Manfredi* ruling of the European

---

25 The Turkish Supreme Court, General Assembly of Civil Law, E:2007/5-233 K:2007/221, 18.04.2007.

26 15 USC §15 provides, '. . . any person who shall be injured in his business or property by reason of anything forbidden in the antitrust laws may sue. . . .'

27 Aksoy, *supra* note 8, p. 50; Topcuoglu, *supra* note 7, p. 304; Oz, *supra* note 13 at 181; E. Badur (2001), Agreements Restricting Competition in Turkish Competition Law, Ankara: Competition Authority, p. 62. See further: '[t]he preferred position of the consumer has seemed well settled' Jones, *supra* note 24, p. 180. '. . . In this case, however, the Union was neither a consumer nor a competitor in the market. . . .' 459 US 519 (1983) at 539.

28 Decisions of the 19th Civil Law Chamber: E:1999/3350 K:1999/6364, 01.11.1999; E:2002/2827 K:2002/7580, 29.11.2002.

29 See Aksoy, *supra* note 8, p. 50; Oz, *supra* note 13, p. 181; Topcuoglu, *supra* note 7, p. 304; E. Badur, *supra* note 28, p. 162.; M. Ikizler (2005), Concerted Practices in Competition Law, Ankara:Seckin, p. 364; D. Cengiz (2006), Concerted Practices in Turkish Competition Law and its Legal Consequences, Istanbul: Beta, p. 421.

30 A.P. Komninos (2008), EC Private Antitrust Enforcement, Oxford: Hart Publishing, p. 202.

31 *Hanover Shoe, Inc. v. United Shoe Machinery Corp.*, 392 US 481 (1968).

32 *Illinois Brick Co. v. Illinois*, 431 US 720 (1977). In this case the US Supreme Court prohibited the indirect purchasers of goods or services from recovering antitrust damages from antitrust violators.

33 Cumming, *supra* note 23, p. 230. See also: Jones, *supra* note 24, p. 193; Komninos, *supra* note 30, p. 202. See generally: F. Cengiz (2007), Passing-On Defense and Indirect Purchaser

Court of Justice made the standing of indirect purchasers stronger.[34] The ECJ's judgment in *Manfredi* confirmed a third party's ability to claim compensation, including loss of profit, for harm caused by anti-competitive behavior. The EC Commission welcomed this decision in the White Paper.[35] However, it must be noted that even *Manfredi* ruling did not put an end to the matter.[36]

With respect to the Turkish judiciary, however, the *Illinois Brick* rule may not apply, given the broad language of Article 58 of the Competition Act,[37] which suggests that all victims of competition law violations – including indirect purchasers – have a private damages remedy.[38]

c. Competitors

The term 'competing undertakings' in Article 58 of the Competition Act leaves no doubt that competitors have standing. In fact, competitors can claim a variety of damages while other plaintiffs can only claim for overcharges. The injury, however, should be carefully considered with respect to competitors.[39] In particular, it is necessary to carefully examine claims of competitors to determine whether the contended damage has a link of unlawfulness with the infringement charged.[40] This adds up to the concept of antitrust injury.

d. Suppliers and other third party claimants

There are conflicting views on the standing of third party claimants such as suppliers, creditors, contractors or vendors who may have suffered indirect damage.[41] In general, indirect damage incurred by third parties does not satisfy the causation link between unlawful act and injury.[42] Because indirect damage does not seem to be the type of injury the Competition Act aims to prevent,[43] the author believes that suppliers and other third party claimants should not have standing for an antitrust damages case.

Standing in Actions for Damages against the Violations of Competition Law: What Can the EC Learn from the US? CCP Working Paper No. 07-21, available at SSRN: http://ssrn.com/abstract=1038521.

34 Case C–295/04 *Vincenzo Manfredi v Lloyd Adriatico Assicurazioni SpA*, ECR [2006] I–06619.

35 Commission White Paper on Damages Actions for Breach of the EC Antitrust Rules, COM(2008)165 final, 4.

36 See F. Cengiz, *supra* note 34, p. 28 *et seq.*

37 The preamble to the Competition Act states, '[i]t is provided in the article that natural or legal persons who may or may not be of a nature of undertaking can claim compensation . . .' On the other hand, it should be noted from the comparative point of view that 'restrictive [US] rules on standing cannot be automatically transposed to the EC Law.' Komninos, *supra* note 31, p. 191.

38 See: D. Cengiz, *supra* note 30, p. 422; M. Ikizler, *supra* note 30, p. 364.

39 See for a detailed discussion Jones, *supra* note 24, p. 173. The link of unlawfulness may be deemed the Turkish equivalent of this concept. See Sanli, *supra* note 18, p. 224.

40 See Sanli, *supra* note 18, p. 224.

41 Opposing: Sanli, *supra* note 18, p. 238; D. Cengiz, *supra* note 30, p. 376; Z. Ari (2004), The Concept of Collusion in Competition Law and Legal Consequences, Ankara:Seckin, p. 232. Favoring: Topcuoglu, *supra* note 7, p. 303.

42 F. Eren, (2001), Law of Obligations, Istanbul: Beta, p. 496.

43 Ari, *supra* note 42, p. 232.

3. Competent courts

There are no special courts or tribunals competent to try cases resulting from competition infringements. As there is no specific provision in the Competition Act concerning jurisdiction and venue, general rules of the Code of Civil Procedure apply.[44] The Act on the Establishment, Jurisdiction and Competency of the Courts of First Instance and the District Courts of Appeal provides that the civil courts of first instance have jurisdiction in all cases except for cases exclusively allocated to the courts of peace and other specializing courts.

In practice, the jurisdiction of the courts of peace will be very limited due to relatively low monetary value threshold. On the other hand, all cases go to commercial courts of first instance if both parties are tradespersons or the subject is of an exclusively commercial nature in terms of the Commercial Code. Therefore, as a rule, actions for damages are tried in the civil courts of first instance other than those which fall under the jurisdiction of commercial courts of first instance.[45]

4. Venue

Article 9 of the Code of Civil Procedure stipulates that all cases may be filed in the court of the defendant's domicile if there is no statutory provision to the contrary.[46] Under Article 21 of the Code of Civil Procedure, tort actions may also be filed in a court where the tortious act occurred. Actions concerning the protection of personality, which includes moral damage, may be filed in the jurisdiction where the plaintiff is domiciled.[47]

5. Aggregation of claims

Class actions currently are not recognized in Turkish jurisprudence, but the topic demands proper attention given the goal of facilitating access to justice for aggrieved parties.[48] Some commentators assert that the concept of a class action will eventually be adopted into Turkish law.[49]

In fact, Article 23 of the Act on the Protection of Consumers[50] provides a clear standing to 'consumers' organizations' exclusively in cases that arise from that very same Act. However, this exceptional standing could not be extended to actions for damages. To date, the Turkish Supreme Court has been silent on the availability of class actions in other types of actions.

---

44 Ikizler, *supra* note 30, p. 359.

45 Ari, *supra* note 42, p. 235.

46 Ikizler, , *supra* note 30, p. 359.

47 M.R. Karahasan (2003), Law of Damages: Damages Actions and Trial Procedure, 6th ed. Istanbul: Beta, p. 386.

48 Project Summary of the Public Research Program for Turkish Law, Ministry of Justice, 2006, www.tubitak.gov.tr/tubitak_content_files/ARDEB/kamag/Turkiye_Hukuk_Kamu_Arastirma_Programi.pdf.

49 M. Ozbek (2002), 'Developments Occurred with the Worldwide Movements for Access to Justice and Alternative Dispute Resolution', Journal of Ankara University Faculty of Law, Vol. 51, No. 2, 121–161, p. 134.

50 Law No. 4077 of 23.02.1995.

6. Procedural defenses

Antitrust damages cases are subject to the Code of Civil Procedure. An action begins when the plaintiff files a petition in the court's registry.[51] After the exchange of the petition and defendant's reply, both parties are bound by their submissions. Further adjustments are subject to a prohibition on changing or extending the case[52] or the defense[53] respectively.

After the parties exchange pleadings, the examination (investigation) phase begins, during which the judge may invite the parties for a hearing at any time. If the judge decides that the case can be resolved based on the pleadings alone, pursuant to Article 214 of the Code of Civil Procedure, the judge may declare the end of the examination and invite parties to a final hearing at which judgment may be entered. Under no circumstances may the judge enter a final judgment without holding a hearing.[54] In practice, however, there is virtually no case that ends after the exchange of pleadings. The Code of Civil Procedure does not provide a tool similar to the concept of summary judgment.

After being notified of the petition, the defendant may raise preliminary objections[55] through which an interruption in the proceedings may be obtained. Procedural preliminary objections could be made concerning: a request of guaranty deposit from a plaintiff who does not have a domicile in Turkey;[56] the venue;[57] a pending case;[58] a connection to a pending case; or a deficiency in the petition. Defendants must lodge their preliminary objections in the responsive pleading because they cannot raise such objections in later stages of the case.[59]

7. Available devices to obtain evidence

Private actions arising out of the Competition Act are subject to the general rules provided in the Code of Civil Procedure. There are no pre-action obligations upon parties with regard to evidence in the Code of Civil Procedure, as Turkish law does not recognize

---

51 Article 178 of the Code of Civil Procedure.

52 Article 185 of the Code of Civil Procedure. Compare with the French procedure: Cumming, *supra* note 23, p. 194.

53 Article 202 of the Code of Civil Procedure.

54 However, there may be legal exceptions to that rule. See Article 73 of the Code of Civil Procedure.

55 Preliminary objections are different from conditions of action. Conditions of action which may prevent going into substance of a case are jurisdiction, venue, standing, *res judicata* effect, and the requirement of legal interest. Conditions of action should be examined by the judge *ex officio* before the proceedings start. See B. Kuru, *et al.* (2001), The Law of Civil Procedure, 13th ed. Ankara: Yetkin, pp. 307–321.

56 According to Article 32 of the Act on the International Private Law and Procedural Law, foreign plaintiffs have to give a guaranty deposit that will be determined by the judge *ex officio*, except in certain situations mentioned in the foregoing Act.

57 Venue may be agreed upon by the parties as long as it is not contrary to the absolute or non-absolute rules on the venue relating public order. If the venue is not related to public order, objection may only be filed as a preliminary objection and may not be raised again. See Kuru, *supra* note 56, p. 689.

58 The two cases must be identical in respect of the parties, subject matter and cause of action.

59 Kuru, *supra* note 56, p. 696.

the concept of pre-trial disclosure. Therefore, potential plaintiffs must rely upon available information to prove the existence of an antitrust violation in a stand-alone case.

The search for and seizure of relevant evidence requires significant time, money and professional manpower, particularly in cartel cases. This could be one of the most important reasons for establishing an independent administrative authority responsible for detecting competition problems. In light of the aforementioned difficulties, by requiring a TCA decision prior to affirming a lower court judgment on a damages action, the Supreme Court appears to have implicitly refused to get the lower courts involved in evidence probing. Consequently, the Supreme Court admits TCA decisions as direct evidence absolving plaintiffs from finding further evidence seeking on the infringement.

Obtaining proper evidence to prove an antitrust violation is a clear obstacle for private litigants because 'competition law disputes are characterized by wide information inequalities and asymmetries between the litigants.'[60] Private plaintiffs are in a rather weak position to obtain evidence in order to get into a legal struggle over competition matters.[61]

Turkish private law is based on the adversarial system in which the court is bound by evidence presented by the parties.[62] As a rule,[63] the plaintiff bears the burden to prove the defendant's liability in a damages action.[64] Therefore, the powers of the judge in a civil action for damages are relatively restricted because the parties are primarily responsible for submitting their cases.[65]

However, in order to reach a sound judgment, the judge should use the power granted in Article 75 (3) of the Code of Civil Procedure, which creates an exception to the party disposition principle whenever necessary. According to Article 75 (3), acting *ex officio*, the judge may decide to obtain an expert witness statement, conduct discovery, or order the parties or third parties to submit necessary evidence provided it is relevant to the contentions of the parties.[66] If a party does not comply with such an order, the court may make a negative inference on the disputed subject.[67] In cases where the submission of documents to the court creates undue difficulties, the judge may order an expert witness to examine those documents at the place where they are stored.[68] In practice, judges use these powers aggressively to force defendants to produce evidence.

---

[60] Komninos, *supra* note 30, p. 225.

[61] See Sanli, *supra* note 18, p. 240; Aslan, *supra* note 3, p. 796. See also R. Stürner (2007), 'Duties of Disclosure and Burden of Proof in the Private Enforcement of European Competition Law' in Private Enforcement of EC Competition Law, ed. J. Basedow, Alphen aan den Rijn: Kluwer Law International p. 171 and Commission Staff Working Paper Annex to the Green Paper – Damages Actions for Breach of the EC Antitrust Rules, COM(2005)672 final, para. 54.

[62] See Sanli, *supra* note 18, p. 240. Similarly Cumming, *supra* note 23, p. 41 and p. 243; Komninos, *supra* note 30, p. 225.

[63] Article 6 of the Civil Code.

[64] Kuru, *supra* note 56, p. 425; Karahasan, *supra* note 48, p. 416.

[65] The principle of party disposition. Compare with the French and German procedures: Cumming, *supra* note 23, pp. 21–24; Stürner, *supra* note 62, pp. 174–175.

[66] The Turkish Supreme Court, 4th Civil Law Chamber, E: 2003/2424, K: 2003/6935, 26.05.2003.

[67] Kuru, *supra* note 56, p. 464. Compare Cumming, *supra* note 23, p. 247; Stürner, *supra* note 62, p. 176.

[68] M.A. Tutumlu (2000), Presentation of Evidences, Ankara: Seckin, p. 40.

Article 75 (3) may effectively be used where commercial records of the parties are seen as indispensable in establishing an antitrust violation that is asserted with reasonable support. Specifically, if the plaintiff reasonably demonstrates the existence of documents or information related to the alleged infringement, the judge may order the defendant to produce all such relevant books and records even if they include incriminating information.[69]

Furthermore, there may be situations where important evidence is subject to possible loss or destruction before the court proceedings take place, therefore requiring the court to make an expedited determination of the available evidence. According to Article 368 of the Code of Civil Procedure, the plaintiff must reasonably show that there is a legal interest in making such a determination. Legal interest generally means urgency of the situation caused by the possibility of losing evidence. Determination of evidence may be requested before the filing of the action or during the proceedings.[70] According to the Code of Civil Procedure, witness and expert witness statements are also admissible as discretionary evidence.[71] Appointment of experts depends on the discretion of the judge. In practice, judges usually appoint a scholar or a lawyer who has an academic reputation in the matter in question.

The Draft Act No. 1/636, pending in the Parliament, provides that 'the civil court may request an expert witness statement from the TCA concerning economic facts required in finding the existence of an infringement. President [of the TCA] shall appoint sufficient competition experts for the preparation of an expert witness statement by taking the principles of impartiality into account.' This provision, if passed, may bring some advantages as there could be more focused expert witness statements. Nevertheless, there would be some drawbacks as well. Involvement of TCA officials in judicial affairs might cause a question of objectivity and there could be possible conflict between those expert views and the TCA decisions. In the author's opinion, the best solution could be the appointment of an independent academician with established expertise in competition law.

8. Illegal practices and elements of proof

Article 4 of the Competition Act prohibits all agreements between undertakings that prevent or distort competition. Single firm conduct that amounts to an abuse of a dominant position is prohibited by Article 6 of the Competition Act. Plaintiffs may be able to gather evidence proving illegal vertical restraints and abuse of dominant position with significantly less effort as such behaviors are typically part of a given defendant's ordinary business practices. Nevertheless, the Turkish Supreme Court has been reluctant to affirm lower courts granting damages in stand-alone actions.[72] Accordingly, it is most

---

69 Kuru, *supra* note 56, p. 462.

70 *Id.* at 718.

71 See Sanli, *supra* note 18, p. 241; A.C. Budak (2003), 'Evidences and Proof in Competition Law' in 1st Symposium on Recent Developments in Competition Law, Ankara: Competition Authority, 45–62, p. 52.

72 *Etibank* case, The Turkish Supreme Court, 19th Civil Law Chamber, E:1999/3350 K:1999/6364, 01.11.1999.

efficient for a private plaintiff to initiate a damages action following a decision of the TCA.

Vertical restraints seem to be the type of infringement that is most promising for plaintiffs to bring suit for. In one vertical restraints case, a trial court awarded double damages to the plaintiff, though that judgment did not survive appeal.[73] Horizontal restraints are more difficult to prove because they are conducted surreptitiously, as in cartel agreements. It is an uphill battle for a plaintiff to claim a damages award, particularly in a stand-alone action. To date, there have not been any follow-on actions in this context.

Article 59 of the Competition Act addresses concerns about the difficulties inherent in proving antitrust violations by easing the plaintiff's burden of proof. Article 59 provides as follows:

> Should the injured person submit to the courts the evidences such as, particularly, the actual partitioning of markets, the stability observed in the market price for quite a long time, the price increase within close intervals by the undertakings operating in the market, which give the impression of the existence of an agreement, or the distortion of competition in the market, then the burden of proof is for the defendants to prove that the undertakings are not engaged in concerted practice.
>
> The existence of agreements, decisions and practices limiting competition may be proved by any kind of evidence.

Three important conclusions may be inferred from this Article: 1) factual evidence, such as simultaneous price increases, is preferable for the convenience of the plaintiff; 2) the burden of proof shifts to the defendant if the plaintiff submits this kind of evidence indicating illegal behavior; and 3) any kind of evidence, for instance witness statements, is acceptable for proving the infringement.

Even if the Supreme Court were to permit stand-alone actions, the fact that parties are not obligated to disclose relevant documents and other information could continue to be an obstacle for plaintiffs in stand-alone actions. There were several examples of evidence requests by private parties even at the 'preliminary investigation' and the investigation stages at the TCA. Those potential plaintiffs could not be regarded as 'followers' since there was no final decision by the TCA. However evidence obtained by the TCA in investigations may not be completely available to plaintiffs due to trade secrets.

Disclosure of evidence obtained by the TCA is subject to the relevant provisions in the Code of Civil Procedure.[74] If the claimant directly requests the TCA for access to a file, the request may be accepted in a very restricted form or may be totally rejected as the disclosure could undermine the confidentiality of TCA proceedings generally or specific third parties' trade secrets. In this scenario, an ordinary claimant demonstrating a rightful interest in accessing the file may at most examine only non-confidential information. On the other hand, if the plaintiff directly files an action for damages, the court itself may order the TCA to submit relevant files for court examination.

---

73 *Ford* case, The Turkish Supreme Court, 19th Civil Law Chamber, E:2002/2827 K:2002/7580, 29.11.2002.

74 See Articles 322, 323 and 324 of the Code of Civil Procedure. Compare R. Nazzini (2004), Concurrent Proceedings in Competition Law, Oxford: Oxford University Press, p. 245.

Further, the TCA may just send a warning to undertakings according to Article 9 of the Competition Act. In those cases, there will be no final decision establishing infringement. However, the TCA would have to have serious findings in order to send such a warning. Third parties may want to use those findings to support their stand-alone cases. Moreover, although there has been no such demand regarding the two leniency applications so far, third parties may request information disclosed to the TCA on leniency applications, which include unconditional confession of participation in a cartel. However, pursuant to Article 6/3 of the Regulation on Active Cooperation for Detecting Cartels,[75] documents submitted during a leniency application are kept confidential until the release of the investigation report. There is no clear statement about the access rights of potential private plaintiffs concerning leniency applications.

In the author's opinion, the kinds of evidence described above might be sufficient to convince the Supreme Court not to overrule the lower court's decision to award damages in a stand-alone case.[76] Given the evidentiary difficulties faced by plaintiffs, follow-on actions – which depend on the decision of competition authorities – are the most efficient vehicle for private enforcement of the antitrust laws. Therefore, the decisions of competition authorities are of key importance in damages actions brought by the victims of an infringement.[77] In this light, given the recent approach of the Turkish Supreme Court, decisions of the TCA establishing an infringement would be the most convenient tool for obtaining damages awards in practice.

9. Remedies

a. Single/treble damages

As a general matter, damages awards are designed to restore injured parties to their position prior to the damage by replacement in kind or full compensation.[78] Article 43 of the Code of Obligations gives the judge broad discretion in deciding the appropriate remedy.[79] Since Turkish law recognizes the notion of compensatory damages in principle, the amount of compensation cannot exceed the amount of the damage suffered as it should not cause unjust enrichment to the injured party.[80]

In the competition law context, however, Turkey has opted to allow a judge the discretion to award treble damages. Although Turkish jurisprudence has long adopted civil law principles and followed EC jurisprudence in competition law, it has adopted the US treble damages concept into Article 58 of the Competition Act and thereby departed

75 Regulation published in the Official Gazette No. 27142 on February 15, 2009.

76 Turkish leniency policy has no requirement such as 'restitution of injured parties' as is the case in the US DOJ's Corporate Leniency Policy.

77 Commission Staff Working Paper Annex to the Green Paper on Damages Actions for Breach of the EC Antitrust Rules, COM(2005)672 final, paras. 97–98.

78 Eren *supra* note 43, p. 717.

79 M.K. Oguzman and M.T. Oz (2000), Law of Obligations, Istanbul: Filiz, p. 554.

80 S.S. Tekinay, *et al.* (1993), Law of Obligations, Istanbul: Filiz, p. 583; Eren, *supra* note 43, p. 723; The Turkish Supreme Court, 4th Civil Law Chamber, E:1978/3173 K:1978/15053, 29.12.1978.

from the continental European system. Contrary to the US system, however, the decision to award treble damages is left completely to judicial discretion.[81]

b. Calculation of damages

The Competition Act does not provide specific rules concerning the calculation of damages. Therefore, general rules of the Code of Obligations are used.[82] Relying on decisions of the Supreme Court and doctrinal opinions of different scholars may be useful in this regard.

In theory, damage caused by competition infringements is overcharge damage, lost profits and damage resulting from a terminated or disadvantaged business.[83] According to Article 58 of the Competition Act, competitors are entitled to recover all kinds of damages including actual loss, lost profits and terminated business, while purchasers may recover only overcharges.[84] Determining the amount of overcharges imposed by the conspiring undertakings has its own difficulties, however.[85] 'The ability to measure the overcharge accurately depends upon how reliably and precisely the analysis can distinguish the collusive effect on prices from other influences that are unrelated to the anticompetitive conduct.'[86]

Several methods can be utilized to ascertain the 'but-for' price[87] that would have existed absent the restricting agreement.[88] The yardstick[89] method, which benchmarks the allegedly collusive price with other markets that are not affected by the agreement, has been suggested to be reasonable.[90]

Article 58 of the Competition Act accepts the pre-post model for calculating lost profits. This method compares data from the same market and same undertakings before and after the infringement.[91] According to Article 58 '[i]n determining the damage, all expected profits of the injured undertakings shall be calculated by taking the balance sheets of the previous years into account.'

Furthermore, the Code of Obligations grants the judge significant discretion in

---

81 There are conflicting views on the discretion of the trial court as to whether it can determine different multiplier like 1, 5 or 2. See for different views: D. Cengiz, *supra* note 30, p. 404.

82 See for a comprehensive work on the issue of calculating damages in Turkish law: A.U. Sahbaz (2009), Determination and Compensation of Damages Arising from Competition Infringements in the Light of American Practice, Ankara: Competition Authority.

83 See Sanli, *supra* note 18, p. 252.

84 A. Akinci (2001), Horizontal Restriction of Competition, Ankara: Competition Authority, p. 310 and p. 381; A.U. Sahbaz, *supra* note 83, p. 46.

85 See Aksoy, *supra* note 8, p. 52.

86 J. Nieberding (2006), 'Estimating Overcharges in Antitrust Cases Using a Reduced-Form Approach: Methods and Issues', Journal of Applied Economics, Vol. 9, No. 2, 361–380, p. 363.

87 L.J. White (1999), Lysine and Price Fixing: How Long? How Severe? New York University, Center for Law and Business, Working Paper No. 99-001, p. 6. The 'but-for' approach is also recognized in Turkish tort law. See Eren, *supra* note 43, p. 732.

88 See Jones, *supra* note 24, p. 216.

89 *Id.* p. 217; Commission Staff Working Paper Annex to the Green Paper on Damages Actions for Breach of the EC Antitrust Rules, COM(2005)672 final, para. 133.

90 See Aksoy, *supra* note 8, p. 52. Compare Cumming, *supra* note 23, p. 207.

91 See Sanli, *supra* note 18, p. 254; Sahbaz, *supra* note 83, p. 53.

determining the existence and amount of damages. Specifically, Article 42 defers to the judge when determining the existence or amount of damages is otherwise impossible.[92] This broad judicial discretion is very important, especially in assessing lost profits and the imperiled economic future of the plaintiff, where such damages typically may not be calculated easily.[93]

c. Interest

Application of interest to damages awards is a firmly established rule in Turkish liability law.[94] 'The judge must add an interest to the amount of the damage. An interest applies from the time at which the damage occurred . . . [b]ecause injured person was entitled to damages at the time of wrongdoing.'[95] Prejudgment interest must be included in the judgment of the trial court. After obtaining the judgment, the plaintiff will have a right to execute it. Execution of the judgment can be voluntary or involuntary. In either case, the plaintiff is entitled to claim 'default interest' provided in Act No.3095 starting from the date at which demand of execution was notified to the defendant either by the plaintiff or by the Execution Office.

d. Fees

Article 417 of the Code of Civil Procedure provides that a losing party is obligated to pay all the costs and fees arising from the litigation. The court *ex officio* orders the losing party to pay all costs.

Litigation costs are examined under two categories: adjudicatory fees, which are designated to the governmental treasury, and adjudicatory costs, which include the attorney's fees.[96] Adjudicatory fees are shown in Tariff Schedule 1 of the Act on Fees.[97] In general, they can be fixed or proportional depending on the subject matter of the case. However, in an antitrust case, application fees are fixed while judgment fees are proportional depending on the value of the claim.

Adjudicatory costs are comprised of components listed in Article 423 of the Code of Civil Procedure, including expenditures on notifications, hearings, witnesses and expert witnesses, discovery, determination of evidence, per diem allowances of the parties, fees paid to other official institutions and attorneys' fees.[98] The adjudicatory costs are relatively higher than the fees, and may be seen as the most discouraging factor precluding damages actions. Insurance for adjudicatory fees and/or costs is not available for antitrust damages actions in Turkey.

---

92 See for the concept of impossibility Eren, *supra* note 43, pp. 716–717.

93 See Sanli, supra note 18, p. 251; Tekinay, *supra* note 81, p. 580. Also see Eren, *supra* note 43, p. 719.

94 See The Turkish Supreme Court, General Assembly of Civil Law, E:1990/11-88 K:1990/591, 28.11.1990.

95 Eren, *supra* note 43, p. 722.

96 Kuru, *supra* note 56, p. 835.

97 Act No. 492 of 17.07.1964.

98 Kuru, *supra* note 56, p. 839.

e. Equitable remedies

i. Injunctive relief Under the Code of Civil Procedure trial courts have broad discretion in granting interim injunctions.[99] Interim injunctions are examined under the concept of 'provisional legal protection orders.'[100] Article 103 of the Code of Civil Procedure provides a flexible tool for judges to order all kinds of necessary injunctive measures, stating that '. . . [i]n situations where the possibility of a danger or a significant harm in the event of delay is acknowledged, the judge may order necessary interim measures in order to avert that danger or harm.'

The judge has broad discretion in deciding the type and scope of an interim injunction.[101] As a threshold matter, however, the judge must substantiate that an imminent and significant harm exists to necessitate the injunctive relief awarded.[102]

However, in light of the Supreme Court's decisions requiring a final infringement decision from the TCA in order to grant damages, interim injunctions do not have much value as a remedy for plaintiffs in damages actions. Even if the plaintiffs present a prima facie case in a petition,[103] interim measures would most probably be hard to obtain, as the courts will be inclined to dismiss the case at the pleadings stage. Nonetheless, interim injunctions may be sought in cases where the plaintiff demands preventive relief in order to mitigate the damage arising from an infringement.[104]

Permanent injunctions also may vary in type and scope depending on the broad discretion of the judge. Permanent injunctions are aimed at preventing any future recurrence of the established infringement.[105] In this context, once the court finds an infringement, it may order any necessary permanent injunctions in its final judgment. The TCA usually does not order specific injunctions in its decisions establishing infringement. For example, in a recent decision, the TCA decided that one company had committed a breach by acquiring minority shares in two joint-venture companies. The TCA ordered that those shares be sold within 12 months and anticompetitive practices be avoided.[106] However, potential private plaintiffs may need more certain behavioral injunctions such as continuation of supply. Thus, even in a follow-on case, injunctions that were ordered by the TCA may not suffice to prevent the damage caused to the private parties by the infringement.

ii. Restitution The absolute nullity of contracts predicated upon competition infringements gives rise to the application of unjust enrichment. Unjust

---

[99] E. Yılmaz (2001), Interim Legal Protection Measures, Ankara: Yetkin, p. 170. See §9 of the First Chapter of the Code of Civil Procedure (Articles 101–113/A).

[100] The Turkish Supreme Court, 19th Civil Law Chamber, E:2008/4717 K:2008/6504, 12.06.2008; See for a detailed analysis: E. Yılmaz, *supra* note 99.

[101] The Turkish Supreme Court, 11th Civil Law Chamber, E:2002/8127 K:2003/1169, 17.02.2003.

[102] The Turkish Supreme Court, 3rd Civil Law Chamber, E:1994/10746 K:1994/15362, 21.11.1994.

[103] See Yılmaz, *supra* note 100, p. 893.

[104] See Sanli, *supra* note 18, p. 234, note 400.

[105] American Bar Association Section of Antitrust Law (2007), Antitrust Law Developments, 6th ed., p. 855a.

[106] TCA decision No. 09-28/600-141 of 16.06.2009 (*Erdemir*).

enrichment comes into consideration as a result of unilateral or mutual transfers that were made according to the invalid agreement. With the reference of Article 56 of the Competition Act, the general rules in Articles 63 and 64 of the Code of Obligations apply to restitution claims arising from unjust enrichment in competition cases.[107] There has been no such restitution award so far in an antitrust context.

iii. Declaratory relief Theoretically, a declaratory judgment is available to establish an infringement and has *res judicata* effect. However, the availability of declaratory relief in any given case is subject to strict criteria. The Turkish Supreme Court has ruled on the issue, holding '. . . the plaintiff has no legal interest in filing an independent declaratory action where the legal protection aimed with the declaratory action can be obtained through the action for performance.'[108]

10. Limitation periods

In the author's opinion, because competition infringements are deemed akin to torts, limitation periods for tort claims apply. Article 60 of the Code of Obligations provides two applicable limitation periods.

First, an action for damages should be filed within a year of knowledge of the existence of injury and the identity of the perpetrator. The limitation period does not begin to run simply because the plaintiff was capable of receiving knowledge of his injury – it is required that the plaintiff have actual knowledge of the injury.[109] However, knowledge of the scope and gravity of harm is also required for the period to run if the damage is expected to proliferate.[110]

Second, irrespective of knowledge about the injury and perpetrator, the action must be filed within ten years after the damage occurred.[111] The Turkish Supreme Court has consistently held that the ten-year limitation period starts running from the date the damage occurred.[112]

11. Financing private enforcement

As a general rule, the losing party pays all litigation costs.[113] Attorneys' fees borne by the losing party are determined by the court pursuant to the fixed rate provided

---

[107] See Topcuoglu, *supra* note 7, p. 295.

[108] The Turkish Supreme Court, General Assembly of Civil Law, E:2004/7-411 K:2004/477, 31.03.2004.

[109] See Oguzman and Oz, *supra* note 80, p. 523. Compare Cumming, *supra* note 23, p. 277. See also The Turkish Supreme Court, General Assembly of Civil Law, E: 1999/4-983 K: 1999/995 24.11.1999.

[110] The Turkish Supreme Court, General Assembly of Civil Law, E: 2002/13-1011 K: 2002/1047, 11.12.2002. See further Tekinay, *supra* note 81, p. 719; Eren, *supra* note 43, p. 824.

[111] See Oguzman and Oz, *supra* note 80, p. 525.

[112] See the following decisions of the Turkish Supreme Court, General Assembly of Civil Law: E: 1979/4-548 K: 1982/46, 20.01.1982; E: 1999/1–222 K: 1999/226, 21.04.1999; E: 2003/4-400 K: 2003/393, 04.06.2003; E: 2003/4-603 K: 2003/594, 22.10.2003.

[113] There may be exceptions such as Articles 90, 94, 173 and 253 of the Code of Civil Procedure.

in the Minimum Tariff Schedule of the Act on Attorneyship. However, a lawyer and client may contract for higher fees. Article 163 of the Act on Attorneyship allows free determination of attorneys' fees as long as they do not contravene other provisions of the Act. Specifically, fees must be fixed at a minimum amount but can be subject to increase upon success. Contingency fees may also be agreed at a rate of up to 25 per cent of the monetary value of the claim, besides the minimum fee.

It must be noted that a true contingency fee arrangement is prohibited since a lawyer must charge the minimum amount stated in the schedule of Article 168.[114] If violated, disciplinary proceedings may be initiated by the relevant bar association.[115]

12. Conflicts between private and public enforcement

Commentators on competition law have long anticipated the possibility of concurrent proceedings at the administrative and judicial levels.[116] The TCA's decisions are subject to judicial review by the highest administrative court, whereas private claims are conducted exclusively in civil courts. This dichotomy in judiciary disciplines raised new issues in terms of concurrent proceedings. In *Etibank*,[117] and later in *Ford*,[118] the Turkish Supreme Court overruled lower court decisions, even though there were no pending administrative proceedings. Moreover, the Supreme Court ordered lower courts to wait for a decision by the TCA and decide accordingly. Given the Supreme Court's approach, encountering inconsistency problems associated with concurrent proceedings seems unlikely.[119]

However, in its *Turk Telekom*[120] decision, the Supreme Court went further and said 'It has been decided in the decision of the TCA No. 06-02/47-8 that Turk Telekom is in dominant position and has abused this position. It must be inquired whether there is a case filed against that decision in the Council of State and if there is a case pending, its outcome must be sought.' This approach may further jeopardize efficient private enforcement as it creates another barrier for private plaintiffs: waiting for the outcome of an action for annulment. Considering the average duration[121] of administrative cases

---

[114] For detailed rulings on the issue, see the following remarkable decisions: The Turkish Supreme Court, General Assembly of Civil Law, E: 1993/13-26 K: 1993/95, 03.03.1993; and E: 1998/13-439 K: 1998/363, 27.05.1998; The Turkish Supreme Court, 13th Civil Law Chamber, E: 2006/13050 K: 2008/4281, 27.03.2008.

[115] Kuru, *supra* note 56, p. 847.

[116] See for instance Oz, *supra* note 13, p. 185 *et seq.*; Aslan, *supra* note 3, p. 826 *et seq.*; Aksoy, *supra* note 8, p. 55 *et seq.*; Sanli, supra note 18, p. 242 *et seq.*; Topcuoglu, *supra* note 7, p. 265.

[117] The Turkish Supreme Court, 19th Civil Law Chamber, E:1999/3350 K:1999/6364, 01.11.1999.

[118] The Turkish Supreme Court, 19th Civil Law Chamber, E:2002/2827 K:2002/7580, 29.11.2002.

[119] See Aslan, *supra* note 3, p. 830. For a discussion on interplay between administrative and private enforcement see: G. Oz, *supra* note 13, p. 185 *et seq.*

[120] The Turkish Supreme Court, 19th Civil Law Chamber, E:2007/3229, K:2007/10677, 29.11.2007.

[121] The average duration is 18 months. See www.basin.adalet.gov.tr/bkonusma/hikmetsamitu rk/240201yargininsorunlari.html.

before the Council of State and frequent annulments of TCA decisions due to procedural irregularities,[122] eventually, it could be extremely difficult to obtain redress.

13. Extraterritoriality/arbitrability

Article 2 of the Competition Act adopts the so-called 'effects doctrine'.[123] It provides that 'Agreements, decisions and practices which prevent, distort or restrict competition between any undertakings operating in or affecting markets for goods and services within the boundaries of the Republic of Turkey . . . fall under this Act.' In this regard, irrespective of headquarters location or the physical conduct of business within the Turkish boundaries, all undertakings are subject to the Competition Act provided they have power to affect the Turkish markets.[124] Thus, a Turkish court trying an antitrust damages case should carry out the examination according to the Turkish Competition Act.[125]

The Turkish judiciary has not yet addressed the arbitrability of competition law disputes or which foreign antitrust laws could apply in a given dispute. As a general matter, arbitration may be possible on subjects that are at the disposal of the parties such as contracts. That said, competition law is of an absolute public law nature and therefore involves not only the private interests of the parties but also those of the general public.[126] In this regard, the question of arbitrability should first be answered by the Supreme Court, as the decisions of arbitrators are subject to judicial review.[127] In total, the arbitrability of competition rules needs judicial interpretation to explicate on how the arbitration procedure could work in the competition law context.[128]

Conclusion

Private actions have hardly been developed in the past decade in Turkey. As of June 2009, Turkish courts have not awarded damages in private actions resulting from antitrust infringements. Possible reasons may be summarized as follows:

1. Competition law was somehow unknown to legal professionals and individuals/companies concerned;

---

122 O. Guzel (2006), 'Role of the Judiciary in Turkish Competition Law Practice' in 4th Symposium on Recent Developments in Competition Law, Ankara: Competition Authority, pp. 188–239, at p. 223 *et seq.*

123 G. Oz (2009), 'Turkey', in M. M. Dabbah and B. E. Hawk (eds), Anti-Cartel Enforcement Worldwide, Cambridge University Press, p. 1192.

124 K. Erol (2000), Extraterritorial Application of Competition Laws, Ankara: Competition Authority, p. 157.

125 *Id.* p. 163.

126 See Nazzini, *supra* note 75, p. 326.

127 Article 533 of the Code of civil Procedure. See: Kuru, *supra* note 56, p. 931.

128 For a detailed discussion on arbitrability issue, see: G. Oz (2005), Competition Law and Practice in Turkey, paper submitted in International Arbitration Seminar, ICC Turkish Committee, Ankara, October 4, 2005; E. Ozsunay (2005), Status of the Turkish Competition Law in the Light of New Developments Regarding Arbitrability in Competition Law, paper submitted in International Arbitration Seminar, ICC Turkish Committee, Ankara, October 4, 2005.

2. The Competition Act is designed to be enforced primarily by an administrative agency (the TCA);
3. The TCA's decisions are subject to judicial review by the highest administrative court, whereas private claims fall under the jurisdiction of civil courts. This dichotomy in judiciary disciplines raised new issues in terms of concurrent proceedings; and
4. High adjudicatory costs such as attorneys' fees, expert witness and long duration of cases discourage potential plaintiffs.

Amendments to the Competition Act are expected to be enacted soon which may affect the situation for private remedies. For instance, the dispute over the interpretation of the expression 'those who suffer' may be resolved by changing it to 'those who directly suffer' – which may undermine the standing of consumers and indirect purchasers.

Nevertheless, in the author's opinion, private actions seem destined to emerge gradually over time and damages awards could be obtained by the victims in the future.

PART IV

THE AMERICAS

24 Overview of the Americas

Jonathan W. Cuneo[1]

Antitrust regimes in the Americas fall into three broad categories: (1) the United States (including many states), have antitrust legislation, class actions, and a common law tradition; (2) Canada (and Jamaica) draw heavily on common law traditions and are in proximity to the United States and therefore have hybrid models that draw on American and British legal traditions; and (3) Spanish and Portuguese countries in Central and South America, where private actions are present in inchoate form but are only now beginning to emerge.

Canada[2]

In 1985, as European countries adopted a competition model for their economies in line with the increased pace of globalization of trade, the Canadian parliament passed the Competition Act. That Act creates a claim for a person who has suffered a loss or damage as a result of certain specifically prohibited acts, generally involving collusion or otherwise universally condemned practices; other practices, such as resale price maintenance and abuse of dominant market positions are left to government enforcement. Actions may be maintained both under the common law and under the Competition Act. Canadian courts have entertained class cases on behalf of both direct purchasers and indirect purchasers. Significantly, Competition Act private actions in Canada may proceed in either Federal or provincial court; however, most proceed in provincial court.

More than any other legal system in the world the Canadian system of antitrust resembles ours in the United States.[3] Frequently, class cases are pursued in informally coordinated, parallel and simultaneous, or tandem proceedings in the US and Canada. In the past decade, Canada has begun to develop a sophisticated jurisprudence as its courts systems have produced multimillion dollar recoveries on behalf of affected Canadians.

Jamaica and the Caribbean

The Anglo-American common law antitrust tradition has extended to Jamaica. In 1993, to help promote a competition-based economy, Jamaica passed the Fair Competition Act, which both created the Jamaican Fair Trade Commission and outlawed a series of specifically identified agreements that restrain competition and abuses of market dominance. The Supreme Court of Jamaica has considered a half dozen or more major antitrust cases. The Jamaican law specifically provides for free standing private damage

---

[1] Jonathan W. Cuneo, a former Director of the American Antitrust Institute, is a partner in the Washington, D.C. law firm of Cuneo Gilbert & LaDuca, LLP.

[2] See Chapter 26, Canada, in this *Handbook*.

[3] After World War II, the US and other occupying powers imposed antitrust laws on Japan, which were further strengthened by amendments in 1977. 2 Wilbur Lindsay Fugate, Foreign Commerce and the Antitrust Laws 587–590 (Little Brown & Co. 1996).

actions. Jamaica has a rapidly advancing jurisprudence that frequently looks to the precedents of the United States for guidance. Other Caribbean nations have been urged to adopt a competition law model as well.

Central and South America

No discussion of limiting corporate power in the Spanish and Portuguese speaking countries of the Americas can proceed without first noting the shameful history of exploitation of Central and South America by dominant American corporations, who acted all too often with the support of the host government and the United States. Any attempted antitrust movement would surely have to confront this exploitation by dominant firms, the history of which becomes a backdrop for more current antitrust developments.

For example, American agricultural giants so exploited their might in Central America that they caused conflict and death and rearranged Central American borders, giving rise to the pejorative term 'banana republic.' The advent of the twentieth century brought particularly aggressive use of so-called 'gunboat diplomacy' – 'diplomacy' with the direct threat of forceful intervention – through the so-called 'Roosevelt corollary' to the Monroe Doctrine.

Hand-in-hand with American corporate dominance and Cold War 'diplomacy' was the all-too-frequent support and even sponsorship of totalitarian regimes that crushed dissent even in countries as cosmopolitan as Argentina whose military junta conducted its 'dirty war' to stifle dissent in the late 1970s. In the face of these obstacles, even for those countries that had passed a competition law, effective enforcement was simply not a practical undertaking.

The tools to counteract this exploitation were necessarily more basic – ubiquitous cries of 'Yankee go home,' riots, revolution and nationalizations. Governmental responses included intense protectionism and state-sponsored monopolies.

Argentina was the first Latin American country to adopt competition laws in 1919, followed by Mexico in 1934, Chile and Colombia in 1959, Brazil in 1962, Peru in 1991, Costa Rico in 1994, and Panama in 1996. These laws lay dormant, little understood and were all but a dead letter.

Almost all of the countries that adopted competition laws before 1980 revamped them in the 1990s to reflect the emerging realities of globalization. With some exceptions, identified below, most Central and South American countries follow the European model of using an autonomous government agency to investigate and play the role of primary enforcer in competition law with relatively little emphasis on private rights of action.

Panama

Influenced by the United States, Panama has enacted competition protection laws with an independent cause of action and a statute of limitations period of ten years. Panamanian judicial procedures also contemplate class actions. Significantly, in August 2009, a prominent Panamanian law firm filed a putative class action with respect to the international vitamins cartel.[4] Although Panama has a population of less than 3.5

---

[4] See generally, Memorandum from Rubio, Alvarez, Solis & Abrego, Bulletin: The Tower of Panama (on file with the author; see generally, www.rasalaw.com and Industrias Lacteas, S.A.

million people, its importance as an international center of trade potentially makes this development extremely significant.

Argentina

Argentina overhauled its antitrust laws in 1999. §51 of the Argentinean antitrust law provides for a stand-alone private right of action and contingent fees are allowed. Since that time, the National Commission for the Defense of Competition has focused largely on collusive practices. Significant disincentives to private enforcement exist because Argentina follows a 'loser pays' rule on attorneys' fees and because the plaintiff must put up a bond of 3 per cent of the claim at the outset of the litigation. In 2009, for the first time, an Argentinean court provided a judgment in excess of $10 million US to a competitor (including interest) who was the victim of exclusionary practices.[5]

Argentina is considering class action legislation similar to Federal Rule of Civil Procedure 23 in the United States. In early 2009, the Supreme Court reversed its prior course, and cleared the way for representative or class actions.

Brazil

The largest and by far the most powerful economy in South American belongs to Brazil. Brazil has an active governmental antitrust enforcement program, and is said to be leading the multinational investigation of alleged price fixing among manufacturers of refrigerator compressors. Brazilian law provides a panoply of private remedies through complaints to the administrative body, and through private actions in judicial bodies that provide for both injunctive relief and damages. A complainant may bring an administrative complaint and a private action simultaneously. Because of fee shifting, precedence given to administrative determinations and rigorous standing requirements, there are significant incentives to pursue the administrative remedies, and in fact judicial remedies are seldom used. Brazilian law does provide for collective actions that can be brought by either by public authorities or private parties with standing; significantly, public prosecutors can recover damages on behalf of victims. There has yet to be a successful purely private judicial action for damages in Brazil.[6]

Mexico

Mexico revamped the Federal Economic Competition Law (FECL) in 1994. The law is administered by the Federal Competition Commission. There is no private enforcement in Mexico.

Peru

The National Institute for the Defense of Competition and Protection of Intellectual Property (INDECOPI) enforces competition law. No private rights of action are

---

v. F. Hoffman La-Roche, Ltd. (filed Aug. 31, 2009), Civil Branch of the First Judicial Circuit of Panama.

[5] Memorandum from Allende & Brea, Antitrust News Alert: Argentina's First Case on Antitrust Private Enforcement (Nov. 19, 2009) (on file with the authors; see generally, www.allendebrea.com.ar).

[6] See Chapter 25, Brazil.

provided for unless and until INDECOPI finishes its work. No significant jurisprudence has evolved in Peru in relation to private rights of actions.[7]

Conclusion

The evolution of a competition-based model in the Americas is a remarkable step forward – one that would have been unimaginable 25 years ago.

The next decade will likely determine whether private enforcement of competition laws will emerge as a viable force in Central and South America. Given the pervasiveness of globalized cartels, governments would do well to develop an effective means to provide redress.

7 See Chapter 27, Peru.

25 Brazil

Mauro Grinberg, Camilla Paoletti and Leonor Cordovil[1]

Introduction

This chapter aims to explain the Brazilian system of private antitrust enforcement. One can even say that this chapter tries to explain why it does not work.

There are two lines of private actions concerning antitrust in Brazil: (i) private antitrust actions aiming to deter antitrust violations and (ii) private antitrust actions in order to charge the violators for losses due to such violations.

Article 29 of the Brazilian competition law (Law No. 8.884/94) sets forth these two lines of actions. Notwithstanding the provision of Article 29, Brazilian courts are still learning how to deal with private antitrust enforcement. Despite 15 years of existence, the application of the competition law by courts has still not made any significant progress.

1. How the competition system works in Brazil

Antitrust remedies may be obtained through the administrative level or the judicial level. The administrative level of the Brazilian competition system (SBDC) consists of (i) a body for economic analysis – Secretaria de Acompanhamento Econômico (SEAE), of the Ministry of Finance, (ii) an administrative body – Secretaria de Direito Econômico (SDE), of the Ministry of Justice, thus part of the executive branch and in charge of the investigations, and (iii) a decision making agency – Conselho Administrativo de Defesa Econômica (CADE), which is independent. Together, these three bodies are referred to as the 'Brazilian competition authorities.'

These are governmental or official entities that are governed by the Brazilian competition law and directed by their own initiatives and by complaints.

According to Article 20 of the Brazilian competition law, notwithstanding malicious intent, *any act* in any way intended or otherwise *able to produce the following listed effects, even if any such effects are not achieved*, shall be deemed a violation of the economic order: I – to limit, restrain or in any way or injure open competition or free enterprise; II – to control a relevant market of a certain product or service; III – to increase profits on a discretionary basis; and IV – to abuse one's market control. Article 21 of the same law provides some examples of what can be considered as a violation of the economic order.

In that the defense of the economic order is a public matter, the complainant does not have to show his/her legitimacy and/or interest in an administrative proceeding. The complainant, consequently, is not necessarily a party to the administrative proceeding.

---

[1] Mauro Grinberg is a partner of Grinberg Cordovil e Barros Advogados, a traditional firm founded in 1954 and located in São Paulo, Brazil. He was a commissioner of CADE, the Brazilian antitrust agency, from 1986 to 1990, a time when CADE began to assume greater importance in the Brazilian economy. Camilla Paoletti and Leonor Cordovil are associate lawyers at Barcellos Tucunduva Advogados.

Instead, the complainant can be someone who brings notice of an antitrust violation to the Brazilian competition authorities and is able to supply information and evidence for the administrative investigation.

However, according to Article 29 of the Brazilian competition law,[2] the complainant may go to the judiciary instead of the Government, and here there is the possibility of a private antitrust action aiming to deter an antitrust violation. In this case, the complainant will be a plaintiff. Article 29 also provides that complaints in the Judiciary may not only aim to deter an antitrust violation, but they may also seek the award of damages in connection therewith.

Accordingly, in Brazil, these two lines of antitrust complaints can be simultaneously brought to the Brazilian competition authorities – administrative level – and also to the judiciary. However, what may seem odd is the fact that actions that seek recovery for damage caused by anticompetitive practices can be brought to the judiciary irrespective of the correspondent administrative proceeding. This leads to court actions claiming for damage recovery when there is still no final administrative determination from CADE. In these cases, judges usually stay the judicial suit until a final determination is reached by CADE.

2. Civil actions before the judiciary

In Brazil the two lines of actions mentioned in Article 29, i.e. antitrust actions in courts aiming to deter antitrust violations and antitrust actions in order to charge the violators for losses due to such violations, can be brought either (i) individually or (ii) collectively by parties that have standing under the law to sue.[3]

a. Private actions

One should start by private antitrust actions in court aiming to deter anticompetitive practices. These actions can be brought by direct consumers, final consumers, indirect consumers or competitors. Civil associations may also bring private civil actions regarding antitrust cases, especially civil associations that do not fall within the criteria for filling a public collective action.

The fact remains that this possibility is seldom used; the few cases are not able to be understood as jurisprudence. So, there is no valid and reliable case law. By the way, this sentence will be repeated at other times throughout this chapter because, in fact, nothing has yet been decided by the highest courts.

The main reason for the perplexity surrounding using the judicial alternative is the lack of knowledge of competition law and what constitutes a violation of the economic order as stated in Article 20 and 21 above. Most of the law schools in Brazil still do not teach competition law; many lawyers are not even aware of it.

---

[2] Not only Article 29, but also Article 5, item XXXV, of the Brazilian Federal Constitution (1988) states that the law shall not exclude any injury or threat to a right from the consideration of the Judicial Power.

[3] Article 82 of the Consumer Defense Code (Law No. 8.078/90) states that the following parties have standing to sue collectively to enforce the rights and interests of consumers and victims: (i) the Public Prosecutor's Office; (ii) administrative agencies; and (iii) civil associations (such as class unions and cooperative associations).

Another key factor is costs and difficulties for a party to prove the anticompetitive practice; the standard of proof in such cases is very challenging. And there are also filing costs, attorneys' fees etc. In Brazil, private actions are not encouraged like public collective actions; here if the plaintiff loses the action, he/she has to pay all the costs incurred by the defendant as well. With all these odd conditions, it is unlikely that injured parties feel encouraged to bring such actions.

This is a time-consuming endeavour and there is still a long way to go. Complainants are usually not encouraged to seek the judiciary in the first place if they face an antitrust violation. But on the other hand complainants in the administration have no control over the file and, even worse, if an accused party is convicted by CADE, a judicial dispute over such decision is always available. For example, if an accused party decides to appeal CADE's decision, the Judiciary may stay such administrative decision and, then, the complainant will have to wait for a long judicial dispute resolution that may take years to reach a final determination.

In order to show that things can always get worse, the judicial file in an appeal starts from point zero. The difference here is that the case is against CADE – the entity which issued the decision convicting a party – and not against another party. The complainant here is not a party, although he/she may be called for depositions.

CADE is usually challenged in court not to repeat the production of evidence; the argument has not been accepted so far by the judges. Again, and as usual, there is no valid or reliable case law.

So, this is the dilemma for a potential complainant: (i) go to the administration, see the case being conducted by the administration itself and, at the end of the day, see the accused party (if convicted) go to court and face an almost endless case; or (ii) go directly to court and, besides facing the burden of proof, have the case decided by a possibly unprepared (in antitrust law) judge. Anyway, appeals (for better or worse) are always available.

This is an unresolved dilemma which, so far, has seen by far the highest preference for the administration, because it (i) has specific knowledge, (ii) does not charge the complainants costs and (iii) itself faces the burden of proof.

At this point it is important to move to the other possible purpose of private antitrust enforcement, which is related to charges of losses due to antitrust violations. This is obviously cumbersome to explain because, again, we do not have a valid and reliable case law.

In fact, just about all antitrust violations which ended in CADE's convictions have been taken to the judiciary and have not, so far, reached the highest courts. This means that, even with a conviction imposed by CADE, the judiciary may suspend the enforcement of such decision until the highest courts have reached a final and enforceable verdict. As this has not happened so far, damages have not been charged. Of course, with the passing of time in a case, plaintiffs will face an ever increasing difficulty in demonstrating losses.

There is a possibly (although only partially but significantly) changing situation because, with some leniency agreements already signed and with the files in progress, in some cases there are settlements, which are only accepted by CADE (when there are leniency agreements) if the settler pleads guilty.

This is a real confession of a wrongdoing and, as such, it makes it easier for eventual plaintiffs to show the causal link between losses and conduct. Of course, a plaintiff will still have to demonstrate the losses, which are never self-explanatory. Besides, another discussion – which is already well developed in tax law – will arise: some or all of these losses may have been charged already to clients in the consumer chain. In Brazil, there is still no case law to rely on in settlements agreements. It is a very recent possibility that has been adopted by CADE, and most of the settlements agreements have been signed in cases where there is a leniency agreement.

b. Public collective actions

As mentioned above, antitrust actions either to deter an antitrust violation or to charge for losses can also be brought by parties[4] that have standing under the law to sue; and they must bring these actions on behalf of others.

These actions are public and collective; therefore they have their own characteristics and benefits, differing in some aspects from the private antitrust actions explained above. For example, in the procedures of collective actions, there is no payment of fees and any other expenses up front, and at the end of the proceeding, if the plaintiff wins or loses the case, he/she cannot be condemned to pay attorneys' fees and court costs, unless his/hers malicious prosecution is proven.

The Brazilian legislature limited who could bring collective actions on behalf of others. There was concern about the proper use of collective actions so as not to turn them into an instrument of personal profit for those who propose, instead of fulfilling the social objectives which was the aim.

In Brazil, there are no legal provisions providing for control by the courts of 'adequate representation' of the party; however, this often occurs in practice. The judge can determine, in each case, the inadmissibility of the collective action and may do so, for example, when there are collective actions brought by associations which, while complying with the legal requirements, do not have the credibility, reliability, economic capacity and the ability to produce a valid procedural complaint – all factors which are essential to an adequate and proper representation.

Jurisdiction to file collective actions for damages lies with the federal courts in cases where the Federal Government, federal agencies or federal public companies have an interest as plaintiffs, defendants or third parties. A recent decision issued by the Brazilian Superior Court of Justice (STJ) held that if the wrongdoing has effects over more than one Federal state, the Federal Government has jurisdiction. Besides these examples, the jurisdiction will be decided according to the Brazilian Code of Civil Procedure.

The most common type of collective action in Brazil is the civil public action brought by the Federal or State Prosecutor's Office. They can bring an action to either (i) deter an antitrust violation or (ii) determine civil liability for losses and damages recovery.

---

4 Article 82 of Law No. 8.078/90 states that the following parties have standing to sue: i. the Public Prosecutor's Office; ii. the Federal Government, States, Municipalities, and the Federal District; administrative agencies or departments (such as the PROCONs); and civil associations (such as class unions and cooperative associations).

In the second case, the Public Prosecutor's Office brings an action for the determination of the defendant's civil liability. After the finding of liability, a determination of remedial damages takes place, requiring the injured parties to qualify individually.

Considering that the judge's determination does not quantify the individual losses, the individual qualification proceeding can be very challenging once the injured parties have to (i) start a new action (qualification proceeding), (ii) prove that they were injured by the antitrust violation and (iii) quantify their losses. Therefore, the individual qualification proceeding is not usual once the private agents have to face a new proceeding with a challenging burden of proof and with additional costs.

In view of the above, when no injured party qualifies individually, the amount of the remedial damages must go to the Fund for Diffuse Rights (Law No. 7.347/85).[5] The Fund will then use the money for purposes other than reparatory ones.

3. Relationship between Brazilian competition authorities and the judiciary

a. Conflicts

As stated, in Brazil, the two lines of civil antitrust actions can be filed at the judiciary and at the administrative level at the same time. This leads to concurrent and independent analysis of the same wrongdoing both by the Brazilian competition authorities and by the judges, raising two main problems: (1) possible conflicting decisions from CADE and from the courts and (2) the possibility of duplicate convictions for the same wrongdoing (*bis in idem*).

Of course, private and collective actions are encouraged, but here one is not talking about filing a civil complaint subsequent to the final administrative determination, but rather about filing a civil complaint at the administrative level and the judiciary simultaneously. And not only that, but one is saying that it is possible for a court to analyze and decide civil liability and remedial damages, irrespective of an ongoing administrative analysis by the Brazilian competition authorities on the same case.

In Brazil, according to the hierarchy of the laws, a court determination prevails over an administrative determination; therefore, if CADE issues a determination different from what the court states, the court decision must prevail. In a case like this, CADE, which is the agency that has the technical knowledge to verify antitrust wrongdoings, will have its authority undermined. Therefore, in order to avoid conflicting determinations, what has been seen in practice is that some judges often wait for CADE's final determination to issue their decisions.

Notwithstanding that there is no legal provision barring the judiciary from analyzing the merits of antitrust wrongdoings concurrently with the Brazilian competition authorities, there is a debate regarding this conflict of attributions. Although there are judges, attorneys and public prosecutors who defend the argument of the concurrent attributions, others practitioners argue that Brazilian competition law states that CADE is the sole authority entitled to determine and fine an antitrust wrongdoing and that courts should only determine the civil liability and remedial damages in civil actions subsequent to CADE's final determination.

---

[5] The amount of the fines imposed by CADE also goes to this fund.

This is an ongoing, extensive discussion because of its potential to have a larger impact on the interpretation of Brazilian law provisions. At the moment, it is only possible to say that Brazil does not yet have a reliable body of case law.

b. Public enforcement

Brazilian competition authorities have an important role in providing technical knowledge of competition law and publicizing their decisions in antitrust violation cases.

Article 89 of the Brazilian competition law states that when there is a judicial discussion involving the application of the competition law, the court should notify and invite CADE to assist the proceeding.

To avoid the appearance of impropriety or unfair prejudgment, CADE prefers not to take part in court cases when there is still an ongoing administrative proceeding on the same matter.

According to CADE's former Commissioner, Mr. Roberto Pfeiffer, this is one of the reasons why 'the Council has consistently chosen not to intervene in lawsuits as co-principal or plaintiff's assistant until it has issued a final decision in the correspondent administrative proceeding.'[6]

The study 'Competition Law and Policy in Brazil – A peer review', published in 2005 by the Inter-American Development Bank ('IDB's report') recommended that:[7]

> For cases in which CADE has no proceeding of its own, CADE should consider treating such invitations as opportunities for competition advocacy. Particularly with respect to private cases that involve attacks on such conduct as predatory or abusively high prices, CADE could provide useful advice to the court about how to evaluate such claims under law 8884. In this respect, CADE should also undertake to develop a database containing information about the volume, nature, and outcome of civil suits for antitrust damages filed under Article 29 of Law 8884 and under other laws, such as the Consumer Defense Code and the Collective actions Law, that provide a basis for antitrust damage claims.

If effectuated, the IDB's recommendation may help to legitimate antitrust private suits and to reduce inconsistent judgments. However, for this recommendation to be effective, administrative investigations and decisions will have to be better publicized, and competition advocacy will have to be encouraged, so that private parties and official agents can access and collect information about anticompetitive behavior to legitimize their claims.

Another point that was already mentioned briefly above is the exposure of leniency participants to civil damages awards resulting from antitrust violations. Under the Brazilian competition law, leniency program participants receive no protection from civil damages suits and Brazil has still not adopted any measure to reduce the beneficiary's exposure to civil actions. It is difficult to know how the courts will treat leniency agreements, as no cartel investigations initiated by means of such agreements

---

[6] Pfeiffer, Roberto (2003), 'Tutela Coletiva da Livre Concorrência', Revista da Procuradoria Geral do Estado de São Paulo, São Paulo.

[7] (2005), Competition Law and Policy in Brazil – A peer review, IDB and OECD Competition Division (www.oecd.org), p. 112.

and involving big companies and powerful parties have thus far reached a judicial conclusion.[8]

In short, the interaction of Brazilian competition authorities and courts is very important for the development of antitrust civil actions in Brazil, but there is still much to be improved in this regard.

4. Brazilian challenges in private antitrust enforcement

Besides the lack of interaction between the Brazilian competition authorities and courts, there are other issues deterring the development of private antitrust enforcement in Brazil; most of them were already mentioned above.

Firstly, the lack of knowledge of the Brazilian competition law, mainly by private attorneys and judges.[9] As mentioned, competition law is still not taught in most of the Brazilian law schools. And, another interesting point to raise here is that it is somewhat difficult for common law attorneys to understand the implications of using a common law inspired law in a civil law country, mainly with a Portuguese formalistic origin. For example, the mere basic notion of relevant market is difficult to understand in Brazil (except, of course, in the limited antitrust community) because there is no law explaining what it is.

Secondly, in Brazil, as in many other jurisdictions, private parties are often deterred from filing civil actions for damages due to the inherent cost, delay, uncertainty and risk, with the result that many victims remain uncompensated.[10] Also most of CADE's final determinations are being reviewed by courts that may or may not overrule them; therefore it is possible to say that in these cases there is not yet a valid administrative decision.

Finally, the Brazilian courts lack technical knowledge. In Brazil, most of the judges are still not prepared to deal with competition issues. It is clearly a new subject for them; no important cases regarding competition matters have reached final decisions. Preliminary injunctions to stay either the anticompetitive practice or the effect of CADE's final rulings are often granted by the judges (provided that a comprehensive guarantee is offered); however Brazilian courts usually postpone the issuance of ultimate decisions.

In this regard, the IDB's report[11] stated that:

> Brazilian courts will nonetheless confront antitrust questions in adjudicating criminal cases under the Economic Crimes Law and civil suits seeking antitrust damages. Although there are constitutional constraints on the creation of specialized courts, the chief judge of a regional appellate court may designate specialized panels to hear appeals of antitrust cases and may also suggest to the first instance courts in the region that specialized judges be designated to hear first

---

[8] The cartel case involving the conviction of companies providing surveillance services in the State of Rio Grande do Sul, Brazil, started with a leniency agreement. However, it did not involve big and powerful companies. Administrative Proceeding No. 08012.001826/2003-10.

[9] Except, of course, in the limited antitrust community, where there is an adequate cadre of trained private attorneys and expert economists.

[10] European Commission White Paper on damages actions for breach of the EC antitrust rules, 2008.

[11] (2005), Competition Law and Policy in Brazil – A peer review, IDB and OECD Competition Division (www.oecd.org), p. 112.

instance antitrust cases. If judges are designated for service as specialists, they should receive appropriate training in the analysis of economic issues, which could then also be employed in resolving cases that involve sector regulatory agencies or that otherwise raise economic issues.

Therefore, one can say that training of judges is a real challenge to be faced by the Brazilian courts in the next coming years.

Conclusion

One can see that much is left to improve and develop in the Brazilian system of civil actions. This will take place with more advanced and comprehensive education and with the consolidation in practice of this kind of action and the case law of CADE. In a word: advocacy.

Notwithstanding the development that will take place naturally within the next few years, the Brazilian antitrust authorities already recognize the importance of private enforcement and have decided to stimulate civil suits seeking damages for anticompetitive behavior. The main agency in this new battle is SDE.

According to SDE, private enforcement makes indemnification of injured parties more effective, and it is also a way to show companies that punishment goes beyond the administrative fine.[12]

In view of the above, one will have to wait a few more years to discuss more completely the law and the practice of civil actions in Brazil.

[12] '*Governo afirma que processará empresas – União cobrará na Justiça prejuízo em compras públicas causado por empresas condenadas pelo Cade por prática de cartel*'. Folha de São Paulo. November 11, 2007. Dinheiro, B9.

26 Canada

Charles M. Wright[1]

Introduction

Class proceedings are relatively new to Canada, and prior to their introduction the ability to pursue damage claims for competition violations was seemingly more theoretical than real. This was presumably because of the expense associated with bringing such claims on a non-class basis. Competition law class actions are now becoming increasingly prevalent and judicial commentary is beginning to clarify some of the parameters of those proceedings.

Competition law class actions can be brought pursuant to the common law or the federal *Competition Act*.[2] Section 36 of the *Competition Act* creates a cause of action for any person who has suffered loss or damage as a result of conduct that is contrary to any provision of Part VI of the *Act*. Part VI of the *Act* deals with matters such as price-fixing conspiracy, bid-rigging, false or misleading representations, and pyramid schemes. Actions commenced pursuant to section 36 can be brought before a federal or provincial court.

The *Competition Act* gives the Competition Tribunal jurisdiction over certain matters addressed in the *Act*, such as mergers, refusal to deal, price maintenance, exclusive dealing, and abuse of dominate position.

The Competition Bureau is an independent law enforcement agency that investigates complaints and monitors businesses for unfair practices, including illegal cartels.

1. How does a damages action case get started?

a. Meeting clients

Generally, solicitation of clients is not prohibited. However, there are some common sense exceptions to this rule. For example, lawyers cannot solicit clients with a view to creating a claim that does not already exist. In *Arabi v. Toronto Dominion Bank*,[3] class counsel trawled their files to find possible representative plaintiffs and caused one of the

---

[1] Charles M. Wright is a partner at Siskinds LLP. His practice focuses predominantly on price-fixing conspiracy and securities class actions. Charles is a co-author of Class Actions Law and Practice (Butterworths 1999). Charles is the Vice Chair of The Canadian Bar Association National Competition Law Section, Private Actions Committee. He is also an Advisory Board Member of the American Antitrust Institute (Washington, D.C.). Charles is an International Advisory Board Member for the Institute for Consumer Antitrust Studies (Loyola University, Chicago School of Law). Charles, along with his partner Andrea DeKay and their associate Linda Visser, make up the only group of plaintiff lawyers in the country whose practices have such a distinct focus on competition law.

[2] R.S., 1985, c. C-34.

[3] [2006] O.J. No. 2072 (S.C.J.).

proposed representative plaintiffs to take action to create a claim. For this reason, the proposed representative plaintiff was found to not be suitable.

Rules governing solicitation of clients generally distinguish between clients who are represented by a lawyer and those who are not. They also distinguish between general solicitation and solicitation of a specific client.

For clients already represented by counsel, there is a distinction between trying to lure individual clients away from their current lawyers and general firm promotion. In Ontario, lawyers are not permitted to solicit individuals who have retained a lawyer for a particular matter to change lawyers for that matter.[4] Wider marketing campaigns do not generally fall within this prohibition.

For clients not already represented by counsel, some law societies try to protect those who are vulnerable and therefore susceptible to exploitation.[5]

Law society rules generally prohibit any type of solicitation that is false or misleading, that amounts to coercion, duress, or harassment, or that otherwise brings the profession or the administration of justice into disrepute.

b. Investigative tools

In Canada, most competition law cases commenced have followed announcements of a criminal investigation initiated in Canada, the United States and/or the European Union. Where the investigation is commenced outside Canada, plaintiffs have to consider whether the conduct extended to Canada and the size of the implicated Canadian market.

Even where there are guilty pleas and/or convictions, plaintiffs will want to obtain additional evidence, including expert reports examining the industry and establishing the impact of the unlawful conduct.

The ability to bring stand-alone actions depends on the capacity of plaintiffs to discover the wrongdoing through their own means. For example, in a horizontal price-fixing conspiracy, there is often no public information available about the conspiracy until criminal charges are brought and no alternative means for plaintiffs to become aware of such conduct. In a price-maintenance case or vertical price-fixing conspiracy case, there is greater opportunity for plaintiffs to discover the wrongdoing through their own means.

c. Obstacles in commencing a competition law case

Competition law cases are still relatively novel in Canada and many of the legal issues, including the evidentiary requirements at class certification, are unclear or have not yet been settled by the appellate courts. This makes it difficult for plaintiff's counsel to know the standard that they have to meet at certification. Counsel litigating these cases are therefore undertaking considerable risk.

---

4 The Law Society of Upper Canada (Ontario), Rules of Professional Conduct, Rule 3.01(2)(d).

5 See, for example, The Law Society of Upper Canada (Ontario), Rules of Professional Conduct, Rule 3.01(2)(c); and Quebec Code of ethics of advocates, Rule 5.05.

2. Who may pursue a private claim?

a. Direct and indirect purchasers

At present, there is nothing in Canadian law to prevent both direct and indirect purchasers from seeking recovery in a price-fixing conspiracy case.

In the settlement context, the Canadian courts have been willing to allow the claims of indirect purchasers to be pursued in tandem with the claims of direct purchasers. The settling defendants will consent to certification for settlement purposes of a broader class (generally consisting of all purchasers of the price-fixed product, including manufacturers, distributors, intermediaries and consumers) in order to achieve a more comprehensive release.[6] The settlement proceeds are distributed to direct and indirect purchasers based on an estimate of the extent to which the alleged overcharge has been passed through the distribution chain.

Contested competition law cases have, to date, received relatively little judicial comment in Canada. While numerous *Competition Act* class actions have been commenced, only a small number of these cases have proceeded to a contested certification motion. In the few cases that have proceeded to certification, the results have been mixed.[7] In the cases denying certification, the class has been comprised entirely or almost entirely of indirect purchasers, and the quality of the evidentiary records has been called into question. In each case, the courts found that the experts' conclusions were not supported by the necessary industry analysis or empirical evidence.[8]

---

[6] See for example: *Alfresh Beverages Canada Corp. v. Hoechst AG et al.*, [2002] O.J. No. 79 (S.C.J.); *La Cie McCormick Canada Co. v. Stone Container Corp. et al.*, (May 24, 2006), London, 43669 (Ont S.C.J.) (unreported); *Bona Foods Ltd. et al. v. Ajinomoto U.S.A., Inc. et al.*, [2004] O.J. No. 908 (S.C.J.); *Vitapharm Canada Ltd. v. F Hoffmann-La Roche Ltd.*, [2005] O.J. No. 1118 (S.C.J.); *Randall Klein Inc. v. Nan Ya Plastics Corp. et al.*, (June 29, 2005), London, 41309CP, (Ont. S.C.J.) (unreported); *Stone Paradise Inc. v. Bayer Inc. et al.*, (November 16, 2005), London, 45604CP, (Ont. S.C.J.) (unreported); *Luigi Del Guercio o/a Westown Shoe Clinic v. Bayer Inc. et al.*, (November 16, 2005), London, 46517CP, (Ont. S.C.J.) (unreported); and *Luigi Del Guercio o/a Westown Shoe Clinic v. Bayer Inc. et al.*, (May 30, 2006), London, 46460CP (Ont. S.C.J.) (unreported).

[7] See for example: *Irving Paper Ltd. v. Atofina Chemicals Inc.*, [2009] O.J. No. 4021 (S.C.J.) (Certification granted), leave to appeal refused [2010] O.J. No. 2472 (S.C.J.); *Axiom Plastics Inc. v. E.I. DuPont Canada Co.*, [2007] O.J. No. 3327 (S.C.J.) (Certification granted), aff'd [2008] O.J. No. 1973 (Div. Ct.); *Pro-Sys Consultants Ltd. v. Infineon Technologies AG*, [2008] B.C.J. No. 831 (S.C.) (Certification denied), [2009] B.C.J. No. 2239 (C.A.) (Certification granted), additional reasons [2010] B.C.J. No. 293 (C.A.), leave to S.C.C. denied [2010] S.C.C.A. No. 32; *Chadha v. Bayer*, (1999), 45 O.R. (3d) 29 (Gen. Div.) (Certification granted), (2001), 54 O.R. (3d) 520 at 549 (Div. Ct.) (Certification denied), appeal dismissed [2003] O.J. No. 27 (C.A.), leave to appeal to S.C.C. denied; *Price v. Panasonic Canada Inc.*, [2002] O.J. No. 2362 (S.C.J.) (Certification denied); *Harmegnies v. Toyota Canada*, [2007] J.Q. No 1072 (S.C.) (Certification denied); *2038724 Ontario Ltd. v. Quizno's Canada Restaurant Corp.*, [2008] O.J. No. 833 (S.C.J.) (Certification denied); reversed [2009] O.J. NO. 1874 (Div. Ct.) (Certification granted), aff'd [2010] O.J. No. 2683 (C.A.); and *Steele v. Toyota Canada Inc.*, [2008] B.C.J. No. 1496 (S.C.J.) (Certification denied).

[8] See for example: *Chadha v. Bayer*, (1999), 45 O.R. (3d) 29 (Gen. Div.) (Certification granted), (2001), 54 O.R. (3d) 520 at 549 (Div. Ct.) (Certification denied), appeal dismissed [2003] O.J. No. 27 (C.A.), leave to appeal to S.C.C. denied; *Price v. Panasonic Canada Inc.*, [2002] O.J. No. 2362 (S.C.J.); *Harmegnies v. Toyota Canada*, [2007] J.Q. No 1072 (S.C.); and *Steele v. Toyota Canada Inc.*, [2008] B.C.J. No. 1496 (S.C.J.).

In *Chadha v. Bayer Inc.*,[9] the Ontario Court of Appeal did not foreclose the possibility of indirect purchasers advancing claims. However, the Court of Appeal held that the motions judge did not adequately address the underlying reasoning of the US Supreme Court in *Illinois Brick Co. v. Illinois*[10] in disallowing indirect claims, namely the complexity of proving the extent to which the illegal overcharge was passed through the chain of distribution.

In *Vitapharm Canada Ltd. v. F. Hoffmann-La Roche Ltd.*,[11] a case involving claims by direct and indirect purchasers of various vitamins, the court endorsed a system whereby all levels of purchasers could claim for their losses in a single proceeding. In the context of a contested carriage motion, with one counsel team seeking to act for consumers only and another counsel team seeking to act for all purchasers, direct and indirect, the court held that *Illinois Brick* was 'not relevant to the case at hand',[12] as section 36 of the *Competition Act* provides that 'any person who has suffered loss or damage'[13] can bring an action, 'including it would seem, retail purchasers.'[14] The court further held that 'upon a determination of the common issues, including the global damages with respect to a product, the plaintiffs would seek directions as to the appropriate manner and means of distribution amongst the class members.'[15] This distribution of damages would involve further economic analysis and it may be necessary to form subclasses at this stage so that the interests of claimants at any given level on the chain of distribution are properly represented. Until determination of the common issues, including the assessment of global damages for each product, there is no divergence of interests among class members, and through the 'common pursuit of the common issues, all class members are more likely to maximize the quantification of their overall, global damages and achieve their ultimate, shared goal of a fair and just resolution of the claims of all class members.'[16]

Irving Paper Ltd. v. Atofina Chemicals Inc.[17] is the first decision by a Canadian court in a contested case certifying a price-fixing class action on behalf of a class that includes both direct and indirect purchasers. In certifying the class, the Ontario Superior Court of Justice rejected the defendants' arguments that the proposed class was overly broad in that it may include virtually all individuals and businesses in Canada. The Court held that 'it is no response to the plaintiffs' proposed class definition that because it is so large, it is unsuitable. If that were so, defendants engaged in "bad behaviour" affecting large numbers of the population could do so with relative immunity, knowing that class proceedings were not available and individuals affected would be most unlikely to bring an individual action.'[18] The Court also rejected the

---

9 (2003), 63 O.R. (3d) (C.A.), leave to appeal refused [2003] S.C.C.A. No 106.
10 431 US 720 (1977).
11 [2000] O.J. No. 4594 (S.C.J.).
12 *Ibid.* at para. 44.
13 *Ibid.*
14 *Ibid.*
15 *Ibid.* at para. 41.
16 *Ibid.* at para. 45.
17 [2009] O.J. No. 4021 (S.C.J.), leave to appeal refused [2010] O.J. No. 2472 (S.C.J.).
18 *Ibid.* at para. 105.

defendants' arguments that the proposed representative plaintiffs (a direct purchaser and an indirect purchaser) have an inherent conflict and are therefore unsuitable. The Court agreed that there may be a conflict between the direct and indirect purchasers arising from the impact of passing-on, but was not persuaded that this disqualifies the proposed representative plaintiffs from acting as representatives for the class. Plaintiffs' counsel was aware of the issue and, when settlement was achieved with the other defendants, plaintiffs' counsel took steps to ensure that any conflict between the two groups was resolved.[19]

In *Pro-Sys Consultants Ltd. v. Infineon Technologies AG*,[20] the British Columbia Court of Appeal overturned the certification judge's decision denying certification. The Court of Appeal certified a class consisting of all levels of purchasers of DRAM (a semiconductor memory chip). The Court of Appeal did not agree with the certification judge that the appellant was not a suitable representative plaintiff because of the potential that the plaintiff passed the overcharge along to its customers. The Court of Appeal saw this as a 'minor issue that may never be reached.' The Court held that the appellant shared a common interest with all class members in establishing the respondents' wrongful conduct and maximizing the aggregate award.[21]

b. Availability of the passing-on defense

Plaintiffs in price-fixing conspiracy actions are commonly faced with arguments by the defendants that the action should not be certified as a class proceeding because fact of harm (a requirement for establishing a claim under the *Competition Act* or the tort of conspiracy) and/or aggregate damages cannot be established on a class-wide basis as direct purchasers may have passed on any unlawful overcharge to others in the chain of purchase. Typically, the argument is that determining the extent of pass-on will be so complex that it will make determining who suffered damage unmanageable.

In *Pro-Sys Consultants Ltd. v. Infineon Technologies AG*,[22] on the pass-through issue, the British Columbia Court of Appeal held that, at the certification stage, the appellant was only required to show a credible or plausible methodology for demonstrating that the alleged overcharge was passed through the chain of distribution. The appellant's expert satisfied this requirement – it was common ground that statistical regression analysis 'is in theory capable of providing reasonable estimates' of the extent of pass through.[23]

Whether defendants have a passing-on defense available to them in a price-fixing case is not clear. In its most recent decision on the issue, decided outside the competition law context, the Supreme Court of Canada rejected the passing-on defense in its entirety, noting that the defense is economically misconceived and creates serious difficulties of proof.[24]

In assessing at the certification stage whether the availability of the passing-on defense

---

19 *Ibid.* at para. 158.
20 [2008] B.C.J. No. 2239 (C.A.).
21 *Ibid.* at para. 78.
22 [2008] B.C.J. No. 2239 (C.A.).
23 *Ibid.* at para. 68.
24 *Kingstreet Investments Ltd. v. New Brunswick (Finance)*, [2007] S.C.J. No. 1.

would affect the ability of direct purchasers to establish fact of harm, the Ontario court, in *Axiom Plastics Inc. v. E.I. DuPont Canada Co.*,[25] held that the 'possibility that the defen[s]e of passing on might prevail at trial does not mean that there cannot be some basis in fact for finding that class members suffered loss.'[26] In *Irving Paper Ltd. v. Atofina Chemicals Inc.*,[27] the court held that the plaintiffs ought be allowed to advance their arguments on the passing-on defense at trial on the basis of a full evidentiary record.[28]

There are no examples in Canada of competition law claims being brought by competitors, suppliers or other members of the public. However, there is nothing at law precluding these claims from being brought provided the claimants can prove that they were injured by the alleged conspiracy.

3. In what forum does a plaintiff initiate a private claim?

Although price-fixing conspiracy cases may be brought to the provincial or federal courts, most cases are brought to the provincial courts.[29] Plaintiffs can generally select which province they pursue their claims in. The province selected will generally depend on the location of the representative plaintiff, the location of the defendant(s), and whether the jurisdiction has opt-in or opt-out legislation.

It is possible that there could be multiple or overlapping proceedings. Where multiple class actions are commenced in the same province, counsel will either agree to pursue the actions together or will bring a carriage motion to the court, wherein the court will decide which counsel group is best positioned to pursue the matter. Where class actions are commenced in multiple provinces, counsel for the various actions may agree to pursue the claims on a national basis, with litigation focused in one province, or counsel may pursue the claims only on behalf of persons in their province. A more difficult situation arises where actions have been commenced in multiple provinces, each seeking to represent a 'national' class.[30] There is no system in Canada for resolving this situation. In *Canada Post Corporation v. Lépine*,[31] the Supreme Court of Canada commented on the need for legislative reform in this area:

> As can be seen in this appeal, the creation of national classes also raises the issue of relations between equal but different superior courts in a federal system in which civil procedure and the administration of justice are under provincial jurisdiction. This case shows that the decisions made may sometimes cause friction between courts in different provinces. This of course often involves problems with communications or contacts between the courts and between the

---

[25] [2007] O.J. No. 3327 (S.C.J.), aff'd [2008] O.J. No. 1973 (Div. Ct.).

[26] *Ibid.* at para. 131.

[27] [2009] O.J. No. 4021 (S.C.J.), leave to appeal refused [2010] O.J. No. 2472 (S.C.J.).

[28] *Ibid.* at para. 150.

[29] All Canadian provinces, with the exception of Prince Edward Island, have class action legislation.

[30] The Vioxx litigation is illustrative of this problem. See: *Setterington v. Merck Frosst Canada Ltd.*, [2006] O.J. No. 376 (S.C.J.); *Tiboni v. Merck Frosst Canada Ltd.*, [2008] O.J. No. 2996 (S.C.J.) appeal dismissed; *Mignacca v. Merck Frosst Canada Ltd.*, 2009 CanLII 10059 (Div. Ct) (all cases are part of the same proceeding, but style of cause was amended); *Wuttunee v. Merck Frosst Canada Ltd.*, [2008] S.J. No. 324 (Q.B.), appeal allowed [2009] S.J. No. 179 (C.A.).

[31] [2009] S.C.J. No. 16.

> lawyers involved in such proceedings. However, the provincial legislatures should pay more attention to the framework for national class actions and the problems they present. More effective methods for managing jurisdictional disputes should be established in the spirit of mutual comity that is required between the courts of different provinces in the Canadian legal space. It is not this Court's role to define the necessary solutions. However, it is important to note the problems that sometimes seem to arise in conducting such actions.[32]

Recent amendments to the Saskatchewan class proceeding legislation address some of these concerns. The new legislation provides that if there is a multijurisdictional class action or a proposed multijurisdictional class action commenced elsewhere in Canada dealing with the same subject matter, the court must, at the class certification stage, consider whether it would be preferable to have all or some of the claims or common issues raised by the proposed class determined in that action.[33]

Although uncommon, there are some examples of plaintiffs 'forum shopping'. *R. v. Brooks*,[34] was one of thirteen proceedings (including eleven with the Merchant Law Group acting as plaintiff's counsel) commenced in Canada relating to the testing and application of herbicides (e.g., agent orange) at a Canadian Forces base in New Brunswick. Plaintiff's counsel focused its efforts in different jurisdictions at different times based on which jurisdiction had the more favorable class action legislation at the time. As Saskatchewan is now a 'no costs' jurisdiction with 'opt-out' class actions, plaintiff's counsel is now focusing its efforts in Saskatchewan. The court refused the defendants' motion to stay the Saskatchewan action for abuse of process, noting that the defendants' concerns were statutorily required to be addressed at certification and that the Saskatchewan class is defined differently from the Newfoundland and New Brunswick actions (where certification had already been heard).

4. How may claims be aggregated?

a. Collective redress

In Canada, class actions can be commenced on behalf of an 'identifiable' class of two or more persons. Subclasses may be created where the members of the subclass have claims that raise common issues not shared by all class members, such that they require separate representation in order to protect their interests. British Columbia, Alberta, New Brunswick and Newfoundland require that subclasses be formed for non-resident class members. In these provinces, resident class members are included in the class unless they opt out and non-resident class members are included in the class only if they opt in. Manitoba allows, but does not require, subclasses to be formed for non-resident class members. Ontario, Manitoba, Saskatchewan, Quebec and Nova Scotia have opt-out regimes.

Joinder, consolidation and test cases are other procedural mechanisms designed to promote judicial economy. Joinder and consolidation are processes whereby claims arising from the same event(s) or involving the same question of law or fact are heard

---

32 *Ibid.* para. 57.
33 *The Class Actions Act*, R.S.S. c. C-12.01, s. 6.
34 [2009] S.J. No. 62 (Q.B.).

together. Joinder and consolidation require the involvement of each plaintiff. Test cases involve a process whereby one case is heard by the court and other persons with similar claims agree to be bound by the result.[35]

In Quebec, consumer protection organizations may pursue remedies on behalf of Quebec consumers.

b. Joint and several liability and the related rights of contribution and indemnity

In Canada, it is clear that there is joint and several liability among co-conspirators. Additionally, provincial negligence laws provide for rights of contribution and indemnity among co-defendants. However, as recognized in *Crosslink Technology, Inc. v. BASF Canada*,[36] it is unclear whether the contribution and indemnity provisions apply with respect to intentional torts or criminal behavior, such as violations of the *Competition Act*. As a result, in partial settlements, bar order provisions are often drafted to accommodate for this present uncertainty in the law, and provide that plaintiffs will reduce their claims against the non-settling defendants if the court ultimately finds a right of contribution and indemnity does exist. The court order granting settlement approval may accommodate for this uncertainty as well. The court order will typically contain a provision to the effect of:

> THIS COURT ORDERS that if the Courts ultimately determine that there is a right of contribution and indemnity between the Defendants, the Plaintiffs and the Settlement Class Members shall restrict their joint and several claims against the Non-Settling Defendants such that the Plaintiffs and the Settlement Class Members shall be entitled to claim and recover from the Non-Settling Defendants on a joint and several basis only those damages (including punitive damages) arising from and allocable to the sales or conduct of the Non-Settling Defendants.

Where there is joint and several liability, defendants cannot assume that their liability will be a direct function of their sales. *Crosslink Technology, Inc. v. BASF Canada*[37] recognizes the possibility that there are other bases upon which to allocate liability. Allocating liability in a manner that focuses on the conduct of the defendants is consistent with the behavior modification objective of the class proceeding legislation.

5. What procedural defenses are available short of trial?

In Canada, there are several procedural defenses available short of trial including: (1) motions to strike; (2) certification; (3) motions for summary judgment; and (4) motions for determination of a legal issue.

At the pleading stage, motions can be brought to strike all or part of a statement of claim or statement of defense. Defendants in price-fixing conspiracy cases have generally been unsuccessful at bringing motions to strike. Recognizing the secretive nature of price-fixing conspiracies, the courts have adopted a generous approach when assessing

---

35 Ward K. Branch, *Class Action in Canada*, Western Legal Publications, 1996–2002; Canada Law Book, 2003-at 2.110–2.120.

36 (November 30, 2007), London, 50305CP (Ont. S.C.J.) (unreported).

37 *Ibid.*

the adequacy of pleadings.[38] For example, in *Chadha v. Bayer Inc.*,[39] the court refused the defendants' motion to strike despite the 'very general'[40] nature of the allegations. In *Stone Paradise Inc. v. Bayer Inc.*,[41] the court again refused to strike the conspiracy claim, noting that the details of the alleged conspiracy would be within the knowledge of the defendants and largely unavailable to the plaintiffs.

The main pre-trial procedural hurdle for plaintiffs in pursuing competition law cases in Canada has been the motion for certification. The main difficulty in certifying these cases has been showing that loss can be proven on a class-wide basis and that a class proceeding is the preferable procedure even if an aggregate assessment of damages is not possible. Defendants will often argue that due to various market conditions loss cannot be proven on a class-wide basis, such that individual inquiries would be needed and a class proceeding would not be the preferable procedure.

Through a summary judgment motion, the court may issue judgment without a trial provided that the court is satisfied that there is no genuine issue for trial with respect to a claim or a defense, or the parties agree to have all or part of a claim determined by summary judgment and the court is satisfied that it is appropriate to grant summary judgment.

Parties may also move for a determination, before trial, of a question of law raised by a pleading in the action where the determination of the question would dispose of all or part of the action, substantially shorten the trial or result in a substantial cost savings.

6. What devices are available to obtain evidence?

In Canada, as discovery does not occur until after the certification hearing, there is limited ability for plaintiffs to obtain evidence pre-certification from defendants. Possible sources of evidence for plaintiffs include: settling defendants, expert economists, discovery documents in related US proceedings, former employees of the defendants, and the related criminal investigation.

Evidence can be obtained through early settlements with a defendant(s), which require the defendant(s) to provide cooperation in the continuing prosecution of the action against the non-settling defendants. Defendants will seek discounted settlements in exchange for providing such information. The cooperation provisions typically require the settling defendant(s) to produce documents relevant to the litigation, require company representatives to attend at examinations and/or trial, and provide general information about the competition law violation. Plaintiffs ideally want to enter into a first settlement with a party who is at the core of the unlawful activities – such parties will have better information about the nature and scope of the alleged misconduct. Balanced against this is the desire to enter into a first settlement with a defendant with a small market share, as the first settlement is often discounted to account for the benefit of the cooperation and settling with a small defendant helps keep a greater amount of sales in

---

[38] See for example: *Chadha v. Bayer Inc.*, 1998 Carswell Ont 5225 (S.C.J.); *Axiom Plastics Inc. v. E.I. Dupont Canada Co.*, [2007] O.J. No. 3327 (S.C.J.); *Stone Paradise Inc. v. Bayer Inc.*, [2005] O.J. No. 5657 (S.C.J.).

[39] 1998 Carswell Ont 5225 (S.C.J.).

[40] *Ibid.* at para. 5.

[41] [2005] O.J. No. 5657 (S.C.J.) at paras. 9–10.

play in the litigation. The cooperation provisions often provide that the documents and information obtained pursuant thereto are to be treated as confidential and can only be used for the purposes of the litigation. The cooperation provisions will protect the settling defendant(s) from being obligated to disclose privileged information. Canadian courts have recognized that cooperation is valuable consideration in approving such settlements as being fair and reasonable for the class.[42]

Experts provide the economic evidence required at the certification hearing and later at the common issues trial. Expert evidence is typically used at the certification hearing to provide information about the affected market(s) and to establish that the fact of harm and/or damages can be proven on a class-wide basis.

Where there is a related case ongoing in the United States, Canadian plaintiffs will sometimes seek intervenor status in the US proceeding for the limited purpose of gaining access to the documents provided during the discovery process.[43] Canadian courts have held that this practice is not in contravention of any rules.[44] The Canadian court may issue a sealing order to preserve the confidentiality of the US documents referenced in the plaintiff's materials.[45]

In some circumstances, information can be obtained through former employees. Professional investigative agencies can be retained to contact former employees of the defendants, and sometimes employees will come forward on their own initiative.

Evidence can also be obtained through related criminal proceedings. This is limited to publicly available information and does not extend to information gathered by antitrust authorities through leniency/amnesty applications.

7. What practices are illegal and what are the elements of proof?

The *Competition Act* is the governing legislation. Section 36 of the *Competition Act* creates a right of action for any person who has suffered loss or damage as a result of conduct that is contrary to Part VI of the *Act*. Part VI governs various anticompetitive matters, including price-fixing conspiracies, bid-rigging, and pyramid schemes. Of the matters provided for under Part VI, horizontal price-fixing is the anticompetitive conduct that is most commonly pursued through private enforcement. Price maintenance, which is now addressed under a different part of the *Act*, has been pursued through private enforcement as well, albeit on a less frequent basis.

Under the current provisions, in order to establish a price-fixing conspiracy, it is necessary to show that the alleged agreement resulted in an 'undue' lessening of competition

---

42 *Irving Paper Limited et al. v. Atofina Chemicals Inc et al.*, (October 15, 2008) London, 47025 (Ont. S.C.J.) (unreported) at ¶26; and *Crosslink Technology, Inc. v. BASF Canada et al.*, (November 30, 2007), London, 50305CP (Ont. S.C.J.) (unreported).

43 See for example: *In Re Vitamins Antitrust Litigation*, MDL 1285, 2001 WL34088808 D.D.C., 2001; *In Re Linerboard Antitrust Litigation*, 333 F.Supp.2d 333 (E.D.Pa., 2004); and *In Re Neurontin Marketing, Sales Practices, and Products Liability Litigation*, MDL 1629, order issued October 20, 2006.

44 See: *Ford v. F. Hoffman-LaRoche Ltd. et al.*, (2001), 11 C.P.R. (4th) 230 (S.C.J.); (2002), 212 D.L.R. (4th) 563 (Div. Ct.); (2002), 223 D.L.R. (4th) 445 (C.A.); leave to the Supreme Court of Canada denied, (2003), 29 C.P.R. (4th) vii (S.C.C.).

45 *La Cie McCormick Canada Co. v. Stone Container Corp. et al.*, (December 22, 2005), London, 43669CP, (Ont. S.C.) (unreported).

or an unreasonable enhancement of price. Amendments not yet in force will eliminate the undue and unreasonable qualifiers. Under the amendments, a conspiracy is established where there is an agreement '(a) to fix, maintain, increase or control the price for the supply of the product; (b) to allocate sales, territories, customers or markets for the production or supply of the product; or (c) to fix, maintain, control, prevent, lessen or eliminate the production or supply of the product.'

The amendments to the price maintenance provisions, already in force, repeal the previous provisions which created a cause of action under section 36 and create new provisions whereby affected persons can seek redress before the Competition Tribunal.

There is a limited exemption under the *Competition Act* for government entities. The *Competition Act* is binding on government corporations only to the extent that they are engaged in commercial activities in competition with other persons.[46] The price-fixing provisions do not apply in respect of certain specified agreements between federal financial institutions or certain specified agreements between teams and clubs engaged in professional sport as members of the same league. Furthermore, several of the provisions under Part VI exclude agreements entirely between affiliate companies.

Plaintiffs can also bring a claim under the common law. The most commonly pursued claim at common law is in the tort of conspiracy. In *Canada Cement LaFarge Ltd. v. British Columbia Lightweight Aggregate Ltd.*,[47] the Supreme Court of Canada set out the elements of the tort of conspiracy:

(1) whether the means used by the defendants are lawful or unlawful, the predominant purpose of the defendants' conduct is to cause injury to the plaintiff; or,
(2) where the conduct of the defendants is unlawful, the conduct is directed towards the plaintiff (alone or together with others), and the defendants should know in the circumstances that injury to the plaintiff is likely to and does result.

In situation (2) it is not necessary that the predominant purpose of the defendants' conduct be to cause injury to the plaintiff but, in the prevailing circumstances, it must be a constructive intent derived from the fact that the defendants should have known that injury to the plaintiff would ensue. In both situations, however, there must be actual damage suffered by the plaintiff.

8. What do plaintiffs get if they win?

a. Available remedies and distribution of damages

In Canada, there are no 'treble' damages. Plaintiffs can seek general, special and punitive damages. The court has jurisdiction to award both pre-judgment and post-judgment interest.

To date, no competition law class action case has proceeded to trial. The cases have been resolved through settlements or discontinuances prior to the trial. However, in

---

46 *Competition Act*, R.S.C. 1985, c. C-34, s, 2.1.
47 [1983] 1 S.C.R. 452.

Axiom Plastics Inc. v. E.I. DuPont Canada Co.,[48] a vertical conspiracy case, the court indicated that the aggregate damages provisions of the Ontario *Class Proceeding Act, 1992*[49] could be relied upon in a competition law case to calculate damages. *Irving Paper Ltd. v. Atofina Chemicals Inc.*[50] held that the aggregate provisions are available where the plaintiffs have established 'potential liability' or, in other words, that the defendants acted unlawfully.[51]

Section 23 allows for the use of statistical information not otherwise admissible as evidence for determining the amount or distribution of an award. Section 24 allows the court to determine aggregate damages where: (a) monetary relief is claimed on behalf of class members; (b) no questions of fact or law other than those relating to the assessment of monetary relief remain to be determined; and (c) the aggregate or a part of the defendant's liability can reasonably be determined without proof by individual class members. In both *Axiom* and *Irving*, the plaintiffs' expert proposed to calculate aggregate damages using a 'benchmark' analysis. The expert first contemplated using the 'before and after approach' to determine the 'but for' price and then using a multiple regression analysis to account for any other factors that might have influenced the supply and demand of the relevant product.

In terms of allocating damages, in *Pro-Sys Consultants Ltd. v. Infineon Technologies AG*,[52] the British Columbia Court of Appeal held that once the common issues trial judge has determined the aggregate amount of the loss suffered by the class, it would then be open to the trial judge to distribute the award by assessing loss on an individual basis, an average or proportional basis,[53] or a *cy pres* basis.[54] *Pro-Sys* held that after the determination of the aggregate award, the participation of the defendants would not be required.[55]

In the settlement context, experts may be retained to opine on the quantification of damages, the appropriateness of the settlement amount and an appropriate allocation of the settlement amount as between different levels or types of purchasers. Mediators may also be used to help determine an appropriate allocation, with different class counsel groups representing the interests of different purchaser groups. In the settlement context, it is not uncommon for some levels of indirect purchasers to be compensated through

48 [2007] O.J. No. 3327 (S.C.J.), aff'd [2008] O.J. No. 1973 (Div. Ct.).

49 S.O. 1992, c.6, ss. 23 and 24.

50 [2009] O.J. No. 4021 (S.C.J.), leave to appeal refused [2010] O.J. No. 2472 (S.C.J.).

51 *Ibid.* at para. 118.

52 [2008] B.C.J. No. 2239 (C.A.).

53 The class action legislation provides that where it is impractical or inefficient to identify the class members entitled to share in a damages award or to determine the exact shares that should be allocated to individual class members, damages can be awarded on an average or proportional basis. See: *Class Proceeding Act, 1992*, S.O. 1992, c.6, ss. 23, 24; *Class Proceedings Act*, R.S.B.C. 1996, c. 50, ss. 29, 30, 31; *Class Proceedings Act*, S.A. 2003, c. C-16.5, ss. 30, 31; *Class Actions Act*, S.S. 2001, c. C-12.01, ss. 31, 32, 34; *Class Proceedings Act*, C.C.S.M. c. C130, ss. 29, 30, 31; *Class Proceedings Act*, S.N.B. 2006, c. C-5.15, ss. 31, 32, 33; *Class Proceedings Act*, S.N.S. 2007, c. 28, ss. 32, 33, 34; and *Class Actions Act*, S.N.L. 2001, c. C-18.1, 29, 30, 31.

54 *Pro-Sys Consultants Ltd. v. Infineon Technologies AG*, [2008] B.C.J. No. 2239 (C.A.) at para. 70.

55 *Ibid.*

a *cy pres* distribution. Usually, *cy pres* distributions will be made to organizations that benefit the class members indirectly. This is in keeping with the meaning of *cy pres*, 'next best', and the principle that funds should generally be distributed for a purpose as near as possible to the objectives underlying the lawsuit, the interests of the class, and the interest of those similarly situated. However, the court has approved *cy pres* distributions where the class members benefit only as members of the public.[56]

If monies remain after distribution of the aggregate damages award or the settlement fund, they are often distributed *cy pres*. If there is a significant amount remaining, there may be a second distribution.

In competition law cases, plaintiffs may seek an equitable remedy in the form of declaratory relief. For example, in a price-fixing case, plaintiffs may ask for a declaration that the defendants have engaged in an unlawful conspiracy or that the defendants hold any illegal overcharge in trust for class members. Restitution is not available as a remedy for competition law claims. However, there may be some cases where plaintiffs seek restitution by framing their case as unjust enrichment.[57] In theory, plaintiffs could seek injunctive relief precluding or prescribing certain conduct on the part of the defendants, but I am not aware of any such orders having been granted in the competition law context.

Plaintiffs in a 'costs' jurisdiction (a jurisdiction where the regular costs rules apply and the losing party is required to pay the winning party's costs; these jurisdictions include Ontario, Alberta, Nova Scotia, Quebec and New Brunswick) who are successful at certification or the common issues trial may be entitled to a costs award from the defendant(s).[58] Costs recoveries are generally in the range of 60 per cent of all time incurred, plus nearly full reimbursement for expenses incurred. Plaintiffs in a 'no costs' jurisdiction cannot recover for their costs. In these jurisdictions (British Columbia, Saskatchewan, Manitoba and Newfoundland), the class action legislation precludes the court from awarding costs to any party, apart from in exceptional circumstances or where there has been improper conduct by a party in pursing the litigation.

b. Limitation periods

The limitation period for bringing a claim under the *Competition Act* is two years from the latter of the day on which the conduct was engaged in and the date on which any criminal proceedings relating thereto were finally disposed of.[59]

The limitation period for bringing a claim under the common law is generally two years. In Canada, limitation periods are based on discoverability principles. This means

---

[56] See for example: *Currie v. McDonald's Restaurants of Canada Ltd.*, 2006 Carswell Ont 1213 (S.C.J.); *Alfresh Beverages Canada Corp v. Hoechst AG et al.*, [2002] O.J. No. 79 (S.C.J.); and *Sutherland v. Boots Pharmaceutical PLC*, [2002] O.J. No. 1361 (S.C.J.).

[57] *Pettkus v. Becker*, [1980] 2 S.C.R. 834 at 848 sets out the three requirements for unjust enrichment: (1) an enrichment to the defendant; (2) a corresponding deprivation in the plaintiff; and (3) the absence of juristic reason (such as contract, disposition of law or donative intent) for the enrichment.

[58] Section 31(1) of the *Ontario Class Proceedings Act, 1992* provides that in exercising its discretion in awarding costs, the court may consider whether the class proceeding was a test case, raised a novel point of law or involved a matter of public interest.

[59] *Competition Act*, R.S.C. 1985, c. C-34, s. 36(4).

that the two-year limitation period does not begin running until the earlier of the day the person first knew that she or he has a cause of action against the defendant or the day that a reasonable person under the circumstances would first know that she or he has a cause of action against the defendant. In considering when a reasonable person would first know that he or she has a cause of action, the court will consider factors such as: the level of purchases by the plaintiff, the plaintiff's involvement in the industry, whether the plaintiff had the means to learn about the competition law claim earlier, and whether the plaintiff was aware of misconduct in related industries.[60]

9. How does a plaintiff's lawyer finance private enforcement?

Competition law cases in Canada are almost without exception financed by plaintiff's counsel through contingent fee arrangements. In Ontario, plaintiffs can apply to a public fund to help finance certain expenses associated with pursuing a class action. Plaintiffs who receive funding and are successful have to repay the fund for any funding received, plus a percentage of any settlement and/or award achieved.[61]

In the 'costs' regime provinces (Ontario, Alberta, Nova Scotia, Quebec and New Brunswick), more retainer agreements are starting to provide that class counsel will indemnify the representative plaintiff for any adverse costs award. In *Poulin v. Ford Motor Co. of Canada*,[62] the Ontario court indicated that the absence of an indemnity agreement between a proposed representative plaintiff and class counsel is 'a significant matter in the context of the plaintiff's capacity to be a representative plaintiff for a class proceeding'.[63]

Contingency fees awarded are generally within the 20 per cent to 30 per cent range, plus disbursements and applicable taxes. The reasonableness of class counsel fees is often tested using the multiplier approach, whereby fees are calculated as a multiple of docketed time. Multipliers usually range between slightly greater than one at the low end and three to four in the most difficult cases.[64] Fees can also be determined on a straight time basis[65] or a fixed-sum approach.[66] A fixed-sum approach is more common where the settlement benefits vary based on the number of claims forms submitted.[67]

Under the class proceeding legislation, class counsel's fees must be approved by the

---

[60] *Sun-Ripe Products Ltd. v. Archer Daniels Midland Co.*, [2008] B.C.J. No. 1298 (C.A.).

[61] In Ontario, where a plaintiff receives funding from the Class Proceedings Fund, he or she must pay 10 per cent of any award or settlement to the Fund, together with a return of any funded disbursements. Plaintiffs receiving funding are indemnified for costs that may be awarded against them. See www.lawfoundation.on.ca/cpcabout.php. Plaintiffs can also apply for funding in Quebec. See: *An Act Respecting the Class Action*, R.S.Q. c. R-2.1.

[62] [2006] O.J. No. 4625 (S.C.J.).

[63] *Ibid.* para. 93.

[64] *Gagne v. Silcorp.*, [1998] O.J. No. 4182 (C.A.).

[65] See for example: *Smith v. Labatt Brewing Co.*, [2009] O.J. No. 117 (S.C.J.).

[66] See for example: *Nantais v. Teletronics Proprietary (Canada) Ltd.*, [1996] O.J. No. 5386 (Gen. Div.); leave to appeal denied (1996), 28 O.R. (3d) 523n (C.A.) and *Parsons v. Canadian Red Cross Society*, [2001] O.J. No. 214 (C.A.).

[67] See for example: *Wong v. Sony Corp.* 2009 Carswell Ont 17 (S.C.J.) at para. 12; *Waddell v. Apple Computer Inc.*, 2008 Carswell Ont 4674 (S.C.J.) at paras. 25–28; and *Donnelly v. United Technologies Corp.*, 2008 Carswell Ont 3999 (S.C.J.) at para. 14.

court. In deciding whether to approve class counsel's fees, the court will take into account the following factors: the time expended by the solicitor; the legal complexity of the matters to be dealt with; the degree of responsibility assumed by the solicitor; the monetary value of the matters in issue; the importance of the matter to the client; the degree of skill and competence demonstrated by the solicitor; the results achieved; the ability of the client to pay; and the client's expectations as to the amount of the fee.[68] Where the court considers the fees sought to be excessive, it will award a lower amount.[69]

10. How does private enforcement interact with public enforcement?

In Canada, there is no interaction between private and public enforcement. The leniency program in Canada does not provide for any assistance to private plaintiffs. Plaintiffs only have access to information that is publicly available, which in most cases is limited. There is no obligation on the Competition Bureau or plaintiffs to inform one another when a case is commenced. The Competition Bureau does not have any right to participate in a civil action.

There is no state of action defense in Canada. In Canada, where there is overlapping jurisdiction over a subject matter of legislation, and the federal and provincial laws overlap and conflict, the doctrine of paramountcy provides that the federal law takes precedence over the provincial law. The *Competition Act* is federal legislation and would therefore take precedence over any provincial law purporting to deal with competition law matters.

The *Competition Act* provides that a conviction of an offense under Part VI of the *Act* is, in the absence of any evidence to the contrary, proof of conduct contrary to a provision of Part VI. Also, any evidence given in the criminal proceedings about the effect of the conduct on the plaintiff is evidence thereof.[70]

Conclusion

Although competition law class actions remain relatively novel in Canada, in that most have been resolved through settlement rather than contested proceedings, the approach being adopted by Canadian courts in adjudicating such cases is fair, balanced and pragmatic. The Canadian courts appear to be moving towards a system whereby all levels of purchasers affected by the defendants' wrongdoing can recover for their damage but there would not be duplicative recoveries. Canadian courts are also requiring evidence before enabling cases to proceed as class actions, but in doing so are adopting a realistic approach to the level of detail required at the certification stage.

---

[68] *Serwaczek v. Medical Engineering Corp.*, (1996), 3 C.P.C. (4th) 386 at 393 (Ont. Gen. Div.).

[69] See for example: *Maxwell v. MLG Ventures Ltd.*, [1996] O.J. No. 2644 (Gen. Div.) and *Martin v. Barrett,* [2008] O.J. No. 2105 (S.C.J.).

[70] *Competition Act*, R.S.C. 1985, c. C-34, s. 36(2). Some provinces have evidentiary rules to the same effect. See for example: *Ontario Evidence Act*, R.S.O. 1990 c. E. 23, s. 22.1(1); *Evidence Act*, R.S.B.C. 1996, c. 124, s.71; and *Alberta Evidence Act*, R.S.A. 2000, c. A-18, s. 26.

27 Peru

Alfredo Bullard[1] *and Alejandro Falla*[2]

Introduction

Competition law and policy was formally introduced to Peru in 1991 with the enactment of Legislative Decree 701. It was replaced in 2008 with the Law for the Repression of Anticompetitive Conduct, Legislative Decree 1034 (the Competition Law).[3]

Competition law in Peru follows the European model in several significant ways. An administrative and autonomous governmental agency, the National Institute for the Defense of the Competition and Protection of Intellectual Property (INDECOPI), is the primary enforcer of competition law. Its primary enforcement tools are administrative sanctions. INDECOPI has no authority to award damages.

Unlike other jurisdictions, the jurisdiction of INDECOPI is exclusive, not allowing individuals to resort before or simultaneously to any other administrative authority or court before the exhaustion of administrative proceedings in the agency.

The model does not promote private actions. Even though antitrust damages actions are contemplated in the Competition Law, they do not have an important role in this model. INDECOPI has no jurisdiction to award damages. There are no direct private actions before courts as actions before courts are conditioned upon the exhaustion of administrative proceedings at INDECOPI. In addition, the Competition Law does not encourage damages actions with measures such as punitive or treble damages.

Private actions are restricted even within proceedings brought before INDECOPI. These proceedings are always initiated ex officio, whether or not a private party has filed a complaint.

The Peruvian model is based on a public enforcement action by INDECOPI. The enforcement of the Competition Law and compliance are basically achieved by the imposition of administrative sanctions by INDECOPI.

1. Private actions

Direct private actions to enforce the Competition Law before ordinary courts are not allowed. Courts can review decisions of the competition agency once the administrative procedure is concluded. Then the sanctioned firm or the person who filed the

---

[1] Lawyer. Master of Laws (LL.M.), Yale Law School. Principal Professor at Pontificia Universidad Católica del Perú. Visiting Professor of Competition Law, Master Program, at Universidad Torcuato di Tella, Argentina. Bullard, Falla & Ezcurra Law Firm Partner.

[2] Lawyer. Master (Msc) in Regulation, London School of Economics and Political Sciences. Professor of Competition and Regulation at Pontificia Universidad Católica del Perú. Visiting Professor of Competition Law, Master Program, at Universidad Torcuato di Tella, Argentina. Bullard, Falla & Ezcurra Law Firm Partner.

[3] Published in the Official Gazette on June 25, 2008.

administrative claim can file a judicial action so the decision made by INDECOPI can be reviewed by the ordinary courts.

Private damages actions may be filed directly by the injured parties only when the administrative procedure before the competition agency is finished, never before or concurrently.[4]

During the 18 years of existence of the Competition Law, there is no record of a successful claim for private damage.[5] In this matter, the situation is very similar to the European one.[6]

The judicial precedents are very few and poor; therefore, it is impossible to make conclusions or establish important principles. In general, courts have not participated actively in the application of the Competition Law and in the revision of INDECOPI's decisions. Partly because the Competition Law is rather recent, the number of cases pursued by INDECOPI is small and even smaller is the number of INDECOPI's resolutions appealed before the courts by private parties. In addition, the extensive delay in the review process of the courts impedes one having a good record of court decisions on antitrust matters. For example, to date, the final court decision on the well known Chicken Cartel Case sanctioned by INDECOPI in 1997[7] is still pending.[8] Finally, the information

---

[4] Legislative Decree 1034. Article 49 – Compensation for Damages: Once the administrative procedure is finished, any person that has suffered damages as a result of anticompetitive conduct declared by the Commission or by the Tribunal, even if he or she is not party to the procedure followed before INDECOPI, may claim compensation for damage before the judiciary provided he or she is capable of showing a connection with the declared anticompetitive conduct.

[5] OECD (2004), 'Competition Law and Policy in Peru, A Peer Review', p.52, http://www.oecd.org/dataoecd/34/12/34728182.pdf. As noted on the OECD Peer Review 'Even when INDECOPI proceedings are initiated by a private party claiming that the defendant's illegal conduct has caused injuries, the Commissions are not authorized to order payment of damages. However, if a Commission finds that a defendant has engaged in illegal conduct, the Commission's finding will be conclusive proof of the violation if a complainant files suit in civil court for damages. It is unclear whether any such cases have ever been brought.'

[6] http://ec.europa.eu/competition/antitrust/actionsdamages/index.html.

[7] Redondos S.A, Avícolas Asociadas S. A., Asociación Peruana de Avicultura, Molinos Mayo S.A. F. Car. S.A. , Corporación Ganadera S.A, Agropecuaria del Pilar S.A., El Palomar EIRL, Granja Avícola Galeb EIRL, Alimentos Protina S.A., Molinera San Martin de Porres S.A., German Orbezo Suarez y Avicola San Fernando S.A. contra INDECOPI y otro. Exp 878-2008. Supreme Court's Constitutional and Social Chamber. For a general description of the case, see: OECD (2001) 'Global Forum on Competition', http://www.oecd.org/dataoecd/18/20/23716869.pdf.

[8] OECD (2004), 'Competition Law and Policy in Peru. A Peer Review', p. 52, http://www.oecd.org/dataoecd/34/12/34728182.pdf. 'INDECOPI's most impressive case is the well-known 1997 Chicken Case, which found that Peruvian poultry firms and their association engaged in price fixing by agreeing to prevent new entries, excluded some existing competitors, and limit the availability of live poultry for sale in order to raise or maintain prices. Total fines were initially set at slightly over USD 5 million, but were later reduced to slightly over USD 2 million. Unfortunately, the Chicken Case is also a good example of the serious deficiencies in Peru's judicial system. The case was appealed to the Courts in 1997, and there still has been no decision. The slow nature of judicial review is not a substantial problem with respect to most of INDECOPI's functions because relatively few cases are appealed, but 90 percent of the competition law enforcement cases are appealed.'

system on judicial decisions is quite limited, making access to the decisions issued by the Peruvian courts on antitrust matters very difficult: there are no public records of private claims for damages or for review of decisions rendered by INDECOPI; also, there are no public records of final court decisions on these cases.

2. Antitrust legislation

In 2008, the Peruvian Government launched an initiative to introduce changes in several laws with the purpose of making the current internal market regulation compatible with the Free Trade Agreement entered into by Peru and the US.[9]

The proposal included quasi-mandatory arbitration for damages actions arising out of anticompetitive conduct declared as such by the competition agency.[10] This proposal was not accepted by the Executive and the arbitration mechanism for damages was removed from the draft prepared by INDECOPI and does not appear in the enacted Competition Law.

It is expected that proposals for improving the ability to bring private claims for damages will emerge in the future in order to strengthen private actions as a mechanism of enforcement of the Competition Law. The recent elimination of criminal sanctions for anticompetitive conduct[11] makes the reinforcement of private actions vital so as to avoid weakening the incentives of compliance with the Competition Law. Today the only effective deterrence mechanism is the administrative fine, because there are no criminal sanctions and private damages actions are ineffective.

3. Development of the competition law 1991–2008

Competition law and policy were formally introduced to Peru in 1991 with the enactment of Legislative Decree 701.

The first Competition Law, enacted in 1991, was replaced in June 2008 by the Law for the Repression of Anticompetitive Conduct approved by Legislative Decree 1034.

The prohibitions included in the Competition Law are similar to Articles 81 and 82 on the European side.[12] There is no pre-merger control except for transactions involving the electricity market.[13]

The essential enforcement model set forth in the Competition Law enacted originally

[9] The United States–Peru Trade Promotion Agreement (April, 2006).

[10] In the explanatory statement of Legislative Decree 1034 drafted by INDECOPI and sent to the Executive for its revision and approval was pointed out the following: 'Article 49 of the Bill regulates damage compensation resulting from anticompetitive practices sanctioned by the competition agency'.

[11] The Competition Law enacted in 2008 – Legislative Decree 1034 – repealed the criminal sanction for antitrust violations in force since 1991.

[12] The new Competition Law enacted in June 2008 – Legislative Decree 1034 – is applicable to all individuals and entities that engage in economic activity as well as to all individuals who direct or represent such entities. On December 1, 2009, the Treaty of Lisbon came into effect, amending the Treaty Establishing the European Community (EC Treaty) that is now called the Treaty on the Functioning of the European Union (TFEU). Therefore, all references to Articles 81 and 82 of the EC Treaty now reference Articles 101 and 102 TFEU.

[13] Both under Legislative Decree 701 and under Legislative Decree 1034.

in 1991 was not amended in 2008 reform: it is focused more on public instruments and agents (INDECOPI) than on private actions. [14]

Proceedings are not of a private nature and do not aim to compensate private parties for damage caused by anticompetitive conduct. INDECOPI has no authority to award damages to the complainants.

Decisions of the Commission may be appealed by the parties – third parties cannot appeal INDECOPI's decisions – to the Competition Tribunal also of INDECOPI – the second administrative instance. The INDECOPI Tribunal's decisions may also be challenged (on administrative and constitutional grounds), first in the Administrative Chamber of the Superior Court of Lima, and secondarily in the Civil Chamber of Peru's Supreme Court. Exceptionally, there may be third-instance appeals to the Supreme Court's Constitutional and Social Chamber.

4. Private damages actions

The Peruvian Competition Law, without prejudice to the administrative sanctions, provides for civil liability in tort cases as applied to claims for economic and non-economic damages in antitrust. The Law provides for the possibility of initiating private damages actions. There is no direct private action for damages before courts: actions before courts are conditioned to the exhaustion of administrative proceedings before INDECOPI.[15]

Article 49 of the Competition Law regulates the recovery of damages relating to antitrust actions. This article sets forth the victim's right to recover damages, that is, to claim compensation for economic and non-economic damage resulting from anticompetitive behavior, and establishes the cause of action.

There is no specific regulation as to possible defenses or how damages shall be

---

[14] OECD (2004), 'Competition Law and Policy in Peru. A Peer Review', p. 13, http://www.oecd.org/dataoecd/34/12/34728182.pdf.

[15] In a recent case the Supreme Court has declared that private damages actions related to tort liability based on antitrust violations can only be initiated once the proceedings before INDECOPI have been concluded. The judgment issued by the Second Civil Court of the Superior Court of Callao on March 14, 2007 in Fábricas de Productos Lave S.R. LTDA vs. Clorox Perú S.A., Químpac S.A. and others (Case No 1273-2006) revoked the decision issued at first instance declaring inadmissible the exception filed by the defendants for not concluding the administrative procedure. Hence, the court sustained that: 'NINTH: The Organization and Functions Law of the National Institute for the Defense of the Competition and Protection of Intellectual Property – INDECOPI, Law No. 25868, provides in its Article 16 that "In issues related to competition of any of its functional bodies it is not allowed to resort to the Judiciary while the administrative procedure has not been previously exhausted. For these effects it is understood that the administrative procedure is exhausted only when the Tribunal of the Defense of the Competition and Intellectual Property issues its resolution"'.

This criterion was confirmed in the Resolution of the First Civil Court of the Supreme Court on December 2007 (Civil Cassation No. 2761-2007) that declared groundless the cassation resource filed by Fábricas de Productos Lave S. R. LTDA, sentencing the claimant with a sanction of Three Procedural Reference Units plus costs and expenses. For additional reference see: Santistevan de Noriega, Jorge, 'Responsabilidad Extracontractual Derivada de Conductas Anticompetitivas: Tipicidad, Antijuricidad y calificación previa por parte de la Administración', Revista de la Competencia y la Propiedad Intelectual Nº 6, http://www.indecopi.gob.pe/ArchivosPortal/boletines/recompi/castellano/articulos/otono2008/Santistevan.pdf.

assessed or proven. As a consequence, antitrust damages actions are treated as ordinary civil liability cases (basically tort actions), and thus civil liability rules and procedure apply.

According to Article 49, once the administrative proceedings brought before INDECOPI are concluded, any individual or entity that has been injured by a breach of the Competition Law and that can prove causation between the infringement and the damage, can seek compensation under the civil liability rules before judicial civil courts.

If the agency has found that a defendant was engaged in illegal conduct, the finding will be conclusive proof of the violation if a complainant files suit for damages before the courts. INDECOPI's decision is binding for the court which is adjudicating the claim on damages and it cannot modify the conclusions reached by INDECOPI in its decision. The court's decision will be limited to identifying the alleged damage and determining the appropriate compensation.

The Law does not contemplate the direct or indirect participation of INDECOPI in private tort actions for damage compensation arising from an antitrust violation. INDECOPI's participation to assist the court is a theoretical possibility, but it does not appear to have been considered. It is likely that INDECOPI may be reluctant to voluntarily participate in this type of proceedings 'of private interest', unless it is expressly required to do so by the court.

Several obstacles make it difficult for victims to recover damages stemming from anticompetitive conduct. One is the undeveloped rules governing private tort actions for Competition Law violations. Another is the failure to allow joint actions in single proceedings both to determine a breach of the Antitrust Law and to compensate the victim for the antitrust injury – victims must initiate separate actions, one before INDECOPI and, later, a compensation action before judicial civil courts – together with the lack of appropriate coordination between such proceedings, which explains to a great extent the limited progress that private damages actions have had in our country. Since damages actions can only be initiated once the administrative decisions are final, the system condemns antitrust victims to wait no less than three to five years before they can initiate an action for damages, and at least four to six additional years before they can receive some compensation for the damage suffered. The waiting period for the victim can increase significantly if INDECOPI's decision is challenged before the judiciary.

In practice, all of the above results in no enforcement of antitrust damages actions, weakening the Competition Law enforcement system. There is no record of a successful damages action during the 17 years since the enactment of Legislative Decree 701. As a matter of fact, it is unclear how many damages actions have ever been brought under this Law since 1991.[16]

At least two proceedings for damage compensation arising from a violation of the Competition Law filed before the court by victims are unofficially known about. In the first case (Fábricas de Productos Laive S. R. LTDA), the victim resorted directly to the courts claiming damage compensation for anticompetitive conduct committed by

[16] See OECD (2004), 'Competition Law and Policy in Peru. A Peer Review', p. 52, http://www.oecd.org/dataoecd/34/12/34728182.pdf.

Clorox Perú SA and Quimpac. In this case, the victim had not previously filed a claim before INDECOPI nor had INDECOPI issued any decision on the alleged conduct prior to its submission to the courts. As already mentioned, the First Civil Court of the Supreme Court on December 2007 (Civil Cassation No. 2761-2007) upheld the judgment issued by the Second Civil Court of the Superior Court of Callao on March 14, 2007 that revoked the decision issued in first instance declaring inadmissible the exception filed by the defendants for not concluding the administrative procedure. Hence, the criterion that victims cannot file direct actions before the courts for damage compensation resulting from violations to the Competition Law was confirmed; they must previously exhaust a proceeding before INDECOPI.

In the second case, the victim (Depósitos Santa Beatriz S.R.L.) resorted to court claiming damage compensation for anticompetitive conduct by Distribuidora Norte Pacasmayo S.R.L. In this case, INDECOPI had previously issued its decision sanctioning the anticompetitive conduct of Distribuidora Norte Pacasmayo S.R.L for violation of the Competition Law (price discrimination and tied clauses). The action was initiated by the victim at the same time as the sanctioned company (Distribuidora Norte Pacasmayo S.R.L.) initiated action before the court appealing INDECOPI's decision (*contencioso administrativo*, administrative proceeding). Final resolution in both proceedings is pending.

5. Active legitimacy and class actions

An action for damages is open to any individual able to prove the damage and causation, regardless of its prior participation in the administrative procedure before INDECOPI. There is no limitation to the direct or indirect participation of purchasers, competitors, suppliers, consumers or other members of the public; they all have standing to initiate a damages action. The determination of such link will be made under the general liability rules of the Civil Code (Tort Law).[17]

The Peruvian Civil Procedure Law allows for two forms of collective actions: '*Intereses difusos*' (diffuse interests) and '*intereses colectivos*' (collective interests).[18] Diffuse interests relate to cases where it is impossible to determine who is entitled to the rights at issue, due to the great number or difficulty in identifying all of the stakeholders. Collective interests refer to the cases in which there is a class or a group of people or entities entitled to the right.[19] Under these categories, Peruvian legislation provides for the existence of class actions in order for consumers to claim personal injury and monetary losses before the judiciary.

Under Peruvian law class actions may be filed by communitarian entities authorized to litigate on behalf of such interests. Since 1996, consumer protection class actions may be filed by INDECOPI itself on behalf of consumers,[20] or by any public or private entity

---

[17] Civil Code, Articles 1969 to 1988.

[18] José Ovalle Favela 'Popular Actions For the Protection of Collective Interests', General paper presented during the 7th International Seminar on Formation and Characteristics of the Latin American Legal System and Problems of Civil Proceedings, May, 2002, available at: http://info8.juridicas.unam.mx/cont/mlawr/5/arc/arc7.htm#N*.

[19] Civil Procedure Code, Article 82.

[20] Legislative Decree 716, Article 51, as amended by Legislative Decree 807 of 1996.

empowered by INDECOPI (through registration) to fulfil this role.[21] These actions may include those for antitrust damages.[22]

Registration by INDECOPI is required for consumers' associations interested in representing consumers in collective actions brought before the institution. Registration is automatic. However, the Commission for Consumer Protection of INDECOPI is in charge of assessing the documentation submitted for the registration and can annul registrations if the association does not fulfil the legal requirements.

In addition, INDECOPI can directly file class actions before ordinary courts, to claim for damage caused to consumers. INDECOPI will represent all consumers affected by the alleged claim provided that the latter do not express their will to initiate private actions within 30 days after the publication of the summary of the claim in the Official Gazette. A summary of the statement of claim will be published in order to afford consumers not wishing to be represented an opportunity to opt out.

The final decision by the ordinary courts may order compensation, the refund of amounts already paid, and whatever is necessary to protect consumers' interests. If the respective judge or court orders the payment of compensation, it will be collected and the amount will be divided by the court among the consumers attending the proceedings and proving their injury.

In the case of collective actions pursued by INDECOPI on behalf of consumers, INDECOPI manages the distribution and payment of damages. Under the Consumer Protection Act, if the court or judge awards the payment of damages, the amount will be transferred to INDECOPI. INDECOPI will then distribute the compensation among the consumers that can prove a legitimate interest together with their injury before INDECOPI. In these cases, once one year has elapsed the unclaimed balance will be set aside and used to finance education for consumers and to promote new class actions. The destination and use of those unclaimed funds have not yet been regulated. The answers to some relevant questions, for example who can use those funds (INDECOPI, private lawyers) remain uncertain.

De facto, since 1996,[23] INDECOPI has not exercised directly or indirectly its ability to file class actions. Therefore no precedents exist on such matter. In general, to date no one has filed class actions for tort claims in antitrust.

Again, the undeveloped law governing class actions in Competition Law, the failure to join actions in single proceedings and the lack of appropriate coordination between the proceedings stemming from antitrust violations (administrative proceeding at INDECOPI, '*contencioso administrativo*' at the appellate courts and private actions for damages) can explain to a great extent the minimal development that private damages actions have had in Peru.

---

21 Directive No. 001-2003-INDECOPI/DIR on Regulations for the Intervention of Consumer Associations in Administrative Procedures before the Consumer Protection Commission and other Functional Bodies of INDECOPI, provides that consumers' associations may legally participate in proceedings of violations of the Competition Law except for those cases subject to the Antimonopoly and Antioligopoly Law in the electricity sector.

22 Legislative Decree 716, Article 51, as amended by Legislative Decree 807 of 1996.

23 This power was given to INDECOPI through the enactment of Legislative Decree 807 in 1996.

6. Statute of limitation

The statute of limitations applicable to antitrust injury is two years, if the cause of action for an antitrust liability lawsuit is based on a tort action.[24] The Competition Law does not impose any limitation on the duration of such action.

There are no rules established under the Law on how to calculate the beginning or suspension of such term. This fact hinders the development of private actions for damages due to the possibility that the administrative procedure before INDECOPI and the lawsuit before a court may last more than two years. The private damages action may be affected by the delay in such proceedings: administrative proceedings before INDECOPI may last at least three years. Private damages actions may be affected or impeded because of the delay in INDECOPI proceedings.[25]

7. Civil procedure and damages claim: jurisdiction and venue

In Peru, civil procedure is ruled by the Civil Procedure Code (CPC), in force since 1993, applicable throughout the country. Cases are decided by the civil Courts of First Instance; by the Superior Courts (*Cortes Superiores*) in the second instance; and, finally, by the Peruvian Supreme Court, located in Lima.[26]

Civil courts also handle damages actions arising out of antitrust injury. These cases follow the same private damages rules as any torts or contractual liability matter and are thus governed by civil liability procedural rules and jurisdiction.

The parties cannot select the judge to be in charge of their case; whenever a claim is submitted, it is assigned randomly to a certain judge. The Peruvian procedural system is similar to the majority of Latin American procedural systems which do not have a federal governmental structure; there is no difference between national or state court and there are no courts or special commissions to deal with this type of action either. The action should be initiated – according to the claimant's choice – before the civil judge on duty of the actual domicile of the defendant or of the place where the event that caused the damage occurred.[27]

Actions initiated by several victims may be joined in a single damages proceeding (either at the beginning or in the course of the proceeding) provided such actions deal with claims arising from the 'same title' (INDECOPI's Condemnatory Resolution), relate to the same object (claim for compensation), have a connection among them and are within the jurisdiction of the same judge. They may not be contradictory to one another.[28]

---

[24] Civil Code, Article 2001, paragraph 4.

[25] The term begins once there is a final decision by INDECOPI establishing that there was an infringement of the Competition Law.

[26] The Courts of First Instance are the trial courts. Each has jurisdiction over one of the 195 Peruvian provinces. There are more than 480 Courts of First Instance throughout the country. They are presided over by only one judge, whose jurisdiction varies according to the defendant's domicile and the amount in dispute. The Superior Courts are the courts of appeal on the decisions of the Courts of First Instance. The Superior Courts have jurisdiction over an entire Judicial District. There are 28 Judicial Districts in Peru. The Supreme Court of Justice in Lima is the highest judicial court in Peru. Its jurisdiction extends over the entire territory of the nation.

[27] Civil Procedure Code, Article 24.

[28] Civil Procedure Code Articles 85 and 89.

8. Civil Procedure Rules

According to the CPC, the lawsuit is initiated with the filing of the claim, that is, when the plaintiff submits its complaints in writing indicating who will be the defendant. After the judge assigned to the case approves the claim, summonses are issued in order for the defendant to submit its answer or its counterclaim, as the case may be, which must be answered by the plaintiff. All these pleas must be based on factual and legal grounds to be admitted and to be subject of the judge's determination of the merits of the case. In all cases, summonses are served simultaneously with the pleas.

Preclusion is a very important principle in the CPC. Thus, the claim must be answered within a deadline, upon expiration of which the defendant will be charged with civil contempt. Additionally, the evidence must be submitted or requested on time, that is, together with the claim, the answer to the claim, the counterclaim and the answer to the counterclaim. Usually, evidence submitted or requested by the parties after the first stage of pleadings has concluded will be rejected.

At the pleadings stage, the defendant, besides answering the claim, is allowed to raise its defenses which in the civil law system are known as *exceptio dilatoria* (a dilatory exception – 'one which defeated the action for a time and created delay'[29]) or *exceptio peremptoria* (a peremptory exception – 'one which forever destroyed the subject-matter or ground of the action'[30]).

The pleadings stage concludes when the judge decides on all pending motions, either rejecting or accepting them. If any motion is accepted then the judge invites the parties to attempt to settle the action, and if this does not occur the judge proceeds to determine the matters at issue.

9. Obtaining evidence: discovery system

Evidence production in Peru is governed by the preclusion principle. Evidence must be submitted together with the claim, the answer to the claim, the counterclaim and the answer to the counterclaim. All evidence submitted after the conclusion of the pleadings stage will be rejected.

However, there are exceptions to this rule: if the party was not able to submit or request the evidence from the defendants or third parties during the pleadings stage, this new evidence will be accepted. Likewise, if new facts relevant to solving the controversy arise, the evidence meant to credit those facts will also be accepted.

Generally, evidence can be introduced to the trial by the parties (*ex parte*) or if the judge orders it, even though neither of the parties requested the introduction of the additional evidence to the process (*ex officio*).

All evidence introduced must be used by the court to determine the facts of the lawsuit, regardless of whether it affects or benefits the party submitting such evidence. However, unlike the general obligation of exchanging documentation subject to disclosure, in the Peruvian system the documentation in the possession of one of the parties or of a third party is disclosed only if one of the parties explicitly requests it and the judge orders its presentation. The court *ex officio* may also order its presentation. In short, in

---

29 Henry C. Black, Black's Law Dictionary, definition of 'Exceptio Dilatoria'.

30 Henry C. Black, Black's Law Dictionary, definition of 'Exceptio Peremptoria'.

Peru the documents disclosure needs to be made through the court and is subject to its approval.

According to the CPC, all evidence for the purpose of determining the facts of the case will be admitted, including witnesses, expert opinions, visual inspection of material evidence by the judge, parties' sworn statements and documents. Likewise, in accordance with the CPC, the trial court is entitled to use presumptions and circumstantial evidence to supplement the failure of a party to introduce direct evidence. Nevertheless, the tendency of the Peruvian courts is not to use circumstantial evidence.

If during the civil procedure in court the evidence previously produced in the proceeding before INDECOPI is required, the court has the obligation to keep confidential the information that was declared and kept confidential during the proceeding before INDECOPI.[31]

The Competition Law expressly creates a mechanism for the exoneration from sanctions (administrative sanction) of those individuals furnishing evidence that helps to identify and prove the existence of an illegal practice (leniency).[32] Such exoneration does not release the petitioner from liability for damages.[33]

The documents submitted as part of the leniency program cannot be used as evidence in these proceedings. INDECOPI and its officials are obligated to keep confidential the identity of the individuals who apply for leniency, as well as the negotiations related to the granting of such benefit.[34] The privilege does not apply to evidence furnished during the INDECOPI proceedings.

Leniency programs have not been very successful. There are very few cases where the program was effectively activated, and we cannot say that it is an important tool in competition law enforcement.

There are no provisions under the Competition Law providing for a specific privilege with respect to communications between the client and his lawyer. There are, however, several provisions in other regulations that allow the affected party (the lawyer or the client) to exercise such privileges in the proceedings brought before INDECOPI and the courts for violations of the Competition Law.[35]

---

[31] Directive No. 001-2008/TRI-INDECOPI, subparagraph 4.6, Confidentiality of Information in the Procedures followed by the Functional Bodies of INDECOPI.

[32] Legislative Decree 1034, Article 26.

[33] Legislative Decree 1034, Article 26.4.

[34] Legislative Decree 1034, Article 26.

[35] The Constitution recognizes the right to keep professional secrecy (Article 2, subparagraph 18); the Competition Law itself establishes INDECOPI's obligation to keep confidential all information disclosure of which may cause harm to the titleholder (Article 32 of the Law). In addition, the criteria of the Law of Transparency and Access to Public Information (Law 27806) should be applied by INDECOPI in the evaluation of the information that must be declared confidential. Article 32 of the Law establishes as confidential information – except for the right of access to public information – 'The information prepared or obtained by legal counsels or lawyers of public entities which publicity may disclose the strategy to adopt in the processing or defense of an administrative or judicial procedure, or any kind of information under professional secrecy that the lawyer must keep in respect of his client. This exception expires at the conclusion of the proceeding' (Law 27806. Article 15-B subparagraph 4).

10. Gathering of evidence

Once the evidence is admitted, the court starts the collection of information through the hearings. There is a special hearing for this purpose, called 'Evidence Retrieval Hearing'. This hearing opens with the experts' opinions, followed by the witnesses' sworn statements, the documents discovery requested by the parties and, finally, the parties' sworn statements.

Prior to the hearing, the parties' statements are not recorded in writing. On the contrary, if during the pleadings stage one of the parties requests a sworn statement of the other party or a sworn statement of a witness, the latter is obligated to submit such statement in a sealed envelope. This envelope is to be opened by the judge at the hearing. On the basis of this sworn statement the judge interrogates the deponent party and/or the witness. During the pleadings stage, cross-examination is permitted. As opposed to the litigating parties, the trial court has subpoena powers over the witnesses.

With respect to experts' opinions, the CPC allows each party to hire its own expert, provided that during the pleadings that right has already been reserved. The parties may also request the trial court to appoint an expert. Such request must be made during the pleadings stage. Normally, experts' reports are discussed during the hearing and must be delivered in writing to the trial court and the parties prior to the hearing, in order for the parties and the judge to be able to cross-examine the experts during the hearing.

11. Damages

In the Peruvian legal framework, damages are mainly treated as a mechanism to compensate the victim for a particular injury and not to deter unlawful actions. The principle of full compensation applies, implying that the award must place the victim in a position as close as possible to that in which it would have been had the damage not occurred. Damages must be limited to compensate the loss actually suffered or direct damage (*damnum emergens*) and loss of profits (*lucrum cessans*). There are no punitive damages in the Peruvian system. In very limited cases, moral damages for individuals are admitted as part of the compensation.

Pursuant to both the Competition Law and Article 1985 of the Civil Procedure Code, victims are entitled to compensation for property damage resulting from antitrust violations. There is no rule establishing restrictions for the recoverable amount of damages, other than that those damages have to be proven to have been caused by the antitrust violation.

There are no special rules related to damages distribution. The only exception is related to the class actions conducted by INDECOPI on behalf of consumers or by any public or private entity authorized by INDECOPI. In this case, the following special arrangements apply.[36]

In accordance with Article 46 of the Competition Law,[37] INDECOPI may implement corrective measures aimed at reestablishing the competitive process.[38] According to

---

[36] Legislative Decree 716, Article 51.

[37] Legislative Decree 1034, Article 46.

[38] In recent years, the Constitutional Tribunal, Peru's highest judicial authority for interpreting the Constitution and deciding the constitutionality of Laws and regulations, has acknowledged INDECOPI's authority to order 'corrective measures' even when the measures affect the

the Competition Law these may consist of, but are not limited to, the following: (1) an order to do or cease doing, or not to engage in a particular form of conduct, which may be conditioned to certain circumstances; (2) an order to deal under certain conditions; (3) a determination concerning the unenforceability of contractual provisions, or other private provisions deemed anticompetitive; and (4) an order to allow access to a party to an association or organization.

In its precedents, INDECOPI has classified its 'corrective measures' as either structural – when divestiture is implied in the decision – or behavioral – when they refer to a duty to behave in a certain way or to refrain from a certain behavior.[39] INDECOPI has only rarely ordered corrective measures such as requiring one party to deal with another. Examples of behavioral corrective measures ordered by the Commission include termination of tying and bundling agreements.[40] Recently, in a case involving the railway industry, INDECOPI ordered a behavioral measure consisting of a duty to deal, by leasing railway assets to competitors.[41] Structural measures, for example a division or reorganization of a firm, have never been ordered by INDECOPI.

Corrective measures can only be taken by INDECOPI in an administrative procedure or by the court in a lawsuit initiated to review INDECOPI's decision. These measures cannot be taken by the court in a proceeding for damages.

12. Costs and funding

The losing party is usually required to pay the lawyer's fees of the winning party, the costs of evidence gathering, and, in general, all additional expenses related to the trial. In some cases, courts exonerate the losing party from paying the trial expenses if it deems that (1) the plaintiff who has lost had sufficient and reasonable grounds to file the claim, or (2) the defenses raised by the defendant who has lost were based on reasonable grounds and therefore the plaintiff's claim was not fully accepted: Articles 410[42] and 411.[43]

In the case of claims for damages it is possible to arrive at a settlement putting an end to the claim. This settlement may include part or cover all of the lawyer's fees. In Peru contingency fees are permitted, so the settlement of those fees is also accepted. The only restriction is in the Code of Ethics of the Lima Bar Association that establishes that the amount received by the lawyer may not exceed that of his client.[44]

---

infringing party's freedom of contract, an aspect which is adjudicated in ordinary courts (Case N° 1963-2006-AA/TC (Ferretería Salvador S.R.L.).

[39] Ferrocarril Santuario Inca Machu Picchu S.A.C., Organismo Supervisor de la Inversión en Infraestructura de Transporte de Uso Público – Ositran v. Ferrocarril Trasandino S.A. (Case 1122-2007/TDC-INDECOPI).

[40] Depósitos Santa Beatriz S.R.L. , Eleodoro Quiroga Ramos E.I.R.L., Comercial Quiroga S.R.L. v. Distribuidora Norte Pacasmayo S.R.L. (Case N° 256-2005/TDC).

[41] Ferrocarril Santuario Inca Machu Picchu S.A.C., Organismo Supervisor de la Inversión en Infraestructura de Transporte de Uso Público – Ositran v. Ferrocarril Trasandino S.A.. (Case 1122-2007/TDC-INDECOPI).

[42] Procedural Civil Code, Article 410.

[43] Procedural Civil Code, Article 411 provides a definition of the costs and expenses as well as the rules for their distribution.

[44] Code of Ethics of the Peruvian Bar Associations, Article 35, http://www.cal.org.pe/Inst_codigo_etica_abo_cal.html.

Conclusion

As it can be inferred from the discussion above, in the field of damages actions for violations of the antitrust legislation everything is yet to be developed. There are no specific cases in torts or civil liability that can be worthy of special mention and, in actuality, those injured by such practices do not file actions for damages before the courts. In the authors' opinion, there are two causes for that:

1) In general, the minimal use of tort actions is mainly due to the reduced amount of the compensation obtained in these actions, including the costs of conducting the lawsuit (ordinary courts in Peru are known for awarding clearly below compensatory damages in tort actions), and the extremely long periods for which the processes brought in the ordinary courts last; and
2) The legal framework is not favorable towards damages lawsuits for violations of the Competition Law, including the long wait for the conclusion of the administrative procedures before a civil damages action can be initiated.

It is rather unlikely that there will be significant developments in this matter in the coming years if a reform of the Competition Law is not considered. However, we hope that, due to the relevance that the Competition Law has gained in recent years, the interest in introducing the necessary reforms will increase.

PART V

ASIA, AFRICA AND AUSTRALIA

28 Overview of Asia and Africa

Byung Geon Lee[1] *and Ke Li*[2]

The intensity of private antitrust enforcement across the Asian and African nations has a wide range of variation. In Australia, Israel, Japan, and Korea, the number of private damages actions has gradually increased. Many private actions in those nations are initiated following the competition agencies' finding of antitrust violations. For example, the Korea Fair Trade Commission (KFTC) annually finds approximately 40 cartels guilty, and private parties have commonly brought damages actions after the KFTC's corrective measures. In contrast, private antitrust enforcement of many other countries in these regions remains inactive in tandem with the comparatively weak public enforcement regimes. To the extent that private enforcement is restrained, this seems to be in large part the result of the limited ability of private parties to gather evidence independently.

Asian and African nations' private antitrust enforcement procedures also have broad variations. For example, class action procedures, which can provide workable litigation mechanisms for the mass wrongs of competition law, are varying. The opt-out class action mechanism is available in Australia, Israel, Indonesia, and South Africa; however, no antitrust damages actions have been filed in the latter two countries utilizing this opt-out device as of May 2009. Most other Asian and African jurisdictions have a traditional opt-in class action mechanism, under which each injured party must individually express his or her interest in participating in the action. As a third method, Indonesia, Japan, Korea, and Taiwan permit an association lawsuit which certain qualified associations can bring on behalf of aggrieved consumers. It remains to be seen whether this method will be vigorously utilized in antitrust matters.

This overview addresses the current state of Asian and African jurisdictions' private antitrust enforcement, with a focus on recent institutional improvements that could provide policy implications to other similarly situated countries. We do not necessarily limit this review to the countries covered by chapters in this book.

Two noteworthy private enforcement cases

The international vitamins cartel (Vitamins) case of Australia and the school uniform cartel (School Uniform) case of Korea are particularly noteworthy in light of the recent development of private antitrust enforcement in these regions.

The Vitamins case is notable because it is the first opt-out antitrust class action initiated within Asia and Africa.[3] In 1999, an Australian law firm initiated this class action

[1] Research Fellow, The American Antitrust Institute.

[2] Summer Research Fellow, The American Antitrust Institute.

[3] *See* Kim Parker, *Class Actions*, International Class Actions Conference 2007, Sydney, Australia (25–26 October 2007), *available at* http://www.mauriceblackburn.com.au/news/newsletters/pdfs/KParker_paper.pdf. Further illustrations of the Vitamins case in this overview are based on the same article.

against the three defendants for price-fixing and market sharing arrangements in the Australian animal vitamins market, after the Australian Competition and Consumer Commission (ACCC)'s initiation of the investigation. The class member was defined as a person who bought more than AUD2,000 worth of defendants' vitamin products between 1992 and 1999. In 2006, the court approved the proposed settlement by which the defendants paid compensation of AUD30.5 million and paid additional AUD10.5 million as litigation costs.

The School Uniform case is noteworthy in light of both the active initiatives of consumers' associations and the large number of consumers participating through the opt-in class action mechanism.[4] A group of consumers' associations initiated the class action in 2002 against three school uniform manufacturers, which together possessed more than 50 per cent market shares in the Korean school uniform market. The KFTC's finding of violation in 2001 motivated this damages suit. Approximately 3,500 parents who bought school uniforms from the defendants signed up for the litigation. In 2007, the court ruled that the defendants were liable for KRW 240 million to the parents. The number of plaintiffs who signed up for the claim is believed to be the largest in terms of opt-in mechanism in Asia as of May 2009.

Statutory basis for private enforcement of competition law

Most Asian and African competition laws provide a specific statutory basis for private enforcement irrespective of civil law or common law tradition. For example, in Japan, a civil law country, Articles 24 and 25 of its Anti-Monopoly Act provide the basis for private parties' rights to injunctive relief and damages. In Australia, a common law country, Articles 80 and 82 of its Trade Practices Act provide for the same private rights. China, a civil law country with a socialist heritage, enacted its own Anti-Monopoly Law, Article 50, in August 2008 and endorsed similar civil liabilities.[5] Other countries, including Egypt, India, Israel, Kenya, Korea, Saudi Arabia, South Africa, and Taiwan, also have specific provisions for private enforcement in their competition laws.[6]

When private damages rights are provided under both the general civil code and the competition law in parallel, substantial differences may exist with respect to litigation procedure, burden of proof, etc. For example, the Japanese and Korean competition laws alleviate the claimants' burden of proof. In Japan, the claimants do not need to prove the defendants' intention or negligence if they pursue damages rights under the Anti-Monopoly Act.[7] In exchange for this benefit, a damages action cannot be initiated prior to the issuance of a cease and desist order by the Japan Fair Trade Commission

---

4 *See* the Korean Chapter.

5 Anti-Monopoly Law of P.R. China, art 50.

6 *See generally* Law on the Protection of Competition and the Prohibition of the Monopolistic Practices of Egypt, art. 25; Competition Act of India, sec. 53N; Restrictive Trade Practices Law of Israel, sec. 50; Restrictive Trade Practices, Monopolies and Price Control Act of Kenya, sec. 21(3); Commerce Act of New Zealand, arts. 81 & 82; Monopoly Regulation and Fair Trade Act of Korea, art. 56; Competition Law of Saudi Arabia, art. 18; Competition Act of South Africa, art. 65; and Fair Trade Act of Taiwan, arts. 30 & 32.

7 Anti-Monopoly Act of Japan, arts. 26 & 84.

(JFTC).[8] On the other hand, if claimants want to bring damages actions under the general civil code and prior to the JFTC's decision, they must prove the defendants' intention or negligence, as required by Japanese tort law.[9]

In Korea, on the contrary, the claimants can seek compensation under the competition law even prior to the KFTC's finding of violation. In fact, Korea used to have similar procedural limitations to those of Japan, but the Congress abolished the prior-decision system in 2005 for purposes of facilitating private antitrust enforcement. In Korea, the claimants' burden of proof is alleviated under the competition law. They do not need to prove the defendants' willfulness or negligence of the alleged violation, but the defendants may still be exonerated from liability by proving the nonexistence of either.[10]

The general civil code in some countries may also impede private antitrust claims. In Taiwan, for example, the Fair Trade Act grants a right to pursue civil liabilities if violations of the Act injure a party. What constitutes injury is governed by the Taiwanese general civil law, which stipulates that only direct injuries confer standing to sue. This leads some Taiwanese scholars to speculate that indirect purchasers will be precluded from pursuing antitrust claims against sellers.[11]

In some countries, the scope of the competition law is inclusive enough to cover unfair trade practices, which are elsewhere ordinarily addressed as consumer protection issues. For example, in India, there have been a fairly high number of claims with respect to the unfair trade practice aspects of the Monopolies and Restrictive Trade Practices Act, but genuine private antitrust claims have not yet arisen.[12]

The scope of private remedies

Although most competition laws of Asian and African countries provide a statutory basis for pursuing private damages actions, variations exist with respect to private injunction claims.

New Zealand, Singapore, and Taiwan allow private parties to seek injunctions on a broad basis. The Fair Trade Act of Taiwan has separate provisions for private injunctions under which private parties can seek termination of specific conduct for violation of the Act.[13] The Commerce Act of New Zealand allows private injunctions on both restrictive trade practices and business acquisitions.[14] In Singapore, private parties are also entitled to seek a full range of injunctive and declaratory reliefs under its Competition Act.[15] In Australia, private parties are allowed to seek injunctions for any antitrust violation except mergers.[16]

The competition laws in China, Israel, and Korea have no specific provisions governing private injunction claims. Israel, however, allows private parties to seek injunctions

---

8 Masako Wakui, *Antimonopoly Law: Competition Law and Policy in Japan*, 297 (2008).
9 OECD, *Regulatory Reform in Japan* 26 (1999).
10 Article 56 of the Monopoly Regulation and Fair Trade Act.
11 *See* the Taiwan Chapter.
12 *See* the India Chapter.
13 Fair Trade Act of Taiwan, art. 30.
14 Commerce Act of New Zealand, secs. 81 & 84.
15 Competition Act of Singapore, art. 86(8).
16 Trade Practices Act of Australia, sec. 80.

under its general laws. In Korea, debate sometimes arises on whether private parties can seek injunctions under the general civil code. Korean courts have refused to recognize private injunctions on the grounds that the Korean competition law does not specifically provide for them.[17]

The recent amendments to the Japanese Anti-Monopoly Act are noteworthy in that the private injunction mechanism has been partially adopted for purposes of facilitating private antitrust enforcement. Prior to 2001, Japan did not recognize private injunctions for violations of the competition law. [18] The Japanese Diet amended the Act in 2001 to allow private parties to seek injunctions under limited circumstances, such as unfair trade practices.[19] When an injunction suit is filed with a civil court, the court must notify the JFTC of the suit, and may seek advice from the JFTC on how to apply the Act.[20]

The prerequisites for pursuing private enforcement

When private antitrust actions are brought before the civil courts, a conflict of judgments between a civil court and an administrative court or an antitrust agency may be a realistic concern. To minimize the risk of inconsistent judgments, many jurisdictions commonly impose prerequisites for initiating private actions in civil courts.

In some countries, follow-on actions are the only option. In South Africa, for example, private parties' right to damages actions in civil courts arises only after the Competition Tribunal's conclusive determination on the same subject matter, and civil courts are obliged to apply the decision of the Tribunal on the same legal issues.[21] In Singapore, private parties may bring damages actions only after the Competition Commission's cease and desist order or certain payment orders have become final and binding.[22] In India, the Competition Tribunal can hear private damages actions only after the Competition Commission or the Tribunal itself has found violations under the Competition Act, and no further investigation will be permitted for this purpose.[23]

In some countries, the prior-conclusion restriction may be bypassed. In Japan, private parties may bring damages actions under the Anti-Monopoly Act only after the JFTC issues a cease and desist order.[24] Private parties, however, may still bring damages actions under the Japanese general civil code without having to await the JFTC's decisions.[25] As noted earlier, a stand-alone damages action under the general civil code requires the proof of additional elements.

---

[17] Yi, Sang-Seung & Youngjin Yung, *A New Kid on the Block: Korean Competition Law, Policy, and Economics*, Competition Policy International, vol.3, no.2, 153–183 (2007), *available at* http://papers.ssrn.com/sol3/papers.cfm?abstract_id=1075324.

[18] Masako Wakui, *supra*, at 50.

[19] Annual Report (January–December 2000), Japan Fair Trade Commission 3 & 14 (2001), *available at* http://www.jftc.go.jp/e-page/reports/annual/japan2000.pdf. *See also* Wakui, *supra*, at 298.

[20] Act Concerning Prohibition of Private Monopolization and Maintenance of Fair Trade of Japan, art. 84(3).

[21] *See* the South Africa Chapter.

[22] Competition Act of Singapore, art. 86(2).

[23] *See* the India Chapter.

[24] Anti-Monopoly Act of Japan, art. 26(1).

[25] Wakui, *supra*, at 298.

Some other countries have recently lifted the restriction. In 2005, Korea abolished the prior-conclusion restriction. Private parties can now bring damages actions directly before the civil courts under the competition law without having to await the KFTC's decisions. Despite this legislative development, most current private damages actions in Korea still piggyback on the KFTC's findings of liability. This is probably because private parties have very limited means of gathering evidence in a civil action in Korea.[26]

In China, the statutory language of the new Anti-Monopoly Law appears to allow private parties to simultaneously pursue litigations in civil courts and administrative complaints with the enforcement authority. The Supreme People's Court, however, will likely eventually issue a judicial interpretation of the Law, binding on all Chinese courts with respect to litigation procedures of private damages claims. Although administrative proceedings are routinely required before private litigation in certain complicated areas of law in China, such as securities, the Supreme People's Court has unofficially stated that there should be no prerequisite for commencing a private damages action.[27]

Representative actions

There are three types of representative action mechanism across the Asian and African nations: (1) the opt-out class action, (2) the traditional opt-in representative action, and (3) the association lawsuit. Australia, Indonesia, Israel, and South Africa have all adopted the opt-out class action mechanism, although its actual usage has been limited. The US-style opt-out class action has been available in Australia since 1992.[28] Its uniqueness lies in that there is no separate procedure for class certification. The court, however, may order the suspension of the proceeding at any stage of the litigation when it ceases to satisfy the threshold requirements for representative proceedings.[29] The lack of certification requirement has led to interlocutory warfare in Australian class action proceedings. As of May 2009, only three antitrust claims have been reported utilizing this opt-out mechanism in Australia.

In Indonesia, a group of consumers may bring damages actions against companies pursuant to the consumer protection law and the Supreme Court Regulation.[30] As of 2006, no antitrust class action has been reported. The Indonesian government is reportedly drafting an amendment bill to the Civil Procedure Act, in which detailed procedures for the opt-out class action mechanism will be provided.[31]

Israel adopted the opt-out class action mechanism for securities in 1988. It applied it in the antitrust area in 1996, by amending its Restrictive Trade Practice Law. In 2006, the Class Actions Law, which governs general procedures for the opt-out mechanism, was established. The class action mechanism of Israel is different from that of Australia

---

[26] *See* the Korea Chapter.

[27] *See* the China Chapter.

[28] Federal Court of Australia Act, Part IVA.

[29] FFCA, sec. 33N.

[30] Mas Achmad Santosa, *Indonesia*, 3 & 6 (2007), *available at* http://www.law.stanford.edu/library/globalclassaction/PDF/Indonesia_national_report.pdf.

[31] *Id.* at 11.

because, in Israel, class certification by the court is needed before the commencement of a class action.[32]

In South Africa, Article 38 of the Constitution established the opt-out class action mechanism in 1996, stipulating that 'anyone acting as a member of, or in the interest of, a group or class of persons' can claim rights before the courts.[33] No antitrust case has been reported utilizing this provision to date.

As of May 2009, the legislatures in New Zealand and Korea are reviewing bills contemplating adoption of the opt-out class action mechanism.

Japan, Korea, China, Taiwan, and most other countries in these regions have the traditional opt-in representative action regime. In these jurisdictions, multiple claimants with common interests may appoint one or more representatives to bring actions. Each claimant needs to express his or her own intention to participate in the action. The result binds the participating parties only.[34] To date, several cases have been reported in these countries utilizing the opt-in representative action mechanism.

Many countries, including Australia, Indonesia, Japan, Korea, South Africa, and Taiwan, also have the association lawsuit mechanism, which allows certain qualified associations to seek injunctions on behalf of aggrieved consumers. In Australia, the ACCC can seek damages on behalf of aggrieved consumers.[35] It prevailed in several representative actions with respect to consumer protection, but no case has been reported involving antitrust matters.

In Japan, Korea, and Taiwan, certain qualified associations can seek injunctions, but not damages, on behalf of aggrieved consumers. In addition, the association lawsuit is commonly available only for consumer protection matters, so the availability to antitrust matters is often uncertain.

South Africa endorses 'public interest' actions, where a single plaintiff can bring suit on behalf of others having a common interest in the subject matter of the suit.[36] In a public interest action, the standing requirement is relaxed; a plaintiff can initiate an action even if he or she does not have a direct interest in its outcome. Also, the judgment of a public interest action does not bind the parties whose interest is merely represented.[37] Having these differences from the class action mechanism, its application in antitrust matters so far remains obscure.

Actual or punitive damages

Most nations in the Asian and African regions only award actual damages in antitrust matters. This is probably based on a legislative intent that is more compensation-oriented,

---

32 Class Actions Law of Israel, §8(a).

33 For class actions, see §38(c) of the Constitution of the Republic of South Africa 1996, and for association action, see §38(e) of the Constitution of the Republic of South Africa 1996.

34 In China, the court's decision is binding on nonparticipants who bring suit within the prescribed litigation period. *See* Benjamin Liebman, *Class Action Litigation in China*, fn. 31, 111 Harv. L. Rev. 1523 (1998).

35 Trade Practices Act of Australia, §75AQ.

36 Constitution of the Republic of South Africa 1996, §38(d).

37 *See* the South Africa Chapter.

as opposed to deterrence-oriented. In a handful of nations, such as Kenya, New Zealand, and Taiwan, however, there are statutory bases for punitive or exemplary damages awards. For example, Kenya's competition law stipulates that the defendants may be liable for up to twice the monetary value of the actual damages.[38] In New Zealand, the competition law allows courts to order punitive damages awards even when defendants have been ordered to pay pecuniary penalties.[39] As of April 2009, there is no report of punitive damages awards in New Zealand. In Taiwan, the competition law prescribes that, in maximum, treble damages may be awarded if the violation is intentional.[40]

Legal costs and funding

In the Asian and African nations, no competition law has specific provisions on the distribution of legal costs, and thus general civil procedure rules commonly apply in private antitrust actions. Many nations in these regions, such as Australia, China, Japan, Kenya, and Korea, have the 'loser-pays' rule. [41] In China, the losing party bears the court fees in a class action where the number of plaintiffs or defendants is not fixed at the time of filing, but class representatives may nevertheless be dissuaded from litigating due to practical concerns over the difficulty of collecting fees from class members if the claim is unsuccessful.[42] In Australia, however, class members are immune from adverse cost awards; only class representatives will stand this risk due to the operation of the Federal Court of Australia Act.[43]

As for attorneys' fees, Japan, Korea, and Taiwan allow contingent fees, while Australia, China, and Malaysia prohibit such arrangements.[44] In China, despite tight fee regulations, the use of contingency fees was unofficially widespread.[45] The 2006 Measures on Litigation Fees now expressly prohibits contingency fees in class actions, but it remains unclear whether this rule will be closely observed.[46]

Australian lawyers frequently work on a 'no win no fee' basis in class actions, but success fees may not be calculated as a percentage of the actual recovery and uplifts are allowed only in some Australian jurisdictions.[47] Although Australian law forbids contingent fees charged by legal professionals, it does not bar commercial litigation funders from receiving a percentage of the litigation proceeds as a result of their investment. In

---

[38] Restrictive Trade Practices, Monopolies and Price Control Act of Kenya, §21(3).

[39] Commerce Act 1986 of New Zealand, §82A.

[40] Article 33 of the Fair Trade Act of 2002.

[41] UNCTAD (2005), Voluntary Peer Review on Competition Policy, http://www.unctad.org/en/docs/ditcclp20056_en.pdf.

[42] *See Interpretation of the Supreme People's Court on Questions Concerning the Implementation of the Civil Procedure Law of the People's Republic of China,* 1992 SPC Gaz., No. 3, at 70, art. 59; *see also Class Action*, 111 Harv. L. Rev. (1998) at 1534.

[43] Sec. 43 of the Federal Court of Australia Act 1976.

[44] Choong and Balan, *Class Action in Malaysia: Principles and Procedural Obstacles, The Globalization of Class Actions Conference* (2007) p. 14.

[45] *See Class Action*, 111 Harv. L. Rev. (1998) at 1537.

[46] Art 12, Measures on the Payment of Litigation Fees (promulgated by the State Council on Dec. 19, 2006, and in effect on Apr. 1, 2007).

[47] *See* the Australia Chapter.

Japan, it has been observed that public funding is needed in order to facilitate consumer association actions.[48]

Conclusion

In Asia and Africa, the majority of private civil actions are brought after the national antitrust authorities' finding of violations. In most countries, this restriction is imposed by statute, as there are realistic concerns over inconsistent judgments. Even in a very few countries, such as Korea, where stand-alone cases are theoretically possible, claimants continue to bring civil actions in conjunction with the KFTC's finding of violations. The lack of an expansive discovery mechanism in civil actions is a major hurdle to initiating stand-alone cases. In this sense, the further development of private antitrust enforcement depends on changes not only in the antitrust laws themselves, but also in civil procedures.

The incentive structure in Asia and Africa has not been conducive to private antitrust enforcement. Recoveries are generally limited to single damages. Compensation for plaintiffs' lawyers is often not commensurate with the level of work and investment required. In a class action, where individual claimants have relatively small stakes, it is of particular importance that plaintiffs' lawyers are properly compensated for their work. In Australia, while the legal profession cannot receive contingent fees, commercial funders routinely finance class actions, relieving plaintiffs' lawyers of the burden of upfront costs. This is a development worth watching.

On a more general level, public awareness of the benefits of competition and the role of competition policy should be raised, especially in countries like China, where competition laws are new, or India, where the law has recently been modernized. In much of Asia and Africa, there are many issues left to be worked out. There is no doubt, however, that we will see the development of private antitrust enforcement drive in the fast lane, motored by the vibrancy of many Asian economies.

48 Ikuo Sugawara, *The Current Situation of Class Action in Japan*, 5, *available at* http://www.law.stanford.edu/display/images/dynamic/events_media/Japan_National_Report.pdf.

29 Australia

Brooke Dellavedova, Vince Morabito and Brendan Sweeney[1]

Introduction

Private actions for breaches of competition law have been available in Australia since 1975 when the *Trade Practices Act* came into force.[2] The *Trade Practices Act* is the cornerstone of a competition law system that is designed (so far as permitted by the Constitution) to be national in scope and application. As a result, the same substantive competition provisions apply federally and in the states to the vast majority of business entities (including public entities to the extent that they are engaged in carrying on a business). The substantive provisions cover horizontal and vertical arrangements, as well as unilateral conduct. In keeping with the aim to create a national scheme, most private actions are decided in the federal courts.[3] The overall legislative aim of Australian competition law is to enhance the welfare of Australians through the promotion of competition. The regulator is the Australian Competition and Consumer Commission (ACCC).

Class actions are a relatively new phenomenon in Australian antitrust enforcement.[4] Only one antitrust class action has been successfully concluded to date,[5] against the global vitamins price-fixing cartel. In 2006 settlement was approved in the sum of AUD30.5 million plus costs. A wide range of businesses, from small-scale livestock producers to large animal nutrition companies, received average compensation of AUD143,000, generally regarded as an excellent result. At the time of writing, there are three further antitrust class actions pending, all involving price cartels.[6]

---

1 Brooke Dellavedova is a Principal, Maurice Blackburn, Lawyers; Vince Morabito is a Professor and Brendan Sweeney is an Associate Professor at Monash University.

2 An earlier statute, the *Australian Industries Preservation Act 1906* (Cth), which provided for treble damages, was almost completely ignored by both public and private actors. It was repealed in 1965.

3 As part of an agreement between the Commonwealth and the states, the states have agreed that where an antitrust case is brought in a state court it will be transferred to the Federal Court. See further at text accompanying n 31.

4 This matter is discussed further at text accompanying n 41.

5 Another representative proceeding brought in respect of an alleged cartel for pre-mixed concrete was discontinued as a representative proceeding: *Gold Coast Council v Pioneer Concrete (Qld) Pty Ltd* (1997) ATPR 41-585.

6 The actions involve the fibreboard packaging industry, international air freight services and the rubber chemicals industry.

1. What practices are illegal and what are the elements of proof?

a. Horizontal restraints

The *Trade Practices Act* prohibits a range of concerted activities involving competitors including fixing prices, restricting outputs, market sharing, bid rigging and concerted refusals to deal.[7] These activities are prohibited irrespective of any adverse effect on competition. In addition, any contract, arrangement or understanding that has the purpose or effect of substantially lessening competition is prohibited.[8] This provision is not limited to arrangements between competitors.[9] Exemptions are discussed below.

Naked horizontal restraints are normally secretive arrangements. In the absence of a confession the main forensic issue in establishing an infringement is proving the existence of the unlawful arrangement. This may be proved by circumstantial evidence, although, as in most jurisdictions, parallel conduct, including conscious parallel conduct, is not sufficient. The most difficult area tends to be where there is evidence of conduct (for example, various forms of price signalling) that falls short of proving an agreement but which facilitates outcomes not inconsistent with collusion. The trend in Australian cases is to require evidence of a commitment to the arrangement.[10]

b. Vertical restraints

Minimum resale price maintenance is prohibited per se.[11] There is no requirement to establish any adverse effect on competition. Third line forcing is also prohibited per se.[12] Again, there is no requirement to establish any adverse effect on competition. Other types of vertical restraints (exclusivity arrangements, minimum quantities arrangements, loyalty rebates, bundling and tying arrangements) are prohibited if they substantially lessen competition in the supplier's or the buyer's market.[13] Exemptions apply as discussed below.

c. Single firm conduct

A firm that has a substantial degree of market power is not permitted to take advantage of that power in that or any other market for the purpose of:

- eliminating or substantially damaging competitors,
- preventing a person from entering any market, or
- preventing a person from engaging in competitive conduct in any market.[14]

---

7 *Trade Practices Act 1974* (Cth) (TPA) Part IV. Price fixing, output restrictions, market sharing and bid rigging attract criminal and civil penalties as well as damages.

8 TPA, §45(2).

9 Vertical restraints are excluded from this provision. They are dealt with under separate provisions.

10 *Apco Service Stations Pty Ltd v ACCC* [2005] FCAFC 161; *ACCC v Leahy Petroleum Pty Ltd* [2007] FCA 794.

11 TPA, §48.

12 TPA, §47. Third line forcing is defined in §§47(6) & (7).

13 TPA, §47.

14 TPA, §46(1).

In 1988 Australia's highest court (High Court of Australia) held that a supplier with the requisite degree of market power could be ordered to supply a willing buyer even where the supplier had a policy of not supplying the product to anyone but its own wholly-owned subsidiary.[15] The court applied a counterfactual test to determine that if the supplier had faced more competitive market conditions, it would not have refused to supply the applicant. As its reason for refusing supply was to protect its subsidiary's hold over the downstream market, the supplier had breached the *Trade Practices Act*. The question of remedies was settled out of court.[16]

The expansive approach to single firm conduct suggested by this case has not eventuated. Both the regulator and private applicants have found it extremely difficult to establish breach, which requires a showing of market power, conduct constituting use of the market power, and unlawful purpose. In particular, it has been extremely difficult to establish the necessary causal connection between the existence of market power and the conduct said to constitute its use, without which the elements of breach are not proven. The counterfactual test by itself is insufficient. The regulator or a private applicant must offer additional proof showing that the impugned conduct was in fact materially facilitated by the firm's market power.[17]

There has been considerable political pressure from small business to expand the ambit of unlawful single firm conduct. This resulted in the introduction of a new predatory pricing provision in 2007. A firm that has a substantial share of a market must not supply products for a sustained period at a price less than the relevant cost to the firm for the purpose of eliminating or substantially damaging competitors, or preventing a person from entering any market, or preventing a person from engaging in competitive conduct in any market.[18] No case has yet been decided under this provision.

d. Exemptions

Conduct that has been authorised by the ACCC or is the subject of a valid notification is exempt.[19] Export cartels are exempt (subject to notification). Certain joint venture arrangements and collective buying groups are exempt from the per se price fixing provisions. Some marketing boards for primary products are exempt. Finally, certain industries protected under state laws are exempt (e.g., local transport in certain states).

---

15 *Queensland Wire Industries v Broken Hill Proprietary Co. Ltd* (1989) 167 CLR 177.

16 In *ASX Operations Pty Ltd v Pont Data Australia Pty Ltd* [1991] FCA 158 the court had to settle the supply price.

17 *Melway Publishing Pty Ltd v Robert Hicks Pty Ltd* [2001] HCA 13.

18 TPA, §46(1AA).

19 Conduct may be authorised by the ACCC on the basis that there are public benefits flowing from the conduct which outweigh any adverse effects on competition. Notification is available for collective bargaining arrangements (between small businesses) and all types of vertical exclusive dealing. These arrangements are exempt from the competition prohibitions provided they have been notified to the ACCC. This involves advising the ACCC of the intended conduct and paying a fee. The ACCC will withdraw the notification if it determines that the conduct will substantially lessen competition and that any public benefits that may flow from the conduct will not be sufficient to offset the adverse competitive effects.

e. Elements of a claim for damages

To obtain damages for a breach of any of these provisions the applicant must establish:

(a) the existence of the unlawful conduct, and
(b) that the applicant's loss was caused by the unlawful conduct.[20]

2. Commencing a damages action

Except where the plaintiff has deep pockets, the majority of significant damages claims in the future are likely to be class actions. In such cases, the risks – which are significant given Australia's cost rules and the complexity of antitrust actions[21] – are typically borne not only by the plaintiff, but also the plaintiff's lawyers and the litigation funder[22] (pursuant to the terms of any funding and retainer agreements entered into). These risks will only be assumed if there are excellent prospects of success, the potential damages are significant and those affected are committed to taking action.

During the investigative phase, class lawyers will contact likely claimants to notify them of the proposed action and gauge interest. There are no restrictions on lawyers identifying and contacting potential claimants, who may be identified by various means. Lawyers may contact their existing or previous clients to bring a matter to their attention, provided that, in respect of individuals, they comply with the relevant privacy laws.[23] Trade industry associations provide an important means of providing information to potential claimants, as do the media. Plaintiffs' lawyers will typically make information and materials regarding the action available via the internet.

The most immediate sources of information during preliminary investigation will be decisions and findings of fact from local and overseas competition regulators. Documents filed in foreign civil proceedings may indicate avenues for further inquiry. Witnesses are obviously critical, but may be reluctant to speak, located in a foreign jurisdiction or bound by confidentiality obligations (as discussed below). Other important tools include preliminary discovery,[24] company documents, and preliminary econometric analysis of price data.

---

[20] TPA, §82. Compensation is also available under §87(1). This is a discretionary remedy.

[21] In general, the successful party in any litigation is entitled to have their costs paid by the unsuccessful party. For a comment on the cost of antitrust cases see, e.g., *Seven Network Limited v News Limited* [2007] FCA 1062 which involved a battle for national television rights to Australian rules football. The trial judge commented, 'In my view, the expenditure of [AUD]$200 million (and counting) on a single piece of litigation is not only extraordinarily wasteful, but borders on the scandalous'.

[22] See text accompanying n 81.

[23] *The Privacy Act 1988* (Cth) incorporates the National Privacy Provisions which restrict the use of personal information, such as contact details, collected by an organisation.

[24] *Federal Court Rules*, Order 15A. Preliminary discovery may be ordered (at the discretion of the court and subject to the rules of privilege) either (a) to identify a potential defendant, or (b) to discover information that will enable a prospective plaintiff to determine whether to commence proceedings against a particular defendant. In each case the discretion is subject to a number of provisos. For example, in respect of the second instance, the discretion may only be exercised if there is reasonable cause to believe that the prospective plaintiff has or may have a right to obtain the relief sought from the defendant, and that there is reasonable cause to believe that the defendant has or had a document in its possession relating to that issue and that inspection of the

3. Gathering evidence

Former and current employees of the defendants who were involved in or knew about the alleged unlawful conduct are likely to be important sources of evidence. However, they may be subject to strict obligations of confidence, imposed by express contractual provision (under a written confidentiality agreement), implied contractual obligation (in an employment contract) or equity.[25] Where a potential witness is bound by obligations of confidentiality, a lawyer who receives or uses confidential information from the witness may be found to have committed the tort of inducing breach of confidence,[26] notwithstanding that the witness is compellable by subpoena to give evidence at trial.[27] This places the plaintiffs' lawyers in a difficult position: first, in terms of compliance, it may be impossible to know whether a witness will divulge confidential information until he or she has done so: second, as a matter of trial practice, it is risky to subpoena a witness without knowing the substance of his or her evidence. In contrast to the United States, there is no general power in Australia to compel witnesses to provide evidence on deposition.

Where a witness is unable to appear at trial (for example, for health reasons or because the witness is outside Australia), the court may order the witness' evidence to be taken under oath by an examiner appointed by the court (or in the case of letters rogatory by a person appointed by the relevant foreign authorities).

Company documents are an important source of evidence, and these may be obtained through the corporate regulator (Australian Securities & Investment Commission) or equivalent in the home jurisdiction of the defendant, or they may be publicly available on the internet. Indeed, the defendants' own publications regarding their operations can be a significant source of evidence.

Expert witnesses, and in particular expert economists, play an important role in antitrust actions. Use of expert evidence is governed by specific rules[28] and by a Federal Court Practice Direction. The purpose of the Direction is to facilitate the admission of opinion evidence, to assist experts to understand what the court expects of them and to 'assist individual expert witnesses to avoid the criticism that is sometimes made (whether rightly or wrongly) that expert witnesses lack objectivity, or have coloured their evidence in favour of the party calling them.'[29]

In cartel cases, for instance, economists will be retained to identify and quantify

---

document would assist in making the decision. Although the rule is to be beneficially construed in the plaintiff's favour, it is clear that there must be more than a 'mere assertion, suspicion or conjecture' that the plaintiff has a right to relief. The plaintiff must demonstrate that there is reasonable cause to believe that the elements of the cause of action exist. The court may also order discovery from a third party.

[25] *AG Australia Holdings Ltd v Burton & Anor* (2002) 58 NSWLR 464 at [73].

[26] *AG Australia Holdings Limited v Burton & Anor* (2002) 58 NSWLR 464, cited with approval in *Rapid Metal Developments (Australia) Pty Ltd v Anderson Formite Pty Ltd* [2005] WASC 255 and *Richards v Kadian by his tutor Kadian & Ors* (2005) 64 NSWLR 204. An exception applies where the information disclosed reveals an iniquity (narrowly construed).

[27] At common law, confidentiality is not of itself a ground for refusing to give evidence: *AG Australia Holdings Limited v Burton & Anor* (2002) 58 NSWLR 464 at [129] to [140].

[28] *Federal Court Rules*, Order 34A.

[29] Practice Note CM 7 – expert Witnesses in Proceedings in the Federal Court of Australia, at http://www.fedcourt.gov.au/how/practice_notes_cm7.html.

any price inflation, usually using econometric techniques including multiple regression analyses. Economists may also be retained to provide opinion evidence as to the relevant market and its characteristics (such as barriers to entry), the extent of any passing-on of cartel overcharges, the impact of the alleged conduct on competitors and the appropriateness of any proposed remedy or settlement scheme.

Econometric analysis is likely to require significant price data, usually obtained from class members, the defendants (by subpoena or discovery), trade associations, private research companies or other sources. Additional information is available from government bodies such as the Australian Bureau of Statistics (trade data) or the Australian Customs Service (import data requested pursuant to freedom of information legislation).[30]

Discovery in antitrust class actions is typically large, time consuming, expensive and attended by lengthy interlocutory proceedings as to scope and form. The types of documents requested of defendants include direction communications (minutes, agendas, directions) and documents relating to market shares, total sales figures, production capacity and utilisation, and of course documents evidencing the destruction of relevant documents.

4. Attorney/client privilege

Some evidence generated for use in legal proceedings is likely to be protected from pre-trial production to the opposing party by legal professional privilege, which may be claimed in respect of a document produced or brought into existence with the dominant purpose of obtaining legal advice or preparing for existing or anticipated legal proceedings.[31]

5. Who may pursue a claim?

An action for damages may be brought by any person who suffers loss or damage by the conduct of another in contravention of the antitrust provisions.[32] Actions in Australia have been commenced by and on behalf of direct and indirect purchasers of cartel affected products and services: claims by both direct and indirect purchasers were allowed under the vitamins class action settlement. It is doubtful that there is any scope for the application in Australia of an *Illinois Brick*-style standing rule.

An application for injunctive relief may be made by the ACCC or 'any other person'.[33] 'Any person' may commence a proceeding for declaratory relief.[34]

The court has the power to make a variety of ancillary orders (including monetary compensation) on the application of any person who is a party to the proceedings.[35] These orders may be made in addition to any injunction, declaration or order for damages.[36]

---

30 *Freedom of Information Act 1982* (Cth).

31 *Esso Australia Resources v FCT* (1999) 201 CLR 49.

32 TPA, §82.

33 TPA, §80.

34 TPA, §163A. See *Re Tooth & Co Ltd* (1978) 31 FLR 314.

35 TPA, §87.

36 An order for monetary compensation would not be made if the person has been fully

Anyone with a personal claim may bring a representative proceeding on behalf of other persons.[37] The ACCC may also commence representative proceedings on behalf of persons who have suffered loss or damage, provided those persons are identified in the proceedings and have consented.[38] For a variety of reasons the entitlement is rarely used.[39]

6. In what forum does a plaintiff initiate a private claim?

Australia's antitrust laws are an attempt to produce, so far as is permitted by the Constitution, a uniform federal regime with the Federal Court as the judicial arm. Antitrust actions brought in state courts will be transferred to the Federal Court.[40]

7. How may claims be aggregated?

Various mechanisms exist for bringing together multiple claims, including traditional joinder and consolidation and the use of test cases, but we focus here on representative proceedings.

'U.S.-style' class actions have been available in the Federal Court of Australia since March 1992.[41] The class action provisions are found in Part IVA of the *Federal Court of Australia Act*.

Australia's federal class action regime does not impose on potential class representatives any requirement to seek leave from the court before proceeding with a class action; that is, there is no certification device. Defendants may, however, seek the intervention of the court if they feel that the proposed litigation does not comply with the threshold requirements[42] for the institution of a class proceeding.[43] The threshold requirements are:

- that there are seven or more persons who have claims against the same person (the numerosity requirement),
- that the claims of all those persons are in respect of, or arise out of, the same, similar or related circumstances (the connectivity requirement), and

---

compensated by an award of damages. An order for compensation under s 87 becomes important, for example, where damages under §82 are not available, or not available in full, due to the rules relating to limitations periods.

37 *Federal Court of Australia Act 1976* (Cth) (FCAA), s 33D.

38 TPA, §87(1B).

39 The fact that this regime adopts an opt-in device (see n 45 below) appears to be a major reason for its limited use and for the fact that on several occasions the ACCC has employed, instead, the Part IVA regime with its opt-out device: see V Morabito, *Group Litigation in Australia – 'Desperately Seeking' Effective Class Action Regimes* (National Report for Australia prepared for *The Globalisation of Class Actions Conference* held at Oxford University in December 2007), 21.

40 *Jurisdiction of Courts (Cross-Vesting) Acts*. For constitutional reasons, there are a limited number of cases that must be brought in state courts. However, such cases are likely to be rare.

41 FCAA, Part IVA. Class actions are also available in the Supreme Court of Victoria, but not in other states. See Part 4A of the *Supreme Court Act 1986* (Vic) which is virtually identical to Part IVA.

42 See *Wong v Silkfield Pty Ltd* (1999) 165 ALR 373, 381; and *Philip Morris (Australia) Ltd v Nixon* (2000) 170 ALR 487, 514 .

43 FCAA, §33C(1).

- that they give rise to a substantial common issue of law or fact (the commonality requirement).[44]

Provided these requirements are met, a class proceeding may be commenced by one of the seven or more claimants 'as representing some or all of them'. There are no restrictions as to the persons and entities that may commence a class proceeding on behalf of similarly situated claimants.

Part IVA employs the opt-out device.[45] Claimants that fall within the description of the group represented by the class representative (the represented group) will be bound by the outcome of the litigation unless they take the positive step of excluding themselves from the litigation, by signing and sending to the court an opt-out form.

A class proceeding may be discontinued, as a class proceeding, by the trial judge if one of the scenarios specified in the Act is found to exist.[46] Thus, the trial judge may discontinue class proceedings if, in the opinion of the judge,

(a) it is in the interests of justice that a proceeding no longer continue as a class proceeding; and
(b) one or more of the following circumstances exist:
  (i) the costs that would be incurred if the proceeding were to continue as a class proceeding are likely to exceed the costs that would be incurred if each class member conducted a separate proceeding;
  (ii) all the relief sought can be obtained by means of a proceeding other than a class proceeding;
  (iii) the class proceeding will not provide an efficient and effective means of dealing with the claims of the class members; or
  (iv) it is otherwise inappropriate that the claims be pursued by means of a class proceeding.[47]

8. What procedural defences are available short of trial?

a. General

It is essential that the applicant plead a factual basis that discloses the necessary elements of the alleged breach. This has been important in cases involving unlawful cartels and

---

44 *P Dawson Nominees Pty Ltd v Multiplex Limited* [2007] FCA 1061 at [14].

45 Section 87(1B), on the other hand, employs an opt-in device by requiring the ACCC to furnish the written consents of the claimants in question. See n 38. It is interesting to note that the first empirical study of the operation of the Part IVA regime, which is currently in progress, has revealed that some class members, who have opted out of Part IVA proceedings, have done so because of confusion as to the nature of a class action proceeding, their liability for costs and/or the practical and legal effect of lodging an opt-out form: see V Morabito, 'Revisiting Australia's First Shareholder Class Action' in Justice KE Lindgren (ed), *Investor Class Actions* (Sydney; 2009) 34, 43–44. To date, this scenario has not resulted in any disputes between parties to Part IVA proceedings or had other formal impact on the progress of the litigation.

46 See FCAA, §§33L, 33M, 33N.

47 FCAA, §33N.

abuses of market power. Failure to plead such facts is grounds for having the case struck out.

The Federal Court may give summary judgment to one party if the court is satisfied that the other party has no reasonable prospect of successfully prosecuting/defending the proceeding.[48] The relevant statutory provision provides that a proceeding need not be hopeless or bound to fail for it to have no reasonable prospect of success.[49] The Federal Court has general power to dismiss an action that is oppressive, vexatious, frivolous or an abuse of process of the court or where there are vexatious litigants.[50] This power, and the power to summarily dismiss, appear to have been exercised rarely with respect to Part IVA proceedings[51] (see next section with respect to the types of disputes that have frequently taken place in Part IVA proceedings and which have required the intervention of the court).

b. Class action proceedings

Unlike North American class action regimes, Australian class action rules do not employ a certification device. The object of this was to avoid expending excessive time and resources on preliminary issues. Unfortunately that object has not been achieved. Instead, many class proceedings, including antitrust actions, have tended towards interlocutory warfare as defendants mount every possible interlocutory challenge available to them. Defendants routinely argue that Part IVA's 'threshold requirements', discussed above,[52] have not been satisfied or that the court ought to exercise its discretionary powers to terminate the class proceedings (as discussed above). Defendants also regularly challenge every aspect of the pleadings. In particular, defendants invariably seek removal of cartel class actions on the basis that the plaintiff has failed to plead material facts sufficient to give rise to a cause of action, and has failed to provide proper particulars. Plaintiffs in turn argue that precise pleadings and particulars should not be required at the early interlocutory stage where concealed conduct is alleged.

The resulting profusion of time-consuming and costly interlocutory hearings has often been criticised by Federal Court justices.[53]

---

48 FCAA, §31A. This section does not expressly restrict the exercise of this power only to those cases where an application has been lodged by one of the parties to the litigation.

49 FCAA, §31A(3). As recently noted by Rares J of the Full Federal Court of Australia, 'by enacting s 31A, the Parliament broadened the categories of case in which the power summarily to determine proceedings could be exercised': *Jefferson Ford Pty Ltd v Ford Motor Company of Australia Ltd* [2008] FCAFC 60 at [45].

50 *Federal Court Rules*, Order 20 Rule 5. These powers are expressly preserved, with respect to Part IVA proceedings, by §33ZG.

51 For a very recent example see *Byrnes v Brisconnections Management Company Limited* [2009] FCA 736.

52 See above at text accompanying n 44.

53 In the vitamins class action (Australia's first anti-cartel class action) Finkelstein J said that 'many class actions become bogged down by interminable and expensive interlocutory applications and protracted and even more expensive appeals from interlocutory orders': *Bray v F Hoffmann-La Roche Ltd* (2003) 200 ALR 607, 660. See also *Bright v Femcare Ltd* (2002) 195 ALR 574, 607; *Milfull v Terranora Lakes Country Club Limited (In Liquidation)* [2004] FCA 1637 at [1], [17]; Justice Lindgren, 'Class Actions and Access to Justice' (Keynote Address given at the International Class Actions Conference 2007 organised by Maurice Blackburn Lawyers

9. What do the plaintiffs get if they win?

a. Damages and other remedies

Australian competition law does not provide for treble damages. Nor does it provide for punitive damages. Any damages award is based on the loss or damage suffered by the claimant.[54] As a result there is probably limited scope for adopting the US approach to passing-on, although the matter has not yet been judicially examined.[55] Prejudgment interest is available on a damages claim.[56]

The court has no power to order contribution or an indemnity.

The court may on the application of *any* person grant interim and final injunctions. Injunctions are discretionary, but quite common where a breach has been established. The court has a wide variety of remedial powers including power to declare a contract void, wholly or in part, to vary a contract (both prospectively and retrospectively) and to order restitution.[57]

Finally, the court may make a declaratory order.[58]

b. Measuring damages

Very few reported cases (and none by an appellate court) have considered the issue of how damages should be measured in antitrust cases. The most likely method is an approach similar to that used in tort law.[59] Thus, in assessing damages the court will compare the applicant's actual position with the position the applicant would have been in but for the breach.[60]

The majority of large damages cases are likely to involve price fixing cartels. In the case of a price-fixing cartel, there are at least two ways of measuring the applicant's loss. The first method is to calculate the applicant's lost profits flowing from the unlawful cartel. The second method is to calculate the amount of the overcharge: that is, the difference between the price actually paid by the buyer and the price that would have been paid but for the collusion (adjusted to account for the amount of the higher price that the buyer was able to pass on to its buyers). Australian courts must apply the approach that is most likely to produce a measurement of the actual loss or damage suffered by the applicant. Adopting tort terminology, this means putting the applicant in the position

---

in Sydney – 25–26 October 2007), 2 (it is a familiar feature of representative proceedings in the Federal Court that the respondent attacks the form of the application or statement of claim or both).

[54] TPA, §82.

[55] Views differ as to whether and how a passing on rule might apply in Australia. For a sceptical view see B Sweeney, 'The Role of Damages in Regulating Horizontal Price-Fixing: Comparing the Situation in the US, Europe and Australia' (2006) 30 *Melbourne University Law Review* 837, 871–2.

[56] FCAA, §51A.

[57] TPA, §87(2).

[58] TPA, §163A.

[59] The tort approach has been held to be a useful analogue when assessing damages for resale price maintenance: see *Hubbards Pty Ltd v Simpson Ltd* (1982) 41 ALR 509.

[60] This interpretation of §82 has been applied to the calculation of damages in misleading or deceptive conduct cases: see *Marks v GIO Australia Ltd* (1998) 196 CLR 494.

in which it would have been if the contravention had not occurred. This is effectively the lost profits approach.

Lost profits could include losses other than those directly related to the overcharge, for instance, the value of any provable lost commercial opportunity.[61] This would include losses suffered by competitors. For example, an amount for lost profits suffered by the defendants' competitors formed part of the settlement in the vitamins class action case.[62] In the case of a retailer, it could also include lost sales on products other than the product which is subject to price-fixing.[63]

10. Class action settlements

In approving class action settlements the courts will accept quantifications based on the overcharge method.[64] In the vitamins class action the court approved a complex settlement regime which provided for distribution of an aggregate damages award to both direct and indirect purchasers.[65] Entitlement to compensation was calculated by reference to a range of factors including the proportion of overcharge estimated to have been 'absorbed' by any claimant, that is, not retained upstream or passed further downstream. Tax incidence analysis[66] was used to estimate the overcharge 'absorption' for categories of claimants, grouped by industry, to avoid the need for individual assessment.

Under the 'vitamins' settlement scheme, competitors of the cartel were compensated for loss of market share caused by the cartel.[67] Competitor-plaintiffs who purchased vitamins in the process of manufacturing and selling vitamin premix (the independent premix manufacturers) during the cartel period suffered loss of sales as a result of the overcharge, but also (importantly) a loss of market share as a result of being put at a serious competitive disadvantage *vis-à-vis* the defendants' premix businesses. The defendants were able to significantly undercut the prices offered by the independent premix manufacturers because they were taking inflated profits in the upstream market.

Although end-consumers are theoretically able to claim damages, it is unlikely that they would be included in a class action where their individual losses are small. In fact, the Australian class action regime is not particularly well-suited to such groups. A class action seeking compensation for a multitude of small claimants would be vulnerable to being discontinued as a representative proceeding on the basis that the cost to the defendants of identifying the group members and distributing to them identified amounts would be excessive having regard to the likely total of those amounts.[68] In practice, a minimum expenditure threshold is likely to be imposed for group membership. This will

---

61 The High Court has recognised that the loss of a commercial opportunity may have a present value and therefore be compensatable: see *Sellars v Adelaide Petroleum NL* (1994) 179 CLR 332, 355–6.

62 See below at text accompanying n 67.

63 See *Hubbards Pty Ltd v Simpson Ltd* (1982) 41 ALR 509, 518.

64 See, eg, *Darwalla Milling Co Pty Ltd v F Hoffmann La Roche Ltd (No 2)* [2006] FCA 1388.

65 Ibid.

66 A supply and demand analysis which measures the impact of a change to price by using elasticities of supply and demand.

67 AUD $7m of the total damages pool of $30.5m.

68 FCAA, §33M.

exclude small value end-consumers. Distribution of settlement funds under Part IVA is restricted to group members who have established an entitlement to compensation. Cy-pres distribution is not available.[69]

11. Fees and court costs

Subject to the court's discretion, the successful party is generally entitled to their legal costs and disbursements ('costs follow the event' rule).[70] Costs awards are based on a scale and typically comprise about 50 to 70 per cent of the successful party's total legal costs. Disbursements are recoverable to the extent to which they have been properly and reasonably incurred and paid.

As most large private actions will involve a class action settlement, the question of costs will depend on the terms of the settlement as approved by the court. In the vitamins class action settlement, for example, the court approved 'reimbursement payments' to be paid out of the settlement sum to the prosecuting claimants as recompense for their valuable time and out-of-pocket expenses incurred on behalf of the group members.[71]

12. Limitation periods

A damages action 'may be commenced at any time within 6 years after the day on which the cause of action that relates to the conduct accrued'.[72] A cause of action accrues when the applicant suffers loss or damage. Whether this occurs, in the case of cartel price-fixing, at the time of purchase or at the time when the cartel's activities are discovered has not yet been finally determined. In one case the Federal Court accepted that it was at least arguable that loss or damage is only suffered when the anti-competitive conduct in question comes to light.[73]

Where a party to proceedings for an injunction (which have no time limit) seeks compensation ancillary to that injunction, there is no limitation period.[74] This applies whether or not the court grants the injunction.

13. Distribution of damages

As most cases will involve class action settlements, distribution will depend on the terms of the settlement or court order. As is the case with class actions in the US and Canada, Part IVA proceedings may not be settled without the approval of the court.[75] The relevant statutory provision, s 33V, provides no guidance to trial courts as to the factors that are to be considered when determining whether to approve a settlement proposed

---

69 *Cauvin v Philip Morris Limited* [2002] NSWSC 736 revised – 04/09/2002, at [34].

70 There are court filing fees for initiating a claim in the Federal Court including a representative proceeding. These fees, however, represent a very small proportion of the total costs of an action. The fees are AUD $1881 for a corporation, $785 for others.

71 *Darwalla Milling Co Pty Ltd v F Hoffmann La Roche Ltd* [2006] FCA 1388.

72 TPA, §82(2).

73 *Energex Ltd v Alstom Australia Ltd* (2004) ATPR (Digest) ¶46-251 at [179] per Weinberg J; *Energex Ltd v Alstom Australia Ltd* [2005] FCAFC 215 at [51]–[63], per French, Hely and Merkel JJ.

74 *Mayne Nickless Limited v Multigroup Distribution Services Pty Limited* [2001] FCA 1620 interpreting TPA, §87.

75 FCAA, §33V.

by the representative plaintiff and the defendant. The general approach that is applied in relation to s 33V applications by trial judges is that the court is to determine whether the proposed settlement is fair and reasonable, having regard to the claims of the class members who will be bound by the settlement.[76] The fairness and reasonableness of the settlement are, in turn, usually determined by the application of the following criteria, enunciated by Justice Goldberg of the Federal Court in 2000:

> The amount offered to each group member, the prospects of success in the proceeding, the likelihood of the group members obtaining judgment for an amount significantly in excess of the settlement offer, the terms of any advice received from counsel and from any independent expert in relation to the issues which arise in the proceeding, the likely duration and cost of the proceeding if continued to judgment, and the attitude of the group members to the settlement.[77]

14. How does the plaintiff's lawyer finance private enforcement?

The 'costs follow the event' rule means that the losing party needs to pay not only its own legal costs but also a significant proportion of its opponent's costs. In the class action context, however, Part IVA expressly confers upon class members an immunity from adverse cost awards.[78]

This means that, in many circumstances, it would not be financially rational for aspiring class representatives to institute class actions, unless they are able to shift to others the liability for (a) the fees and disbursements of the class representative's lawyers; (b) any costs awarded to the defendants in the event of a loss for the class; and (c) any security for costs orders granted to the defendants. Thus, the class representative's solicitors have frequently funded class actions by acting on a 'no win no fee' basis.[79] However, it is important to note that in Australia the conditional fees, received by plaintiff solicitors, may not be calculated as a percentage of the amount recovered on behalf of the client. Only uplift fees may be charged, and even then only in some Australian jurisdictions.[80]

Litigation funding, a relatively new phenomenon in Australia, is becoming more

---

76 See, for instance, *Lukey v Corporate Investment Australia Funds Management Pty Ltd* [2003] FCA 1602 at [7] (per Emmett J); *Tongue v Council of the City of Tamworth* [2004] FCA 972 at [22] (per Allsop J); and *Courtney v Medtel Pty Limited (No 5)* [2004] FCA 1406 at [39] (per Sackville J).

77 *Williams v FAI Home Security Pty Ltd (No 4)* (2000) 180 ALR 459 at [19]. See also *Wong v Silkfield Pty Ltd* [2000] FCA 1421 at [18] (per Spender J); *Neil v P & O Cruises Australia Limited* [2002] FCA 1325 at [6]–[9] (per Weinberg J); *Tongue v Council of the City of Tamworth* [2004] FCA 972 at [22] (per Allsop J); *Lukey v Corporate Investment Australia Funds Management Pty Ltd* [2003] FCA 1602 at [7] (per Emmett J); and *Crawford v Bank of Western Australia Ltd* [2005] FCA 949 at [20] (per Lee J).

78 FCAA, s 43(1A).

79 It is important to note that in Australia only two plaintiffs law firms – Maurice Blackburn and Slater & Gordon – have regularly commenced class actions. This stands in stark contrast to the class action landscape in the US and Canada.

80 See, e.g., R Mulheron, *The Class Action in Common Law Legal Systems: A Comparative Perspective* (Oxford; Hart Publishing; 2004), 476. In Victoria, for instance, the *Legal Profession Act 2004* (Vic) provides that a costs agreement may provide for uplift fees being a premium not exceeding 25% of the legal costs (excluding unpaid disbursements) otherwise payable.

common.[81] Commercial litigation funders have funded many class proceedings over the last three years or so in exchange for, in the event of a victory by the plaintiff class, reimbursement of their expenditures as well as the payment of between 20 per cent and 45 per cent of the compensation that the class members will be entitled to receive from the litigation.[82] Their ability to receive a percentage of the damages or settlement proceeds received by the litigants stems from the fact that they are not lawyers and the prohibition against contingency fees only applies to the legal representatives of the litigants.[83] This is not the only controversial aspect of the involvement of commercial litigation funders. In fact, the restriction of the group represented by the class representative to those claimants who are willing to enter into funding agreements with litigation funders (as well as fee and retainer agreements with the class representative's solicitors) has been an integral part of their involvement in class proceedings.[84]

It is interesting to note that the judicial responses to the two developments noted above – the ability of third parties to fund legal proceedings in exchange for a share of the proceeds and the ability of such third parties (and/or the solicitors acting on behalf of the class representatives) to implement limited class mechanisms – have been conflicting. But in 2006 and 2007 the High Court of Australia[85] and the Full Federal Court of Australia,[86] respectively, held that these two emerging features of Australia's class action landscape were not illegal. An interesting ramification of the judicial approval of the involvement of commercial litigation funders, on the basis of contingency fee agreements, has been that 'both plaintiff and defence lawyers are asking why they should be prevented from entering into arrangements that function in the same way'.[87]

15. Interaction of public and private enforcement

Local antitrust actions, particularly class actions in cartel cases, rely heavily on regulatory action to reveal and articulate the alleged anticompetitive conduct. The ACCC has very broad powers to investigate potential antitrust breaches, including power to require the giving of information and the production of documents.[88] The ACCC is under no

---

[81] *Multiplex Funds Management Limited v P Dawson Nominees Pty Limited* (2007) 244 ALR 600 at [113]. See also *Kirby v Centro Properties Limited* [2008] FCA 1505 at [4] (in Australia it is becoming increasingly common for a litigation funder to cover the costs of the action).

[82] *Dorajay Pty Ltd v Aristocrat Leisure Limited* (2005) 147 FCR 394 at [77]; and *P Dawson Nominees Pty Ltd v Multiplex Limited* [2007] FCA 1061 at [32].

[83] As recently pointed out by Clark and Harris, this is due to the fact that the prohibition in every jurisdiction only extends to 'law practice': S Clark and C Harris, 'The Push to Reform Class Action Procedure in Australia: Evolution or Revolution?' (2008) 32 *Melbourne University Law Review* 775, 789 n 79. This prohibition has its origin in the common law offences and torts of maintenance and champerty: see V Morabito, 'Federal Class Actions, Contingency Fees, and the Rules Governing Litigation Costs' (1995) 21 *Monash University Law Review* 231, 243.

[84] See generally V. Morabito, 'Class Actions Instituted only for the Benefit of the Clients of the Class Representative's Solicitors' (2007) 29 *Sydney Law Review* 5.

[85] See *Campbells Cash & Carry Pty Ltd v Fostif Pty Ltd* (2006) 229 CLR 386.

[86] See *Multiplex Funds Management Limited v P Dawson Nominees Pty Limited* (2007) 244 ALR 600.

[87] Clark and Harris, above n 83, 789.

[88] TPA, §155. Employees cannot refuse to answer questions on the basis that the information is confidential.

obligation to provide this information to private plaintiffs. Indeed, it is under an obligation not to share certain types of information so obtained. The recent trend is for the ACCC (and other regulators[89]) to be generally reluctant to provide information to private litigants.[90]

The ACCC's reticence to cooperate with private claimants is attributable in part to its cartel immunity policy. The immunity policy is the key weapon in the ACCC's regulatory armoury against cartels.[91] To qualify for immunity from civil penalty proceedings brought by the ACCC the applicant must

- be the first to apply for immunity,
- not have coerced others to participate,
- not have been the clear leader of the cartel,
- have ceased the cartel conduct,
- provide full disclosure to the ACCC, and
- be prepared fully to cooperate with the ACCC.

The immunity policy does not oblige the applicant to pay damages or make restitution.[92] An immunity application may be made orally.[93] This is specifically to avoid discoverable admissions or to assist others (including private claimants).

Parliament has recently introduced criminal sanctions for serious cartel conduct.[94] Under the new provisions the ACCC's ability to cooperate with private litigants will be even further curtailed.[95]

The ACCC has power to intervene in civil proceedings with the leave of the court (whether as a party or as amicus curiae).[96] It will normally only do so where it considers that the matter involves an issue of significant public interest (for example, a critical question of statutory interpretation).

In any event, the ACCC will not subsidise private actions. Where it does intervene the ACCC will share information with the applicant to the extent permitted by law, but this will normally be done subject to conditions of confidentiality.[97] In this way the ACCC maintains control over the use of the information.

---

[89] For example, the Australian Securities and Investment Commission.

[90] See, eg, *Cadbury Schweppes Pty Ltd v Amcor Ltd* (2008) 246 ALR 137; *ACCC v Cadbury Schweppes Pty Ltd* [2009] FCAFC 32; *Jarra Creek Central Packing Shed Pty Ltd v Amcor Limited* [2008] FCA 554 at [37] – [38]; *ACCC v Visy Industry Holdings Pty Ltd (No 2)* [2007] FCA 444 at [103]–[108]; *Visy Industries Holdings Pty Ltd v ACCC* [2007] FCAFC 147 at [94]–[113]; *Australian Securities & Investment Commission (ASIC) v P Dawson Nominees Pty Ltd* [2008] FCAFC 123.

[91] ACCC, *Immunity Policy for Cartel Conduct* (2005). A new version will soon take effect.

[92] The ACCC's *Leniency Policy for Cartel Conduct* (2003) contained a vague requirement to make restitution to injured parties. No such requirement, however, is contained in the 2005 version or in the proposed new version.

[93] ACCC, *Immunity policy interpretation guidelines* (2008).

[94] See *Trade Practices Amendment (Cartel Conduct and Other Measures) Act 2009* (Cth). Other types of anti-competitive conduct do not attract criminal sanctions.

[95] See *Trade Practices Amendment (Cartel Conduct and Other Measures) Act 2009* which sets out a new regime for protecting cartel information supplied to the ACCC.

[96] TPA §87CA. See ACCC, *Intervention in Private Proceedings* (July 2002).

[97] See ACCC, *Intervention in Private Proceedings* (July 2002).

In a damages action a finding of fact by a court in a previous proceeding that a person has contravened the antitrust provisions is prima facie evidence of that fact.[98] The preferred view, however, is that this only applies to findings made as a result of a full hearing into the evidence. An agreed statement of facts is not sufficient.[99]

16. Extraterritoriality

Australia does not apply a US-style effects doctrine to its antitrust provisions. In Australia statutes are presumed not to have extraterritorial application, unless the legislature has otherwise indicated. The *Trade Practices Act* provides that the competition provisions extend to offshore conduct engaged in by, inter alia:

- companies incorporated in Australia, and
- companies carrying on business in Australia.

This leaves little room for an effects doctrine.

Where an applicant for damages intends to rely on the extraterritorial provisions of the Act the applicant must obtain the consent of the relevant government minister before initiating proceedings. The minister must give that consent unless, in her opinion, the conduct was required or authorised by the state in which it occurred and it would not be in Australia's national interest for the case to proceed.[100] The restrictive nature of Australia's extraterritorial provisions has been the subject of criticism.

As a result of having no effects doctrine, jurisdiction in the case of a global cartel will usually depend on the manner in which multinational corporations conduct their business in Australia. It is unlawful in Australia to make or *give effect* to a price fixing arrangement. If there is evidence that the multinational defendants engaged in unlawful conduct in Australia, then the extraterritorial provisions are not required. This happened in the vitamins case.[101] The foreign defendants' hands-on approach to implementing the cartel in Australia (e.g. communicating directly with local personnel and directing them in the implementation of the cartel) amounted to giving effect to the cartel in Australia.

In the absence of such evidence, however, the critical question is whether foreign defendants were carrying on business in Australia. Unlike Europe where the group economic unit doctrine extends jurisdiction to catch subsidiaries of foreign cartel members, Australian courts tend to apply a fairly strict version of the corporate veil.[102] Thus, in the vitamins cartel case, the court held that there was insufficient evidence to conclude

---

98 TPA, §83.

99 *ACCC v ABB Transmission and Distribution Limited (No 2)* (2002) 190 ALR 169; *ACCC v Monza Imports Pty Ltd* (2001) ATPR 41-843; *ACCC v Leahy Petroleum Pty Ltd (No 3)* [2005] FCA 265.

100 TPA, §5.

101 *Bray v F. Hoffman-La Roche Ltd* [2002] FCA 243 upheld on appeal: *Bray v F. Hoffman-La Roche Ltd* (2003) 200 ALR 607.

102 The test is whether the 'parent company is so directly and intimately connected with the conduct of the subsidiary that it is proper to regard the conduct of the subsidiary as that of the parent company as well'. *Bray v F. Hoffman-La Roche Ltd* [2002] FCA 243 upheld on appeal: *Bray v F. Hoffman-La Roche Ltd* (2003) 200 ALR 607.

that the multinational defendants were carrying on business in Australia through their subsidiaries.

17. Effect of court/ACCC decisions on the disposition of private proceedings

Private litigants may rely on findings of fact in proceedings brought by the ACCC as *prima facie* evidence of those facts.[103] However, a statement of agreed facts tendered to the court in penalty proceedings but not subject to any critical analysis is almost certainly not a 'finding of fact' for this purpose.[104] Statements of agreed facts may vary significantly from the scope of alleged conduct in the civil matter.[105] Therefore, while statements of agreed facts are likely to assist private litigants to plead otherwise obscured conduct and to provide markers for further inquiry, their evidentiary usefulness is limited.[106]

Where the ACCC has authorised conduct or where there is in place in respect of the conduct a valid notification, the conduct is lawful.[107] No civil proceedings would lie.

Conclusion

Private actions have been a regular part of the Australian competition law landscape for many years. Until recently, however, these cases were fought as party against party actions (competitor against competitor or commercial buyer against commercial supplier), not as representative proceedings. Given the costs rules in Australia and the often protracted nature of competition proceedings, the cases tended to revolve around establishing grounds for injunctive relief. Damages followed normally as an out-of-court settlement. This scene has changed with the use of class actions. Unless there are significant legislative changes to the class action rules, private actions are likely to play an important role in antitrust enforcement in the next five years.

---

103 TPA, §83.

104 *ACCC v Leahy Petroleum Pty Ltd (No 3)* [2005] FCA 265; *ACCC v ABB Transmission and Distribution Limited (No 2)* [2002] FCA 558; *ACCC v Monza Imports Pty Ltd* (2001) ATPR 41-843.

105 See for example *ACCC v Roche Vitamins Australia Pty Ltd* (2001) ATPR 41-809 cf *Darwalla Milling Co Pty Ltd v F Hoffman-La Roche Ltd (No 2)* (2006) 236 ALR 322.

106 See, eg, *ACCC v Pratt (No 3)* [2009] FCA 407.

107 See above n 19.

30 China

Zou Weining[1] *and Ma Chunsheng*[2]

Introduction

The Antimonopoly Law of the People's Republic of China (Antimonopoly Law) was passed on August 30, 2007 and took effect on August 1, 2008. The Antimonopoly Law regulates the monopolistic acts of monopoly agreements, abuse of dominant market position, concentration of business operators and abuse of administrative power to eliminate or restrict competition. However, the Antimonopoly Law mainly focuses on substantive provisions and administrative enforcement proceedings. The Chinese administrative authorities in charge of antimonopoly investigations are now drafting its implementation rules and guidelines.

For disputes related to properties and personal relationships between natural persons, juristic persons and other organizations, a civil action may be taken in the court. However, private antimonopoly enforcement in China is still in a preliminary phase. Because the Antimonopoly Law is not particularly clear on substantive and procedural issues related to private enforcement, the Supreme People's Court (Supreme Court) has unofficially clarified certain issues and is currently drafting an official judicial interpretation on private enforcement. In China, judicial interpretations of the Supreme Court are binding on all Chinese courts.

1. Legal basis for private rights of action

The Antimonopoly Law allows companies, organizations and persons (consumers), if adversely affected by monopolistic acts under the Antimonopoly Law, to sue for civil damages. Article 50 of the Antimonopoly Law states that 'the business operators that carry out the monopolistic conducts and cause damages to others shall bear the civil liability according to law.' Accordingly, if an interested party brings a civil action on the grounds of monopolistic acts, the action should meet the requirements of both the Civil Procedure Law and the Antimonopoly Law.

In order to facilitate the trial of private antimonopoly cases, the Supreme Court unofficially clarified several issues related to private enforcement in China, including jurisdiction, qualified plaintiffs, civil liability, the relationship between administrative and private enforcement, determination of monopolistic acts and intellectual property protection.

2. Jurisdiction of private antimonopoly cases

The Supreme Court has clarified that all antimonopoly cases, including private cases, are to be tried at the Intellectual Property Court within the people's court. However, it

---

[1] Zou Weining, Partner of Jun He Law Offices.
[2] Ma Chunsheng, Associate of Jun He Law Offices.

remains unclear which level of courts will be granted jurisdiction to try private antimonopoly cases. Some commentators believe that due to the multifarious nature of antimonopoly cases and their influence on business and the economy, private antimonopoly cases should be tried at an intermediate court specifically appointed by the Supreme Court in order to ensure the quality of the trial.

3. Qualified plaintiffs

Any person may bring a civil action in the court according to the Procedure Law. However, in private antimonopoly enforcement, the scope of business entities qualified to be plaintiffs and whether consumers are qualified to be plaintiffs remain unclear because the Antimonopoly Law does not clarify these issues. Before the Supreme Court issues an opinion on these issues, different courts may implement different standards at their discretion in practice.

4. Civil liabilities

Regarding the forms of civil liability for monopolistic practices, the Supreme Court has clarified that, in addition to compensation for damage, a court may also grant injunctive relief. However, the procedure for calculation of damages in private antimonopoly cases is still unresolved. Some commentators believe that the Supreme Court would further clarify the method to calculate the compensation for damage caused by monopolistic acts.

5. Relationship between public and private enforcement

In China, administrative proceedings may be required prior to private litigation in certain complicated areas of law, such as cases involving securities. There were expectations that private antimonopoly enforcement might also require administrative proceedings before private litigation.

According to a statement of the chief justice of the Intellectual Property Department of the Supreme Court at a press interview, there would be no prerequisite of administrative proceedings to start private antimonopoly litigation. The Supreme Court further stated that coordination between administrative antimonopoly enforcement and private antimonopoly enforcement should mainly consist of the finding of facts and establishing the existence of monopolistic practices, and the Supreme Court would research and issue its opinions on whether the findings in administrative proceedings bind private actions. In the views of some commentators, it is progress to abandon such prerequisite in private antimonopoly enforcement, but it would be very difficult for private entities and/or end consumers to collect sufficient evidence to prove monopolistic acts.

6. Determination of monopolistic practices

The determination of monopolistic practices is the most important part of private antimonopoly cases, which mainly includes the questions of how to allocate the burden of proof in private enforcement and how to analyze monopolistic practices. Issues such as defining the relevant market, assessment of market shares and the investigation of the competing relationship between plaintiff and defendant are all very complicated and important to private antimonopoly cases, and must be further clarified by the Supreme Court.

7. Intellectual property protection and antimonopoly

The delicate balance between intellectual property protection and monopolistic acts, i.e. the abuse of intellectual property under Article 55[3] of the Antimonopoly Law, is another important issue remaining to be resolved by the Supreme Court.

There is still no private case in practice on the grounds of monopolistic acts by abusing intellectual property rights. In the views of the commentators, the Antimonopoly Law should apply if the business operators abuse their intellectual property rights, including but not limited to horizontal restraints, price discrimination, tying arrangements, exclusive dealing, cross-licensing and pooling arrangements, grantbacks, exclusive dealing.

8. Private antimonopoly cases

Private antimonopoly cases typically involve private business entities in the competing position rather than business entities and consumers. There have been no completed private cases in China to date.

However, there are two private cases – one is still pending – that may ultimately help clarify how private actions will be handled. First, in Li Fangping v. China Netcom (Group) Company Beijing Branch, the plaintiff, a consumer of a fixed-line telephone, filed suit for price discrimination in business resulting from his lack of Beijing citizenship. Second, in Beijing Pan-Pass Info Tech Co. Ltd. v. General Administration Quality Supervision Inspection and Quarantine of PR China, the plaintiffs filed suit for administrative monopolistic practices through compulsory implementation of the 'Electronic Supervision Network.'

a. Li Fangping v. China Netcom (Group) Company Beijing Branch (August 1, 2008)

Li Fanping is a registered attorney who had worked and lived in Beijing for over 10 years at the time of the litigation. Li's domicile, however, was not registered as a Beijing citizenship. In China, the domicile of a person is registered and administered by the Public Security Bureau of the local government and the domicile is the basis to exercise most of political and social rights, such as voting and other welfare provided by local government. However, Chinese people are not allowed to move their domicile without the permission of government authorities. Li filed an application for a fixed-line telephone in Beijing and was told that he must provide a guarantee from a person with a local domicile; otherwise, he could only apply for a pre-paid telephone. Li ultimately applied for the pre-paid telephone because he could not provide such a guarantee.

In May 2007, China Netcom (Group) Company Beijing Branch ('Beijing Netcom') started a set broadband network service to provide some favorable selectable packages in the telephone rate (called 'Family 1+'). In 2008, Beijing Netcom further promoted an updated version of 'Family 1+' activity including the service of 'family gateway of network, net print' etc. However, such benefits were limited to fixed-line telephone clients, making Li ineligible for the benefits.

---

[3] Article 55 of the Antimonopoly Law provides that 'this law shall not apply to the conduct of business operators to exercise their intellectual property rights according to the laws and relevant administrative regulations on intellectual property rights; however, this Law shall apply to the conduct of business operators to eliminate or restrict market competition by abusing their intellectual property rights.'

On August 1, 2008, the first day that the Antimonopoly Law took effect, Li filed a complaint against Beijing Netcom, claiming it had committed a monopolistic practice by abusing its dominant market position under the Antimonopoly Law in discriminating against pre-paid telephone clients, as the practice was made possible by its dominant market position in Beijing.

The case was officially established by the Court for Beijing Chaoyang District, where it is still pending, and was the first private antimonopoly case in China. In the view of some commentators, this is a classical private monopoly enforcement case involving abuse of dominant market position which violates the Antimonopoly Law. And this case is also an opportunity for the court to clarify certain ambiguous issues relating to the Antimonopoly Law.

b. Beijing Pan-Pass Info Tech Co. Ltd. et al v. the General Administration Quality Supervision Inspection and Quarantine of PR China (August 1, 2008)

Also on the first day that the Antimonopoly Law took effect, Beijing Pan-Pass Info Tech Co. Ltd. and three other companies (collectively 'Pan-Pass') filed a complaint against the General Administration Quality Supervision Inspection and Quarantine of PR China ('AQSIQ') for administrative monopoly in the compulsory implementation of the 'Electronic Supervision Network.'

Pan-Pass and the other plaintiff companies manufacture anti-counterfeiting products, such as anti-counterfeiting labels. Beginning in April 2005, AQSIQ promoted a system called the Electronic Supervision Network, requiring relevant manufacturers to attach a code to their products and join the Network system for public query purposes.

In November 2007, AQSIQ circulated an official notice to implement the Electronic Supervision Network, requiring all producers of foods, domestic electrical appliances, artificial slabs, electrical wires and cables, farm materials, gas devices, labor safety supplies, electrothermal blankets and cosmetics to attach an electronic supervision code before the sale of such products.

The Electronic Supervision Network was operated by a company named CCIT China, which is controlled by the AQSIQ. Companies applying for access to the system must pay for the data maintenance service, and consumers seeking information also must pay the information fees.

Pan-Pass claimed that AQSIQ violated the Anti-Unfair Competition Law and Antimonopoly Law by promoting the Electronic Supervision Network system and requiring companies to attach a product code and join the Network. By promoting the electronic supervision business of CCIT China and granting it sole rights to run the system in the anti-counterfeit products market, AQSIQ caused serious damage to the competitive rights of other companies manufacturing anti-counterfeit products.

This case was rejected by the Beijing First Intermediate Court for being outside the statute of limitations of two years. Since the Anti-Unfair Competition Law also regulates the abuse of administrative power to eliminate or restrict competition, and overlaps with the Antimonopoly Law in this regard, it is noteworthy that Pan-Pass based its claim on both the Anti-Unfair Competition Law and the Antimonopoly Law for abuse of administrative power, and Pan-Pass, however, did not sue its competitor, the CCIT China, in its complaint.

9. Resources of private antimonopoly enforcement

In China, the administrative authorities in charge of antimonopoly investigations include the Antimonopoly Commission, the Ministry of Commerce, the National Development and Reform Commission and the State Administration for Industry and Commerce. The courts have jurisdiction over the trial of antimonopoly cases.[4]

Conclusion

In the views of commentators, more and more private enforcement cases involving the Antimonopoly Law will arise in the future, since there are so many companies with dominant market positions in many industry areas in China. Claims for damages for monopolistic acts will also be filed in the private enforcement cases pursuant to Article 50 of the Antimonopoly Law. However, it would be a very complicated issue for the court to award and calculate the damages.

Further, commentators believe that the administrative agencies' decisions should be subject to judicial review by courts and the findings in administrative proceedings should bind in the private monopoly cases.

[4] For more information about the above administrative agencies and the Supreme Court of China, please visit their respective official websites: State Council: http://www.gov.cn/; Ministry of Commerce: http://www.mofcom.gov.cn/; National Development and Reform Commission: http://www.ndrc.gov.cn/; State Administration for Industry and Commerce: http://www.saic.gov.cn/; Supreme People's Court: http://www.court.gov.cn/; and People's Court Daily: http://rmfyb.chinacourt.org/.

31 India

Pradeep S. Mehta[1] *and Cornelius Dube*[2]

Introduction

The Indian case with respect to private antitrust enforcement offers a unique example, given that private enforcement has to be administered by the same institutions tasked with public enforcement of competition law. The Monopolies and Restrictive Trade Practices Commission (MRTP Commission), established by the Monopolies and Restrictive Trade Practices Act, 1969 (MRTP Act), was the sole body responsible for the enforcement of competition law in India until 20 May, 2009, when the Competition Commission of India (CCI), established by the Competition Act, 2002 (Competition Act), became effective. The Competition Appellate Tribunal (CAT), which is also provided for under the Competition Act, was inaugurated on 19 October 2009. The CAT is established to hear appeals against orders of the CCI and to preside over compensation claims relating to violations of the Competition Act. In terms of the Competition Act, the MRTP Commission was expected to continue to prevail for two years after the Competition Act took effect to handle pending cases, although not entertaining any new cases.[3]

However, in a surprising turn of events, the MRTP Commission came to a premature demise on October 14, 2009 when the President of India promulgated the Competition (Amendment) Ordinance, 2009 amending section 66 of the Competition Act. In terms of the Ordinance, from October 14 all monopolistic or restrictive trade practices pending before the MRTP Commission would be transferred to the CAT. However, the MRTP Act will still be in force, given that in deciding these outstanding cases, the CAT would only apply the provisions of the MRTP Act.

Private enforcement of competition law, in the Indian context, refers to situations where private agents use the provisions of the MRTP Act and/or the Competition Act to seek compensation for damage suffered as a result of anticompetitive behaviour. Although there have been numerous applications for receiving compensation from violators of the MRTP Act's provisions related to unfair trade practices, the same cannot be said about applications relating to violations of restrictive and monopolistic trade practices. For example, during the period April–December 2004, there were 1,231 applications for compensation being considered under section 12B (of which only 75 were filed during the same period and others were brought forward from previous period). During the period April–December 2006, there were 1,323 cases being considered (114 were fresh applications) while for the period April–December, 2007, there were 1,187 applications

[1] Secretary General, CUTS International (psm@cuts.org and www.pradeepsmehta.com), India.

[2] Economist, CUTS CCIER, (cd@cuts.org) India. Significant contribution came from Dr S Chakravarthy, a civil servant by profession and formerly Member, MRTP Commission.

[3] This is as per the provisions of §66 of the Competition Act, 2002.

being considered (79 cases were new applications).[4] It can be established however that these applications related largely to unfair trade practices, with cases relating to anti-competitive practices cropping up once in a while. Thus in India private enforcement of competition law has generally not been pursued.

Section 12B of the MRTP Act was the legal basis for private enforcement of competition law in India, while under the Competition Act, private action for damages is provided for under section 53N of the Competition Act, 2002.

This chapter is an analysis of the various issues on private enforcement of competition law in India. Private enforcement will be discussed with respect to provisions of both the MRTP Act and the Competition Act to reflect the current position where both pieces of legislation are operational.[5]

1. What practices are illegal and what are the elements of proof?

The MRTP Commission was actively involved in competition enforcement for decades, although its performance has never been satisfactory, with cases remaining pending for long periods. With respect to cartels and abuse of dominance, the lack of private actions for damages following these prolonged investigations compounded the problem of public under-enforcement. Under the MRTP Act, there are three categories of cases that are illegal. These are classified as monopolistic trade practices, restrictive trade practices and unfair trade practices.

In terms of section 2(i) of the MRTP Act, monopolistic trade practices include practices which have or are likely to have the following effects:

(a) maintaining the prices of goods or charges for services at an unreasonable level by limiting, reducing or controlling the production, supply or distribution of goods;
(b) unreasonably preventing or lessening competition in the production, supply or distribution of goods or services;
(c) limiting technical development or capital investment or allowing the quality of any goods or services produced, supplied or distributed in India to deteriorate;
(d) increasing unreasonably the cost of production of goods or charges for provision or maintenance of services;
(e) increasing unreasonably the price at which goods and services are provided or increasing unreasonably the profits which may be derived in production, supply or distribution of goods and services.

On the other hand, restrictive trade practices are defined in section 2(o) of the MRTP Act to mean trade practices which have or may have the effect of preventing, distorting or restricting competition in any manner, particularly:

---

4 The statistics were extracted from the annual reports of the Ministry of Corporate Affairs, India, for the periods 2004–05; 2006–07 and 2007–08. The choice of periods is just arbitrary.

5 Although the MRTP Act is only applicable to outstanding cases, the new Act has just started operations and the only experience on private enforcement can be obtained from the MRTP era, hence the inclusion. In addition, any outstanding case on compensation from the MRTP era also has to be addressed by the CAT.

(a) which tend to obstruct the flow of capital or resources into the stream of production;
(b) which tend to bring about manipulation of prices, conditions of delivery or affect the flow of goods and services supply in such a manner that they impose on the consumers unjustified cost or restrictions.

This generally covers all kinds of agreements, which must all be registered with the MRTP Commission, as per sections 33 and 35 of the MRTP Act.

Unfair trade practices are defined to mean trade practices which adopt any unfair method or unfair or deceptive practice for the purpose of promoting the sale, use and supply of any goods or services. These provisions, which also fall under the Indian Consumer Protection Act, 1986 (COPRA), are not discussed in this chapter.

Although using different terms, abuse of dominance provisions generally are covered under monopolistic trade practices, while anticompetitive agreements are classified under restrictive trade practices. Mergers and acquisitions are not covered under the MRTP Act.

The MRTP Act does not list any elements that can be used as proof of occurrence for each case besides giving definitions. Instead the MRTP Act calls upon the MRTP Commission to undertake enquiries, which include any hearings it may think fit to hold, to make factual findings.

Under the Competition Act, private actions for damages can be pursued in respect to cases falling under Chapter II of the Act, covering sections 3 to 6. In Chapter II, unlike the MRTP Act that lumps various practices under monopolistic and restrictive practices, anticompetitive practices have been disaggregated to cover anticompetitive agreements (both horizontal and vertical), abuse of dominance and anticompetitive combinations (mergers and acquisitions). For business combinations, the scope for private action probably would be in instances where the parties do not abide by the pre-merger notification requirement provided for in terms of the Competition Act and it is later proven that the combination was anticompetitive. Private parties, typically customers of the business combination, can seek damages for the period in which the combination was in place.

It is difficult to predict at this stage whether cartels, business combinations or abuse of dominance are most likely to give rise to successful private action, as the Competition Act has just taken effect. However private action is likely to be comparatively easier than under the MRTP Act, as provisions on anticompetitive agreements and abuse of dominance are well articulated in sections 3 and 4 respectively of the Competition Act. Section 19 of the Competition Act also lays out the various aspects that are to be taken into account in determining dominance and its abuse, as well as whether any agreement is anticompetitive. Arguing a case for damages will be easier for claimants and their attorneys using these provisions as references, unlike under the MRTP Act scenario.

2. How does a damages action get started?

Under the MRTP Act, section 12B required the aggrieved parties to apply for compensation to the MRTP Commission and granted the Commission exclusive authority over deciding these claims. In this regard, the MRTP Commission had dual functionality: finding of contravention and calculation of damages.

The MRTP Act provides only for follow-on cases in which claimants wait for MRTP

Commission judgments to file for compensation claims. Although claimants can also seek compensation on cases that have not yet been investigated by the MRTP Commission when they believe there have been violations and they have suffered damage, that can only be done if they also provide details to necessitate an investigation to prove occurrence, as the claim would be considered only after the Commission has established the contravention. There is no time limit provided by the MRTP Act for investigation and response and the MRTP Commission uses its discretion in each case.

Although the compensation quest was unsuccessful, the case of *Narang Store v T.T. Krishnamachari and Co. (1999)* can be used to substantiate this. Narang Stores filed a complaint with the MRTP accusing TT Krishnamachari of restrictive trade practices such as discriminatory pricing, refusal to deal and exclusive dealing among others. In the same application, Narang Stores pursued compensation for losses suffered due to some of these practices under section 12B. In its judgement, the MRTP Commission dismissed the restrictive trade practices on which these compensation claims were based, and on that basis, dismissed the compensation claim without any further analysis. However, the company was found guilty of area restrictions, a charge to which the claimant had not linked his compensation claims. [6]

Under section 53N of the Competition Act, damages actions can be pursued through applications to the Competition Appellate Tribunal and not to the Competition Commission, a slightly different set-up from the MRTP Act. The explanation to section 53N explicitly states that such applications can only be made after the Commission or Tribunal has found evidence of violations and no compensation application requiring new investigations would be permitted. The claimants are therefore requested to attach the findings of the CCI or the Tribunal with respect to public enforcement in their application.

Private parties can also pursue injunctive relief, given that an injunction may be granted both under the Competition Act and the MRTP Act pending a final decision on the main application.

3. Who may pursue a claim?

Under both the MRTP Act and the Competition Act, any party who has suffered loss or damage as a result of the practices may pursue a claim. This includes Central Government, State Government, Local Authority, any enterprise, trader or class of traders or any consumer. Thus the determinative factor is having suffered losses or damage as a result of a practice that is in contravention of the competition law rather than the status of the claimant.

4. How may claims be aggregated?

Under both the MRTP Act and the Competition Act, where any loss or damage is caused to multiple parties having the same interest, one or more of such parties may make an application on behalf of others in accordance with the terms of the Code of Civil Procedure, 1908 (5 of 1908). Under Rule 8 of Order 1 of the First Schedule to the Code of Civil Procedure, 1908 a person may request the permission of the court to claim

---

[6] MRTP Commission Judgment found at http://indiankanoon.org/doc/876664/.

on behalf of other parties, after which the court will notify the parties of the intended suit, either individually or through advertisement, at the plaintiff's expense. The Code provides that people may be joined in one suit as plaintiffs where a right to relief arising out of the same act is alleged to exist in such persons or where, if such people brought separate suits, any common question of law or fact would arise. Thus the Code provides for an 'opt-in' system to class action, where no person can be added as a plaintiff without seeking his/her consent. It is unclear whether an 'opt-out' system for claims aggregation may be adopted in the future.

5. What procedural defences are available short of trial?

Once the MRTP Commission ruled that the practice engaged in was a monopolistic or restrictive trade practice, it was difficult to stop the initiation of a damages suit with respect to the offending practice. One of the grounds upon which private enforcement was dismissed short of a trial was the period that elapsed between the time that an individual purchased the product and the time that the claim for compensation was sought.

In the case of *Shiva Motors v TVS Suzuki Ltd 2002 CTJ 292 (MRTP)*, the applicant was aggrieved by the termination of a dealership agreement by the respondent on October 14, 1997 and filed a section 12B application with the MRTP Commission in the year 2001. The Commission dismissed the compensation claim as being time barred, placing reliance on a Supreme Court decision in the case of Corporation Bank v. Navin Shah, which stated a maximum time limit of three years after the offence.

6. What devices are available to obtain evidence?

While evidence gathering in the case of public enforcement is provided for under both the MRTP Act and the Competition Act, there are no separate provisions on evidence gathering for private enforcement. During hearings on compensation cases relating to unfair trade practices under section 12B of the MRTP Act, the onus was largely on the claimant to provide evidence on how s/he suffered damage. No court procedure has been laid down in India for gathering evidence by private parties.

Provisions on evidence gathering for public enforcement include section 12 of the MRTP Act, empowering the MRTP Commission to summon defendants or witnesses and to request any document for use as evidence in its investigations. Where it believed documents might be hidden, destroyed, altered or mutilated, the Commission was empowered to enter storage facilities and search and seize any document from an undertaking for use in its preliminary investigation. Similarly, under section 36 of the Competition Act, the CCI has the power to summon witnesses and respondents and can order them to produce any documents it feels are necessary for its investigations. Moreover, the section empowers the CCI to call upon experts from the fields of economics, commerce, accountancy, international trade or from any other discipline as it deems necessary to assist the Commission in the conduct of any inquiry by it. Information gathered in such a manner can also be used for private enforcement.

The explanation to section 53N of the Competition Act makes it clear that compensation decisions by the Tribunal would be based on the evidence obtained under public enforcement, and the task of the Tribunal would be only to determine the eligibility and quantum of the compensation due. Thus public enforcement evidence would guide private enforcement.

7. What do plaintiffs get if they win?

Under both the MRTP Act and the Competition Act, plaintiffs get compensation if they win, where the compensatory award equals the damage shown to have resulted from the contravention. Claimants receive only actual damages, as opposed to the punitive or treble damage regimes in other countries.

The methods for determining the damages amount have not been provided for under both set of laws. Going by the previous cases handled by the MRTP Commission on unfair trade practices, the claimants submit their own calculation on how much they have suffered but the MRTP Commission has the final say in how much should be awarded. There are no established cases where the MRTP Commission resorted to ordinary civil laws or code in determining damages.

The same is the case under the Competition Act, as the Tribunal makes the final decision on the damages amount based on the amount that it feels is 'realisable' from the enterprise as well as 'any loss or damage shown to have been suffered' by the plaintiffs.

8. How does the plaintiff's lawyer finance private enforcement?

Given the dearth of private enforcement in India, it is difficult to ascertain how plaintiffs' attorneys finance private enforcement efforts. While both the MRTP Act and the Competition Act provide that the claimants should claim for compensation for amounts relating to damage suffered, there appears to be nothing that can prevent the claimants from including legal costs incurred in recovering the damages in their application.

9. How does private enforcement interact with public enforcement?

In India, private enforcement interacts closely with public enforcement. As has already been explained, under both the MRTP Act and the Competition Act, private enforcement is based on public enforcement outcomes. Private enforcement becomes possible only after cases have been investigated and concluded through public enforcement.

Conclusion

Although there has been a basis for private enforcement of competition law in India due to the insertion of section 12B provisions into the MRTP Act in 1984, the level of private enforcement two decades later is troublingly almost non-existent. The paltry number of private actions may be the result of systematic under-enforcement on the part of the MRTP Commission.

The MRTP Act itself was very weak, with no mention of anticompetitive practices such as abuse of dominance and cartels, rendering it less effective in containing them. The MRTP Commission was poorly resourced, and unable to meet the expectations of a big country such as India. The biggest failure of the MRTP Commission was in the prosecution of cartels, where it has failed to take action amid allegations of cartels in various sectors, including cement, steel, tyre, trucking and family planning services.[7] Some competition cases involving abuse of dominance, which are resolved expeditiously in other jurisdictions, would take more than five years for the MRTP Commission to handle.

In such an environment, it is inevitable for a similar trend to be witnessed for private

---

[7] See CUTS (2007), Competition and Regulation in India, 2007, CIRC, Jaipur.

enforcement, which is entirely dependent on the outcomes of public enforcement actions.

As a deterrent tool, private enforcement can play a bigger role in India than public enforcement, given that the MRTP Commission could only pass cease and desist orders for violation of the law (except in resale price maintenance, for which fine is provided for under section 51), and could only impose fines if its orders were not followed. In addition to cease and desist orders, the CCI is empowered to impose financial penalties of up to 10 per cent of turnover for the last three preceding financial years for violations of the Competition Act. However more private enforcement action would have a greater deterrent effect on would-be offenders than public enforcement.

The role of private action is likely to become more prominent during the next few years with the newly-effective Competition Act. The current arrangement where the CCI is not responsible for private enforcement (unlike the MRTP Commission) would allow the CCI to concentrate only on public enforcement while the CAT is responsible for hearing private claims. Moreover, the CCI has more teeth compared to the MRTP Commission, given its stronger legislative framework; hence this is likely to stimulate private players into action, as their chances of getting compensation would be enhanced. Thus in the next five years, private enforcement is likely to gather momentum.

Increased private enforcement is only possible if the public is made aware of the important role of private actions in deterring anticompetitive practices. The consumer practitioners and movements need to be active in building the capacity of consumers and public-minded lawyers in bringing more compensation claims.

32 Israel

Niv Zecler, Michal S. Gal and Yariv Ilan[1]

Introduction

Private antitrust enforcement in Israel has been on the books for many years. Indeed, the first Israeli Restrictive Trade Practices Law, dating from 1959, stated that a breach of the Law's prohibitions can serve as a basis for a private damages claim.[2] This provision was later incorporated into the new version of the Restrictive Trade Practices Law, dating from 1988[3] ('the Competition Law' or 'the Law'). In practice, however, private damages suits were seldom invoked. One of the main reasons was that collective redress was unavailable. This situation changed markedly in 1996 when class actions on antitrust issues were allowed.[4]

Today private antitrust enforcement is an integral part of the Israeli antitrust arena, attracting growing awareness from the general public and the legal community. It is thus rightly perceived as a potential pivotal enhancement to the Rashut Hahegbelim Haiskiim's (Israeli Antitrust Authority or IAA) enforcement toolkit. Indeed, the IAA has often indicated the importance of invigorating private enforcement initiatives, aimed at deterring antitrust infringements as well as securing redress for private parties' damage.[5] The role of private actions in Israeli antitrust enforcement is enhanced by the limited powers of the IAA to sanction most antitrust violations in practice.[6]

Private litigants' increasing consciousness of antitrust issues and the possibility for private redress, alongside significant advancements in economic and legal analysis, have led to an increased number of private claims for damages in recent years. In general, private antitrust actions are available for almost all forms of infringements under the Competition Law, namely, horizontal and vertical anti-competitive restraints of trade, abuse of dominance and mergers consummated without receiving prior approval or

---

1 Respectively partner and founder, Weinstock, Zecler Attorneys; LL.B., LL.M., J.S.D., Vice-Dean, Associate Professor and Co-Director, Center of Law and Markets, Haifa University School of Law; Ph.D. Associate Weinstock, Zecler Attorneys.

2 The Restrictive Trade Practices Law , 1959, S.H. 286.

3 The Restrictive Trade Practices Law, 1988, S.H. 1258.

4 Chapter VI1 of the Israeli Competition Law 1988 (repealed).

5 See, *e.g.*, IAA, Annual Report 2008, *available at* http://archive.antitrust.gov.il (hereinafter: 'Antitrust'), decision number 5001419. Note that most of the decisions quoted herein can be found on the IAA website just cited, by using their assigned serial numbers.

6 Under the Competition Law the IAA is not empowered to impose a fine. It has three main remedial options which are further elaborated below: criminal proceedings (by delegation from the Attorney General), publishing a declaration that an antitrust violation has occurred and reaching a consent decree with the accused violator. It is interesting to note that under the Israeli Class Actions Act 2006 the IAA is also empowered to bring a class action based on an antitrust violation. However, the IAA has never used this power and has never announced its intentions of doing so in the future.

without meeting the conditions imposed by the IAA. Yet while the number of private damages suits is steadily growing, it is still limited relative to its potential. In addition, to date, only a small number of damages cases have been concluded. Some of the reasons for such limited private enforcement will be elaborated throughout this chapter. One reason, worth mentioning at the outset, is the length of the proceedings. For example, in 2007 monetary compensation was awarded by the District Court to three foreign airlines, injured by a restrictive arrangement between wholesale suppliers of jet refueling services for the aviation sector.[7] This litigation, which lasted more than a decade, marked the first private action in which pecuniary compensations were sought.

Another important basis for private enforcement in Israel involves contractual claims. Under the Competition Law, a breach of the law's provisions constitutes a criminal offense.[8] Under the Israeli Contract Law an illegal contract is automatically void.[9] The combination of these provisions enables a party to an illegal contract to contend that the agreement is void and thus it does not have to meet its contractual obligations. Indeed, most private antitrust claims in Israel center around contractual disputes, whereby a party to an agreement seeks to elude its unprofitable contractual obligations.[10] Although the contractual remedy is not pecuniary, it oftentimes has significant pecuniary effects. It is noteworthy that since the disputed contracts generally have a small effect on competition, if at all, and the conduct may have been caught under the prohibition only because of its too-wide wording, the risk that the contractual dispute will lead to criminal charges against the contracting parties or to other actions taken by the IAA is generally insignificant. Accordingly, in the past decade most antitrust disputes that reached the Israeli Supreme Court were contractual disputes.[11] This affected the interpretation of the Competition Law. Given the clash between its wide and inflexible prohibitions against unauthorized restrictive arrangements on the one hand, and the perceived attempts of parties to take advantage of this fact and elude contractual obligations by arguing that the contract infringes the prohibition against restrictive arrangements and thus is void, on the other, the result was a narrow and sometimes problematic interpretation of the Law by the Court.[12]

The rest of this chapter focuses mainly on private damages suits. It will first provide a general review of the relevant legal framework and then delve into more detailed issues involved in bringing such suits. In particular, the chapter will focus on the unique

---

[7] CC (Hi) 1114/99 *Tower Air v. Flight Serv. Ltd.* IsrDC, 2007 Antitrust 5000590.

[8] Sections 47 and 47A of the Competition Law.

[9] Section 30 of the Contract Law (General Part), 1973, 694 S.H. 118. See also, *e.g.*, Rehearing 4465/98 *Tivall (1993) Ltd. v. Chef Hayam (1994) Ltd.* [2001] IsrSC, 56(1) 56; CC 666/97 *Ahmed Naser v. Delek the Israel Fuel Corporation Ltd.*, IsrDC (March 3, 2005); PCA 5622/90 *Refaeli v. Camp Israel Ltd.* [1991] IsrSC, 45(2) 104.

[10] See, e.g. 626/70 *Shimoni v. Ulamei L'echaim Ltd.*, [1971] IsrSC, 25(1) 824.

[11] See, e.g., Rehearing 4465/98 *Tivall (1993) Ltd. v. Chef Hayam (1994) Ltd.*, [2001] IsrSC, 56(1) 56; CA 3700/98 *A.M. Hanayot (Jerusalem) 1993 Ltd. v. Municipality of Jerusalem* [2003] 57(2), 59; PCA 6233/02 *Axtel Ltd v. Kalma Way Indus. Mktg. Aluminum Glass & Metal Fixtures Ltd.* [2004] IsrSC, 58(2) 634.

[12] See, e.g., Michal S. Gal, 'Separating the Wheat from the Shaft: Restrictive Agreement in Light of the Supreme Court's Recent Decisions', 1 *University of Haifa L. R. (Din Udvarim)* 533 (2004) (Hebrew).

challenges faced by potential private litigants. Some of these challenges arise because of Israel's legislative framework and some result from the unique characteristics of the Israeli economy.

1. The general legislative framework

a. Conduct prohibited by the law

The Competition Law covers three practices: restrictive arrangements, abuse of dominance, and mergers. Below we provide a broad-brush analysis of the Law's prohibitions. Israeli law is a combination of mostly common law, with some civil law influences as well as some unique Israeli legal constructs. The Competition Law of 1959 was largely based on the British model, with some American and European influences.[13] Later changes in the law, most notably modifications in the monopolization prohibitions, followed the European model.

i. Restrictive arrangements The Competition Law forbids restrictive arrangements unless they fulfill one of the following two conditions:

(A) THEY HAVE BEEN EXEMPTED BY THE DIRECTOR GENERAL OF THE IAA The Director General is empowered to exempt restrictive arrangements only if they do not harm competition significantly. The Director General publishes Block Exemptions that specify categories of cases which are deemed to have an insignificant harmful effect on competition. Should the arrangement fulfill all of the conditions of a Block Exemption, it is automatically exempt.[14] Otherwise, the parties can request that the Director General grant them a specific exemption. The Director General will only grant such an exemption if the parties convince him that the arrangement has insignificant effects on competition.[15] The decisions of the Director General are subject to appeal to the Beit Hadin LeHegbelim Iskiim (the 'Antitrust Tribunal').

(B) THE RESTRICTIVE ARRANGEMENT WAS APPROVED BY THE ANTITRUST TRIBUNAL The Tribunal may approve an arrangement, following a request by affected parties, if the public interest benefits outweigh any harms to competition and no less restrictive option is available to achieve such benefits.[16] A potential example of such an arrangement could be one where a research and development joint venture is created that is likely to increase consumer welfare.

The exemption or the approval must be obtained prior to the commencement of the arrangement. This system has many similarities to the European notification system that existed before 2003.

A restrictive arrangement is defined as follows:[17]

---

[13] Lionel Kestenbaum, 'Israel's Restrictive Trade Practices Law: Antitrust Misadventures In a Small Developing Country', 8 *Isr. L. Rev.* 411, 417 (1973).
[14] Section 15A of the Competition Law.
[15] Section 14 of the Competition Law.
[16] Section 9 of the Competition Law.
[17] Section 2(a) of the Competition Law.

> An arrangement entered into by persons conducting business, pursuant to which at least one of the parties restricts itself in a manner likely to prevent or reduce competition in the marketplace between it and the other parties to the arrangement, or any of them, or between it and a person not party to the arrangement.

The Law further includes a list of instances in which a restrictive arrangement is deemed to harm competition. These cases create an irrefutable presumption of harm:[18]

> an arrangement involving a restraint that relates to one of the following issues shall be deemed to be a restrictive arrangement:
> (1) The price to be demanded, offered or paid;
> (2) The profit to be obtained;
> (3) The allocation of all or part of the market, in accordance with the location of the business or in accordance with the persons or type of persons with whom business is to be conducted;
> (4) The quantity, quality or type of assets or services in the business.

Accordingly, any restrictive arrangement which meets this definition is deemed illegal, unless one of three conditions is met: (a) the arrangement falls within a list of nine statutory exemptions enumerated in the Law, such as an arrangement between a parent company and its subsidiary or an arrangement mandated by another law;[19] (b) the arrangement received an exemption from the Director of the IAA or came under a block exemption issued by the IAA; or (c) the parties to the arrangement obtained the approval of the Antitrust Tribunal.

ii. Monopolization Monopoly is defined as the possession of 'more than half of the total supply or acquisition of an asset,' or of 'the total provision or acquisition of a service.'[20] This definition may reduce evidentiary burdens, since it does not require an in-depth analysis of entry barriers into the market.

The Law does not proscribe monopolies, but rather prohibits the abuse of monopoly power. Accordingly, a monopoly is prevented from 'unreasonably refus[ing] to provide or purchase an asset or a service over which the monopoly exists.'[21] In addition, the Law includes a provision which follows Article 82 of the EC Treaty.[22] Under this provision the monopolist is prohibited from abusing its dominant position in a way which reduces competition in the marketplace or that injures the public.[23] The provision also establishes

---

18 Section 2(b) of the Competition Law.

19 Section 3 (5) and § 3(1) of the Competition Law, respectively.

20 Section 26 of the Competition Law.

21 *Id.*, §29 of the Competition Law.

22 See, e.g., Michal S. Gal, 'The "Cut and Paste" of Article 82 of EC Treaty in Israel: Conditions for a Successful Transplant', 9 *European Journal of Law Reform* (2007). On December 1, 2009, the Treaty of Lisbon came into effect, amending the Treaty Establishing the European Community (EC Treaty) that is now called the Treaty on the Functioning of the European Union (TFEU). Therefore, all references to Articles 81 and 82 of the EC Treaty now reference Articles 101 and 102 TFEU.

23 The term 'public injury' was not, as of yet, clearly defined in Israeli law. Accordingly, it is not yet settled by the Supreme Court whether public injury relates to consumer or to total welfare. Nonetheless, most courts interpret the law as requiring that consumers be harmed.

a number of categorical behaviors, under which the monopolist is presumed to abuse its position:[24]

> (1) The establishment of an unfair buying or selling price of an asset or a service over which a monopoly exists;
> (2) A reduction or increase in the quantity of the assets or the scope of the services offered by the monopoly, not within the context of fair competitive activity;
> (3) The establishment of different contractual conditions for similar transactions in a manner which is likely to confer upon certain customers or suppliers an unfair advantage vis-à-vis their competitors; and
> (4) The inclusion in a contract regarding an asset or a service over which a monopoly exists of conditions that, by their nature or according to accepted trading practices, are unrelated to the subject matter of the contract.

Abuse was defined by the courts as an objective concept, detached from the monopolist's intention or success in hampering competition.[25]

iii. Merger regulation The IAA is authorized to prohibit a proposed merger if it creates 'a reasonable risk of significant harm' to competition.[26] Any merger that does not receive the approval of the IAA or does not meet the conditions that the IAA previously imposed on the merging parties may be subject to fines or even separation.[27]

The conditions for submitting and reviewing mergers are twofold. First, a transaction must qualify as a 'corporate merger' as defined by the Law. A corporate merger is presumed to exist, inter alia, where one corporation acquires more than 25 per cent of one or more of the following rights in another corporation: stock, voting rights, the right to nominate directors or the right to dividends of the other corporation. Second, the merger must meet certain thresholds, based on the turnover or market shares of the parties, which are designed to ensure the existence of a public interest in scrutinizing the transaction.[28] Transactions which meet the relevant threshold must still receive IAA approval prior to their consummation. The decision of the IAA is then subject to appeal before the Antitrust Tribunal.

An illegal merger may serve as a basis for a private right of action, if it harmed the plaintiff. However, a private party cannot bring a private damages suit if the merger was duly notified and approved.

b. Private damages suits – the legal framework

Section 50 of the Competition Law provides that 'any act or omission in violation of the provisions of the Law constitutes a tort, with accordance with the Tort Ordinance.' The Tort Ordinance authorizes the courts to grant compensatory damages or make other orders designed to remedy a tortuous injury.[29]

---

24 Section 29A of the Competition Law.

25 See, e.g., AT1/93 *Gen. Dir. v. Dubek Co. Ltd.* ATTRIB, 1995 Antitrust 3005459.

26 Section 21 of the Competition Law.

27 *Id.*, §25.

28 *Id.*, §17.

29 Section 71 of the Israeli Tort Ordinance [New Version], 5728-1968, 10 LSI 266 (1968) (ISR).

Individuals filing private antitrust actions under §50 of the Competition Law must prove three cumulative conditions:[30] (1) an infringement of the Competition Law such as participation in a restrictive arrangement or abuse of a dominant position; (2) a causal link between the damage and the antitrust violation; and (3) quantification of the ensuing damages.

Damages suits are heard in the regular court system – the district or magistrates' courts – rather than before the Antitrust Tribunal. They are brought in accordance with the general jurisdictional rules applied to tort claims, and are based on the extent of the remedy requested as well as the locus of the parties and the offense (either where the violation was conducted or where the damage occurred).

Most damages suits based on competition law violations are class actions.[31] The Competition Law was one of the first pieces of legislation to include class action provisions, which came about as early as 1996. The newly promulgated Class Action Law – 2006, which repealed and replaced the Competition Law's treatment of class actions, serves today as the platform for launching class actions.[32]

In order to warrant a class action certification, several conditions must be satisfied:[33] (1) generally, it is required that the individual plaintiff bringing the class action has incurred the alleged injury. However, the law extends the list of people who can bring such claims.[34] Most importantly, an antitrust class action can be brought under some conditions by qualified entities, such as consumer associations, on behalf of identified victims which suffered an injury as long as certain conditions are met;[35] (2) the action must manifest issues of law and fact which are central to the case and which are shared by all class members, and must display a reasonable likelihood that the case at hand would be determined in favor of the class members;[36] (3) it is reasonable to presume that the plaintiff will adequately represent the interests of all class members; and (4) a class action is the most favorable and efficient course of action, given the issues involved.

In a recent ruling pertaining to alleged price abuses by dominant credit card companies in Israel, the Supreme Court addressed the requisite evidentiary threshold for certification of a class action.[37] It specified that only substantiated applications, supported by adequate evidence such as submission of a verified economic expert opinion, would be certified by the court. An additional case, which is currently pending before the Supreme

---

30 See, e.g., CC (Hi) 1114/99 *Tower Air v. Flight Serv. Ltd.* IsrDC, 2007 Antitrust 5000590.

31 For an analysis of antitrust class actions see Amir Israeli, 'The Power of the Market: On Antitrust Class Actions', 37 *Hebrew Univ. L. Rev.* 131 (2007) (Hebrew).

32 Section 3(a) of the Class Action Law, 2006, 2054 S.H. 264 (hereinafter: 'Class Action Law').

33 See, e.g., CC (Motion) 1895/05 *Amir v. Tadiran* [2008] IsrDC (not published).

34 Section 8 and 4 of the Class Action Law, 2006.

35 Section 4 of the Class Action Law, 2006.

36 PCA 2616/03 *IsraCard Ltd. v. Rise* IsrSC [2005] 59(7) 701, 2005 Antitrust 5000073 (hereinafter 'Reis').

37 See, e.g., *Reis*, *id.* (stressing the need to *prima facie* substantiate the claim, for instance, by submitting an expert opinion). The same rationale was recently echoed in CC (Motion) (TA) 21953/02 *Vasli Communication and Production Ltd. v. Pelephone Communication Ltd.* IsrDC [2008] (not published).

Court, involves the level of preliminary proof necessary to certify a class action.[38] The Israeli case is relatively similar to the one addressed by the US Supreme Court in *Bell Atlantic Corp. v. Twombly*.[39] The issue is whether proof of parallel pricing, by itself, is sufficient to initiate a claim of a restrictive arrangement, where the alleged evidence that the parallel conduct resulted from such an arrangement is held by the defendants. The Tel-Aviv District court certified the class action, and the appeal is still pending before the Supreme Court.

Under the Class Action Law, class actions principally follow the opt-out model. Once the action has been certified and the group of class members is defined by the court and published to the wide public, a member who wants to opt out must notify the court within 45 days. Furthermore, a member of the class who does not wish to be governed by a particular settlement may request that the court allow it to opt out within 45 days from the date such a settlement was submitted to court.[40]

In the past courts generally did not intervene in settlements reached by the parties. As a result, several settlements approved by the courts ended up harming competition.[41] One example pertains to the settlement reached in the case of *Morad and Goldberg v. Aloni* which involved the floor tiles cartel.[42] The remedy agreed upon granted future buyers of tiles the opportunity to receive price reductions from the cartel members. This, of course, served to increase future demand for their products. Today there is much closer scrutiny of settlements, to ensure that they benefit the plaintiffs and do not harm competition. Under the Class Actions Law the court should not approve a settlement before it receives the opinion of an external examiner, who has expertise in the relevant field, unless good reasons exist for not nominating such an examiner.[43]

In civil claims which are not class actions, pursuant to the Civil Procedure Regulation,[44] the court is authorized to order aggregation of claims, following a party's request or by its own discretion, if the submitted claims raise similar questions of law or fact. If such claims were submitted to different courts of similar authority, they may be aggregated by an order of the President of the Supreme Court. In class actions the timing is crucial.[45] The court to which a consequent class action is submitted must transfer it to the court to which the first-in-time class action was submitted. The second-in-time action is most likely to be dismissed if the first has already been certified and both actions raise similar questions of fact and law.

Under the Israeli tort law, joint and several liability applies. These rules also apply in tort cases which are based on antitrust violations. The Israeli law also applies the

---

38 CC(TA) 2133/06 (motion 19230/06) *Sharnoa Computerized Machines Tel Aviv Ltd. v. Bank Hapoalim B.M.* IsrDC [2008] (not published).

39 *Bell Atl. Corp. v. Twombly*, 127 S.Ct. 1955, 1964 (2007).

40 Section 18(f) of the Class Actions Law 2006.

41 For such criticism see Israeli, *supra* note 30.

42 CC (TA) 2021/02 *Morad and Goldberg Inc. v. Aloni et al.*[2002] IsrDC (not published).

43 Section 19(b)(1) of the Class Action Law 2006.

44 Section 520 of the Civil Procedure Regulation, 1984, KT 4685, 2220.

45 Section 7(a)(1) of the Class Actions Law 2006. *See also* CC(Motion) (TA) 7376/03 *Oren Sfizer v. Golden Channels* [2006] IsrDC (not published) (maintaining that the aggregation of class actions is aimed at circumventing conflicting rulings in class actions sharing mutual legal and factual grounds).

concept of contributory negligence, where compensation might be reduced if the plaintiff contributed to the violation or did not take reasonable steps to limit its harm.

3. Methods for obtaining private relief

There are two main methods for obtaining private relief. The first is more unique and pertains to indirect benefits derived by private parties from proceedings undertaken by the IAA. The second involves private damages lawsuits, pursuant to section 50 of the Competition Law.

a. Involvement in governmental proceedings

Under the first course of action, a private party may obtain private relief as an indirect effect of the IAA proceedings. Such relief generally does not compensate the complainers for the loss incurred, but it often serves as a quick and effective way to prevent or limit anti-competitive conduct by competitors, suppliers or buyers. Most importantly, a private party may file a complaint with the IAA which, in turn, will scrutinize the complaint and may eventually decide to take action in order to prohibit the complained-of conduct. Under the Correction of Administrative Procedures Law[46] the IAA must respond to any request for inquiry sent by a private party within set time limits. Generally, should the IAA not respond within three months, such silence will be regarded as a rejection of the request and can then be appealed to the court.[47] In addition, under Israeli constitutional and administrative law an individual can bring a case before the Supreme Court, claiming that the IAA acted unreasonably or outside the legal boundaries of its authority or power.

Furthermore, the Law allows private parties to voice their concerns regarding the harm to competition in several of the actions taken by the IAA. For example, the Law mandates the IAA, before reaching a consent decree with an alleged violator, to publish a draft of the consent and grant hearing to all parties interested, before submitting it for the approval of the Antitrust Tribunal.[48] In addition, private parties may, under certain circumstances, acquire standing before the Antitrust Tribunal, provided that they are likely to be injured by a pending application for approval of a restrictive arrangement or a merger.[49] The Law further empowers consumer organizations[50] to appeal to the Tribunal certain IAA decisions.[51]

Taking such actions might be the best way to get expedited redress, as well as avoid

---

46 Amendment to the Administrative Procedures Law (Decisions and Reasoning), 1958, S.H. 264.

47 *Id.*

48 Section 50(d)(1) of the Competition Law.

49 Sections 8(b) and 15(a) of the Competition Law.

50 A 'Consumer Organization' is defined in §1 of the Competition Law as 'an organization representing consumers, approved by the Minister of Justice for the purposes of this Law.'

51 Consumer organizations are allowed to appeal to the IAA or the Antitrust Tribunal in order to exempt a restrictive arrangement (§8(b) of the Competition Law), to apply to the General Director of the AAI in relation to an amendment or annulment of a Tribunal approval (§12(b)), to appeal to the Tribunal an IAA exemption of a restrictive arrangement (§15(a)), to appeal to the Tribunal an IAA approval of a contemplated merger (§22(b)), and to appeal to the Tribunal the IAA Instructions to a monopoly (§30(f)).

the often-significant legal costs of a private action. The private party will benefit from the prohibition or the limitation of the anti-competitive conduct. It might also indirectly benefit from other restrictions imposed on the infringer, such as one prohibiting its Directors from continuing to serve as such for a set period. Pecuniary compensation, however, has so far only been given to the state treasury and not to private parties.

b. Civil Proceedings

A second course of action, undertaken where the first one is inefficient[52] or where significant damage has been suffered (either by an individual or in the aggregate), involves private damages proceedings. Such proceedings can benefit from government action as well. The vast majority of private claims follow the IAA's or the Attorney General's enforcement actions. This is because private parties often lack the information or the resources to independently undertake antitrust investigations. The case of *Morad and Goldberg v. Aloni*, mentioned previously, illustrates such a scenario.[53]

In order to appreciate the nature of follow-on suits, it is important to first understand the governmental actions available. The government can take three main types of actions. The first involves bringing criminal proceedings against parties to an antitrust violation.[54] Such suits are quite rare, however,[55] and have only been brought where the violation was egregious and involved a hard-core horizontal cartel with potentially significant effects on competition in the relevant market or a vertical agreement with significant effects on competition in a horizontal market. Follow-on private suits which are based on successful criminal prosecutions are, of course, the strongest. This is because the level of proof in criminal cases (beyond a reasonable doubt) is higher than in civil cases (preponderance of evidence), and thus the former can be used as a basis for the latter, and there is no need to prove the violation once again. Accordingly, pursuant to the Evidence Ordinance, a final criminal conviction of the defendant is conclusive evidence of an infringement.[56] It follows that the convicted party is prohibited from exhibiting evidence contradicting the criminal verdict, unless it receives a special permission to do so from the court.[57]

Although the Law empowers the Attorney General to bring a criminal case based on abuse of dominance, in the past twenty years or so a case has never been brought.[58] Thus, criminal findings are currently relevant as a basis for private suits only in cases involving hard-core cartels. This option is further limited by the fact that the high burden of

---

52 For example, where the remedy imposed by the IAA is not sufficiently prohibitive. For a list of the IAA's enforcement powers see infra.

53 CrimA 2929/02 *State of Israel v. Svirski* [2003] IsrSC 57(3) 135, 2003.

54 *Id.* See also CrimA 7068/06 *State of Israel v. Ariel Elec. Eng'g, Traffic Light & Control Ltd.* [2006] IsrSC (not published), Antitrust 5000597.

55 In the past 15 years only 25 criminal proceedings have been brought.

56 Section 42A of the Evidence Ordinance, 5731-1971, 18 ISL 421 (1971) (Isr).

57 *Id.*

58 There was one instance in which the IAA considered bringing such a case against Strauss Group, alleging that the firm tried to exclude its competitor Carmit Candy Industries Ltd. from the market. Eventually, the issue was settled in a consent decree. *See* Consent Decree between the IAA and Strauss (Antitrust Tribunal, 2006), Antitrust 5000610.

proof required in criminal proceedings might create situations in which a criminal case is dismissed, whereas a civil one would have succeeded. An additional barrier to the use of criminal convictions as a basis for private suits involves the often lengthy proceedings in criminal matters. The limitations period, which is seven years from the time the tortious conduct took place or was revealed, often ends during or quite soon after the criminal proceedings terminate. Since no stay can be granted by the courts in civil cases until the criminal proceedings come to an end, the usefulness of criminal convictions as a basis for civil suits is often very limited.

The second type of action that the government may take is an issuance of a declaration by the IAA that the Competition Law has been breached or that a certain firm holds a monopoly position.[59] Such a declaration does not carry any immediate remedial results. Nonetheless, it can be used in civil courts as *prima facie* evidence of an antitrust violation or of the existence of monopoly.[60] It thus serves to shift the burden of proof that an antitrust violation has occurred, that a firm holds a monopoly position, or that damage resulted, from the plaintiff to the defendant, who can then bring evidence to rebut the presumption.[61] A party so declared may choose to challenge the declaration before the Antitrust Tribunal. If the Tribunal overturns the declaration then the declaration loses, of course, its evidentiary value.[62] In class actions the declaration will most likely serve as *prima facie* evidence of the violation, which is one of the conditions required to approve a class action suit.

The third option open to the IAA is to reach a settlement with the alleged infringer and submit a consent decree to the Antitrust Tribunal for its approval. In such cases, however, the decree cannot serve as a basis for a private suit as it does not involve an admission of guilt.

Given the usual competition to be the first to bring a class action and the constraints imposed by the limitation period, oftentimes the plaintiff does not wait until the governmental proceedings come to an end.[63] For example, in 2008 the District Court certified an antitrust class action in *Sharnoa*.[64] The case involved alleged price-fixing and information exchanges among the largest banks in Israel, and was brought in the midst of the IAA's massive and long-awaited investigation of such antitrust violations. The IAA Director General issued a declaration concerning the existence of a restrictive arrangement among the banks in May 2009.[65] This declaration is expected to strengthen the force of that part of the private suit which raises similar issues as the declaration, if it is

---

59 Section 43 of the Competition Law. There is no administrative fine available.

60 *Id.*

61 *Id.*

62 CC (Jm.) 8011/06 (motion 250/06) *Discount Bank v. Harel Shopping Mall Ltd* [2006] IsrDC.

63 See, e.g., Civil Case *Limor Pupick v. Paz Gaz et al* IsrDC (pending) (the class action involves an allegation of a nation-wide cartel in the market for liquefied petroleum gas); Civil Case 12275-09-08 *Itay Laniel v. Tnuva et al* [2009] IsrDC (not published) (the class action was withdrawn).

64 CC(TA) 2133/06 (motion 19230/06) *Sharnoa Computerized Machines Tel Aviv Ltd. v. Bank Hapoalim B.M.* IsrDC [2008] (not published). An appeal is currently pending.

65 General Director, Determination (Restrictive Arrangement Among Banks), 2009, Antitrust 5001411 (April 26, 2009).

not overturned by the Tribunal in the pending appeal. The fact that the two proceedings are conducted in parallel creates, in effect, a race between the parties, since the defendant is attempting to speed the proceedings and bring them to an end before the governmental proceedings end, while the plaintiff is attempting to lengthen them, hoping to use a favorable decision in the civil suit.

It is interesting to note that in several major cases in which the government found anti-competitive conduct, no successful private actions followed. Probably the most notable case is one involving a cartel among the major insurance companies in Israel. The government reached plea bargains with most defendants which did not involve admissions of guilt but instead imposed fines on the insurance companies. However, two small insurance companies brought the case to trial and lost. The Supreme Court affirmed the decision of the District Court that the insurance companies' conduct was cartelistic rather than pure oligopolistic coordination.[66] Despite the significant damage incurred by most of those insured in Israel, no successful private suits were initiated, despite one attempt. One of the main reasons behind this perplexing lack of action was that in the relevant period class actions were not available, and thus bringing a suit that included a sufficient number of insured individuals was a Herculean and highly costly task.

The size of the Israeli economy may be a relevant factor in deciding whether to bring a case. In general, the smaller the market, the lower the absolute size of remedies granted. This is because generally the smaller the market, the smaller the number of consumers and thus the fewer the potential plaintiffs. At the same time, the costs of litigation are generally not affected by size. Therefore, the lower the level of the compensation, the weaker the motivation to bring private suits. This conclusion further strengthens the importance of governmental proceedings both as a deterrence of anti-competitive conduct and as a means for lowering the costs of bringing private suits.

4. Key elements of a private damages action

a. Standing: who may pursue a claim

Any individual who suffered harm caused by an antitrust infringement is entitled to bring an action and to assert damages before a civil court.[67] A well-established prerequisite for obtaining legal standing, analogous to the one recognized in US jurisprudence, is that the plaintiff must demonstrate an antitrust injury, that is, interests or rights protected by the antitrust rules which have been compromised.[68] The plaintiff must also prove that the damage is derived from the defendant's antitrust offense.

Israeli law is, however, still unclear on the exact standing criteria which govern private

---

[66] CrimC (Jer) 417/97 *State of Israel v. Israel Phoenix Ins. Co.*[2001] IsrDC, Antitrust 5000788; CrimA 4855/02 *State of Israel v. Burovitch* [2005] IsrSC, 59(6) 776. For the Supreme Court's decision see CrimA 4855/02 *State of Israel v. Burovitch* [2005] IsrSC, 59(6) 776.

[67] Section 3 of the Tort Law and §50 of the Competition Law.

[68] AT 5/98 *Edgar Invs. and Dev. Ltd. v. Gen. Dir.* [1998] ATTrib, Antitrust 3001816; CC (Motion) 515/08 (A.T. 803/08); *Terraflex Compaunds 1994 Ltd. v. General Director* [2008] ATTrib, Antitrust 5001266; CC (Motion) 802/08 *Home Centre (DIY) v. Gen. Dir.* [2009] ATTrib, Antitrust 5001405.

antitrust actions.[69] In particular, the issue of whether indirect purchasers may initiate an action has yet to be settled by the courts. The case of *IsraCard Ltd. v. Reis* is the only case in which it has been discussed thus far.[70] In *Reis*, the plaintiff, a pharmacy owner, contended that the major credit card undertakings in Israel had abused their dominant position by charging excessive interchange fees. The District Court certified the class action. The Supreme Court, however, vacated the plaintiff's motion, based, *inter alia,* on the assertion that the evidence provided by the plaintiff did not suffice to substantiate its damage. The court further noted that the damage incurred could not be adequately categorized as direct, as it was partly passed on to end consumers, and thus could not serve as a basis for a tort suit.[71] Nonetheless, since the issue of direct purchasers was not fundamental to the Court's reasoning, in accordance with Israeli law its statement does not serve as an established and mandatory rule, although it will likely still carry some weight in lower court decisions, even if not formally, given that some Supreme Court judges have revealed their opinion on the matter.

Under Israeli law, there is no general limitation on the type of relationship that must exist between the plaintiff and the defendant. Thus suppliers, competitors or purchasers can all bring a private action. Purchasers and suppliers are the most likely parties to bring such suits.

As noted above, class actions are also allowed under Israeli law. Consumer organizations may bring class actions on behalf of a group of people, provided that: the cause of action pertains to one of the public objectives of the organizations' operation; the claim raises substantial legal and factual issues shared by all the group members; it would be difficult for an individual to bring the case alone;[72] and the organization was certified by the Minister of Justice for the purpose of representing consumers against violations of the Competition Law.[73] Where the claim is brought by the Israel Consumer Council,[74] there is no need to prove the difficulty that an individual would encounter in bringing the case.[75]

b. Ethical restrictions

A lawyer who represents the group is strictly prohibited from acting as a representative plaintiff for the class action.[76] Under the ethical rules of the Israel Bar Association lawyers cannot solicit plaintiffs.[77]

---

69 The issue of whether shareholders have standing is unsettled. See, e.g., CC (Motion) 11129/00 *Tambur Ltd. v. Iry Gaash* [2004] IsrDC (not published).

70 *Reis, supra* note 35.

71 *Id.*, at para. 31.

72 This term has not been elaborated upon in the law. Nonetheless, we believe it will include, inter alia, situations in which the damage to each plaintiff is small and no plaintiff wishes to organize a class action.

73 Section 3 of the Class Action Law.

74 The Israel Consumer Council is a government corporation established and financially supported by the Ministry of Industry and Trade. One of the Council's main goals is 'to protect consumer rights and respond to individual consumer complaints'. Additional information is available at: www.tamas.gov.il/NR/exeres/2244BFAA-6074-4129-B004-948C33A7887C.htm.

75 Section 4(a)(3)of the Class Action Law.

76 See, e.g., Gil Lotan & Eyal Raz, *Class Actions* Part I, 199–200 (2006).

77 Section 56 of the Bar Association Law, 1960. S.H. 347.

5. Procedural defenses short of trial

a. Claim dismissal

Short of trial, a claim may be dismissed for numerous reasons. Most importantly, it may be dismissed if the statement of a claim indicates no legal cause. Pursuant to the Civil Procedure Ordinance, a statement of a claim reveals a cause if, upon substantiation of all the proclaimed facts, the plaintiff is entitled to the requested remedy.[78] Accordingly, in a claim dismissal proceeding the court is not required to scrutinize or to affirm the alleged facts, but merely to determine whether a remedy may be granted if all the alleged facts are proven. If the answer is negative, the claim will be dismissed. Yet such a harsh measure necessitates a great deal of caution, and will be exercised only in situations in which the plaintiff clearly cannot obtain the requested remedy on the basis of his allegations and cannot easily rectify his claims in a way which does not create significant injustice.[79]

In class action suits, the existence of a cause of action is one of the conditions for class action certification. In such cases, a petition to dismiss the motion for certification of a class action will not ordinarily be heard other than in rare and exceptional circumstances, when the motion evidently reveals no merit. Furthermore, the court can approve the class action and replace the representative plaintiff if the plaintiff does not have a private claim of action yet all the other conditions for the approval of the class action have been fulfilled.

b. Class action certification denial

A motion to certify a lawsuit as a class action may be denied in the following instances: 1) the claimant failed to show a *prima facie* cause of action; and 2) a causal link between the antitrust violation and the proclaimed damages cannot be established.

6. Devices for obtaining evidence

a. General discovery rules

The Civil Procedure Regulations[80] set the rules for discovery and are aimed at revealing the evidence that may shed light on the issues under dispute, with the purpose of advancing the truth.[81] The general principle in civil procedures is one of maximum scope of disclosure which is rooted in the notion of a fair and efficient litigation process, whereby the parties 'unveil their cards'.

The main vehicle for discovery is document disclosure.[82] The right to present other parties with a questionnaire serves as an additional mechanism to gather requisite information. The party seeking disclosure can send a direct request to the other party. Only if a disagreement arises do the parties go to court to decide the dispute. A failure

---

[78] Section 100 of the Civil Procedure Regulation, 1984, KT 4685, 2220. See also Uri Goren, *Issues in Civil Procedure*, 171 (2009).

[79] Uri Goren, *Issues in Civil Procedure*, 171 (2007).

[80] Civil Procedure Regulation, 1984, KT 4685, 2220.

[81] See, e.g., CC 4999/95 .*J. S. Alberici Construction Co. et al v. State of Israel* [1996] IsrSC 50(1), 39.

[82] See, e.g., CC 6546/94 *Union Bank of Israel v. Henry Azulai at al* [1995] IsrSC 59(4), 54.

to comply with a court order to reply to the questionnaire or to disclose the requested documentation may result in dismissing the party's statement of action or defense.[83]

There are several limitations on the scope of disclosure.[84] Most importantly, confidential information is not automatically communicated to the other parties. A trade secret is defined in the Commercial Wrongs Law as 'business information, of any kind, which is not publicly known nor easily detected by others, and its confidentiality gives its holder a business advantage over its rivals, and the owner has taken reasonable measures to protect the confidentiality of this information'.[85] The court possesses the discretion to prohibit the misappropriation and disclosure of commercial or trade secrets, recognizing the pivotal public interest in preserving business incentives to engage in competitive activity. Accordingly, the court will generally refrain from ordering the disclosure of commercial secrets unless it finds that there is a solid basis for the need for disclosure. Even then, disclosure will only include the most relevant documents essential for establishing the legal claim. The court may also instruct the party to reveal the confidential information only to the opposing party's attorney. Finally, in the stage of class action approval, discovery is limited to specific documents which are relevant to the approval procedures of the class action and general disclosure is not allowed.

b. Searches

While searches are available in proceedings brought by the government, they are not available in private enforcement initiatives.

c. Information obtained from the IAA

Governmental actions play an important role in amassing sufficient evidence. Beyond the use of court findings and IAA determinations as a basis for evidence, elaborated above, parties often request information and documents possessed by the IAA in order to facilitate private action. Indeed, plaintiffs have attempted to use information gathered by the IAA during the course of a variety of proceedings, including indictments, consent decrees,[86] declarations of monopoly, declarations of anti-competitive conduct, and the separation of a merger consummated without prior authorization.[87] This is not surprising, given the wealth of discovery tools possessed by the IAA, including searches, warrants for questionings, requests for information from all market participants, etc.

As a governmental authority, the IAA is subject to the Freedom of Information

---

[83] Section 122 of the Civil Procedure Regulation, 1984, KT 4685, 2220. For further discussion *see, e.g.* Goren, *supra* note 51, at 194–5.

[84] For a profound discussion see *Goren, id.*, at 202. Attorney–client relationships also limit the scope of disclosure. Section 48 of the Evidence Ordinance [New Version], 5731-1971, 18 LSI 241 as well as §90 of the Bar Association Law, 1960. S.H. 347. The non-disclosure obligation extends only to documents (e.g. correspondence, legal advice) exchanged between counsel and a client in the course of the professional services bestowed upon the latter.

[85] Section 5 of the Commercial Wrongs Law, 1999, 1709 S.H. 146.

[86] See, e.g., the consent decree in *Strauss, supra* note 49. Following the settlement, a competitor, Carmit Candy Industries Ltd., requested the IAA to provide it with the documentations collected in the course of its investigation in order to facilitate a private antitrust action.

[87] 407/07 *General Director v. Prinir (Hadas 1987) Ltd.*, [2009] ATTrib, Antitrust 5001400.

Law, which mandates the disclosure of non-confidential information to third parties.[88] The statute specifies the circumstances in which a governmental entity may not disclose the required information. Such circumstances include, *inter alia*, instances in which the information consists of trade secrets and materials accumulated in the course of a criminal investigation. Accordingly, these provisions exempt some of the information gathered by the IAA from mandatory disclosure.

The courts have exhibited a recent tendency to require the IAA to adhere to wide disclosure. In the *Pazgas case* the court stated that while the law explicates the disclosure of certain types of information, it should not be interpreted to exclude the possibility that additional information will be disclosed to the public.[89] In the words of the court:

> §14(a)(8) of the Freedom of Information Law exempted the transfer of materials related to an investigation . . . but didn't prohibit the authority from transferring information, whilst exercising a discretion, even in the absence of an obligation to do so by the Freedom of Information Law.[90]

Accordingly, the IAA might be required by the courts to disclose information beyond that mandated by the Freedom of Information Law. As noted above, it should be in the interest of the IAA to assist private parties to bring successful private cases, given the IAA's relatively limited remedial powers and their relatively weak deterrent effects.

So far, leniency applications have not been a source of information. The IAA's Leniency Program empowers the IAA to exempt a party to a restrictive arrangement from criminal liability if it is the first to provide information on the existence of a restrictive arrangement and such information is sufficient to bring all other parties to trial.[91] The program does not, however, exempt the leniency applicant from any civil remedies. Thus the incentives of parties to come forward are reduced. This may be one of the reasons why, to the best of our knowledge, no applications have been made under the leniency program so far.

d. Expert opinions

The Evidence Ordinance authorizes the court to accept an expert opinion on issues that do not involve purely legal questions, which are presumed to be within the expertise of the court.[92] Private litigants often make use of expert opinions in order to substantiate their claims and prove actual damage. Accordingly, expert economists play an important role in most antitrust cases. They often analyze the economic effects of a certain type of conduct or compute the damage from it. Expert testimony is also brought to delineate the relevant antitrust market, determine various elasticities (e.g., demand, supply or cross), establish a causal link between the cause of action and the damage incurred, and

---

88 Freedom of Information Law, 1998, S.H. 226; CC 605/06 (Motion 110/06) *El Al Ltd. v. Gen. Dir.* [2006] ATTRIB, Antitrust 5000471.

89 See also the Attorney General's Guidelines Concerning the Disclosure of Investigatory Materials to Third Parties (1994); The IAA Guiding Principles for Evaluating a Disclosure of Information Obtained Through Its Investigations to Third Parties (2007).

90 AP 204/03 *Paz Gaz Ltd. v. The Ministry of National Infrastructures* ISRDC (not published).

91 IAA, Leniency Program, 2005 Antitrust 5000097E (in English).

92 Section 20 of the Evidence Ordinance [New Version], 5731-1971, 18 LSI 241.

compute pre- and post-merger prices. Yet the courts do not always follow the expert testimony brought before them. In the case of *Tower Air vs. Sherutei Teufa,* for example, the court relied on the expert evidence brought by the plaintiff with regard to price discrimination, but it rejected both parties' experts' testimonies with regard to the height of the pecuniary damage caused by the violation. Instead the court calculated the damages on its own, based on information presented.[93]

7. Remedies

a. Damages

The Israeli Competition Law, unlike its American counterpart, does not enable plaintiffs to receive treble damages in private actions. Rather, compensation is intended to enable the plaintiff to recover the harm suffered as a result of the antitrust violation. However, courts are allowed to recompense plaintiffs to the full extent (including both actual loss and the loss of profit) of their antitrust injury.

The largest damages awarded in an antitrust lawsuit was in the case of *Tower Air,*[94] in which the court ordered the payment of approximately 3.5 million US dollars to several airlines which paid a high sum for fuel, resulting from a restrictive arrangement that lasted for many years. In the recent case of *Oved v. Paz,*[95] which involved a restrictive arrangement that included several resale price maintenance clauses, compensation of approximately 1.8 million US dollars was awarded to the plaintiffs.

Class actions have also not succeeded thus far in proving large damages. Nonetheless, the class action that is currently pending against the major Israeli banks is based on significantly larger potential damage. As noted above, one of the obstacles to large damages awards is the size of transactions in the Israeli market. Another involves the difficulties in proving the size of the damage and its causal connection to the antitrust injury.

In the case of *Reichart* the Supreme Court considered the different methods of calculating and proving damages.[96] It ruled that where individual damages are awarded to each member of the class, each member must prove the amount of damage it suffered.[97] The Court also approved determination of damages by estimation based on the information presented before it. However, it stated that such a method should be reserved for exceptional cases.[98]

b. Injunctive relief

Obtaining injunctive relief for antitrust injuries is subject to the general rules for such relief under Israeli law. A private plaintiff seeking injunctive relief must prove an impending harm resulting from an antitrust violation. Private parties, however, rarely invoke this measure, and only a few plaintiffs have successfully obtained injunctive relief

93 *Tower Air, supra* note 7.
94 *Tower Air, supra* note 7.
95 CC (TA) 986/96 *Oved v. Paz Oil Co. Ltd.* [2006] IsrDC, at para. 2.5, Antitrust 5000860.
96 CA 345/03 *Dan Reichart v. The Heirs of Moshe Shemesh* [2007] IsrDC (not published).
97 *Id.*, pp. 41–44.
98 *Id.*, p. 48.

based on antitrust allegations.[99] This is because courts generally decline to accommodate antitrust apprehensions at the initial stages of the proceedings, especially if possible damage can be remedied later by monetary compensation.[100] At the conclusion of the case the court can issue mandatory injunctions, both positive and negative, in order to restore competition.

c. Attorneys' fees

In regular lawsuits attorneys' fees are agreed upon with the client, either as an hourly fee, or as a contingent fee – a percentage of the monetary value of the judgment or settlement.

Parties bear their own legal costs incurred for the duration of the proceedings. Yet at the end of the proceedings the court can determine whether the prevailing party will be entitled to reasonable compensation for its litigation costs, including attorneys' fees, from its opponent. In practice, however, the legal costs granted by the courts seldom cover the actual costs incurred.

In class actions the attorneys' fees are determined solely by the court.[101] The court bases its decision on several indicia including inter alia the inherent benefits derived from the class action, the complexity of the legal proceedings, and the indispensability of the class action to the public interest. Yet to date attorneys' fees have been relatively modest in most class actions, though a recent increase in the fees is evident. The increased number of class actions brought in recent years may serve as an indicator that fees are sufficiently high, at least in cases which involve significant damages claims, to bring class actions. Should the class action fail, the plaintiff or its lawyers are not responsible for paying defense fees and costs, unless they engaged in unsuitable conduct, such as bringing a case with no legal basis.

d. Prejudgment interest

In accordance with the Interest Rate Law,[102] prejudgment interest will be calculated commencing from the date the claim was submitted to the court, or the date in which the cause of action materialized.[103]

---

99 CA (TA) 1617/93 (Motion 13006/93) *Vulcan Batteries Ltd. v. Israel Garage Ass'n* [1994] IsrDC, Antitrust 3005679. For further discussion, see Gal Rozent & Ben Ami, 'Establishing A Restrictive Arrangement in the Motion for Preliminary Remedies', 4(1) *Corporations* 20 (2007) (Hebrew).

100 Motion 24813/05 (TA) *Shefi, Insur. Agency for the Eng'g and Architecture Indus. v. Madness Insur. Agency Ltd.* [2006] IsrDC, Antitrust 5000866; PCA 4933/01 *Superpharm Ltd. v. Edomim Mall Ltd.* [2001] IsrSC, Antitrust 5000869; PCA 10910/02 *Paz Oil Co. v. Peretz* [2003] IsrSC, Antitrust 5000870; *cf.* Civil Case (Motion) 250/06 *Israel Discount Bank Ltd. v. Harel Mall Ltd.* (Supreme Court, October 30, 2006) Antitrust 5000591. CC (Jer) 8011/06 (Motion250/06) *Israel Discount Bank Ltd. v. Harel Mall Ltd.* [2006] IsrDC, Antitrust 5000591.

101 Section 23 of the Class Action Law 2006.

102 Interest Rate Law, 1961, S.H. 348.

103 With regard to attorneys' fee, interest should be calculated commencing from the date in which the verdict was delivered until the date of payment, as determined by the court.

e. Limitation period

The regular rules on limitation periods, found in the Statute of Limitations,[104] apply. The statute provides for a seven year limitation period commencing from the date the cause of action materialized or was revealed.[105] The limitation period creates a major obstacle to the use of criminal convictions as a basis for private suits. This is because criminal proceedings are often lengthy and no stay can be granted in the civil court until the criminal proceedings have been completed.

8. Extraterritoriality

The Effects Doctrine (often referred to as the 'Objective Territoriality Principle'), which permits a country to apply its domestic laws to foreign individuals or entities under certain circumstances when their conduct affects a domestic jurisdiction, most likely applies in Israel.[106] The doctrine broadens the application of domestic laws to acts performed outside the territorial boundaries, even by foreign entities.

The Effects Doctrine was applied as a basis for the application of the Law to foreign firms by the Director General of the IAA in the matter of *James Richardson.*[107] James Richardson, an Israeli corporation, held a franchise to operate a duty-free store at the national airport. It reached agreements with perfume manufacturers to maintain price margins of 30 per cent between its store and other stores located in Israel. The perfume manufacturers, who were party to these agreements, were all foreign companies located overseas. The Director General applied the Law to the perfume manufacturers by using the Effects Doctrine as a basis for such application. The *James Richardson* decision was not appealed and thus was not subject to the scrutiny of the court. However, one may presume that the Effects Doctrine will also be applied by Israeli courts in relevant cases as part of established customary international public law, especially in the area of antitrust.[108]

One may also assume that Israeli courts will condition the application of the Competition Law on the conditions that are applied elsewhere, and are sufficiently respected, such that they may be regarded as sources of customary public international law. All jurisdictions that adopted the Objective Territoriality Principles have applied significant limiting factors to their application. Extraterritorial jurisdiction is regularly recognized only if the alleged conduct has 'substantial, direct and intentional' anti-competitive effects on competition in the jurisdiction. These conditions were specifically acknowledged in the *James Richardson* decision.[109]

Where conduct constitutes a criminal offense under the Israeli law – as in the case of cartels, abuse of dominance and mergers without approval – Chapter C of the Israeli

---

104 Statue of Limitations, 1958, S.H. 251.

105 See also §89 of Torts Ordinance [New Version], 5728-1968, 10 LSI 266 (1961) (Isr).

106 For an extended discussion see M. S. Gal, 'Extra-territorial Application of Antitrust – The Case of Small Economy (Israel)', *in* Andrew Guzman ed., *Cooperation, Comity, and Competition Policy* (forthcoming, 2010).

107 *Re: Premium Fragrance (James Richardson PTY Israel)* (General Director), Antitrust 3002438.

108 Gal, *supra* note 84.

109 *Id.*

Penal Law[110] sets out several principles for the territorial reach of the law. Chapter C dictates that for Israeli penal laws to apply, some factual element of the offense must take place within the territory of Israel.[111] The theoretical application of this requirement in the abuse of dominance offenses was recognized by the IAA General Director in the matter of *James Richardson:*[112]

> Where a monopolist acts in a way that might reduce competition among domestic businesses in Israel or might harm the Israeli public – this is an internal offense which may be tried in Israel.

Conclusion

Private antitrust claims play an increasingly important role in antitrust litigation in Israel. In recent years a growing number of private damages lawsuits have been filed. This resulted, inter alia, from the increased awareness of the plaintiffs, the improved expertise of the lawyers and the economic experts, and the reduction of some legal obstacles in bringing and successfully conducting such suits.

Yet private antitrust damages actions are still relatively under-developed and obstacles to their successful conclusion are still quite high. Some factors that shape this outcome have been elaborated throughout the chapter. First, the small size of the Israeli economy and the resultant relatively low absolute size of damage reduce incentives to bring such suits. Nonetheless, reductions in the costs of bringing such suits may increase motivations to sue. For example, the stronger the ability of private litigants to use information obtained by the IAA during the course of its investigations, and the more decisions and declarations issued by the IAA which can serve as a *prima facie* basis for a private suit, the lower the costs of bringing such suits. Second, the disinclination of some courts to award significant compensation to private plaintiffs serves to reduce incentives to bring such suits. Yet, the winds may be changing, creating stronger incentives for bringing such actions in the future. Third, discovery opportunities in the first stages of approving class actions are quite limited. A change may thus be required, given that some of the most egregious forms of anti-competitive conduct are performed covertly.

---

110 Israeli Penal Law [New Version], 1977, 864 S.H. 622.

111 S. Z. Peller, *Elements of Criminal Law* (1, 5744-1984) 260. See also *James Richardson, supra* note 9, pp. 43–4.

112 *James Richardson, id.*

33 Japan

Hiromitsu Miyakawa[1]

Introduction

Under the Japanese laws, which are primarily based on civil law systems, antitrust violations, including acts of private monopolization, unreasonable restraint of trade and unfair trade practices, are considered to constitute torts. Private antitrust enforcement seeking damages against corporations violating the antitrust law has been gradually increasing in Japan since the government promoted and expanded the civil antitrust litigation system by introducing injunctive relief and expanding the scope of anticompetitive conduct subject to strict liability. Moreover, section 83-4 of the 2009 amendments to the Anti-Monopoly Act (AMA) newly established a special rule for an order to produce documents for an injunction in order to help antitrust plaintiffs to collect evidence. Nevertheless, the status of private antitrust enforcement in Japan is not very active yet, particularly compared with the United States.

It is widely recognized that private antitrust enforcement has great significance in that: (i) monetary and injunctive relief are available for victims of anticompetitive practices; (ii) private enforcement may cover illegal activities not detected by the Japan Fair Trade Commission (JFTC) and thereby can supplement public enforcement; and (iii) the accumulation of judgments may play an important role in establishing clearer guidelines and increasing transparency.[2] It is expected that private antitrust enforcement will further expand into more diverse areas, such as monopolization and unfair trade practices, although most private litigation filed so far relates to unreasonable restraint of trade, such as cartels and bid riggings. The JFTC has expressed its intention to increase the disclosure of information in response to requests from courts and relevant parties in order to make private antitrust enforcement function effectively by reducing the burden of proof on plaintiffs.[3]

1. Damages actions

Section 25 of the AMA provides that any undertaking which has committed private monopolization, unreasonable restraint of trade, or unfair trade practices in violation of section 3, 6 or 19, and any trade association which engaged in substantial restraint of

---

1 Attorney-at-Law, Jones Day, Tokyo; admitted in Japan and New York; LL.B., Keio University 1992; LL.M., University of Virginia School of Law 2002.

2 Takayuki Soda (2008), Private Antitrust Litigation, Japan: LexisNexis Japan, pp. 327–328. One of the issues in the field of antitrust law in Japan is the lack of legal precedents because corporations have rarely challenged administrative orders issued by the JFTC. Therefore, the accumulation of legal precedents may help establish clearer guidelines to distinguish illegal activities and increase transparency in the antitrust enforcement.

3 Koichi Higashide (2000), 'Amendments to the Antimonopoly Act with regard to Improvements of the Civil Relief System', Fair Trade, No. 597, pp. 27–33.

competition or any other acts prohibited under section 8, shall be liable for damages.[4] The AMA also provides several special rules facilitating the recovery of damages by antitrust plaintiffs and thereby deterring anticompetitive practices. For example, strict liability[5] applies to defendants of antitrust cases and a court is required to seek the opinion of the JFTC when calculating damages. Nevertheless, a plaintiff is only allowed to file suit at the Tokyo High Court, one of the eight appellate courts under the Supreme Court in Japan, after the issuance of an administrative order by the JFTC. On the other hand, a three-year statute of limitations applies under the AMA, whereas general tort actions are subject to a three or twenty-year statute of limitations.

In addition, a plaintiff may choose to file a tort action for antitrust violations under section 709 of the Civil Code. This procedure is beneficial for plaintiffs, particularly where illegal activities are continuing and the victims are continuously suffering damage, because they are able to bring civil suits before the issuance of an administrative order by the JFTC. Moreover, such actions may supplement public enforcement of antitrust violations as the JFTC is unable to detect all anticompetitive practices in the market due to its limited resources.

In principle and in the absence of a specific statute, the elements a plaintiff in a civil damages case under section 709 of the Civil Code must prove are: (i) the illegal activities; (ii) the amount of damage incurred; (iii) a causal relationship between the illegal activities and damage; and (iv) intent or negligence. It is difficult for antitrust plaintiffs to prove all of the requisite elements, particularly when a court requires strict proof. Recognizing this, the AMA introduced the special rules for private antitrust litigation mentioned earlier. However, in practice, plaintiffs often choose to bring damages actions based on section 709 of the Civil Code. One of the possible reasons for this trend is that plaintiffs may be able to file suits at local district courts without waiting for the JFTC's actions. This suggests that the existing special rules for civil litigations under section 25 of the AMA are not so effective or beneficial for antitrust plaintiffs. In order to improve this situation, in 2005, the JFTC published its revised policy for providing information regarding the existence of illegal conduct, a causal relationship, the amount of damages and other relevant matters.[6]

---

4 Private monopolization is defined as business activities by which any corporation, individually or collectively with others, excludes or controls business activities of other corporations, thereby causing substantial restraint of competition in the relevant market and prohibited under section 3 of the AMA. Unreasonable restraint of trade is any concerted action, including contracts and agreements, with other corporations which mutually restrict or conduct, their business activities, thereby causing substantial restraint of competition in the relevant market in violation of section 3 of the AMA. Unfair trade practices are any act which tends to impede fair competition and is designated by the JFTC in violation of section 19 of the AMA. In addition, section 8 of the AMA provides that no trade association shall engage in any activities which fall within any of the following acts: substantially restraining competition; entering into an international agreement which substantially restrains competition; limiting the present or future number of corporations in the relevant market; unjustly restricting the functions or activities of the member corporations; and causing corporations to employ any act constituting unfair trade practices.

5 The defendant may not be freed from responsibility by arguing and proving that there was no intent or negligence.

6 The JFTC originally issued the notice of the secretary general, 'Provision of Information for Damage Actions regarding Violation of the Antimonopoly Act' in 1991, and the notice was revised in 2005.

2. Standing to sue for damage actions

A person or entity, including indirect purchasers, has standing to sue under both section 25 of the AMA and section 709 of the Civil Code. For example, in the Tsuruoka Toyu case in 1989, a group of consumers filed a complaint alleging that oil companies conspired to fix prices for kerosene and other petroleum products. The Supreme Court held that indirect purchasers have standing to bring private antitrust suits against cartel participants so long as there is a causal relationship between the illegal activity and damage that the indirect purchasers incurred.[7]

3. Proof of antitrust violation

There is no specific statute or provision under Japanese law by which an administrative order issued by the JFTC or any other government decision creates a legal presumption of an antitrust violation. However, Japanese courts have established a rule that a JFTC order shall be prima facie evidence. As a result, when a suit is filed following the issuance of cease and desist orders by the JFTC under either section 25 of the AMA or section 709 of the Civil Code, the burden of proof on the plaintiff is significantly reduced. Moreover, in the event that a defendant initiates an administrative hearing at the JFTC to challenge the order, relevant parties, including victims of the anticompetitive conduct, are allowed to access the JFTC's file in order to obtain evidence for private litigation according to section 70-15 of the AMA.

If a party suffering damage from anticompetitive practices initiates a civil suit before the JFTC issues an administrative order, the violation must be proven without relying on the findings of government investigation. In such a case, plaintiffs often face difficulties in gathering evidence since the wide range of discovery measures available in the United States is not available in Japan. For example, in 1994, although the JFTC had not issued an administrative order, the United States filed suit against Japanese construction companies, alleging they manipulated the bidding procedure for a series of construction projects at a US military base in Japan. The Tokyo District Court ruled that the plaintiff failed to establish a material fact and submit evidence proving the illegal bid-rigging.[8] The Tokyo High Court upheld the district court decision in 2006.[9]

4. Amount of damages

One of the most controversial issues in private antitrust enforcement is the proof and calculation of damage caused by antitrust violations. There has been a suggestion that a presumptive provision regarding the amount of damages should be introduced, but such a provision has not been adopted because it is difficult to correctly estimate the amount of damages, given that the nature of the violations, and victims may vary significantly in antitrust cases.[10] In practice, the difference between the envisaged price or estimated profit

---

[7] Case No. Showa 60 (O) 933, MINSHU vol. 43, No. 11, p. 1259 (Supreme Court, Dec. 8, 1989). The Court refused to award damages to the plaintiffs in this case.

[8] Case No. Heisei 6 (Wa) 18372, 49 SHINKETSUSHU 720 (Tokyo District Court, Jul. 15, 2002).

[9] Case No. Heisei 14 (Ne) 4622, HANREI JIHO No. 1960, p. 28 (Tokyo High Court, Oct. 5, 2006).

[10] Higashide, supra note 2.

without violation and the actual price or actual profit earned with the illegal activity is generally considered the amount of damages in antitrust cases. However, in cartel cases, it is very difficult to predict what would have been the contractual price if there had been no conspiracy. The courts recognize this issue and adopt the theory that prices charged just before the start of cartel activity are considered the true market prices.[11]

In this regard, a new provision, §248, was introduced in 1996 in the Civil Procedure Law providing that a court may determine a reasonable amount of damages based on the entire import of the oral argument and the result of the examination of evidence where it is found that some damage has occurred and it is extremely difficult, due to the nature of the damage, to prove the amount thereof.[12] Subsequently, many courts awarded damages to antitrust plaintiffs based on section 248 of the Civil Procedure Law. Most courts accepted approximately 5 to 10 per cent of rigged contract prices as the reasonably estimated amount of damages based on the surcharge rate provided in the AMA (previously 6 per cent, and 10 per cent after the 2005 amendments) and the average rate of decline in contract prices after the cessation of cartels. Some courts adopted 15 or 20 per cent as the base rate to calculate a reasonable amount of damages.[13] In 2001, the Osaka High Court upheld a lower court decision that recognized 5 per cent of the value of contracts for public utility works as the estimated amount of damage incurred by the local government.[14] In 2003, the Tokushima District Court stated that the damages arising from bid-rigging on public work projects are generally recognized as the difference between the rigged contract prices and the potential prices under fair competition, but mentioned the difficulty in proving the supposed competitive price. Based on section 248, the court awarded 20 per cent of the actual contract prices to the plaintiff based on the fact that comparable contract prices without conspiracy were more than 20 per cent lower than the rigged prices.[15]

5. Damages actions in areas other than cartels

In recent years, private actions in the areas of private monopolization and unfair trade practices have increased as antitrust enforcement in such areas by the JFTC grows. In 2002, approximately 85 per cent of the administrative measures issued by the JFTC were related to bid-rigging and price-fixing, whereas in 2006 cartel cases accounted for approximately 70 per cent of administrative measures.[16]

For example, in 2005, the largest cable broadcasting company in Japan, Usen, filed suit against the second largest broadcasting company, Can System, arguing, among

---

11 Takaji Kanai, Noboru Kawahama and Fumio Sensui (eds) (2004), Antimonopoly Act, Japan: Kobundo, pp. 491–494. In cases where a cartel lasted for a long time and it is difficult to identify when the illegal activity started, the courts may recognize the prices charged after the cessation of a cartel as the possible market prices. In most cases, the cessation of a cartel may lead to sharp price declines and plaintiffs try to calculate damages based on such price declines.

12 Minji Soshoho [Civil Procedure Law], Law No. 109 of 1996, art. 248.

13 Kanai, Kawahama and Sensui, supra note 9, p. 494. See also Kenji Ito (2005), 'Current Situation of Damage Actions regarding Bid-Rigging', Fair Trade, No. 652, pp. 20–26.

14 Case No. Heisei 11 (Gyo Ko) 94, 47 SHINKETSUSHU 748 (Osaka High Court, Mar. 8, 2001).

15 Case No. Heisei 12 (Gyo U) 3 (Tokushima District Court, Jun. 13, 2003).

16 Fair Trade Commission (2008), Annual Report for Fiscal Year 2007.

other things, that Can System was taking away Usen's customers by predatory pricing in violation of the AMA. In response, Can System filed a counterclaim alleging that Usen was infringing upon Can System's interests by illegally headhunting their employees and taking away customers by implementing a discriminatory pricing scheme constituting private monopolization in violation of the AMA. In December 2008, the Tokyo District Court found in favor of Can System, stating that the discriminatory pricing scheme implemented by Usen to deprive the customers of Can System substantially restrains competition in the market and constitutes private monopolization in violation of the AMA.[17] Prior to the filing of the lawsuit, in 2004, the JFTC issued a cease and desist order against Usen, finding it excluded the business activities of Can System by offering discount prices only to Can System customers, thereby increasing its market share from 68 per cent to 72 per cent while Can System lost 6 per cent of its market share in one year.[18]

Two damages actions initiated by AMD Japan in 2005 have also received broad attention. In April 2005, the JFTC issued a cease and desist order upon finding that Intel gave rebates to major computer manufacturers on condition that these manufacturers bought all or almost all CPUs from Intel to exclude its competitor. Subsequently, under section 25 of the AMA, AMD Japan filed suit against Intel at the Tokyo High Court based on the findings included in the administrative order issued by the JFTC. AMD brought another damages action to the Tokyo District Court, alleging that Intel engaged in practices, other than the illegal anticompetitive practices found in the administrative order issued by the JFTC, in order to restrict trade and interrupt business activities of AMD.[19]

6. Injunctions

In general, purchasers are forced to accept higher prices as a result of cartels due to price-fixing and market division, making monetary damages an effective form of relief for victims of cartel activities. However, vertical restraints, such as refusal to deal, tying arrangement and exclusive dealing, are also utilized as a way to exclude competitors and monopolize the market. For example, when a distributor is excluded from the market or barriers to entry are established by incumbents through vertical restraints, such exclusionary conduct must be swiftly removed to restore fair competition in the market.

In order to reinforce antitrust regulation through private enforcement, injunctions were introduced in the 2000 amendments to the AMA. Section 24 of the AMA provides that any person whose interests are infringed or likely to be infringed by unfair trade practices prohibited under sections 8 and 19 and is thereby suffering or likely to suffer serious damage is entitled to demand suspension or prevention of such infringements. When a suit seeking an injunction is filed, the court is required to notify the JFTC. The

---

[17] K.K. USEN v. Can System K.K., HANREI TAIMUZU No. 1288, p. 112 (Tokyo District Court, Dec. 10, 2008).

[18] K.K. Usen Broadband Networks, K.K. Nihon Network Vision, 51 SHINKETSUSHU 518 (FTC, Oct. 13, 2004).

[19] Press Release, AMD (June 30, 2005), 'AMD Japan Files Claim for Damages Arising from Violations of Japan's Antimonopoly Act Against Intel K.K. in Tokyo High Court and Tokyo District Court', www.amd.com/us-en/Corporate/VirtualPressRoom/0,,51_104_543_13743~99765,00.html, accessed 15 May 2009.

court may request the opinion of the JFTC with respect to application of the AMA and other necessary matters, and the JFTC is also able to submit its opinion with court approval, although such opinion is not binding on the court. Moreover, there is a special rule with regard to jurisdiction under which the Tokyo District Court and the other seven district courts located where high courts exist all have jurisdiction in addition to other district courts which have jurisdiction based on the general rules of civil procedure. In an action for an injunction, a court may order the plaintiff to deposit a bond as security when the defendant submits prima facie evidence to show that the plaintiff filed for the injunction to interfere with business activities of its competitors or for any other abusive purpose.

7. Illegal practices

A plaintiff may seek an injunction against unfair trade practices either by entrepreneurs in violation of section 19 or by trade associations in violation of section 8 of the AMA. Section 2-9 of the AMA defines unfair trade practices as any act falling within any of the following categories, which tends to impede fair competition and which is designated by the JFTC notice: (i) discriminatory dealing; (ii) dealing with unjust consideration; (iii) unjust customer inducement; (iv) restrictive dealing; (v) abuse of superior bargaining position; and (vi) unjustly interfering with a transaction of a competitor. Pursuant to §2-9, the JFTC published the notice which includes a list of designated unfair trade practices which provides a more detailed description of practices prohibited under the AMA.[20] In principle, unfair trade practices are vertical restraints including, among other things, refusal to deal, discriminatory practices, tying, exclusive dealing and resale price maintenance. Such practices are also recognized as a means to monopolize the market. Thus, in practice, an act constituting private monopolization also becomes subject to injunction.[21]

For example, in 2001, a group of engineers filed a lawsuit seeking an injunction against interference with a transaction, predatory pricing, deceptive customer inducement and tying implemented by the seller of a remote monitoring system for electronic equipment. It was alleged that (i) the seller tried to convince purchasers of the remote monitoring system to cancel maintenance agreements with the plaintiffs; (ii) engineers managed by the seller offered fees below cost; (iii) the remote monitoring system sold did not have its performance indicated in advertisements thereby deceptively inducing customers; and (iv) the remote monitoring system was sold to purchasers on the condition that the purchasers conclude maintenance agreements with engineers managed by the seller.[22] Although the case was dismissed by the Tokyo District Court, it nonetheless captured attention because the court provided its judgment in an area where there has been little precedent.

---

20 Designation of Unfair Trade Practices (Fair Trade Commission Public Notice No. 15 of June 18, 1982).

21 Kanai, Kawahama and Sensui, supra note 9, p. 496.

22 Case No. Heisei 13 (Wa) 18139, HANREI TAIMUZU No. 1155, p. 161 (Tokyo District Court, Mar. 18, 2004).

8. Standing to sue for injunctions

As provided in section 24, any person whose interests are infringed or likely to be infringed by unfair trade practices and is thereby suffering or likely to suffer serious damage has standing to file for an injunction. Competitors, consumers and indirect purchasers have standing to sue if they are suffering or likely to suffer serious damage, but there is no collective lawsuit mechanism, and consumer groups are not authorized to file for an injunction on behalf of consumers unless such groups are actually suffering damage.[23]

9. Serious damage requirement under section 24

The meaning of 'serious damages' provided in section 24 has been vigorously debated and, in practice, no injunction has been granted thus far, in part because proving serious damage is very difficult. In the Kansai International Airport newspaper sales case, the Osaka District Court stated that an injunction is to be granted when the illegal act has a higher degree of detrimental effect and causes more severe damage than a case in which victims are effectively compensated by monetary damages, since a wide range of activities may be recognized as unfair trade practices and injunctions attempt to cover only those practices which should be eliminated immediately.[24] In other words, the court adopted the view that an injunction should only be granted if damage incurred by victims may not be recovered by monetary compensation.

10. Scope of injunctive relief

Courts may issue an injunction which suspends or prevents infringements constituting unfair trade practices in violation of the AMA. While an administrative order may prohibit the entire illegal transaction, the scope of injunctive relief is limited to measures necessary to recover damages incurred by the plaintiff due to the nature of civil litigation.[25] Among the issues currently being discussed is whether a court may order a defendant to desist from engaging in ancillary activities securing the anticompetitive effect of illegal practices or take any affirmative action to remove the effect of unfair trade practices. For example, where a defendant forced third parties to refuse to deal with a plaintiff by punitive measures, the issue is whether a court may order the defendant not only to stop such coercion against third parties but also to take any affirmative action to encourage third parties to engage in transactions with the plaintiff. It is generally recognized that a court is allowed to order any necessary measures to effectively suspend or prevent infringements.[26] However, some courts stated that section 24 does not authorize a court to impose a duty to take affirmative action on a defendant.[27]

---

23 Higashide, supra note 2.

24 Airport Press Service K.K. v. Kansai Kokusai Kuko Shinbunhanbai K.K., 51 SHINKETSUSHU 935 (Osaka District Court, Jun. 9, 2004).

25 Kanai, Kawahama and Sensui, supra note 9, p. 500.

26 Higashide, supra note 2.

27 Kanai, Kawahama and Sensui, supra note 9, p. 501.

11. Relationship between courts and the JFTC

Since private parties suffering serious damage may file suit for an injunction in addition to reporting the same infringement to the JFTC, there might be discrepancies between judgments of courts and the JFTC. In order to avoid such problems, the systems for notification of filing of suit and request for opinion of the JFTC were implemented. However, it has been noted that those systems for notification and request for opinion have not been functioning effectively and it is necessary to establish a better framework for their operation.[28]

Conclusion

Japan introduced the leniency program in 2005, which has been very effective and successful. Under the Japanese leniency program, the first applicants before the initiation of a JFTC investigation are awarded immunity from surcharges and criminal liabilities, and up to three applicants, including those who applied for leniency after the initiation of investigation, can receive a reduction in surcharges if they provide necessary information.[29] As described above, this program is based on the idea that such leniency would create sufficient incentive for cartel participants to disclose information regarding illegal activities to the authorities by granting immunity from administrative and criminal liabilities or reduction of punishments. It means that the success of the program depends on whether the government offers potential applicants enough of an incentive to confess illegal activities and disclose relevant information. At the present time, the leniency program does not provide any favorable treatment or protection to applicants with respect to civil litigation, but this produces no appreciable negative effect on the program because private antitrust enforcement is not very active and, unlike in the United States, there is no treble damages system under Japanese law. However, if private antitrust enforcement were expanded and enhanced, cartel participants would face greater civil liabilities, potentially making them less willing to admit to cartel activities and disclose information to the authorities. Thus, the government might consider establishing some mechanisms to mitigate negative effects on the leniency program arising from potential civil liabilities if private enforcement is expanded.

Meanwhile, as seen from the discussion above, antitrust plaintiffs, especially under the injunctive procedure, may often face great difficulty in proving illegal activities by defendants since private parties do not have at their disposal compulsory measures to collect evidence. Furthermore, specialized or technical information with regard to relevant markets and business activities may be necessary to prove antitrust violations. As stated earlier, the 2009 amendments are trying to improve private antitrust enforcement by introducing a special rule for the order to produce documents under the injunctive procedure. It is expected that such newly established system may enhance private antitrust enforcement and ensure consumer welfare. While courts should carefully analyze whether to grant an injunction because injunctive relief may have a significant impact

---

[28] Kyozo Suzuki (2005), 'Reality and Some Problems regarding Injunctions under §24 of the Antimonopoly Act', Fair Trade, No. 653, pp. 46–49.

[29] The 2009 amendments to the AMA increased the maximum number of leniency recipients from three to five.

on a broad range of business activities of firms in the market, it is also important to further reduce the burden of proof on antitrust plaintiffs by utilizing existing measures and introducing new systems in order to allow private antitrust enforcement to function effectively.

34 Korea

Hwang Lee[1] *and Byung Geon Lee*[2]

Introduction

During the last few years, there has been a gradual increase in Korea of private damages actions in conjunction with the intensifying Korea Fair Trade Commission (KFTC) public enforcement of the Monopoly Regulation and Fair Trade Act (MRFTA). This has been particularly so in the areas of cartel and abuse of dominance cases.[3] A Korean newspaper recently reported that, as of the end of 2008, approximately 12-16 cases were pending at the Seoul Central District Court, most of which were follow-on actions from KFTC proceedings.[4]

More recent private damages actions of significance include those on military-use gasoline bid rigging (2001), school uniform price fixing (2002), local phone call price fixing (2005), flour and sugar price fixing (2006), and Microsoft's tying case (2008).[5] The military-use gasoline case was particularly striking because of the large damages award, approximately KRW 81 billion, declared by the district court in 2007. The Ministry of National Defense brought this suit following the KFTC's imposition of a KRW 190 billion surcharge on five cartel members in 2000, which was the largest fine at that time. The school uniform case is also noteworthy because of the large number of opt-in plaintiffs under the representative action system. In that case, 3,525 parents who had bought school uniforms participated in the litigation with the help of several consumers' groups. During the course of litigation, as shown below, significant limitations of the opt-in mechanism became obvious and the case had important policy implications that are at the center of the debate on the development of private antitrust enforcement in Korea.

In an effort to encourage private damages actions, MRFTA was amended in 2005 in two respects. First, the National Assembly abolished the requirement that the KFTC render a conclusion prior to the commencement of private suits. This amendment permits stand-alone suits. Second, the National Assembly gave judges a certain degree of discretion in awarding damages, which lessened plaintiffs' burden of calculating precise

---

1 Associate Professor, Korea University School of Law; Secretary, Innovation, Competition and Regulation Law Center. The author can be reached at hwang_lee@korea.ac.kr.

2 Research Fellow, American Antitrust Institute. Byungkun1@gmail.com. The authors thank Sung-Mook Kim, Partner of DeRyook & Aju and Kenneth M. Vorrasi, Attorney of Drinker Biddle & Reath LLP for useful comments.

3 As the Korean leniency program has been vigorously utilized since 2005, over 40 cartel cases have been annually uncovered and surcharged by the KFTC. For details of Korea's cartel enforcement and leniency program, *see* KFTC (2009), '11 Years after Introduction of Leniency Program; Performance and Agenda' (Korean). *See also* KFTC's annual report (2009), p. 19, *available at* http://eng.ftc.go.kr/bbs.do?command=getList&type_cd=16.

4 The Law Times, Dec. 21, 2008. (Korean).

5 Since many of the cited cases are still ongoing, only years of complaint filing are shown for cases except where noted otherwise.

damages. In addition to these amendments, the National Assembly is considering several bills that would further facilitate private antitrust enforcement, which are discussed in detail below.

1. How does a damages action case get started?

a. Meeting clients and ethical restrictions

The Attorney-at-Law Act and the Ethics Code of the Korean Bar Association prohibit lawyers from directly contacting potential clients and from letting their employees solicit clients. Advertisements are permitted, but the manner and content of advertising are heavily restricted. As a result, lawyers most often develop clients through recommendations and reputation. This is true for competition law matters as well. In addition, the lack of an opt-out class action mechanism discourages lawyers from initiating class actions in Korea.

b. Investigative tools: follow-on or stand-alone actions

Most private antitrust damages actions occur after the KFTC has found that a person or entity has violated the law. Despite the elimination in 2005 of the requirement that private actions could only be initiated after a KFTC liability determination, which was regarded as a major obstacle to bringing damages actions, few stand-alone private actions have thus far been filed in civil courts without the KFTC's prior finding of violation. This primarily occurred because claimants could rely on the KFTC's liability finding and could concentrate their efforts on proving the amount of damages. The difficulties claimants face in gathering evidence and conducting discovery in civil actions contribute to the lack of stand-alone cases.[6]

Only a small number of stand-alone civil damages actions have occurred without the KFTC's finding of a violation. In these few instances, the plaintiffs are usually large companies with the resources to bring suit and to hire competent lawyers and experts. One of the most well known cases was a refusal-to-deal case in 2005 where Incheon Oil Refinery pursued approximately KRW 159 billion in damages against Hyundai Oil Bank. The plaintiff brought the lawsuit after the KFTC had dismissed the complaint against Hyundai on the grounds that the alleged refusal was merely a civil dispute. The Supreme Court ruled in favor of the defendant in 2008.[7]

c. Amassing sufficient evidence

In follow-on actions, with the benefit of the KFTC's decision, plaintiffs face relatively less of a burden to establish violations unless the KFTC's findings of facts and law are seriously challenged. When an administrative complaint is filed before the Seoul High Court, which has exclusive jurisdiction over appeals from KFTC decisions, civil courts usually wait and respect the outcome. This tradition stems from the general perception

---

[6] Yi, Sang-Seung and Y. Jung (2007), 'A New Kid on the Block: Korean Competition Law, Policy, and Economics', Competition Policy International, Vol. 3, No. 2, 153–183, p. 178, available at SSRN: http://ssrn.com/abstract=1075324.

[7] Supreme Court, 2004da39238, February 14, 2008.

that the Seoul High Court possesses superior expertise about antitrust matters to the general civil courts. However, when a violation seems to be clear enough (for example, in a case where a leniency filing was made), civil courts may make their own judgments.

As a result, the main issue in civil antitrust proceedings usually is the calculation of damages. Because the damages amount is not the main concern of the KFTC or the subject matter of the Seoul High Court, claimants need to gather additional evidence on damages. The Korean Civil Procedure Act (CPA) stipulates that it is the parties' responsibility to produce evidence and a court will intervene, on its own accord, only when judges cannot be confident about their expected decision or when they acknowledge the need to find truth.

2. Who may pursue a claim?

Under the CPA, claimants generally have standing to bring suits for damages. While, in the United States, there are limitations on who has standing to sue in order to prevent excessive litigation and limit the risk of multiple liabilities, Korea's civil procedures address these concerns at the stage of adjudicating on the merits, such as, the existence of damages or causation.

Accordingly, all alleged victims of a violation of MRFTA, such as transaction partners, end-consumers, and even government agencies that are engaged in private transactions, have standing to sue for damages. Indirect purchasers have standing to sue in principle, but the difficulty in establishing causation and the amount of damages poses obstacles to recovery.

So-called public interest litigation – when a claim is brought by a third party person or association on behalf of the public – is not allowed in Korea.

There are no established precedents on which types of harm are redressable by damages awards. The antitrust academy in Korea, however, is receptive to the 'antitrust injury' doctrine developed in the U.S.[8] According to the doctrine, only damages suffered as a result of another's anticompetitive conduct may be redressable.

3. In what forum does a plaintiff initiate a private claim?

A three-tiered judicial review system applies to antitrust damages suits. Depending on the amount claimed, a single judge or a three-judge panel adjudicates cases in the first instance. Under the CPA, personal jurisdiction is based on where the defendant is domiciled, where the defendant's main office is located, or where the unlawful conduct occurred.[9]

There are no meaningful differences among district courts in terms of local bias because judges periodically transfer between different jurisdictions on a national basis and the Supreme Court's precedents play a crucial role in the judgments of local courts owing to *de facto* binding effects. As a result, forum shopping rarely occurs in Korea. As a matter of practice, however, most claims are brought before the Seoul Central District Court because many large companies' headquarters are located in Seoul.

The Seoul High Court has exclusive jurisdiction in a two-tier system with respect to

---

[8] Yim, Young Chul, Competition Law (2008), pp. 520–521 (Korean).

[9] Article 2 of the Civil Procedure Act.

appeals against the corrective measures of the KFTC. The Seoul High Court operates in two special exclusive divisions for competition law matters. For this reason, it is common that the same alleged violation is adjudicated in two different courts; one in Seoul High Court in association with the KFTC's decision and another in general civil courts.

4. How may claims be aggregated?

As a general matter, the CPA provides that a single plaintiff files one complaint. When multiple parties believe they have been injured by the same conduct, multiple claimants can sign up for one complaint or the court may consolidate the claims for purposes of judicial economy. When individual damages are too small to justify each member's litigation costs, however, this scheme may not be economically viable.

The recent local phone call price fixing case (2005) shows the actual problems with the current opt-in mechanism.[10] In this case, a consumers' organization initiated a damages action after the KFTC instituted corrective measures against two telecommunication companies. Though the total number of affected subscribers was approximately 20 million, only 484 consumers gathered to file a claim and each paid KRW 10,000 as litigation fees. According to plaintiffs' counsel, they worked on a *pro bono* basis because the participation fee they were paid could not even cover the attorneys' fees besides other costs. As the case proceeded, consumers' unwillingness to participate in the claim appeared to be economically reasonable because the Seoul Central District Court awarded each subscriber only KRW 12,000, which was almost the same amount as the pre-paid litigation fees. To address such problems, discussions about introducing a new system are going on, as noted below.

a. Representative actions

Article 53 of the CPA provides the 'representative action' mechanism under which multiple claimants can jointly bring a damages action. The central aim of this mechanism is to improve the economies of litigation by aggregating individual claims that have common issues of fact and law. Under this mechanism, multiple litigants can designate one or a small number of representatives. The judgment binds all litigants who opted into the action. This mechanism is also known as the 'opt-in class action'. A representative action aggregates individual claims where numerous claimants entrust their claims to a small number of representatives. Accordingly, each claimant needs to formally express his or her entrustment to the representatives and also share any individual evidence, such as receipts for purchased products to prove the individual damages amount. Injured victims who do not sign up independently need to file separate complaints if they also want to recover their damages.

The representative action is not widely utilized in competition matters involving widespread harm because there is no meaningful difference, in terms of time, expenses, and legal effects, from an action consolidating multiple plaintiffs and designating common counsel, as occurred in the local phone call price fixing case.

---

[10] Seoul Central District Court, 2005gahap88973, 109504 (consolidated), January 18, 2008.

b. Association lawsuit

The recent amendment to the Framework Act on Consumers has established the 'association lawsuit' device under which qualified consumers' associations can seek injunctive relief commencing in January 2008.[11] But the association lawsuit has several procedural restrictions that could discourage consumers' associations from utilizing it. For example, associations may seek injunctive relief only; damages claims are not allowed. Further, a court's prior permission is required to initiate an action. The association lawsuit mechanism needs to be significantly modified to be useful as a tool for the private enforcement of competition law.

c. Debate over introduction of opt-out class action

To facilitate private damages actions, several alternatives are being discussed in Korea. Many scholars and consumers' groups support the adoption of an opt-out class action mechanism, especially under the competition law and the Product Liability Act (PLA).[12] Private companies and business associations, however, tend to oppose these reforms on the grounds that the opt-out device is not compatible with the traditional civil law regime and may cause excessive litigation, the cost of which will be passed on to end-consumers.

To date, the opt-out class action has been adopted only in the securities law area beginning in 2005.[13] As of July 2009, the bill of the Class Action Act, which includes a general opt-out mechanism, was introduced in the National Assembly. In light of the strong opposition from businesses, however, it is unlikely that this bill will pass the National Assembly soon.

d. Joint and several liability

Defendants are liable for damages on a joint and several basis for violations of the MRFTA. In other words, each defendant is liable for the full amount of damages even though multiple defendants jointly may have committed the alleged violation. Each defendant's liability, however, is evaluated in accordance with its individual contribution to the plaintiff's injury, such as a proportion of relevant sales volume affected by a cartel. Thus, if a defendant is ordered to pay damages exceeding its actual contribution, then the defendant may pursue indemnification from other defendants.

5. What procedural defenses are available before trial

A claim can be dismissed before trial if certain prerequisites are not met, such as jurisdiction, interest of litigation, limitation period, and so on. In private antitrust damages litigation, however, those prerequisites are usually not onerous because they are easily satisfied in most cases that are filed right after disclosure of violations by direct victims.

---

11 Section 3 of the Framework Act on Consumers.

12 Citizens' Coalition for Economic Justice (CCEJ), one of the major civil associations in favor of the opt-out class action device, fulfilled a focus group survey on 156 legal experts in March 2007. According to the survey, 76.3% responded in favor of the adoption of the opt-out class action mechanism.

13 The Class Action Act on Securities Matters.

Furthermore, because Korea has no jury trial system in civil litigation, arguments on the prerequisites and on the merits are commonly adjudicated at the same stage.

6. What devices are available to obtain evidence?

It is hard for plaintiffs to gather evidence in civil actions, especially in antitrust cases, because Korea does not have expansive discovery rights as in the US. As stated earlier, parties should submit arguments and relevant evidence. As a result, it is very difficult to bring private antitrust damages claims without a prior KFTC finding of a competition violation. However, the CPA and the MRFTA provide some limited evidence-gathering devices as described below.

a. Request for transfer of documentary evidence

The MRFTA, along with the CPA, provides that a court may ask the KFTC to transfer relevant records and evidence.[14] Parties can also directly request the KFTC to provide relevant evidence. However, parties frequently resort to the court's authority. The KFTC has stated expressly that its general policy is to cooperate actively with injured victims with regard to collecting evidence.[15]

b. Order for submission of documentary evidence

Parties may request that courts order opposing parties or third parties to submit any specified documentary evidence. To make such a request, a party should name the title of specified documents along with the name of their custodians. The court will order the submission of named documents if deemed appropriate. The CPA articulates types of documents that parties are obliged to deliver to the opposing parties, including certain documents supporting their own arguments. The CPA was amended in 2002, in response to the criticism that the scope of disclosure described above is too narrow. As with the discovery rules of the US the amendment has made it mandatory to submit all documents beyond the traditional types of documents by the request of opposing parties, as long as deemed appropriate by the court. But the problem remains that courts lack the authority to compel submission in this situation. Accordingly, some experts propose the adoption of the US-style broad discovery device in the Korean civil procedure regime.[16]

c. Witness and examination

Expert witness testimony is primarily used for damages calculations in civil courts. As described above, expert witnesses retained by plaintiffs usually face difficulty in securing relevant data from defendants because they usually are not able to name the necessary documents exactly and courts lack the authority to compel broad production without specification. As a result, expert reports requested by parties and designated by the court are mainly used for purposes of damages calculations. Despite the limitations, voluntary submissions of data were well utilized in the military-use gasoline bid rigging

---

14 Article 56-2 of the MRFTA.

15 KFTC, 'Introduction to Policy; Damages Claim under the MRFTA', available at http://blog.korea.kr/app/log/anticartel/40470755 (Korean).

16 Lee, Ki Jong (2006), 'A Study on the Economic Analysis in Antitrust Damage Suit', Commercial Law Research, Vol. 25, No. 3, p. 316 (Korean).

case,[17] where the district court requested damages calculation from an economic-analysis institute under agreement between the parties. The court articulated several important criteria in light of evaluating econometric analysis: correctness and consistency of data process; robust economic theory and practical foundation of the estimating equations; and appropriate reflection of reality. This judgment of 2007 is expected to be a significant precedent in terms of econometric analysis on damages calculations.

7. What practices are illegal and what are the elements of proof?

In principle, private parties are entitled to seek damages for all violations of the MRFTA, such as cartel, abuse of dominance, and unfair trade practices. In parallel with the KFTC's active enforcement of cartels and abuse of dominance in recent years, the number of damages actions against these unlawful practices also has been increasing.

There are three types of exemptions stipulated in the MRFTA under which no damages can be sought. First, the MRFTA does not apply to legitimate conduct pursuant to laws, its subordinate decrees, or corresponding agency actions. In reality, defendants in heavily regulated industries, such as finance or telecommunications, attempted to utilize this exemption, arguing that the regulatory agencies compelled them to act in accordance with certain statutes.[18] To date, however, courts have not been receptive to this argument.

Second, the MRFTA does not apply to cartels authorized in advance by the KFTC for purposes of overcoming the recession, establishing joint research, and so on. Currently, there has been no cartel authorized by the KFTC under this provision.

Third, the MRFTA does not apply to the legitimate exercise of intellectual property rights under the Patent Act and Copyright Act.[19] Anticompetitive or unfair trade practices that exceed the legitimate purview of intellectual property rights and are considered abusive are not exempted from the MRFTA.[20]

a. Burden of proof in damages claim

Damages claims for violation of the MRFTA may be brought either under the Civil Code or under the MRFTA. If claimants choose to pursue damages under the Civil Code, they must prove each element of tort; that is, the existence of alleged behavior, the defendant's willfulness or negligence, the illegality of alleged behavior, the existence of damages, and finally, the causation between alleged conduct and damages.

In comparison with the Civil Code, the MRFTA has a lower buren of proof in two respects. First, the burden of proof shifts from plaintiffs to defendants regarding the defendant's willfulness or negligence element.[21] Second, the MRFTA confers on judges a certain degree of discretion in deciding damages amount and thus judges may consider

---

[17] Seoul Central District Court, 2001gahap10682, January 23, 2007.

[18] Recently, this exemption argument was the core issue in the following two cases: (1) the local phone call price fixing case (KFTC Case No 2004Danchae3830); (2) the 10 Insurers' cartel case (KFTC Case No. 2007seoka0740).

[19] Article 59 of the MRFTA.

[20] KFTC, Guidelines of Reviewing Undue Exercise of Intellectual Property Rights, Article 1 (August 30, 2000).

[21] Article 56 of the MRFTA.

certain relevant arguments even when the plaintiff fails to prove the exact sum.[22] It is an important exception to a general principle of tort law to acknowledge the overall purport of pleading as complementary or separate elements for damages calculation; this is assessed to have significant impact in alleviating the plaintiffs' burden of proof.

As for causation, the MRFTA has no specific provisions; hence the general theory of tort law, the so-called 'reasonable causation relationship' principle, applies and the plaintiff bears the burden of proof.[23]

8. What do plaintiffs get if they win?

As an established principle, the amount of compensation is limited to actual damage. Punitive or exemplary damages awards are not acknowledged in Korea, but a group of consumers' associations and scholars have been proposing the introduction of punitive damages.[24] As of July 2009, a bill to amend the MRFTA by introducing punitive damages is pending in the National Assembly. It is uncertain whether the bill will be approved in the near future.

With respect to prejudgment interest, the CPA stipulates the interest to be applied for the gap between the damage-occurred date and the damage-award date. The prejudgment interest is 5% from the date of violation to the judgment date, while it becomes 20% from the next day after judgment to the full payment date.

a. Criteria for damages calculation

The courts held that damage means a disadvantage caused by the infringement, assessed by the differences between the asset in the absence of violation and the asset reduced by the infringement. This is the so-called 'differential amount' theory and is similar to the before-and-after method of the US court.

With respect to damage caused by a cartel, the courts calculate damages by considering the difference between the competitive price in the absence of the cartel and the inflated price caused by it. For example, in the school uniform cartel judgment in 2007, the Seoul High Court held that the competitive price in the absence of the alleged cartel was 85% of the actual purchase price, considering the sales volume, margin ratio, etc. The military-use gasoline bid-rigging judgment in 2007 has been known as a more sophisticated ruling in terms of damages calculation. The court determined the damages amount as KRW 81 billion by using a regression method based on 'difference-in-differences' analysis. The court further held that the surcharge imposed by the KFTC should not be considered in

22 *Id.*, Article 57.

23 In the two judgments in June 2009 about Microsoft's tying conduct, each about media server and internet messenger software products, an identical bench of the Seoul Central District Court made it clear that a plaintiff should establish causation elements. In the two cases, the Court admitted that Microsoft's tying conduct was illegal; however, no reasonable causation was established and plaintiffs could not be awarded damages.

24 Kim, Doo Jin (2007), 'Introducing Punitive Damages into Competition Law and Consumer Law, Korea Legislation Research Institute', p. 103 (Korean).

According to the CCEJ survey *supra*, 75% of the respondents were in favor of the adoption of punitive damages.

calculating the damages amount because it is intrinsically different from civil damages liability.

b. Pass-on defense

To date, there is no established doctrine concerning the pass-on defense, under which defendants could argue that plaintiffs passed an anticompetitive overcharge onto the end consumers. A recent district court judgment in a flour price fixing case affirmed the need to avoid double compensation to achieve fairness. Accordingly, the amount that the plaintiff (bread maker) passed on to the end consumers was deducted from the awarded damages.[25]

c. Moral damages

In Korea, damages are basically awarded in the form of monetary compensation. Case law generally holds that the compensation for financial loss compensates moral damage inflicted by infringement of properties. Thus, it is rare that plaintiffs are separately awarded moral damages when courts award financial damages.

d. Contributory negligence and offset of profits/losses

Under the Civil Code, when deciding the damages amount, the courts consider the plaintiff's own negligence. Precedents also provide that benefits the plaintiffs received from the unlawful conduct should be deducted from damages awards to achieve fairness. For example, in a refusal-to-deal case, the court held that the plaintiff's benefits, generated from the defendant's resale price maintenance onto other competing companies, should be deducted.[26]

e. Legal costs

The CPA subscribes to the principle that 'costs of a lawsuit shall be borne by the losing party.'[27] In practice, however, courts do not base litigation costs on actual costs, such as filing fee, travel expenses of witnesses, attorneys' fees, etc, but on the Supreme Court's Notice.[28] According to the Notice, for example, if the amount sought is KRW 1 million, courts acknowledge 10% as litigation costs, that is, KRW 0.1 million. The result is not sufficient to cover the actual costs, especially attorneys' fees, and this valuation method serves to discourage private damages actions.

f. Limitation periods

The statute of limitations of an antitrust damages claim follows the rule of the general tort law; no private damages claim can be made after the lapse of three years from the day when the plaintiff becomes aware of such damages and the wrongdoer, and after the

---

25 In addition to the flour judgment in May 2009, at least two civil cases are currently pending before courts involving the assertion of a pass-on defense; price fixing cases over sugar (2006) and Value Added Network service fee for credit cards (2007).

26 Supreme Court, 89daka29075, April 10, 1990.

27 Article 98 of the CPA.

28 The Supreme Court Notice No. 1829, 'The Rule on Renumeration of Attorney and Calculation of Litigation Costs'.

lapse of ten years after the date when the wrongdoing was committed.[29] Thus, if plaintiffs intend to bring damages actions in conjunction with a KFTC's decision, they should bring actions within the statute of limitations and should move the court to toll it until the KFTC reaches a decision.

9. How does the plaintiff's lawyer finance private enforcement?

Plaintiffs and their attorneys can freely decide a retaining fee and a contingent fee on top of the litigations costs, with no ceiling limitation.[30] The amount of attorneys' fees in the antitrust damages litigation is reportedly similar to those of ordinary damages lawsuits. In practice, the proportion of the retaining fee and the contingent fee is adjustable based on the degree of difficulty and the possibility of prevailing. In addition, as explained above, the attorneys could be awarded the litigation costs by the court's ruling under the Supreme Court Notice.

10. How does private enforcement interact with public enforcement?

a. Extraterritoriality

By adopting the 'effects' doctrine, the MRFTA applies to activities committed overseas if they have *influence* on the Korean domestic market.[31] Accordingly, injured victims can bring damages actions in domestic courts even though the alleged cartel operates exclusively on foreign soil. To date, no private damages action has reportedly been brought against cartels formed overseas, even though the KFTC has prosecuted three international cartels as of July 2009.[32]

b. The effect of the KFTC's decisions on civil courts

The Supreme Court has held that the KFTC's decision has no binding effects on civil courts. With respect to factual findings, however, the Supreme Court held in 1990 that the KFTC's fact findings could be presumed as *prima facie* evidence. The *prima facie* presumption effects of KFTC's fact-findings may vary in individual cases according to the types of corrective measures and the actual adjudication process within the KFTC.[33]

c. Interplay with leniency programs of the national authority

The application of Korea's leniency program has significantly increased over the past ten years. Potential leniency recipients may be disincentivized to apply for the program because statements or materials they disclose to the government could be used in civil lawsuits against the recipients' interests. Though this issue is rare in Korea due to the

---

29 Article 766 of the Civil Code.

30 In a few cases, excessive attorneys' fees for poor legal service were found violative of the ethics code of the Korean Bar Association. However, there do not exist clear standards and it is to be decided case by case.

31 Article 2-2 of the MRFTA.

32 Graphite electrodes price fixing (2002), Vitamin price fixing (2003), Copy paper price fixing (2008), Marine hose bid-rigging (2009).

33 Hong, Dae Sik (2003), 'Damage Claim under the Korean Antitrust Law – From the Perspective of Practice', Business Law, Vol. 13, No. 2, p. 254 (Korean).

rarity of damages actions, it may be problematic for foreign businesses in places where the application of damages actions is vigorous and the KFTC is known to study the issue. As for damages liability, no mechanism exists under which the liability of leniency recipients could be reduced.

d. Adoption of private injunction
Courts generally do not allow private parties to seek injunctive relief beyond financial compensation, for they are concerned that individual freedom of activity might be unduly restricted. The National Assembly is currently reviewing a bill to amend the MRFTA, which introduces the possibility of injunctive relief. The bill has not passed as of July 2009.

Conclusion
In sum, the number of follow-on private enforcements is gradually increasing while the level of stand-alone private enforcements remains low. Over the years, the KFTC has taken several initiatives to facilitate private enforcement, but it is generally viewed that Korea's private antitrust enforcement is far from robust and several institutional impediments hamper changes in this regard. It is a generally shared notion in the Korean antitrust community, however, that private antitrust enforcement should be enhanced to achieve optimal deterrence, supplementing public enforcement by the KFTC.[34] Academia and consumer groups have been proposing several measures, such as the introduction of private injunctions, punitive damages awards, an opt-out class action mechanism, public interest actions, and finally the extension of the scope of association lawsuits. Indeed, the National Assembly has before it several relevant bills. Despite these efforts, however, it is unlikely that the proposed reforms will be adopted in the near future, due to the strong opposition from the business sector and the inherent legal conflict in deviating from the general civil law regime.

Given that both the opt-out class action and the limited association lawsuit device have already been adopted in the securities law and the consumer law areas respectively, the possibility of adopting the opt-out class action mechanism would be relatively higher than the proposal of the broader US-style discovery system; the opt-out style association lawsuit could be considered as a stepping-stone in this reform.

In sum, thanks to vigorous public enforcement and diverse efforts to remove hurdles for plaintiffs in civil antitrust actions, private enforcement is expected to gradually increase in the years ahead.

---

[34] Lee, Byung Joo (2008), Discussion Paper of Seoul Int'l Competition Forum Session 1, attached at the KFTC Press Release (Sep. 2, 2008).

35 South Africa

Kasturi Moodaliyar[1]

Introduction

Private enforcement in antitrust cases is a rarity in South Africa. The Competition Act,[2] which governs the rules and regulations of competition law in South Africa, allows for parties to seek reparation for damage in the civil courts only after the competition authorities (that being the Competition Commission, Competition Tribunal and if there is an appeal, the Competition Appeal Court) have investigated and made a final determination as to whether anti-competitive conduct has taken place. Thus parties seeking damages in antitrust cases have to wait for the outcome of that decision before pursuing redress. Many additional factors work against the private plaintiff. Claiming damages can be an expensive exercise due to the time and costs required. The anti-competitive conduct may have caused the aggrieved party to suffer significant economic loss, thereby limiting the resources available to a claimant to underwrite litigation. Injured parties can seek legal assistance on a contingency basis (although there may not be too many willing litigators).

Since the inception of the Competition Act in 1999, there has in fact been just one damages case. In this case, which occurred in 2008, Nationwide Airlines (a company that is currently being liquidated) sued South African Airways (SAA) after the Tribunal had made a finding that SAA had abused its dominant position.[3] Nationwide Airlines subsequently settled for an undisclosed amount.[4] Since this case, there has not been much development in the area of private enforcement in antitrust cases in South Africa. Instead there have simply been rumors and rumblings about possible damages claims which have not yet come to light.

1. Public enforcement in South Africa

In South Africa, restrictive anticompetitive practices are prohibited by the Competition Act section 89 of 1998 (as amended). The Act created the Competition Commission, which investigates restrictive practice complaints.[5] Private parties may file complaints

1 B.Proc. LLB.LLM (Natal) M.Phil (Cambridge). Programme in Economics and Public Finance (UNISA). PhD Candidate. Senior Lecturer in Law, University of the Witwatersrand, Johannesburg. The chapter on Private Enforcement in South Africa contains extracts from my pending PhD thesis registered at the University of Witwatersrand.

2 Section 65 of the Competition Act 89 of 1998 (as amended), hereafter referred to as the 'Competition Act' or 'the Act'.

3 Case no: 83/CR/Oct04 available at www.comptrib.co.za . See also Tamara Dini, 'Nationwide settles damages claim for SAA's abuse of dominance', February 19 2008, at www.bowman.co.za/Law/Articles/Law-Articles.asp?id=2132417250.

4 www.bowman.co.za/LawArticles/Law-Article.asp?id=2132417250/.

5 Section 19(2) stipulates that the Minister [of the Department of Trade and Industry] appoints the Commissioner and one or more Deputy Commissioners. The posts are held for one term (5

with the Commission or the Commission can initiate a complaint.[6] If the Commission has sufficient evidence of anticompetitive conduct, it will refer the case to the Competition Tribunal for adjudication.[7] If the respondent is found to have contravened the Act, the Tribunal may impose an administrative penalty of up to 10% of the respondent's annual turnover (sales) in South Africa for the preceding year.[8] The Tribunal has in some cases based its penalty on the annual turnover in other affected markets as well. In order to determine the penalty, the Tribunal has to consider the following factors:

- the nature, duration, gravity and extent of the contravention;
- any loss or damage suffered as a result of the contravention;
- the behavior of the respondent;
- the market circumstances in which the contravention took place;
- the level of profit derived from the contravention;
- the degree to which the respondent has co-operated with the Competition Commission and the Competition Tribunal; and
- whether the respondent has previously been found in contravention of this Act.[9]

There has been much publicity in recent years concerning the investigation of restrictive, anticompetitive practices and fines imposed by the Competition Tribunal. While the fines, the largest being over R200m,[10] may serve as a punishment and deterrent to violators, these fines do not compensate the aggrieved parties who have been directly affected by anticompetitive behavior. An infringed upon party or group of parties only has recourse to the civil court to claim damages. One possible avenue of relief in the civil court is a class action. There has been an attempt to introduce legislation to provide better guidance on class action procedure in courts, but there has been no such enactment to date.

The Competition Act provides:

> A person who has suffered loss or damage as a result of a prohibited practice-
> (a) may not commence an action in a civil court for the assessment of the amount or awarding of damages if that person has been awarded damages in a consent order confirmed in terms of section 49D(1);[11] or
> (b) if entitled to commence an action referred to in paragraph (a), when instituting proceedings, must file with the Registrar or Clerk of the Court a notice from the Chairperson of

---

years) and can be renewed for a second term. The posts are not renewable for a third term. The Commission also comprises a number of economists and lawyers who hold either contract or permanent positions in the various departments.

6 The Commissioner is given the power to initiate a complaint in terms of §49B of the Act.

7 Section 26(3).

8 Section 59(2).

9 Section 59(3).

10 'Competition Commission increases Sasol's fine' www.mg.co.za/article/2009-05-19-competition-commission-increases-sasols, accessed on 10 June 2009.

11 It will be up to the High Court to determine the basis on which damages can be awarded. Section 49D(1) does not appear to specify or restrict the type of applicant who may make a claim for damages. The applicant could be the party who brought the initial complaint. This would be an obvious choice. However, it is uncertain that a party who did not bring the initial complaint can claim damages. This has yet to be tested in court.

the Competition Tribunal, or the Judge President of the Competition Appeal Court, in the prescribed form-

i. certifying that the conduct constituting the basis for the action has been found to be a prohibited practice in terms of the Act;
ii. stating the date of the Tribunal or Competition Appeal Court finding; and
iii. setting out the section of this Act in terms of which the Tribunal or the Competition Appeal Court made its finding.[12]

Since its inception, the Commission has investigated a number of complaints related to restrictive practices under chapter two of the Competition Act. Such prohibited practices include: (a) restrictive horizontal practices (that is, restrictive agreements between competitors as well as hard core cartels that engage in price fixing, market allocation and bid rigging),[13] (b) restrictive vertical practices (that is, restrictive agreements between parties in a vertical relationship as well as restrictions on minimum resale price agreements),[14] and (c) abuse of dominance, which includes prohibitions against excessive pricing, refusing a competitor access to an essential facility, engaging in exclusionary acts, such as inducing a customer or supplier not to deal with a competitor, refusing to supply a scarce good to a competitor, tying or bundling, predatory pricing, and buying up scarce goods required by a competitor.[15] The provisions also prohibit a dominant firm from price discrimination where, amongst other things, it has the likely effect to substantially prevent or lessen competition.[16]

Although the Tribunal has imposed fines or granted consent orders in a number of these cases, there has only been the one civil action claim mentioned earlier, which was settled before a hearing for an undisclosed amount. The civil courts are yet to have a full hearing for a case for damages. The granting of consent orders does not preclude a private party from seeking damages once those cases are finalized by the Competition Authorities. Damages claims have had a slow start in South Africa and this may be due to the barriers to bringing claims, such as the lack of procedural clarity, single damages (as opposed to treble damages), legal costs and the significant time it takes to reach a resolution. More recently, however, aggrieved parties have been threatening to make claims for civil damages, but these parties will still have to wait for the outcome of Competition Authority findings before pursuing private litigation, in accordance with the Act.

2. Who can bring a claim

The Competition Act allows a very general category of persons who have suffered loss or damage as a result of anti-competitive conduct to bring civil actions for damages.[17] There is no jurisprudence in either statute or case law identifying parties who may or may

---

[12] Section 65(6).

[13] Section 4 of the Competition Act.

[14] Section 5.

[15] Section 8.

[16] Section 9.

[17] It is difficult to give accurate estimates of the number of billable hours and the percentage of attorneys who represent defendants/claimants predominantly. In addition, it is not just law firms that represent clients. Sometimes these firms hire advocates to litigate, and in many instances an advocate may represent firm A in one case and then act against firm A in another case.

not be entitled to claim damages. Plaintiffs can apparently be direct purchasers, indirect purchasers, suppliers or competitors, provided they have not been participants in the anti-competitive conduct. It should also be noted that 'the more remote a claimant's loss is from the infringement, the less likely it may be to obtain damages'.[18] The claimant thus has to prove that there is a direct, significant link between the anti-competitive conduct and the loss suffered.[19]

In South Africa, a claimant must file a civil action within 3 years of the date on which the cause of action arose.[20] In a damages claim arising under the competition law, the claimant must wait for the outcome of the decision by the competition authorities before proceeding.[21] It is unclear whether this requirement in conjunction with the statute of limitations infringes the claimant's right to due process because the claimant cannot make a claim for damages without the Competition Authorities deciding on the case first.[22] Another barrier to bringing a civil claim is the prospect of a prolonged delay before such a claim can be filed. The competition authorities may spend years finalizing a matter, especially if the case goes on appeal, and the claimant must wait for that final decision before proceeding. Even though the Tribunal/Appeal Court's findings may be persuasive in the civil courts, the information that the competition authorities receive may be confidential. Therefore the information that the competition authorities are allowed to share with the clamant is limited to non-confidential information, which may not be sufficient to carry a damages case forward. The parties who have submitted the confidential information may be asked to waive confidentiality; however this is far from guaranteed. These delays can be a prohibiting factor for claimants who may be out of business by that time, or may not have the resources to wait, or may simply lose interest in the matter.

A law review article on private damages concludes, 'In many cases, potential claimants may consider that the lengthy procedure, uncertainty of outcome, and relatively low level of damages that are likely to be available (at least when compared to the US) outweigh the potential benefits of bringing an action'.[23] This is possibly due in part to the fact that, unlike in the US, only single damages can be claimed, and punitive damages are not available.

a. Standing

In South Africa, a claimant may have *locus standi* (standing) to bring a civil action if two tests are satisfied. First, the party concerned must have a direct and substantial interest

---

18 David Harrison and Rachel Cuff, 'Private Damages actions in Competition Law', The In-House Lawyer, September 2007 p. 52 at p. 55.

19 See *S v Mokgethi* 1990 1 SA 32 (A).

20 Prescription Act 68 of 1969.

21 Section 65 of the Competition Act.

22 Section 34 of the Bill of Rights states that: 'Everyone has the right to have any dispute that can be resolved by the application of law decided in a fair public hearing before a court or, where appropriate, another independent and impartial tribunal or forum.' Constitution of the Republic of South Africa Act 108 of 1996.

23 David Harrison and Rachel Cuff, 'Private Damages actions in Competition Law', The In-House Lawyer, September 2007 p. 52 at p. 54.

in the matter and, second, the party must have legal capacity to litigate in the matter.[24] In *Ferreira v Levin*, the Constitutional Court held that these tests are to be broadly applied to ensure that prospective parties fully enjoy their constitutional rights.[25]

In competition-related cases, as in other cases, a party generally has the capacity to litigate as a person or as a company.[26] Under the common law, a partnership, association or firm was not considered a legal person and therefore did not have standing.[27] However, the High Court rules went beyond the common law and permitted standing for an association ('any unincorporated body or person, not being a partnership'[28]) or a firm ('a business carried on by a body corporate, carried on by the sole proprietor thereof under a name other than his own'[29]). However, a third party, even one that has a direct financial interest in the company (for example a shareholder), does not have standing in South Africa unless it has an interest that was directly and substantially affected by the conduct. Under South African rules of civil procedure, a direct and substantial interest requires:

(a) the plaintiff/applicant for relief must have an adequate interest in the subject-matter of the litigation, which is not a technical concept but is usually described as a direct interest in the relief sought;
(b) the interest must not be too far removed;
(c) the interest must be actual, not abstract or academic;
(d) the interest must be a current interest and not a hypothetical one.[30]

The South African Constitution broadens the scope of 'direct and substantial interest' with regard to actions taken under the Chapter 2 Bill of Rights. Section 38 specifies who may be a claimant in these circumstances. The claimants may include:

- anyone acting in their own interest;
- anyone acting on behalf of another person who cannot act in their own name;
- anyone acting as a member of, or in the interest of, a group or a class of persons;
- anyone acting in the public interest, and

---

24 Steve Pete, David Hulme, Max du Plessis and Robin Palmer, Civil Procedure: A Practical Guide, 2005, New Africa Books (Pty) Ltd: Claremont, at p. 14.

25 Justice Chaskalson: 'It is my view that we should adopt a broad approach to standing. This would be consistent with the mandate given to this court to uphold the Constitution and would serve to ensure that constitutional rights enjoy the full measure of the protection to which they are entitled.' *Ferreira v Levin NO* 1996 (1) SA (CC) ¶165.

26 The Companies Act, No. 61 of 1973, s. 34 and the Close Corporations Act s 2(4) of Act 69 of 1984 give companies the legal right to litigate.

27 Jones and Buckle, *The Rules*, Rule 54-2. Jones, Buckle, Erasmus and Van Loggerenberg, *The Civil Practice of the Magistrates Court in South Africa: The Rules Vol 2* (Juta Legal and Academic Publishers, 9th ed., 1997).

28 High Court rule 14(1).

29 High Court rule 14(1).

30 Jones, Buckle, Erasmus and Van Loggerenberg, *The Civil Practice of the Magistrates' Courts in South Africa: The Rules Vol 2* (Juta Legal and Academic Publishers, 9th ed., 1997), *The Rules*: Rule 6-7 in Pete et al., *Civil Procedure: A Practical Guide*, p. 15. See also *Voget v Kleynhans* 2003(2) SA 148 (C) at 151E and *Judin v Wedgwood* 2003(5) SA 472 (W) at 475 H-476 A, *Natal Fresh Produce Growers' Assocation v Agroserve (Pty) Ltd* 1990 (4)SA 749 (N).

- an association *acting in the* interest of its members.[31]

A prospective plaintiff in a competition-related damages action can bring suit in accordance with these provisions only if the suit raises constitutional issues implicating the Bill of Rights.[32] Some of the issues that could be raised would be, for example, the right to equality (section 9), the right to freedom of trade, occupation and profession (section 22), the right of access to information (section 32), the right to just administrative action (section 33) and the right of access to courts (section 34). There has not been a case thus far where such issues have been raised in the context of an antitrust matter. Commentators believe these provisions should be extended to civil courts in class action cases where the Bill of Rights has not been infringed,[33] but there are no guidelines instructing the civil courts as such. It has been argued that, 'In view of the lack of adequate protection of collective interests under our traditional civil procedure model, the innovation under consideration [that is, the proposed extension of §38 provisions to the civil courts] must be hailed as a major development in the quest for effective access to justice for all in the new South Africa.'[34] The question of standing and identifying the correct plaintiff becomes increasingly important when issues such as the pass-on defense are raised. The concept of passing-on has yet to be considered in South African antitrust cases.

b. Class action in South Africa

In the *Ngxuza* case,[35] Supreme Court Justice Cameron described South African class actions generally:

> In the type of class action at issue in this case, one or more claimants litigate against a defendant not only on their own behalf but on behalf of all other similar claimants. The most important feature of the class action is that other members of the class, although not formally and individually joined, benefit from, and are bound by, the outcome of the litigation unless they invoke prescribed procedures to opt out of it.[36]

Class action suits may be brought against companies or individuals in South Africa. They are usually initiated when joinder is impractical, but where the parties nonetheless seek to avoid spending unnecessary time and money on individual claims. Class actions are thus intended to enhance '(1) judicial economy and efficiency; (2) protection of defendants from inconsistent obligations; (3) protection of the interests of absentees;

---

31 Section 38 of The Constitution of the Republic of South Africa Act 108 of 1996.

32 See for example *Competition Commission v Clover Industries* et al., Case no 103/CR/Dec06, available at www.comptrib.co.za, where points in question regarding the constitutionality of summons issued by the competition authorities were called into question.

33 See *S v Saib* 1994 (2) BCLR (D) at 55 C–F, *Bate v Regional Magistrate Randburg* 1996 (7) BCLR 974 (W) at 984 C–I, *Congress of Traditional Leaders of South Africa v Minister for Local Government, Eastern Cape* 1996 (2) SA 898 (TKA) at 905 E–H.

34 De Vos W le R, 'Reflections on the introduction of a class action in South Africa', 1996 (4) Journal of South African Law 639 at 641.

35 *Permanent Secretary, Department of Welfare, Eastern Cape Provincial Government v Ngxuza* 2001 (4) 1184 (SCA). This was not a competition law-related case, but instead illustrates the issues in class action cases.

36 Ibid at 1192–1194.

(4) access to judicial relief for small claimants; and (5) . . . [enforcement of the] laws and [deterrence of] wrongdoing.' [37]

i. Defining the class It is imperative that the parties bringing the action first define the class of people included in the action. Although there are no antitrust class actions to refer to, it is generally necessary for the class to be defined first and for the Court to certify that such class has standing before the case can proceed on the merits. Exactly what is required is unclear.

In the paper produced by the South African Law Reform Commission in its 1998 report to the Department of Justice,[38] it recommended that a class action be defined as 'an action instituted by a representative on behalf of a class of persons in respect of whom the relief claimed and the issues involved are substantially similar in respect of all members of the class and certified as a class action . . . .'.[39] This definition has not been formally entrenched in our law, which is why this remains an unresolved debate.

ii. How to bring a class action suit To date, there has been no class action suit for damages under Competition Law in South Africa. Even though there have been class action cases decided at the Constitutional Court, there are no formalized procedures or guidelines on how to bring a class action for a competition related case.

The South African Law Reform Commission[40] recommended that a class action may be brought when:

- there is an identifiable class of person;
- a cause of action is disclosed;
- there are issues of fact or law which are common to the class;
- a suitable representation is available;
- the interests of justice so requires; and
- the class action is the appropriate method of proceeding with the action.[41]

In this Report, the Law Commission advocated for legislation to be drafted to serve as a guide in defining the roles and procedure for class action and public interest suits, especially in non-constitutional cases.[42] The South African Constitution is the supreme

---

37 Ian Simmons and Alexander Okuliar, 'Private Enforcement of the US Antitrust Laws through Class Actions', in ICLG Competition Litigation 2009. www.iclg.co.uk; and see Alba Conte and Herbert B. Newberg, 1 *Newberg on Class Actions* (Thomson/West, 4th ed., 2002), sec 1.1.

38 South African Law Commission, *Report on the recognition of class actions and public interest actions in South African law*, Project 88, August 1998, www.doj.gov.za/salrc/reports/r_prj88_classact_1998aug.pdf.

39 Ibid.

40 A statutory body enacted under the South African Law Reform Commission Act 19 of 1973. This Commission has established various working committees, projects and writes discussion and research papers as well as making recommendations for legislation to the Minister of Justice. See www.doj.gov/za/salrc/docs_gen/function.htm.

41 Ibid at xv.

42 South African Law Commission, *Report on the recognition of class actions and public interest actions in South African law*, Project 88, August 1998, www.doj.gov.za/salrc/reports/r_prj88_classact_1998aug.pdf, ¶3.1.1.

law of the land and all law must be consistent with the provisions of the Constitution. If it is not, it will be rendered invalid by the Constitutional Court. The Constitutional Court only hears matters of a constitutional nature (i.e. that fall within the Constitution Act) and all other matters can be ultimately appealed to the Supreme Court of Appeal, the final court of appeal in non-constitutional matters. Unfortunately, at this stage, there has been no legislation enacted to iron out these issues.

iii. Giving notice to members of a class action As has been defined above, judgment in a class action affects everyone in the class who has not opted out. It is therefore imperative that members of the class be aware of the impending damages claim. The outcome of the claim could be rewarding to that member, or it could be detrimental if the member is not able to take further action and would be liable for the costs of the action. Court costs are not automatically required from the losing party. It is usually up to the Court to decide if costs should be awarded, but the fact that the claimant may be required to cover his or her opponent's legal fees if he or she loses may also be a deterrent to bringing damages suits.

Currently there is no prescribed form for giving notice of class actions. Plaintiffs can individually contact members of the class, publish the notice in the Government Gazette, or advertise using different media such as newspapers or the internet.[43] Considering the lack of formal guidance available for how to notify class members of the action, it has been submitted that the courts should make notice compulsory, and all reasonable forms of advertisement to prospective class members be utilized.

iv. Option to opt out As in many other jurisdictions, South African courts give parties the option to opt out of a class action.[44] Individuals may opt out of a class action suit for various reasons. For example, they may not have the financial resources or time to see the action through, they may not have a large financial stake in the suit, they may believe that they are not part of the 'class' or that the legal representative is not acting in their best interest, or they may believe they have a better chance of success if they sue for damages independently.[45] In such cases, the individual may give written notice to the plaintiffs' attorneys or the court indicating their desire to opt out of the action. The cut-off date to opt out is unclear.

3. Jurisdiction

a. Jurisdiction of South African courts

It is necessary to determine which court has the power to hear a civil claim for damages in a competition law matter. The Competition Act applies to 'all economic activity within,

---

[43] See for example, a notice to join a class action suit advertised on the internet: www.southafrica.to/transport/Airlines/SAA-flights/anti-SAA/SAA-strike/SAA-strike.php5 and www.fly-africa.info/forums/showthread.php?s=18f51163a3dbe0feefb87c5e47b0b950&t=13124.

[44] *Permanent Secretary, Department of Welfare, Eastern Cape Provincial Government v Ngxuza* 2002 (2) SA 609 (E) at 630 C–J.

[45] See www.lawsuitsearch.com/class_action_opt_out.aspx.

or having an effect within the Republic'.[46] Because the Act allows private claimants to sue in civil court once the South African Competition authorities make their final decision, it is presumed that the South African civil courts would thereafter have jurisdiction over private claims. The High Court would also have automatic jurisdiction over claims exceeding R100,000 (approximately $12,500).[47] Likewise, the High Court has jurisdiction if there is a claim for injunctive relief without the alternative of damages.[48] There is no room for forum shopping to choose a magistrates court over the High Court, or choose one High Court over another. There are currently no High Courts with so-called 'expertise' in antitrust cases.

There are a number of High Courts that exist in the various provinces in South Africa, and it will likely always be a question of which High Court in South Africa has jurisdiction over which case. High Court jurisdiction is governed by §19 of the Supreme Court Act which states that, inter alia: 'A provincial or local division shall have jurisdiction over all persons residing or being in and in relation to all causes arising and all offenses triable within its area of jurisdiction and all other matters of which it may according to law take cognizance . . .'[49]

There may be instances where the South African competition authorities have jurisdiction over the conduct of a foreign entity where the High Court does not. This is because the competition authorities have jurisdiction over economic activity that affects South Africa. South African civil courts, however, will not have jurisdiction over foreign entities unless the courts are able to exercise control over the person or property. In such cases, it is likely that the claimants would ask the court to attach the respondent's person or property to confirm jurisdiction.[50] These rules would also apply in antitrust cases for damages heard in the civil courts.

When considering claims for money damages where there may be a foreign party, the South African courts also distinguish between:

- a person who is either resident and domiciled within the court's jurisdiction,
- a person who is peregrinus or foreign to the court's jurisdiction but resident and domiciled within South Africa; and
- a person who is resident and domiciled in a foreign country.[51]

In order for the plaintiff to proceed against a foreign party it must bring an application to find or confirm jurisdiction by attaching the defendant or its property if the cause of action arose within the South African Court's jurisdiction. In order to succeed with the attachment claim, the defendant or its property must be physically present within South Africa.[52] The foreign party may also consent to jurisdiction. In *American Flag*, the court held that it was not necessary to bring an application to attach or confirm jurisdiction if

46 Section 3(1) of the Competition Act.
47 Magistrates Court Act 32 of 1944.
48 Section 46(2)(c) of the Magistrates Court Act.
49 Section 19(1)(a) of the Supreme Court Act 59 of 1959.
50 Section 26 of the Supreme Court Act.
51 Pete et al., p. 84.
52 Section 19(1)(c) of the Supreme Court Act., See Pete et al., p. 87.

the respondent, who is a foreign party, consented to jurisdiction.[53] One should also note that in cases where both parties are foreign, the 'parties cannot by agreement confer on a court jurisdiction which it could not otherwise have.'[54] Bringing these provisions within the competition law context, section 3(1) of the Competition Act stipulates that the South African courts have jurisdiction if the respondent's activity has an economic effect that is felt within South Africa.

The civil courts are not as definitive when it comes to assessing jurisdiction of foreign companies based on economic effect. Therefore, in the context of a South African competition law civil claim, the plaintiff will have to provide the information listed above. If the defendant refuses to consent to jurisdiction, the claimant can seek to attach a local South African office of the defendant or the income generated in South Africa by the defendant's economic activity.

4. Damages

A successful claimant will be entitled to single damages. South African law does not permit punitive damages. In many cases the general rule is that the losing party may be ordered to pay the plaintiff's attorney's fees.[55] This means that the unsuccessful plaintiff may have to pay the attorney's costs as well as the cost of two counsel. Such a possibility may dissuade a potential claimant for damages from pursuing an action.[56] However, depending on the facts of the case, a court may exercise its discretion and not award costs to the successful party.[57]

Conclusion

As the competition authorities gain momentum with investigations and reach successful outcomes, the interest in pursuing civil claims for damages will also heighten. This will in turn promote a symbiotic relationship between the private and public enforcers who will rely on each other for evidence gathering and information. Whether that exchange of information would include submissions from leniency applicants is still to be determined, as these are untested waters. However, what remains clear is that confidential information given to competition authorities cannot automatically be handed over to parties in a damages suit. Only when confidentiality is waived can the information enter the public domain. One of the major obstacles that potential claimants face is the lack of clear procedural direction, which will in time be ironed out by much needed guidelines.

A number of lawyers stand ready to represent claimants. In South Africa, even though there is a relatively small niche of lawyers who practice antitrust law, many of them come from the largest law firms in the country where these law firms have specialized antitrust law departments. There are also less-specialized advocates who have worked on many cases in which they have developed a fair amount of antitrust expertise. It is envisaged

---

53 *American Flag plc v Great African T-Shirt Corporation CC* 2000 (1) SA 356 (W) at 377.

54 D. Pistorius, Pollack on Jurisdiction (second edition), 1993, Juta & co, p. 9.

55 *Skotnes v SA Library* 1997 (2) SA 770 (SCA).

56 Costs may be awarded either on 'party-and-party costs' incurred during the course of litigation (and not pre-trial costs) or 'attorney-and-client' costs which include pre-trial and trial costs. Costs in South Africa are usually awarded on party-and-party costs.

57 See *Mahomed v Nagdee* 1952 (1) SA 410 (A).

that the driving force behind damages claims will be the mid-sized companies (perhaps those below the market power threshold of 45 per cent) who have been affected by anti-competitive conduct or consumers' groups that are able to mobilize and take on these antitrust damages claims as class action litigants. For a consumers' organization to have a right to bring a representative action, however, amendments would have to be made to the Competition Act. The cost and risks of litigation are always a major factor. Although parties have been encouraged to sue for damages, there has been no active role played by government authorities in the form of, for example, guidelines on private damages. What is needed is a strengthened relationship between public and private enforcement, which will benefit competition in South African markets.

36 Taiwan

Lawrence S. Liu[1] *and Frank S. Chang*[2]

Introduction

Taiwan's Fair Trade Law (FTL) of 1992, as amended, is highly influenced by EU- and German-style competition legislation. The two salient components of the FTL are antitrust law and unfair competition law. The FTL's legislative goals are 'maintaining trade order, protecting consumers' interests, ensuring fair competition, and promoting economic stability and prosperity'.[3] To this end, the enforcement mechanism of FTL imposes civil liability, criminal sanctions and administrative enforcement.

1. How does a damages action case get started?

Damages actions under Taiwan's FTL are relatively rare, because the legislative focus is administrative enforcement by Taiwan's Fair Trade Commission (TFTC). In the view of some commentators, a damages suit may result from business disputes, such as termination of a dealership. It may also result from large-scale consumer complaints. There is a very small 'antitrust bar', if one exists at all. This is because most lawyers treat FTL cases as part of their existing corporate, intellectual property or litigation practice. Also, there is no US-style opt-out class action mechanism, nor is a civil jury or discovery allowed in Taiwan. In light of these limitations, an attorney may have limited incentive to indentify and seek to represent parties injured by anticompetitive acts. In addition, a lawyer cannot solicit clients by using methods which are against public policy, morals, or lawyers' respect and credibility, as prescribed by the Norm of Lawyers' Ethics.[4]

As far as an antitrust claim is concerned, there is no requirement to pursue a claim with a prior or simultaneous governmental action. Initiating a stand-alone civil action is allowed. If a claim follows a governmental action, it will be easier for the plaintiff to collect evidence, as there is no extensive US-style 'discovery' mechanism in Taiwan.

When a plaintiff considers initiating a damages action, he or she may be concerned with costs and time. Unless a fact alleged by a party is admitted by the opposing party or it is proved by a prior governmental action, the plaintiff must consider whether he or she can amass sufficient evidence to prove actual damage and proximate causation between the defendant's violation and the resulting injury. It is not easy to submit all necessary evidence to the court, because it is costly and time-consuming.

---

1 Executive Vice President, China Development Financial Holding Corporation, Taipei.
2 Vice President, Grand Cathay Securities Corporation, a CDFH affiliate.
3 See FTL Article 1.
4 See the Norm of Lawyers' Ethics Article 13.

2. Who may pursue a claim?

Any enterprise that violates any of the provisions of the FTL and thereby infringes upon the rights and interests of another shall be liable for damages.[5] What constitutes injury under the FTL will be guided by general principles of civil law in Taiwan. Under Taiwan's civil law, injuries must be direct in order to give a person standing to sue. That means any injured persons, normally including direct purchasers, competitors and suppliers, may pursue a claim if they can prove they have directly suffered damage. However, some commentators opine that (despite lack of case law) indirect purchasers and other members of the public are not persons who have direct injuries, so they rarely can pursue an antitrust claim.

3. In what forum does a plaintiff initiate a private claim?

All courts in Taiwan are national courts, and the first instance of civil litigation is within the jurisdiction of district courts. Therefore, forum shopping is not possible in Taiwan. As far as the venue is concerned, an individual defendant may be sued in the court covering the place of the defendant's domicile, and a private juridical person may be sued in the court covering the location of its principal office or principal place of business, according to The Code of Civil Procedure (CCP).[6]

4. How may claims be aggregated?

The CCP traditionally allows a joinder of parties and claims, and follows an 'opt-in' approach for aggregating claims and parties. As a result of a recent amendment to the CCP, it now also permits 'representative claims', but not the US-style class action or 'collective claims'. Any individual plaintiff in a representative claim must be identified and named. According to the CCP, multiple parties with common interests may appoint one or more persons from themselves to sue or to be sued on behalf of them. Multiple parties with common interests who are members of the same incorporated charitable association (such as a consumers' association) may, to the extent permitted by the association's purpose prescribed in its bylaws, appoint the association to sue on behalf of them. Moreover, when multiple parties whose common interests have arisen from the same product defect or the same transaction appoint one or more persons from themselves to sue for the same category of legal claims, the court may publish a notice so that other persons with the same common interests may join the action by filing a pleading within a designated period of time.[7] Theoretically, antitrust claims can be aggregated by representative claims, but so far there has been no case filed this way in Taiwan.

In addition, there is a similar mechanism under the Consumer Protection Law. A consumers' protection group that has met certain requirements, such as government certification, may bring in its own name an action for damages with the approval of the government-appointed consumer ombudsman. Where multiple consumers are injured as the result of the same incident, a consumers' protection group may accept assignment

---

5 See FTL Article 31.
6 See CCP Article 1 and 2.
7 See CCP Articles 41, 44-1 and 44-2.

of the rights of claims from 20 or more consumers and bring litigation in its own name. Consumers may revoke such assignment of rights (opt-out system).[8]

Regarding public interest litigation, there is similar mechanism in the CCP that allows an incorporated charitable association or a foundation to initiate an action for injunctive relief when an enterprise has violated the interests of the general public. The incorporated charitable association must receive permission from the relevant governmental business authority, such as the Consumers' Foundation (Chinese Taipei). A plaintiff may claim and prove specific acts of an enterprise which has violated the interests of the general public, and this is determined by the court. For public interest litigation purposes, the incorporated entity can initiate an action only for injunctive relief, but not for damages. There has been, however, no such public-interest antitrust litigation, perhaps because of the TFTC's enforcement program.

In accordance with the FTL, any enterprise that violates any provisions of this law and thereby infringes upon the rights and interests of another shall be liable for damages. This may be characterized as a special type of tort. General tort principles under the Civil Code, therefore, may apply. If several enterprises have jointly and wrongfully damaged the rights of another, they may be jointly and severally liable for the injury.[9]

5. What procedural defenses are available short of trial?

Theoretically, the defendant may propose a motion to dismiss the plaintiff's claim. If the plaintiff's claim, considering the facts he or she alleges, is manifestly without legal grounds, the court may, without oral argument, issue a judgment dismissing the action with prejudice.[10] However, in business litigation, courts rarely render such de facto summary judgments for fear of being criticized for irresponsible judging or reversed by appeal.

In addition, since there is no US-style class action, 'class denial' is not available for the defendants. Plaintiffs bear the initial burden of aggregating their claims under the 'opt-in' approach. A summary proceeding may apply to actions regarding proprietary rights where the price or the value of the claim is not more than NT$500,000.[11]

6. What devices are available to obtain evidence?

Though the Judicial Yuan (that is, Taiwan's judicial branch) has studied the US 'discovery' mechanism in previous years, it has not adopted US-style discovery rules into the CCP. Each party generally needs to find its own way to gather evidence without compelling the opposing party to produce evidence. The CCP, nevertheless, allows an order for the preservation of evidence. If evidence may be destroyed, or its use in court may be difficult, or requires the consent of the opposing party, a party may request the court to preserve such evidence. Meanwhile, the party who has legal interests in ascertaining the status quo of a matter or object may move for expert testimony, or inspection or preservation of documentary evidence.[12]

A plaintiff may propose a motion for taking expert testimony. Expert witnesses shall

---

8 See Consumer Protection Law Articles 49 and 50.
9 See Civil Code Article 185.
10 See CCP Article 249, para. 2.
11 See CCP Article 427.
12 See CCP Article 368.

be appointed by the court in which the action is pending, and the number of expert witnesses shall also be determined by the court.[13] Note, however, that expert witness practice is not well developed in Taiwan because its civil and criminal justice system is more inquisitorial than adversarial in nature.

Normally, the courts and plaintiffs cannot search defendants and their domicile for evidence-gathering purposes in civil litigation, but an exception lies with a special proceeding named 'supplementary civil litigation in tandem of criminal prosecution'. According to the Code of Criminal Procedure, a person injured by a criminal act may initiate a supplementary civil litigation in the criminal procedure to claim his damages.[14] Since some antitrust practices are criminalized, theoretically the plaintiff may 'piggyback' on the criminal prosecutions, and use evidence gathered by criminal investigations.

7. What practices are illegal and what are elements of proof?

Illegal antitrust practices may be divided into 4 categories under the FTL: monopolistic and oligopolistic enterprises' actions, enterprises' concerted actions (horizontal cartels), resale price maintenance, and impeding fair competition. No industry is exempt from the FTL.

Monopolistic and oligopolistic enterprises' actions are highly regulated. No monopolistic enterprises shall: 1) directly or indirectly prevent any other enterprises from competing by unfair means; 2) improperly set, maintain or change the price for goods or the remuneration for services; 3) make a trading counterpart give preferential treatment without justification; or 4) otherwise abuse its market power.[15] According to the FTL, the definition of 'monopolistic' enterprise is any enterprise that faces no competition or has a dominant position which enables it to exclude competition in a relevant market; two or more enterprises, in other words, oligopolies shall be deemed monopolistic enterprises if they do not in fact engage in price competition with each other and they as a whole have the same status by definition as a monopoly.[16] Therefore, the 4 prohibitions apply to oligopolistic enterprises as well.

The FTL sets out a general 'per se' illegality principle by stating that competing enterprises may not engage in concerted action to restrict prices, quantities, customers, territories, or otherwise restrict each other's commercial activities. The primary difficulty in this case is one of proof – to obtain evidence showing actual agreement among competitors. Extensive exceptions (somewhat similar to a 'rule of reason' approach), however, are made to this prohibition, legalizing a concerted action if it meets one of the following requirements. Those exceptions must be determined by the TFTC to be beneficial to the economy as a whole and in the public interest, and an application with the TFTC for such concerted action must be approved for purposes of:

1) unifying the specifications or standards of goods for the purpose of reducing costs, improving quality, or increasing efficiency;

---

13 See CCP Articles 325 and 326.
14 See Code of Criminal Procedure Article 487.
15 See FTL Article 10.
16 See FTL Article 5.

2) joint research and development on goods or markets for the purpose of upgrading technology, improving quality, reducing costs, or increasing efficiency;
3) developing a separate and specialized area for the purpose of rationalizing operations;
4) entering into agreements concerning solely the competition in foreign markets for the purpose of securing or promoting exports;
5) joint acts in regards to the importation of foreign goods for the purpose of strengthening trade;
6) 'joint acts limiting the quantity of production and sales, equipment, or prices for the purpose of meeting demand in an orderly fashion during an economic downturn, or setting the market price of products lower than the average production costs so that enterprises in a particular industry will have difficulty maintaining their business' (generally known as a 'recession cartels');
7) joint acts for the purpose of improving operational efficiency or strengthening the competitiveness of small and medium enterprises.[17]

To prevent resale prices from being manipulated, where an enterprise supplies goods to its trading counterpart for resale to a third party or such third party makes further resale, the trading counterpart and the third party shall be allowed to decide their resale prices freely; and any agreement contrary to this provision shall be void.[18] This 'resale price maintenance' is a kind of anti-vertical restraints rule. This rule is perhaps the only rule for per se illegality in the FTL; it only requires proof that resale price maintenance exists, which the TFTC can easily obtain from provisions in distribution agreements of less legally sophisticated producers.

To facilitate competition, no enterprise shall engage in any of the following acts which are likely to lessen competition or to impede fair competition:

1) cause another enterprise to discontinue supply, nor purchase from or engage in any other business transaction with a particular enterprise for the purpose of injuring such particular enterprise;
2) treat another enterprise discriminatively without justification;
3) cause the trading counterpart(s) of its competitors to do business with itself by coercion, inducement with interest, or other improper means;
4) cause another enterprise to refrain from price competition, or to take part in a merger or any other concerted action by coercion, inducement with interest, or other improper means;[19]
5) acquire trade secrets, information concerning trading counterparts, or other technology related secret of any other enterprise by coercion, inducement with interest, or other improper means; or
6) limit its trading counterparts' business activity improperly by requiring such limitations as a requirement for doing business.[20]

---

17 See FTL Article 14.
18 See FTL Article 18.
19 A violation of which would entail refusal to supply products, monetary penalties, or other improper restrictions on the trading partners' business activities.
20 See FTL Article 19.

As of March 2009, there were approximately 194 FTL-related civil judgments awarded by the Taiwan Supreme Court,[21] but only seven cases can be deemed antitrust in nature: three concerned monopolistic and oligopolistic actions, two concerned concerted actions and the other two are related to impeding fair competition. The reasons why there were so few antitrust cases include difficulties related to gathering evidence of illegal practices, judges' unfamiliarity with economics or industry practices, and motivation by injured parties to urge the TFTC to take administrative measures or punishments to enjoin illegal actions rather than filing civil litigations.

The CD-R case is one of the leading judgments.[22] The plaintiff, Digital Storage Technology, a Taiwan licensee of Philips, N.V., Sony, and Taiyo-Yuden, alleged that the joint licensing program related to CD-R products by the three foreign companies was anticompetitive. The defendants adopted a joint licensing arrangement, by which Sony and Taiyo-Yuden first licensed their patent rights to Philips, and then Philips bundled the rights together for purposes of licensing to other companies. The plaintiff alleged that the defendants had overwhelming market power in CD-R patent techniques and their licensing method violated the FTL provisions regarding price maintaining and abuse of a dominant position. Taiwan Supreme Court reversed the previous judgment in favor of the plaintiff by the Taiwan High Court, and remanded the case for clarification on issues whether the defendants had a dominant market position, whether there was any relation between CD-R price under the previous contract and that under the new contract, and whether such prices constituted improper price maintenance.[23] The case is important because it is the only case in Taiwan's very limited case law on antitrust regarding monopolistic and oligopolistic actions, especially in the CD-R high-tech industry which Taiwan enjoys more than 70% of the global market.

8. What do plaintiffs get if they win?

Under Taiwan's general principles for civil liabilities, a compensation claim should be primarily for nonmonetary restitution. Concerning the damages measure, Taiwan's judicial practices usually compare the injured party's total assets after the infringing party's act and the total assets the injured party would have if the infringement had not occurred. If there is a difference (that is, a loss), then the injured party has suffered a compensatable injury. In brief, all compensation is for actual harm.

In response to the request of a party injured by an anticompetitive act and taking into consideration the nature of the infringement, a court is authorized by the FTL to award more than actual damages if the violation is intentional, provided that no award shall exceed three times the amount of proven damage.[24] In judicial practice, thus far the Taiwan Supreme Court has encountered four cases in which the plaintiffs claimed treble awards, but these cases involve other issues and the Court so far has not ruled on any treble damages claims.

The FTL also utilizes a gains-based method to calculate the damages resulting from

---

21 According to the Judicial Yuan's website there were approximately 194 FTL-related civil judgments awarded by the Taiwan Supreme Court.

22 See Taiwan Supreme Court Judgment: 95-Tai-Shang-No. 20.

23 See Taiwan Supreme Court Judgment No. 95 Tai-Shang 20.

24 See FTL Article 32, ¶1.

antitrust violations, where the injured party may request an assessment of the damages exclusively based on the infringing party's monetary gains.[25]

In general, the losing party shall bear the litigation expenses.[26] This usually means court fees. In Taiwan, the plaintiff must bear the court fees, which for the district court are within the 1% to 0.6% range of the value of the claims (based on a sliding scale).[27] Attorneys' fees, however, do not count as part of the litigation expenses, unless: 1) the court has duly appointed an attorney to act as the special representative or advocate for a party;[28] 2) compensation is paid to the attorney in the court of third instance[29] (the Supreme Court)[30]. The plaintiff's attorneys' fees, therefore, usually cannot be shifted to the defendant in a victorious case. Since plaintiffs in Taiwan have to pre-pay court fees as a pre-condition of filing the law suit, and attorneys' fees usually cannot be shifted to the defendant, these fees constitute a potential deterrent against bringing private antitrust suits.[31]

If an enterprise violates FTL provisions and thereby infringes upon the rights and interests of another, the injured party may request the removal of such infringement; if there is a likelihood of future infringement, prevention may also be claimed.[32] If the existence of infringement is in dispute, the injured party may apply for a provisional injunction for purposes of securing the satisfaction of compulsory execution.[33]

In terms of the limitations period, no damages claim in antitrust cases shall be allowed unless the right is exercised within two years after the claimant knows about the violation and the identity of the person(s) liable for the damages; nor shall the claim be allowed after the lapse of ten years from the time of infringing conduct.[34]

Concerning distribution of damages, if there is more than one infringer, each of them is liable to the injured party for the full obligation, jointly and severally. Meanwhile, unless otherwise provided by the law relating to internal recourse among joint tortfeasors based on relative fault or the contract, all of the joint and several debtors shall bear the obligation equally. The damages and the costs for which one of the joint and several debtors is personally responsible, however, shall be borne by that debtor.[35]

---

25 See FTL Article 32, ¶2.

26 See CCP Article 78.

27 See CCP Article 77-13.

28 See CCP Article 77-25.

29 Taiwan has adopted a three-level and three-instance court system, comprising: (1) district courts (which conduct trials of fact); (2) a High Court (also conducts trials of fact, but in principle does not allow new allegations or defense methods); and (3) a Supreme Court (conducts trials of law, does not usually hold session). If the Supreme Court finds a High Court judgment to be in violation of the law, it will remand it to the High Court for further investigation of the facts and a rehearing.

30 See CCP Article 466-3.

31 A plaintiff should pay court fees up front. Once he win the case, then he can collect them back from a defendant.

32 See FTL Article 30.

33 See CCP Article 532.

34 See FTL Article 33.

35 See Civil Code Article 272 and 280.

9. How does plaintiff's lawyer finance private enforcement?

The total attorneys' fee for each instance in civil litigation should be lower than NT$500,000, according to Taipei Bar Association's Standard. If the value of a claim is more than NT$5 million, attorneys' fee can be raised to 3% of that value. The Standard, however, is only for recommendation purposes, and has no binding force on member lawyers. Contingency arrangements or success fees are allowed in civil litigation. Such arrangements are so far rare in antitrust cases in light of the limited case load and difficulty in bringing such cases.

10. How does private enforcement interact with public enforcement?

As mentioned earlier, starting a stand-alone antitrust action is allowed. If a claim follows a governmental action, it will have a higher rate of success.

Regarding cooperation of private and public officials with courts, the court may request an agency, a school, a chamber of commerce, an exchange or any other organization to conduct necessary investigations; the organization being requested is under a duty to comply. Where the court considers it appropriate, it may also request a foreign agency or organization to conduct necessary investigations.[36]

Based on the Constitution, judges shall try cases independently, in accordance with law, and free from any interference.[37] Even though there are already administrative orders of statutory interpretation by the government agencies, a judge shall, based on his or her fair and honest belief in the accurate interpretation of the law, give a lawful and legitimate legal opinion on a controversy which requires an accurate judicial interpretation. Orders and decisions made by administrative agencies, therefore, do not necessarily bind the courts.[38] In order to prevent conflicts of judgments by civil and administrative courts, a civil court shall, by a ruling, stay its own proceeding until the corresponding administrative proceeding is concluded.[39]

There is no leniency program in the FTL and Taiwan administrative legal system at the moment, but the TFTC has drafted a bill to introduce it. Commentators suspect that a leniency program, if implemented, may not affect courts' decisions on actual damages, but may affect courts' decisions in granting discretionary treble damages in the future.

Conclusion

Taiwan's near two decades of enforcing the FTL offers an important example of fostering competition law. However, some mechanisms make it harder to pursue civil (as opposed to administrative) enforcement in Taiwan. This is caused more by features of Taiwan's civil justice system, which is similar to many civil law jurisdictions, rather than substantive competition law. On the other hand, the TFTC's administrative enforcement has produced an emerging body of antitrust jurisprudence that may be of interest to other jurisdictions recently adopting competition laws.

---

36 See CCP Article 289.
37 See Constitution Article 80.
38 See Interpretation No.137 of the Justices of the Constitutional Court.
39 See Code of Administrative Procedure Article 12.

PART VI

THE FUTURE OF PRIVATE ENFORCEMENT

37 International settlements

Laurence T. Sorkin[1]

Introduction

Many jurisdictions, including the United States and the European Union, devote considerable enforcement resources to detecting and prosecuting cartels. At the governmental level, the response to cartels has become increasingly global. Antitrust enforcement agencies throughout the world are cooperating in their efforts to detect and punish cartel behavior, and at the governmental level, the war against cartels has been characterized by increased cooperation, coordination of resources, and convergence of best practices.[2]

Companies that find themselves the subjects or targets of multi-jurisdictional cartel investigations also tend to respond globally to the risks posed by such investigations.[3] Companies will often seek to make simultaneous amnesty applications in multiple jurisdictions, or, if amnesty is not available, will seek to negotiate plea agreements or other dispositions in all of the affected jurisdictions. Counsel representing these companies will typically coordinate their efforts in all of the relevant jurisdictions, and although plea agreements or other dispositions may have to be negotiated on a jurisdiction by jurisdiction basis, counsel dealing with multiple investigations at the governmental level will typically adopt a global strategy for trying to resolve their clients' potential exposures.

This process of trying to resolve potential exposures for cartel violations at the governmental level should be contrasted to what typically happens with respect to the resolution of private antitrust claims arising out of the same conduct. In the United States, where there is a well-developed tradition of private enforcement, and where the treble damages remedy is seen as a proper additional deterrent to governmental enforcement, class actions are frequently brought against cartel violators. These actions are typically brought by classes of direct and indirect purchasers. It is not uncommon for cartel defendants in direct purchaser class actions in the US to at least consider settlement, particularly where those defendants have negotiated plea agreements with the Department of Justice and been fined. This is because the guilty plea will typically be preclusive (in the collateral estoppel sense) on the question of liability,[4] at least with respect to the period of time alleged by the DOJ. In contrast, outside the US (and Canada), class actions are rarely brought against cartel violators, and there have been few collective settlements of

---

[1] Mr. Sorkin is Senior Counsel in the law firm of Cahill Gordon & Reindel LLP in New York City and an adjunct professor of law at Fordham University School of Law, where he teaches a course on comparative cartel enforcement. The author is grateful to Lawrence A. Reicher for his invaluable assistance in the preparation of this chapter.

[2] Scott D. Hammond, *Recent Developments, Trends, and Milestones in the Antitrust Criminal Enforcement Program*, Speech at the Fifty-Sixth Annual Spring Meeting of the ABA Section of Antitrust Law (Mar. 26, 2008).

[3] For further discussion of global cartels, see Chapter 2 of this *Handbook*.

[4] 15 U.S.C. §16(a) (2006).

private cartel claims in other jurisdictions, even where defendants have been fined by the competition authority in those jurisdictions.

Settlements in US-style class actions depend for their utility on a judicial finding that a collective redress mechanism – a litigation class or a settlement class – is proper. Among the considerations that affect the decision of cartel defendants to settle is the amount of the overcharge claimed by the plaintiffs (and the likelihood that they can establish the claimed level of overcharge at trial), the fact that liability in private treble damages actions in the US is joint and several with no right of contribution, and the extent to which large purchasers may opt out of the settlement and bring lawsuits of their own (in which case the settling defendant is deprived of one of the main benefits of the settlement – the prospect of purchasing 'global peace,' at least from potential direct purchaser plaintiffs in the US).

Some of the same considerations that influence a defendant's decision to settle antitrust class actions – the high cost of defending antitrust actions, the impossibility of predicting with confidence how antitrust juries will decide cases, and the possibility that a judgment entered in favor of a class may exceed a defendant's ability to pay or may be reversed on appeal – also affect the decision of plaintiffs and/or class counsel to consider settlement. From the plaintiffs' perspective, settlements are attractive because they ensure that class members will recover at least some portion of the alleged cartel overcharge, and because they relieve class counsel of the cost and burden of protracted discovery and motion practice and minimize the risks associated with complex class action litigation, including the risks of certifying a class, establishing liability (including causation and antitrust injury), and proving damages. Settlements also relieve plaintiffs' counsel of the substantial cost of having to finance the litigation through trial and appeal. Settlements also assure that class counsel, who typically work on a contingent fee basis, will be financially rewarded for their efforts in bringing the action. Because plaintiffs and defendants both have substantial incentives to settle without a trial, settlements have become the predominant method of resolving US antitrust class actions where a class has been certified by the district court.

Some commentators have suggested that given the global nature of cartel behavior, there ought to be a mechanism for permitting victims of global cartels to assert claims collectively and to settle those claims.[5] These same commentators suggest that from an efficiency and fairness point of view, there should be a mechanism that would permit global claims to be asserted in a single forum. In this chapter, we explain why, given the state of private antitrust remedies in most jurisdictions outside the United States – (1) the absence of a single forum in which multi-jurisdictional claims could be adjudicated; (2) the lack of any effective mechanism for collective redress of such claims; and (3) the lack of any developed consensus on how cartel overcharges should be apportioned among different classes of purchasers – we think it unlikely that there will be global settlements of private cartel claims on a collective basis in the short term. This is not to say

---

5 *See generally* Note, Jonathan T. Schmidt, *Keeping US Courts Open to Foreign Antitrust Plaintiffs: A Hybrid Approach to the Effective Deterrence of International Cartels*, 31 Yale J. Int'l. L. 211 (2006); Michael D. Hausfeld and Brian A. Ratner, *A Proposal for a Transitional Forum*, presented at Antitrust Claims Against Foreign Firms and Cartels Conference (2006).

that large multinational corporations who purchase in multiple jurisdictions will not be successful in settling their own claims as direct purchasers on a global basis, but this is likely to happen on a case-by-case basis and is not the same as the collective settlement on behalf of a broader class of cartel victims. This is also not to say that there will not be settlements such as the recent and highly innovative *Marine Hose* settlement, but the most significant aspect of that settlement is that it is an extrajudicial settlement in the sense that it is not administered by a court at all.

The quest for a single forum

United States

One of the principal obstacles to global settlements of private claims in the context of a global cartel that caused injury to purchasers in multiple jurisdictions is the current lack of a single forum where these claims can be brought. The litigation that has taken place to date suggests that foreign plaintiffs had hoped that the United States would be this forum. Some of the reasons why foreign plaintiffs prefer the US courts are obvious. As the great British jurist Lord Denning famously remarked, 'As a moth is drawn to light, so is a litigant drawn to the United States. If he can only get his case into their courts, he stands to win a fortune.'[6]

The US antitrust laws provide for the award of treble damages, while many other jurisdictions, including Canada, for example, provide only for single damages or hold that punitive damages are not available in private damage actions. In the US, there is no right of contribution, so plaintiffs' counsel have greater bargaining leverage in trying to negotiate settlements with defendants than they would have in those jurisdictions that effectively limit damages to a defendant's own sales. Because of the Supreme Court's decision in *Illinois Brick*, direct purchasers are presumed to have suffered all of the cartel overcharge, and there is thus no issue of pass-on or the need to quantify the level of overcharge at each level of the distribution chain in treble damages actions brought in federal courts in the US.[7] Unlike many foreign jurisdictions, which do not allow class actions or impose strict limits on collective actions, the US courts are seen as a hospitable forum because class actions are a familiar feature of the US legal landscape, and the most common type of class action in private antitrust cases is the opt-out class action. This means that plaintiffs' counsel do not have to persuade potential class members to join the class, thus resulting in the aggregation of claims with a much higher value than if counsel had to persuade potential class members to join the class. Beyond this, the US courts allow far-reaching discovery in civil litigation, and discovery in antitrust cases is much broader than the discovery that is allowed in many other jurisdictions. Funding of private litigation is generally not an issue in the US because, unlike the rules that apply in other jurisdictions with respect to fee shifting and contingent fee arrangements, the US legal system does not ordinarily require the losing party to pay the other side's legal fees and allows plaintiffs' counsel to be compensated on a contingent fee basis.

---

6 *Smith Kline & French Laboratories Ltd. v. Bloch*, [1983] 1 W.L.R. 730, 733 (C.A.).

7 *Illinois Brick Co. v. Illinois*, 431 US 720 (1977). For further discussion of the rights of direct and indirect purchasers under US federal and state law, see Chapter 6 of this *Handbook*.

One of the earliest efforts to establish the United States as the single forum for the adjudication of claims arising from a global cartel was the *Den Norske* case,[8] which, interestingly, was not brought as a class action.[9] The plaintiff was a Norwegian oil company that had contracted for marine construction services to be provided in the North Sea off the coast of Norway. The plaintiff was what we will refer to in this chapter as a 'foreign-cubed' plaintiff – a foreign plaintiff that purchased the cartel product or service in a foreign market and, to the extent that it was injured by the cartel, suffered only foreign harm in the sense that its injury was not caused by the US domestic effects of the cartel.[10] Nonetheless, the plaintiff in *Den Norske* sued in the federal District Court in Houston, alleging that because it was injured as the result of a single unitary international cartel which operated in US waters in the Gulf of Mexico and also injured domestic oil companies, there was subject matter jurisdiction under the US antitrust laws. The District Court dismissed the complaint for both lack of subject matter jurisdiction and lack of antitrust standing, and the Fifth Circuit affirmed by a 2–1 vote.[11]

The same issue then arose in both the *Auction House*[12] cases and *Empagran,*[13] where the appellate courts reached decisions in conflict with the Fifth Circuit's *Den Norske* decision, resulting in the Supreme Court's decision to grant certiorari and decide the question of the ability of foreign-cubed plaintiffs to sue in the US courts. The plaintiffs in *Empagran* were direct purchasers of vitamins in Ecuador, Panama, Australia, and Ukraine. They had purchased the allegedly price-fixed vitamins outside the US and had no nexus whatever to the US. They advanced three theories for the assertion of jurisdiction of their claims by the US courts. First, they argued that there was jurisdiction under the Foreign Trade Antitrust Improvements Act of 1982,[14] because the conduct alleged – the global cartel – had caused direct and foreseeable effects in the US and because US purchasers as well as the foreign plaintiffs had been injured by that conduct. They also argued that the US courts could exercise supplemental jurisdiction over the foreign

---

8 The author's law firm represented defendants in both the *Den Norske* and *Empagran* cases.

9 *Den Norske Stats Oljeselskap As v. Heeremac VoF*, 241 F.3d 420 (5th Cir. 2001), *cert. denied,* 534 US 1127, *and rehearing denied*, 535 US 1012 (2002).

10 The term 'foreign-cubed' is borrowed from securities law where a 'foreign-cubed' action refers to an action brought against a foreign issuer on behalf of a plaintiff class that includes, in addition to US investors who purchased the securities in question on a US securities exchange, foreign investors who purchased the securities on a foreign securities exchange. *See, e.g., Morrison v. National Australia Bank Ltd.,* 547 F.3d 167, 172 (2d Cir. 2008), *aff'd*, 130 S. Ct. 2869 (2010); *see generally* Hannah L. Buxbaum, *Multinational Class Actions Under Federal Securities Laws: Managing Jurisdictional Conflict*, 46 COLUM. J. TRANSNAT'L L. 14, 17 (2007). The question in the foreign-cubed securities case is whether the foreign purchasers who purchased securities on a foreign exchange can sue the foreign investor in the US for violations of the US securities laws. In the antitrust context, the question is whether foreign purchasers who are alleged to have been injured by the same international cartel that injured US purchasers can sue for damages under the US antitrust laws for injuries occurring outside the US.

11 *Id.*

12 *Kruman v. Christie's International PLC*, 284 F.3d 384 (2d Cir. 2002).

13 *Empagran S.A. v. F. Hoffmann-LaRoche, Ltd.*, 315 F.3d 338, 359 (D.C. Cir.), *cert. granted,* 540 US 1088 (2003) *and judgment vacated*, 542 US 155 (2004).

14 15 U.S.C. §6a (2006). For further discussion of courts' analysis of the FTAIA, see Chapter 9 of this *Handbook*.

claims, because they arose out of the same common nucleus of facts as the claims of US purchasers. Under the supplemental jurisdiction theory, however, the US court would have been obliged to apply foreign law to the foreign purchasers' claims, something the District Court declined to do because 'these foreign law claims raise novel and complex issues of foreign law' and because of 'comity and efficiency reasons.'[15] They also argued that there was subject matter jurisdiction because under customary international law, the defendants' actions were torts committed in violation of the law of nations. The same argument had been advanced unsuccessfully in the *Auction House* cases, where the District Court held that 'there is no substantial support for the proposition that there is an international consensus proscribing price fixing that fairly might be characterized as customary international law, much less an international consensus that price fixing gives rise to tort claims on behalf of victims,' [16] and was similarly rejected by the District Court in *Empagran*.[17]

The Supreme Court's decision in *Empagran* effectively closed the door to the US courts to foreign-cubed plaintiffs.[18] Writing for the Court, Justice Breyer held that it would be unreasonable to apply US antitrust law in situations where foreign anticompetitive conduct causes independent foreign harm and where that foreign harm alone gives rise to the plaintiff's claim. 'Why,' he asked, 'should American law supplant, for example, Canada's or Great Britain's or Japan's own determination about how best to protect Canadian or British or Japanese customers from anticompetitive conduct engaged in significant part by Canadian or British or Japanese or other foreign companies?'[19] The United States Department of Justice and numerous foreign governments had filed *amicus* briefs in the *Empagran* case arguing that the extension of the US antitrust laws to claims based on injuries suffered by foreign purchasers in foreign markets would undermine the DOJ leniency program (as well as leniency programs in foreign jurisdictions, including the EU's highly successful leniency program) because potential amnesty applicants would be deterred from seeking amnesty if they faced the prospect of large follow-on damages actions in the US for conduct that caused injury in global markets.[20] The foreign government *amici* also argued that extending the US antitrust laws to claims

---

15 *Empagran, S.A. v. F. Hoffman-LaRoche, Ltd.*, 2001 WL 761360 (D.D.C. 2001).

16 *Kruman v. Christie's International plc*, 129 F. Supp. 2d 620, 627 (S.D.N.Y. 2001), *aff'd in part and vacated in part*, 284 F.3d 384 (2d Cir. 2002).

17 *Empagran, S.A. v. F. Hoffmann-La Roche, Ltd.*, 2001 WL 761360 (D.D.C. 2001).

18 *F. Hoffmann-La Roche Ltd. v. Empagran, S.A*, 542 US 155 (2004).

19 *Id.* at 165.

20 As the Department of Justice stated in in its amicus brief in *Empagran:*

'The court of appeals' interpretation of [the Foreign Trade Antitrust Improvements Act of 1982, 15 U.S.C. 6a] would undermine the effectiveness of the government's amnesty program. Even those conspirators who come forward and receive amnesty from *criminal* prosecution still face exposure to private treble damages actions under 15 U.S.C. 15(a). Potential amnesty applicants therefore weigh their civil liability exposure when deciding whether to avail themselves of the government's amnesty program. The court of appeals' interpretation would tilt the scale for conspirators against seeking amnesty by expanding the scope of their potential civil liability. Faced with joint and several liability for co-conspirators' illegal acts all over the world, a conspirator could not readily quantify its potential liability. The prospect of civil liability to all global victims would provide a significant disincentive to seek amnesty from the government' (Brief for the United States as Amicus Supporting Petitioners, at 20; emphasis in original).

suffered by foreign purchasers outside the US could undermine the efforts of foreign jurisdictions to develop effective private antitrust remedies of their own. Although the *Empagran* Court did not explicitly rely on these arguments, Justice Breyer's opinion makes plain that comity considerations weighed heavily in the Court's decision to decline to extend the reach of the US antitrust laws to situations where private purchasers are injured in transactions having no causal nexus to the US.

Since the Supreme Court's decision in *Empagran,* efforts by foreign-cubed plaintiffs to plead their way into US courts by advancing a 'global' or 'inter-related' market theory of harm have generally not succeeded.[21] Most courts have applied a proximate cause standard consistent with the test applied by the DC Circuit in *Empagran* on remand,[22] and have held that foreign-cubed plaintiffs cannot rely on indirect or 'but for' causation theories to remain claimants in US courts. 'Global indivisibility jurisdictional' theory is a rejected concept.[23] Plaintiffs hoping to find a forum where they can establish subject matter jurisdiction over foreign-cubed claims – with a view toward settling those claims after jurisdiction has been established – must now look beyond the United States.

United Kingdom

Some commentators have suggested that the United Kingdom might possibly be a logical alternative forum where multi-jurisdictional private cartel actions could be brought. A decision by the High Court in the 2003 *Provimi* case adopted an expansive notion of personal jurisdiction and held that the UK courts could obtain personal jurisdiction over foreign parent companies in cartel cases if the foreign parents had UK subsidiaries, even if those subsidiaries had no nexus to the challenged cartel behavior.[24] The UK courts also allow discovery in civil cases, which, although not as far-reaching as in the US, is considerably broader than in other European jurisdictions. The availability of pre-judgment interest is also seen as an attractive feature of the UK legal system, as is the relatively favorable statute of limitations for torts in the UK. Some have suggested that the UK fee-shifting rules, which allow claimants to recover their costs if they are able to recover some damages, might also favor plaintiffs in private cartel actions, particularly those who sought to rely on fining decisions by the European Commission where liability has already been established.

However, despite these features of the UK legal system and despite *Provimi*, the UK courts have not proved to be particularly welcoming to plaintiffs in private cartel actions to date. In two recent cases, plaintiffs have suffered serious setbacks, suggesting that the UK courts may not be the logical alternative forum that some had hoped. In *Devenish,* the Court of Appeal held that exemplary damages and restitutionary awards were not

---

21 *See, e.g., Latino Quimica-Amtex S.A. v. Akzo Nobel Chemicals B.V.*, 2005 WL 2207017 (S.D.N.Y. 2005); *In re Monosodium Glutamate*, 2005 WL 2810682 (D.Minn. 2005); *In re Dynamic Random Access Memory (DRAM) Antitrust Litig.*, 2006 WL 515629 (N.D.Cal. 2006), *aff'd*, 538 F.3d 1107 (9th Cir. 2008); *In re Intel Corp. Microprocessor Antitrust Litig.*, 476 F. Supp. 2d 452 (D. Del. 2007); *CSR Ltd. v. CIGNA Corp.*, 405 F. Supp. 2d 526 (D.N.J. 2005).

22 *Empagran, S.A. v. F. Hoffmann-La Roche, Ltd.*, 417 F.3d 1267 (D.C. Cir. 2005), *cert. denied,* 546 US 1092 (2006).

23 *In re Graphite Electrodes Antitrust Litig.,* 2007 WL 137684, at *5 (E.D. Pa. 2007).

24 *Provimi Ltd. v. Roche Products, Ltd.*, [2003] EWHC 961 (Comm).

available to cartel victims, and that only compensatory damages could be awarded.[25] *Devenish* would appear to make it unlikely that direct purchasers suing in the UK would be able to recover a substantial portion of any cartel overcharge, since, given the principle of compensatory damages under UK law and the right of recovery for indirect purchasers recognized by EU law,[26] defendants in cartel cases in the UK – unlike defendants in the US in actions brought under federal law – would be able to assert a pass-on defense.

A second case, *Emerald Supplies v. British Airways plc,* declined to permit a class action to proceed under the English Civil Procedure Rules because the members of the class could not be identified at the time the action was brought.[27] There, the named claimants were importers of cut flowers from Colombia and Kenya, and they brought claims on behalf of all direct and indirect purchasers of air freight services from British Airways and the other airlines alleged to be part of the cartel. The class sought to be represented consisted of all direct and indirect purchasers during the period from 1999–2006. The High Court declined to allow the action to be maintained as a class action, holding that the identity of the class with the common interest could not be properly ascertained until the court determined which prices had been inflated and thus 'the criteria for inclusion in the class cannot be satisfied at the time the action is brought because they depend on the action succeeding.'[28]

European Union

In the United States, direct purchasers are not required to bring actions in each of the 50 states to obtain damages for cartel overcharges, because they can sue for damages in federal court. This, coupled with the availability of the opt-out class action under Rule 23 and the absence of a right of contribution – which means that there are not cross-claims or other intramural litigation between class members regarding the proper allocation of settlement amounts paid by them – has contributed to the healthy development in the US of known rules by which plaintiffs' counsel and defendants can settle private cartel cases. A logical question is whether, if such a system can be developed in the US, it could not happen in the EU? In other words, instead of requiring EU purchasers who were the victims of cartel conduct to bring damages actions in 27 Member States, why not create a mechanism by which all of the claims could at least be heard in a single court in the EU?

Under the framework established by the EU Treaty, damages claims for violations of Community competition law must be pursued exclusively at the Member State level. There are no Community courts or other Community institutions where a private claimant can pursue a damages action for cartel overcharges. As a practical matter, this means that if damages actions are brought by different plaintiffs (either individually or as collective or representative actions) against the same cartel defendants, these actions are likely to be pursued – quite possibly simultaneously – in the national courts of the different

---

25 *Devenish Nutrition Ltd v. Sanofi-Aventis SA (France),* [2008] EWCA Civ 1086.

26 Joined Cases C–295/04 to C–298/04, *Manfredi v. Lloyd Adriatico Assicurazioni SpA*, [2006] ECR I–6619; C-453/99, *Courage Ltd. v. Crehan,* [2001] 5 CMLR 28.

27 *Emerald Supplies Ltd v. British Airways plc,* [2009] EWHC 741 (Ch).

28 *Id.*

Member States, even though all of the claims will be based on the same violation of Community law. There is currently no mechanism, however, for consolidating these claims in the national courts of a single Member State. The creation of a Community court – or a series of Community courts – to hear private damages claims in cartel cases would require an act of the EU Parliament and the concurrence of the Member States, but is considered to be politically unfeasible. It would also require the adoption of procedural rules by the EU to govern the adjudication of such claims. Some may say that it is paradoxical to provide that a breach of the Community's competition laws should give rise to a private right of action for damages, but that aggrieved parties should be required to rely on inconsistent and conflicting (and in some jurisdictions, undeveloped) procedural rules established in the legal systems of the 27 Member States in the pursuit of their remedy. In its White Paper on private damages remedies in cartel cases, however, the European Commission makes clear that there is currently no political consensus for creating a private remedy for cartel violations at the Community level or for creating special Community-wide tort rules for cartel violations that would supersede the tort remedies currently available under the national law systems of each of the Member States.

The need for a collective redress mechanism

Global settlements are also not likely to occur in the absence of an effective collective redress mechanism. Without such a mechanism, which has the effect of aggregating individual claims and increasing a defendant's potential exposure dramatically, defendants have little incentive to settle outside the US. As Commissioner Kroes has put it, 'Of course out-of-court settlements can be even simpler, fairer and cheaper than just one court case, but what if the company is not willing to settle? Out-of-court settlements can only really work if they are coupled with a realistic chance of effective court action. The threat must be real if we are to achieve fair settlements.'[29]

Private settlements of cartel cases occur with some frequency in the US because the collective redress mechanism in the US – the Rule 23 class action device – contains features that are attractive to both plaintiffs and defendants. Class actions permit plaintiffs to aggregate individual claims, thus representing a large number of claimants and leveraging their bargaining power. Plaintiffs prefer a settlement because it guarantees a recovery without a long-drawn-out discovery period, trial, and possible appeal. Defendants find class actions an acceptable way of extinguishing large potential exposures, minimizing legal costs, and limiting the number of individual actions that they will have to defend. For settlements to be attractive, however, there must be an effective way to bind absent class members.

None of the Member States has mechanisms that would allow class actions or collective redress mechanisms on the scale of those permitted in the US. Most Member States, to the extent that they permit collective actions at all, do not provide for opt-out class actions. Regardless of whether one agrees that the opt-out class action is an abusive feature of the US legal system or creates an unlevel playing field by increasing

---

[29] Neelie Kroes, *Consumers at the Heart of the EU Competition Policy,* Address at BEUCC Dinner, Strasbourg (Apr. 22, 2008) *available at* http://europa.eu/rapid/pressReleasesAction.do?reference=SPEECH/08/212&format=HTML&aged=0&language=EN&guiLanguage=en.

the hydraulic pressures on defendants to settle,[30] the fact remains that the opt-out class action – or some other mechanism that incorporates most of its features – is a necessary condition for any settlement where the defendant faces massive exposure from the aggregation of individual claims, because without the assurance that absent class members will be bound by the settlement, no defendant will have the incentive to enter into such a settlement. Under Rule 23, absent class members are ordinarily bound by a class settlement so long as they receive notice of the settlement and the opportunity to opt out and object to the settlement. Provided that the notice that they receive comports with fundamental notions of due process, they cannot later bring an action of their own or collaterally attack the settlement.

From the perspective of a defendant who wants to settle, opt-in class actions such as those proposed in the European Commission's White Paper,[31] are much less attractive than the opt-out variety, because they do not bind absent class members who choose not to participate in the settlement. Depending on the number of those who do not opt in, a settling defendant faces the prospect of future litigations, litigation expenses, and uncertainty as to the amount of its potential liability.[32]

EU settlements: complicating factors

In the United States, defendants in class actions alleging cartel violations are at least open to the possibility of settling, because the potential liability to a class of direct purchasers (assuming a class can be certified) can be staggering. Even if a class is not certified, defendants may still be willing to settle with large direct purchasers whose claims, individually or in aggregate, are substantial. This should be contrasted with the situation in the EU, where defendants have been slow to settle private damages claims arising out of cartel conduct. A number of different factors appear to influence the decision-making of defendants in the EU, but certainly one of the considerations is the absence of effective class action mechanisms, which, because the defendant does not face market-wide exposure, tends to eliminate the main financial incentive to settle. A second factor is the absence in many EU jurisdictions of effective discovery, and so the asymmetry of information tends to favor defendants who do not want to settle. A third factor is that private plaintiffs in the EU cannot rely on the fining decision of the European Commission until the decision has been fully appealed through the European Community Courts, and this process can take anywhere from 6 to 10 years. Until the fining decision has been fully appealed, it may not be used in private litigations in the national courts of the Member States. A fourth factor is that most EU jurisdictions allow for a right of contribution

---

[30] Contrary to what some critics have suggested, the standards for obtaining class certification in antitrust cases are becoming more stringent in the US. *See, e.g., In re Hydrogen Peroxide Antitrust Litig.*, 552 F.3d 305 (3d Cir. 2008) (reversing grant of class certification in antitrust conspiracy case and holding that each of the elements of Rule 23 must be established by preponderance of the evidence; some of the defendants in that case had pled guilty in the US to cartel violations and had been fined by the European Commission).

[31] Commission of the European Communities, *White Paper on Damages Actions for Breach of the EC Antitrust Rules*, COM(2008)165 (*'White Paper'*).

[32] *See generally* J. Thomas Rosch, Commissioner of the Federal Trade Commission, *Striking a Balance? Some Reflections on Private Enforcement in Europe and the United States*, Speech at International Chamber of Commerce Annual Meeting, at 7–10 (Sept. 24, 2008).

in tort cases, including competition cases, and so even if a defendant wants to enter into a collective settlement, it runs the risk that it will be sued for contribution by a co-defendant who either settles later for a higher amount or goes to trial and loses. This, of course, is a risk that defendants do not face in negotiating settlements in the US.

Another factor that affects decisions by EU defendants to settle EU cases is the question of the pass-on defense. Pass-on is not an issue in the US in direct purchaser actions, because *Illinois Brick* holds that the direct purchaser is entitled to recover the full overcharge. It is generally thought that pass-on would be a defense in most EU jurisdictions because indirect purchasers can bring claims,[33] and, as a result, the quantification of damages at each stage of the distribution chain is a much more difficult and daunting exercise in EU cases than in the US. This tends to make even individual settlements more difficult, but also has the possibility of enormously complicating any collective settlement where there are not only direct purchasers but different levels of indirect purchasers. There is also the question of whether there comes a point in the distribution chain where the amount of the potential recovery to indirect purchasers is less than the cost of administering the individual claim. In the US, some indirect purchaser settlements have provided that the settlement amounts shall be paid not to the class, but to *cy pres* beneficiaries. Other settlements have distinguished between 'commercial' and 'consumer' indirect purchasers, and have provided that the settlement amounts would be paid to commercial claimants who submitted claims but not to consumers, whose share of the settlement would be subject to a *cy pres* distribution.

EU White Paper

A more basic obstacle, at least in the short term, to global settlements of private cartel claims is the absence of any well-developed body of law dealing with private enforcement in the EU. A 2004 study by the European Commission characterized the body of law at that time as one of 'total underdevelopment.'[34]

The shortcomings of the substantive law remedies in the Member States are well documented in the European Commission's 2005 Green Paper and in its 2008 White Paper setting forth its recommendations. The Commission notes the absence of an effective collective remedy mechanism, the asymmetry of information available to plaintiffs and defendants in cartel cases, the lack of discovery tools in many Member States, and limitations on the ability to fund private cases as constituting major obstacles to robust private cartel enforcement efforts in the EU. The White Paper also expresses a general antipathy for US opt-out class actions, recommending opt-in class actions or representative actions instead.[35] Europeans are particularly concerned that opt-out class actions are in part responsible for a 'litigation culture' in the US.[36] Rather than borrowing some of the more

---

33 Joined Cases C–295/04 to C–298/04, *Manfredi v. Lloyd Adriatico Assicurazioni SpA*, [2006] ECR I–6619.

34 Denis Waelbroeck, Donald Slater and Gil Even-Shoshan, *Study on the Conditions of Claims for Damages in Case of Infringement of EC Competition Rules*, at 1 (Aug. 31, 2004), *available at* http://ec.europa.eu/competition/antitrust/actionsdamages/comparative_report_clean_en.pdf.

35 *White Paper* at 4.

36 Neelie Kroes, *Collective Redress – Delivering Justice for Victims,* Address at ALDE Conference, European Parliament, Brussels (Mar. 4, 2009), *available at* http://europa.eu/rapid/

distasteful elements of the US model, the White Paper recommends the adoption of 'balanced measures that are rooted in European legal culture and traditions.'[37]

The White Paper provides a graphic illustration of why even the prospects for EU-wide cartel settlements are not good, at least in the short term. The White Paper points to the crazy quilt of differing rules in the 27 Member States that would govern private damages actions brought in those jurisdictions. The absence of a common body of procedural rules – or a mechanism for consolidating claims in a single EU Member State – make it unlikely that a defendant would have any financial or other incentive to want to settle claims by EU claimants on an EU-wide level. It is more likely, given that the EU Member States have their own procedural rules governing the adjudication of private claims and that these rules have not been subject to harmonization on the EU level so far, that defendants will wait to see who sues them and then assess their potential exposures at that time. Only when defendants face a litigation threat in the EU roughly comparable to that of a direct purchaser class action in the US will they likely be incentivized to consider a global settlement option.

Alternative possibilities for international antitrust settlements

In the current climate, and particularly in the aftermath of *Empagran,* it seems unlikely that the US courts will become competition courts for the world, or that Congress will amend the US antitrust laws to allow foreign-cubed plaintiffs to sue here. For different reasons, based on the structure of the European Community, its strong preference for tort law enforcement at the Member State level, and an aversion to perceived evils of the US system, it seems equally unlikely that a single forum will emerge in the EU where private cartel claims can be asserted on an EU-wide basis. Parties interested in negotiating truly global settlements will thus have to look to more non-traditional mechanisms to structure such settlements.

To date there has been only one settlement that can be fairly described as a limited global settlement, and that is the *Marine Hose* settlement, announced in February, 2009. The *Marine Hose* settlement combines a traditional Rule 23 settlement class for direct purchasers in the US (which, like other US settlements, will be binding on absent class members who do not opt out of the settlement) and an opt-in approach for direct and indirect purchasers located in the rest of the world (ROW) who purchased from the settling defendant.[38] What makes the *Marine Hose* settlement unusual is that it is essentially a private, consensual mechanism for the resolution of the potential claims of ROW claimants. There is no judicial oversight of the ROW component of the settlement, and the settlement was negotiated without the ROW plaintiffs having filed a complaint in a court in any non-US jurisdiction anywhere in the world. Hausfeld LLP, a global plaintiffs' law firm that represented the plaintiffs in the settlement, has described the settlement as 'the first private resolution of a company's global cartel liability without any arbitration, mediation or litigation – creating opportunities never possible

---

pressReleasesAction.do?reference=SPEECH/09/88&format=HTML&aged=0&language=EN&guiLanguage=en.

[37] *White Paper* at 3.

[38] Information with respect to the *Marine Hose* settlement can be found at the Marine Hose Worldwide Settlement web site, www.marinehoseclaims.com.

before for dispute resolution and providing a new model for global cartel settlements going forward.'

The settlement was entered into between Hausfeld LLP on behalf of a number of claimants and Parker ITR, one of the smaller members of the marine hose cartel. Under the terms of the settlement, Parker ITR has agreed to pay 16 per cent of its ROW sales of marine hose for a specified period of time into a settlement account, which will be an interest-bearing account. Non-US customers who purchased marine hose from Parker ITR between 2002 and 2007 can submit claims, which will be paid from the settlement fund. Unlike the traditional Rule 23 settlement in private cartel cases in the US, which allows direct purchasers who purchased from any of the cartel defendants to file claims to be paid from the settlement class fund, the Parker ITR settlement is limited to direct and indirect purchasers who purchased marine hose from Parker ITR. The settlement also provides that purchasers who purchased marine hose from other co-defendants, if they settle with Parker ITR (presumably by releasing their claims against Parker ITR in return for no economic consideration), 'will obtain the benefit of extensive co-operation from Parker ITR in pursuing claims against other cartelists.' Parker ITR's obligations under the settlement require it to 'make available interviews, declarations and affidavits, depositions, testimony at trial and production and authentication of documents that prove the cartel.'[39]

Because the ROW settlement mechanism is in the nature of an opt-in settlement, and because any ROW claimant wanting to participate in the settlement would be required to execute a release, there would be no issues as to the adequacy of notice, since the settlement would not bind absent class members. Only those claimants who filed a claim and executed a release would be bound by the settlement.

The ROW fund will be administered by an independent expert, who will determine how much of the fund goes to each Parker ITR claimant. Claimants must sign on to the settlement and release their claims against Parker ITR in order to receive its benefits. The settlement creates a presumption that ROW direct purchasers are entitled to an overcharge amount equal to 16 per cent of their purchases unless they have passed on some or all of the overcharge. In the event of claims by the indirect purchasers, the independent expert will presumably determine the amount of the portion of the overcharge (capped at 16 per cent) to which the indirect purchaser would be entitled.

It is probably too early to know if the *Marine Hose* settlement structure will prove to be a model for other global cartel settlements. Because it is a private settlement, its terms are not public, and it is not known whether, or how, it addresses questions that have proved to be obstacles to global private settlements in the past, including exposure to potential plaintiffs who did not opt in and possible contribution claims from co-defendants who chose to litigate and lose. It is not known, for example, how many of Parker ITR's customers will choose to opt in to the settlement, or whether some customers may think that the 16 per cent overcharge percentage offered in the settlement is a 'floor' and that a higher percentage might be available if they were to sue. It is also not known whether direct purchasers who purchased from co-defendants will assert claims against Parker ITR, or whether, as the settlement seems

---

39 *Id.*

to contemplate, they will release their claims in return for the cooperation that Parker ITR has offered.

It is also difficult to know at this time whether the *Marine Hose* settlement structure would be appealing to defendants with large market shares. Given its small market share, Parker ITR may have been willing to enter into a global settlement to the extent that its liability would be limited to its own customers. It is unclear, however, whether a larger defendant, say a company with a 40 per cent market share, would have found it attractive to settle for 16 per cent of its non-US sales for the conspiracy period if there was no realistic likelihood that the claims of its customers could be aggregated and consolidated in a single forum and then successfully pursued to judgment. It is also unclear whether a larger defendant would want to settle without some protection that it would not be sued on a joint and several liability theory by potential plaintiffs who bought only from its co-conspirators, because it is generally thought that even with contribution, there would be some liability under EU law for sales made by co-conspirators. A larger defendant would also likely take into account the prospect – and cost – of litigation in cases brought by individual customers in multiple jurisdictions, as well as the magnitude of the potential judgments, including the award of pre-judgment interest in most EU jurisdictions. It is not clear whether all defendants, applying their own risk–reward analysis, would reach the same conclusion as did Parker ITR, which reportedly paid an amount in the 'high seven figures' to settle its ROW claims.[40]

While the *Marine Hose* settlement represents an intriguing first step, and is certainly a creative solution to the problem created by the lack of any collective redress mechanism in the EU or in most ROW jurisdictions, the fact remains that global settlements of cartel claims will happen only if defendants want to settle on a global, class-wide basis, and to date there is scant evidence that defendants are clamoring to settle. What they prefer instead is to settle with direct purchasers (and occasionally with indirect purchasers) on a class-wide basis in the US, thus extinguishing their exposure in the jurisdiction which poses the great potential liability. Some defendants will also settle individual claims, typically the claims of large customers, on a global basis, but these settlements are ordinarily private, and no good information exists as to the extent to which the amounts paid in private settlements outside the US are more or less than a comparably situated plaintiff in the US could expect to receive in a judicially approved class action settlement.

The *Marine Hose* settlement was a private opt-in contractual agreement requiring no court approval. Defendants who want the certainty of an opt-out settlement subject to judicial oversight and approval will have to look to other possible solutions. A comparatively little used procedure under Dutch law for the settlement of mass damages claims may provide an alternative structure for settling private cartel claims.[41] This procedure was recently utilized to settle massive securities law claims brought by foreign shareholders against Royal Dutch Shell. The foreign shareholders, who purchased their shares on foreign exchanges and held approximately 70 per cent of Royal Dutch Shell's shares, originally sued in the US, together with the US shareholders, but as

---

40 Erik Larson, *Parker Agrees to Out-of-Court Price-Fixing Accord*, Bloomberg (Mar. 6, 2009), *available at* www.bloomberg.com/apps/news?sid=adNkajZuGbUk&pid=20602099.

41 Dutch Code of Civil Procedure, §7:907.

foreign-cubed plaintiffs they were dismissed from the US action. In anticipation that the foreign shareholder claims would be dismissed by the US court, and without any action being filed in The Netherlands, the parties to the US litigation filed a request with the Amsterdam Court of Appeal for a binding settlement for non-US purchasers. In May 2009, the Amsterdam Court of Appeal approved a securities settlement of $352.6 million between Royal Dutch Shell and several foundations organized for the purpose of the settlement. The claimants included over 150 institutional investors and possibly more than 500,000 individuals from 17 European countries, plus Canada and Australia.[42] Under the provisions of the Dutch mass claims settlement statute, the settlement was structured as an opt-out class action. Notice was given to the foreign shareholders through direct mailings and publication in newspapers and on websites, and they were given a period of time in which they could opt out of the settlement.

To date, the Dutch mass claims settlement statute has not been applied to a collective antitrust action. It has been used in settling at least two other securities actions in addition to *Royal Dutch Shell*, as well as mass torts. In all of the cases where it has been used, the identity of class members appears to have been readily ascertainable. Because notice was not an issue, questions as to the ability to bind absent class members were not an obstacle to settlement. The situation would obviously be different in collective antitrust actions in which indirect purchasers were asserting claims. It is also unclear to what an extent the challenged conduct must have a nexus to The Netherlands for the Dutch statute to apply. More significantly, however, the statute does not appear to independently confer jurisdiction on Dutch courts or authorize Dutch courts to apply Dutch law (or EU law) to the claims of non-EU claimants, and it would appear that the statute only provides a mechanism for judicial oversight and approval of a private, consensual settlement where a defendant wants, for whatever reason, to settle with a class of claimants. In the cartel context, most defendants have not wanted to settle with EU purchasers on a class-wide basis.

Conclusion

Settlements happen only when there are incentives for both plaintiffs and defendants to want to settle. To date there have been no multijurisdictional settlements of cartel claims on a collective basis, except for the *Marine Hose* settlement. In the US, the aggregation of claims through the opt-out class action device – and the resulting potential treble damages exposure – creates huge pressures on defendants to settle. At present there is little incentive for cartel defendants to settle on a collective basis globally, because plaintiffs in most jurisdictions outside the US have no realistic prospect of aggregating their claims and raising the stakes sufficiently for defendants to consider settlements. In this sense, the absence of a single forum may be less important than the absence of an effective collective redress mechanism. Unless jurisdictions adopt procedural rules allowing for the aggregation of claims through representative or other collective actions at least at the national level, the prospect of global settlements will continue to be an elusive goal.

42 Information with respect to the *Royal Dutch Shell* settlement can be found at the Shell Reserves Compensation Foundation website, www.shellsettlement.com, and at the Claims Administration website, www.royaldutchshellsettlement.com.

In the short term, a more realistic goal would be to see collective redress mechanisms developed in a number of jurisdictions, so that when a cartel is detected and punished at the governmental level, coordinated private actions can be brought in those jurisdictions on behalf of aggrieved purchasers. Once enough jurisdictions develop effective collective redress mechanisms, there will be no need for a single forum, because an organized network of plaintiffs' counsel should be able to exert sufficient pressure on defendants through the commencement of simultaneous actions in multiple jurisdictions to at least consider settlement as a serious option. It may also be that if collective mechanisms were to develop in a number of jurisdictions, particularly some of the EU Member States, cartel defendants in those jurisdictions, when faced with the prospect of ongoing litigation costs (including the cost of plaintiffs' legal fees if plaintiffs should ultimately prevail) in multiple jurisdictions and the possibility of substantial damages awards (which, in most EU Member States, can include an award of pre-judgment interest, thus magnifying the size of any damages judgment), might actually prefer a single forum in which their Community-wide cases could be consolidated and tried (or settled) and would seek to exert political pressure at the Community level for the creation of such a forum.

In the meantime, there may be some settlements based on variants of the *Marine Hose/Royal Dutch Shell* settlement paradigm, but these settlements are likely to happen only where the defendant has a compelling incentive to settle rather than to resist settlement. However, under the legal systems currently in place in most jurisdictions in the EU and the ROW, there are no effective collective redress mechanisms for aggregating individual claims, and so long as there is an imbalance in bargaining leverage that favors defendants, we are not likely to see collective settlements of private damages claims in those jurisdictions, much less truly global settlements of such claims.

38 Toward an effective system of private enforcement

Albert A. Foer and Jonathan W. Cuneo[1]

Preliminary considerations

In this final chapter, we attempt to pull together a variety of observations, ruminations, and recommendations that derive from our immersion in the chapters that constitute this *Handbook*.

Of rights and remedies

States that have adopted competition laws have created what is increasingly seen as a right to participate in a competitive, market-based economy. When that right is diminished by the illegal anticompetitive behavior of one or more persons, the victims include specific individuals or businesses as well as the diffuse general public. The latter's interest is represented by the government's competition authority. However, once a regime has determined that its economy will be framed by a competition law, there should be strong expectations not only that anticompetitive behavior will be stopped by the government, but that private victims will have a right to compensation for injury caused by illegal anticompetitive behavior. The question is how these expectations may best be met.

Government should not do it all

Why not rely completely on the government, i.e., more specifically, on the national competition authority, to provide compensation to injured victims? Currently, the authority for providing a damages remedy has been given to a few governments in various forms, but such authority has rarely been exercised. The US Federal Trade Commission ('FTC'), for example, has twice exercised authority to seek a 'disgorgement' remedy through which it can distribute funds to persons injured by unfair methods of competition. The FTC reviewed its limited experience with disgorgement[2] and published a policy statement delimiting the occasions in which it might use disgorgement in the future,[3] offering something less than a stinging declaration of this remedy's feasibility. There are nations (e.g., Brazil) that have delegated to the competition authority power to bring

[1] Albert A. Foer is President of the American Antitrust Institute. Jonathan W. Cuneo, a former Director of the American Antitrust Institute, is a partner in the Washington, DC law firm of Cuneo, Gilbert and LaDuca, LLP.

[2] The AAI has advocated increased use of disgorgement by the US FTC primarily for purposes of increasing deterrence, not for compensation. See Comments of the American Antitrust Institute Submitted to the Federal Trade Commission on the Use of Disgorgement in Antitrust Matters (March 29, 2002), www.ftc.gov/os/comments/disgorgement/landeroberth.htm.

[3] See FTC Policy Statement on Monetary Equitable Remedies, www.ftc.gov/opa/2003/07/disgorgement.shtm. The Commission noted, 'We will take pains to ensure that injured persons who recover losses through private damage actions under the Clayton Act not recover doubly for the same losses via FTC-obtained restitution.'

a class action on behalf of injured citizens, but we are not aware of this power having resulted in the award of damages. Among the reasons why it is not wise to rely on the government alone or even primarily to provide compensation to persons injured by antitrust violations are the following:

- If the goal is full compensation for the injured, there is little incentive for the government attorneys (as opposed to private attorneys looking toward a success fee) to seek to maximize damages payments to individuals. Indeed, there can be a conflict of interest, in that such payments may displace fines and penalties that could go instead into the public treasury.
- The determination of what damages amounts should be distributed to what claimants is detailed and time consuming. This is not the kind of work that a competition authority's staff is typically interested in undertaking or trained to do. Only to a limited degree could it be contracted out to private specialists in claims administration[4] or to a separate government administrative agency.
- Taking on the responsibility for compensation would reduce the government's ability to pursue violators and to deter violations, unless additional resources were to be made available to the competition authority.
- A government's limited resources and political commitments keep it from pursuing all violations that create private injury.
- If there is a desire to create a private mechanism for remedies, then the ability of the government to step in and take this function away from or minimize the role of private attorneys will undermine the development of a private mechanism.[5]

On the optimal amount of deterrence

In the US, private enforcement is very clearly intended to deter as well as to compensate. Plaintiffs' antitrust attorneys are commonly referred to as 'private attorneys general' and injured persons are given the statutory incentive of treble damages. The losing plaintiff is not responsible for the attorneys' fees or for the costs of a victorious defendant. Settlements are encouraged by joint and several liability and the absence of a right of contribution. This package of incentives in support of private remedies is unique in the world. In some jurisdictions, the expectation is rather clear that private remedies are (or will be) only compensatory; some advocates go so far as to urge that previously implemented government fines be reduced by any subsequent damages awards.

The problem is that no one knows and no one can know the optimal level of deterrence that is needed to influence persons not to violate the antitrust laws without at the same time chilling legitimate pro-competitive behavior. This results largely from the secretive nature of many collusive or otherwise anticompetitive strategies and from the difficulty of ascertaining clear causation between antitrust enforcement and corporate

---

4 See Chapter 14, Class notice and claims administration.

5 In the US, the Securities and Exchange Commission has been authorized to distribute civil penalties to defrauded investors. For a critique of this function, which is generally handled by the private bar, see Barbara Blach, 'Should the SEC Be a Collection Agency for Defrauded Investors?' 63 Bus. Lawyer 317 (Feb., 2008).

decision-making. Deterrence – seen in the calculated decision by a business to not do something because it may later be determined to be illegal – is reflected in the combination of the perceived likelihood of being caught and the severity of the punishment that can be anticipated. In performing the cost-benefit analysis, the business strategist would likely compare the various risks to the gains envisioned from the anticompetitive activity. All other things being equal, the more people searching for violations (whether government, private, or a combination) and the greater the combination of imprisonment, injunctions, fines, and private remedies, then the fewer violations will occur and the economy will on the whole be more competitive. What no one knows at an aggregate level is how many illegal strategies are pursued without subsequent prosecution and how many potentially illegal strategies are actually deterred. We also do not know what the aggregate value lost to society would have been had certain deterred strategies in fact been acted upon and not deemed to be illegal. These data are by their nature impossible to obtain and so we can only base decisions of optimal deterrence on informed instincts, anecdotal data, and reliance on larger cultural and political values.

What we do know, at least in the US, is that despite increased events of imprisonment, increased fines, occasional restructurings, and the robust presence of private remedies, cartels continue to operate, dominant firms continue to abuse their power, and the business of antitrust law thrives in the face of continuing efforts by its opponents to narrow the laws, oppose adequate government resources for antitrust intervention, and extol the virtues of laissez faire economics.

This suggests that it would be folly to conclude that most other nations today, lacking the antitrust tools and resources of the US, are adequately deterring anticompetitive activity. Furthermore, it would be especially poor public policy to try to maintain a steady state of deterrence by subtracting private compensation from public fines. The better policy would be to use private remedies as a supplement to the work of the competition authorities. But what form should private remedies take?

Why there is no ideal model for private enforcement

There is and can be no ideal model for private enforcement. One size will not fit all. Perhaps this is obvious, but it is nevertheless worth stopping to ask why it is true.

With respect to private enforcement of competition law, five factors help us understand why one size cannot fit all:

1. *Differing cultural and moral values lead to different perceptions of what is just and what is proper.* For example, different cultures contribute to attitudes of greater or lesser trust or distrust toward government officials, judges, and business executives, and these attitudes help determine the extent to which a population is comfortable with various mixes of private litigation and government decision-making.
2. *Different political values lead to different perceptions of where authority should lie.* For example, in many civil law jurisdictions there is a sense that because government should play a dominant role in economic life, decisions affecting how the economy operates should be for the most part left to government officials. In other jurisdictions, the US being one, popular sympathies seem to lie much more with private actors. Suspicion of the state runs high; the less interference by government, the better. This broadly shared attitude tends to favor the availability

of stand-alone litigation initiated privately and resolved in independent courts rather than limiting private cases to actions that follow successful government prosecution.

3. *Legal contexts vary.* The distinction between common and civil law may of course be significant in our thinking about private enforcement,[6] but it is also instructive to take into account, for example, whether the purpose of a competition remedy is seen as purely compensatory, as primarily deterrent, or as a mixture of compensatory and deterrent objectives. Another important example of legal context arises in dealing with the aggregation of claims: are collective actions already widely available in the legal system or would they be unique for antitrust and perhaps be perceived as a dangerous precedent that might spill over into the rest of the legal system in undesirable ways?
4. *Economic contexts also vary.* As Michal Gal has elaborated, competition policy for small market economies may necessarily be different from in larger market economies.[7] This could have an impact on a nation's thinking about private enforcement. For example, a nation whose most pressing competition concerns involve monopolies and tight oligopolies may have less need to be concerned about cartel overcharges, which are frequently the cause of consumer-based efforts to recover damages, and more concerned about retaining control over remedies that could affect industry structure in the hands of government officials.
5. *Each nation has its own institutional capabilities at any given point in time.* A regime that has only recently adopted competition policy might well decide to limit or even exclude private remedies for a period while its institutions (enforcement authorities, judges, lawyers and economists, businesses, and media) adjust to a competition regime. A nation whose judges are inefficient, inexperienced in the economics of antitrust, and too frequently corrupt may not have the quality of legal institutions that would facilitate a regime of private enforcement that works fairly. Another institutional capability that is often underestimated is the ability within the population to mobilize political pressure in support of or against the aggressive implementation of competition policy.

These five variables (cultural and moral values, political values, legal context, economic context, and institutional capabilities) go far in explaining why there can be no ideal model of private competition law for all nations. Each nation must develop its own model in light of its own circumstances.

Nonetheless, our study of private antitrust remedies leads us to suggest that there are certain functions that must be handled well if a system of private enforcement is to be effective. In the following section of this chapter, we identify the key decision points for policymakers, offering our suggestions on ways to maximize effectiveness of private enforcement.

---

6 See Chapter 3, Differing traditions.

7 Michal S. Gal, Competition Policy for Small Market Economics (Harvard Univ. Press 2003).

Key structural decisions

How much weight should the remedy system give to deterrence?

An antitrust remedy system increases in effectiveness as it combines additional elements of compensation and deterrence to increase the putative defendant's exposure to risk. Consider the array of antitrust remedies in Figure 38.1, The Strength of Remedies as a Function of the Private/State Mix. As each new feature is added, the cumulative effect of the remedies increases.

The left end of Figure 38.1 features a competition regime in which the government competition authority has injunctive powers and perhaps, in addition, the ability to levy civil fines. There is no mechanism for compensating private injury.

Moving rightward, we come to two 'follow-on' models within a minimalist private remedy regime. The first model rests on the assumption that the government has already determined both antitrust liability and the correct overall imposition that should be levied upon the defendant, with this fine representing a fund that can be invaded by private claimants, whether acting through the competition agency or a special tribunal or court. In other words, in this model any private remedy that is awarded would be subtracted from the government's fine. This model does not increase the defendant's monetary liability above that represented in a government fine, but it raises the ante by exposing the defendant to suppliers, customers or rivals – which can entail the undermining of business relationships and undesirable public relations effects as well as increased litigation costs.

In the second and more powerful follow-on model, any fine levied by the government is distinct from private damages that may be pursued after liability for an antitrust violation has been established. In this category, even though there are no multiple or punitive damages available, deterrence is clearly added to the system simply because a defendant has to face the possibility of additional expenses over and above a government

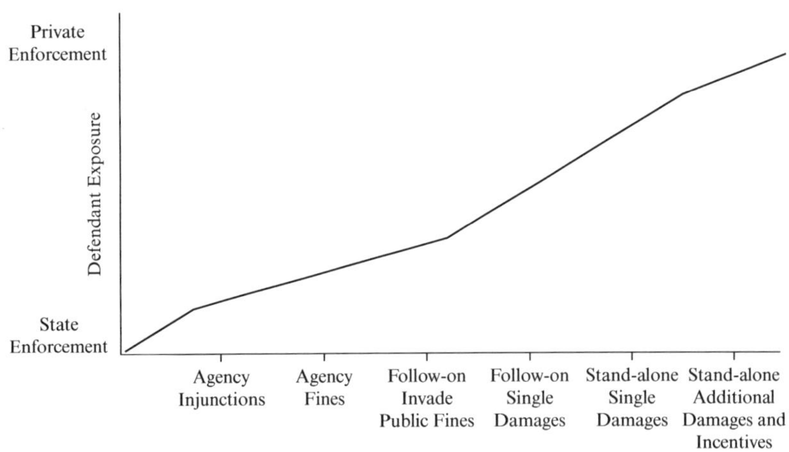

Note: This graph does not contemplate criminal penalties which would raise the starting point of the curve, but would not affect its trajectory.

Figure 38.1 The Strength of Remedies as a Function of the Private/State Mix

fine. Obviously, the availability of aggregated claims would increase the exposure of a defendant. This will also be the case with each of the remaining models.

Moving further rightward in Figure 38.1 we posit two stand-alone regimes. In the first, stand-alone cases may be brought before an agency or a court or a special tribunal, without having to wait for a government case to first establish a violation of the law. Damages in this model are single, that is, limited to the harm proved. In this category, a substantially greater level of deterrence is achieved, because potential lawbreakers need to consider the possibility of 'private attorneys general' initiating litigation, even if the government competition authority takes no action.

Finally, at the right extreme, there would be stand-alone cases that may include additional features, such as treble damages, punitive damages, joint and several liability, limits on contribution, fee-shifting, and/or other incentives to claimants and their attorneys. In this maximal regime, the compensation and deterrence functions are intermixed, with deterrence playing an intentionally significant role.

This last model, described in our chapters on the US system, maximizes deterrence. For completeness, we could add that the US model also includes criminal sanctions for certain hard-çore violations and the possibility of investigation by states as well as two agencies of the federal government.

What we characterized as the starting point actually represents a government monopoly over competition policy, and what we characterized as the maximally deterrent point provides the largest role for the private sector in determining how competition policy will be applied. Notice that it is difficult to apply the standard 'left–right' terminology of politics to the 'left–right' array in Figure 38.1. On the one hand, the enlarged role of deterrence could be considered more politically leftist, in that it reflects a greater degree of intervention in the economy than the purely compensatory regime, a regime that would likely be more appealing to large businesses seeking maximum freedom to pursue their strategies without worry about intervention by agencies or courts. On the other hand, a governmental monopoly in competition policy might also be thought of as leftist because of the large government and small private role. In both cases, however, the prevalent intervention is after-the-fact rather than regulatory. That is, most decisions on strategies and tactics are made by the competitive entities themselves rather than as a result of government mandate and are challenged only after they have been perceived to have caused harmful competitive effects. The political sense of right and left, for this and other reasons, is not particularly helpful in the conversation about the best mix of state and private antitrust remedies.

As have said, there is no ideal model. We believe that corporate decisions are influenced by the prospect of potential lawsuits brought by customers, suppliers, rivals, and/or consumers and that this perception of exposure to risk can be at least as influential in terms of encouraging careful obedience to the law as the presence of a government competition authority. Our advice to reformers, therefore, is to nurture a climate supportive of deterrence while building structures that approach maximal deterrence as nearly as the polity permits.

What should be the relationship between the public and private sectors?

A private remedy system needs to reflect a viable working relationship between the public and private sectors. In many competition law jurisdictions today the government holds a monopoly on antitrust enforcement. This may seem ironic in that a political economy that has a role for antitrust is by definition based to a large degree on a substantial role for the private (i.e., non-governmental) sector. In theory, day-to-day decisions are intended to be made in decentralized ways by buyers and sellers who make the vast majority of decisions on how to allocate their own (and, in aggregate, the nation's) resources. It may be a spillover from history that central governments outside the US have often tended to be reluctant to allow private lawyers and their clients to make decisions about antitrust enforcement.

Businesses need a degree of certainty as to what conduct is likely to be challenged. A single centralized government agency can, at least in theory, provide clear guidance as to what actions it will take if a company follows a particular course. (There are limits, however, because general principles have to be applied to specific factual contexts.) The situation becomes more complicated if the centralized government agency shares enforcement responsibility with subsidiary governments. And, of course, it becomes considerably more complicated if decisions to initiate lawsuits involving competition are decentralized to any person who deems himself to be injured by a competition law violation, with decisions as to what constitutes a violation in the hands of various courts rather than a single antitrust authority.

But there is more at stake here than clarity of rules. Antitrust has the potential of substantially affecting a nation's economy. Decisions affect more than an exchange of money. They can affect the structure of an industry, its ability to compete with other industries both domestic and international, and the nation's employment patterns. In short, antitrust decisions can have severe consequences for the national economy (and, of course, regional and local economies), and – consequently – for politics. Despite efforts to construct walls of economic theory around antitrust, antitrust is fundamentally political, affecting directly and indirectly the 'who gets what, when, and how' that is the title of a classic political treatise.[8] At least in democracies, a government will ultimately be held responsible for what happens in the economy. This is why a nation has to think so carefully about how it will go about decentralizing a highly concentrated antitrust authority. The introduction of effective private remedies is an example of privatization, for better or worse.

Decentralization of decision-making increases deterrence. To the extent that standalone cases are permitted, they also help deal with the problem of limited governmental resources. A competition authority, after all, inevitably must prioritize its activities, which can include a range of tasks such as litigation, advocacy before other government agencies, participation in the legislative process, and public education. It is impossible to conceive today that all antitrust violations could be prosecuted by any government, even if we ignore the well-known reality of the cost to a bureaucrat or even to an agency of government of taking on certain politically potent opponents. If private parties that believe themselves injured can locate and compensate lawyers willing and able to represent them in an antitrust case, the cost-benefit analysis of corporate executives will be adjusted to account for this additional risk exposure, the limitations of government notwithstanding.

---

8 Harold Lasswell, Politics: Who Gets What, When, How (World Publishing Co., 1958).

Experience shows that it is possible to operate an enforcement system that combines public and private elements.[9] A high appellate court is capable of dealing with conflicting lower courts. A central competition authority is able to issue guidelines and other devices (including speeches, advisory opinions, and trial interventions) to make clear its own views and to influence courts. The US system which includes two central competition authorities as well as 50 states and more than ten thousand antitrust lawyers and industrial organization economists, together with a political structure in which quadrennial elections can strongly influence antitrust policy, nevertheless has a workable private antitrust regime where the basic rules are fairly clear and the areas of gray, though undeniably present, are constrained.

It is, of course, possible to design a system that is much simpler than that of the US, one in which the problem of inconsistent policies can be minimized or even avoided altogether. For example, a single specialized competition court could be established to hear all cases, whether brought by the government or by a private party.

To make a private enforcement system workable, it is necessary to have clear rules about whether judicial and/or administrative decisions will be binding in future cases. For example, it is necessary to determine to what extent a competition authority's formal finding of liability (or non-liability) can be utilized in a later private case.[10] If there are stand-alone cases, the opposite situation must also be clarified. And what of findings of fact by a competition authority or a court? Are they to be binding in subsequent actions? Finally, what about evidence supporting an authoritative decision? To what extent can it be obtained and utilized subsequently? We turn now to these questions.

Should all antitrust violations be subject to private enforcement?

The maximal position would be that all activities that are deemed illegal by the competition authority and any relevant courts would be subject to a private remedy, which could include both monetary damages and injunctive relief. This is the general case in the US.[11]

In a jurisdiction where stand-alone cases are not authorized, it is logical that those cases that the government brings successfully would constitute the universe of claims that private parties could pursue in follow-on cases. Where stand-alone cases are authorized, claimants could seek a remedy for activities that the competition authority has not identified as harmful, has chosen for administrative priority or political reasons not to attack, is still in the process of attacking, or has attacked unsuccessfully. A determination must be made, therefore, as to whether major categories of cases such as mergers and abuse of dominance that are most likely to affect industrial structure should be subject to private enforcement and, if so, whether injunctive remedies should be available as well as or in lieu of monetary damages. If consistency of policy is a large concern, it may be possible to design a system where all competition cases are heard by the same expert tribunal.

---

[9] See Chapter 13, Interaction of private and public enforcement.

[10] The European Union is proposing that its own holdings of liability must be accepted in Member States.

[11] Although a merger can be challenged by a private party on a stand-alone basis in the US, this rarely occurs, especially if either the Antitrust Division or the FTC has already made a decision to allow the merger to be consummated.

Our advice, again, is to design a private enforcement system that approaches the maximal position, to the extent that the culture and the polity will permit. Clearly a central question is whether stand-alone cases are intended to be part of that system.

Who may claim a remedy?

The maximal position, once again, would be that any person who is injured by conduct that violates the competition laws should have a right to file a lawsuit against the perpetrator(s) of the illegality. There are some jurisdictions in which this is apparently the law, although one has to look carefully at procedural details such as tests for standing and antitrust injury that may have the practical effect of reducing the universe of claimants.

A much-contested issue is whether an *indirect* purchaser may sue. The answer determines whether end-use consumers (who are often separated from cartel miscreants by middlemen such as wholesalers and retailers) will see themselves as having a stake in the antitrust enterprise.[12] The US experience is particularly noteworthy in that the Supreme Court in the *Illinois Brick* case held that indirect purchasers do not have standing to bring damages actions under the federal antitrust laws. This holding was rejected by states representing more than half of American consumers, which reacted, ultimately with the Supreme Court's blessing,[13] by passing so-called *Illinois Brick* repealer laws that grant indirect purchasers standing under their own state antitrust laws.

The Supreme Court in *Illinois Brick* opted to favor direct purchasers at the expense of indirect purchasers on the ground that this solution would provide more deterrence. An earlier case, *Hanover Shoe*, had held that 'passing on' would not be recognized as a defense. In other words, a cartel defendant who had violated the antitrust law could not defend itself by arguing that the plaintiff direct purchaser did not suffer an injury because it had passed on the price increase to consumers. This holding meant that direct purchasers would have a strong incentive to sue a violator. *Hanover Shoe* left open the question of whether the final consumer could also sue, the question later decided in the negative by *Illinois Brick*.

The *Illinois Brick* decision reasoned that allowing indirect purchasers to sue would be overly complicated and deterrence would be maximized by centralizing the remedy in the direct purchasers who were closer to the violation, were more likely than consumers to learn of it, and had more at stake. If consumers could also bring suits, there would be a risk of multiple damages (e.g., treble damages twice) and complex problems of proof. In reality, critics of this reasoning argue, it is consumers who are primarily injured, not direct purchasers who passed on an overcharge, and as a matter of business reality direct purchasers, having passed on most or all of the overcharge, often have little incentive to sue the companies they work with on an ongoing basis – hence the irony of *Illinois Brick* is that not only is the compensation function not served, but deterrence itself is undermined.

These issues must be considered. In addition, if indirect purchasers are permitted to

---

12 See Chapter 6, Parties entitled to pursue a claim.

13 California v. ARC America Corp., 490 US 93 (1989) held that such state laws were not pre-empted by the federal antitrust laws.

bring claims, is there a point at which a claimant or class of claimants can be too indirect, too far removed from the violation? And how should the question of product components be dealt with, when, for example, the subject of a cartel overcharge is a relatively small item that becomes part of a larger final product as it travels down the multi-stepped lane from manufacturer to consumer? Procedurally, how should cases brought by both direct and indirect purchasers be consolidated to avoid conflicting outcomes and possible multiple damages? Our answer is that a framework including indirect consumers should be set by legislation and that courts can resolve the details on a case-by-case basis. An extensive literature in the US debates precisely how this might be accomplished.[14] The important point, however, is that the objectives of private enforcement will be severely undermined in an antitrust regime that provides no remedy for indirect purchasers.

The argument for including indirect purchasers, despite the inherent complexity, is both moral and political. The moral point is that it is the end-user or final consumer who is very often the ultimate victim, especially when the violation creates a price that is in excess of what a competitive market would have provided. If the objective of private enforcement is to provide compensation to the injured, it is morally wrong to exclude consumers. At the same time, it is important that the system not freeze out direct purchasers, because in many cases they do have legitimate injuries and in systems that do not have well-established histories of recovery by indirect purchasers, too much reliance on indirect plaintiffs could lead to under-deterrence.

The political point in favor of indirect purchasers is that antitrust is a political device as well as an economic one. We know who opposes the expansion of antitrust liability – the largest and most politically powerful companies that do not want the government or courts interfering with their strategies and tactics for maximizing profit. They particularly do not want to be potentially liable for large damages claims by a class of their consumers. They argue that such exposure creates over-deterrence. To offset the influence of these natural opponents of antitrust requires a constituency with a stake in what antitrust can offer.

The roots of competition policy are shallow. While consumers may find some small psychic relief when a government slaps a fine on a large corporate miscreant, this appears to be such a minor and far-removed triumph that it barely registers with the average consumer. To build up a more popular constituency for antitrust, we believe it is necessary for end-use consumers to understand that they have the ability to encounter the miscreant and demand to be made whole.

But, and this is a major 'but', a consumer remedy will only be meaningful if many small claims can be aggregated. Thus the topic of passing on leads very quickly to the controversial questions of whether class actions should exist, whether they should be on an opt-out or opt-in basis, and how lawyers bringing such actions are to be compensated. We will arrive at these questions in due course after discussing several other fundamental decision points.

---

[14] See Antitrust Modernization Commission, Final Report and Recommendations (2007), 265 et seq.

What remedies should be available?
The maximal position on remedies would be to permit the combination of (a) damages that are a multiple of the actual proven loss, (b) pre- and post-judgment interest, and (c) injunctive relief.

Damages could be conceived as single, multiple (e.g., treble as in the US), or, more generally, punitive. Much depends on whether the jurisdiction intends that private enforcement is only for compensation or is also for deterrence. In the US, trebling is often thought of not as punitive but as a reflection of the secrecy with which so many antitrust violations are conducted and as an incentive for private enforcement to occur. If only one in three cartels comes to light,[15] for example, it would arguably be appropriate to triple the fine when a cartel is successfully prosecuted, so that the prospect of an increased penalty will help offset the business decision maker's thought that 'I probably won't get caught, but if I do get caught, the worst that will happen is that I have to give back the extra profits I will have reaped – so let's give price-fixing a try.'

Punitive damages are usually associated with outrageous, intentional wrongdoing when the jury, in its discretion, feels that a lesson must be taught, both to the perpetrator (specific deterrence) and to onlookers (general deterrence). In the US, although treble damages are mandated (but not necessarily deemed punitive), additional punitive damages are not permitted in antitrust cases. Some jurisdictions without the treble damages feature apparently permit punitive antitrust damages, but it is unclear under what circumstances these would be applied and the absence of certainty probably reduces the deterrent value. Virtually all antitrust violations are the result of intentional actions, although the predictability to the actor of what actions will be held to be illegal varies. If punitive damages are to be allowed, it might be best, in nations that are not comfortable with double or treble statutory damages, to restrict them to the type of hard-core violations such as price-fixing and bid-rigging where it is likely that there will be a clear knowledge that an action is deemed illegal together with a belief that the collusion would not be discovered and prosecuted.

Much also depends on how damages are to be calculated. As noted earlier, if a regime permits only single damages but also includes prejudgment interest calculated at market rates, this raises the ante and can perhaps approach the same relief obtainable in the US, where prejudgment interest is not available.[16] Most jurisdictions will consider a wide range of evidence of loss, including lost profits and possibly lost opportunities. Many jurisdictions recognize that evidence of antitrust damages depends on proof of a 'but for' alternative world, i.e. what would have happened in a fairly operating competitive market in the absence of the anticompetitive conduct, and they therefore do not hold claimants to as strict a standard of proof as they might for ordinary tort claims.

---

15 One can only speculate on the size of the cartel iceberg that is submerged. Some estimates suggest that as much as 90 per cent of cartel activity goes undetected. See Chapter 2, The impact of international cartels.

16 Professor Lande has argued that actual damages awards in the US tend not to exceed the amount of harm caused (single damages) because of the exclusion from the damages calculation of interest and several other factors such as the deadweight loss to society. Robert H. Lande, 'Are Antitrust "Treble" Damages Really Single Damages?', 54 Ohio State L. J. 115 (1993), available at http://papers.ssrn.com/sol3/papers.cfm?abstract_id=1134822.

This flexibility seems essential in that a very strict standard could rarely be met. In the absence of perfect proof, fairness and the principle of deterrence require that it be the law violator rather than the injured claimant who should bear the risk of uncertainty in the calculation of damages.

Some jurisdictions contemplate only monetary damages for injured claimants, while others also permit injunctions to be issued in private cases. In some jurisdictions, injunctive and monetary remedies must be pursued in separate forums. Injunctive remedies can be negative or affirmative and they can have a direct influence on industry structure, as in the case of a decision to mandate licensing of intellectual property or to divest specified assets. Some jurisdictions may be reluctant to delegate this authority outside the competition authority.

If injunctive remedies are to be permitted in private cases, the possibilities are (a) all remedies, monetary and injunctive, both positive and negative, would be dealt with in the same case (the most efficient alternative); (b) the only allowable injunctive remedy would be negative, i.e. that the defendant would be ordered to stop doing whatever it was that is illegal; and (c) only monetary damages would be permitted, with injunctive relief to be pursued separately at the competition authority. In jurisdictions where only follow-on cases are authorized, it seems likely that the competition authority would on its own at least order the cessation of whatever activity it had held to be illegal. If there are stand-alone cases, the full range of remedies should be provided in order to assure a pro-competitive outcome. Thus, we return to the matter of follow-on versus stand-alone private enforcement.

Should there be stand-alone cases?

Everyone seems to agree that if there is to be a private remedy for antitrust injuries, such remedy must at least be available in the aftermath of a final government determination of a defendant's liability. A fundamental decision for policymakers contemplating private enforcement is whether, in addition to follow-on remedies, there should also be stand-alone private enforcement. We have already discussed the possible disadvantages of decentralizing enforcement in terms of the government's loss of some degree of control over an element of what might be thought of as national economic policy and of the potential for conflicting signals to be given to companies if cases can be initiated by anyone who claims to have been injured. We have also discussed the benefits of decentralization in terms of justice (in the face of limited government resources and political pressures) and deterrence.

If the objective of an antitrust system is, as a matter of national economic policy, to keep markets open and competitive, what is most important is not that the government investigate or prosecute or that injured parties be fairly compensated, but that business decision-makers make the right decisions in private. What set of policies is most likely to influence private decisions on strategies and tactics that reflect competition on the merits, on a level playing field, as opposed to the kinds of bullying or collusion that are anticompetitive? We assume that the vast majority of business executives would prefer to play by the rules but that a not inconsiderable number will go up to the line or beyond if the rules are not entirely clear, the likelihood of being caught is relatively small, the benefits (e.g., profits for the company, larger income for the executives, elimination of a competitor) are significant, and the sanctions if one is unlucky enough to be caught are not too great. National competition policy can control several of these variables: clarity of rules, likelihood of sanctions, and the severity of sanctions.

As noted previously, the availability of stand-alone cases could reduce the clarity of rules, making it more difficult for business decision makers to predict both whether an action will be challenged and whether a challenge will be successful. The advice of antitrust counsel would presumably be an important factor and it would likely vary according to whether possible private challenges are to be taken into account. It is one thing for specialized antitrust counsel to be able to predict (from experience, from talking to government officials, from reading government statements, etc.) approximately what the government's priorities will be and what or whom it is more or less likely to investigate and with what degree of vigor; it is another to be aware that suppliers, customers, final consumers, and/or rivals who feel themselves to be damaged might initiate a case, regardless of government action or inaction, perhaps along analytical lines that the government would not be likely to pursue. Moreover, in a regime that includes effective stand-alone litigation, private enforcement efforts might even stimulate the government to follow on with its own case. If the realistic possibility of stand-alone cases exists, therefore, the cost-benefit analysis for the business leader becomes more complicated, with additional factors pressing for decisions that are less likely to cross the line.

With respect to the severity of sanctions, the variables appear to be (a) the presence or absence of criminal penalties including imprisonment for individual decision-makers and reputational effects for the business; (b) the predictable impact of government fines and/or injunctive remedies; and (c) the predictable magnitude of private damages, together with the costs of litigation, executive diversion, possible injunctive remedies, and public relations setbacks. The threat of stand-alone cases, while important for achieving goals of just compensation, is likely to be most important for its impact on decisions in the boardroom. What the government does is important, but what private decision-makers do or don't do may be more important.[17] Delegating aspects of antitrust enforcement to private attorneys general through the authorization of stand-alone cases should be viewed not as a relinquishment of government control over economic policy but as a commitment to the effective implementation of competition law.

To the extent that competition authorities are worried about poor public policy being made in the course of private litigation, it is possible to require that copies of all antitrust complaints be filed with the competition authority and that the authority be permitted to appear as *amicus curiae* in private cases at its discretion. A regime that provides only a single tribunal for competition matters, private or public in origin, can also give coherence to public policy. Informed judges and the development of a knowledgeable plaintiffs' bar can help prevent baseless cases from being brought and bad decisions making bad law.

Our advice is for regimes to recognize the advantages of having stand-alone cases in

---

17 For example, if a government antitrust agency convinces private counsellors that it will attack marginally anticompetitive mergers, it is more likely that such mergers will be killed off in the planning stage than if the planners perceived that regulatory intervention is unlikely. Enforcement statistics will not record such non-events, but they would reflect effective enforcement.

addition to cases that follow on government initiatives. But there remains a giant hurdle blocking the way to stand-alone cases: the information barrier.

How can the relevant information be produced in a timely way?
Private enforcement requires access to non-public information. In follow-on cases the typical challenge for the claimant is to prove (a) that the defendant's actions caused the plaintiff's loss and (b) the amount of damage caused. Much of this data are likely to be in the possession of the plaintiff and the problems associated with obtaining evidence may be minimal if the government's establishment of liability can be relied upon during the remedy proceeding. If not, or if stand-alone litigation is permitted, then the need for some form of discovery is far greater, indeed essential. The policy question is how to balance the claimant's need for information against the defendant's legitimate concerns about confidentiality of proprietary information and the legal system's need for limiting the scope and expense of litigation.

The maximal position is probably that of the US. As described in detail in earlier chapters,[18] this system (sometimes the butt of exaggerated critiques)[19] provides both plaintiff and defendant ample opportunity to obtain information prior to a trial, very often leading to settlement without trial as the parties come fully to understand the strengths and weaknesses of their cases. Expert witnesses play a large role and the process is hemmed in by extensive provisions in the Federal Rules of Civil Procedure. The court plays a framing and monitoring role, including the approval of schedules for discovery, but the process is, in the first instance, in the hands of the parties themselves. When they cannot agree, they obtain guidance and orders from the court. Typically the court becomes more involved when there is a demonstrated need for its intervention, but the system is driven by the parties more than the court. Given the complexity of antitrust cases, particularly the need to define markets and market shares and to analyze the dynamics of particular markets, it is not surprising that the discovery process is generally expensive and prolonged. A variety of pre-trial motions can be used by either party to shorten the process.[20]

Outside the US, there is skepticism about the costs of American-style discovery, and even within the US the Supreme Court has been cutting back on the opportunity for discovery by encouraging the dismissal of marginal cases prior to discovery. Although a distinction is frequently made between an adversarial approach to finding truth (as in the US) and an inquisitorial approach (as in much of Europe, where the court is far more involved in asking questions, employing experts, and determining what information will be required), it should be possible to develop a kind of compromise procedure.

In this regard, it should be observed that 'fishing expeditions' are (at least in theory) not permitted by American courts and that judicial intervention in the discovery process is common, even though the process depends heavily on private initiatives. Other nations could develop procedures for private enforcement of competition laws that maintain much of the tradition of tighter judicial control while still allowing claimants

---

18 See Chapters 5, Pre-claim activity, and 10, Obtaining evidence.
19 See Chapter 1, Benefits of private enforcement.
20 See Chapter 9, Procedural defenses short of trial.

an opportunity to obtain evidence necessary to prove the elements of their case. For example, it would be possible to establish a rule whereby the claimant does not have to describe in detail the documents it seeks from the other party (something that is often not even possible), but could identify a category of documents, supported by a rationale connected to the claim being made, and this would be sufficient to obtain an order to produce.[21]

Our advice to nations is not only to provide for stand-alone litigation, but to establish procedures that will permit private antitrust enforcement to actually work. At the heart of most private antitrust cases are hard-to-obtain inherently secretive or proprietary facts. Unless they can be unearthed and analyzed throughout the course of a case, justice will be dubious. It is not necessary to have 'discovery' in the American sense, but some form of 'disclosure' perhaps more tightly controlled by the court than in the US, is required to provide both claimants and defendants a realistic opportunity to present a well-developed case. Such a compromise will facilitate just outcomes for the parties and will likely lead to a higher proportion of settlements than in a system that does not provide some form of pretrial discovery.

Should claims be aggregated?

An effective private enforcement system must include a method of aggregating claims. Why? First, if small claims cannot be aggregated, consumers and small businesses will be left out in the cold because their claims and their resources are usually too small, taken individually, to warrant the expense of seeking recovery. This would obviously be unfair to injured persons who will have no remedy. Second, to the extent that some relatively small claims are nevertheless pursued, it would be inefficient for the system not to allow aggregation, because multiple small claims arising out of the same conduct would be expensive for the courts to administer and for defendants to defend and could result in conflicting outcomes. And third, as argued earlier, failure to provide the large number of end-use consumers with an antitrust remedy would deprive the antitrust system of a potentially strong consumer constituency.

But how should claims be aggregated? The maximal position, once again, is that of the US, which has clear and detailed procedural rules for class actions, applicable not only to antitrust but to civil wrongs generally, with a prominent commitment to an opt-out rather than opt-in default position. The earlier chapters provide a highly detailed look at these features.[22]

The US Federal Rules of Civil Procedure apply broadly to all civil actions, unless specifically excluded by law. Many countries that do not currently allow class actions worry about the 'spillover effects' of permitting class actions for antitrust, being especially concerned that class actions might also be extended to mass torts, environmental, securities, and labor law. Politically, there has been some difficulty in promoting class actions designed only for antitrust law, arising both from the opposition of companies that do not want their antitrust exposure to be expanded and, perhaps more surprisingly, from reformers who want class actions to cover all forms of corporate misconduct.

---

21 See, e.g., Chapter 17, France, fn 8.
22 In particular, see Chapter 8, Aggregation of claims.

What is feasible for a particular country must necessarily be left in the last analysis to its legislators to determine.

Some legislative efforts have created pseudo-class action regimes that have not worked. For example, in a move that avoids American nomenclature in the competition law context, some jurisdictions authorize 'representative actions' in which a single complaint can speak for multiple specifically identified claimants on an opt-in basis. When the default position is for individual claimants to opt in, the British experience[23] and behavioral economics[24] tell us that very few potential claimants will overcome inertia with affirmative steps to become part of the lawsuit. The situation is even less accommodating in jurisdictions where the individual claimants may be held responsible for the defendants' legal fees and expenses if the lawsuit fails and in jurisdictions where ethical considerations are employed to keep the representative from reaching out through advertisements to potential claimants. We have seen no evidence of effective litigation on behalf of a representative class under an opt-in structure.

We have now discussed two ways in which private enforcement has formally been enacted in various jurisdictions, but has failed to provide satisfactory results because of flaws, intentional or unexpected, in the system: namely, lack of workable discovery/disclosure rules and class actions based on opt-in default procedures. A third way private remedies may fail is equally important and seems to have been given relatively little attention in debates over private enforcement: a lack of monetary incentive for an organization or attorney actually to step forward and bring a case. This is a particular problem in regard to class-type actions.

How should private remedy litigation be funded?

There are many ways in which an antitrust suit might be funded. Defendants tend to be represented by attorneys who are paid on an hourly basis. A similar fee arrangement may work for some plaintiffs' claims, especially when the plaintiff is a relatively healthy business that has cash available, e.g. a so-called opt-out client in a class action.[25] Typically, however, the injured party has either been so extensively damaged that it cannot afford an hourly fee or (in the case of a consumer class) individual damages are too small and the number of class members so large that it is not worthwhile for an attorney to try to collect small portions of an overall fee from class members. Complicating all of this is the fact that it is impossible to predict how many hours or, indeed, years of legal time will have to be compensated during the course of investigation, trial preparation, trial, and appeal(s). One solution is to have someone other than the individual plaintiff(s) front the money and take the financial risk, with any payment to the attorneys coming out of the awarded damages.

One model for this is the contingent fee arrangement as utilized in the US, under which

---

23 See Chapter 16, England and Wales.

24 For an introduction to behavioral economics, see, e.g., Richard H. Thaler and Cass R. Sunstein, Nudge (Yale University Press 2008). Nudge emphasizes the importance of default positions (such as opt-in vs. opt-out) in the execution of public policy.

25 An opt-out claimant in the US typically has a relatively large claim and expects to receive more damages, after attorneys' fees and costs, by pursuing the claim individually than as part of a class.

the attorneys advance the costs of litigation and do not get paid for their time unless there is a victory, in which case they will be paid a percentage of the award plus their fees, with the funds coming from the losing party.[26] Other funding arrangements are conceivable and various interesting experiments are under way in Europe. Some jurisdictions require a minimum set fee but allow a success fee (sometimes capped) on top.[27] Others are examining the possibility of allowing a company to buy up claims and then represent them as if brought by a single claimant;[28] or of allowing third-party investors to underwrite a case in return for a percentage of the damages.[29]

As these examples suggest, it is increasingly becoming recognized that the funding of antitrust litigation, especially on behalf of a class, has an investment-type quality. In the US, where outsider investment in a case is prohibited, there is a plaintiffs' antitrust bar, not formally organized, consisting of attorneys who affiliate with law firms that litigate – and therefore fund – contingent fee antitrust cases.[30] In the typical plaintiffs' class action, several law firms will collaborate, with one (or sometimes more) being selected as lead counsel and all firms contributing time and expertise – and direct expenses. At the end of the day, if there is a settlement or a victory at trial, they will share the fee approved by the court, which is typically a significant fraction of the damages recovered (usually ranging from 10 to 30 per cent, depending on the total settlement). Treble damages for a class consisting of millions of consumers or hundreds of companies can obviously represent a substantial motivation.[31]

Firms typically team up to share not only the investment and the payoff, but also the substantial risk, since the future of a plaintiffs' class action antitrust case is uncertain as to the odds of success, the amount of time and effort to be expended, the extent and costs of discovery, and the duration of the case, which is usually measured in years. Because of the risk factor, a law firm generally wants to have a diversified portfolio of plaintiffs' cases at any one time. As in venture capital, many of these cases will lose, a few will return the costs, and hopefully a few will pay premiums. If all goes well, at the end of the day the class action attorneys will earn incomes roughly commensurate with what other antitrust attorneys earn. In short, the system of the American class action contingent fee bears great similarity to venture capitalism, which is premised on the occasional big payday.

The similarity is important in another way: just as venture capitalists look at many

---

26 See Chapter 12, Funding litigation.

27 See, e.g., Chapters 16 on England and Wales and 20 on Netherlands.

28 See Chapter 18 on Germany.

29 See Chapter 16 on England and Wales.

30 Sometimes a law firm will 'work both sides of the table,' representing a defendant in one suit and a plaintiff in a different suit. But combining within the same law firm the two models of hourly fees and contingent fees has often proven difficult and so a kind of dichotomy has developed. See Chapter 12, Funding litigation, generally, on funding an antitrust suit. In many jurisdictions, non-lawyers are not permitted to invest in legal cases, thereby compelling lawyers to be investors if the injured client(s) cannot pay a sufficient fee.

31 The largest antitrust class action fee award for the attorneys came in the massive merchants debit card case, $220 million. The case is described by the lead plaintiffs' attorney, Lloyd Constantine, in his book Priceless (Kaplan Publishing 2009). The claimants in this class action were all businesses, including such large retailers as Walmart.

proposals before settling on the investments that will go into their portfolio, so do plaintiffs' antitrust law firms investigate (often at significant uncompensated expense) each proposal brought to them by potential plaintiffs. Knowing that their own money and time (i.e., the opportunity cost) will be at risk, they can only take on so many cases and can only withstand so many losses; in other words, like the government, they must sift out the cases that are most likely to achieve their objectives. This process renders somewhat dubious the often-heard complaint that 'strike suits'[32] are frequently brought without regard to their merits, as if corporate defendants will automatically spew out cash to settle a case just because a complaint has been filed.

Some jurisdictions have authorized representational cases by certified consumers' associations and trade associations on behalf of their members. Unless this authorization is accompanied by opt-out procedures and motivations for the association and its attorneys, it is not likely to amount to much, as the experience in the UK suggests.[33] One could imagine, however, conditions under which consumers' associations could flourish as advocates of competition law in the interests of consumers. For example: (a) actions could be brought on behalf of all members, without the need to opt in; (b) damages could be distributed to qualified claimants; and (c) any left-over damages could be retained by the association, subject to the jurisdiction of the court.[34]

While we favor a broader availability of class actions, we look upon the possibility of consumers' associations flourishing as the instigators of class actions as a potentially exciting development, not only because it would be a mechanism for achieving justice for consumers and because it could provide an enormous boost to the currently very limited funding available to the consumer movement around the world, but because this could promote the sort of political support for the antitrust enterprise that we have been arguing is essential if that enterprise is to accomplish its mission.

Alternatives to the American approach may be found. But what cannot be ignored in any effective private enforcement framework is the earthy reality that private remedies do not happen merely because a legislature says they are available. Their prosecution must be paid for by somebody, somehow. A private remedy system that does not

---

32 'The frivolous litigation myth is premised on the idea that plaintiffs will bring weak claims in order to obtain settlements and that defendants will settle such claims in order to avoid the costs of discovery ("nuisance settlements" theory) or the small risk of "massive exposure" that may accompany class actions as a result of treble damages, joint and several liability, and fee shifting ("hydraulic pressure" theory).' Both theories are explored and shown to be flawed in Albert A. Foer (ed.), The Next Antitrust Agenda (Vandeplas Publishing 2008), 219, 231–34, available at www.antitrust-institute.org/archives/transitionreport.ashx. Another factor to be considered in the weighing of whether to bring a case is the matter of whether the loser will be required to pay the winner's costs. In the US the defeated plaintiff will not be held responsible for the winner's costs in the absence of an abuse of the process. In jurisdictions where the loser pays, it is important to distinguish whether this responsibility will fall on individual plaintiffs or on their attorneys, particularly in a class or representative action. Either way, however, it is a disincentive to file an antitrust complaint.

33 See Chapter 16, England and Wales.

34 In the US, courts have the equitable authority to award *cy pres* funds at the end of a class action to 'next best' recipients if all of the funds available for distribution exceed the justified claims that are filed or if the transaction costs of distribution are disproportionate to the funds available. See AAI Working Paper 07-11, Albert A. Foer, Cy Pres as an Antitrust Remedy: Suggested Best Practices, www.antitrustinstitute.org/Archives/WP07-11.ashx.

motivate specialized attorneys to litigate on behalf of antitrust plaintiffs will simply not be effective.

Additional institutional issues

The role of expertise

Our review of private enforcement around the world indicates a variety of views on the role of specialized tribunals versus general courts. The chief benefits of a specialized tribunal to handle all antitrust cases are expertise and consistency. This may be especially important in jurisdictions where a market economy is relatively new, expertise in competition law and analysis is rare, rules are still being significantly shaped, and neither courts nor juries can be expected to be facile with antitrust issues. If the number of cases is not too large, a single competition tribunal might be able to handle both government and private cases.[35] As the caseload grows, it may be necessary to create subordinate competition courts, and as the legal community's familiarity with competition law continues to expand, it might be feasible to offload antitrust onto courts of more general jurisdiction.

But expertise has its drawbacks, too. An expert tribunal with long-term incumbents may become captured by a narrow view of competition law. Much of antitrust involves common sense and prediction, which arguably places a premium on a broader experience than might be found on too highly specialized a court.[36]

While juries provide the broadest experience pool, whether juries are deemed appropriate for private antitrust cases may be influenced by the general level of education in the community, the familiarity of the public with the workings of markets, the role of juries in the particular legal system, and the degree to which the polity values expertise as opposed to public participation. While it is the experience in the US that a very high proportion of antitrust cases are settled prior to trial, it is commonly believed that the threat of facing a jury is often an inducement for defendants to settle.[37]

Finality

To what extent should an initial decision by the competition authority and/or the courts be appealable, and which aspects of the decision should be subject to review and under what standard of scrutiny? As the saying goes, justice delayed is justice denied, and this is particularly true for a company that is being destroyed by a competitor's illegal

---

35 See Chapters 16, England and Wales, and 35, South Africa.

36 Questions requiring prediction occur throughout an antitrust case: e.g., in defining a market, forecasting entry, determining competitive effects, developing a remedy that will restore competition or prevent future anticompetitive acts. Note that a court's function of finding the facts that exist or that occurred in the past is rather different from predicting the future, where there is no single truth but only a variety of probabilities with respect to a variety of scenarios that can be imagined. Antitrust systems have not focused on the implications of this difference for decision-making institutions.

37 We are neutral on the question of whether juries should be used in antitrust cases outside the US. Within the US, they are an established and workable part of the overall system, having a constitutional basis, and their presence in an antitrust case requires that the issues be addressed by advocates in an understandable, common sense way.

conduct. But making the first decision necessarily final is not a good idea. Not only can injustice occur at the trial level, but bad policy can be made that will be harmful in the future, especially when important policy lines are being drawn for the first time, as may happen when general antitrust principles are applied to specific and often-complex facts. So at the very least one level of appeal would seem necessary in any effective private enforcement system.

Leniency

In recent years many jurisdictions have initiated leniency programs intended to crack the secrecy of cartels by providing special advantages to the first company to step forward and confess.[38] In the US, under a law referred to as 'ACPERA',[39] successful leniency applicants not only avoid criminal prosecution, but damages in a subsequent private action against the firm will be single rather than treble, provided that the firm cooperates with claimants in such private cases. Some nations express concern that private enforcement will undermine the incentives of cartel members to confess to the government. To the extent this is a concern, it might be possible to adopt provisions like ACPERA and place a cap on civil liability for the whistle-blowing firm. Combining significant private damages with a cap for the whistle-blower might bring greater pressure on cartel members to be the first one to confess, leading to the revelation to both the government and the private sector of a larger number of secret cartels.

Settlements

An effective private enforcement system should also be concerned with arriving at a good mix of settlements and final, well-explained decisions. Too few well-explained decisions by the authorities yield too little authoritative guidance on policy. Too few settlements mean that the incentives and/or mechanisms promoting compromise are insufficient or ineffective. Government settlements need to be largely transparent in order to avoid the perception of corruption and to provide a degree of guidance as to how the government is interpreting the law. There are stronger arguments for protecting the confidentiality of settlements in private cases, and the promise of confidentiality protection may be one incentive for reaching a compromise.[40]

Building the infrastructure of the antitrust enterprise

We have talked about the importance of the role private enforcement can play in developing infrastructure institutions supportive of the antitrust enterprise.[41] Consumers' organizations, having a stake in remedies, can become important supporters. A plaintiffs' bar, likewise, can provide support, either as part of an antitrust section of the local bar association or as an independent entity.

---

[38] The US also provides a lesser degree of leniency to some additional companies that come forward.

[39] The Antitrust Criminal Penalty Enhancement and Reform Act of 2004, P.L. 108-237.

[40] We were impressed, for example, by the mechanisms promoting collective settlements in Chapter 20, Netherlands.

[41] For the term 'antitrust enterprise' we recognize Herbert Hovenkamp, author of a book by that title (Harvard University Press 2005).

A private enforcement system will likely lead to the development of other parts of the infrastructure. For example, with more antitrust activity, additional antitrust training will be needed in law schools, creating or expanding an intellectual cadre that will have a stake in the improvement of antitrust policy and procedures. Also needed will be economists trained in industrial organization and (less frequently) forensic accountants who can assist in the preparation of both sides of antitrust cases. If class actions are allowed, entities specialized in the identification and qualification of class members and in the distribution of damages will be needed.[42] It is also possible that companies providing specialized electronic discovery services will be needed to deal with email and other documents found on computers. The media will also need to develop business and legal reporters who are able to understand antitrust activities and explain them to the public. All of this will be magnified if stand-alone cases are possible.

The roots of antitrust are shallow in most nations. They need to be fertilized and watered. The less recognized role of private enforcement is to help provide this function.

International complexity

Private enforcement obviously complicates the antitrust picture. Domestically, it increases the number of players, the opportunities for conflicting theories to find authoritative support, and the general level of corporate conflict and litigation. It certainly makes life more complicated for businesses that may be subjected to antitrust actions.

More and more, markets can be described as multinational, if not fully global, which raises questions about the liability for damages and the extent of discovery outside the country having jurisdiction. Questions of comity will increasingly arise as well as questions of efficient judicial administration. Is it necessary to create a forum for the resolution of conflicts involving multiple competition jurisdictions? How can a multinational defendant go about settling in a hundred jurisdictions?[43] The antitrust travail of Intel should make a good study, in that the world's dominant microchip firm, operating in a global market, has been challenged more or less simultaneously in Japan, South Korea, the EU, and the US by a mixture of public and private actions.

While we believe that a company should be made to pay for its sins, there is a risk that if everyone around the world piles on, a defendant could be destroyed. This is not desirable, but there is at present no relatively efficient way a global company can admit it was wrong and/or agree to pay up a reasonable aggregate amount that will satisfy all governments, businesses, and consumers who alleged they were harmed by its illegal actions. The absence of a downside brake may not be of much global concern today, but as the antitrust enterprise develops in the ways we are advocating, the need for harmonization will grow and nations will come under greater pressure than they are today to create new institutions that are appropriate for multi-national markets.

It appears that the multi-governmental institutions that focus on competition law – the International Competition Network (ICN), the Organisation for Economic Co-operation and Development (OECD), the World Trade Organization (WTO), and the

---

42 See Chapter 14, Class notice and claims administration.

43 See Chapter 37, International settlements.

United Nations Conference on Trade and Development (UNCTAD) – have not systematically addressed these issues, or for that matter (with the exception of a large study by the OECD[44] and a report to the ICN[45]) devoted significant attention to private enforcement. Yet, in the US, it is estimated that over 90 per cent of antitrust litigation is private rather than governmental; suppose that private enforcement in the rest of the world only multiplies the amount of litigation by a factor of three or five. We strongly favor that development, but what would be the implications?

As long as nations are sovereign, they will find their own ways to deal with the universal problem of how the state should relate to its private sector. Today, the effort to harmonize competition laws around the world focuses on best practices and soft harmonization, in which a common vocabulary is developed and a small but increasing number of practitioners (including primarily government officials, but also lawyers, economists, educators, and judges) are beginning to see themselves as part of a global antitrust community. This is a necessary stage that should not be cooked too rapidly. But we predict that the next stage will be projected to the front of the stove as private enforcement activities take on a dramatic new global role, forcing serious consideration of a world treaty that defines standards, contains a mechanism for prosecuting global cases, and has a court of last resort for both public and private cases that involve cross-border corporate strategies. It is not too soon to begin thinking along these lines.

---

[44] OECD, Policy Roundtables, Private Remedies, 2007, www.oecd.org/dataoecd/24/62/39892177.pdf.

[45] International Competition Network Cartels Working Group Subgroup 1 – General Framework, *Interaction of Public and Private Enforcement in Cartel Cases*, Report to the ICN annual conference, Moscow, May 2007.

Index